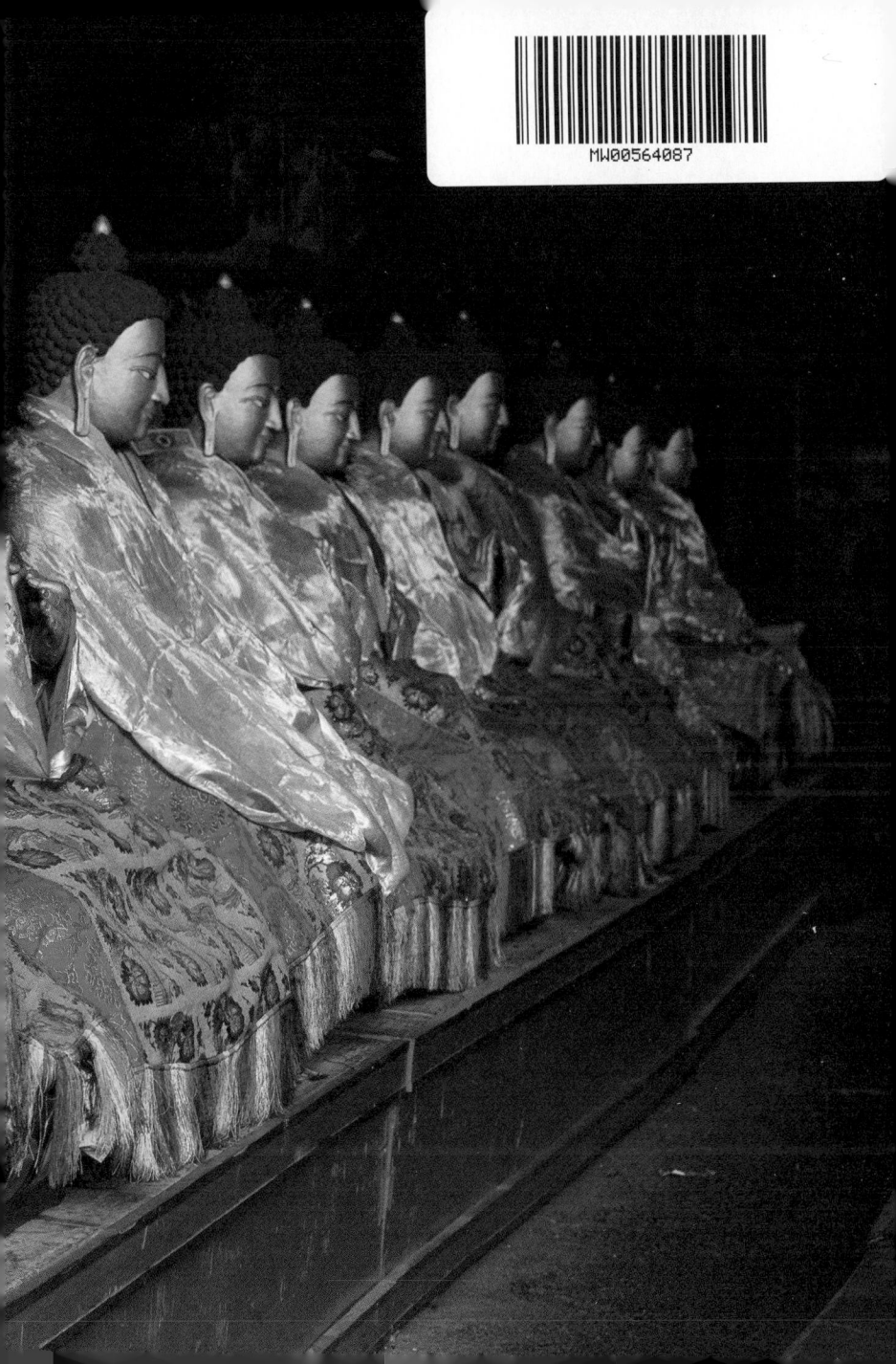

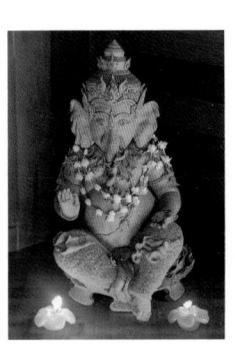

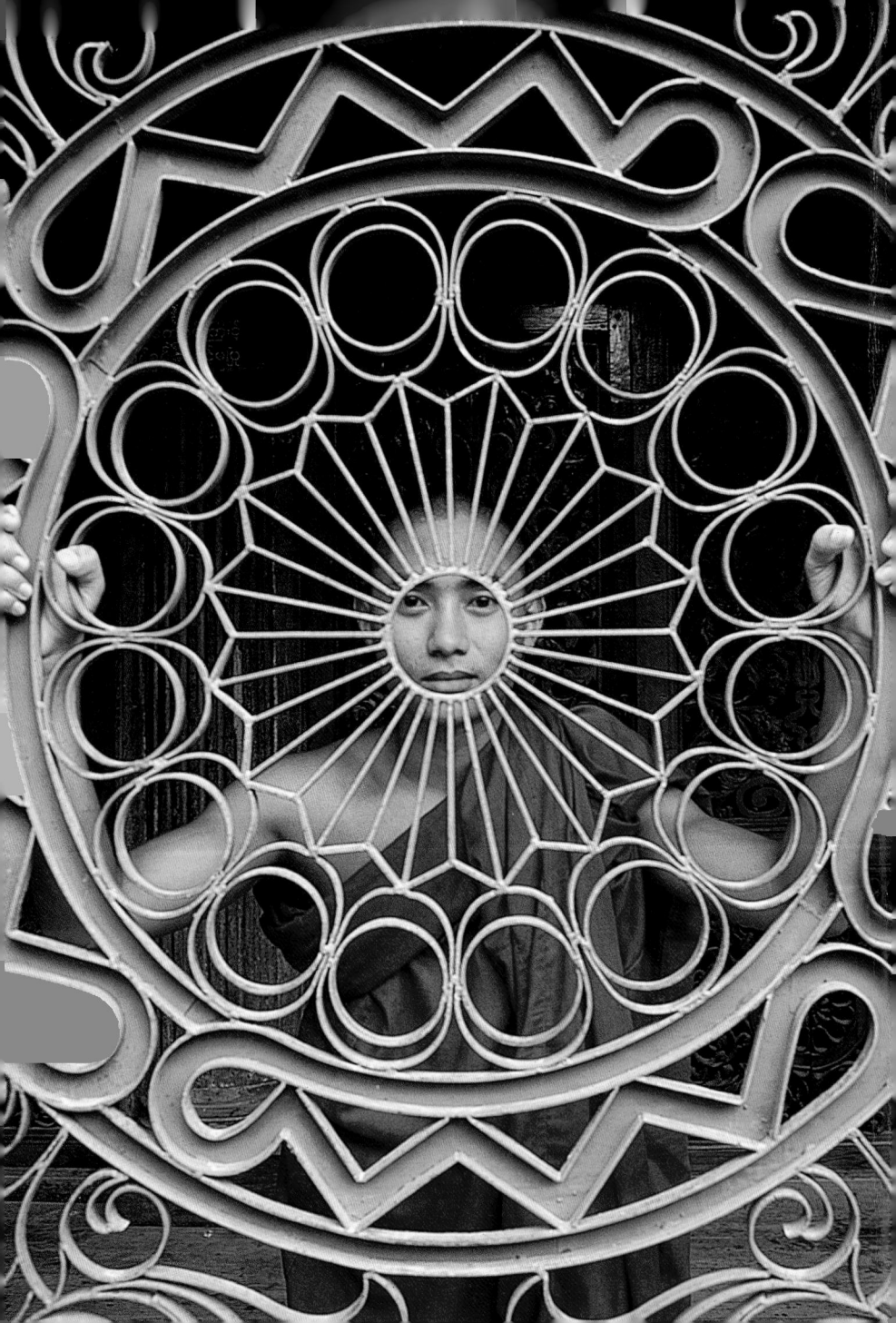

LIVING IN ASIA

Photos RETO GUNTLI
Edited by ANGELIKA TASCHEN
Text by SUNIL SETHI

TASCHEN

Bibliotheca Universalis

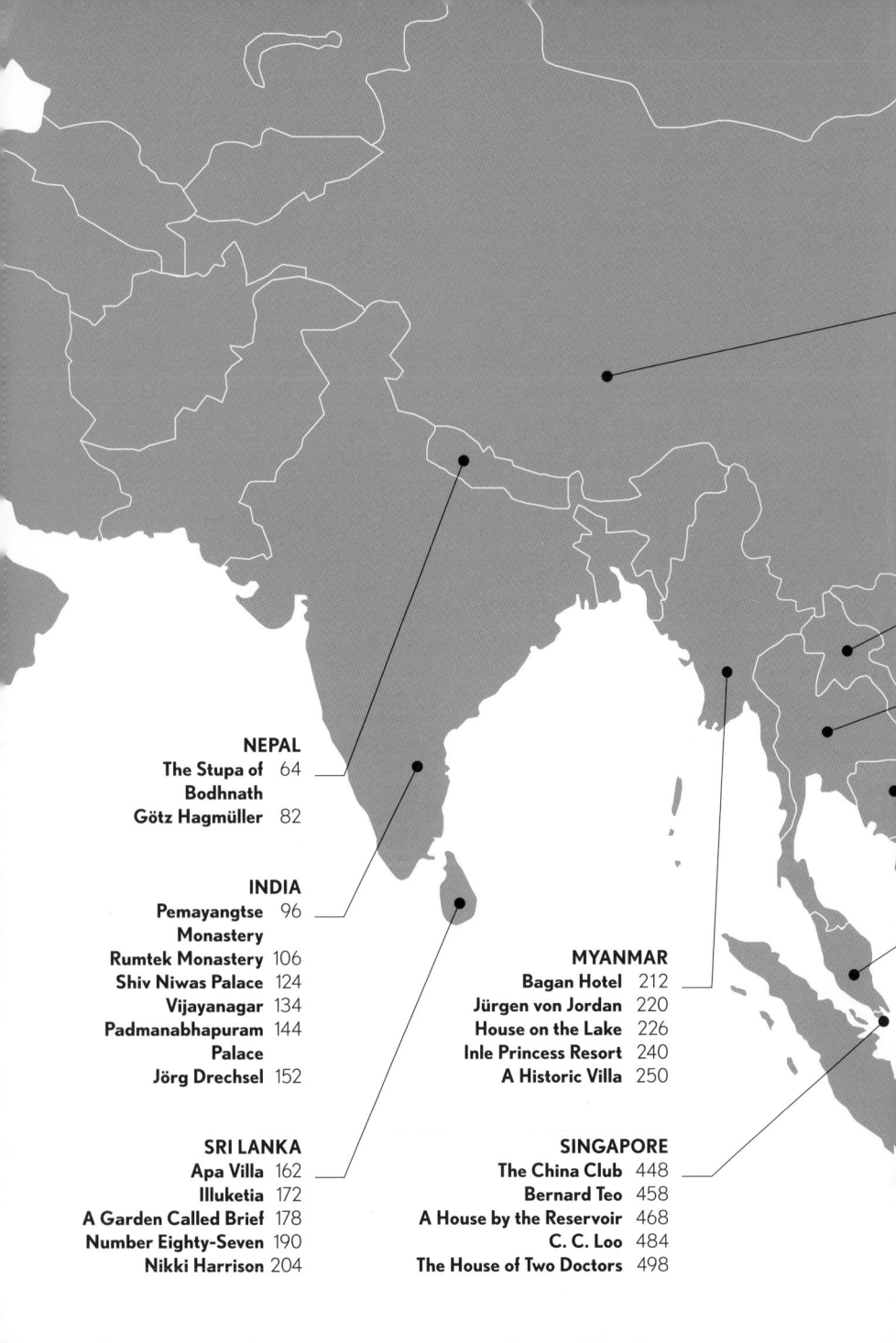

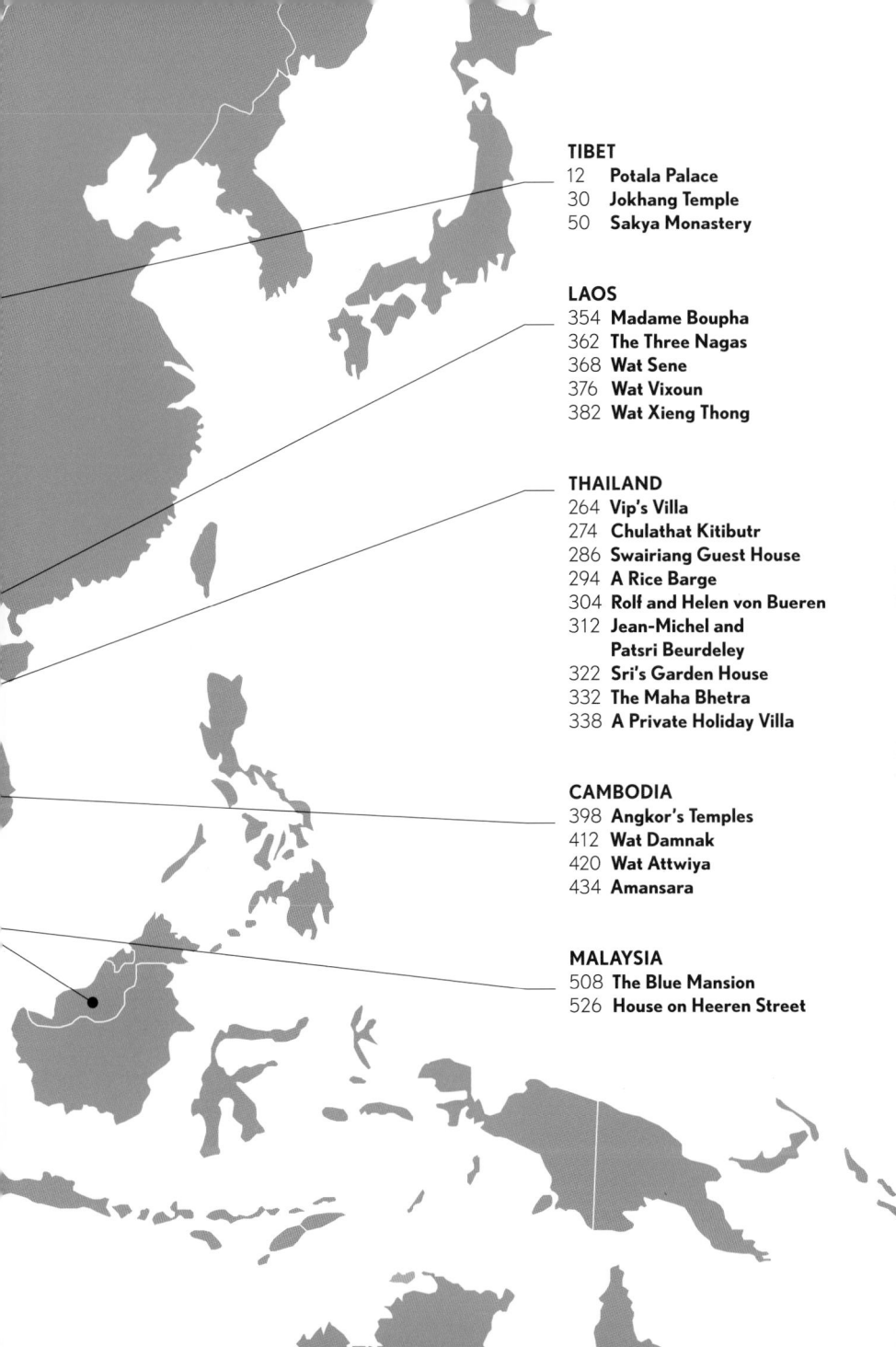

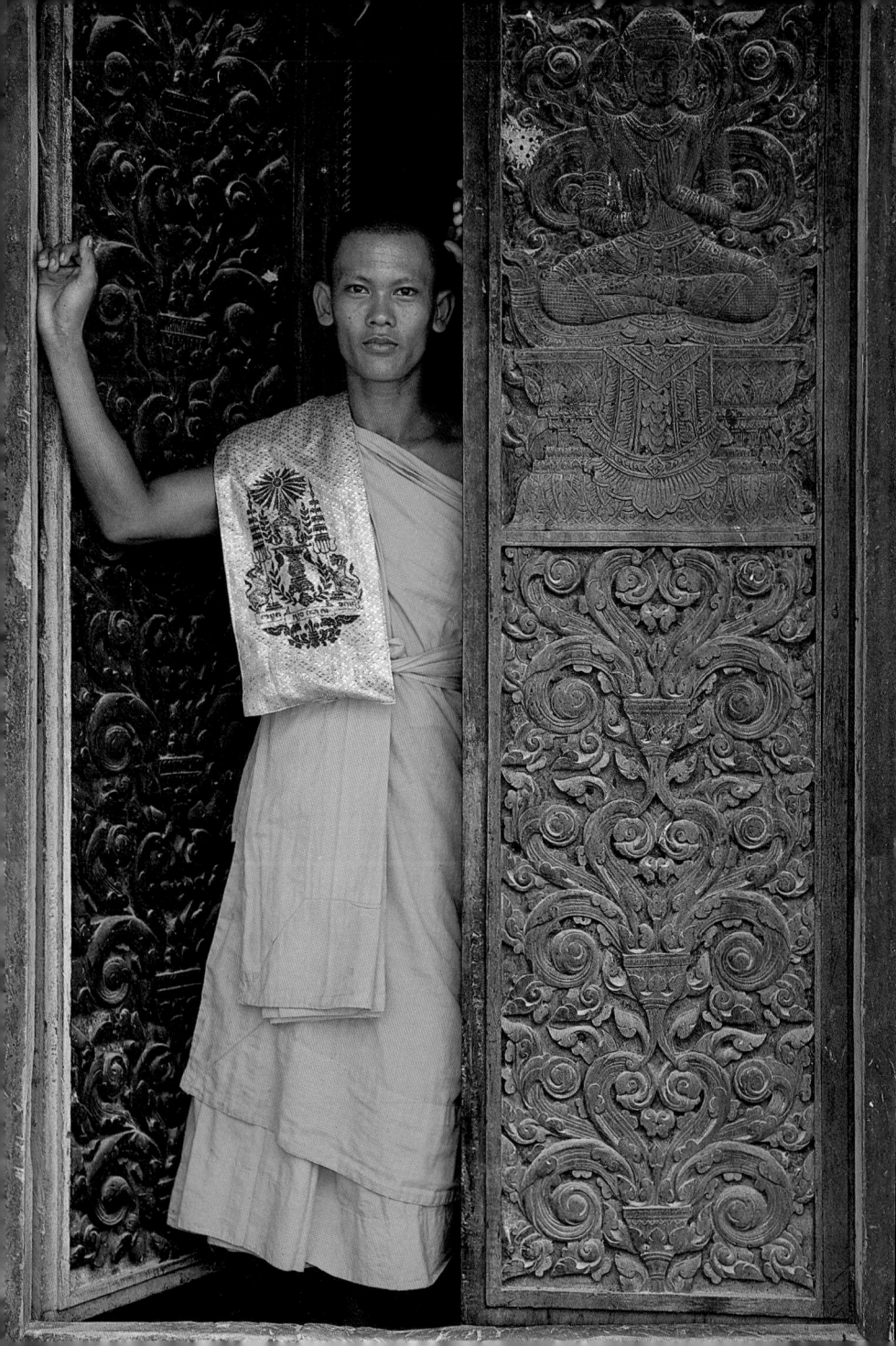

CONTENTS

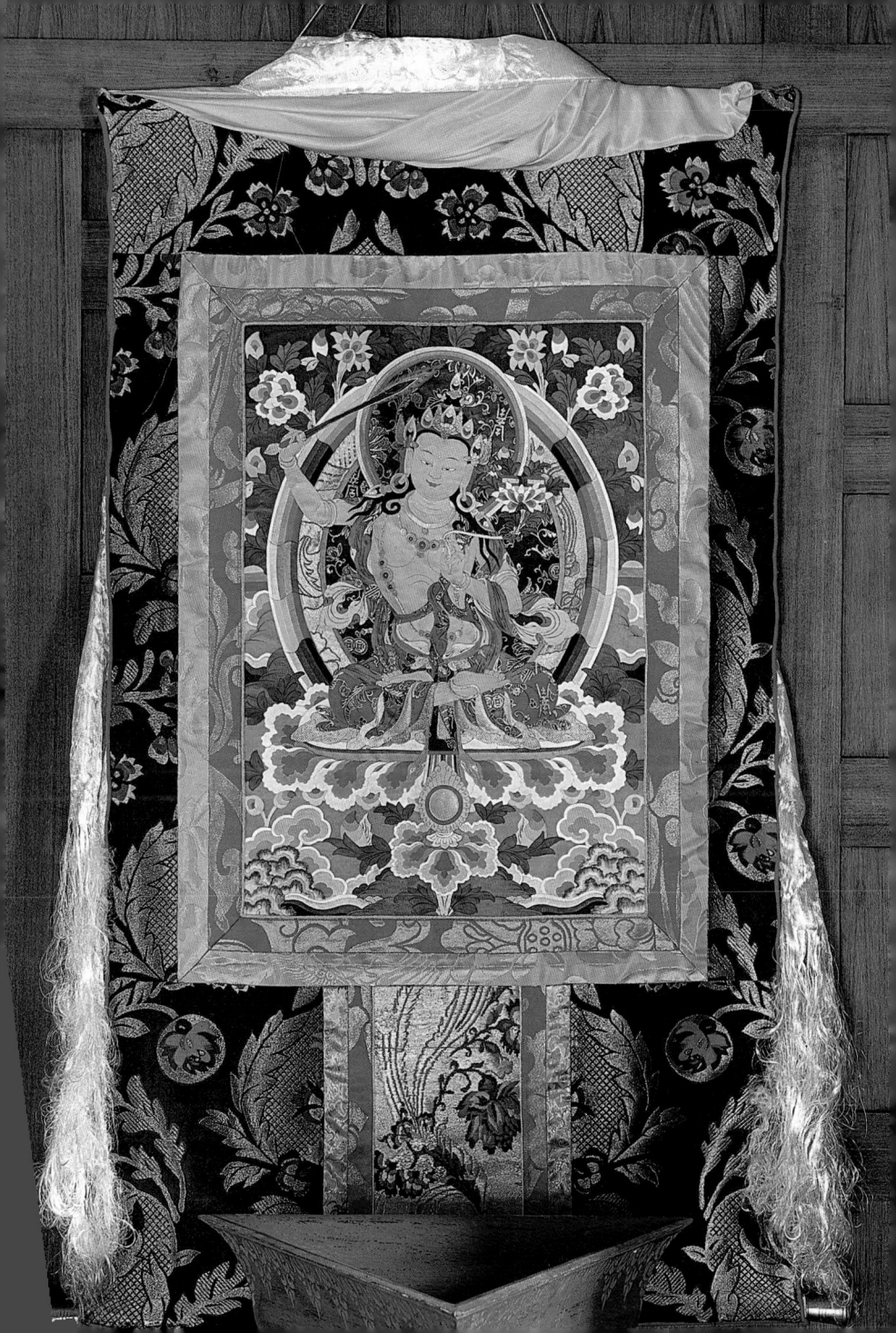

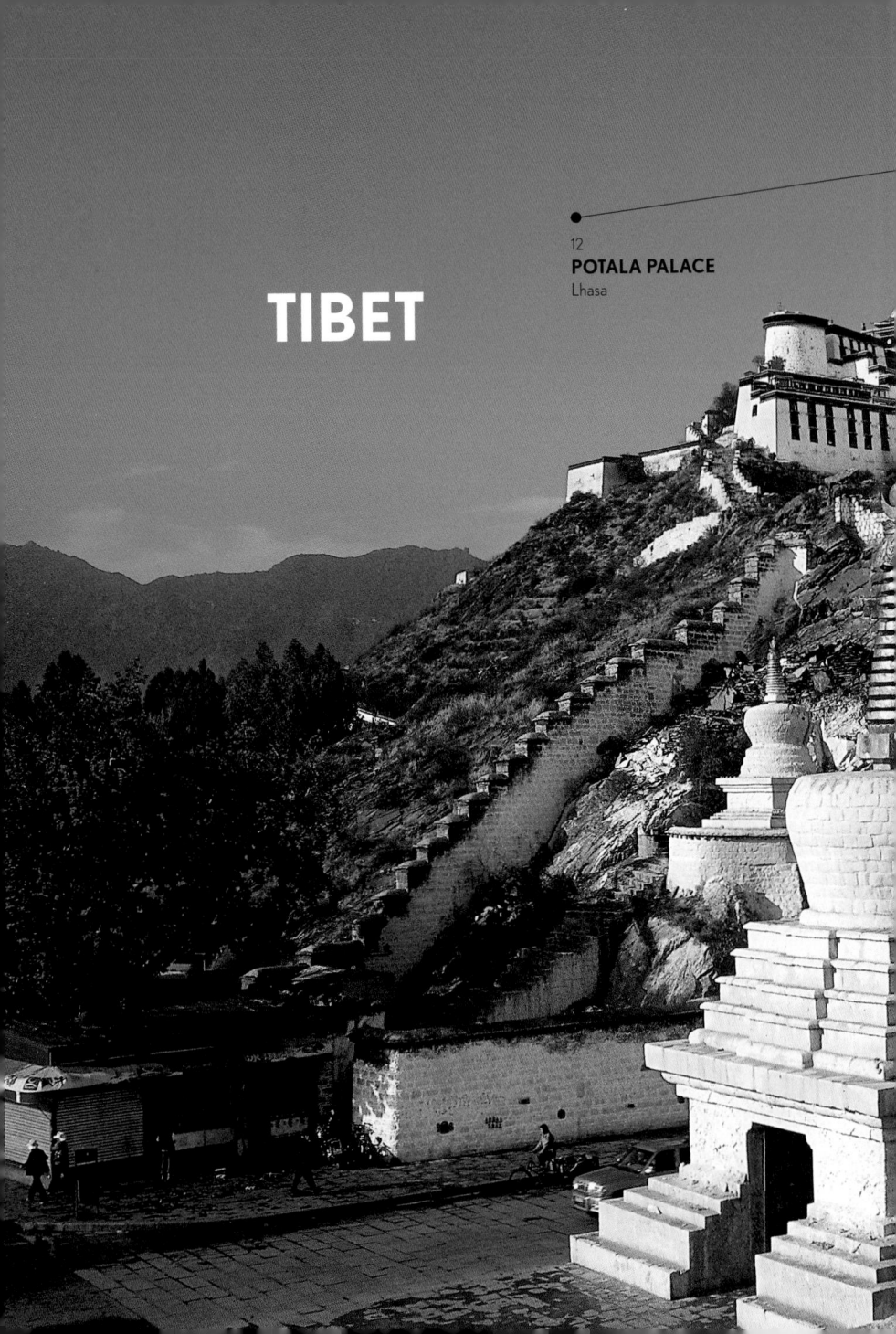

TIBET

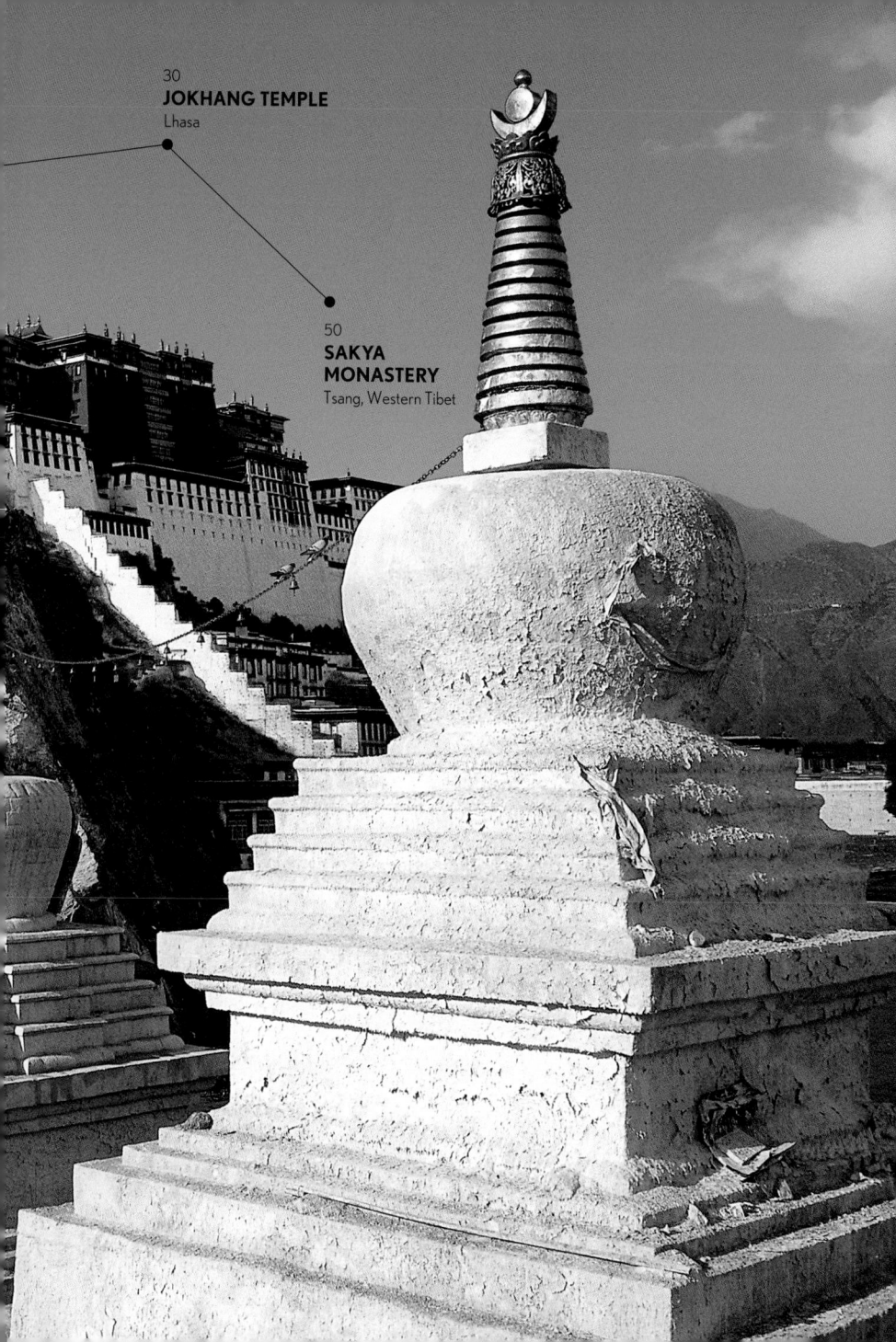

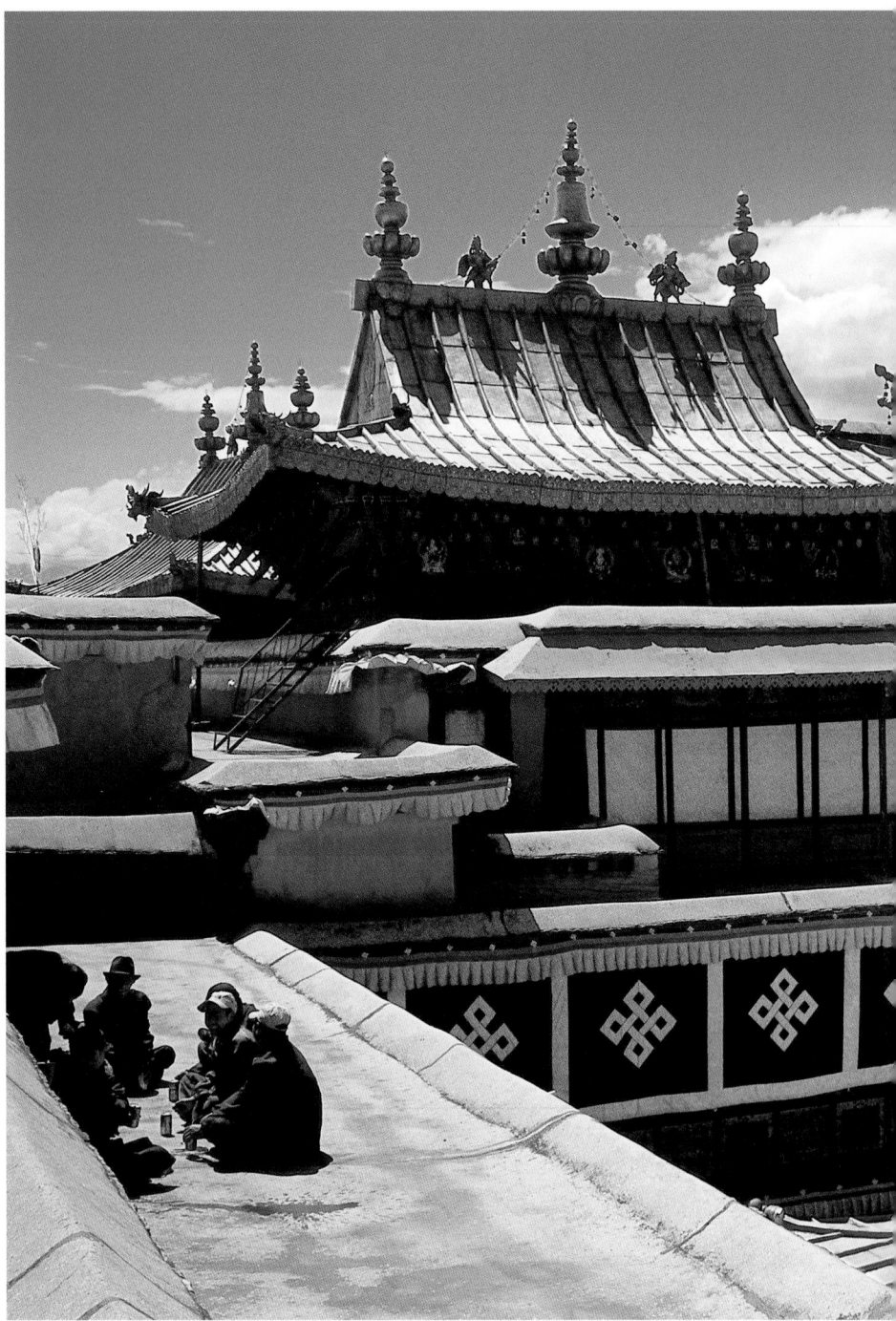

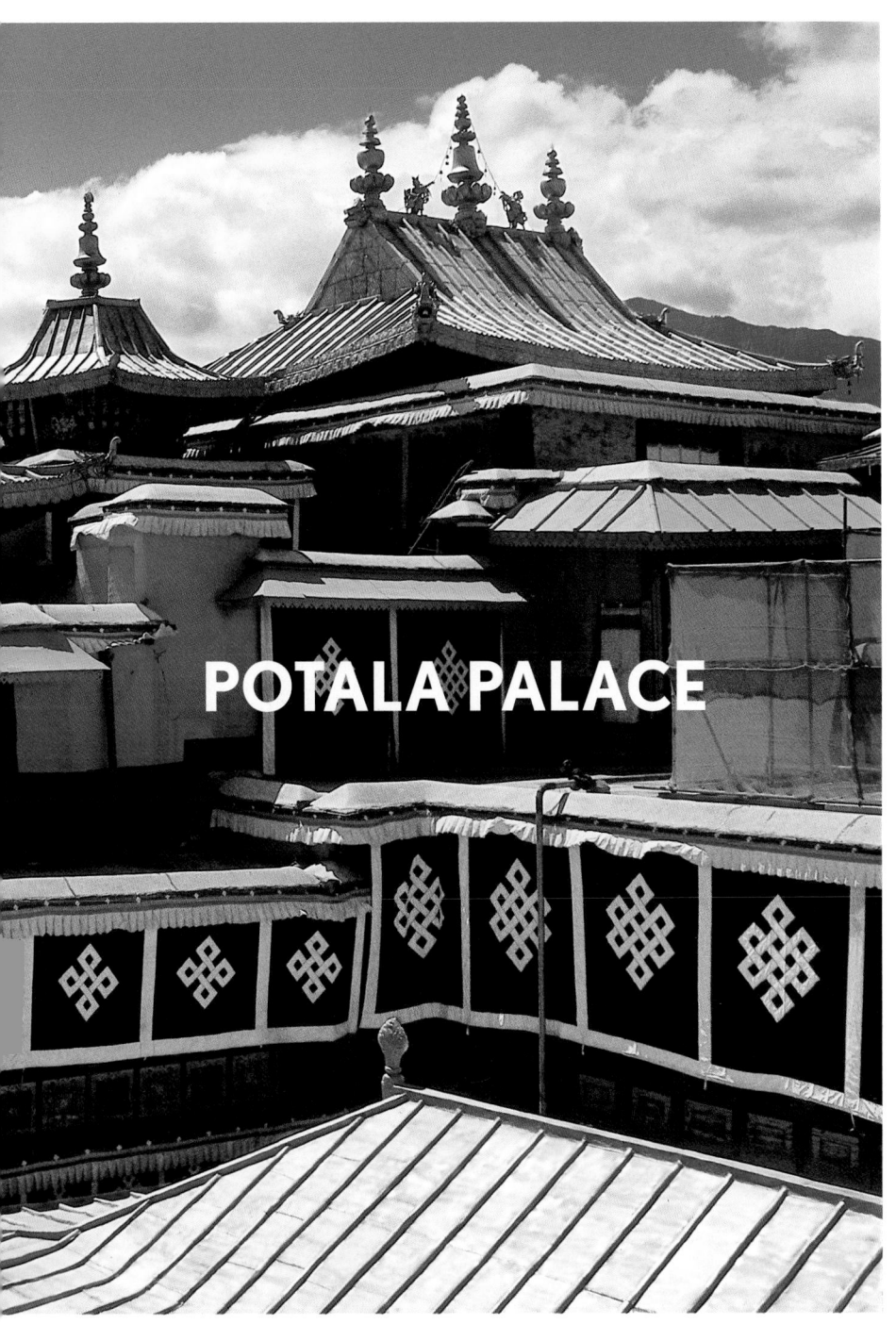

POTALA PALACE

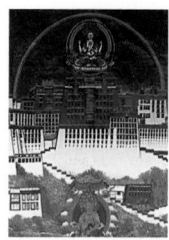

POTALA PALACE

LHASA
TIBET

Soaring above the eminence of Red Hill in the Tibetan capital, the thousand-roomed Potala Palace with its labyrinth of corridors and courtyards is the official seat of the Dalai Lama, Holder of the White Lotus. Tibetans believe the Dalai Lama to be the earthly embodiment of the Bodhisattva of Compassion; for them the Potala is both a symbol of spiritual power and political freedom. Until his exile to India in 1959, the present Dalai Lama, fourteenth in line of reincarnates of the Gelugpa order of Buddhism, lived here. The palace was largely a reconstruction undertaken by the fifth Dalai Lama from 1645 onwards on the site of an earlier palace built by Songtsen Gampo, the king who unified Tibet and ushered in Buddhism early in the seventh century. The Potala was a humming universe of throne rooms, offices, chapels and tombs of earlier Dalai Lamas. After the building of Norbulingka, the summer palace, in the 18th century, it was only used in winter months. But with the God-King gone, both palaces now echo with the drone of tourists.

Hoch über der Anhöhe des Roten Hügels in der tibetischen Hauptstadt ragt der Potala-Palast mit seinen tausend Zimmern und dem Labyrinth aus Gängen und Höfen empor – die offizielle Residenz des Dalai Lama, dem Herrn des Weißen Lotus. Die Tibeter sehen im Dalai Lama die irdische Verkörperung des Bodhisattwa des Mitleids, während der Potala-Palast als Symbol spiritueller Kraft und politischer Freiheit verehrt wird. Bis zum Gang ins indische Exil 1959 lebte hier auch die vierzehnte Inkarnation des buddhistischen Gelugpa-Ordens, der heutige Dalai Lama. Der Palast stellt größtenteils eine Rekonstruktion dar, die der fünfte Dalai Lama ab 1645 an der Stelle eines älteren Palastes vorantrieb. Dieser war von Songtsen Gampo erbaut worden, dem König, der bereits im frühen 7. Jahrhundert Tibet befreit und den Buddhismus eingeführt hatte. Der geschäftige Potala-Palast war ein eigenes Universum – mit Inthronisierungshallen, Amtsstuben und Kapellen sowie Grabstätten ehemaliger Dalai Lamas. Nachdem im 18. Jahrhundert die Sommerresidenz in Norbulingka gebaut worden war, nutzte der Dalai Lama den Potala nur noch im Winter. Da er heute gar nicht mehr in Tibet lebt, sind es die Touristen, die beide Paläste mit Leben füllen.

S'élevant au sommet de la Colline rouge, au cœur de la capitale tibétaine, le palais du Potala, dédale de couloirs, cours et pièces, est la résidence officielle du dalaï-lama, le seigneur du Lotus blanc. Pour les Tibétains, le dalaï-lama est l'émanation terrestre du bodhisattva de la compassion. Aussi voient-ils dans le Potala un symbole de pouvoir spirituel et de liberté politique. L'actuel dalaï-lama, le quatorzième supérieur de l'ordre des gelugpas, y a vécu jusqu'à son exil en Inde en 1959. Le palais est en grande partie une reconstruction commencée en 1645 par le cinquième dalaï-lama sur le site d'un palais ancien, construit par Songtsen Gampo, l'artisan de l'unité tibétaine et l'initiateur du bouddhisme au Tibet au début du 7e siècle. Le Potala, ensemble architectural composé de salles du trône, bureaux, chapelles et sépultures de dalaï-lamas, grouillait de monde jusqu'à la construction, au 18e siècle, du Norbulingka, le palais d'été. Il n'a plus alors été habité que pendant les mois d'hiver. Mais depuis le départ du dieu-roi, les deux palais sont emplis de la rumeur des touristes.

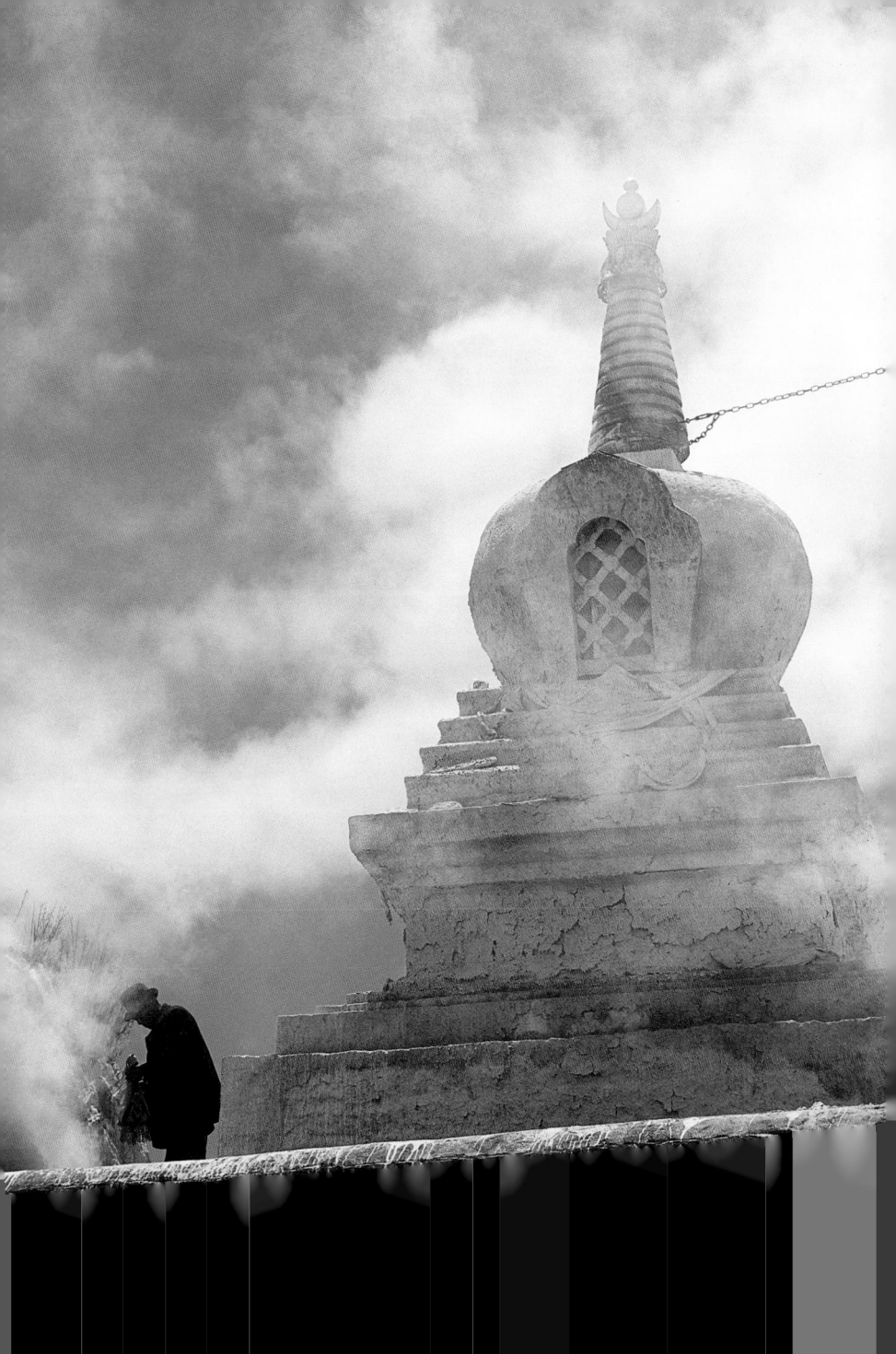

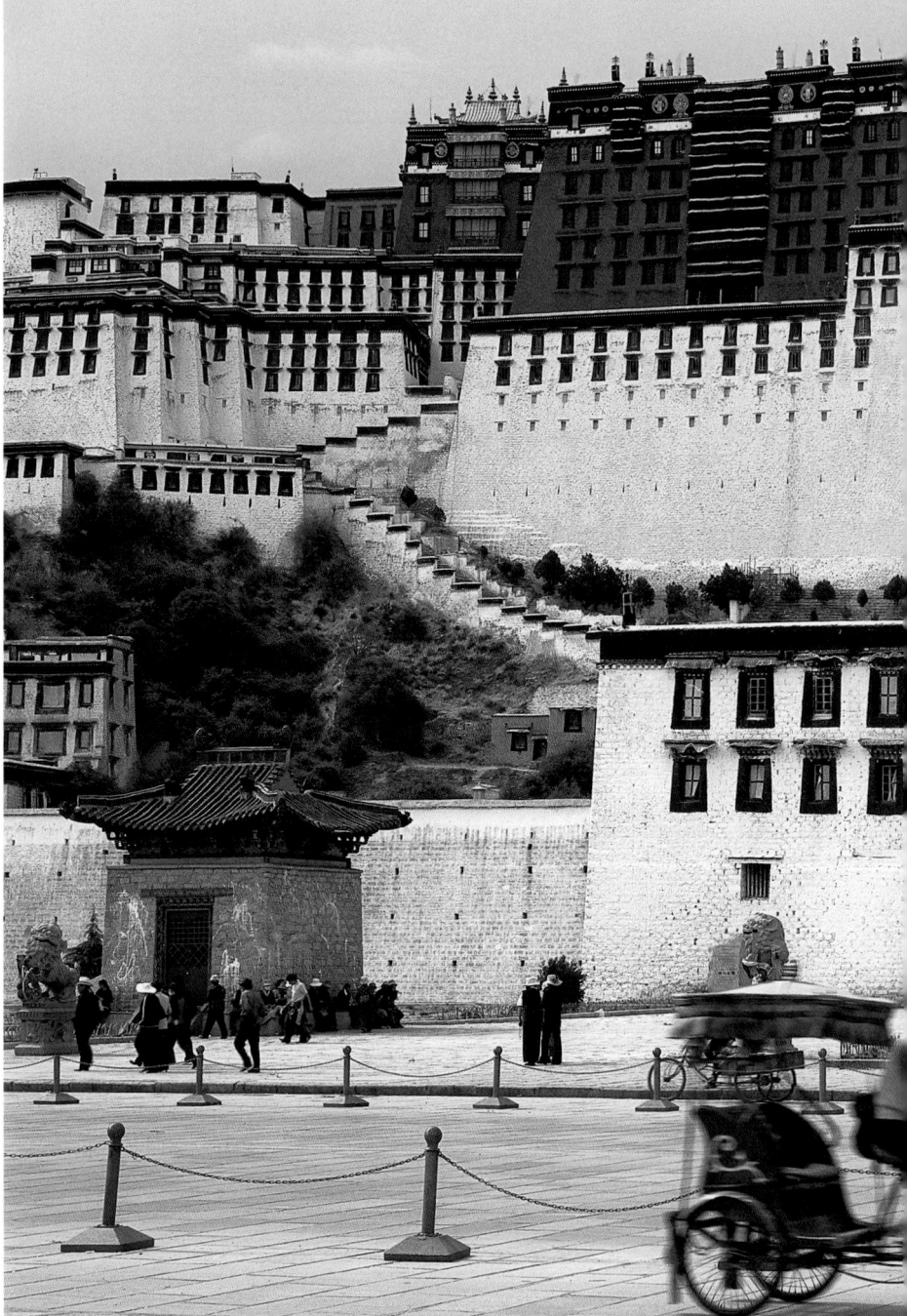

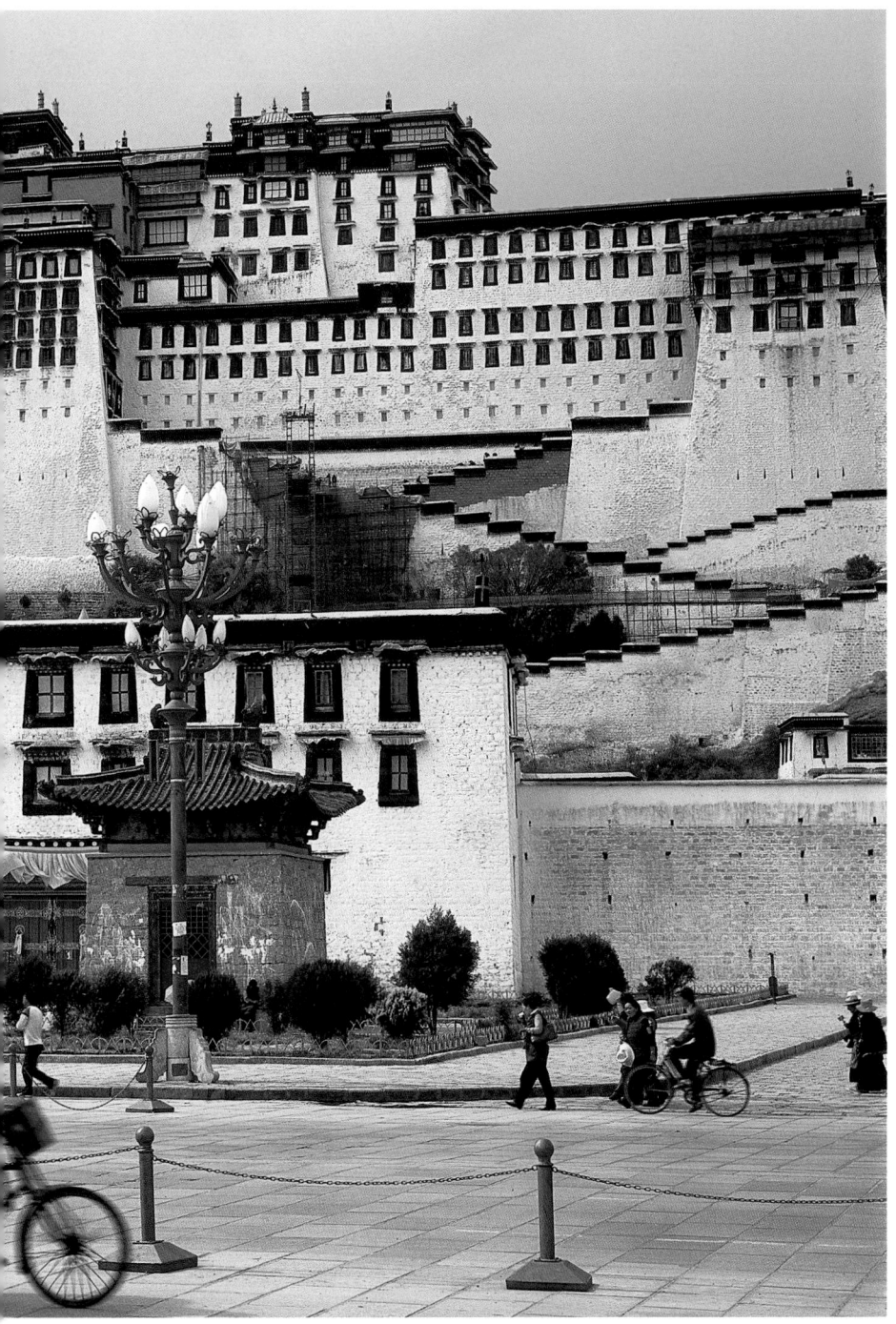

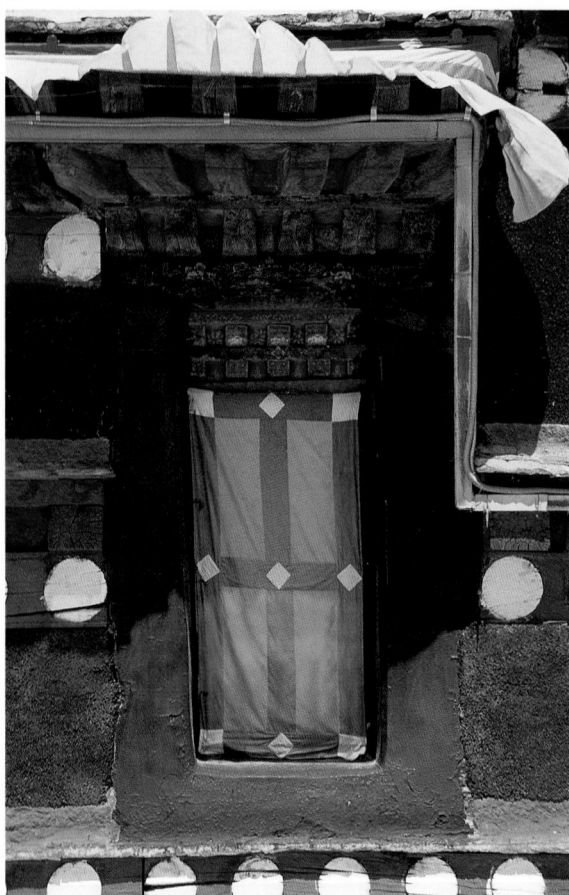

PP. 12–13 The courtyard is hung with black and white banners with the eternal knot, signifying the unity of things. • Der Innenhof ist mit schwarz-weißen Bannern geschmückt, die das Symbol des endlosen Knotens tragen und so an die Einheit der Dinge erinnern. • Les drapeaux noirs et blancs accrochés dans la cour en contrebas arborent le nœud éternel, symbole de l'unité des choses.

P. 15 A worshipper burns fragrant herbs as a votive offering at a stupa, or chorten, at the rear entrance to the palace • Ein Gläubiger verbrennt

Duftkräuter als Weiheopfer vor einem Stupa oder Chörten am Hintereingang des Palastes. • Près de l'entrée arrière du palais, un fidèle brûle des herbes aromatiques en offrande au pied d'un stupa, appelé chörten au Tibet.

PP. 16–17 The massive inward sloping white and ochre walls of the Potala Palace rise to 13 storeys and a height of a thousand feet above the valley floor. • Der 13 Stockwerke hohe Palast mit seinen mächtigen, einwärts geneigten weißen und ockerfarbenen Mauern thront 110 Meter hoch über dem Tal. •

Avec ses murs épais inclinés vers l'intérieur, le palais blanc et ocre de 13 étages domine la vallée, 110 mètres plus bas.

↑ Entrance doorways to the private quarters of the Dalai Lamas are lined with a traditional Tibetan awning. • Die Eingänge zu den Privatgemächern der Dalai Lamas sind mit traditionellen tibetischen Vorhängen verhängt. • Les entrées des appartements privés des dalaï-lamas sont tendues de marquises traditionnelles tibétaines.

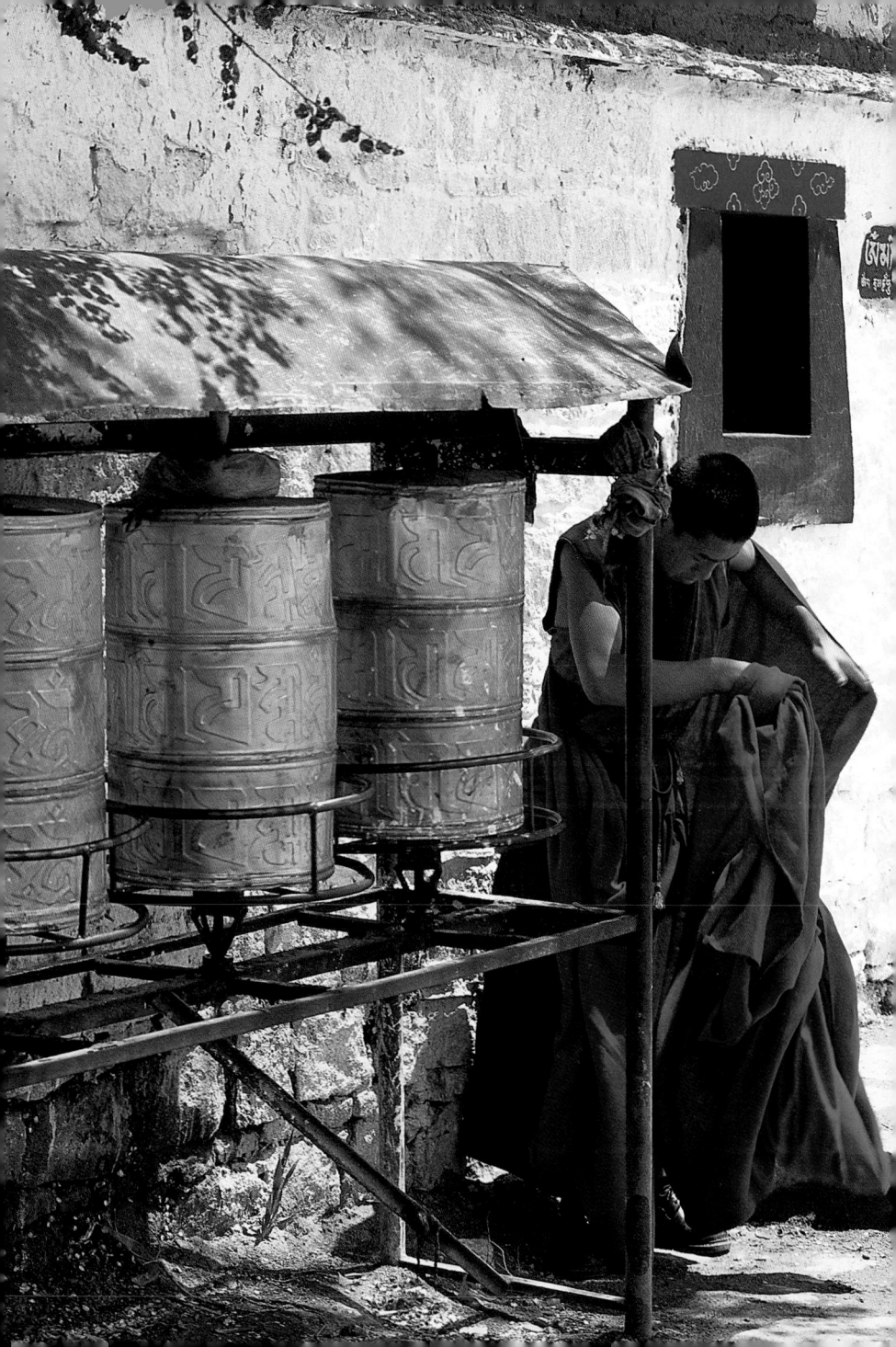

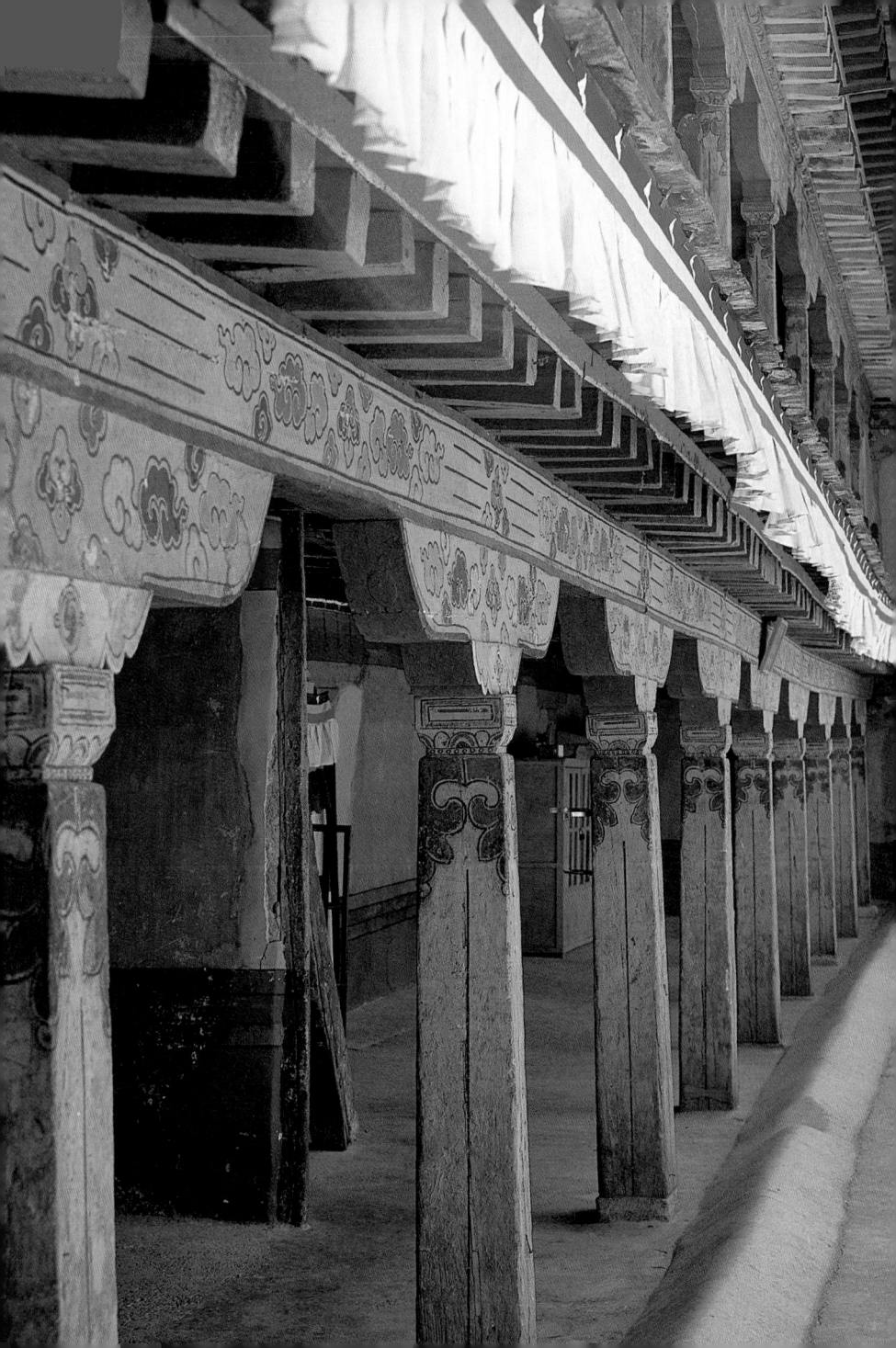

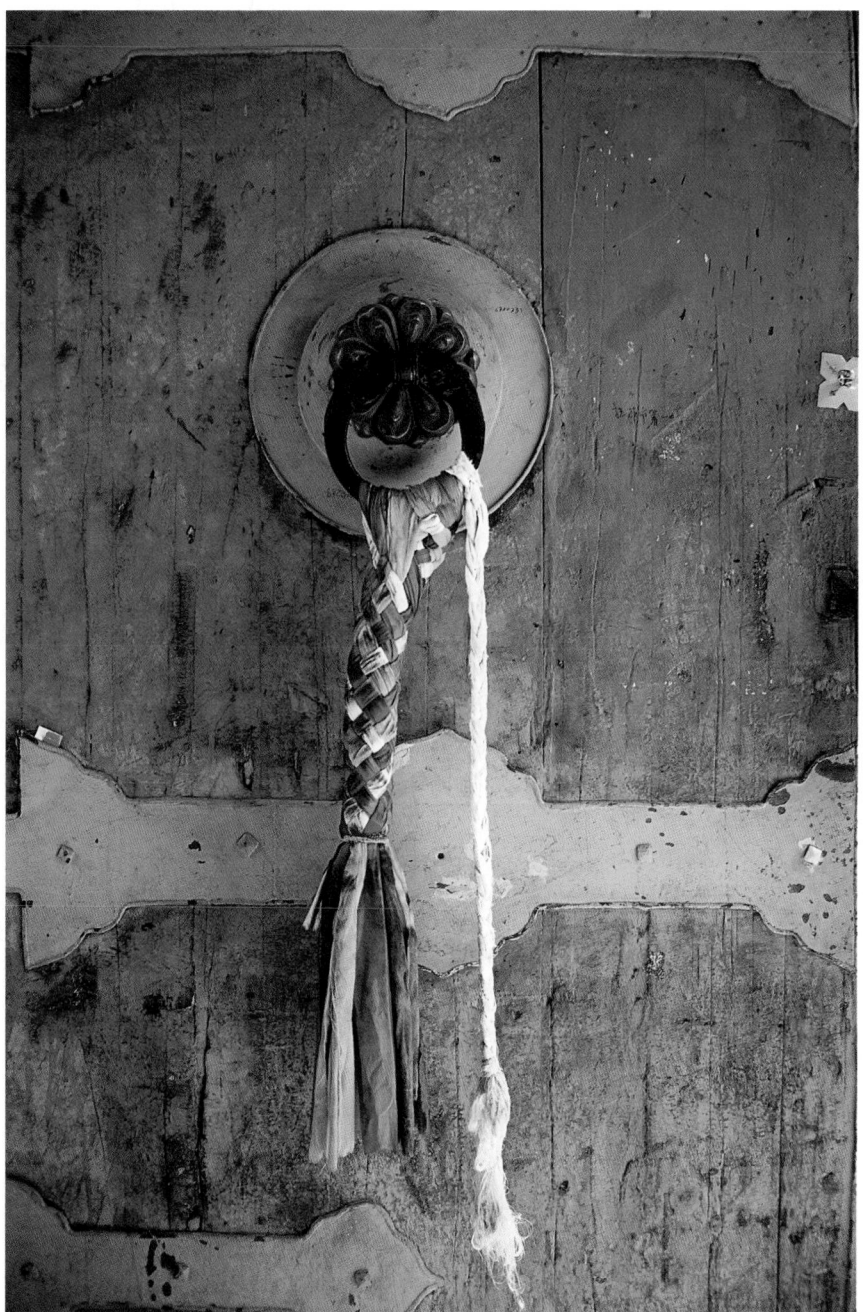

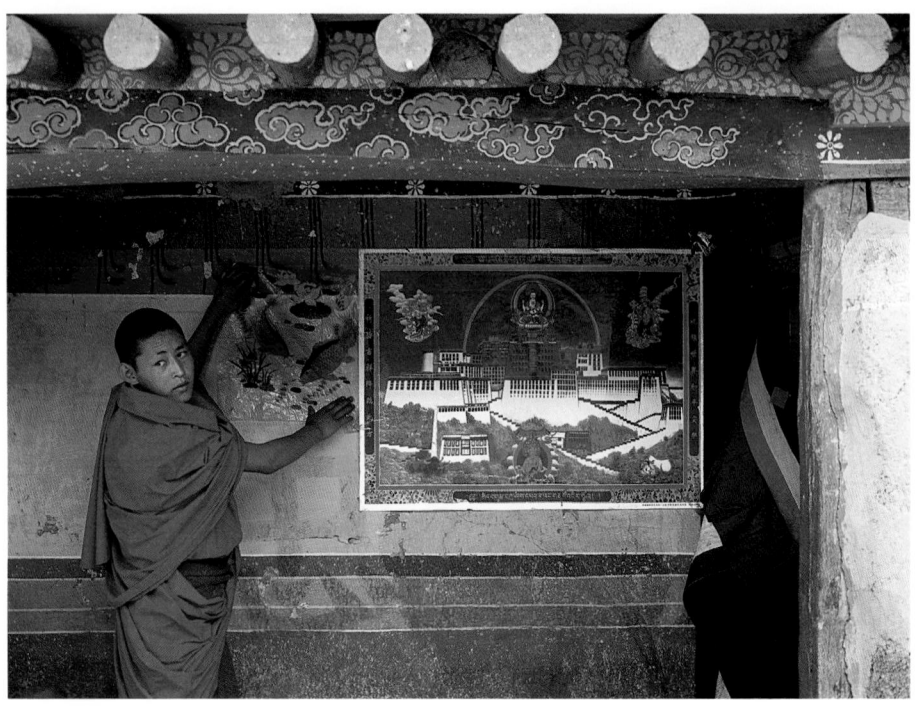

P. 20 A colonnade in the Potala's main courtyard is painted with a pattern of stylised clouds. · Ein Säulengang im Haupthof des Potala ist mit einem Muster aus Wolken bemalt. · Les motifs peints sur la colonnade dans la cour principale du Potala sont des nuages stylisés.

P. 21 A plait of prayer flags hangs from a bronze knocker on a palace gate. · Am Palasttor hängt ein Zopf aus geflochtenen Gebetsfahnen an einem Türklopfer aus Bronze. · Des drapeaux de prière tressés agrémentent un heurtoir de bronze visible sur une porte du palais.

↑ A young monk decorates the terrace outside his room with a popular print of the Potala Palace. · Ein junger Mönch verziert die Terrasse vor seinem Zimmer mit einem beliebten Poster vom Potala. · Un jeune moine décore la terrasse de sa chambre avec une représentation du Potala très prisée au Tibet.

→ An elaborately decorated doorway to the private rooms of the 13th and 14th Dalai Lamas. · Das prächtig geschmückte Tor zu den Privatgemächern des 13. und 14. Dalai Lama. · Cette porte très richement ornée mène aux appartements privés des 13ᵉ et 14ᵉ dalaï-lamas.

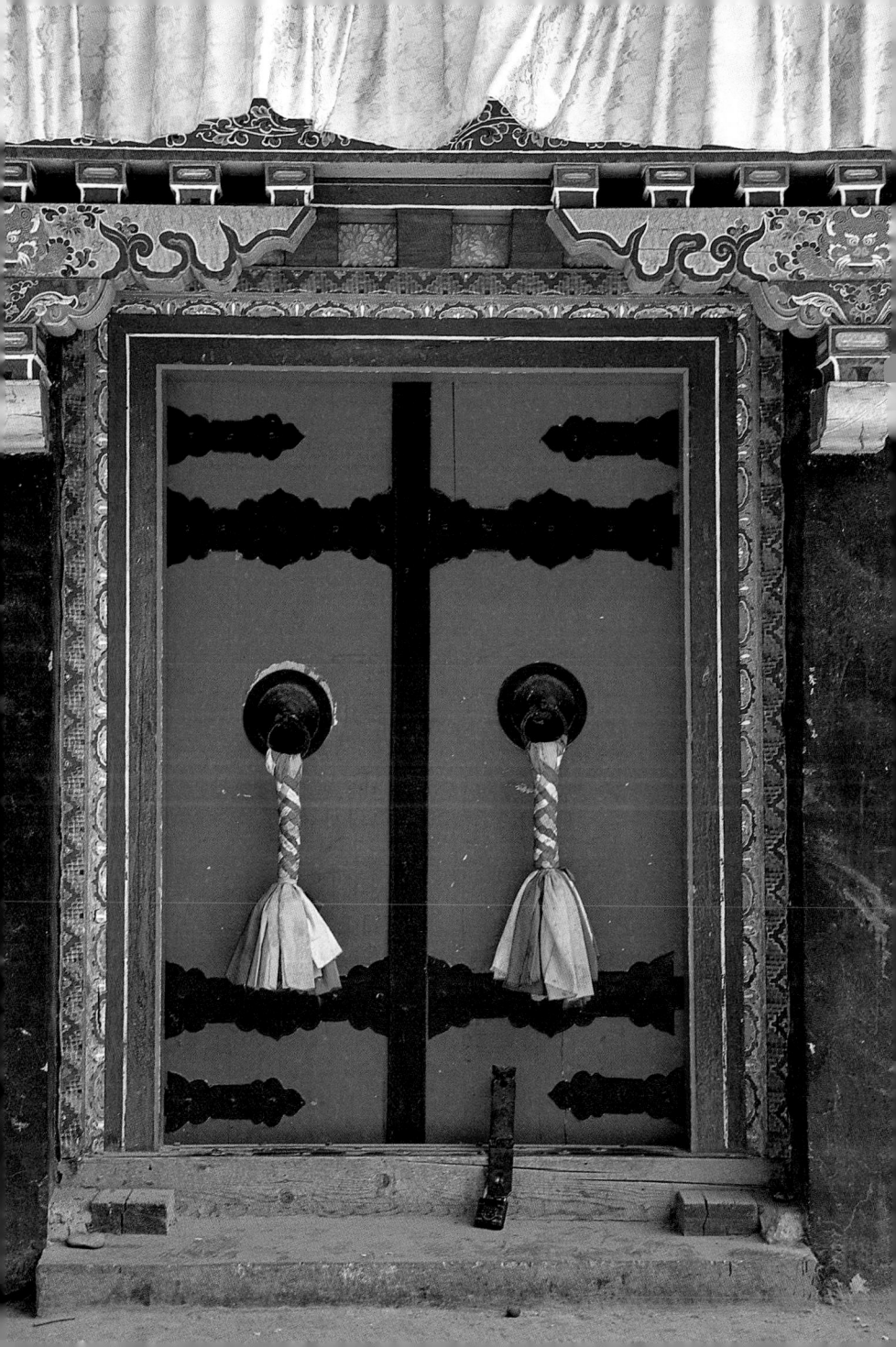

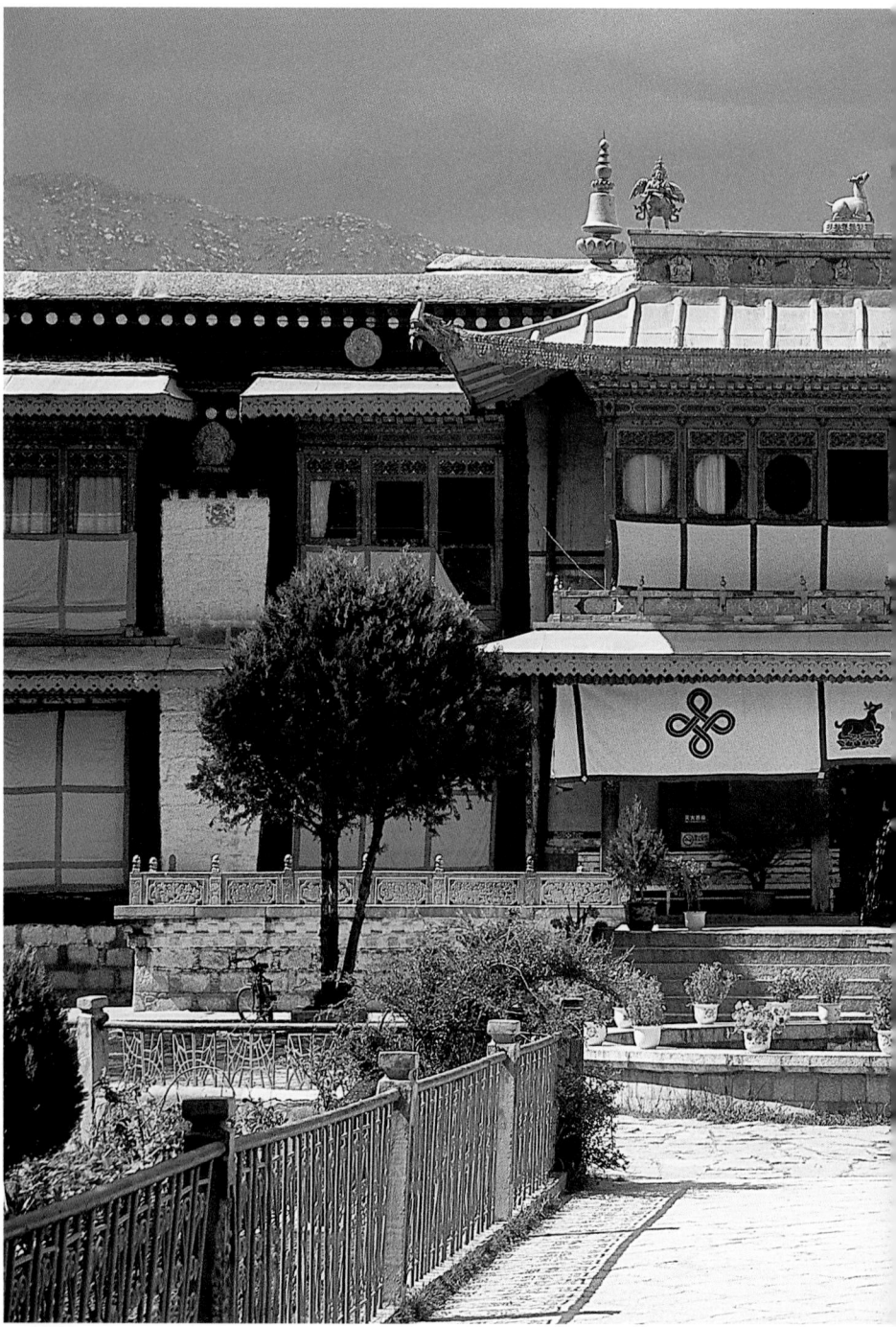

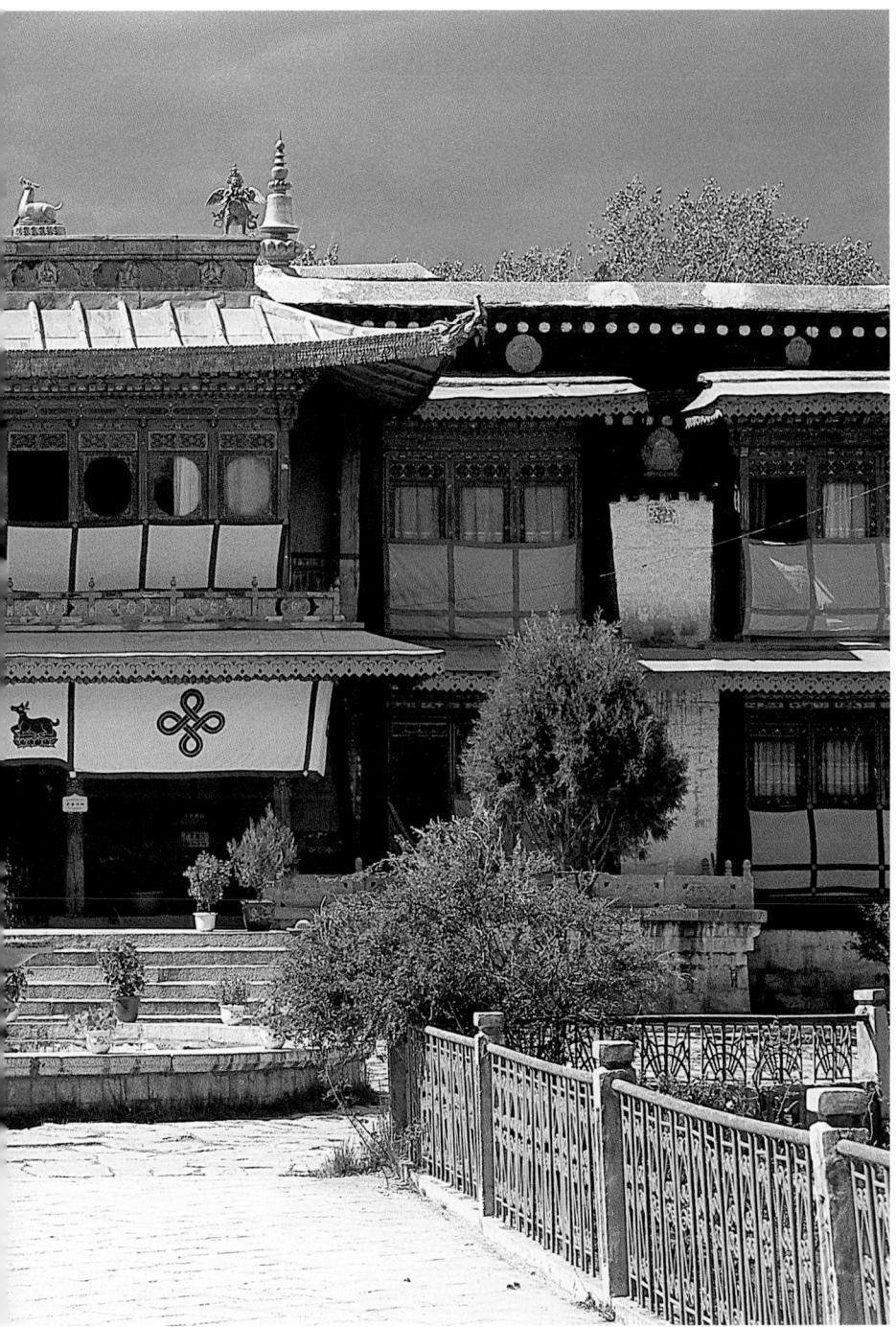

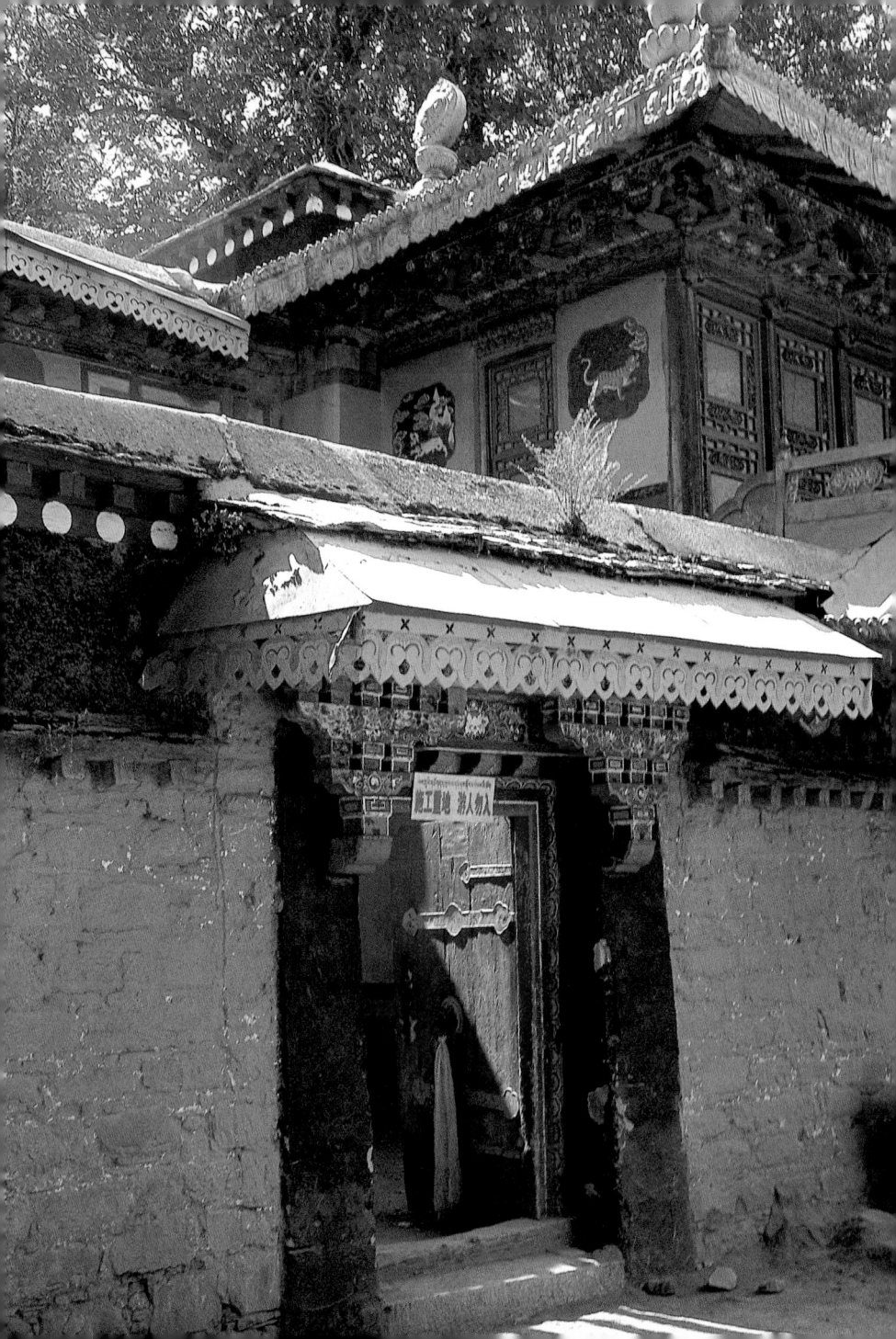

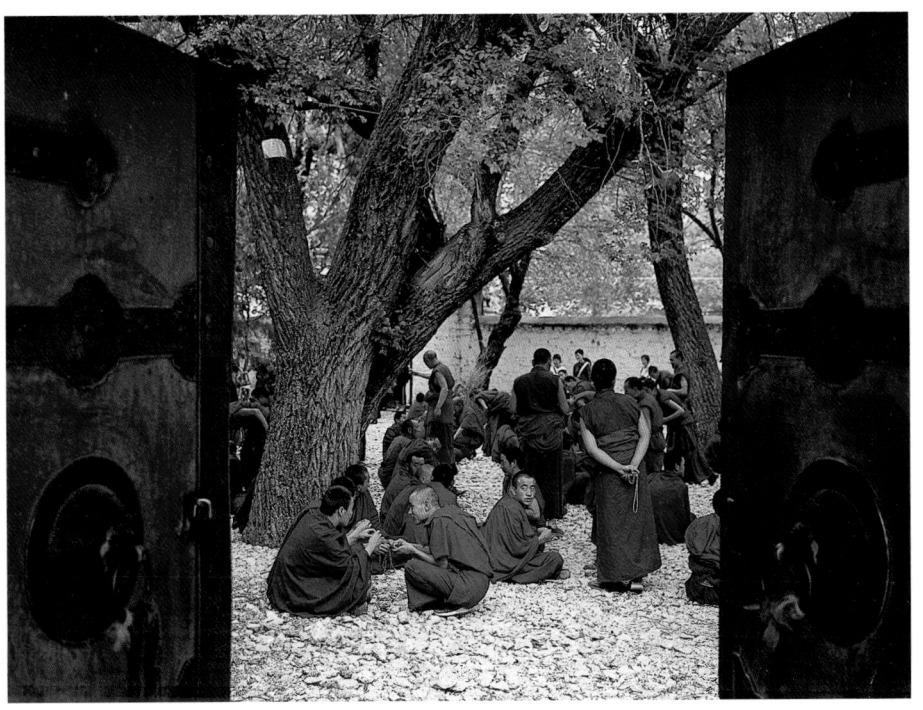

PP. 24–25 and P. 26 Entrance and front view of Norbulingka, the summer palace, built by the seventh Dalai Lama in 1755. Norbulingka means "Jewel Park" and lies two miles west of the Potala Palace. One of Lhasa's great pageants was the annual move of the Dalai Lama from the Potala to Norbulingka each spring. It was from here that the Dalai Lama fled to India disguised as a soldier in March 1959. • Eingang und Fassade des Norbulingka, der Sommerresidenz, die 1755 unter dem 7. Dalai Lama erbaut wurde. Norbulingka bedeutet „Juwelengarten" und liegt etwa drei Kilometer westlich des Potala. Der jährliche Umzug des Dalai Lama vom Potala zum Norbulingka

wurde in jedem Frühling feierlich begangen. Von hier aus floh der Dalai Lama im März 1959 als Soldat verkleidet nach Indien. • Entrée et façade du Norbulingka, le palais d'été, construit par le 7e dalaï-lama en 1755. Le Norbulingka, dit « Parc du joyau précieux », est situé à trois kilomètres à l'ouest du Potala. Tous les ans, au printemps, le déménagement du dalaï-lama pour le Norbulingka était un spectacle fastueux. C'est de ce palais que, déguisé en soldat, le dalaï-lama s'est enfui en Inde en mars 1959.

↑ Entrance to the Sera monastery, established in 1419, on the northern edge of Lhasa. • Der Eingang zum Kloster Sera, 1419 am nördlichen Rand

von Lhasa gegründet. • L'entrée du monastère de Sera, fondé en 1419, à la lisière septentrionale de Lhassa.

PP. 28–29 Novice monks in Sera monastery's famous Debating Garden prepare for monastic examinations by staging mock debates. • Die Novizen bereiten sich im berühmten Disputationshof des Klosters Sera auf die Ordensprüfungen vor, indem sie die Debatten miteinander proben. • Dans le célèbre jardin du monastère de Sera, des novices se préparent à des examens théologiques en simulant des débats dialectiques.

27

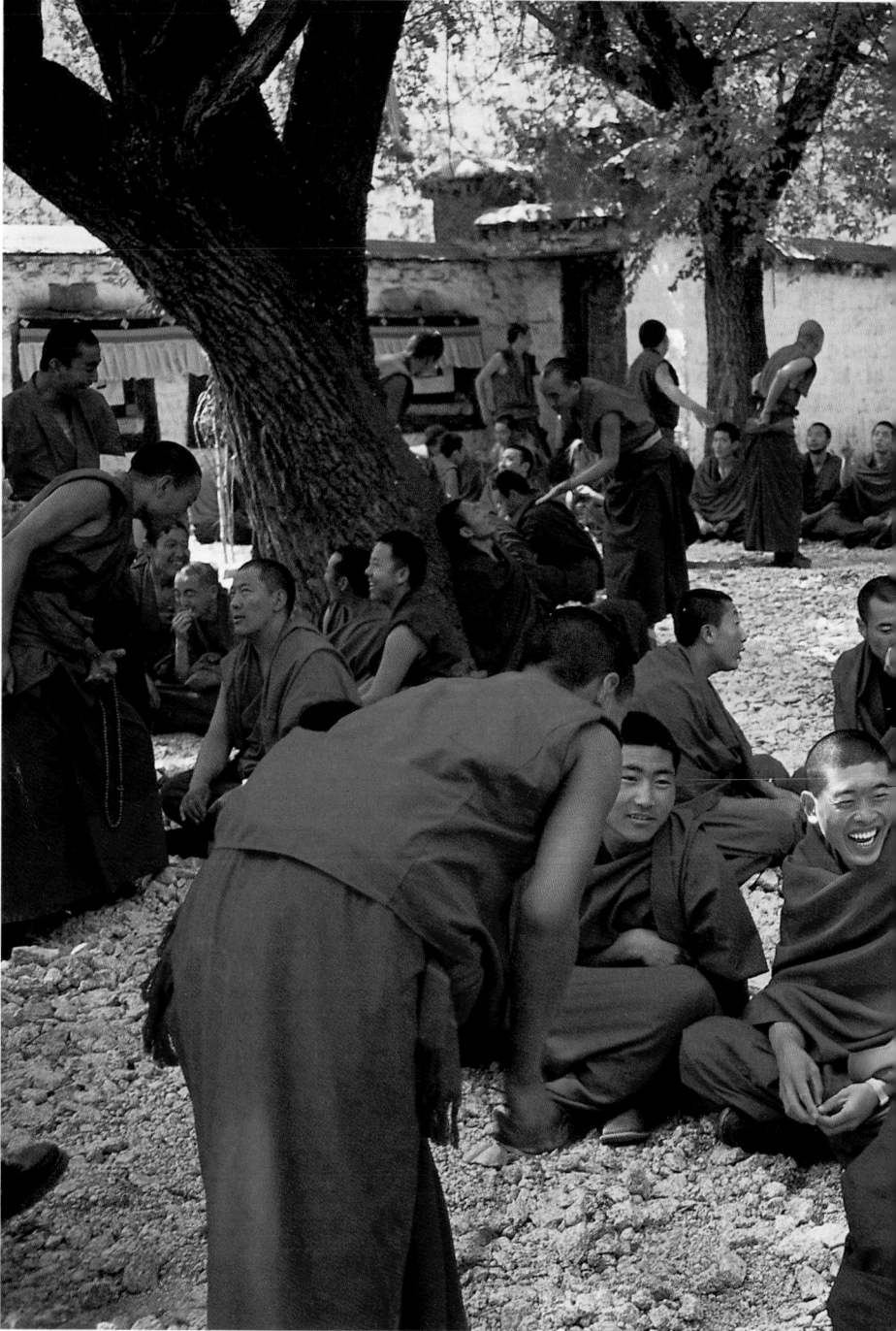

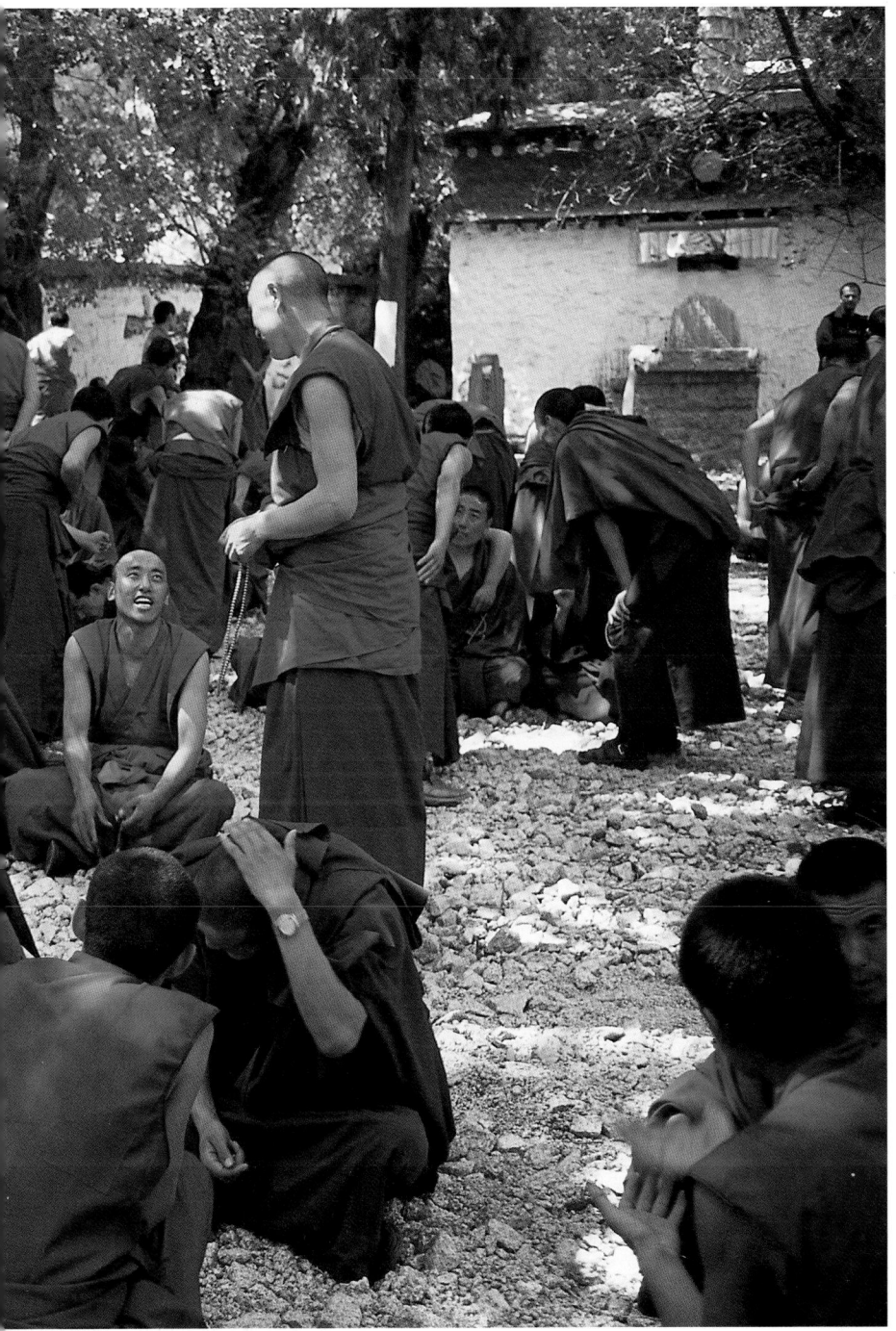

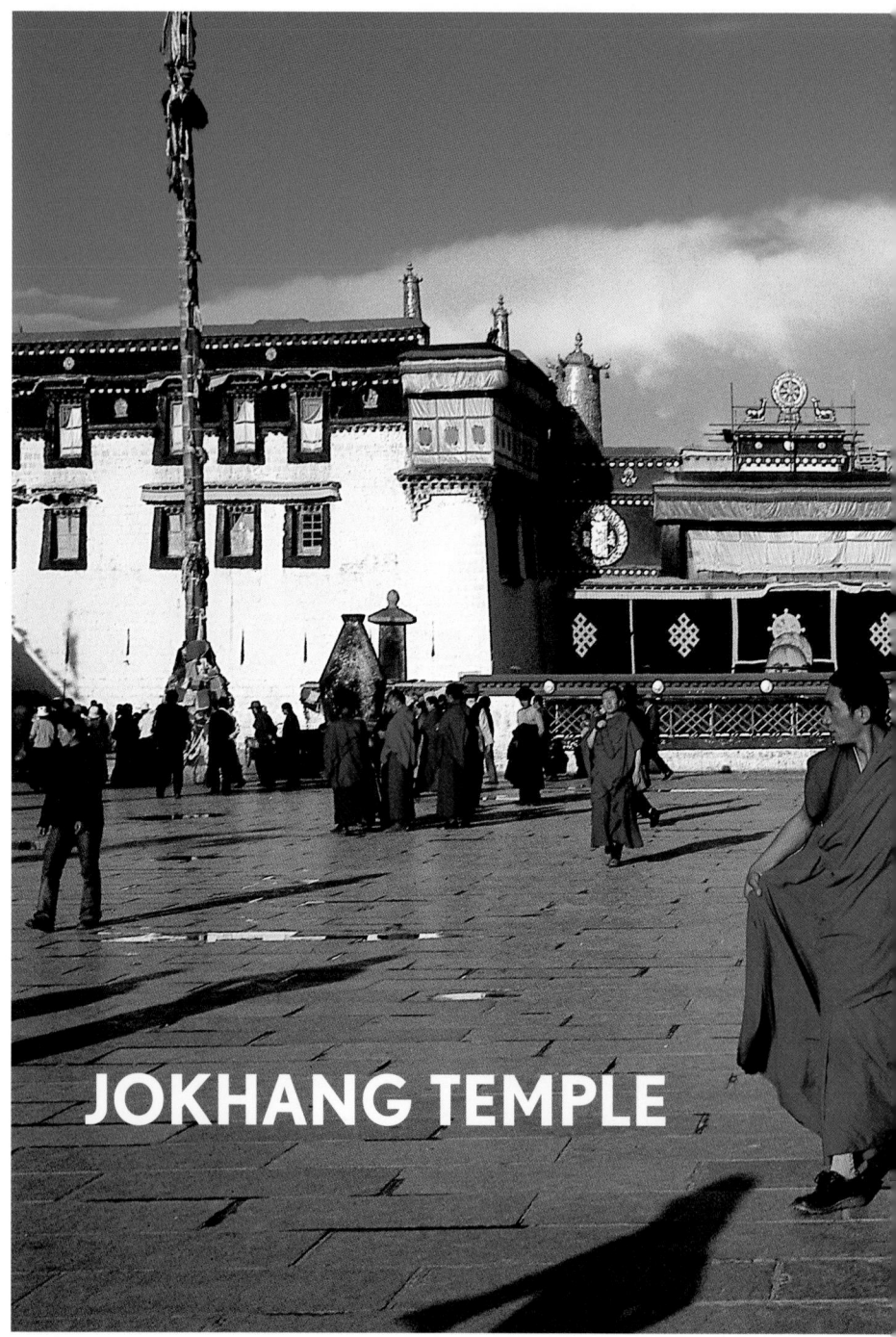

JOKHANG TEMPLE

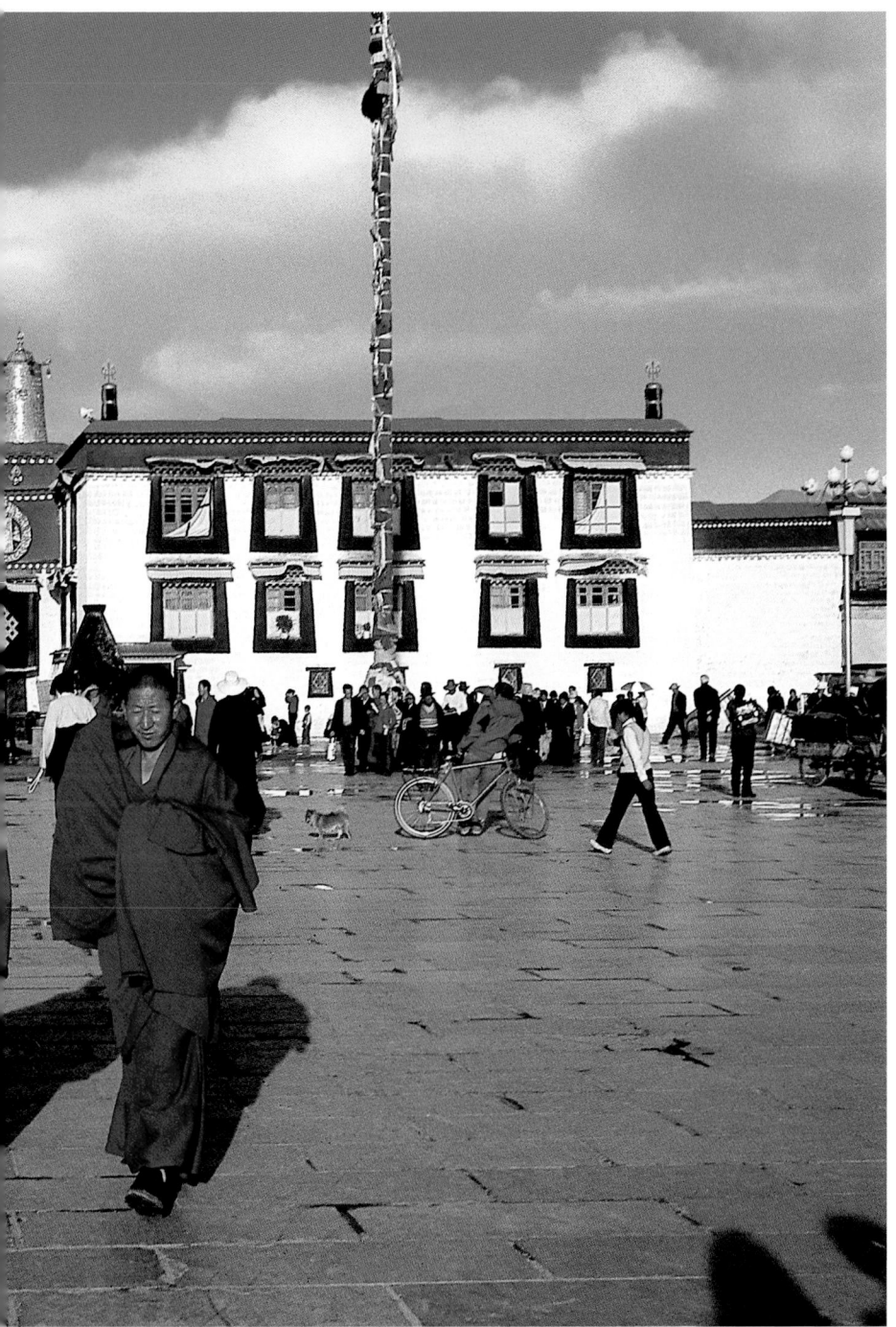

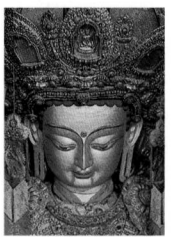

JOKHANG TEMPLE

LHASA
TIBET

Teeming with thousands of worshippers all day long, the continuous press of pilgrims prostrating themselves, lighting butter lamps in chapels, making circumambulatory trips or taking in the view from its gilded rooftops, the Jokhang is the sacred center of Tibet, its holiest of holies. The temple's origins date back to the capital which King Songtsen Gampo established at Lhasa in the seventh century. His two wives, a Chinese and a Nepali princess, are said to have brought images of the Buddha that converted the warrior king and introduced Buddhism to Tibet. The Jokhang is believed to be built on geomantic power points that pin down a sprawling ogress. Its innermost shrine contains the statue of Sakyamuni, the historical Buddha, that came with the Chinese princess. Over the centuries the Jokhang has seen many changes, including much damage done during the Cultural Revolution. That has neither dimmed the fervor of devotees thronging from remote corners of Tibet, nor diluted the palimpsest of intense spirituality that pervades its lamp-lit interiors.

Im Jokhang, dem heiligen Herz und Nationalheiligtum der tibetischen Kultur, trifft der nie versiegende Strom der Pilger auf Tausende von Gläubigen. Die Besucher werfen sich demütig nieder, zünden Butterlampen an, wandeln auf Rundwegen oder bewundern die Aussicht von den vergoldeten Dächern. Der Tempel geht auf die Zeit zurück, als König Songtsen Gampo Lhasa im 7. Jahrhundert zur Hauptstadt ausbaute. Der Legende nach brachten seine beiden Frauen, eine chinesische und eine nepalesische Prinzessin, Buddhafiguren nach Tibet mit, die den kriegerischen König zur inneren Umkehr und Einführung des Buddhismus veranlassten. Der Jokhang soll auf geomantischen Kraftfeldern über einer auf dem Rücken liegenden Riesin erbaut worden sein. Im Hauptheiligtum befindet sich das Standbild des Sakyamuni, des historischen Buddha, das die chinesische Prinzessin mitbrachte. Im Laufe der Jahrhunderte war der Jokhang vielen Veränderungen unterworfen und wurde während der Kulturrevolution schwer beschädigt. Dem Eifer der Gläubigen selbst aus den entlegensten Gegenden Tibets tat dies jedoch keinen Abbruch, und auch die tiefe Spriritualität der verräucherten, geheimnisvollen Innenräume blieb erhalten.

Du matin au soir, le temple du Jokhang accueille des milliers de fidèles et une foule de pèlerins qui se prosternent, allument des lampes à beurre dans des chapelles, font des circumambulations ou admirent les toits dorés. Le Jokhang est le centre sacré du Tibet, son saint des saints. Le temple remonte au 7e siècle, à l'époque où le roi Songtsen Gampo a fait de Lhassa sa capitale. Ses deux épouses, une princesse chinoise et une princesse népalaise, auraient apporté avec elles des représentations du Bouddha. Celles-ci ont amené le roi-guerrier à se convertir et à introduire le bouddhisme au Tibet. Selon une croyance, le Jokhang aurait été bâti sur des points de géomancie clouant au sol une démone. Son sanctuaire intérieur recèle une statue de Sakyamuni, le Bouddha historique, apportée par la princesse chinoise. Au fil des siècles, le Jokhang a connu de nombreux changements, voire des dégradations pendant la Révolution culturelle. Cela n'a cependant jamais fait décliner la ferveur des fidèles qui arrivent en foule des profondeurs du Tibet, ni estompé la spiritualité intense dont sont empreints ses espaces intérieurs brumeux, mystérieux, éclairés à la lueur de lampes.

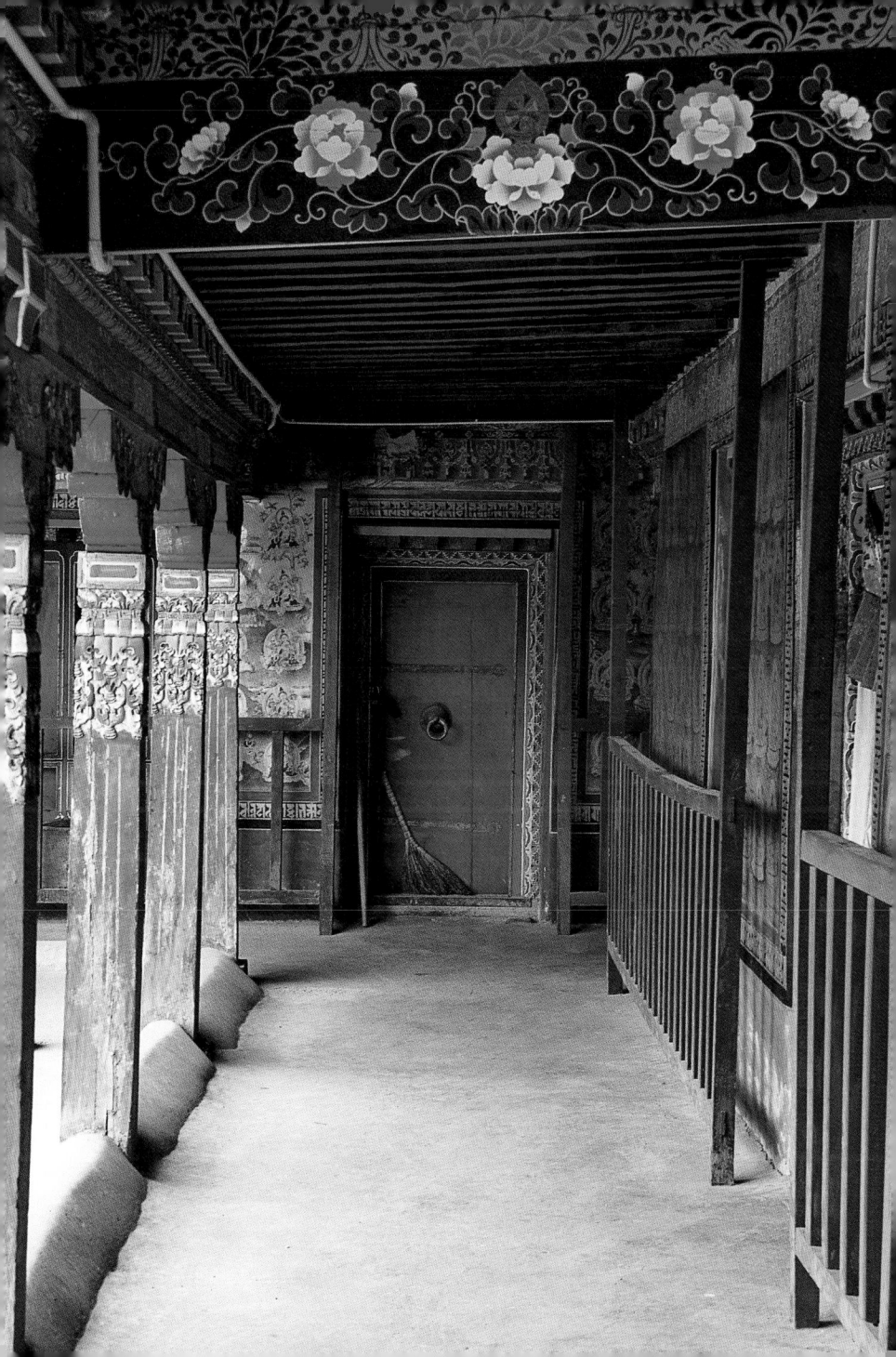

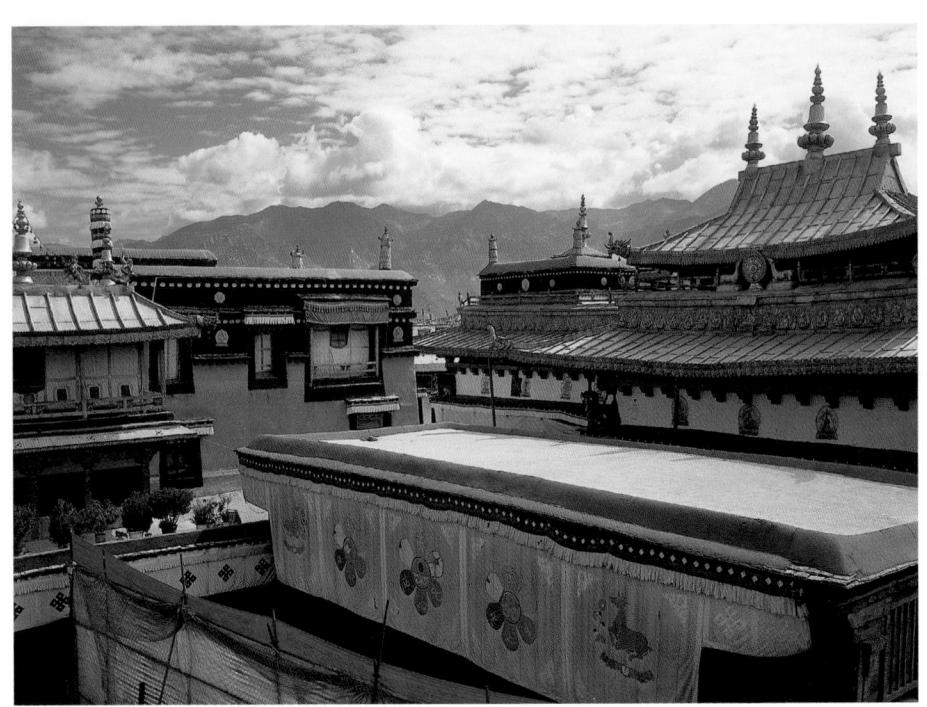

PP. 30–31 The front of the Jokhang
on Barkhor Square. · Die Fassade des
Jokhang am Barkhor-Platz. · La façade
du Jokhang donnant sur la place du
Barkhor.

↑ The Jokhang's rooftops of hand-
beaten copper are gilded with gold. ·

Die Dächer des Jokhang sind aus hand-
gehämmertem vergoldetem Kupfer. ·
Les toits du Jokhang sont en cuivre
martelé à la main et doré.

↗ → Intricately modelled and gilded
finials, images of guardian deities and
sacred symbols decorate three levels of

Jokhang's roofs. · Prachtvoll geformte
Spitzen, Figuren von Schutzgottheiten
und heilige Symbole zieren die Dächer
des Jokhang auf drei Ebenen. · Des
épis de faîtage dorés très travaillés, des
représentations de divinités protectrices
et des symboles sacrés ornent les toi-
tures du Jokhang.

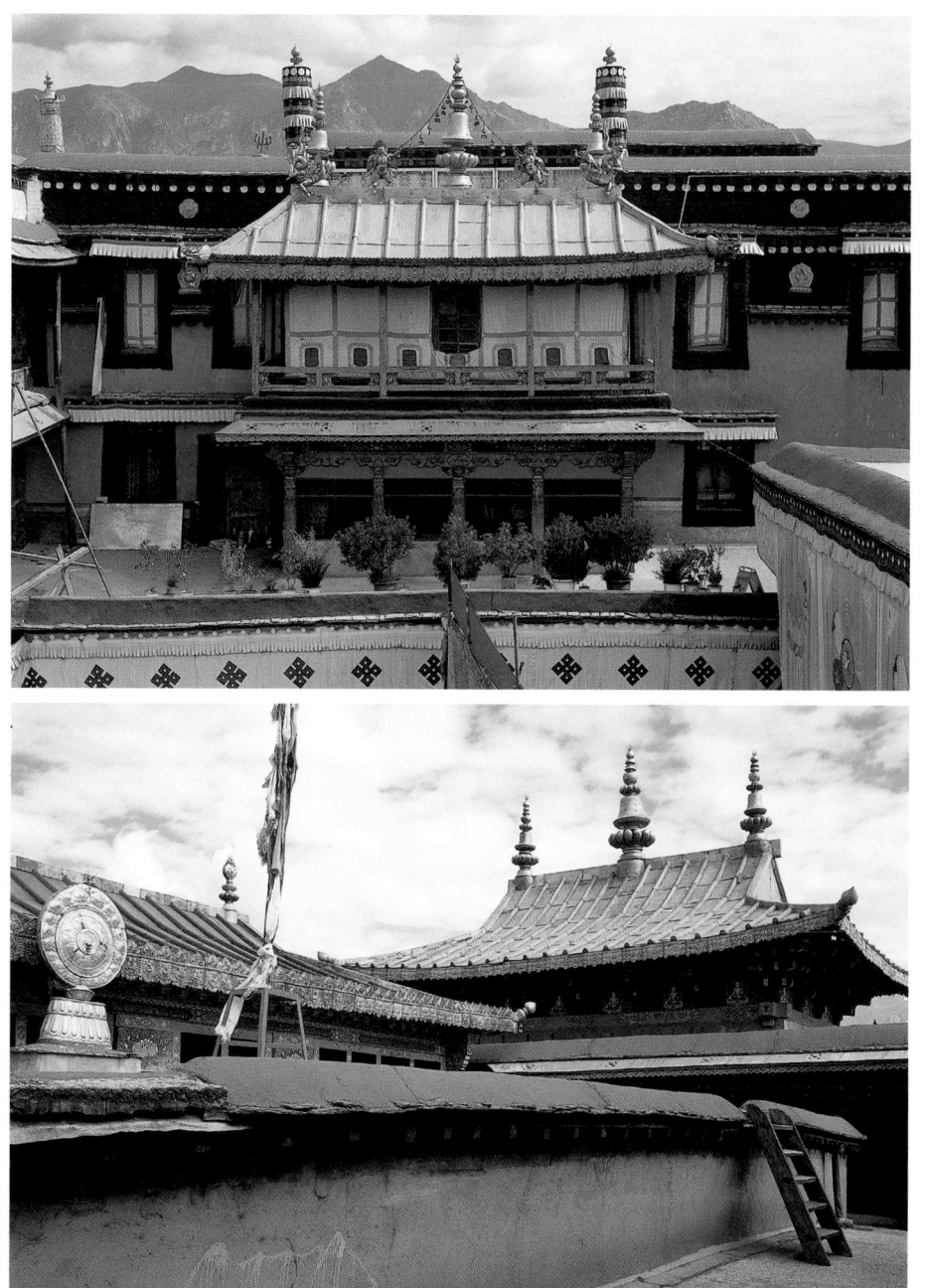

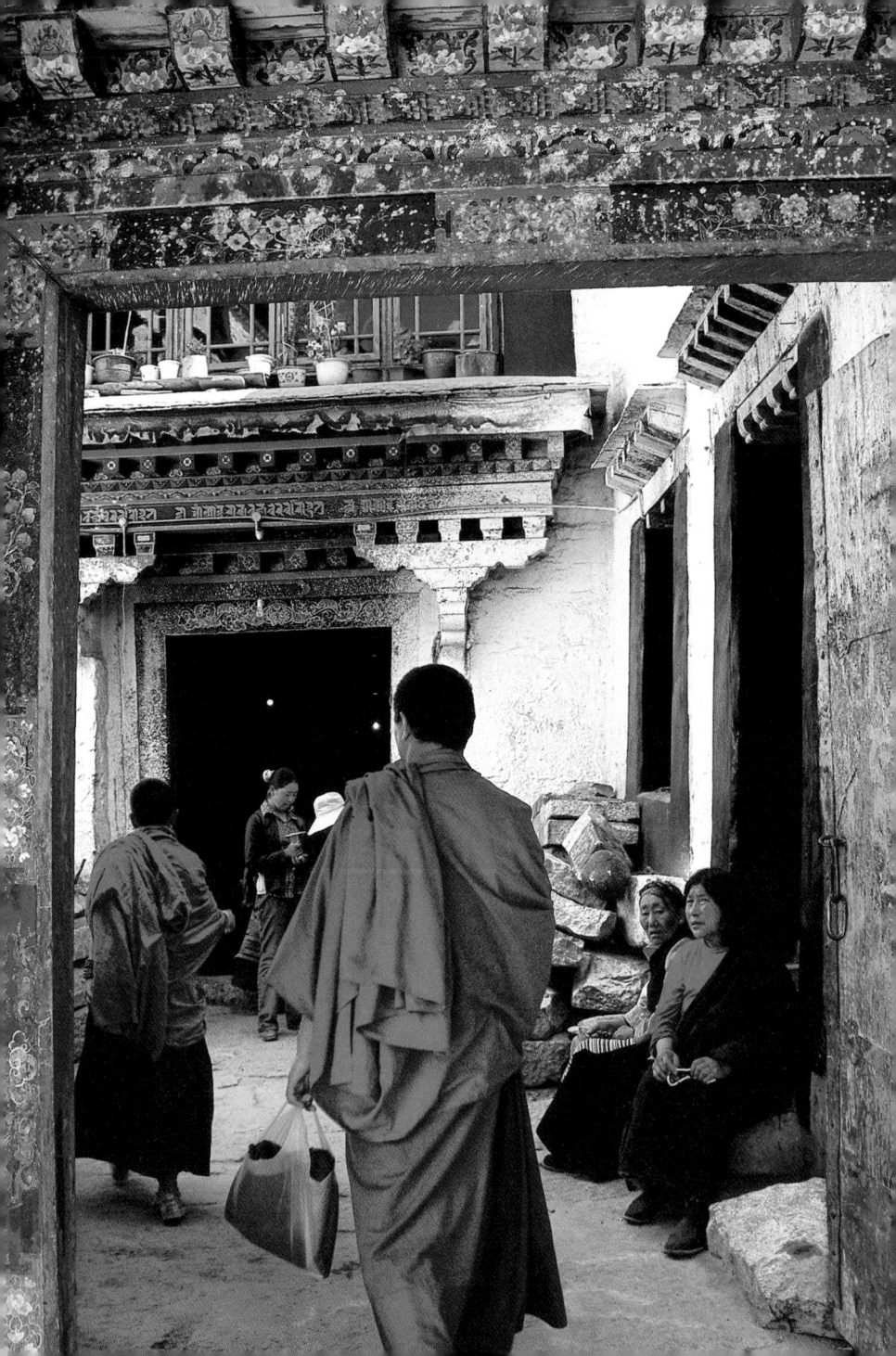

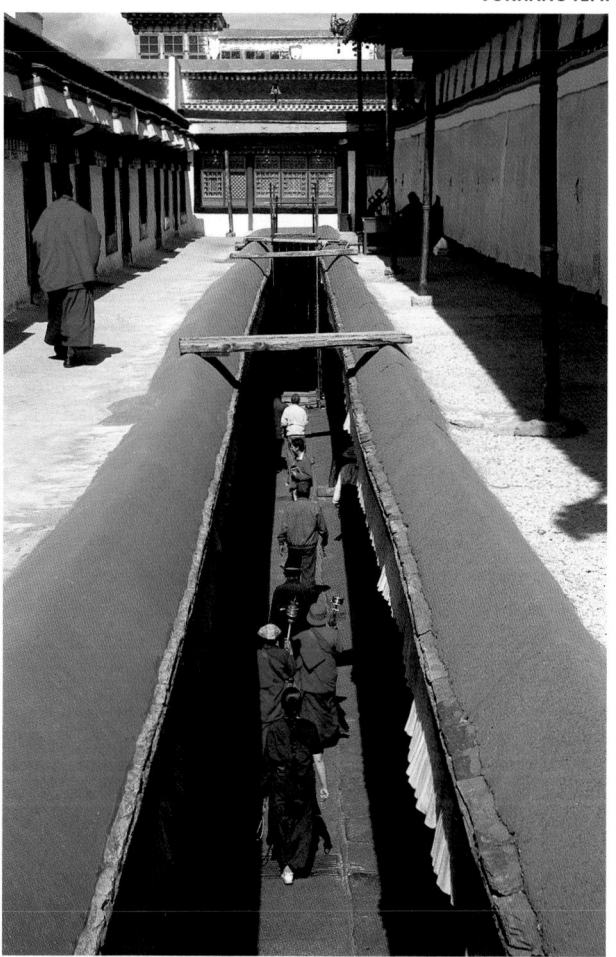

← Pilgrims enter the Jokhang through the southern entrance of the Barkor, the middle of the three ritual circuits that surround the temple and the city of Lhasa. • Die Pilger betreten den Jokhang vom Südeingang an der Barkhor-Straße, dem mittleren der drei rituellen Rundwege um den Tempel und die Stadt Lhasa. • Des pèlerins entrent dans le Jokhang par la porte sud du Barkhor, le parcours intermédiaire des trois circuits rituels entourant le temple et la ville de Lhassa.

↑ The inner passage, known as Nangkhor, goes round the heart of the Jokhang. Each circumambulation is made in a clockwise direction. • Der innere Gang, der Nangkhor, verläuft um das Heiligtum. Jeder Rundgang ist im Uhrzeigersinn zu begehen. • Le circuit intérieur, appelé Nangkor, cerne les chapelles intérieures du Jokhang. Les circumambulations s'effectuent dans le sens des aiguilles d'une montre.

P. 38 Detail of an inner sanctum door with bronze handles cast in the shape of gilded dragons. • Detail einer Tür

zum Hauptsanktuarium mit bronzenen Griffen in der Form vergoldeter Drachen. • La porte du sanctuaire intérieur est pourvue de poignées en bronze doré en forme de dragon.

P. 39 A gold idol of Maitreya, the future Buddha, richly adorned with jewels and silks. • Ein goldenes, prunkvoll mit Edelsteinen und Seide geschmücktes Abbild des in Zukunft erscheinenden Buddha Maitreya. • Une statue dorée de Maitreya, le Bouddha des temps futurs, parée de bijoux et de soieries.

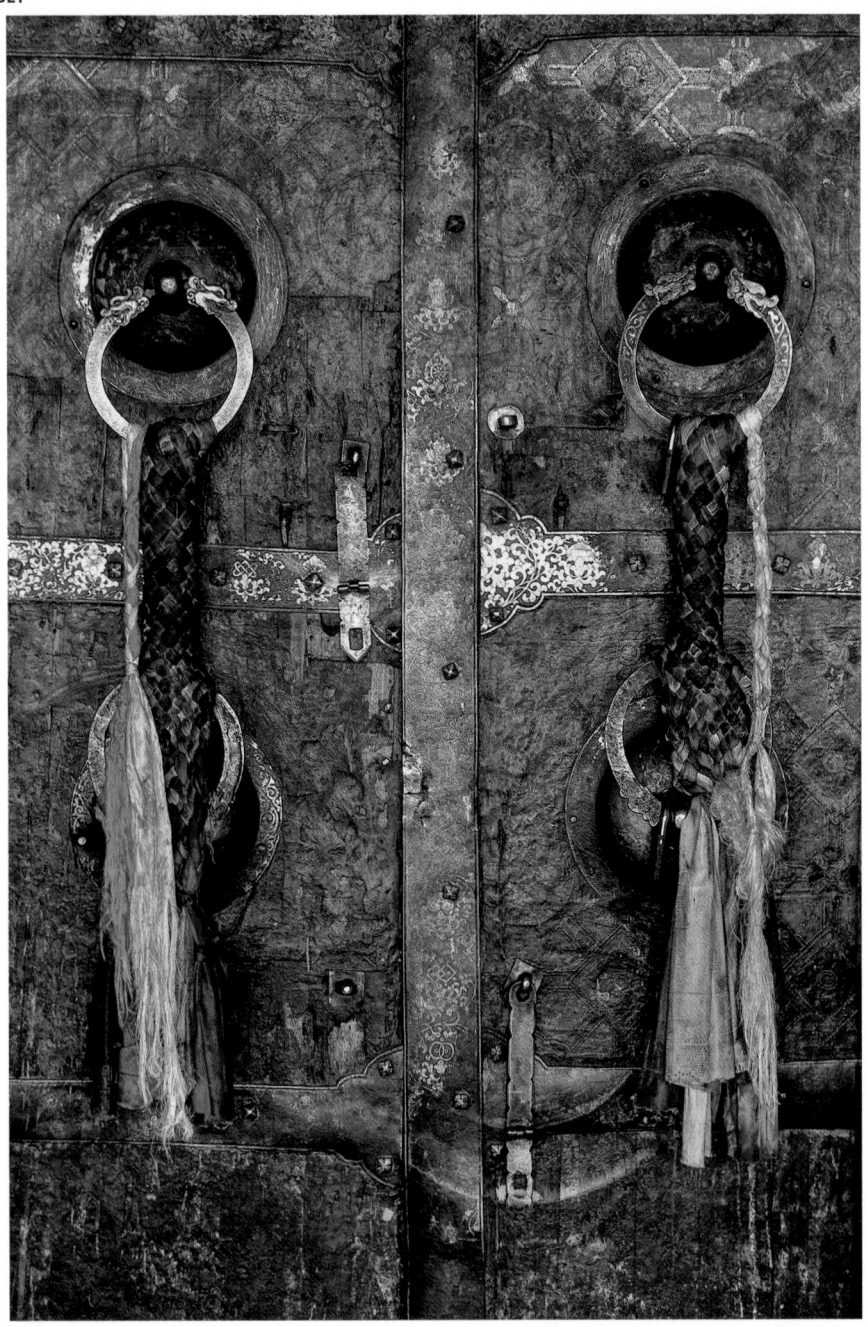

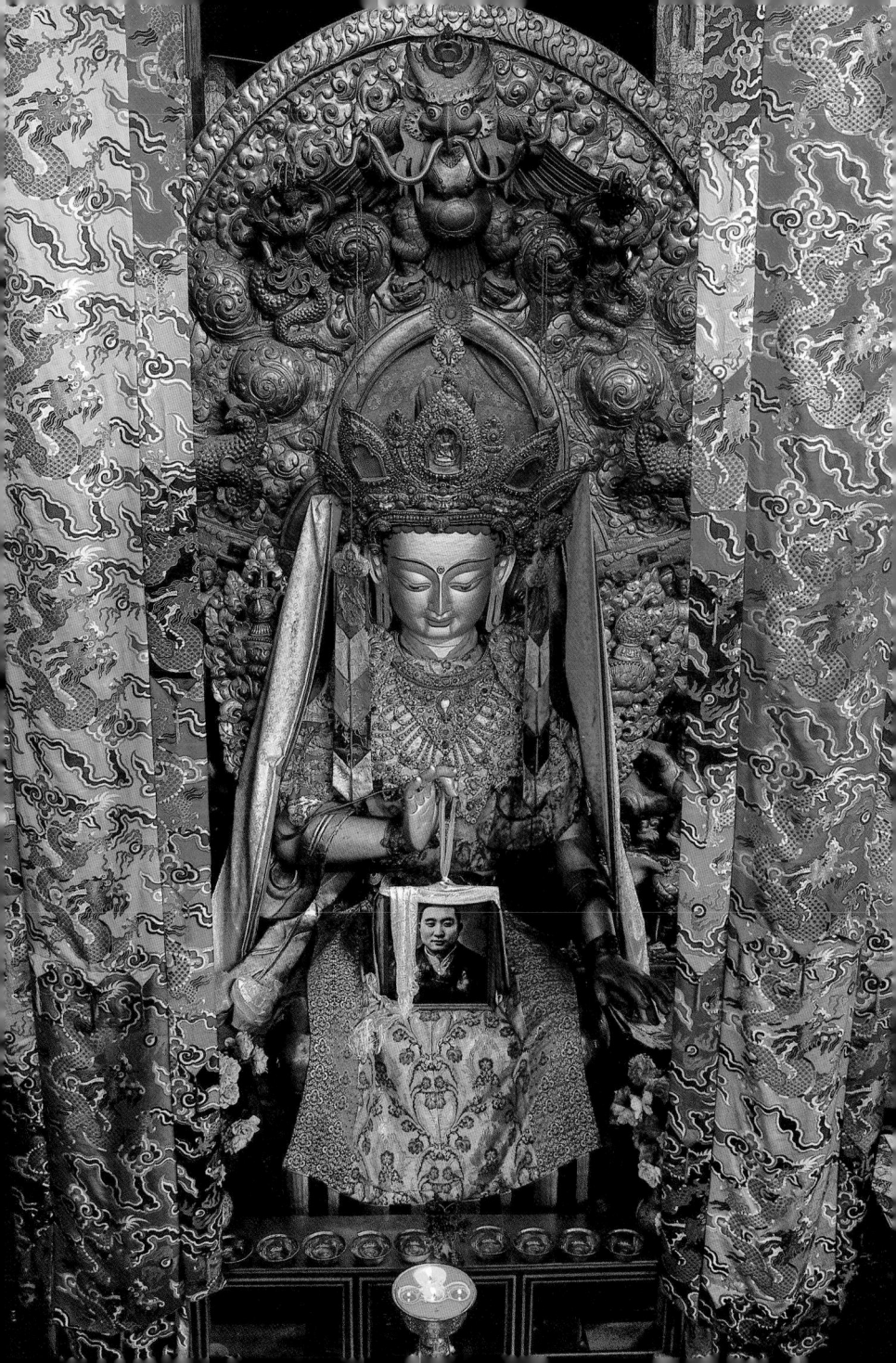

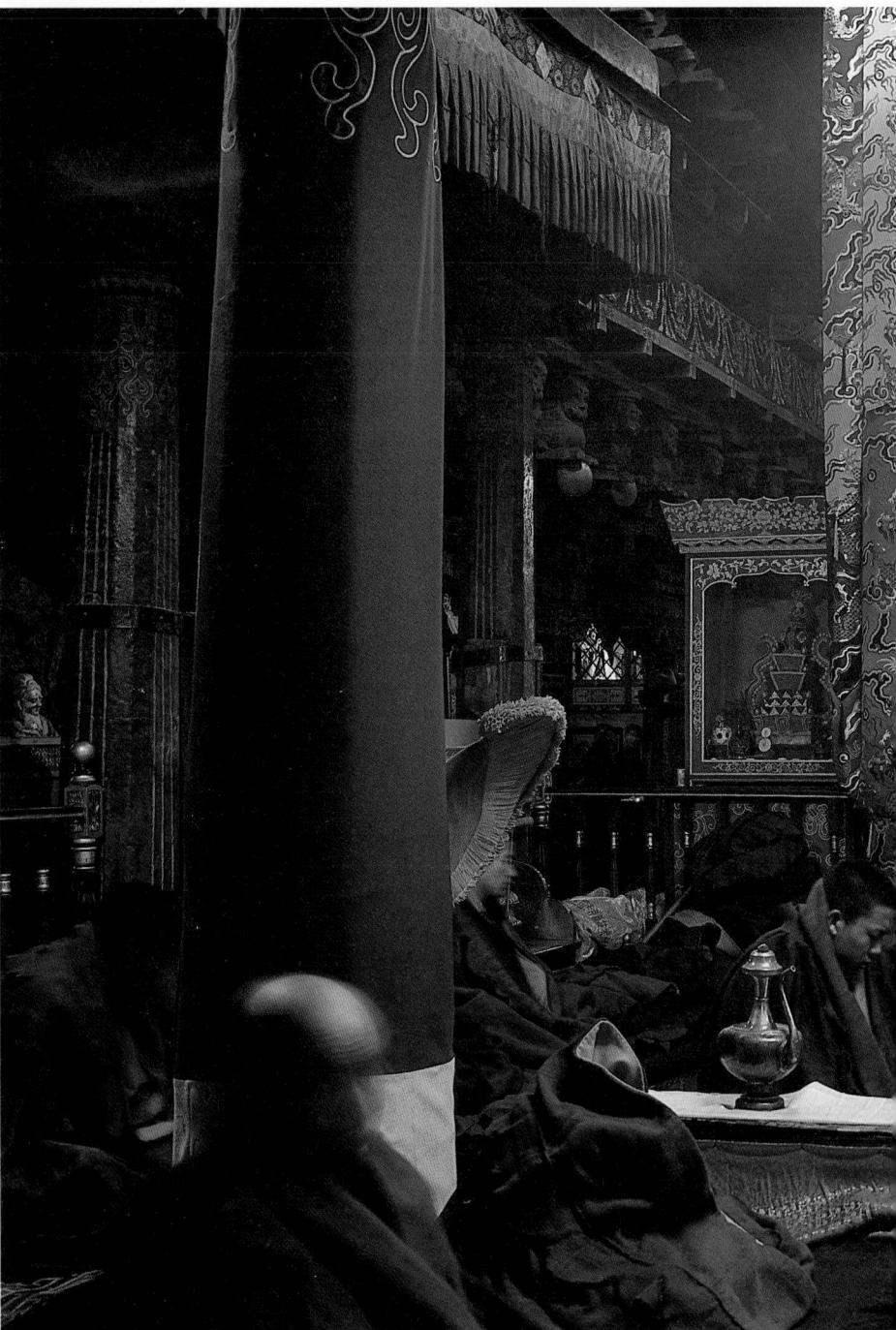

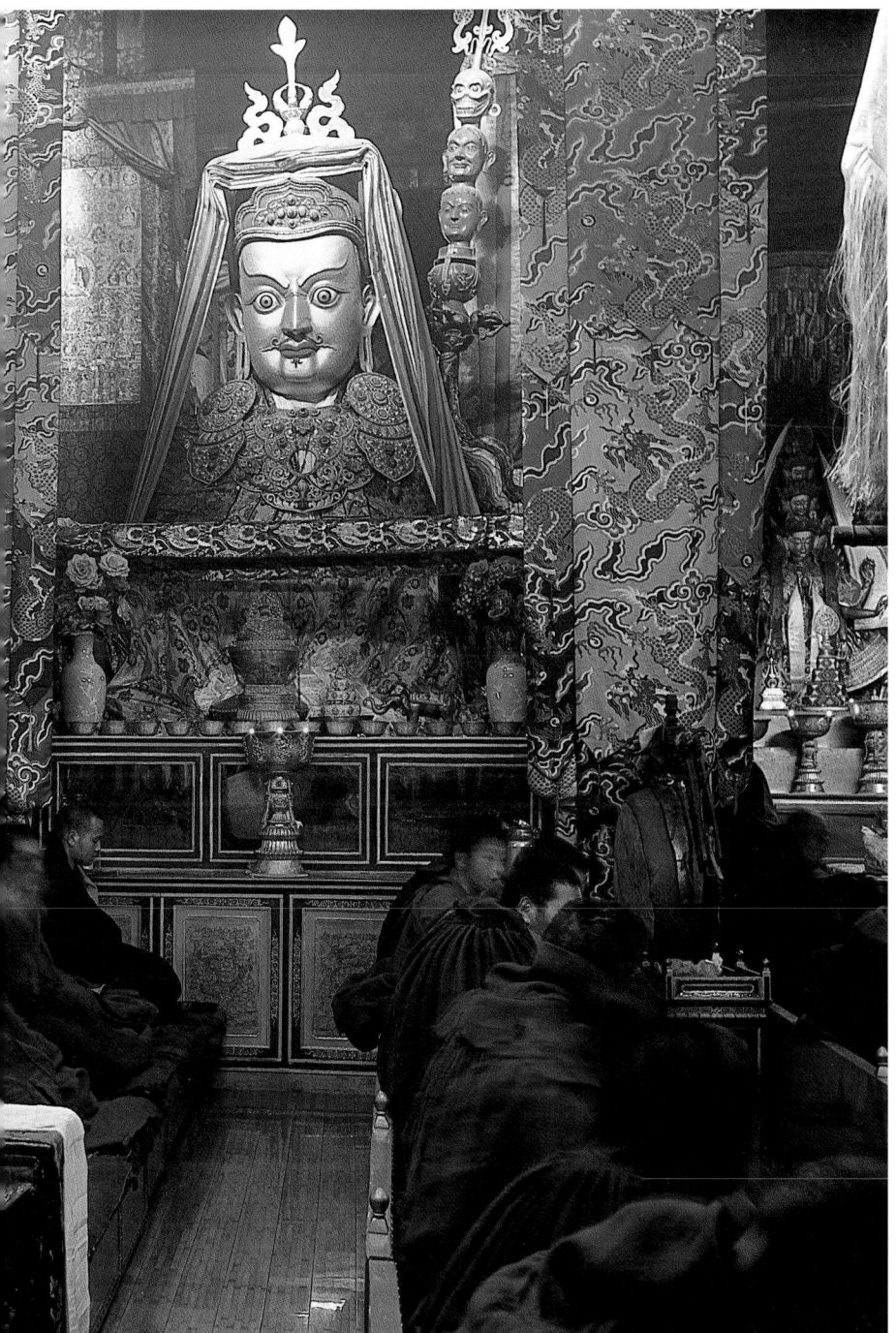

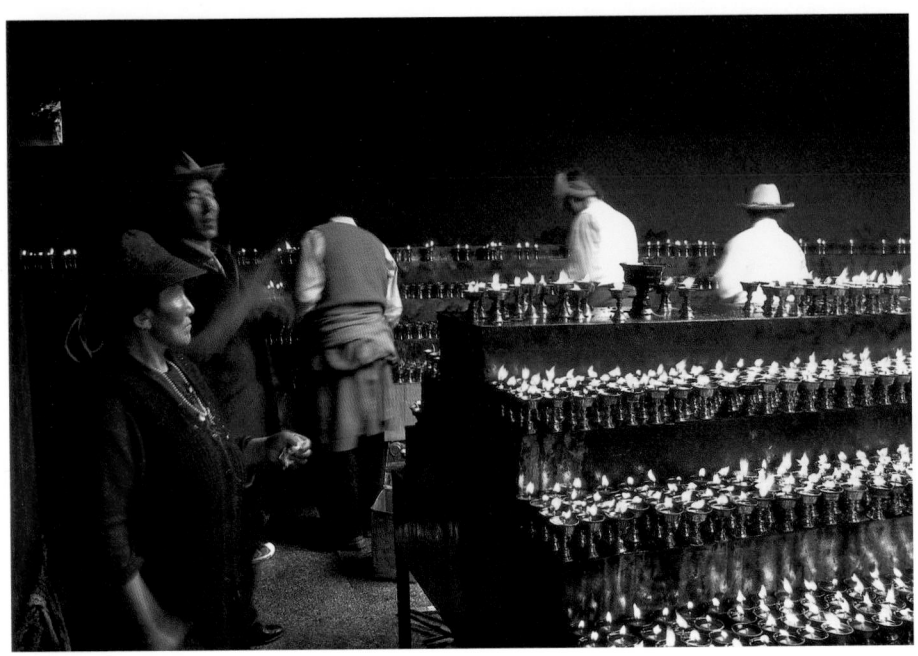

PP. 40–41 Monks at prayer before a jeweled golden idol of Padmasambhava, also known as Guru Rinpoche, the eighth-century adept from the Indian subcontinent who helped to establish Buddhism in Tibet. He is regarded as the second Buddha by the Nyingmapa school of Buddhism. • Mönche beten vor der prachtvoll mit Edelsteinen verzierten, goldenen Statue des Padmasambhava, der auch unter dem Namen Guru Rinpoche bekannt ist und im 8. Jahrhundert als Meister vom indischen Subkontinent dazu beitrug, den Buddhismus in Tibet zu begründen. Die Anhänger der buddhistischen Nyingmapa-Schule bezeichnen ihn als „Zweiten Buddha". • Des moines prient devant une statue dorée et parée de bijoux du Padmasambhava, aussi connu sous le nom de gourou Rinpoché. Ce fidèle originaire du sous-continent indien au 8ᵉ siècle a aidé le bouddhisme à prendre pied au Tibet. La tradition

Nyingmapa le considère comme le deuxième Bouddha.

↑ Pilgrims light oil lamps at a shrine facing the main entrance of the Jokhang on Barkhor Square. • Pilger entzünden Öllämpchen an einem Schrein am Haupteingang des Jokhang am Barkhor-Platz. • Des pèlerins allument des lampes à huile dans un sanctuaire situé face à l'entrée principale du Jokhang, sur la place du Barkhor.

→ They burn fragrant herbs in clay ovens on certain auspicious days in votive offering. • An bestimmten verheißungsvollen Tagen verbrennen sie als Votivgaben Duftkräuter in Lehmöfen. • Certains jours favorables, les pèlerins brûlent, pour témoigner leur reconnaissance, des herbes aromatiques dans des fours en argile.

PP. 44–45 Monks in the Jokhang's inner sanctum bundle currency notes left as offerings. Between the eaves and the colonnade is a row of sphinx-like snow lions, each carved with a human expression. These are thought to have been inspired by Persian images brought via Kashmir. • Die Mönche im Hauptsanktuarium des Jokhang bündeln die Geldscheine, die als Opfergaben gespendet wurden. Zwischen Dachtraufen und Säulengang befinden sich sphinxartige Schneelöwenköpfe mit menschlichem Gesichtsausdruck. Als Vorbild gelten persische Statuen, die über Kaschmir nach Tibet gelangten. • Dans le sanctuaire intérieur du Jokhang, des moines mettent en liasse des billets de banque donnés en offrande. Entre les avant-toits et la colonnade, des lions des neiges aux airs de sphinx surprennent par leur expression humaine. Ils seraient inspirés de miniatures persanes arrivées au Tibet par le Cachemire.

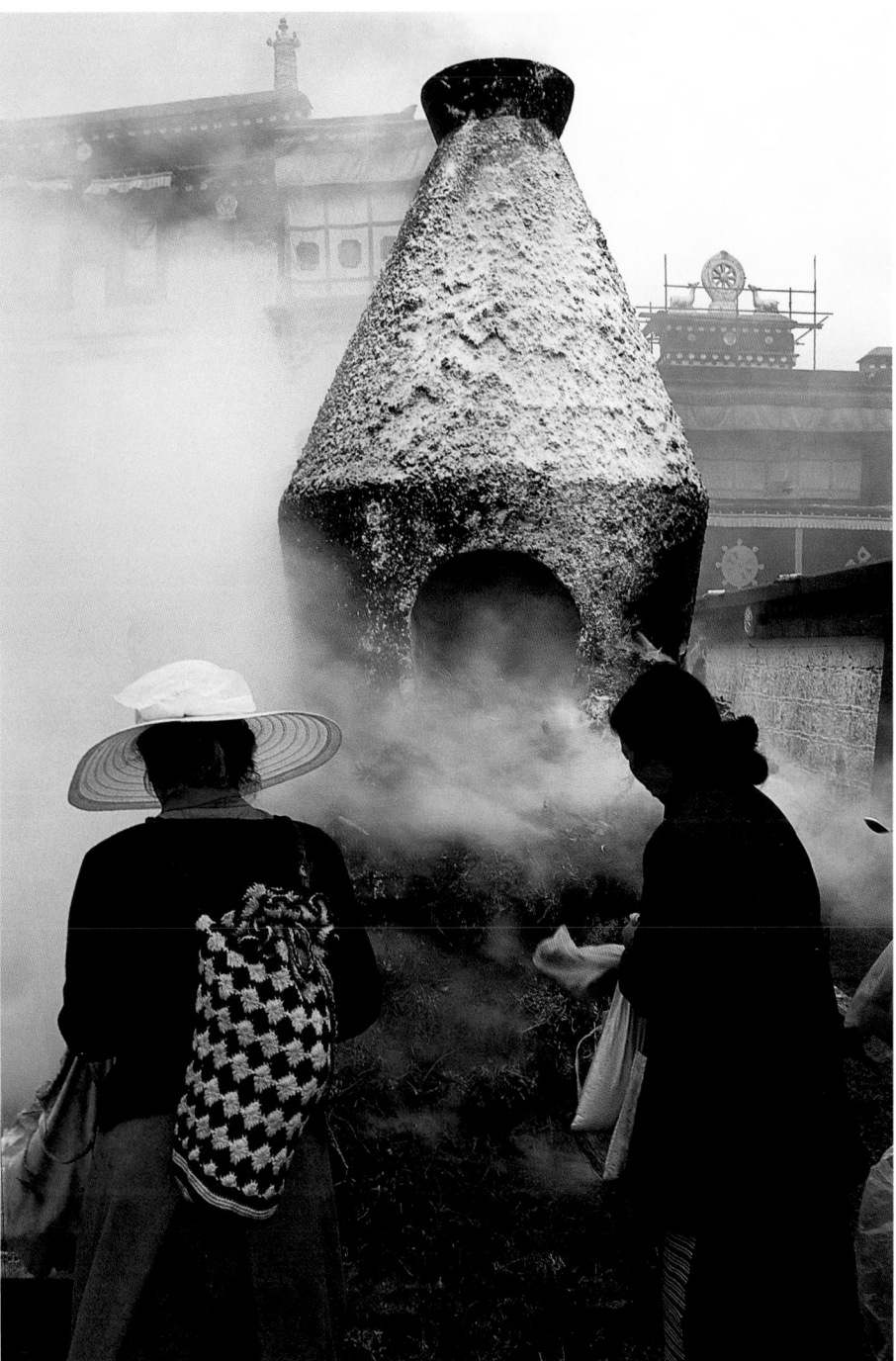

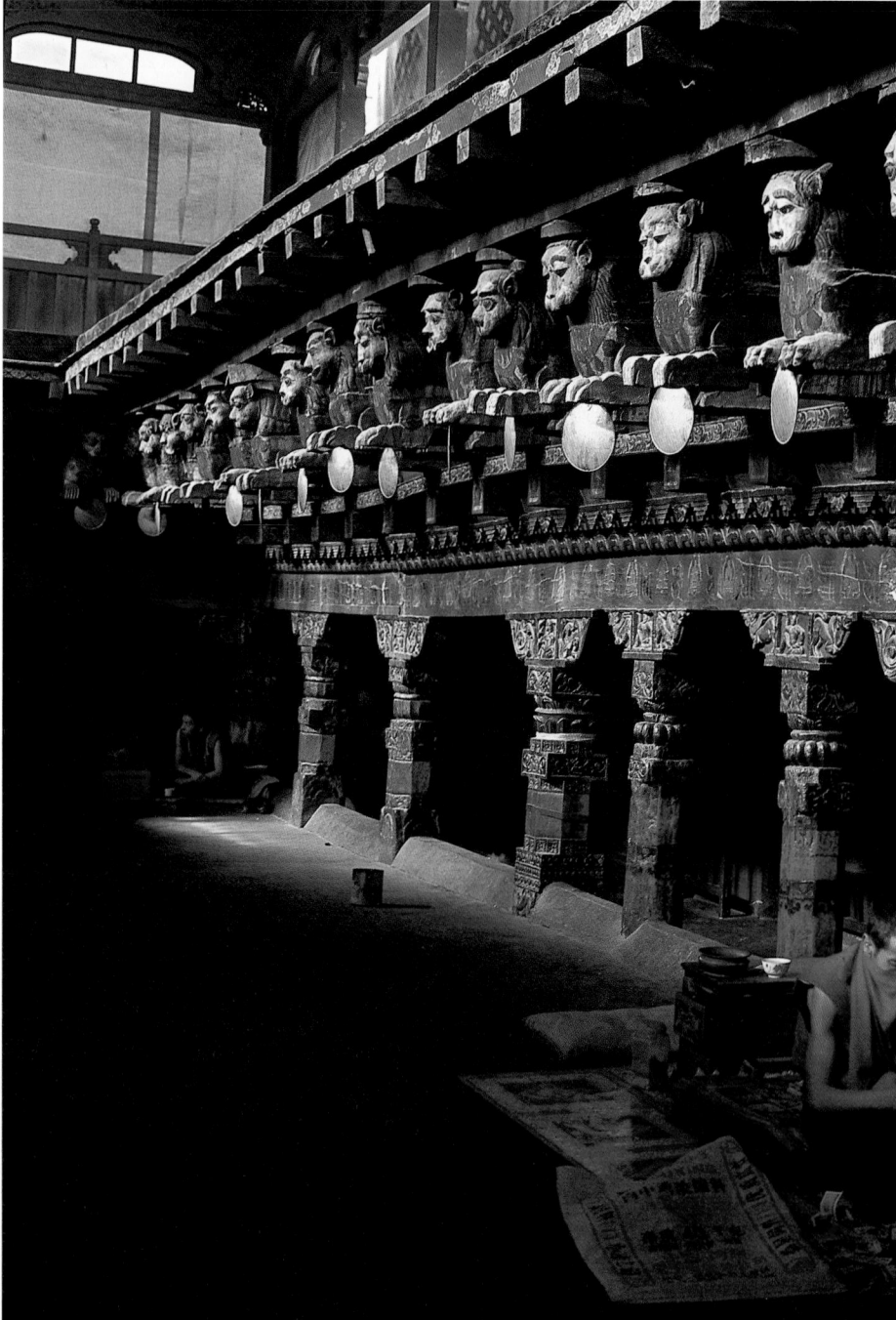

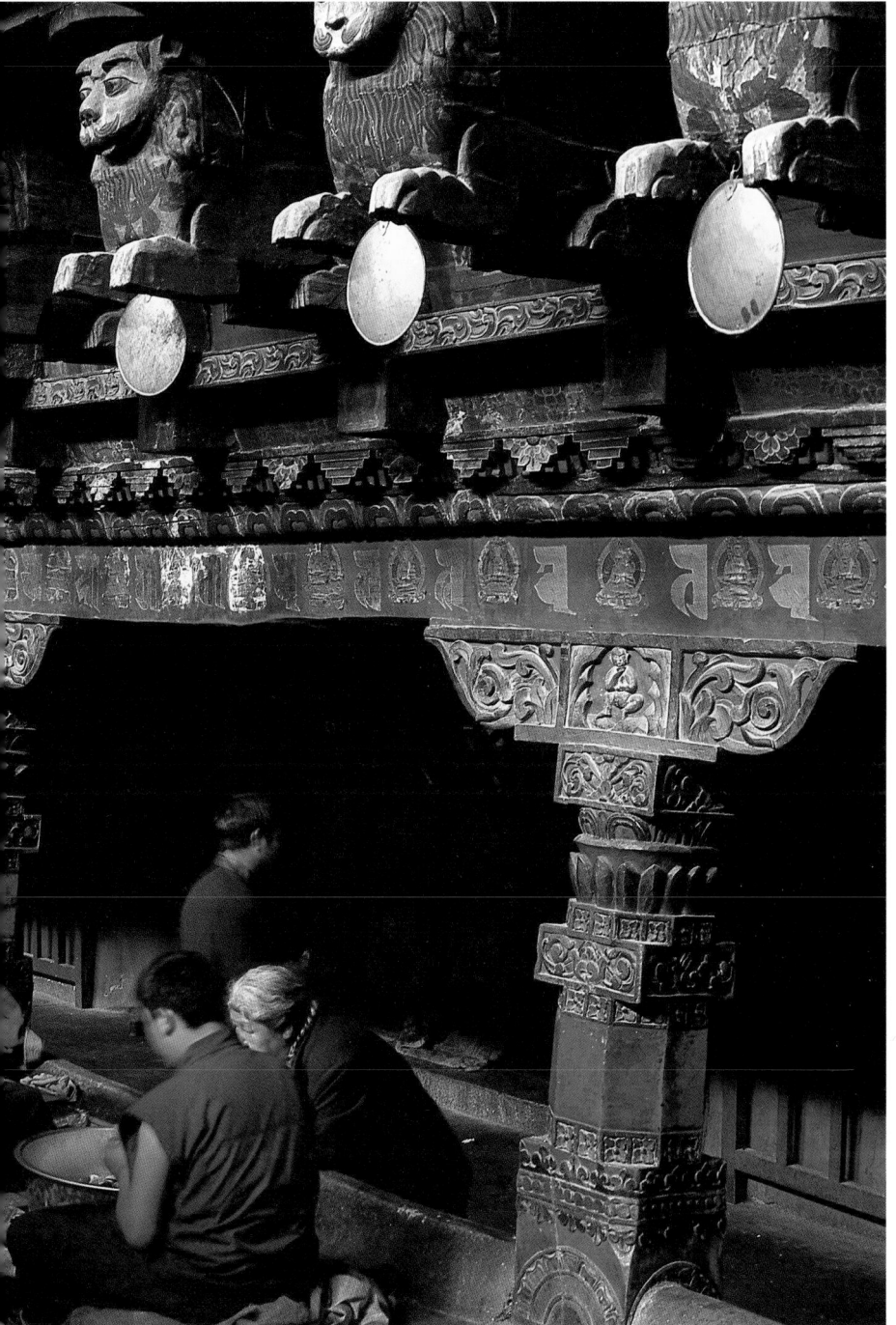

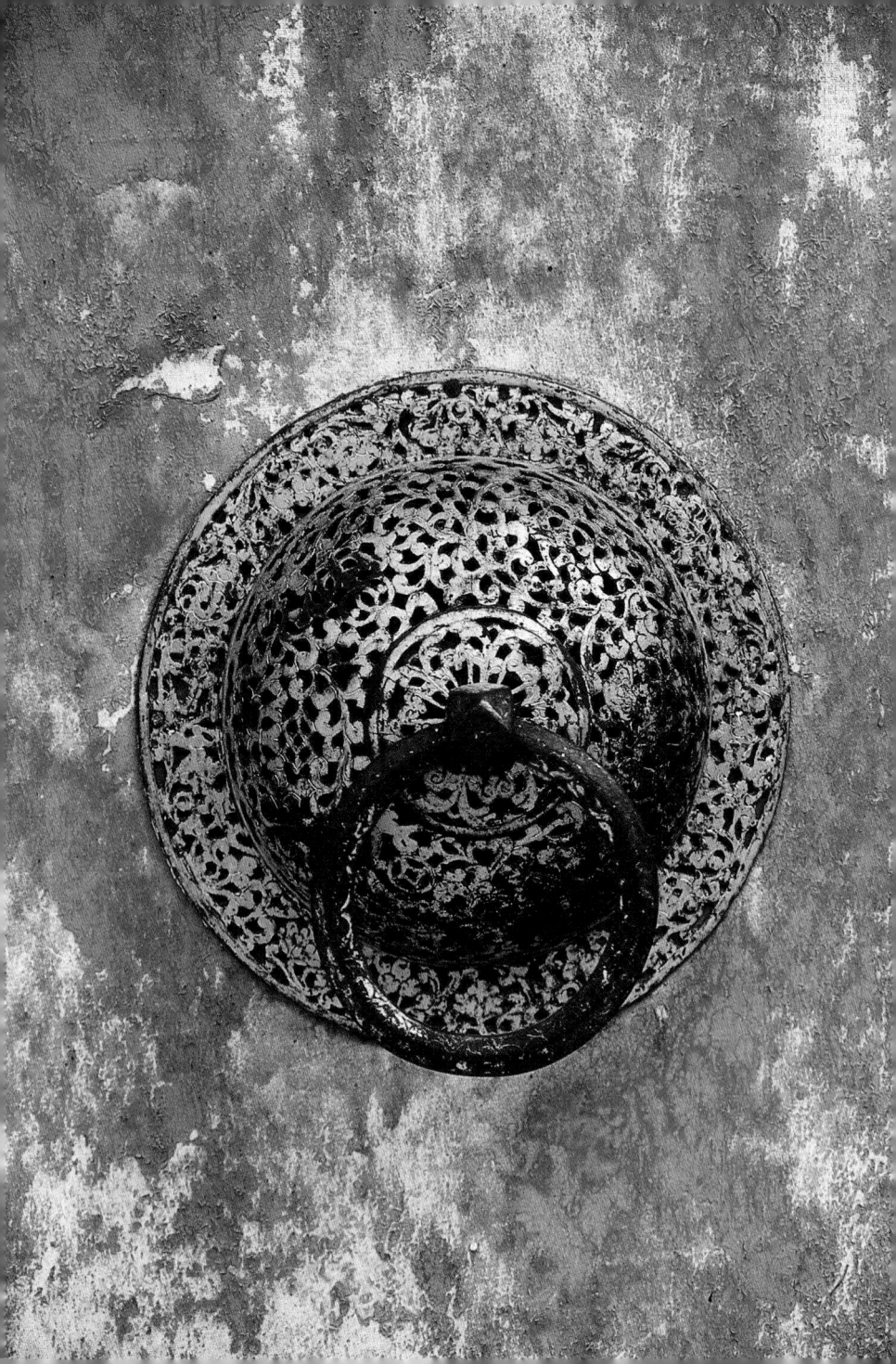

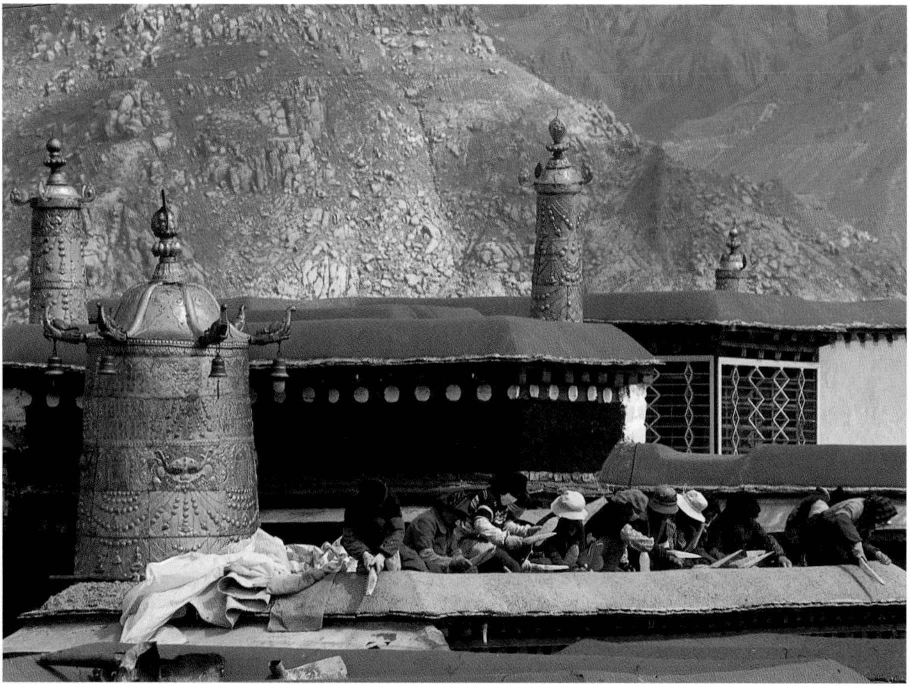

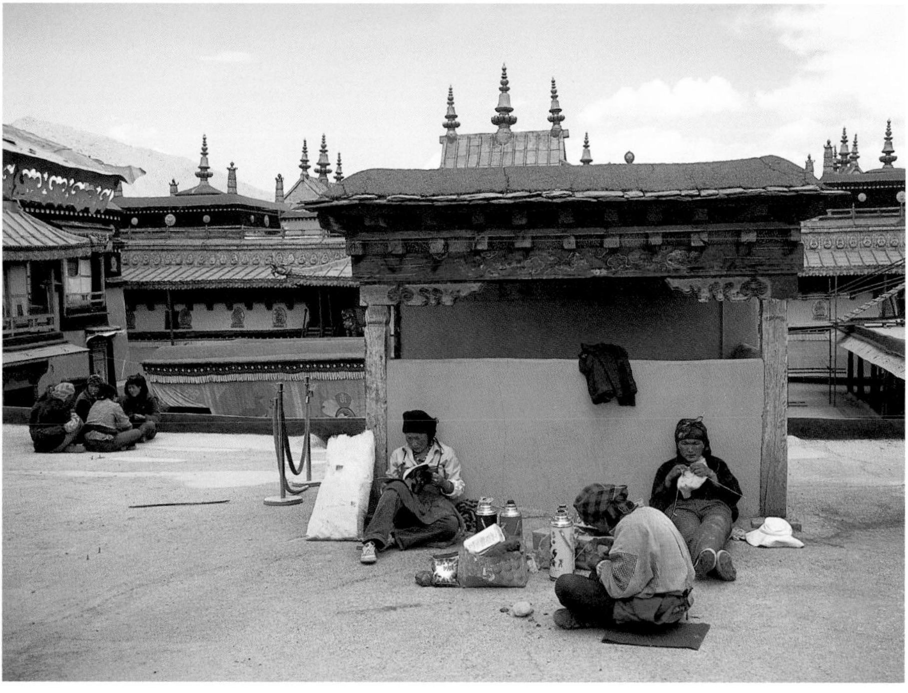

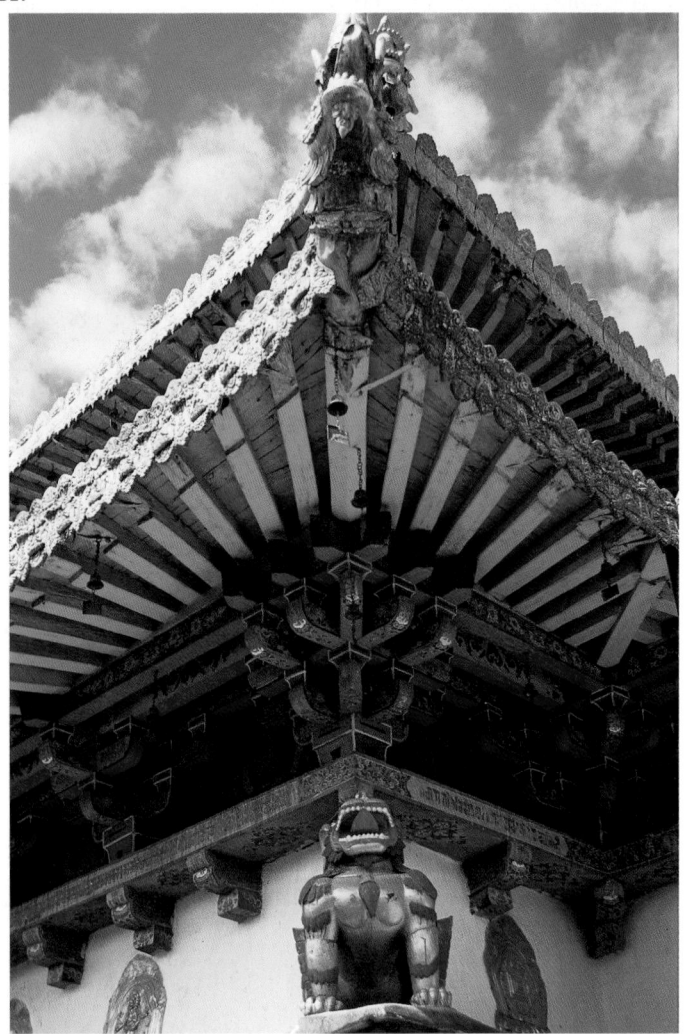

P. 47 Women workers repair the roof of the Jokhang and, later, take an afternoon break. The complex of rooftop pavilions contains monks' quarters and workshops. • Frauen reparieren das Dach des Jokhang, am Nachmittag machen sie eine Pause. In diesem Komplex von Dachpavillons liegen die Wohnräume und Werkstätten der Mönche. • Des ouvrières réparent le toit du Jokhang. On les voit plus tard

dans l'après-midi, à l'heure de la pause. Ce complexe de pavillons aux toits pittoresques abrite les cellules des moines et les ateliers.

↑ Elaborately carved eaves with interlocking wooden joints are typical of classical Tibetan architecture. • Fein geschnitzte Dachtraufen mit zusammengesteckten Holzfugen sind charakteristisch für die tibetische

Architektur. • Ces avant-toits délicatement sculptés constitués de solives entrecroisées sont typiques de l'architecture tibétaine classique.

→ Detail of a snow lion between the wooden brackets and eaves. • Detail eines Schneelöwen zwischen Konsolgebälk und Dachtraufen. • Un lion des neiges entre les consoles et les avant-toits (détail).

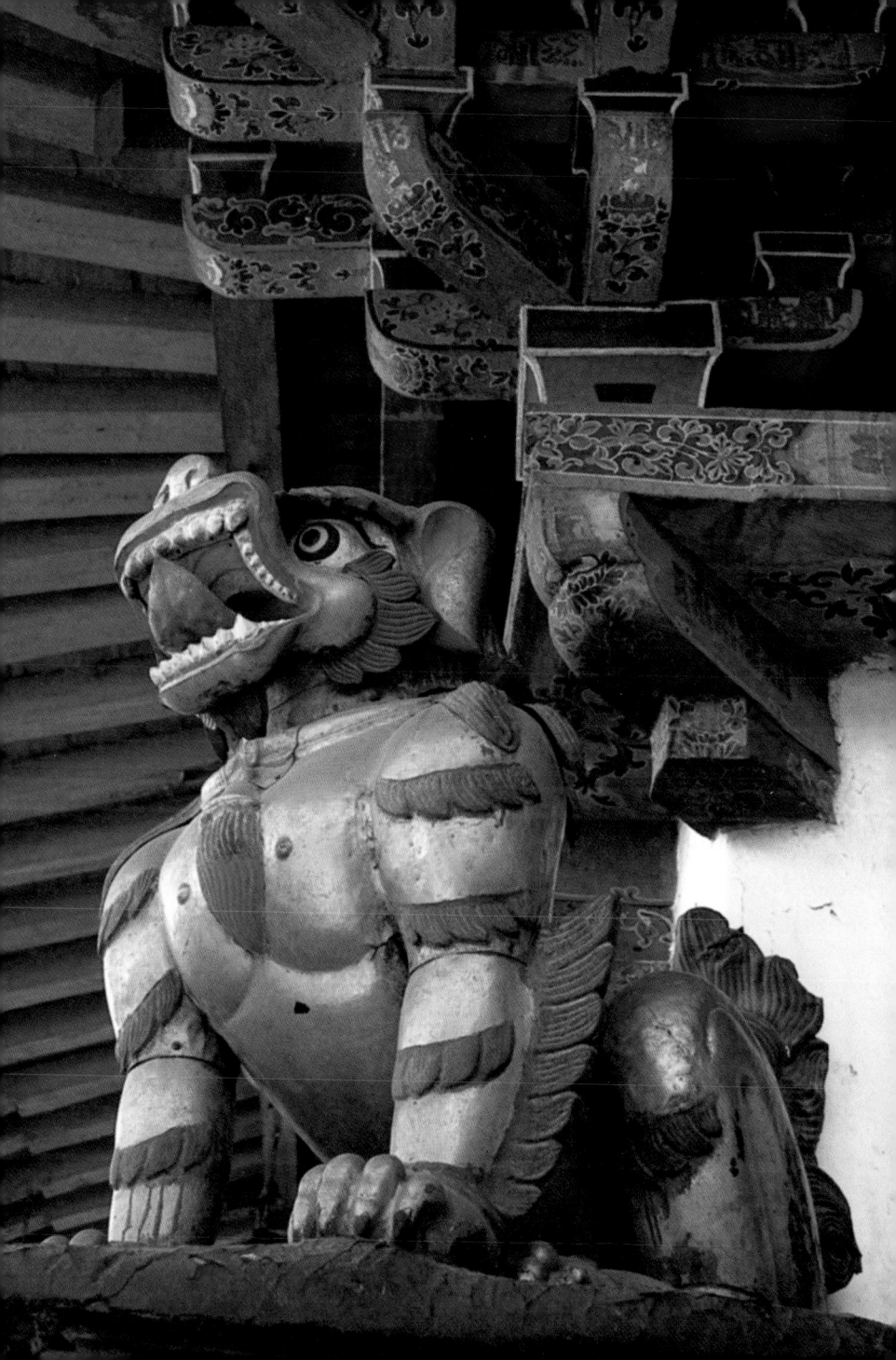

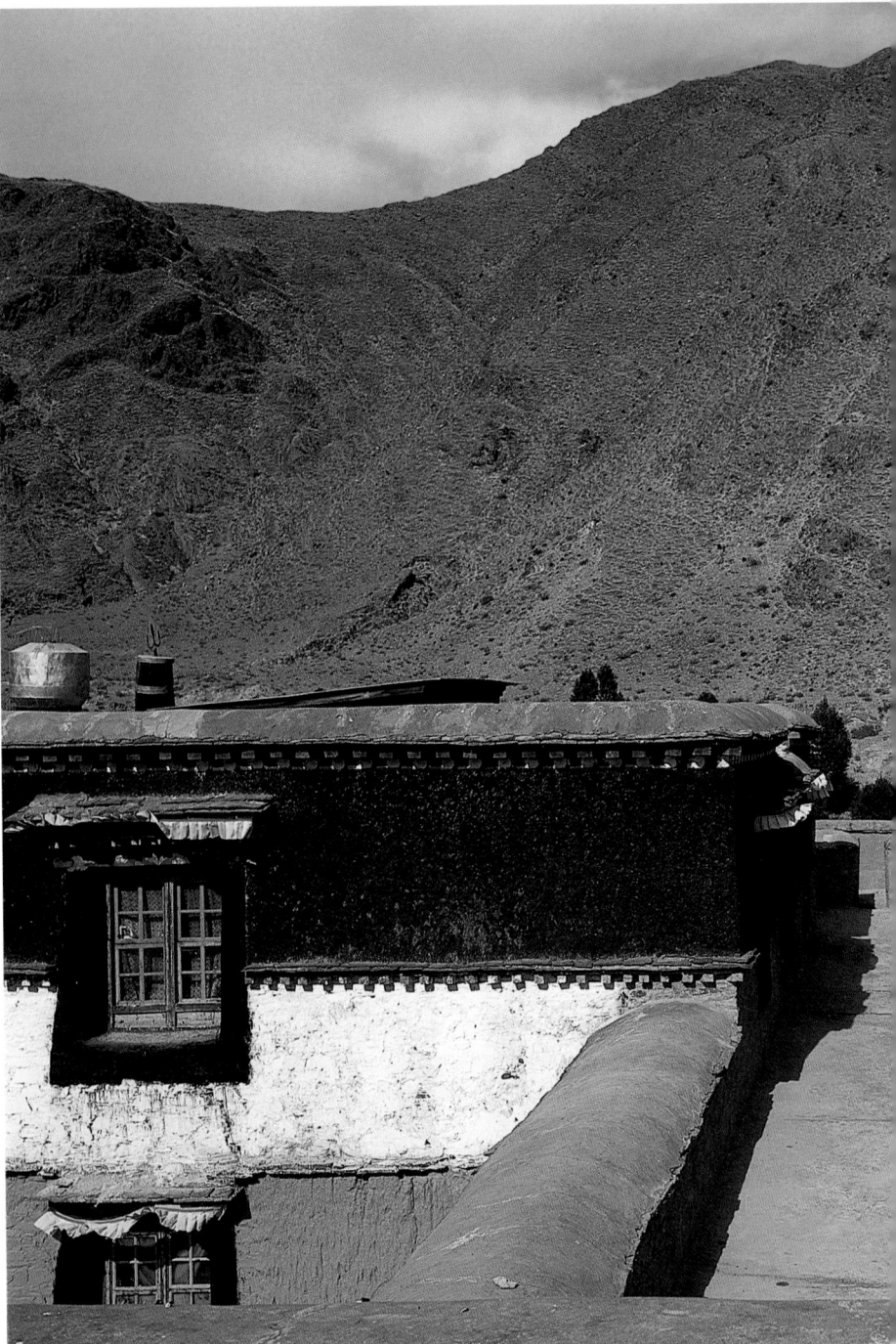

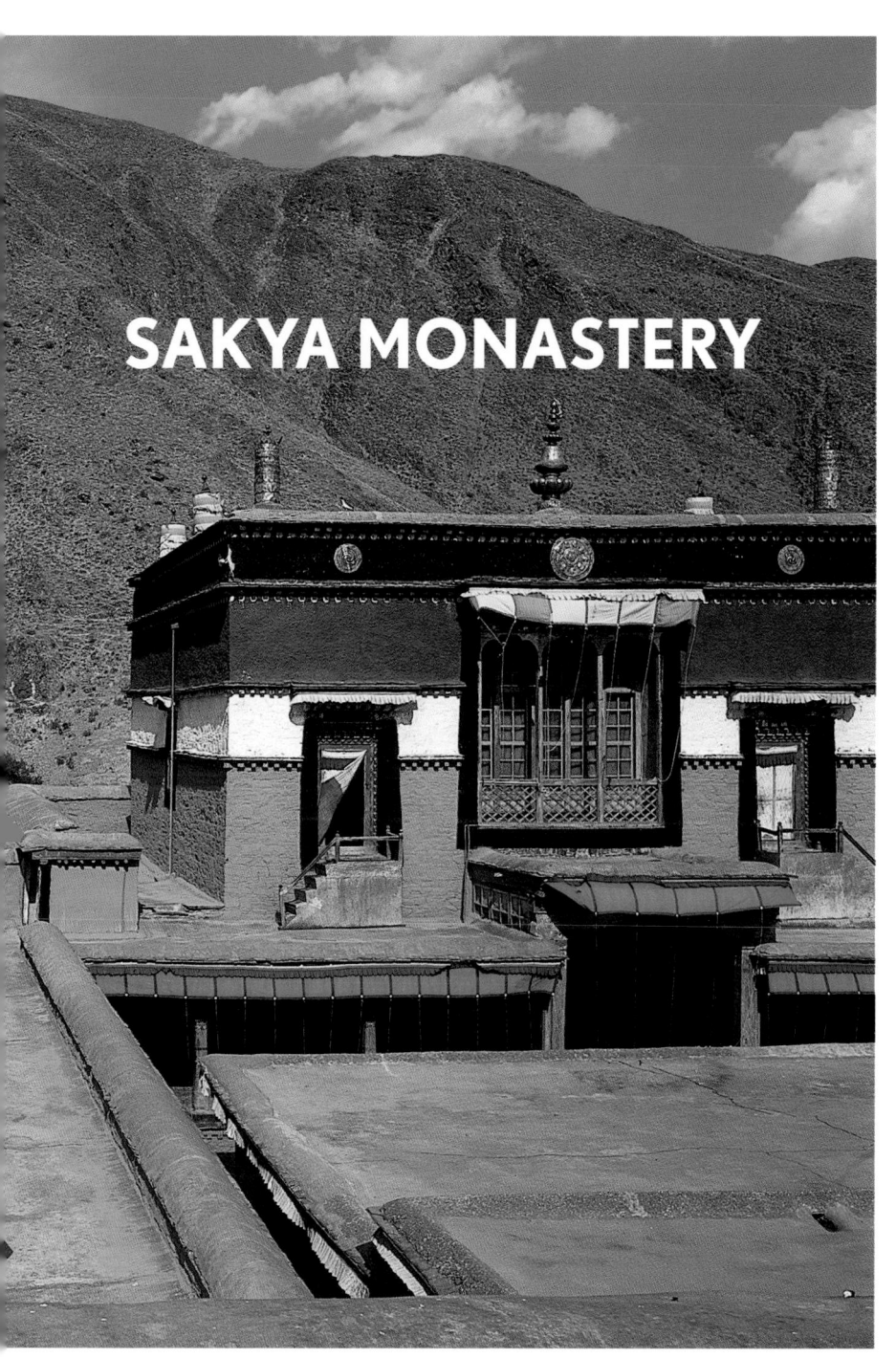

SAKYA MONASTERY

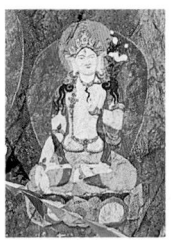

SAKYA MONASTERY

TSANG
WESTERN TIBET

"There was a sense in the little chapel of something timeless, that had kept Sakya going for centuries, regardless of the violent intermissions. I felt this was a remote, independent place, a place that was used to running its own affairs..." recorded the historian Patrick French when he visited Sakya monastery some years ago. Established in 1073 as the seat of the Sakyapa order of Buddhism, the monastery's head Sakya Pandita was the saintly eminence who won the patronage of Godan Khan, grandson of the invading Genghis Khan. Buddhism was declared the state religion of the Mongol empire and for about a hundred years, from the mid-13th century, the lamas of Sakya ruled Tibet. Unlike other Buddhist sects who choose their heads as incarnates, the abbots of Sakya are hereditary and come from one family. Large parts of the monastery were destroyed during the Cultural Revolution and the number of monks is now down to less than a hundred. But its grey walls, marked with distinctive red and white stripes, are a stirring symbol of survival against all odds.

„Die kleine Kapelle strahlte etwas Zeitloses aus, das Sakya jahrhundertelang ausgemacht hat, unabhängig von gewaltsamen Eindringlingen. Ich spürte, dass ich an einen abgelegenen, unabhängigen Ort gelangt war, einen Ort, der seinen eigenen Dingen nachging ...", berichtete der britische Historiker Patrick French, als er vor Jahren das Kloster Sakya besuchte. Sakya Pandita, der dem 1073 als Sitz der buddhistischen Sakyapa-Schule gegründeten Kloster vorstand, stand als heilige Eminenz unter dem Schutz von Dschingis Khans Enkel Göden. Der Buddhismus wurde zur Staatsreligion der Mongolei erklärt, und über hundert Jahre lang herrschten die Lamas von Sakya über Tibet. Im Gegensatz zu anderen buddhistischen Schulen, die ihre Oberhäupter als Inkarnationen wählen, vererben die Äbte von Sakya ihr Amt in der Familie weiter. Im Zuge der Kulturrevolution wurde das Kloster großenteils zerstört, und heute leben nur noch knapp hundert Mönche hier. Doch die grauen Klostermauern, die markant rot-weiß gestreift gestrichen wurden, bleiben das Symbol für das Überleben der Klosteranlage – allen Widrigkeiten zum Trotz.

« Il y avait, dans cette petite chapelle, quelque chose d'atemporel qui avait perpétué Sakya au fil des siècles, en dépit des intermèdes violents. Cet endroit m'a fait l'effet d'être lointain et coupé du reste du monde, de vivre en autarcie... », notait l'historien Patrick French lors de sa visite au monastère de Sakya, il y a plusieurs années. Siège de l'ordre bouddhique des Sakyapas depuis sa création en 1073, ce monastère avait pour supérieur Sakya Pandita, le maître qui avait gagné à la cause du bouddhisme Godan Khan, petit-fils de l'envahisseur Gengis Kahn. Le bouddhisme a été proclamé religion officielle de l'empire mongol et, du milieu du 13e siècle au milieu du 14e siècle, les lamas de Sakya ont gouverné le Tibet. Contrairement à d'autres écoles bouddhistes qui recherchent les incarnations de leur chef, la charge de supérieur est héréditaire à Sakya. Des parties importantes du monastère ont été détruites pendant la Révolution culturelle et le nombre de moines vivant à Sakya est tombé à moins d'une centaine. Mais ses murs gris marqués de bandes rouges et blanches caractéristiques symbolisent la survivance du monastère malgré toutes les vicissitudes de l'Histoire.

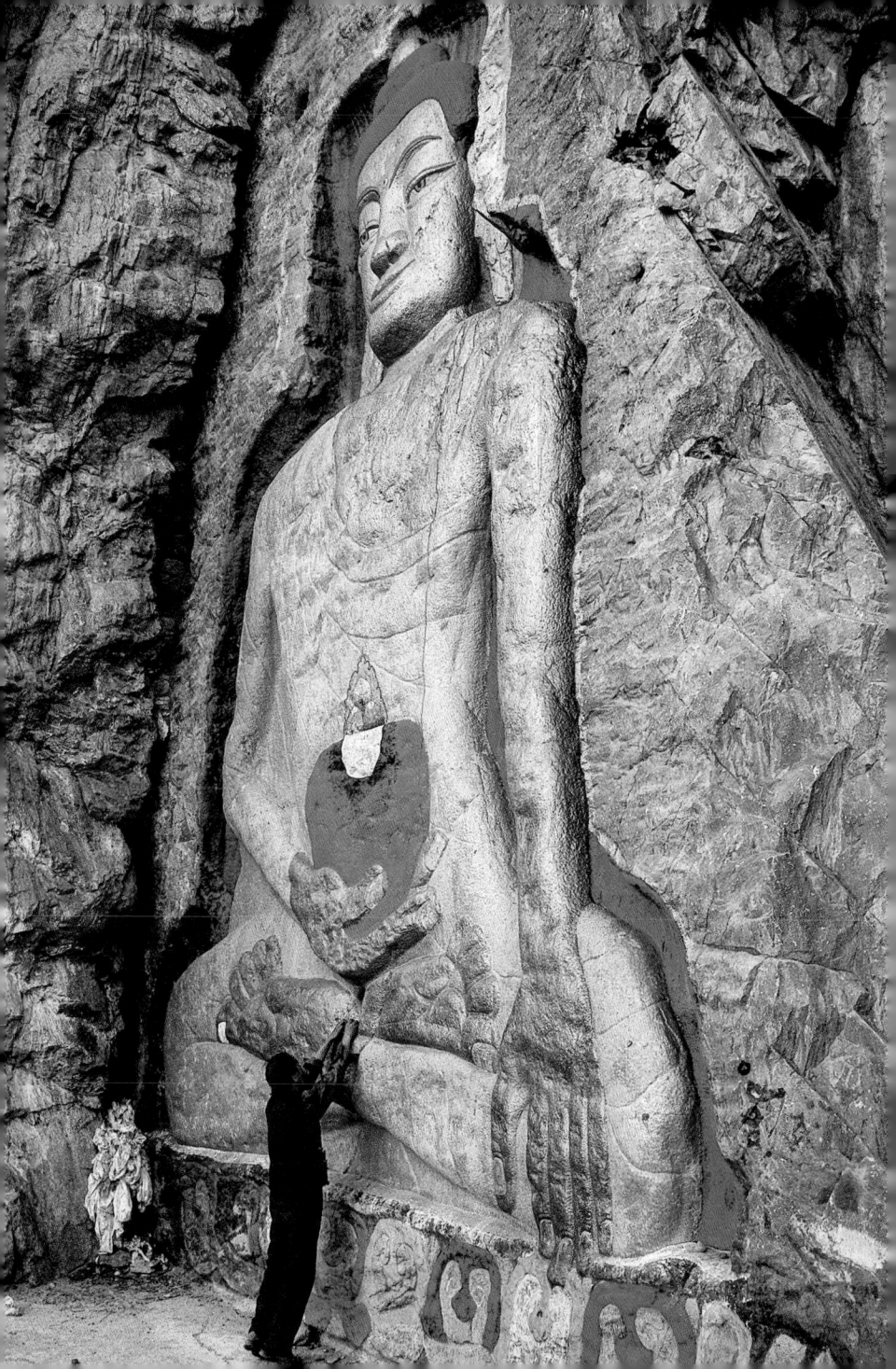

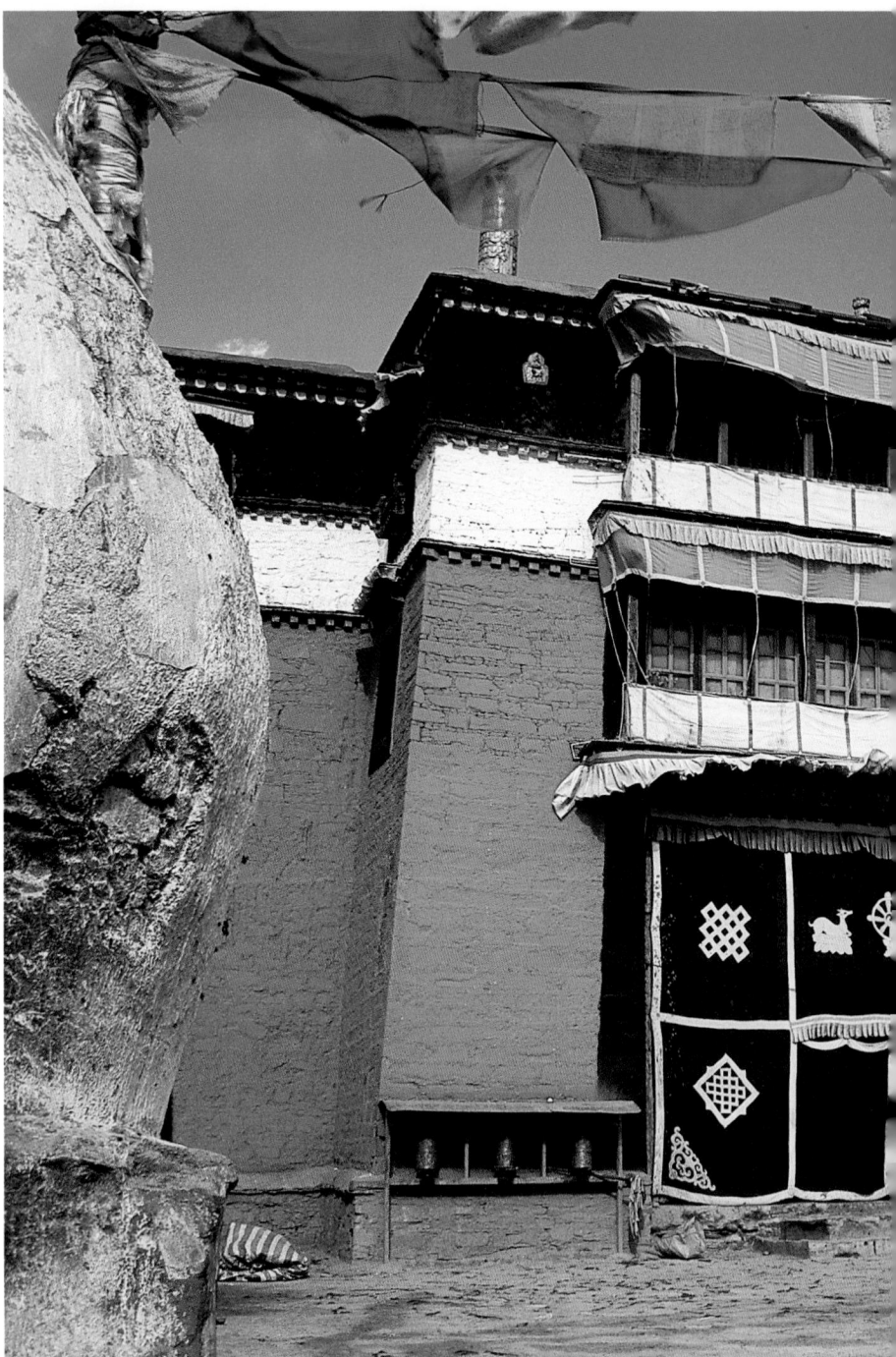

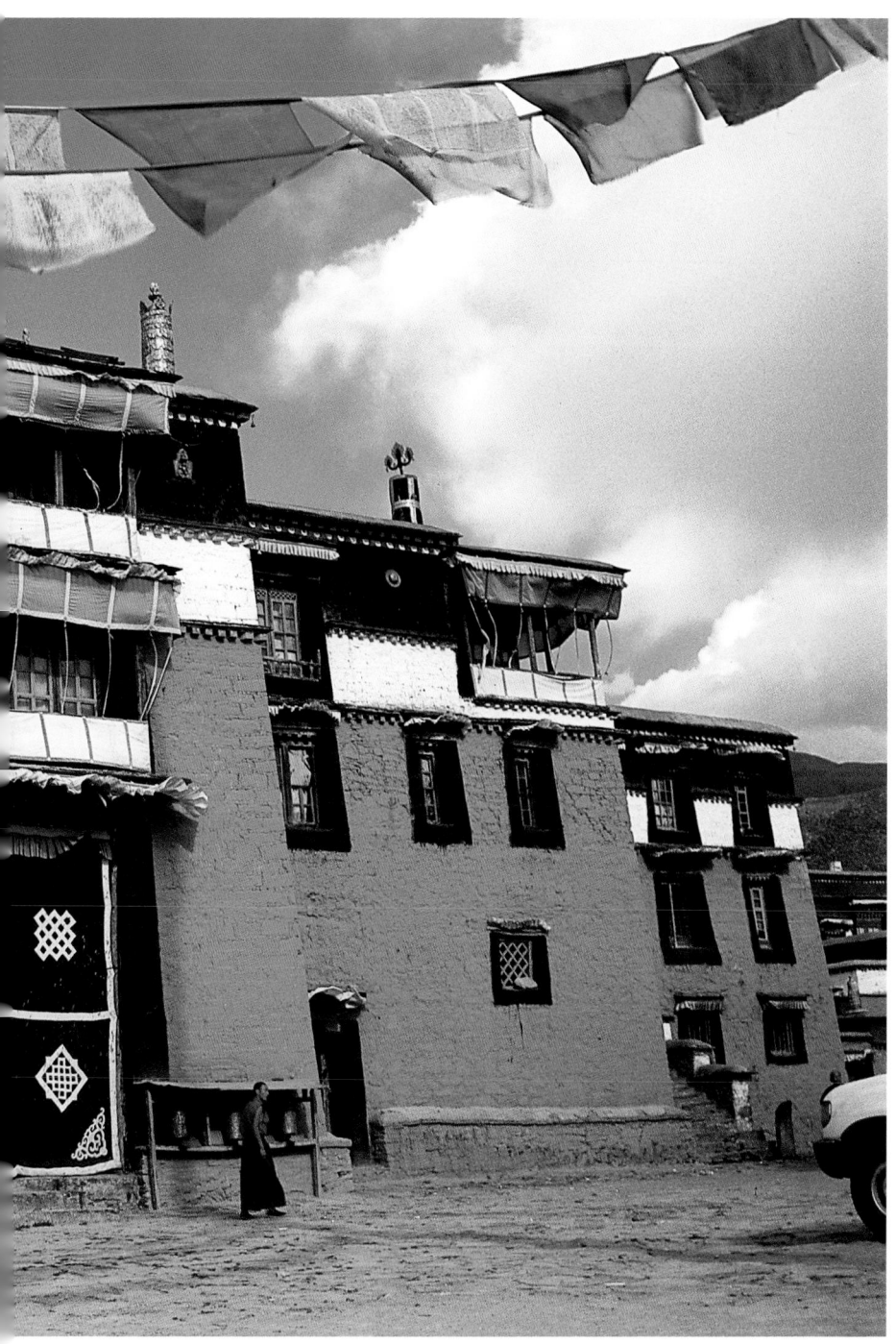

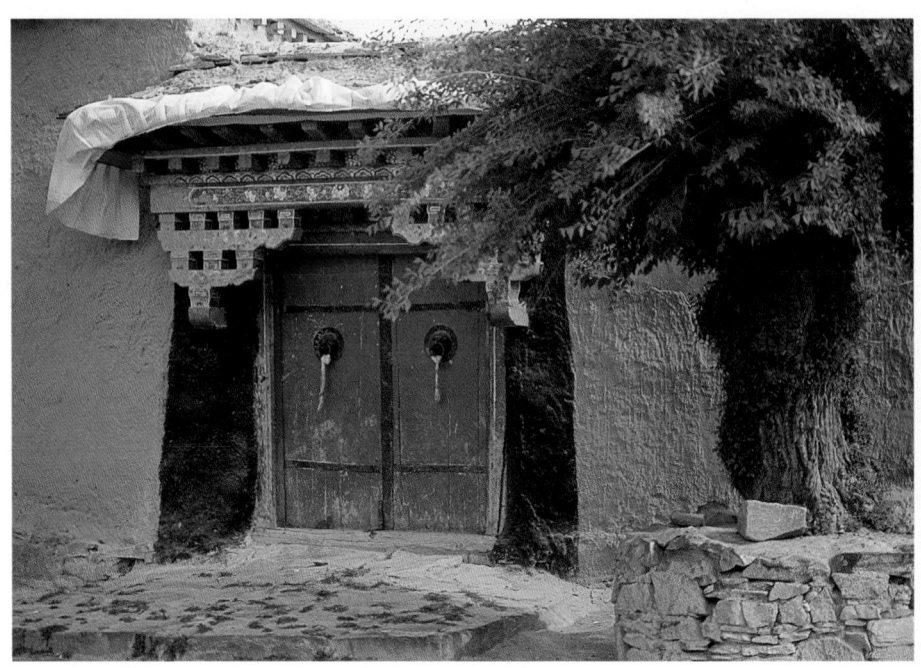

PP. 50–51 Nestled in the Gongkar valley, the rooftops of Sakya look out on rugged views of Mount Khamb La. • Die Dächer des Klosters Sakya schmiegen sich ins Gongkar-Tal; der Blick geht auf den Berg Khamb La. • Au cœur de la vallée de Gongkar, Sakya a vue sur les reliefs accidentés du Khamb La.

PP. 54–55 View from the courtyard to the three-storeyed entrance of the monastery gate, draped with Tibetan banners. • Blick vom Innenhof auf das dreistöckige Klostertor, das mit tibetischen Bannern behängt ist. • Drapée de bannières tibétaines, l'entrée monumentale à deux étages du monastère vue côté cour.

↑ A side entrance to the Sakya monastery. • Ein Seiteneingang ins Kloster Sakya. • Une entrée latérale du monastère de Sakya.

→ A detail of rock relief at Nyethang. • Detail des Felsreliefs in Nyethang. • La falaise sculptée de Nyethang (détail).

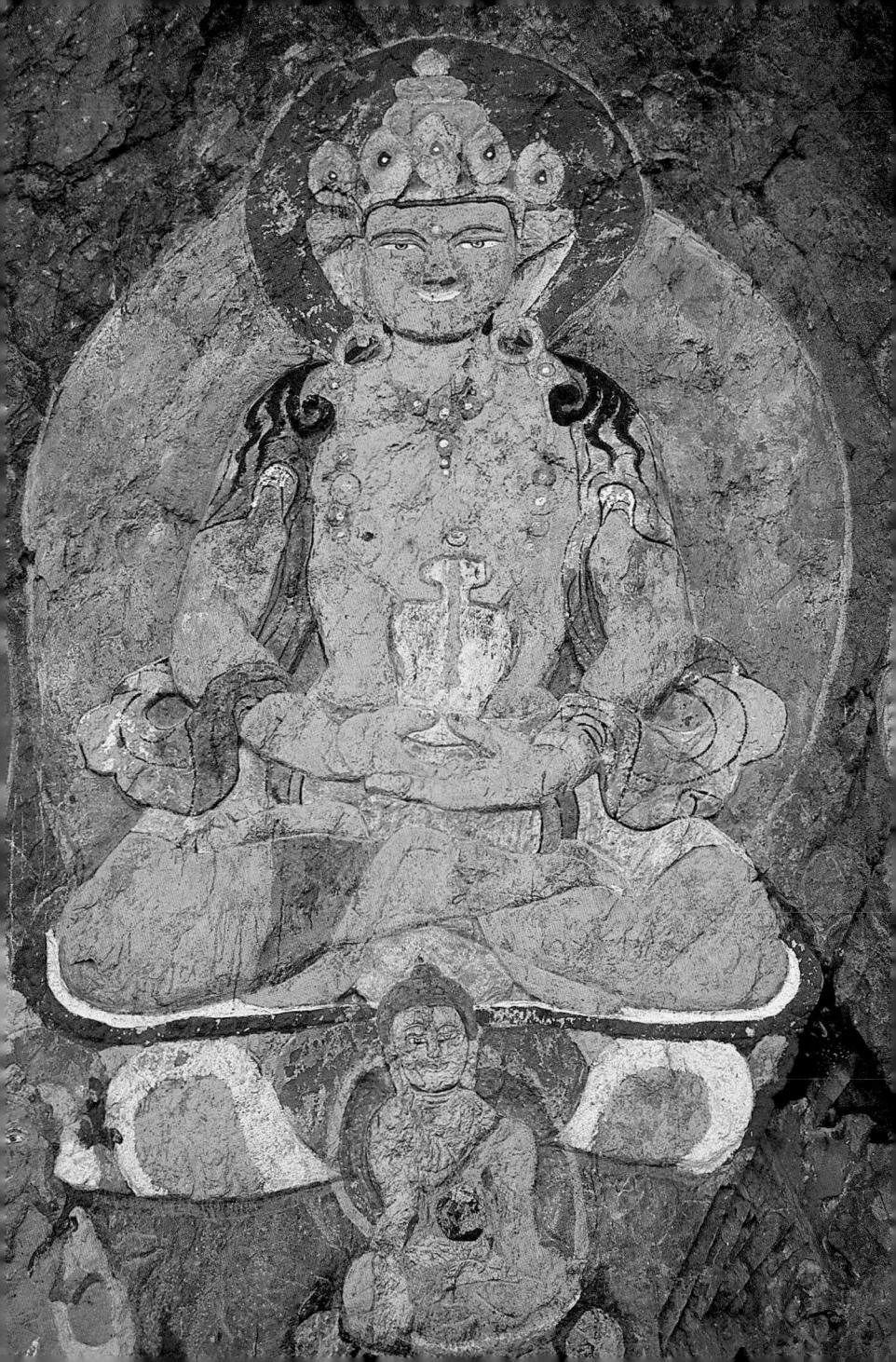

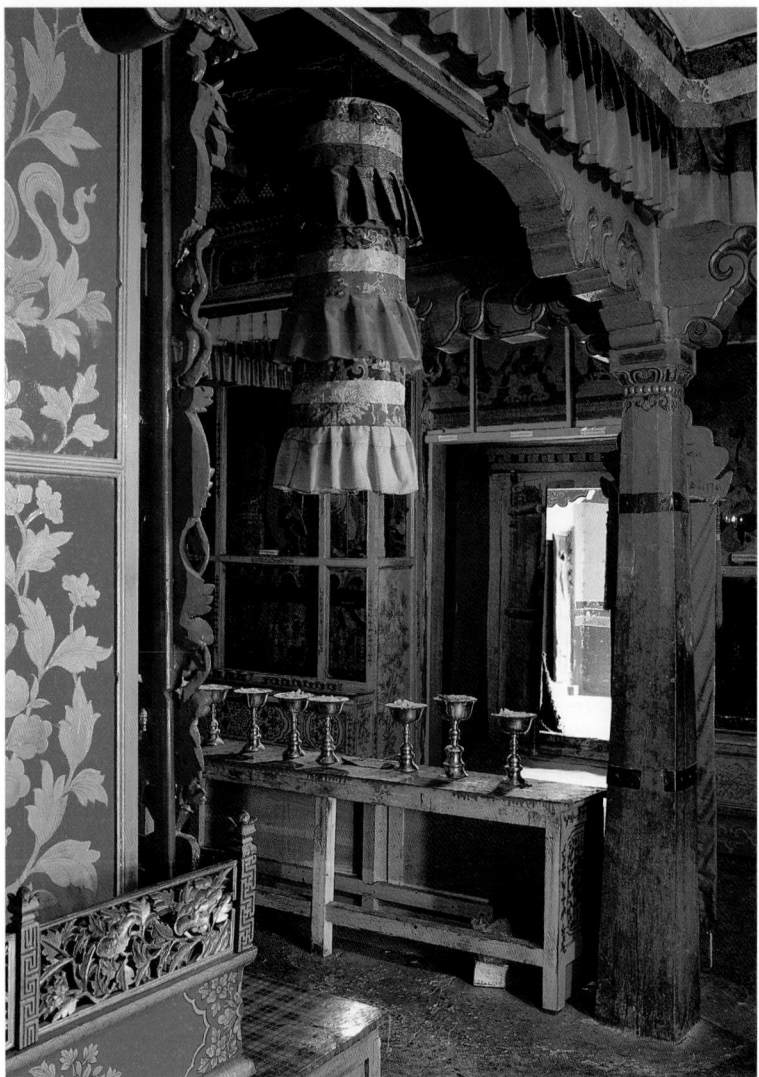

↑ Oil lamps placed before the image
of a goddess in a glass case in the red
and gold chapel. · Öllampen vor der
Statue einer Göttin hinter Glas in der
rotgoldenen Kapelle. · Dans la chapelle
rouge et or, des lampes à huiles éclairent
la statue d'une divinité exposée dans une
vitrine.

→ Monks pose in the exquisitely
painted entrance hall of the monastery.
Frescoes of guardian deities. · Die
Mönche posieren in der großartig aus-
gemalten Eingangshalle des Klosters.
Auf den Fresken sind Schutzgottheiten
dargestellt. · Des moines posent dans
le hall d'entrée superbement orné de
fresques représentant des divinités.

PP. 60-61 Monks during a ceremony
in the main hall. · Mönche während
einer Zeremonie in der Haupthalle. ·
Des moines à l'occasion d'une cérémonie dans le hall principal.

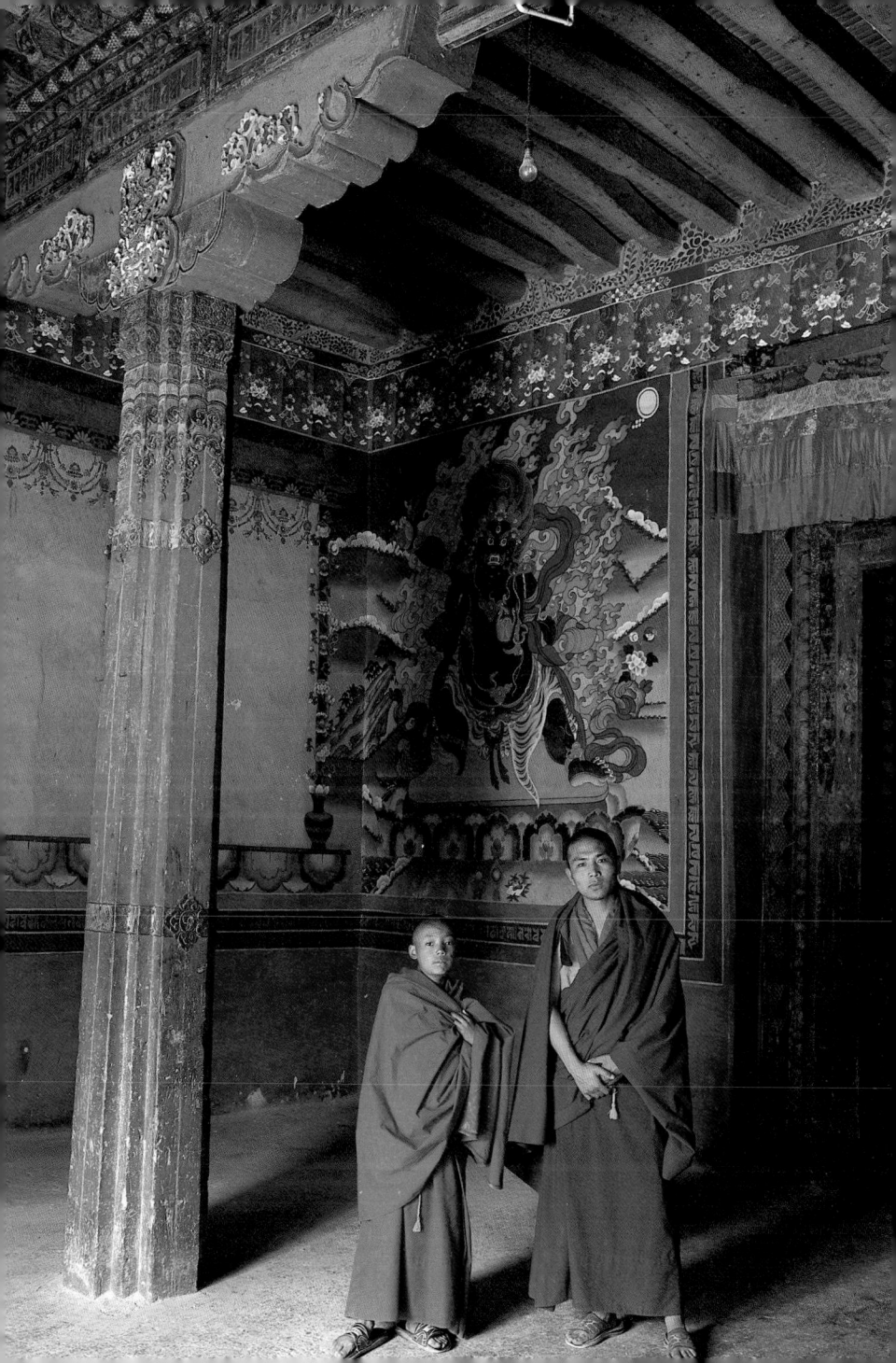

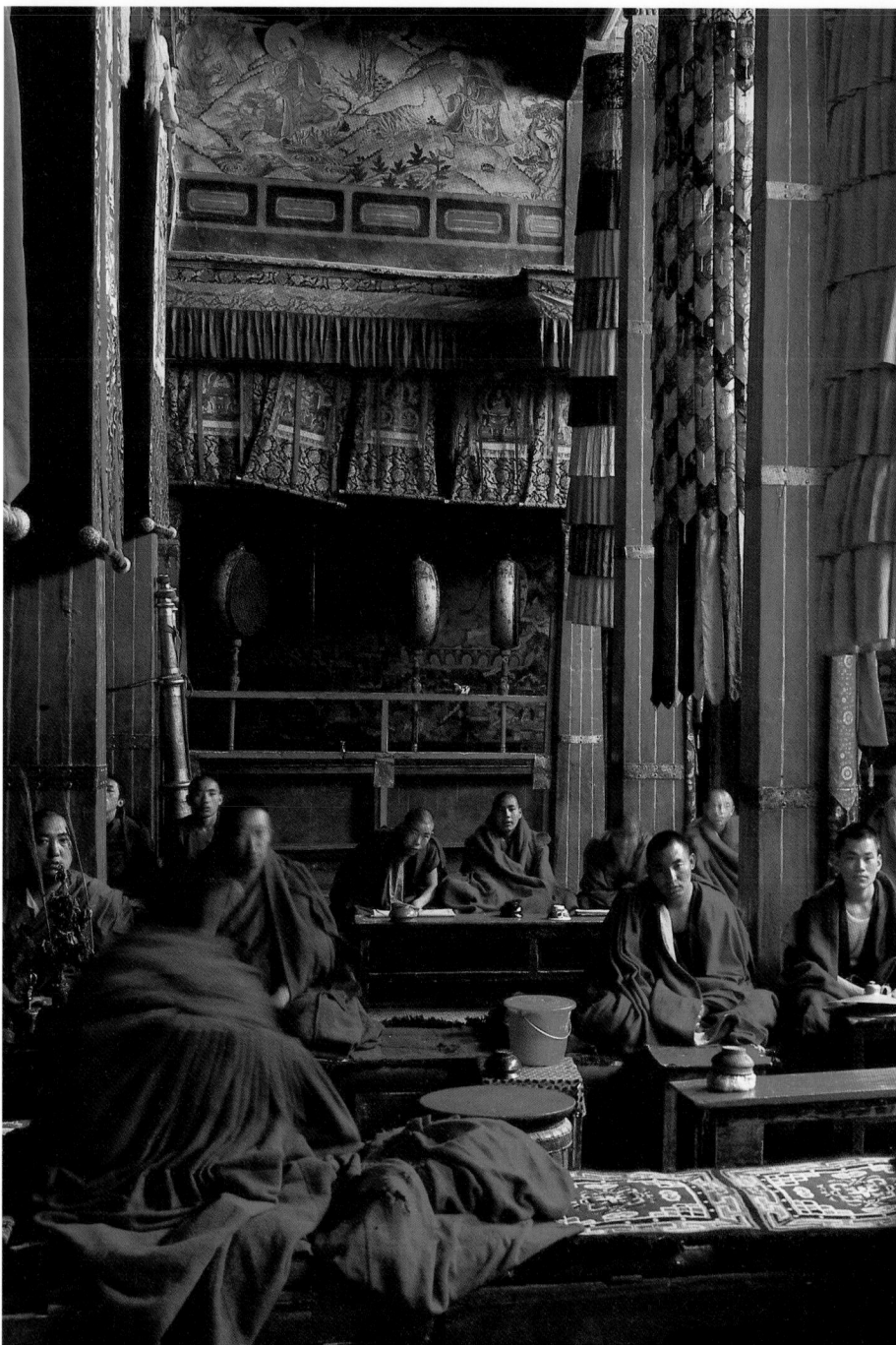

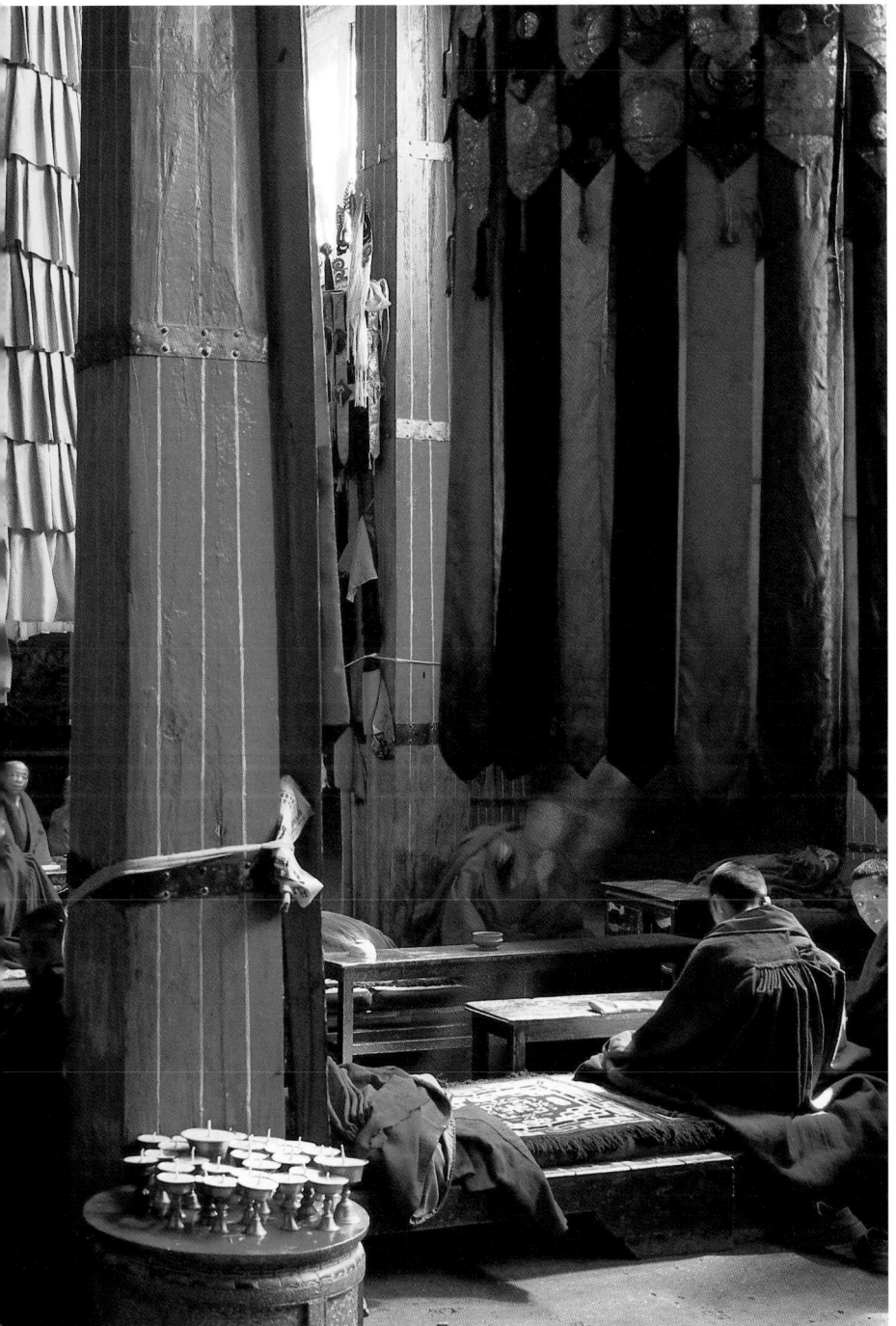

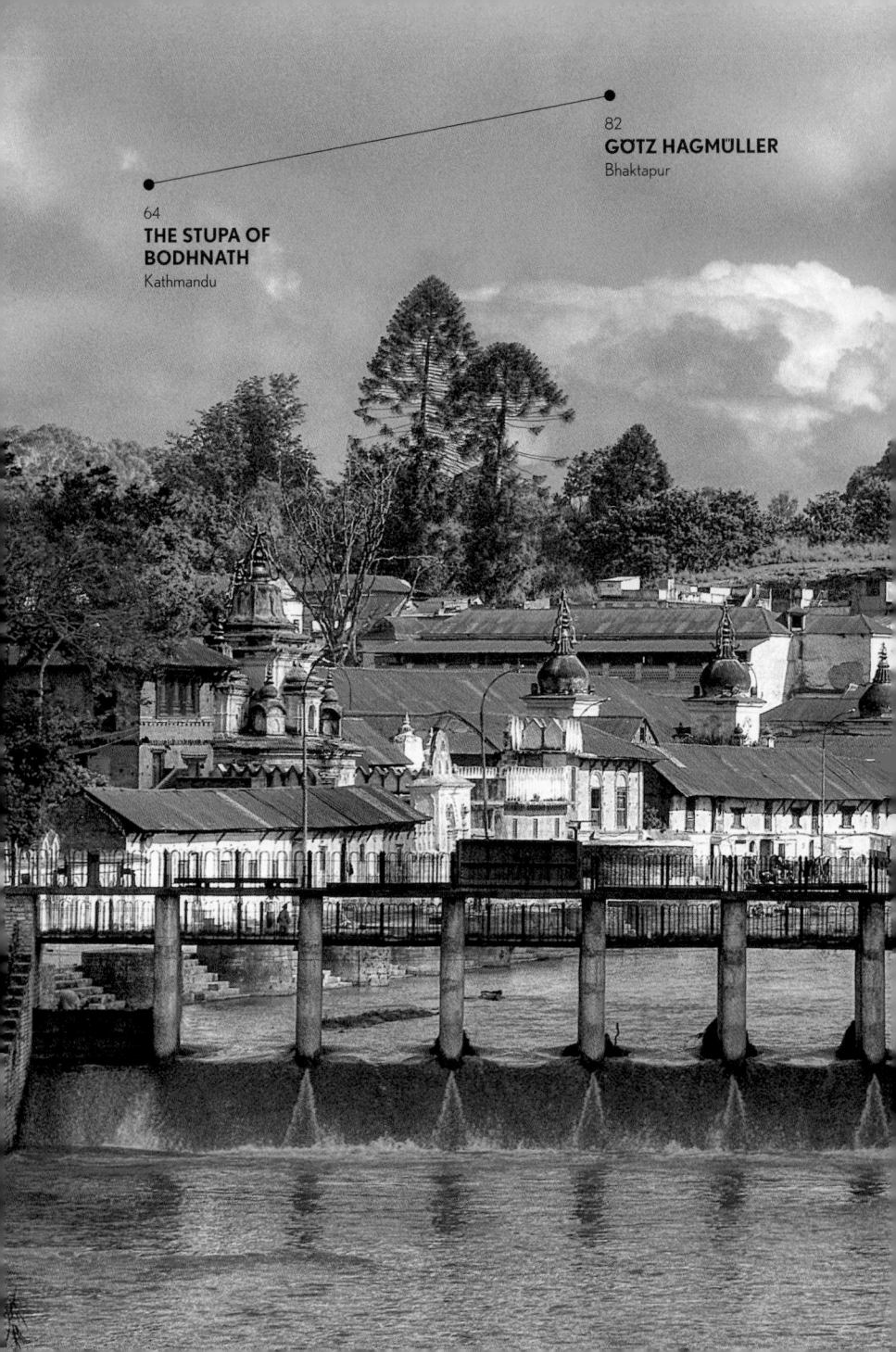

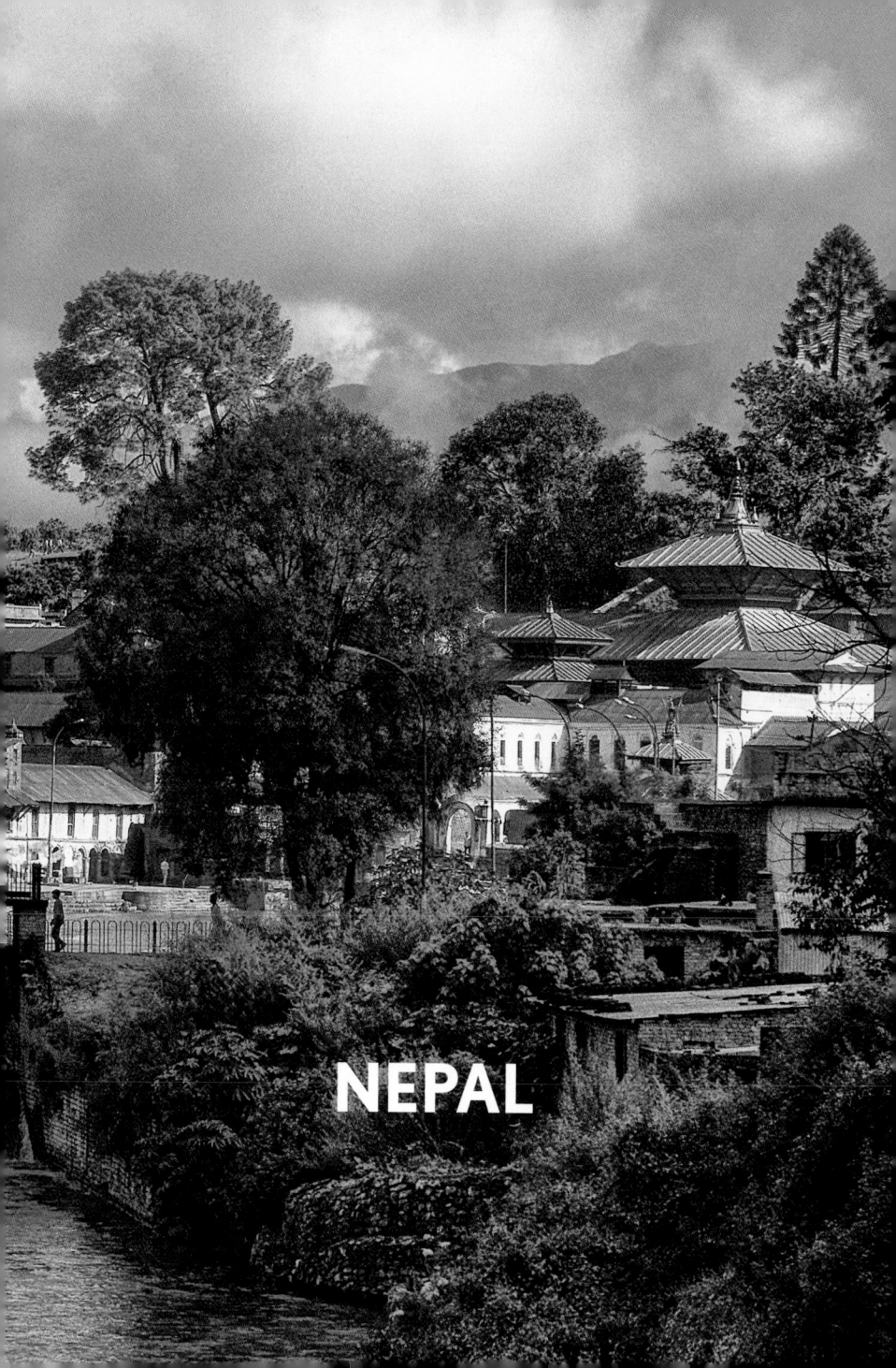

NEPAL

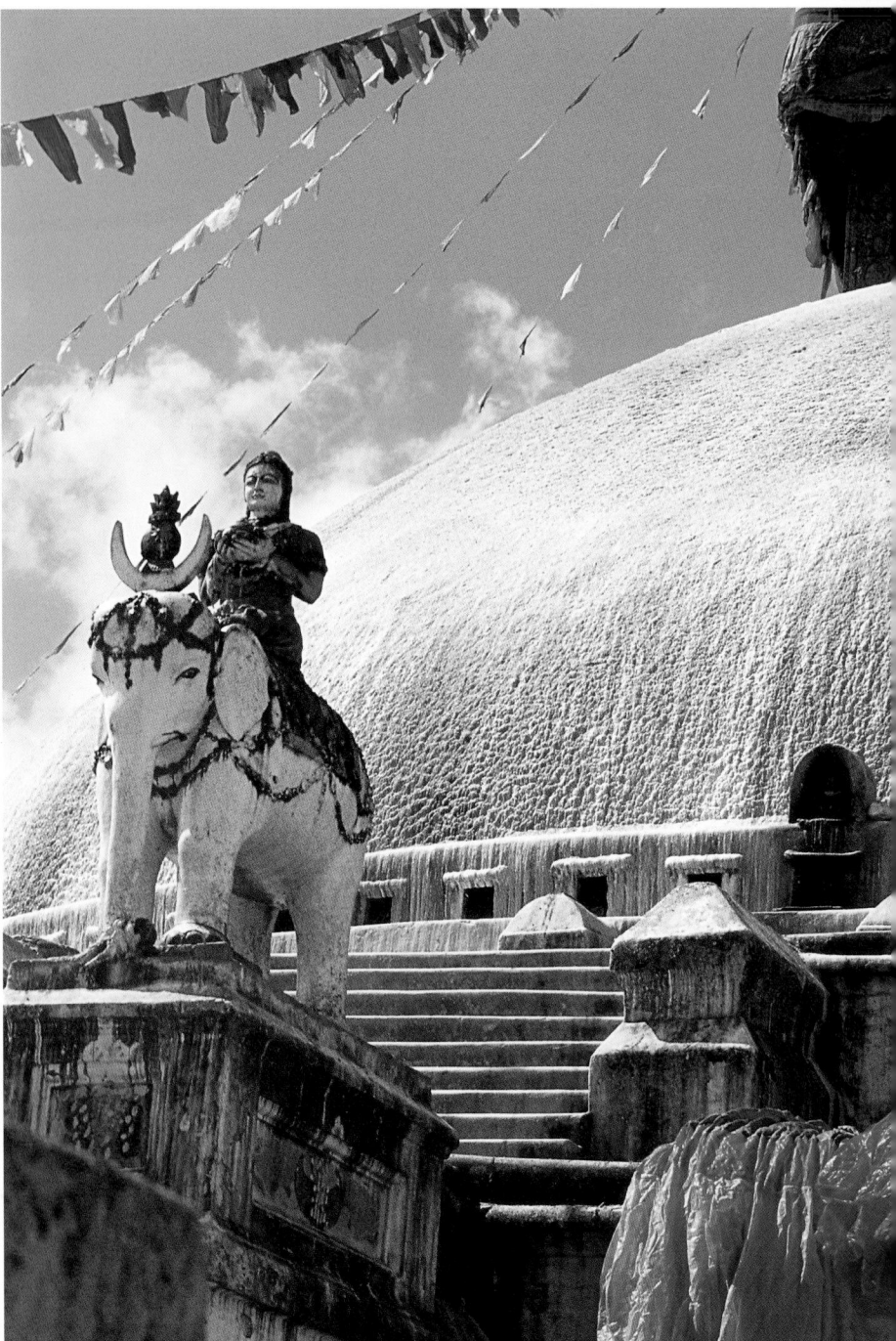

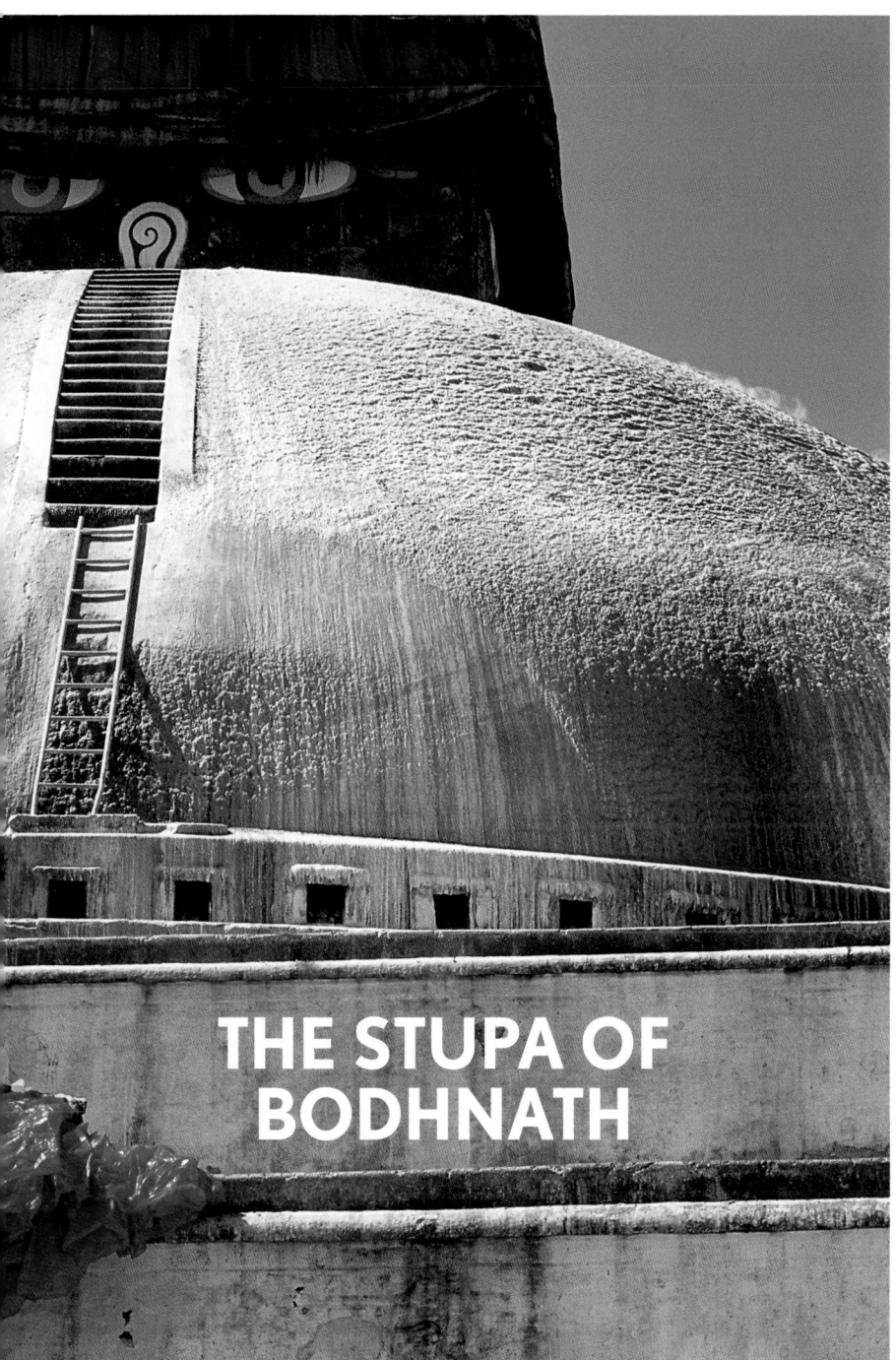

THE STUPA OF
BODHNATH

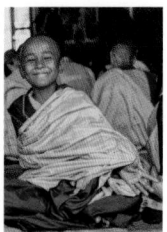

THE STUPA OF BODHNATH

KATHMANDU
NEPAL

If you ask an average Nepali whether he is Hindu or Buddhist the answer often is "Yes". The two religions are deeply intertwined in the Himalayan kingdom and share similar beliefs, rituals, deities and symbols. Officially a Hindu kingdom, the river of Buddhism has flowed through Nepal from the earliest times. The birth of the Buddha in about 566 BC took place in an ancient state that is now part of southern Nepal. Some say that buried in the depths of the stupa in Bodhnath, one of the largest and oldest in the world, is a relic of the Buddha. Around Bodhnath are numerous Tibetan monasteries, including Shechen, whose abbot, Rabjam Rinpoche, is seen on the facing page. Near Bodhnath is the revered temple of Pashupatinath, dedicated to the Hindu god Shiva. Perched on a hill across town is the equally important stupa of Swayambhunath. Between the gilded spires and white-washed domes of the stupas are painted the all-seeing eyes of the Buddha facing all four directions; the question mark-like "nose" stands for the Nepali numeral "one", a reminder that there is only one true path to nirvana.

Fragt man in Nepal jemand, ob er Hindu oder Buddhist ist, so lautet die Antwort häufig: „Ja". Im Königreich des Himalaja sind die beiden Religionen eng miteinander verwoben und teilen ähnliche Glaubenssätze, Rituale, Gottheiten und Symbole. Nepal war zwar zunächst ein hinduistisches Königreich, aber der Buddhismus ist hier seit Urzeiten weitverbreitet. Die Geburt Buddhas um 566 v. Chr. ereignete sich in einem Staat auf dem Gebiet des heutigen Südnepal. Der Legende nach liegt in der Tiefe des Stupa von Bodhnath, der zu den ältesten der Welt zählt, eine Reliquie Buddhas begraben. In der Umgebung sind zahlreiche tibetische Klöster angesiedelt, darunter das Kloster Shechen mit Abt Rabjam Rinpoche (im Bild rechts). Unweit von Bodhnath liegt der Tempel von Pashupatinath, der der Hindugottheit Shiva geweiht ist. Auf einem Hügel vor der Stadt befindet sich der Stupa von Swayambhunath. Zwischen die vergoldeten Spitzen und die weiß getünchten Kuppeln sind die Augen Buddhas gemalt, die in alle vier Himmelsrichtungen blicken. Die dem Fragezeichen ähnliche „Nase" ist das nepalesische Schriftzeichen für „eins" – Mahnung an den einzig wahren Weg zur Erlösung.

Si vous demandez à un Népalais s'il est hindouiste ou bouddhiste, la réponse sera souvent : « Oui ». C'est que les deux religions sont intimement mêlées dans cet État himalayen et qu'elles partagent de nombreux rituels, des croyances, des divinités et des symboles. Si l'hindouisme est la religion officielle de ce royaume, le bouddhisme y est très présent depuis la nuit des temps. En effet, Bouddha est né vers 566 avant notre ère dans un État qui fait désormais partie du Népal méridional. Une relique de Bouddha serait même ensevelie dans les profondeurs du stupa de Bodnath, l'un des plus grands au monde. Dans les environs de Bodnath se trouvent de nombreux monastères tibétains, dont celui de Shechen dirigé par Rabjam Rinpoché (page de droite). Aux abords de Bodnath s'élève le temple de Pashupatinath, dédié à la divinité hindouiste Shiva. Et de l'autre côté de la ville, juché sur une colline, se trouve le stupa tout aussi important de Swayambhunath. Entre les flèches dorées et les dômes peints à la chaux des stupas, rien n'échappe aux yeux de Bouddha tournés vers les quatre points cardinaux. Son nez en forme de point d'interrogation correspond au « 1 » népalais, et nous rappelle qu'une seule voie mène au nirvana.

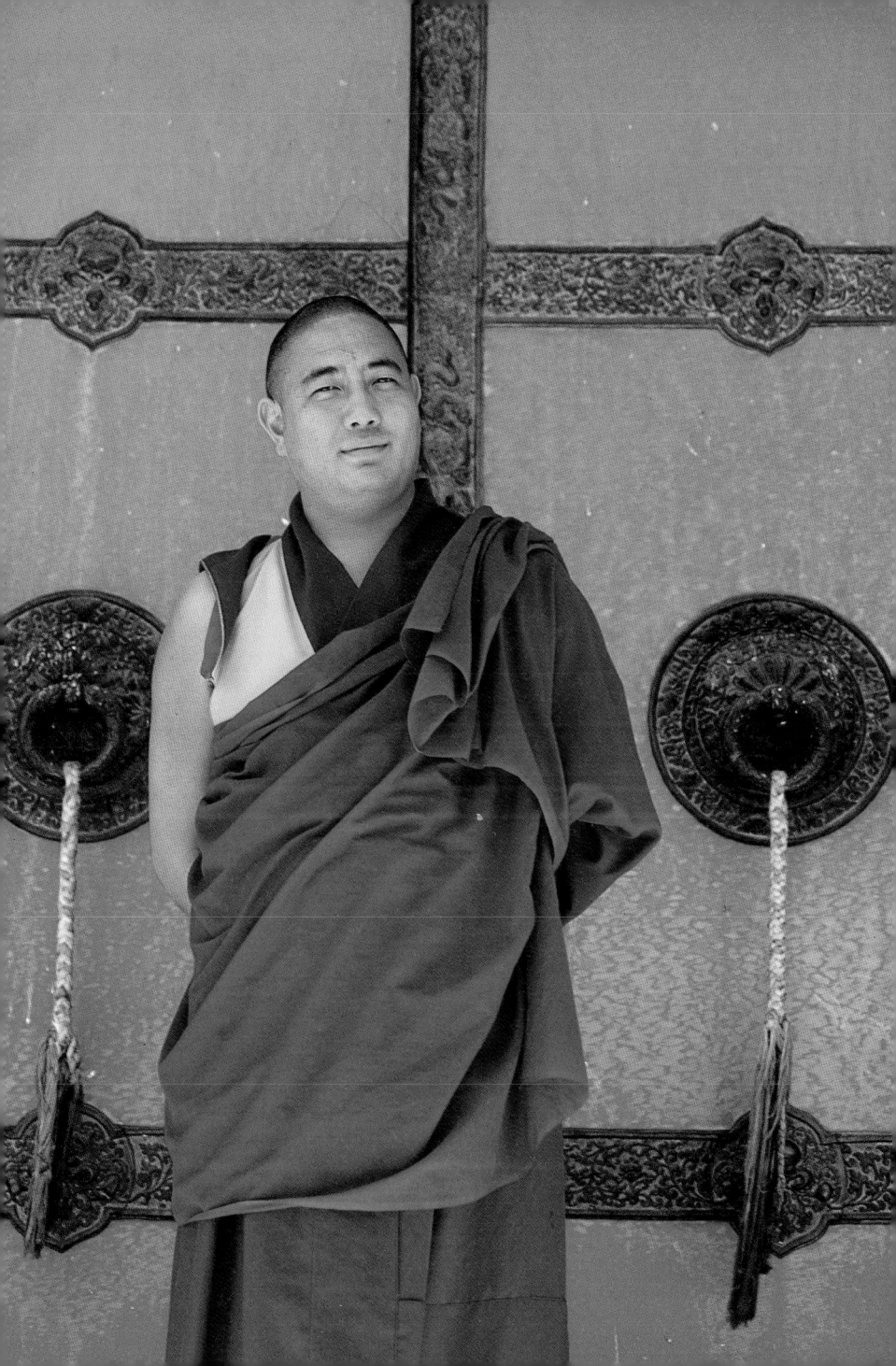

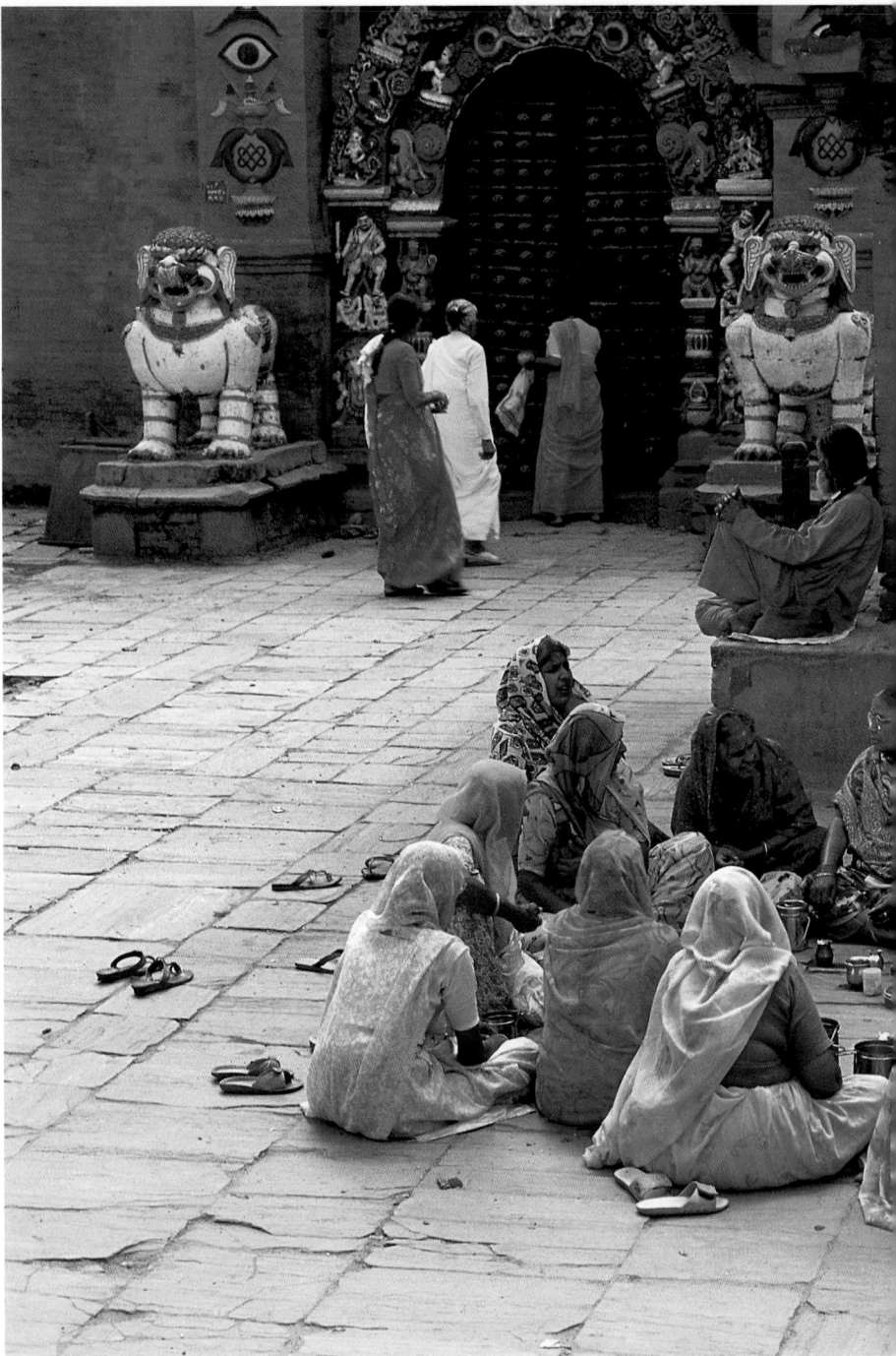

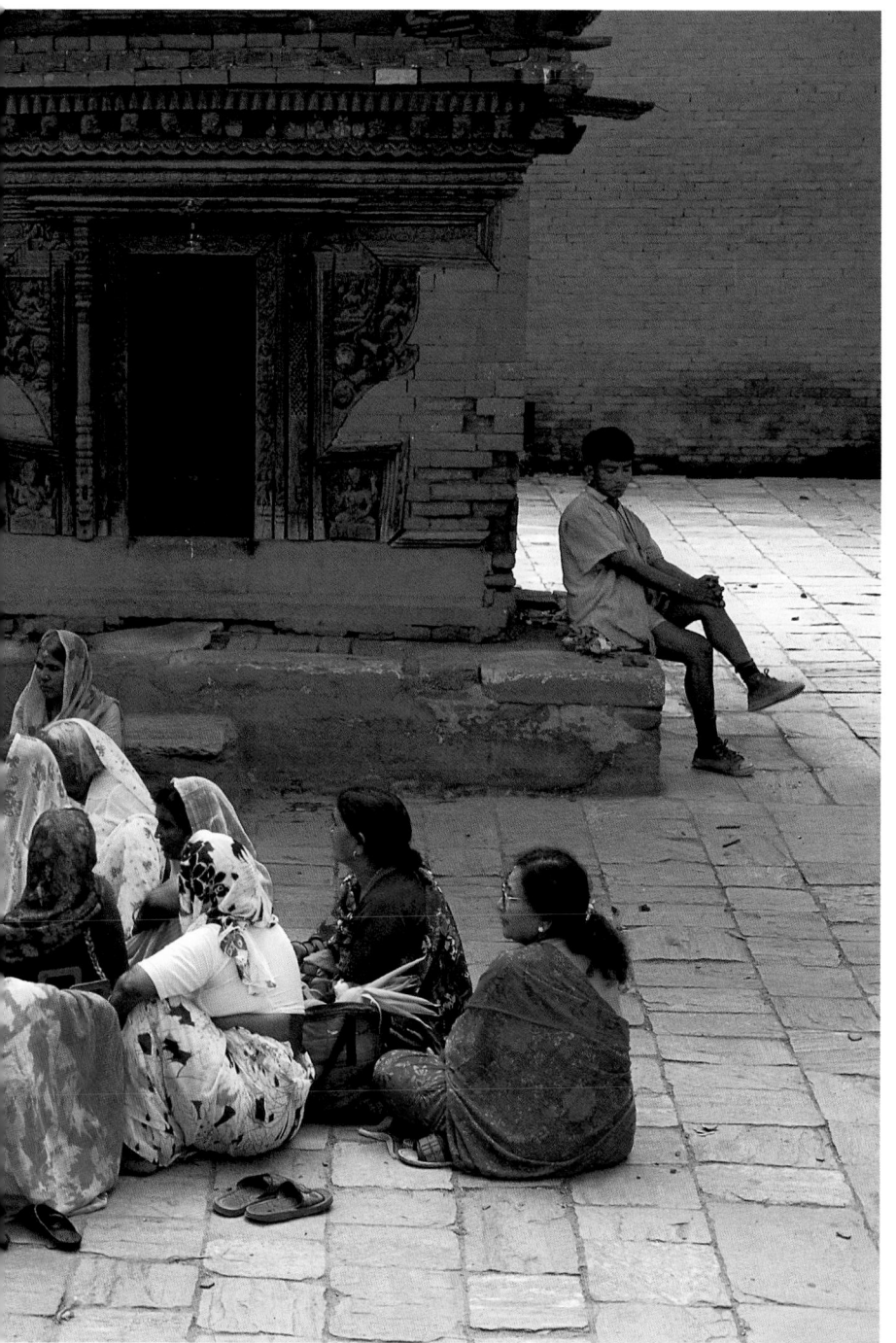

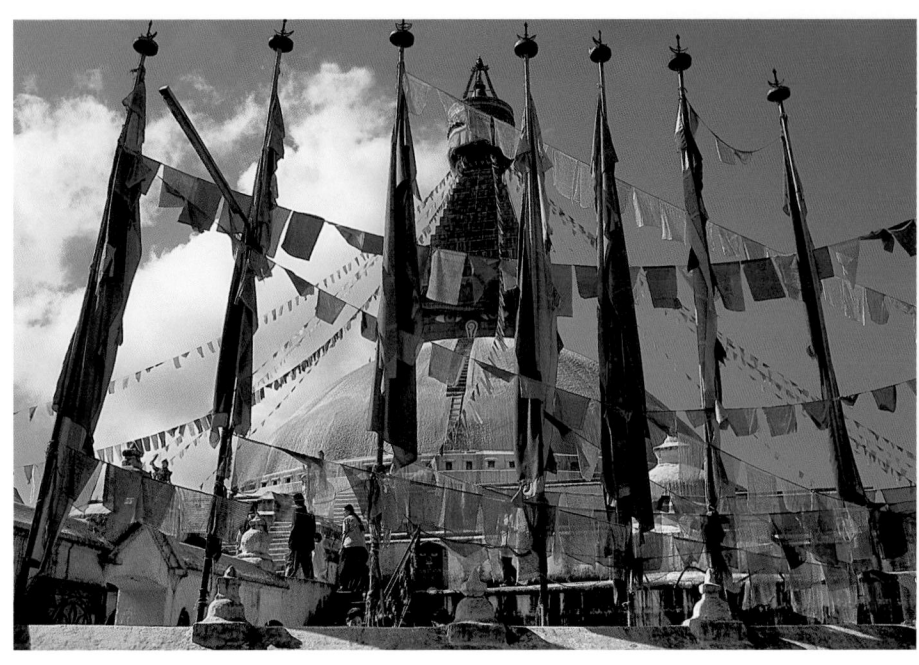

PP. 64-65 A guardian king astride an elephant near the dome. • Ein Schutzkönig rittlings auf einem Elefanten vor der Kuppel. • Un roi gardien sur un éléphant devant le dôme.

PP. 68-69 A group of woman devotees in the temple courtyard. • Eine Gruppe gläubiger Frauen in einem Innenhof des Tempels. • Un groupe de croyantes dans la cour du temple.

↑ Prayer flags planted by worshippers at Bodhnath. • Gläubige hinterlassen

diese Gebetsfahnen in Bodhnath. • Les fidèles ont planté des drapeaux de prière.

→ Placed in niches at the base of Bodhnath's dome are deities daubed with vermilion by devotees. • Platziert in Nischen an der Basis der Kuppel sind Gottheiten, die von Gläubigen mit Zinnoberrot gefärbt werden. • Placées dans des niches au pied du dôme de Bodhnath, des divinités sont colorées en rouge par les fidèles.

PP. 72-73 Hindu deities and Buddhist symbols of snow lions, the eternal knot and the Buddha's all-seeing eyes merge in a decorated gate to Pashupatinath temple. • Hindu-Gottheiten und buddhistische Symbole von Schneelöwen, dem endlosen Knoten und dem alles sehenden Buddha vermischen sich an einem Tor des Pashupatinath-Tempels. • Sur ce portail orné du temple de Pashupatinath, des divinités hindouistes côtoient les symboles bouddhiques des lions des neiges, du nœud éternel, et du Bouddha qui voit tout.

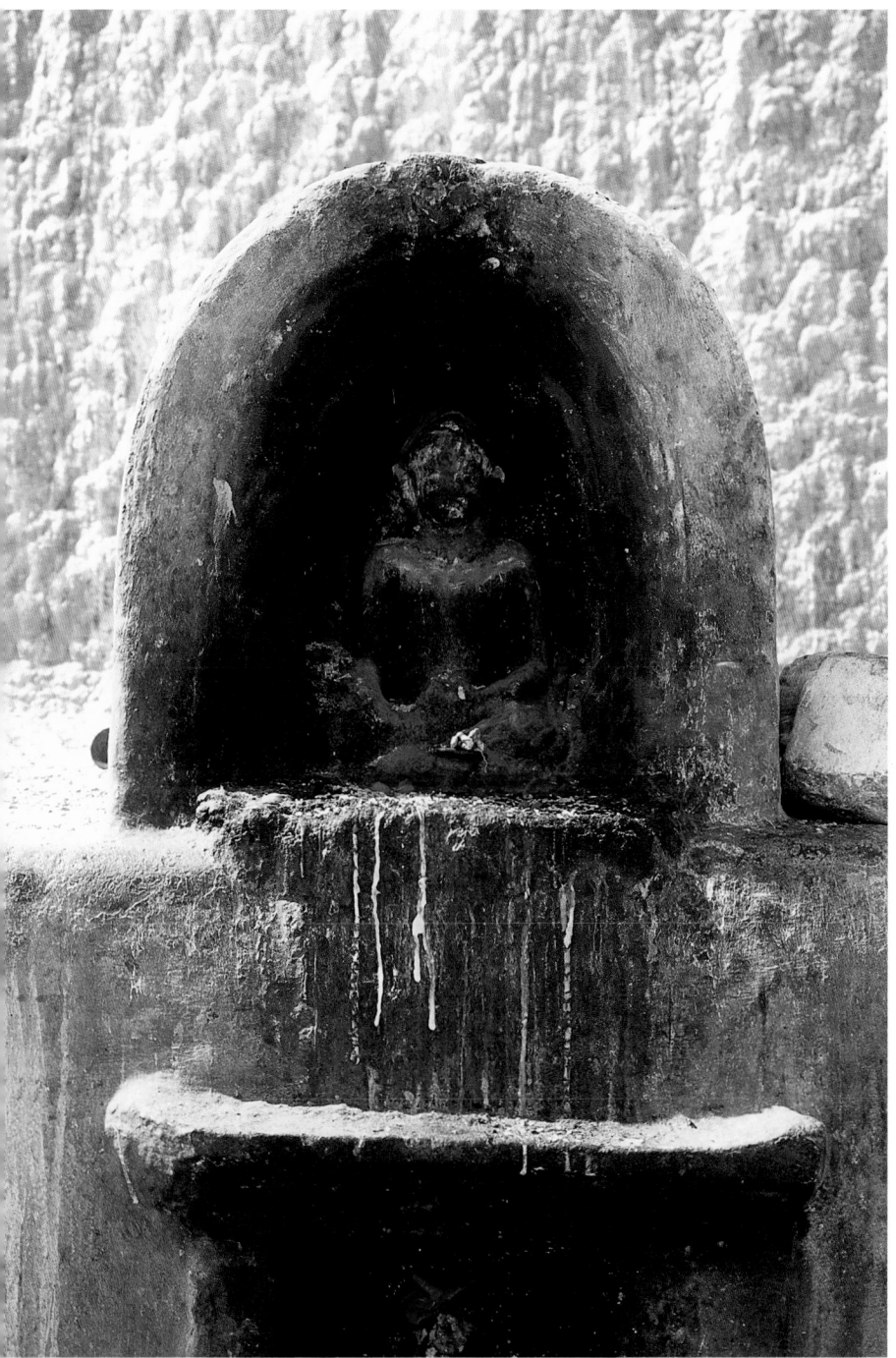

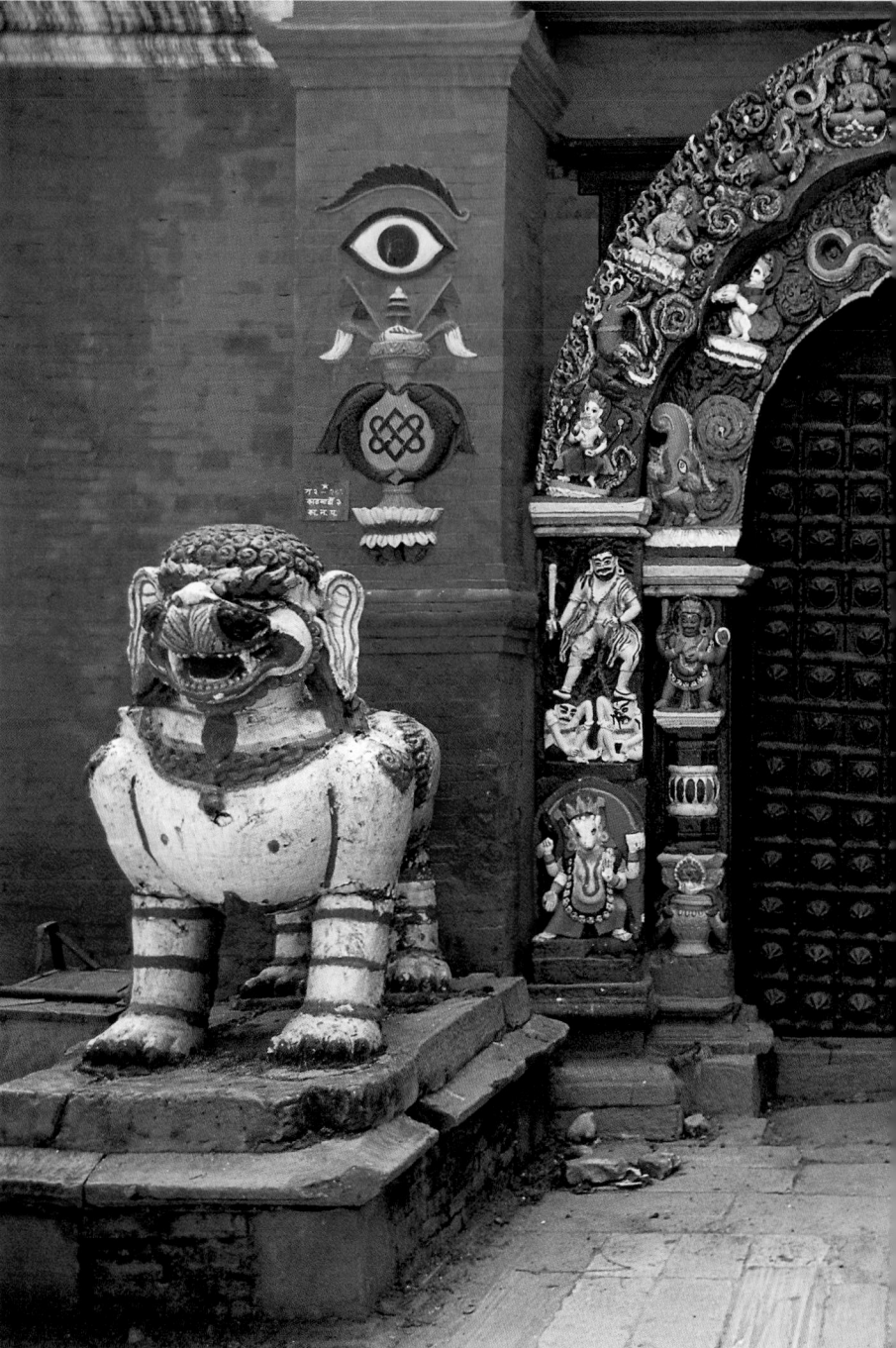

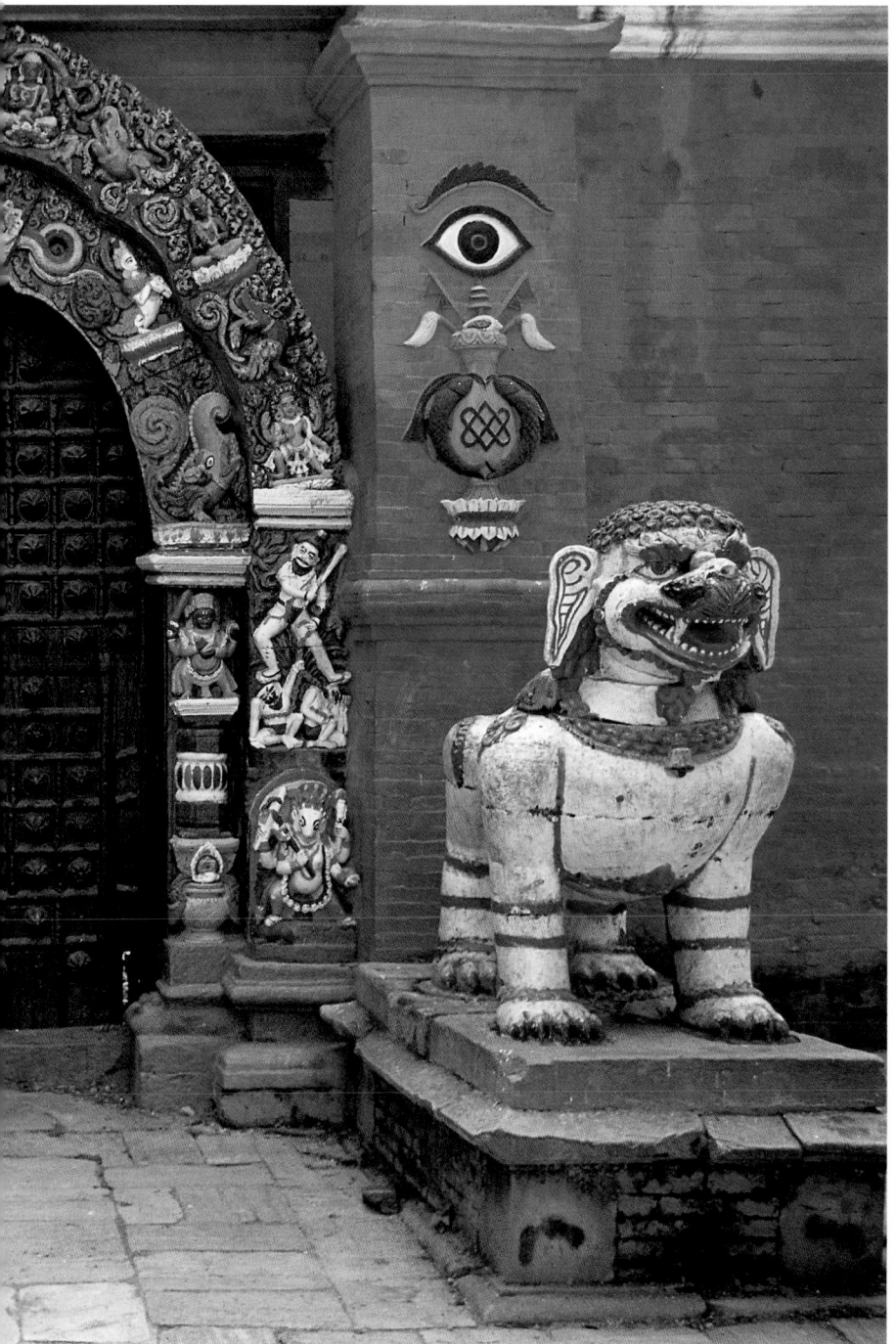

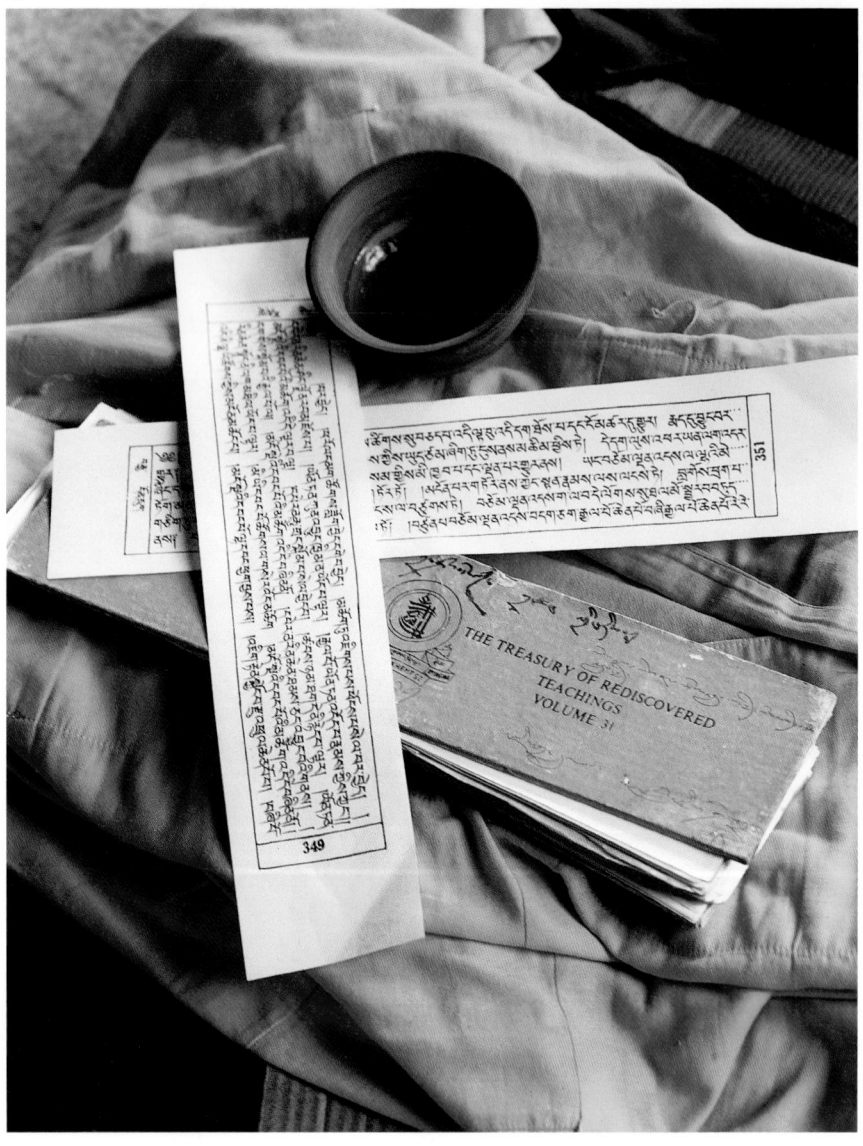

↑ A monk's tea bowl and prayer texts. • Die Teeschale und Gebetstexte eines Mönchs. • Le bol à thé d'un moine et des textes de prière.

→ Hanging from the roof are decorative canopies of brocade patchwork. • Vom Dach hängen dekorative Baldachine aus buntem Brokat. • Les dais en brocart suspendus au toit ont un rôle décoratif.

PP. 76–77 Monks at prayer in the temple of Shechen monastery. • Betende Mönche im Tempel des Klosters Shechen. • Des moines en prière dans le temple du monastère de Shechen.

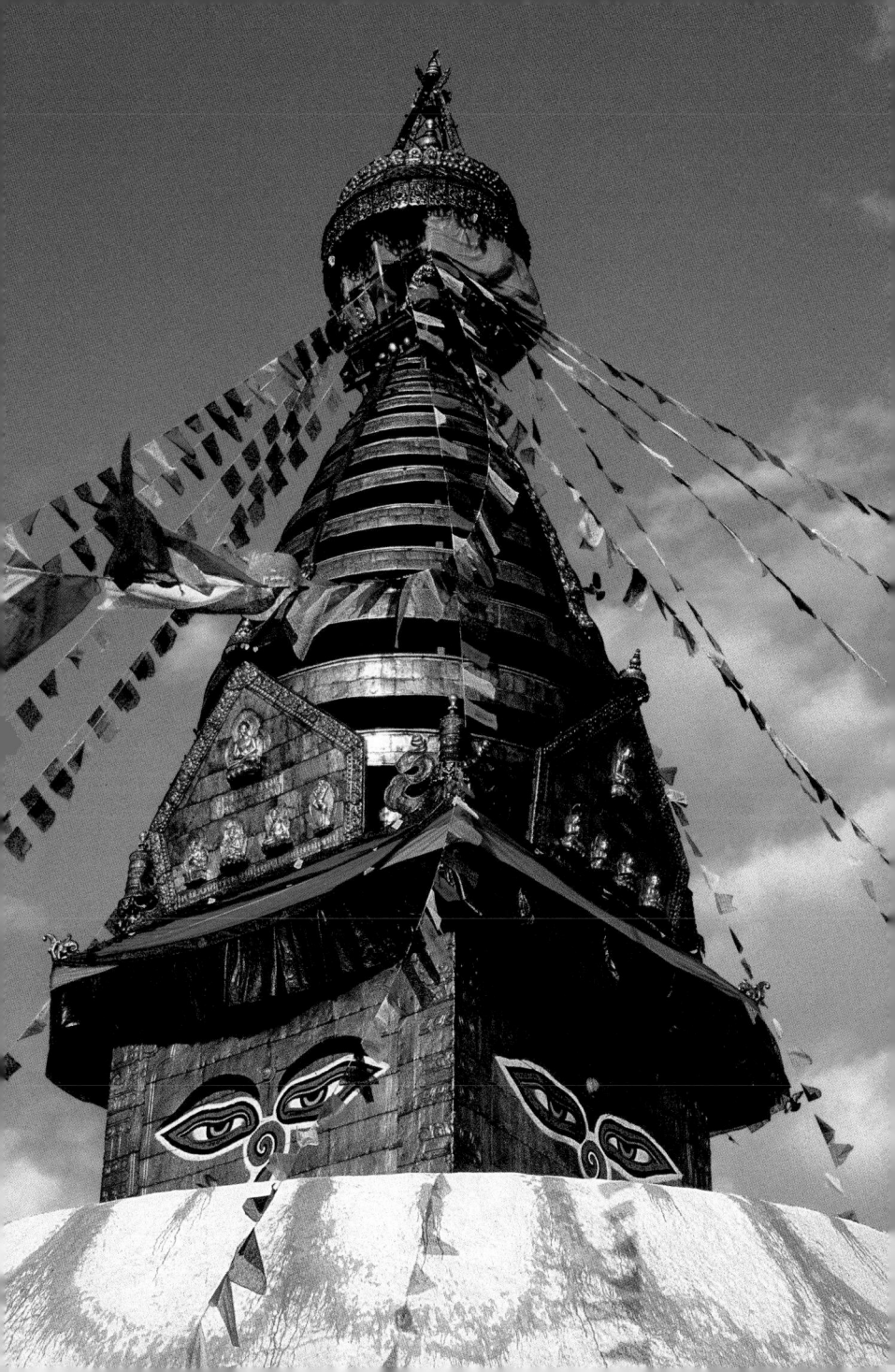

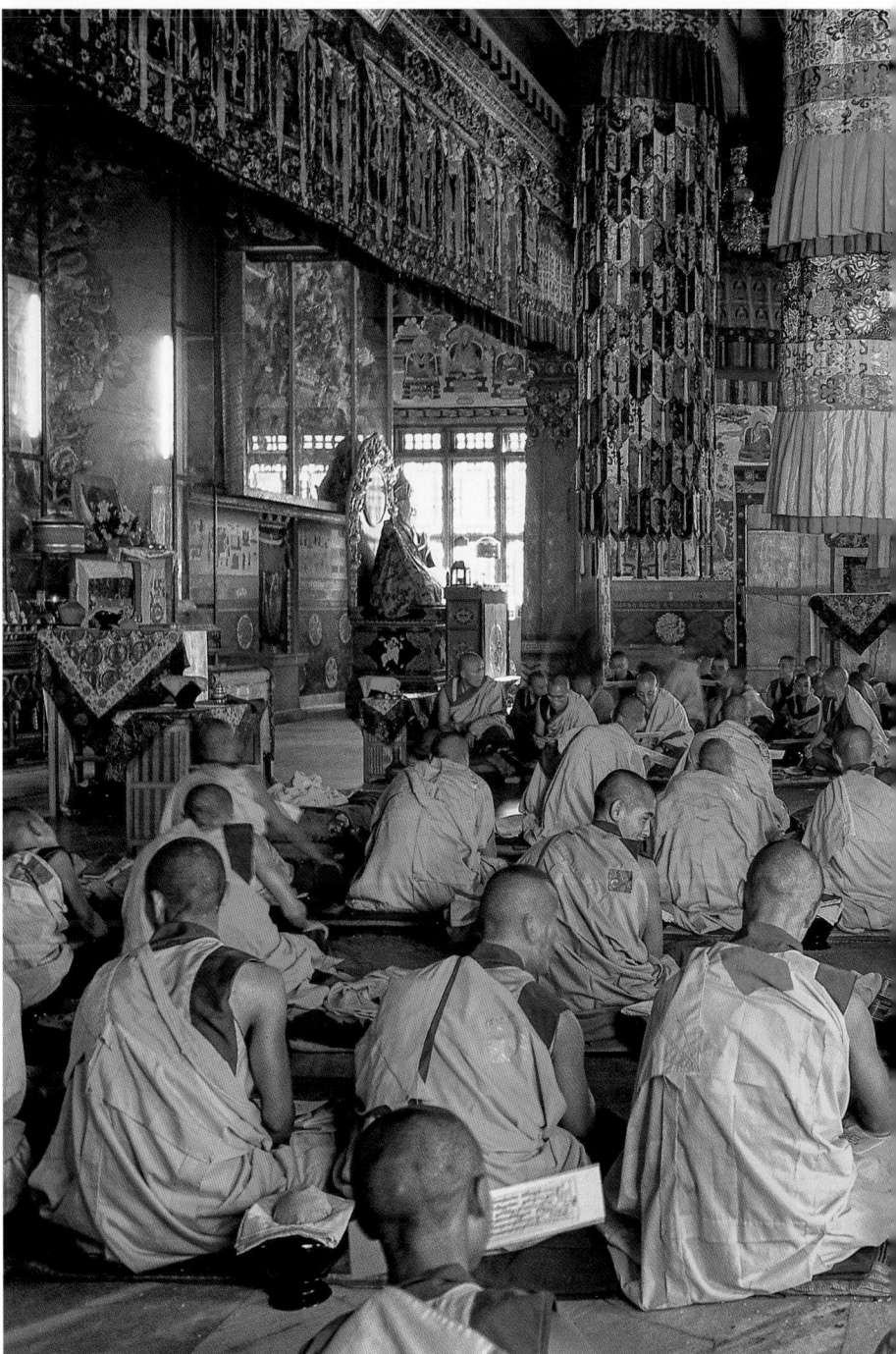

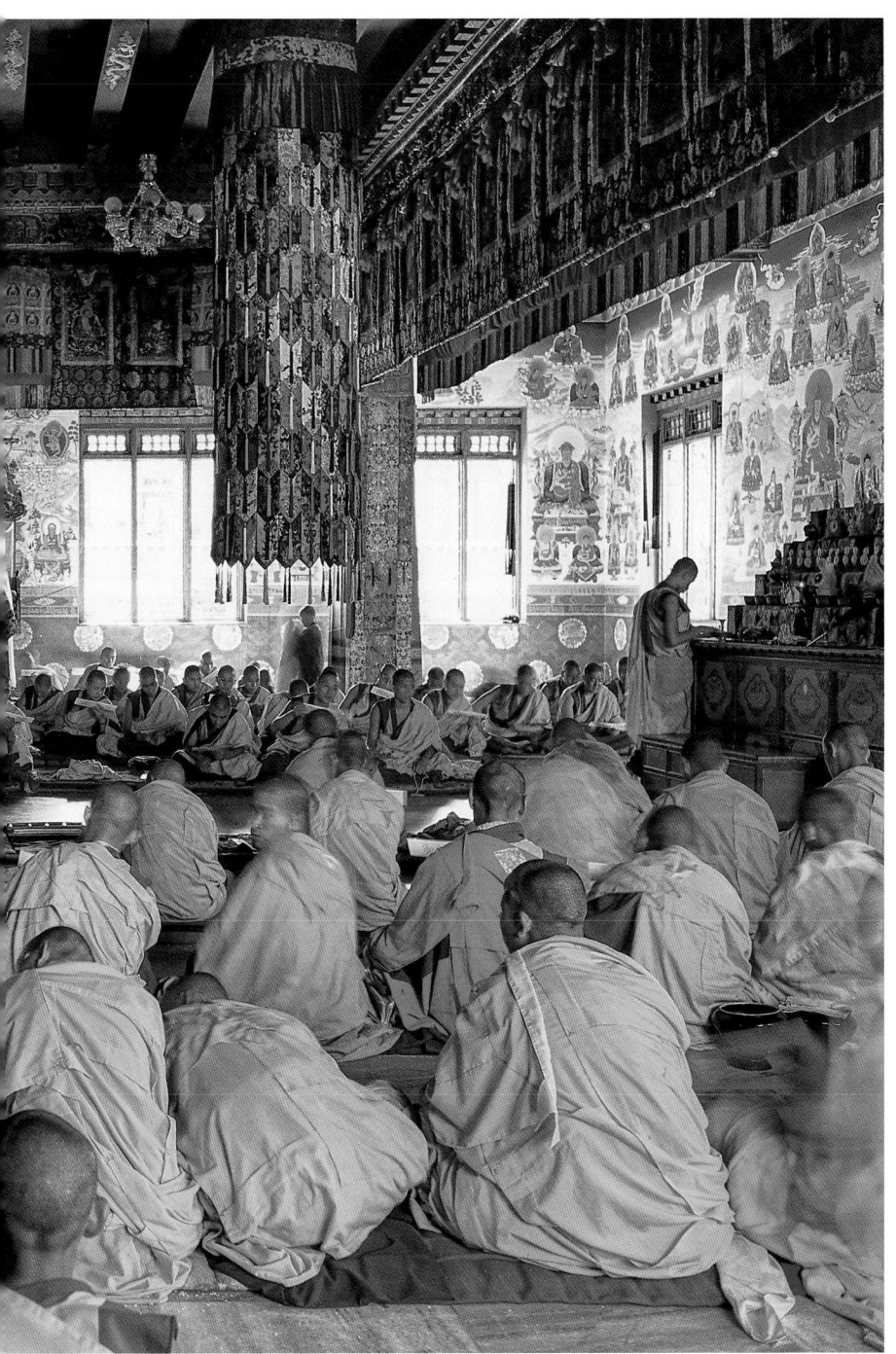

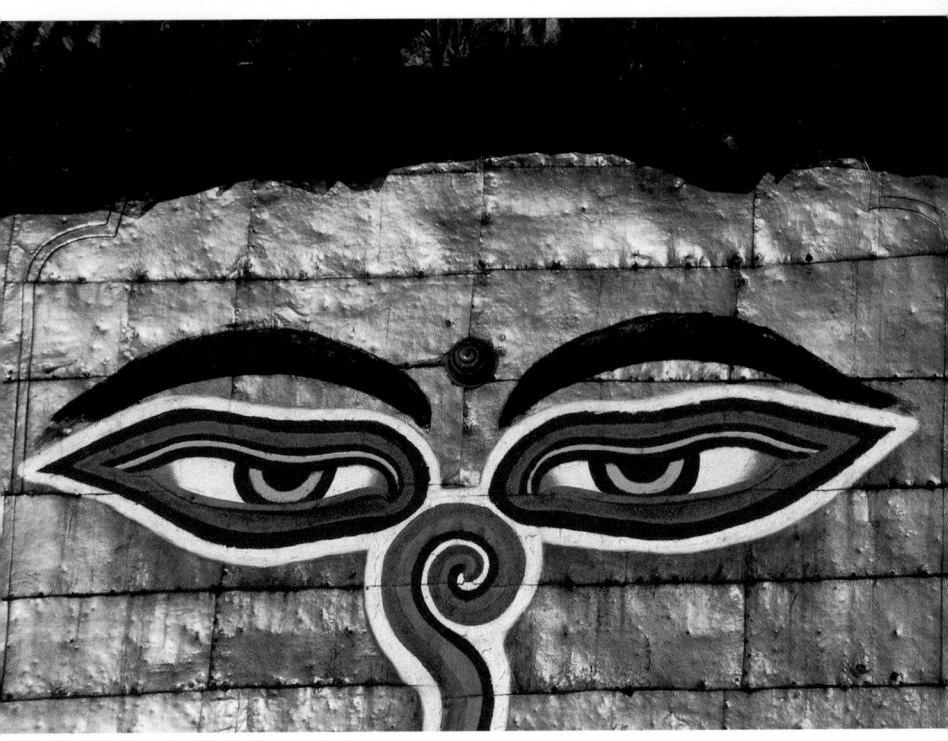

↑ The dot between the two eyes represents the Buddha's "third eye" of perception. • Der Punkt zwischen den beiden Augen repräsentiert Buddhas „drittes Auge" der spirituellen Wahrnehmung. • Le point entre les deux yeux représente le troisième œil du Bouddha, celui de la clairvoyance.

→ An image of the founding guru of a Buddhist sect. • Die Figur des Gründungsgurus einer buddhistischen Sekte. • Le gourou fondateur d'une secte bouddhiste.

PP. 80-81 Frescoes of saints in the temple at Shechen monastery. • Heiligenfiguren im Tempel des Klosters Shechen. • Les fresques du monastère de Shechen représentent des saints.

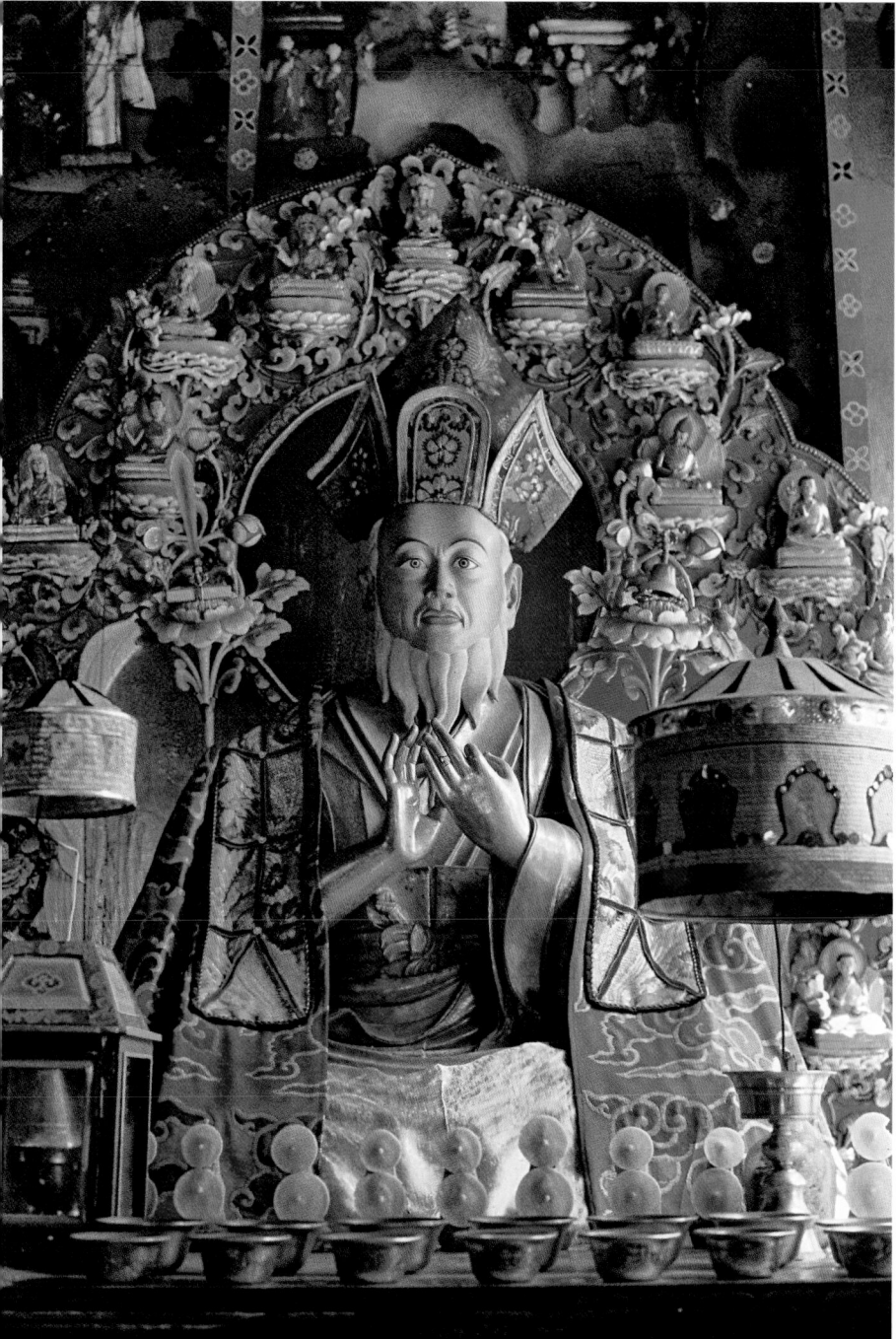

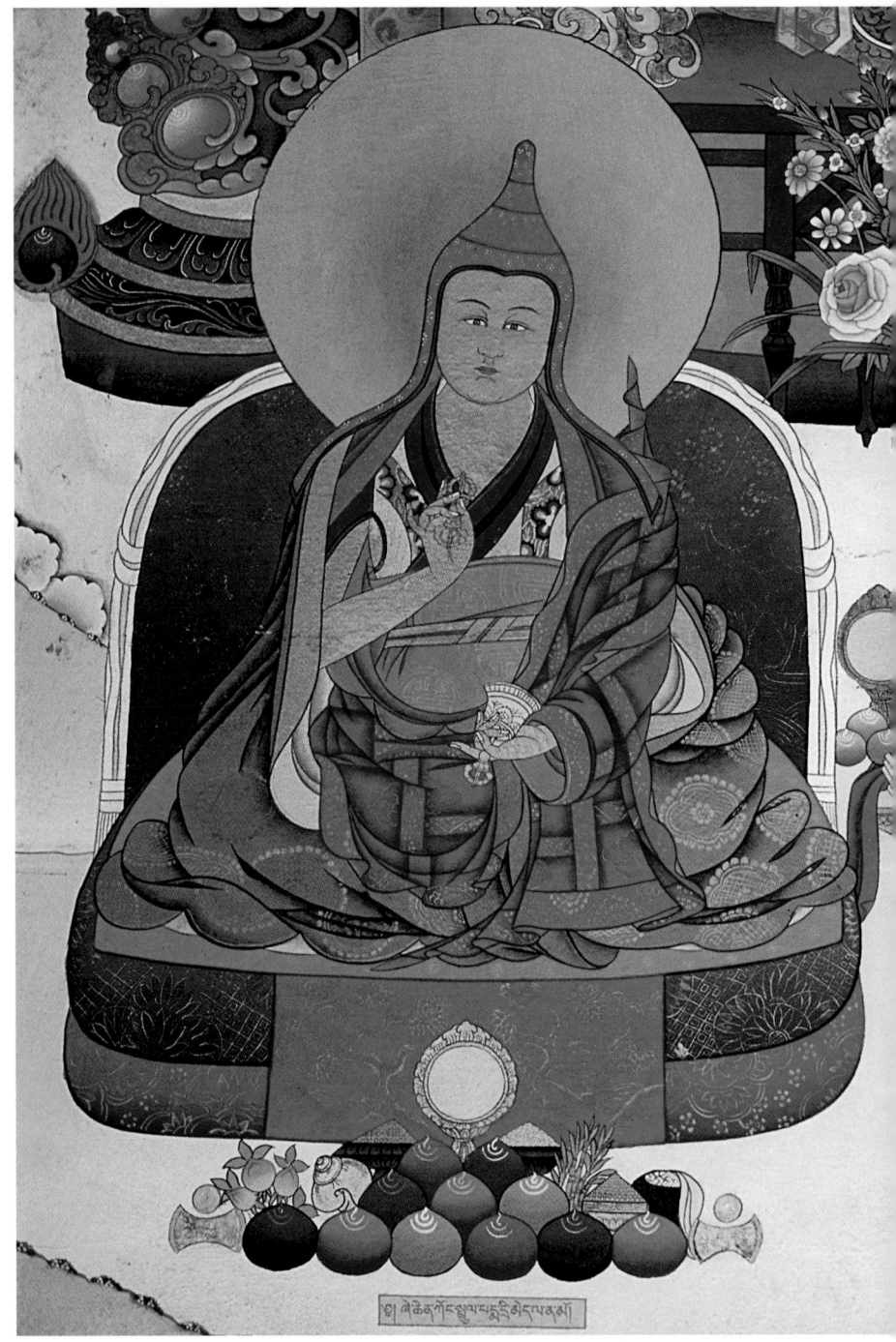

ཨེ་མ་ཧོ། ཤེ་ཆེན་ཀོང་སྤྲུལ་པདྨ་དྲི་མེད་ལ་ཕྱག་འཚལ།

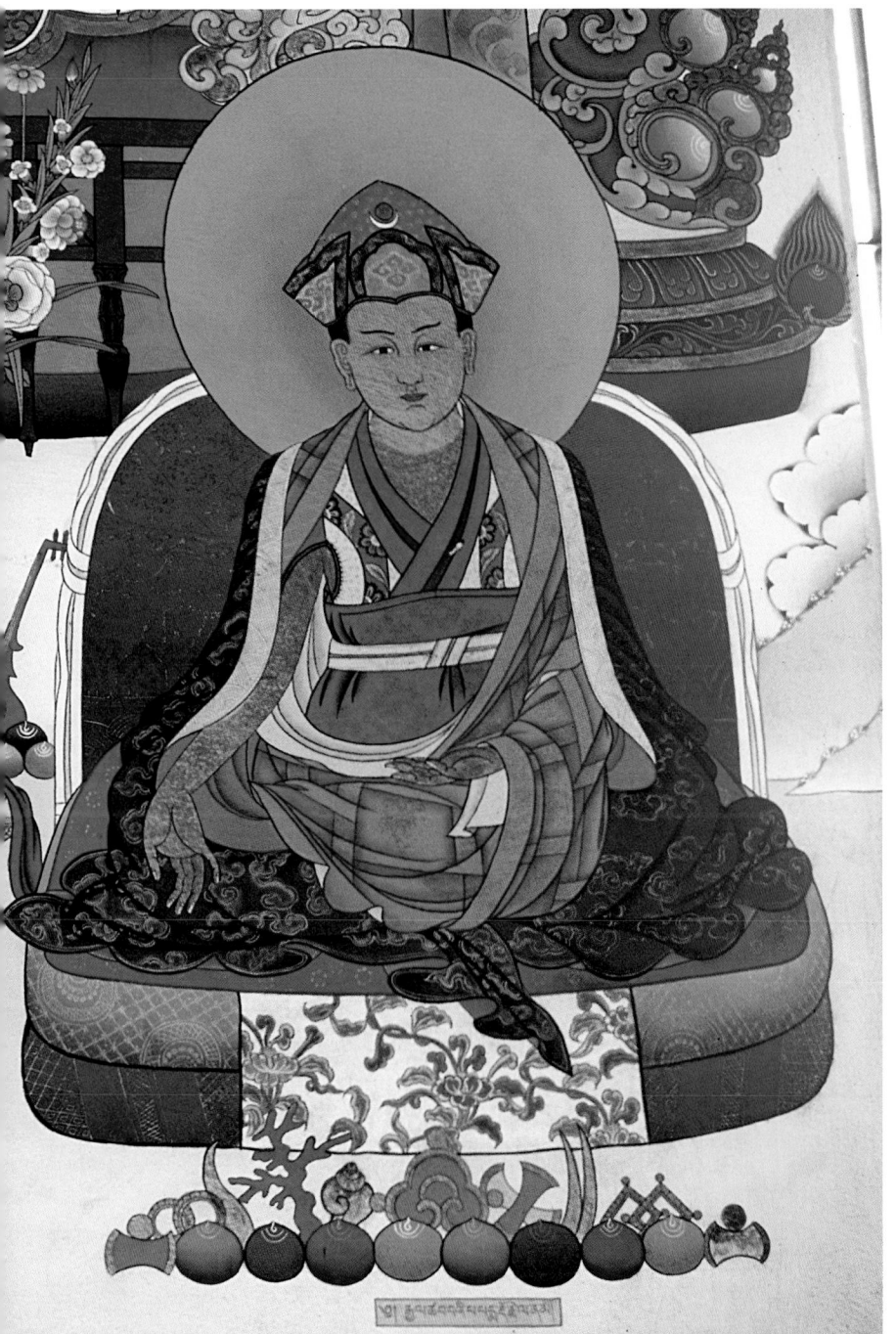

ༀ། རྒྱལ་ཚབ་འགྲོ་མགོན་རྡོ་རྗེ་ཤེས་རབ་ཟེར།

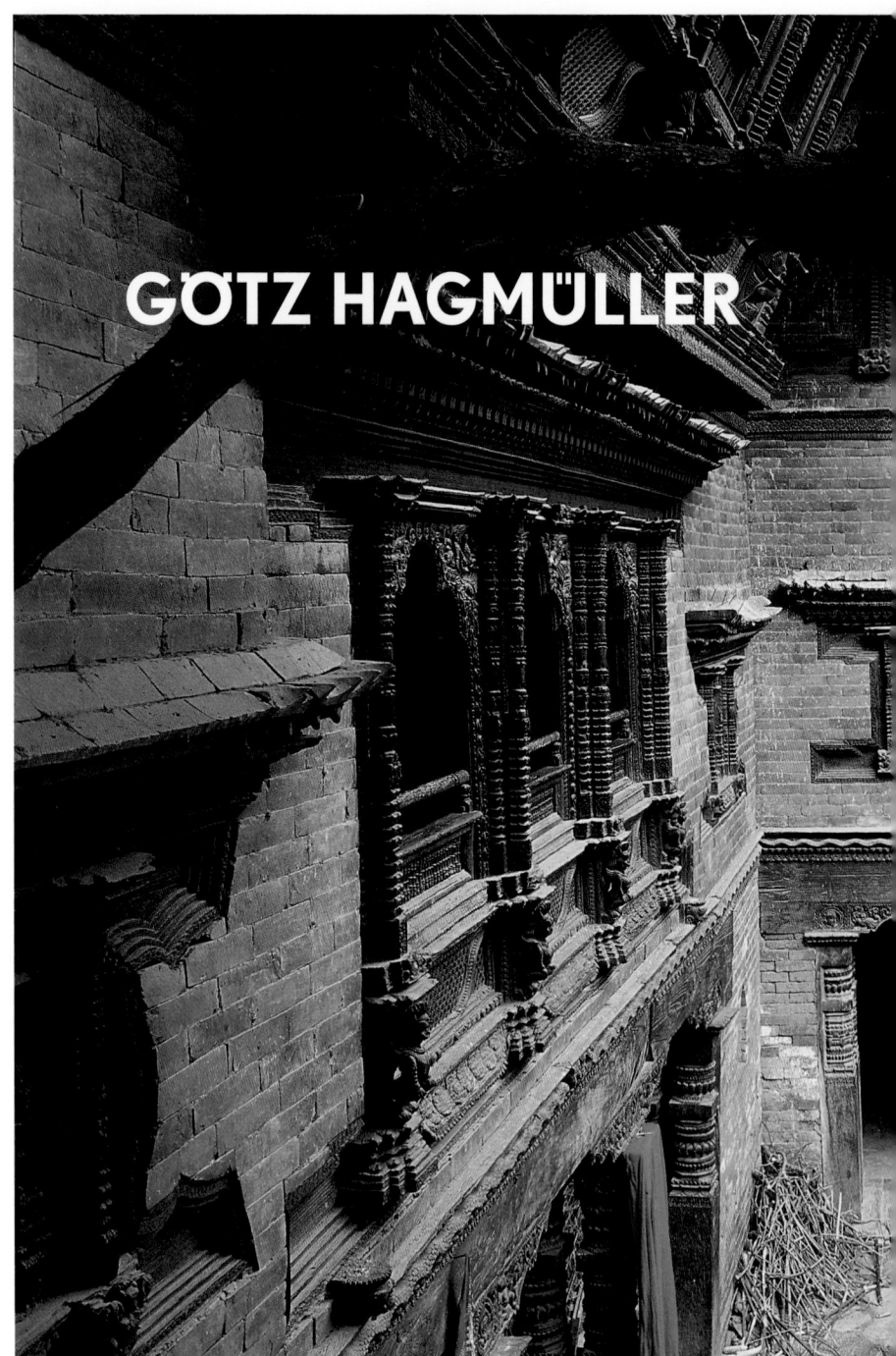

GÖTZ HAGMÜLLER

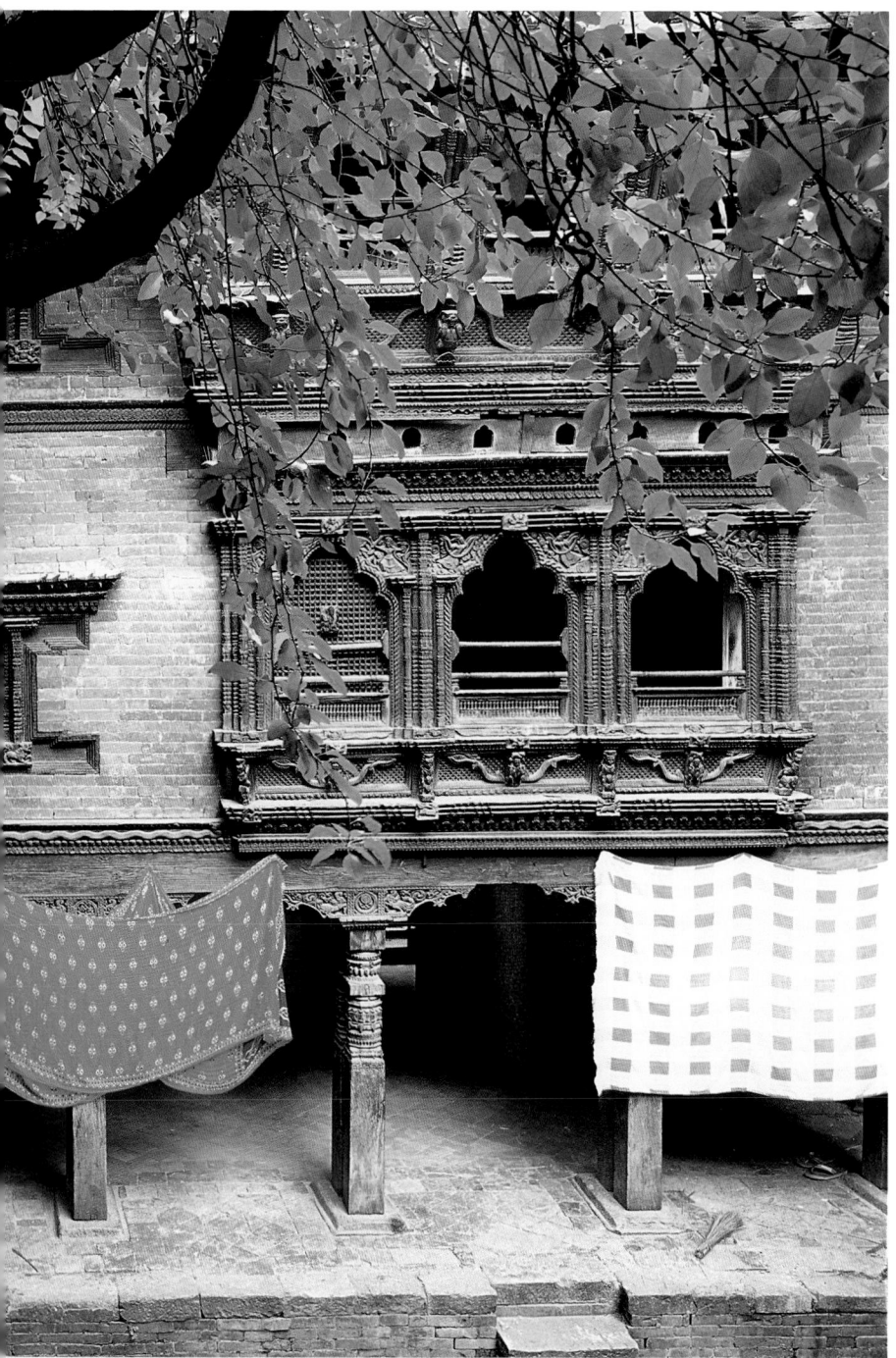

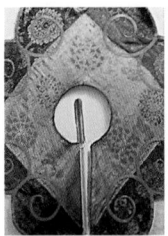

GÖTZ HAGMÜLLER

BHAKTAPUR
NEPAL

One of the abiding pleasures of the medieval town of Bhaktapur, a short drive east of Kathmandu, is that it is a pedestrian preserve. Trucks and buses are forbidden inside city limits. Walking its old cobbled streets that link a series of richly-carved temples, shrines and monasteries, dotted in and around great royal squares, is to breathe the syncretic Hindu-Buddhist culture of the Newari people, the earliest settlers of Kathmandu Valley. The town bustles with the life of traditional artisans – potters, woodcarvers and weavers – who display their wares in the open air. Bhaktapur was saved from ruin by an ambitious German-funded urban conservation project in the 1970s. Götz Hagmüller, an Austrian architect, was part of the effort and formed a deep attachment to Bhaktapur. He rented the two upper floors of a *mat*, a rest house for pilgrims. A typical 17th-century Newari building of narrow rooms, pillared verandas and carved windows built around courtyards, it is now Hagmüller's home from home.

Nur eine kurze Fahrstrecke östlich von Kathmandu liegt die mittelalterliche Stadt Bhaktapur, die zu einer Fußgänger-zone deklariert wurde. Innerhalb der Stadtgrenzen sind Lkw und Busse verboten. Die Straßen mit Kopfsteinpflaster verbinden eine Reihe von Tempeln mit verschwenderischer Holzschnitzerei sowie große königliche Plätze miteinander, wo sich häufig Schreine und Klöster finden. Beim Spaziergang durch diese geschichtsträchtige Stadt spürt man die syn-kretistische, hindu-buddhistische Kultur des Newar-Volkes, das als erstes im Kathmandu-Tal siedelte. Im geschäftigen Bhaktapur bieten traditionelle Handwerker – Töpfer, Holzschnitzer und Weber – ihre Ware unter freiem Himmel an. Die Stadt konnte in den 1970er Jahren dank eines ehrgeizigen, aus Deutschland geförderten Projekts vor dem Verfall gerettet werden. Der österreichische Architekt Götz Hagmüller war damals mit von der Partie und entwickelte eine tiefe Zuneigung zu Bhaktapur. Er mietete die beiden obersten Stockwerke eines *mat*, einer Pilgerpension. Das charak-teristische, um Innenhöfe herum gebaute Newar-Haus aus dem 17. Jahrhundert ist nun mit seinen engen Räumen, den säulengeschmückten Veranden und den holzgeschnitzten Fenstern Hagmüllers zweite Heimat.

Située à quelques heures de route à l'est de Katmandou, la cité médiévale de Bhaktapur offre un plaisir toujours renou-velé : le piéton y est roi. La circulation est interdite aux camions et aux bus. Se promener dans ses rues pavées anciennes reliant de somptueux temples, sanctuaires et monastères disséminés dans de superbes parcs royaux, c'est aspirer une bouffée de la civilisation syncrétique hindouiste-bouddhique des Newari, premiers habitants de la vallée de Katmandou. La ville vit au rythme des artisans traditionnels – potiers, ébénistes et tisserands – qui présentent leurs marchandises en plein air. Bhaktapur a été sauvée de la ruine dans les années 1970 par un ambitieux projet de préservation financé par des fonds allemands. Götz Hagmüller, qui a participé à cette action, a conçu un profond attachement pour la ville. Il a loué les deux étages supérieurs d'un *mat*, relais pour voyageurs. Cet édifice newari typique du 17e siècle, caractérisé par des pièces étroites, des vérandas à colonnade, des fenêtres en bois sculpté et des cours intérieures, est maintenant le chez-soi de l'exilé Hagmüller.

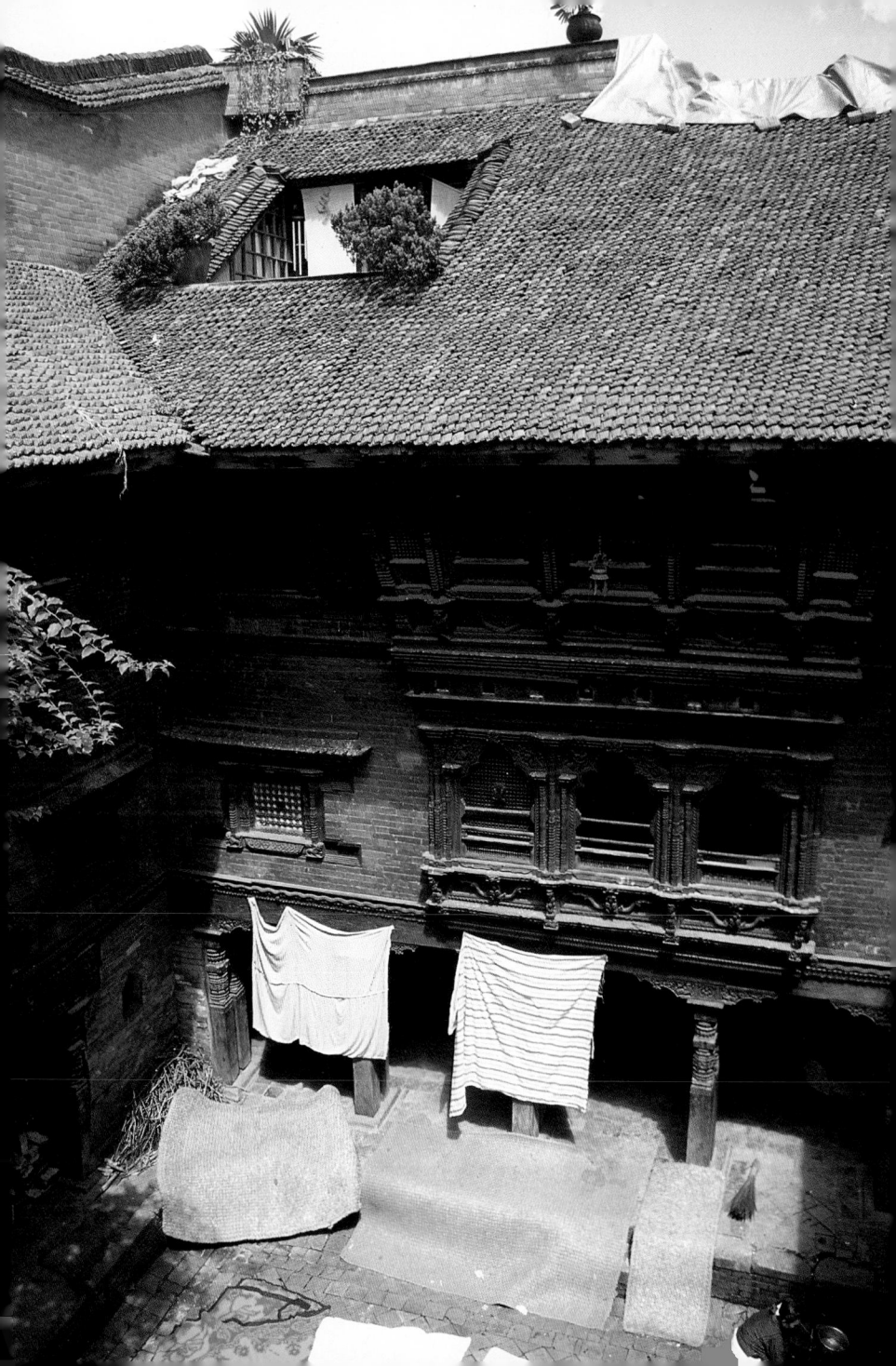

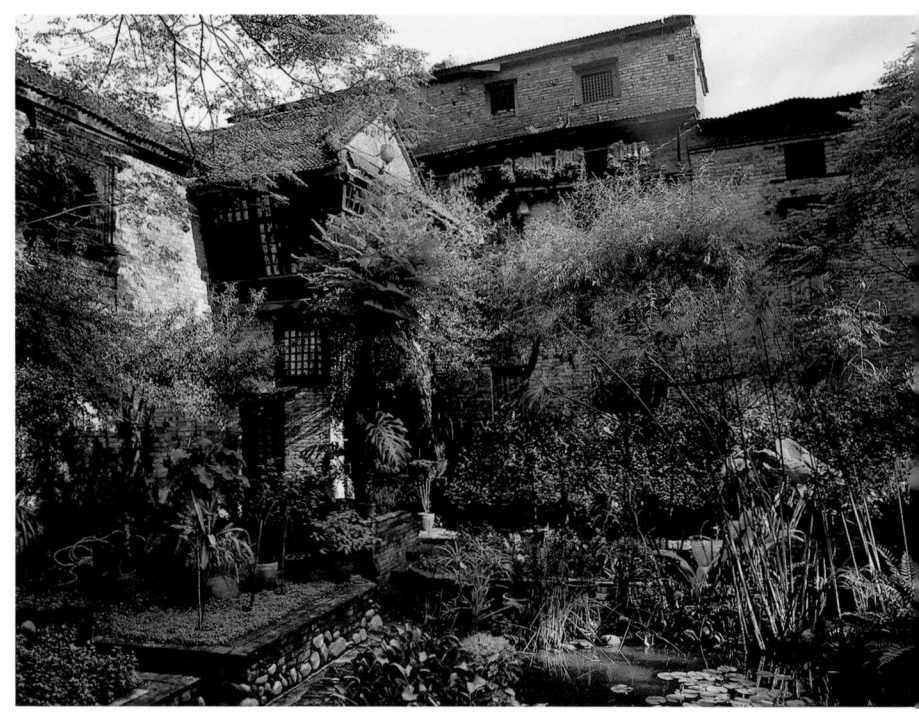

PP. 82–83 and P. 85 The main
courtyard with saris hung to dry on
the elaborately carved woodwork
set in brick walls. • In dem zentralen
Innenhof trocknen Saris an den feinen
Holzschnitzereien, die in das Mauer-
werk integriert sind. • Dans la cour
principale, des saris sèchent accrochés
aux boiseries très ouvragées qui
agrémentent les murs de brique.

↑ Lush greenery drapes a garden
courtyard. • Üppige Pflanzen zieren
einen Innenhofgarten. • La cour-jardin
est envahie par la végétation.

↓ A pergola fashioned from old wooden columns provides shade in the paved garden. • In dem gepflasterten Garten sorgt eine Pergola aus Holz-säulen für Schatten. • Une pergola faite de colonnes de récupération en bois donne de l'ombre dans le jardin pavé.

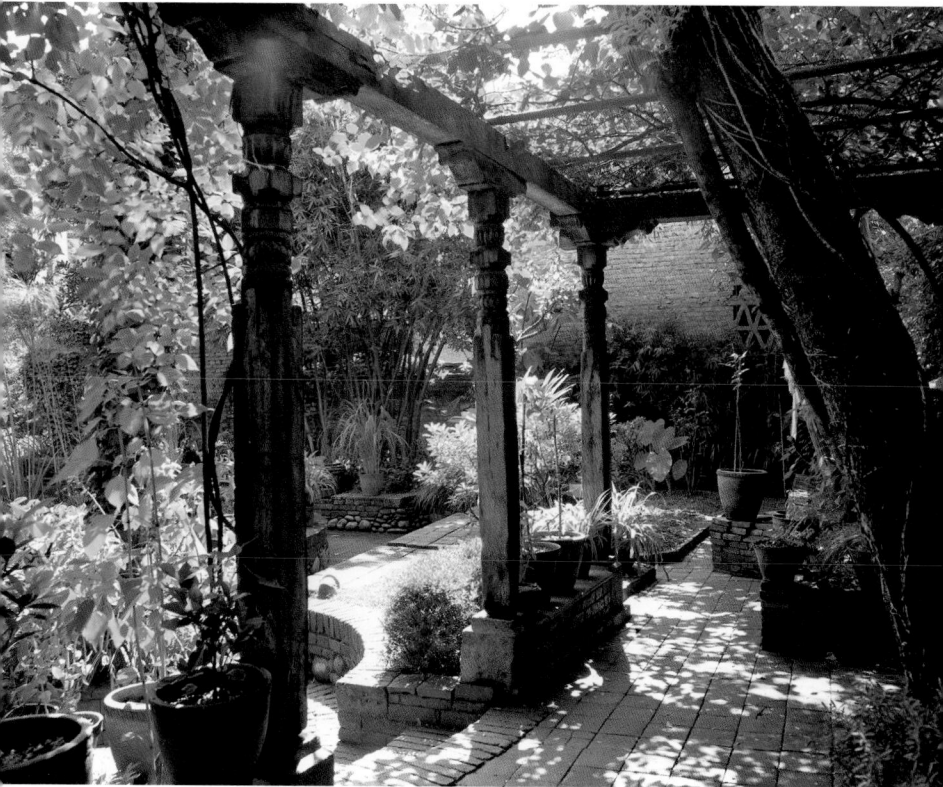

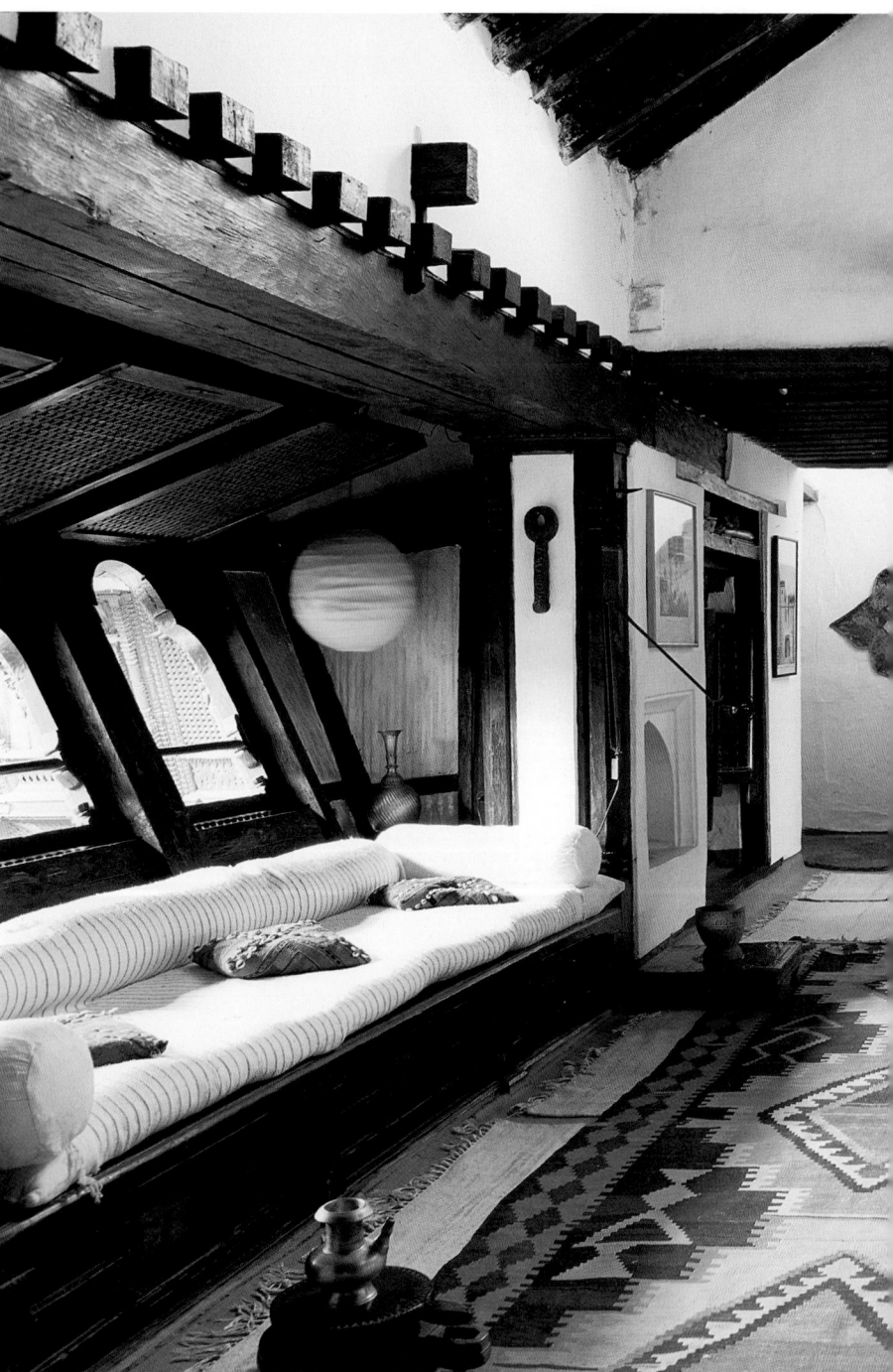

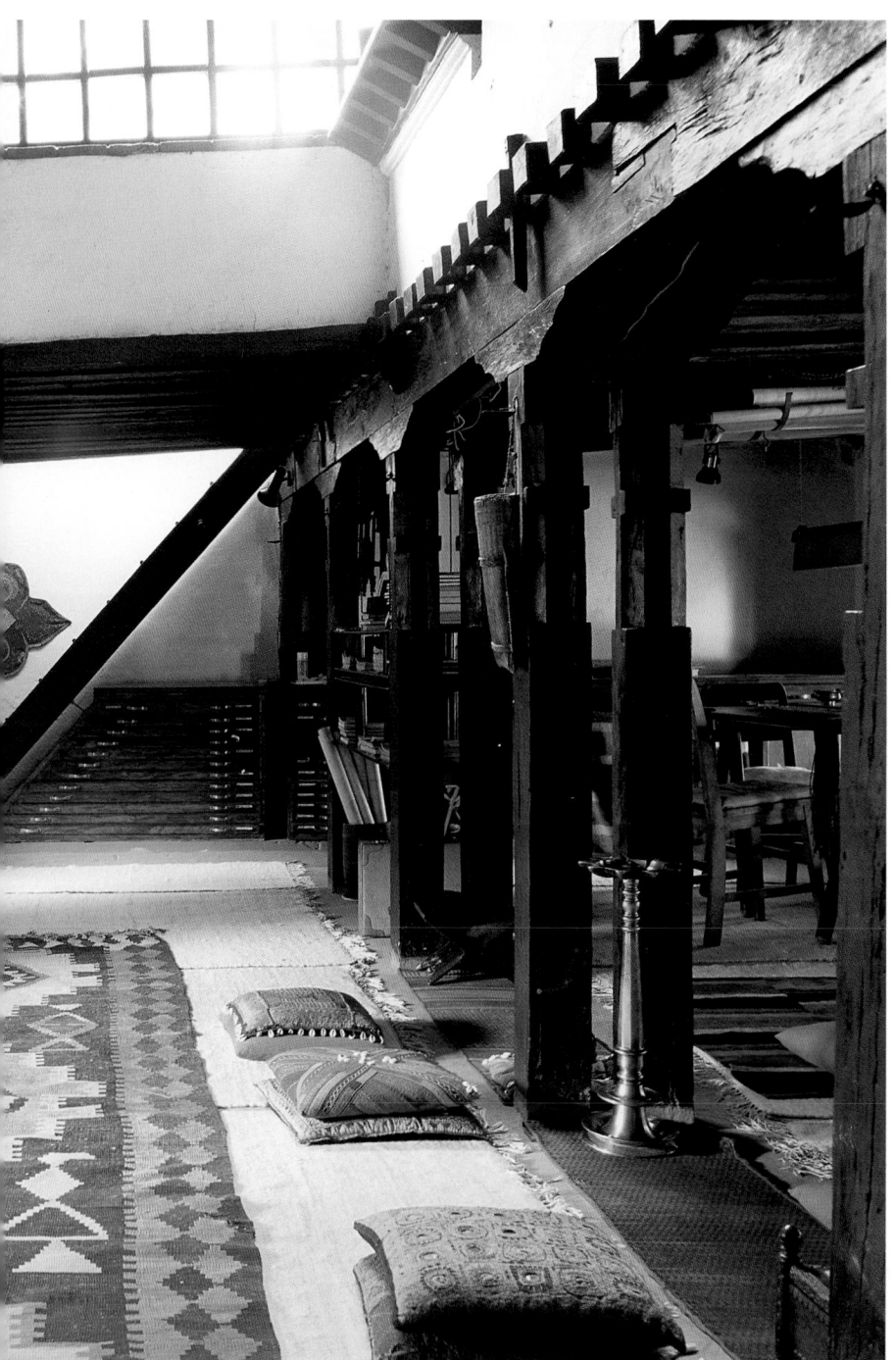

PP. 88–89 The long living room with
its open timberwork. • Das geräumige
Wohnzimmer mit offenem Gebälk. •
Dans ce salon tout en longueur, la
charpente est apparente.

↓ The main seating is a divan placed
against slanting windows that give the
room privacy. • Der große Diwan vor
den schrägen Fenstern, die den Raum
besonders gemütlich erscheinen lassen,
lädt zum Verweilen ein. • Le divan
est adossé à des fenêtres inclinées qui
confèrent à la pièce une certaine intimité.

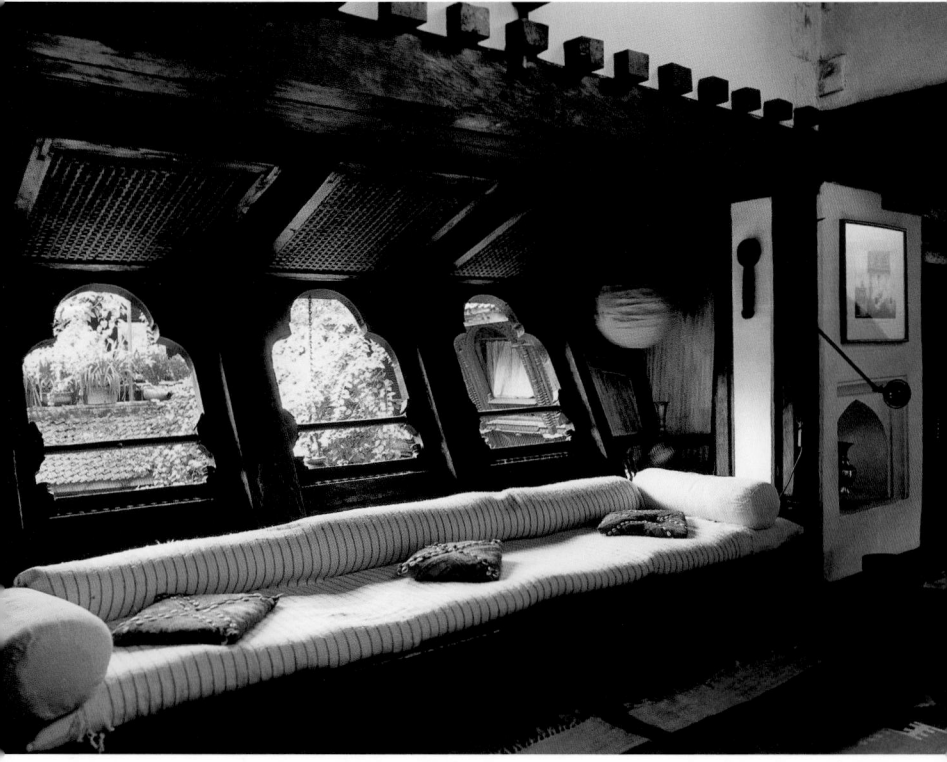

GÖTZ HAGMÜLLER

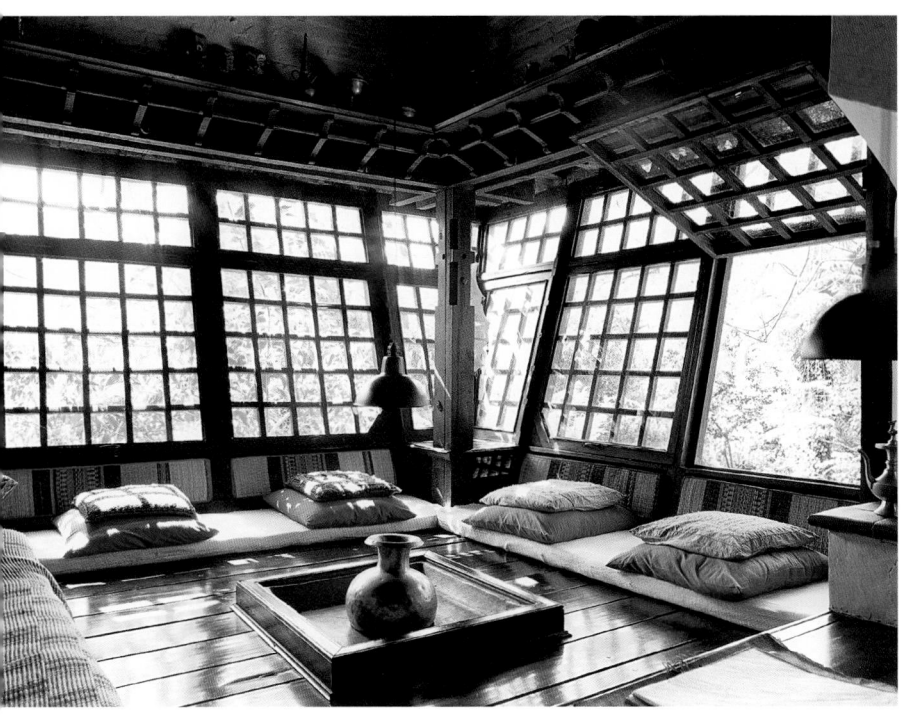

↑ The guest room with its slanted glass-paned windows overlooks the garden. The windows open upwards. • Vom Gästezimmer mit den schrägen Fenstern blickt man in den Garten. Die Fenster werden nach oben geöffnet. • Cette pièce de réception, également dotée de fenêtres inclinées, donne sur le jardin. Les ouvrants des fenêtres se rabattent vers le haut.

PP. 92-93 A scalloped "peacock" arch leads into the dining room decorated with well-scrubbed brass dishes. • Ein muschelförmiger Bogen führt ins Esszimmer, das mit glänzend poliertem Messinggeschirr aufwartet. • La porte de la salle à manger où la vaisselle en cuivre étincelle est surmontée d'un arc polylobé.

91

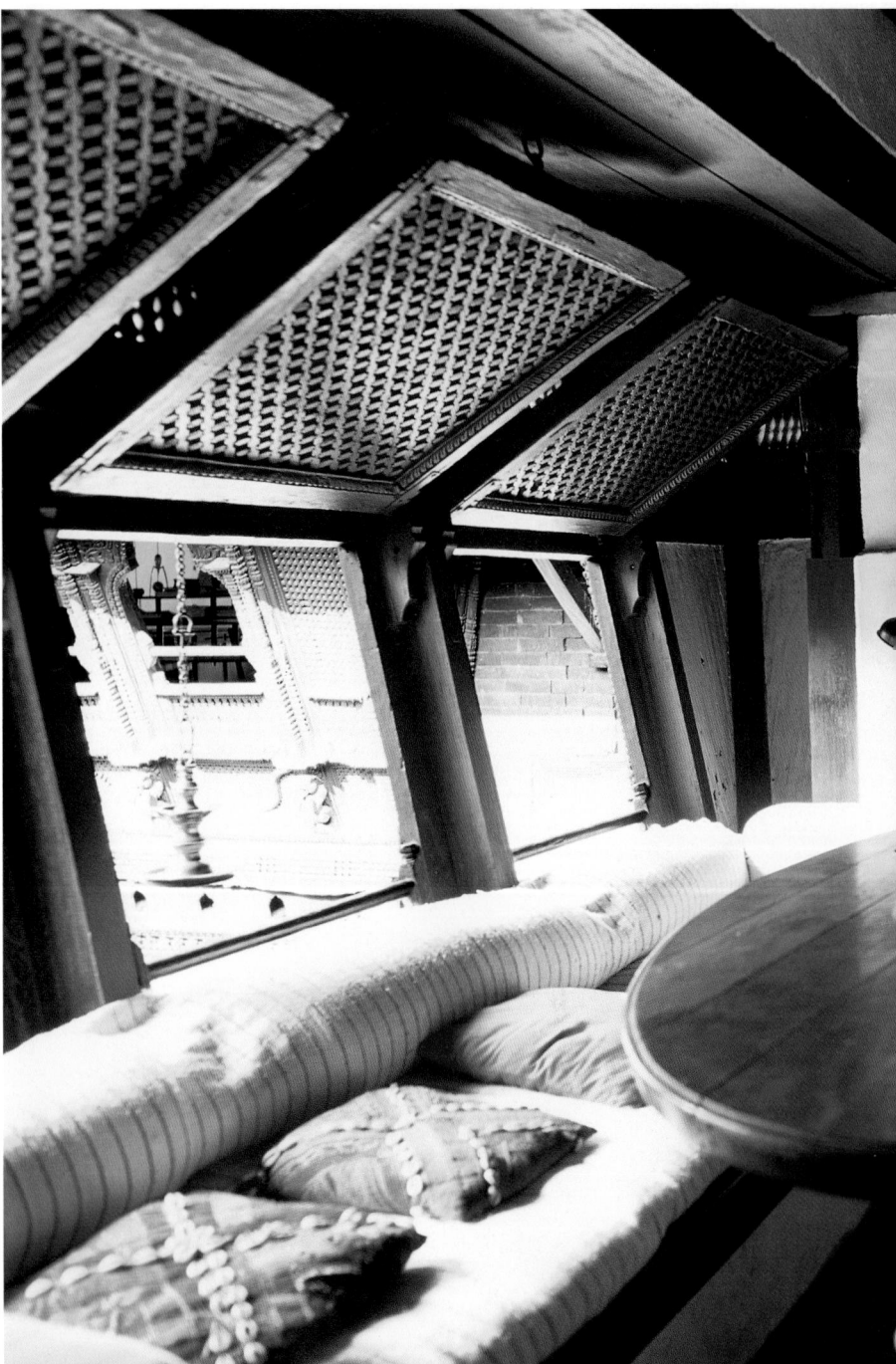

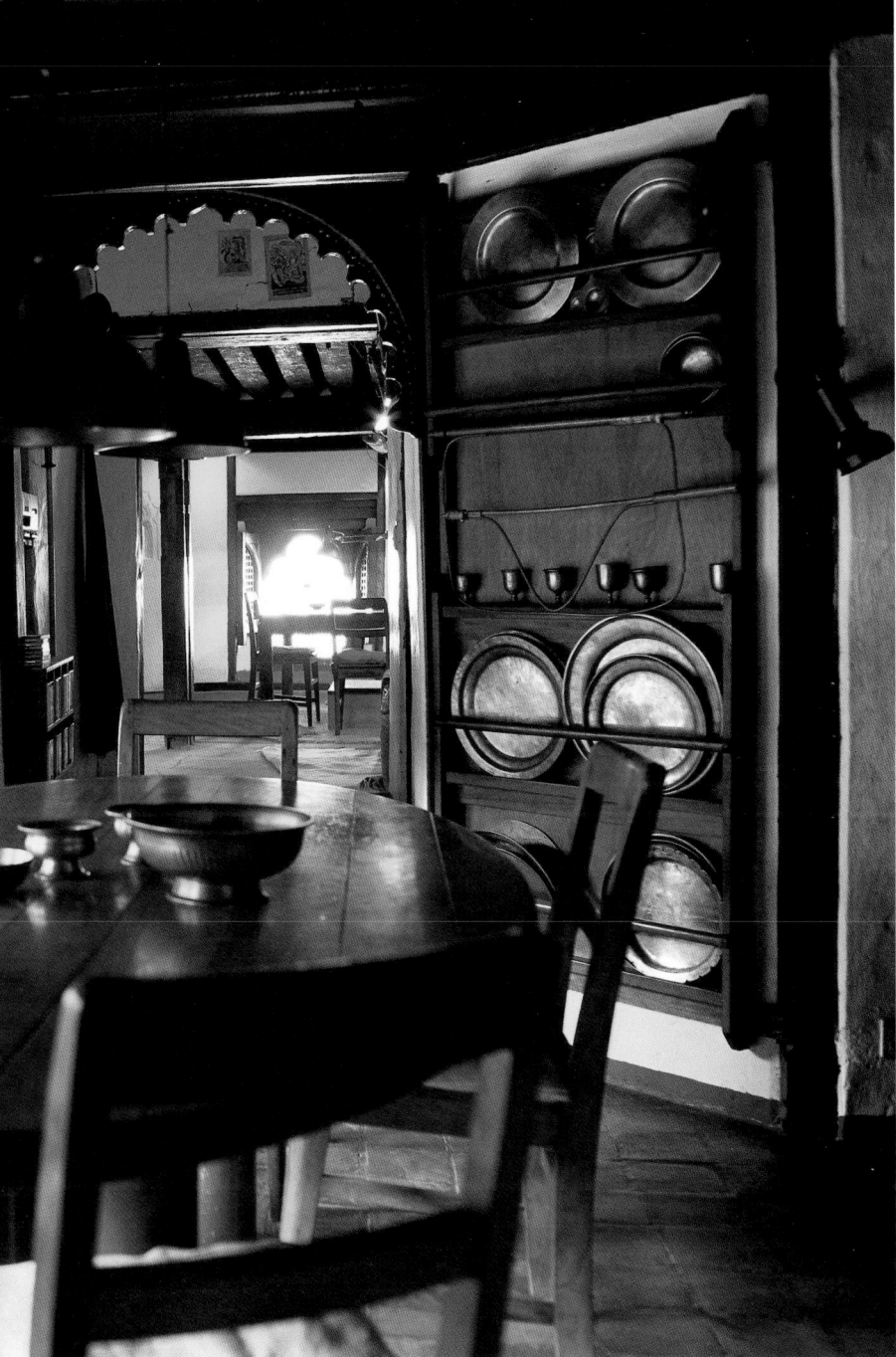

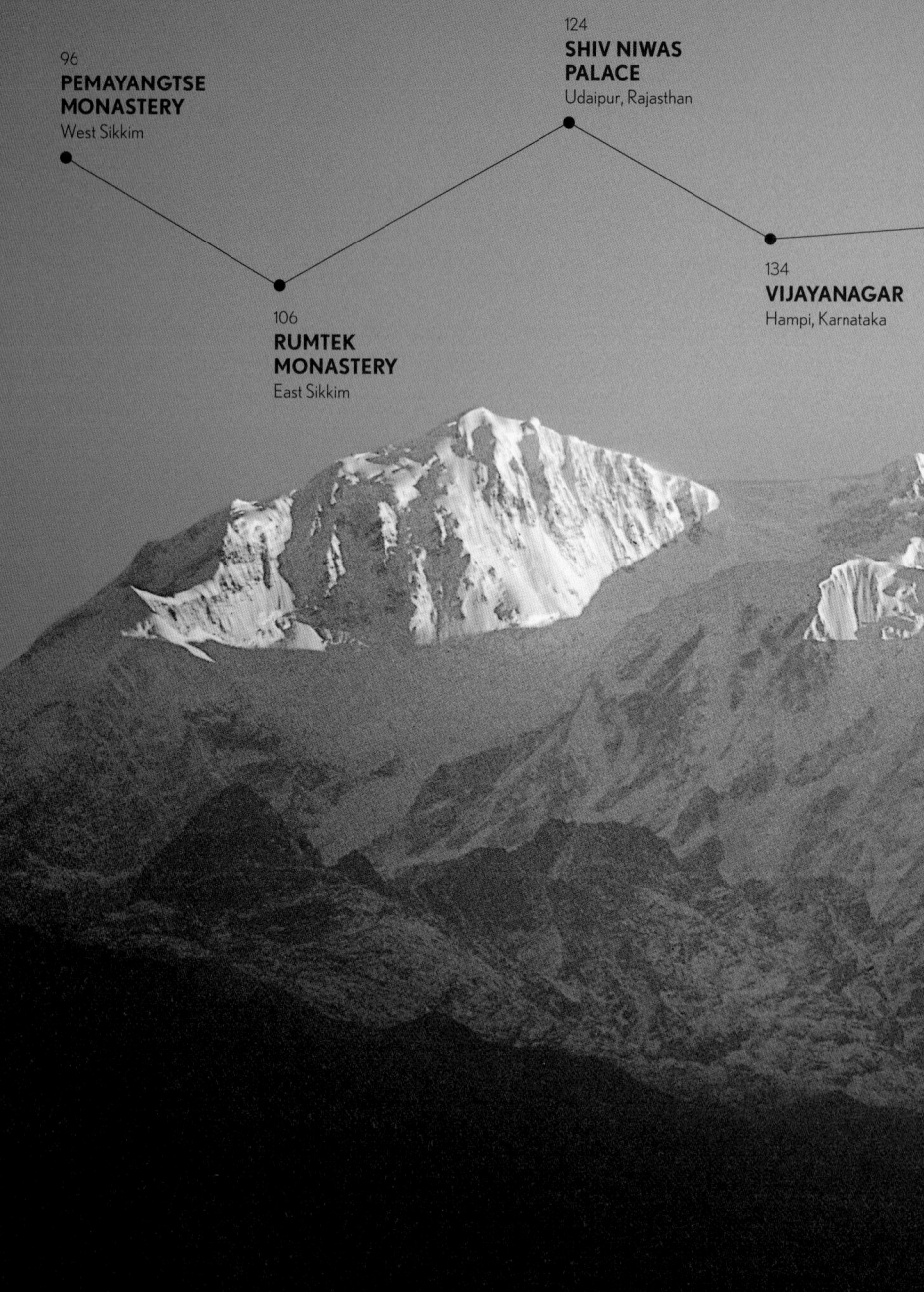

96
**PEMAYANGTSE
MONASTERY**
West Sikkim

124
**SHIV NIWAS
PALACE**
Udaipur, Rajasthan

106
**RUMTEK
MONASTERY**
East Sikkim

134
VIJAYANAGAR
Hampi, Karnataka

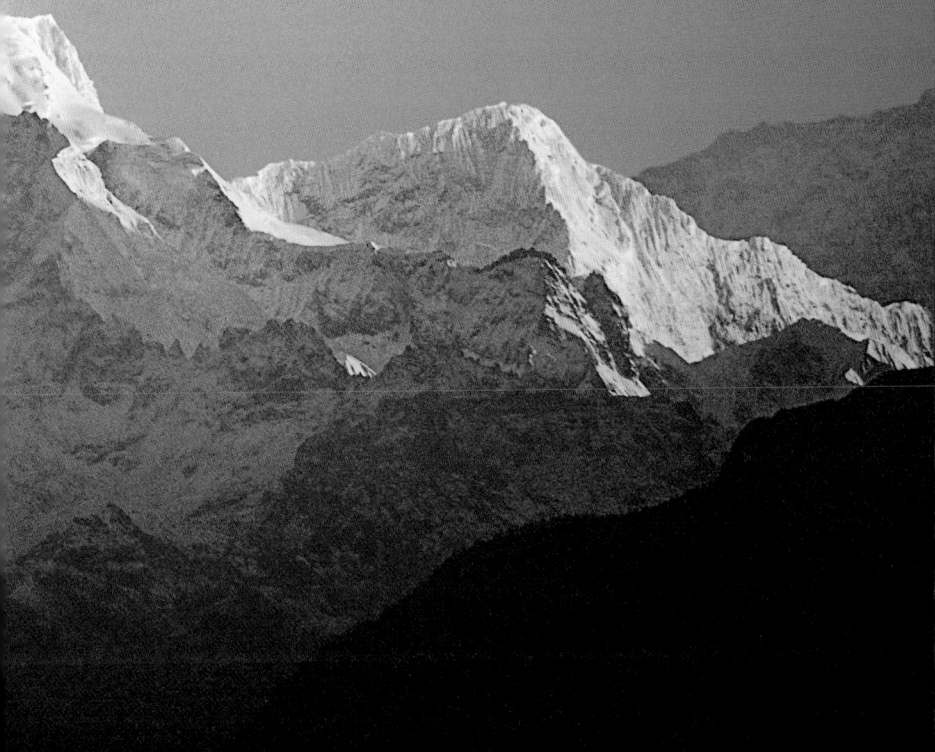

152
JÖRG DRECHSEL
Cochin, Kerala

144
**PADMANABHAPURAM
PALACE**
Nagercoil, Tamil Nadu

INDIA

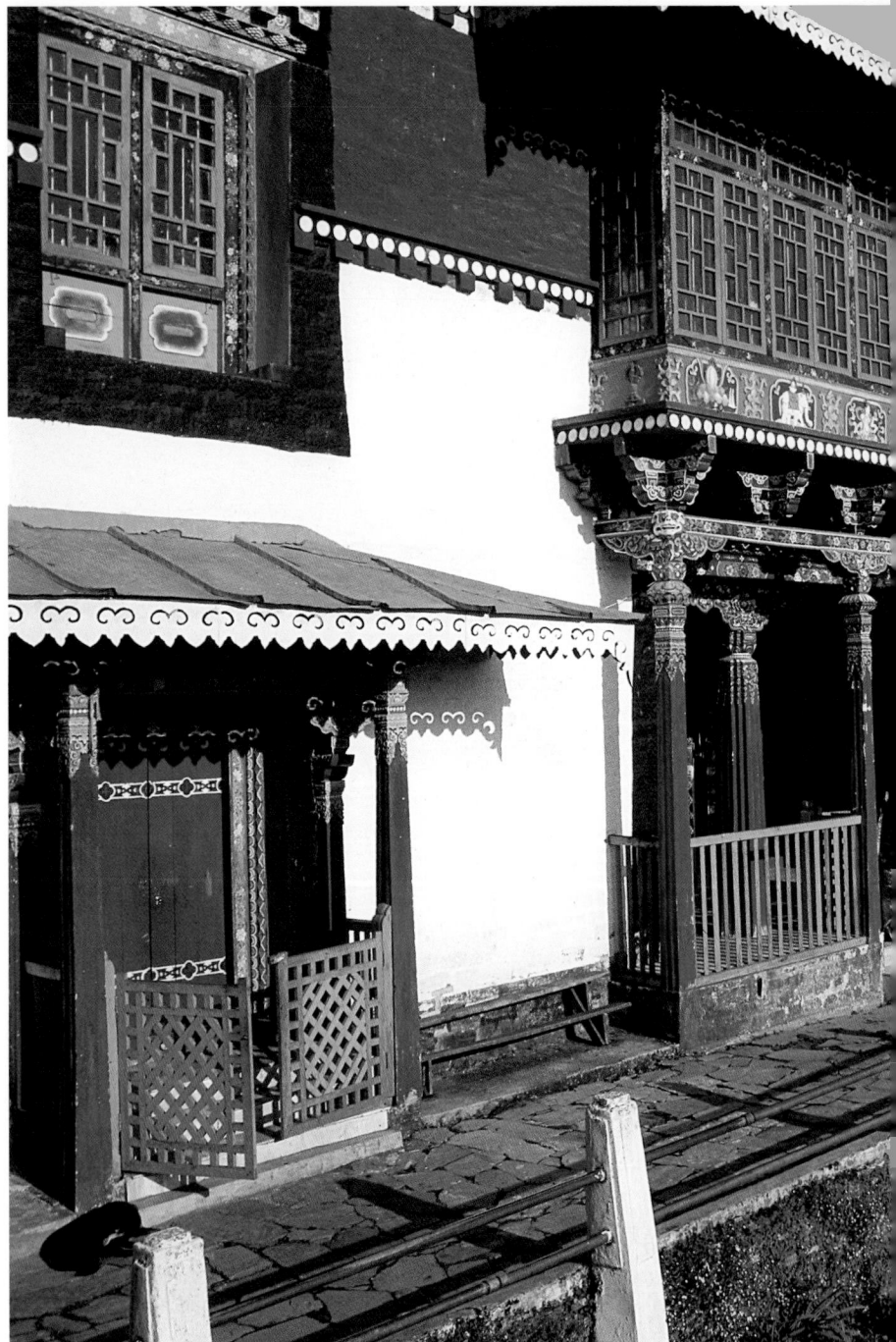

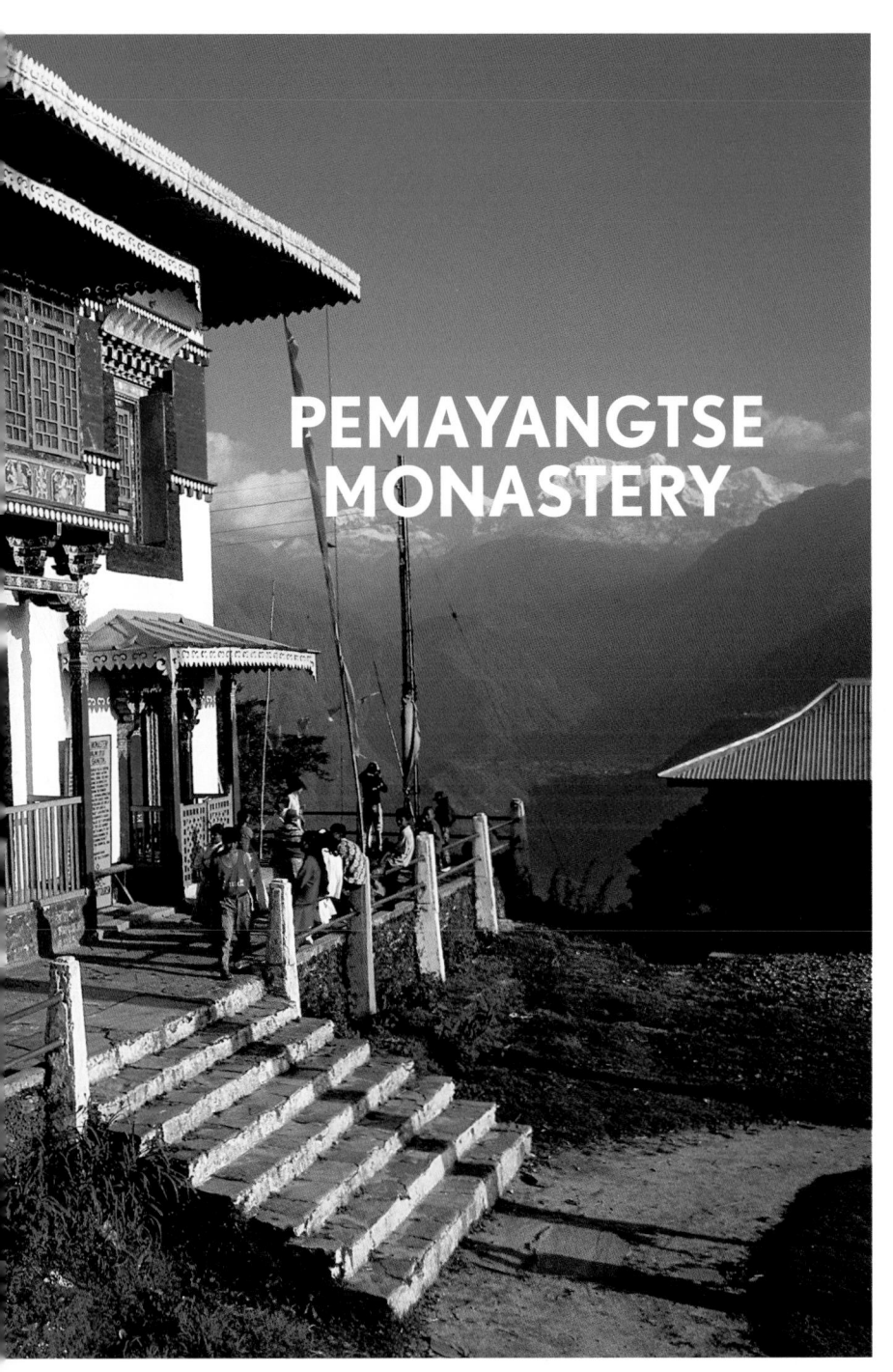

PEMAYANGTSE
MONASTERY

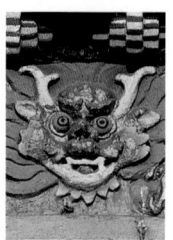

PEMAYANGTSE MONASTERY
WEST SIKKIM
INDIA

Blessed with breathtaking views of Kanchenjunga, the third highest mountain in the world, the Pemayangtse monastery is the most important of more than a hundred monasteries in India's northeastern state of Sikkim. Kanchenjunga in Tibetan means "Five Treasures of the Great Snow" and Pemayangtse translates as the "Perfect Sublime Lotus". High mountain passes at altitudes of 14,000 to 18,000 feet link Sikkim to Tibet in the north, Bhutan and Bengal in the south and Nepal in the west. Padmasambhava, the Indian saint who consolidated Tibetan Buddhism, is said to have passed through Sikkim in the eighth century. Until 1975 the state was ruled by a long line of kings, one of whom established Pemayangtse at the turn of the 18th century. The monastery belongs to the Nyingmapa order of Tibetan Buddhism. More than a hundred monks still live here; at several times in the year – including the Sikkimese New Year in February – Pemayangtse resonates with the sound of masked dancers. Thousands of pilgrims come to worship and watch the spectacle.

Das Pemayangtse-Kloster ist das bedeutendste von über hundert Klöstern in Sikkim im Nordosten Indiens. Vom Kloster, dessen Name „Vollkommene Lotusblüte" bedeutet, bietet sich ein atemberaubender Ausblick auf den Kangchendzönga, den dritthöchsten Berg der Welt. Der tibetische Name des Berges heißt übersetzt „Fünf Schatzkammern des großen Schnees". Hochgebirgspässe auf 4000 bis 5500 Metern Höhe verbinden Sikkim im Norden mit Tibet, im Süden mit Bhutan und Bengalen und im Westen mit Nepal. Der indische Heilige Padmasambhava, der den Buddhismus in Tibet begründete, soll im 8. Jahrhundert durch Sikkim gereist sein. Einer der Könige, die das Land bis zum Jahre 1975 über viele Jahrhunderte regierten, gründete an der Wende zum 18. Jahrhundert das Kloster Pemayangtse. Das Kloster, in dem noch über hundert Mönche leben, gehört zum Nyingmapa-Orden des tibetischen Buddhismus. Mehrmals im Jahr, darunter zum sikkimesischen Neujahrsfest im Februar, werden im Kloster Pemayangtse Maskentänze zelebriert, zu denen Tausende von Gläubigen und Zuschauern strömen.

Bénéficiant d'une vue imprenable sur le Kangchenjunga, le troisième sommet du monde, le monastère de Pemayangtse est le plus important du Sikkim, État du nord-est de l'Union indienne qui en compte une bonne centaine. En tibétain, Kangchenjunga signifie « les cinq trésors de la grande neige » et Pemayangtse « lotus sublime ». Des cols situés à des altitudes allant de 4000 à 5500 mètres relient le Sikkim au Tibet au nord, au Bhoutan et au Bengale au sud, et au Népal à l'ouest. Padmasambhava, le saint d'origine indienne qui a fondé le bouddhisme tibétain, aurait traversé le Sikkim au 8e siècle. Jusqu'en 1975, le pays a été dirigé par une longue dynastie de rois, dont le fondateur de Pemayangtse au début du 18e siècle. Une bonne centaine de moines vivent encore dans ce monastère de l'école bouddhiste tibétaine Nyingma. À plusieurs reprises dans l'année, à commencer par le Nouvel An du Sikkim en février, le monastère vit au rythme de danseurs masqués, spectacle qui attire des milliers de pèlerins.

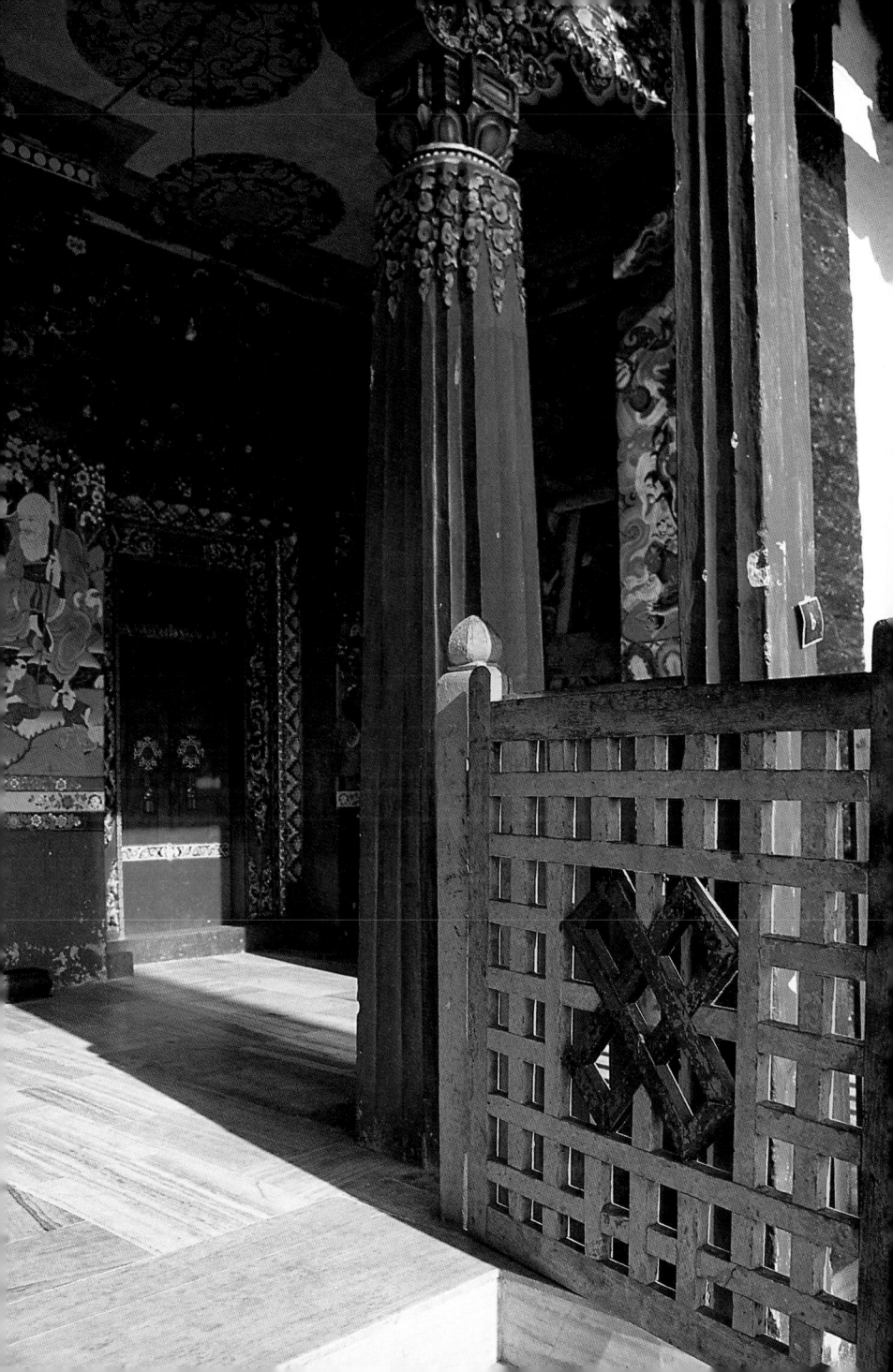

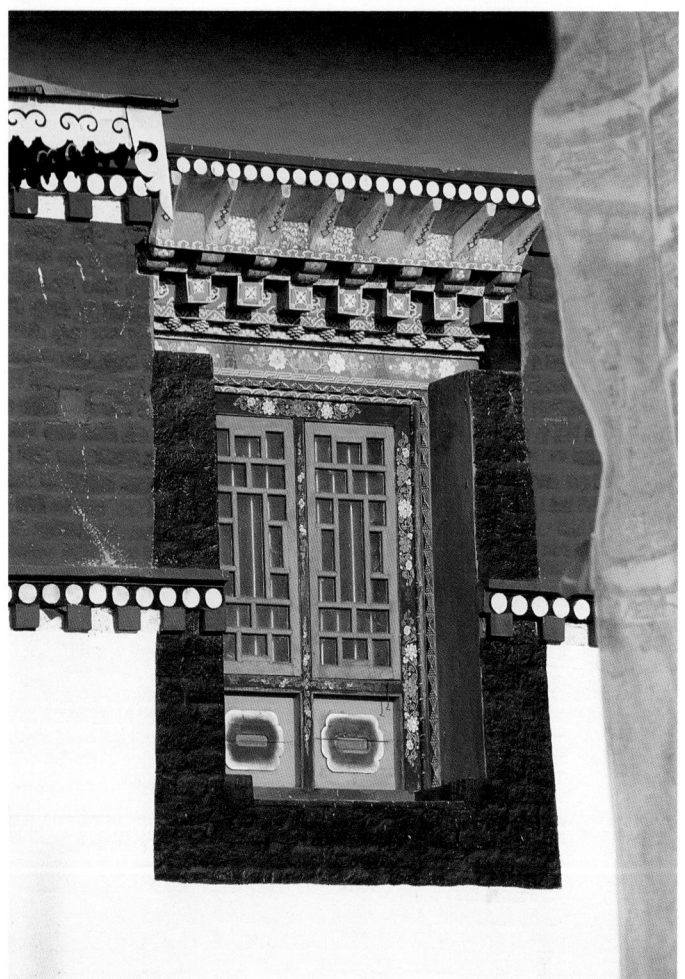

PP. 96-97 Pemayangtse with a spectacular vista of the Kanchenjunga range. • Pemayangtse mit spektakulärem Blick auf das Kangchendzönga-Massiv. • Le monastère se détache sur l'arrière-plan spectaculaire du Kangchenjunga.

P. 99 The gate from the entrance steps leads to a richly-frescoed veranda and the main prayer hall. • Das Tor an den Eingangsstufen führt zu einer üppig mit Fresken verzierten Veranda und zur Hauptgebetshalle. • Le portillon en haut de l'escalier d'entrée mène à une véranda ornée de fresques somptueuses et à la grande salle de prière.

→ Novice monks who join the monastery at a young age. • Die Novizen treten schon im Kindesalter ins Kloster ein. • Les novices entrent très jeunes au monastère.

P. 102 Ornate decorations of flowers, clouds and snow lions on columns and brackets follow a Tibetan iconography. • Die Verzierungen mit Blüten, Wolken und Schneelöwen auf Säulen und Streben richten sich nach der tibetischen Ikonographie. • Sur les colonnes et les poutres, des ornements réunissant fleurs, nuages et lions des neiges relèvent d'une iconographie tibétaine.

P. 103 The doors painted red are a sign of good fortune. • Die rot gestrichenen Türen sollen Glück bringen. • Le rouge des portes est signe de bonheur.

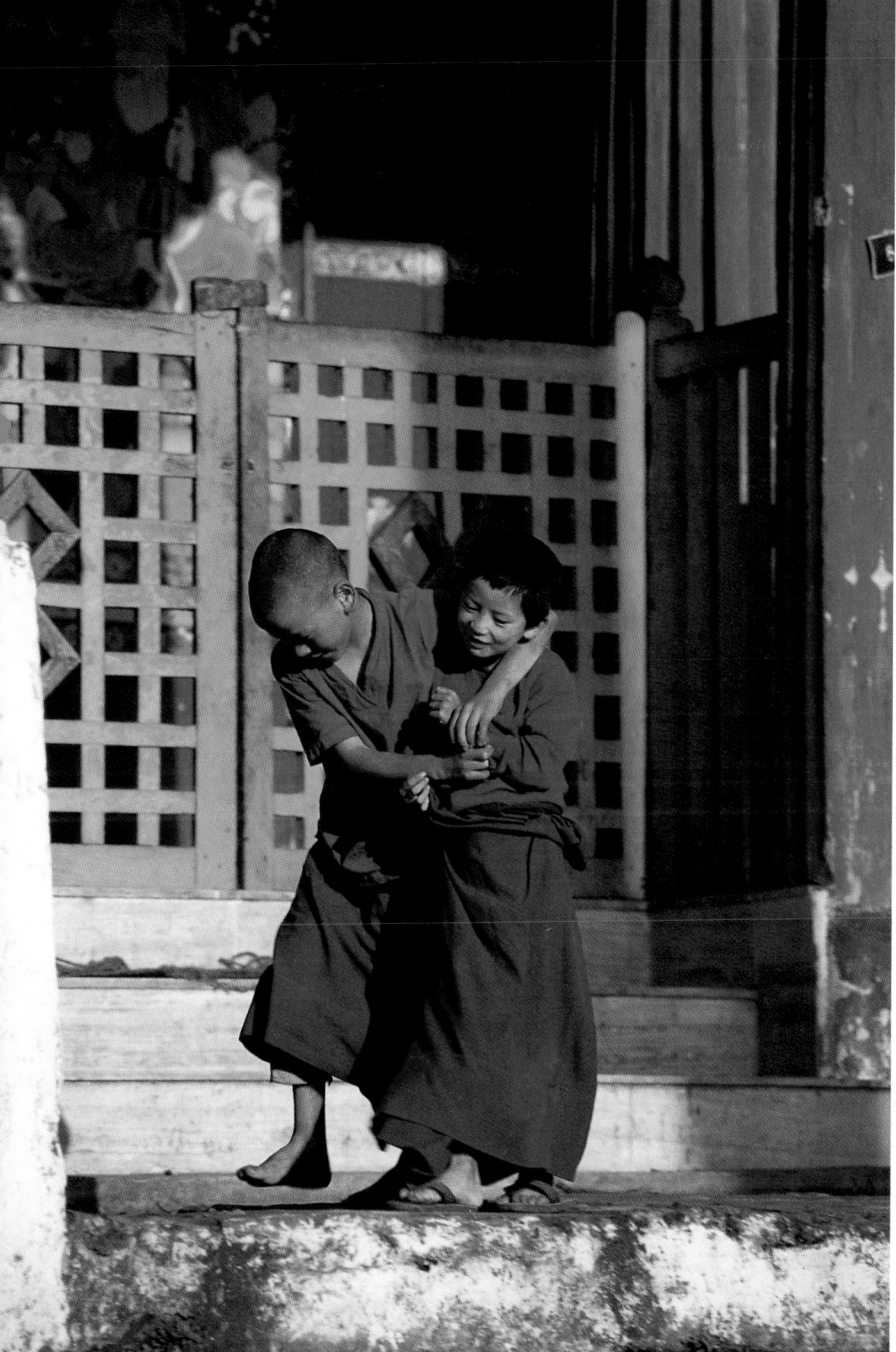

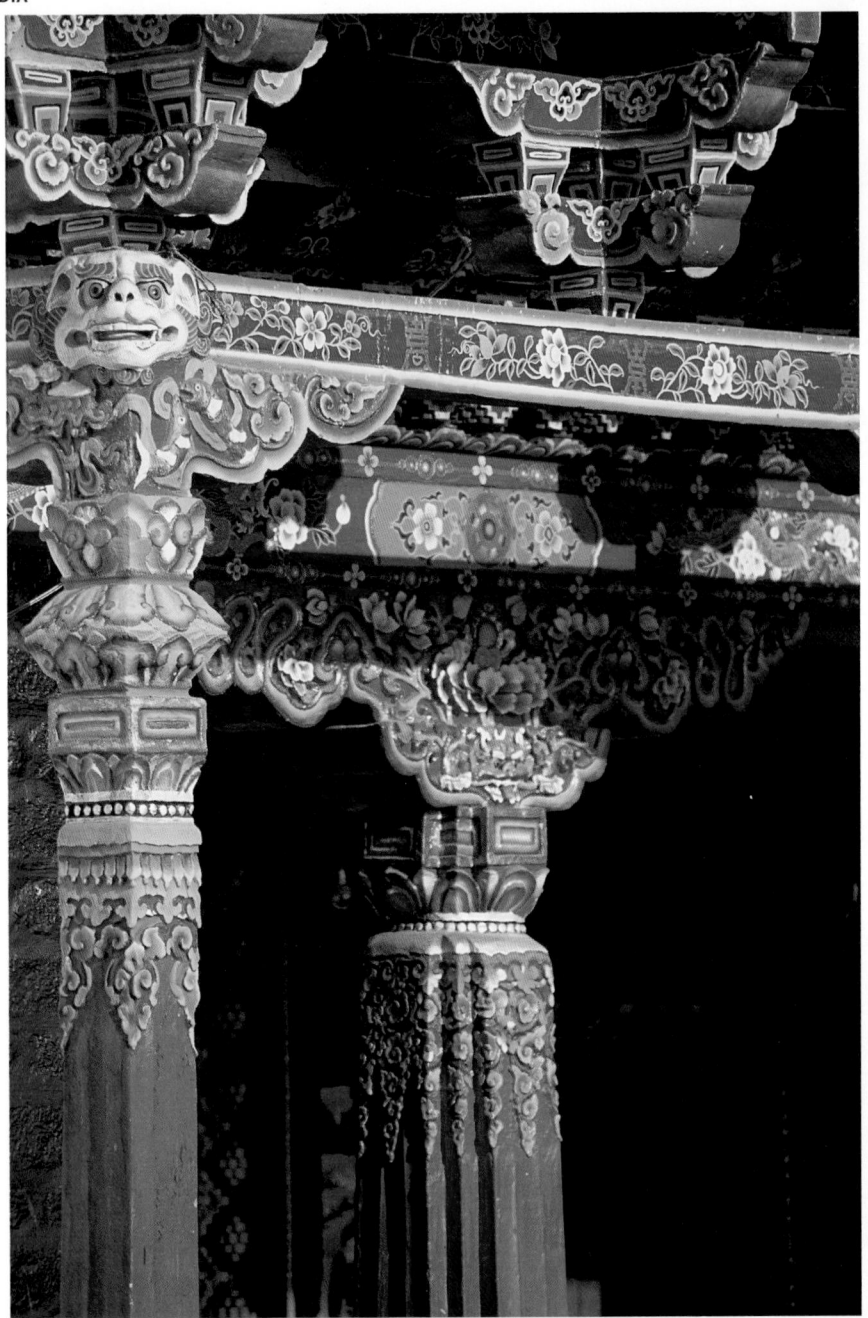

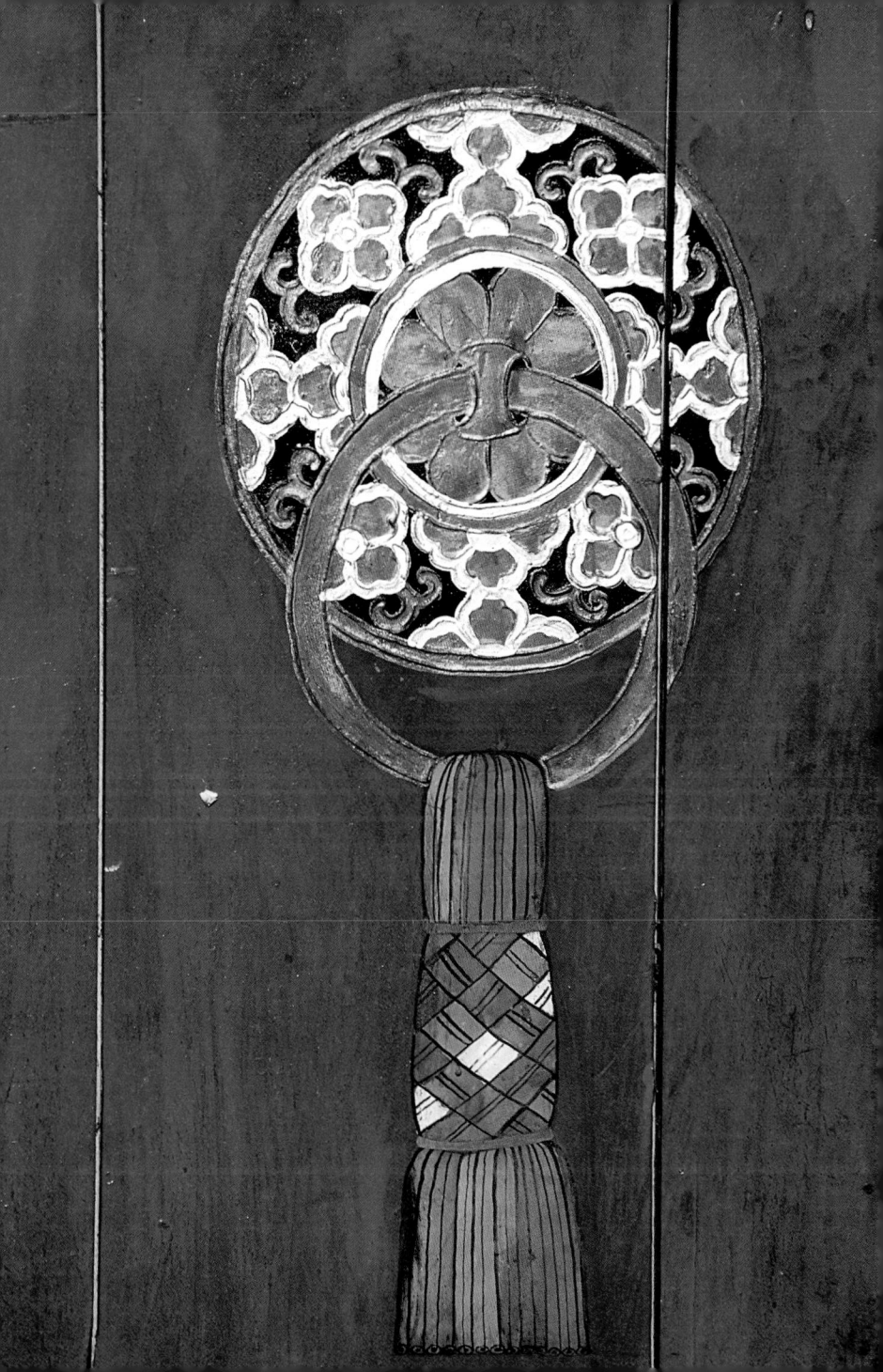

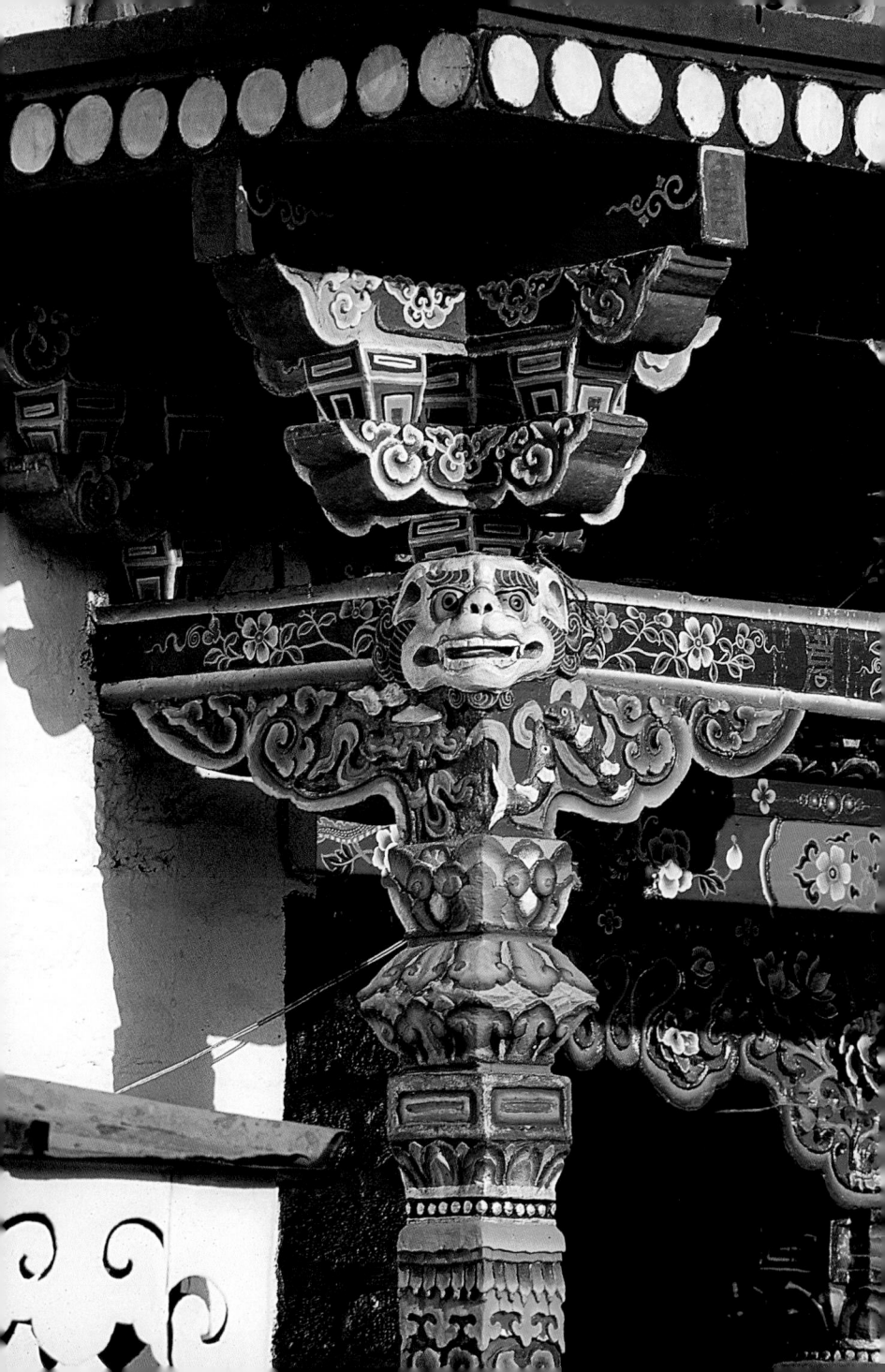

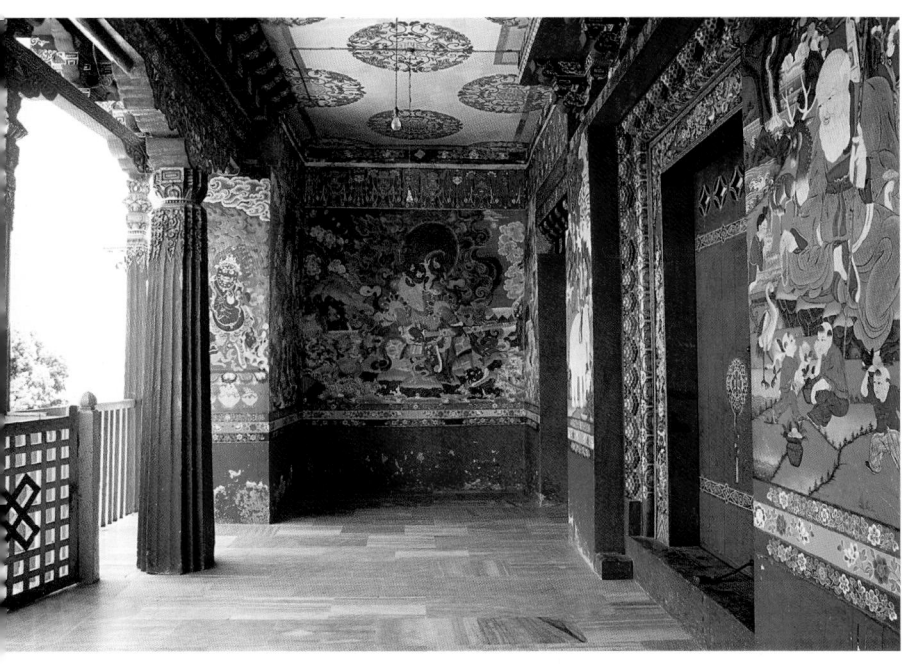

←↑ The repainting and decoration, completed in 2002, a tribute to surviving artistic skills. • Die Restaurationsarbeiten versierter Handwerker wurden 2002 abgeschlossen. •

La restauration des peintures et autres éléments décoratifs, achevée en 2002, est un hommage à des traditions artistiques qui se sont perpétuées jusqu'à nos jours.

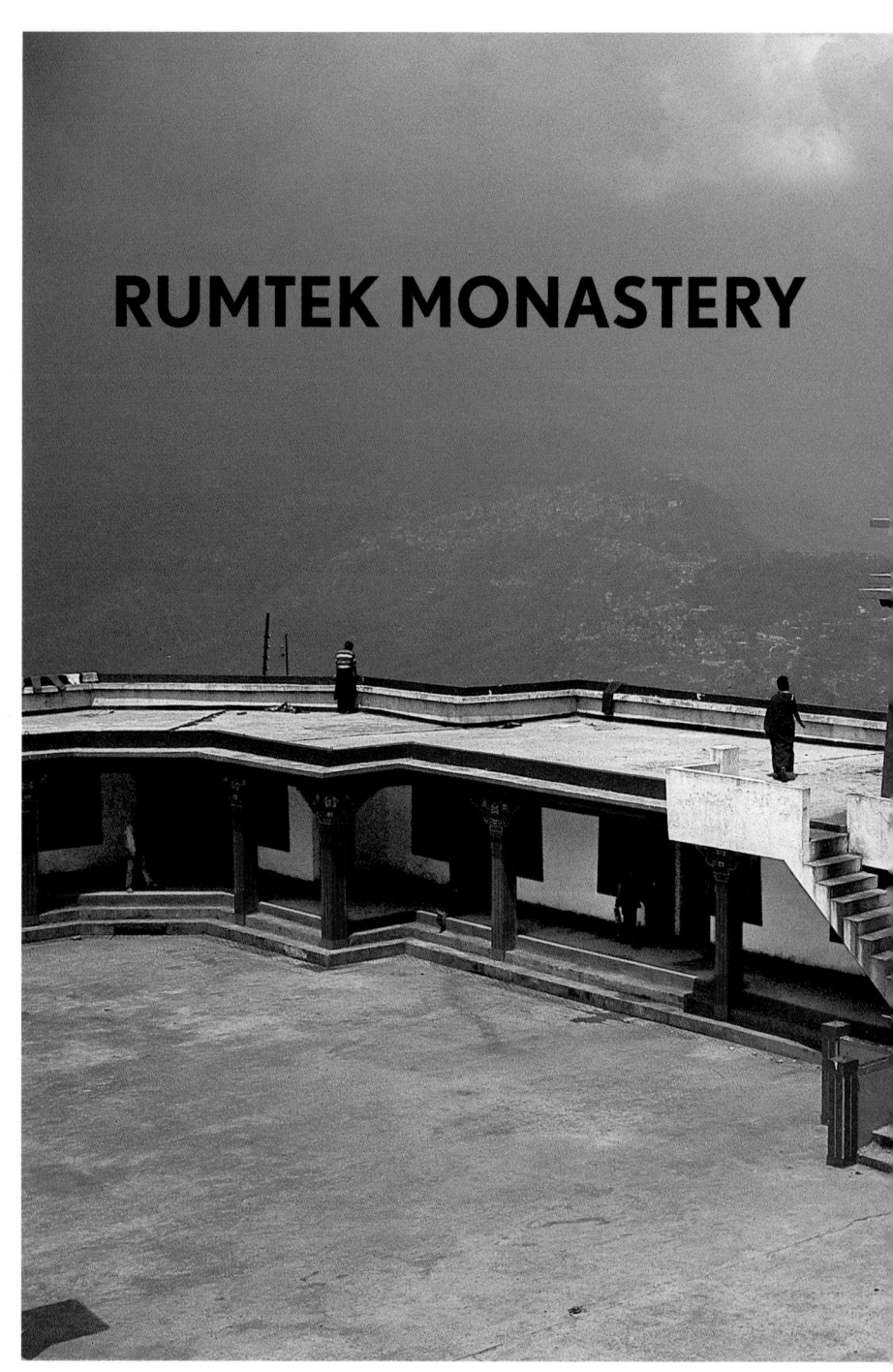

RUMTEK MONASTERY

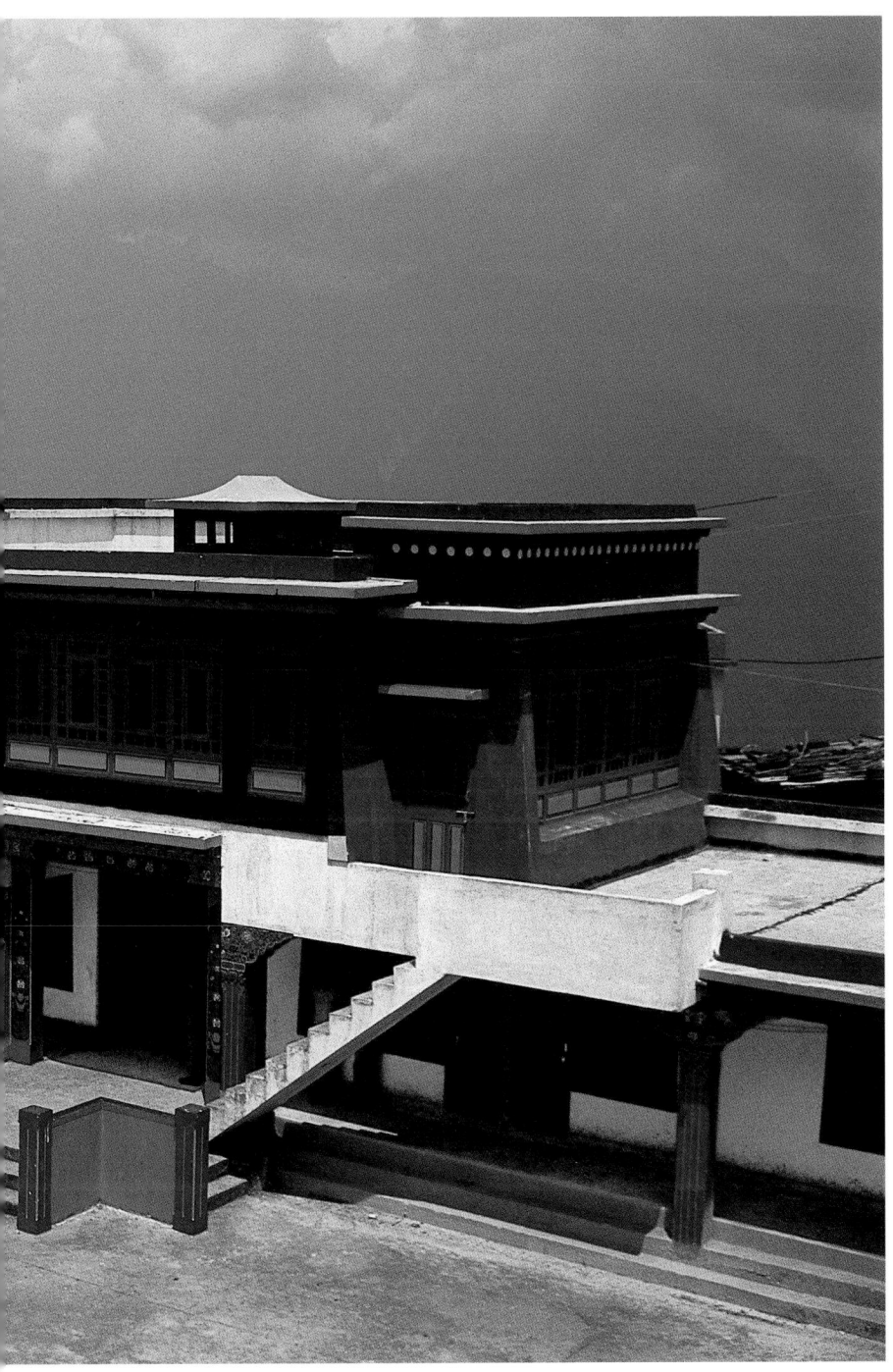

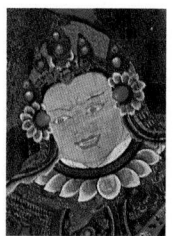

RUMTEK MONASTERY

EAST SIKKIM
INDIA

Buddhists plant prayer flags in the belief that the wind reads the mantras printed on them and scatters them far and wide, bringing merit to all pilgrim souls, not just a single worshipper. In the morning mist, the outlines of Rumtek monastery, 24 km from Gangtok, the capital of Sikkim, appear in a forest of prayer flags. Rumtek is the seat of the Kagyu, or Black Hat, order of Tibetan Buddhism. Devotees believe that when the Karmapa Lama, the leader of the Kagyu sect, performs a secret but spiritually powerful ceremony, the Black Hat, said to be made from the hair of angels, soars above his head. The 800-year-old Kagyu lineage is now headed by the seventeenth incarnation of the Karmapa Lama. The monastery was established in Sikkim in the 16th century but was damaged in an earthquake. An imposing new complex on the lines of the Tsurphu monastery in Tibet was built in the 1960s. The main shrine, monks' quarters, reliquaries, a monastic college and nunnery occupy an entire hillside, integral to the sacred geography of the Himalayas.

Die Buddhisten stellen Gebetsfahnen auf, denn sie glauben, der Wind lese die aufgedruckten Mantras und verstreue sie zum Heil – nicht nur des einzelnen Gläubigen, sondern aller pilgernden Seelen. Das 24 Kilometer von Gangtok, der sikkimesischen Hauptstadt, entfernte Kloster Rumtek erscheint im Morgennebel wie in einem Wald von Gebetsfahnen. Rumtek ist der Sitz des tibetisch-buddhistischen Kagyü-Ordens, auch „Schwarze Hüte" genannt. Seine Anhänger glauben, dass in dem Moment, wenn der Karmapa Lama des Kagyü-Ordens eine geheime, doch spirituell mächtige Zeremonie vollführt, ein schwarzer Hut aus Engelshaar über seinem Kopf schwebt. Als Oberhaupt der 800 Jahre alten Abstammungslinie der Kagyü wird heute die 17. Inkarnation des Karmapa Lama verehrt. Das Kloster besteht seit dem 16. Jahrhundert in Sikkim, wurde aber bei einem Erdbeben beschädigt. In den 1960er-Jahren wurde das heutige Kloster als Replik des Tsurphu-Klosters in Tibet neu errichtet. Der Hauptschrein, der Wohnbereich der Mönche, Stupas, eine Klosterschule und ein Nonnenkloster sind über einen Hügel verteilt und fügen sich in die heilige Landschaft des Himalaja ein.

Les bouddhistes sont persuadés que le vent lit les mantras inscrits sur les drapeaux de prière et qu'il les disperse aux quatre vents, dispensant ses bienfaits à toute la communauté de pèlerins. Dans la brume matinale, la silhouette du monastère de Rumtek, situé à 24 kilomètres de Gangtok, la capitale du Sikkim, s'élève au-dessus d'une forêt de drapeaux de prière. Rumtek est le monastère de l'ordre bouddhiste tibétain de Kagyu, ou Bonnet noir. Les fidèles croient que lorsque leur maître, le lama Karmapa accomplit une cérémonie secrète mais d'une grande force spirituelle, le Bonnet noir, que l'on dit fait de cheveux d'ange, s'élève au-dessus de sa tête. Vieille de 800 ans, la lignée de Kagyu est dirigée à l'heure actuelle par la dix-septième incarnation du lama Karmapa. Ce monastère fondé au 16e siècle a été en partie détruit par un tremblement de terre. Dans les années 1960, on a construit un nouveau complexe monumental sur le modèle du monastère de Tsurphu au Tibet. Le sanctuaire principal, les appartements des moines, les reliquaires, le collège monastique et un couvent couvrent tout un versant de colline, se fondant dans la géographie sacrée de l'Himalaya.

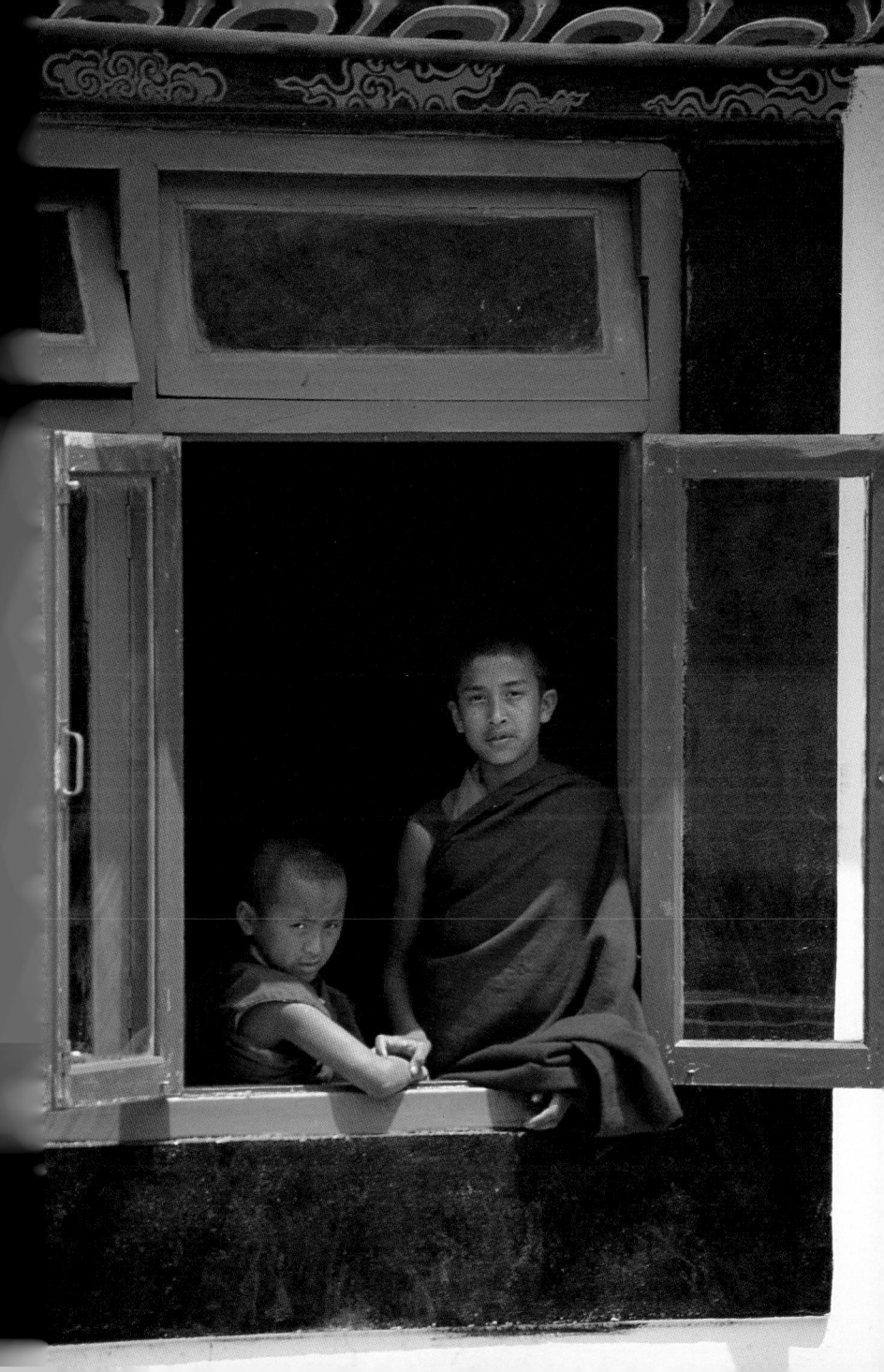

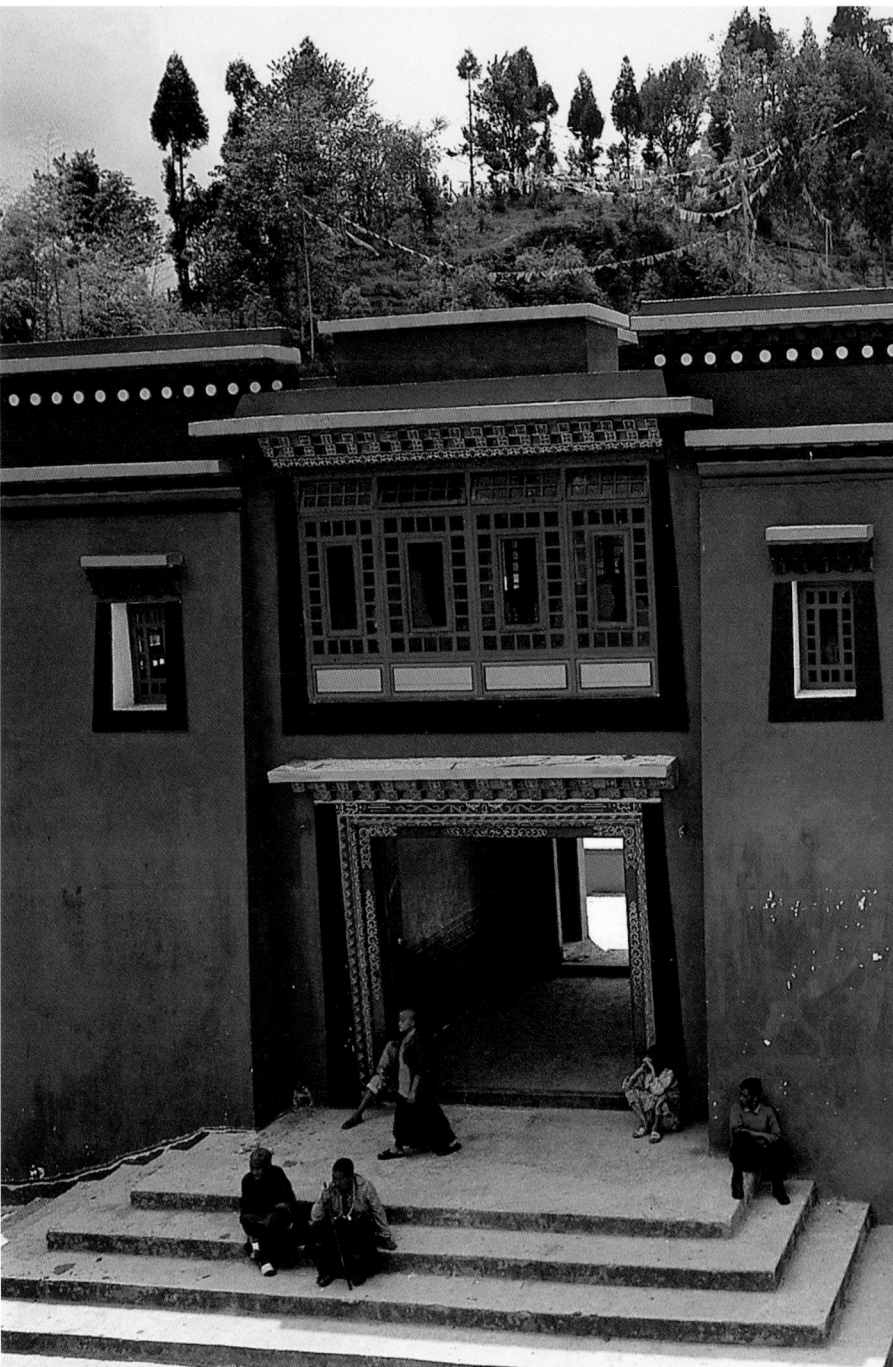

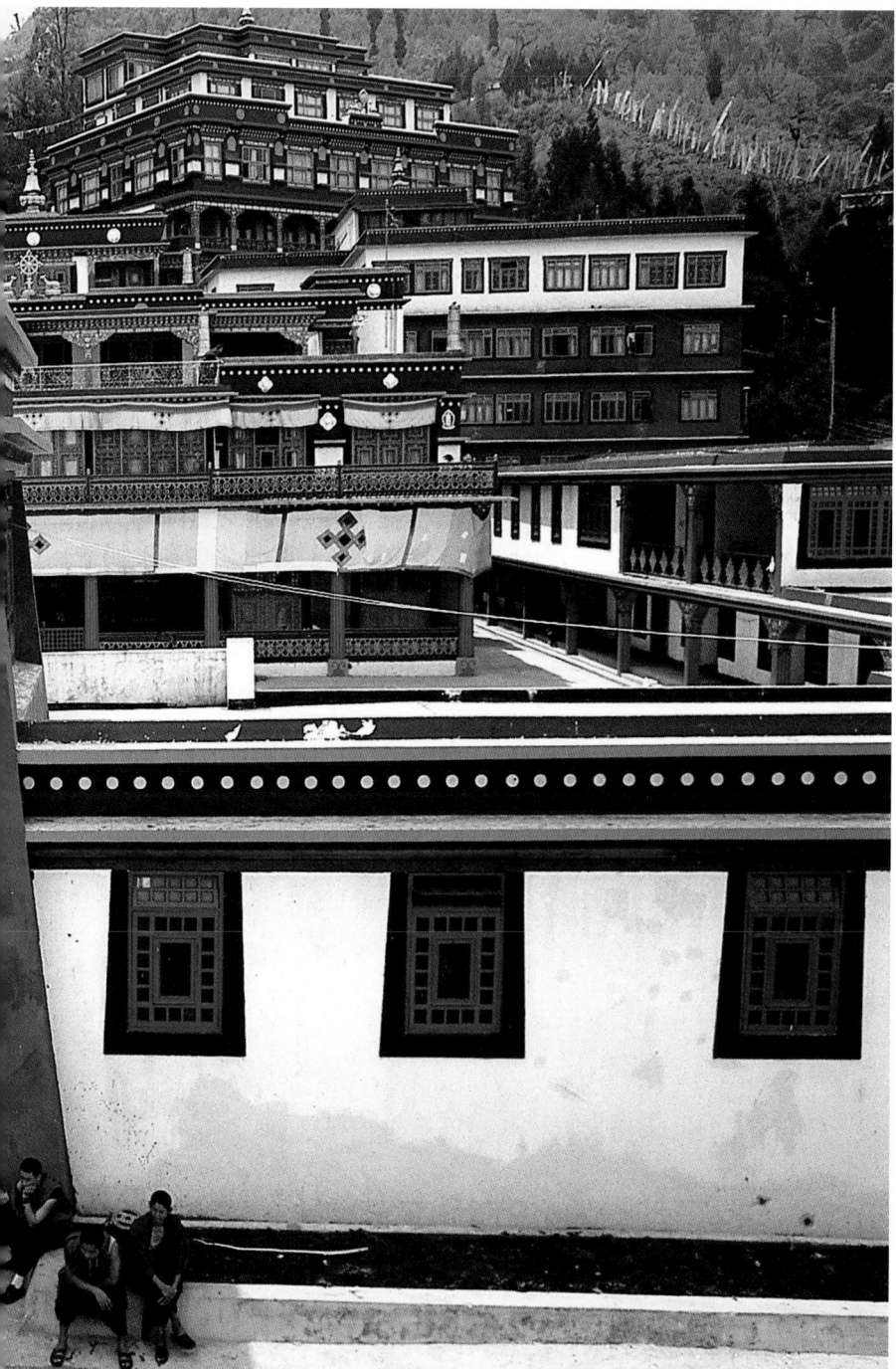

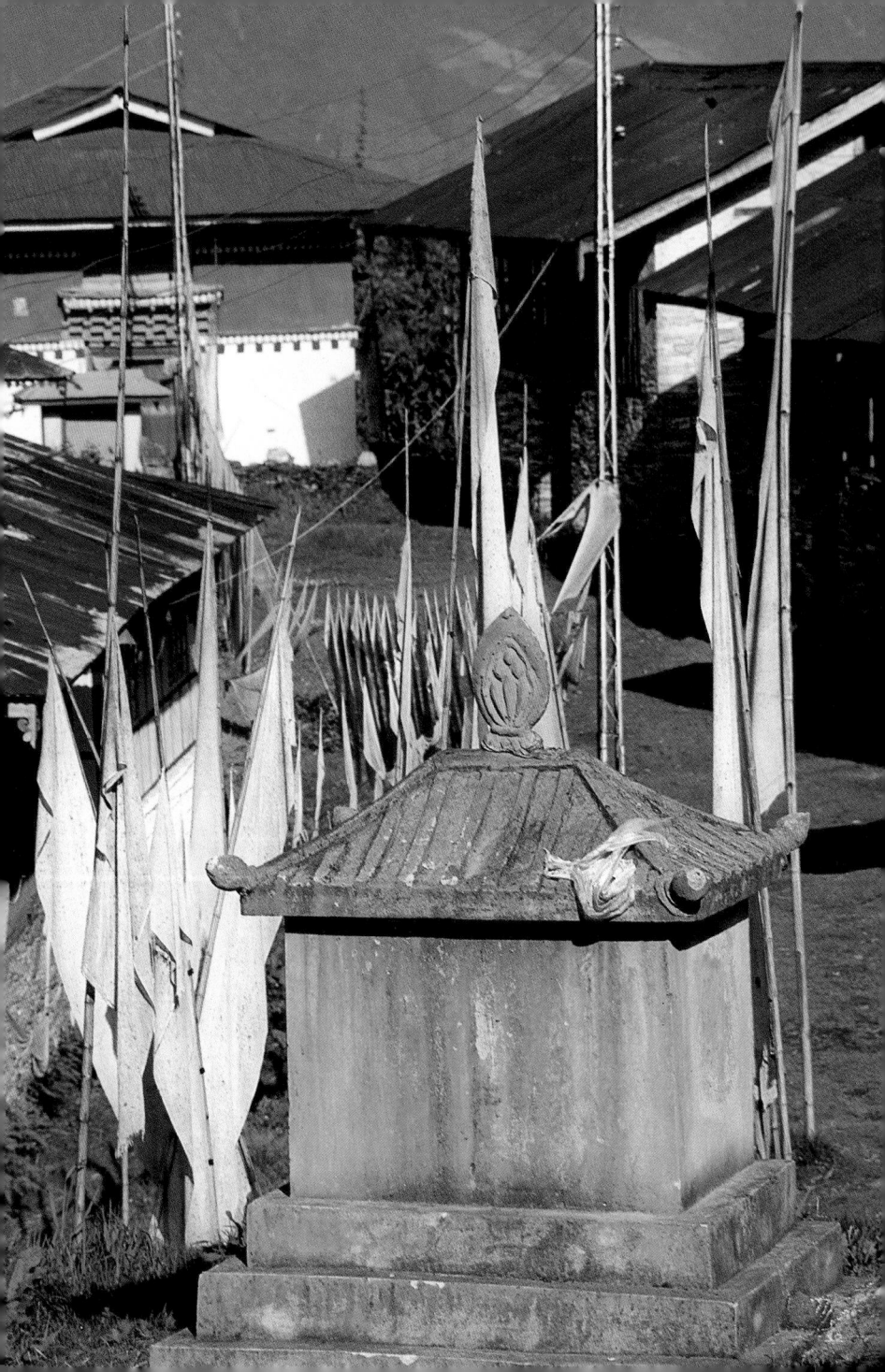

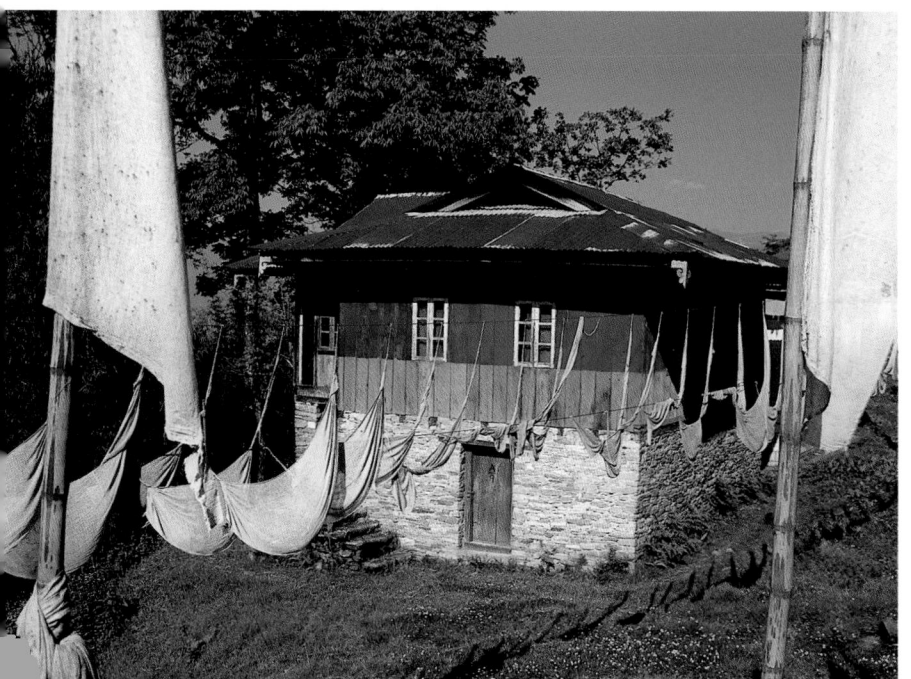

PP. 106–107 and PP. 110–111 The gate house of Rumtek opening into a walled courtyard with a raised walkway is in the classical style of Tibetan architecture. • Das Torhaus von Rumtek, das in einen ummauerten Hof mit einem erhöhten Gang führt, ist charakteristisch für den klassischen Stil der tibetischen Architektur. • Le corps de garde donnant sur une cour ceinte de hauts murs et dotée d'un chemin de ronde surélevé est

caractéristique de l'architecture tibétaine classique.

← Prayer flags with written mantras planted round a container with votive offerings by worshippers. • Gebetsfahnen mit schriftlichen Mantras an einem Häuschen mit Weiheopfern der Gläubigen. • Des drapeaux de prière sur lesquels sont inscrits des mantras signalent cette petite construction

renfermant des offrandes faites par des fidèles.

↑ Rumtek occupies an entire hillside with a series of outbuildings. • Mit einer Reihe von Nebengebäuden nimmt Rumtek einen ganzen Hügel ein. • Le monastère de Rumtek et ses dépendances couvrent tout un versant de montagne.

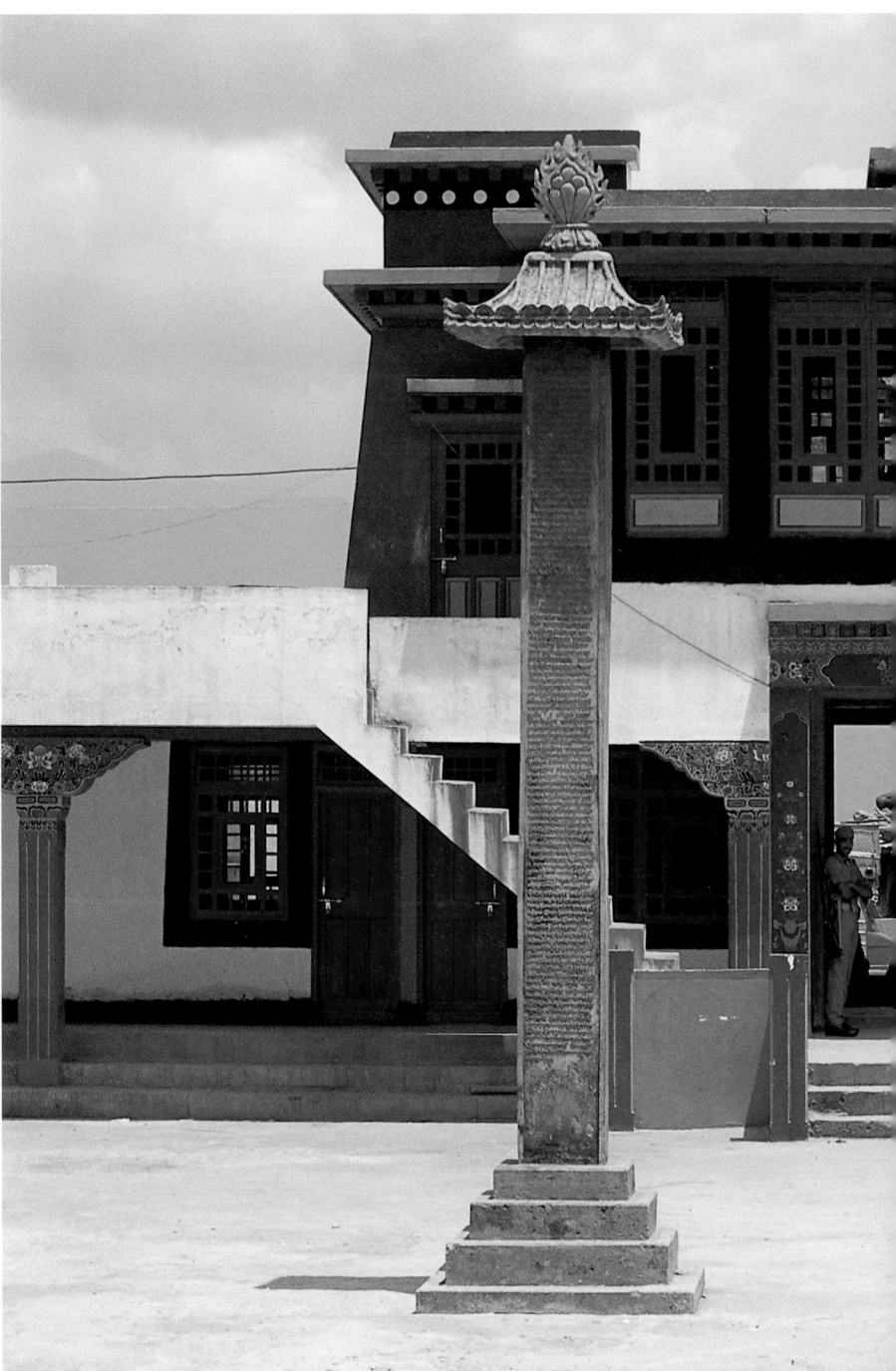

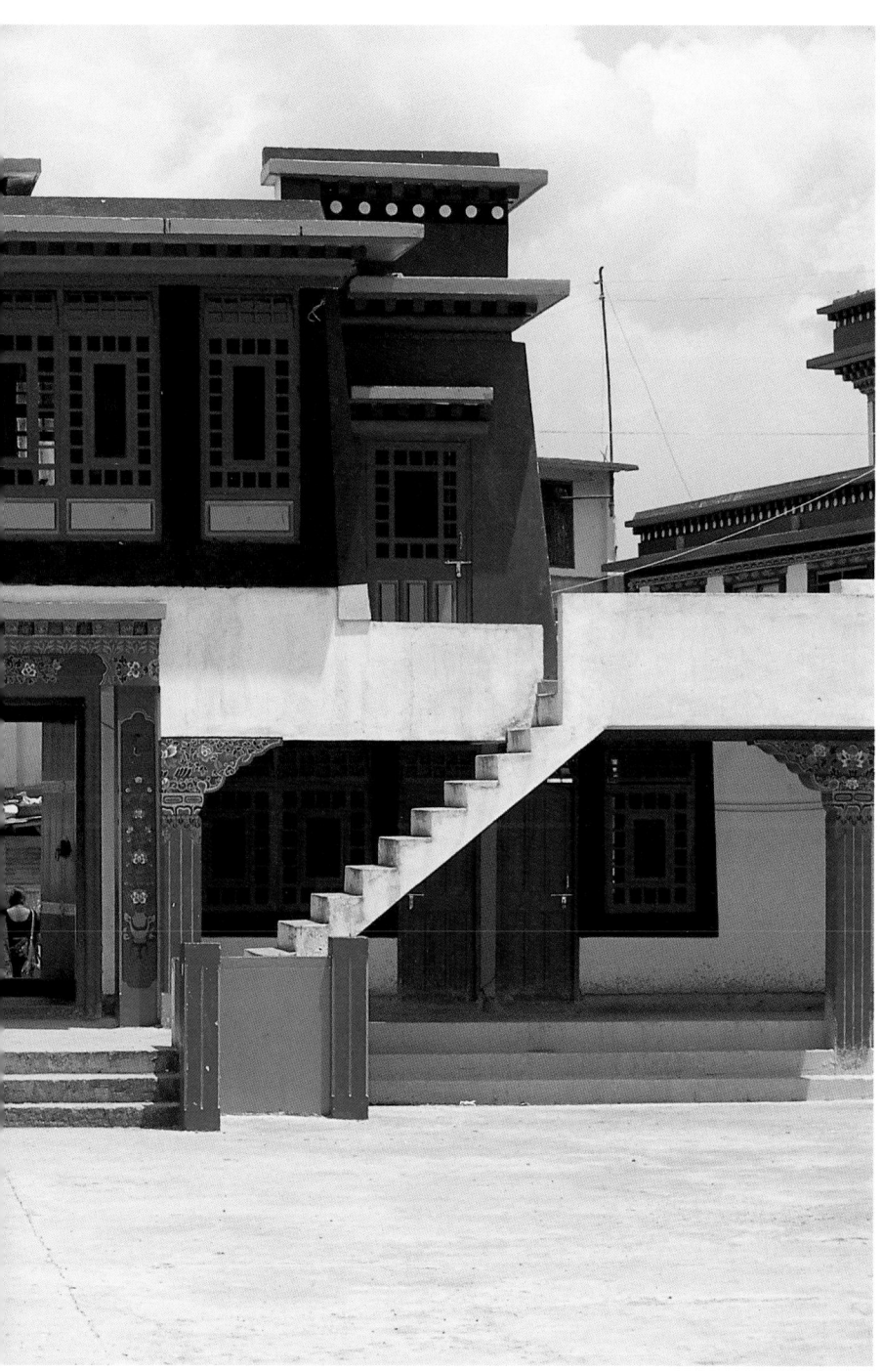

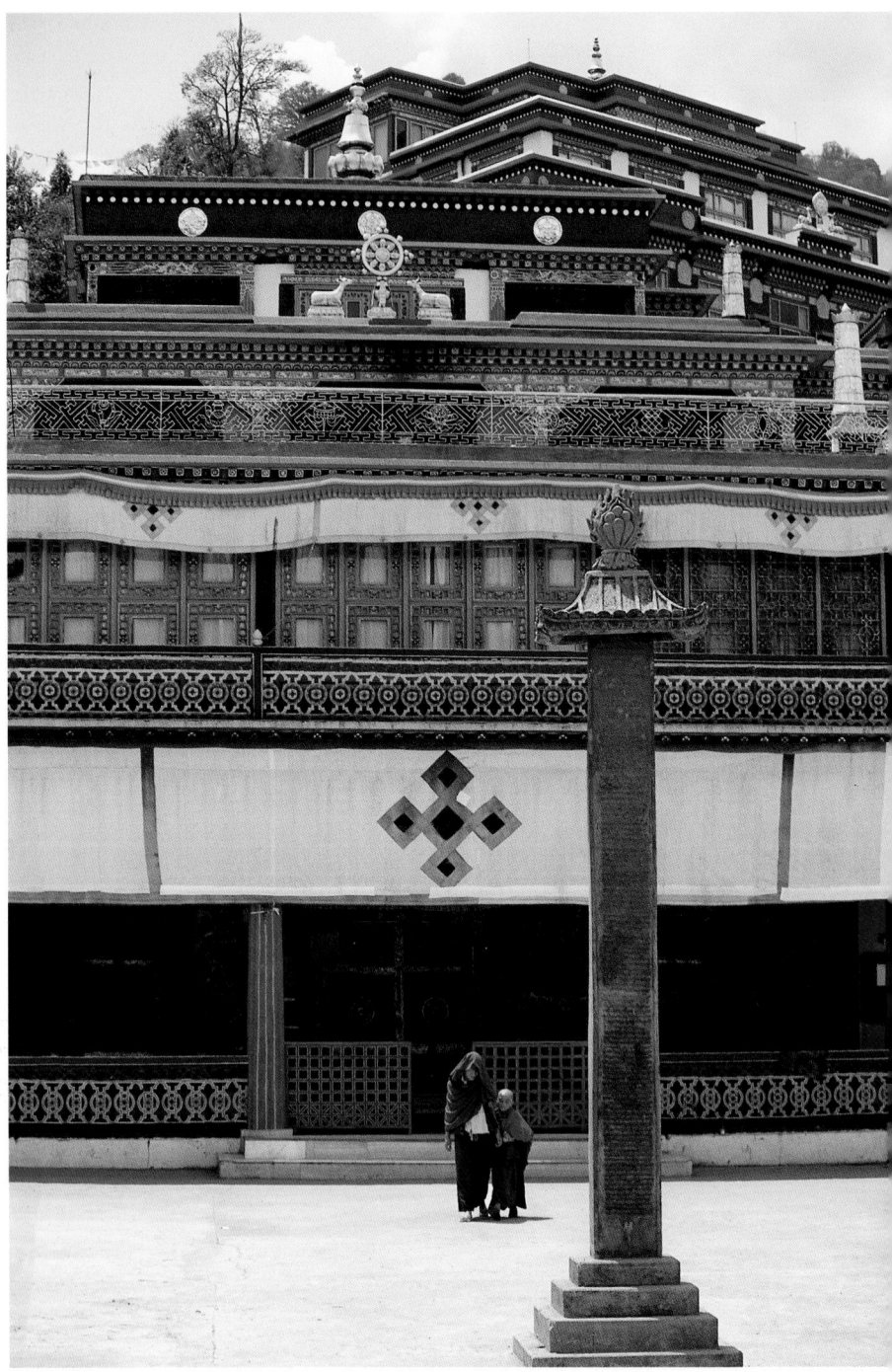

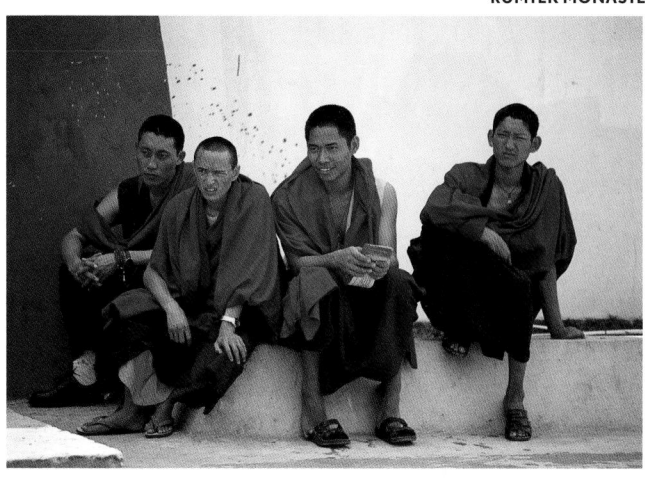

← The banners shielding the verandas are emblazoned with the symbol of the double thunderbolt that represents the indestructible force of truth. • Die Banner vor den Veranden sind mit dem Symbol des Doppelblitzes verziert, der die unzerstörbare Kraft der Wahrheit symbolisiert. • Les bannières protégeant les vérandas des regards indiscrets sont revêtues du double éclair, symbole de la force indestructible de la vérité.

↑ ↓ and P. 120 Rumtek is home to about 200 young monks, of all age groups, for whom it is a place of work and play. • In Rumtek leben etwa 200 Mönche aller Altersstufen, um zu arbeiten und zu spielen. • Quelque 200 jeunes moines, de tout âge, vivent à Rumtek, s'adonnant au travail et au jeu.

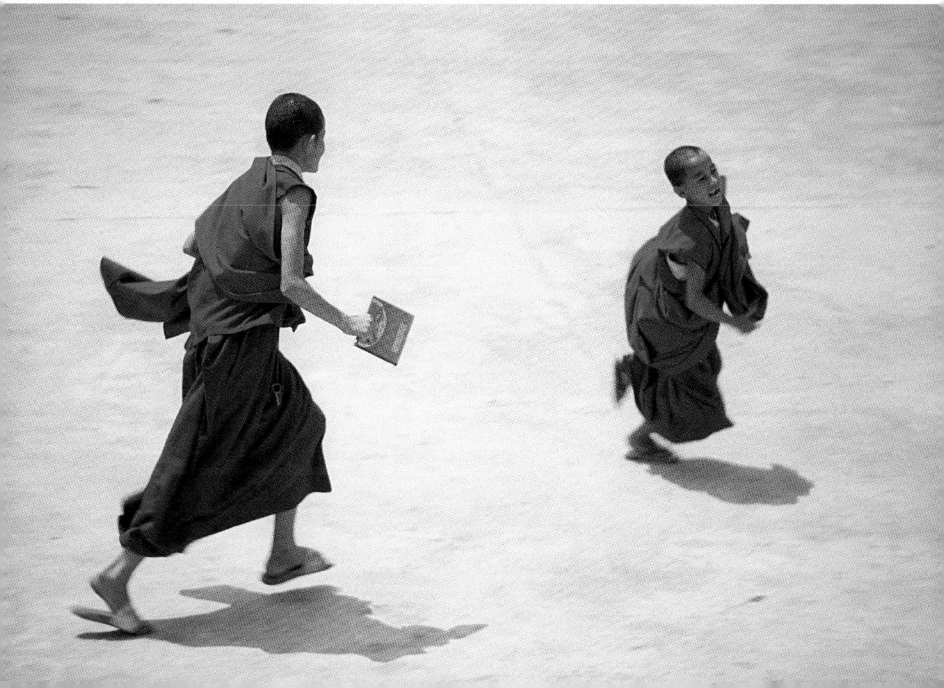

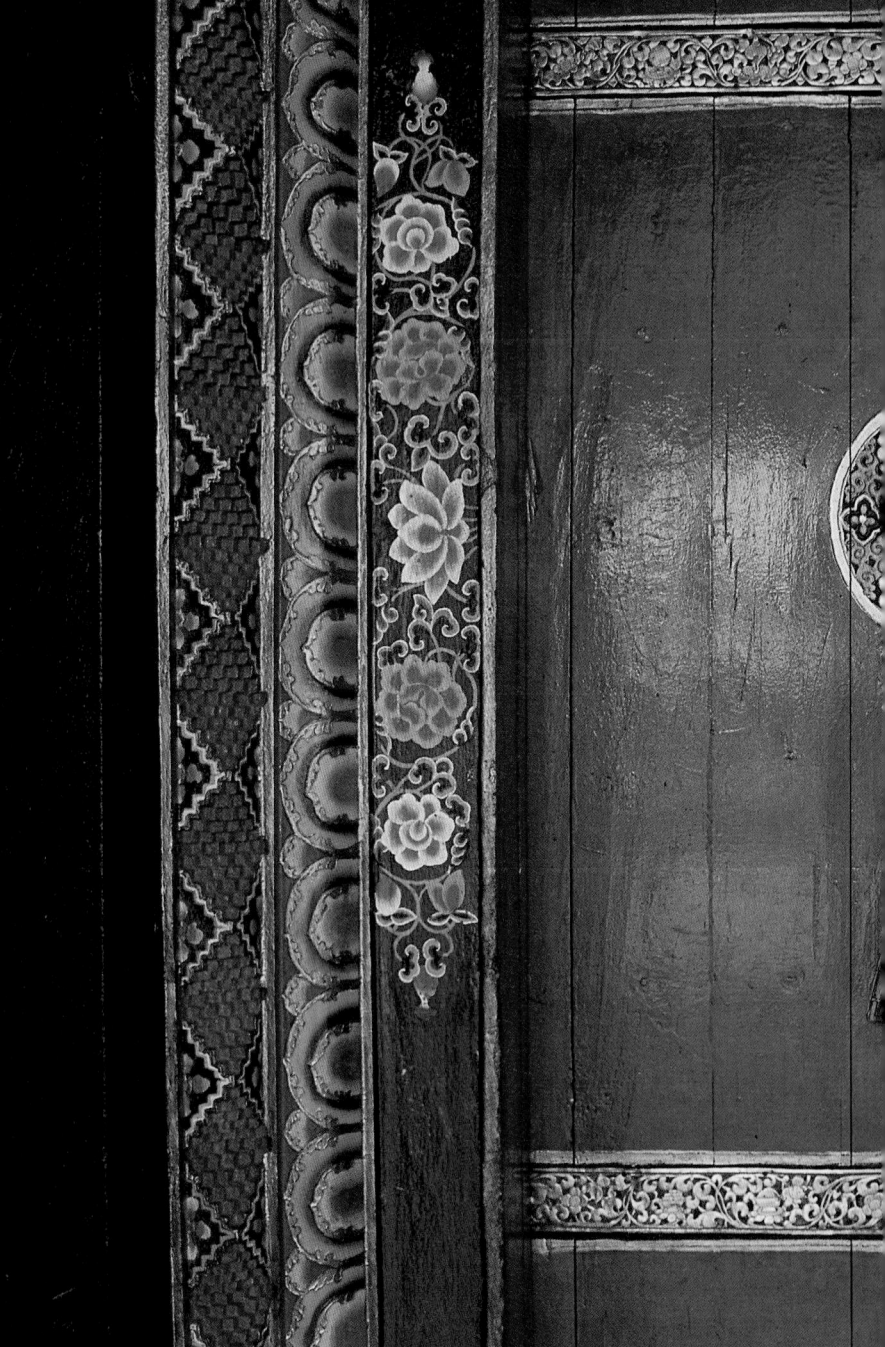

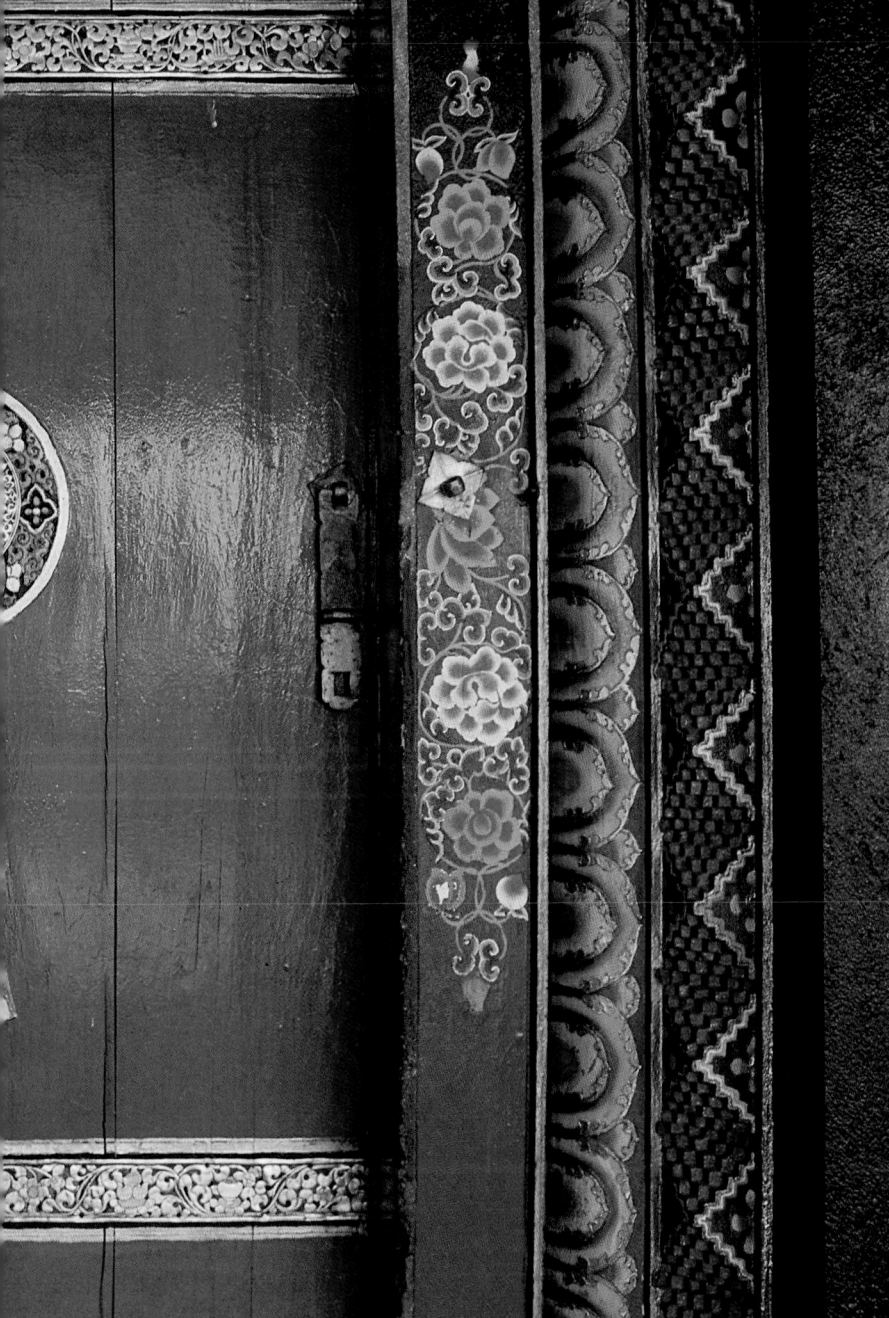

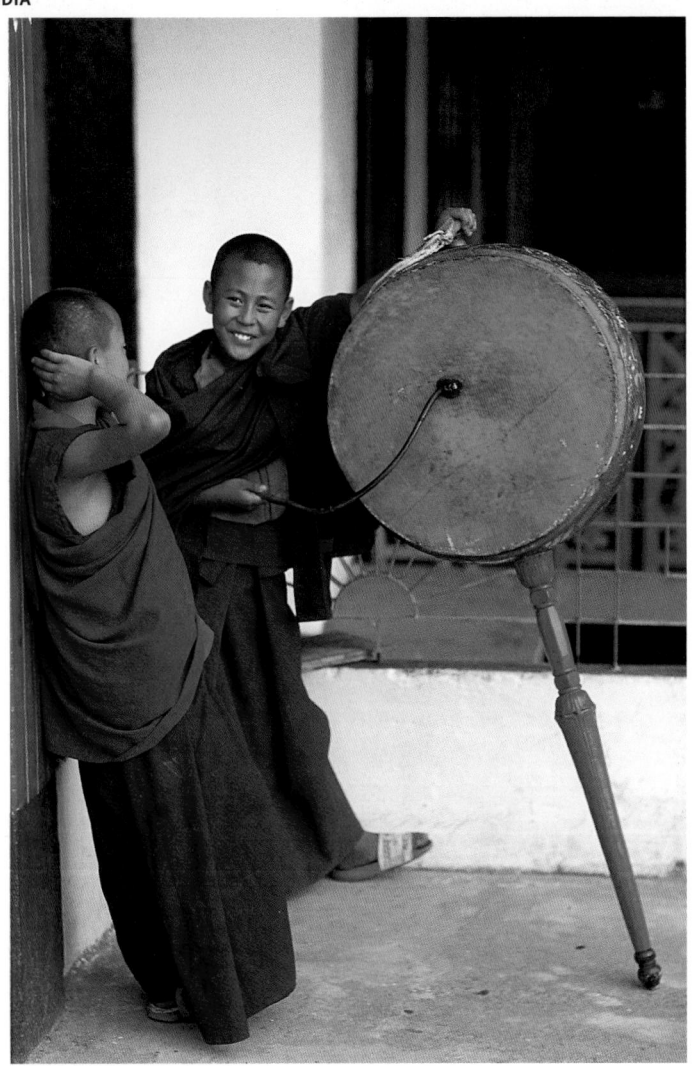

PP. 118–119 A silken tassle hangs from an ornamental doorknob surrounded by a trailing vine of sacred lotus blossoms. • Eine Seidenquaste hängt an einem verzierten Türknauf, während der Türrahmen mit Ranken heiliger Lotusblüten verziert ist. • Un gland en argent agrémente une poignée décorée, sur une porte cernée par les fleurs d'un lotus grimpant sacré.

→ Auspicious snow lions form the capitals of painted columns. • Schneelöwen bilden die Kapitelle der bemalten Säulen. • Des lions des neiges de bon augure constituent les chapiteaux de colonnes peintes.

PP. 122–123 A massive mural of a guardian king stands sentinel near a hanging shield inside the shrine. •

Im Inneren des Schreins hält auf einem mächtigen Wandbild ein Schutzkönig Wache. • À l'intérieur du sanctuaire, une peinture murale impressionnante représentant un roi protecteur monte la garde près d'un blason suspendu.

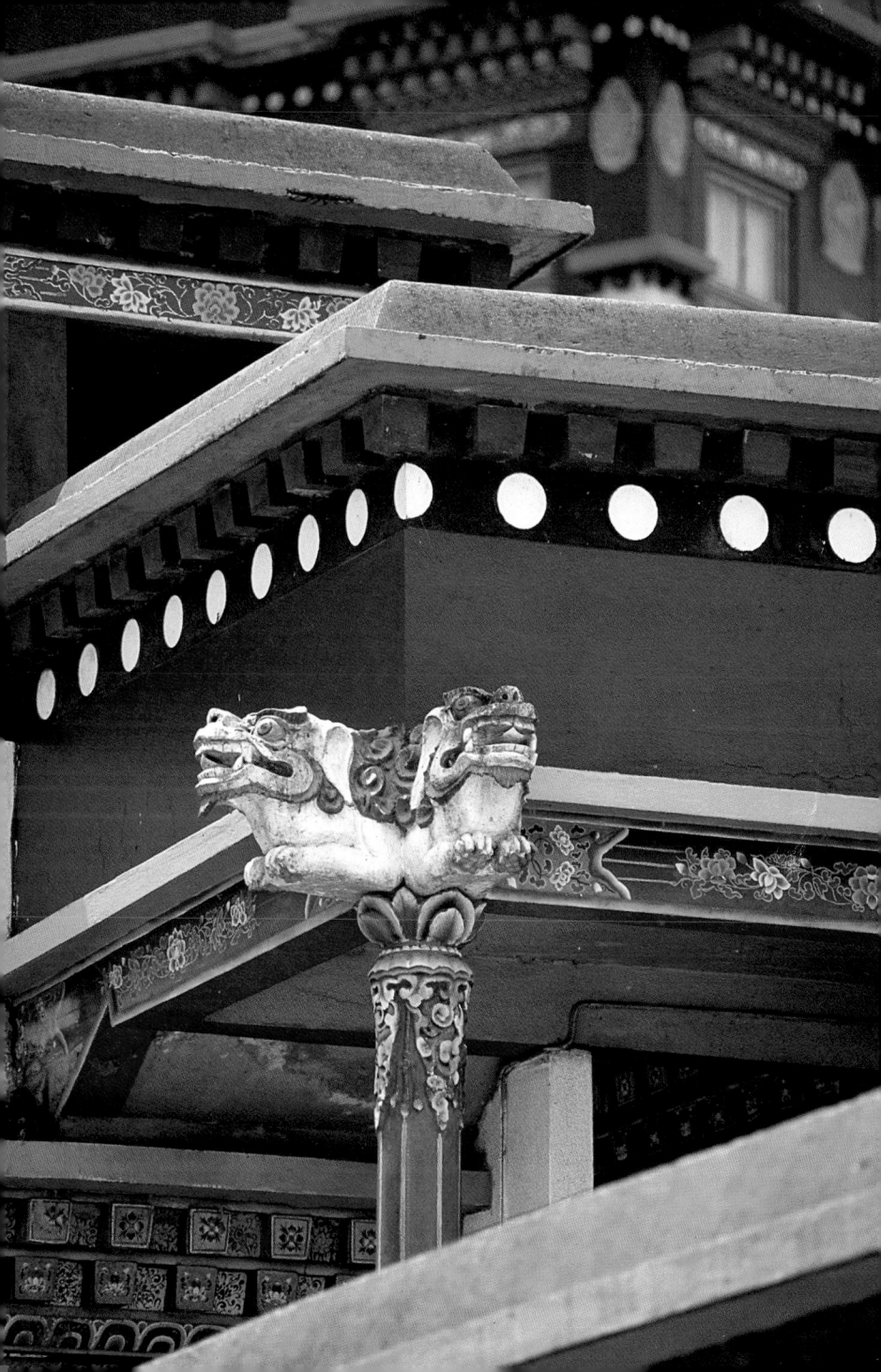

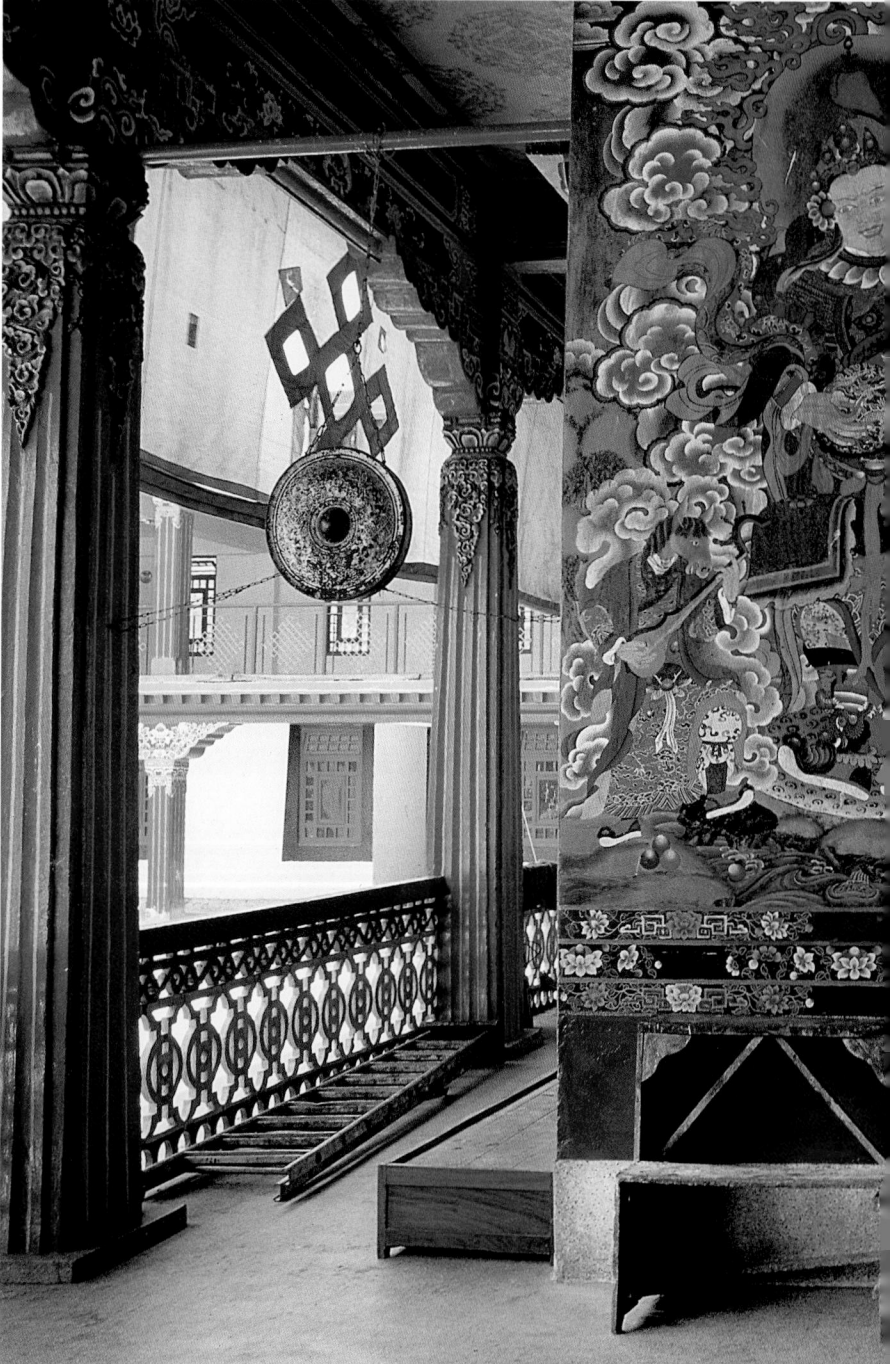

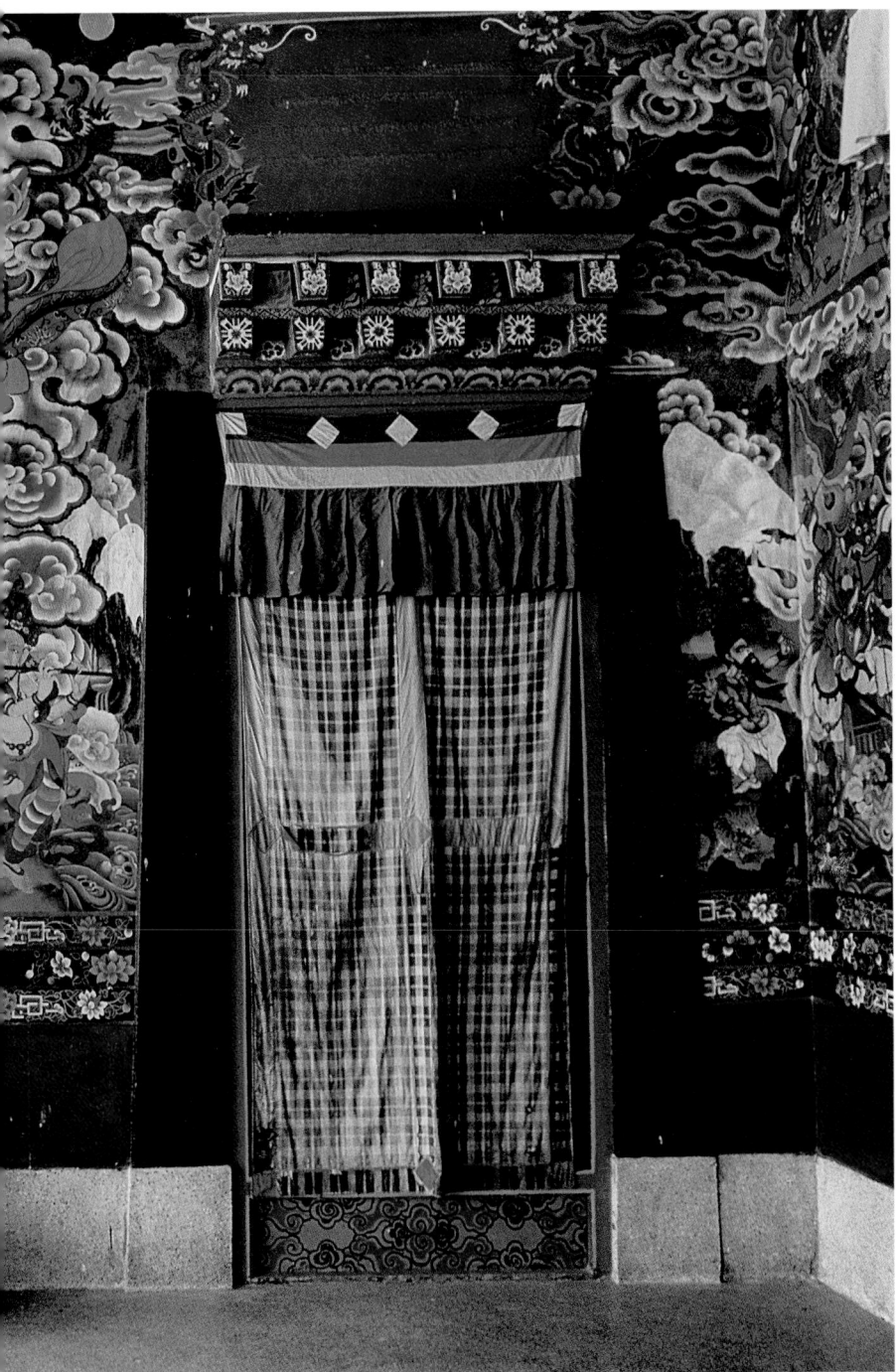

SHIV NIWAS PALACE

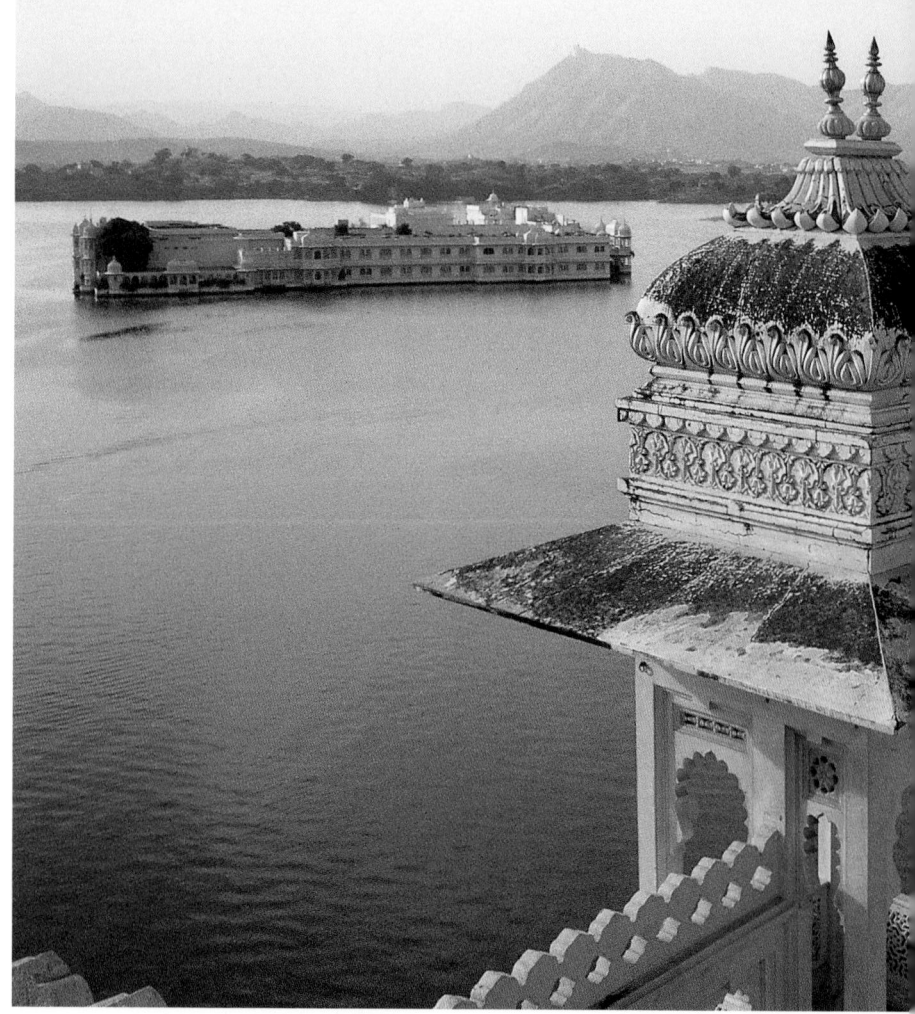

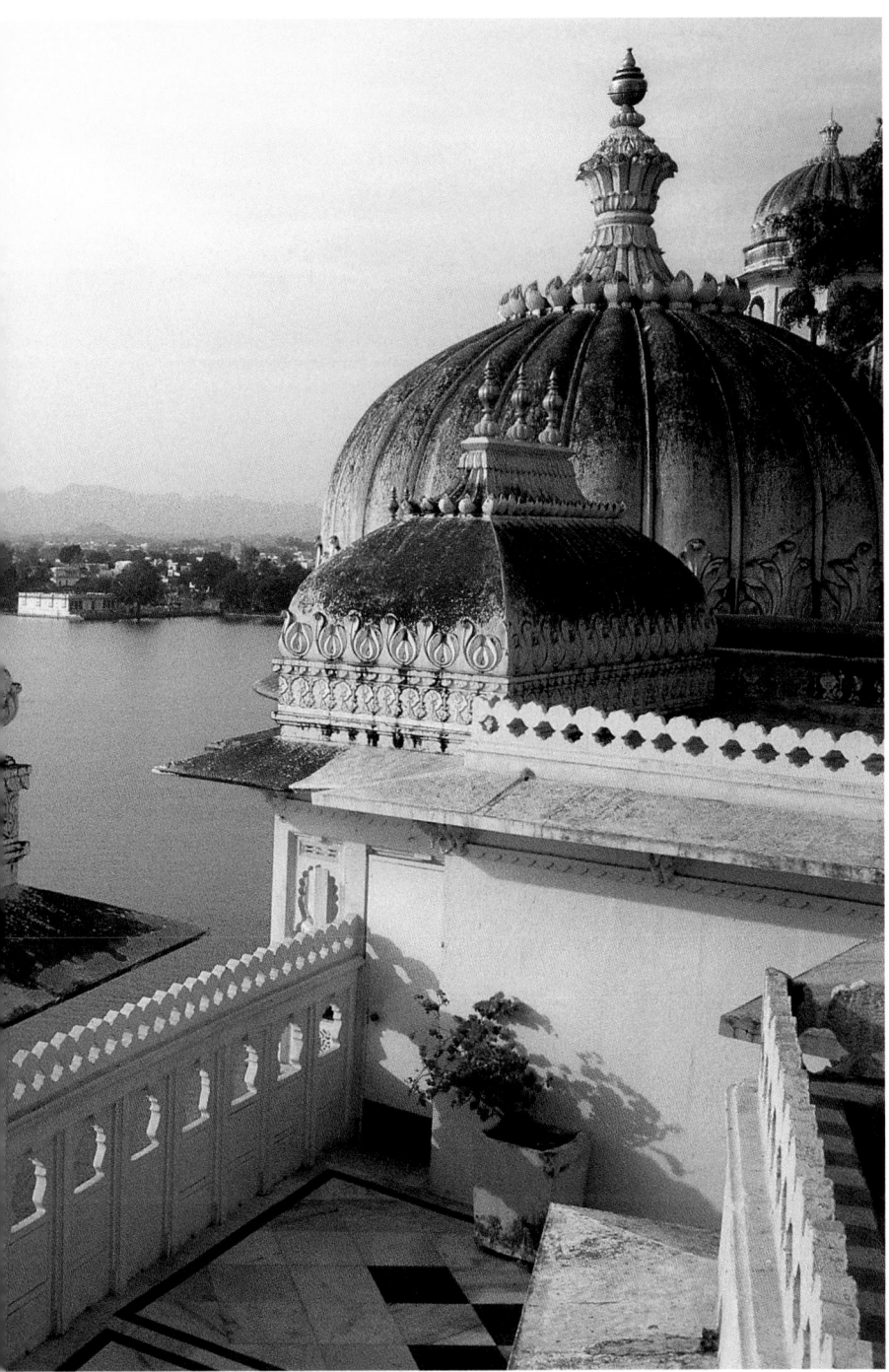

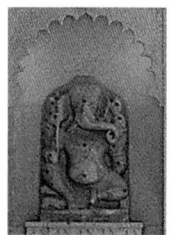

SHIV NIWAS PALACE
UDAIPUR, RAJASTHAN
INDIA

With palaces of breathtaking beauty built on and around lakes and surrounded by a landscape of rugged hills, Udaipur is among the most romantic cities in Rajasthan. The Shiv Niwas Palace is the last of a series of magnificent palaces that Udaipur's rulers built from the 16th century onwards on the crest of a hill overlooking Lake Pichola. The present owner Arvind Singh Mewar's great grandfather Fateh Singh commissioned Shiv Niwas as a private residence in the Indo-European style in the early years of the 20th century. It was presented to his father Bhagwat Singh on the occasion of his marriage in 1939 and Arvind Singh grew up here. Later it served as a private guest house before being converted into a hotel in 1978. A new set of guest rooms was added on the upper storey and the swimming pool in the courtyard was enlarged. James Bond paid an extended visit in 1982 for the filming of "Octopussy". The superb wall ornamentation in colored glass adds to its glittering appeal. It is now a perfect setting for Bollywood stars and the international jet set to stage sumptuous weddings.

Das von zerklüfteten Hügeln umgebene Udaipur mit seinen atemberaubend schönen Palästen auf und an den Seen gilt als eine der außergewöhnlich romantischen Städte in Rajasthan. Der Shiv-Niwas-Palast wurde von den Herrschern über Udaipur als letzter von mehreren prächtigen Palästen gebaut, die ab dem 16. Jahrhundert auf der Spitze eines Hügels mit Blick auf den Pichola-See errichtet wurden. Anfang des 20. Jahrhunderts gab Fateh Singh, der Großvater des heutigen Besitzers Arvind Singh Mewar, Shiv Niwas als Privatvilla im indoeuropäischen Stil in Auftrag. Arvind Singh verbrachte hier seine Kindheit, denn 1939 war die Residenz seinem Vater Bhagwat Singh anlässlich seiner Heirat überlassen worden. Später diente sie als private Gästevilla, bis sie schließlich 1978 in ein Hotel umgebaut wurde. Im oberen Stockwerk wurden mehrere Zimmer hinzugefügt, und der Swimmingpool im Hof wurde vergrößert. 1982 residierte James Bond hier im Film „Octopussy". Nicht nur die herrlichen Wandornamente aus Buntglas verleihen dem Hotel Glanz und Glitter – auch Bollywood-Stars und Berühmtheiten des internationalen Jetsets, die hier rauschende Hochzeiten feiern.

Dans un paysage remarquable, Udaipur, qui s'enorgueillit de palais d'une beauté renversante s'élevant sur des îles lacustres ou sur les rives de lacs, est l'une des villes romantiques du Rajasthan. Le Shiv Niwas est le dernier en date des palais magnifiques que les souverains de Udaipur ont construit à partir du 16ᵉ siècle sur la crête d'une colline surplombant le lac Pichola. Fateh Singh avait fait construire le Shiv Niwas dans le style indo-européen en vogue au début du 20ᵉ siècle et avait offert cette résidence privée en cadeau de mariage à Bhagwat Singh, son fils, en 1939. Son petit-fils Arvind Singh Mewar, l'actuel propriétaire, y a passé son enfance. La résidence a par la suite servi de pension privée avant d'être transformée en hôtel en 1978. À cet effet, de nouvelles chambres ont été créées à l'étage supérieur et la piscine dans la cour a été agrandie. James Bond alias Roger Moore y a séjourné longuement en 1982 pour le tournage du film « Octopussy ». La superbe décoration murale en verre de couleur ajoute à son lustre. C'est pour les stars de Bollywood et la jet-set internationale l'endroit parfait où fêter des mariages somptueux.

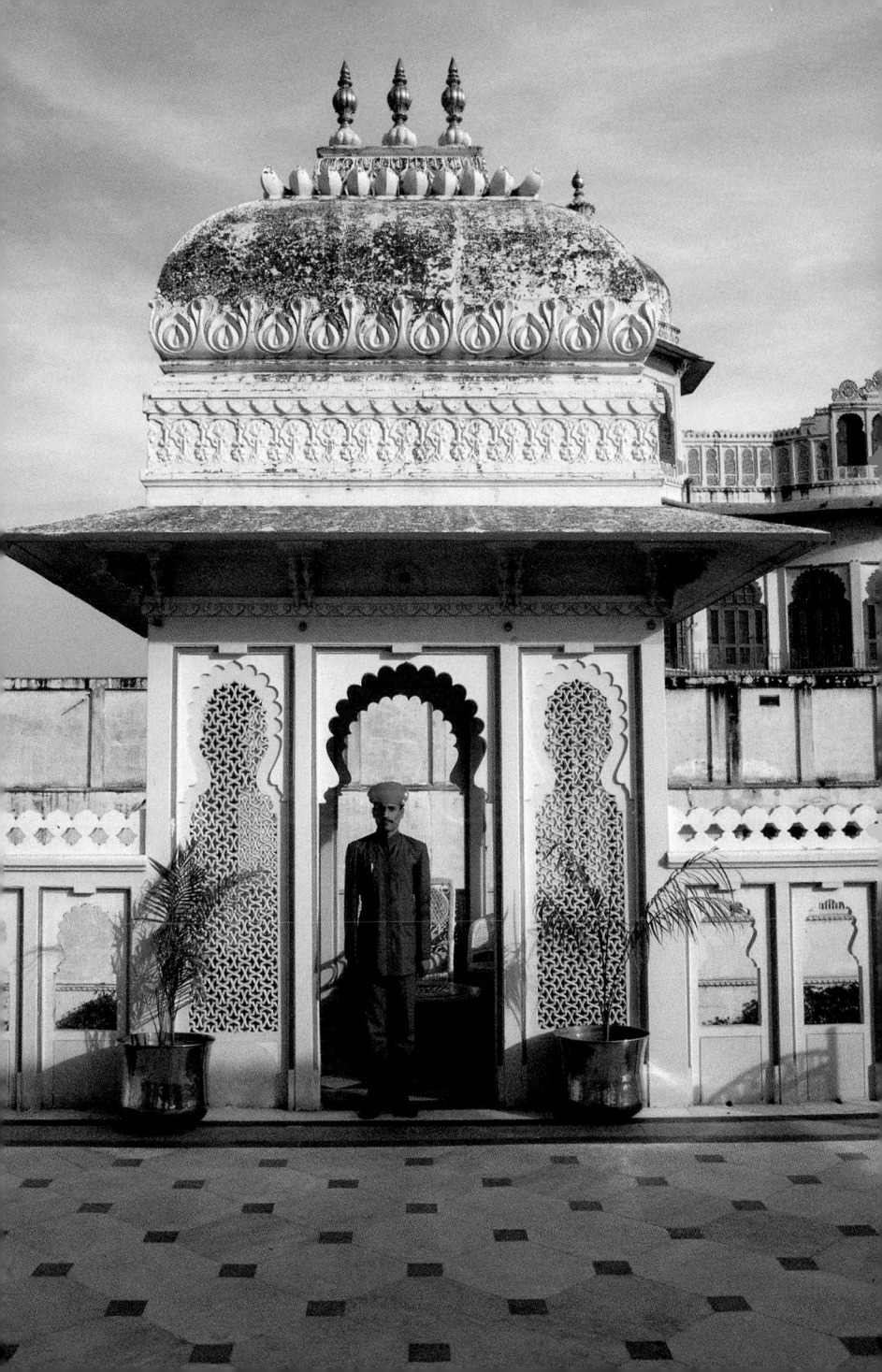

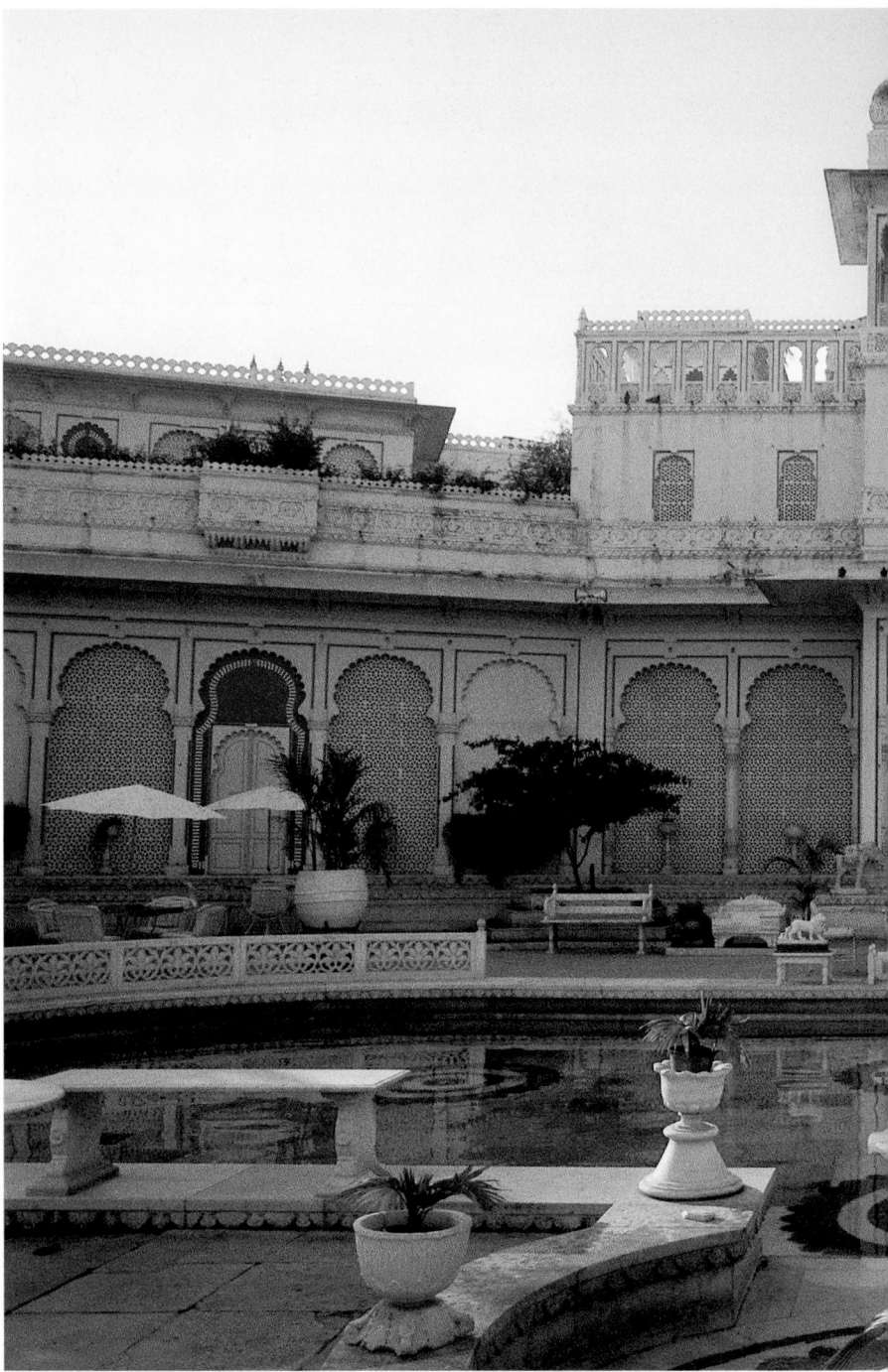

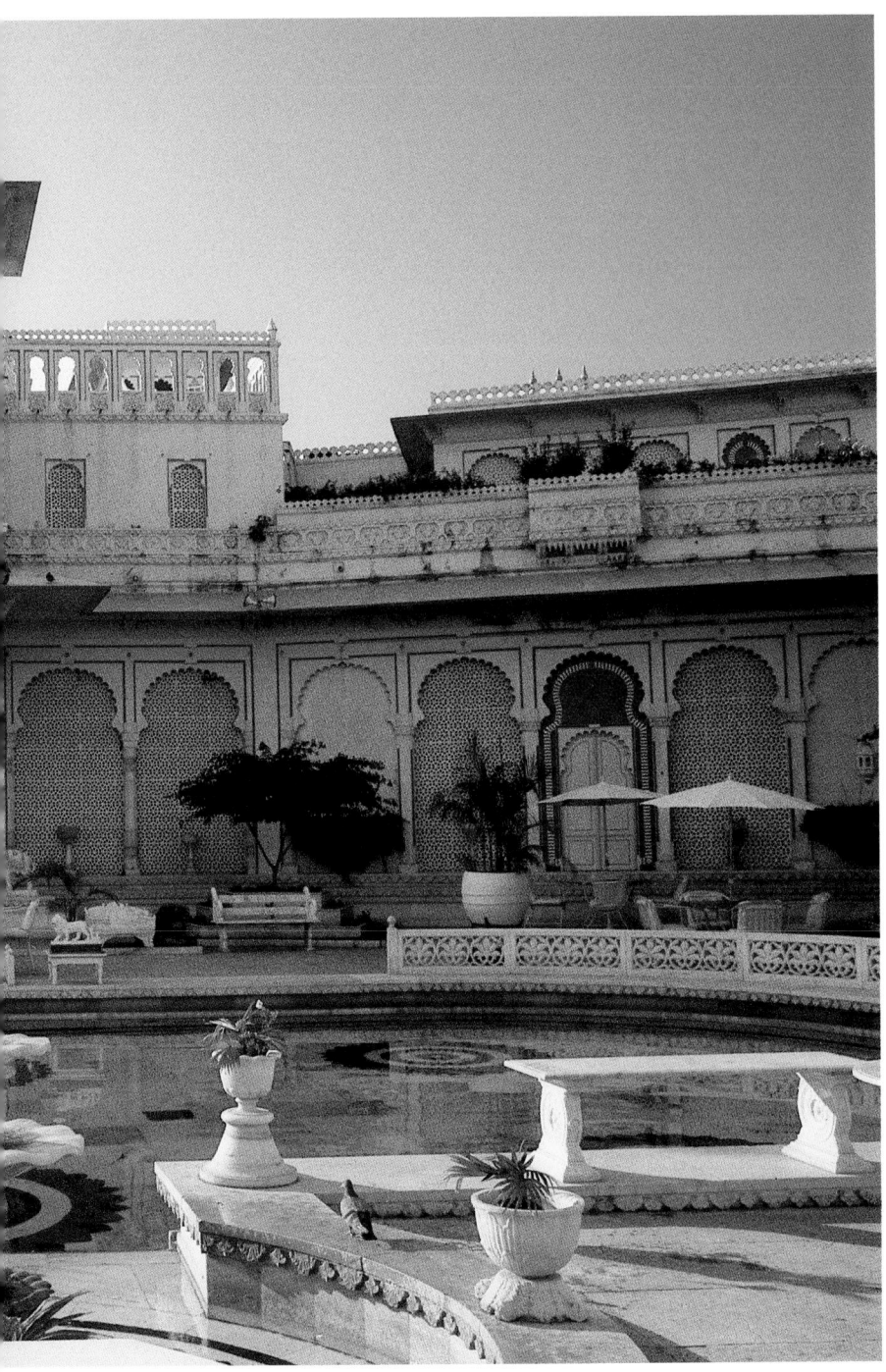

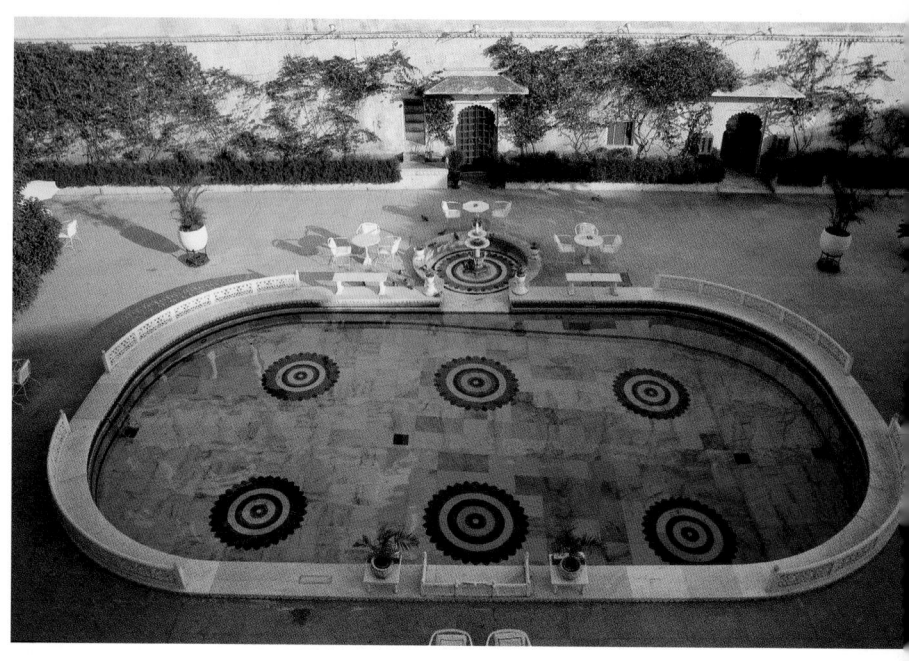

PP. 124–125 View of the Lake Palace Hotel on an island from the roof terrace of the Shiv Niwas Palace. · Blick von der Dachterrasse des Shiv-Niwas-Palastes auf das Lake Palace Hotel. · Le Lake Palace Hotel vu de la terrasse panoramique du Shiv Niwas Palace.

PP. 128–129 The central fountain court at Shiv Niwas Palace. · Der zentrale Innenhof des Shiv-Niwas-Palastes mit Springbrunnen. · La cour centrale du Shiv Niwas Palace et sa fontaine.

↑ The swimming pool, originally a small circular pool, was enlarged when Shiv Niwas was converted into a hotel in 1978. A pattern of lotus flowers in honey-colored Jaisalmer stone inlay was added during the extension. · Der ehemals kleine runde Swimmingpool wurde vergrößert, als Shiv Niwas 1978 in ein Hotel verwandelt wurde. Im Zuge des Ausbaus wurde dieses Lotusblütenmuster als Einlegearbeit aus dem Sandstein der Stadt Jaisalmer hinzugefügt. · La piscine, à l'origine un

bassin circulaire, a été agrandie en 1978, à l'occasion de la transformation du Shiv Niwas en hôtel. Le motif de fleurs de lotus en incrustation en pierre de Jaisalmer couleur de miel date aussi de cette époque.

→ A swimming pool in the ruler's private apartment. · Der Pool im Privatgemach des Herrschers. · Le souverain disposait d'une piscine dans ses appartements privés.

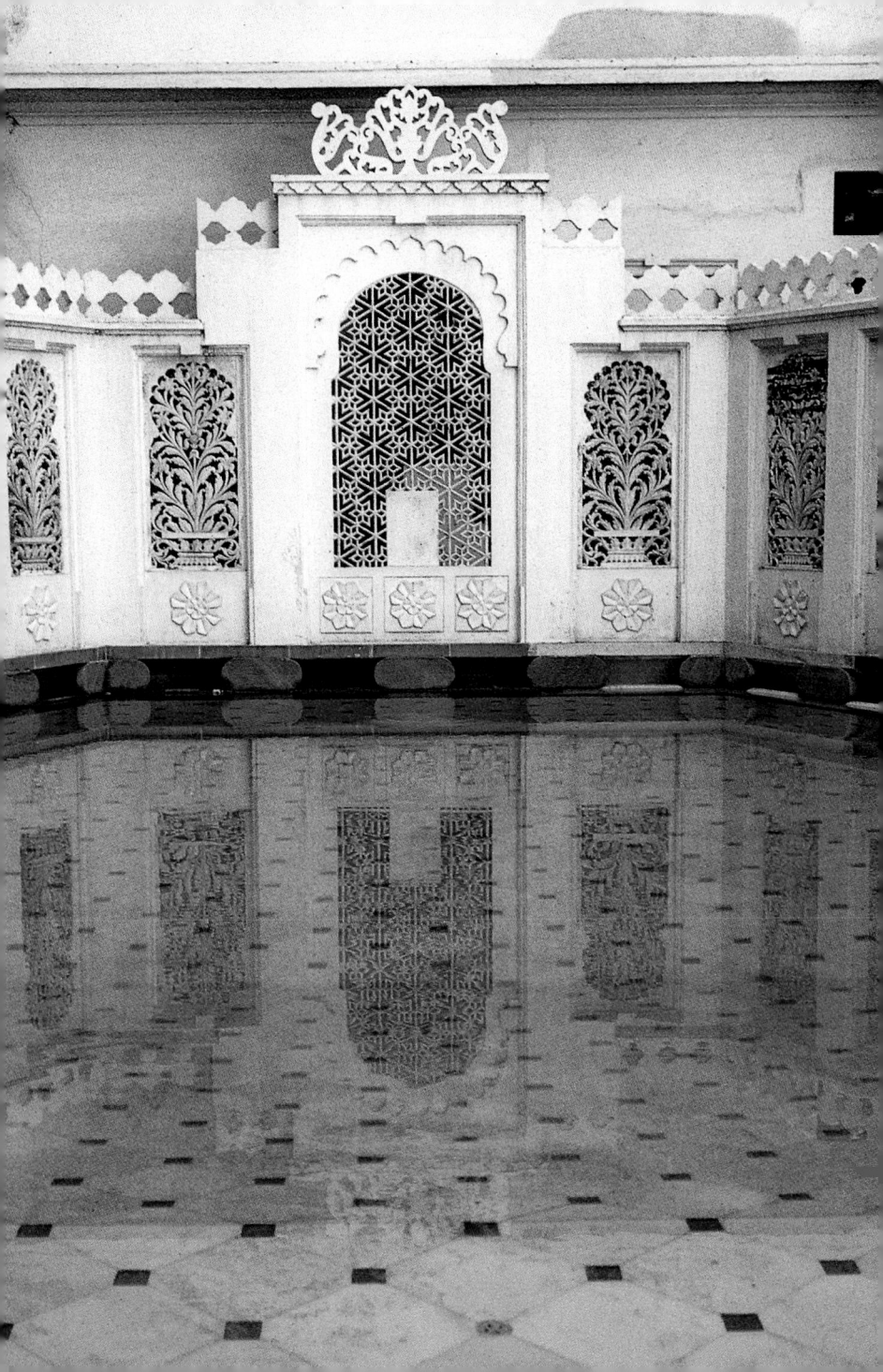

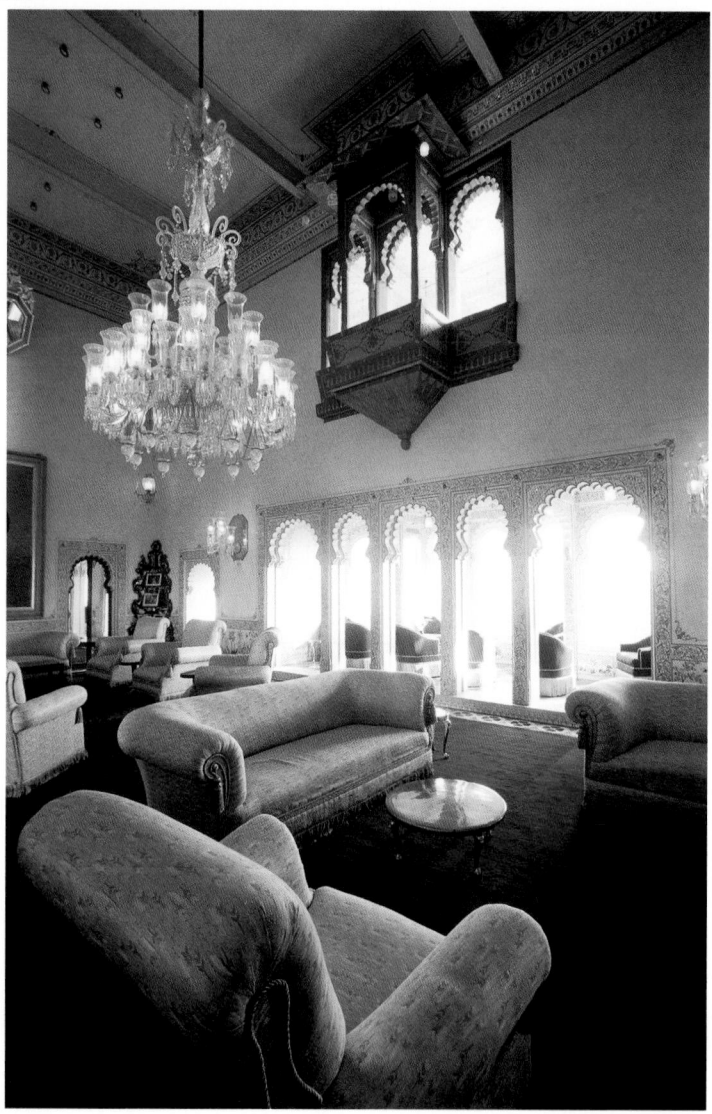

↑ The former drawing room, with a cornice and balcony embellished with patterns in blue and pink glass, is now the hotel bar. • Der ehemalige Salon, dessen Gesims und Balkon mit einem Muster aus blauem und rosafarbenem Glas geschmückt sind, dient heute als Hotelbar. • L'ancien salon, doté d'une corniche et d'un balcon agrémenté d'éléments de verre roses ou bleus, abrite désormais le bar de l'hôtel.

→ The entrance gate to Shiv Niwas in intricately-carved black stone from Dungarpur. • Blick auf den Eingang des Shiv-Niwas-Palastes aus schwarzem Dungarpur-Stein. • La pierre noire de Dungarpur de l'entrée monumentale de Shiv Niwas est taillée comme de la dentelle.

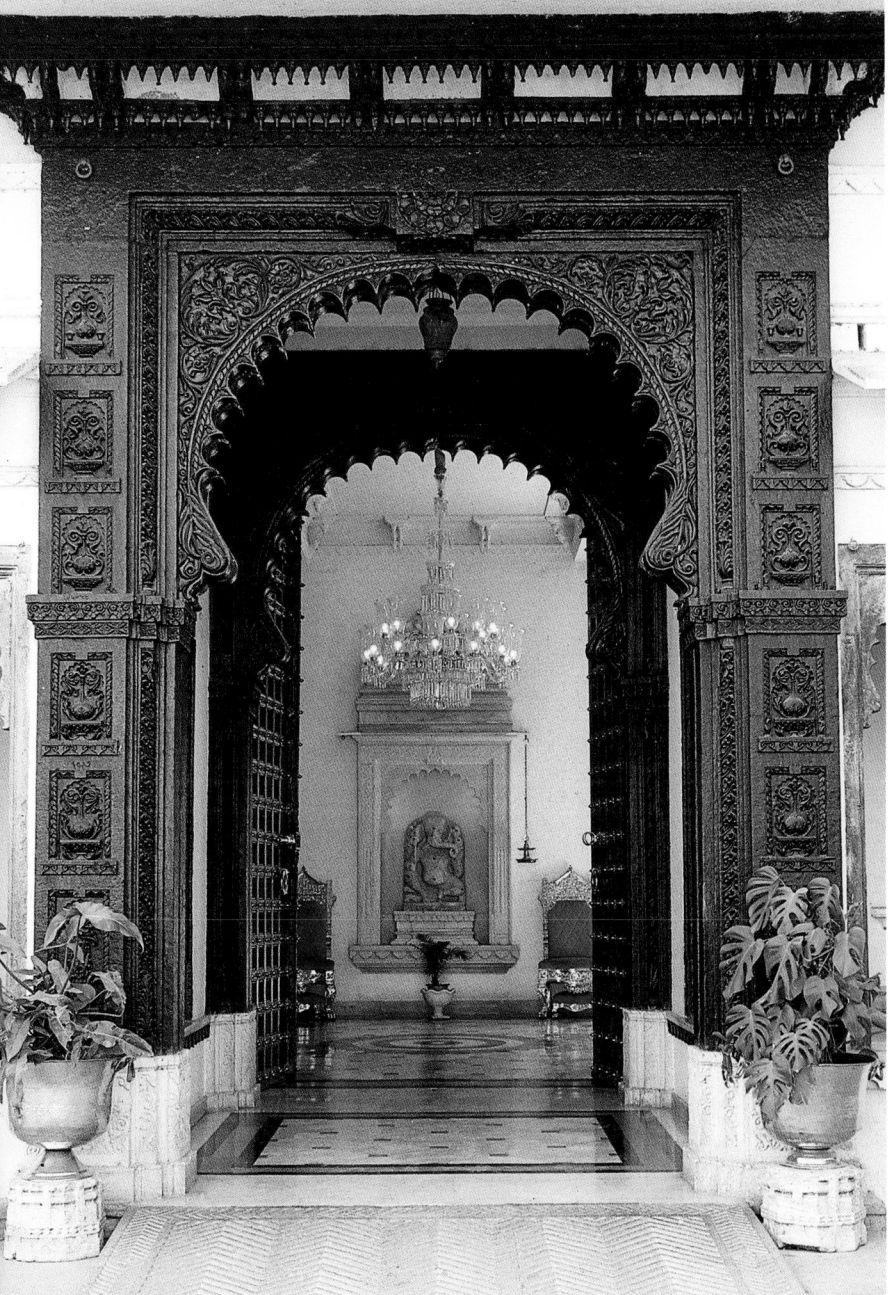

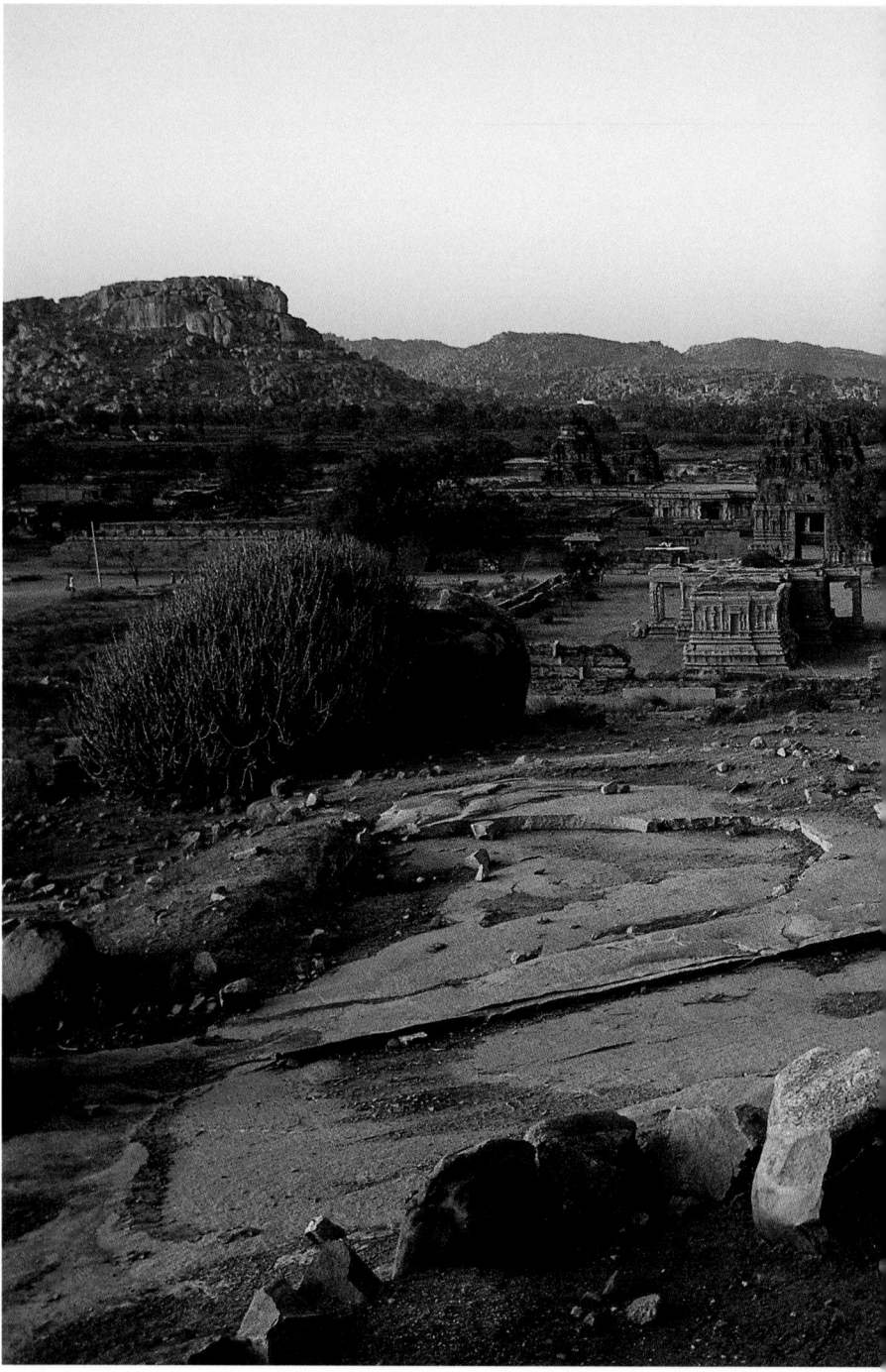

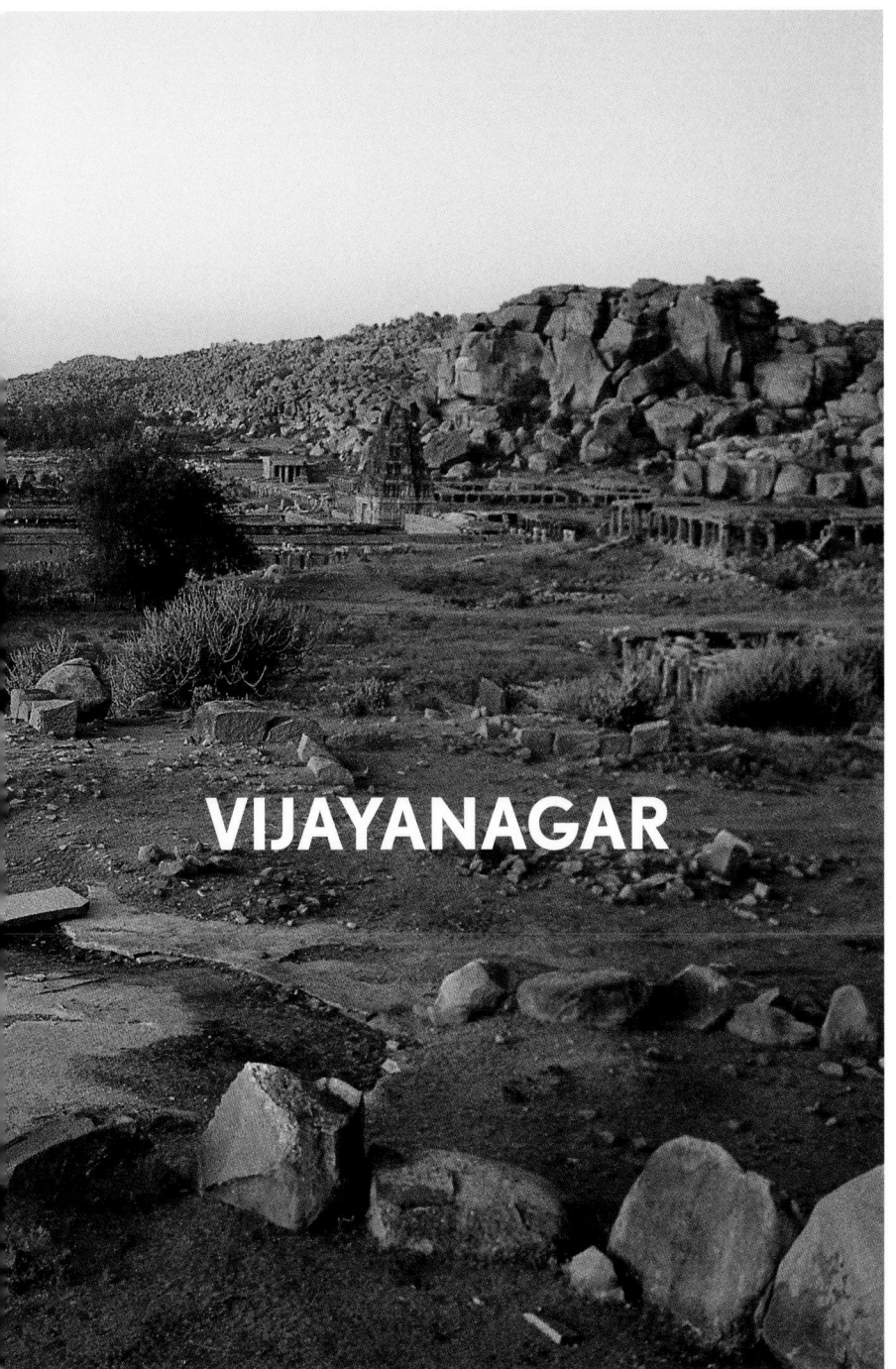

VIJAYANAGAR

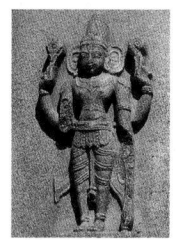

VIJAYANAGAR
HAMPI, KARNATAKA
INDIA

"The king had a thousand elephants with bodies like mountains and miens like demons...the city of Vijayanagar has no equal in the world," wrote Abdur Razzaq, a Persian visitor to the court of Deva Raya II in 1443. For more than 200 years from the mid-14th century onwards until its sack in 1565, a powerful Hindu empire rose on the Deccan plateau in south India. The kings of Vijayanagar – City of Victory – were called "rajas". They established a capital that was also a sacred center, an invocation to the god Vishnu and his incarnation Rama, the hero of the epic "Ramayana". Temples and royal palaces went up on the banks of the River Tungabhadra that snakes its way through a mysterious landscape of rising granite rocks that served as natural fortification. The link between the earthly and the divine conferred a god-like status on the kings; the city grew in the circles of a mandala, a magical diagram representing the universe. Vijayanagar's remains – some preserved, others half-ruined or reduced to rubble – are one of the glories of medieval south Indian architecture.

„Der König besaß tausend Elefanten, deren Leiber wie Berge waren, und ihre Blicke glichen denen von Dämonen ... die Stadt Vijayanagar findet in der Welt nicht ihresgleichen", schrieb der Perser Abdur Razzaq, der 1443 den Hof Deva-rayas II. besuchte. Ein mächtiges hinduistisches Reich entstand von der Mitte des 14. Jahrhunderts bis zu seinem Zusammenbruch 1565 auf dem Dekkan-Plateau in Südindien. Die Könige von Vijayanagar – der Stadt des Sieges – nannten sich Radschas. Sie gründeten eine prächtige Hauptstadt, die auch als Heiligtum für den Gott Vishnu und seine Inkarnation Rama, den Helden des „Ramayana"-Epos, fungierte. Am Ufer des Tungabhadra-Flusses, der sich durch eine geheimnisvolle Landschaft mit Granitfelsblöcken windet, welche als natürliche Verteidigungslinie genutzt wurden, errichteten sie große Tempel und königliche Paläste. Aufgrund der Verbindung von irdischer und göttlicher Macht hatten die Könige einen gottähnlichen Status inne, während sich die Stadt selbst in den konzentrischen Kreisen eines Mandalas, das als magisches Diagramm das Universum repräsentiert, entwickelte. Die erhaltenen, halb verfallenen oder kaum noch sichtbaren Überreste von Vijayanagar zeugen vom Glanz der mittelalterlichen Architektur Südindiens.

« Le roi possédait un millier d'éléphants hauts comme des montagnes et avec des allures de démons... La ville de Vijayanagar n'a pas d'égale au monde », écrivait Abdur Razzaq, Persan en ambassade à la cour de Devaraya II en 1443. Pendant plus de deux siècles, à partir du milieu du 14ᵉ siècle jusqu'à la mise à sac qui a scellé son destin en 1565, un puissant empire hindou dominait le plateau du Deccan, dans le Sud de l'Inde. Les rois de Vijayanagar – la cité de la victoire – portaient le nom de « radjas ». Ils ont fondé une capitale munificente, qui était aussi un centre religieux, dédié au culte de la divinité Vishnou et de son incarnation Rama, héros du poème épique « Ramayana ». Des temples imposants et des palais royaux bordaient les rives de la Tungabhadra qui serpente dans un paysage mystérieux d'affleurements de granite tenant lieu de fortification naturelle. Le lien entre le temporel et le spirituel conférait aux rois un statut de quasi-divinité. La ville s'est développée en cercles concentriques rappelant un mandala, diagramme magique qui représente l'univers. L'ancienne Vijayanagar – dont certains édifices ont été conservés et d'autres à moitié détruits ou sont tombés en ruine – est l'une des gloires de l'architecture médiévale du Sud de l'Inde.

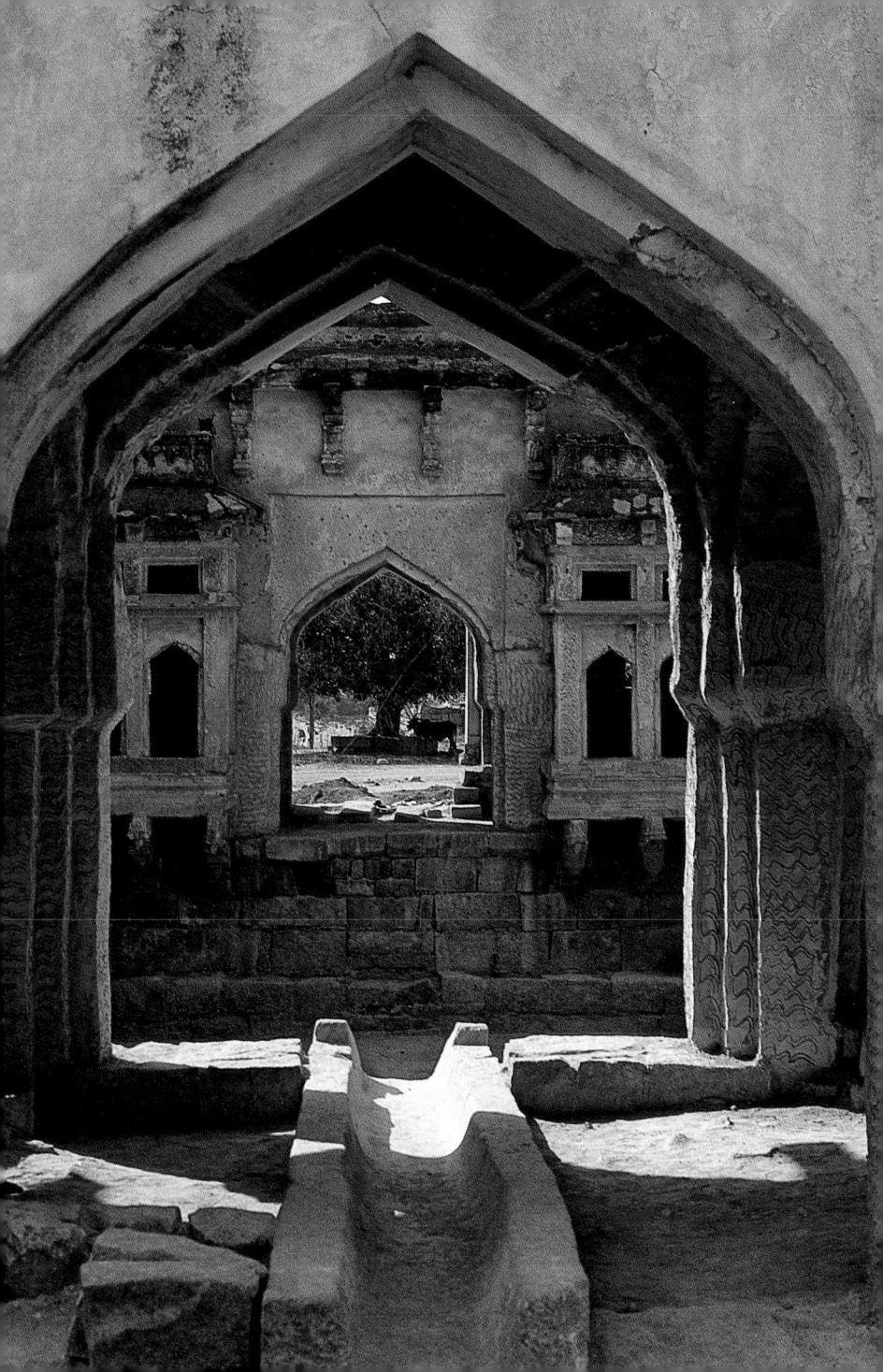

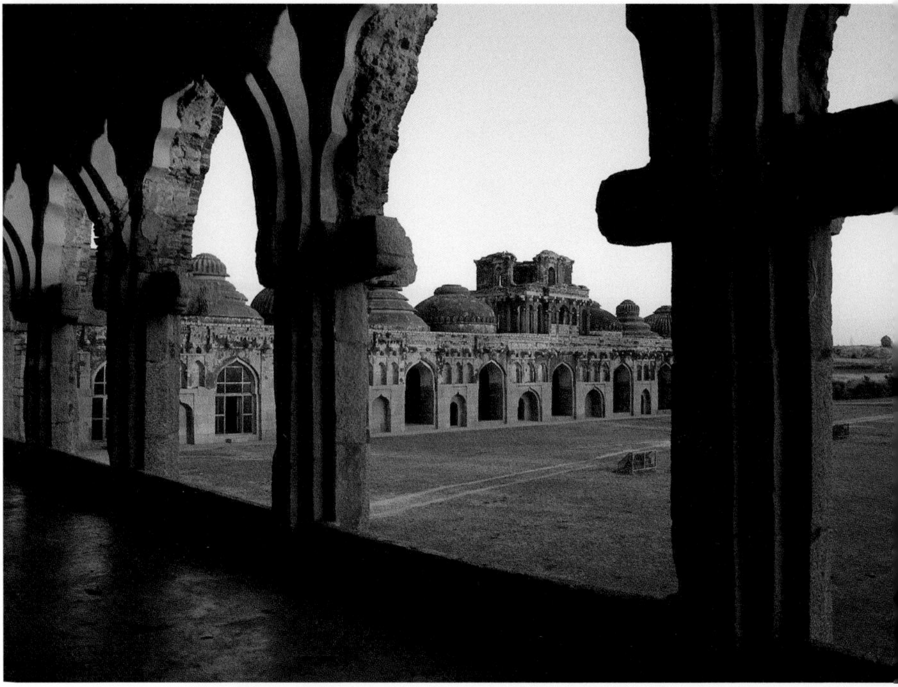

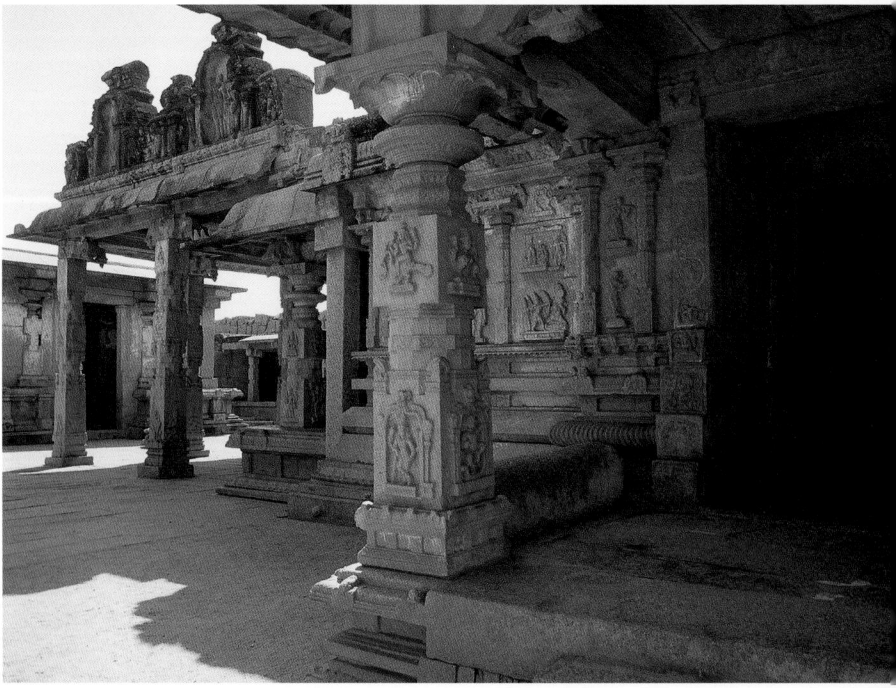

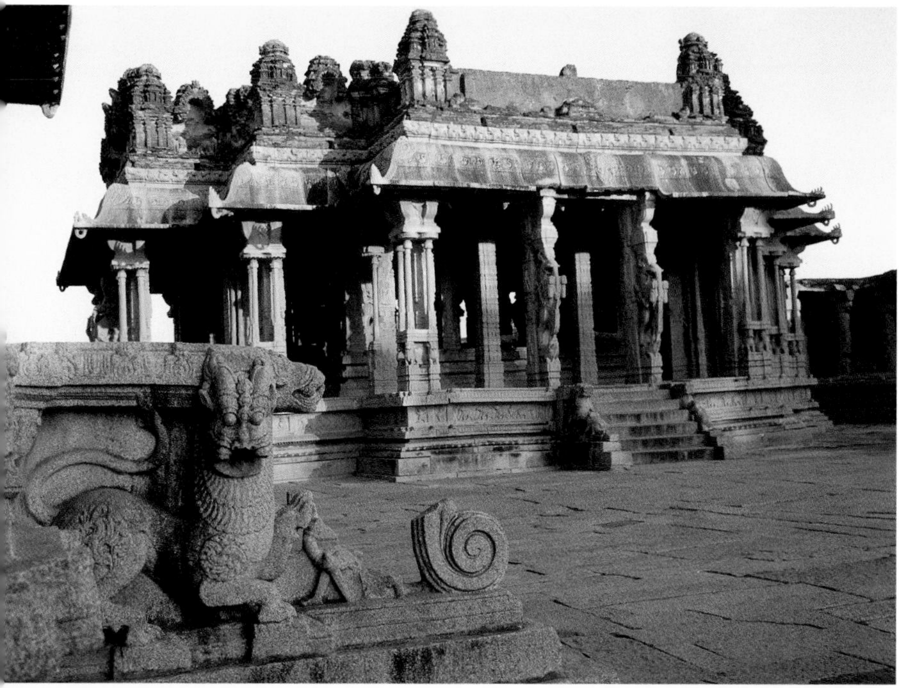

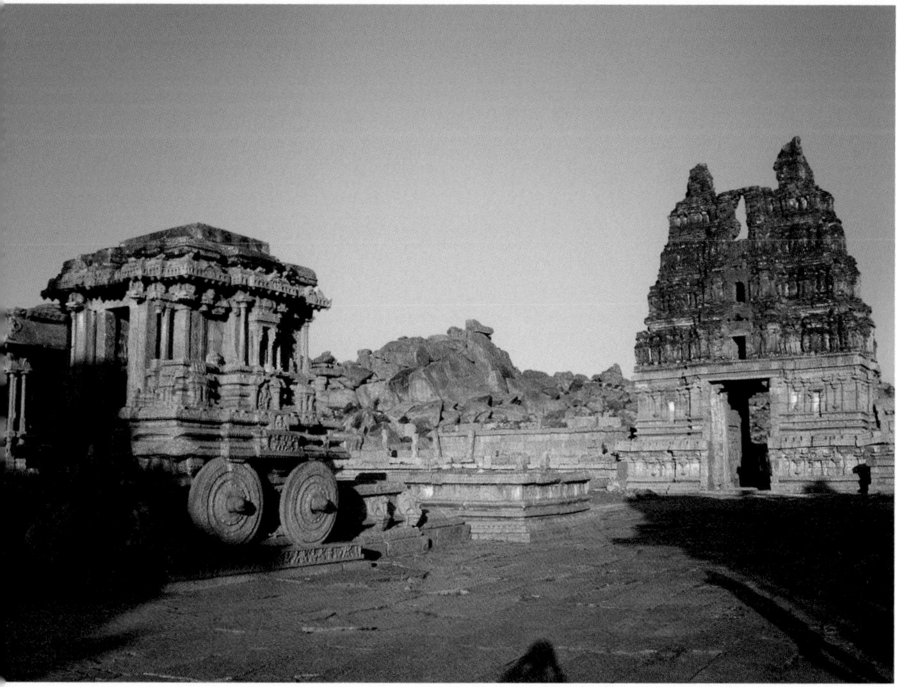

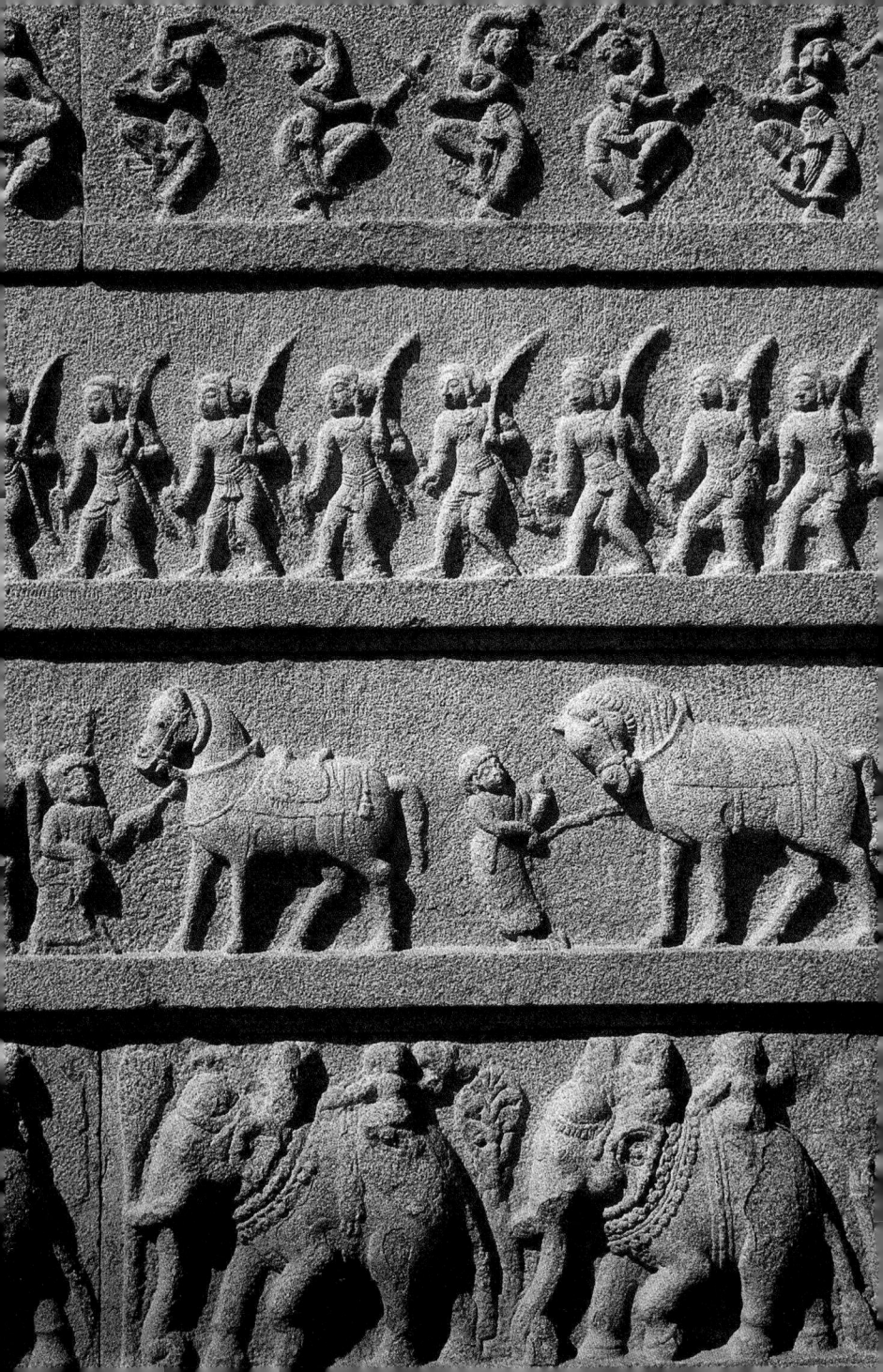

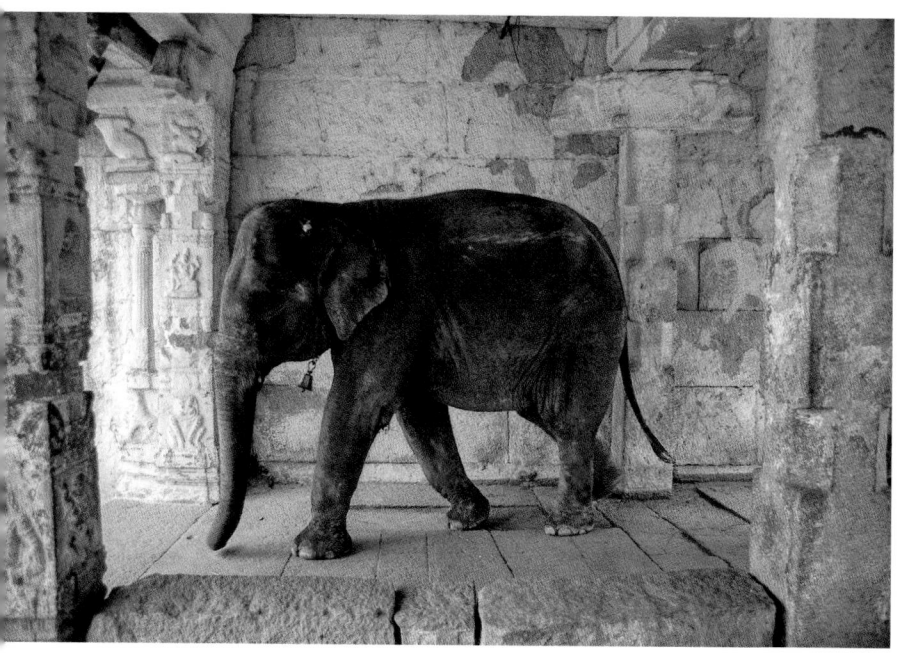

P. 138 ↑ View from an arcaded enclosure of elephants' stables facing a royal parade ground. • Blick von der Einfriedung der Elefantenställe hinter dem königlichen Paradeplatz. • De ces arcades, on aperçoit les écuries pour éléphants.

P. 138 ↓ The richly carved Ramachandra Temple. • Der reich verzierte Ramachandra-Tempel. • Le temple de Ramachandra.

P. 139 ↑ The outstanding 16th-century Vithala Temple. • Der Vithala-Tempel aus dem 16. Jahrhundert. • Le temple de Vithala construit au 16e siècle.

P. 139 ↓ Stone processional chariots for deities. • Steinerne Wagen für die Prozession der Gottheiten. • Les chariots de procession en pierre en l'honneur des divinités.

← Friezes of courtly processions and military campaigns on the walls of Vijayanagar's temples. • Friese mit höfischen Prozessionen und Kampfhandlungen an den Tempelwänden. • Des scènes de processions et de bataille sur les murs des temples de Vijayanagar.

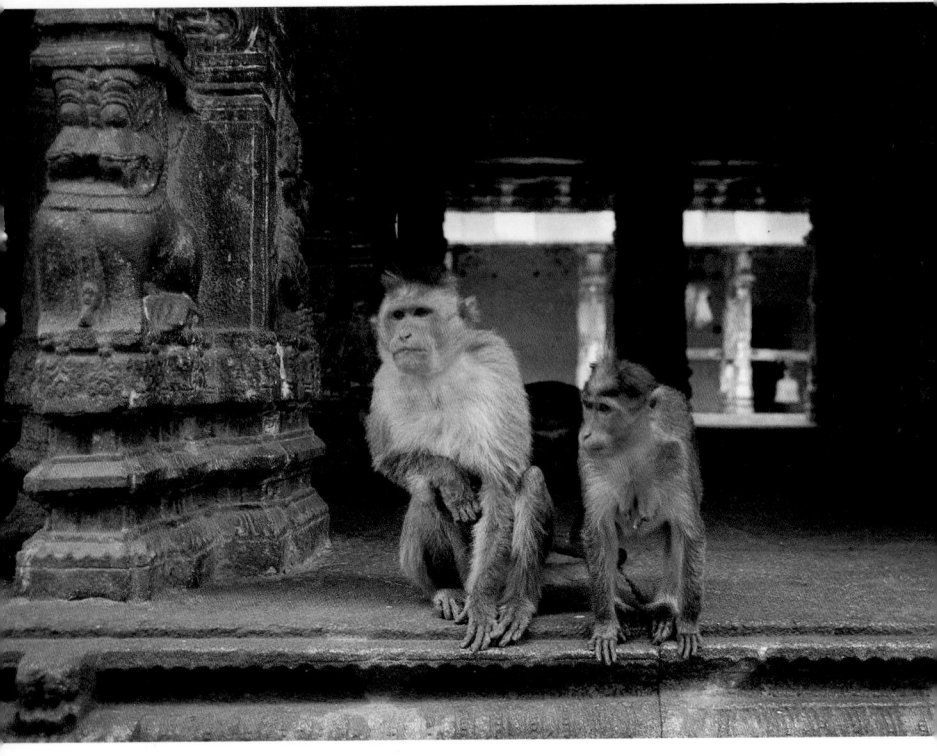

↑ Monkeys run wild among the
ruins of Vijayanagar and are revered
as descendants of the monkey god
Hanuman. • Wilde, als Abkömmlinge
des Affengottes Hanuman verehrte
Affen laufen in den Ruinen von Vijayanagar umher. • Des hordes de singes,
vénérés comme des descendants du
dieu-singe Hanuman, déambulent dans
les ruines de Vijayanagar.

↗ Sacred images of the bull Nandi, the
mount of the god Shiva. • Skulpturen
des heiligen Stiers Nandi, dem Reittier
des Gottes Shiva. • Des statues du
taureau sacré Nandi, monture de Shiva.

→ Carved from granite, the sculpture
was once embellished in rich colors. •
Die aus Granit geschlagenen Skulpturen waren früher bunt bemalt. • Taillées
dans du granite, les sculptures étaient
autrefois parées de couleurs.

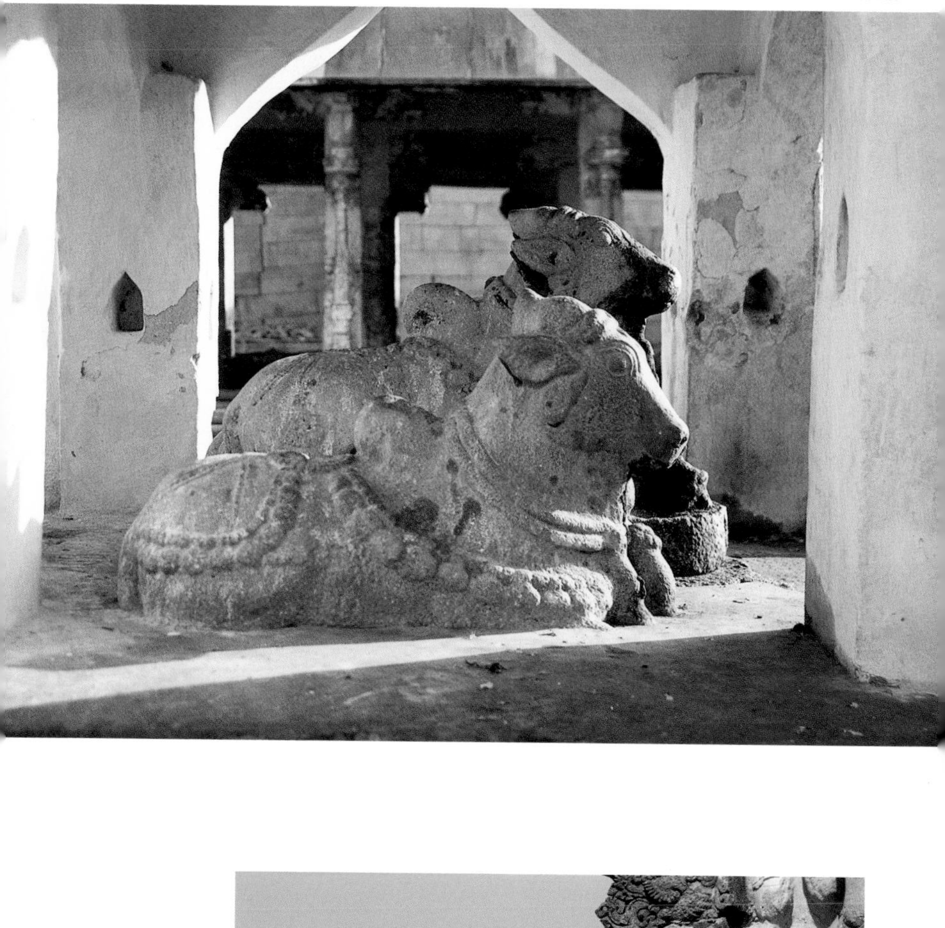

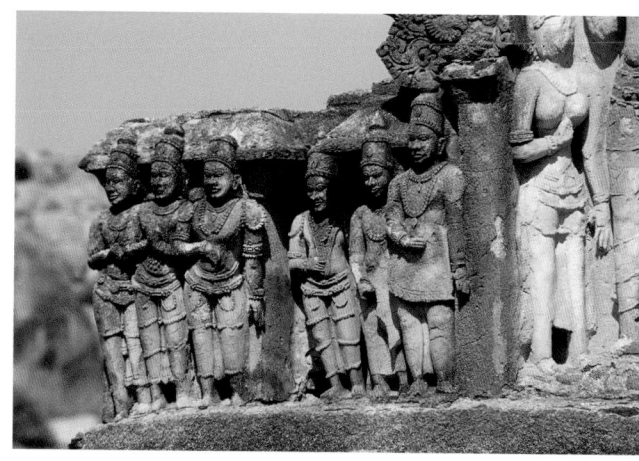

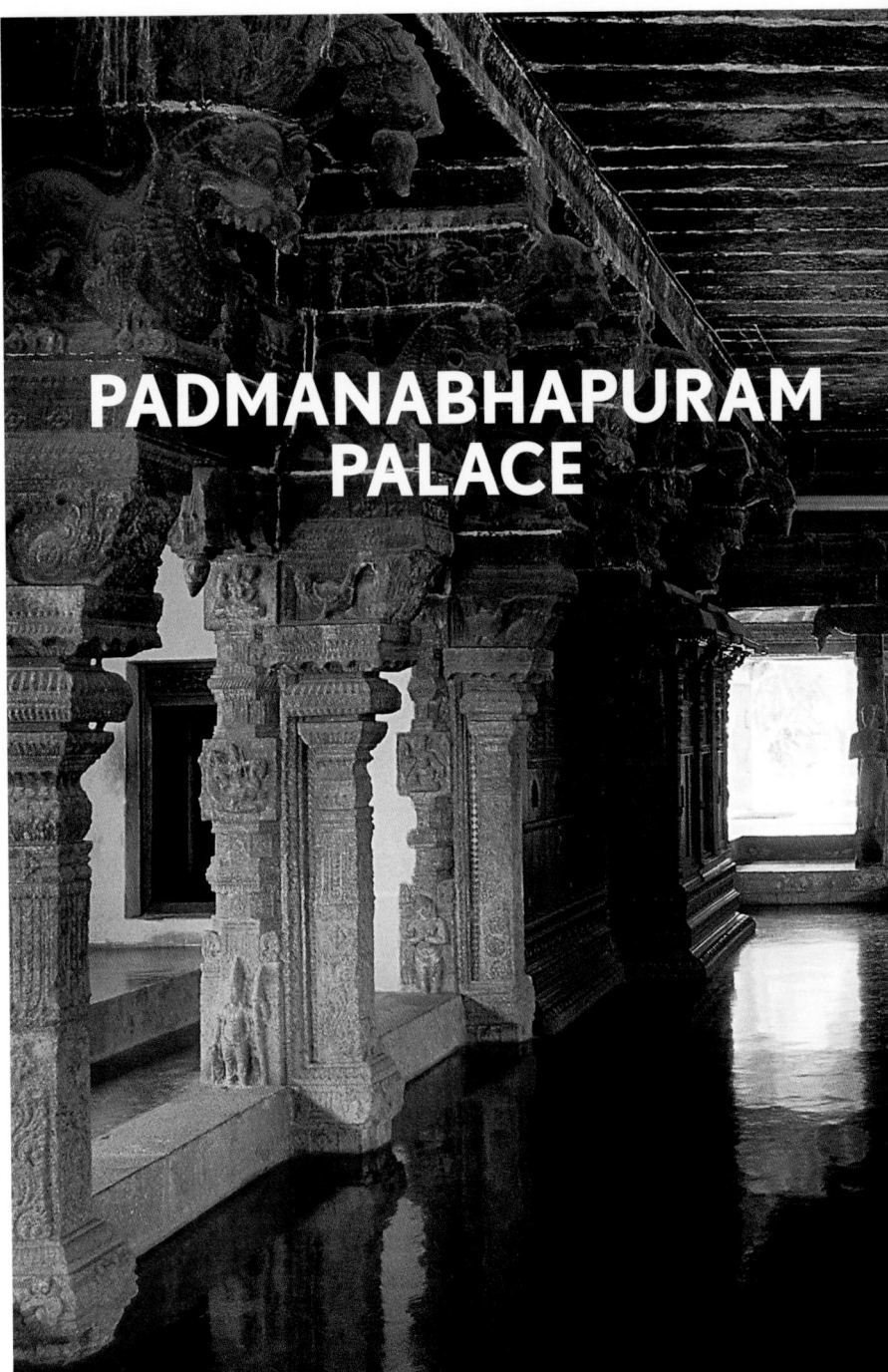

PADMANABHAPURAM PALACE

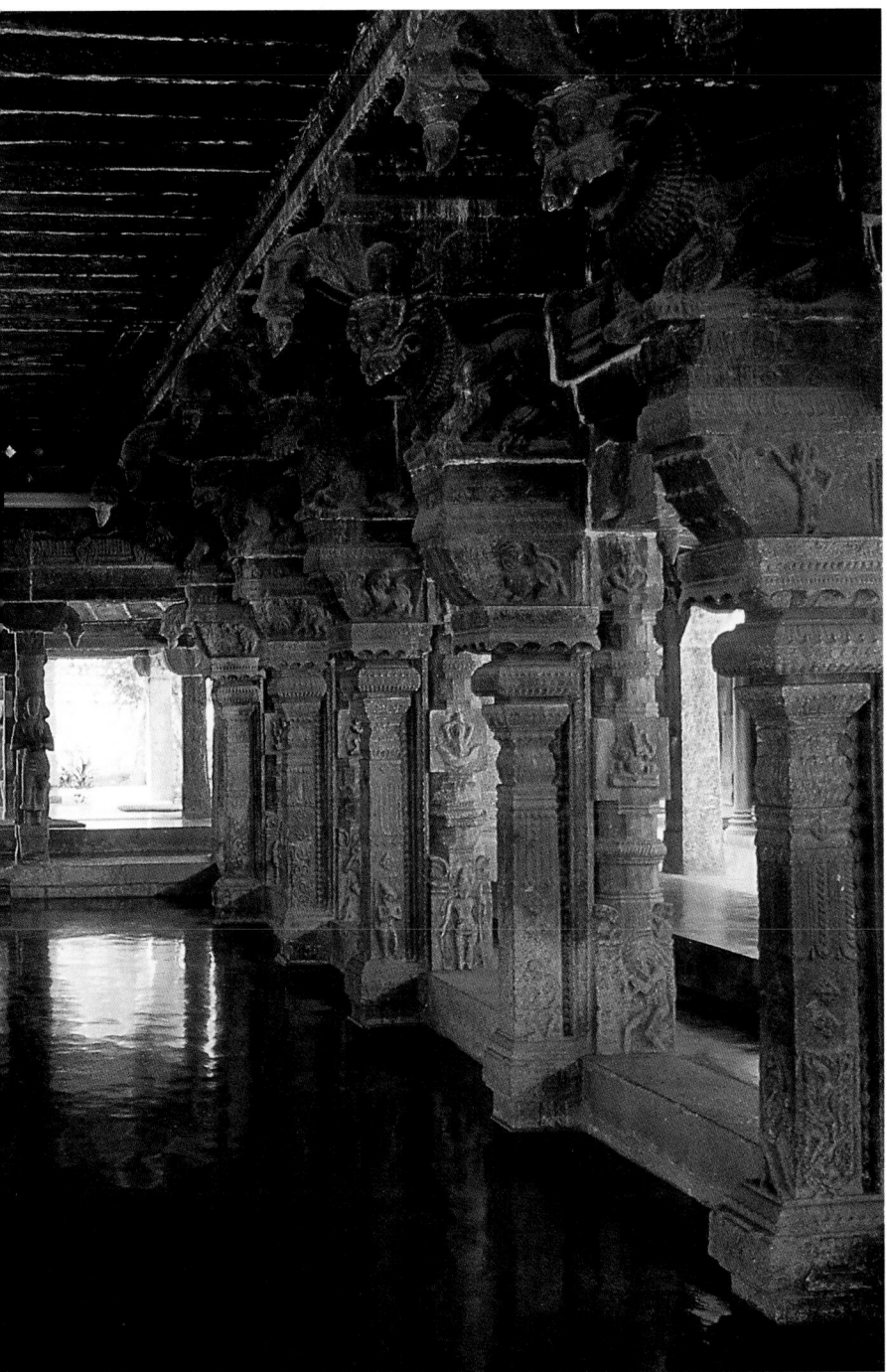

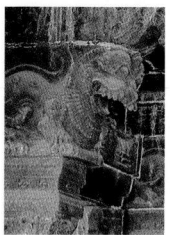

PADMANABHAPURAM PALACE
NAGERCOIL, TAMIL NADU
INDIA

Padmanabhapuram Palace is one of the most outstanding wooden buildings in India, an architectural feat by the master carpenters of Kerala. Built largely in the 18th century by Martanda Varma, ruler of Travancore, the terracotta tiled roofs and gleaming black plaster floors offset its superb woodwork of polished teak. The royal family moved to Trivandrum in 1790 and henceforth it was only used as summer residence. It may be one good reason why it has survived in such good condition. Although built by a great dynasty of Kerala, a shift in boundaries now locates it just over the border in the state of Tamil Nadu. The palace derives its name from the worship of the god Vishnu, the Preserver of the Universe in the Hindu pantheon. Among Vishnu's manifestations is an image of him reclining on a serpent, with the god Brahma, the Creator, seated on a lotus growing out of his navel. *Padma* in Sanskrit is lotus; *nabha* means navel. Padmanabhapuram is thus the citadel of Vishnu from whose navel emerges the lotus and whose preserving radiance fills the universe.

Padmanabhapuram Palace, ein Meisterwerk der Schreiner aus Kerala, ist ein herausragendes Beispiel der indischen Holzarchitektur. Der Palast wurde weitgehend im 18. Jahrhundert unter Martanda Varma, dem Herrscher über Travancore, erbaut. Das Dach aus Terrakottaziegeln und die glänzend schwarzen Gipsböden heben sich von dem prächtigen Schnitzwerk in poliertem Teakholz ab. 1790 zog die königliche Familie nach Trivandrum und nutzte den Palast fortan als Sommerresidenz – daher vielleicht blieb er so gut erhalten. Das Bauwerk wurde von einer mächtigen Dynastie in Kerala erbaut, doch haben sich die Grenzen inzwischen so verschoben, dass es heute im Bundesstaat Tamil Nadu liegt. Sein Name leitet sich von der Verehrung des Gottes Vishnu ab, der im hinduistischen Pantheon die ewige Ordnung des Universums aufrechterhält. Vishnu wird manchmal als liegende Figur auf einer Schlange abgebildet, während der Schöpfergott Brahma auf einem Lotus sitzt, der aus seinem Nabel wächst. Die Wörter *padma* und *nabha* bedeuten Lotus und Nabel. Padmanabhapuram ist dementsprechend die Zitadelle Vishnus, aus dessen Nabel der Lotus wächst und dessen bewahrendes Strahlen das Universum erfüllt.

Le palais de Padmanabhapuram est un des exemples d'architecture en bois les plus spectaculaires d'Inde. On doit cette prouesse architecturale aux maîtres charpentiers de Kerala. Construit en grande partie au 18ᵉ siècle par Martanda Varma, qui régnait sur le Travancore, le palais présente des toits en tuiles de terre cuite et des sols de calcaire noir luisant, qui surpassent en beauté ses superbes boiseries en teck poli. La famille royale ayant fait de Trivandrum sa capitale en 1790, ce palais est devenu une simple résidence d'été, ce qui explique sans doute pourquoi il est encore en si bon état. Bien qu'il doive sa construction à une grande dynastie du Kerala, un déplacement des frontières a fait qu'il est maintenant situé de l'autre côté de la frontière, dans l'État de Tamil Nadu. Le palais tient son nom de la vénération du dieu Vishnou qui est parfois représenté reposant sur un serpent, aux côtés de Brahma, le dieu créateur, assis sur un lotus surgi du nombril de Vishnou. En sanscrit, *padma* signifie lotus et *nabha* nombril. Padmanabhapuram est ainsi la citadelle de Vishnou dont le nombril donne naissance au lotus et dont l'aura protectrice emplit l'univers.

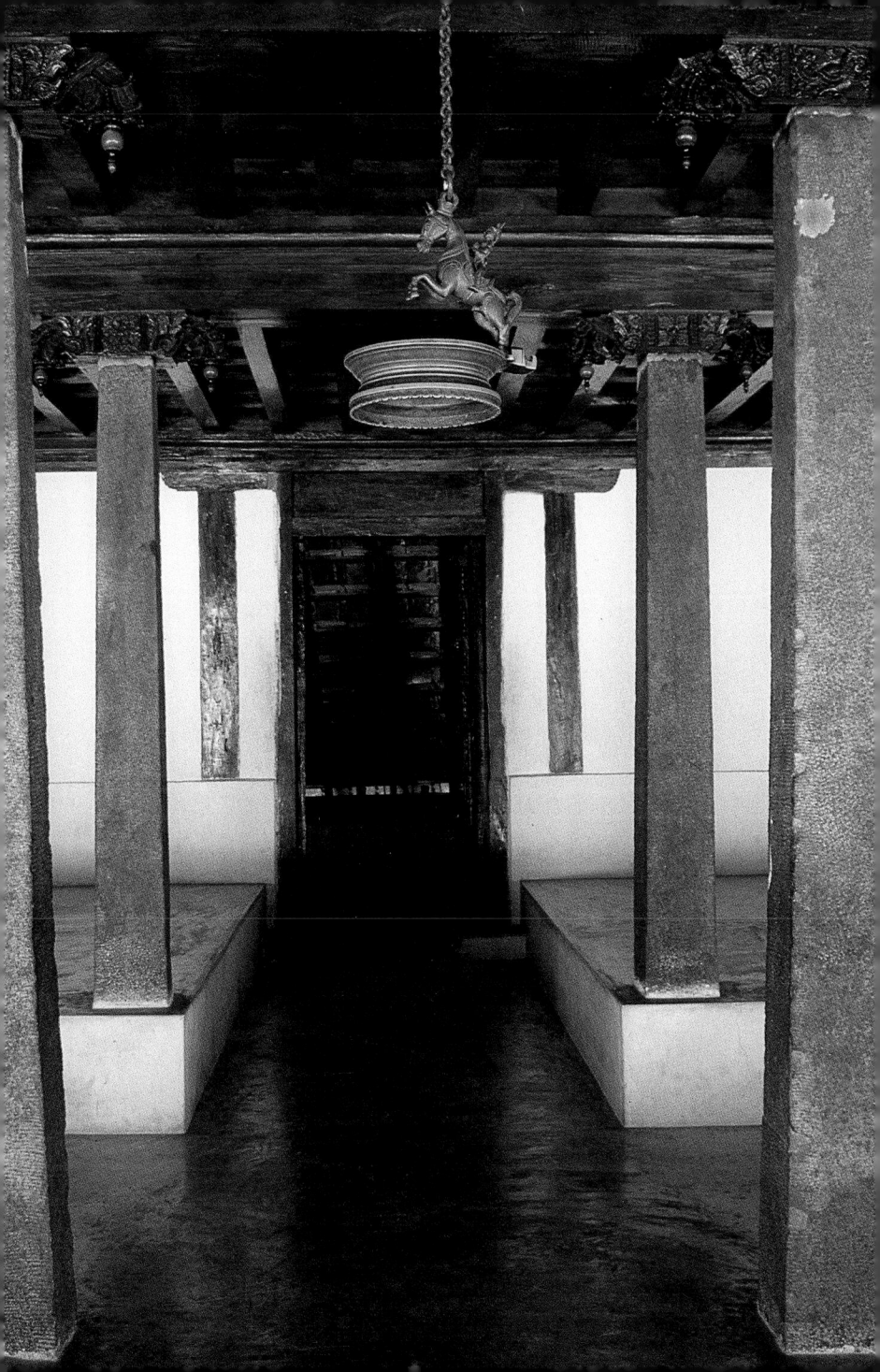

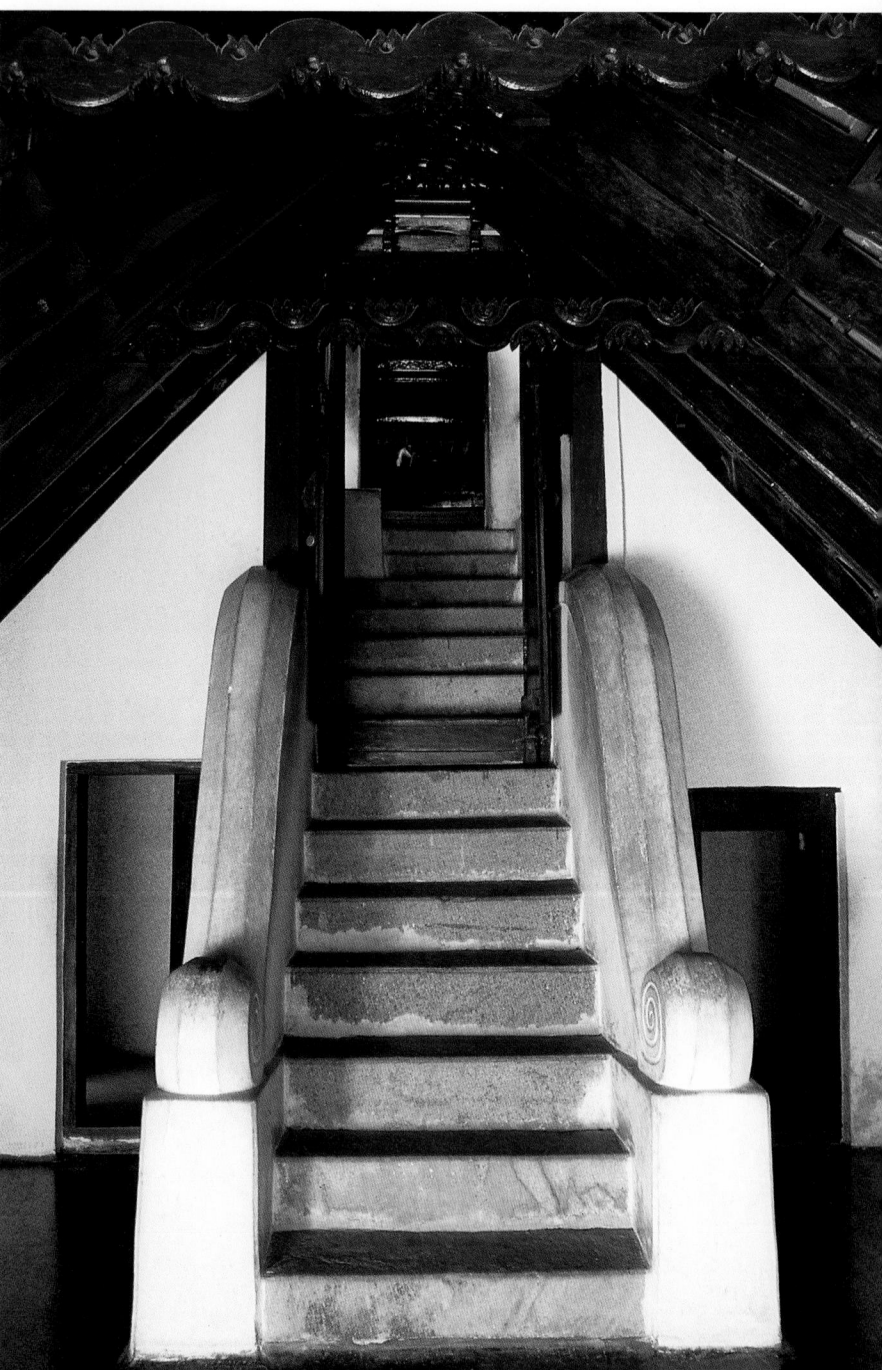

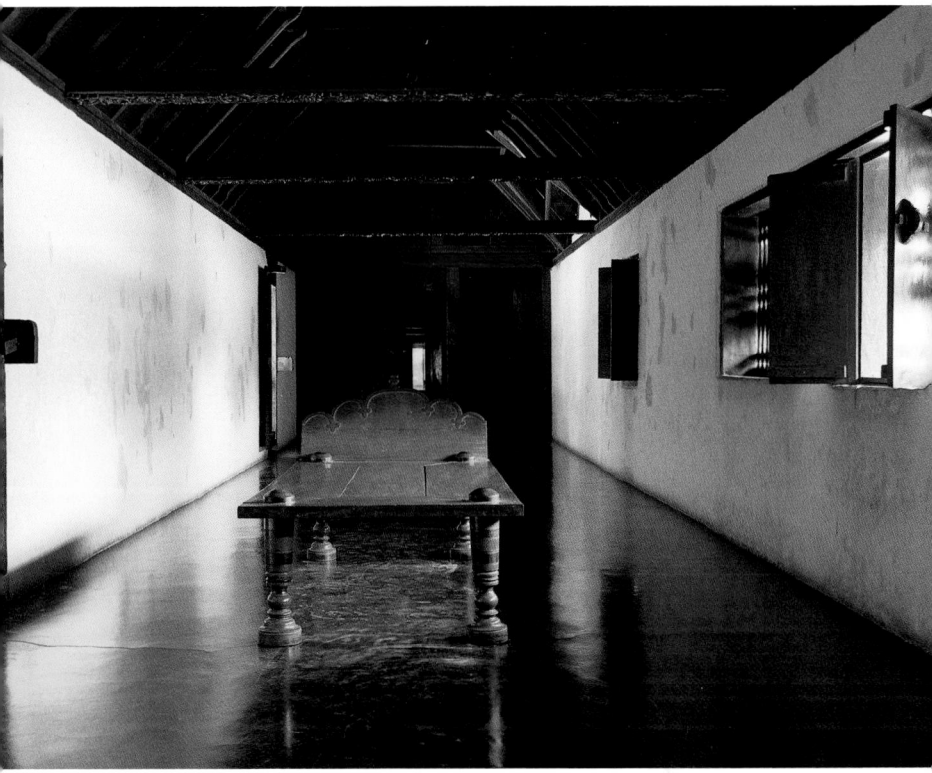

PP. 144–145 Carved stone pillars adorn the dance hall with its polished black floor of lime plaster. • Verzierte Steinsäulen schmücken den Tanzsaal mit dem schwarz polierten Boden aus Gipskalk. • Des piliers sculptés dans la pierre ornent la salle de danse au sol de calcaire noir poli.

← The shape of the staircase parapet is said to be inspired by an elephant's trunk. • Ein Elefantenrüssel diente vermutlich als Inspiration für den Entwurf des Treppengeländers. • La main courante de l'escalier est censée représenter une trompe d'éléphant.

↑ A traditional Kerala bed placed in one of the many palace corridors. • Ein traditionelles Bett aus Kerala steht in einem der vielen Gänge. • Ce lit traditionnel du Kerala trône dans un des nombreux corridors du palais.

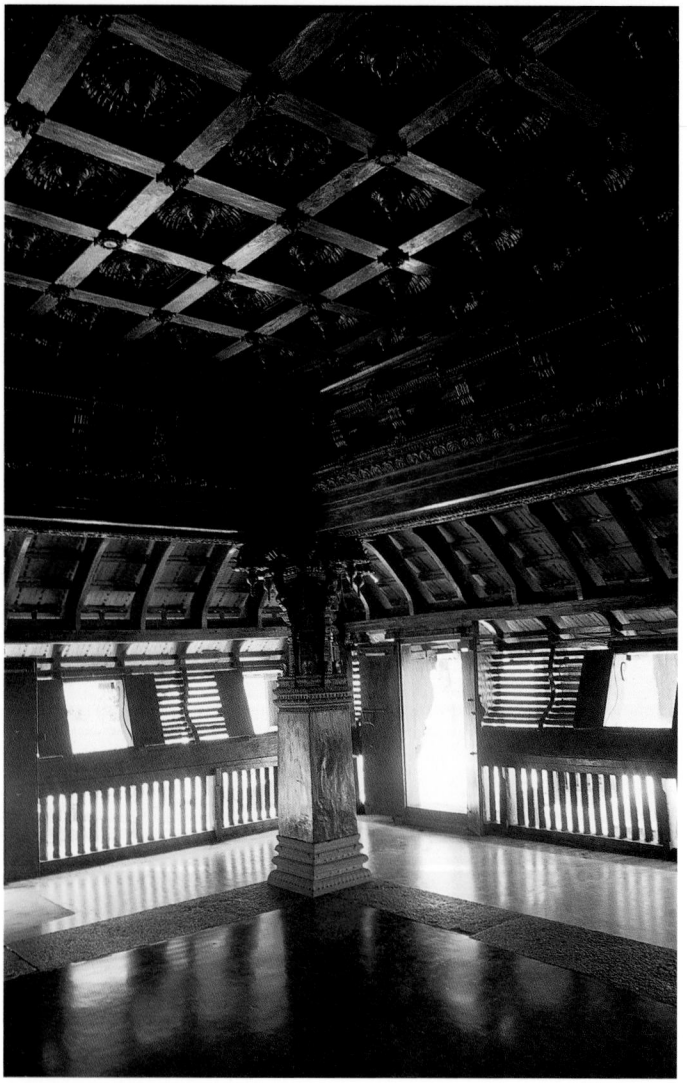

↑ The carved ceiling is held up by ribbed rafters. The outward-sloping slatted windows help to keep out the harsh sunlight and modulate the circulation of air. • Die holzgeschnitzte Decke wird von Rippenbalken gestützt. Die nach außen gewölbten, mit Leisten versehenen Fenster halten das grelle Sonnenlicht ab und regulieren den Luftaustausch. • Le plafond en bois sculpté est supporté par des chevrons travaillés. Les jalousies inclinées filtrent la lumière du soleil et permettent l'aération.

→ The colored glass panes and furniture in the audience chamber were introduced with the arrival of European style. • Buntglasfenster und Möbel im Audienzzimmer verdanken sich dem frühen europäischen Einfluss. • Les vitraux de couleur et le mobilier de la salle d'audience datent de l'arrivée des Européens.

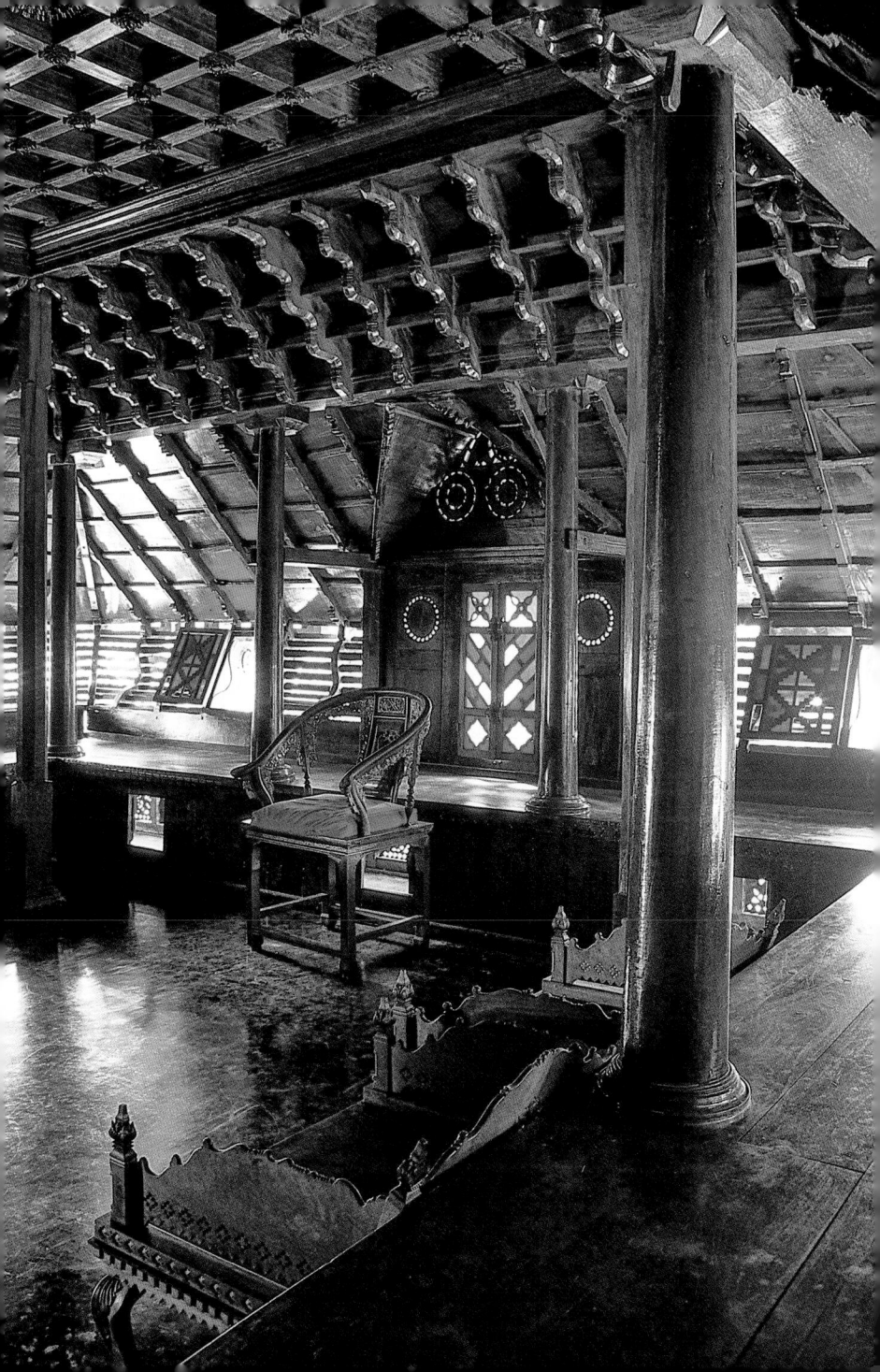

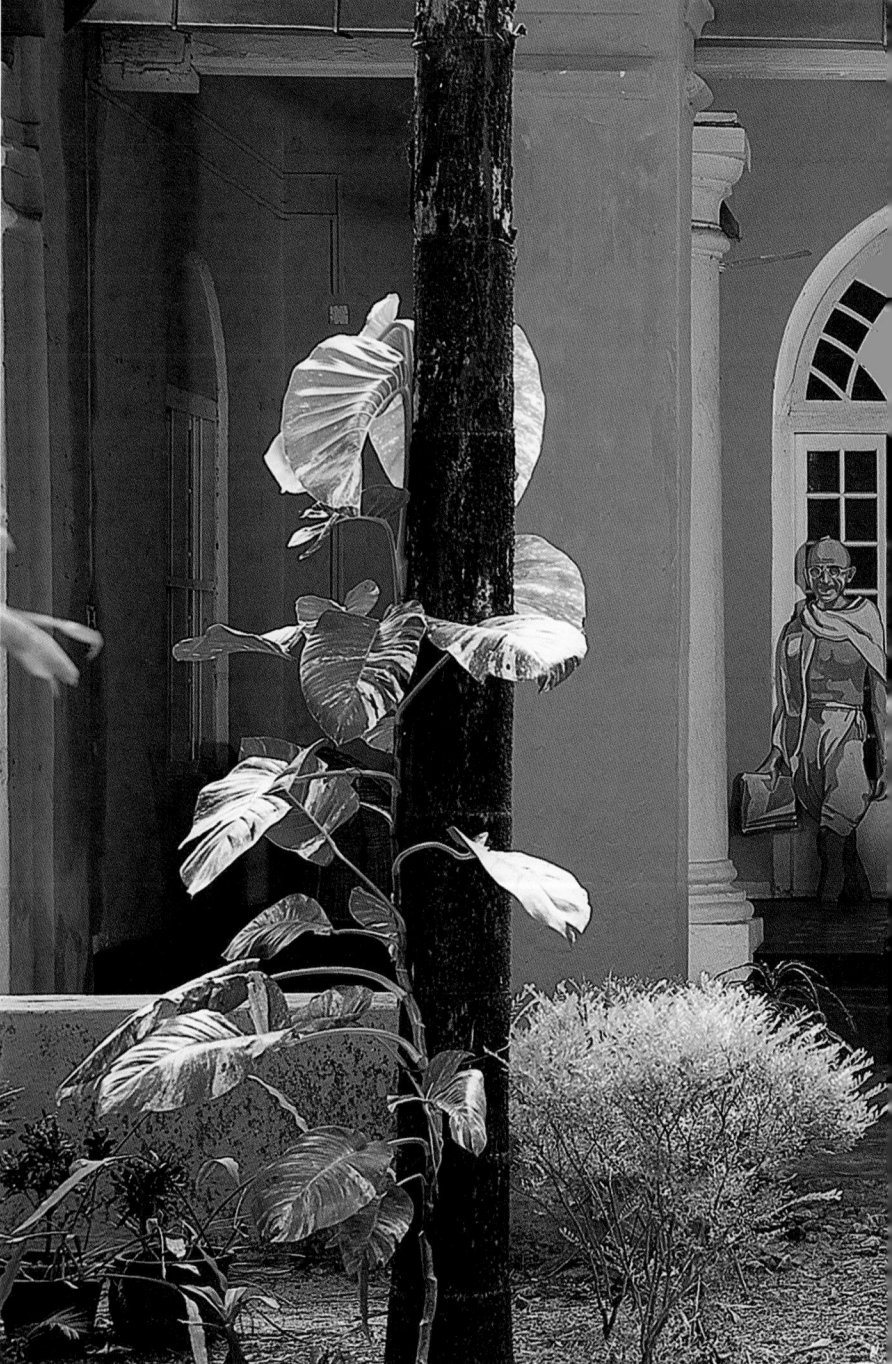

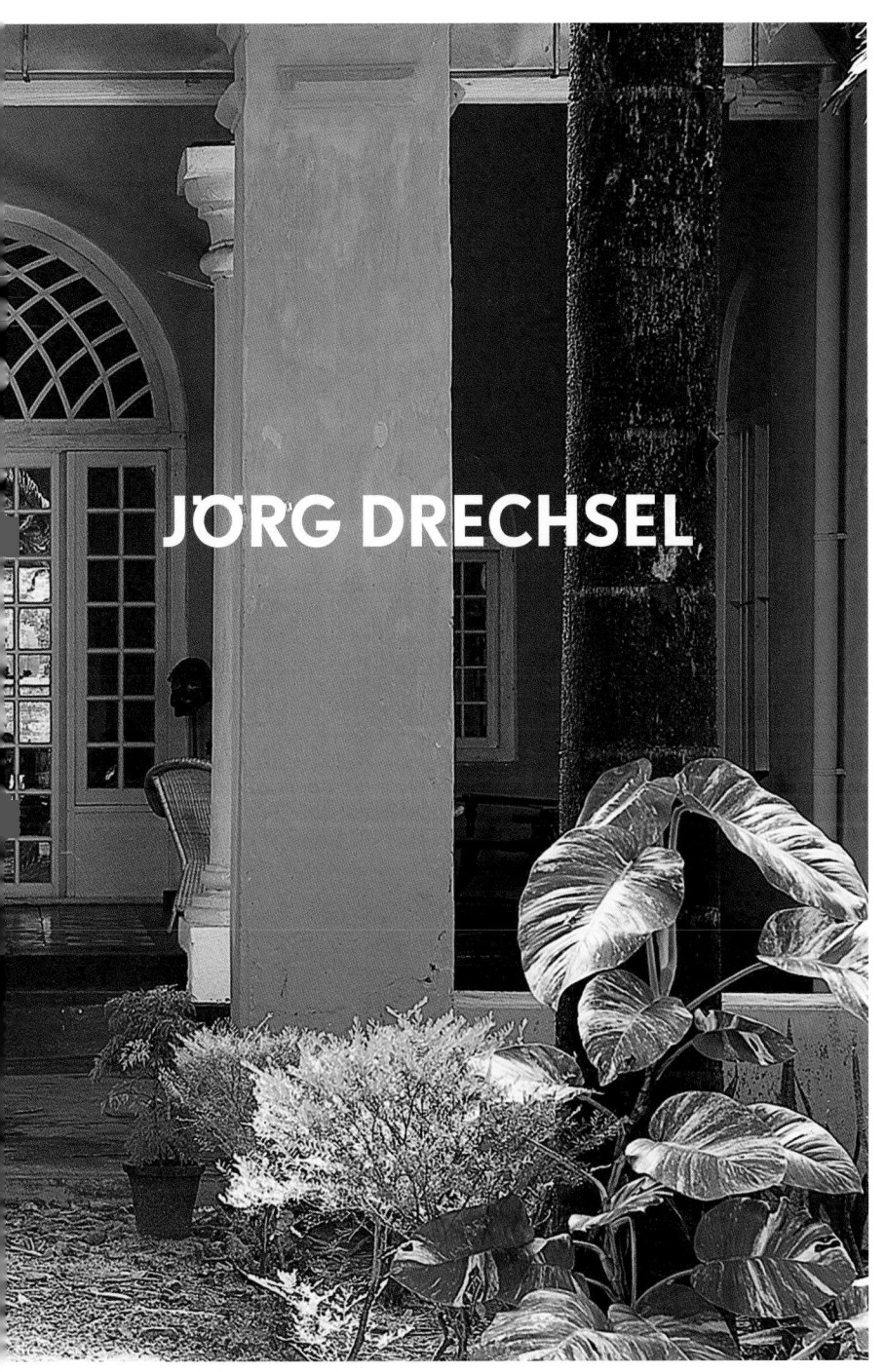

JÖRG DRECHSEL

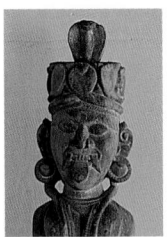

JÖRG DRECHSEL

COCHIN, KERALA
INDIA

With its lagoons, dolphin-filled bays and spice-laden bazaars, Cochin is the most fascinating of cities. The product of India's long encounter with Europe, a medieval church, a synagogue and the tomb of the Portuguese explorer Vasco da Gama are clustered around the historic Fort Cochin area. For Jörg Drechsel, a German-born exhibition designer, Cochin was the place of childhood fantasy when he first visited Kerala in the early 1970s. Over the years it has become his home. Together with his wife Txuku Iriarte, who is Basque, he spent four years transforming the Malabar House, an 18th-century mansion, into the finest small hotel in Fort Cochin. For years Jörg and Txuku had eyed the parsonage of St. Francis Church, a landmark occupied by the English painter Anthony Fry. When Fry moved out in 2001, the Bishop agreed to let them have it, provided they undertook a restoration of the Dutch colonial building. With the welcoming cut-out of Gandhi that he found in a warehouse and select objects, Jörg Drechsel captures some of Cochin's cultural diversity.

Cochin ist eine faszinierende Stadt mit Lagunen, Buchten voller Delfine und duftenden Gewürzbasaren. Auf der Insel mit der historischen Festung Cochin finden sich Zeugnisse europäischer Begegnungen mit Indien: die mittelalterliche Kirche, die Synagoge und der Grabstein des portugiesischen Seefahrers Vasco da Gama. Bereits Anfang der 1970er-Jahre entdeckte der deutschstämmige Ausstellungsdesigner Jörg Drechsel bei seinem ersten Besuch in Cochin die Stadt seiner Kindheitsfantasien. Heute ist er hier zu Hause und hat mit seiner baskischen Frau Txuku Iriarte das Herrenhaus „Malabar House" aus dem 18. Jahrhundert in das feinste kleine Hotel auf Fort Cochin verwandelt. Jörg und Txuku hatten schon früh ein Auge auf das Pfarrhaus der St.-Francis-Kirche geworfen – ein berühmtes Wahrzeichen der Insel, in dem jedoch der englische Maler Anthony Fry wohnte. Als Fry 2001 auszog, überließ der Bischof ihnen das nüchterne holländische Kolonialhaus mit der Auflage, es sorgsam zu restaurieren. Mit dem Konterfei des gastfreundlichen Gandhi, den Jörg Drechsel in einem Lagerhaus entdeckte, und anderen ausgewählten Objekten heißt er seine Besucher in einer Atmosphäre willkommen, die Cochins kulturelle Vielfalt widerspiegelt.

Avec ses lagons, ses baies grouillant de dauphins et des bazars regorgeant d'épices, Cochin est la plus fascinante des villes. Fruits des influences européennes, une église médiévale, une synagogue et la tombe de l'explorateur portugais Vasco da Gama sont regroupées autour du site historique de Fort Cochin. Cochin a nourri l'imagination enfantine de Jörg Drechsel, scénographe d'origine allemande, qui a fait sa première visite au Kerala au début des années 1970. Au bout de quatre ans de travaux, son épouse, la Basquaise Txuku Iriarte, et lui-même ont fait de cette demeure du 18e siècle « Malabar House », le plus bel hôtel de charme de Fort Cochin. Depuis des années, Jörg et Txuku avaient des vues sur le presbytère de l'église St Francis Church, habité par le peintre britannique Anthony Fry. Quand Fry a quitté les lieux en 2001, l'évêque a accepté qu'ils s'y installent, à condition qu'ils restaurent cette austère construction érigée par les colons hollandais. Avec le Gandhi de carton trouvé dans une grande surface, qui réserve un accueil chaleureux aux visiteurs, et des objets choisis, Jörg Drechsel a su capter certaines facettes de la diversité culturelle de Cochin.

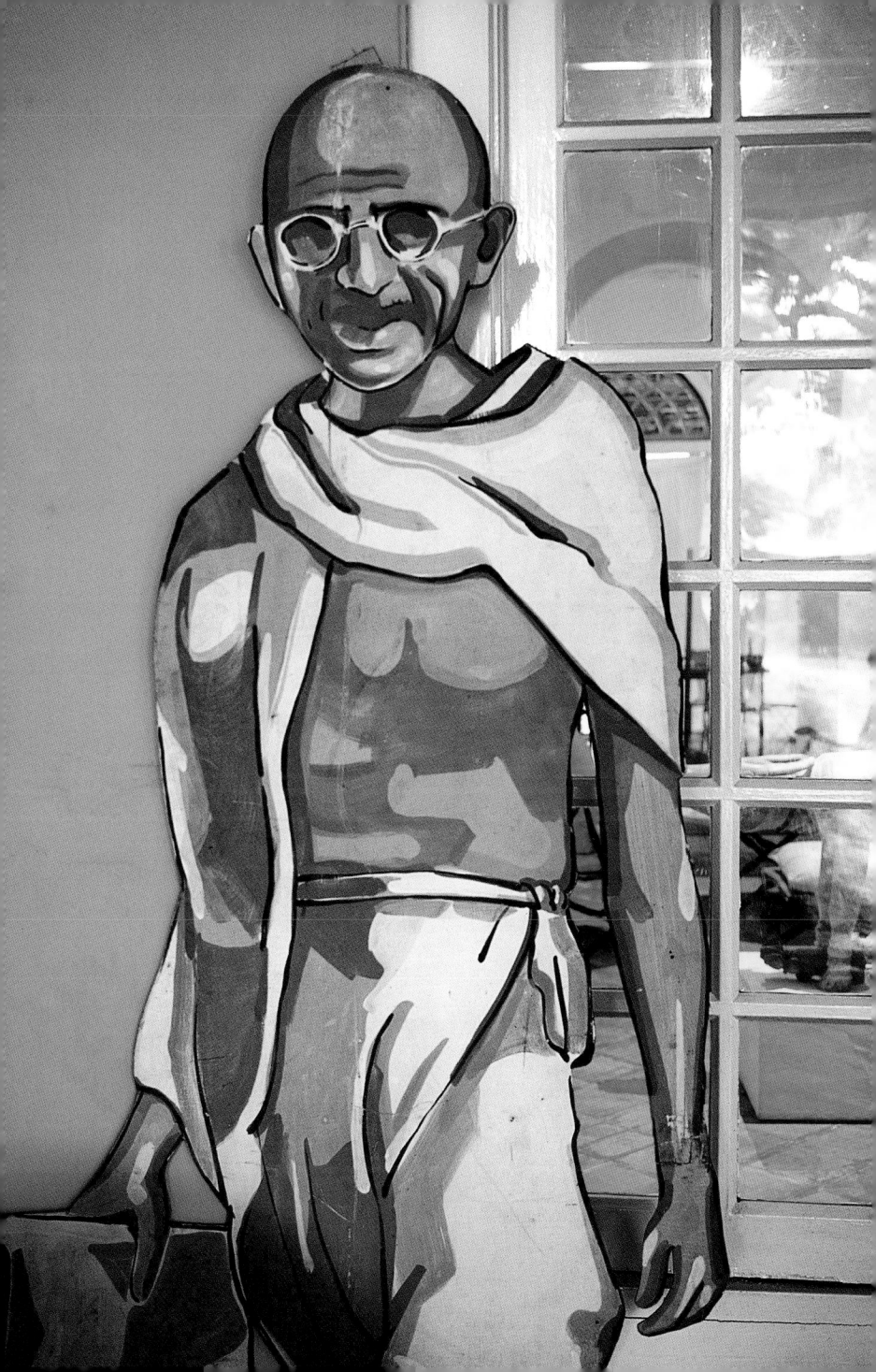

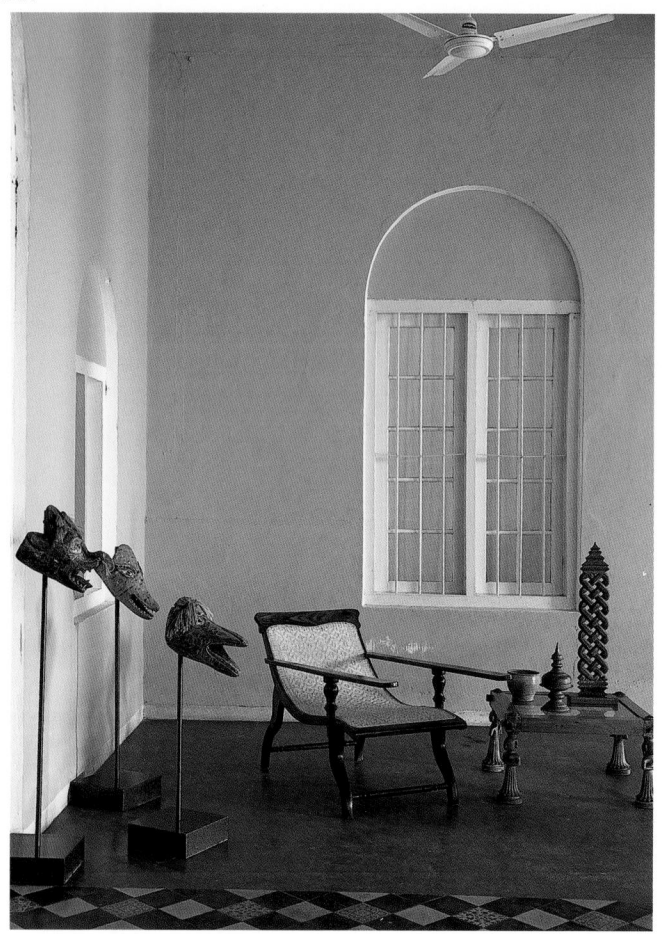

PP. 152-153 The entrance to the parsonage leading to the main hall. • Der Eingang des Pfarrhauses führt in die große Halle. • L'entrée du presbytère, avec la salle principale à l'arrière-plan.

↑ Three traditional masks from north Kerala, for warding off evil spirits, and a planter's chair form a counterpoint in the hall. • In der Halle bilden drei traditionelle Masken aus Nordkerala, die böse Geister abhalten sollen, einen Kontrapunkt zu einem Kolonialstuhl. • Trois masques rituels du Kerala destinés à protéger des mauvais esprits et une

chaise de style colonial forment un contraste saisissant dans cette pièce.

→ A passage to the bedroom is painted in bright pigments. The wooden images are from north Kerala. • Der Gang zum Schlafzimmer ist in leuchtend satten Farben gestrichen. Die Holzfiguren stammen aus dem Norden Keralas. • Le passage menant à la chambre a été peint avec des pigments très lumineux. Les bois sculptés viennent du Nord du Kerala.

PP. 158-159 The dining table with a stone top was made from steel pipes. Against the wall is a tribal sculpture from Karnataka flanked by carved wooden panels from the Deccan. • Der Esstisch mit einer Steinplatte wurde aus Stahlrohr gefertigt. An der Wand steht eine Stammesskulptur aus Karnataka, rechts und links davon lehnen geschnitzte Holztafeln vom Dekkan-Plateau. • La table est constituée d'un plateau en pierre reposant sur des tuyaux en acier. Sur le mur du fond, une sculpture tribale du Karnataka est flanquée de panneaux en bois sculptés provenant du Deccan.

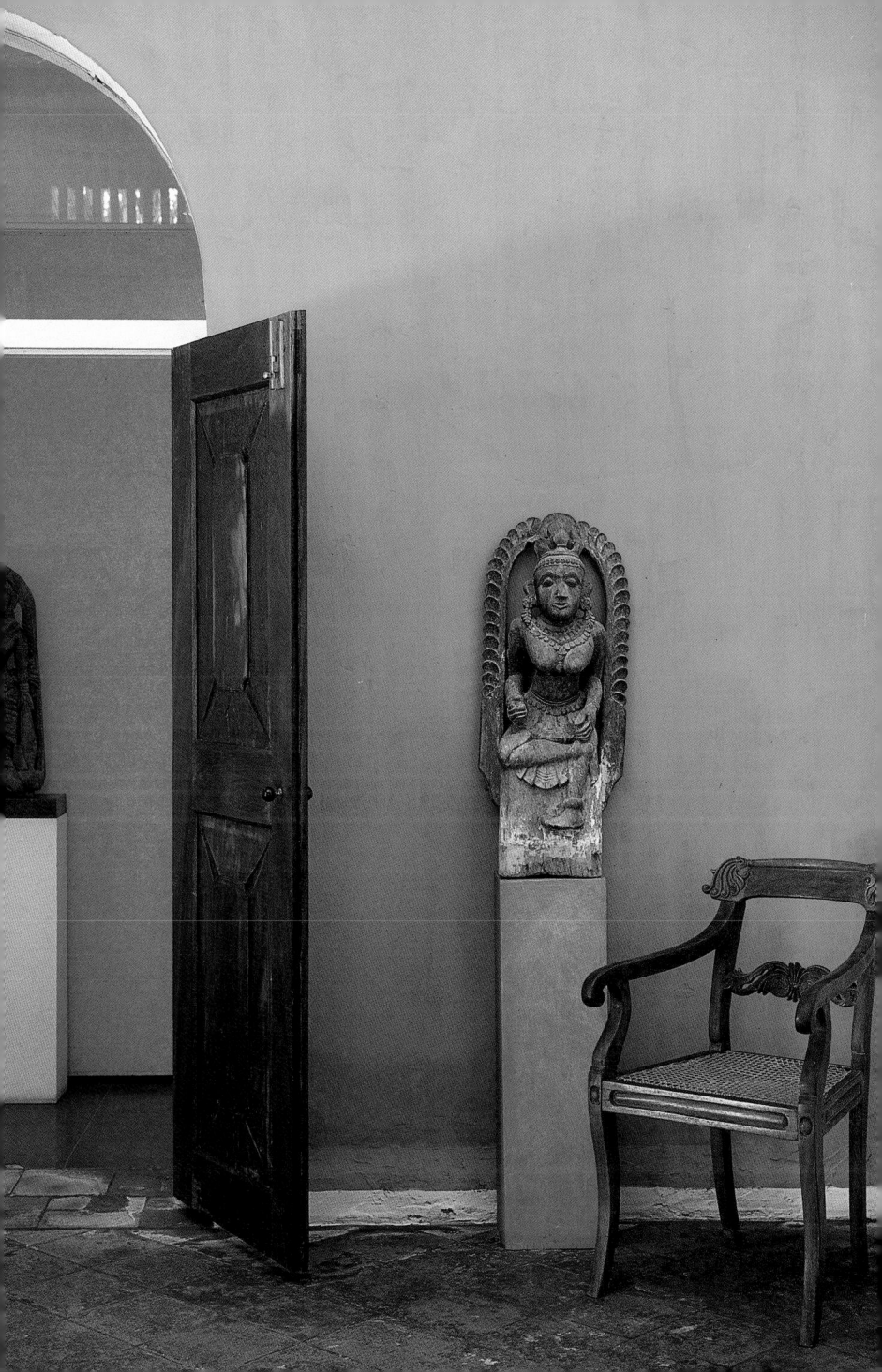

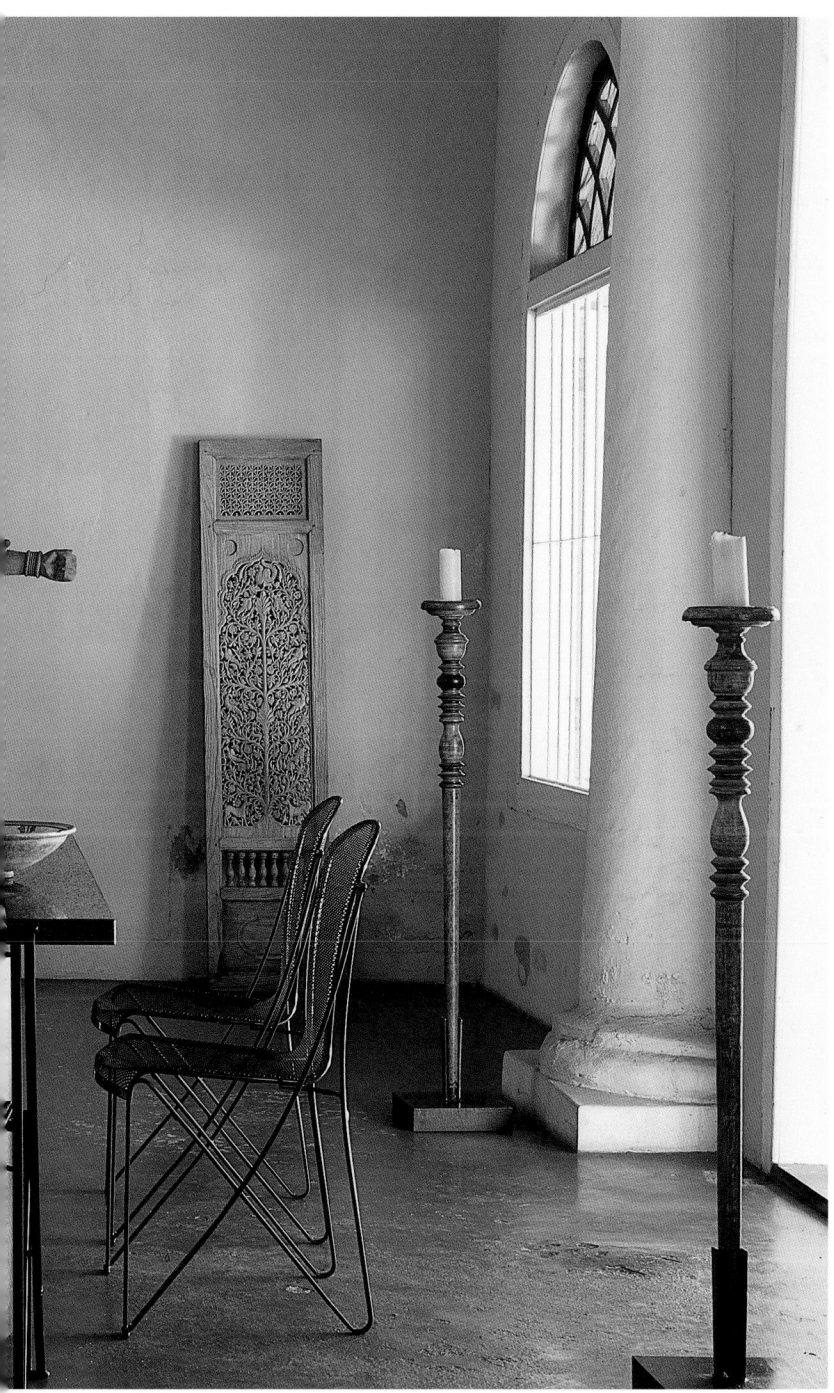

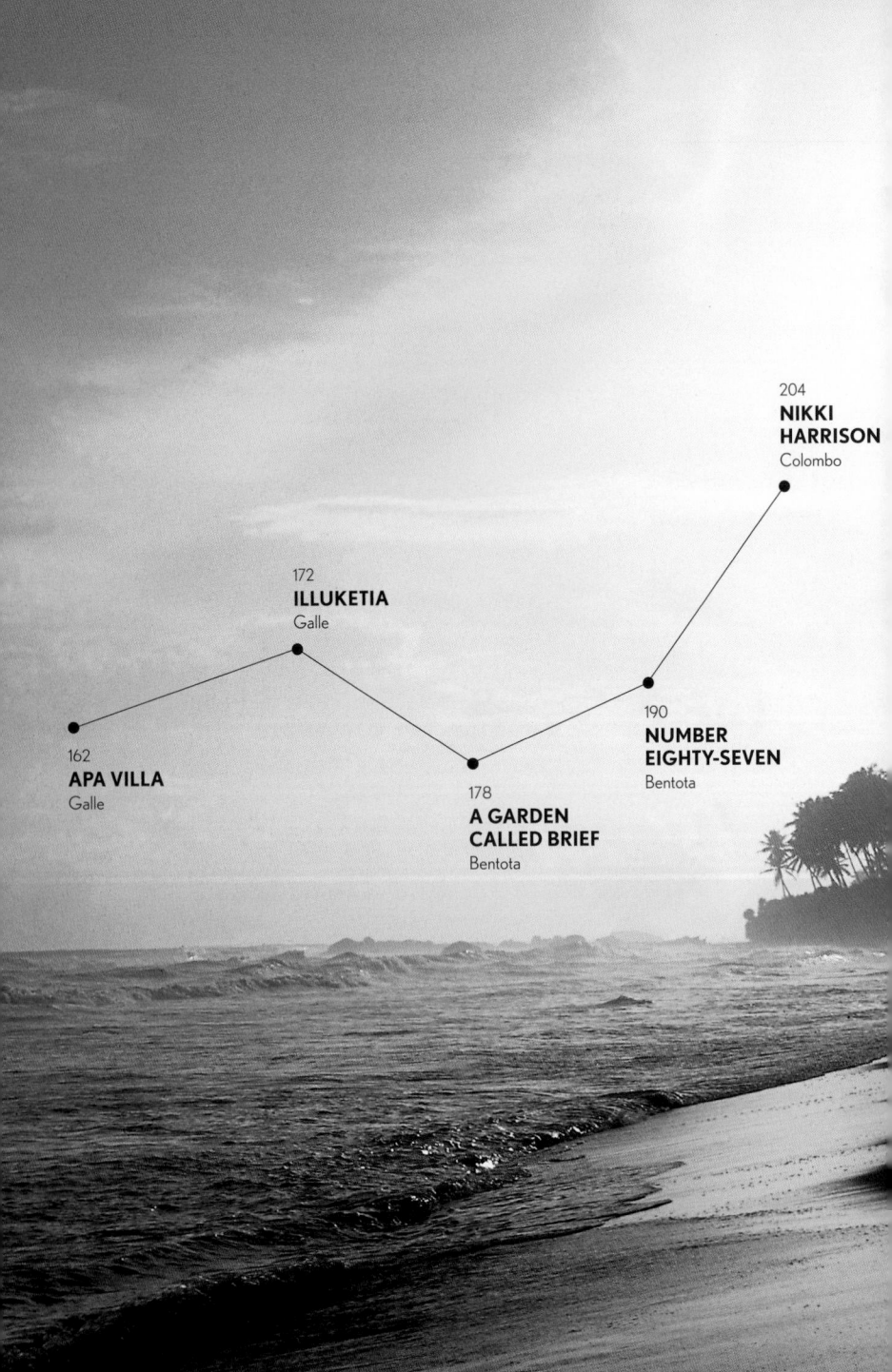

162
APA VILLA
Galle

172
ILLUKETIA
Galle

178
**A GARDEN
CALLED BRIEF**
Bentota

190
**NUMBER
EIGHTY-SEVEN**
Bentota

204
**NIKKI
HARRISON**
Colombo

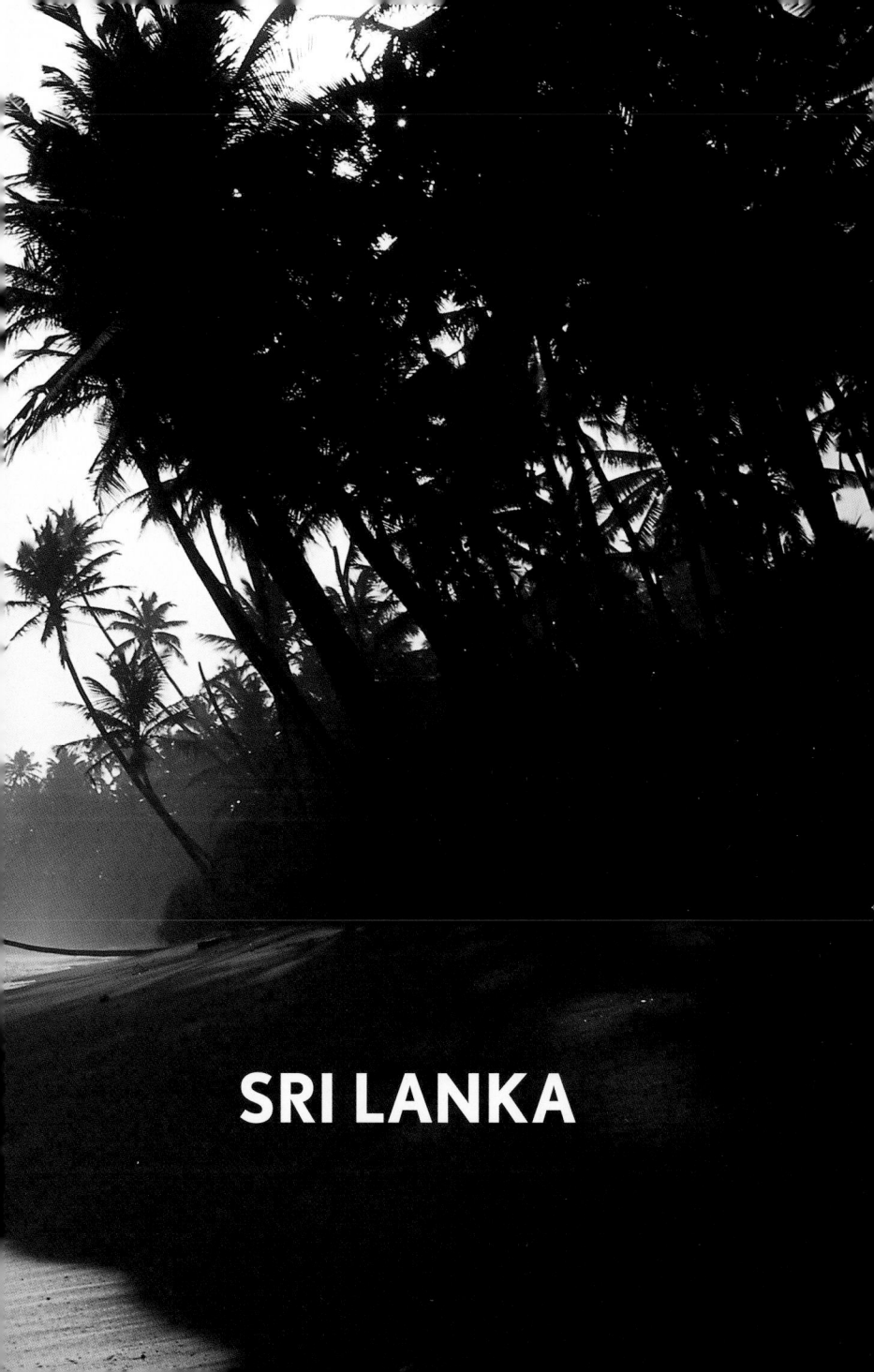

SRI LANKA

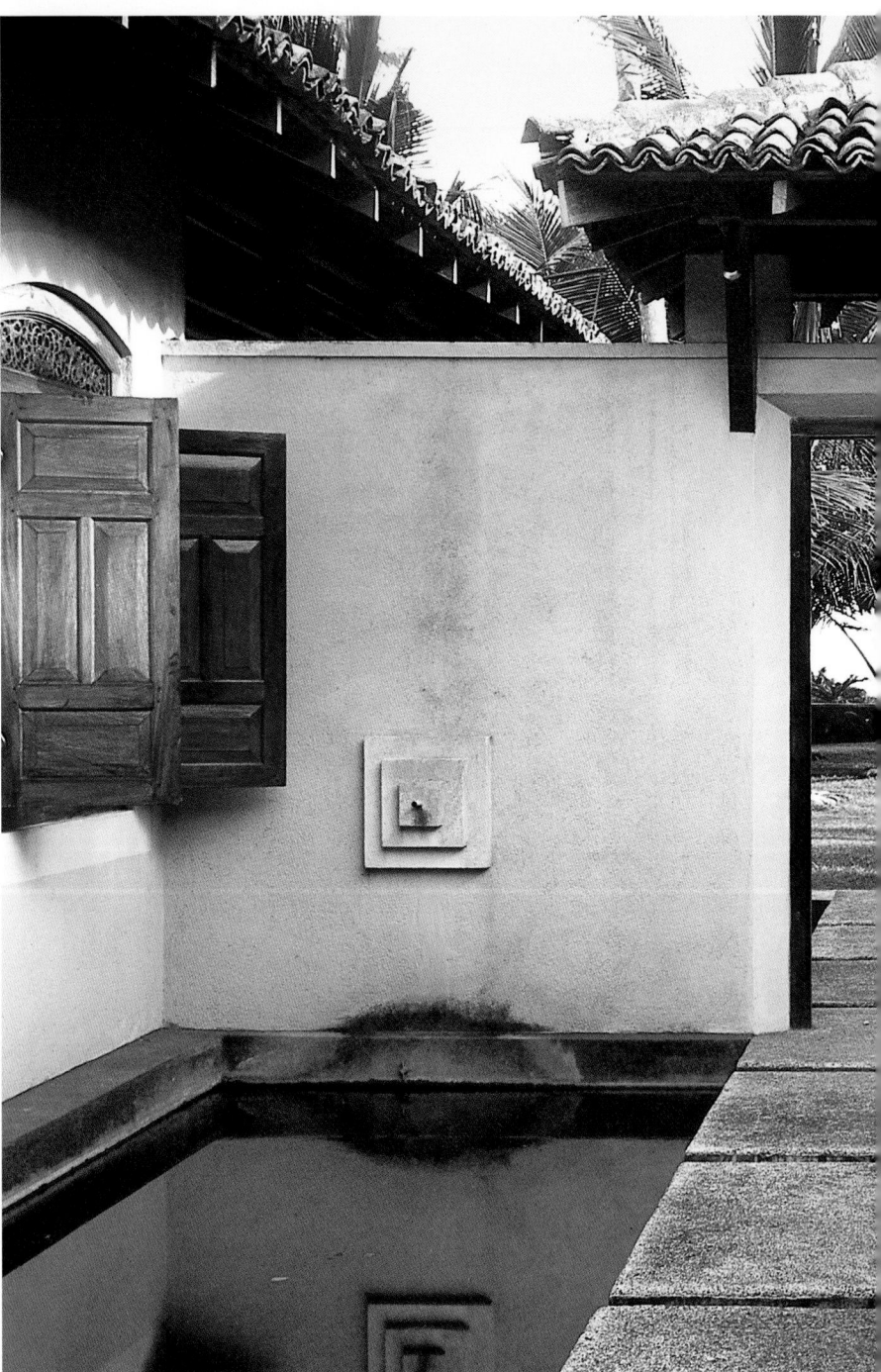

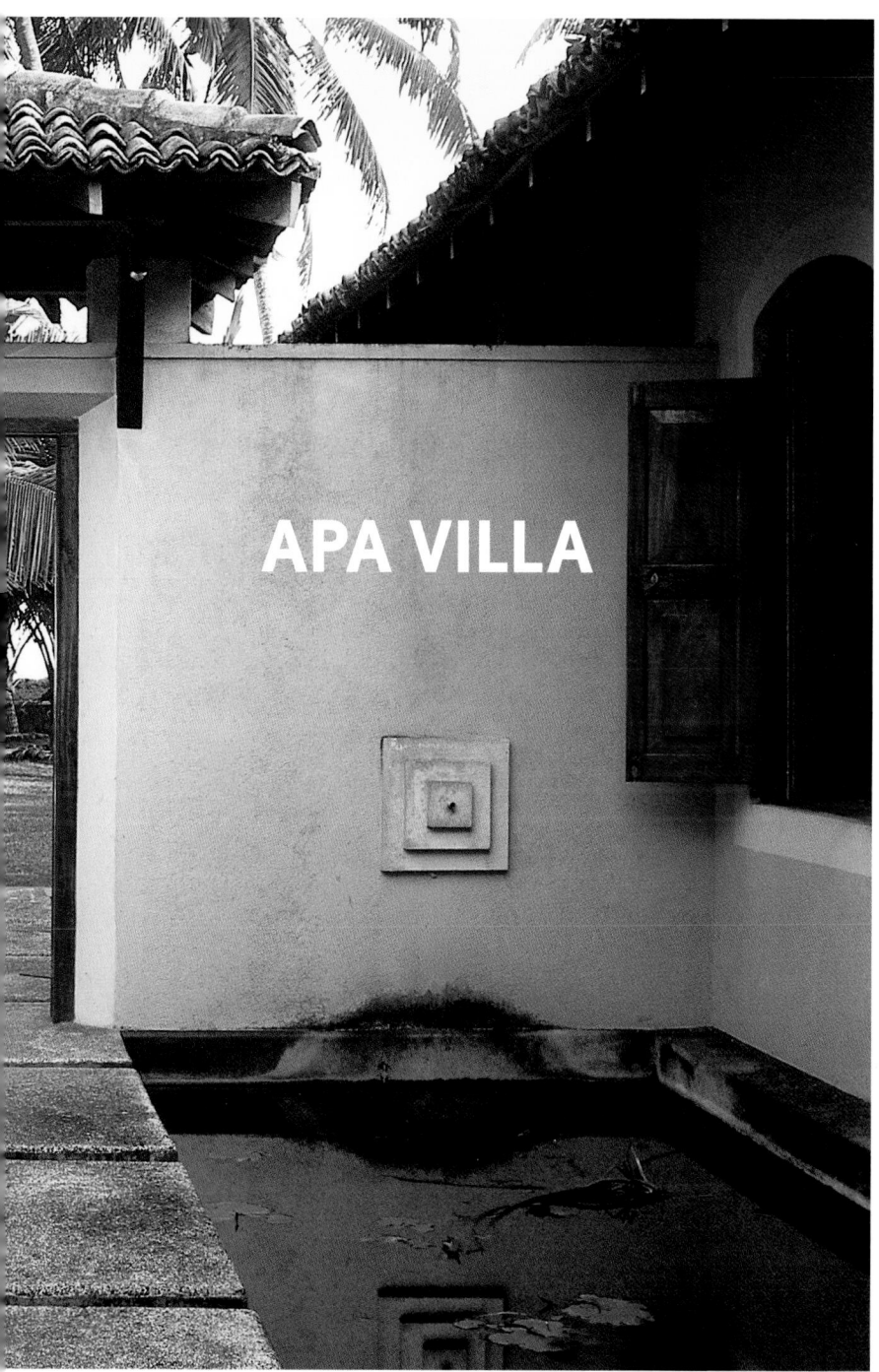

APA VILLA

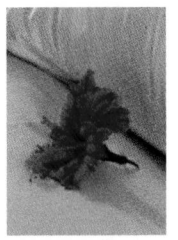

APA VILLA
GALLE
SRI LANKA

Apa is an all-purpose Indonesian word that can mean "how", "why", "what", or "when". When German-born photographer, graphic designer and printer Hans Höfer produced his first guidebook to Bali in 1970 it seemed an apt name for his publishing company. Höfer first visited Sri Lanka in the 1990s and loved it so much that he was soon on a property hunt. Apa was the obvious choice of name for the old guest house he bought on a clear stretch of beach at Thalpe, a few miles south of Galle. After renovation and landscaping, Apa Villa has grown into a series of three ocean-front villas called "Cinnamon", "Cardamom" and "Saffron". Beyond an inner courtyard framed by coconut pillars is the library of the original house and, beyond that, a picture postcard frame of waving palms and the Indian Ocean. The centerpiece of the property is the much-copied swimming pool made of concrete. Between running his business in Singapore and an organic farm in Nepal, Höfer's favorite plaything is a 65-foot yacht called Rising Tide.

Apa ist ein allgegenwärtiges Wort in Indonesien, es kann „wie", „warum", „was" oder „wann" bedeuten. Als der deutschstämmige Fotograf, Grafikdesigner und Drucker Hans Höfer 1970 seinen ersten Reiseführer über Bali veröffentlichte, schien es ihm als Name für seinen neu gegründeten Verlag passend. Als Höfer in den 1990er-Jahren erstmals nach Sri Lanka kam, war er so begeistert von dem Land, dass er sich auf die Suche nach geeigneten Immobilien machte. Für die alte Pension, die er an einem unbebauten Sandstrand in Thalpe wenige Kilometer südlich von Galle erwarb, kam kein anderer Name als „Apa" infrage. Nachdem die Anlage renoviert und gartenarchitektonisch gestaltet wurden war, besteht sie jetzt aus drei Villen mit Meerblick: „Zimt", „Kardamom" und „Safran". Hinter dem mit Säulen aus Kokosholz geschmückten Innenhof liegt die ehemalige Bibliothek mit Postkartenblick auf Palmen und den Indischen Ozean. Im Mittelpunkt der Anlage liegt der häufig nachgeahmte Swimmingpool aus Beton. Höfer, der in Singapur Geschäfte macht und in Nepal einen Bio-Bauernhof betreibt, entspannt sich am liebsten auf seiner 20-Meter-Jacht „Rising Tide".

Apa est un mot indonésien bien utile puisqu'il signifie « comment », « pourquoi », « quoi » ou « quand ». Quand le photographe, graphiste et imprimeur d'origine allemande Hans Höfer a lancé son premier guide sur Bali en 1970, Apa lui a semblé le nom idéal pour sa maison d'édition. Lors de sa première visite au Sri Lanka au début des années 1990, Höfer a été à ce point conquis par le pays qu'il s'est rapidement mis en quête d'une propriété. Apa est le nom qui s'est imposé à lui pour l'ancienne pension qu'il a achetée dans la longue baie de Thalpe, à quelques kilomètres au sud de Galle. À l'issue de travaux de rénovation et d'aménagement paysager, Apa Villa a grandi : elle comprend désormais trois bungalows sur le front de mer portant les noms parfumés de « Cinnamon » (cannelle), « Cardamon » (cardamome) et « Saffron » (safran). Une fois passé une cour intérieure encadrée par des colonnes en bois de cocotier, on traverse la bibliothèque de la maison d'origine pour se retrouver face à une vue de carte postale : une plage de palmiers ondoyants sur fond d'océan Indien. La pièce maîtresse de la propriété est la piscine en béton, souvent plagiée. Hans Höfer consacre les heures de loisir que lui laisse la gestion d'une affaire à Singapour et d'une ferme biologique au Népal à son jouet préféré, un yacht de près de 20 mètres de long appelé « Rising Tide ».

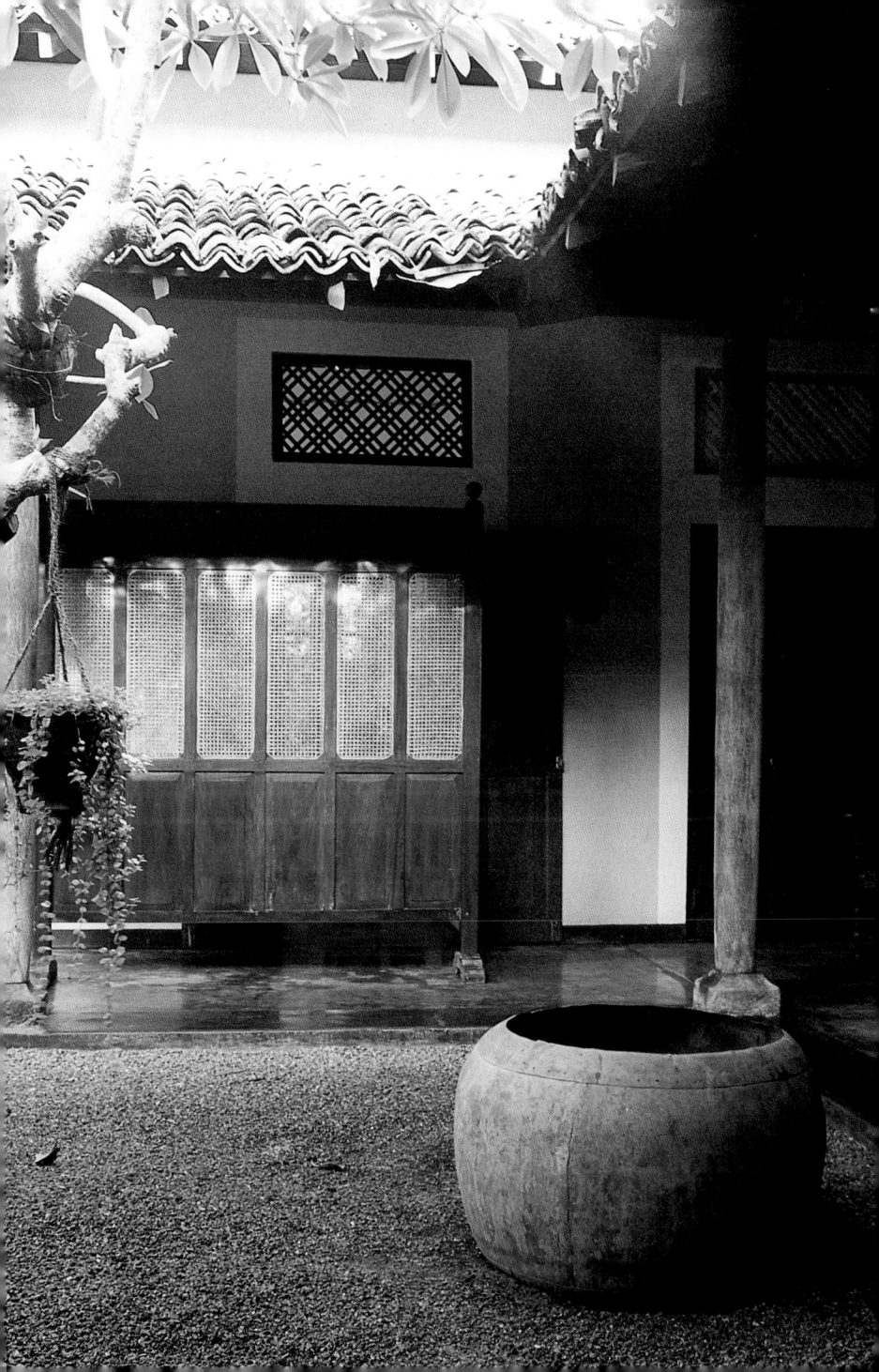

PP. 162–163 In the courtyard of the villa, stone slabs lead across a fishpond through the gate onto the pool and the beach. • Im Innenhof der Villa führen Steinplatten über einen schwarzen Fischteich durch das Tor hinaus zum Pool und zum Strand. • Dans la cour intérieure, des dalles permettent de franchir un vivier noir pour rejoindre, au-delà de la porte, la piscine et la plage.

↓ The 60-foot swimming pool is made entirely from concrete. • Der 18 Meter lange Swimmingpool besteht ganz aus Beton. • La piscine longue de 18 mètres est entièrement en béton.

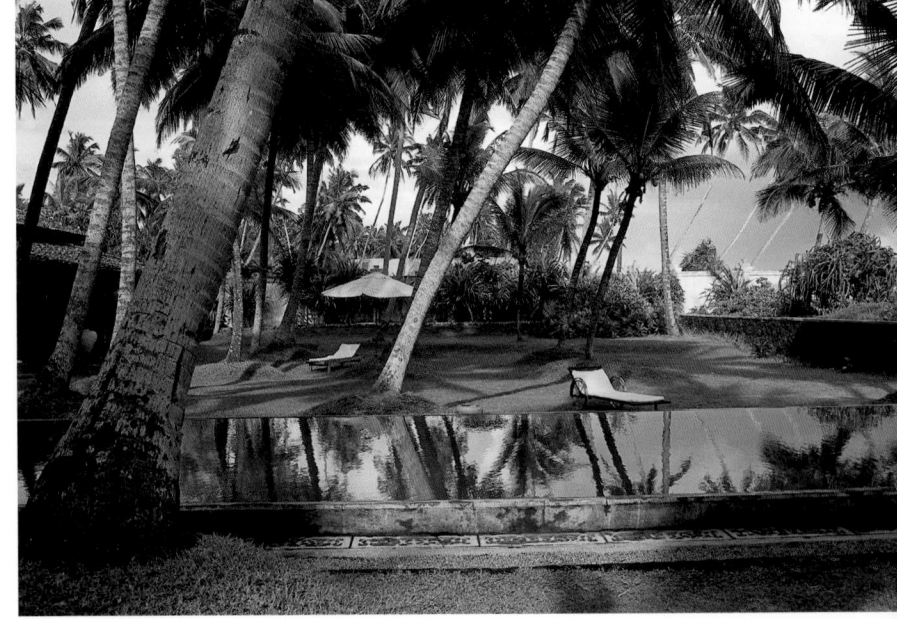

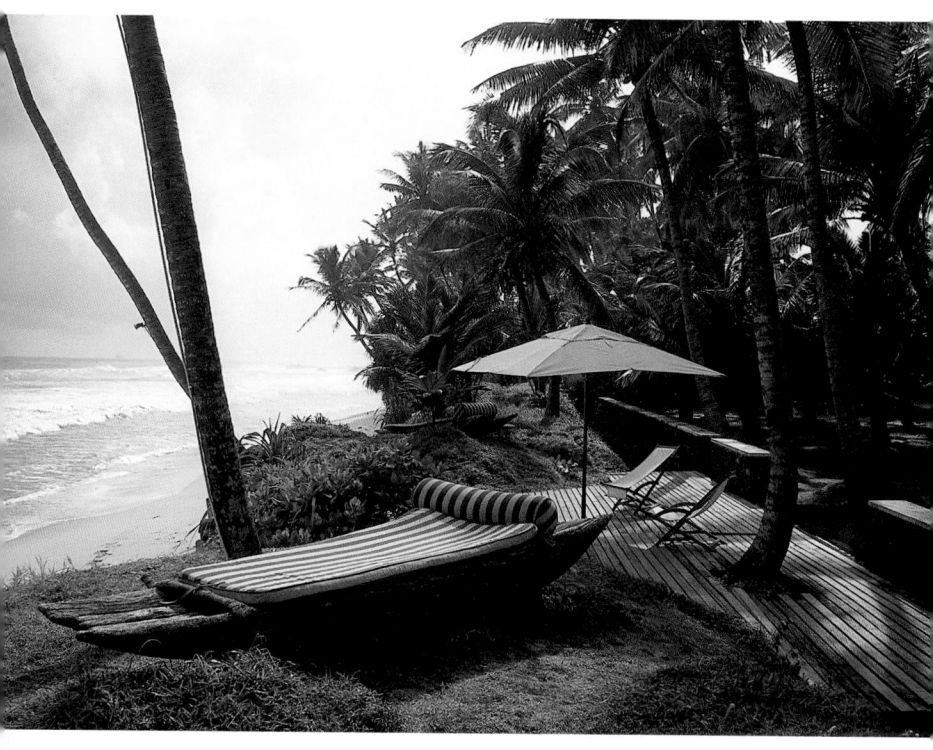

↑ A fishing pontoon from Jaffna converted into a daybed. • Ein Fischerkahn aus Jaffna wurde in ein Ruhebett verwandelt. • Une barque de pêcheur provenant de Jaffna est devenue un lit de repos.

PP. 168-169 The property is on a clear stretch of beach along the Indian Ocean. • Die Anlage liegt an einem feinsandigen Strand am Indischen Ozean. • La propriété n'est séparée de l'océan Indien que par une vaste étendue de sable.

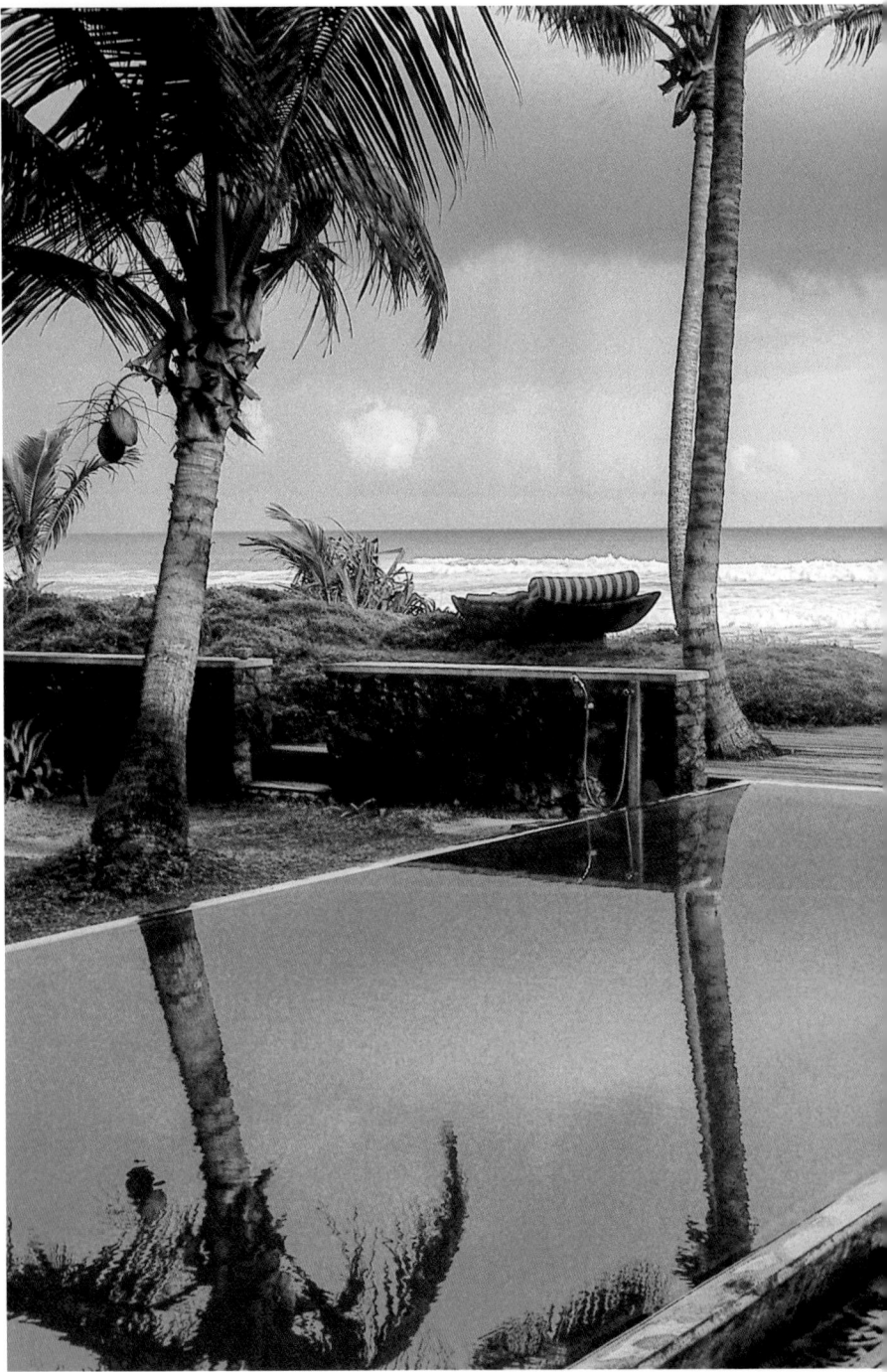

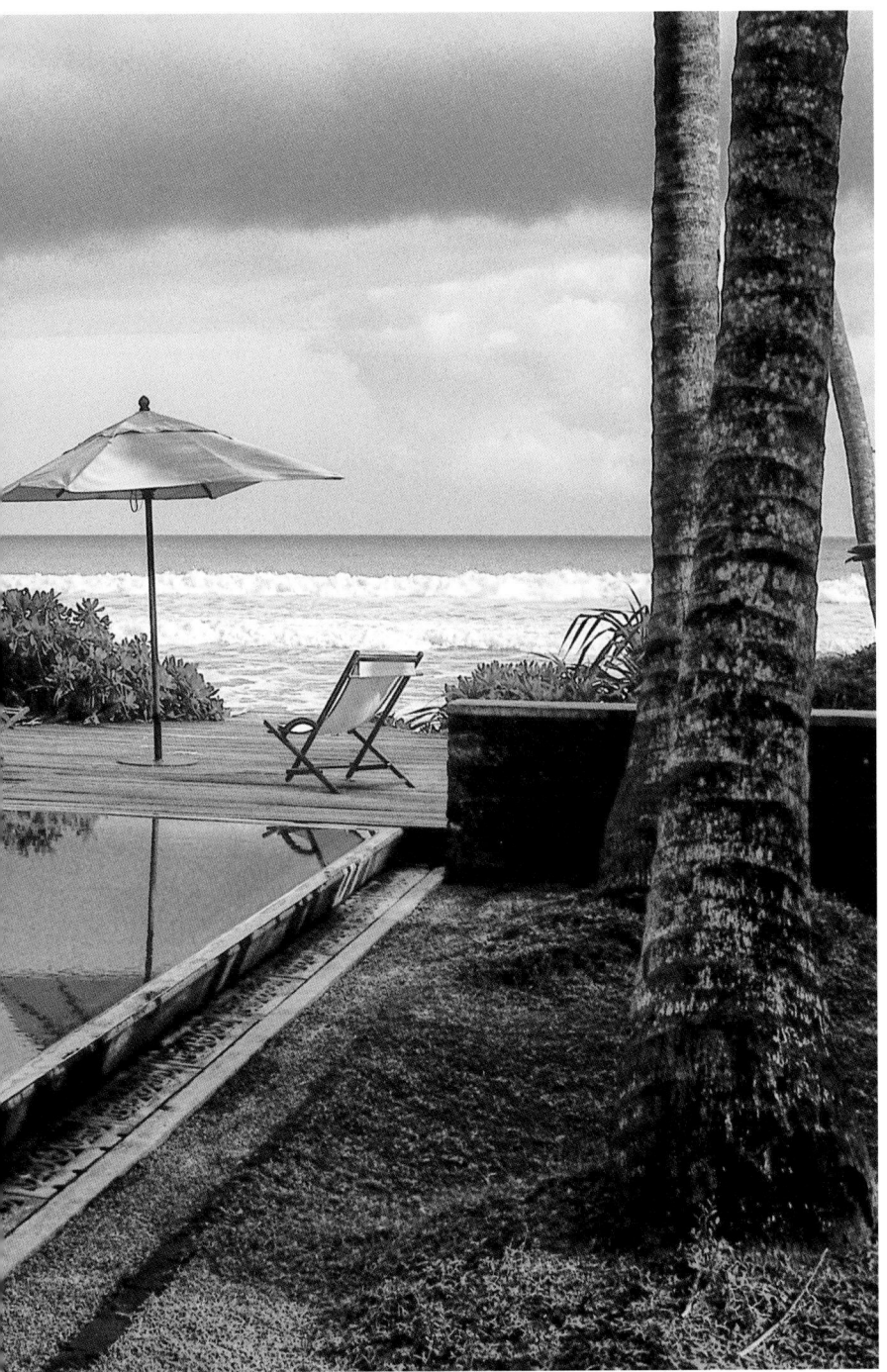

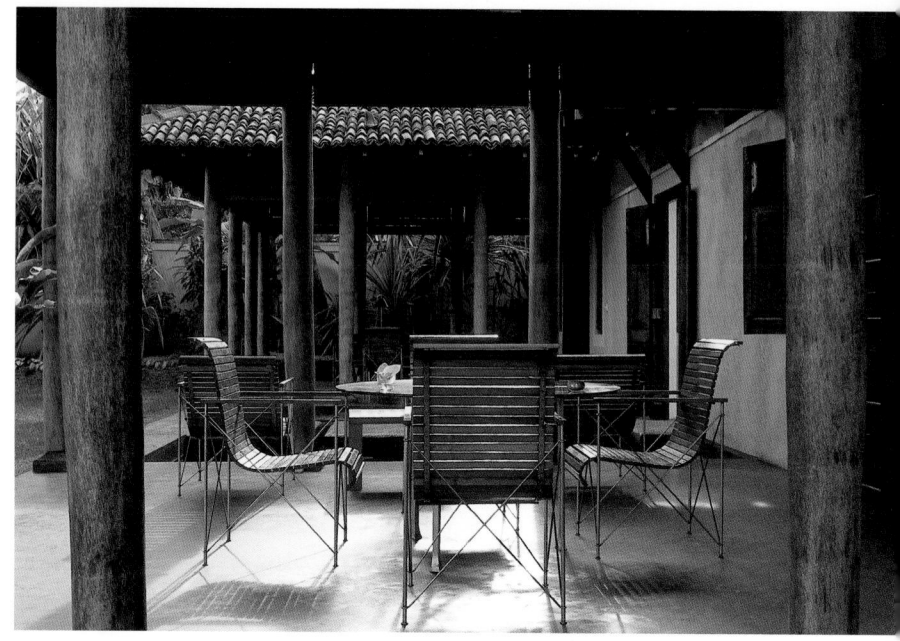

↑ The stainless steel dining chairs with teak slats were inspired by a Geoffrey Bawa design. • Die Esszimmerstühle aus Edelstahl mit Teakholzleisten sind einem Design von Geoffrey Bawa nachempfunden. • Les chaises de salle à manger en inox et lattes de teck sont inspirées d'un design de Geoffrey Bawa.

→ The daybeds in the library. • Ruhebetten in der Bibliothek. • Les lits de repos de la bibliothèque.

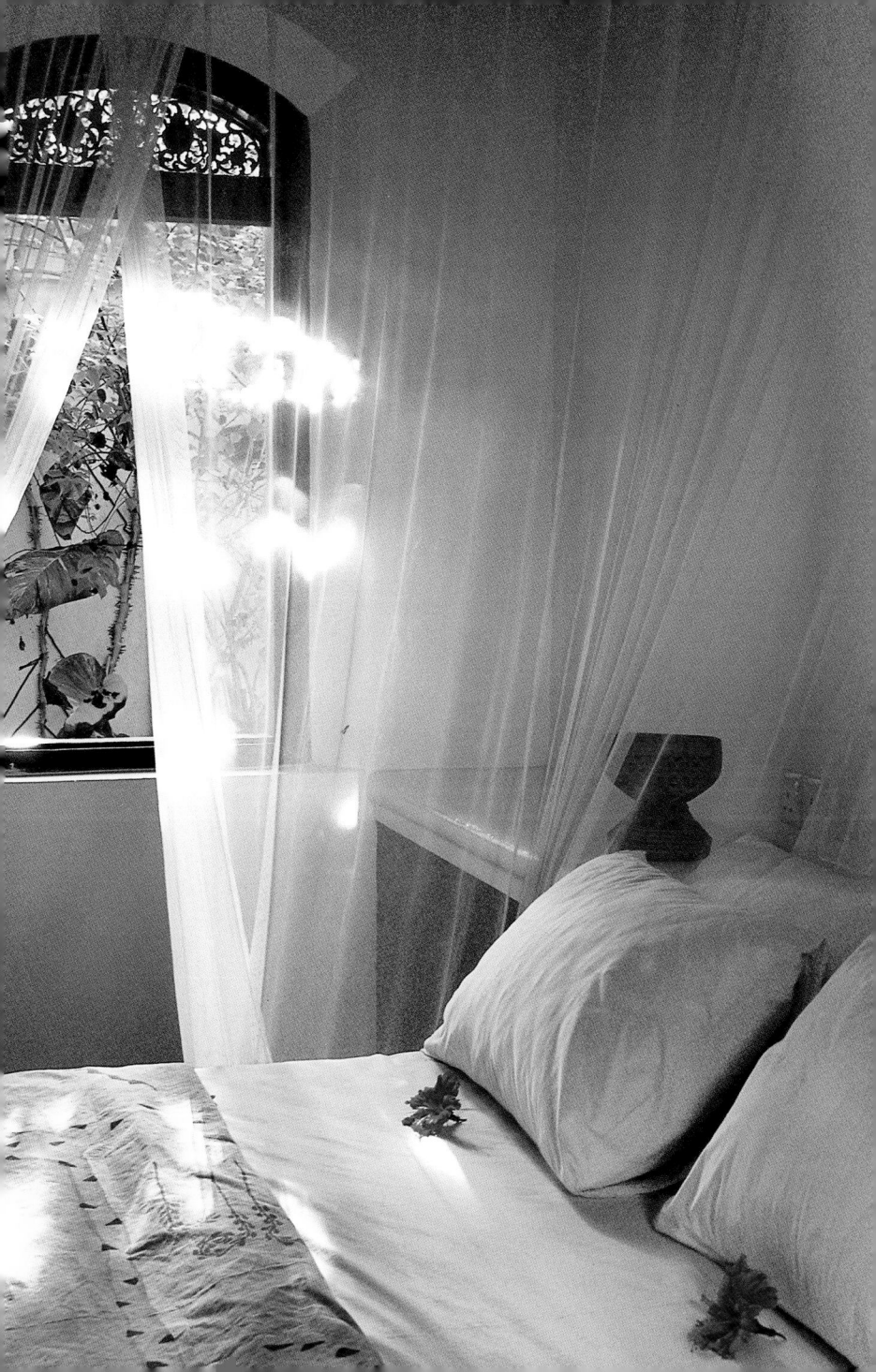

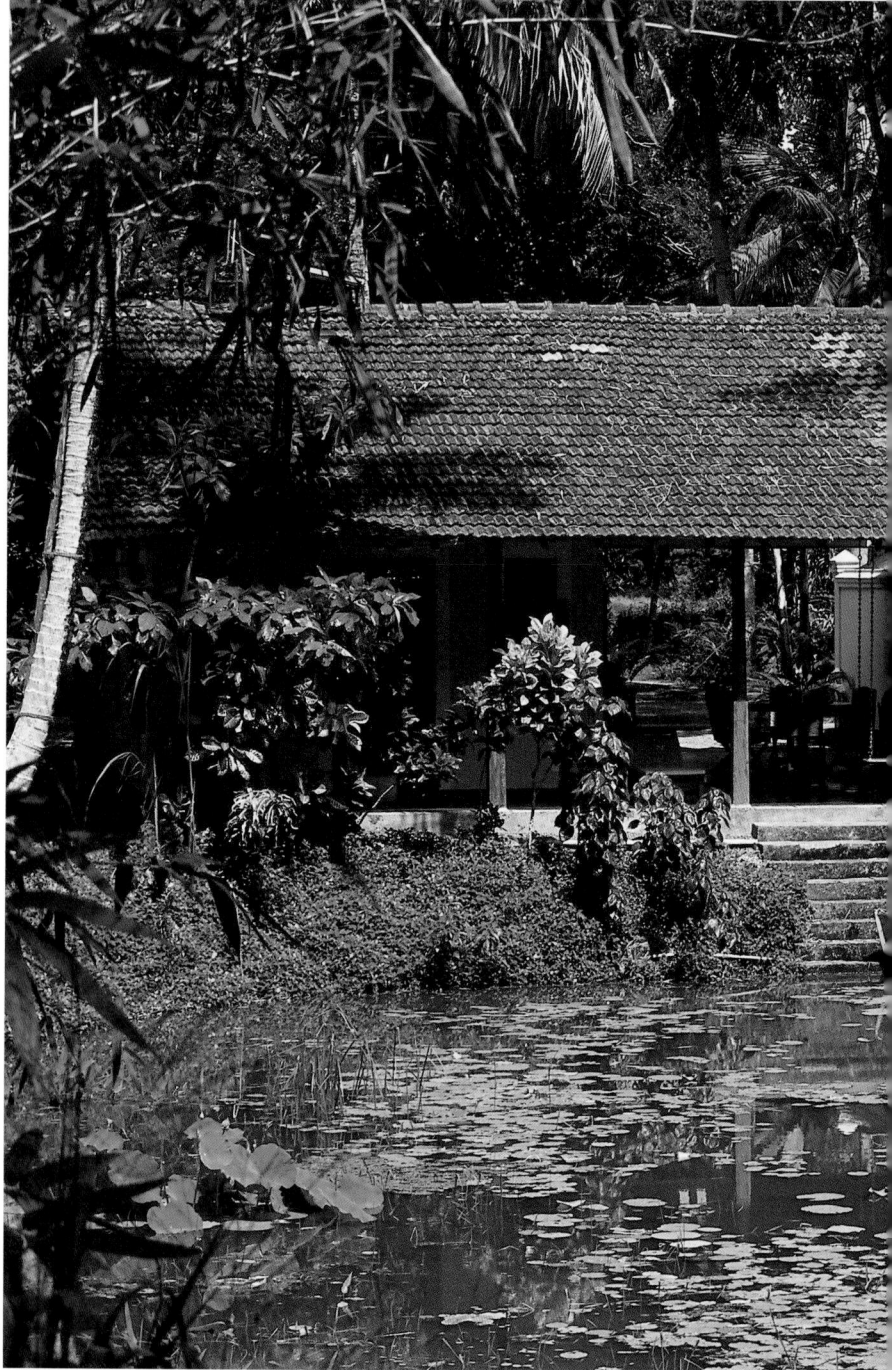

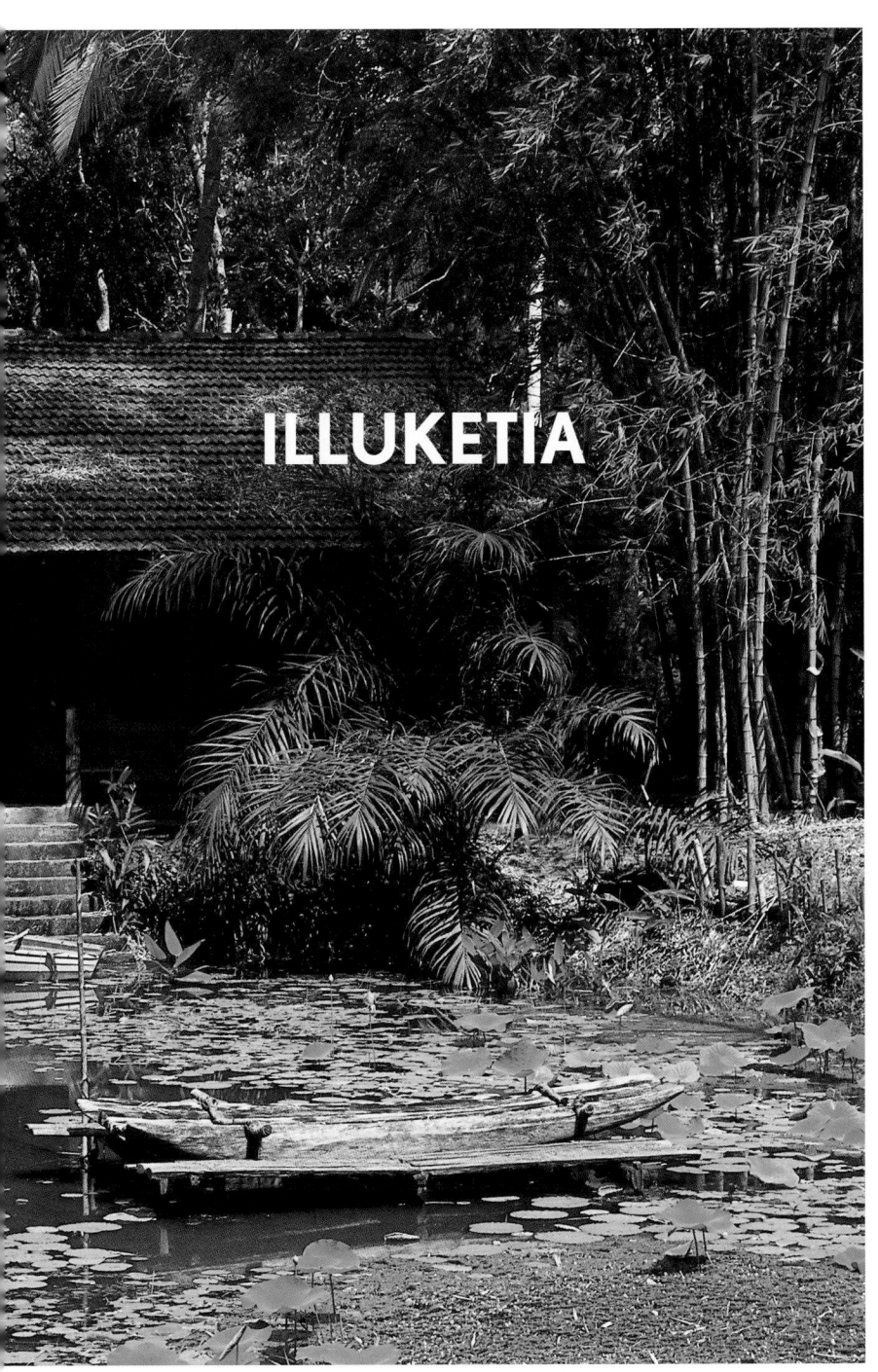

ILLUKETIA

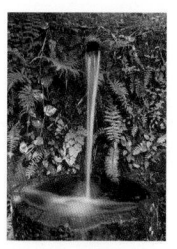

ILLUKETIA
GALLE
SRI LANKA

Moving inland from Galle, through picturesque villages set in a luxuriant tropical landscape, one enters a series of low-lying tea estates and rubber plantations. Although the finest teas are grown in the hills of central Sri Lanka, tea from low-lying areas has a distinctive flavor and is much prized in the Middle East. Near the village of Wanchawala are the gardens of Illuketia. The name derives from a reed-like grass called *illuk*, commonly used as roof thatch, but the soil at Illuketia is doubly blessed. Early in the 19th century it was recorded as a place where rare medicinal plants were grown. Illuketia estate had shrunk to seven acres when Hans Höfer bought it and the old plantation house on a hill was beyond repair. Over the years he has virtually rebuilt it, expanding and renovating to create a boutique hotel. Deep verandas on three sides slope down to swards of lawn, herb gardens, paddy fields, lotus pools and untamed jungle. Surrounding Illuketia for miles are plantations that produce Sri Lanka's famous tea.

Landeinwärts von Galle liegen hinter malerischen Dörfern Tee- und Kautschukplantagen in einer üppigen Tropenland-schaft. Die feinsten Teesorten werden zwar im zentralen Bergland von Sri Lanka angebaut, aber auch der Tee aus die-sen niedrigeren Lagen ist wegen seines besonderen Geschmacks in Asien sehr beliebt. Unweit des Dorfes Wancha-wala liegen die Gärten von Illuketia, so genannt in Anlehnung an das schilffähnliche Gras, *illuk*, mit dem Dächer gedeckt werden. Illuketia war im 19. Jahrhundert zudem für den Anbau seltener Arzneipflanzen bekannt. Das Anwesen war auf drei Hektar geschrumpft, als Hans Höfer es erwarb, und die alte Residenz der Plantage war völlig verfallen. Im Laufe der Jahre errichtete er sie von Grund auf neu und erweiterte die Villa zu einem exquisiten Hotel. An drei Seiten neigen sich tief gelegte Veranden über Rasenflächen, Kräutergärten, Reisfelder, Lotusteiche und wilden Dschungel. Rund um Illuketia erstrecken sich kilometerweit die Teefelder, auf denen Sri Lankas einzigartige Teesorten produziert werden.

L'arrière-pays de Galle abrite des villages pittoresques dans une végétation tropicale luxuriante, parmi des plantations d'hévéas et de thé. Bien que les meilleurs thés soient cultivés dans les montagnes du centre du pays, le thé provenant des zones de basse altitude a une saveur particulière et est très apprécié au Moyen-Orient. Près du village de Wanchawala se trouvent les jardins d'Illuketia, ainsi nommés d'après l'*illuk*, une herbe rappelant le roseau qu'on utilise comme chaume. La terre d'Illuketia est doublement bénie. Au début du 19e siècle, on a constaté que des herbes médici-nales rares y poussaient. Lorsque Hans Höfer a acheté Illuketia, la propriété ne s'étendait plus que sur trois hectares et la vieille maison de planteur juchée sur une colline était complètement délabrée. Au cours des années, il l'a reconstruite et agrandie pour créer un hôtel de charme. Des vérandas profondes sur trois côtés de la maison donnent sur des pelouses, des jardins simples, des rizières, des bassins recouverts de lotus et sur la jungle. Autour d'Illuketia s'étendent à perte de vue des plantations qui produisent le célèbre thé de Ceylan.

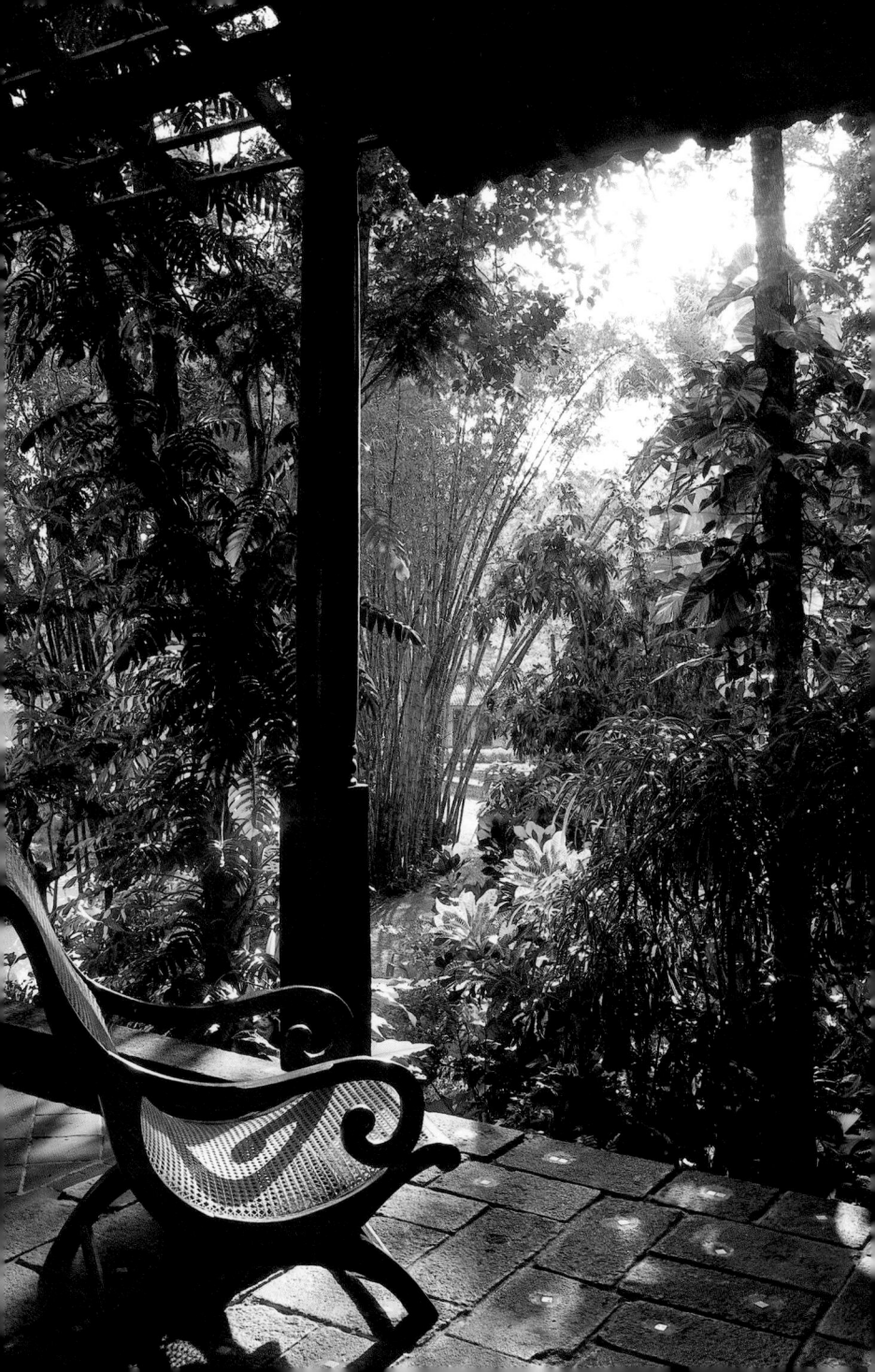

PP. 172–173 The Pond House sits beside the edge of the lotus pool. · Die Zwei-Zimmer-Suite „Pond House" liegt am Lotusblütenteich. · « The Pond House », suite de deux pièces, s'élève au bord du bassin aux lotus.

↓ Light streams through the pyramid roof of the outdoor bathroom. · Das Licht fällt durch das pyramidenförmige Metalldach des Freiluft-Badezimmers. · Dans la salle de bains de plein air, la lumière filtre par la toiture pyramidale.

→ Yellow and olive green cushions on a hand-painted bedspread in the bedroom. · Gelbe und olivgrüne Kissen auf einer handbemalten Tagesdecke im Schlafzimmer. · Des coussins jaunes et vert olive agrémentent un dessus de lit peint à la main.

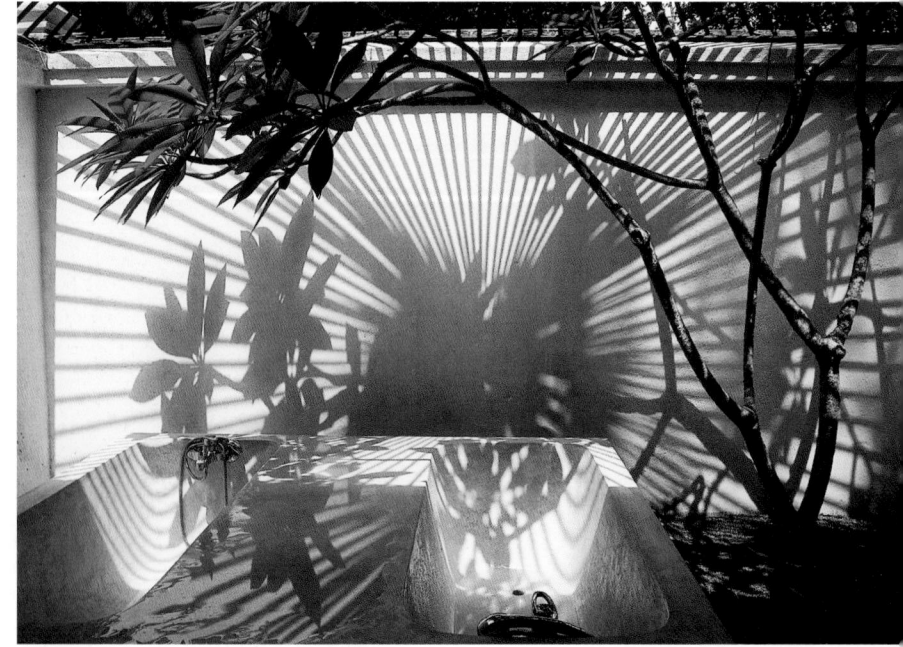

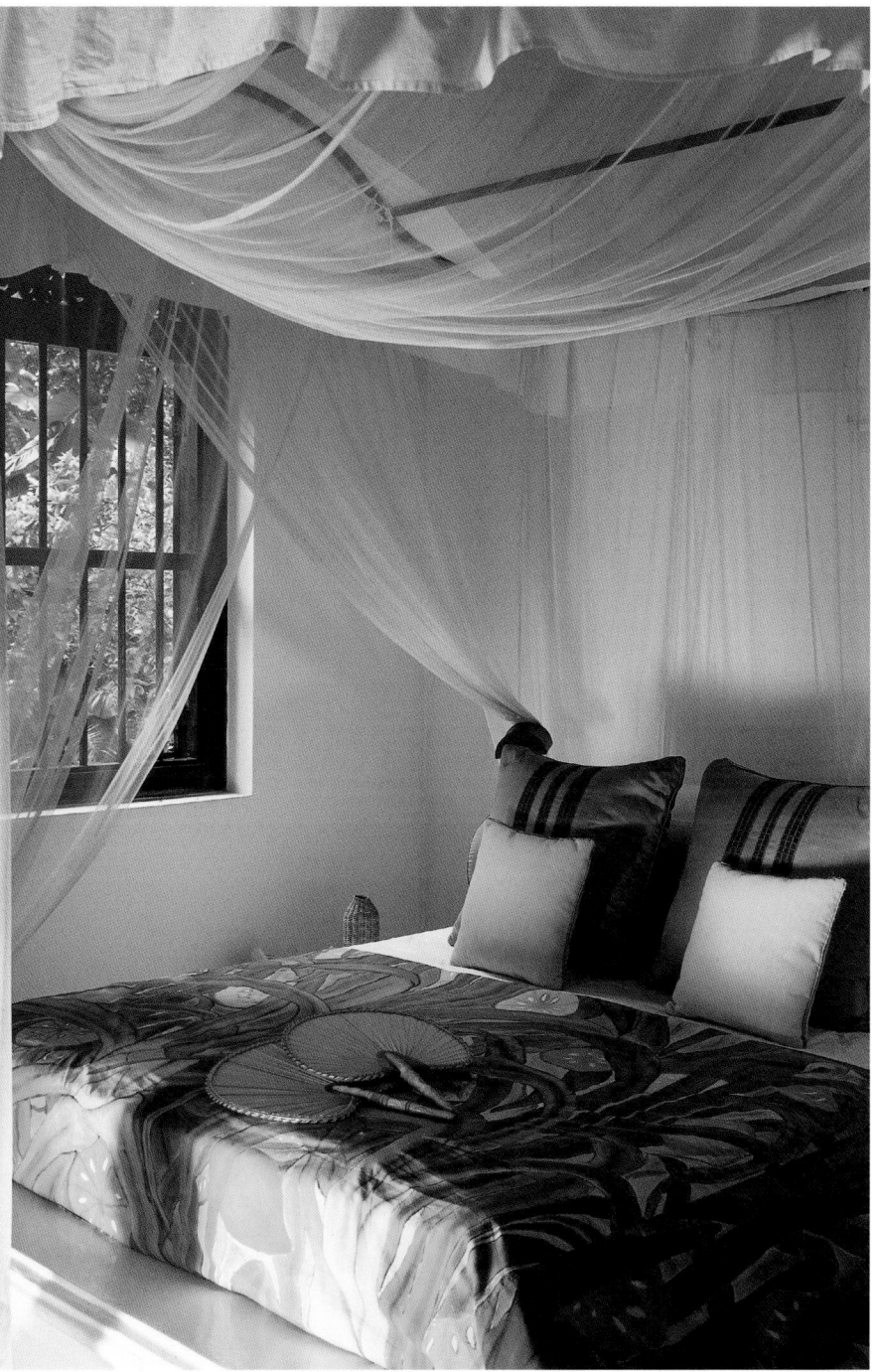

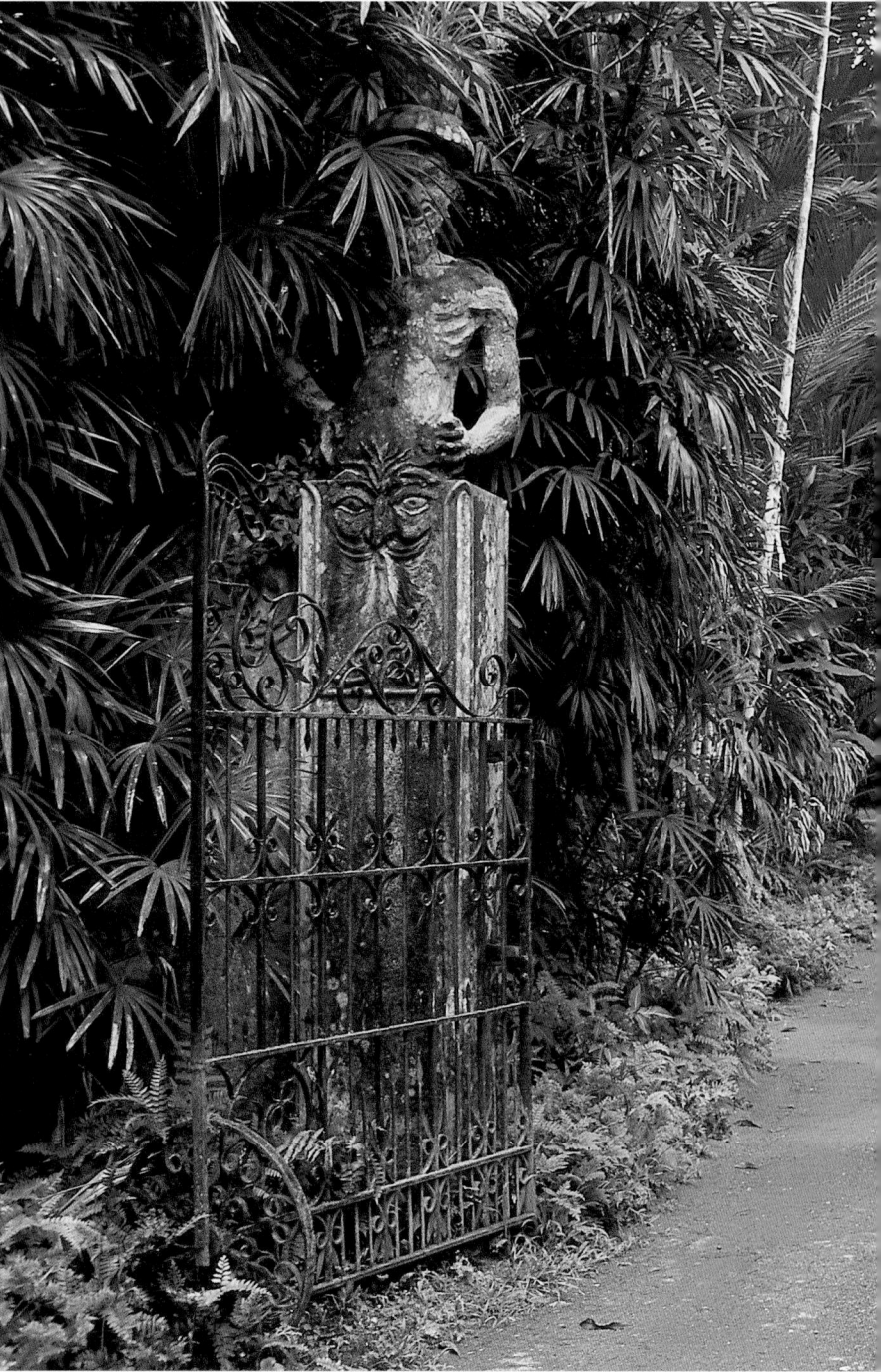

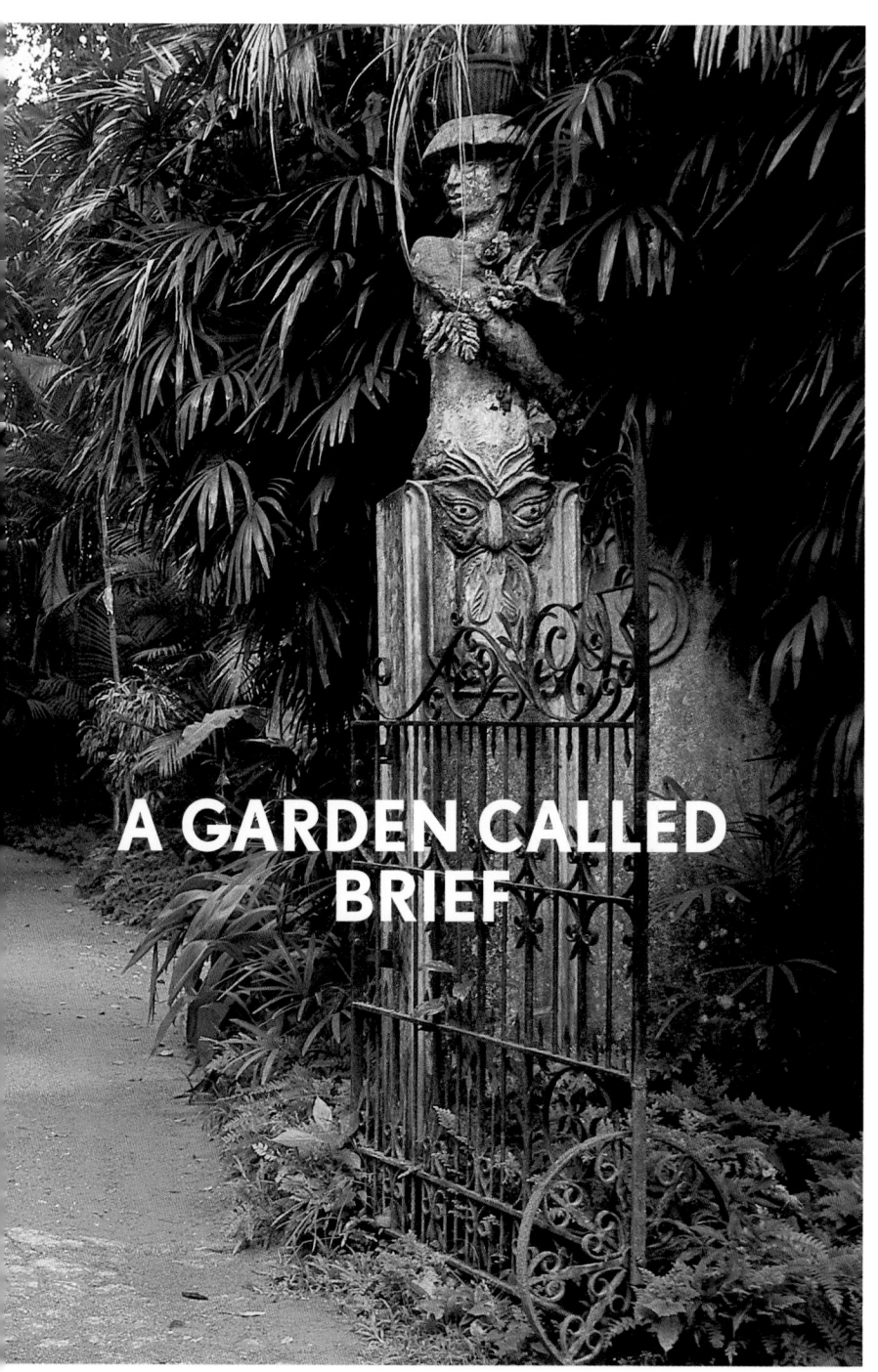

A GARDEN CALLED
BRIEF

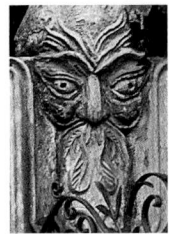

A GARDEN CALLED BRIEF
BENTOTA
SRI LANKA

No account of 20th-century architecture can be complete without the doffing of caps in the direction of the Sri Lankan architect Geoffrey Bawa. "Ceylonese" is probably the word he would have preferred. Along with his brother Bevis, Geoffrey formed a bridge between the dying colonial order and the emerging sensibilities of Asian independence. Born of old Burgher stock, in the years 1909 and 1919 respectively, the Bawa brothers grew up in a snobbish world of rambling Colombo mansions, upcountry estates, European education and an addiction to Rolls Royce cars. But they knew that their allegiance lay in the magical landscape and Buddhist heritage of the Isle of Serendip. Bevis Bawa acquired the rubber plantation called "Brief" – named after the proceeds of a legal brief handled by his lawyer father – outside Bentota in 1929. Here he established a garden that became the precursor to Geoffrey's famous landscape overlooking a lagoon at Lunuganga. Bevis Bawa died in 1993, Geoffrey in 2003. Both brothers have left an indelible impression on the map of modern Sri Lanka.

An dem singhalesischen Baumeister Geoffrey Bawa kommt keine Architekturgeschichte des 20. Jahrhunderts vorbei. Wahrscheinlich hätte ihm die Bezeichnung „ceylonesisch" besser gefallen, denn gemeinsam mit seinem Bruder Bevis verkörperte er die Verbindung zwischen der schwindenden Kolonialordnung und den Empfindlichkeiten asiatischer Unabhängigkeit. Die 1909 bzw. 1919 geborenen Brüder wuchsen in einer alten Burgher-Familie holländischer Kolonialherren auf und bewegten sich in der Welt weitläufiger Herrenhäuser in Colombo, mit Grundbesitz im Hochland, Ausbildung in Europa und einer Leidenschaft für Rolls-Royces. Dennoch fühlten sie sich der Landschaft und dem buddhistischen Erbe der Insel Serendip verbunden. 1929 kaufte Bevis die Kautschukplantage „Brief" vor Bentota, die nach einem Schriftstück ihres Vaters, einem Anwalt, so genannt wurde. Bevis Bawa legte einen Garten an, der Geoffreys berühmter Gartenanlage über der Lagune von Lunuganga als Vorbild diente. Bevis Bawa starb 1993, Geoffrey folgte ihm 2003. Die Brüder haben einen einzigartigen Beitrag zur Gestaltung des modernen Sri Lanka geleistet.

Aucun panorama de l'architecture du 20e siècle ne saurait être complet sans un hommage à l'architecte srilankais Geoffrey Bawa. Encore qu'il aurait certainement préféré qu'on le qualifie de « ceylanais » car avec son frère Bevis, Geoffrey a jeté un pont entre l'ordre colonial moribond et les sensibilités apparues dans le sillage de l'indépendance des anciennes colonies en Asie. Nés respectivement en 1909 et 1919 d'une vieille famille de Burghers, les frères Bawa ont grandi entre des villas construites de manière anarchique à Colombo, des propriétés dans l'arrière-pays, une éducation européenne et une passion pour les Rolls. Mais ils se sentaient proches des paysages magiques et de l'héritage bouddhique de Serendip. En 1929, Bevis Bawa a fait l'acquisition d'une plantation d'hévéas à l'extérieur de Bentota, nommée « Brief », par référence à son père avocat. Il y a créé un jardin qui a été le précurseur du célèbre jardin paysagé de Geoffrey qui surplombe un lagon près de Lunuganga. Bevis Bawa est décédé en 1993, Geoffrey en 2003. Les deux frères ont laissé une marque indélébile sur la carte du Sri Lanka moderne.

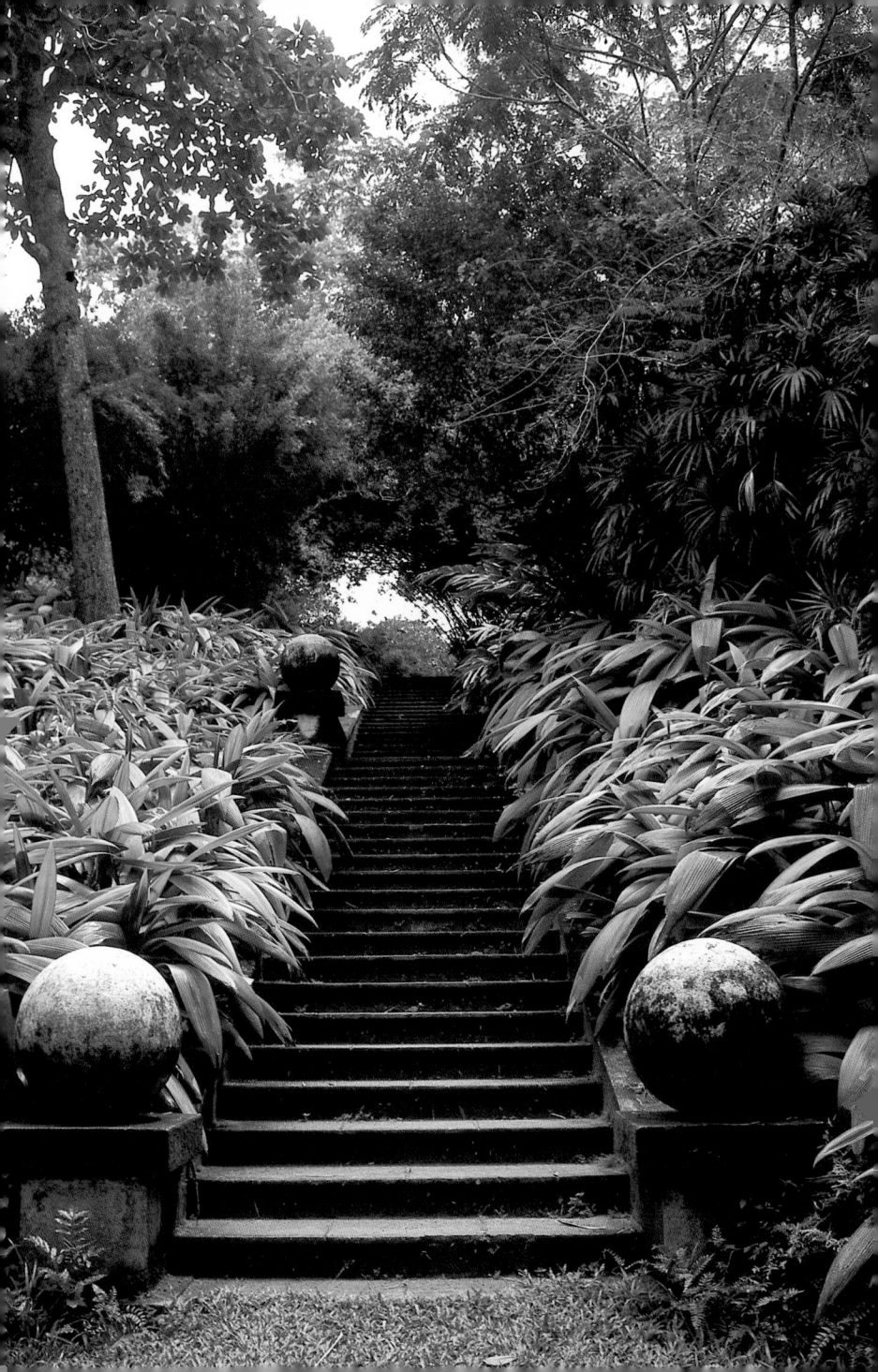

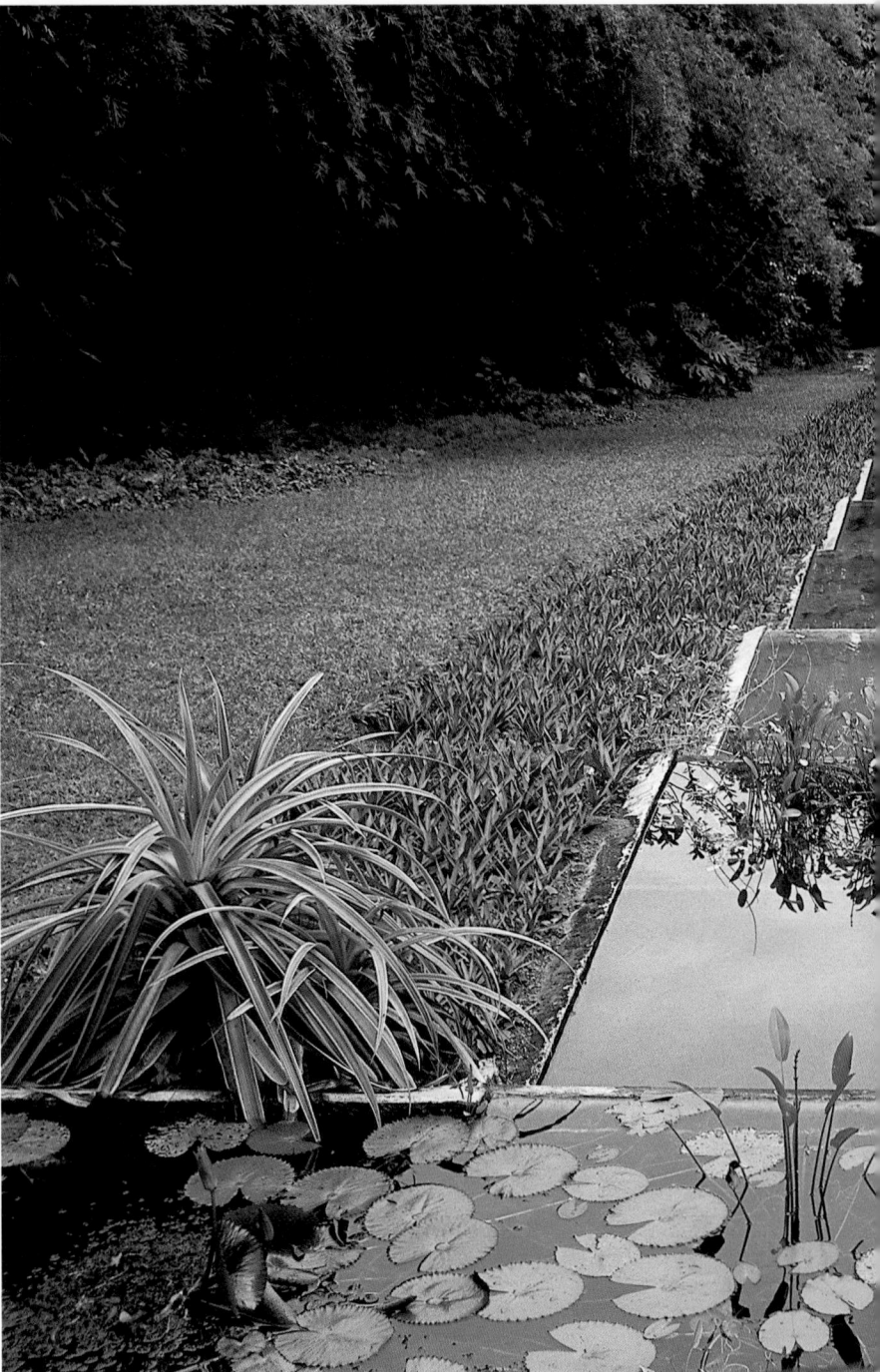

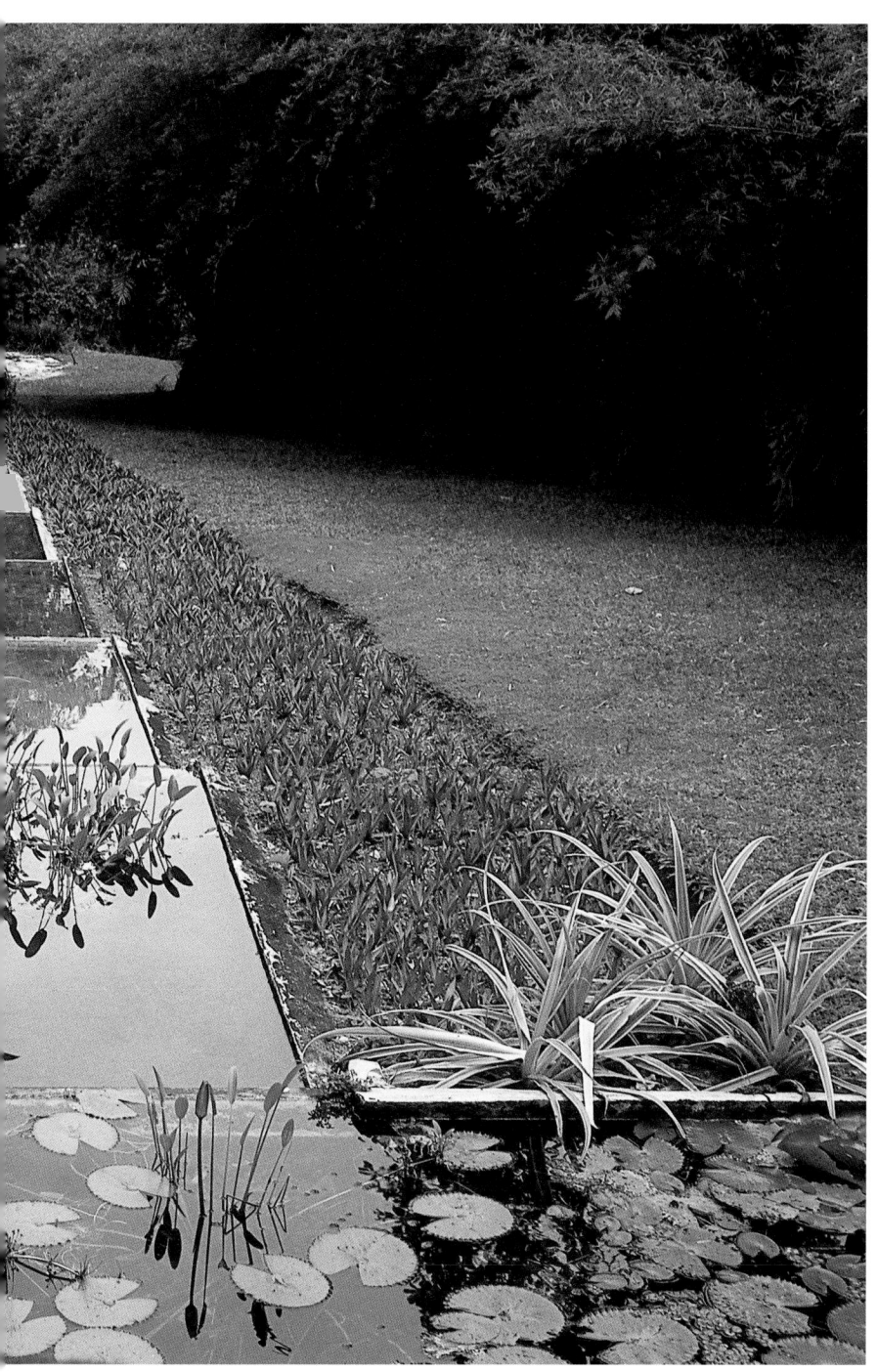

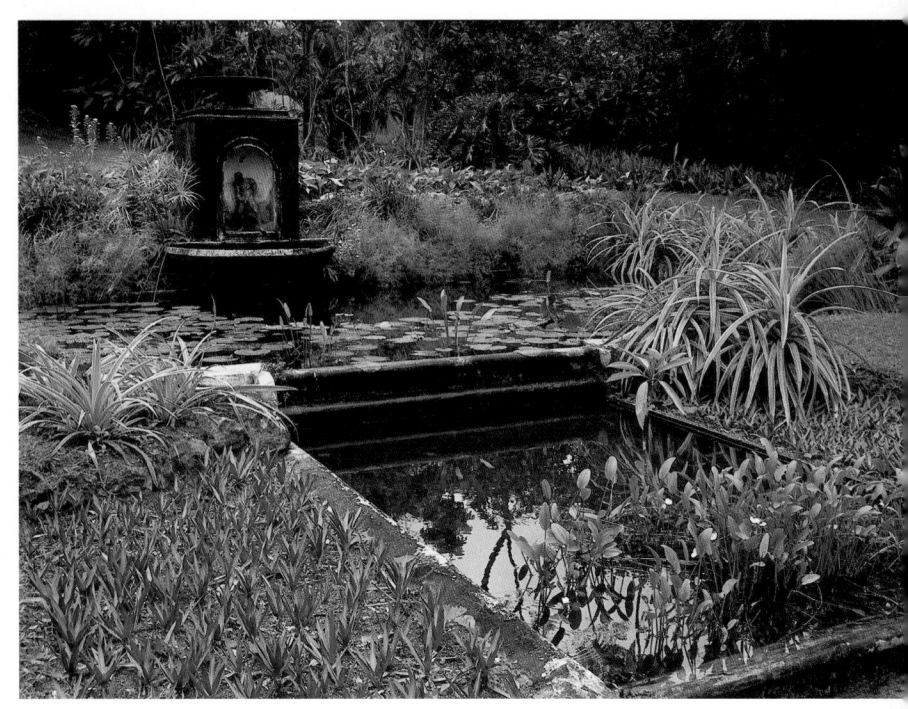

PP. 178–179 The wrought-iron gates and gateposts capped by sculptures were designed by Bevis Bawa. • Die schmiedeeisernen Tore und die Torwächter wurden nach Entwürfen von Bevis Bawa angefertigt. • Les portails en fer forgé surmontés de sculptures ont été dessinés par Bewis Bawa.

P. 181 Entrance to the Japanese garden. • Zugang zum Japanischen Garten. • L'entrée du jardin japonais.

PP. 182–183 and ↑ → Lotus-filled water features and classical sculptures are focal points in many of the garden rooms. The garden has been left exactly as Bevis Bawa designed it and is open to the public. • Teiche mit Lotusblüten sowie klassische Skulpturen sind unverkennbare Bestandteile der Gartenanlage. Der öffentlich zugängliche Garten blieb genau so erhalten, wie Bevis Bawa ihn gestaltet hat. • Des plans d'eau décorés de fleurs de lotus et de sculptures classiques sont les vedettes de bien des chambres de verdure. Le jardin, resté tel que Bevis Bawa l'avait conçu, est maintenant ouvert au public.

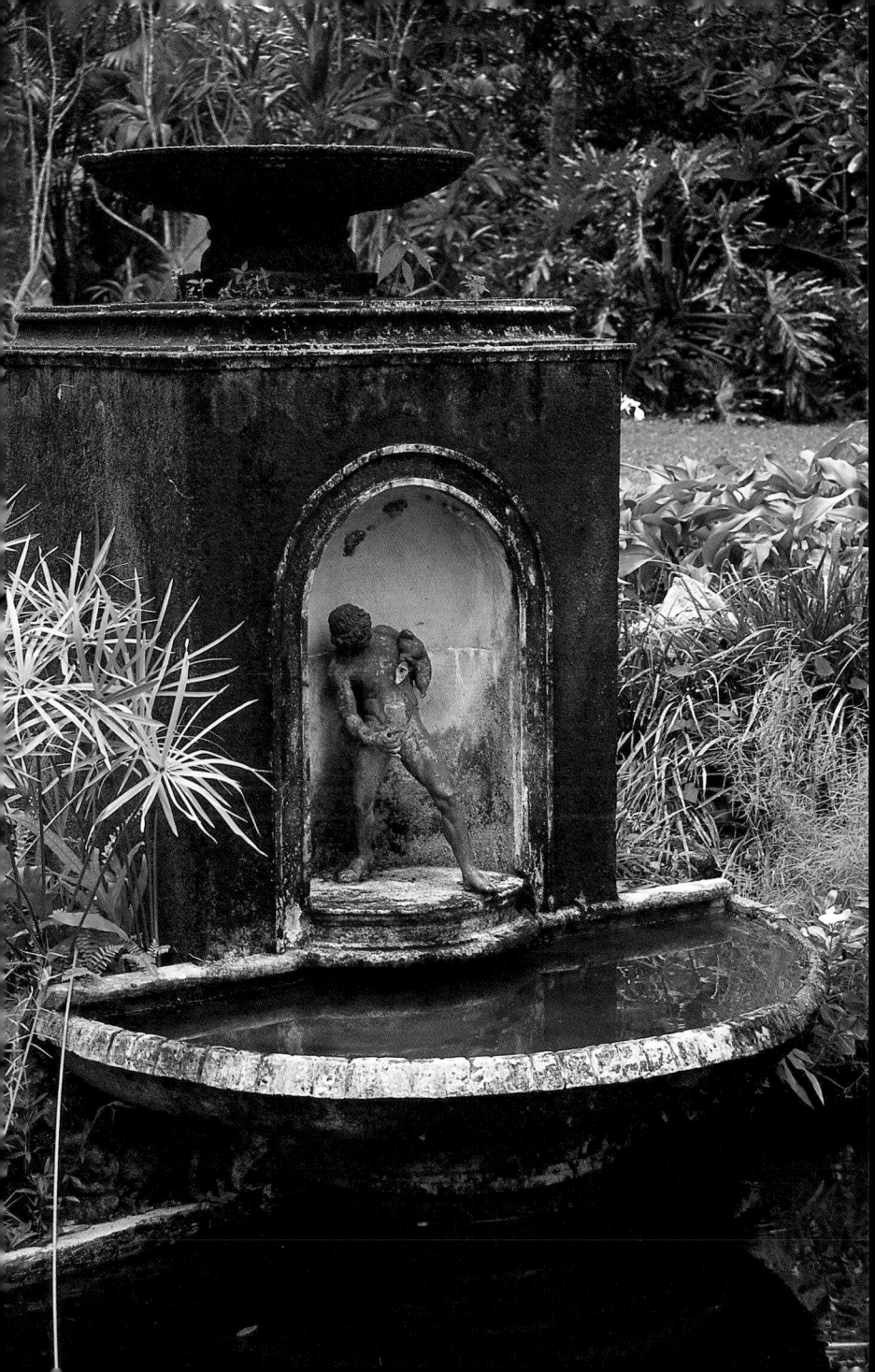

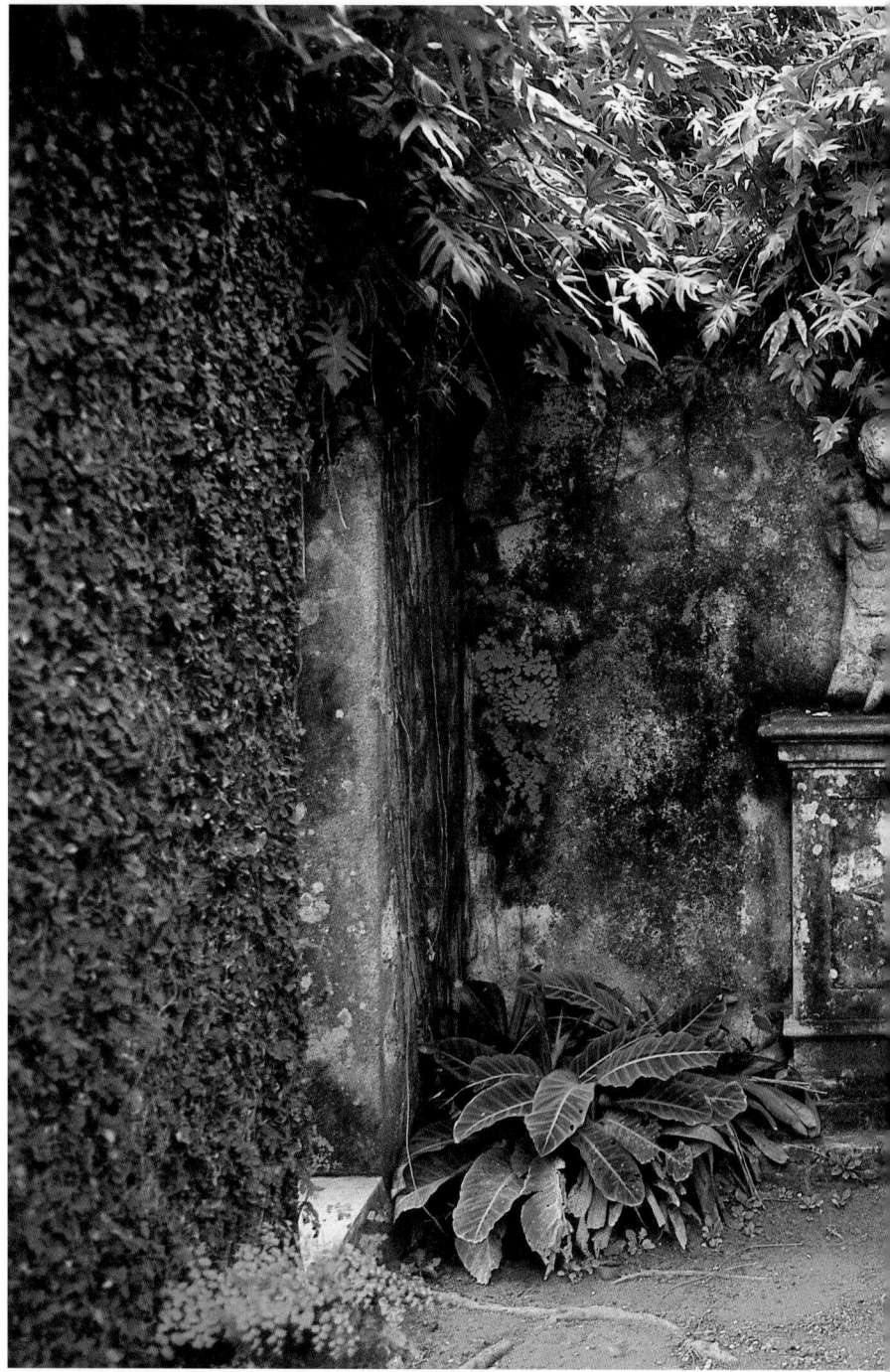

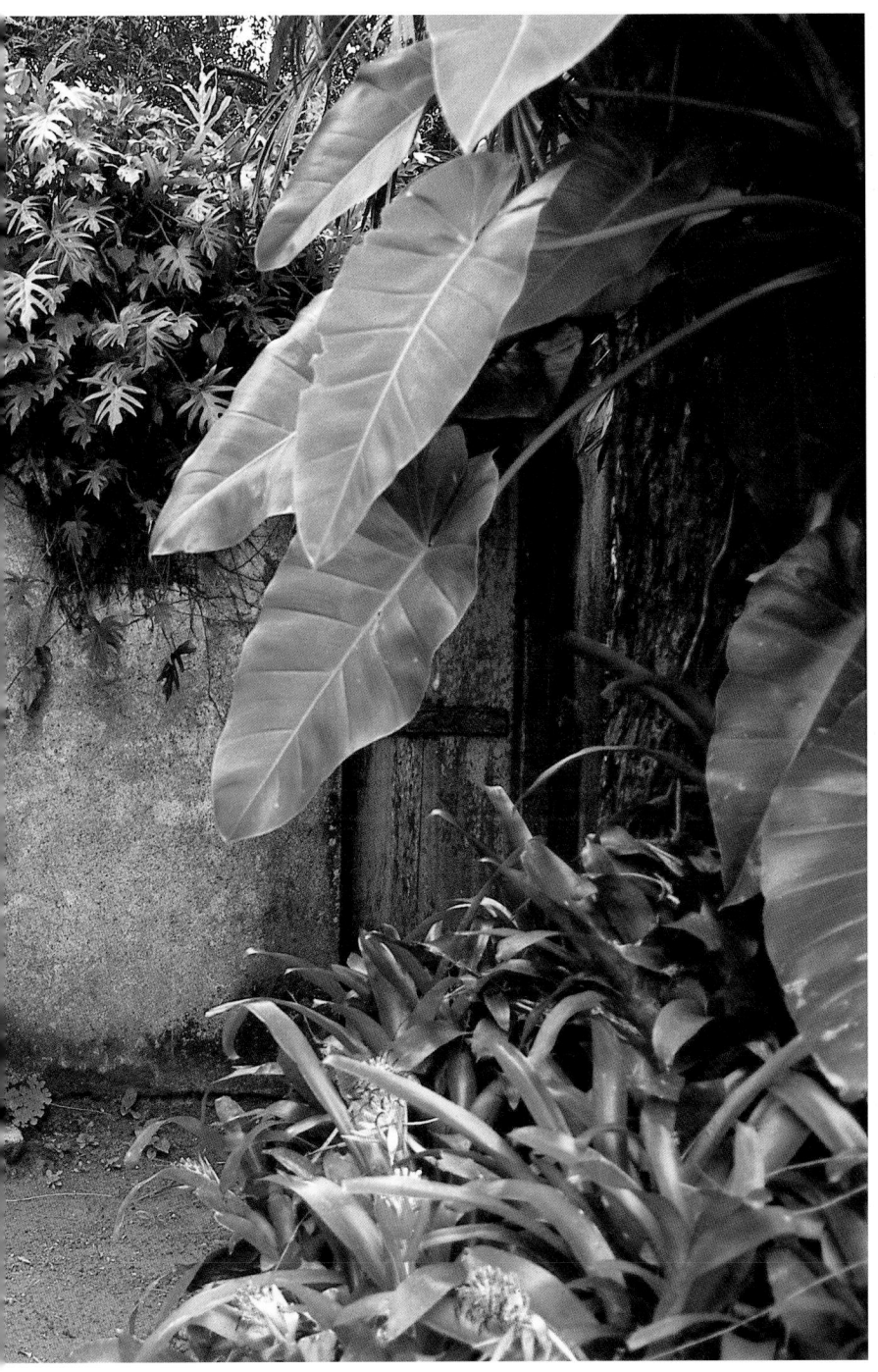

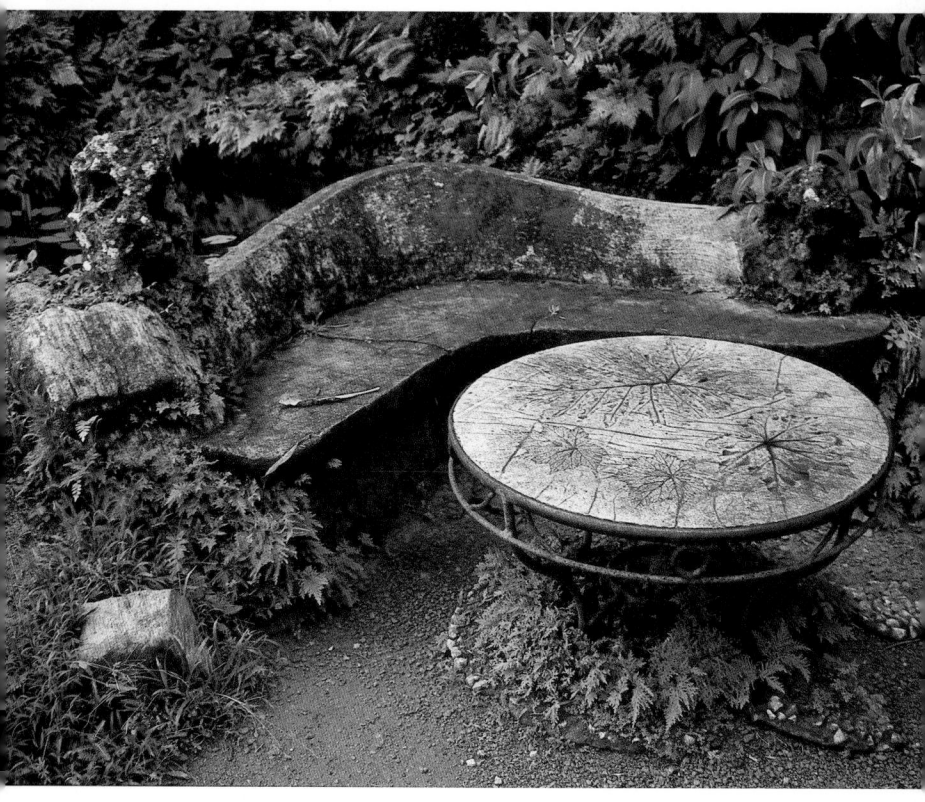

↑ One of the many secluded resting spots. • Eine der vielen lauschigen Rückzugsmöglichkeiten. • L'un des nombreux endroits retirés où l'on peut se reposer.

↗ The waterspout and basin were also designed by Bevis Bawa. • Der Wasser-speier und das Becken wurden ebenso von Bevis Bawa entworfen. • La gargouille et la vasque sont aussi des créations de Bevis Bawa.

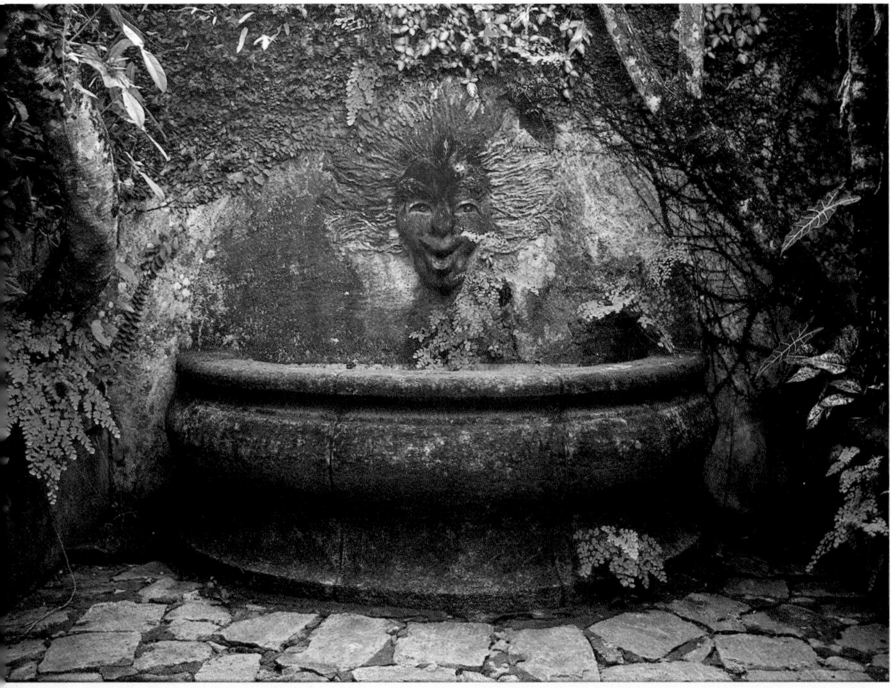
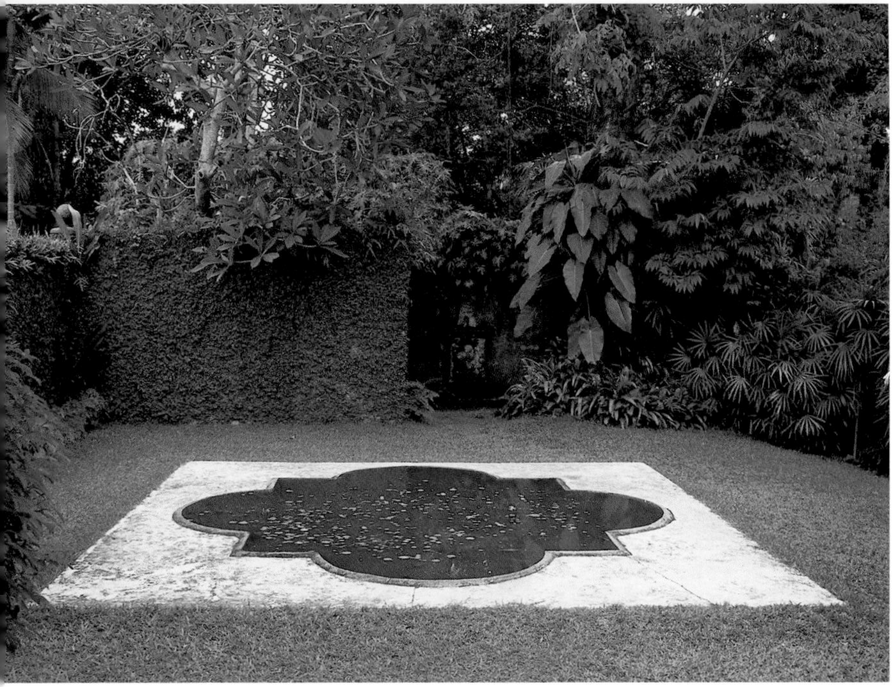

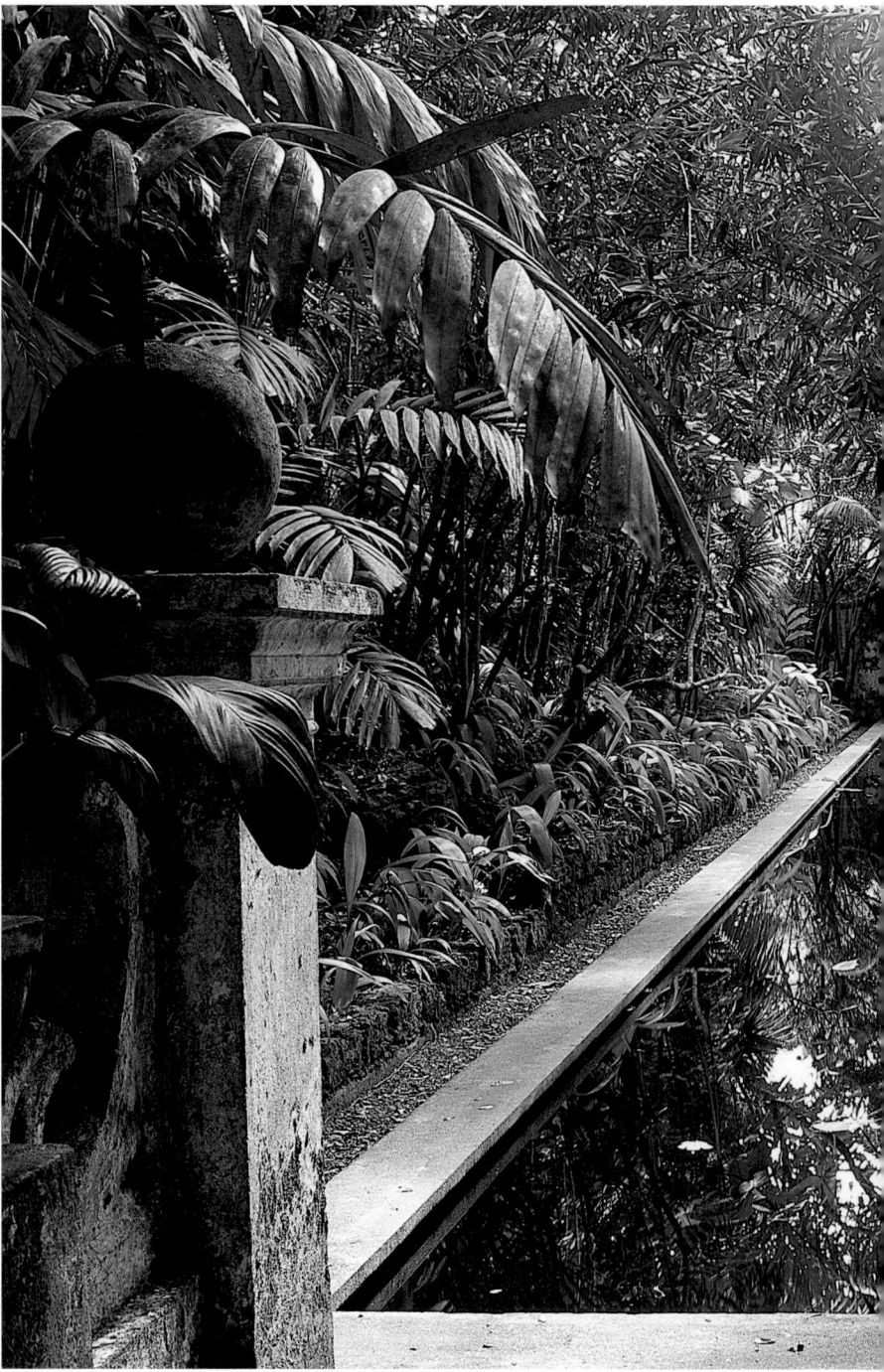

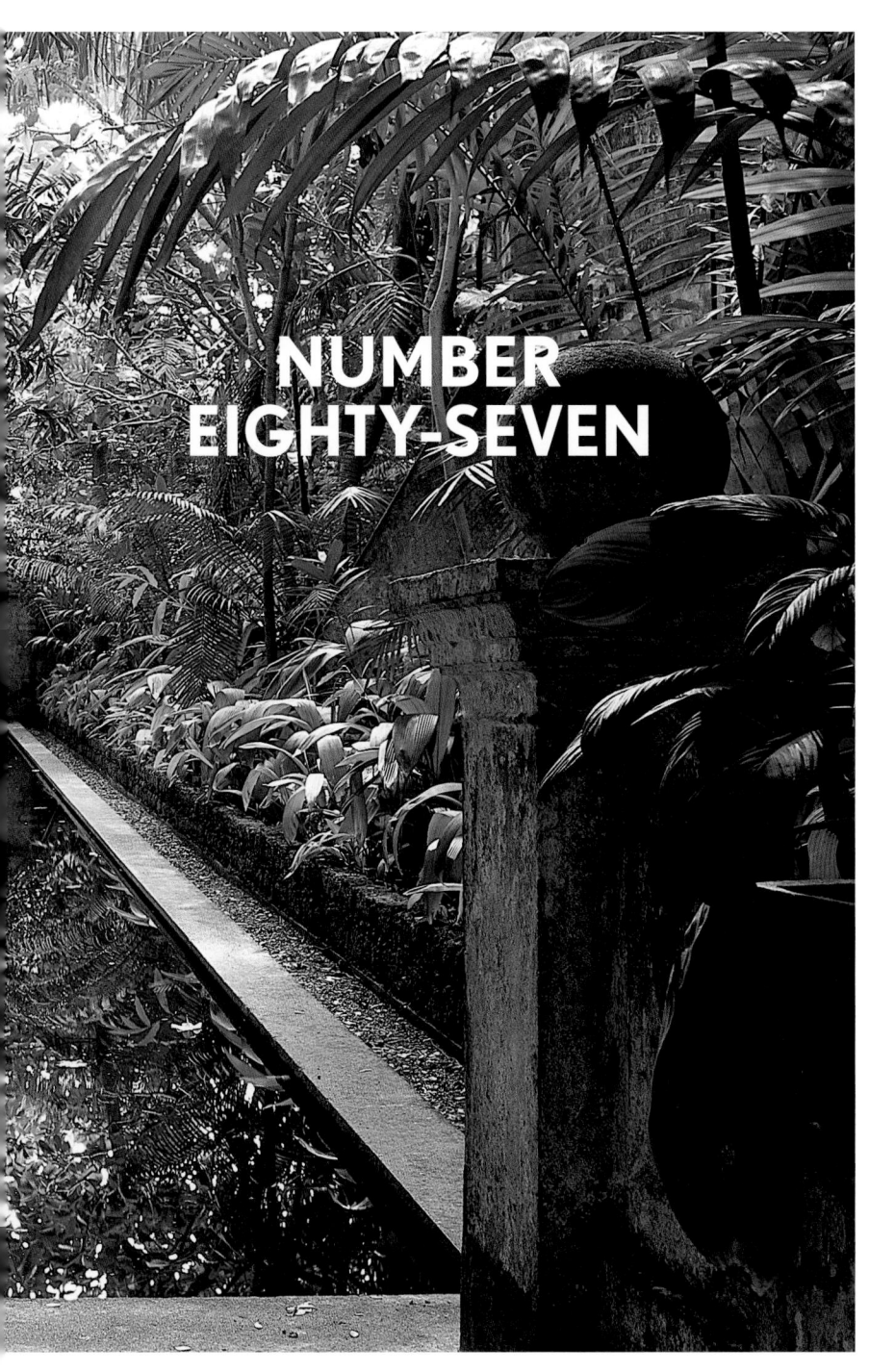

NUMBER
EIGHTY-SEVEN

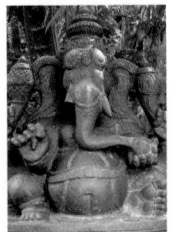

NUMBER EIGHTY-SEVEN

BENTOTA
SRI LANKA

During the 1960s and 1970s architect Geoffrey Bawa was at the height of his powers. Between designing a host of public buildings, from Sri Lanka's parliament to a major university and a series of private houses and hotels for the country's political elite, he longed to indulge in the preservation of small, intimate ruins. Bawa was a trained architect and lawyer and never lost the chance to importune rich or artistic friends to buy properties. He persuaded the Italian sculptor Lidia Duchini, married to a Sri Lankan, to buy two early 18th-century houses sloping towards marshland near the busy coastal road from Colombo to Galle. The plot was called "Number Eighty-Seven". Bawa created a series of terraced water features and pavilions filled with the murmur of the sea. In 1996 Rohan and Dulanjalee Jayakody bought and lovingly restored the private wilderness. Dulanjalee is the daughter of assassinated Sri Lankan premier Ranasinghe Premadasa; Rohan, an art collector and pioneer of floriculture in Sri Lanka, was a friend and admirer of Geoffrey Bawa's. "Number Eighty-Seven" is their homage to Bawa's genius.

In den 1960er- und 1970er-Jahren lag die Glanzzeit des Architekten Geoffrey Bawa. Während eine Reihe öffentlicher Gebäude, wie das Parlament Sri Lankas und eine bedeutende Universität, sowie zahlreiche Privathäuser und Hotels nach seinen Entwürfen gebaut wurden, galt sein wahres Interesse dem Wiederaufbau von Ruinen. Bawa war als Architekt und Anwalt gleichermaßen erfahren und drängte seine Künstlerfreunde gern zum Kauf von Immobilien. Er überredete die italienische Bildhauerin Lidia Duchini, Gattin eines Singhalesen, zum Erwerb zweier Häuser aus dem 18. Jahrhundert, die unweit der Küstenstraße von Colombo nach Galle abschüssig zum Sumpfland lagen. Das Grundstück war als „Number Eighty-Seven" ausgezeichnet. Bawa entwarf mehrere Wasserbecken und Pavillons, die vom Klang des Meeresrauschens erfüllt sind. 1996 ging diese Dschungellandschaft in den Besitz von Rohan und Dulanjalee Jayakody über, die sie liebevoll instand setzten. Dulanjalees Vater war der ermordete Premierminister Sri Lankas, Ranasinghe Premadasa, während Rohan, Kunstsammler und Pionier singhalesischer Blumenzucht, ein Freund und Bewunderer Geoffrey Bawas war. Das Ehepaar betrachtet „Number Eighty-Seven" als Hommage an das Genie Bawas.

Les années 1960 et 1970 ont été les plus fécondes pour l'architecte Geoffrey Bawa. Entre la conception d'une kyrielle d'édifices publics, du parlement national à une grande université, et des maisons particulières et hôtels, il s'est surtout intéressé à la restauration de modestes constructions de charme. Architecte et avocat de formation, Bawa n'a jamais manqué une occasion de travailler au corps ses amis artistes ou fortunés pour qu'ils investissent dans la pierre. C'est ainsi qu'il a persuadé la sculptrice italienne Lidia Duchini, mariée à un Srilankais, d'acheter deux maisons du début du 18e siècle surplombant un terrain marécageux à proximité de la route côtière qui relie Colombo à Galle. La parcelle s'appelait « Number Eighty-Seven ». Bawa y a créé une série de plans d'eau étagés et de pavillons qu'emplit le murmure de la mer. En 1996, Rohan et Dulanjalee Jayakody ont acheté cette propriété. Dulanjalee est la fille de Ranasinghe Premadasa, Premier ministre srilankais assassiné ; Rohan, collectionneur d'art et pionnier de la floriculture au Sri Lanka, était un ami et admirateur de Geoffrey Bawa. « Number Eighty-Seven » est un hommage au génie de ce dernier.

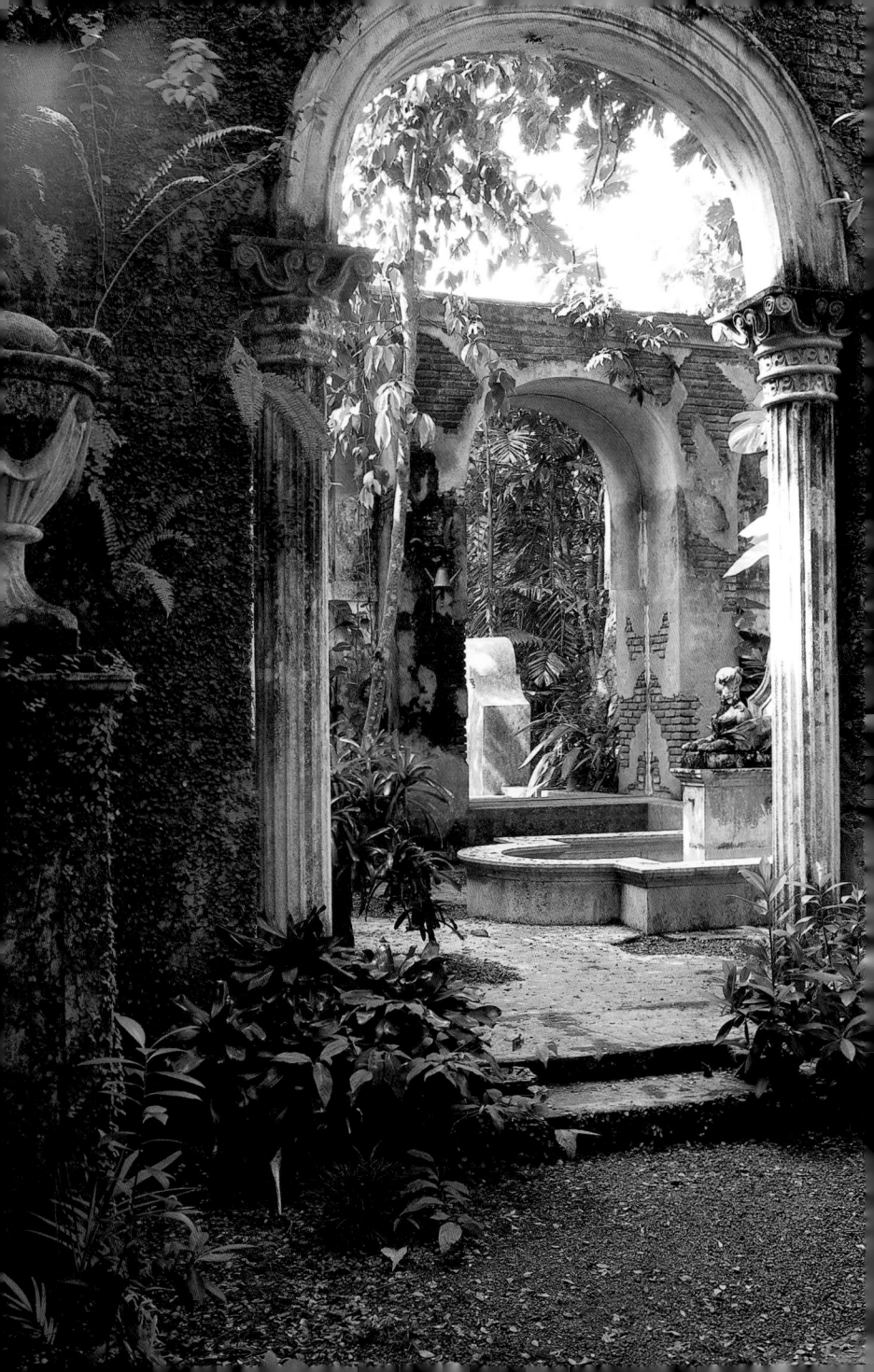

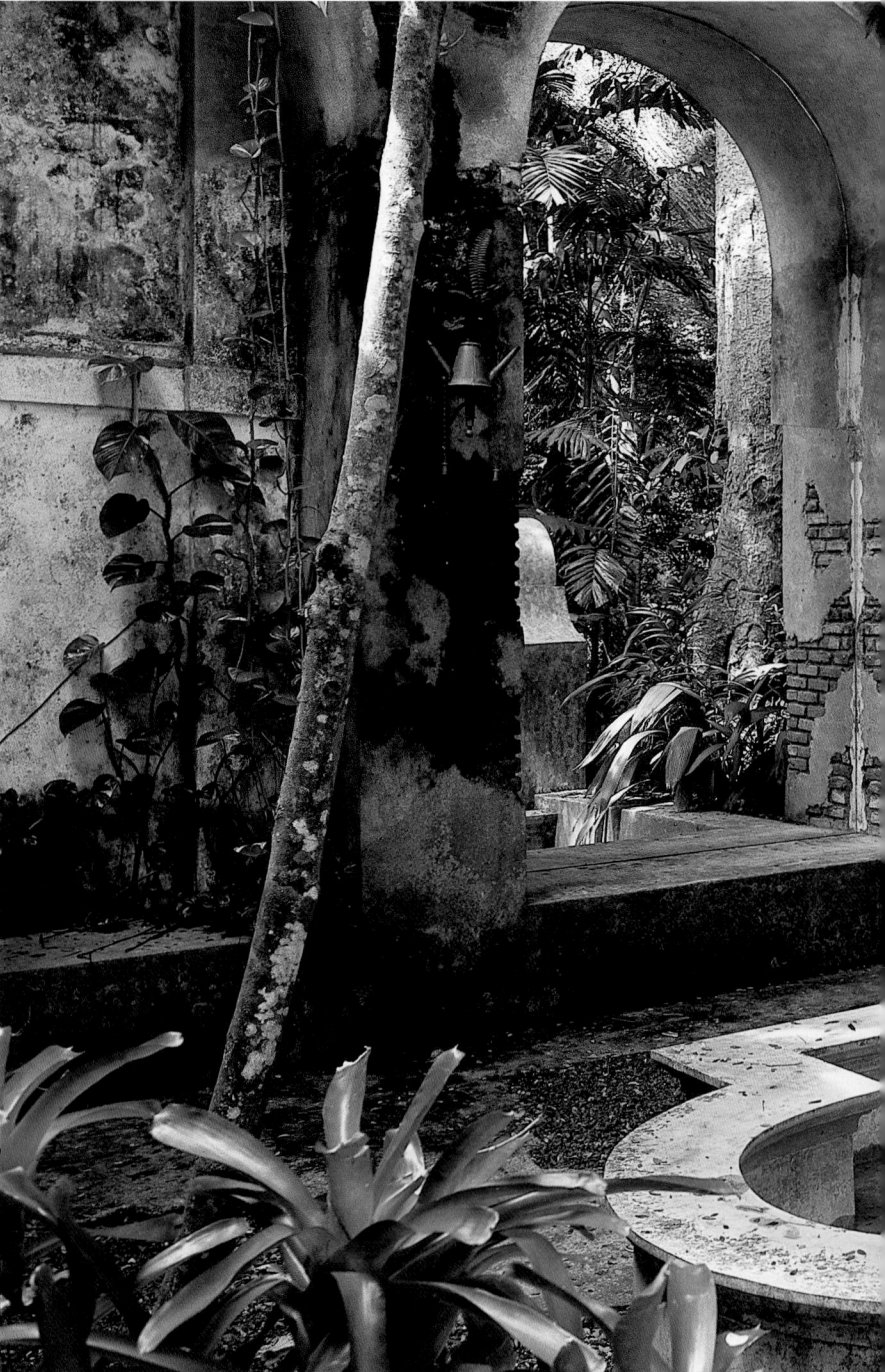

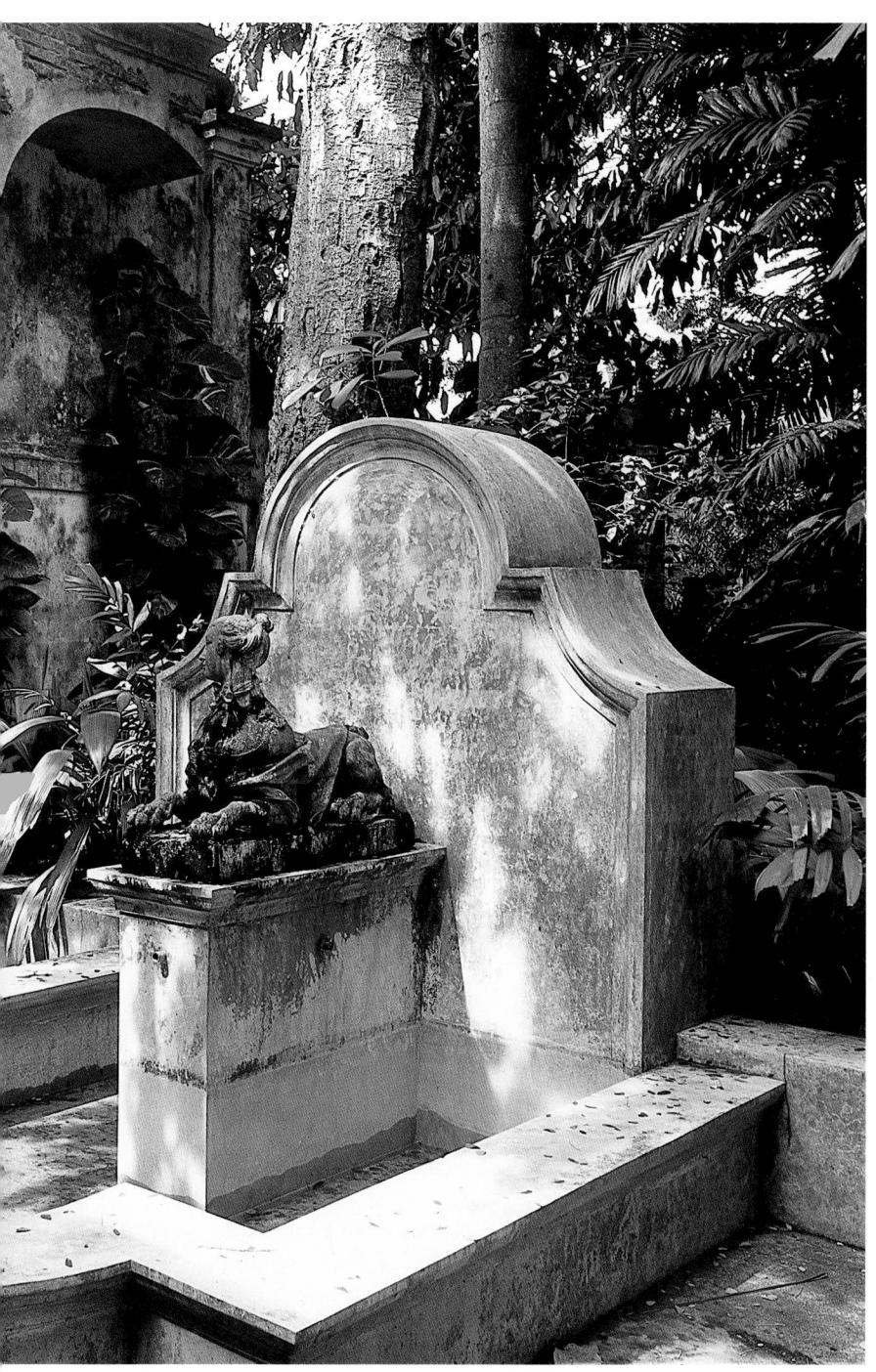

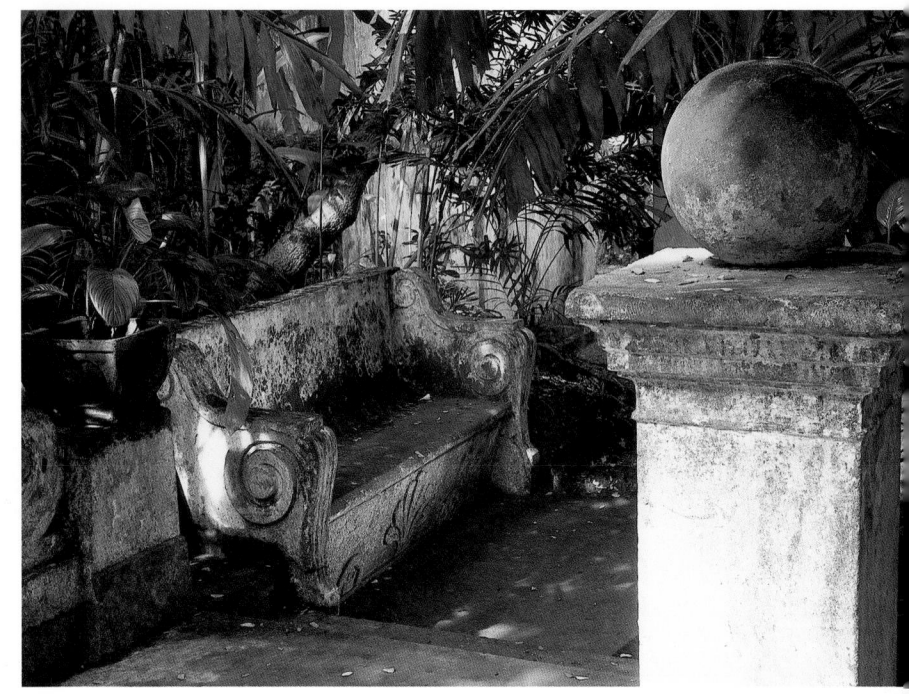

PP. 190–191 The stairs lead to a secluded lap pool that Rohan Jayakody added after acquiring the property · Eine Treppe führt zu einem abgelegenen Swimmingpool, den Rohan Jayakody nachträglich hinzufügte. · La volée de marches conduit à un bassin peu profond, à l'abri des regards, que Rohan a fait construire.

P. 193 and PP. 194–195 Sections of one old house were removed and carefully reassembled to create a garden folly. · Teile eines alten Hauses wurden abgetragen und sorgfältig zu einem Gartenensemble arrangiert. · Une vieille maison a été partiellement démontée et soigneusement remontée pour créer un décor inédit.

↓ A granite grinding wheel in a garden courtyard. • Ein Mahlstein aus Granit in einem bepflanzten Innenhof. • Une meule en granite, élément ornemental du jardin.

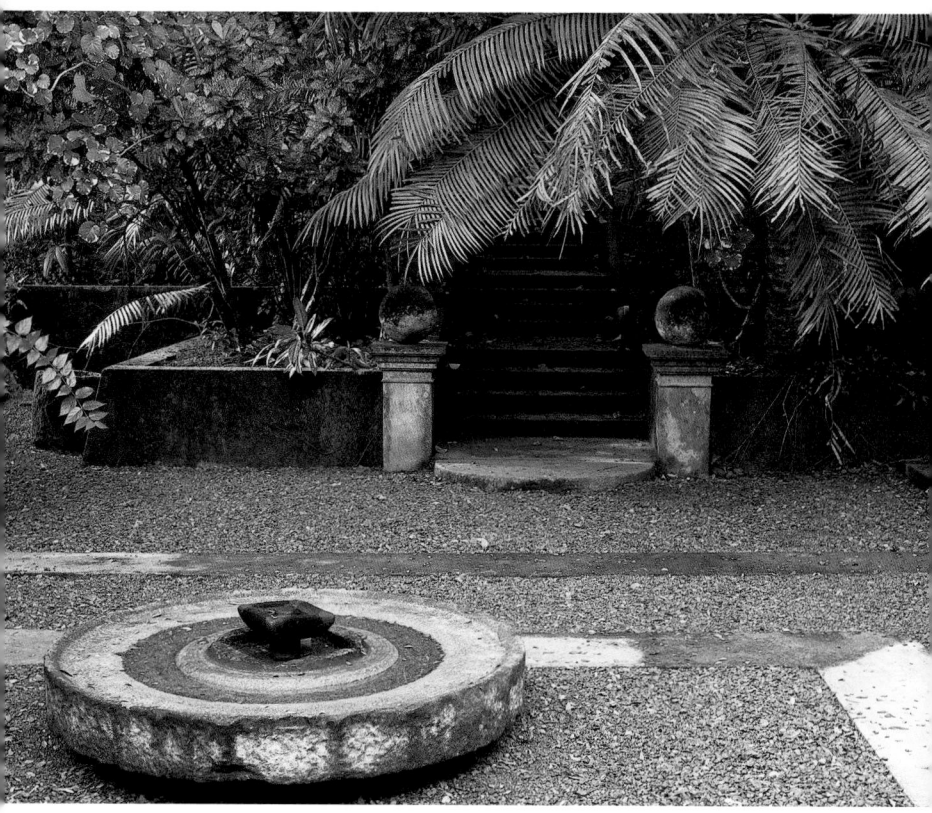

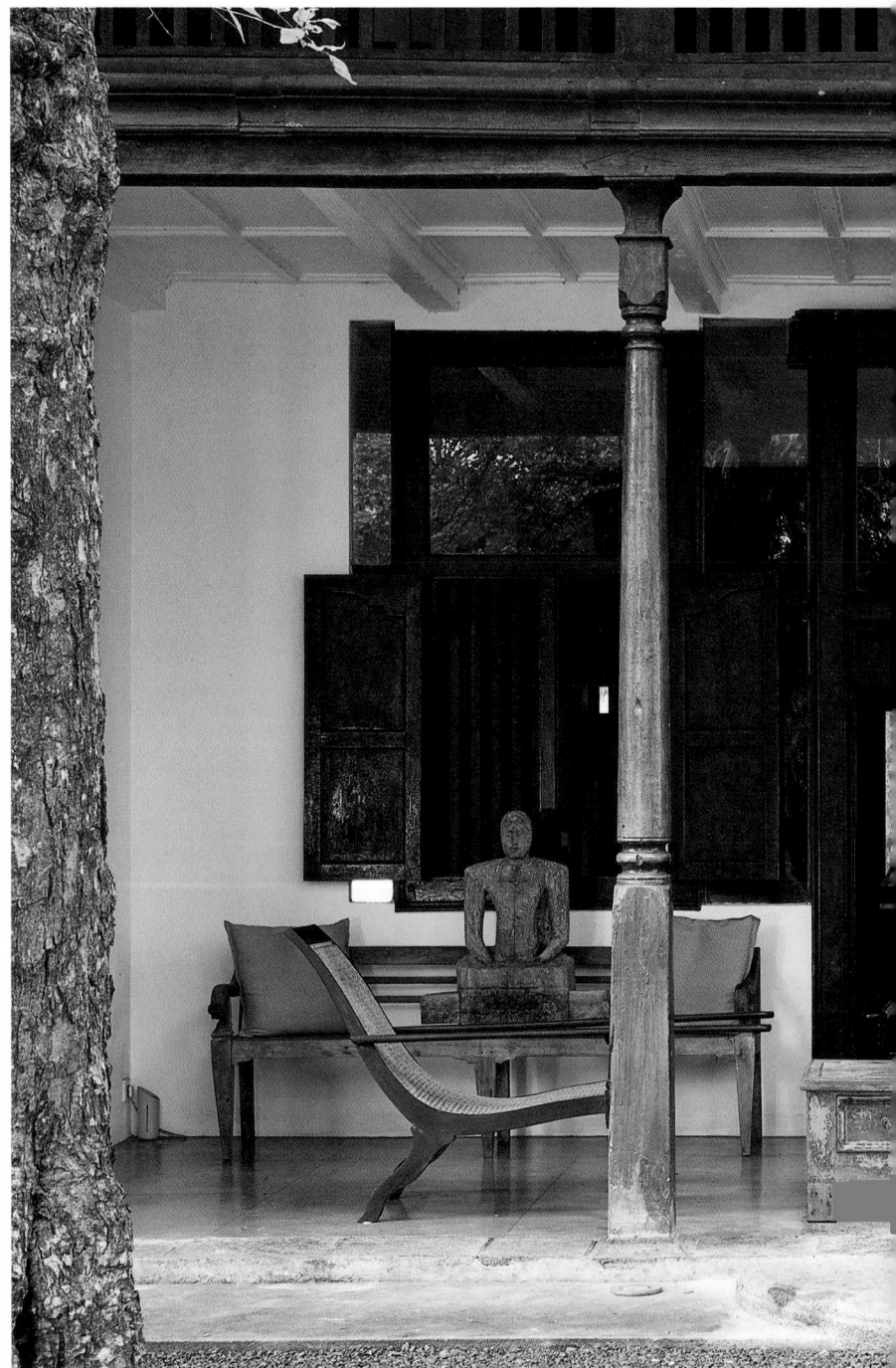

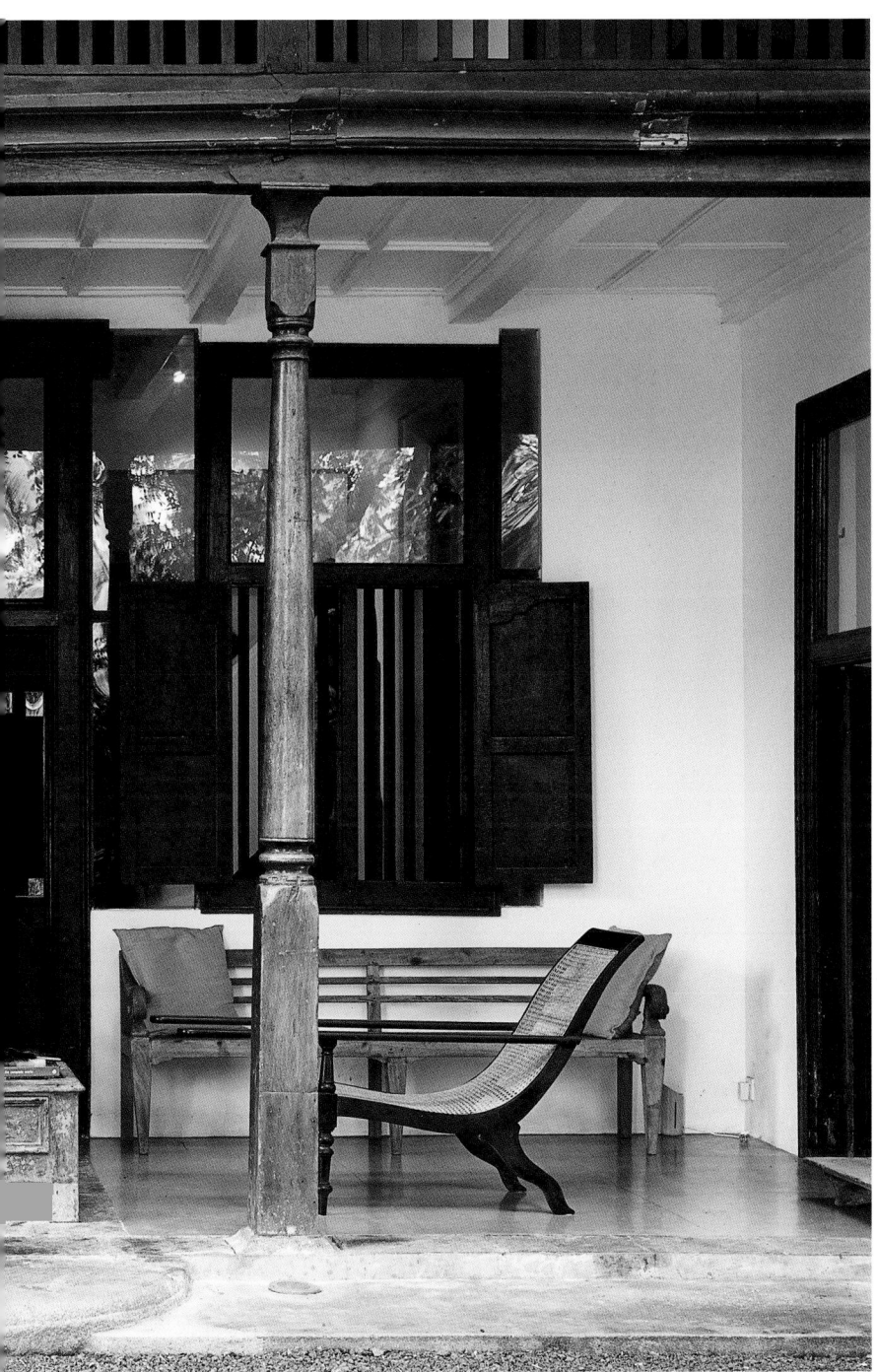

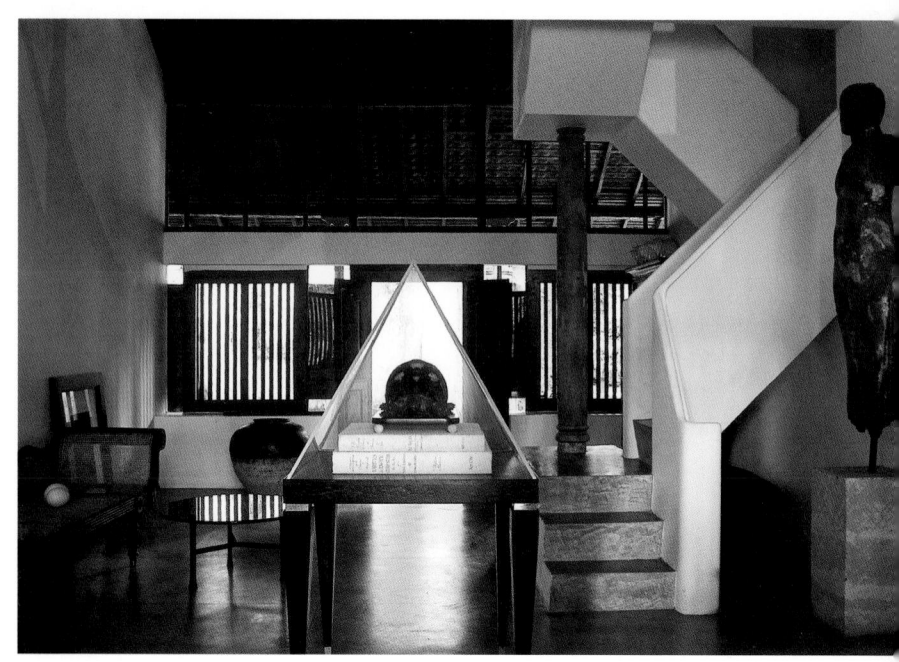

PP. 198–199 Planter's chairs and benches line the veranda with pillars. • Kolonialmöbel auf der Säulenveranda. • Des sièges et des bancs de style colonial invitent au repos sur la véranda à colonnade.

↑ A staircase was added to replace a steep ladder to the floor above. • Die ehemalige steile Leiter ins Obergeschoss wurde durch diese Treppe ersetzt. • Un escalier est venu remplacer une échelle raide par laquelle on accédait à l'étage supérieur.

→ A traditional oil lamp hangs above the dining table. • Über dem Esstisch hängt eine traditionelle Öllampe. • Une lampe à huile traditionnelle éclaire la table de la salle à manger.

PP. 202–203 Rows of Buddhas and stupas in tiers at the Gangaramaya temple near Beira Lake in Colombo. On the lake itself is the Seema Malakaya temple designed by Geoffrey Bawa. • Mehrere Reihen mit Buddhastatuen und Stupas im Gangaramaya-Tempel unweit des Beira-Sees in Colombo. Direkt am

See liegt der von Geoffrey Bawa entworfene Seema-Malakaya-Tempel. • Le temple de Gangarama, sur les rives du lac Beira, à Colombo, est célèbre pour sa composition étagée de bouddhas et de stupas. Au milieu du lac s'élève le temple de Seema Malaka, conçu par Geoffrey Bawa.

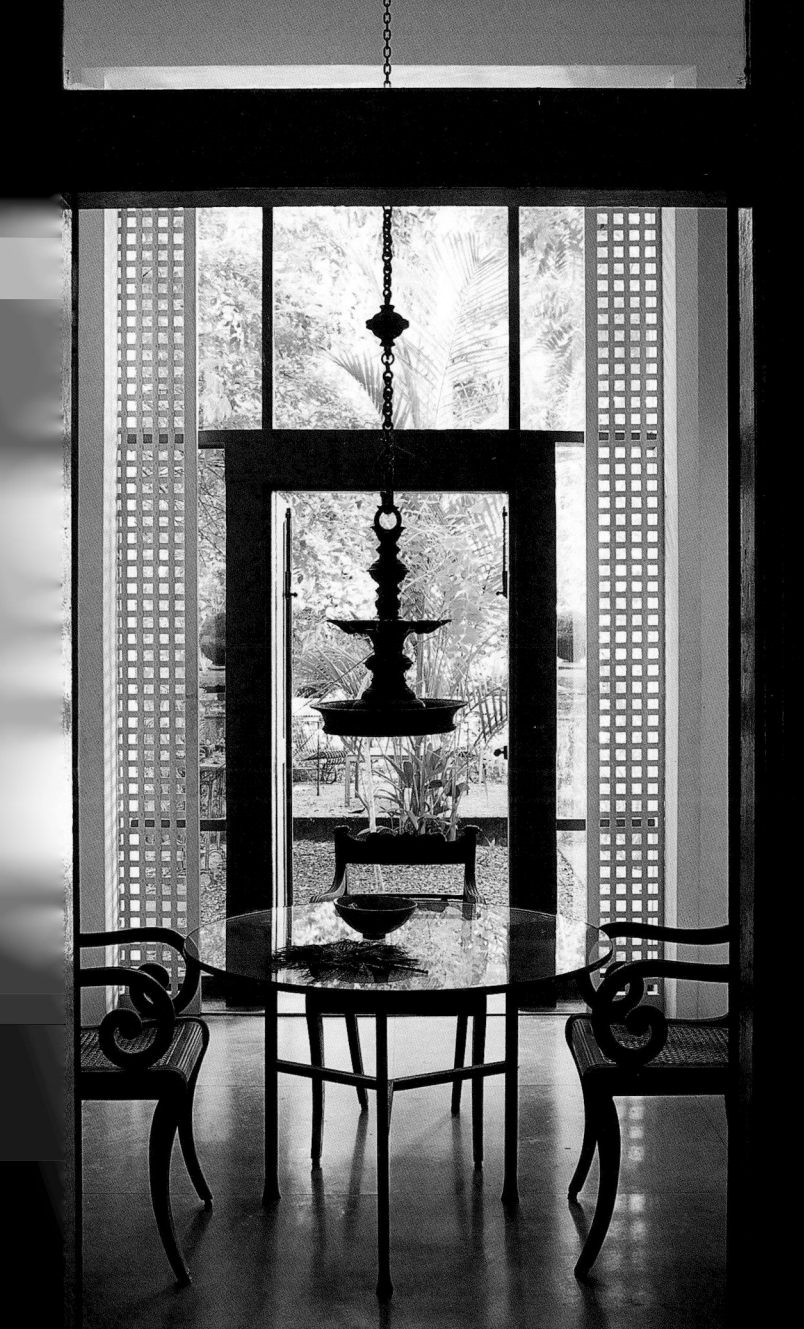

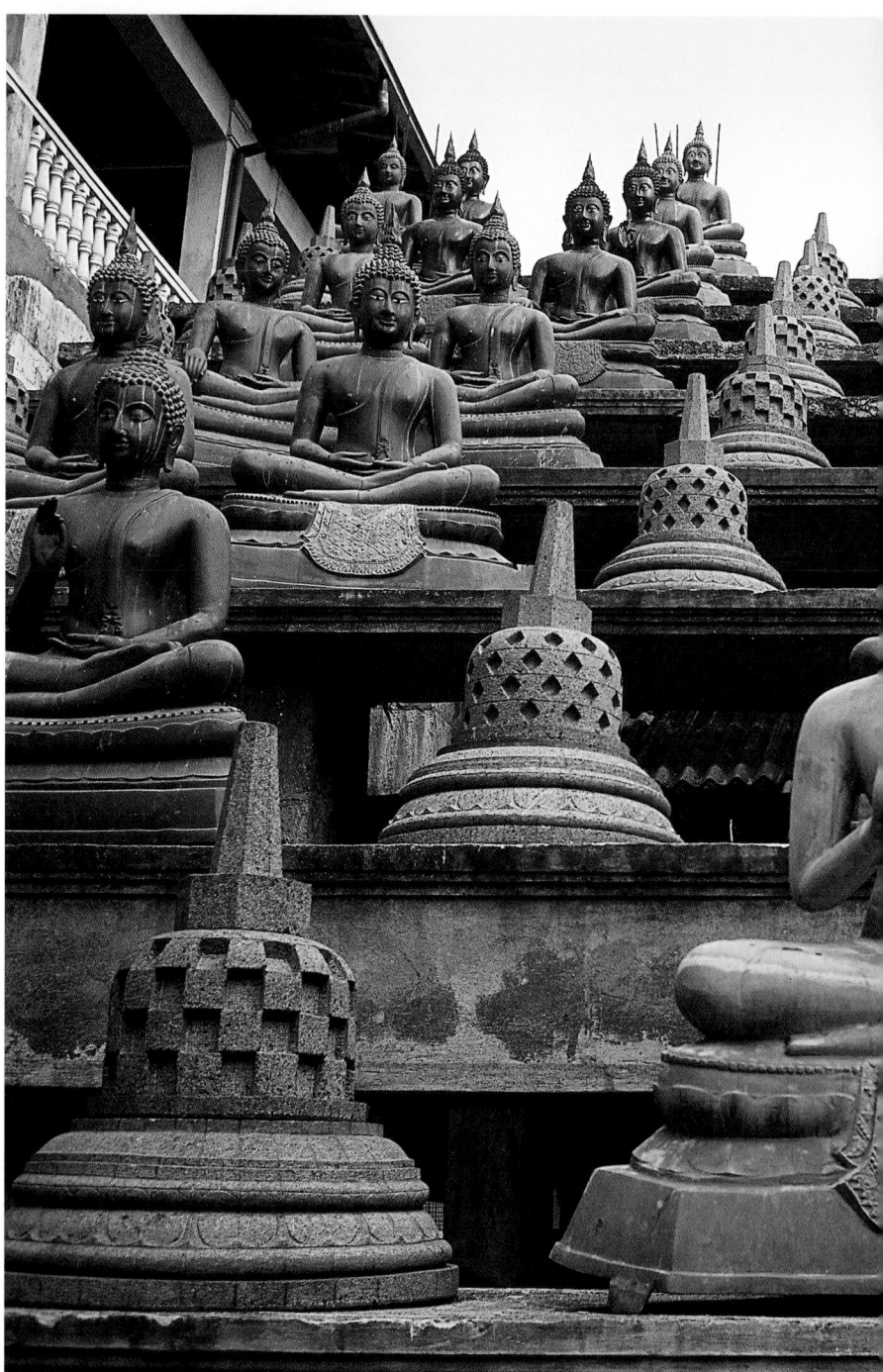

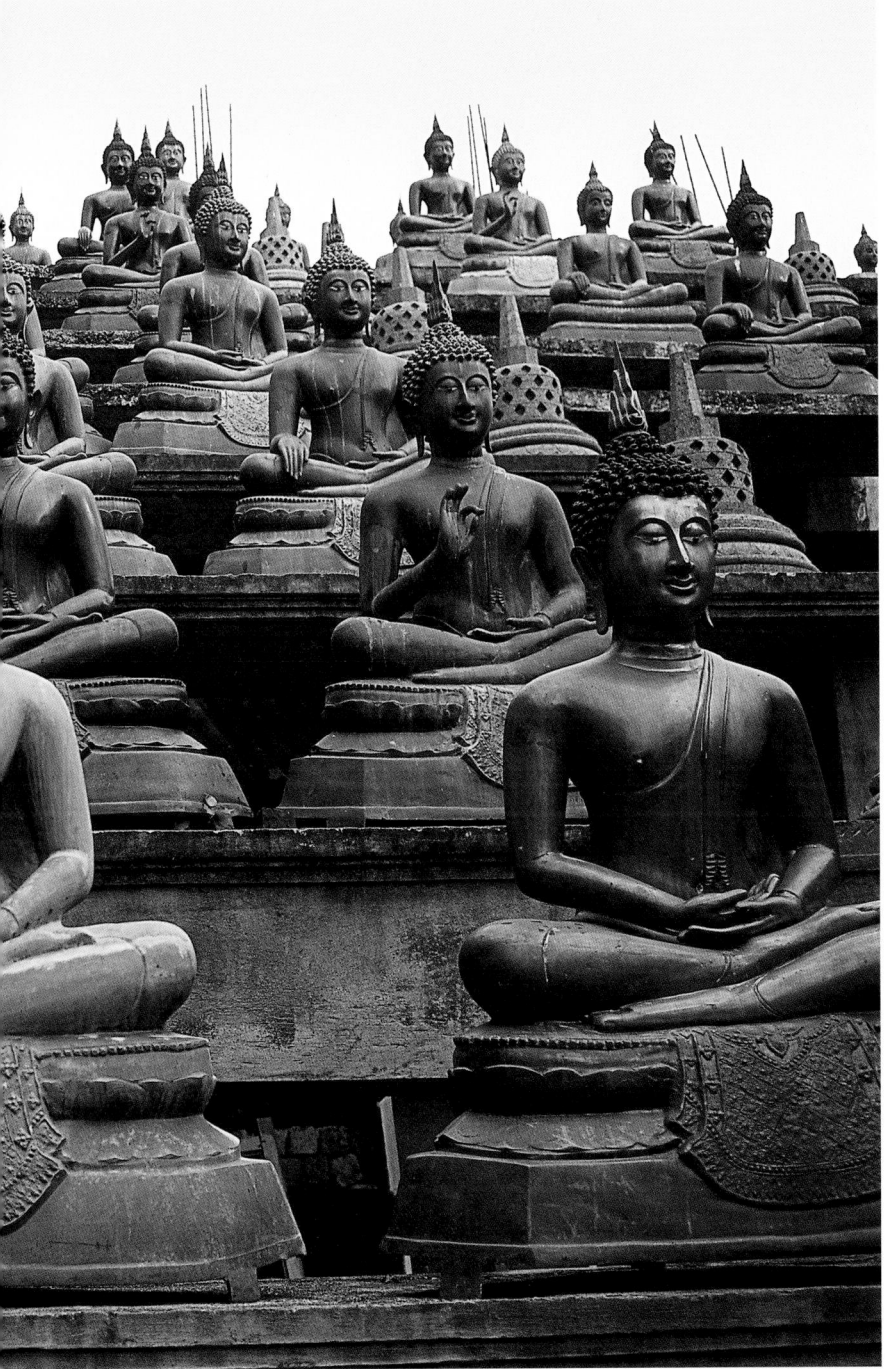

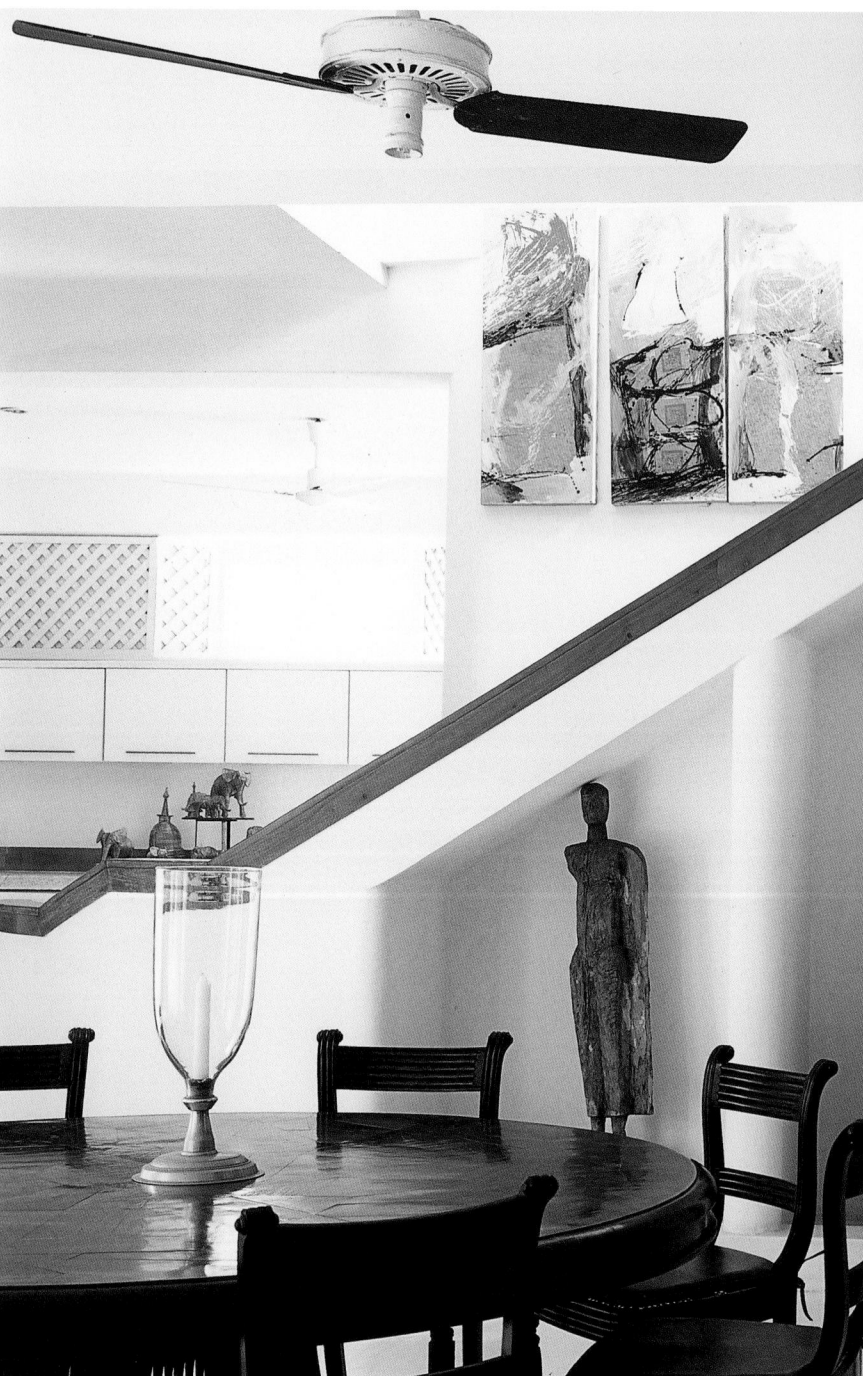

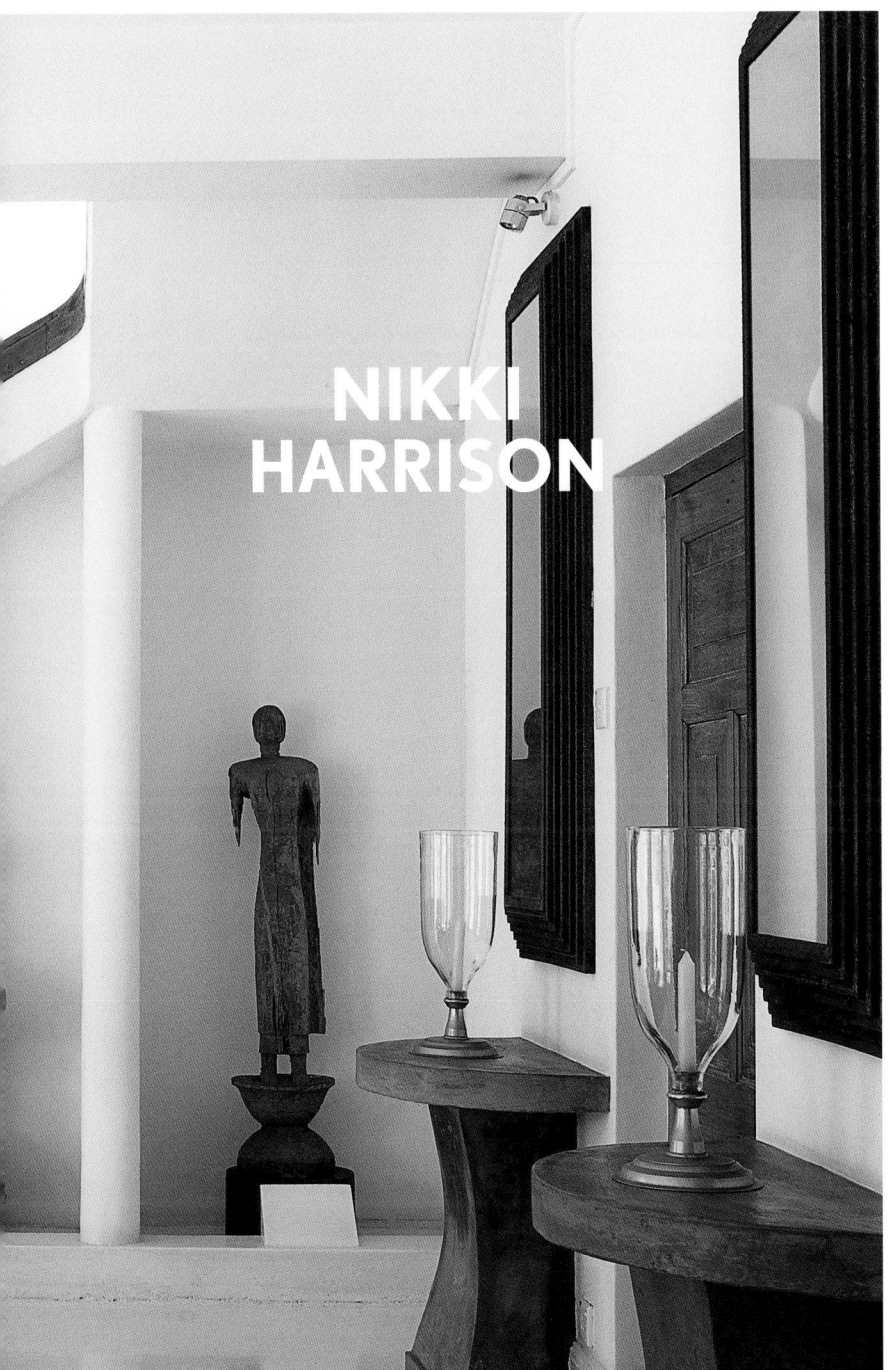

NIKKI
HARRISON

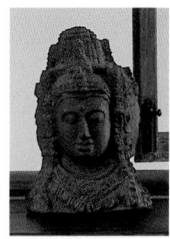

NIKKI HARRISON
COLOMBO
SRI LANKA

Nikki Harrison has been a mistress of many trades. She has worked as a fashion designer, youth counsellor, school head-mistress and PR consultant. No role has fitted her better than taking up designing interiors and managing hotels in Sri Lanka. She arrived from England more than three decades ago as an expatriate wife and stayed on. Her home, a colonial bungalow that she found some years ago, still retained old wooden-blade ceiling fans and a floor of Burma teak in the living room. What Nikki calls "a little tender loving care" was actually a painstaking exercise in removing layers of varnish, opening out the dining room and converting a disused breakfast room into a sleek terrazzo-tiled kitchen. Taking her cue from the lightness of colonial houses, she painted the red concrete floors white, stripped the unusual curved staircase of its handrail and removed wood paneling from the walls. Filling the house with objects collected over the years and furniture designed locally, she has brought back the graceful elegance of its heyday.

Nikki Harrison ist ein Tausendsassa. Sie arbeitete als Modedesignerin, Jugendberaterin, Schulleiterin sowie in der Werbung. Der krönende Höhepunkt dieser Karrieren aber lag in dem Entschluss, als Innenarchitektin und Hotelmanagerin in Sri Lanka tätig zu werden. Mit ihrem Mann wanderte sie vor über 30 Jahren aus England ein und blieb. Als sie ihr jetziges Haus entdeckte, fand sie darin noch Deckenventilatoren mit Drehflügeln aus Holz sowie einen Holzboden aus birmanischem Teak im Wohnzimmer. Es kostete einige Mühe, zahlreiche Lackschichten zu entfernen, das Wohnzimmer zu vergrößern und einen ungenutzten Frühstücksraum in eine schicke Küche mit Terrazzoboden zu verwandeln. Aber Nikki bezeichnet diese Anstrengungen lächelnd als „zärtlichen Liebesdienst". Sie ließ sich von den hellen Kolonialbauten inspirieren und strich die roten Betonböden weiß. Außerdem entfernte sie das Geländer der ungewöhnlich gewundenen Treppe und die Holzvertäfelung von den Wänden. Indem sie das Haus mit Möbeln aus der Umgebung sowie den vielen kleinen Kostbarkeiten dekorierte, die sie über die Jahre gesammelt hat, gab sie ihm seine ursprüngliche Anmut und Eleganz zurück.

Nikki Harrison a exercé avec brio bien des métiers : créatrice de mode, conseillère d'orientation, directrice d'école et consultante en relations publiques. Mais elle a tout bonnement excellé dans celui d'architecte d'intérieur et de directrice d'hôtels au Sri Lanka. Il y a plus de trente ans, elle a quitté l'Angleterre pour suivre son mari et elle est restée au Sri Lanka. Sa maison, un bungalow de style colonial trouvé il y a quelques années, était encore équipée de ventilateurs à pales de bois fixés au plafond et dotée d'un parquet en teck birman dans le salon. Ce que Nikki appelle « aimer d'amour tendre » fut en fait un travail minutieux : elle a décapé les boiseries, ouvert la salle à manger et transformé la salle de petit-déjeuner tombée en déshérence en cuisine dépouillée pourvue d'un sol en terrazzo. Trouvant son inspiration dans la légèreté des maisons coloniales, elle a peint en blanc les sols de béton rouges, débarrassé de sa main courante l'escalier faisant un virage inhabituel et arraché les lambris. Avec des objets collectionnés au fil des ans et du mobilier créé sur place, elle a rendu à la maison l'élégance de ses beaux jours.

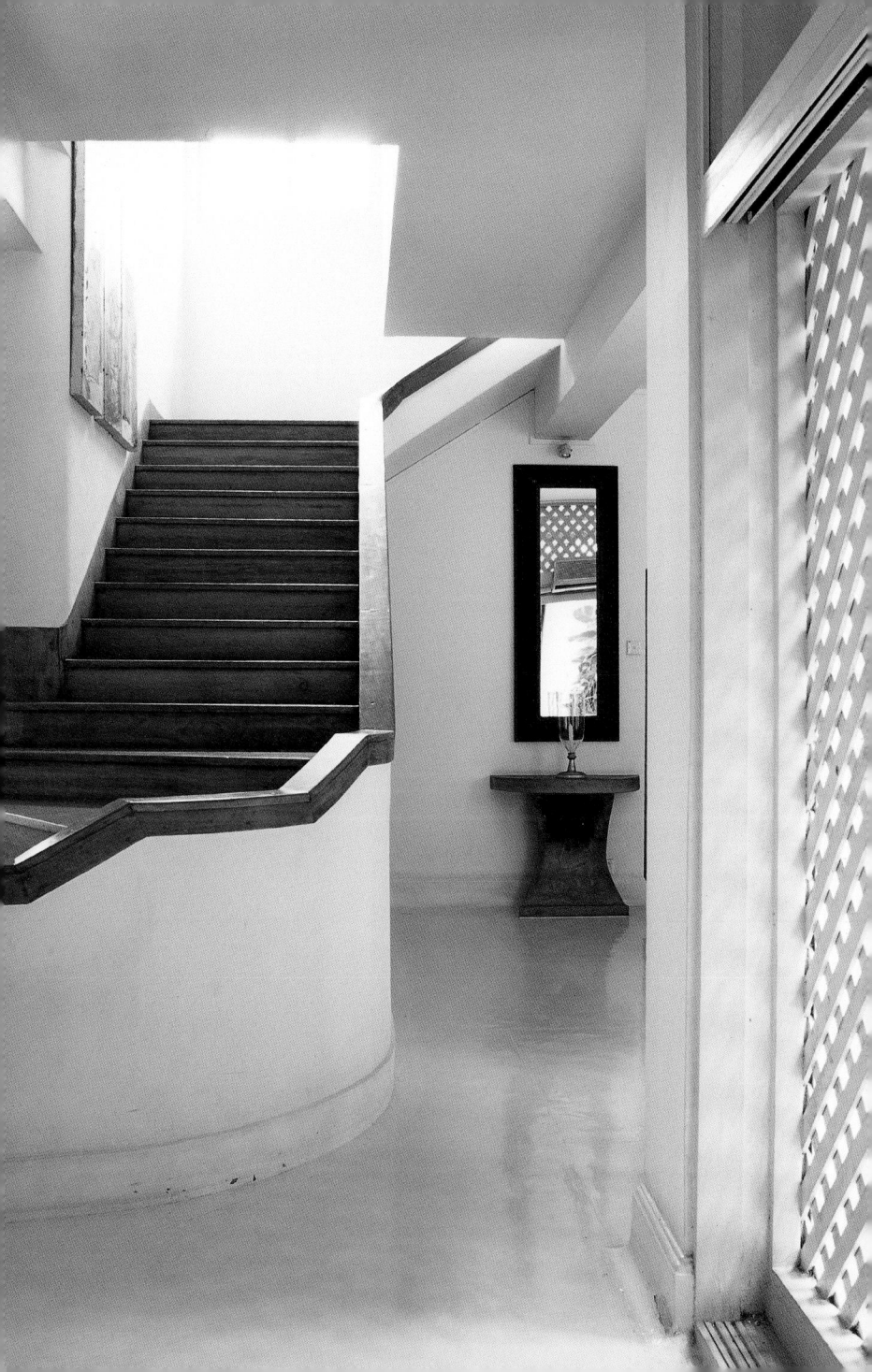

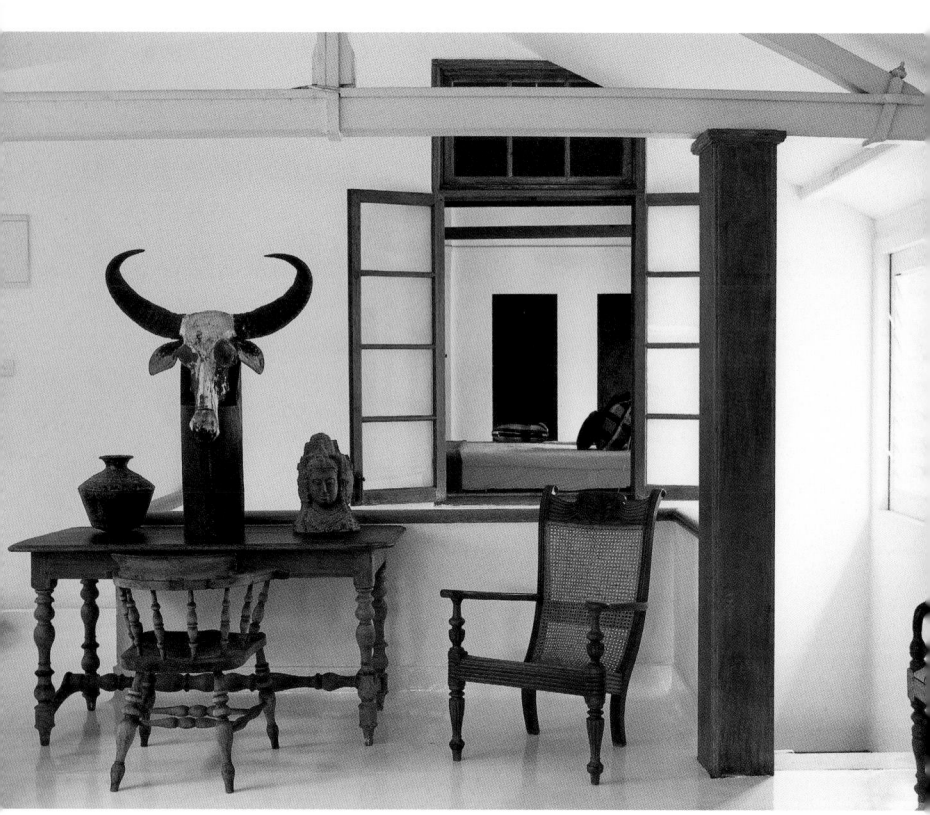

PP. 204–205 Alcoves under the staircase were created by removing old wooden panelling. The two statues are wooden cores of old Buddha images. • Nachdem die alte Holzvertäfelung entfernt wurde, entstanden diese Nischen unter der Treppe. Die beiden Statuen bestehen aus dem hölzernen Kern alter Buddhafiguren. • Nikki Harrison a ménagé des niches sous l'escalier en enlevant les vieux lambris. Les deux statues sont des armatures en bois d'anciennes statues de Bouddha.

↑ The veranda upstairs serves as a living area for the bedrooms. The buffalo head on the table is partly made of wood and was found in an antique dealer's yard. • Die Veranda im Obergeschoss schließt sich als Wohnzimmer ans Schlafzimmer an. Die Eigentümerin erwarb den teilweise aus Holz gefertigten Büffelschädel auf dem Tisch von einem Antiquitätenhändler. • À l'étage supérieur, la véranda sert de salon commun aux chambres. Nikki Harrison a trouvé chez un antiquaire la tête de buffle

complétée par des pièces en bois qui trône sur la table.

→ Old green-painted cupboards add color to the gleaming white kitchen with stainless steel fittings. • Die alten grün gestrichenen Schränke setzen farbliche Akzente in der strahlend weißen Edelstahlküche. • Des buffets anciens peints en vert mettent une touche de couleur dans la cuisine d'un blanc étincelant aux accessoires en inox.

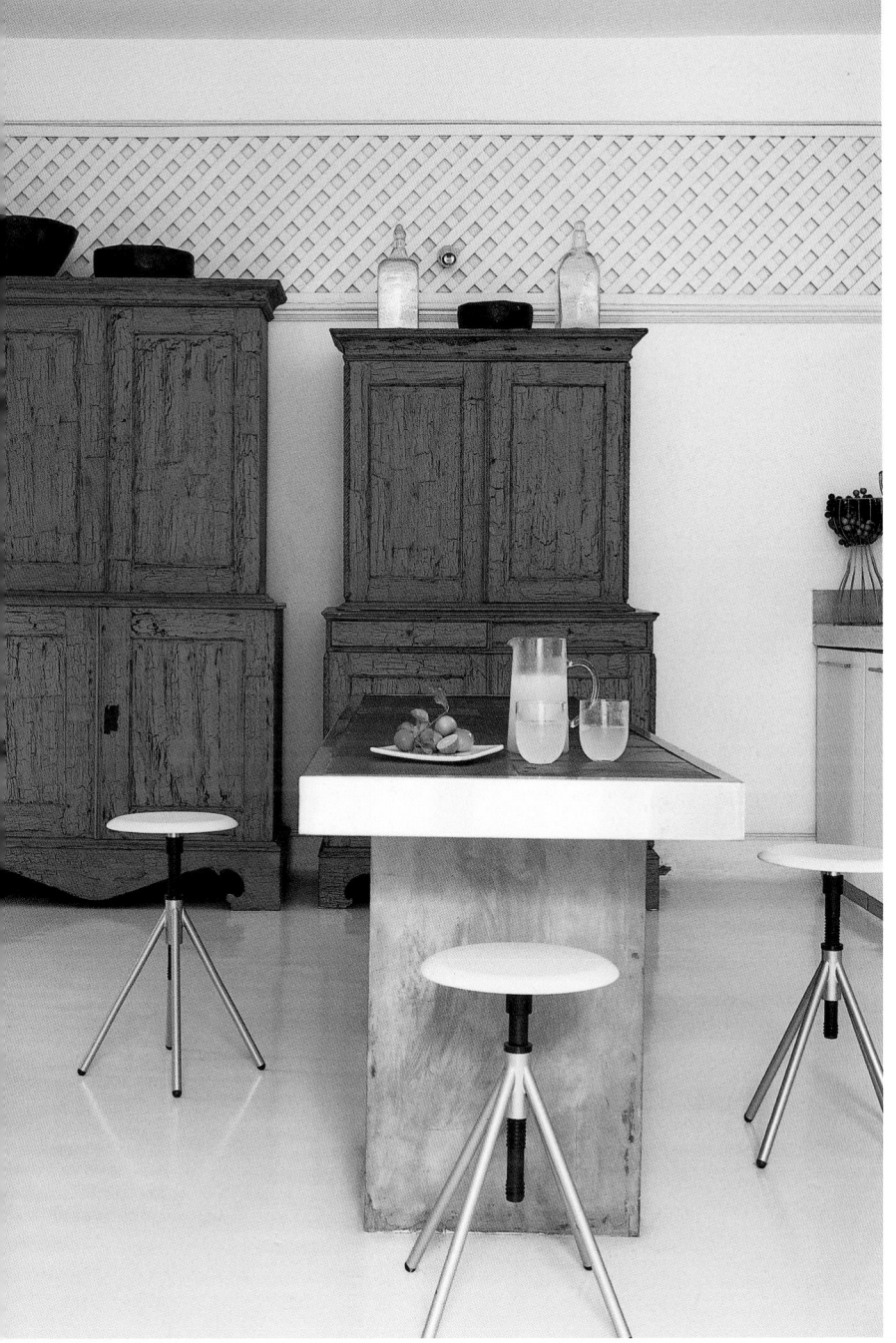

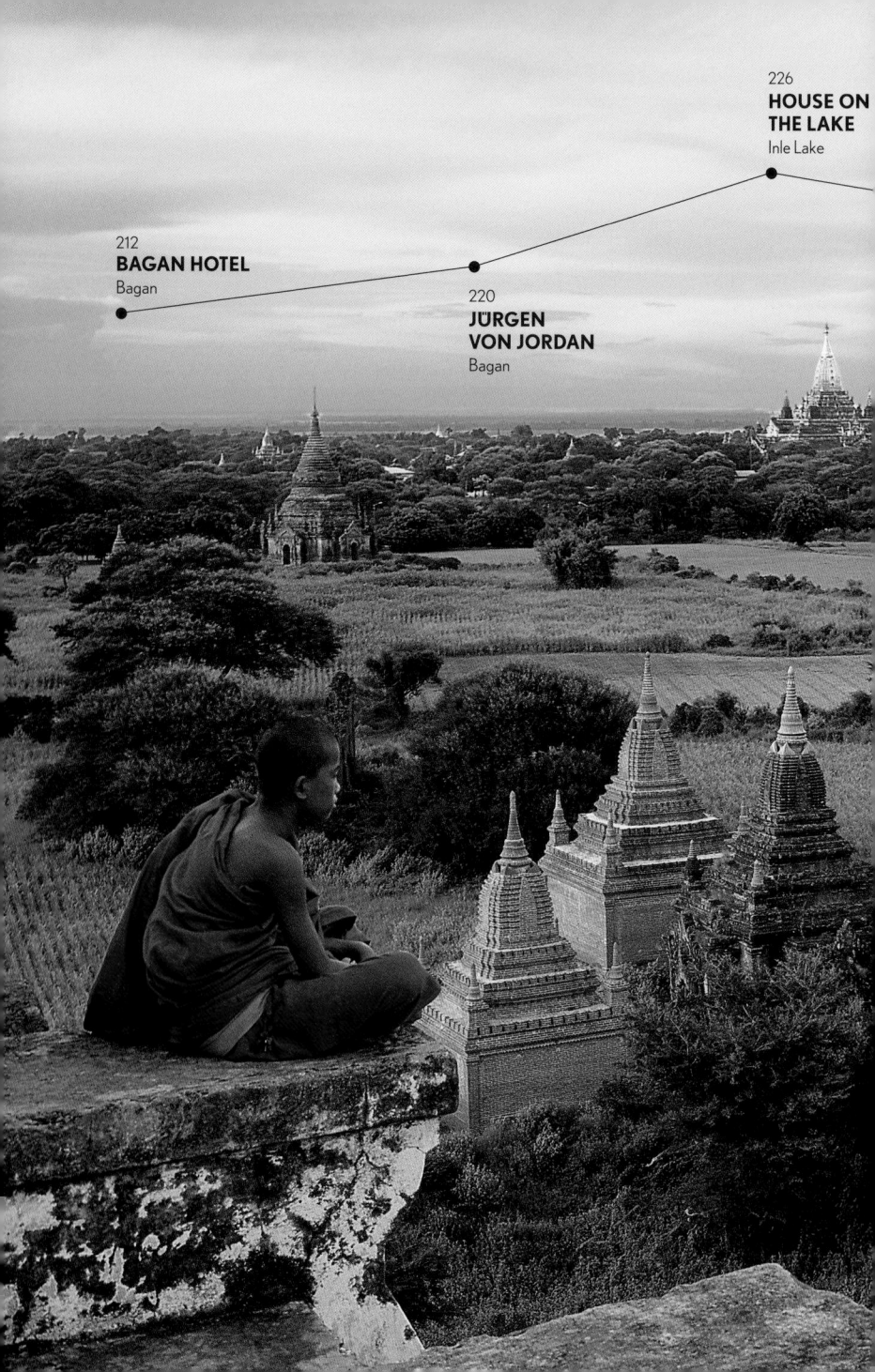

BAGAN HOTEL
Bagan

220
**JÜRGEN
VON JORDAN**
Bagan

226
**HOUSE ON
THE LAKE**
Inle Lake

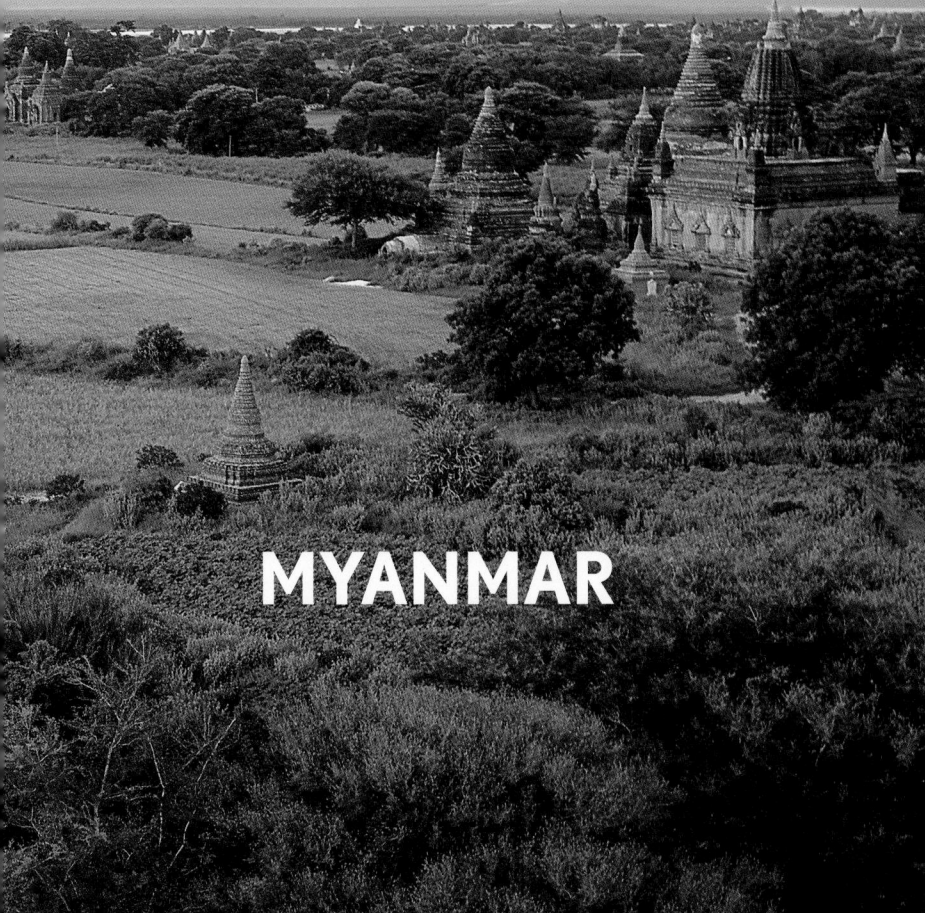

MYANMAR

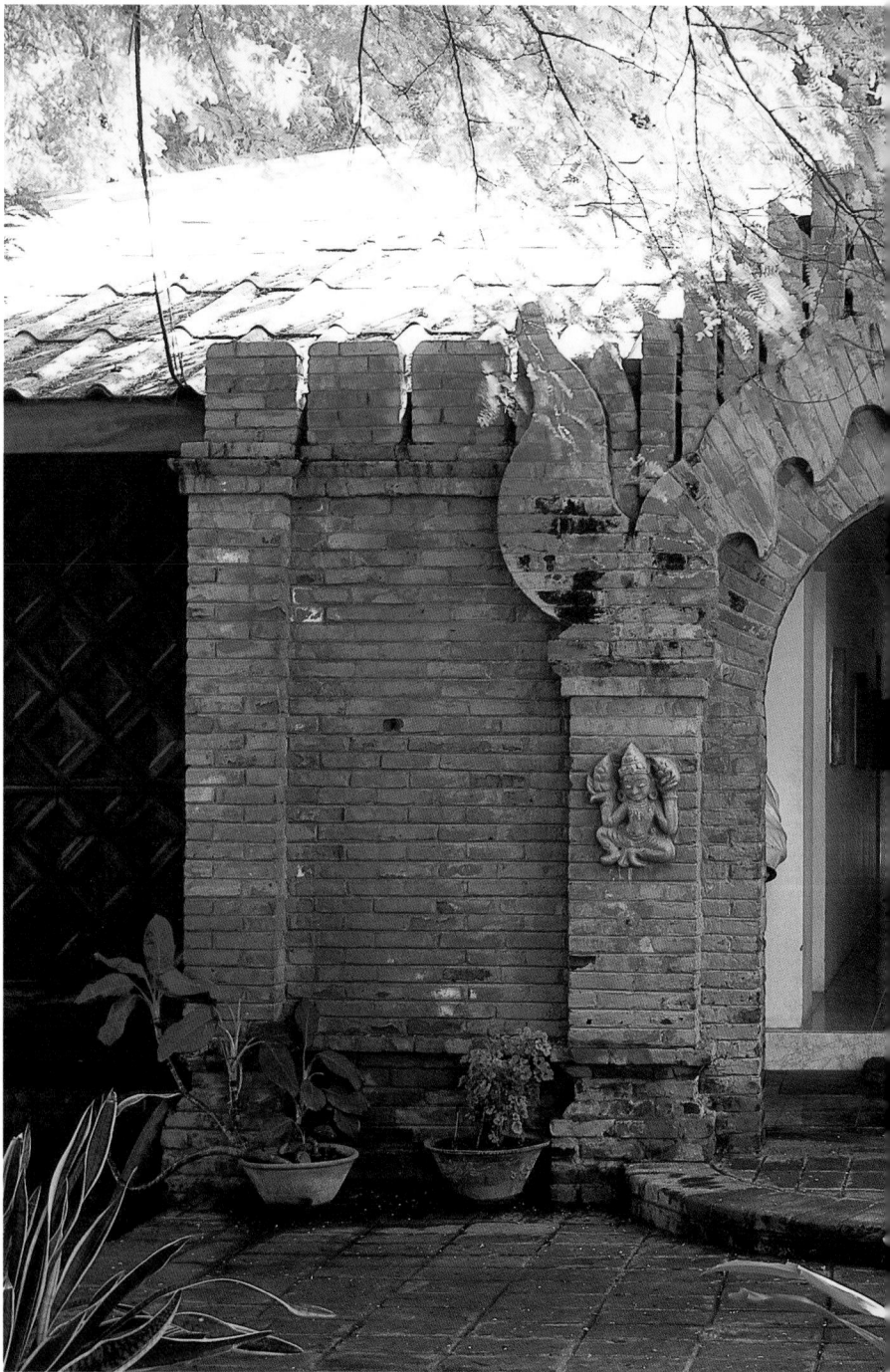

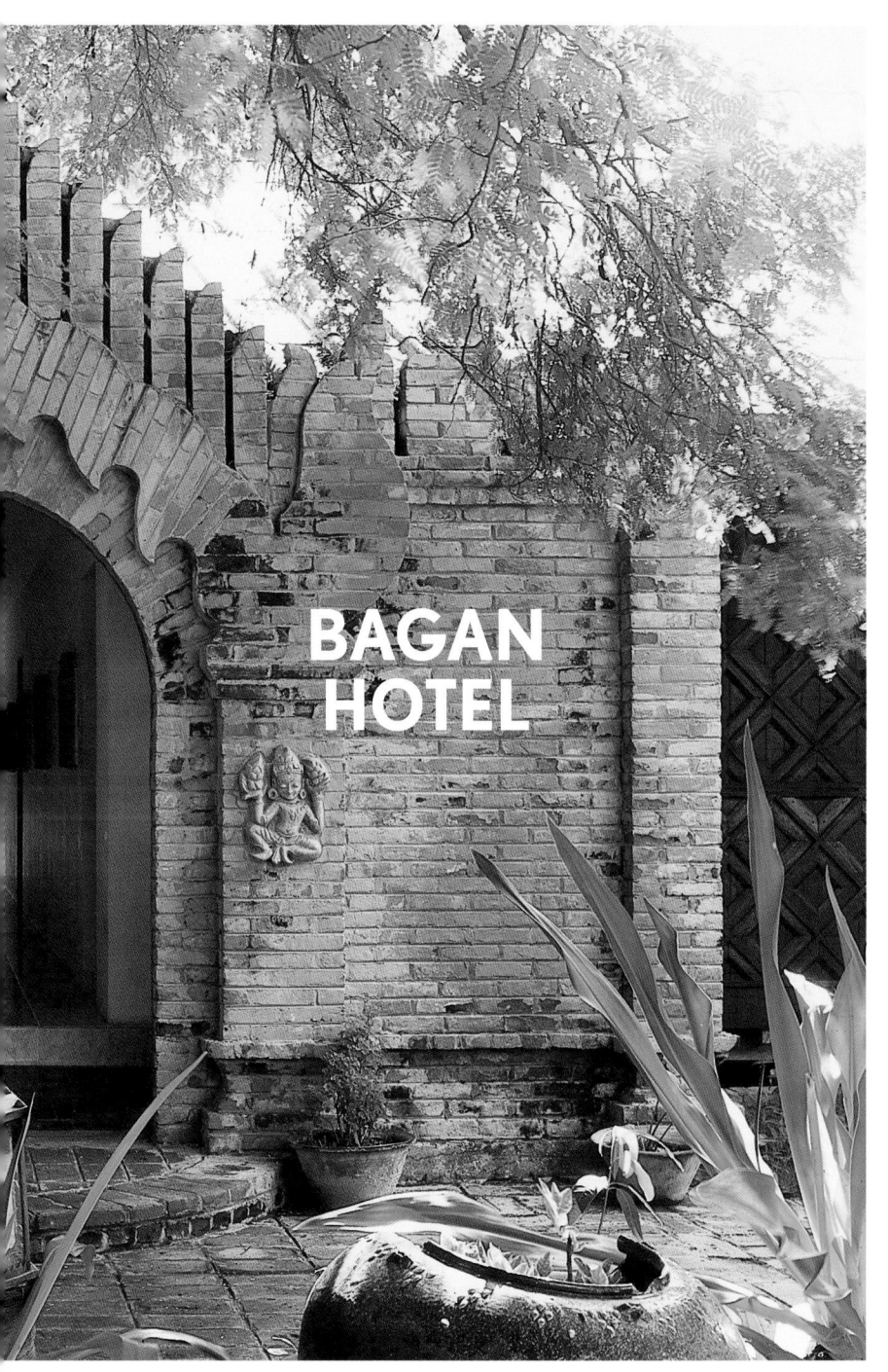

BAGAN
HOTEL

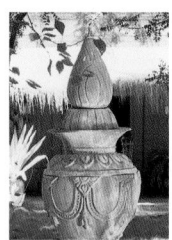

BAGAN HOTEL

BAGAN
MYANMAR

Cradled by the grand sweep of the Ayeyarwady River, the view across the plain of Bagan with its thousands of pagodas, one red-brick Buddhist temple after another, with the occasional white-washed or golden spire reaching heavenwards, is one of the heart-stopping sights of Asia. About a decade after ascending the throne of Bagan in 1044, King Anawrahta was converted to Theravada Buddhism by a young monk. Enthralled by the rationalism of the new doctrine, he embarked on its spread among his people, replacing the forms of animist worship that existed earlier. Some 13,000 pagodas were built between 1057 and 1287, when Bagan was invaded by Kublai Khan's army. More than 2,000 remain today, many of them covered with frescoes and images of the Buddha. There are so many pagodas in Bagan that two, in fact, are within the tree-shaded garden of the Bagan Hotel. Overlooking the river, the hotel was rebuilt in 1997 by Myanmar's leading architect U Myint Han, and commands a superb location in the old town.

Atemberaubend ist die Aussicht am großen Bogen des Ayeyarwady-Flusses – und eine der schönsten Asiens. Der Blick schweift über das Hochland von Bagan mit Tausenden von Pagoden und buddhistischen Tempeln in rotem Backstein sowie hier und da einem weiß gewaschenen oder goldenen Turm, der in den Himmel strebt. Ein junger Mönch über-zeugte König Anawrahta zehn Jahre nach dessen Krönung in Bagan im Jahr 1044 davon, zum Theravada-Buddhismus zu konvertieren. Der König war vom Rationalismus der neuen Lehre so begeistert, dass er sich für ihre Verbreitung im Volk einsetzte und animistische Elemente, die im Volk verbreitet waren, mit dem Buddhismus verband. Von 1057 bis 1287 – als das Heer des Kublai Khan Bagan eroberte – wurden 13 000 Pagoden gebaut, von denen 2000 mit Fresken und Bildern des Buddha erhalten blieben. In Bagan gibt es so viele Pagoden, dass schon allein im Baumschatten des Hotels Bagan zwei stehen. Das Hotel mit Blick auf den Fluss und in bester Lage in der Altstadt wurde 1997 von dem führenden birmanischen Architekten U Myint Han wieder aufgebaut.

Lovée dans le vaste lit de l'Irrawaddy, la plaine de Pagan est l'un des paysages les plus saisissants d'Asie, avec ses milliers de pagodes, ses temples bouddhiques se touchant presque et, çà et là, une flèche blanche ou en or, qui part à l'assaut des cieux. Une dizaine d'années après être monté sur le trône de Pagan en 1044, le roi Anawratha a été converti au bouddhisme theravada par un jeune moine. Séduit par le rationalisme de cette doctrine nouvelle, il a œuvré à sa diffu-sion parmi ses sujets, l'associant aux cultes animistes pratiqués jusqu'alors. C'est ainsi que 13 000 pagodes ont été construites entre 1057 et 1287, année de la prise de Pagan par les armées de Kubilaï Khan. Il en subsiste plus de 2 000, ornées pour certaines de fresques et de représentations du Bouddha. Deux des innombrables pagodes de Pagan se trouvent précisément dans le jardin ombragé du Bagan Hotel. Cet établissement dominant le fleuve et la vieille ville a été reconstruit en 1997 par l'architecte national vedette, U Myint Han.

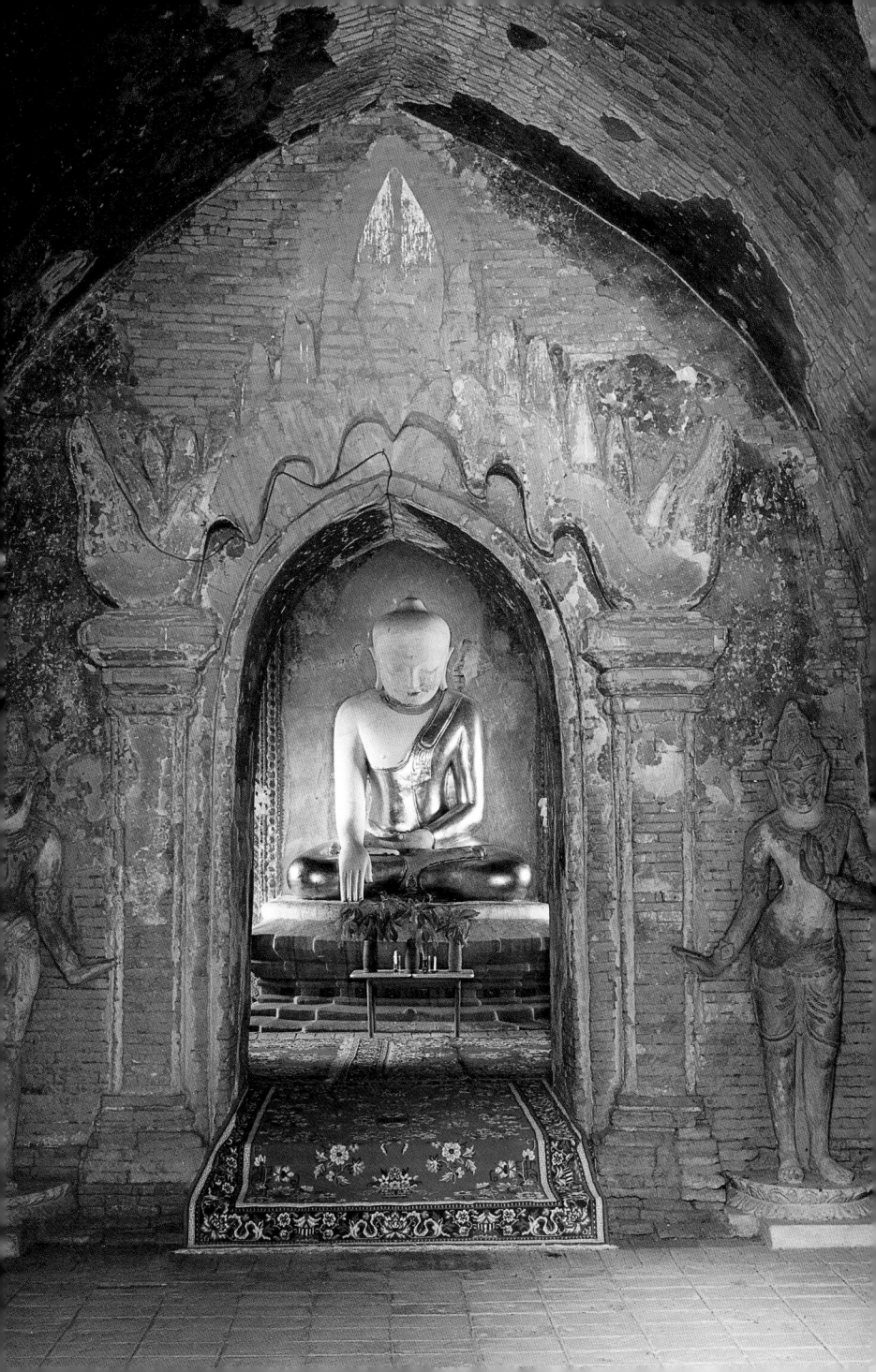

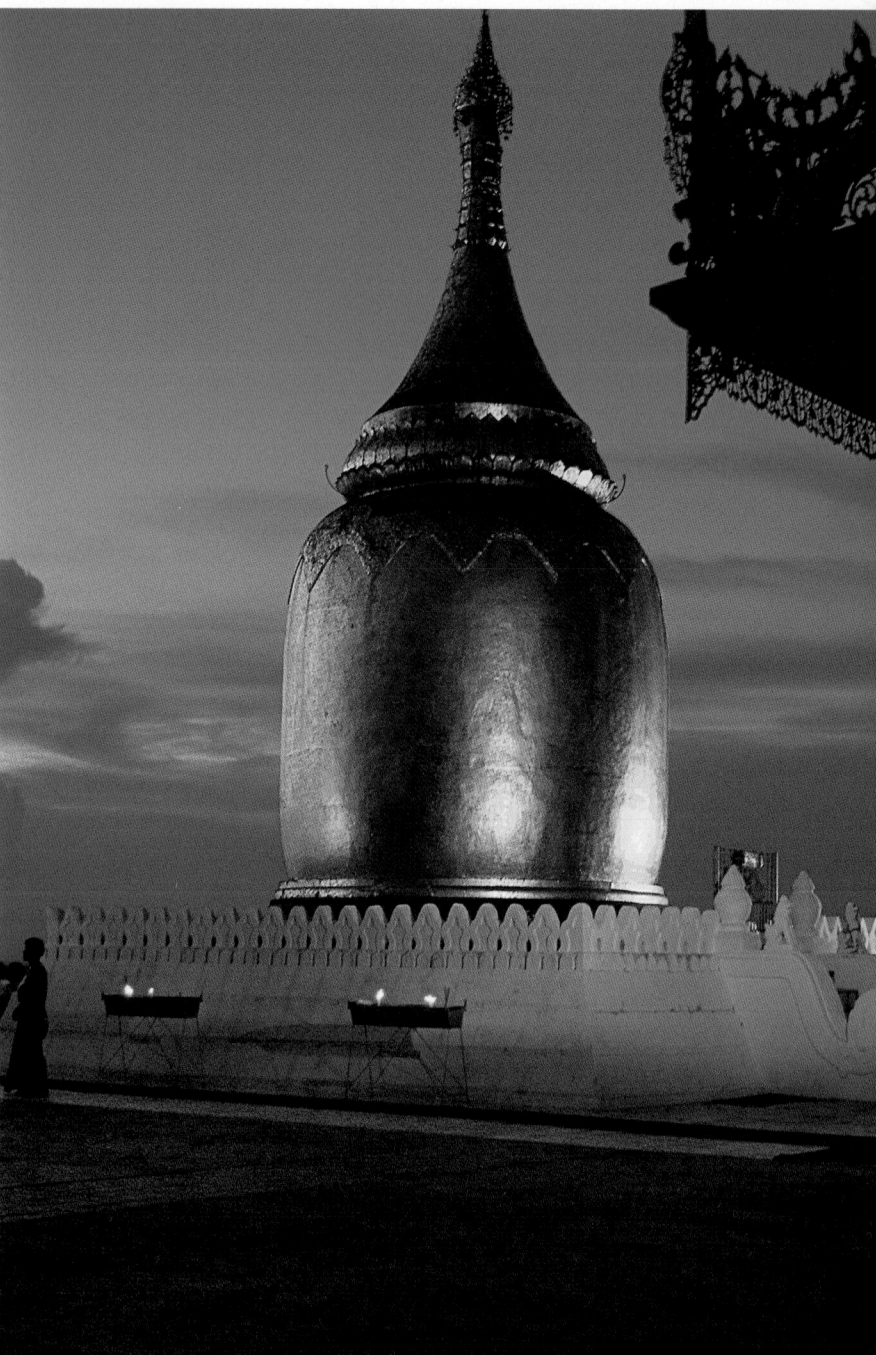

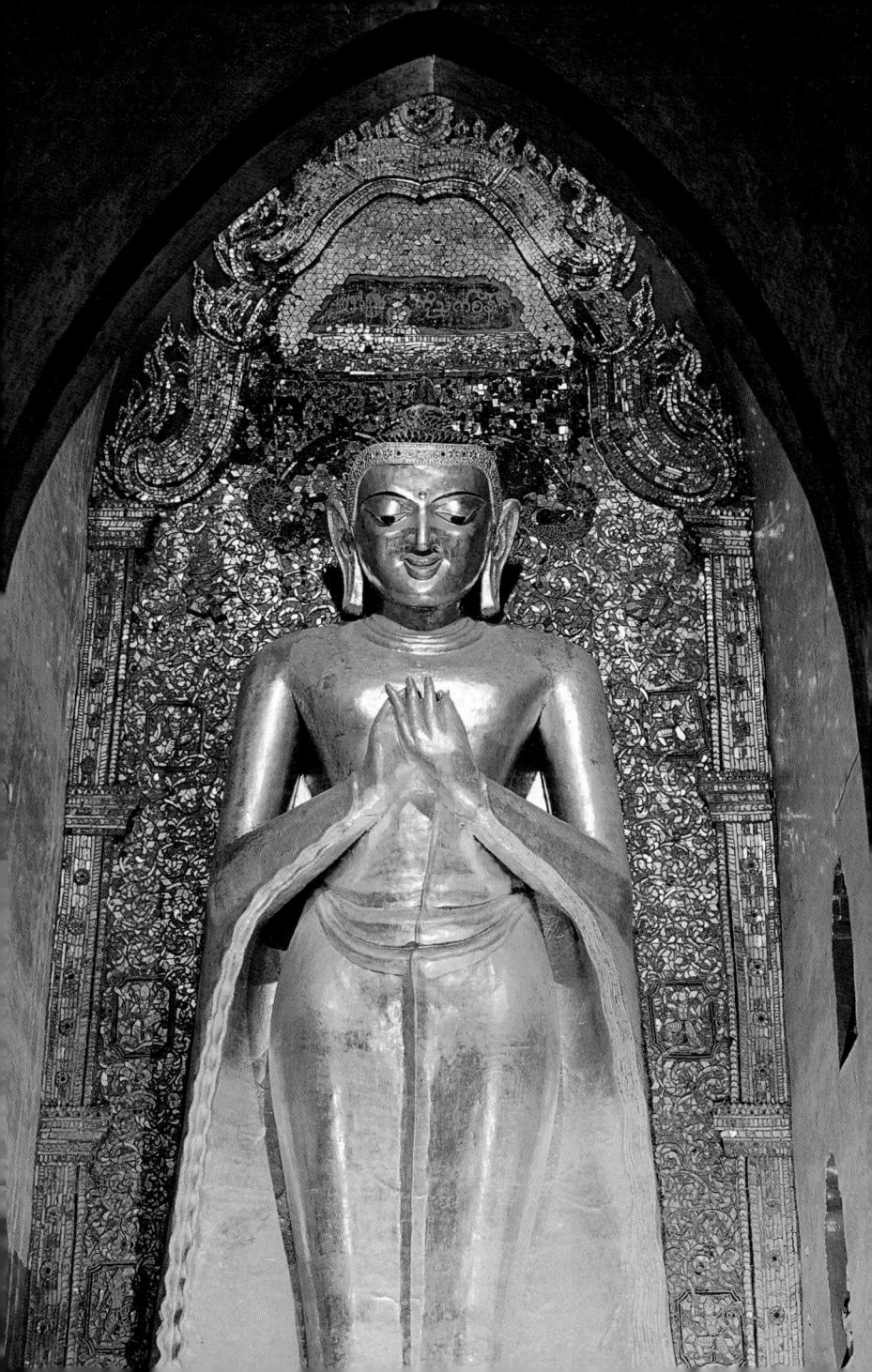

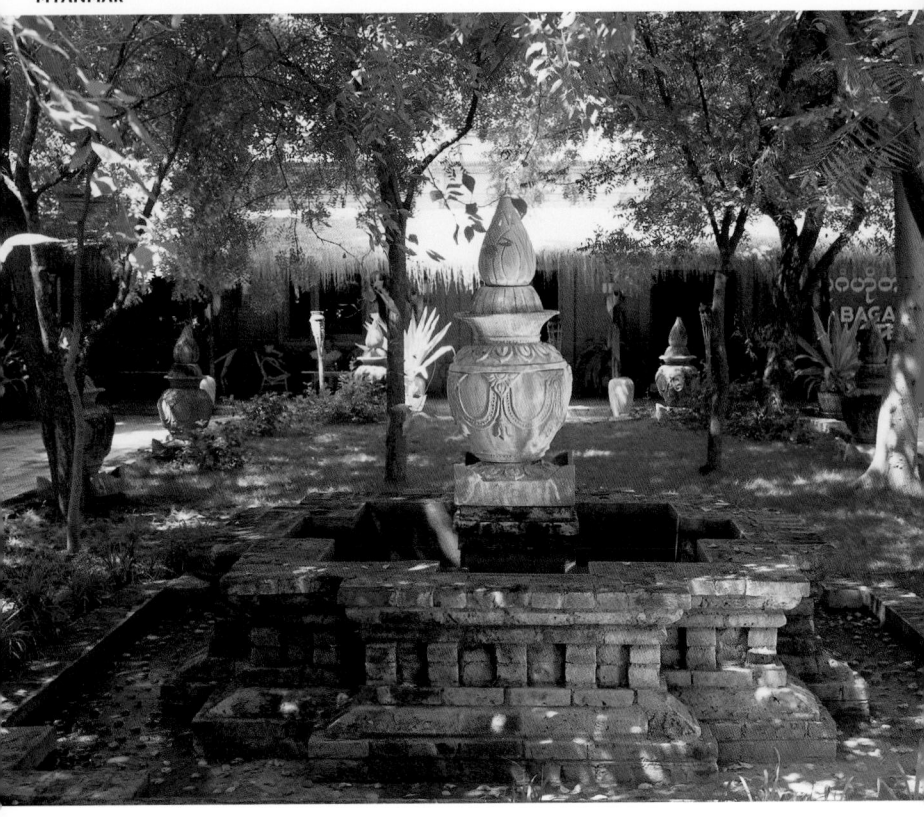

PP. 212–213 An ancient brick pagoda
and glazed Burmese jars near the hotel's
swimming pool. • Eine alte Pagode aus
Backstein und glasierte birmanische
Übertöpfe beim Swimmingpool des
Hotels. • Près de la piscine de l'hôtel,
une pagode ancienne en briques et
des jarres vernissées birmanes.

PP. 215–217 Golden stupas and
gilded images of the Buddha adorn
many of the pagodas scattered on the
riverside plain of Bagan. • Goldene
Stupas und vergoldete Buddhadarstel-
lungen schmücken viele der Pagoden,
die man verstreut im flussnahen Hochland von Bagan findet. • Des stupas
et des bouddhas dorés ornent nombre
des pagodes qui émaillent la plaine
fluviale de Pagan.

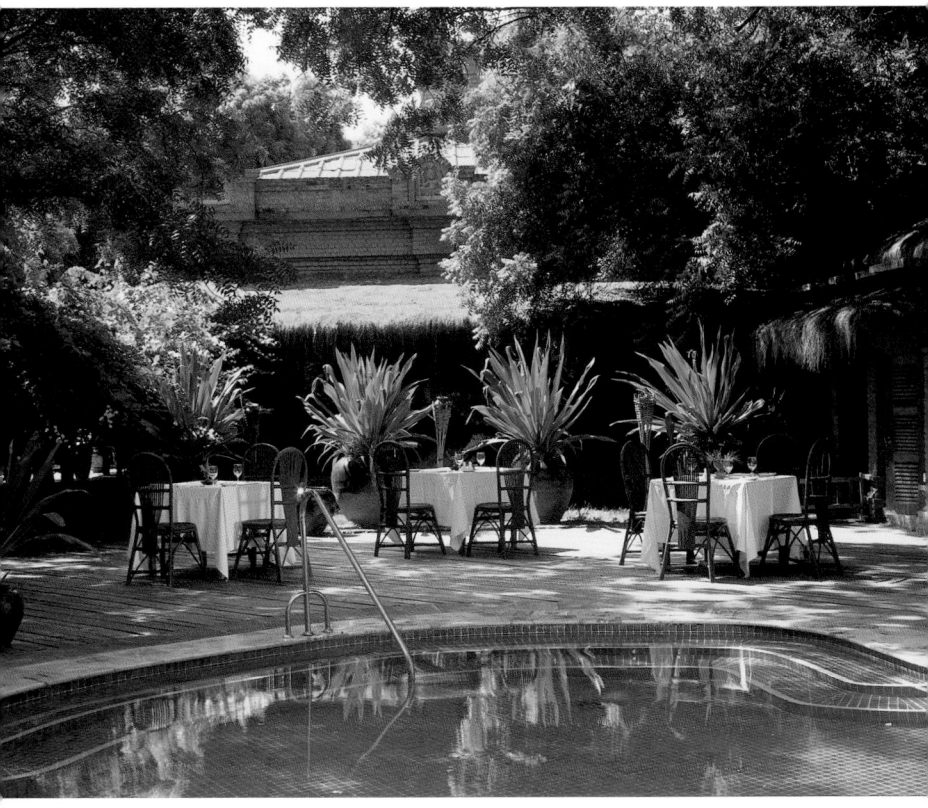

↖ Votive terracotta urns in the garden of the Bagan Hotel. • Votivurnen aus Terrakotta im Garten des Hotel Bagan. • Des urnes votives en terre cuite dans le jardin du Bagan Hotel.

↑ Jars near the hotel's swimming pool. • Übertöpfe am Swimmingpool des Hotels. • Des jarres vernissées birmanes.

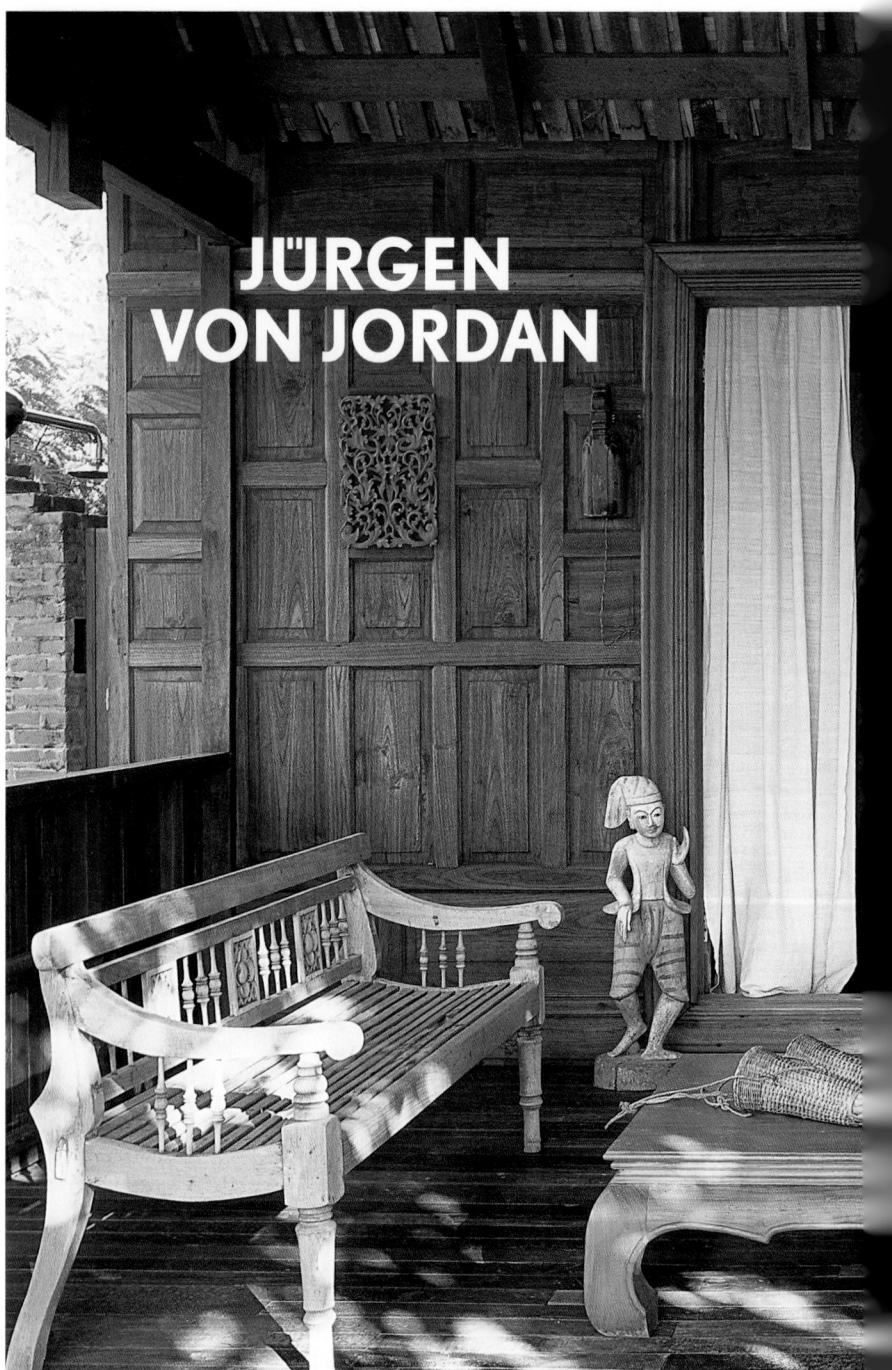

JÜRGEN
VON JORDAN

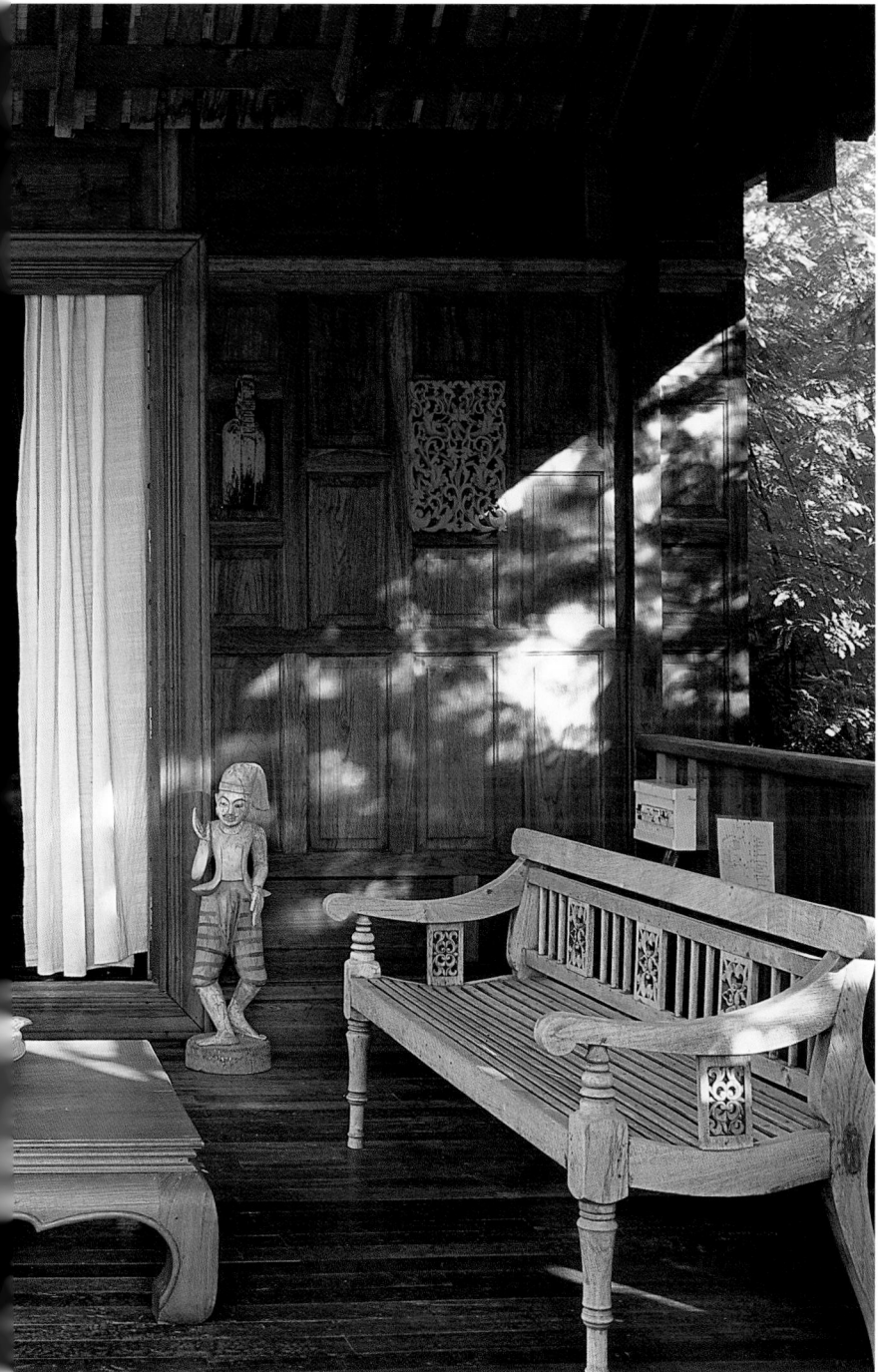

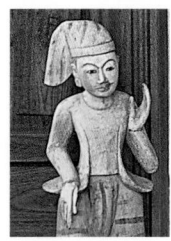

JÜRGEN VON JORDAN
BAGAN
MYANMAR

Jürgen von Jordan grew up in the countryside around the Bavarian Alps. Much of his working life was spent in Bangkok, running a company that sold heavy machinery. Business first took him to Yangon in 1970 and from that visit he was bewitched by Myanmar. For von Jordan, as the cliché goes, there was no looking back. In 1991, many inhabitants of the old town were shifted to a wasteland called New Bagan. Fearing the presence of "bad spirits" many residents refused to move. In partnership with a Burmese friend, von Jordan bought a plot cheaply by the Ayeyarwady River and landscaped a garden. The original bamboo house with verandas on three sides was extended with a new structure in teak. He found gifted local masons and carpenters to create his "sunset garden". Since 1995, von Jordan has run a charitable foundation from here that supports a series of village schools, orphanages and provincial hospitals. He lives here in the dry winter months, enjoying his "quiet refuge in a little-known paradise".

Jürgen von Jordan wuchs in den Bayerischen Alpen auf. In Bangkok leitete er lange Jahre ein Unternehmen für Maschineneinrichtung. Seit seiner ersten Geschäftsreise nach Yangon im Jahr 1970 ist er von Myanmar geradezu verzaubert. Es gab schlichtweg keinen Weg zurück. 1991 sollten viele Bewohner der Altstadt in eine Einöde namens Neu-Bagan umgesiedelt werden. Viele Menschen fürchteten jedoch böse Geister und weigerten sich umzuziehen. Gemeinsam mit einem birmanischen Freund kaufte von Jordan ein preiswertes Grundstück am Ayeyarwady-Fluss und legte dort einen Garten an. Das vorhandene Bambushaus mit Veranden an drei Seiten wurde um einen Neubau aus Teak erweitert. Der Besitzer beauftragte talentierte ortsansässige Maurer und Schreiner mit der Gestaltung seines „Gartens des Sonnenuntergangs". Von diesem Domizil aus leitet von Jordan seit 1995 eine gemeinnützige Stiftung, die Dorfschulen, Waisen- und Krankenhäuser in der Provinz unterstützt. In den trockenen Wintermonaten genießt er hier sein „stilles Refugium in einem Paradies, das nur wenige kennen".

Jürgen von Jordan, originaire des Alpes bavaroises, a passé la majeure partie de sa vie active à la tête d'une entreprise spécialisée dans la vente d'équipements lourds. Ses affaires l'ont amené à Yangon, qui s'appelait alors Rangoon, en 1970. Il est aussitôt tombé sous le charme du Myanmar et, comme c'est très souvent le cas, n'a jamais envisagé de retour en arrière. En 1991, de nombreux habitants de la vieille ville devaient être déplacés vers les terres en friche de la Nouvelle Pagan, mais ils ont souvent refusé de s'y installer à cause des « esprits malveillants » qui pourraient y rôder. Avec un ami birman, von Jordan a ainsi pu acheter pour une bouchée de pain une propriété sur les rives de l'Irrawaddy. Il a chargé d'excellents ouvriers et artisans locaux d'agrandir le bâtiment d'origine en bambou doté de vérandas sur trois côtés en lui adjoignant une construction en teck, et de créer un « jardin du coucher de soleil ». Depuis 1995, la maison héberge les bureaux de l'association caritative dirigée par von Jordan, association qui apporte son soutien financier à divers orphelinats, écoles de village et hôpitaux provinciaux. Von Jordan vit ici pendant les mois secs d'hiver, profitant de son « refuge tranquille dans un paradis méconnu ».

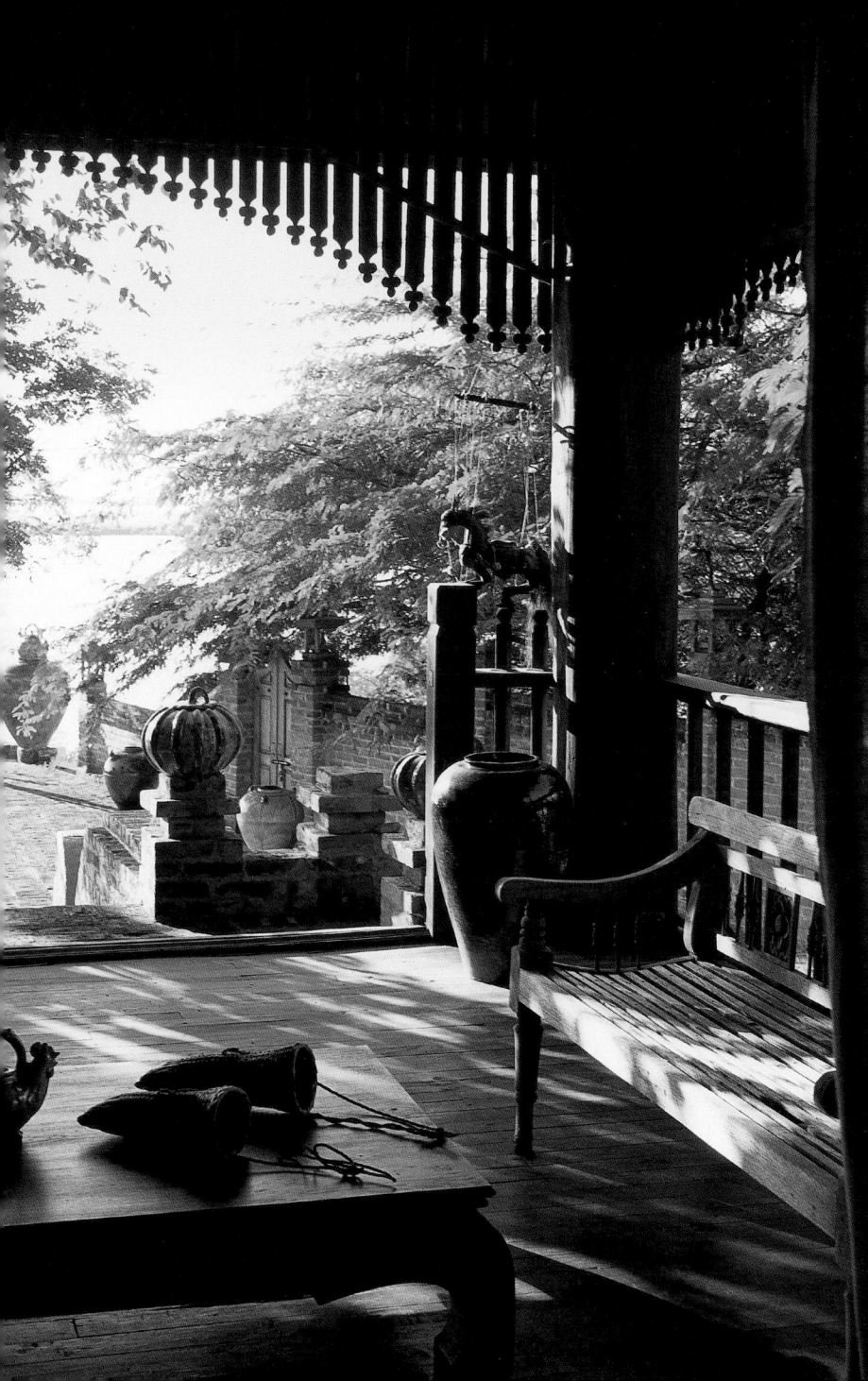

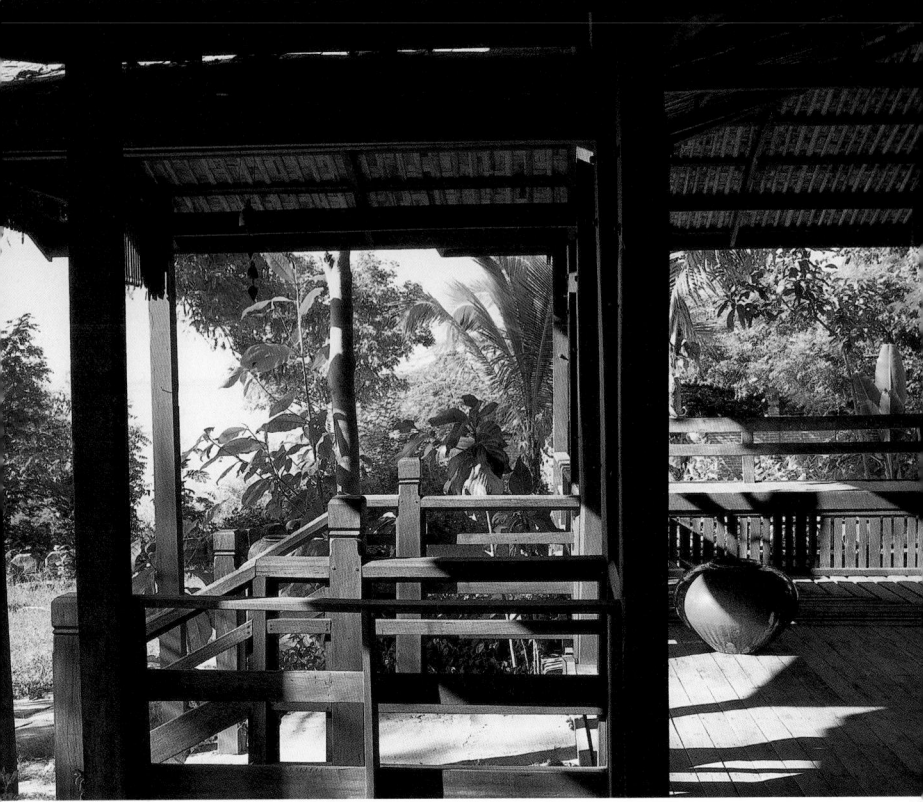

PP. 220-221 The veranda is the main living area, designed as part of the garden. • Meist findet das Leben auf der Veranda statt, die in den Garten integriert ist. • Conçue comme partie du jardin, la véranda est la pièce principale.

↑ Teak posts support the stairways and roof. • Teakholzpfosten stützen die Treppe und das Dach. • Des poteaux de teck soutiennent l'escalier et le toit.

→ A Burmese puppet of a horse hangs in the veranda. • Eine birmanische Pferdemarionette hängt auf der Veranda. • Une marionnette birmane suspendue au plafond de la véranda.

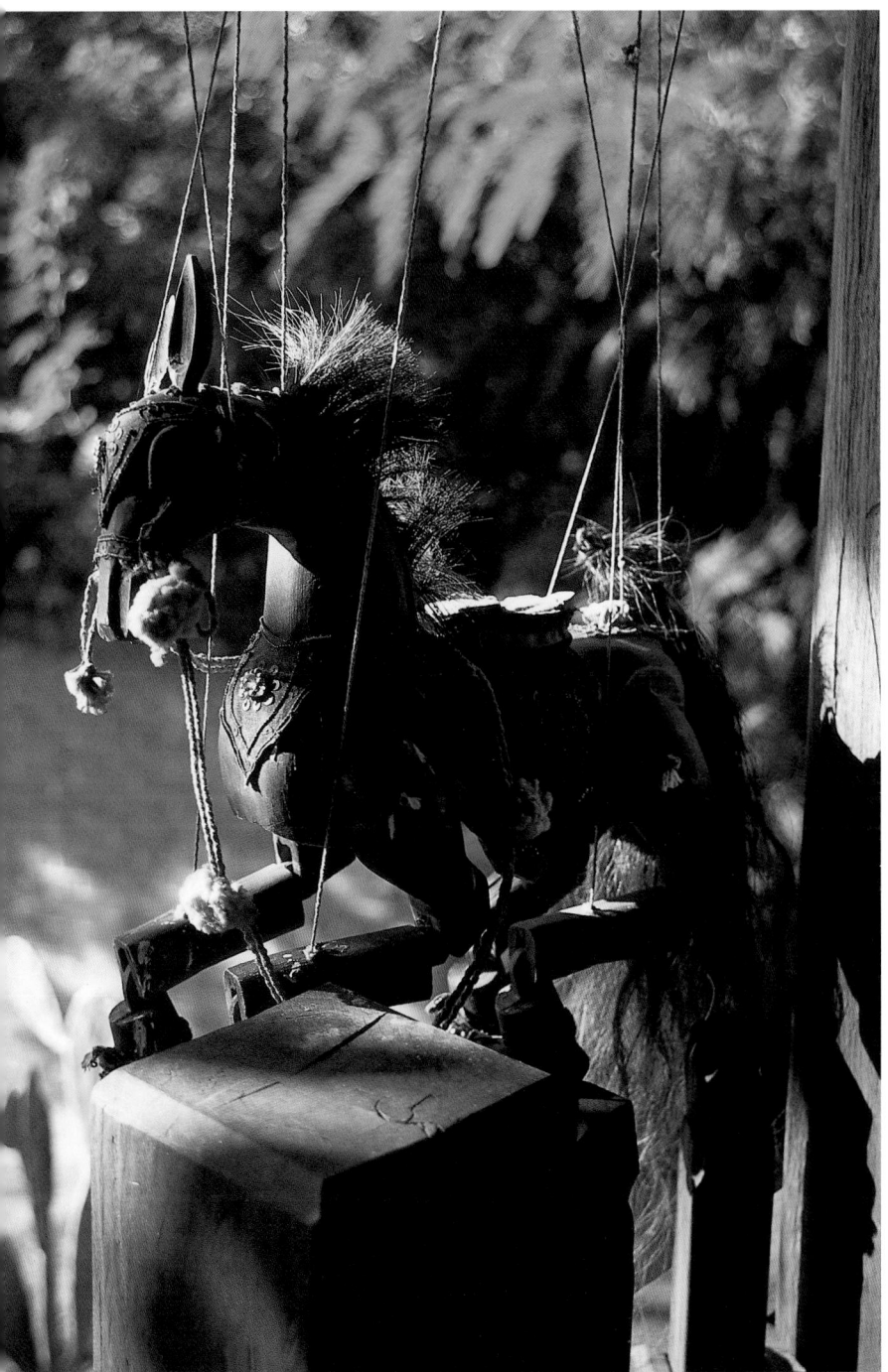

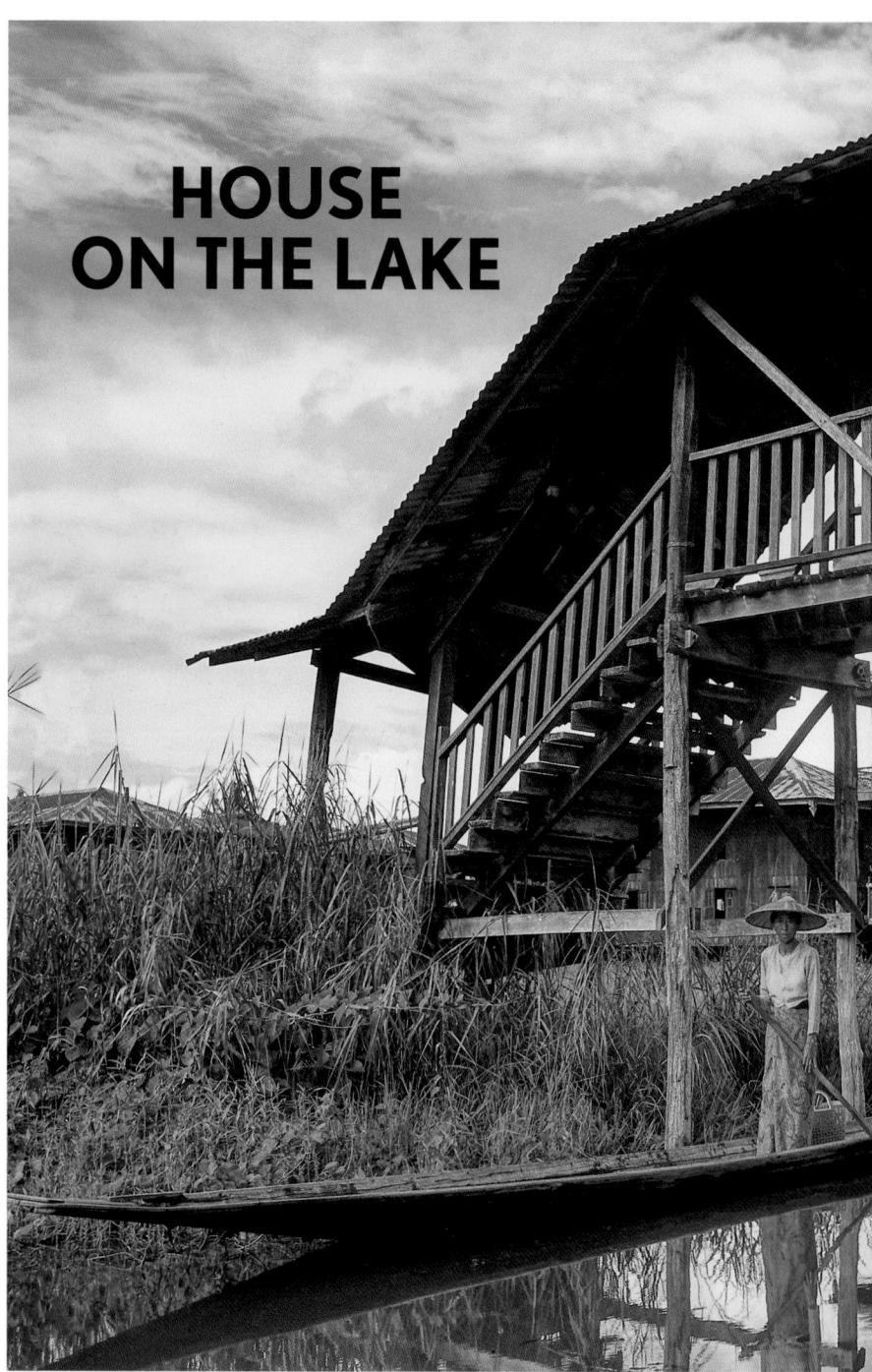

HOUSE
ON THE LAKE

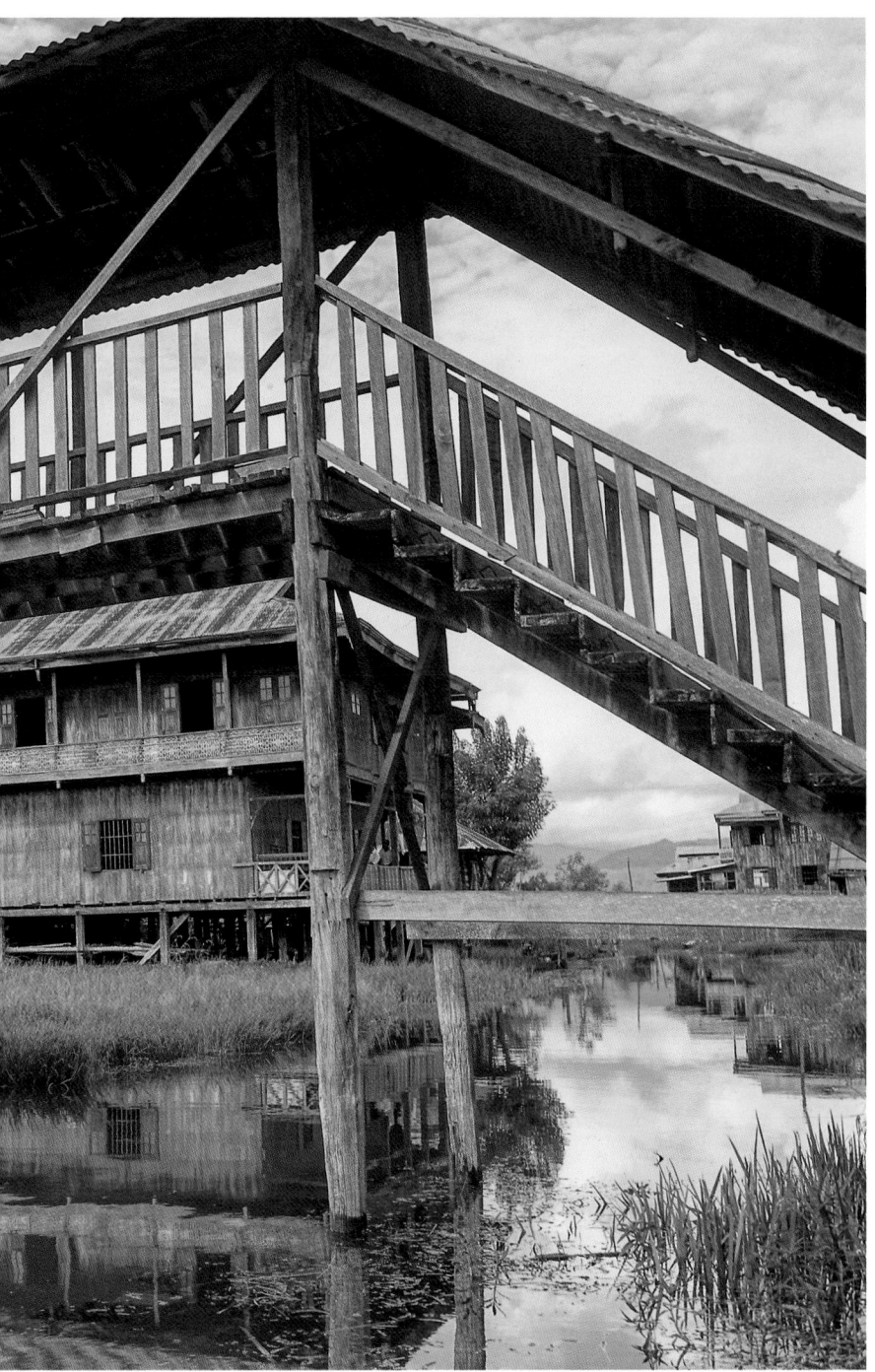

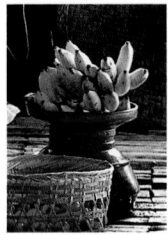

HOUSE ON THE LAKE
INLE LAKE
MYANMAR

When the mists come rolling down the nearby mountains, the flat, shallow expanse of Inle Lake is wrapped in mystery. Here the Intha tribe – *intha* means "sons of the lake" – have evolved an aquatic culture uniquely their own. They build homes on stilts and cultivate floating vegetable gardens, developed from a combination of silt and tangled growths of water hyacinth. The main form of transport is boat; Intha fishermen propel their canoes by twisting a leg around a single oar. They are a prosperous, industrious people: farming, fishing, weaving, cheroot-making and metalwork are common occupations. In the village of In-Chan, U San Khin and Daw Kyin Mee, live in an old house. Their only son died of jaundice leaving behind a widow and son; his photographs are among their treasured memories. For generations the family owned rice paddies in the area. But the landholding has diminished and yields have shrunk. The quiet simplicity of their home holds up a mirror to the dignified survival of a remarkable culture.

Der Nebel aus den nahen Bergen legt sich wie ein geheimnisvoller Schleier auf die ausgedehnte Fläche des Inle-Sees. Der Stamm der Intha – *intha* bedeutet „Söhne des Wassers" – hat hier eine einzigartige Wasserkultur geschaffen. Sie wohnen in Pfahlbauten und bauen Gemüse in schwimmenden Gärten an, die sie aus einer Mischung aus Schlick und ineinander verschlungenen Wasserhyazinthen herstellen. Boote dienen als Haupttransportmittel, und die Inthafischer betätigen das Ruder ihres Kanus, indem sie ein Bein darum schlingen. Die Wirtschaft dieses wohlhabenden, fleißigen Volkes umfasst Ackerbau, Fischerei, Weberei, Metallarbeiten sowie die Herstellung von Zigarillos. U San Khin und Daw Kyin Mee wohnen in einem alten Haus im Dorf In-Chan. Ihr einziger Sohn starb an Gelbsucht und hinterließ eine Frau und einen Sohn – Fotos halten die Erinnerung an sie lebendig. Seit Generationen besitzt die Familie Reisfelder in der Gegend, aber der Grundbesitz hat sich vermindert, und auch die Erträge wurden geringer. Die stille Einfachheit ihres Hauses spiegelt das würdevolle Überleben einer bemerkenswerten Kultur wider.

Lorsque les brumes dévalent les pentes des montagnes voisines, les eaux étendues et peu profondes du lac Inle sont enveloppées de mystère. Les Inthas (« fils du lac ») vivent ici dans des maisons sur pilotis. Les Inthas pratiquent des cultures maraîchères uniques en leur genre sur des jardins flottants – en fait de larges bandes de jacinthes d'eau et autres herbes aquatiques qu'ils ont recouvertes de boue et de terre avant de les ensemencer. Les pêcheurs se déplacent surtout en canoë, et ont une manière bien à eux de manœuvrer en enroulant une jambe autour de la rame. Les Inthas sont un peuple travailleur et prospère qui tire le gros de ses revenus de l'agriculture, de la pêche, du tissage, de la fabrication de cigarillos et du travail des métaux. U San Khin et Daw Kyin Mee habitent une vieille maison dans le village de In-Cahn. Leurs souvenirs les plus chers sont les photographies de leur fils aîné décédé de la jaunisse en laissant une veuve et un enfant. Cette famille de riziculteurs depuis des générations a vu ses terres rétrécir et ses revenus diminuer. La simplicité paisible de leur foyer renvoie l'image de la survivance dans la dignité d'une civilisation remarquable.

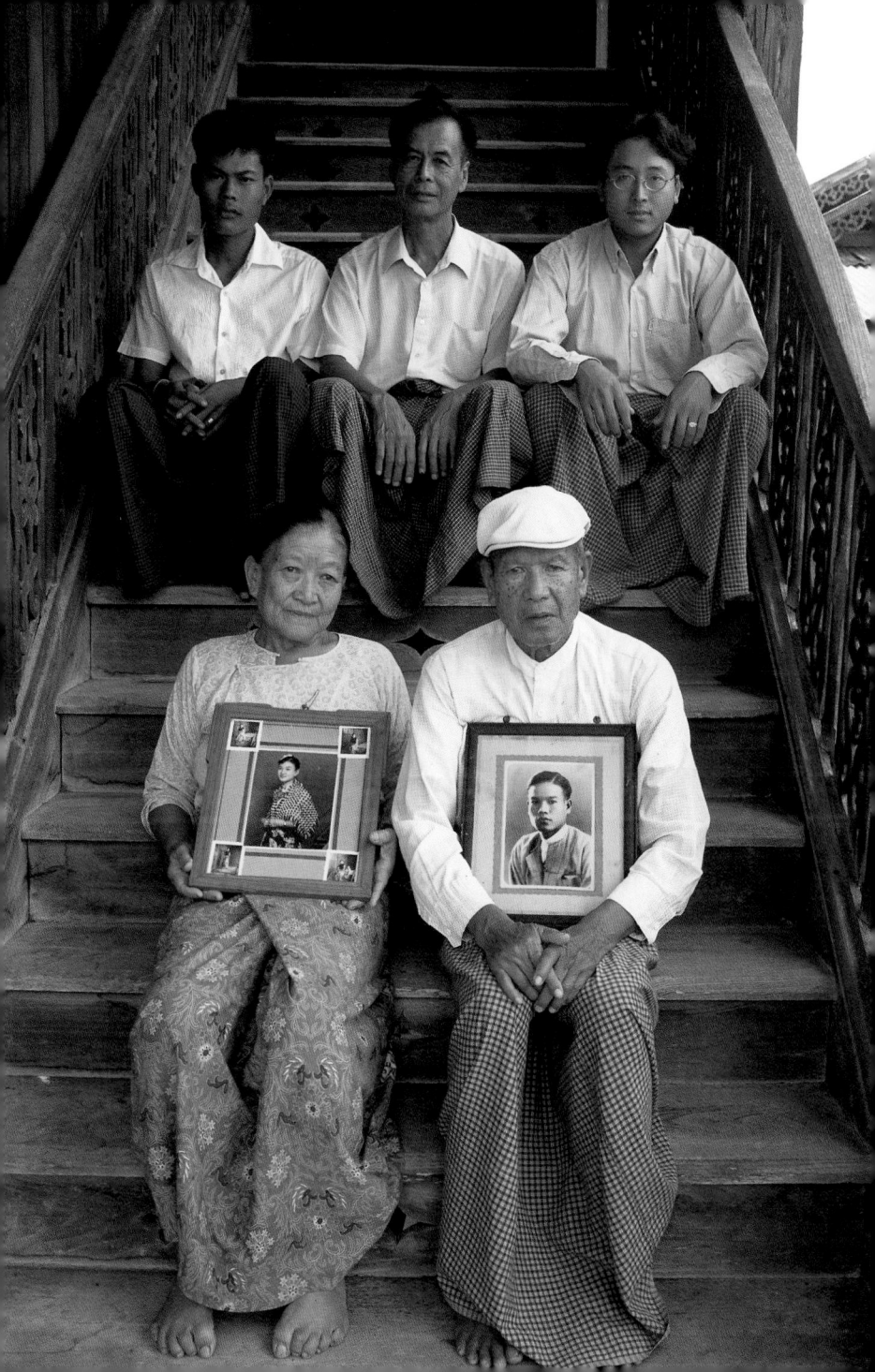

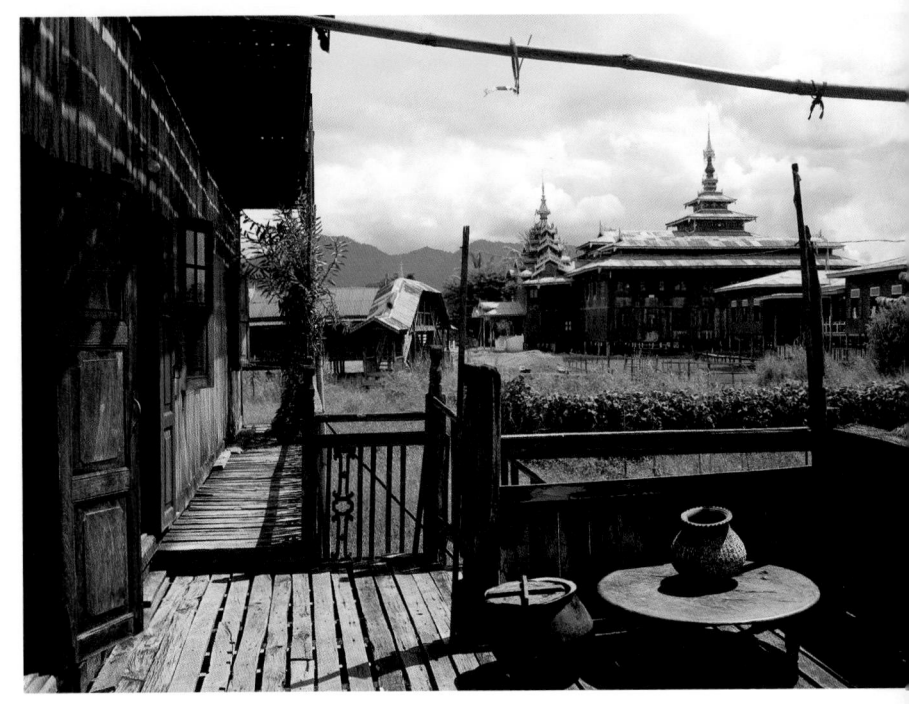

PP. 226-227 A covered wooden bridge links settlements on the lake. • Eine überdachte Holzbrücke verbindet die Siedlungen am See. • Un pont de bois couvert relie entre elles les maisons du lac.

↑ Vegetable gardens cover parts of Inle Lake where the Intha built homes on stilts. • In der Nähe der Intha-Pfahlbauten ist der Inle-See häufig mit schwimmenden Gemüsegärten bepflanzt. • Les cultures maraîchères recouvrent une partie du lac Inle sur

lequel les Inthas ont construit des maisons sur pilotis.

→ A teak staircase leads to the two-story house. • Eine Treppe aus Teakholz führt zu dem zweistöckigen Haus. • L'escalier en teck de la maison à deux étages.

P. 232 Wooden shelving, glazed terracotta urns for drinking water and split bamboo baskets are used for storage in the kitchen. • Die Holzregale, Trinkgefäße aus glasierter Terrakotta und

Bambuskörbe in der Küche dienen der Lagerung. • Dans la cuisine, les denrées sont stockées sur des étagères en bois, dans des urnes en terre cuite et des paniers en bambou fendu.

P. 233 The coal stove is on a platform to reduce the risk of fire in a wooden house. • Der Kohleofen steht erhöht, um das Brandrisiko in dem Holzhaus zu verringern. • Le poêle à charbon est surélevé pour limiter les risques d'incendie.

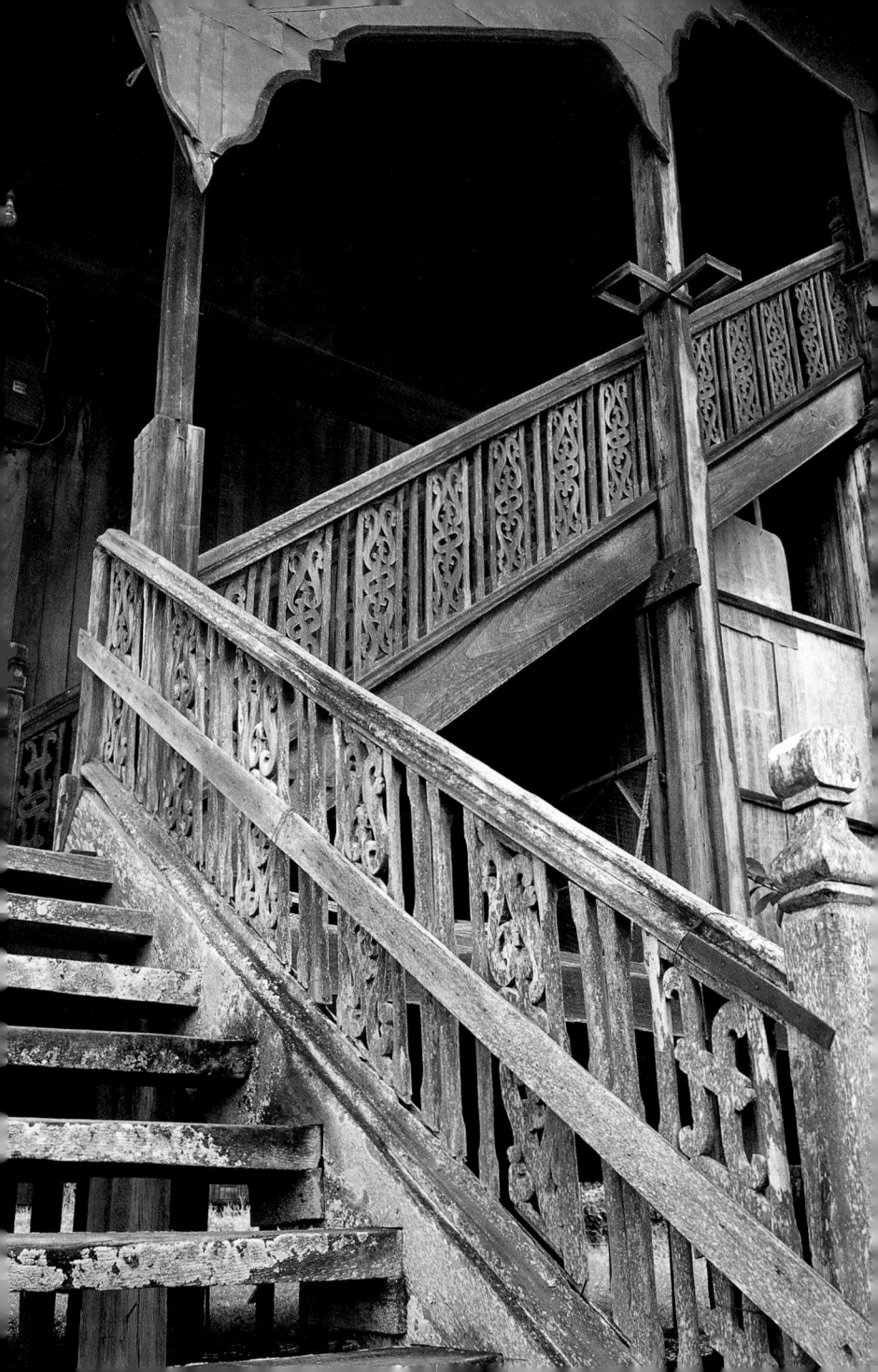

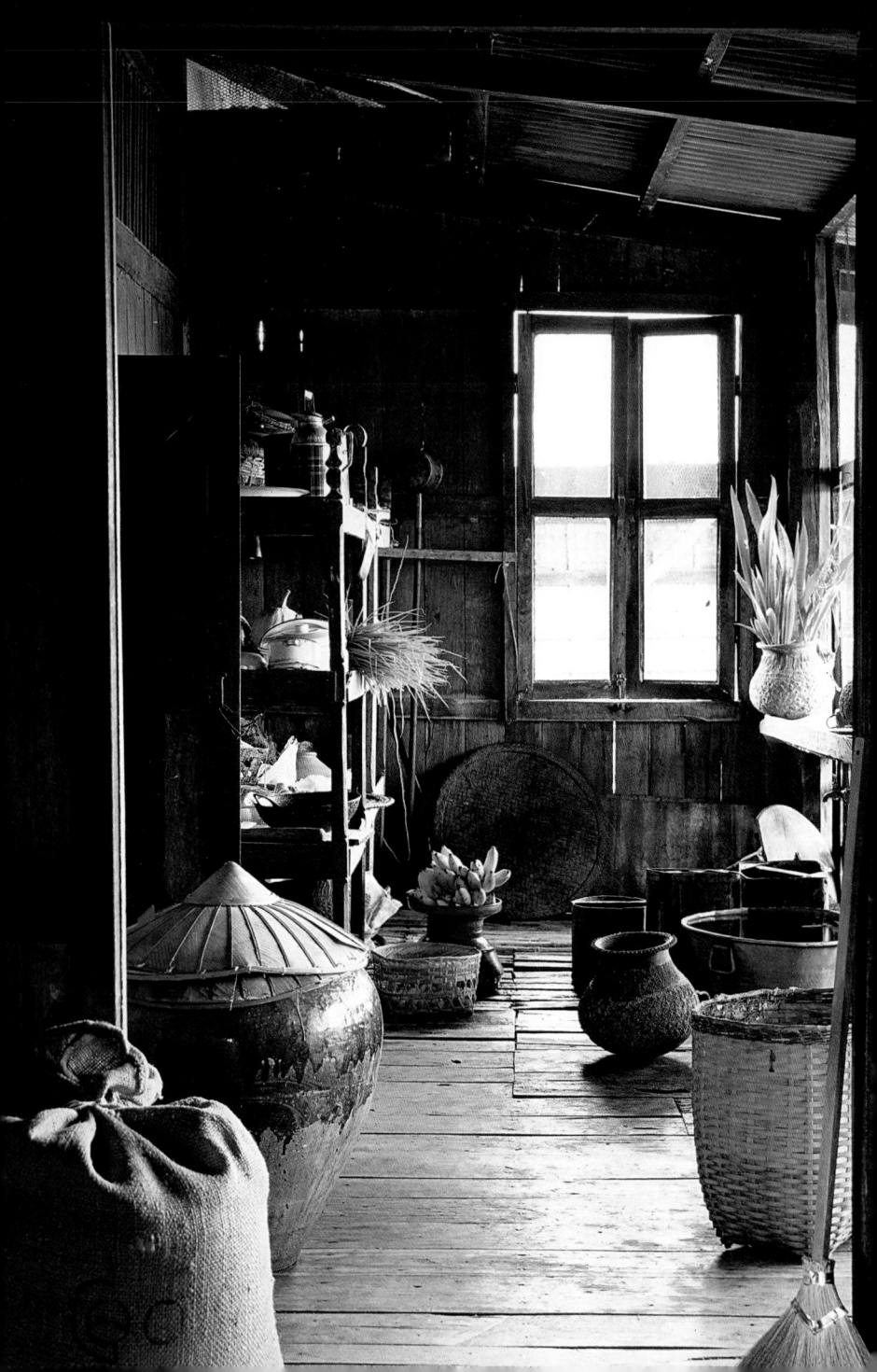

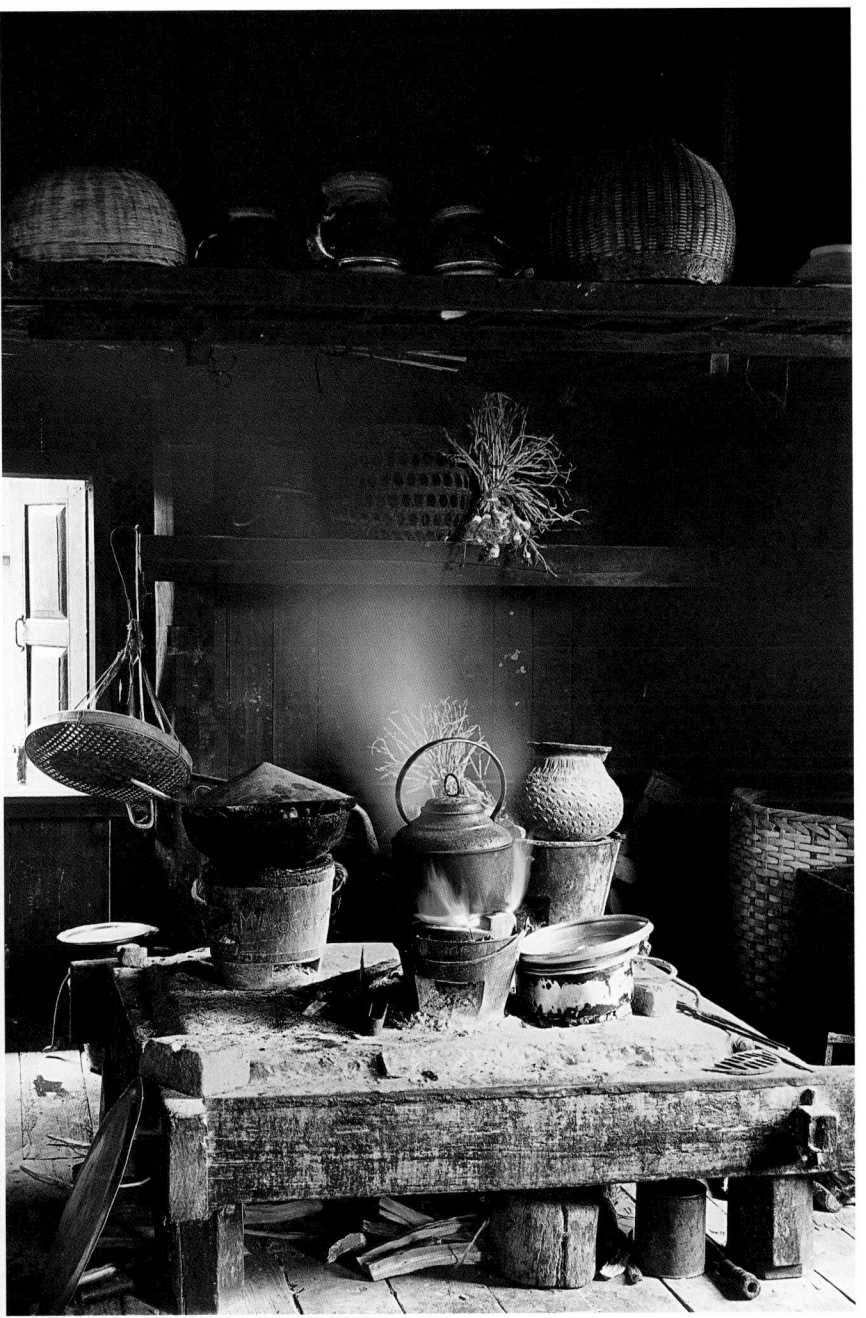

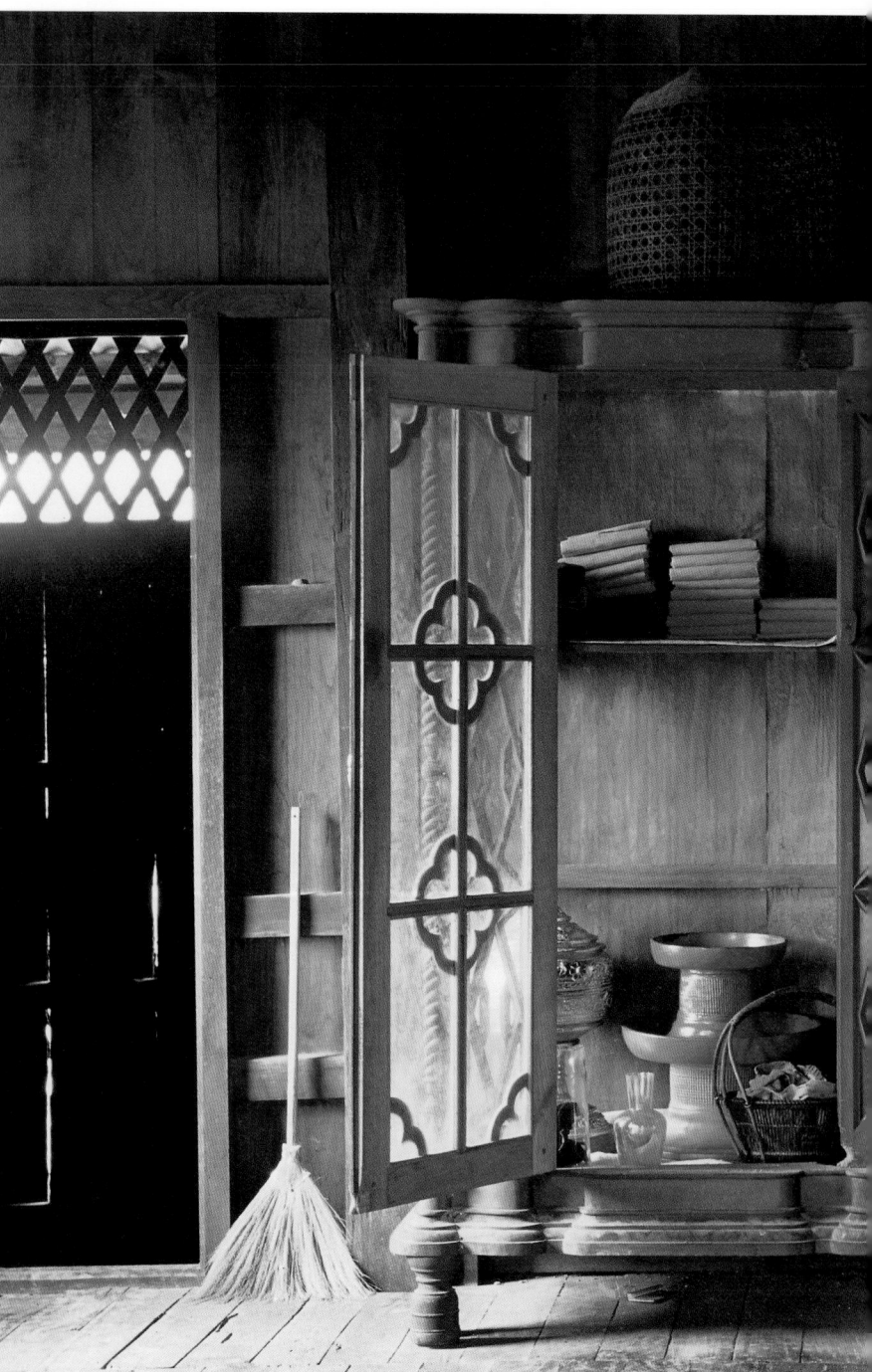

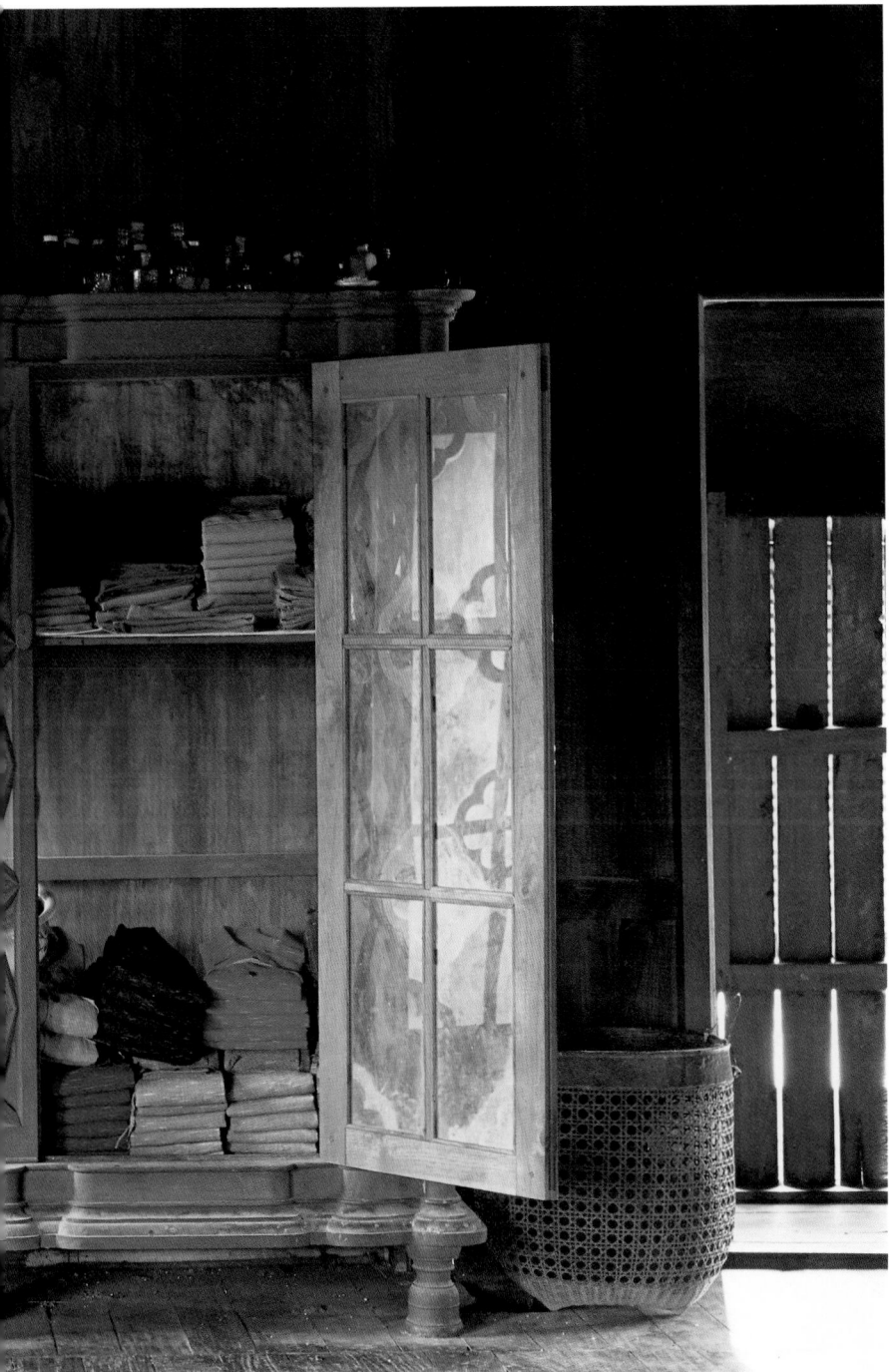

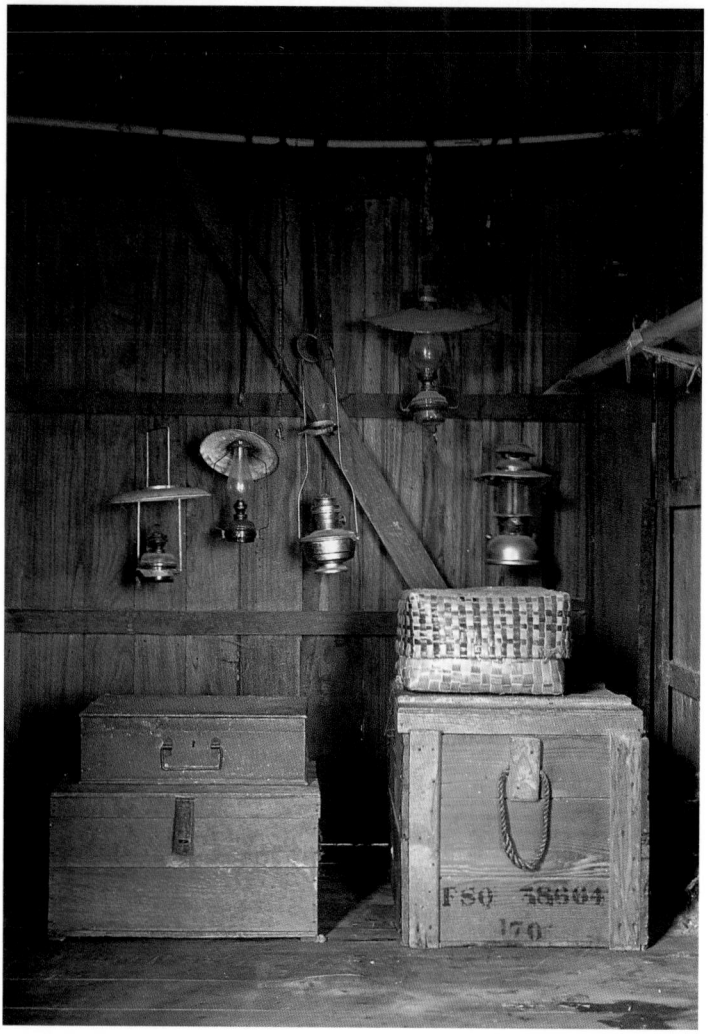

PP. 234-235 A glass-fronted teak cabinet in the main room stores valuables including lacquer dishes and clothes. • Der Vitrinenschrank aus Teak im Hauptraum enthält die Wertsachen, darunter Kleidung und Lackgeschirr. • Dans la pièce principale, les objets de valeur – des plats laqués aux vêtements – sont rangés dans une vitrine en teck.

↑ Kerosene lanterns are the main form of lighting after dark. • Nach Einbruch der Dunkelheit sind Kerosinlampen die Hauptlichtquelle. • Des lampes à pétrole constituent le principal éclairage à la nuit tombée.

→ Large metal trunks are used for storing clothes and bed linen, keeping them safe from termites. • In großen Metalltruhen sind Kleidung und

Bettwäsche sicher vor Termiten. • Les vêtements et le linge de maison sont rangés dans de gros coffres en métal, à l'abri des termites.

PP. 238-239 A mosquito net drapes the bed on the wooden floor. • Ein Moskitonetz ist über dem Schlafplatz gespannt. • Une moustiquaire protège le lit posé à même le plancher.

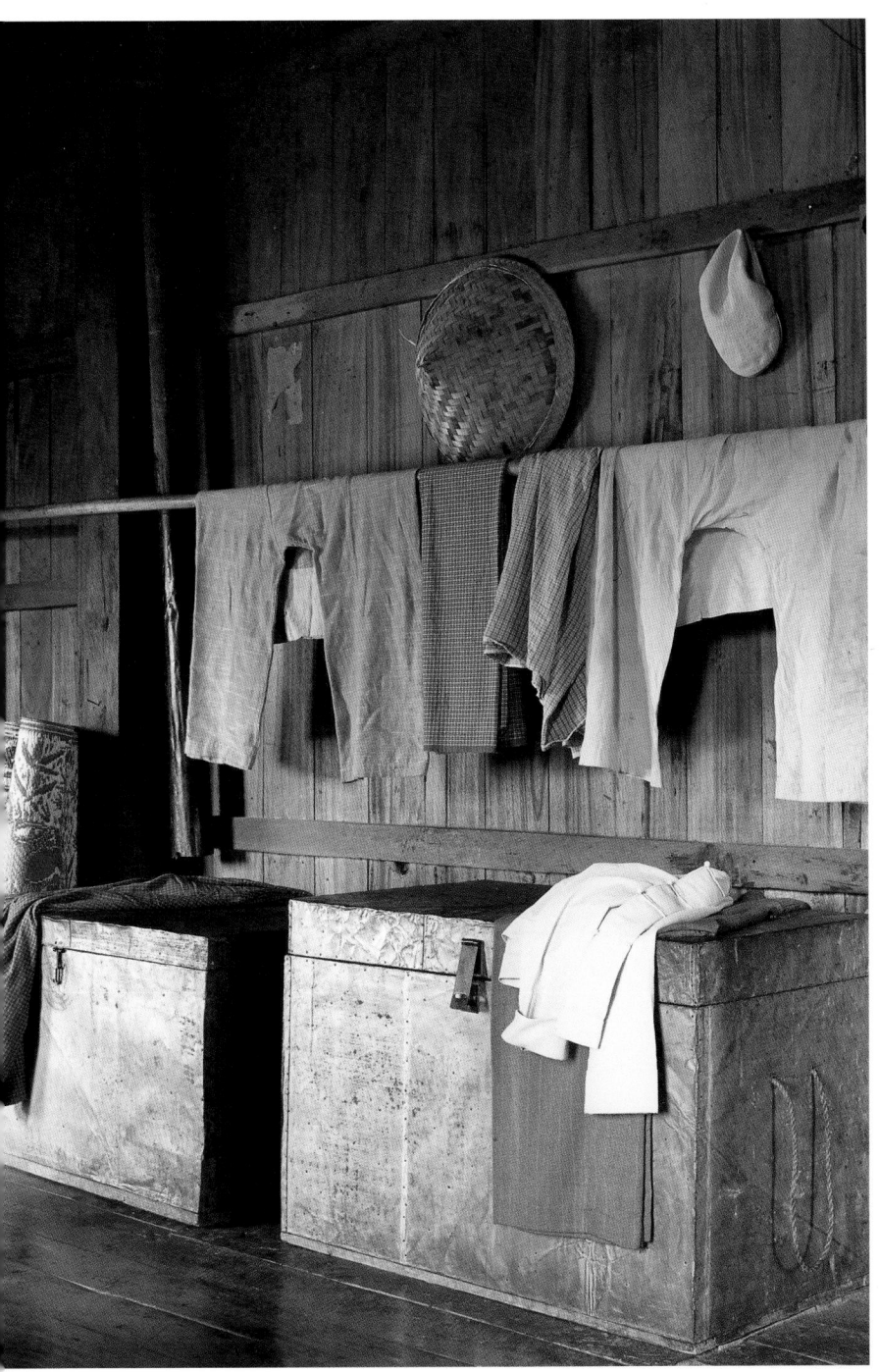

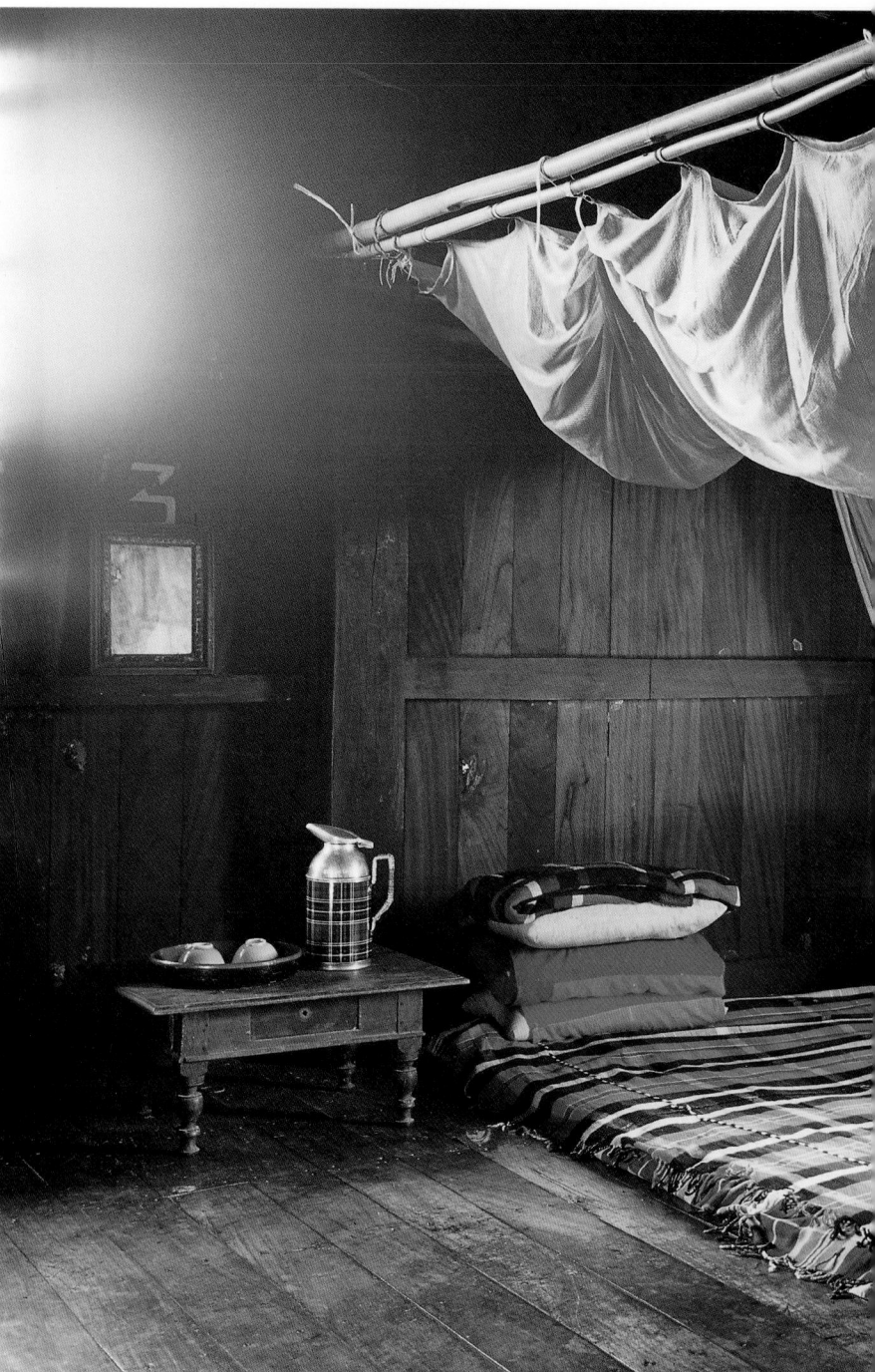

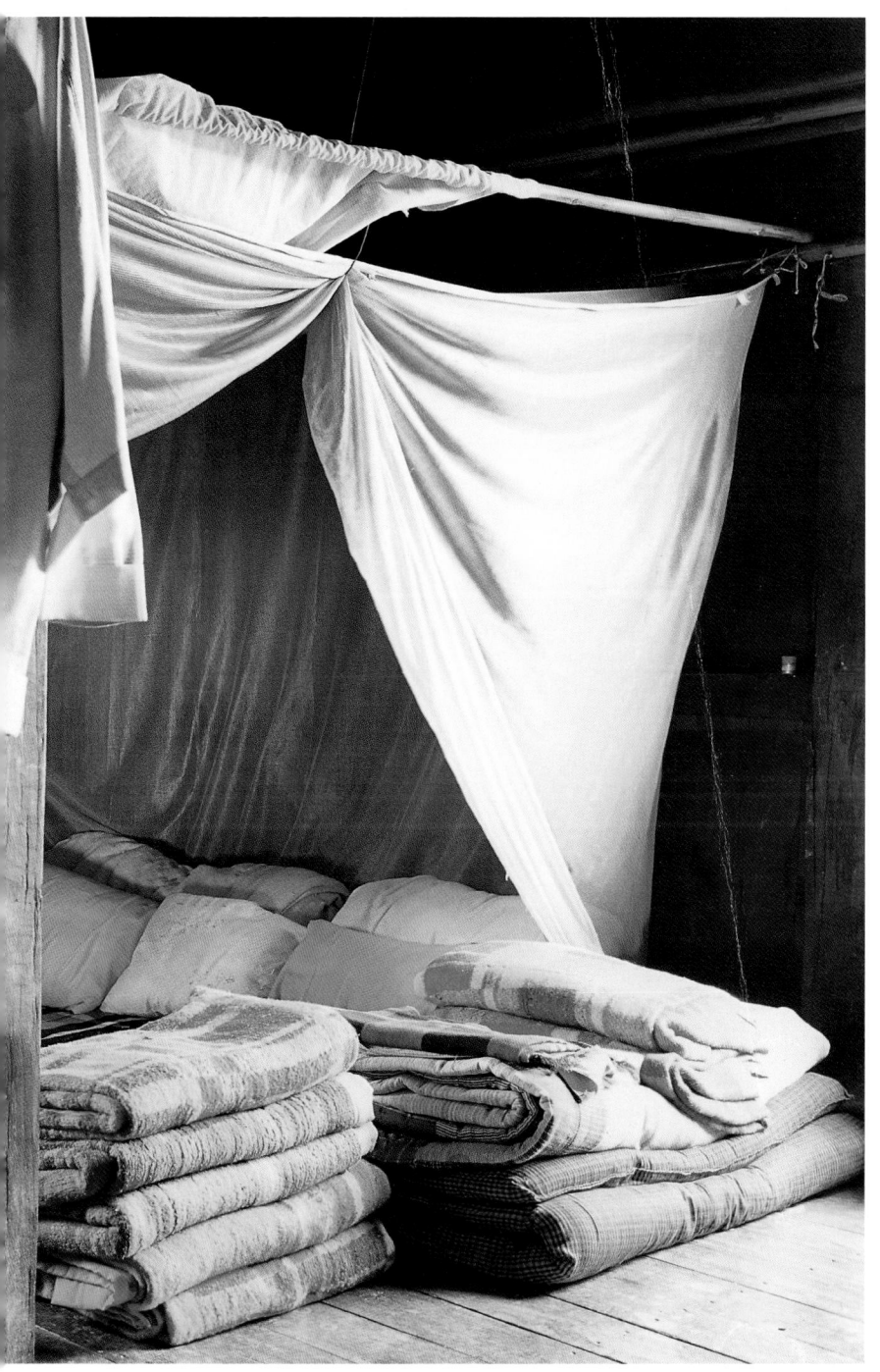

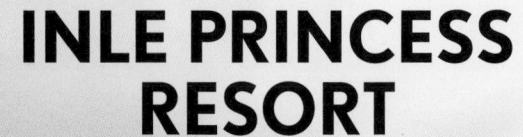

INLE PRINCESS
RESORT

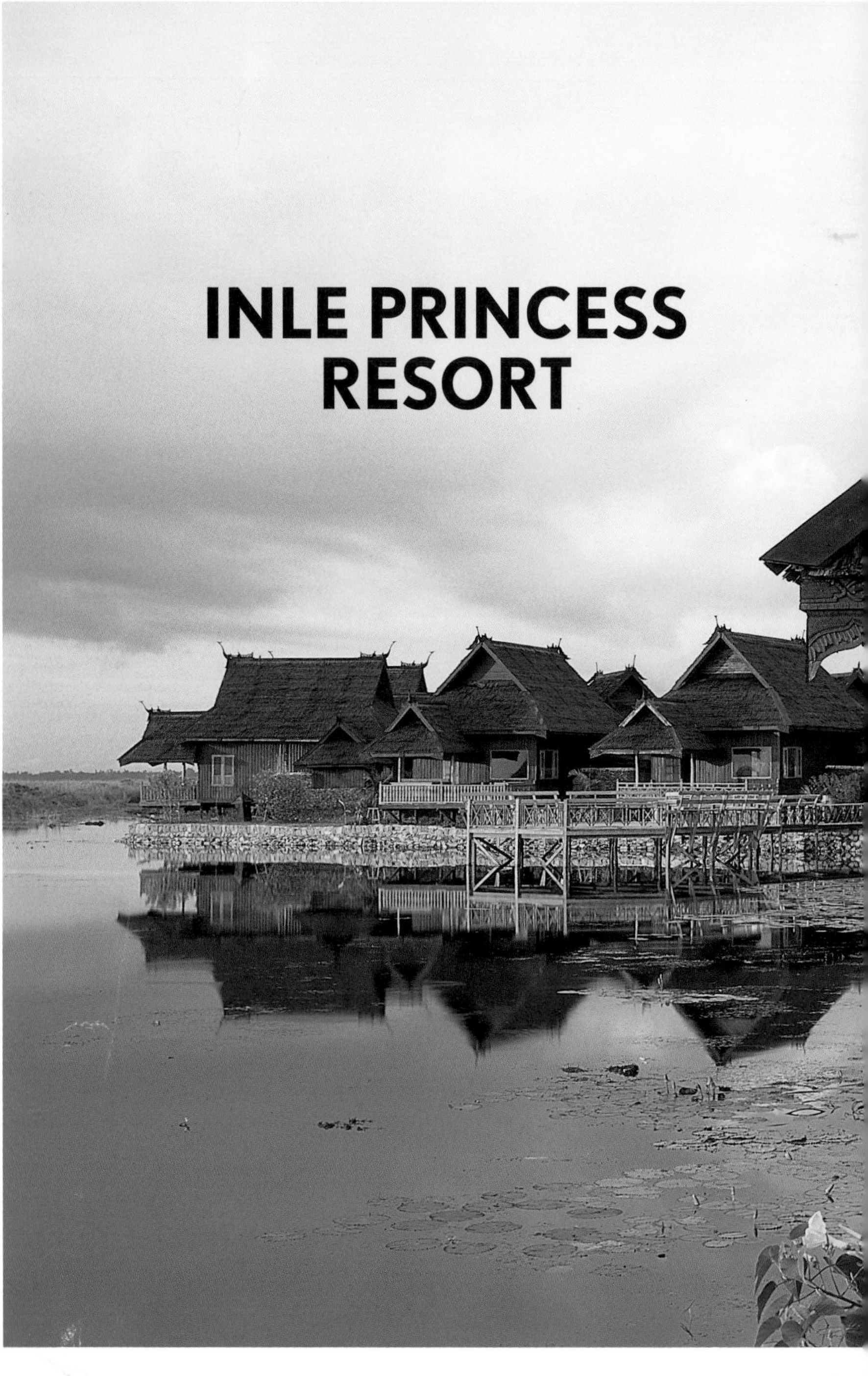

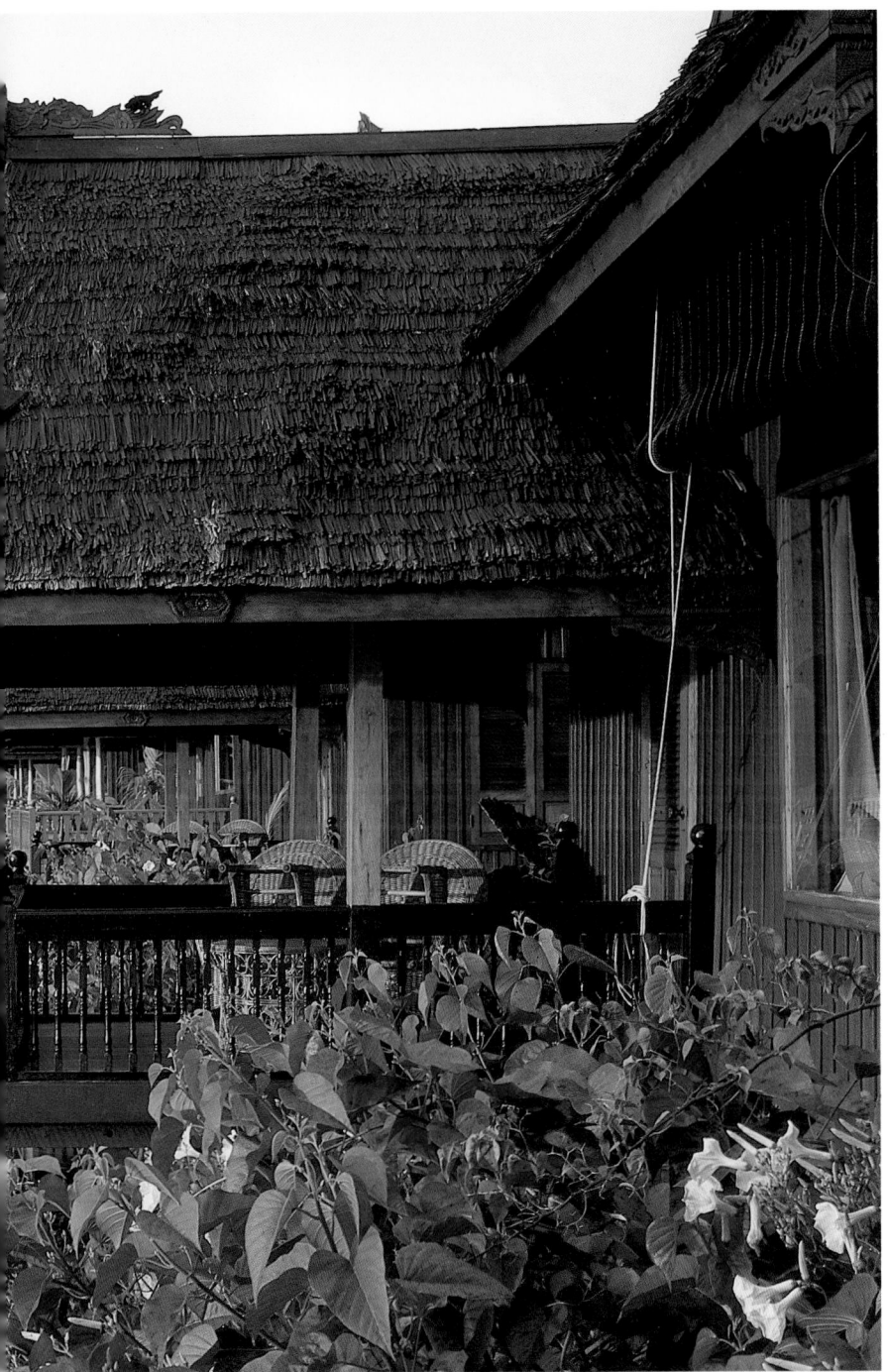

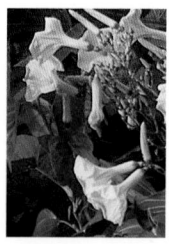

INLE PRINCESS RESORT
INLE LAKE
MYANMAR

Misuu Borit tells the story of the Inle Princess Resort with candor and charm: When she was small her father ran a small guest house in Nyaung Shwe village on Inle Lake. He dreamed of a foreign education for his daughter and hoped that one day she would help him build a professional hotel owned and managed by a local family that would be a symbol of pride for the Shan people. Parental aspiration has been happily rewarded. Misuu returned with both an education and a European husband. In Magyizin village, on the eastern shore of the lake, they built the resort in 1996, basing the design on traditional Intha and Shan architecture. Almost everything in the resort, with its 46 chalets, from the fabrics to the furniture, is indigenous and of their own devising. Misuu and Yannick Borit also produce pottery and handmade paper on the 20-acre property surrounded by tranquil views of rice fields on the water. The resort acquired its name because Misuu's father always referred to her as "my little princess".

Offen und charmant erzählt Misuu Borit die Geschichte des Inle Princess Resort: In ihrer Kindheit leitete der Vater eine kleine Pension im Dorf Nyaung Shwe am Inle-See. Er träumte davon, seiner Tochter eine Erziehung im Ausland zu ermöglichen – in der Hoffnung, dass sie ihm eines Tages bei der Errichtung eines professionell geführten Hotels helfen würde, das, als Symbol für den Stolz des Shan-Volkes, in der Hand von Einheimischen liegen und auch von ihnen geführt werden sollte. Der väterliche Ehrgeiz wurde mehr als belohnt: Misuu kehrte mit einer Ausbildung und einem europäischen Ehemann zurück. Am östlichen Seeufer erbauten sie 1996 im Dorf Magyizin das Resort im Stil der traditionellen Architektur der Shan und Intha. In der 46 Chalets umfassenden Anlage wurde beinahe alles von ihnen selbst entworfen und von Einheimischen hergestellt – von den Stoffen bis zu den Möbeln. Misuu und Yannick Borit produzieren auf dem zehn Hektar großen Gelände überdies Keramik und handgeschöpftes Papier. Die Anlage inmitten von Reisfeldern verdankt ihren Namen der Tatsache, dass Misuus Vater seine Tochter stets „kleine Prinzessin" nannte.

Misuu Borit raconte avec beaucoup de candeur et de charme : quand elle était petite, son père dirigeait une petite pension de famille dans le village de Nyaung Shwe, sur le lac Inle. Il rêvait de voir sa fille faire des études à l'étranger et espérait qu'un jour elle l'aiderait à monter un hôtel digne de ce nom. Cet établissement serait entre les mains d'une famille locale qui serait la fierté du peuple Shan. Et ce rêve s'est réalisé : Misuu est revenue au pays, diplôme en poche, avec un mari européen. C'est à Magyizin, un village de la rive est du lac, que Misuu et son mari ont construit le complexe en 1996, s'inspirant de l'architecture traditionnelle intha et shan. Dans cet ensemble de 46 bungalows, le couple a presque tout conçu lui-même, des tissus au mobilier, à partir de matériaux locaux. Misuu et Yannick Borit fabriquent aussi de la poterie et du papier artisanal sur cette propriété de dix hectares située au milieu d'un cadre paisible de rizières inondées. En souvenir de son père qui l'appelait souvent « ma petite princesse », Misuu a nommé le complexe Inle Princess.

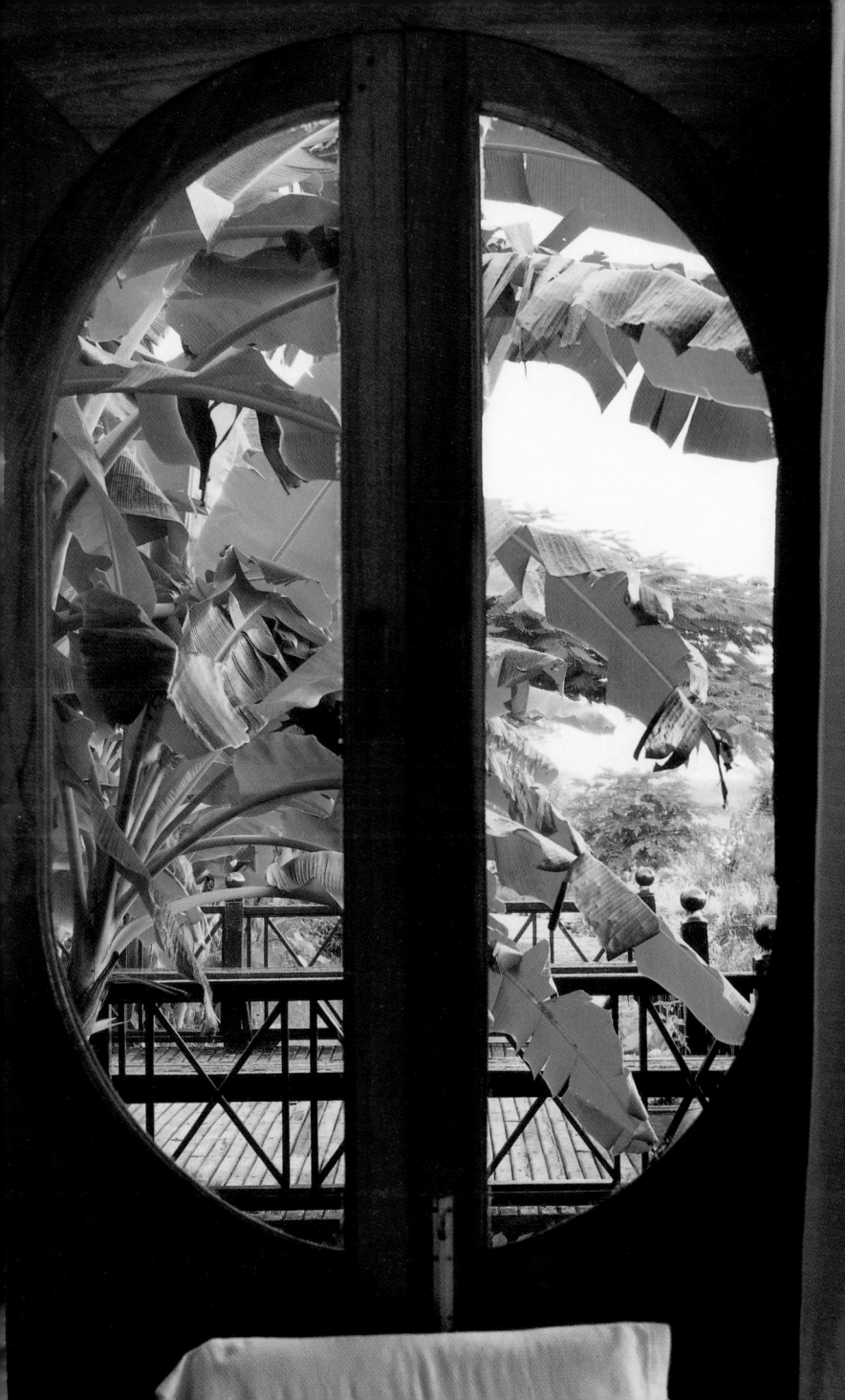

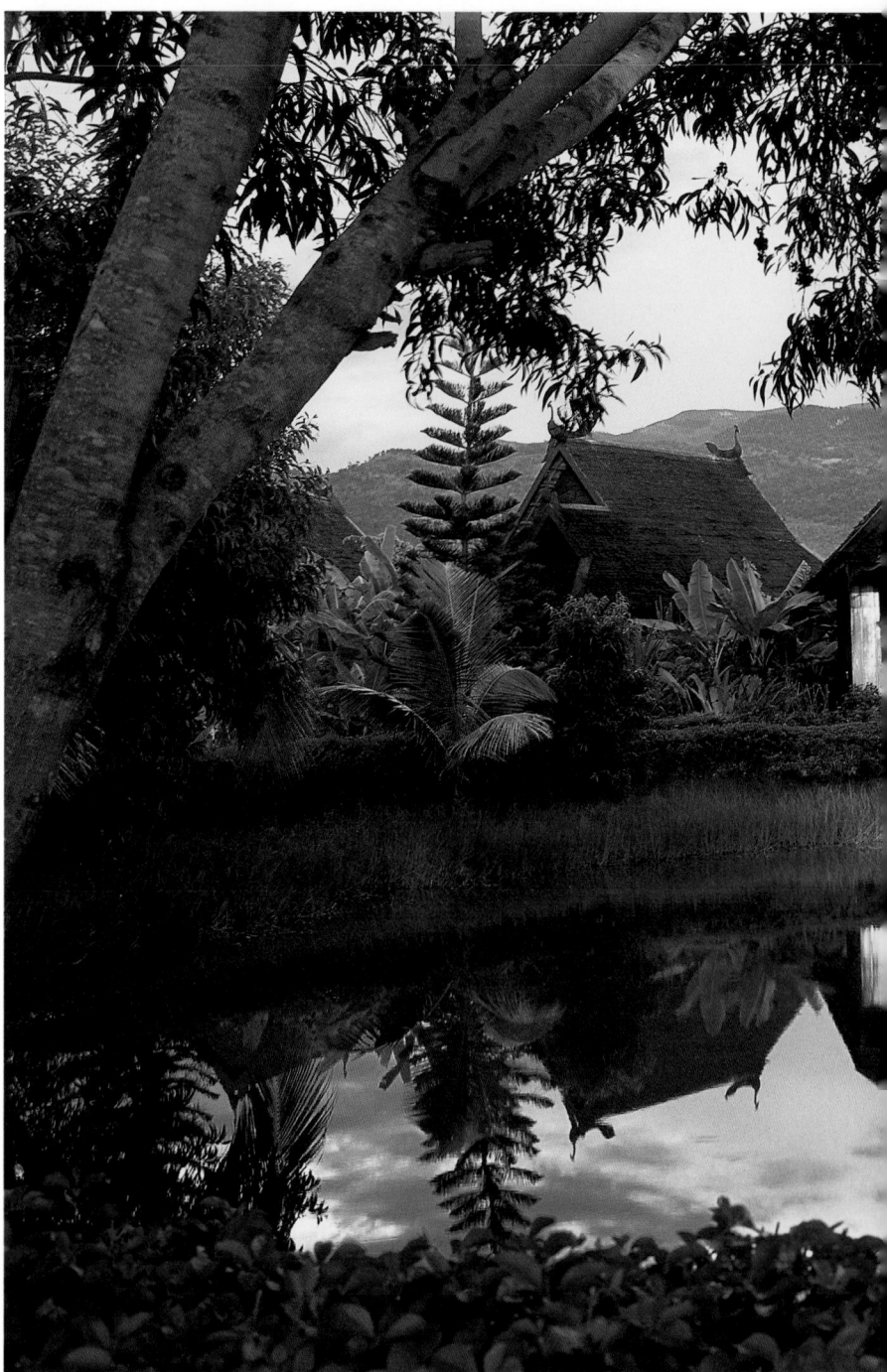

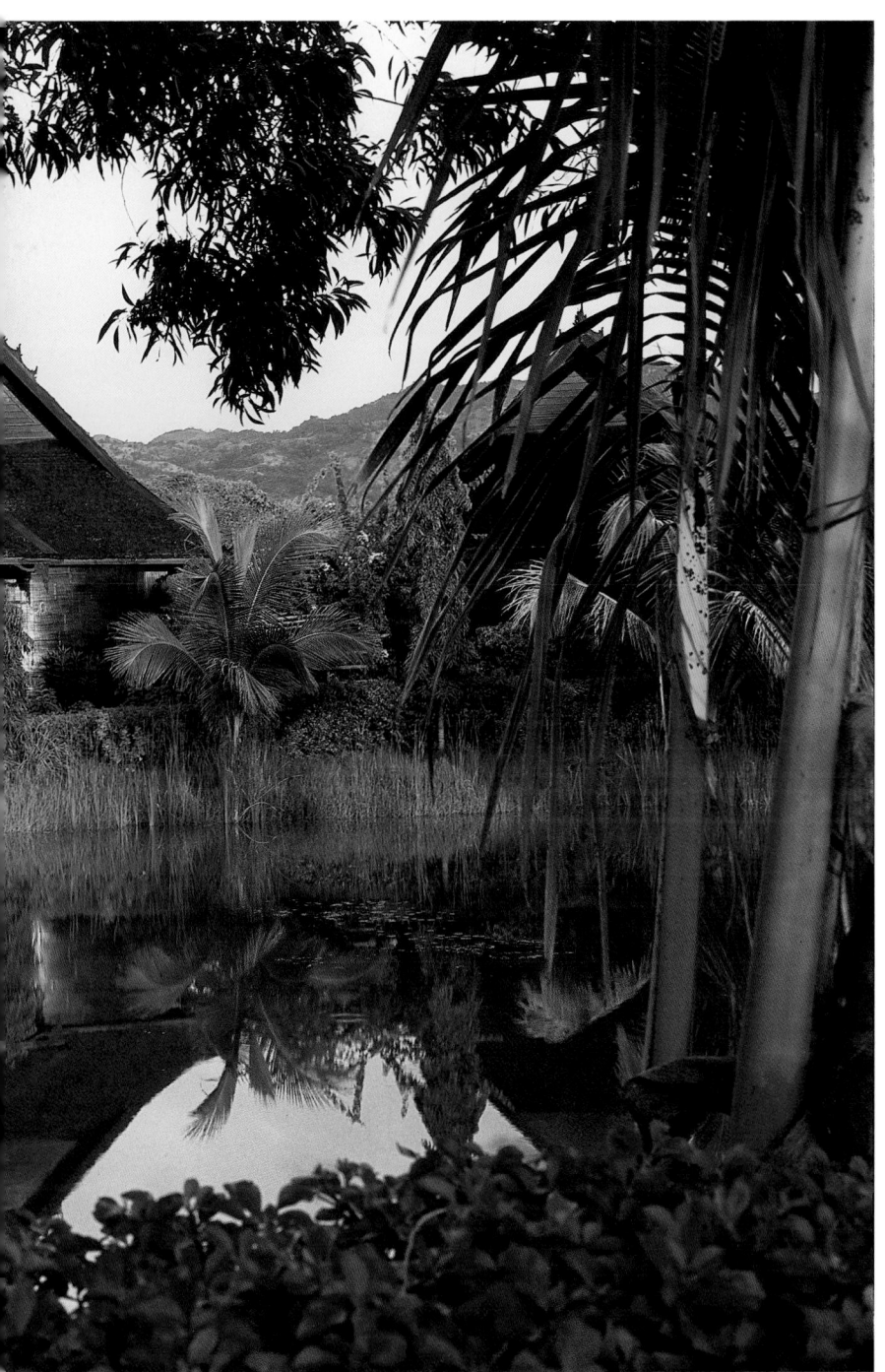

PP. 240-241 Many of the rooms in the resort have private balconies facing the lake. • Viele Zimmer verfügen über einen privaten Balkon mit Blick auf den See. • La plupart des chambres ont des balcons privés donnant sur le lac.

PP. 244-245 Framed by palms and banana trees, the resort's chalets are built in traditional Intha style. • Die im traditionellen Stil der Intha erbauten Chalets liegen inmitten von Palmen und Bananenstauden. • Dans un décor de palmiers et de bananiers, les bungalows construits dans la tradition intha.

↓ The resort's simple interiors were designed by local artisans. • Die schlichte Inneneinrichtung des Resorts haben einheimische Handwerker entworfen. • Les intérieurs simples ont été réalisés par des artisans locaux.

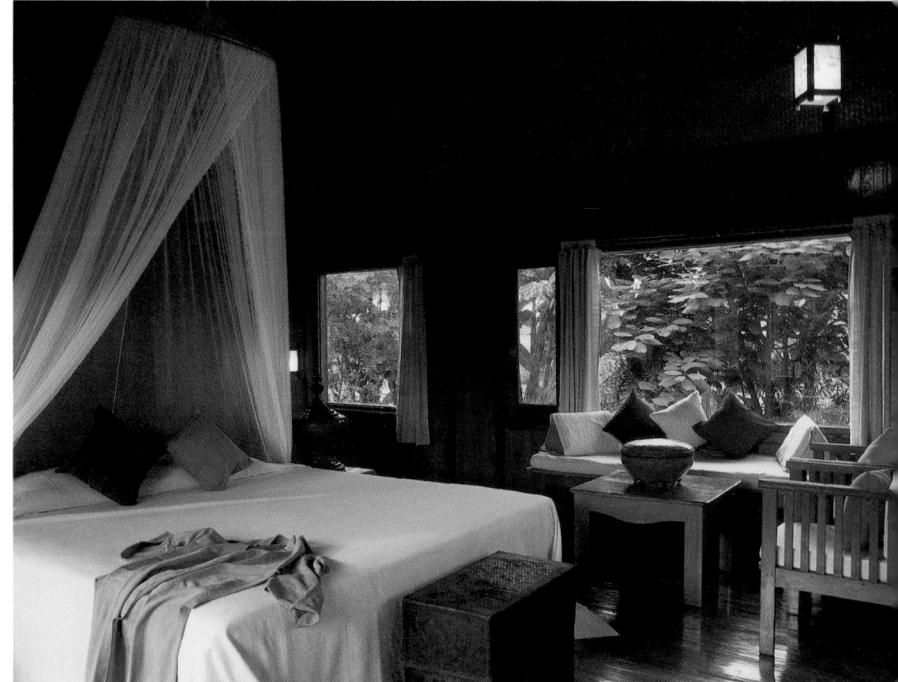

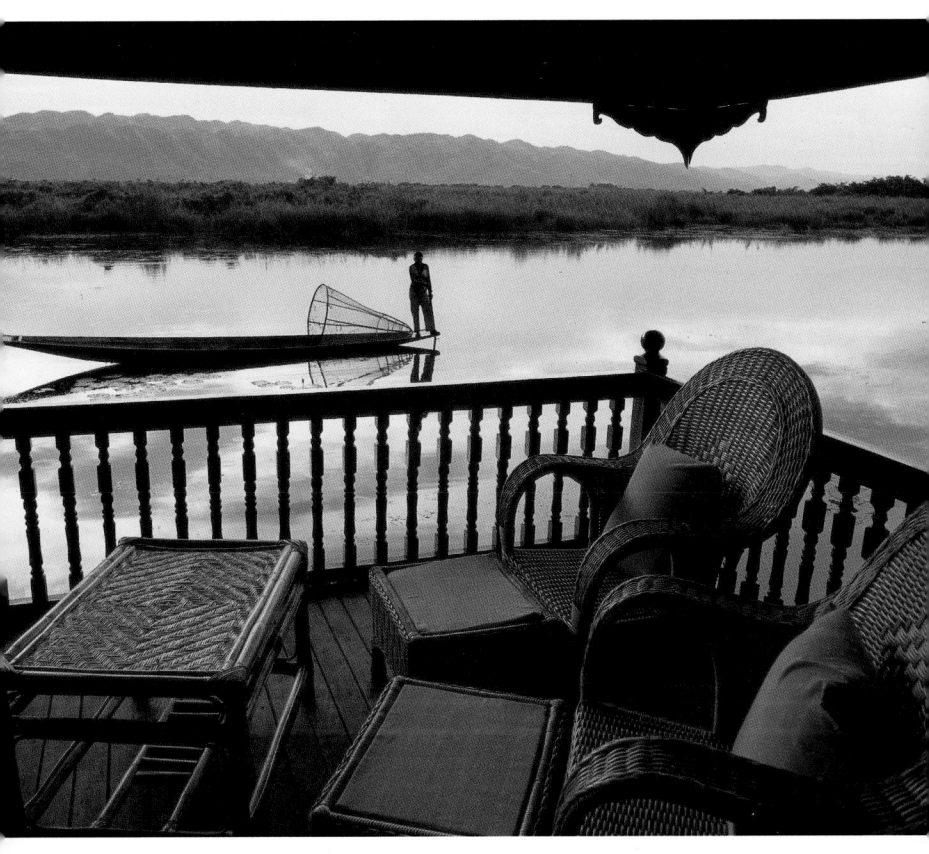

↑ Fishermen glide by with cone-shaped fishing nets. • Fischer mit kegelförmigen Netzen gleiten auf dem See vorbei. • Un pêcheur équipé d'une nasse conique glisse sur les eaux du lac.

PP. 248-249 Monks and pilgrims make a religious boat trip aboard a traditional royal barge with pagoda roofs and a prow in the shape of a mythical bird. • Priester und Pilger auf einer religiösen Bootsfahrt in einer traditionellen

königlichen Barke, deren Bug einem mythischen Vogel nachgestaltet wurde. • Des prêtres et des pélerins en déplacement, sur une barge royale traditionnelle avec des toits en pagode et une proue en forme d'oiseau mythique.

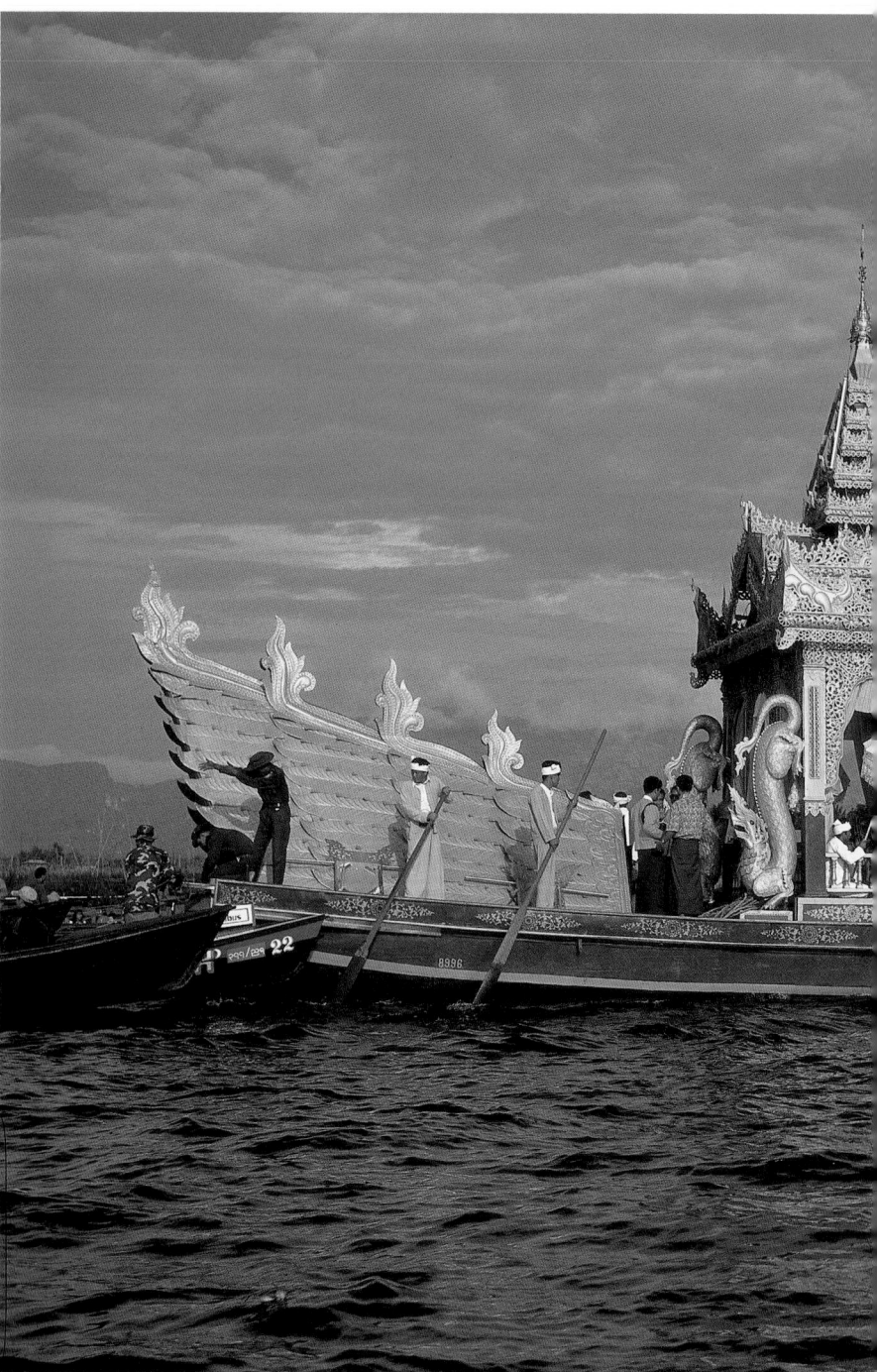

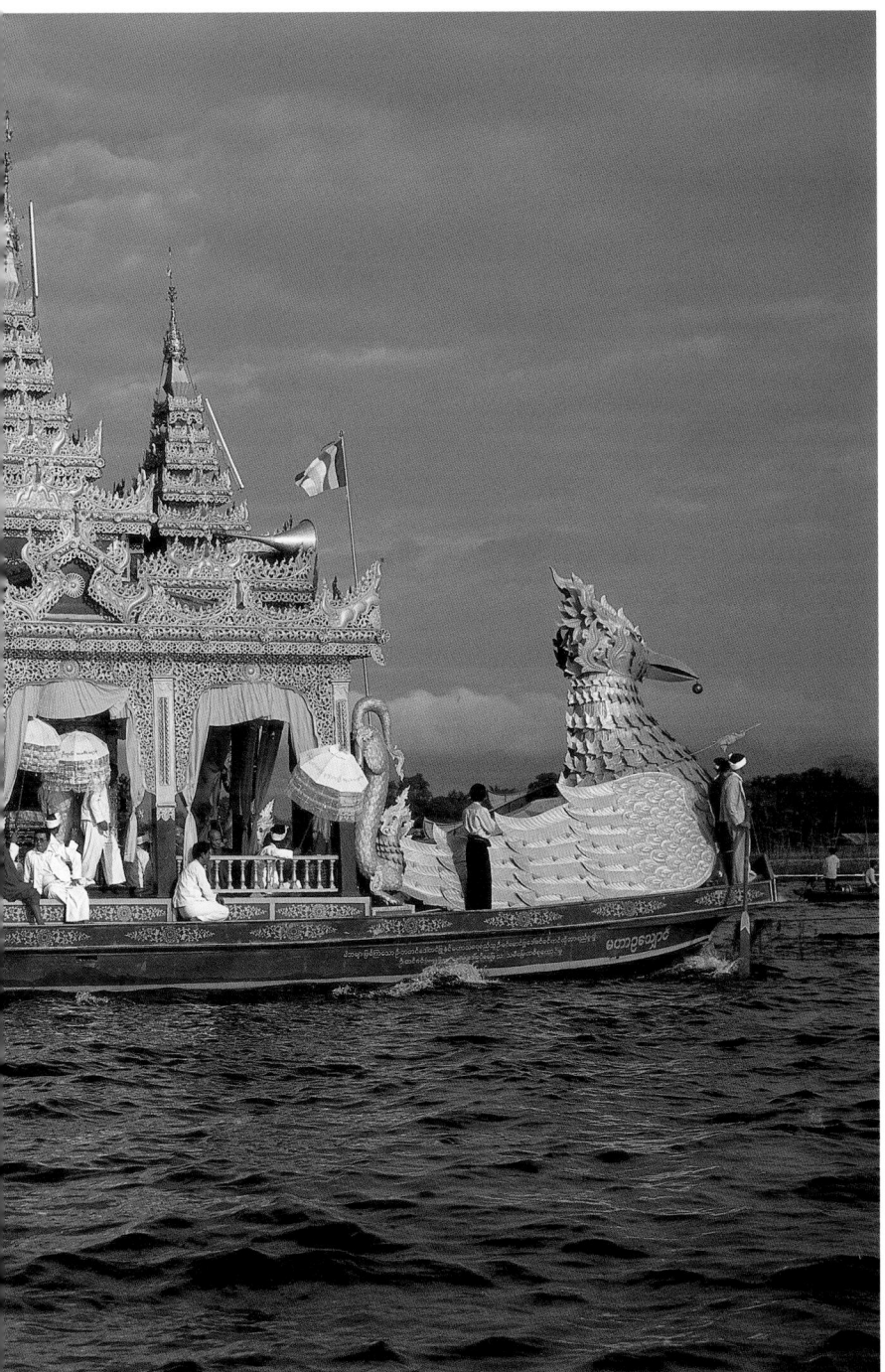

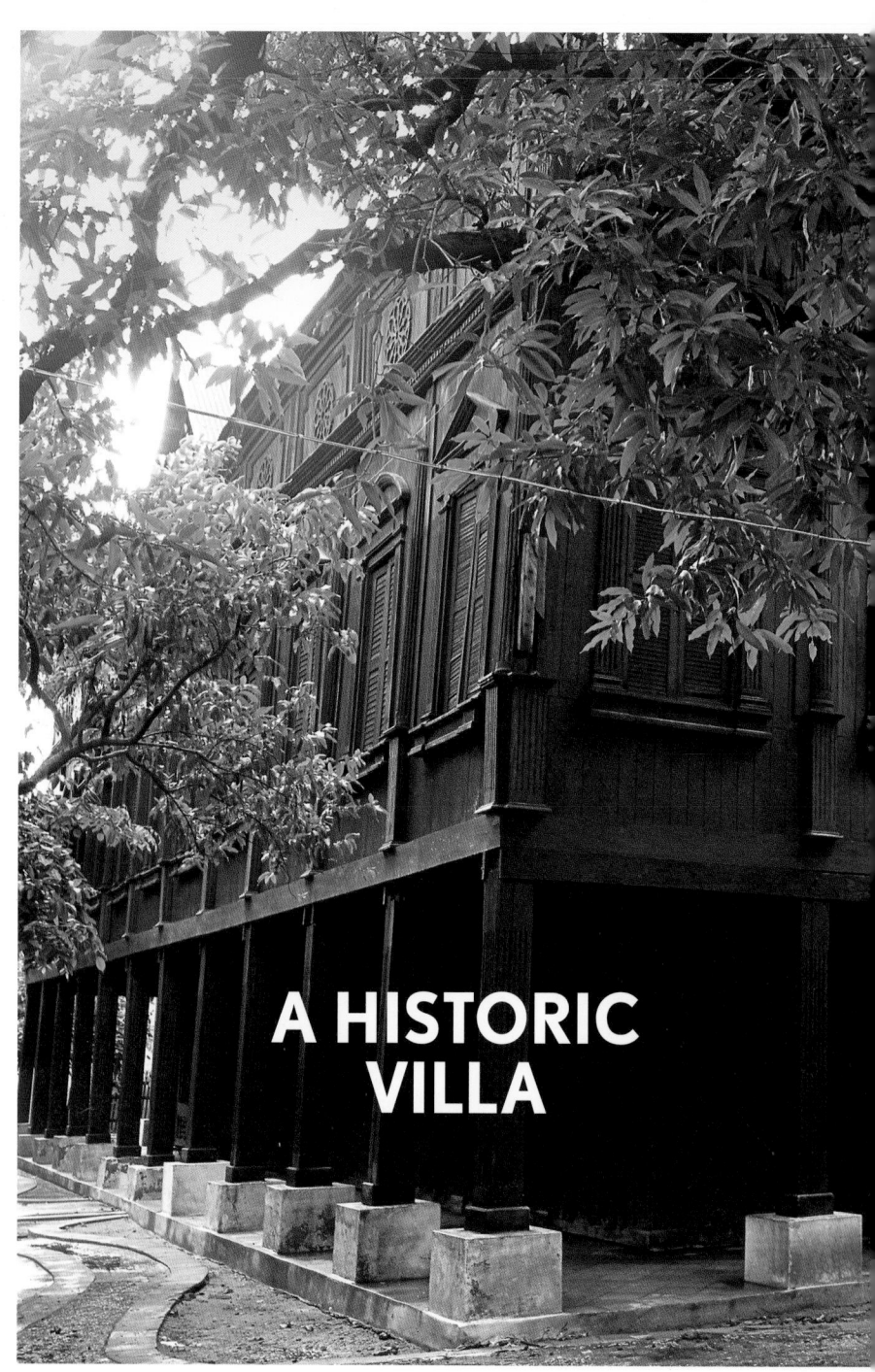

A HISTORIC VILLA

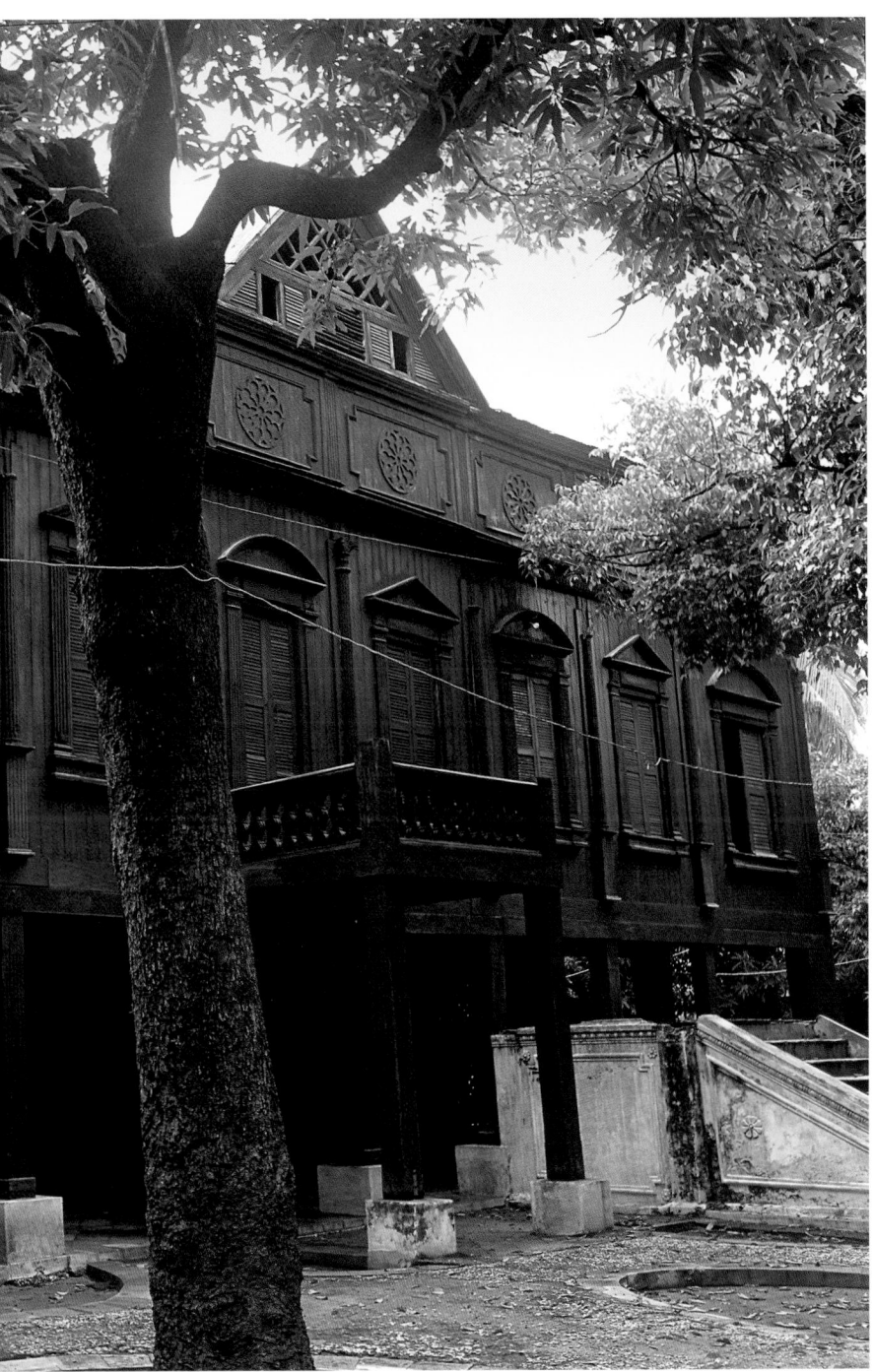

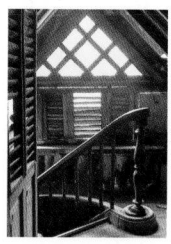

A HISTORIC VILLA
MANDALAY
MYANMAR

Descended from the Buddha, the people of Myanmar believe they are the first inhabitants of the world. That is what the word *Myanmar* actually means. By the mid-19th century however, after a long, often bloody cycle of tribal conflicts, Myanmar was overtaken by the British rulers in neighboring India. Following two Anglo-Burmese wars, benevolent King Mindon ascended the throne in 1853. Deeply religious yet curious about the outside world, he transferred his capital north, from Amarapura to Mandalay. He began to send young men abroad, among them U Kaung. Queen Victoria received Mindon's envoy in Britain. As a minister, U Kaung was later a key figure in the succession of Thibaw, the last Burmese king. Influenced by what he had seen, U Kaung commissioned a European firm to build a Palladio-inspired mansion in Mandalay. Now an adjunct to a Buddhist monastery, the villa's lavishly-carved doors, passages, classical columns and pedimented windows in teak are a haunting reminder of old Burma's passing infatuation with the West.

Die Birmanen sehen sich als Abkömmlinge Buddhas und glauben, sie seien die ersten Bewohner der Erde gewesen. Das ist die eigentliche Bedeutung des Wortes *Myanmar*. Mitte des 19. Jahrhunderts eroberten die Briten vom benachbarten Indien aus Myanmar, das auf eine lange blutige Geschichte von Stammeskriegen zurückblickte. Nach zwei britisch-birmanischen Kriegen bestieg der großherzige König Mindon 1853 den Thron. Der tief religiöse Herrscher interessierte sich auch für fremde Länder und verlegte die Hauptstadt von Mandalay ins nördliche Amarapura. Darauf sandte er junge Männer ins Ausland, darunter auch U Kaung, den Königin Victoria als König Mindons Gesandten in London empfing. Unter dem Einfluss seiner Reiseerlebnisse gab U Kaung einem europäischen Unternehmen den Auftrag, in Mandalay ein von Palladio inspiriertes Herrenhaus zu bauen. Die Villa ist heute an ein buddhistisches Kloster angeschlossen, aber die aufwendig geschnitzten Türen, überdachten Gänge, klassischen Säulen und Fenster mit Giebeln aus Teakholz erinnern an die inzwischen schwindende Anziehungskraft des Westens für das alte Birma.

Descendant du Bouddha, les habitants du Myanmar croient être les premiers habitants du monde, ce que signifie d'ailleurs le nom *Myanmar.* Au milieu du 19ᵉ siècle, les Britanniques, alors souverains aux Indes, ont mis fin aux longues luttes intestines qui avaient souvent laissé le pays exsangue. À l'issue de deux guerres anglo-birmanes, le populaire Mindon est devenu roi de Birmanie en 1853 et a transféré la capitale d'Amapura à Mandalay, plus au nord. Cet homme profondément religieux n'en était pas moins curieux du monde extérieur : il a envoyé de jeunes émissaires à l'étranger, dont U Kaung, qui fut reçu par la reine Victoria. Devenu ministre, U Kaung a par la suite joué un rôle clé dans la succession de Thibaw, le dernier roi birman. Influencé par ce qu'il avait vu à l'étranger, U Kaung a chargé un entrepreneur européen de bâtir une maison de style palladien à Mandalay. Les portes somptueusement sculptées, les circulations, les colonnes d'inspiration classique et les fenêtres en teck à fronton sont autant de détails de cette maison, désormais située dans l'enceinte d'un monastère, qui rappellent de manière obsédante l'engouement passager de l'ancienne Birmanie pour l'Occident.

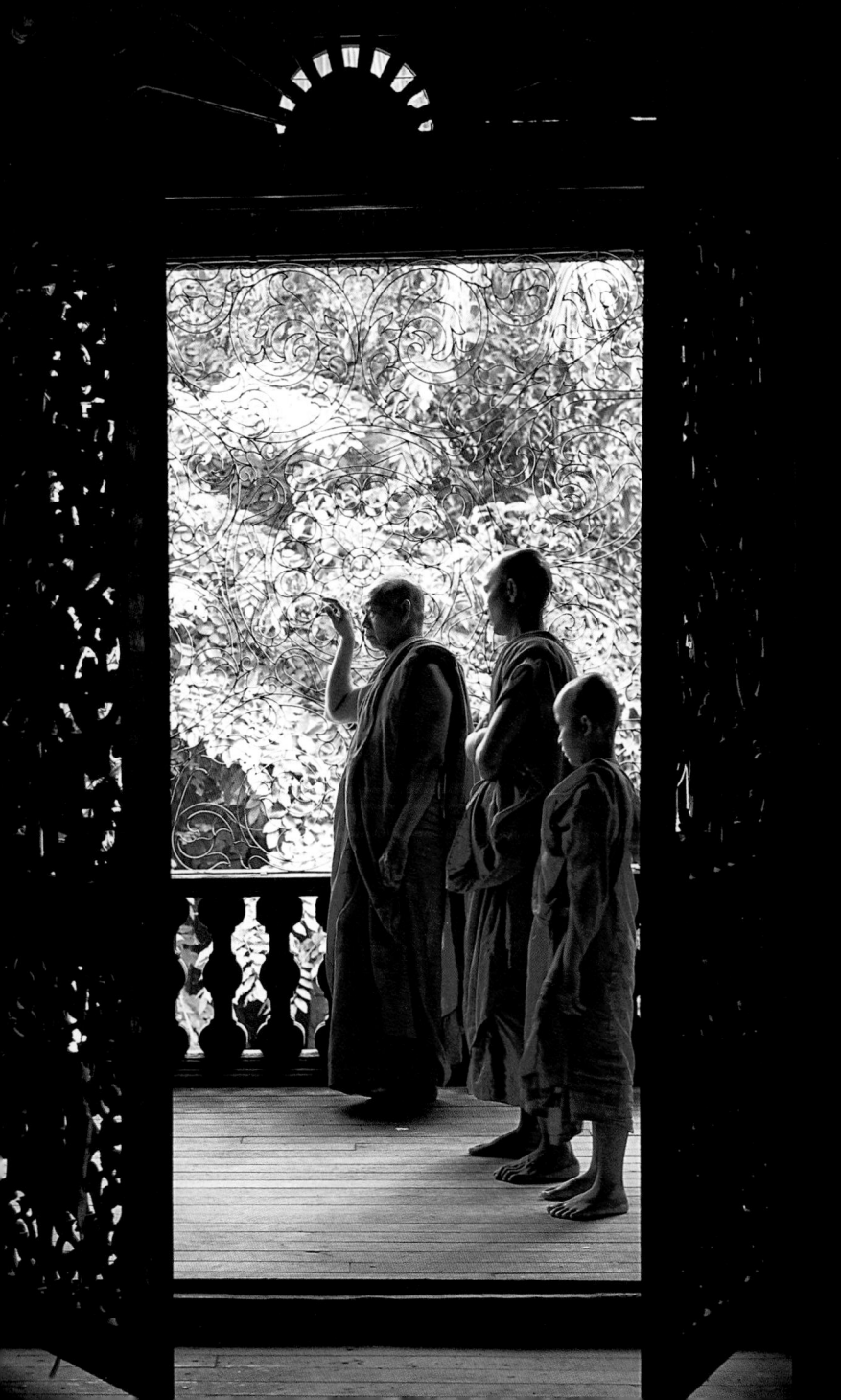

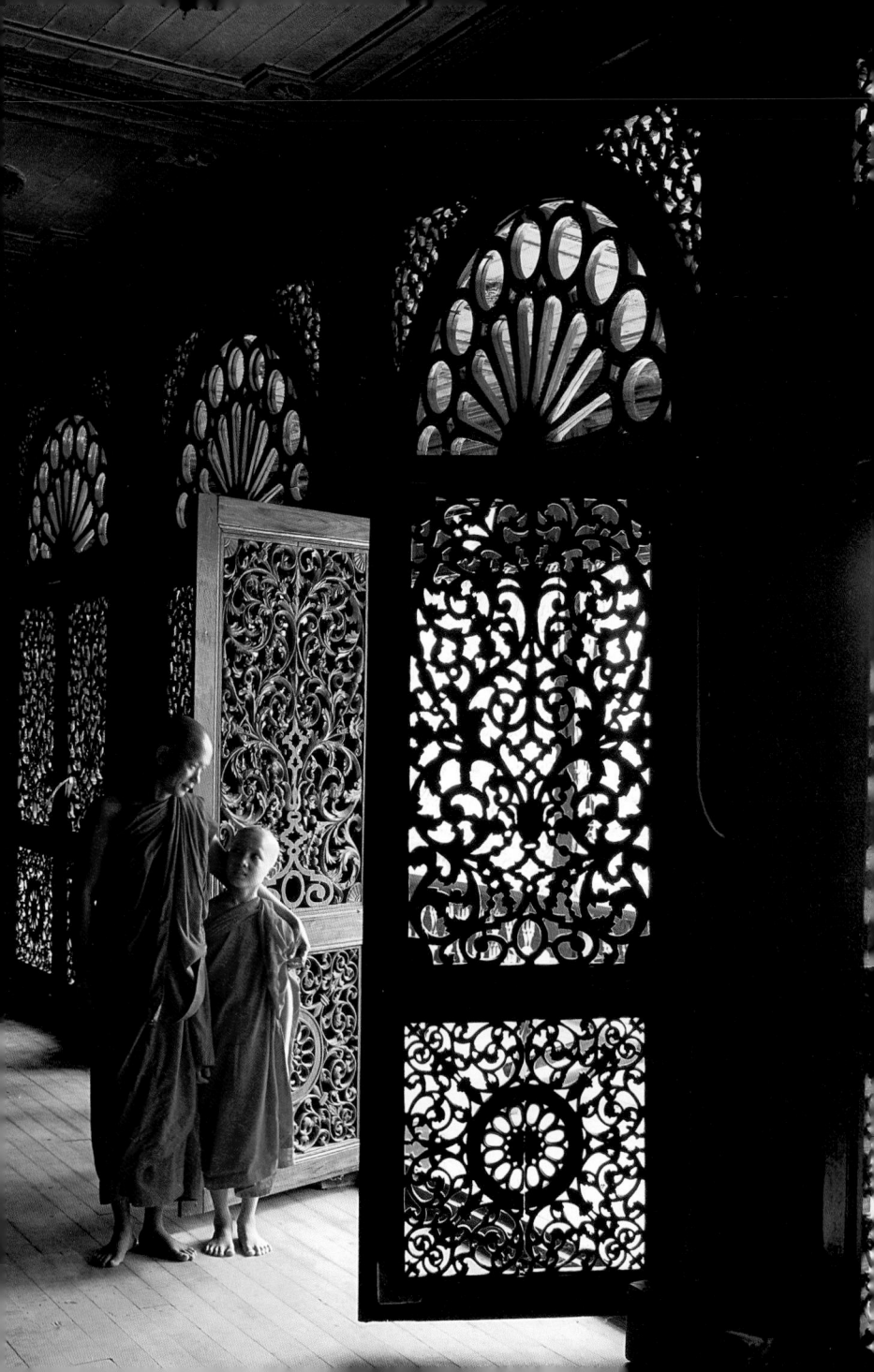

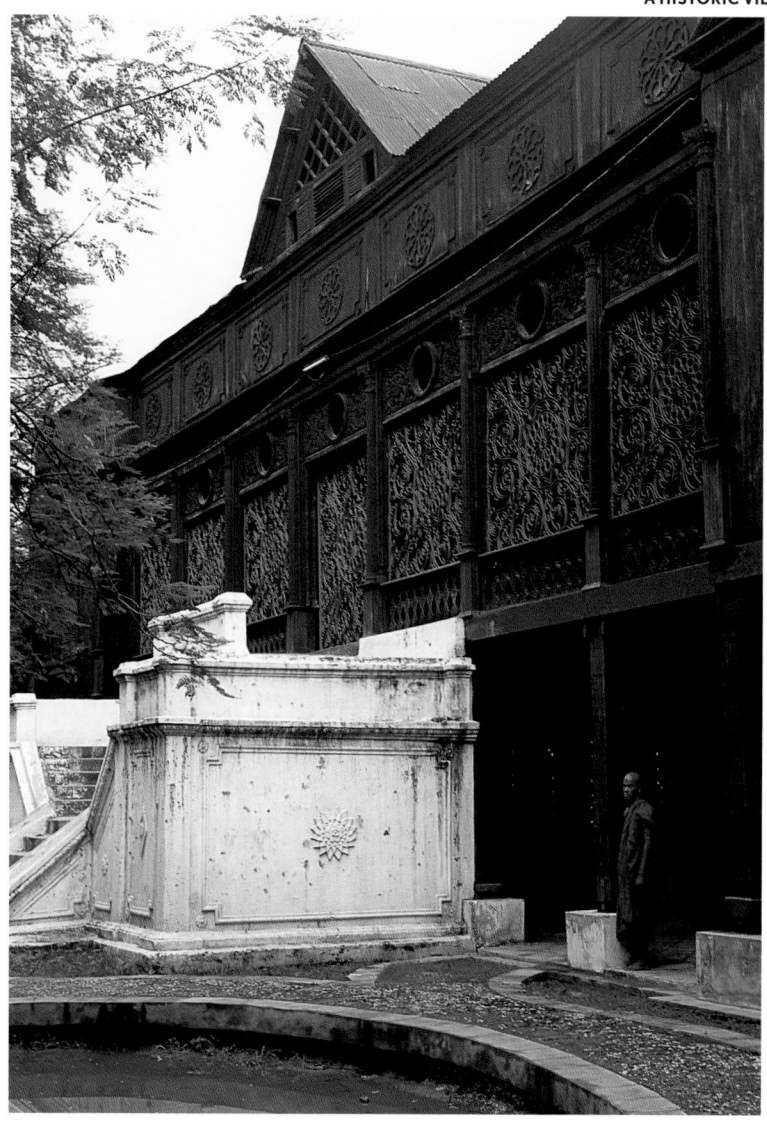

PP. 250–251 Pedimented windows and a gabled terrace dominate the villa's façade. • Giebelfenster und eine Terrasse mit Balkon zieren die Fassade der Villa. • La façade est marquée par des fenêtres à fronton et une terrasse à pignons.

← and P. 253 Monks from a nearby monastery have made the former minister's villa their own. • Die Mönche aus dem nahen Kloster fühlen sich in der ehemaligen Gesandtenvilla wie zu Hause. • Les moines du monastère voisin se sentent chez eux dans cette villa.

↑ A double plaster staircase at the entrance to the villa. • Eine stuckverzierte Doppeltreppe am Eingang zur Villa. • À l'entrée de la villa, un escalier en plâtre à volée double.

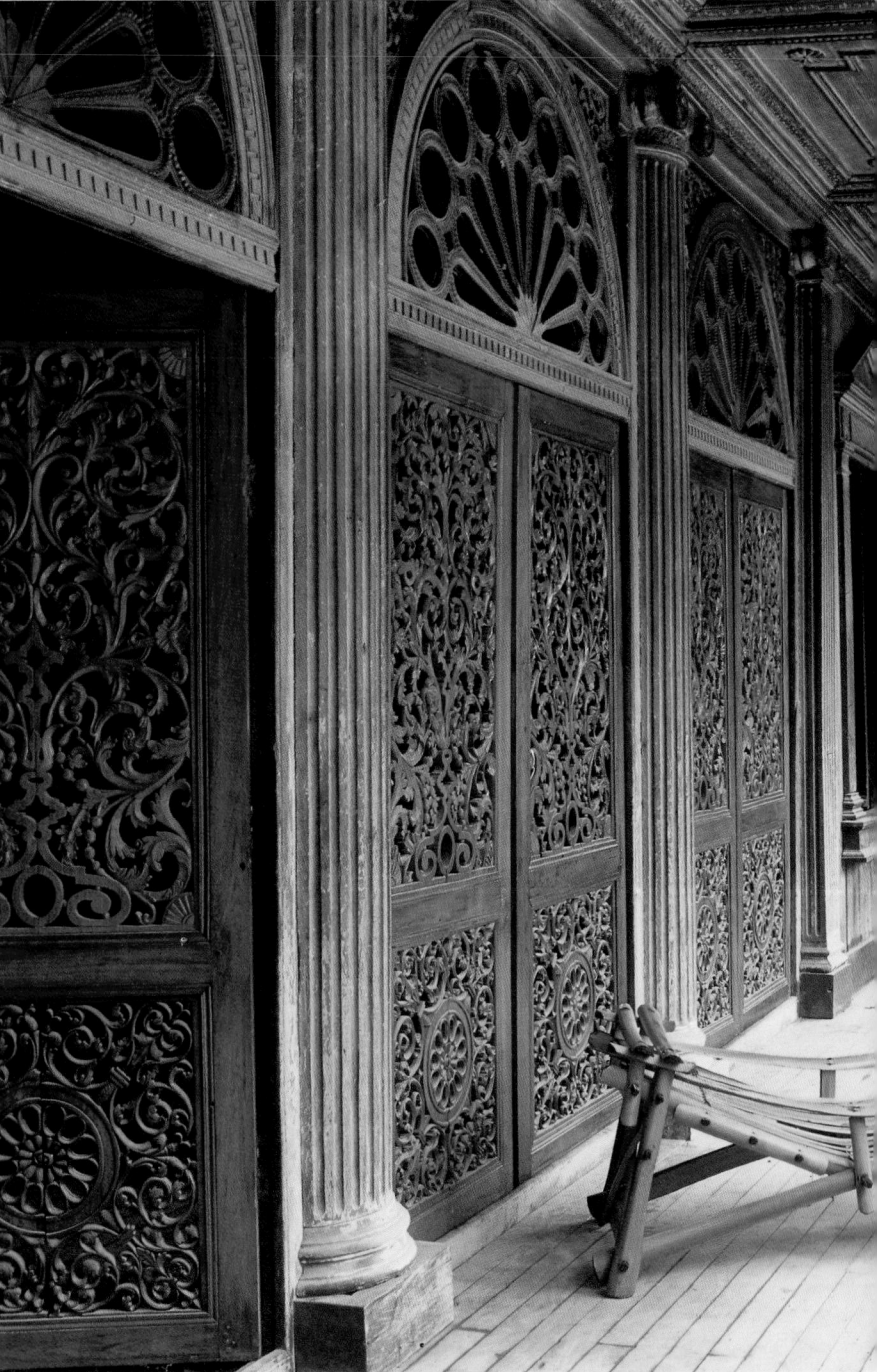

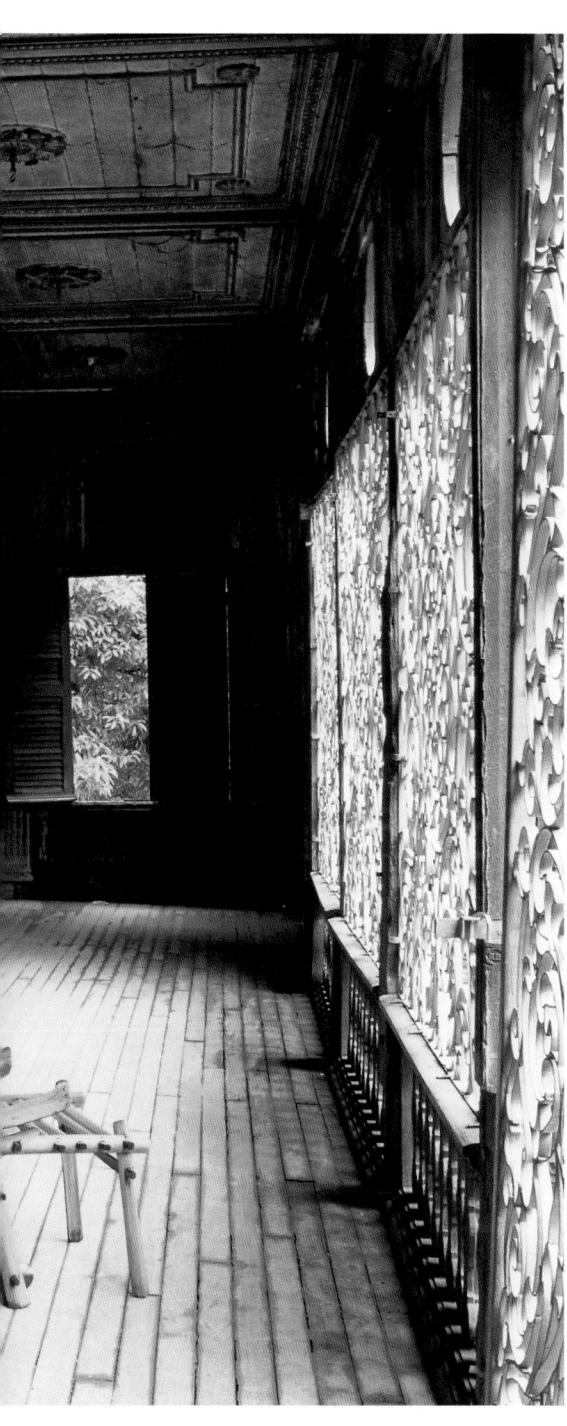

← Doric pillars intersperse with elaborately-carved door panels of Burmese teak. • Dorische Säulen unterbrechen die fein geschnitzten Türfüllungen aus birmanischem Teakholz. • Des pilastres doriques alternent avec des portes finement sculptées en bois de teck birman.

P. 258 A richly-carved transom above ornate doors. • Ein aufwendig geschnitzter Türsturz über prunkvoll verzierten Türen. • Une imposte délicatement ouvragée domine une porte richement ornée.

P. 259 The spiral staircase leading to the roof. • Die Wendeltreppe zum Dach. • Départ de l'escalier en spirale menant aux combles.

PP. 260-261 Novices taking a siesta. • Novizen während der Siesta. • Novices à l'heure de la sieste.

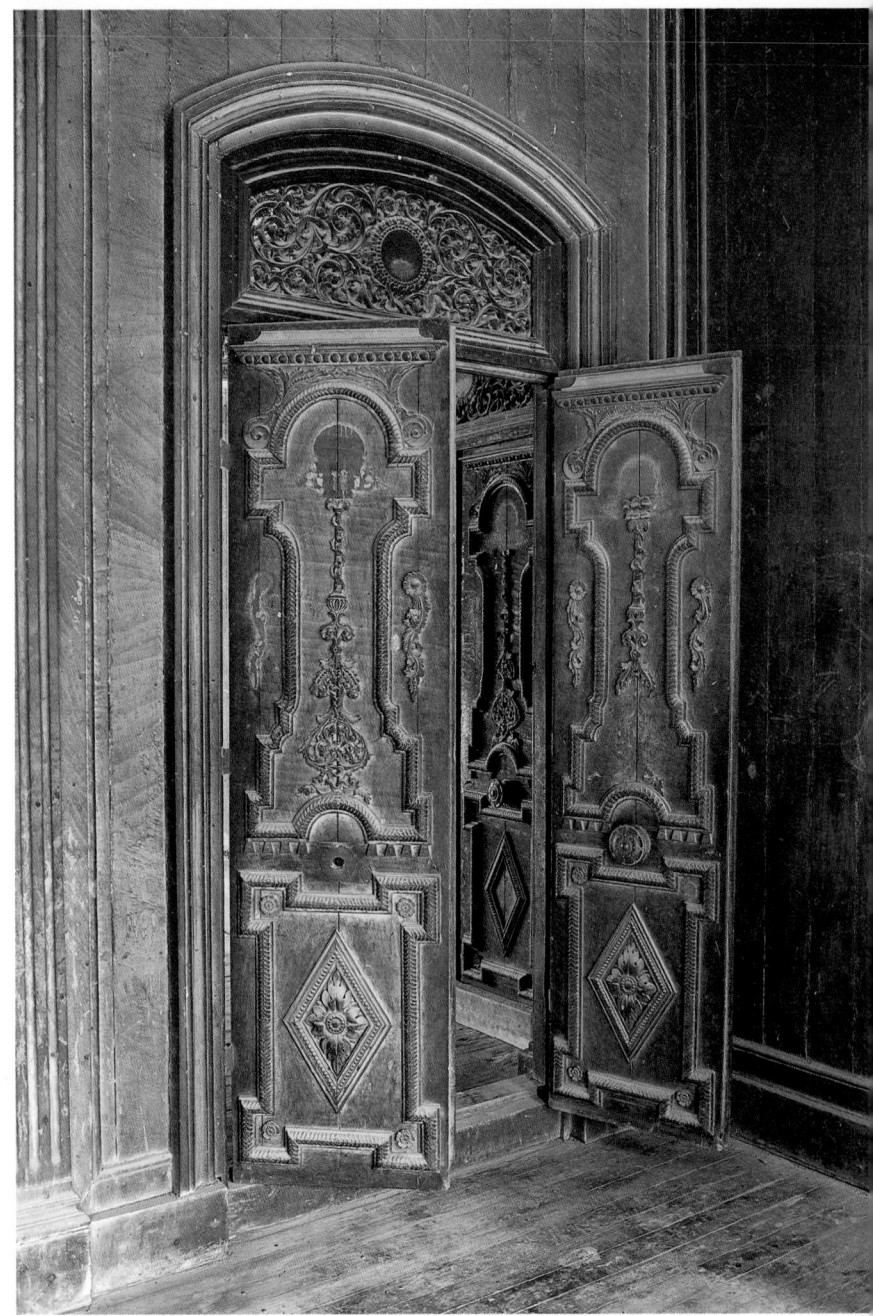

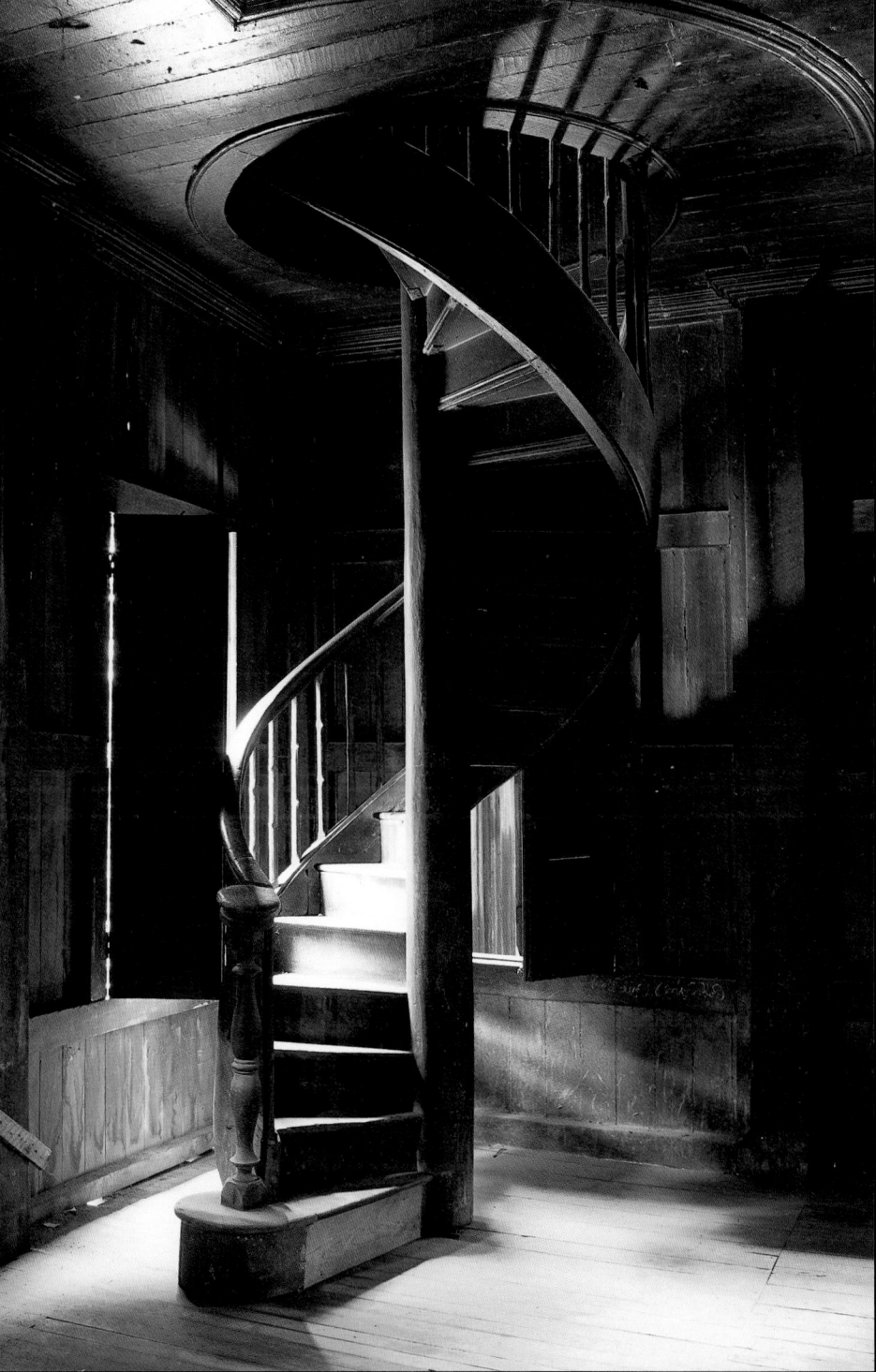

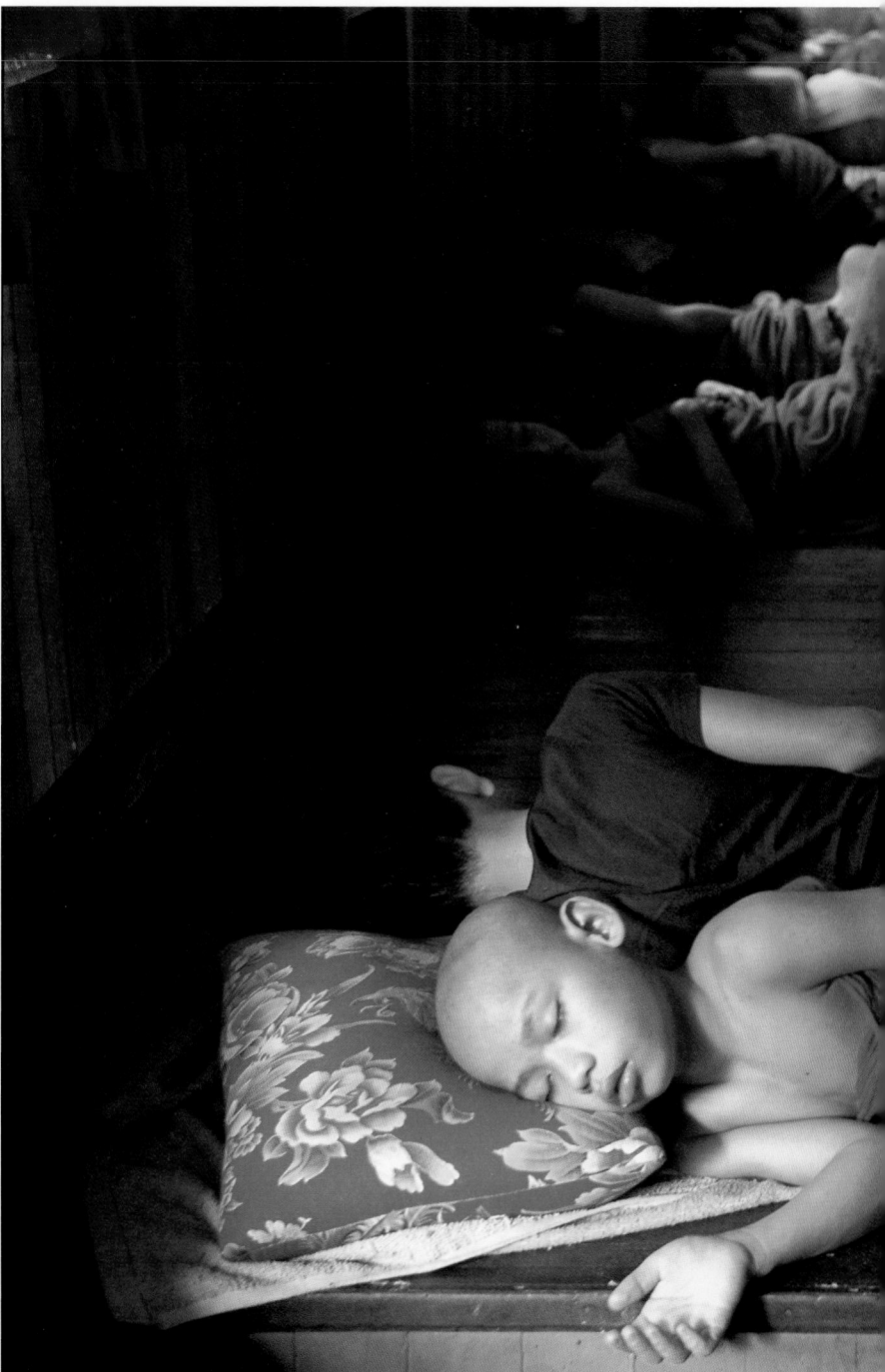

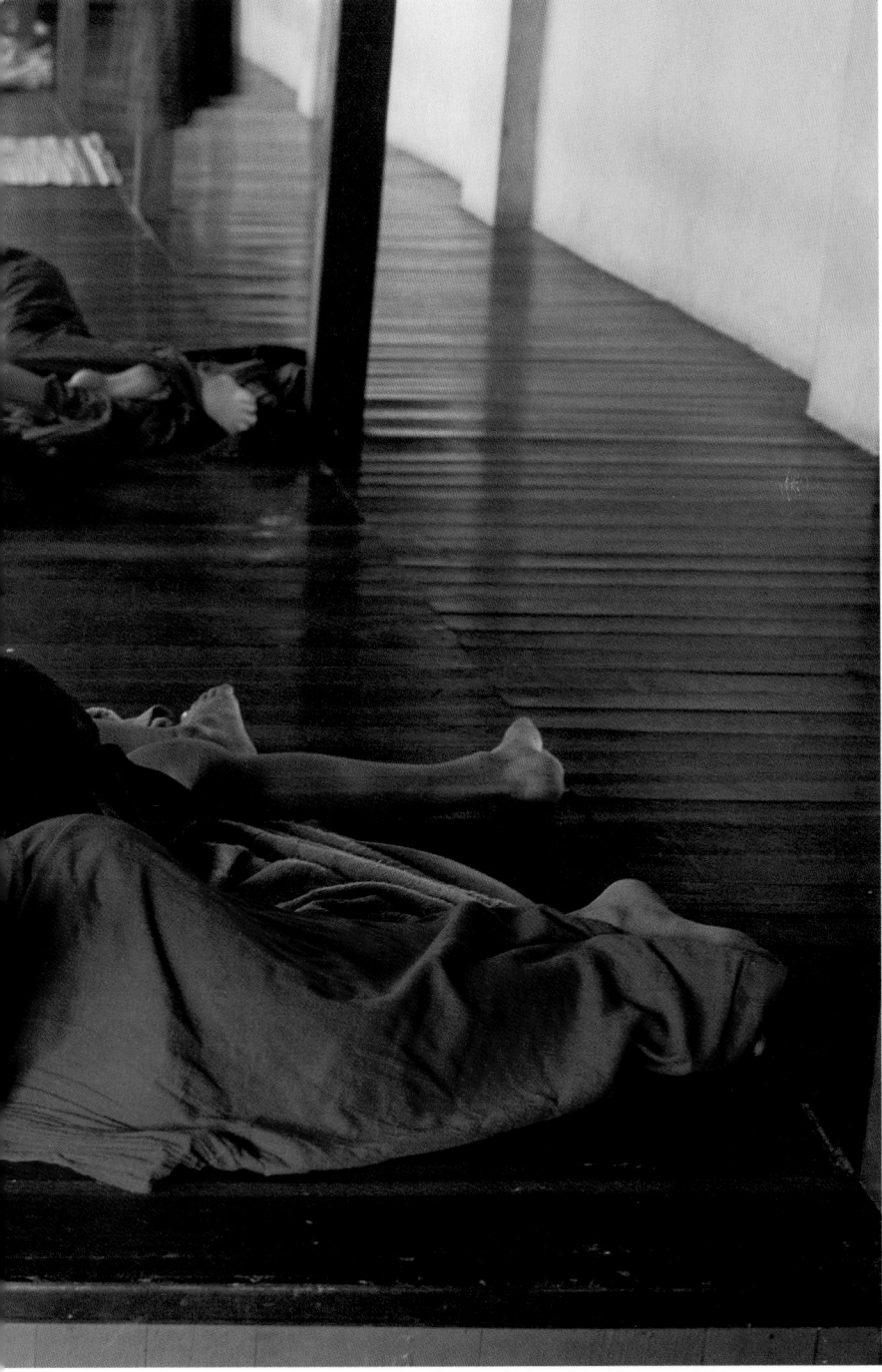

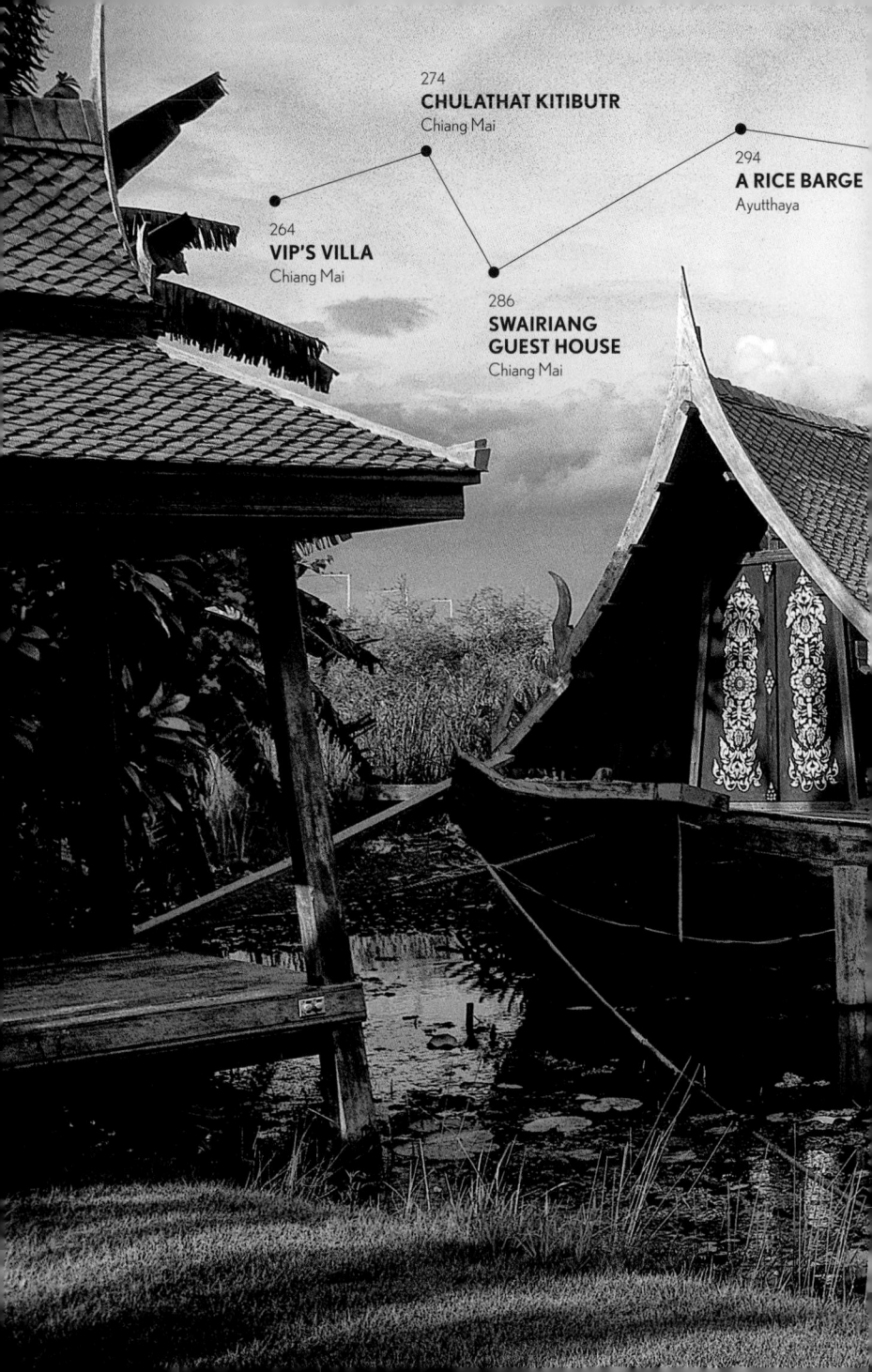

274
CHULATHAT KITIBUTR
Chiang Mai

294
A RICE BARGE
Ayutthaya

264
VIP'S VILLA
Chiang Mai

286
**SWAIRIANG
GUEST HOUSE**
Chiang Mai

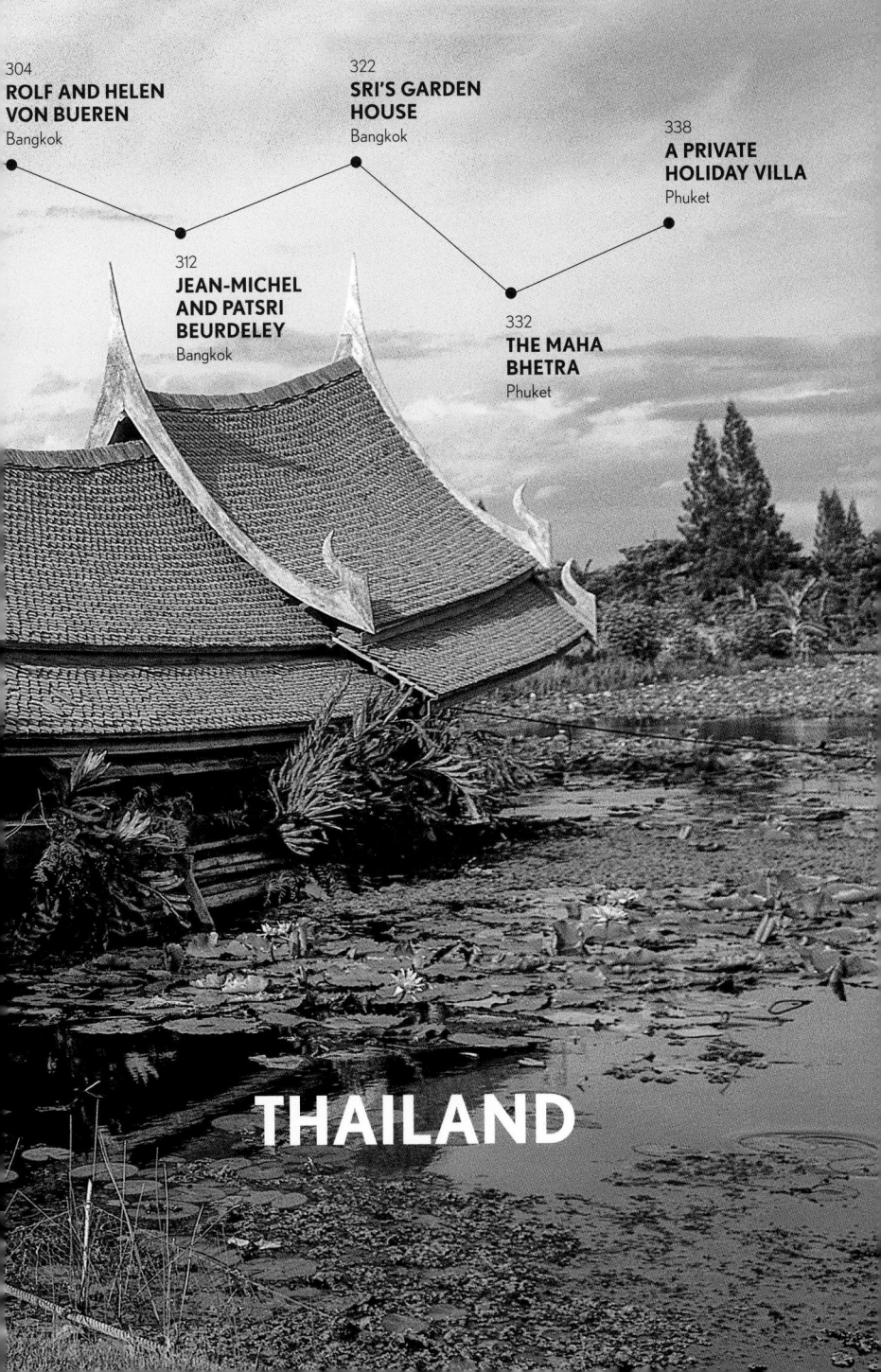

304
**ROLF AND HELEN
VON BUEREN**
Bangkok

322
**SRI'S GARDEN
HOUSE**
Bangkok

338
**A PRIVATE
HOLIDAY VILLA**
Phuket

312
**JEAN-MICHEL
AND PATSRI
BEURDELEY**
Bangkok

332
**THE MAHA
BHETRA**
Phuket

THAILAND

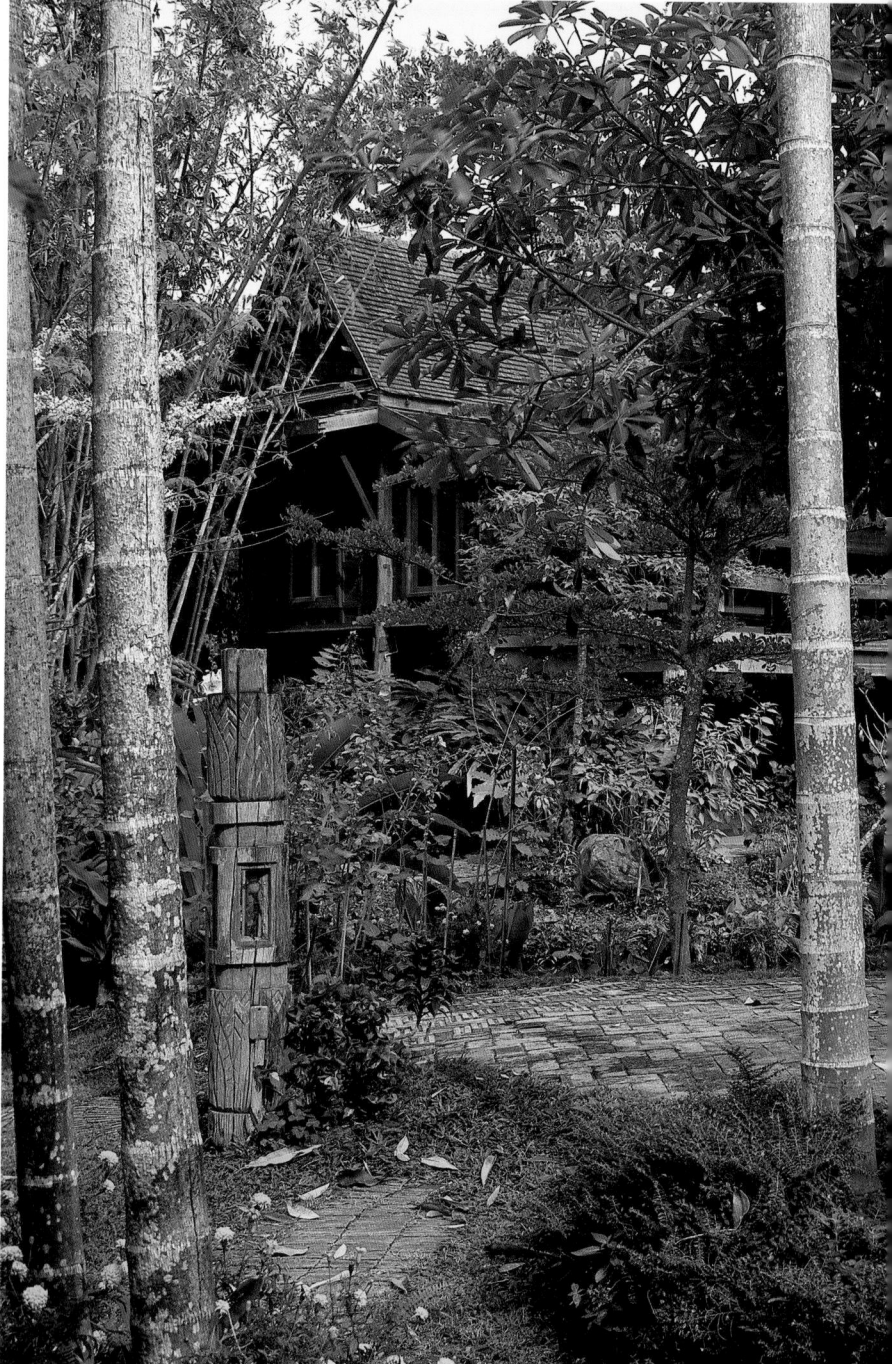

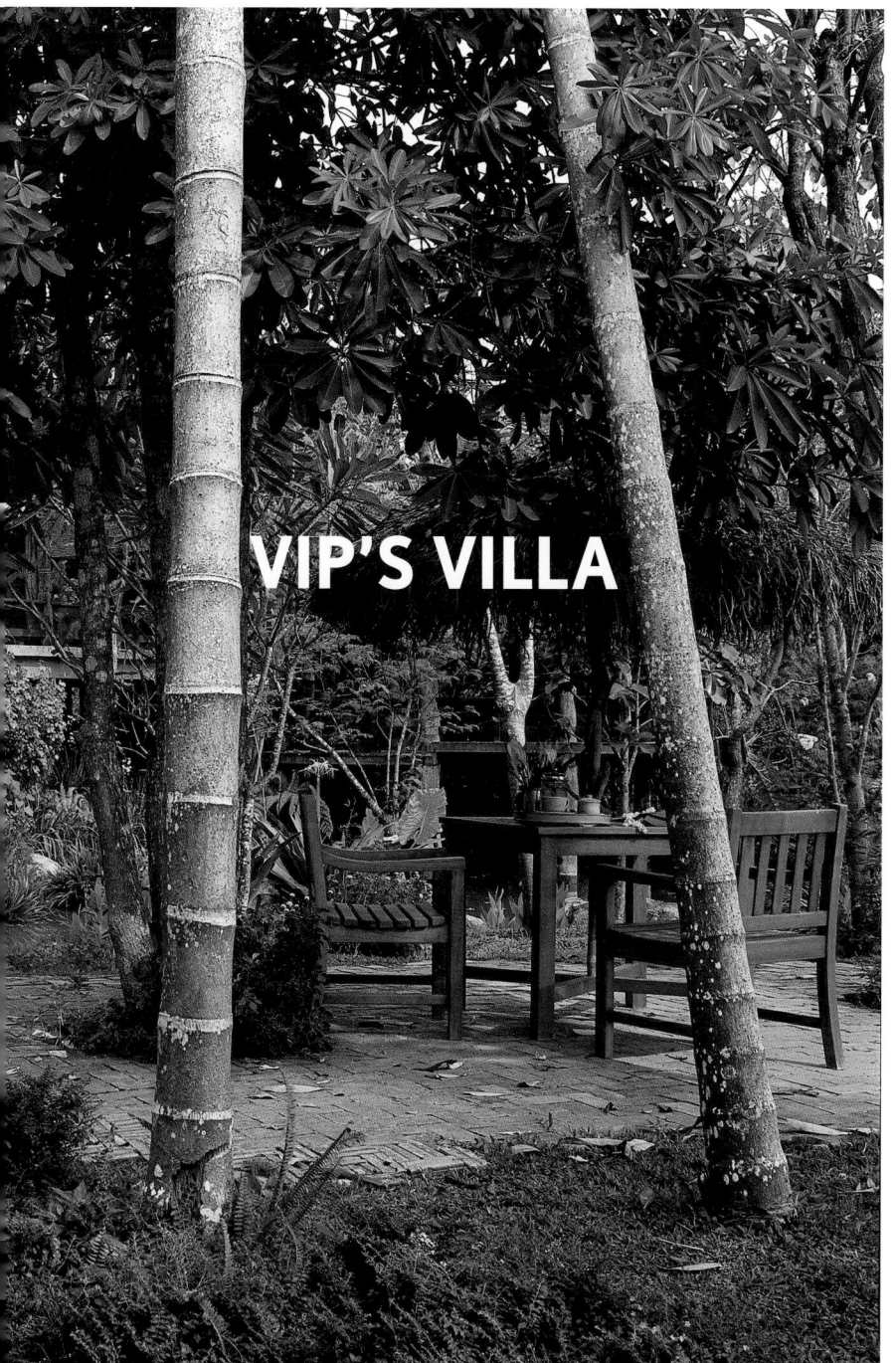

VIP'S VILLA

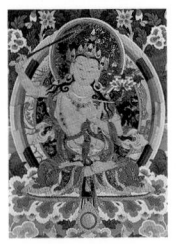

VIP'S VILLA
CHIANG MAI
THAILAND

A fragrant jasmine-like flower, the *kaew* is often grown in Thailand as a hedge. In season, the white blossoms fill the northern hill town of Chiang Mai with a heady scent. *Suan Kaew* means the "Garden of Kaew Flowers". It is the name of a village about 15 miles north of Chiang Mai. It was here that Vibhanand Rangsit – Vip for short – stumbled upon a plot of land amidst rice paddies and wooded hills. He commissioned an architect friend, Archarn Dulphichai, and landscape designer Patraporn Charusorn, who happens to be a cousin, to build him a traditional house in a garden setting. Vip had the foresight not to interfere with their design. With its steeply-pitched roof, the house came up amidst bamboo groves and layered plantings of foliage and flowering plants. Vip works part of the week as an acupuncturist in Bangkok. But Vip's Villa has now grown into a guest house around the garden. Not much enamored of hotel life, he is delighted to find that many people, like him, are always in search of the small, personal, family-run place.

In Thailand wächst die Blume *kaew*, die dem Jasmin ähnelt, häufig als Heckenpflanze. Zur Blütezeit überziehen die weißen Blüten die Hügel im Norden Chiang Mais mit einem berauschenden Duft. Suan Kaew – „Garten der Kaew-Blumen" – lautet der Name eines Dorfes vierundzwanzig Kilometer nördlich von Chiang Mai. In diesem Ort fand Vibhanand Rangsit – kurz Vip – ein Stück Land, umgeben von Reisfeldern und bewaldeten Hügeln. Er gab einem befreundeten Architekten, Archarn Dulphichai, und der Landschaftsarchitektin Patraporn Charusorn, seiner Cousine, den Auftrag, ein traditionelles Haus inmitten eines Gartens zu bauen, und war als Bauherr weise genug, sich nicht in ihre Entwürfe einzumischen. Bambushaine umgeben das Haus mit dem Steildach, das mitten in einem Garten voller verschiedener Blatt- und Blütenpflanzen steht. Mehrmals pro Woche praktiziert Vip in Bangkok als Akupunkteur. Inzwischen hat sich seine Villa mit ihrem schönen Garten zu einer beliebten Pension entwickelt. Er selbst hält nicht viel von dem üblichen Hotelangebot und freut sich, dass es noch mehr Leute seiner Art gibt – die ein kleines, persönlich geführtes Gästehaus zu schätzen wissen.

On voit souvent en Thaïlande des haies de *kaew*, une fleur blanche qui ressemble au jasmin. Lorsqu'elle fleurit, Chiang Mai, ville escarpée au nord du pays, s'emplit de son parfum entêtant. C'est dans le village de Suan Kaew (le jardin de fleurs de *kaew*), à une bonne vingtaine de kilomètres au nord de Chiang Mai, que Vibhanand Rangsit, alias Vip, a découvert un terrain parmi les rizières et les collines boisées. Il a chargé son ami, l'architecte Archarn Dulphichai, et sa cousine, l'architecte paysagiste Patraporn Charusorn, de lui construire une maison traditionnelle dans un cadre de verdure. Il a été bien inspiré de leur laisser carte blanche, car il est désormais l'heureux propriétaire d'une maison au toit très pentu qui s'élève parmi les bosquets de bambou, divers feuillages et des plantes fleuries. Vip, qui travaille une partie de la semaine comme acupuncteur à Bangkok, a fait de sa villa une pension ouverte sur le jardin. N'aimant guère la vie à l'hôtel, il est ravi de voir que d'autres apprécient aussi une petite maison où règne une ambiance familiale.

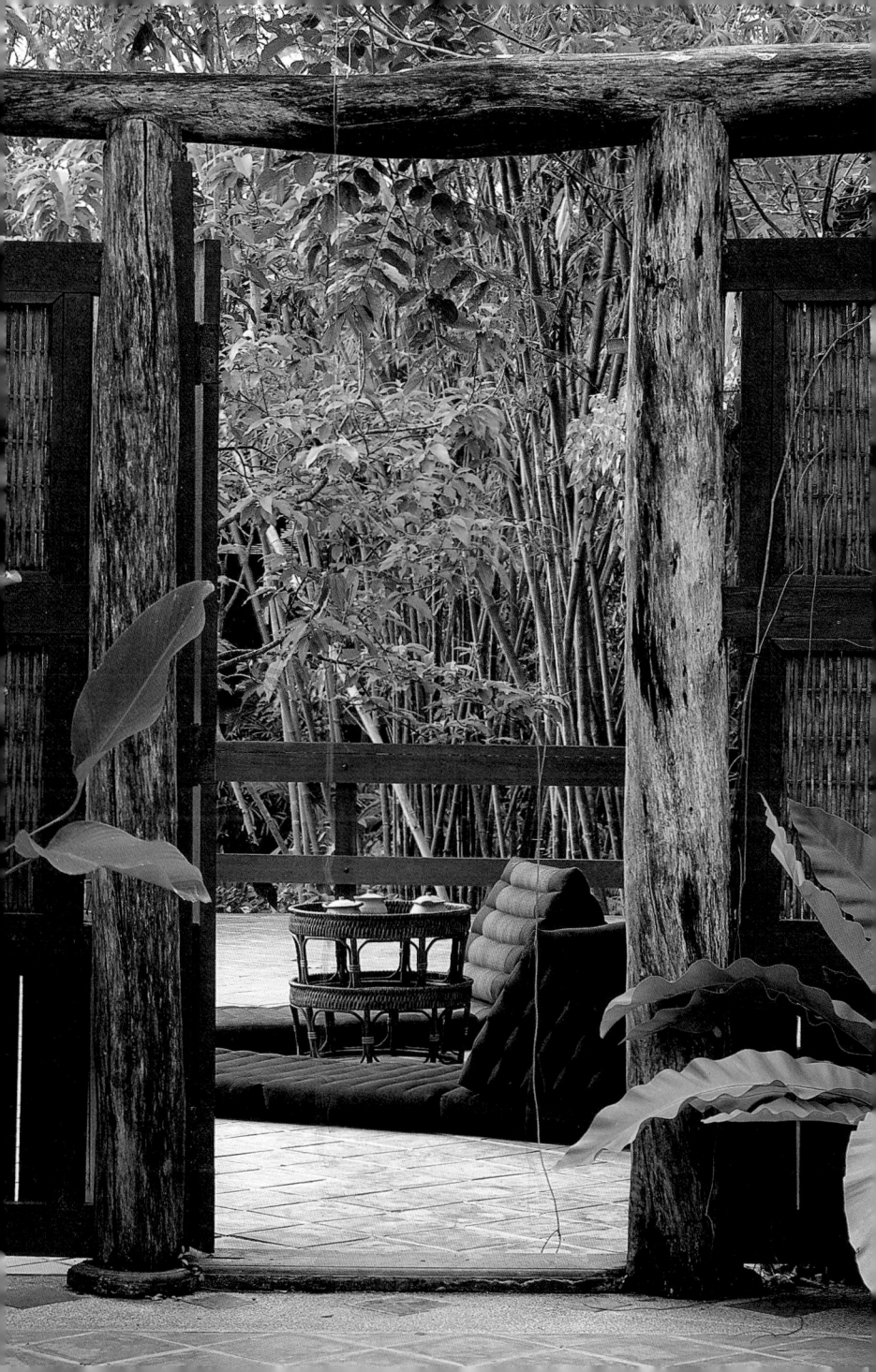

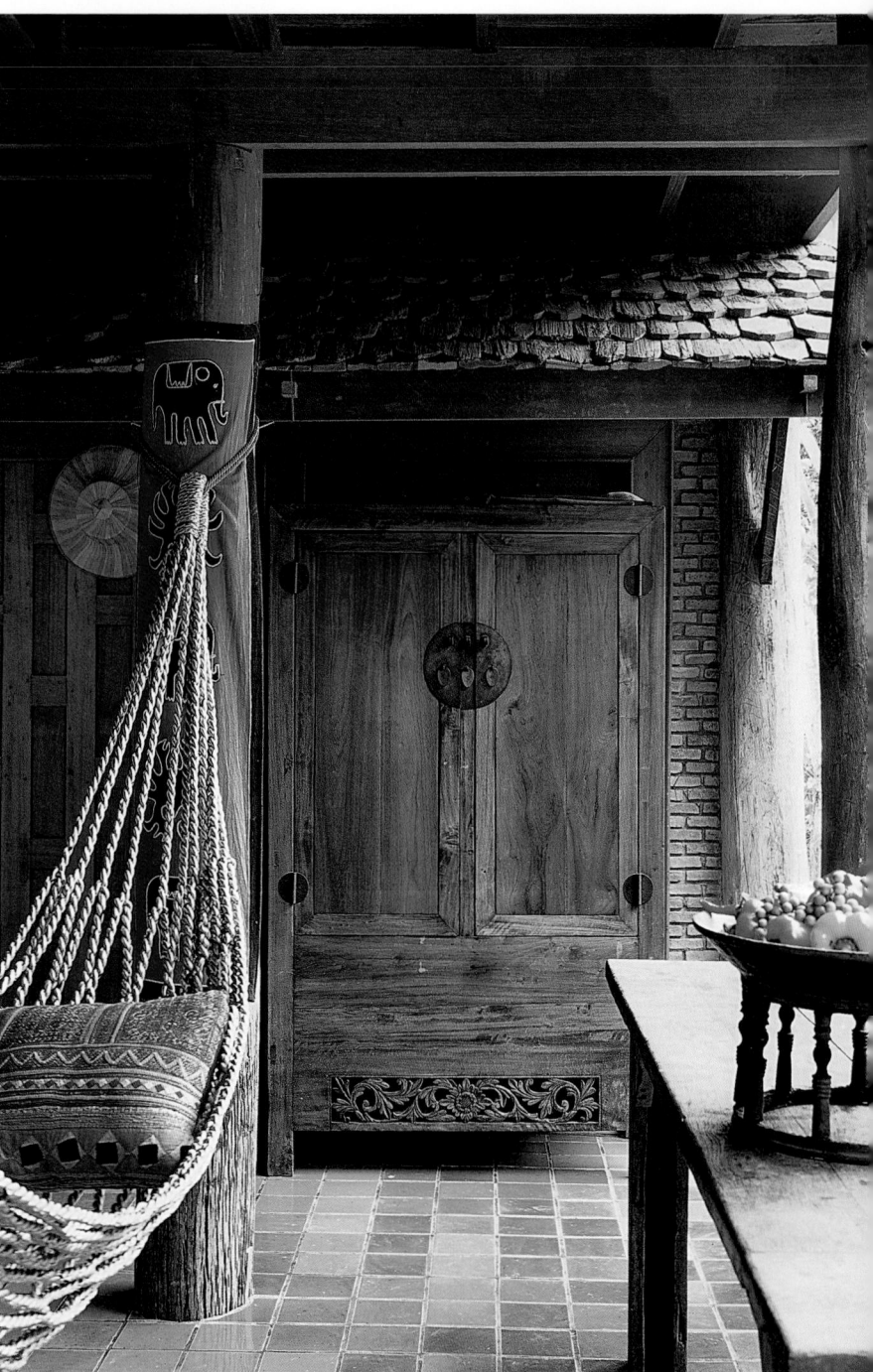

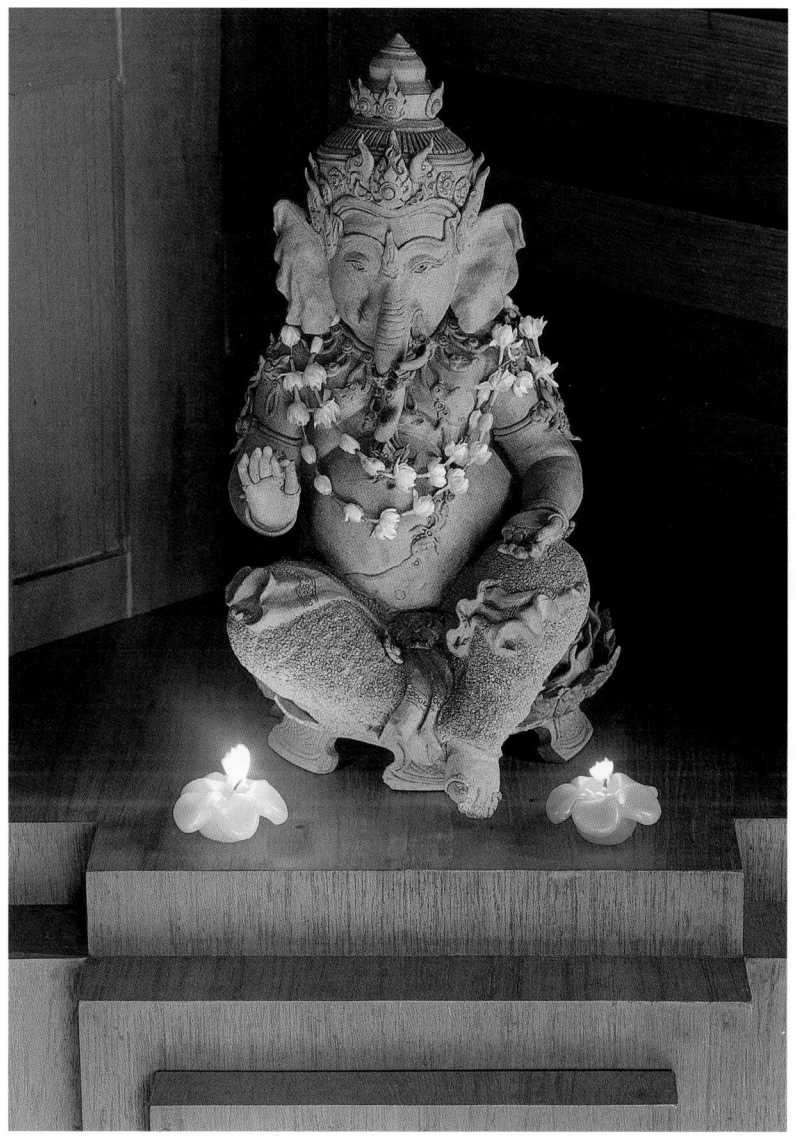

← The veranda floor is lined with locally-made blue tiles. • Der Boden der Veranda wurde mit blauen Fliesen aus dem Dorf ausgelegt. • Le sol de la véranda est couvert d'un carrelage bleu fabriqué sur place.

↑ A clay image of Ganesh, the Hindu god of auspicious beginnings, is adorned with jasmine garlands. • Ganesha, die Hindu-Gottheit der verheißungsvollen Anfänge, als Tonfigur mit Jasmingirlande. • Une statue du Ganesh hindou,

la divinité des débuts prometteurs, arbore un collier de jasmin.

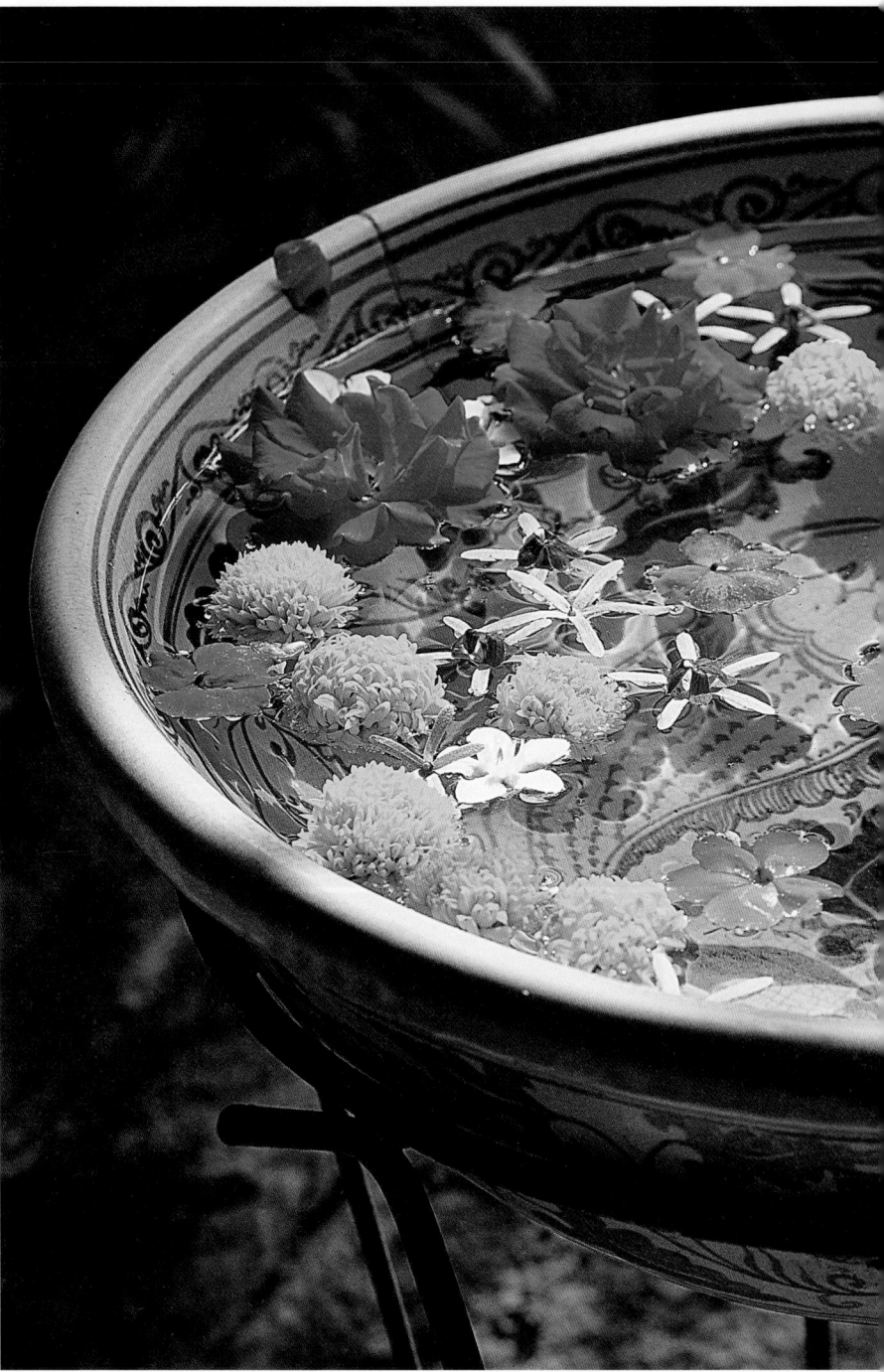

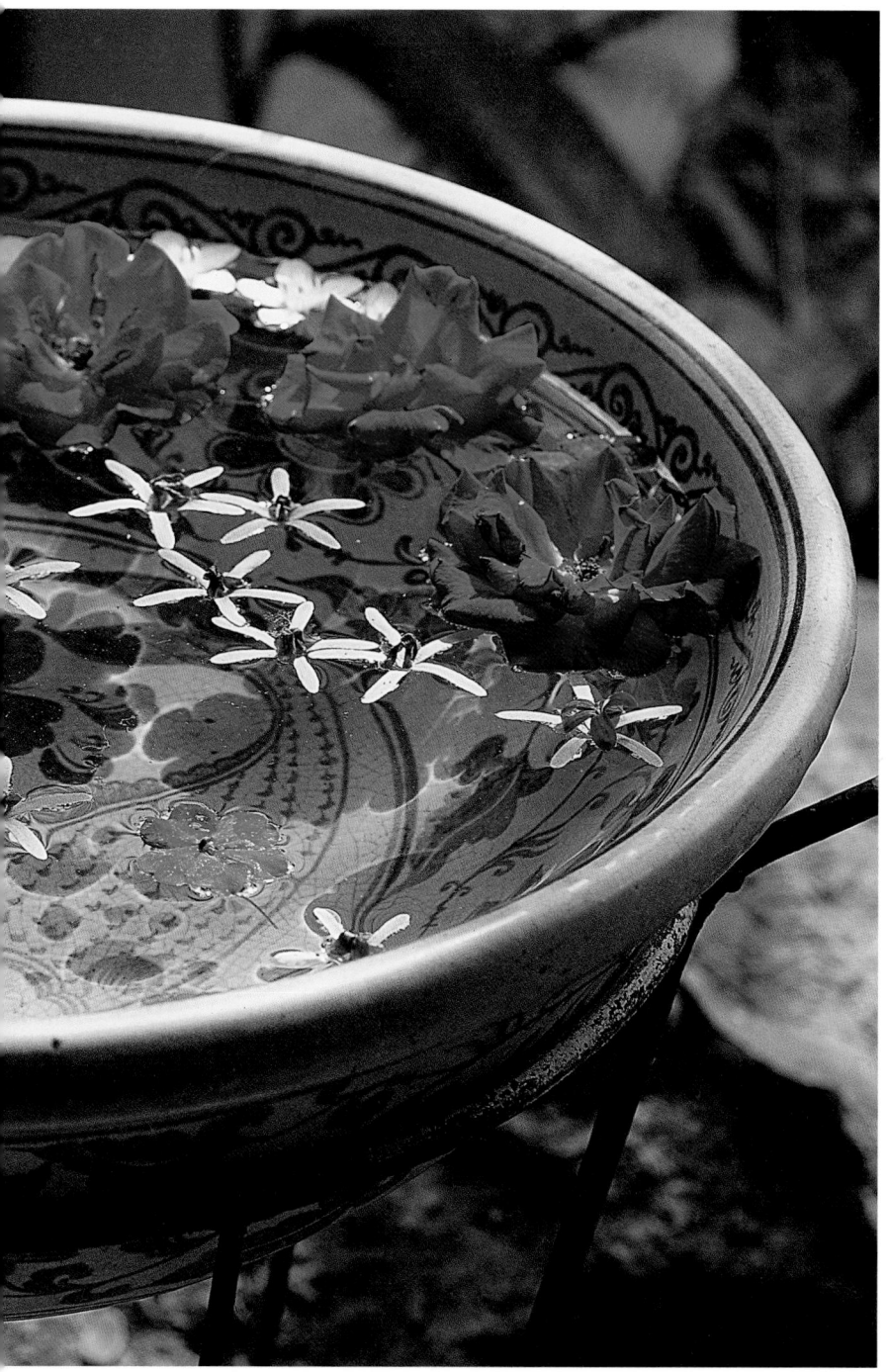

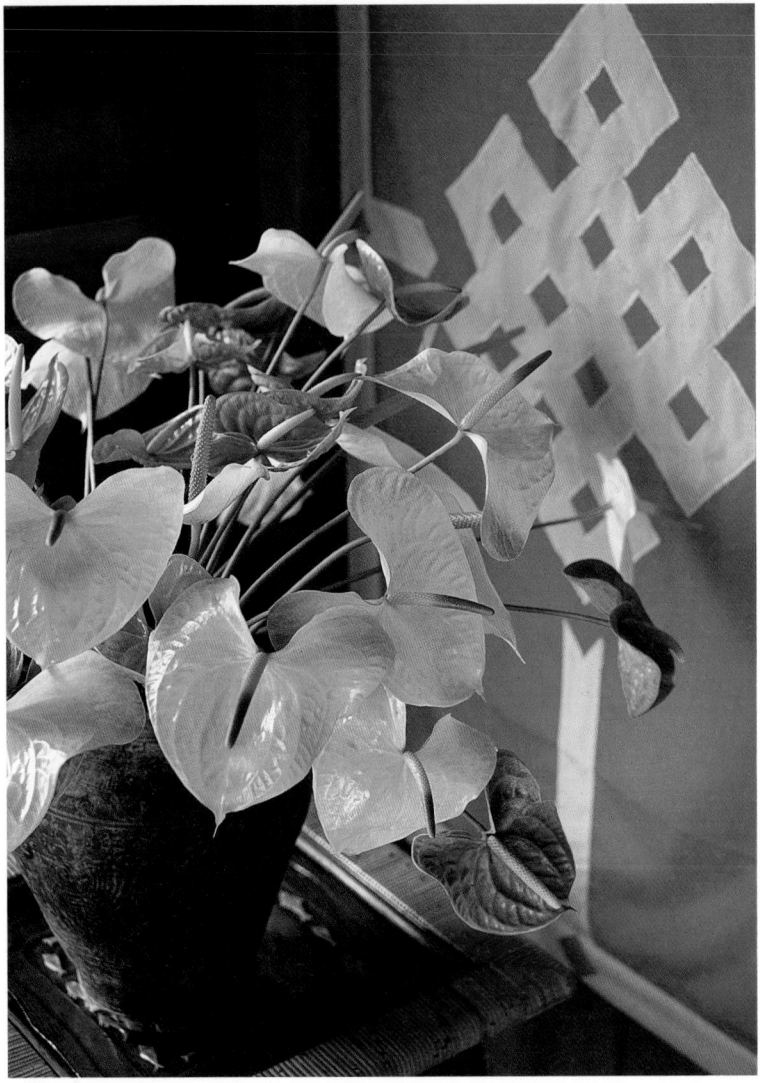

PP. 270–271 Petals floating in a decorative bowl. • Blüten in einer Wasserschale. • Une coupe fleurie.

↑ An arrangement of flowers beside a Tibetan wallhanging with the symbol of the eternal knot. • Ein Blumenarrangement neben einem tibetischen

Wandbehang mit dem Symbol des endlosen Knotens. • Un arrangement floral devant une tenture tibétaine représentant le nœud éternel.

→ A traditional woodcarving above the bed. The carpet and turtle are Tibetan. • Eine traditionelle

Holzschnitzarbeit über dem Bett. Der Teppich und die Schildkröte stammen aus Tibet. • Une sculpture traditionnelle sur bois orne la tête de lit. Le tapis et la tortue proviennent du Tibet.

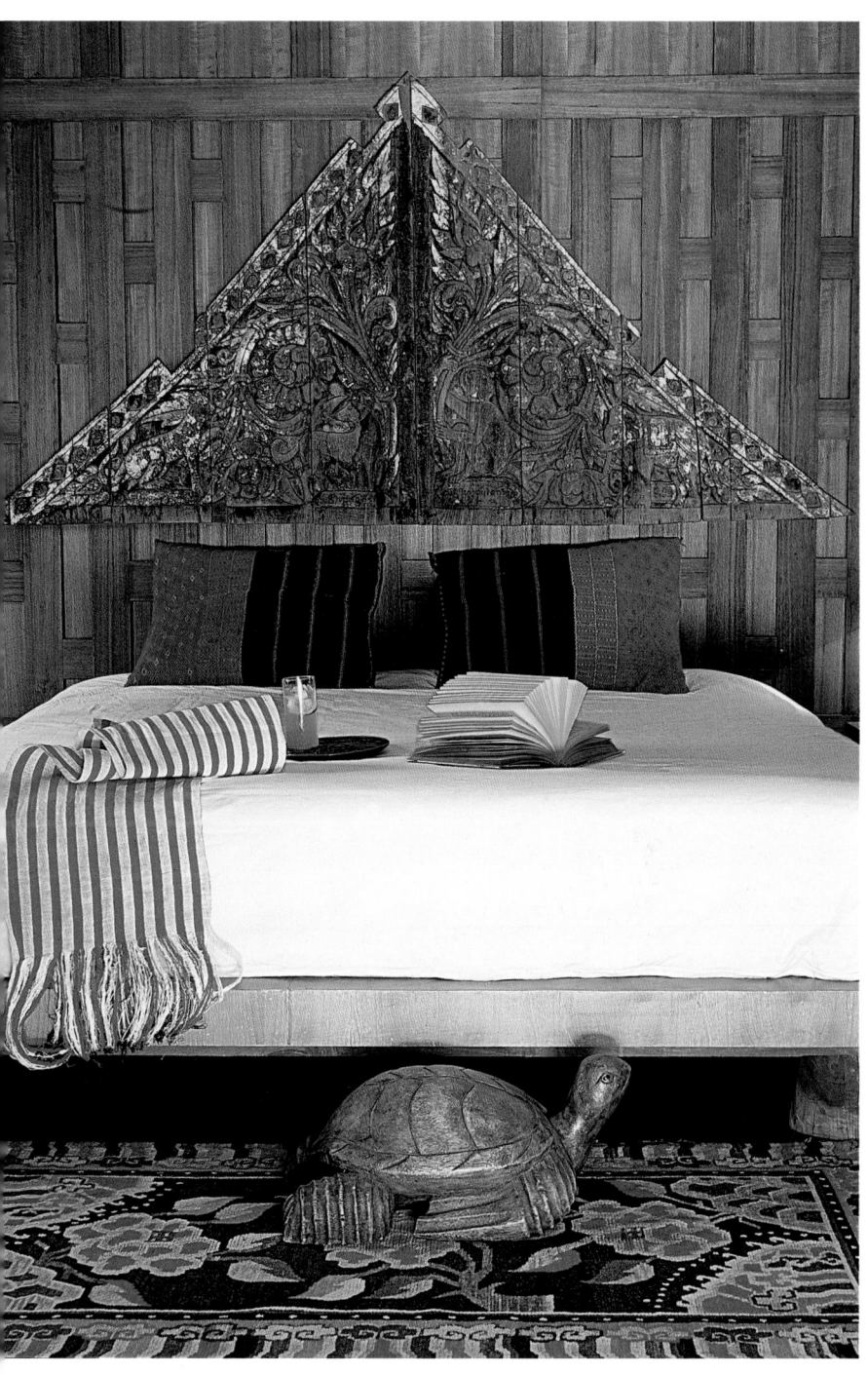

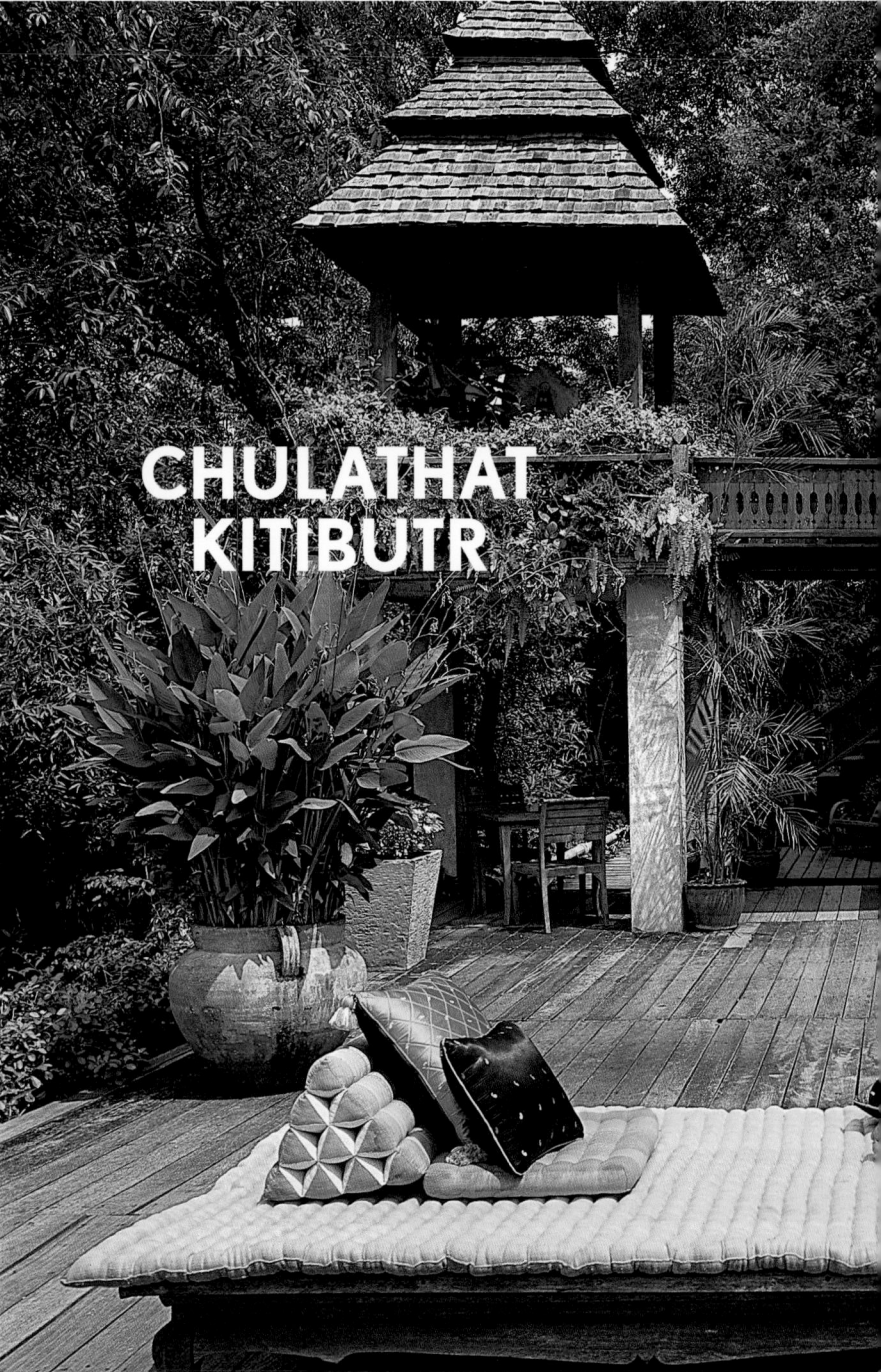

CHULATHAT
KITIBUTR

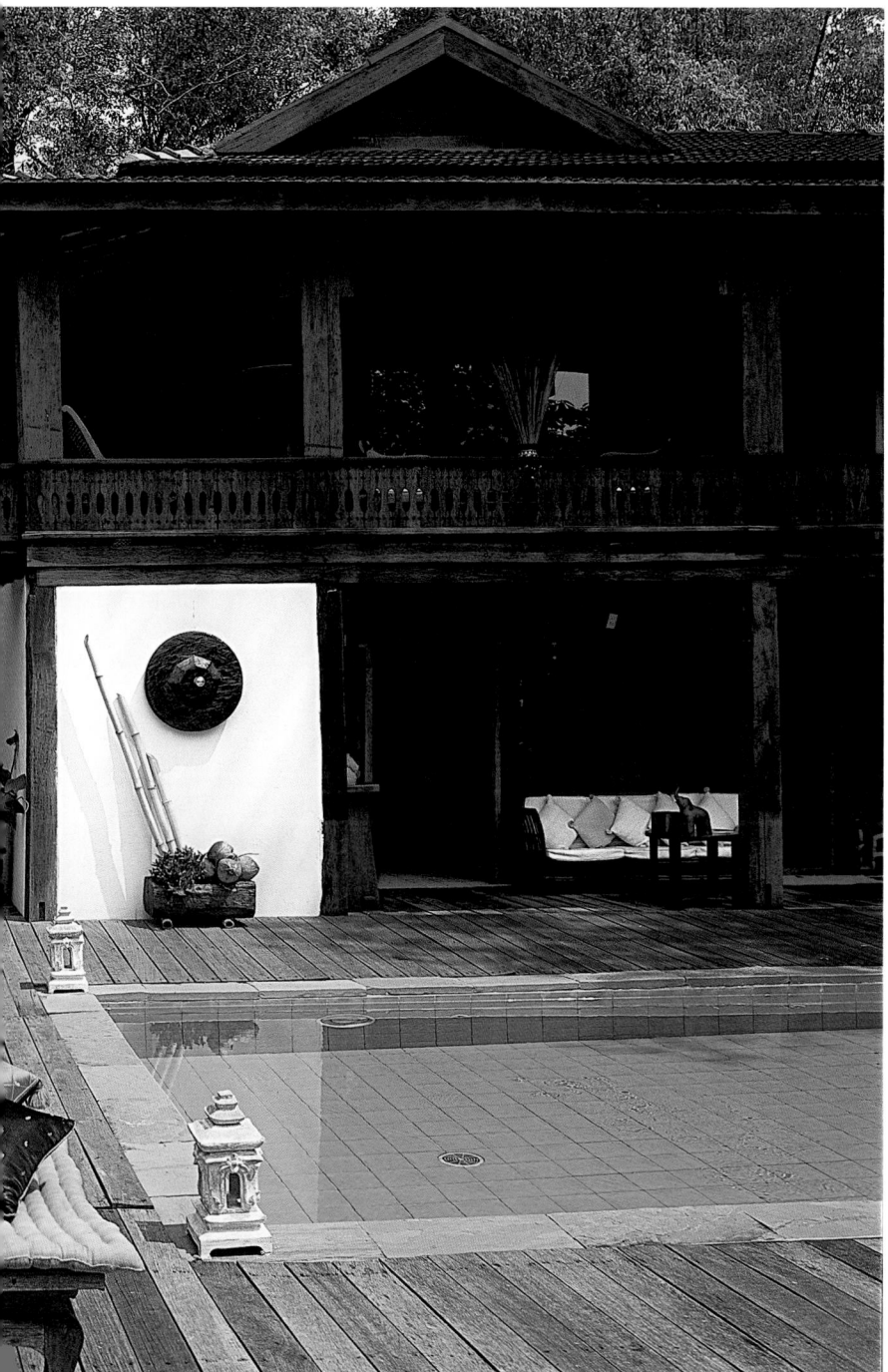

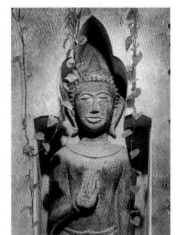

CHULATHAT KITIBUTR

CHIANG MAI
THAILAND

Lamphun province in northern Thailand is culturally one of the oldest, most distinctive parts of the country, a melting pot of picturesque ruins, tribal style and traditional architecture. Historically, the entire region around Chiang Mai was influenced by the traditions of the Shan-Burmese states just west of the border and of Laos to the east. Geographically juxtaposed at the crossroads, the great flowering of this culture took place during the rise of the Lanna dynasty between the 13th and 15th centuries. Lanna-style houses can be spotted a mile off, with their gabled roofs, strong teak timber-work and fretwork balconies. Chulathat Kitibutr, a distinguished professor of architecture at Chiang Mai University, is also famous for establishing the Chiang Mai Architects' Collaborative. He found this old teak house in Lamphun and reconstructed it in the village of San Pi Sear on the outskirts of Chiang Mai. The two-story structure with its three linked pavilions is a restrained adaptation of a Lanna house for modern use.

Aus kultureller Sicht gilt die Provinz Lamphun in Nordthailand als eine der ältesten und bedeutendsten des Landes – mit ihrer aufregenden Mischung aus malerischen Ruinen, alten Stammesbauten und traditioneller Architektur. Historisch gesehen stand die gesamte Region um Chiang Mai unter dem Einfluss der Shan-birmanischen Länder im Westen sowie aus Laos im Osten. Die Blütezeit dieser Kultur war hier, am geografischen Schnittpunkt der beiden Einflüsse, an den Aufstieg der Lanna-Dynastie vom 13. bis zum 15. Jahrhundert gekoppelt. Häuser im Lanna-Stil sind von Weitem an ihren Giebeldächern, dem mächtigen Holzgebälk aus Teak und den durchbrochenen Balkonen zu erkennen. Chulathat Kitibutr lehrt als Architekturprofessor an der Universität von Chiang Mai und gründete ebendort auch eine Architek-tengemeinschaft. Der weithin anerkannte Gelehrte fand sein Haus in der Provinz Lamphun und ließ es in San Pi Sear, einem Dorf am Stadtrand von Chiang Mai, wieder aufbauen. Das zweistöckige Gebäude mit den drei Pavillons verbin-det die zurückhaltende Version eines Lanna-Hauses mit den modernen Bedürfnissen seiner Bewohner.

Sur le plan culturel, la province de Lamphun, dans le nord de la Thaïlande, est l'une des régions les plus anciennes et les plus caractéristiques du pays. Elle marie des ruines pittoresques, le style tribal et l'architecture traditionnelle. Au fil des siècles, la région de Chiang Mai a subi l'influence des États shan birmans à l'ouest, et du Laos à l'est. Carrefour de civili-sations, cette région a été florissante pendant l'âge d'or du royaume de Lan Na, entre les 13e et 15e siècles. Les maisons de style Lan Na, avec leurs toits à pignons, leur solide charpente de teck et leurs balcons aux rambardes richement ouvragées se remarquent à une lieue à la ronde. C'est Chulathat Kitibutr, éminent professeur d'architecture à l'univer-sité de Chiang Mai et fondateur de l'association regroupant les architectes de cette ville, qui a déniché cette vieille mai-son de teck à Lamphun et l'a reconstruite dans le village de San Pi Sear, à la périphérie de Chiang Mai. Cette construc-tion sur deux niveaux, à laquelle sont reliés trois pavillons, correspond à une typologie traditionnelle légèrement adaptée pour un usage moderne.

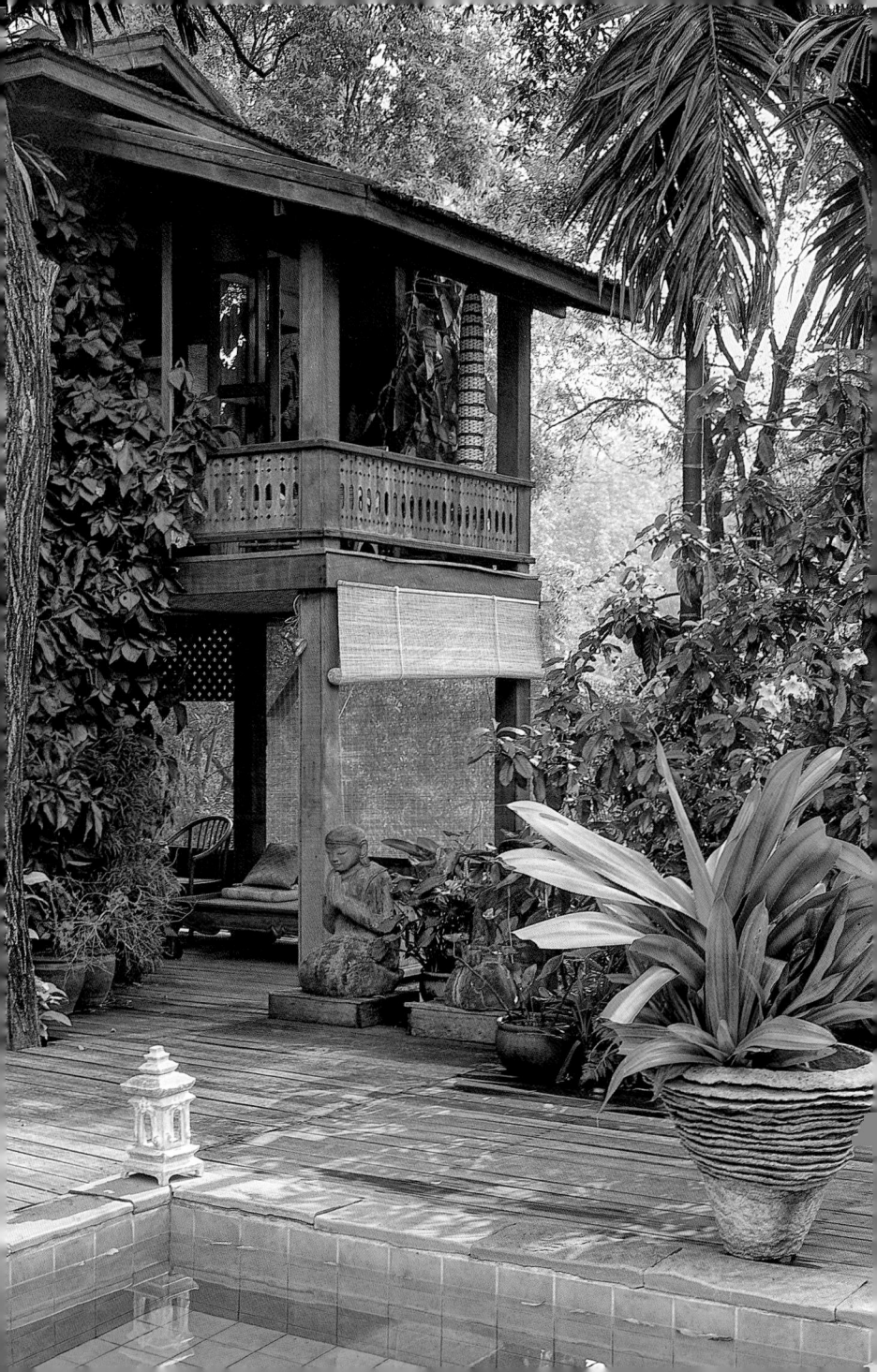

THAILAND

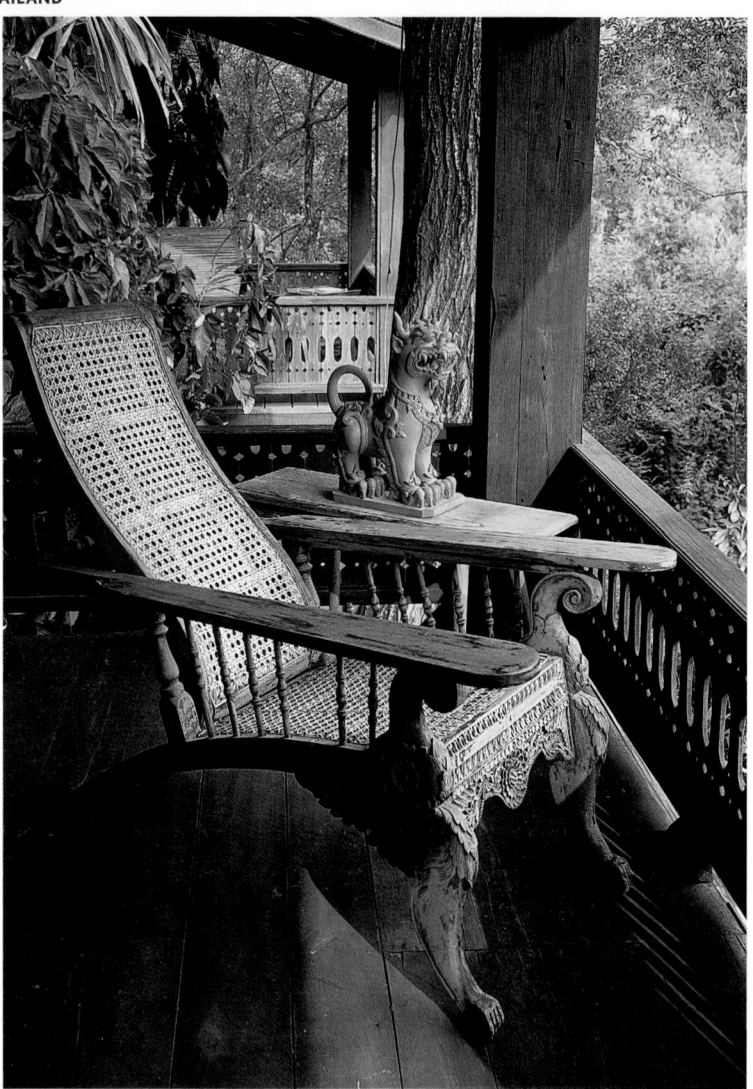

PP. 274–275 A comfortable daybed
on the wooden deck that surrounds
the swimming pool. · Ein bequemes
Ruhebett auf der Holzterrasse am
Swimmingpool. · Un confortable lit
de repos sur la terrasse de la piscine.

P. 277 At the back, a wooden walkway
links the upper storey of the main house
to a Lanna-style pavilion. · Im Hinter-
grund verbindet ein Laufgang aus Holz
das Obergeschoss des Haupthauses
mit einem Pavillon im Lanna-Stil. · À
l'arrière-plan, une passerelle en bois
relie l'étage supérieur du bâtiment principal à l'un des pavillons de style Lan Na.

→ The main staircase to the house
joins the wooden walkway above. · Die
Haupttreppe zum Haus stößt auf den
erhöhten hölzernen Gang. · Le grand
escalier débouche sur la passerelle de
bois à l'étage.

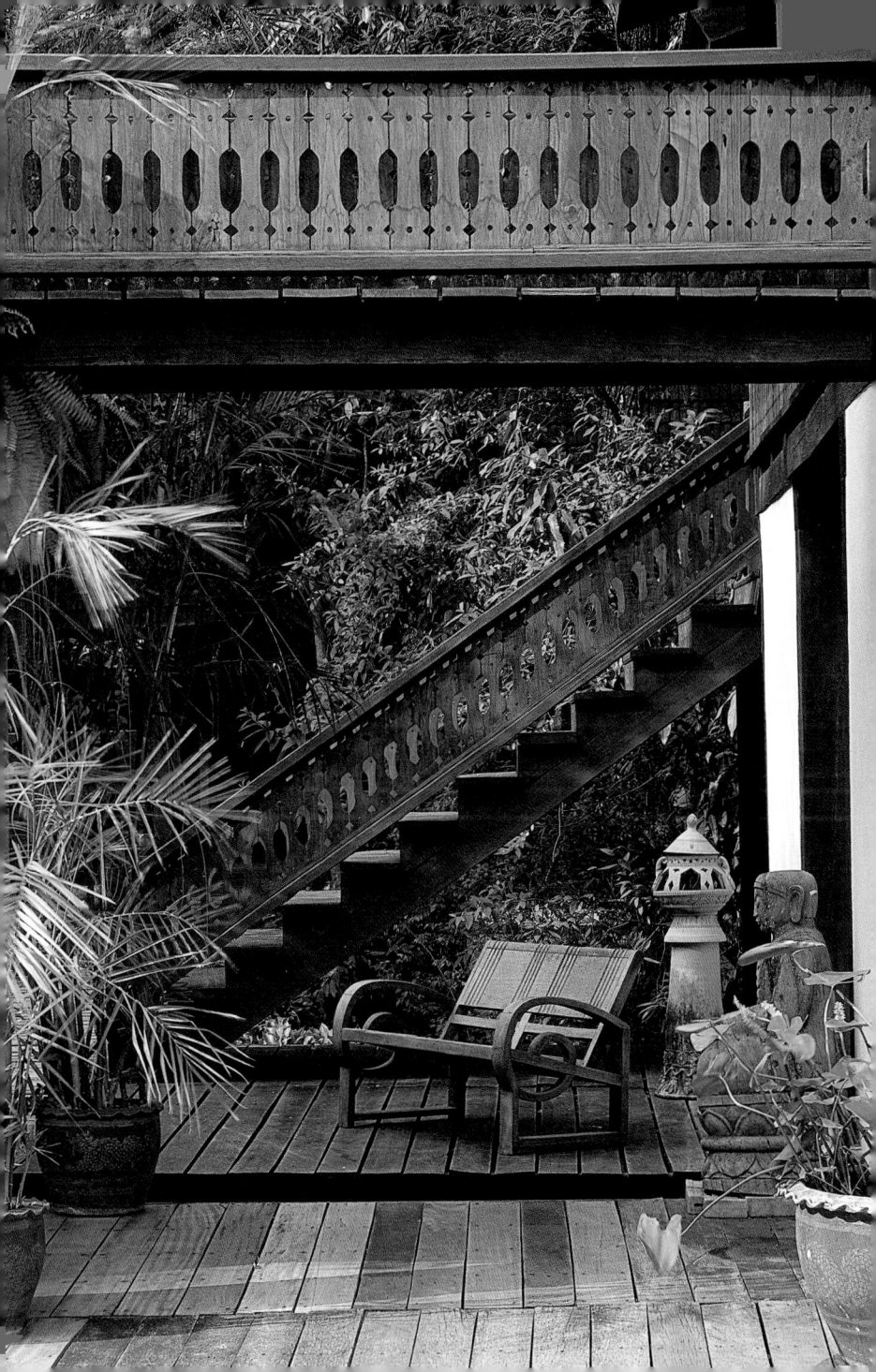

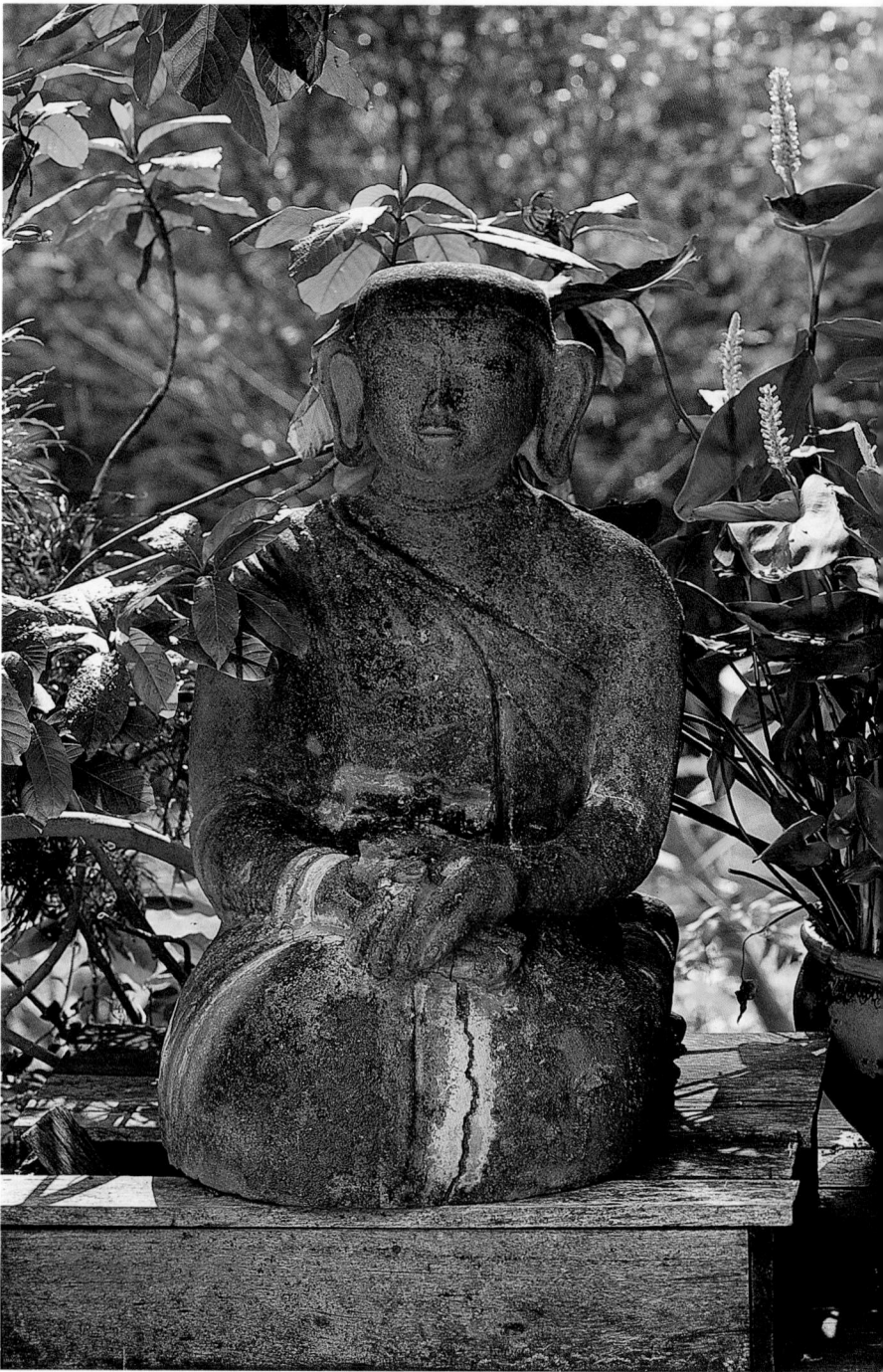

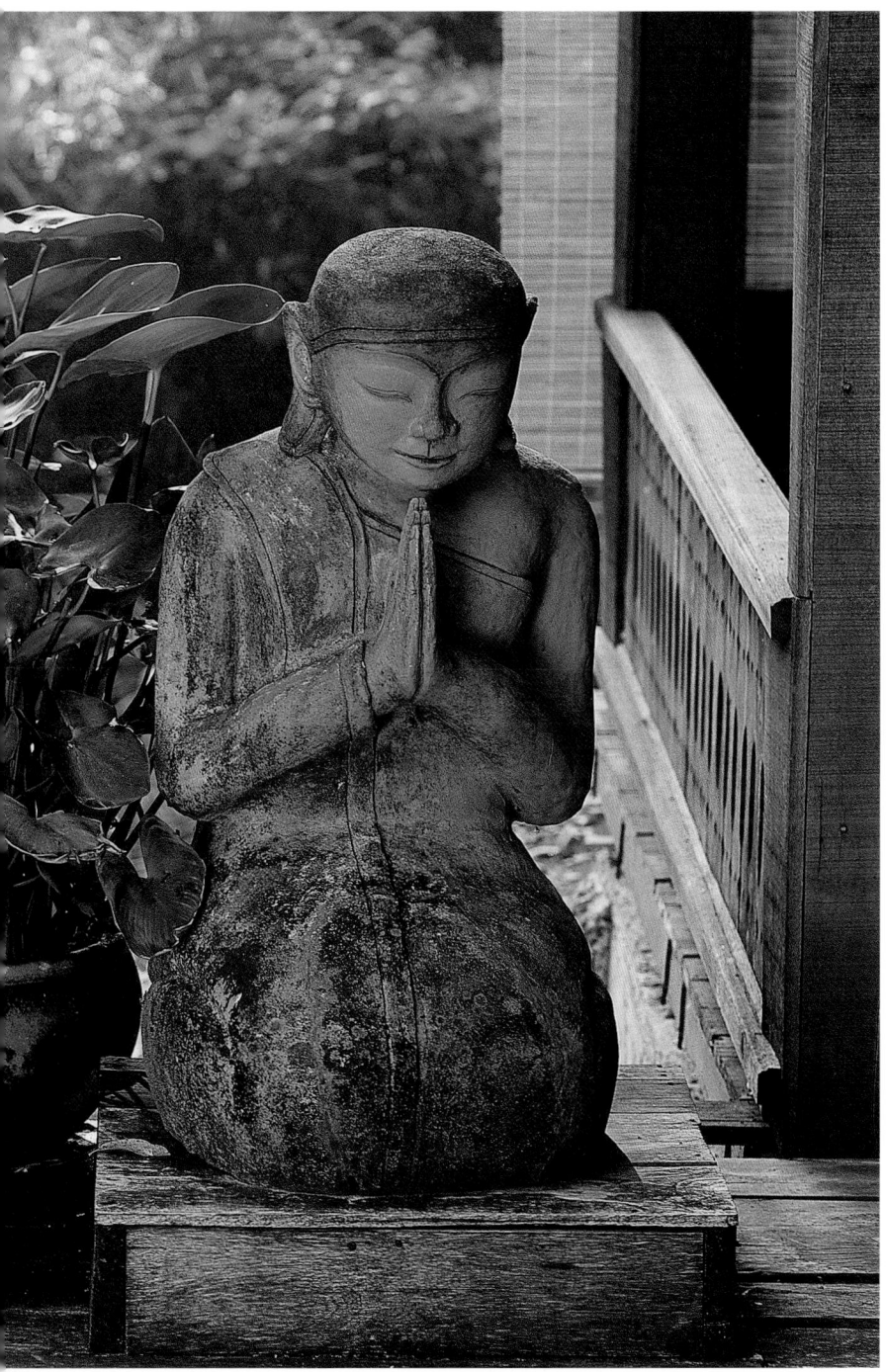

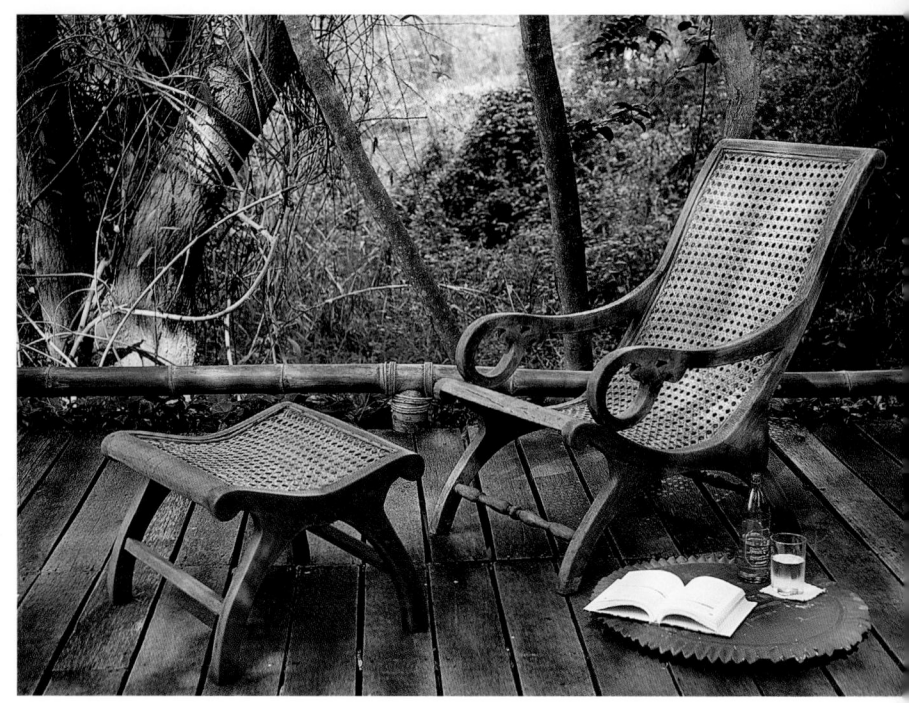

PP. 280–281 The terracotta statues were crafted by local potters. • Die Terrakottafiguren wurden von einheimischen Töpfern hergestellt. • Les statues en terre cuite sont l'œuvre de potiers locaux.

↑ The caned reclining chair and stool were made in Chiang Mai. • Liegestuhl und Hocker wurden in Chiang Mai von Rohrflechtern gefertigt. • Le fauteuil et le repose-pied cannés ont été fabriqués à Chiang Mai.

→ The black bathtub with a wooden surround gives onto a balcony overlooking the swimming pool. • Um die schwarze Badewanne herum wurde Holzboden verlegt. An das Bad grenzt ein Balkon mit Blick auf den Swimming-pool. • La baignoire noire est sertie dans un habillage de bois. Du balcon adjacent, on a vue sur la piscine.

PP. 284–285 Lanna-style Buddha images stand in niches. • Zwei Buddhafiguren im Lanna-Stil werden in Nischen ausgestellt. • Dans des niches, deux bouddhas dans le style de Lan Na.

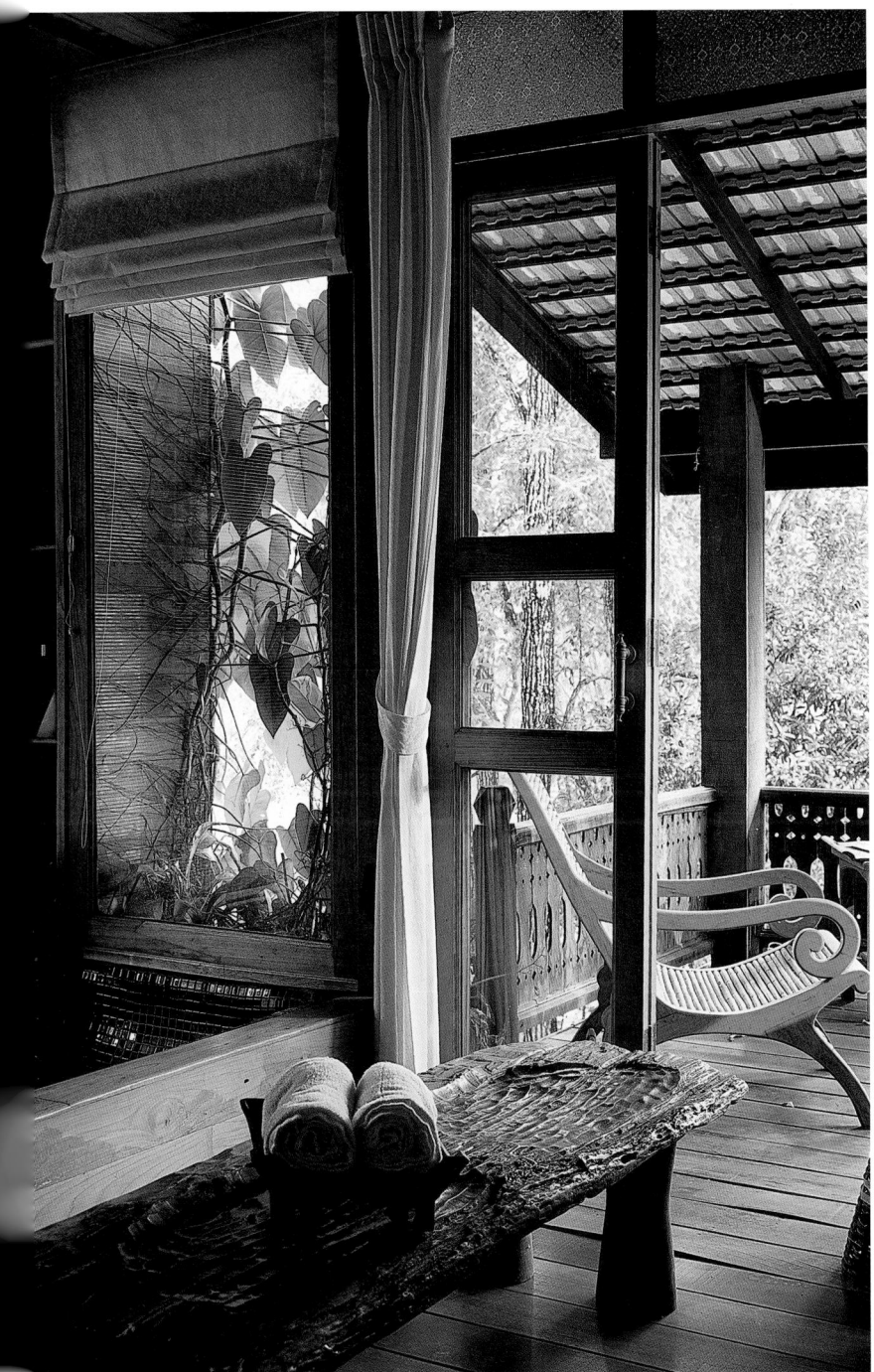

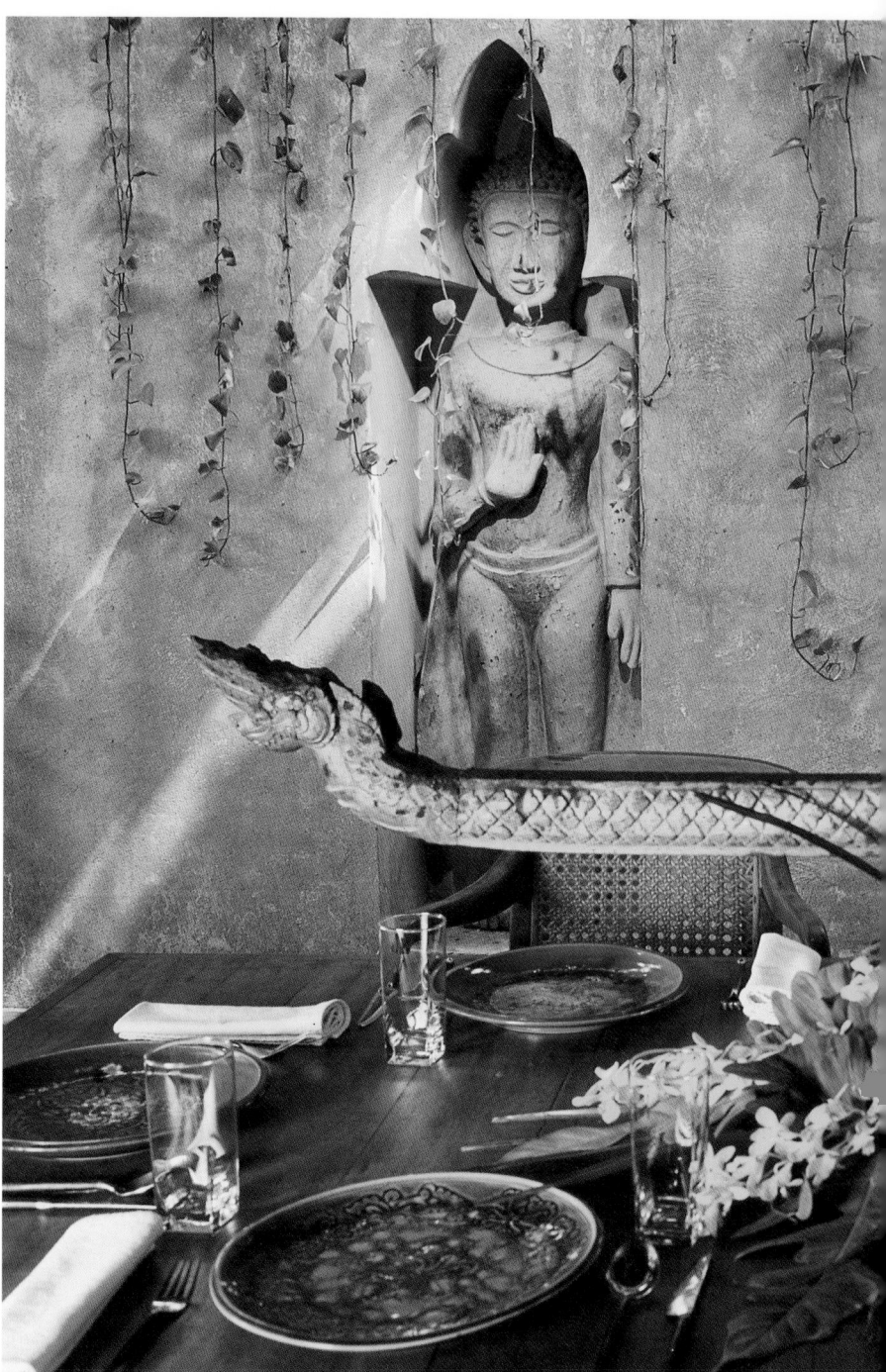

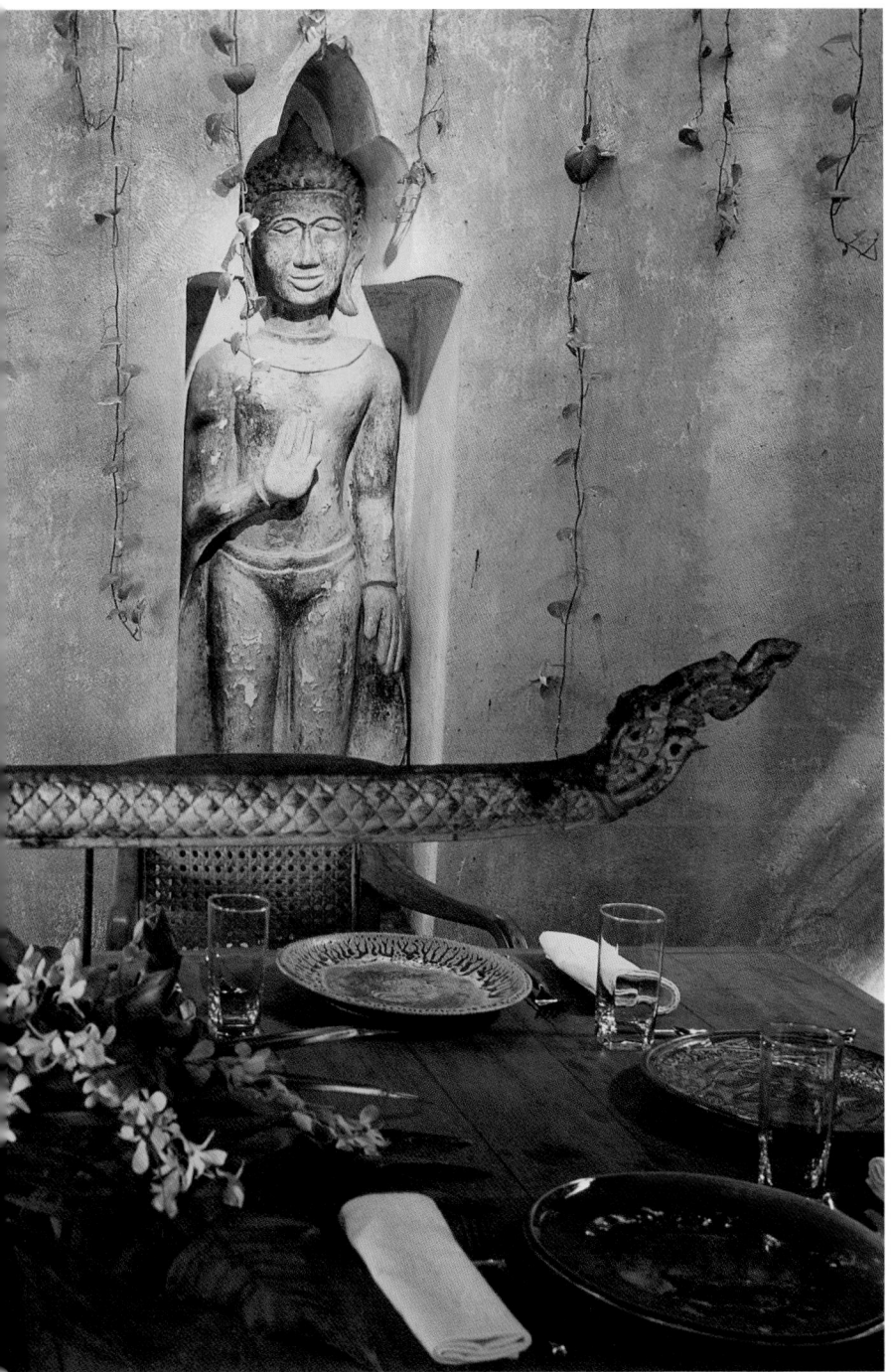

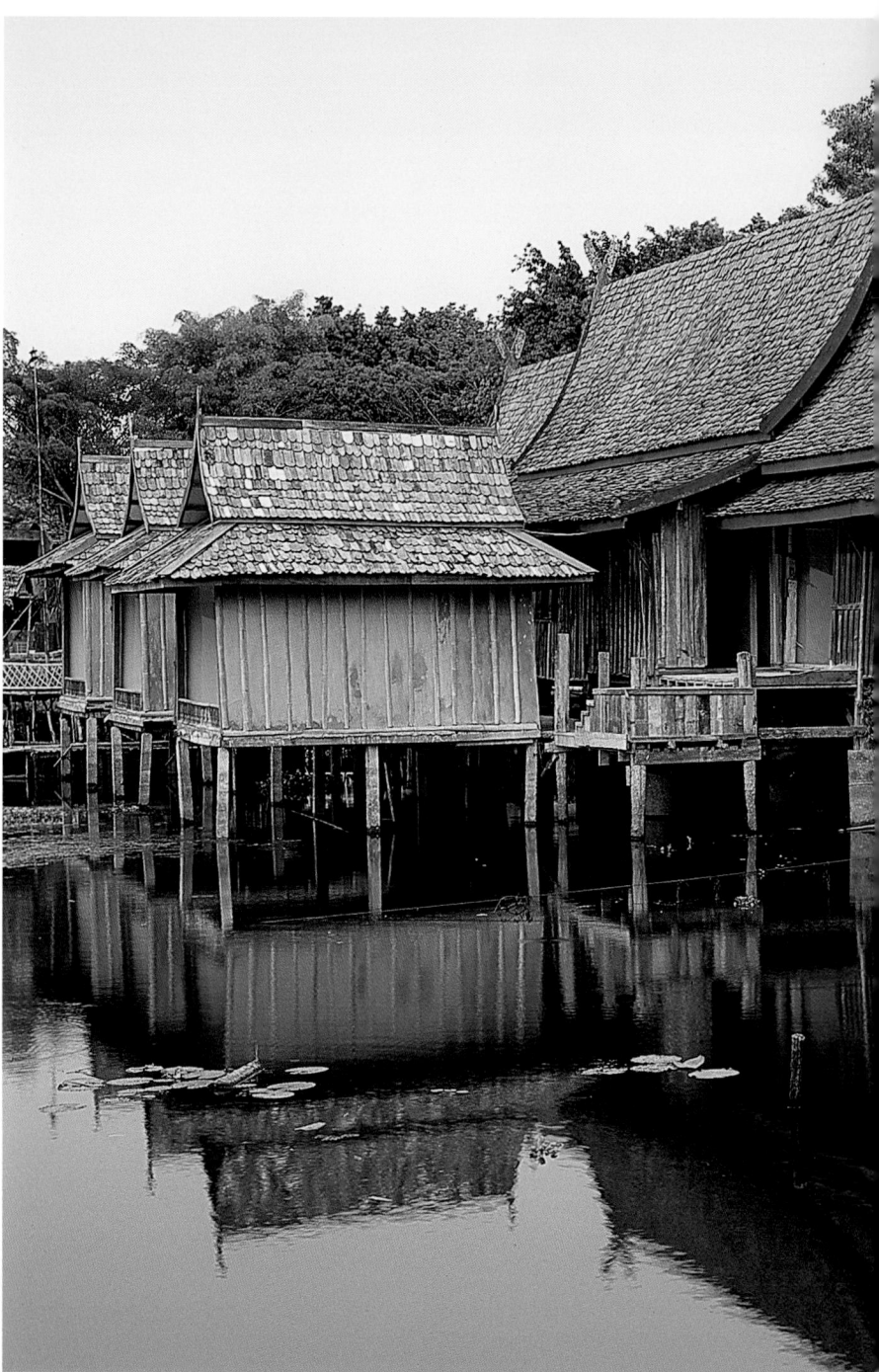

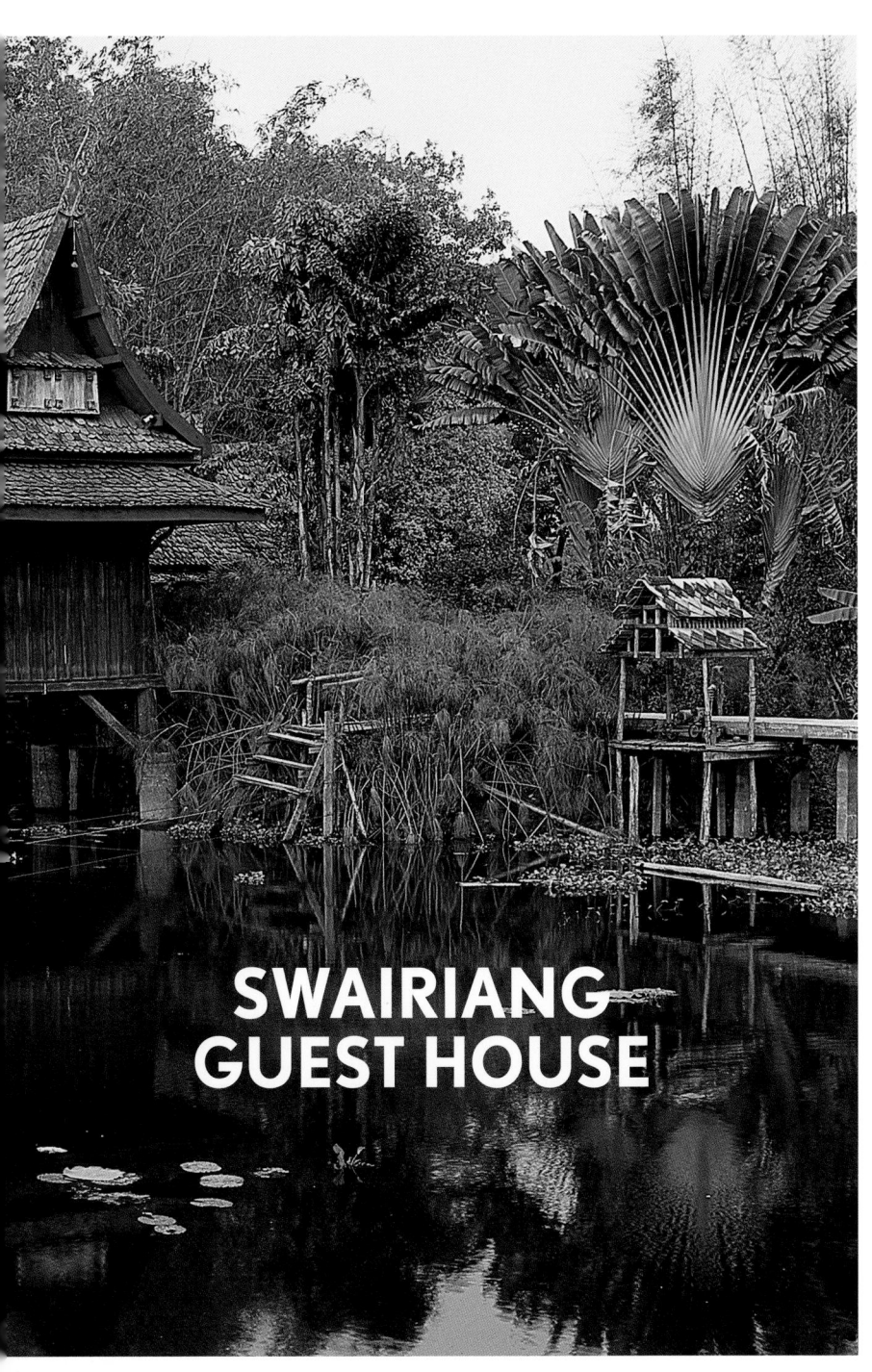

SWAIRIANG
GUEST HOUSE

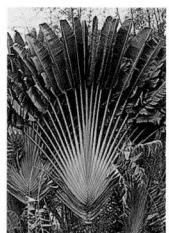

SWAIRIANG GUEST HOUSE
CHIANG MAI
THAILAND

The moated city of Chiang Mai grew on the banks of the River Mae Nam Ping as a prosperous trading post on the medieval caravan route between China's Yunnan province and the ports of Myanmar. Further south along the riverbank, a short drive from the city center, are older excavated ruins at Wiang Kum Kam that date from an earlier kingdom established by Burmese Mon kings in the eleventh century. The landscape is an amateur archaeologist's delight – remains of Mon-style temples, old stones and bricks from crumbling stupas litter the landscape. One of the attractions of Wiang Kum Kam is the pleasant waterside Swairiang Guest House, its cottages and rooms set around a lotus-filled pond. Swairiang is composed of old Lanna-style houses and pavilions with thatched roofs restored by a Bangkok-based architect. Wiang Kum Kam is an idyllic village getaway from bustling, tourist-filled Chiang Mai. One quick way of getting there is by bicycle or on one of the motorized local three-wheelers known as *tuk-tuk*.

Die von einem Wassergraben umgebene Stadt Chiang Mai entwickelte sich am Ufer des Mae Nam Ping aus einem aufstrebenden Handelsplatz auf der mittelalterlichen Karawanenroute, die die chinesische Provinz Yunnan mit den birmanischen Häfen verband. Nur eine kurze Autofahrt vom Zentrum entfernt liegen weiter südlich am Ufer die ausgegrabenen Ruinen von Wiang Kum Kam. Sie stammen aus dem 11. Jahrhundert, der Zeit des Königreichs der birmanischen Mon-Dynastie. Amateurarchäologen kommen in dieser Landschaft auf ihre Kosten, denn sie ist reich an Tempeln im Mon-Stil sowie alten Steinen und Ziegeln bröckelnder Stupas. In Wiang Kum Kam befindet sich direkt am Wasser das angenehme Swairiang Guest House, dessen Häuschen und Zimmer um einen Teich mit Lotusblüten gruppiert sind. Swairiang besteht aus alten Häusern im Lanna-Stil sowie strohgedeckten Pavillons, die von einem in Bangkok ansässigen Architekten restauriert wurden. Ein Kurztrip mit dem Fahrrad oder einem der motorisierten Dreiräder namens *tuk-tuk*, und im Nu erreicht man das idyllische Dorf Wiang Kum Kam und kann sich von dem geschäftigen Treiben in Chiang Mai erholen.

Située sur les rives de la Mae Nam Ping, Chiang Mai était un comptoir florissant sur la route que les caravanes empruntaient au Moyen Âge entre la province chinoise du Yunnan et les ports birmans. À quelques kilomètres du centre ville, plus au sud, on a mis au jour sur le site de Wiang Kum Kam les ruines d'un royaume plus ancien fondé par les rois Môn de Birmanie au 11e siècle. L'archéologue amateur y est comblé : des vestiges de temples dans le style Môn et des pierres et briques provenant de stupas en ruine émaillent le paysage. L'une des attractions de Wiang Kum Kam est la pension Swairiang, un ensemble de bungalows et de villas disposés autour d'un étang recouvert de lotus. L'architecture de Swairiang, avec ses toits en chaume restaurés par un architecte de Bangkok, est typique du style de Lan Na. Wiang Kum Kam est un village idyllique où l'on peut fuir la très touristique et trépidante Chiang Mai. Le moyen de transport le plus rapide pour s'y rendre est la bicyclette ou le *tuk-tuk*, un tricycle motorisé.

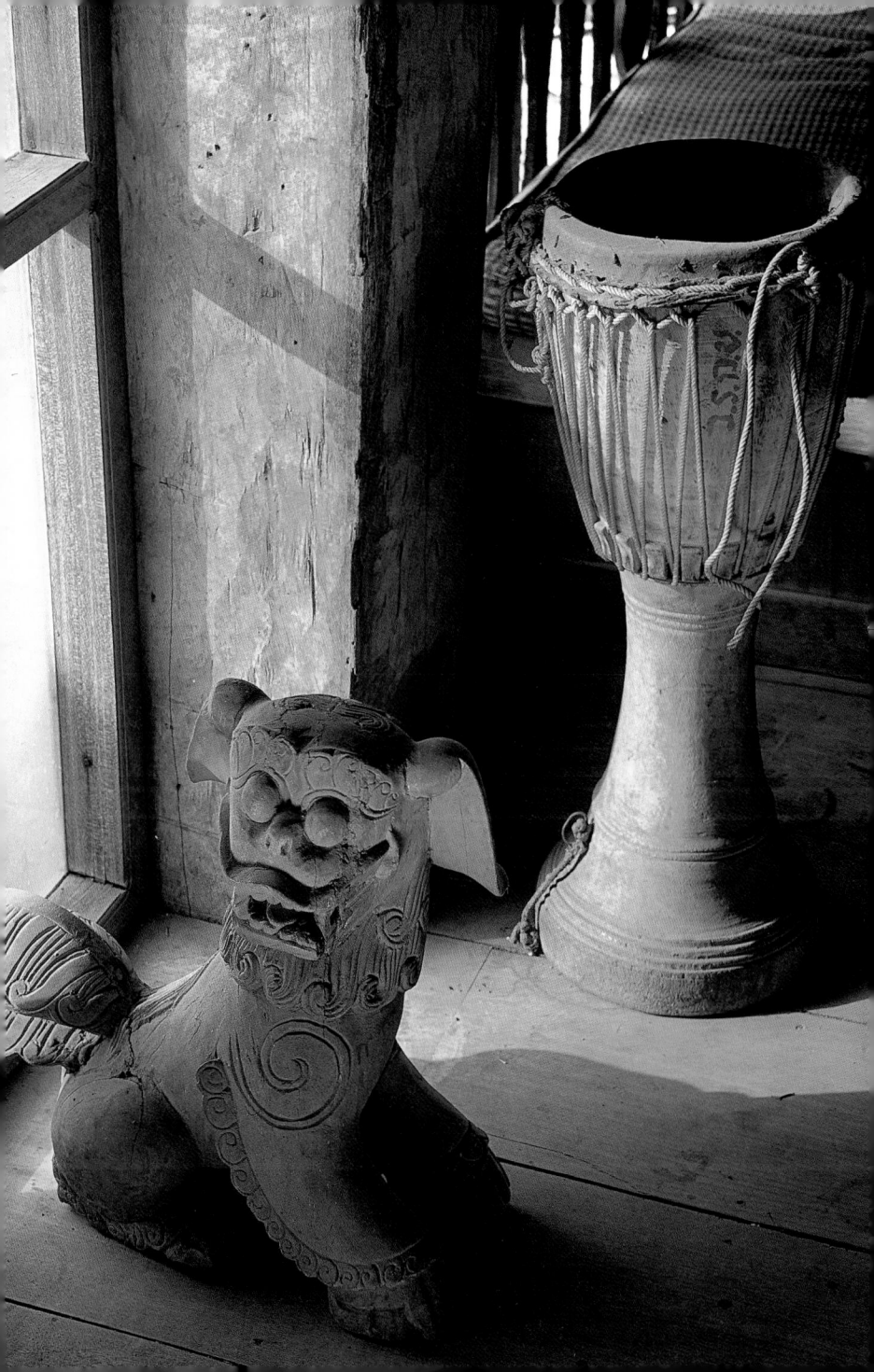

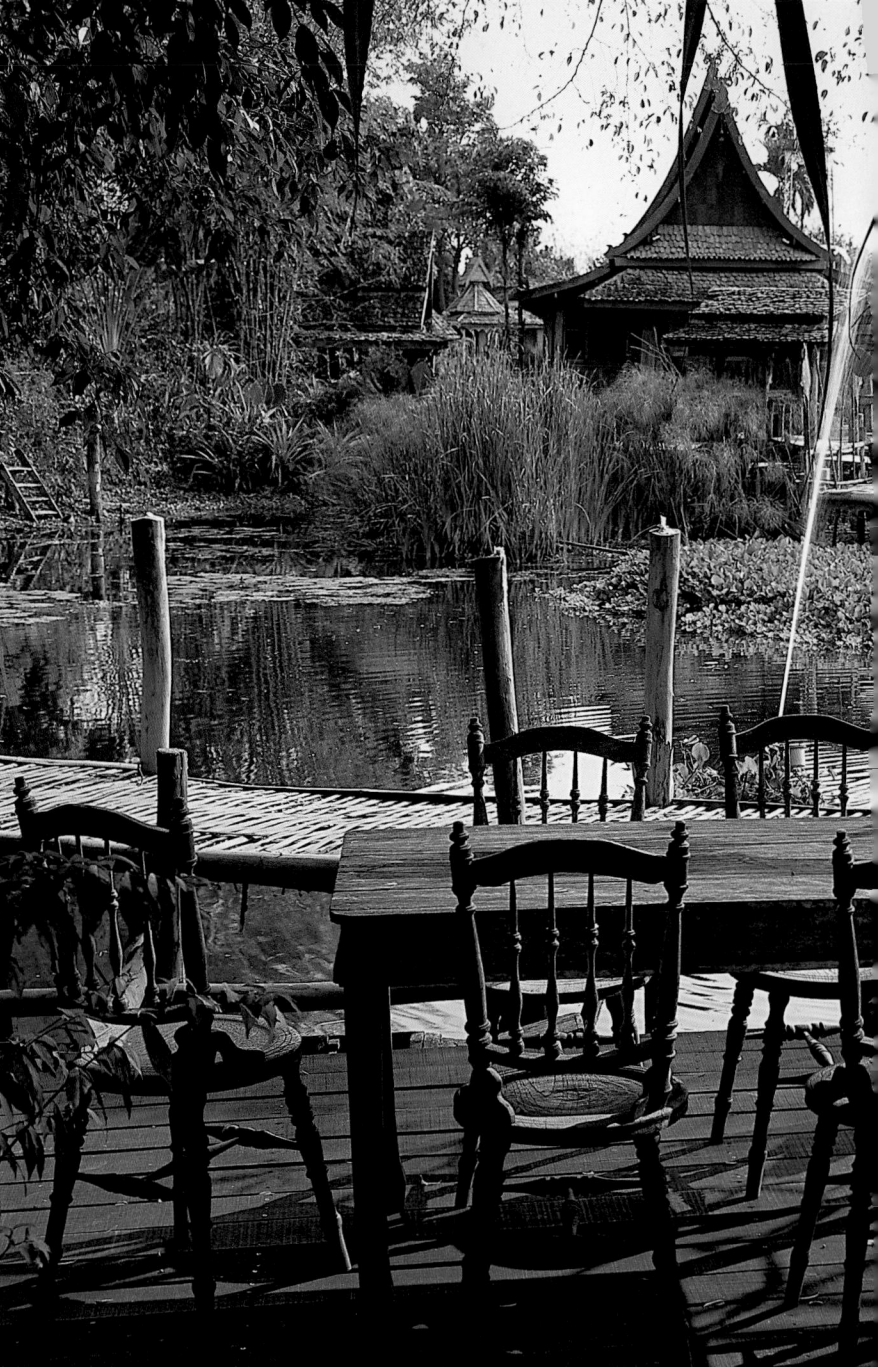

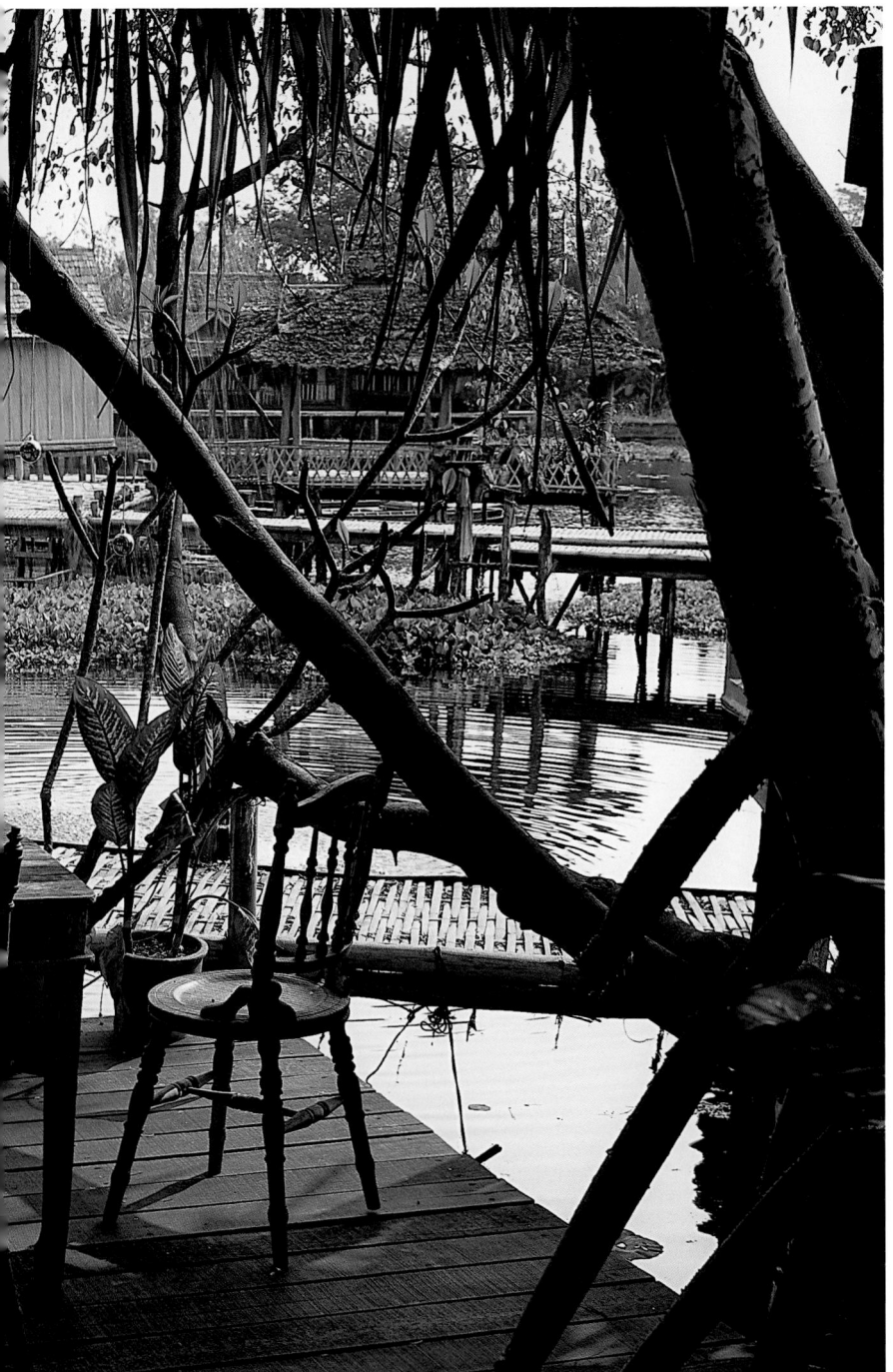

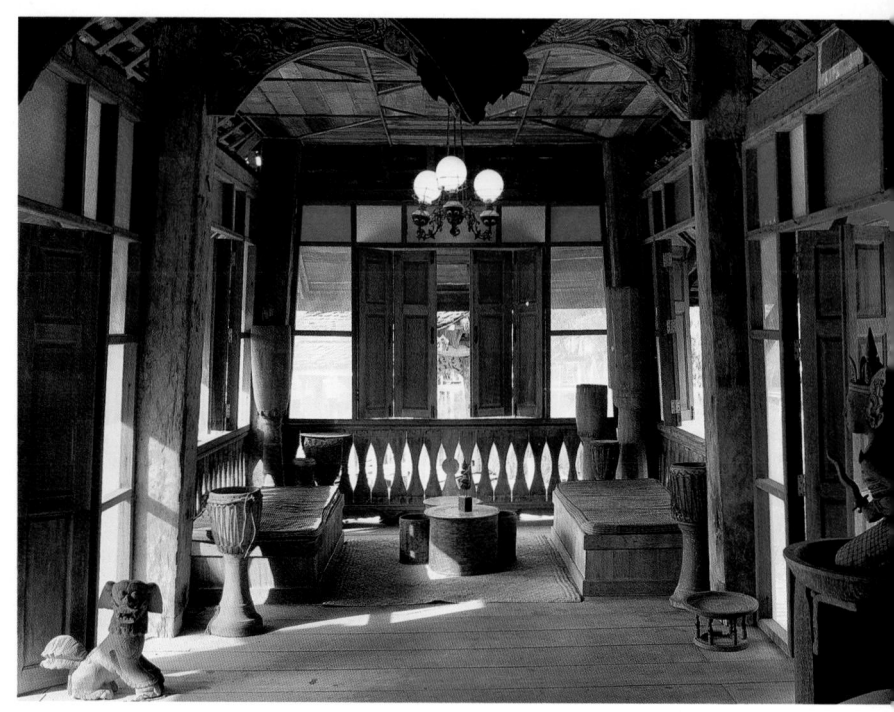

PP. 286–287 Swairiang's special suites are raised above the lotus pond on strong wooden stilts. • Mächtige Holzpfeiler stützen die Suiten über dem Lotusteich. • Reposant sur de robustes pilotis, les suites spéciales de la pension semblent flotter au-dessus des lotus.

PP. 290–291 The restaurant extends to a wooden terrace by the lotus pool for outdoor dining. • Auf der Holzterrasse des Restaurants am Lotusteich kann man unter freiem Himmel speisen. • Sur la terrasse en caillebotis du restaurant, on peut prendre son repas en contemplant le bassin aux lotus.

↑ The entrance hall of Swairiang Guest House is decorated with local artifacts from the Chiang Mai region. • Die Eingangshalle des Swairiang Guest House ist mit einheimischen Objekten aus der Gegend von Chiang Mai dekoriert. • Des objets fabriqués dans la région de Chiang Mai sont exposés dans le hall d'entrée.

→ An antique lamp hangs from a hexagonal glass-paned skylight inspired by the roofs of Buddhist temples. • Eine antike Lampe hängt von einem sechseckigen Oberlicht aus Milchglas. Das Dach wurde den Dächern buddhistischer Tempel nachempfunden. • Une lampe ancienne descend de la lucarne vitrée hexagonale, emprunt aux toits des temples bouddhiques.

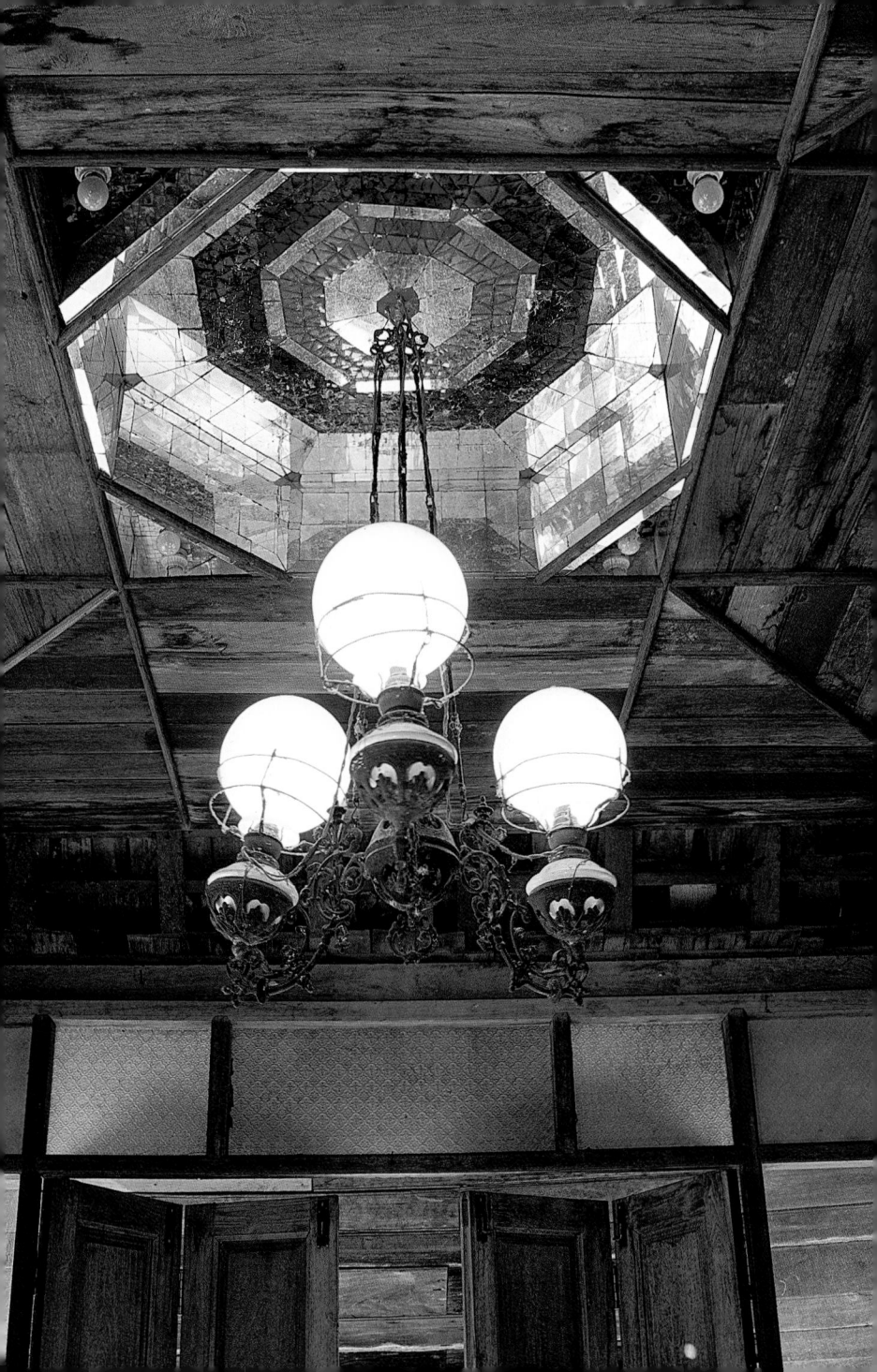

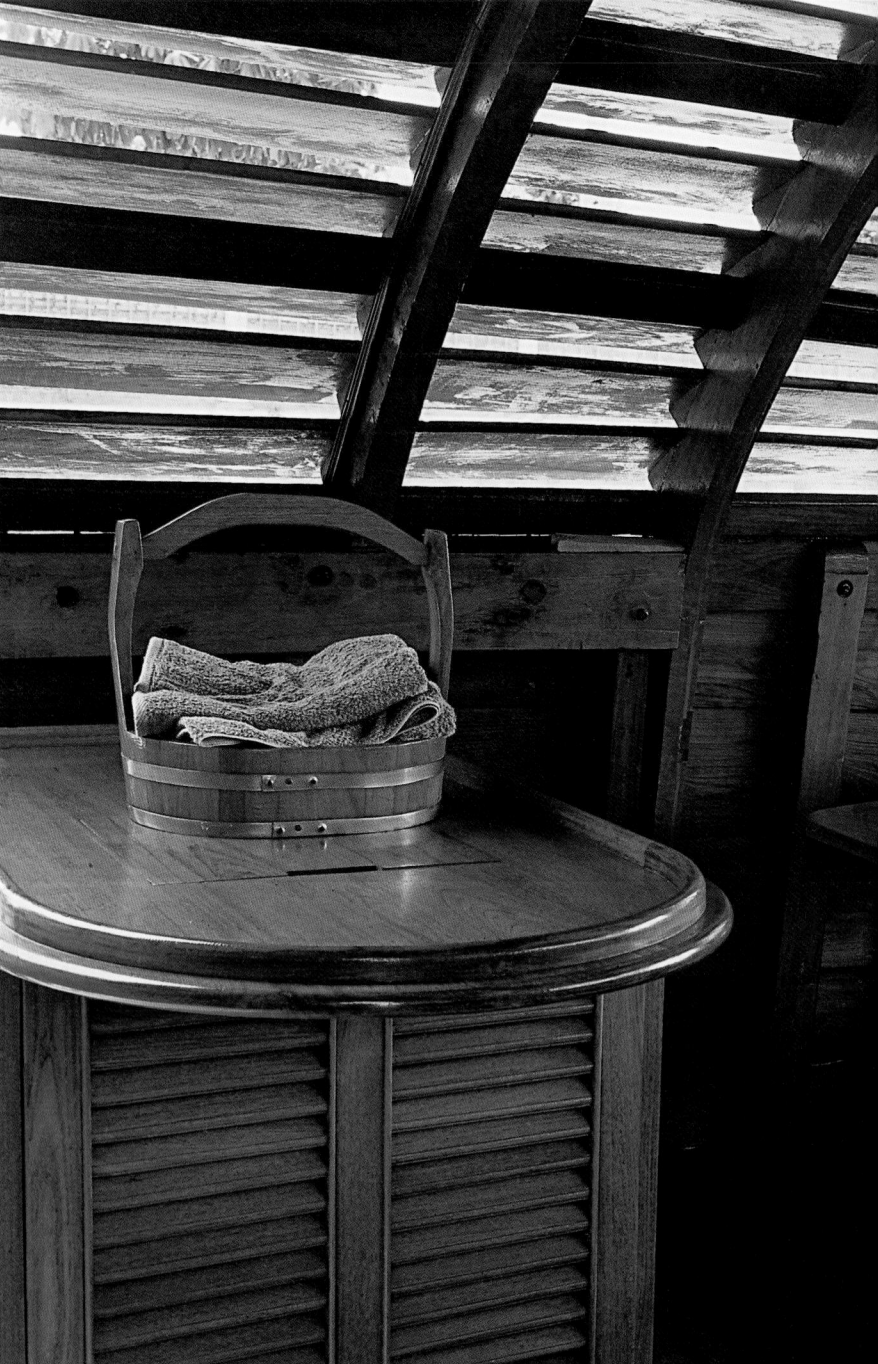

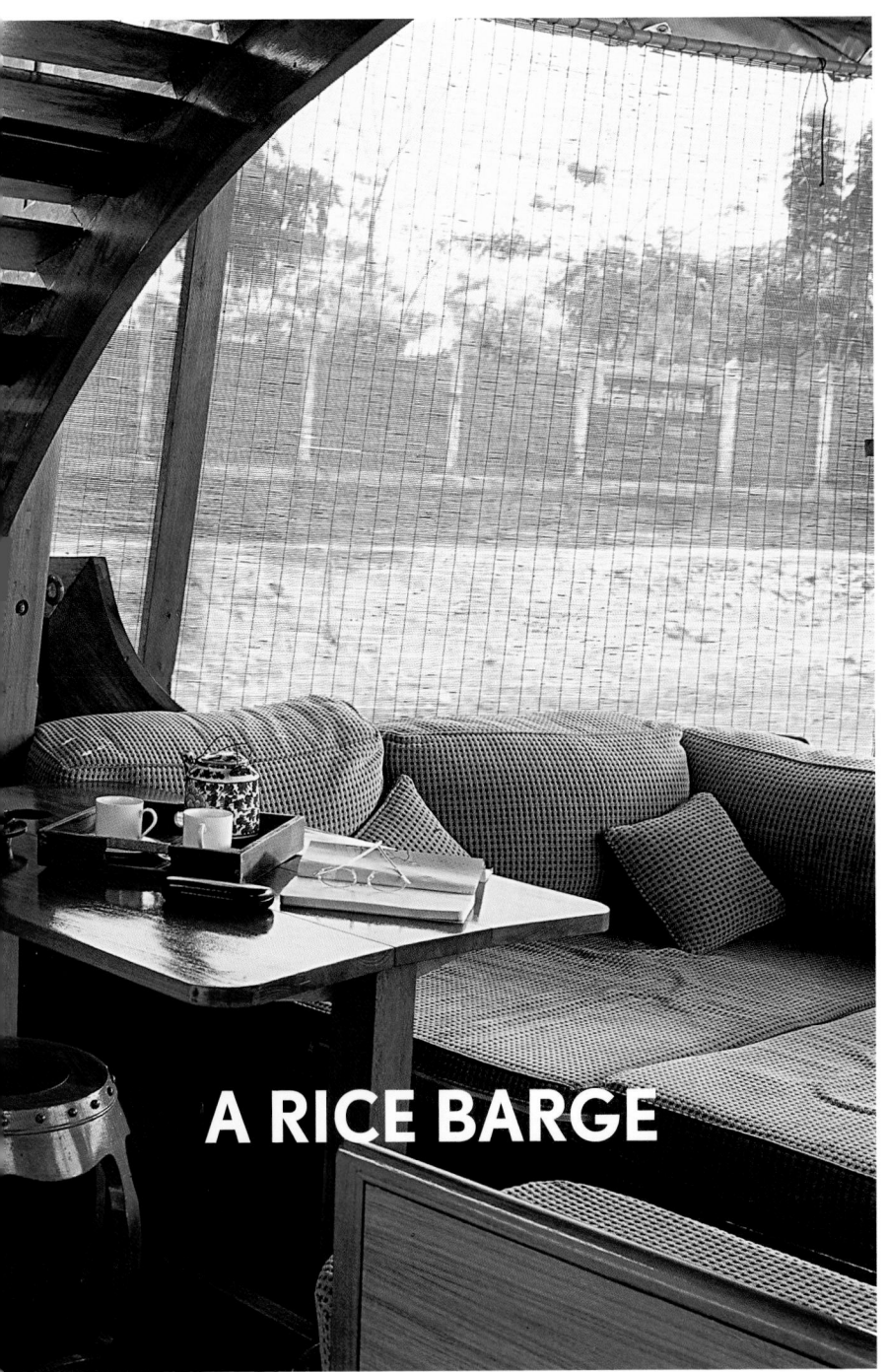

A RICE BARGE

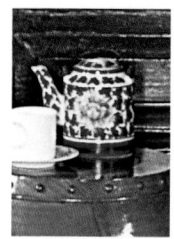

A RICE BARGE
AYUTTHAYA
THAILAND

For about four hundred years the city of Ayutthaya, north of Bangkok, was the royal capital of Siam. Three rivers and a canal cradle the city in a holy circle; images of Buddha, cast in bronze and stone, are consecrated among the scattering of temples and shimmering, painted stupas in the surrounding countryside. Long-tailed barges once carried cargoes of rice harvest downstream to Bangkok; now they ferry visitors to the temples or on leisurely trips to view scenes of river life. "The Golden Naga" is one such barge that Jean-Michel Beurdeley, a longtime resident of Thailand, bought in 1999 and restored as a houseboat powered by a diesel engine. The hold was converted into a master bedroom and two smaller rooms added to create an elegant suite. Passengers can move around the galley for fresh air or lounge on the roof in the evenings. The barge, built from a superb golden teak, gleams with renewed health after its facelift.

Vierhundert Jahre lang war Ayutthaya im Norden von Bangkok Hauptstadt des Königreiches Siam. Drei Flüsse und ein Kanal fließen in einem heiligen Kreis um die Stadt herum. In den Tempeln der Stadt stehen zahlreiche Buddhastatuen aus Bronze oder Stein. Auf dem Land dagegen finden sich glänzend bemalte Stupas. Die langen Reisbarken, mit denen einst die Reisernte flussabwärts nach Bangkok transportiert wurde, dienen inzwischen als Fähren zu den Tempeln oder als Ausflugsboote, von denen aus man das Leben am Fluss bestaunen kann. Jean-Michel Beurdeley lebt seit Langem in Thailand und kaufte 1999 eine solche Barke namens „The Golden Naga". Er baute sie zu einem dieselbetriebenen Hausboot um. Der Lagerraum wurde in ein großes Schlafzimmer verwandelt, das mit den beiden kleineren Räumen eine elegante Suite bildet. Die Passagiere können sich auf der Barke aus feinem goldschimmerndem Teakholz frei bewegen, frische Luft schnappen oder die Abende auf dem Dach verbringen.

Ayutthaya, au nord de Bangkok, a été la capitale du royaume de Siam pendant quatre siècles. Trois rivières et un canal forment un cercle sacré autour de la ville. On peut admirer des statues de Bouddha, en bronze ou en pierre, dans les temples, et des stupas peints aux couleurs chatoyantes dans la campagne environnante. De longues barges acheminaient autrefois du riz vers Bangkok, en aval : maintenant, elles amènent les visiteurs aux temples ou les emmènent en excursion. En 1999, Jean-Michel Beurdeley, qui réside depuis longtemps en Thaïlande, a fait l'acquisition d'une barge de ce type, et l'a transformée en house-boat équipé d'un moteur diesel. La cale de « The Golden Naga » a été convertie en une suite élégante, composée d'une chambre principale et de deux chambres plus petites. Les passagers peuvent se promener sur l'embarcation pour prendre l'air ou passer leur soirée sur le pont. Une fois restaurée, cette barge, construite dans un superbe teck blond, a retrouvé toute sa splendeur passée.

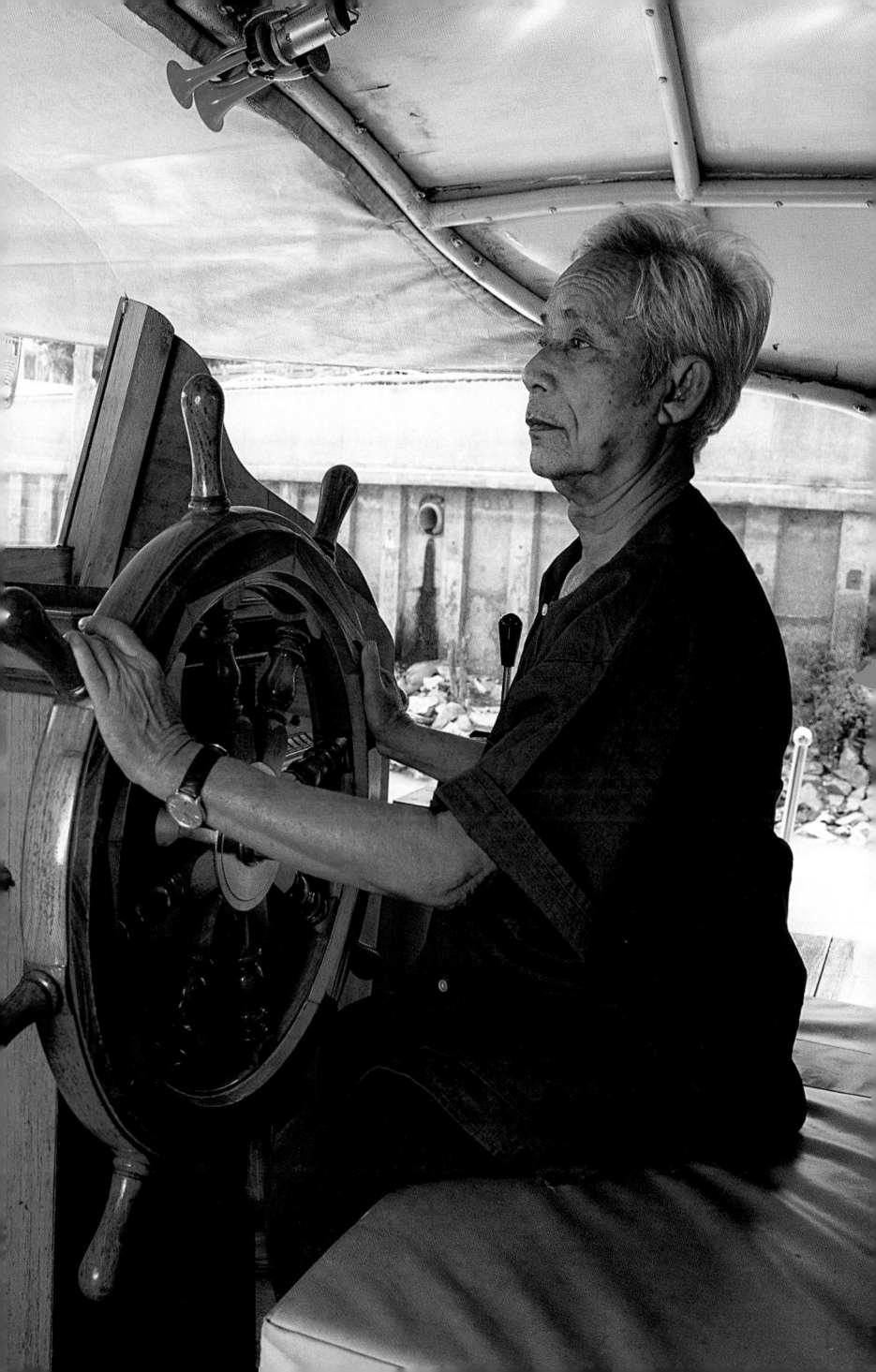

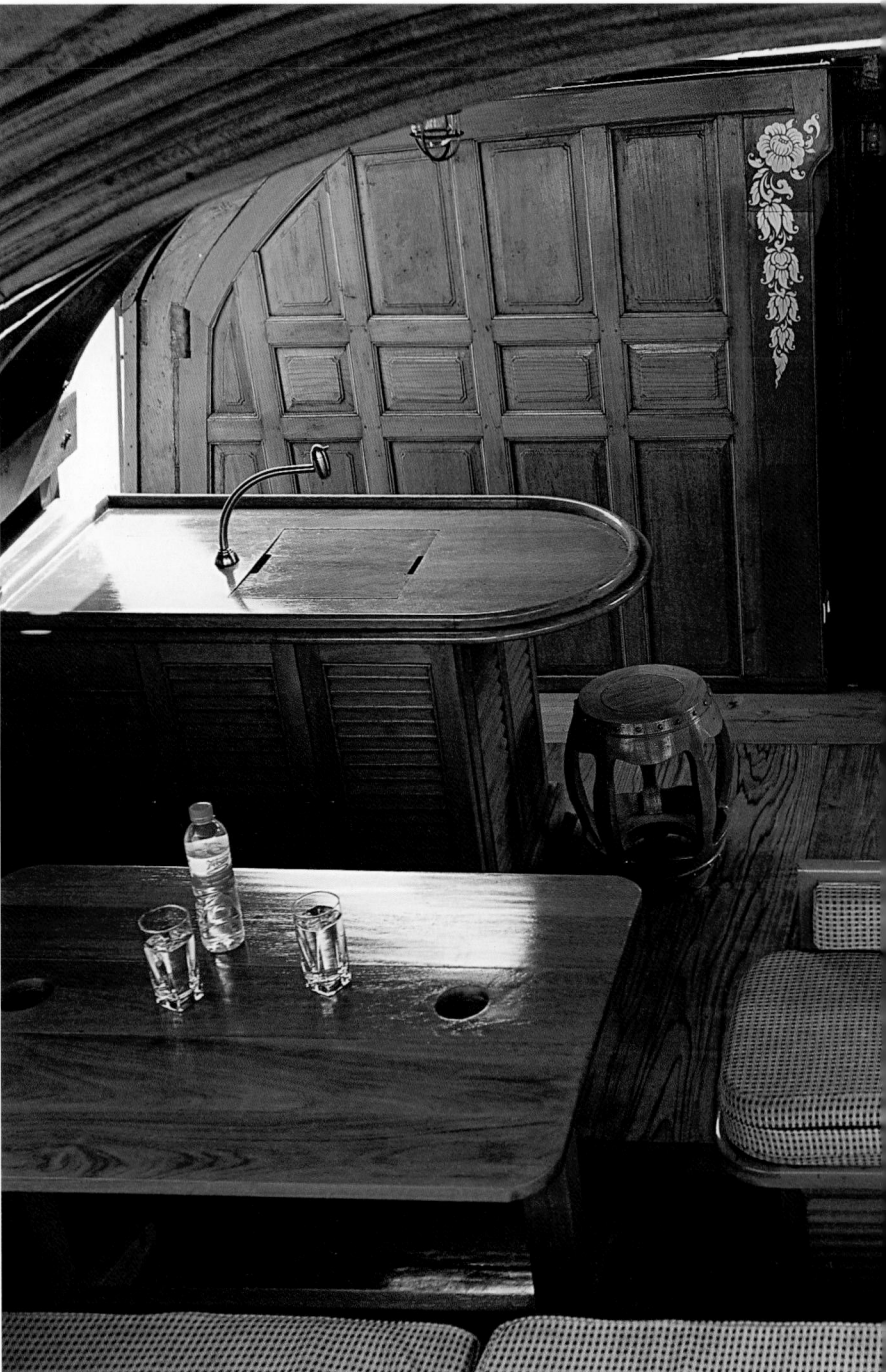

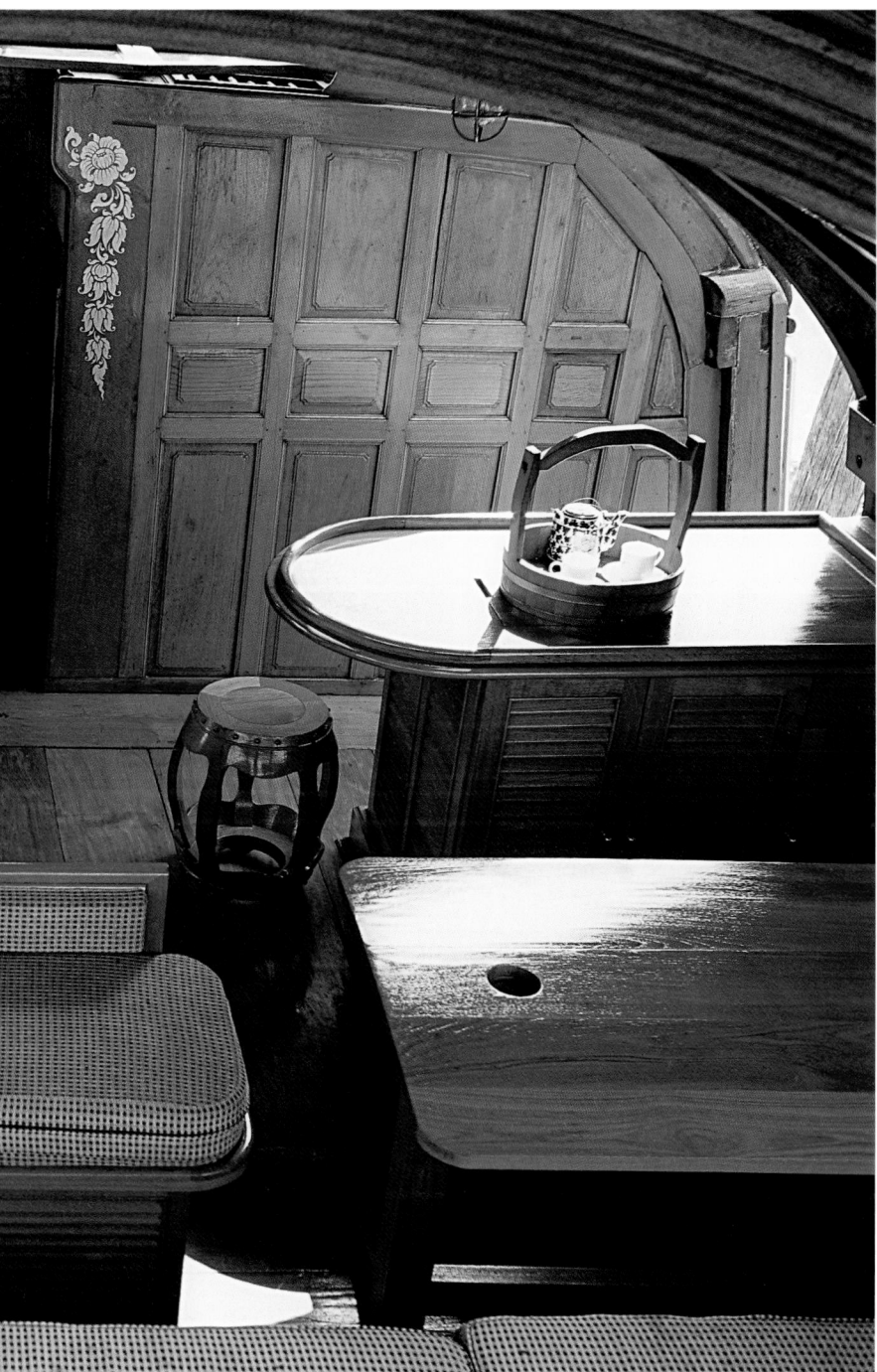

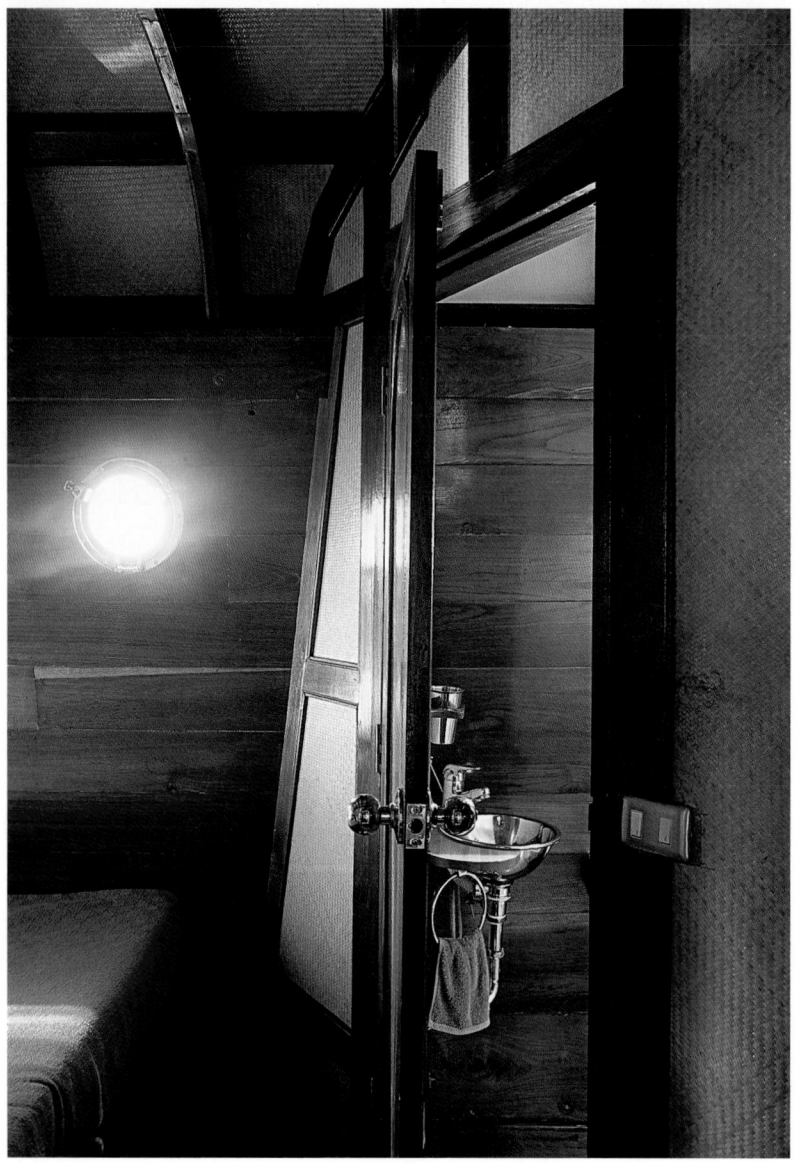

P. 297 Captain and caretaker of the
"Golden Naga" in attendance. • Im
Dienst – der Kapitän und Verwalter der
„Golden Naga". • Le capitaine et le
gardien du « Golden Naga » en service.

PP. 298–299 The dining and lounge
areas. • Speisesaal und Lounge. •
Espace salon–salle à manger.

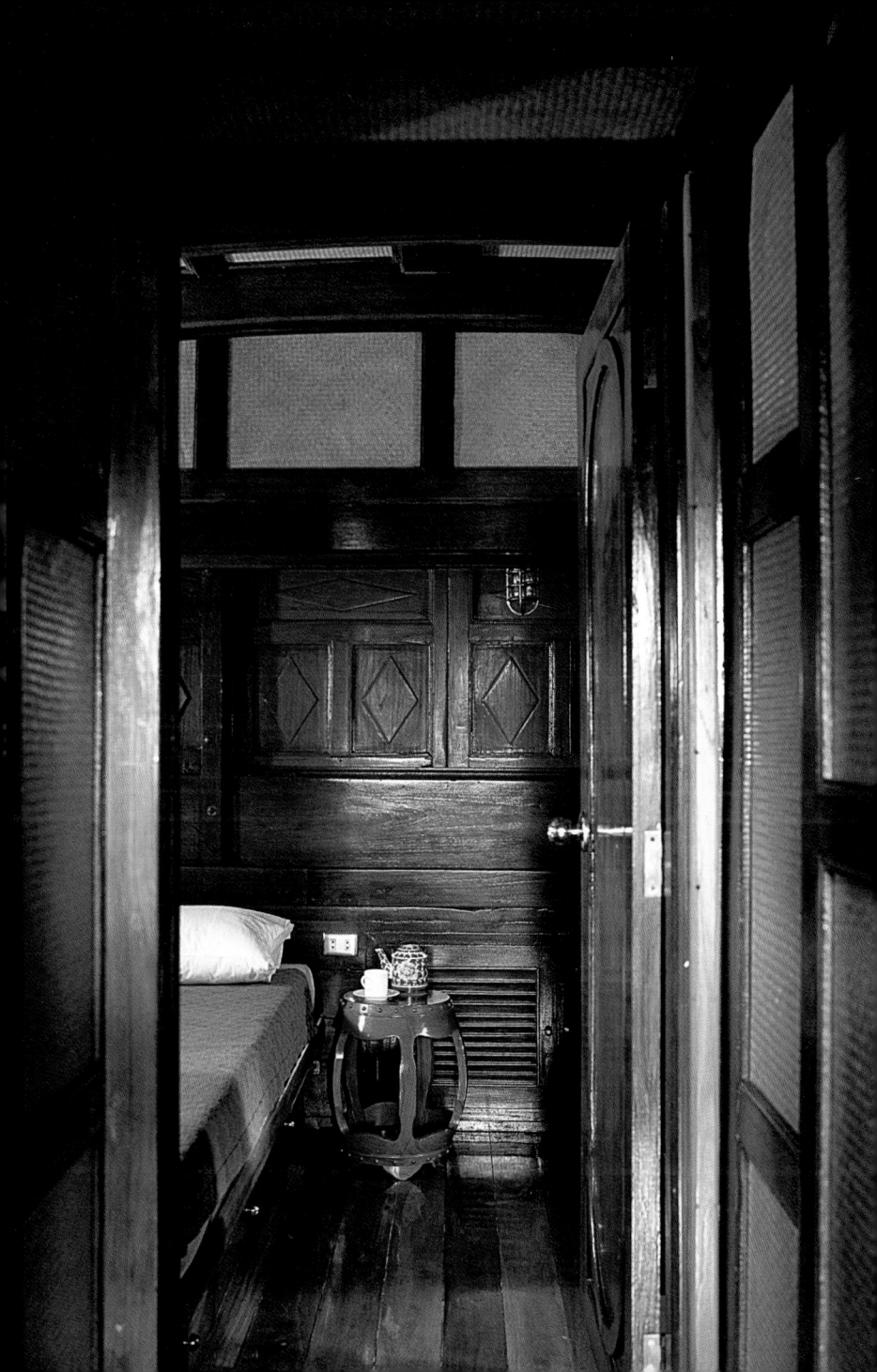

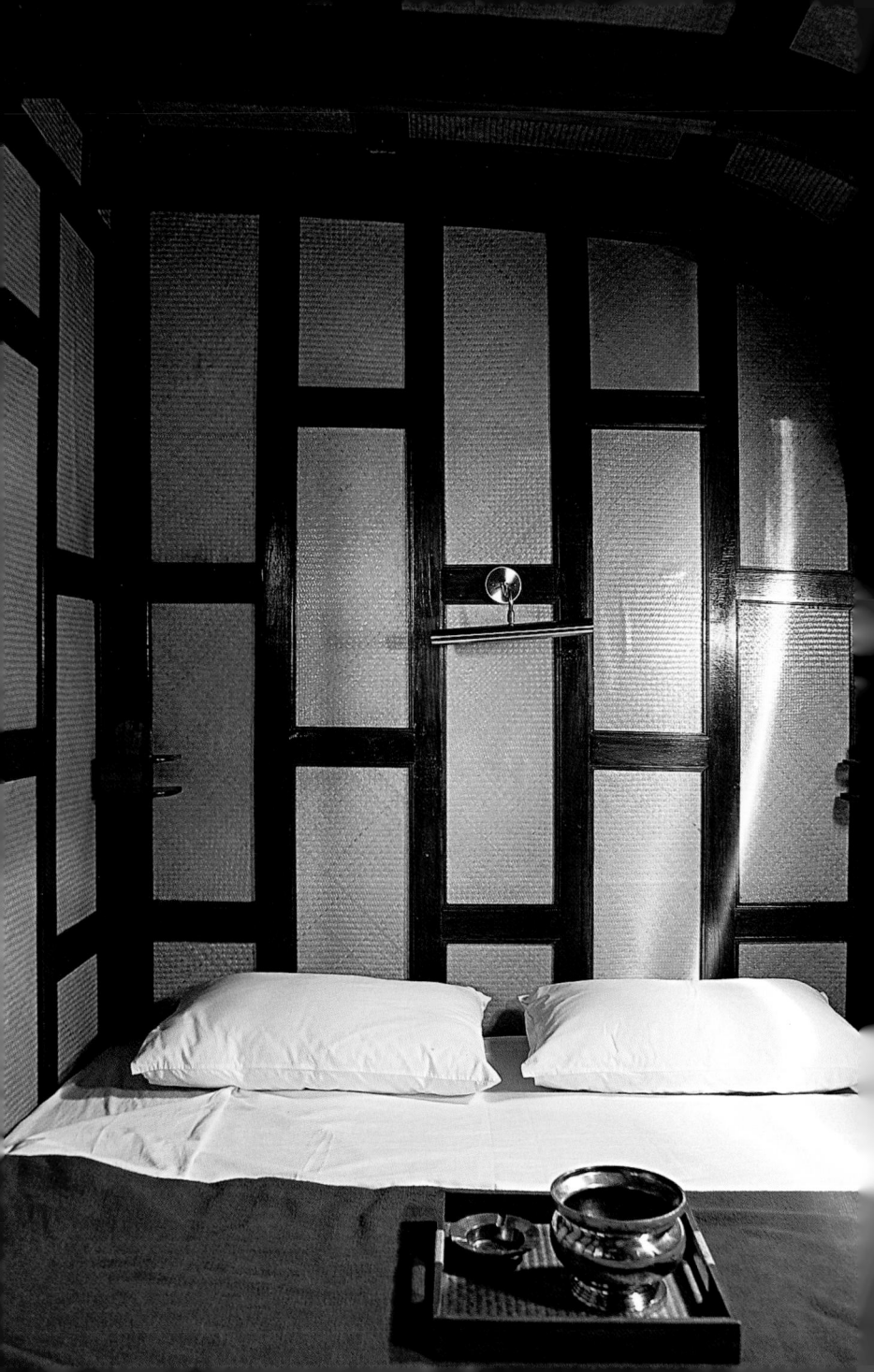

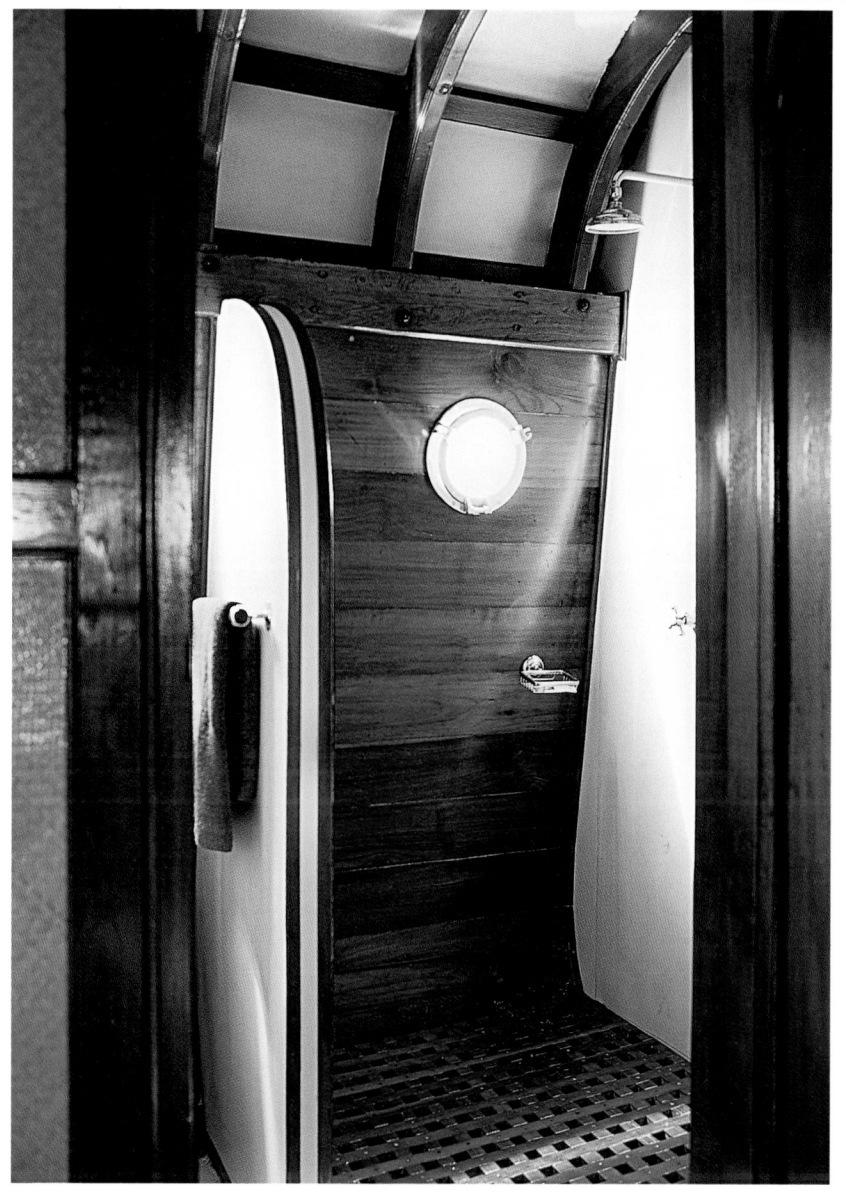

↑ Cabin bathroom with shower. •
Die Kabine hat ein Badezimmer mit
Dusche. • Cabine avec douche.

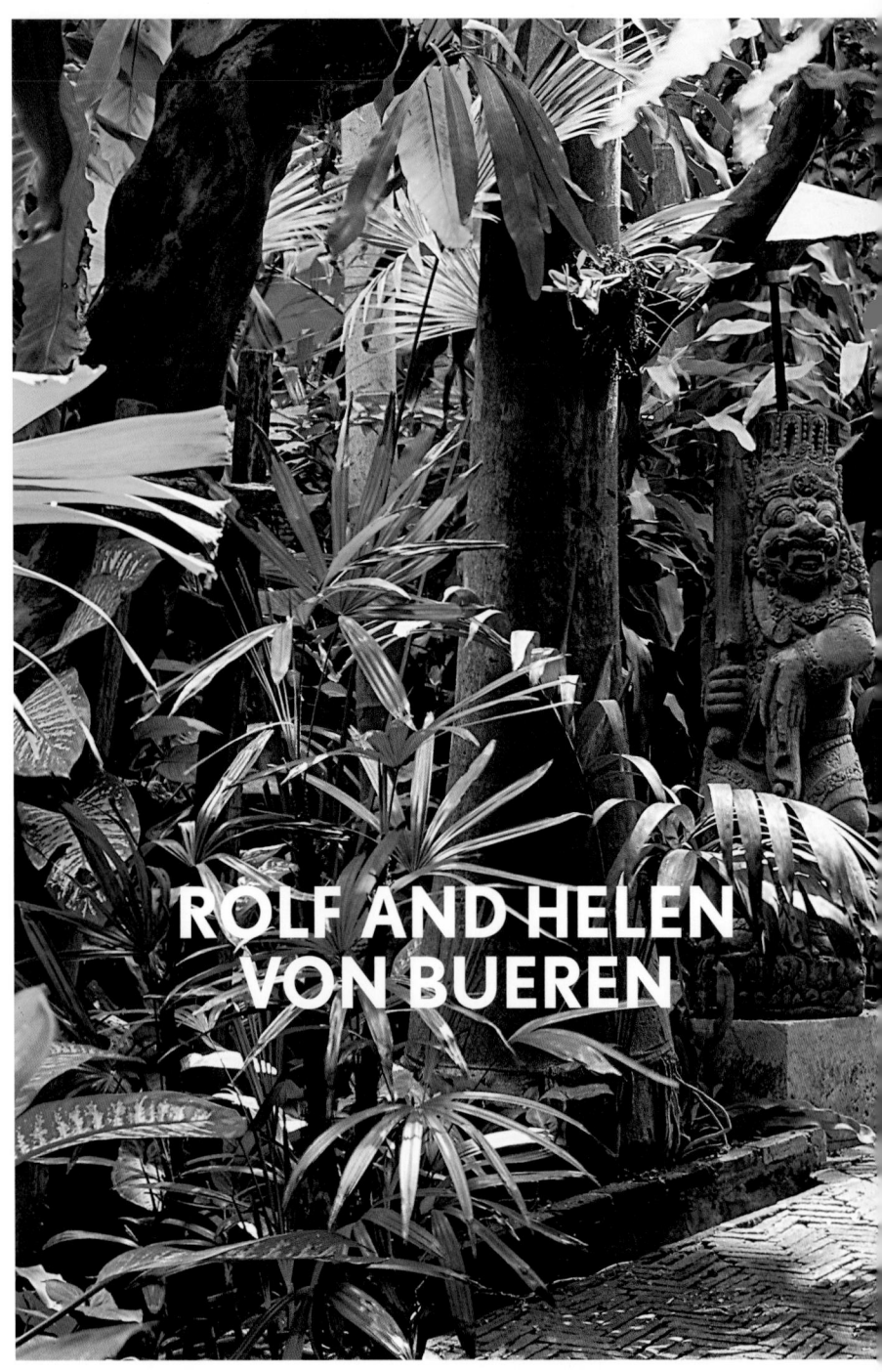

ROLF AND HELEN
VON BUEREN

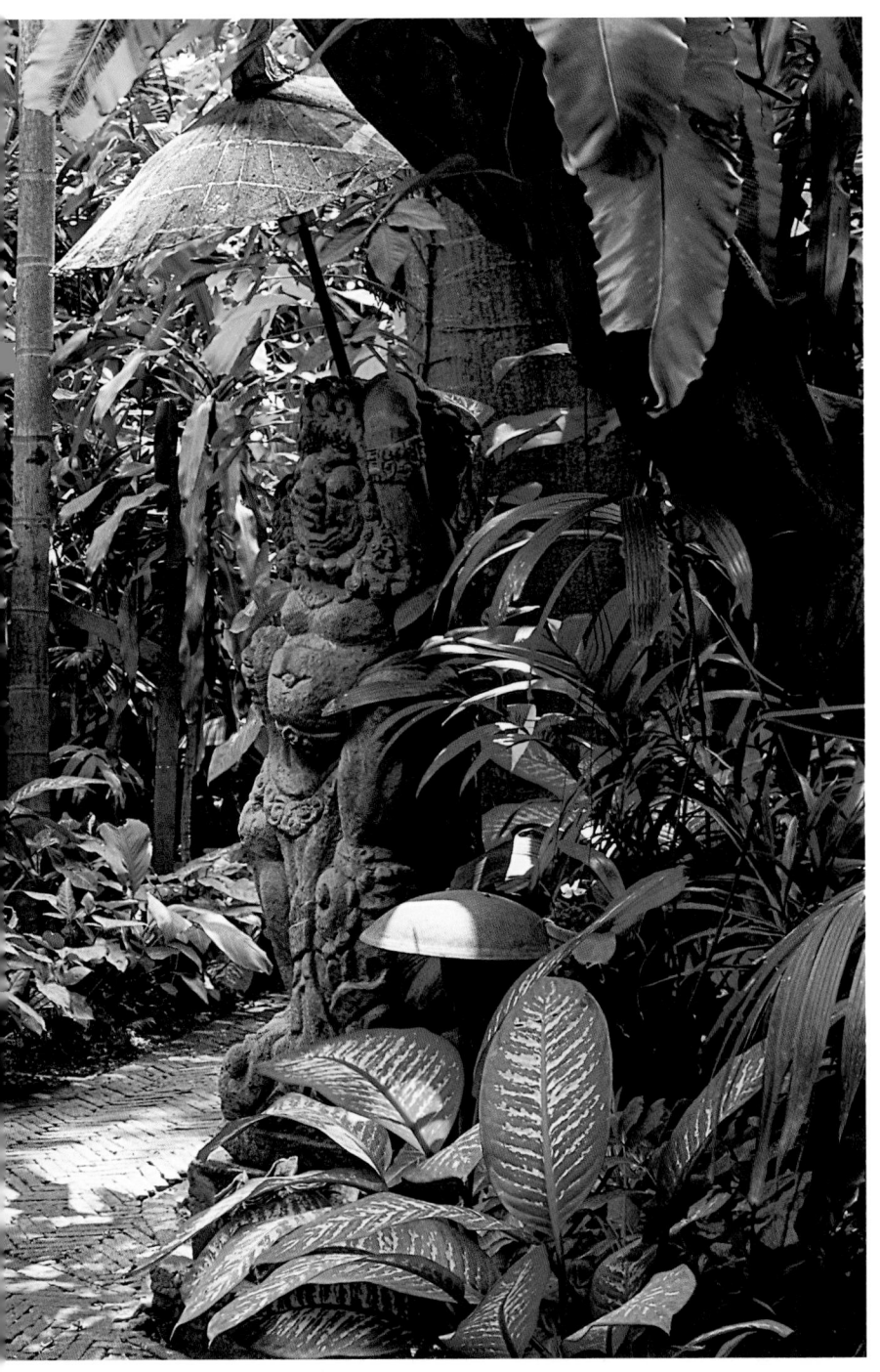

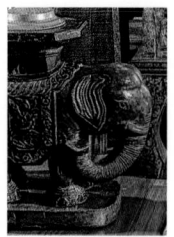

ROLF AND HELEN
VON BUEREN
BANGKOK
THAILAND

With their mixed Thai and European ancestry, and their reputation as collectors and designers of fine handcrafted jewelery and objets d'art in long-established "Lotus Arts de Vivre" outlets in Asia, Rolf and Helen von Bueren, together with their two sons Sri and Nicklas, represent the best of international taste and Asian family values. Their remarkable work – a jade mouse with ruby eyes or a tortoiseshell box with filigreed gold clasp – is produced as a series of individual treasures; it is only matched by the enchantment of their homes in Bangkok and Bali or their life-enhancing hospitality and exuberant high spirits. German-born Rolf came to Thailand more than five decades ago but it was his Thai wife Helen who originated the family business. In the heart of Bangkok, four generations of the family live in a series of traditional Thai houses arranged in a garden estate – a tribute to continuity and the changing fashions of cosmopolitan style.

Rolf und Helen von Bueren repräsentieren, zusammen mit ihren Söhnen Sri und Nicklas, aufgrund ihrer thailändischen und europäischen Wurzeln und ihrem Ruf als Sammler und Designer eine ausgezeichnete Mischung aus international geprägtem Geschmack und asiatischen Familienwerten. Unter dem Markennamen „Lotus Arts de Vivre" entwerfen sie in Handarbeit hergestellte Schmuckstücke und Kunstgegenstände. Ihre bemerkenswerten Arbeiten – beispielsweise eine Maus aus Jade mit Augen aus Rubinen oder ein Kästchen aus Schildpatt mit filigranem Goldverschluss – werden sorgfältig zu einzigartigen Wertgegenständen gefertigt und höchstens noch übertroffen von der Atmosphäre in ihren Häusern in Bangkok und Bali. Im Einklang mit ihren Kreationen stehen ihre großzügige Gastfreundschaft und ihre mitreißend gute Laune. Der deutschstämmige Rolf kam bereits vor mehr als fünfzig Jahren nach Thailand, aber es war seine Frau Helen, die das Familiengeschäft ins Leben rief. Vier Generationen dieser Familie leben in einer Gartenanlage mitten in Bangkok in mehreren traditionellen thailändischen Häusern – ein Tribut an Beständigkeit und Wechsel kosmopolitischen Stils.

Avec leur double ascendance européenne et thaïe et leur solide réputation de collectionneurs et de créateurs de bijoux et d'objets d'art pour la chaîne Lotus Arts de Vivre solidement établie en Asie, Rolf et Helen von Bueren, et leurs fils Sri et Nicklas, représentent le meilleur du goût international et des valeurs familiales asiatiques. Leurs créations remarquables, par exemple une souris en jade aux yeux de rubis ou une boîte en écaille de tortue dotée d'un fermoir en or ouvragé, sont des trésors uniques qui n'ont d'égal que le charme de leurs résidences à Bangkok et Bali ou leur hospitalité chaleureuse et leur formidable entrain. Né en Allemagne, Rolf est arrivé en Thaïlande il y a une bonne cinquantaine d'années. Son épouse Helen, thaïlandaise, est à l'origine de l'entreprise familiale. Quatre générations de la famille vivent au cœur de Bangkok, dans des maisons thaïes traditionnelles disséminées dans une propriété paysagère, – un hommage à la continuité et aux modes cosmopolites changeantes.

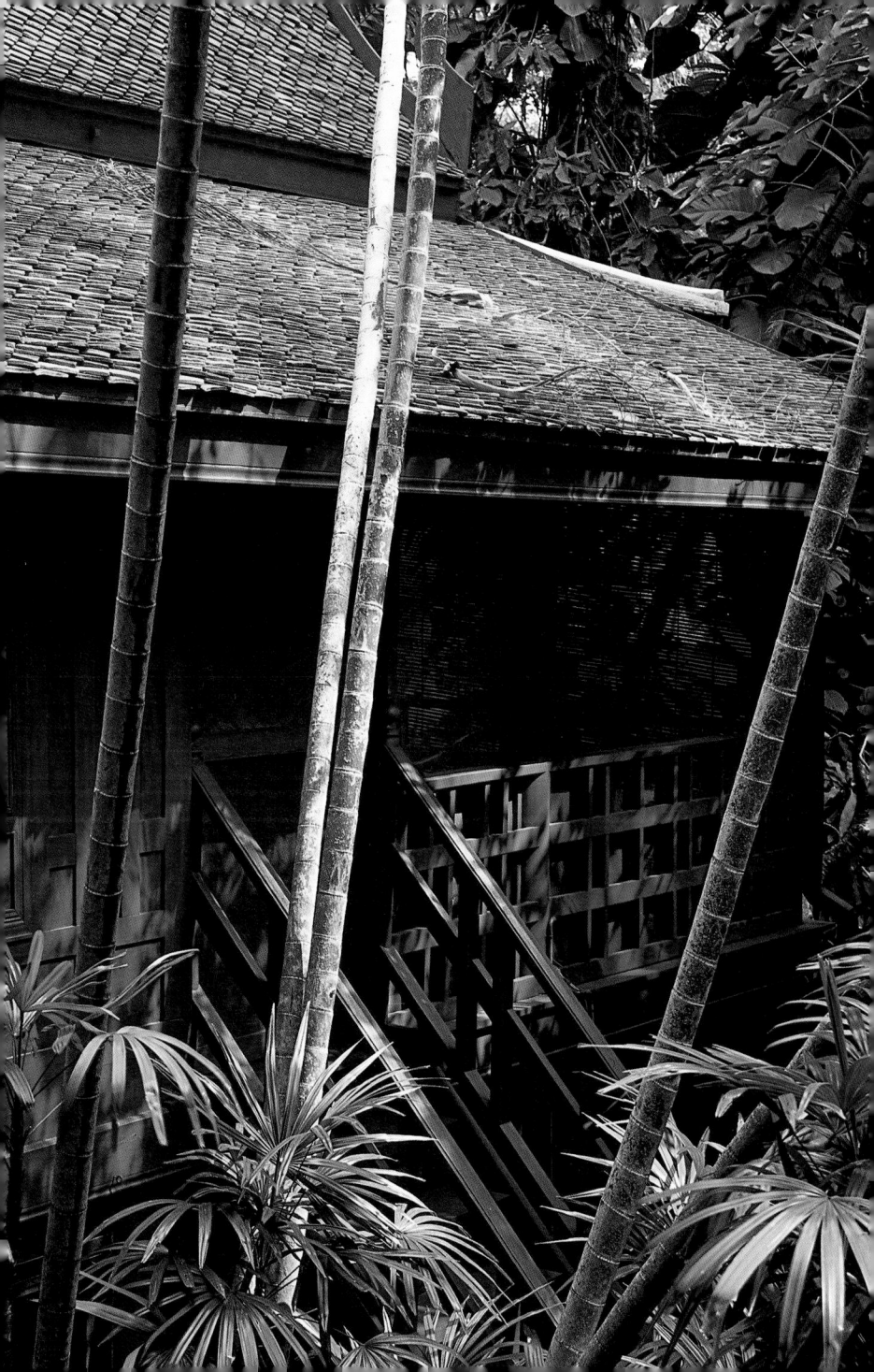

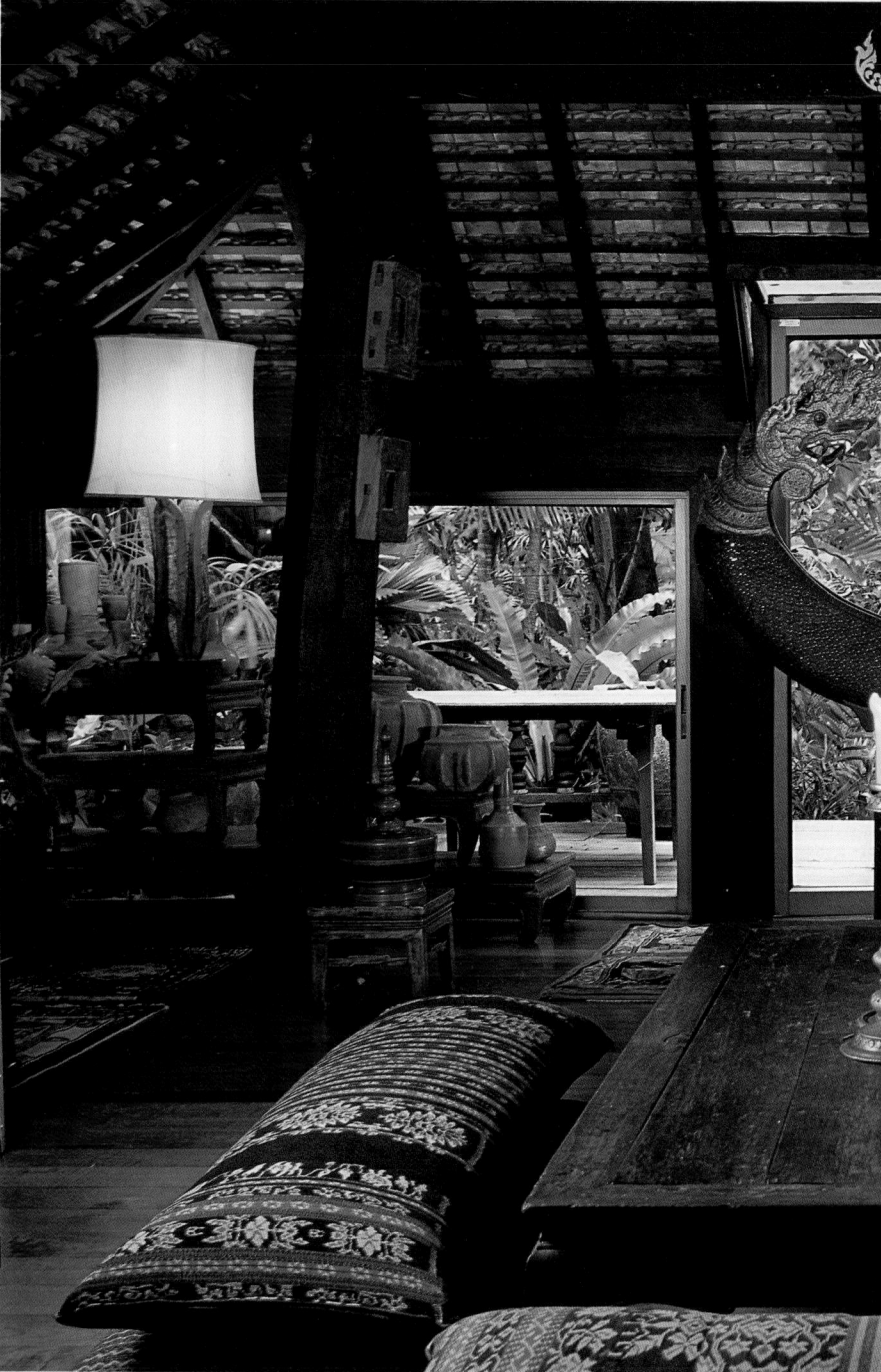

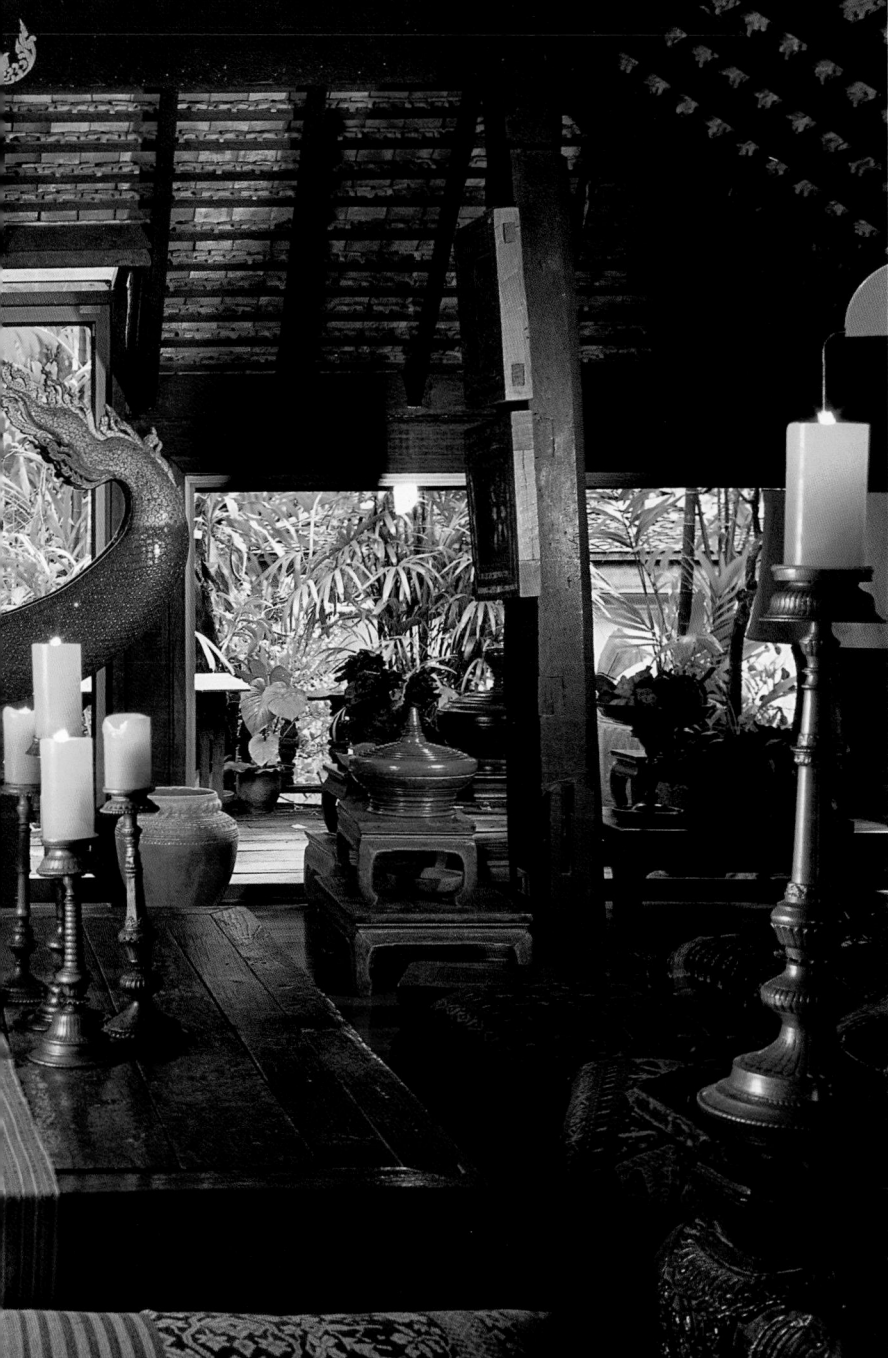

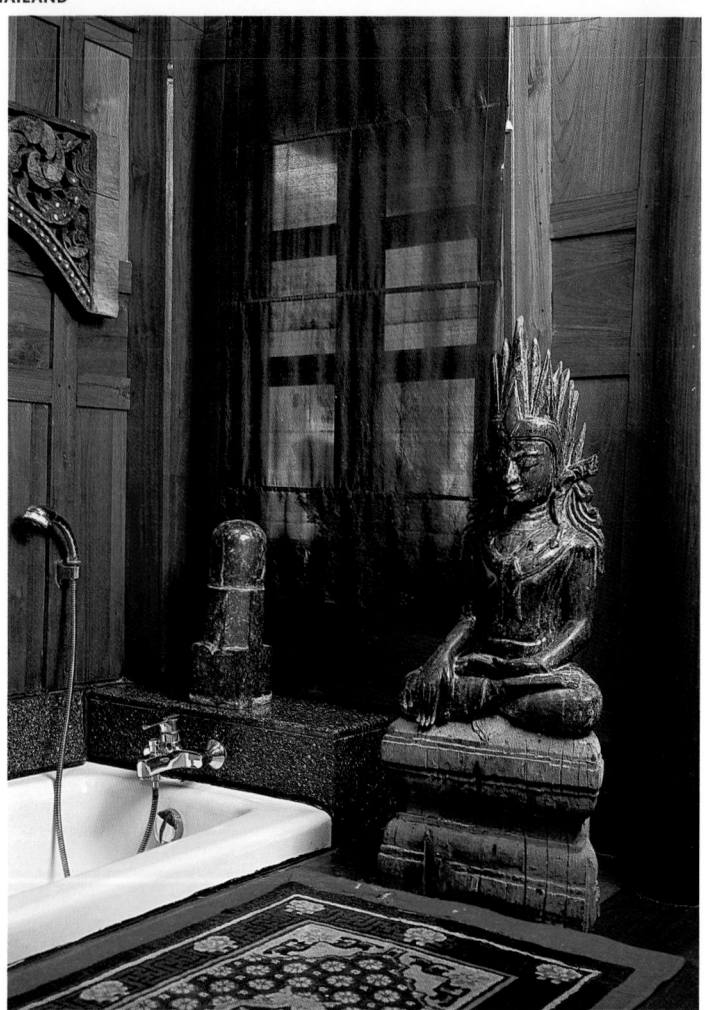

P. 307 Stairs lead to a traditional house elevated on stilts. • Eine Treppe führt zu einem traditionellen Haus auf Pfählen. • Un escalier mène à cette maison traditionnelle sur pilotis.

PP. 308–309 A former rice barn is converted into the dining room with low seating. A Burmese musical instrument in the form of a *naga* dominates the setting. • Eine ehemalige Reisscheune wurde in ein Speisezimmer mit niedrigen

Sitzgelegenheiten verwandelt. Im Zentrum steht ein birmanisches Musik-instrument in Form einer *naga*. • Cette salle à manger où l'on prend ses repas assis sur des coussins est un ancien grenier à riz. Un instrument de musique en forme de *naga* (serpant) constitue la pièce maîtresse de la décoration.

↑ Tibetan rugs and antique images in the bathroom. • Tibetische Teppiche und antike Statuen im Badezimmer. •

Des tapis tibétains et des antiquités agrémentent la salle de bains.

→ Burmese lacquer bowls on a gilt Thai cabinet in a dining room corner. • Birmanische Lackschüsseln auf einem vergoldeten thailändischen Schrank in einer Ecke des Speisezimmers. • Dans un coin de la salle à manger, des réci-pients laqués birmans sont exposés sur un meuble doré thaï.

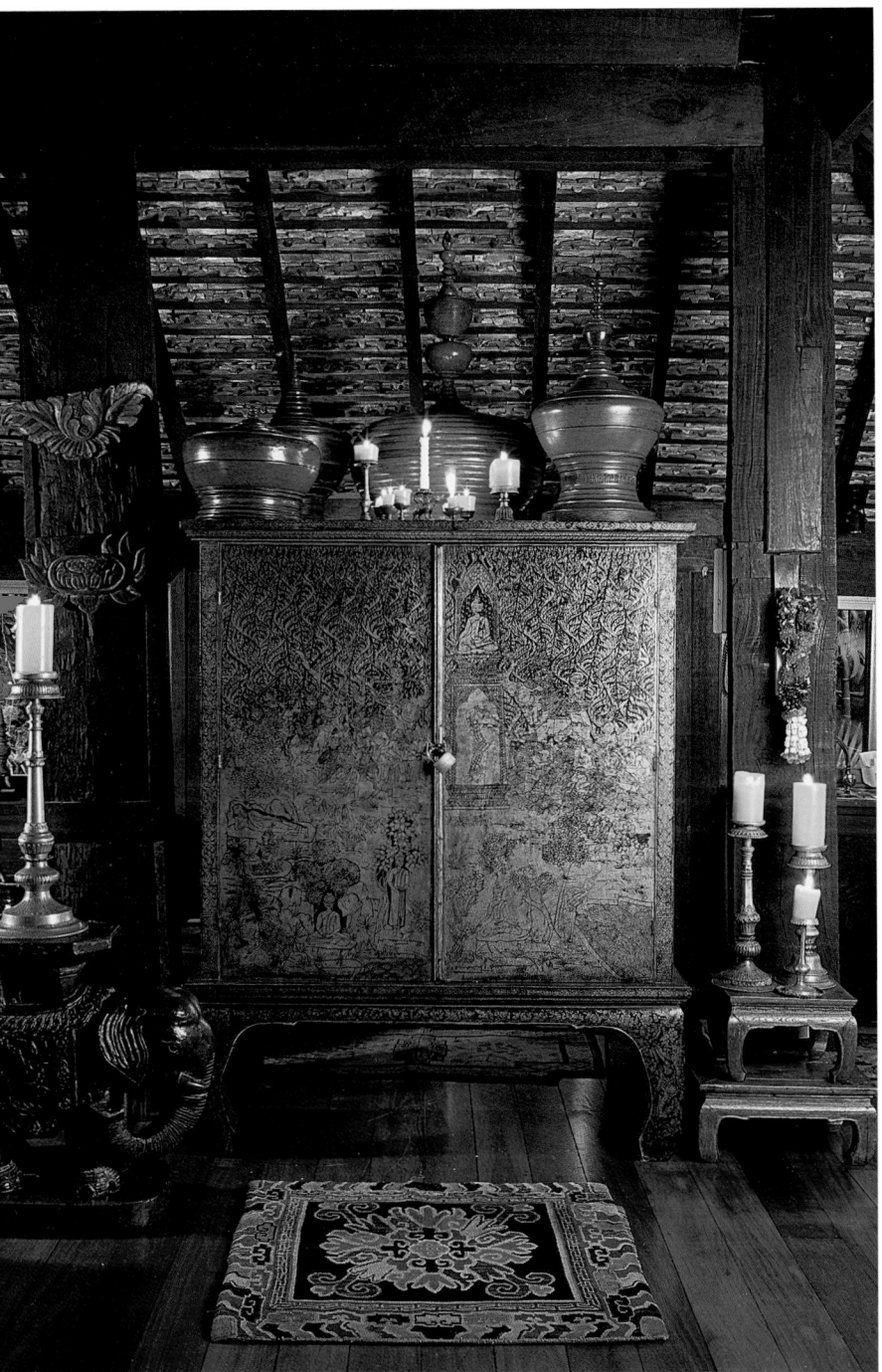

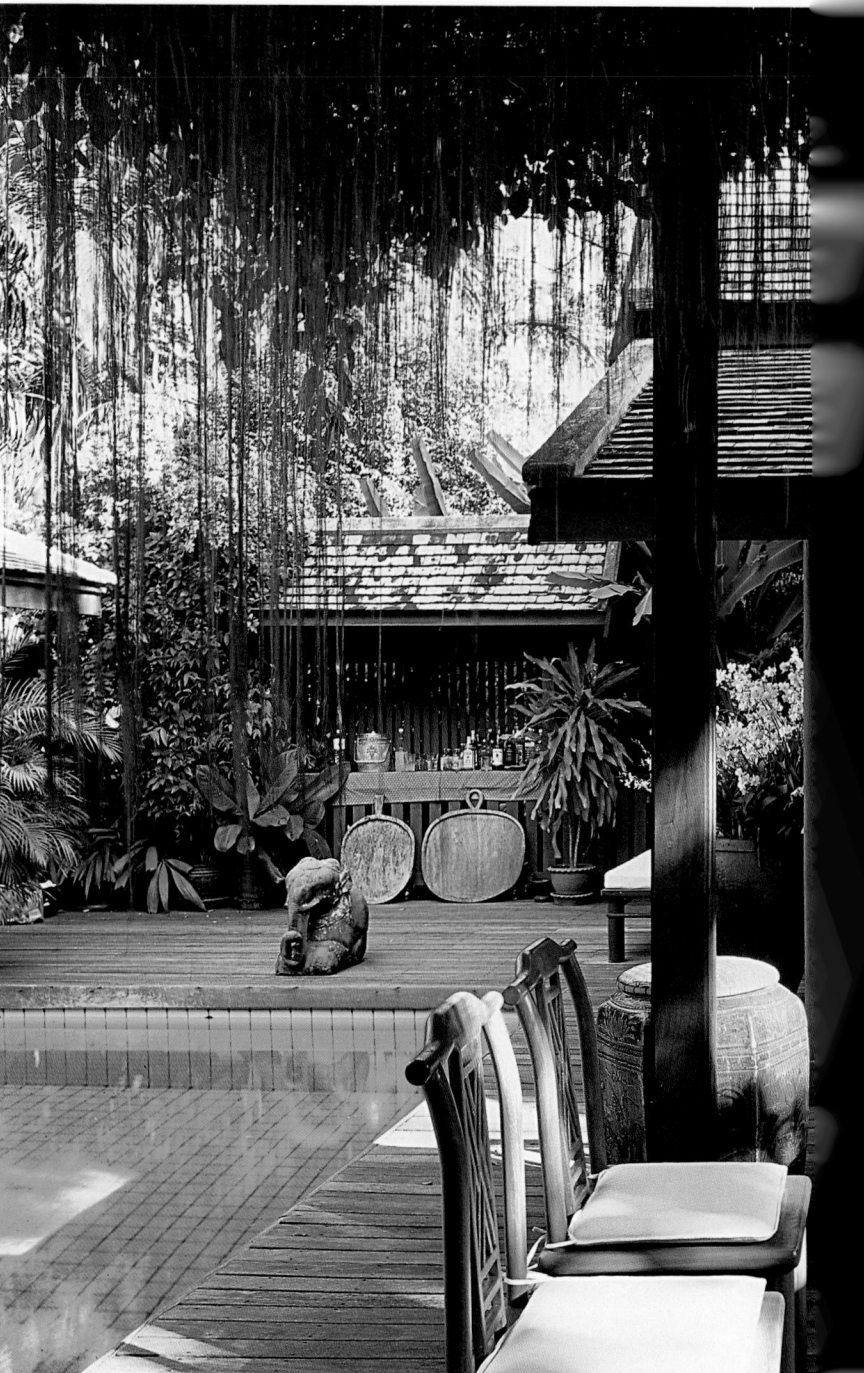

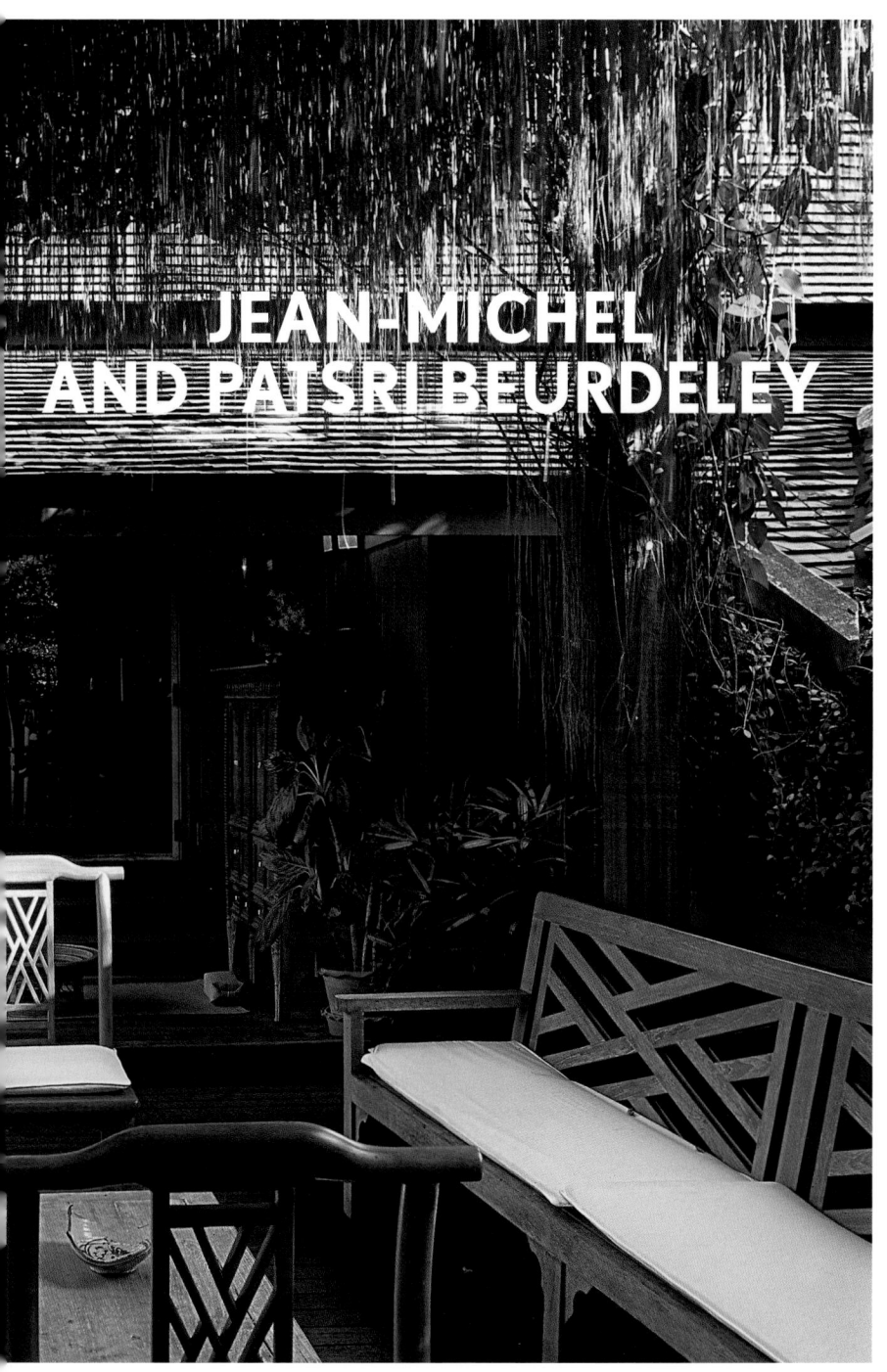

JEAN-MICHEL
AND PATSRI BEURDELEY

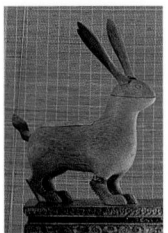

JEAN-MICHEL AND PATSRI BEURDELEY

BANGKOK
THAILAND

In the early 1970s, Jean-Michel Beurdeley's wife Patsri received an unexpected gift from her mother: a plot near Ramkhamhaeng University. Like a great deal of land in Bangkok, the property was a swamp. The Beurdeleys decided to build a traditional house on stilts to prevent damage from flooding, going for the strong, big-roofed style characteristic of architecture in northern Thailand. A fourth-generation art collector, the Paris-born Beurdeley has a weakness for homes that open into courtyards and gardens. The couple was also influenced by Japanese sliding doors with their easy access to the outdoors. Eventually the house grew in four separate sections around a central courtyard and swimming pool with shady terraces. For many years Beurdeley ran a successful gallery of Asian art in Paris. It was inevitable that one section would become a gallery. The box-like structure, also on stilts, has a roof made of cables, not tiles. Creepers form a natural ceiling to displays of modern art by Thai artists.

Anfang der 1970er-Jahre erhielt Jean-Michel Beurdeleys Frau Patsri ein unerwartetes Geschenk von ihrer Mutter: ein Grundstück in der Nähe der Ramkhamhaeng-Universität. Allerdings bestand es, wie viele andere in Bangkok, zunächst vor allem aus Sumpfland. Die Beurdeleys beschlossen, dort einen in Nordthailand üblichen Pfahlbau in Form eines mächtigen Gebäudes mit einem großen Dach zu bauen. Beurdeley, der ursprünglich aus Paris stammende Kunstsammler in vierter Generation, hat eine Vorliebe für Häuser mit Innenhöfen und Gärten. Außerdem bevorzugt das Paar japanische Schiebetüren, die den Übergang zwischen Drinnen und Draußen ineinander gleiten lassen. Schließlich wurde das Haus in vier verschiedenen Teilen rund um einen Innenhof mit Swimmingpool und schattigen Terrassen gebaut. Da Beurdeley in Paris lange Jahre erfolgreich eine Galerie mit asiatischer Kunst leitete, wurde in einem Teil des Hauses ebenfalls eine Galerie eingerichtet. Der Kastenbau steht ebenfalls auf Pfählen und hat ein Dach aus Kabeln statt aus Ziegeln. Kletterpflanzen bilden, passend zu den ausgestellten modernen Kunstwerken thailändischer Künstler, eine natürliche Decke.

Au début des années 1970, Patsri, la femme de Jean-Michel Beurdeley, a eu la surprise de se voir offrir par sa mère un terrain situé près de l'université de Ramkhamhaeng. Comme c'est généralement le cas à Bangkok, il était situé dans une zone marécageuse. Les Beurdeley ont choisi une construction sur pilotis – pour éviter les risques d'inondation –, qui présente le toit massif traditionnel, caractéristique du Nord de la Thaïlande. Issu de trois générations de collectionneurs d'art, ce Parisien aime les maisons donnant sur des cours et des jardins et partage avec son épouse le goût pour les portes coulissantes japonaises, qui permettent d'accéder facilement à l'extérieur. Ainsi leur demeure est composée de quatre bâtiments disposés autour d'une cour centrale et d'une piscine ombragée. Jean-Michel Beurdeley ayant dirigé avec succès pendant de nombreuses années une galerie d'art asiatique à Paris, il allait de soi qu'un des bâtiments deviendrait une galerie. Cette construction en forme de boîte reposant sur des pilotis est surmontée d'un toit en câbles, et non en tuiles. Les plantes grimpantes mettent en valeur des œuvres d'art moderne réalisées par des artistes thaïs.

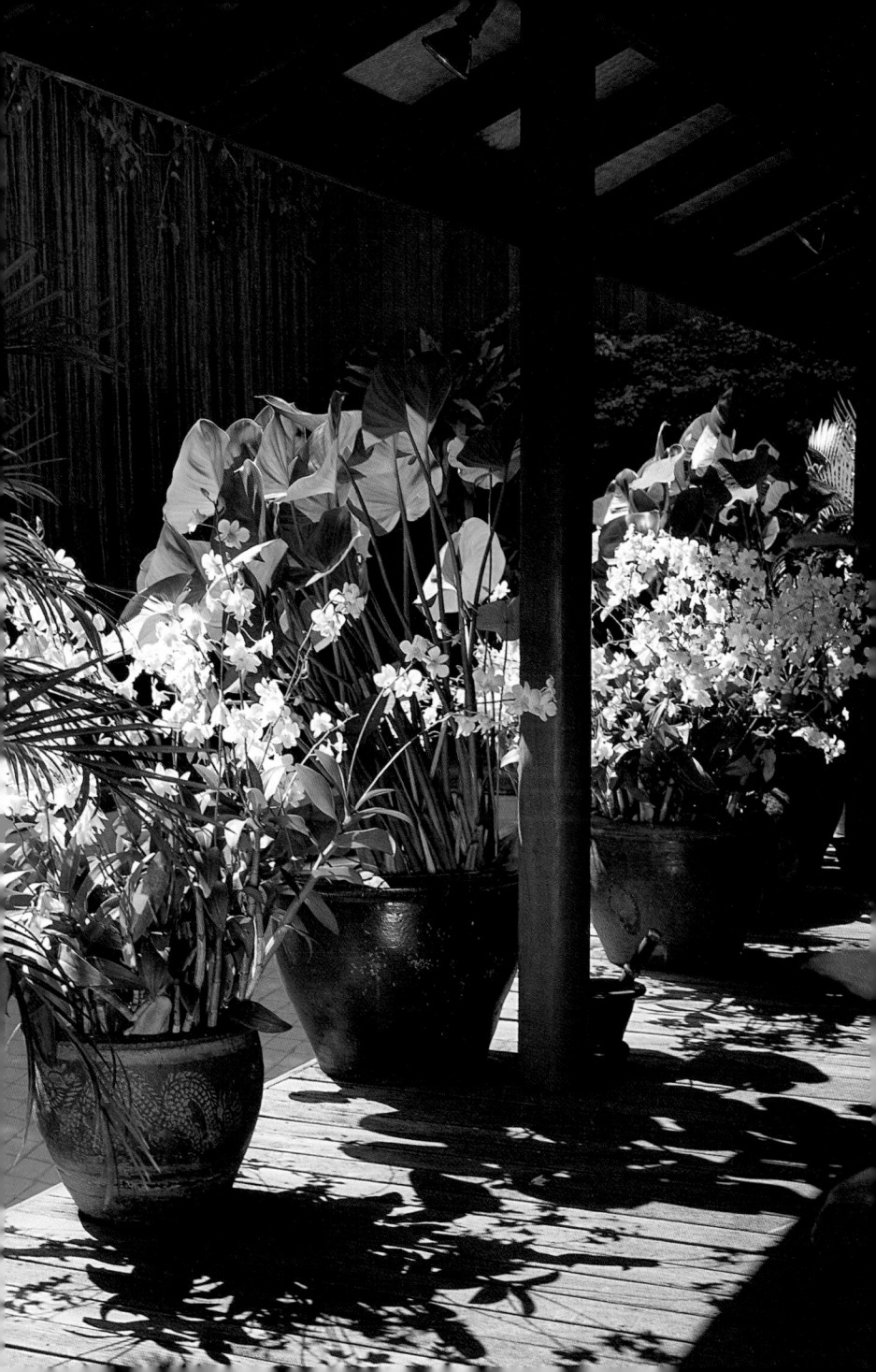

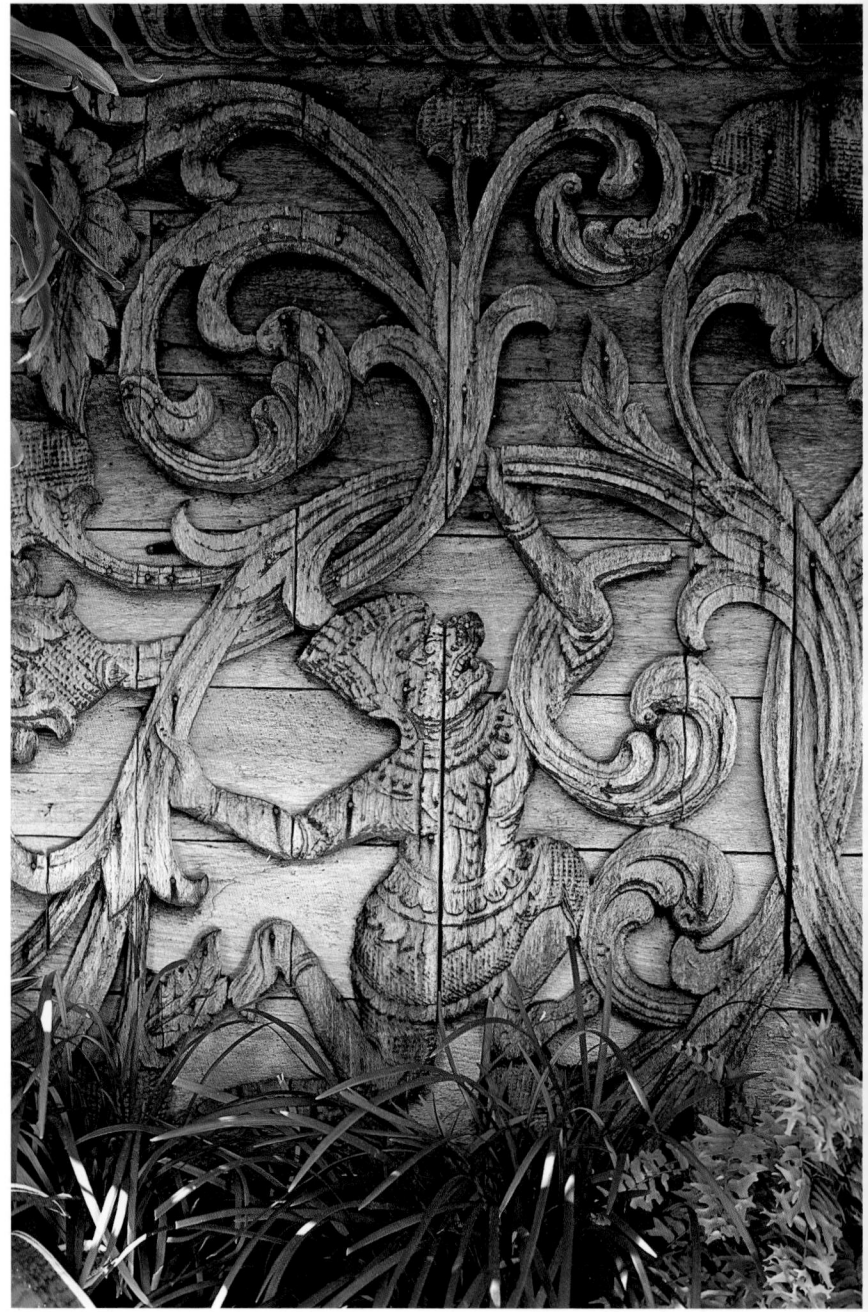

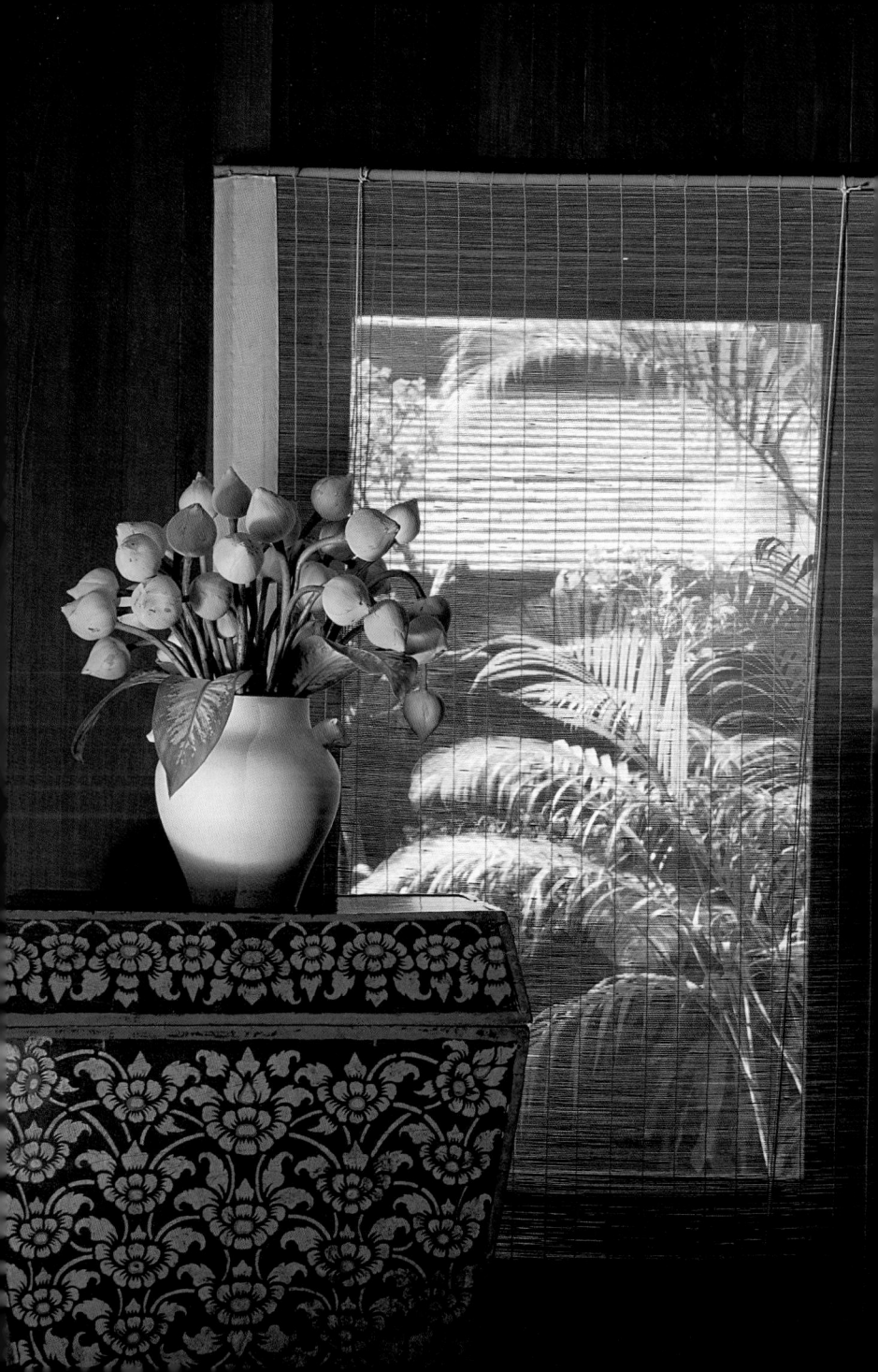

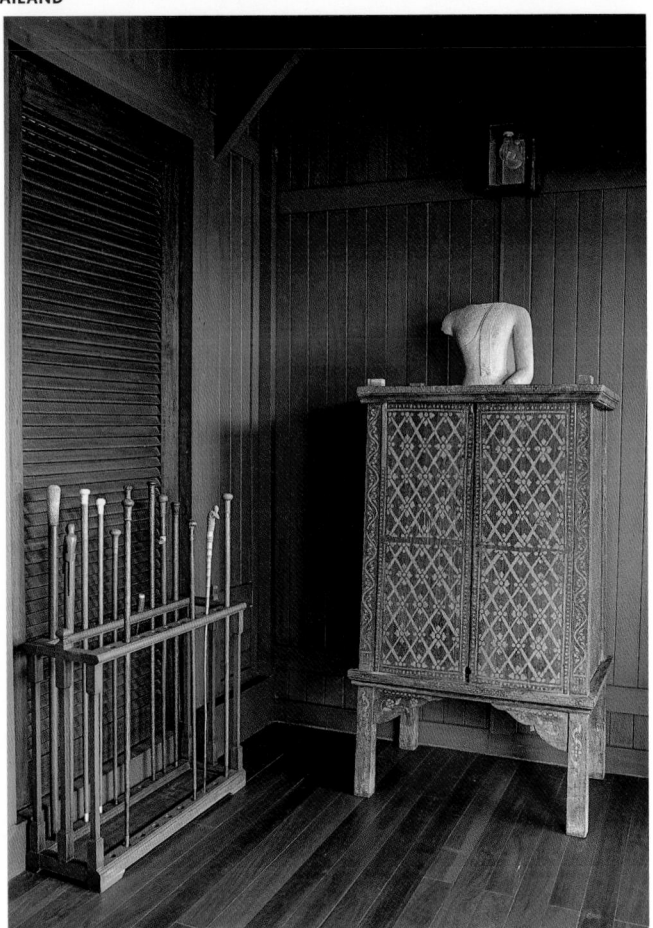

PP. 312-313 The seating area by the swimming pool is covered with trailing vines. • Reben geben in der Sitzecke am Swimmingpool Schatten. • Un coin repos sous la treille près de la piscine.

P. 315 Orchids in glazed urns line a terrace by the swimming pool. • Orchideen in glasierten Töpfen schmücken die Terrasse am Swimmingpool. • Des orchidées dans des pots vernissés bordent la piscine.

P. 316 The 19th-century wood carving of the monkey god is from northern

Thailand. • Die holzgeschnitzte Darstellung des Affengottes stammt aus Nordthailand. • Ce dieu-singe sculpté sur bois provient du Nord du pays.

PP. 320-321 A painting by Thai artist Tawan Dachanee covers an entire wall of the living room. • Das Gemälde des thailändischen Künstlers Tawan Dachanee nimmt im Wohnzimmer eine ganze Wand ein. • Un tableau de l'artiste thaï Tawan Dachanee couvre un mur du salon.

↑ → A stone Buddha's torso on a Thai cabinet. Temple shutters from northern Thailand and a Burmese copper chandelier in the guest room. • Der steinerne Torso einer Buddhafigur thront auf einem thailändischen Schrank. Fensterläden aus Tempeln in Nordthailand und ein birmanischer Kronleuchter aus Kupfer im Gästezimmer. • Sur une armoire thaïe trône le buste en pierre d'une statue de Bouddha. Dans la chambre d'amis, des panneaux provenant de temples du Nord de la Thaïlande et un lustre birman en cuivre.

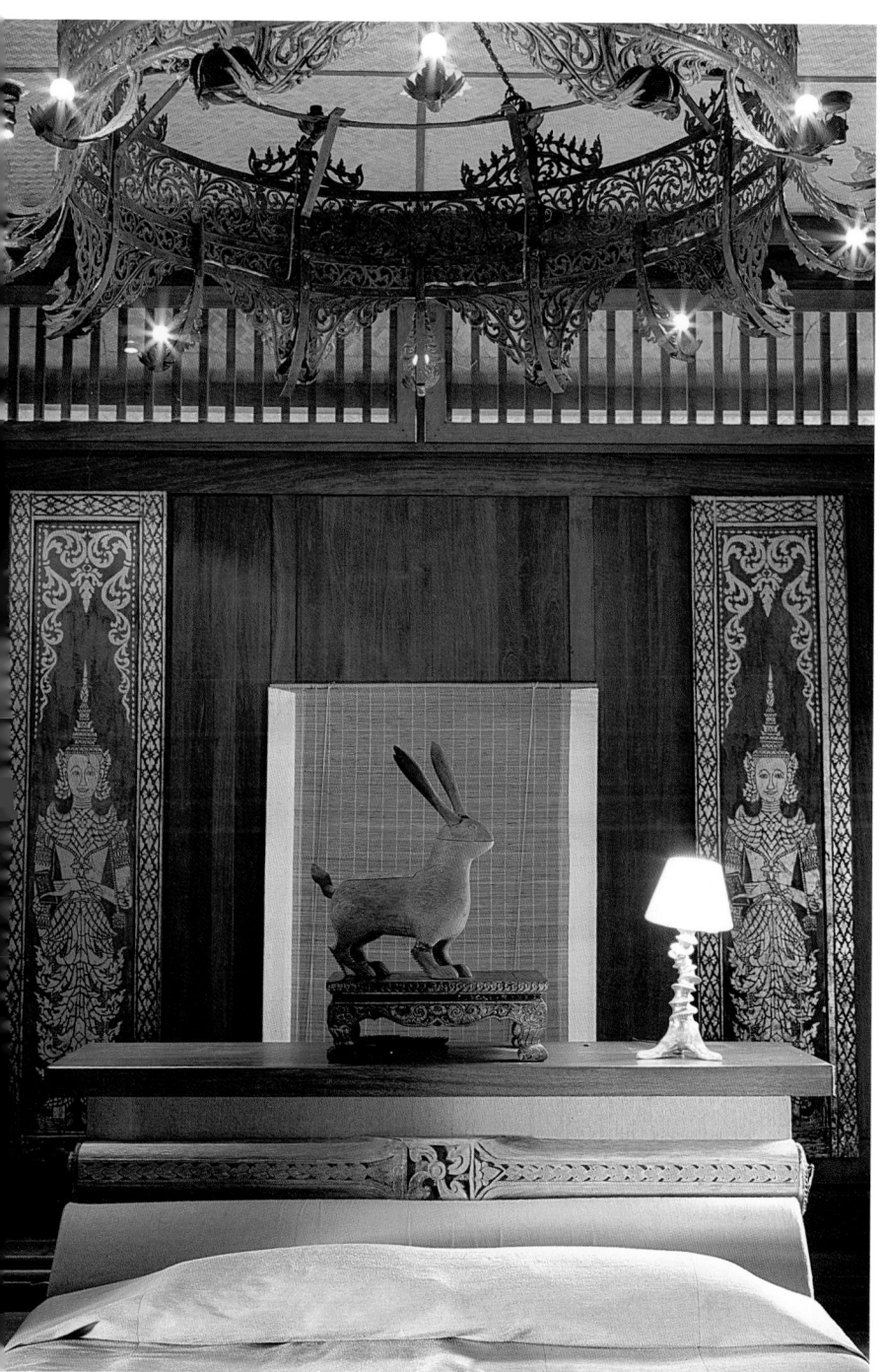

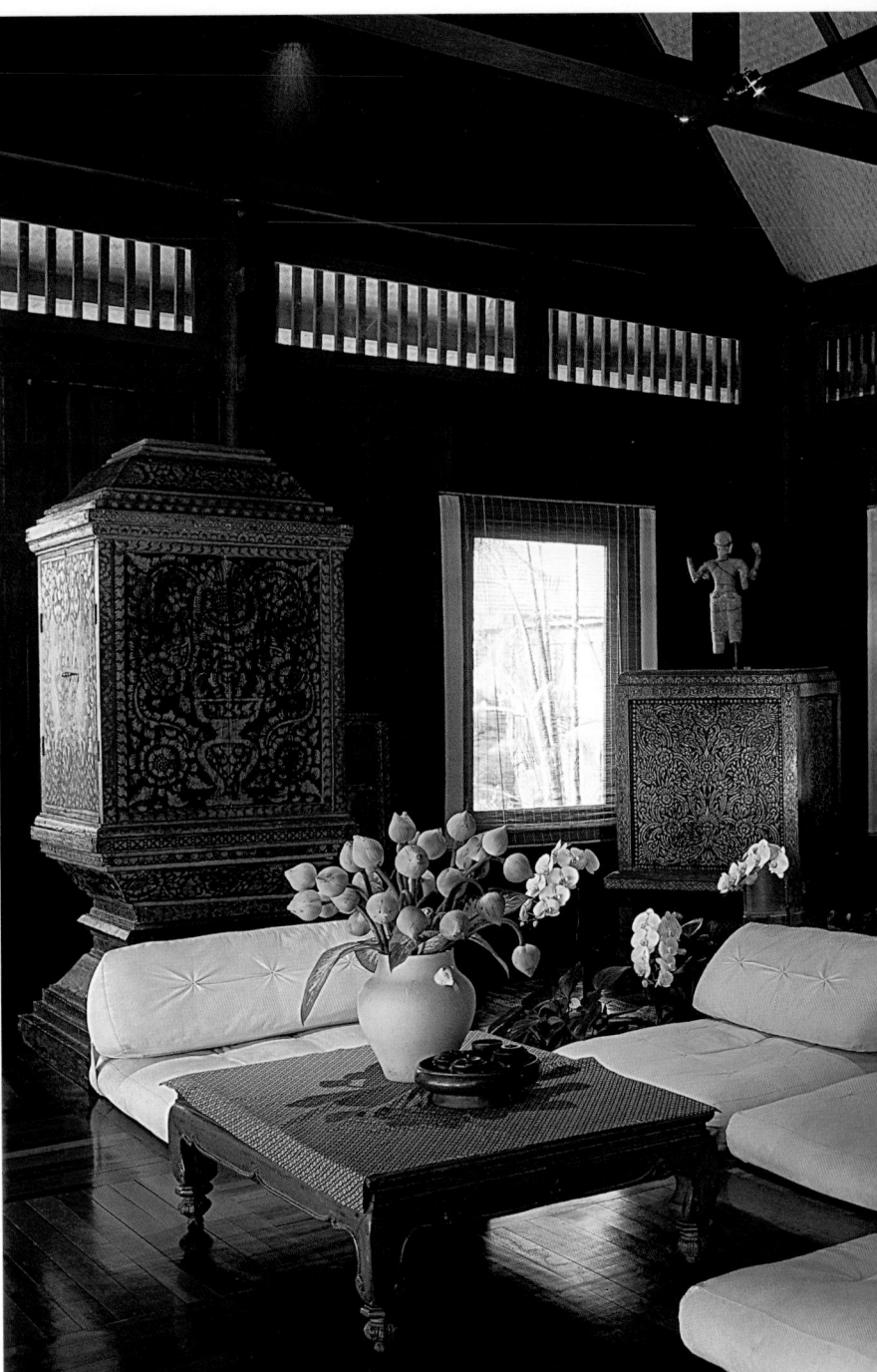

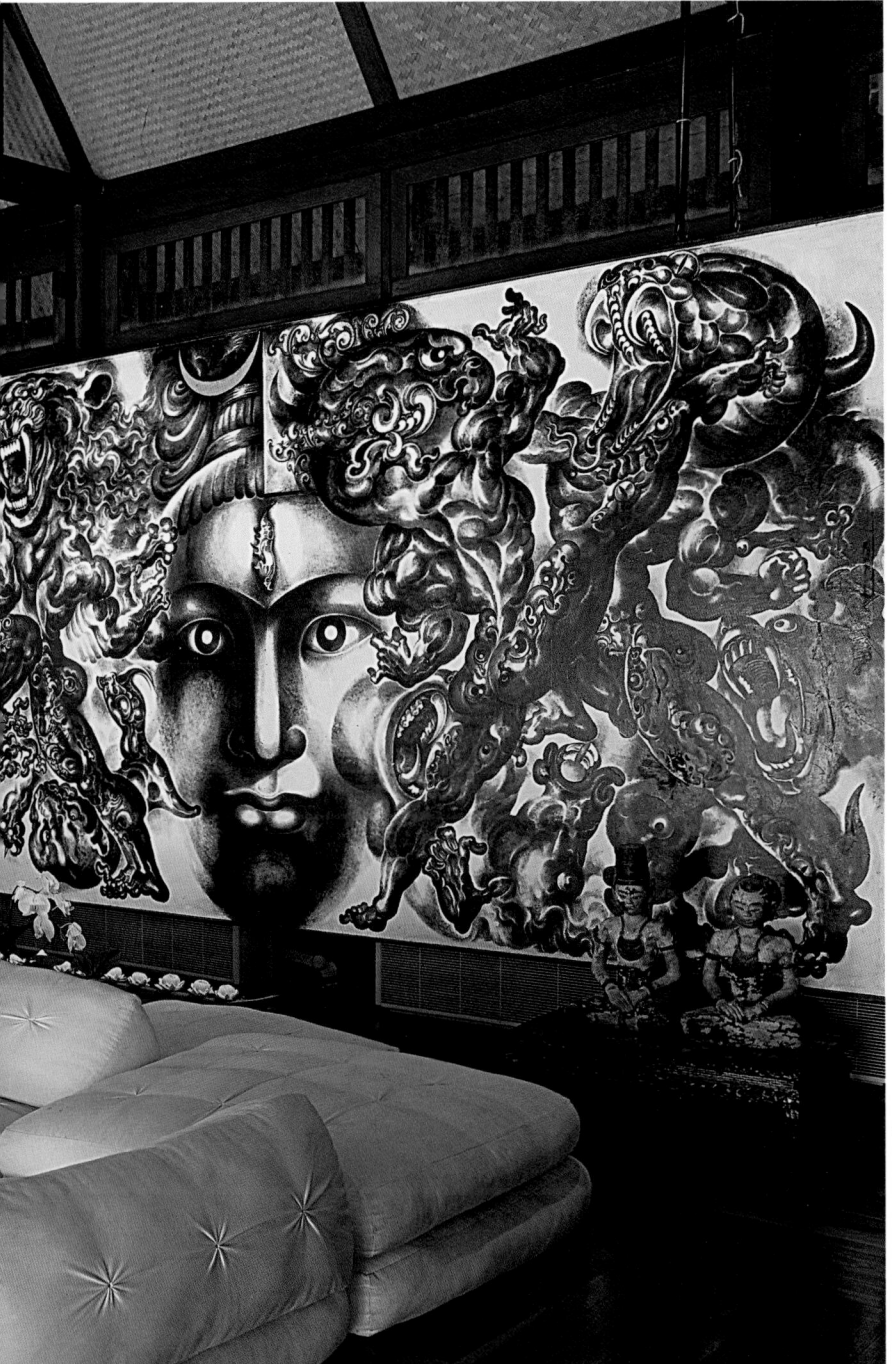

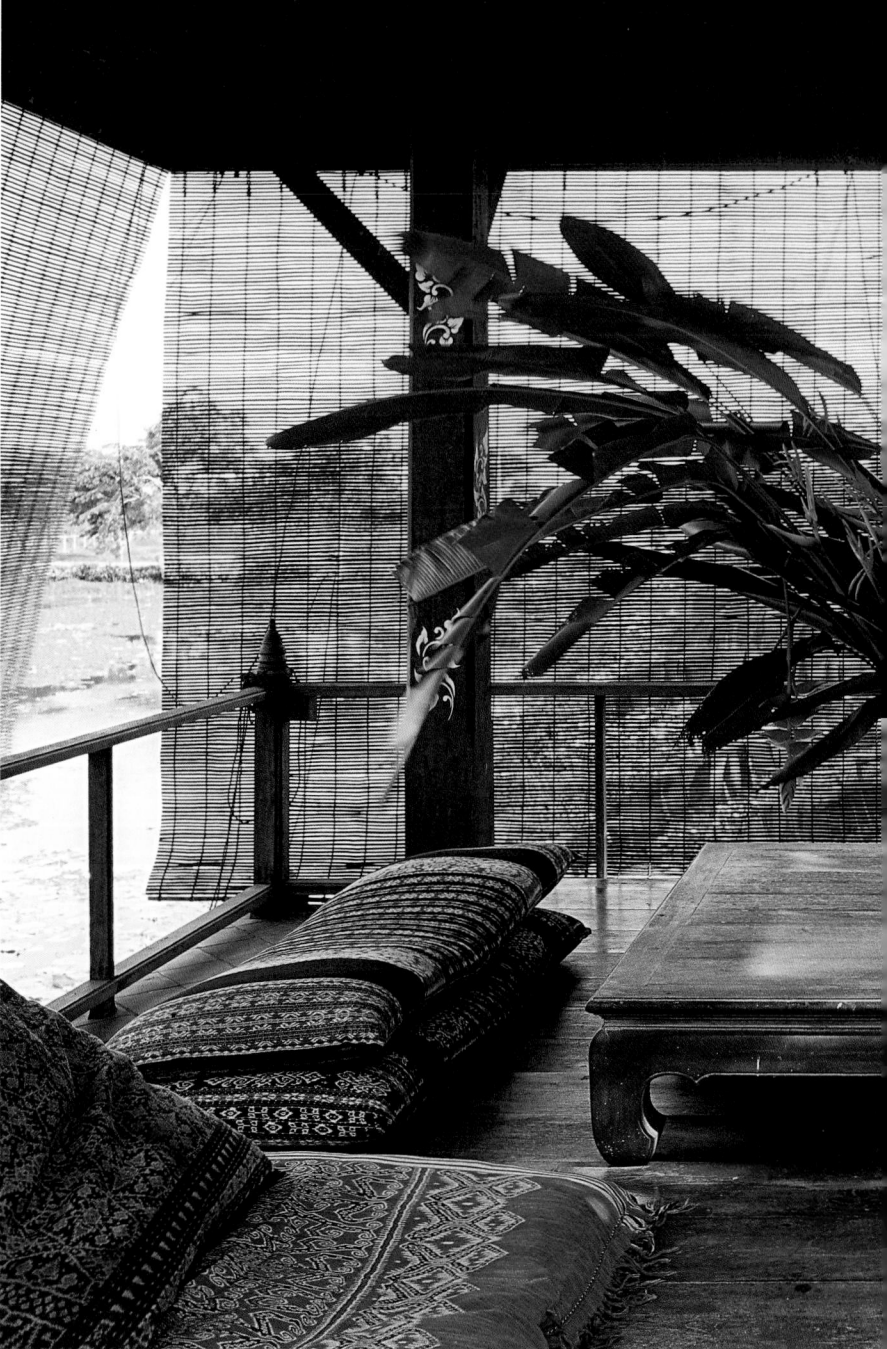

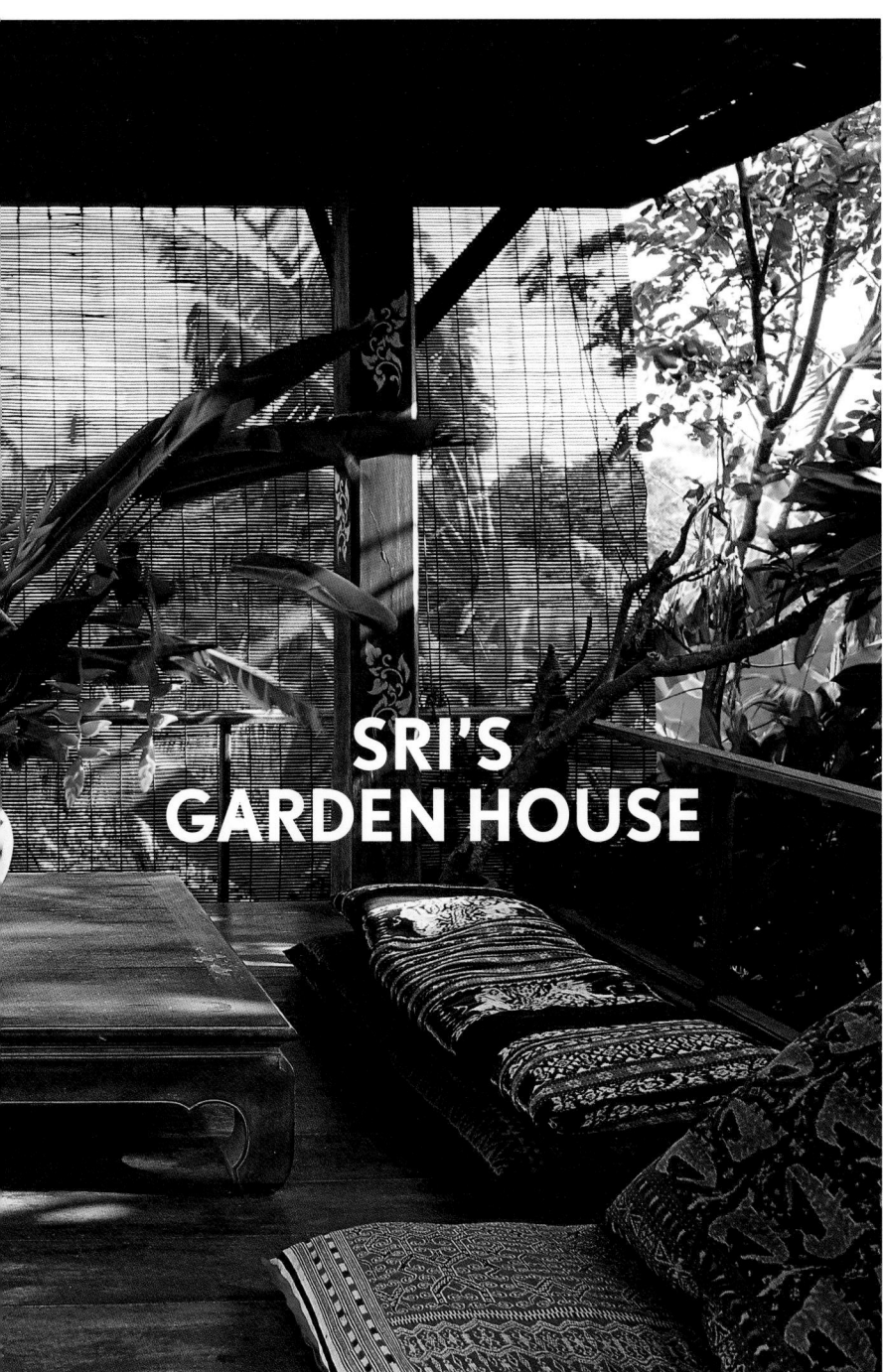

SRI'S
GARDEN HOUSE

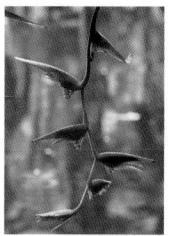

SRI'S GARDEN HOUSE
BANGKOK
THAILAND

Stepping from the heat and dust of Bangkok into the private preserve of the von Bueren family in the heart of the city, visitors are often stunned. It is like entering a magic garden, with trees and trailing vines draping old Khmer and Ming statuary. Hidden here and there are traditional houses and pavilions, and the whole exquisitely ordered jungle overlooks a lotus-filled lake with an old rice barge, converted into a small guest house. Sri von Bueren, elder son of Rolf and Helen von Bueren, lives with his wife Rai and their two boys in a house called *Suan Sai Tan* which is Thai for "garden". Although the von Bueren family occupies separate houses in different parts of the compound, the parent house remains the center of activity. "It's the traditional way of living in Asia," says Bangkok-born Sri, who handles the creative side of the family business. "My mother is a great cook so all the boys hang out in the kitchen. We are so lucky – to live, work, travel and have fun together."

Besucher staunen, wenn sie, mitten aus der Hitze und dem Staub Bangkoks, in die Privatdomäne der Familie von Bueren eintauchen – als beträten sie einen Zaubergarten, in dem sie unter Bäumen und Ranken manch alte Statue aus der Zeit der Khmer und Ming finden. In diesem wohlgeordneten Dschungel verteilen sich traditionelle Häuser und Pavillons um einen See mit Lotusblüten, in dem eine alte Reisbarke in ein kleines Gästehaus umgebaut wurde. Sri von Bueren, der ältere Sohn von Rolf und Helen von Bueren, wohnt mit seiner Frau Rai und ihren beiden Jungen in einem Haus namens *Suan Sai Tan*, was auf Thai „Garten" bedeutet. Obwohl die von Buerens mehrere Häuser in verschiedenen Winkeln des Anwesens bewohnen, findet das wahre Leben noch immer im Elternhaus statt. „Das entspricht der traditionellen asiatischen Lebensart", erklärt Sri, der in Bangkok geboren wurde und den kreativen Bereich des Familiengeschäfts leitet. „Meine Mutter ist eine großartige Köchin, deshalb treffen sich alle Jungs immer in der Küche. Wir haben das unglaubliche Glück, dass wir zusammen leben, arbeiten, reisen und Spaß haben können."

Les visiteurs quittent la touffeur et la poussière de Bangkok pour entrer dans le petit paradis de la famille von Bueren, au cœur de la ville, sont souvent ébahis. C'est comme s'ils entraient dans un jardin enchanté abritant des statues anciennes Khmer et Ming sous les arbres et les treilles. Dissimulés çà et là dans cette jungle admirablement ordonnée, des pavillons et maisons traditionnels sont groupés autour d'un lac où fleurissent les lotus. Une barge pour le transport du riz y a été convertie en petit appartement pour les invités. Sri von Bueren, l'aîné de Rolf et Helen von Bueren, vit avec son épouse Rai et ses deux fils dans une maison appelée *Suan Sai Tan*, « jardin » en thaï. Bien que chaque membre de la famille ait son foyer dans un endroit retiré de la propriété, la maison des parents reste le point de convergence. « C'est le mode de vie traditionnel en Asie », explique Sri, né à Bangkok, le créatif de l'entreprise familiale. « Ma mère est si bonne cuisinière que tous les garçons sont toujours pendus à ses basques. Nous avons beaucoup de plaisir à vivre, travailler et voyager ensemble. »

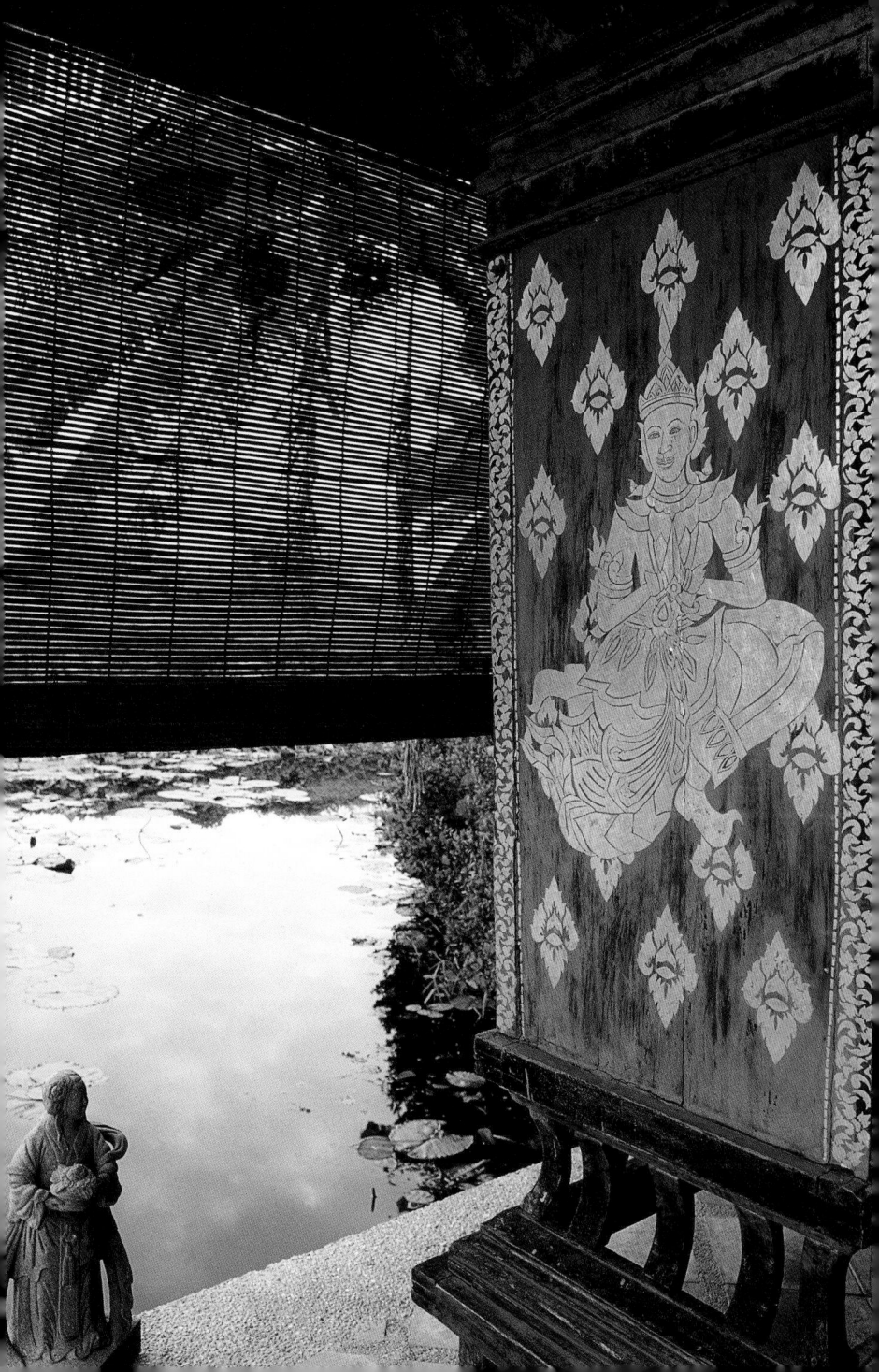

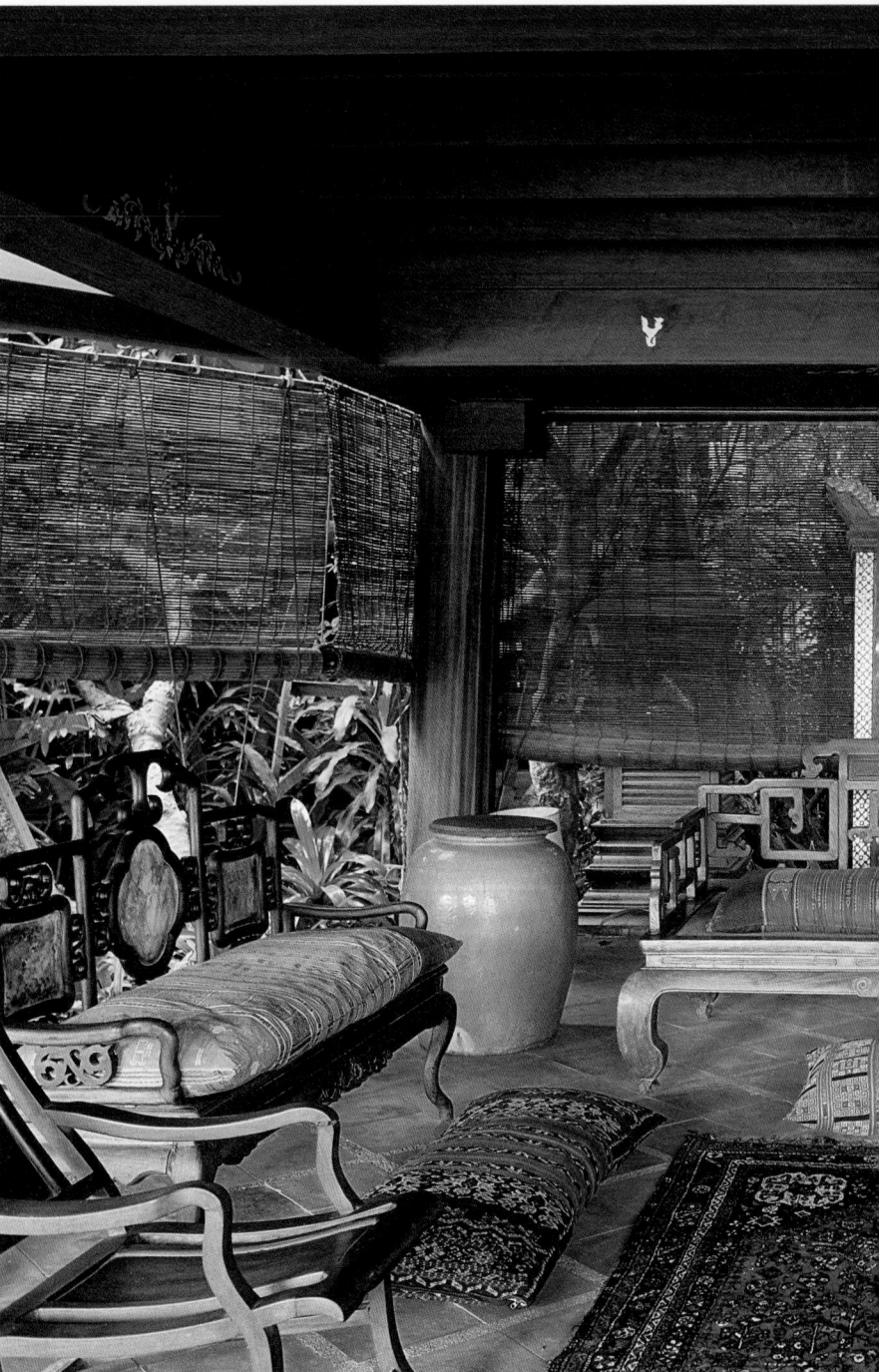

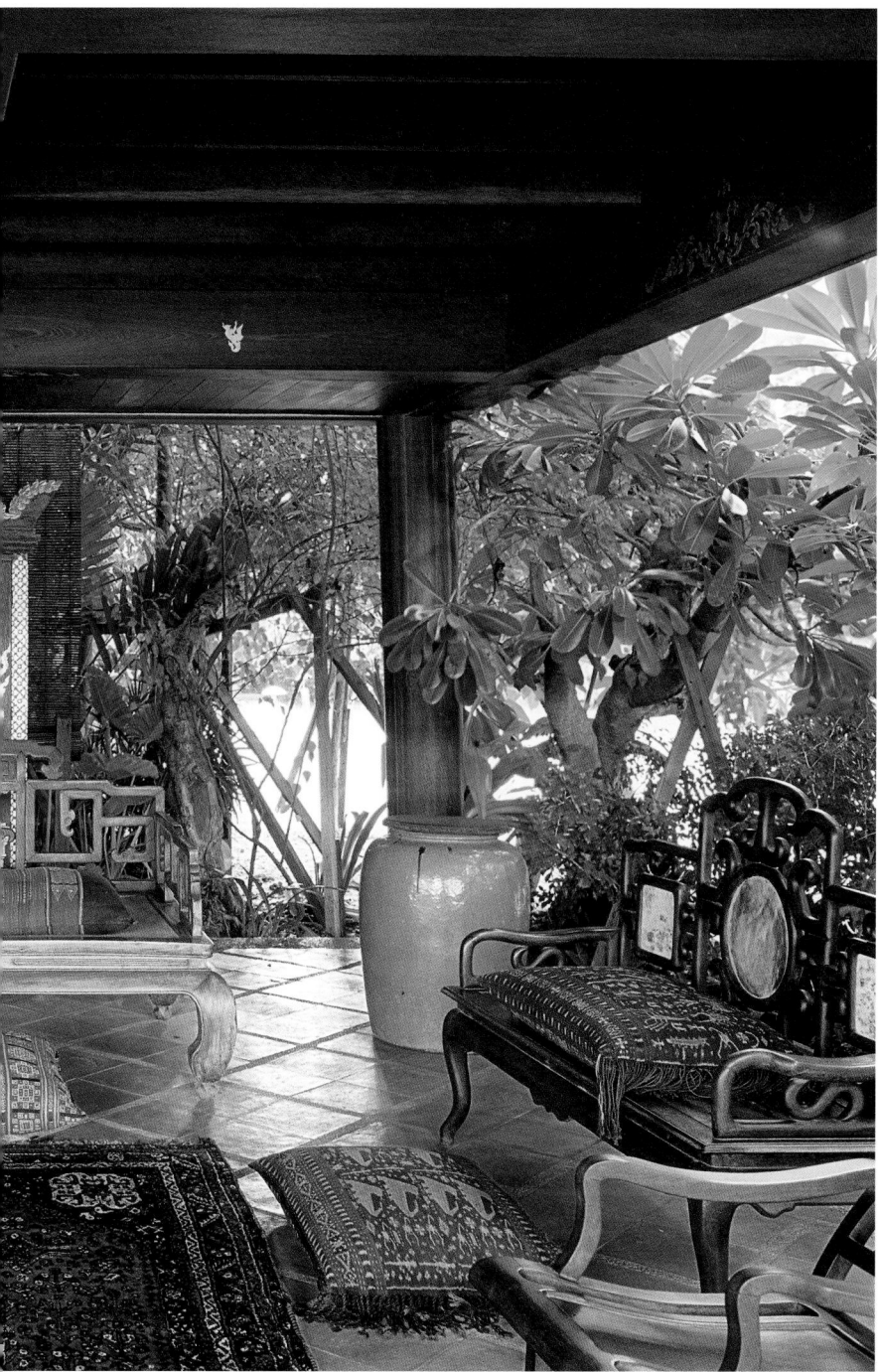

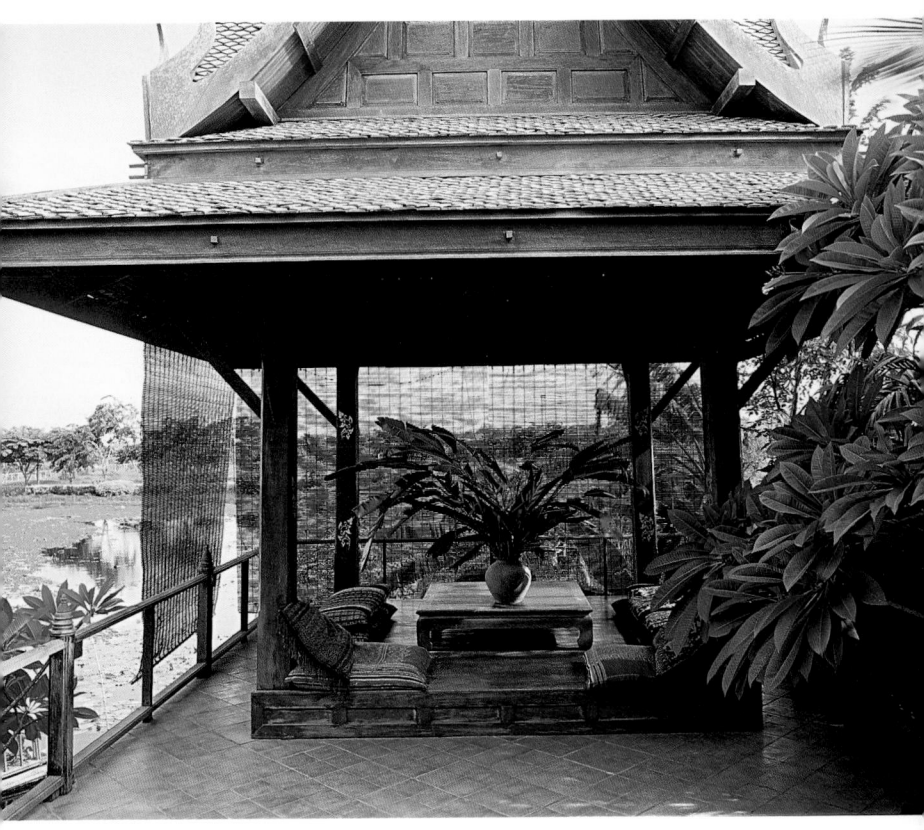

PP. 322–323 The dining area on the lotus-filled lake is a wooden pavilion screened with bamboo blinds. • Im Holzpavillon mit Bambusrollos über dem Lotussee liegt der Essbereich. • La salle à manger au-dessus du lac a été aménagée dans un pavillon en bois protégé par des stores en bambou.

PP. 326–327 A dramatic cabinet from northern Thailand stands at the far end of the living room. • Ein reich verzierter Schrank aus Nordthailand steht ganz hinten im Wohnzimmer. • Un meuble spectaculaire provenant du Nord de la Thaïlande occupe le fond du salon.

← Another view of the pavilion. • Weitere Ansicht des Pavillons. • Le pavillon vu sous un autre angle.

↓ A low carved bed in the bedroom also overlooks the lake. • Ein niedriges holzgeschnitztes Bett im Schlafzimmer, das ebenfalls auf den See hinausgeht. • Du lit bas en bois sculpté, on peut aussi contempler le lac.

PP. 330-331 The walls and floor of the interiors are of teak panels. • Innen sind Wände und Böden mit Teakholz verkleidet. • Les murs et les parquets sont en teck.

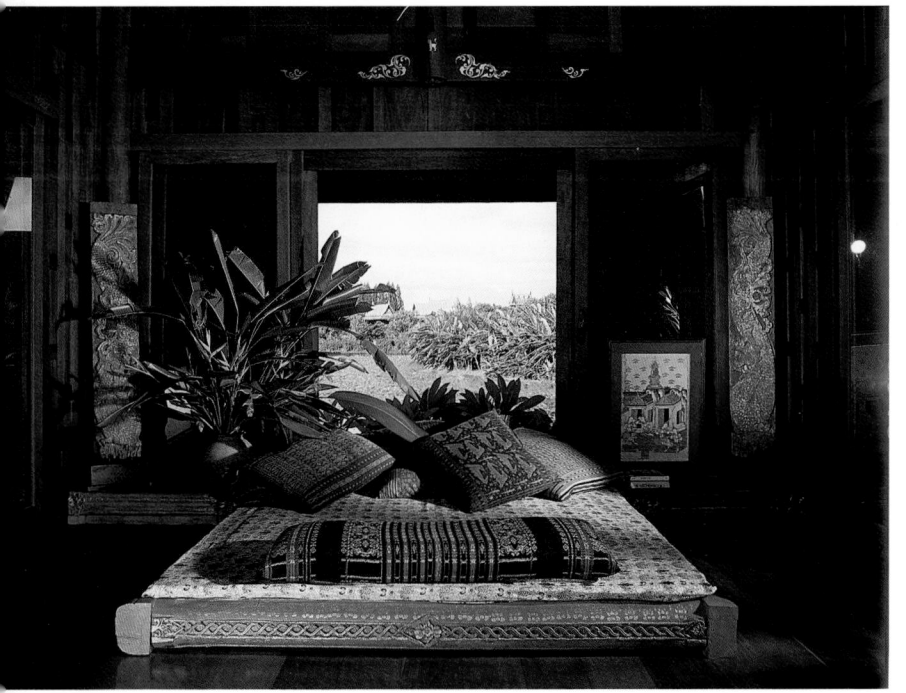

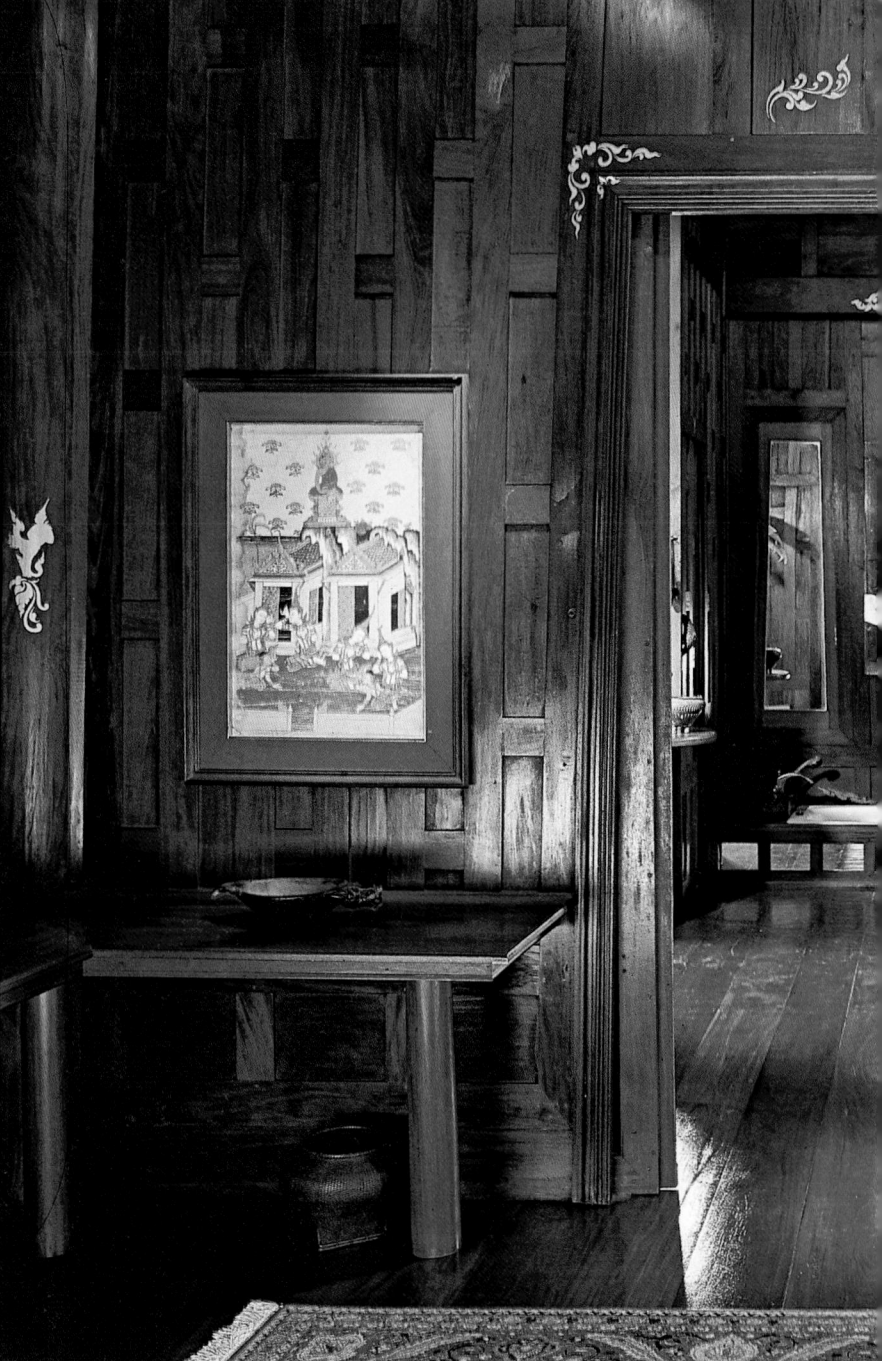

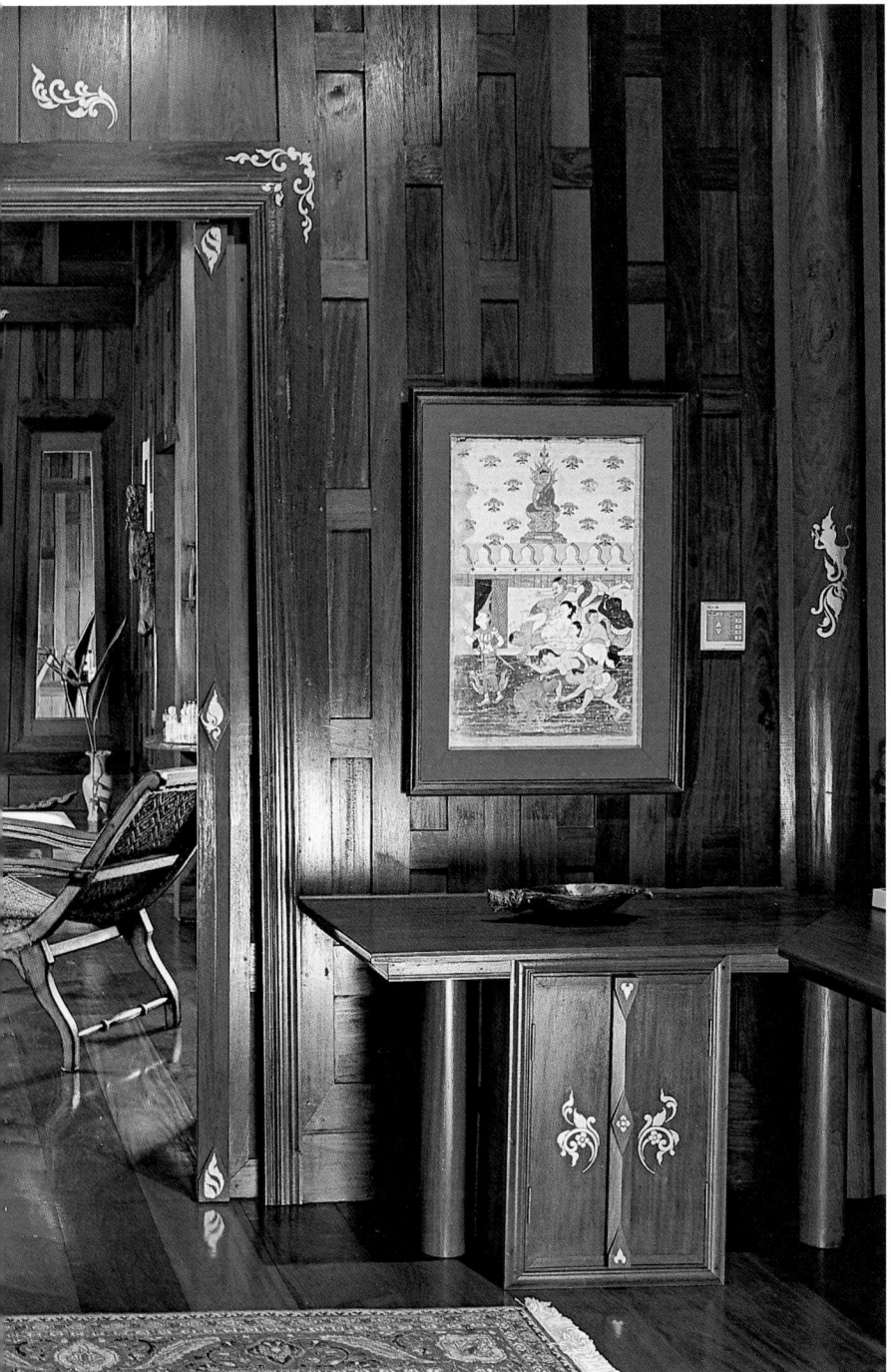

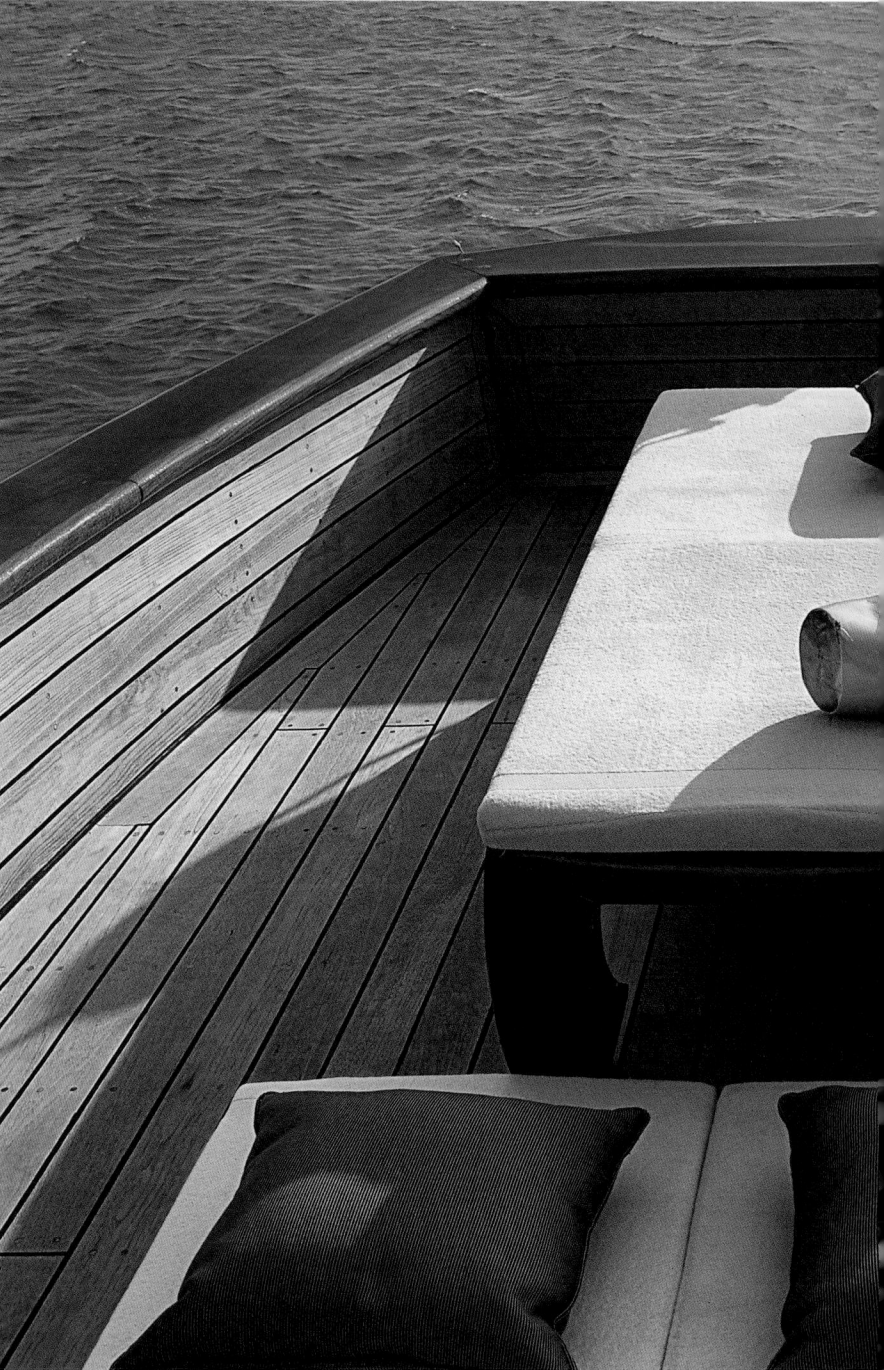

THE MAHA
BHETRA

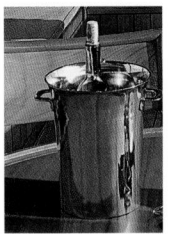

THE MAHA BHETRA

PHUKET
THAILAND

Paris-based American architect Ed Tuttle has moved between Europe and Asia for 30 years, and is distinguished for his design of several hotels and resorts. Asked to design a yacht for a private client to be moored on the west coast of Thailand, he couldn't see the point of a high-tech cruiser; Tuttle is a firm believer in combining indigenous skills with a harmony of materials. In creating the *Maha Bhetra*, which means "Boat" in Thai, he literally went with the flow. The 90-foot wooden motor yacht was crafted by traditional boat-builders in Phuket from local varieties of teak. It has three identical main cabins with woven cane panels set in teak frames; the upper deck has a covered seating and dining area that opens on to a sun deck. Tuttle's interiors are a stylishly simple tribute to quality materials and local antiques. The Maha Bhetra sails among the many uninhabited islands near the border to Myanmar and the Malaysian peninsula.

Der in Paris ansässige amerikanische Architekt Ed Tuttle reiste dreißig Jahre lang zwischen Europa und Asien. Verschiedene Ferienanlagen und Hotels tragen die Handschrift des hochgelobten Designers. Als er darum gebeten wurde, eine Jacht zu entwerfen, die an der Westküste Thailands ankern sollte, lehnte Ed Tuttle es ab, einen weiteren Hightech-Cruiser zu bauen. Da er stets die Geschicklichkeit der Einheimischen mit harmonischem Baumaterial in Verbindung bringen möchte, schwamm er beim Entwurf der *Maha Bhetra*, was auf Thai „Boot" bedeutet, buchstäblich mit dem Strom. Traditionell ausgebildete Bootsbauer zimmerten die neunzig Meter lange Jacht in Phuket aus verschiedenen Teakhölzern. Das Schiff hat drei identische Kabinen mit geflochtenen, in Rahmen aus Teakholz gefassten Rohrplatten. An Deck wurde ein Bereich überdacht, der zum Sitzen und Speisen einlädt. Daran schließt sich ein Sonnendeck an, und auch die Innenräume wurden von Tuttle schlicht, aber mit allem Komfort, aus wertvollem Baumaterial und mit Antiquitäten aus der Umgebung eingerichtet. Die Maha Bhetra segelt zwischen den vielen kleinen Inseln unweit der birmanischen Grenze und der malaysischen Halbinsel.

Ed Tuttle, architecte américain établi à Paris et connu pour ses nombreux hôtels et stations balnéaires, a passé 30 ans de sa vie entre l'Europe et l'Asie. Un jour, un particulier lui a commandé les plans d'un yacht censé avoir son port d'attache sur la côte ouest de la Thaïlande. Fervent adepte du savoir-faire local et d'une harmonie des matériaux, Ed Tuttle a écarté l'idée d'un bateau de croisière high-tech. Et en concevant le *Maha Bhetra* – « bateau » en thaï –, il n'a fait que suivre ses penchants. C'est ainsi que cette embarcation à moteur de 30 mètres de long a été fabriquée dans des essences locales de teck par des artisans de Phuket. Les trois cabines principales du Maha Bhetra sont dotées de cloisons de rotin tressé montées sur des cadres en teck ; sur le pont supérieur, on trouve un espace salon et repas couvert. Les intérieurs conçus par Tuttle sont un hommage d'une grande simplicité aux matériaux de qualité et aux antiquités locales. Le Maha Bhetra vogue entre les milliers d'îlots inhabités qui émaillent la mer aux abords de la frontière birmane et de la péninsule malaisienne.

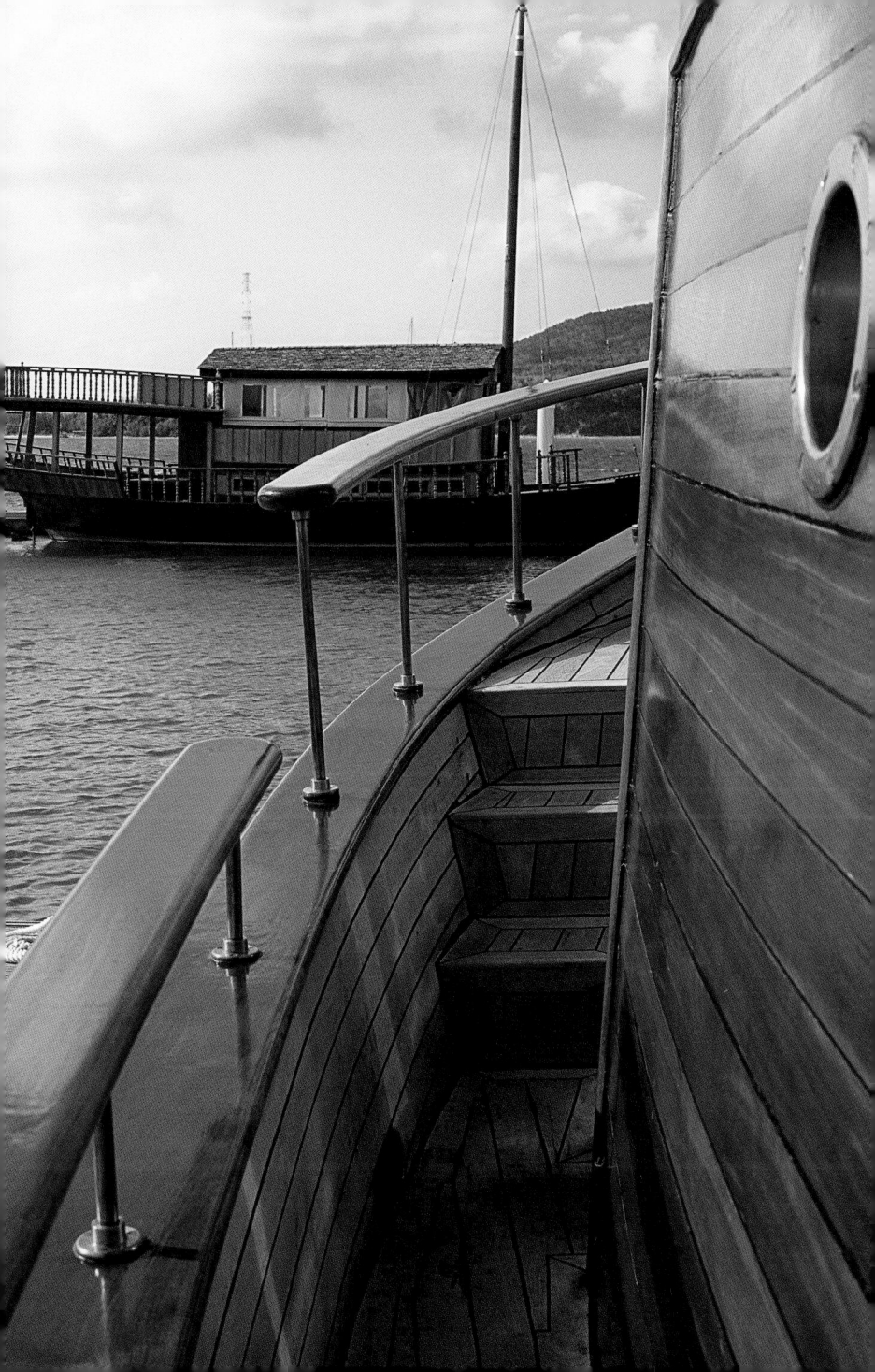

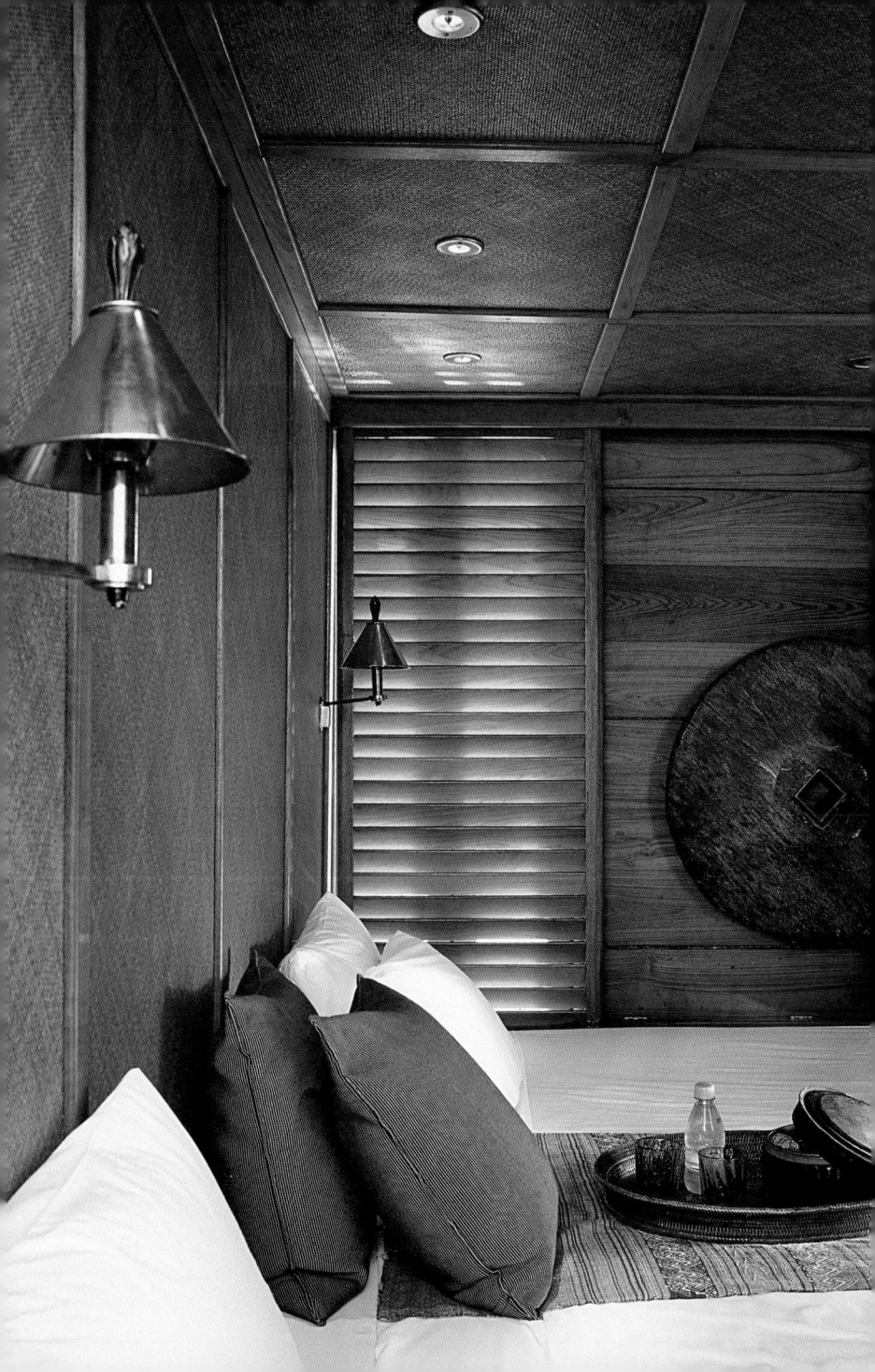

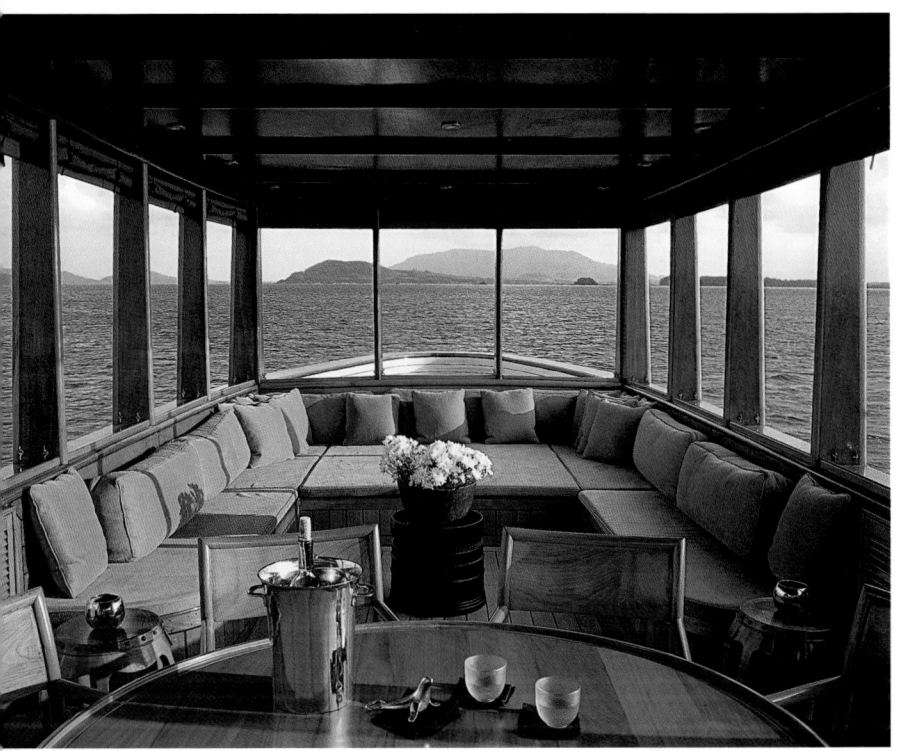

PP. 332-333 An antique spot lamp in the sunning area. • Ein antiker Strahler auf dem Sonnendeck. • Un projecteur ancien sur le solarium du pont supérieur.

← A wooden cart wheel hangs between sliding window panels. • Zwischen den Schiebefenstern in der Kabine hängt

ein hölzernes Wagenrad. • Une roue de charrette est accrochée entre les fenêtres coulissantes de la cabine.

↑ Banquettes covered in Jim Thompson fabric along the covered dining area on the upper deck. • Die Bänke im über-dachten Essbereich an Deck sind mit

Jim-Thompson-Stoffen gepolstert. • Des banquettes recouvertes de tissus signés Jim Thompson courent le long des parois de l'espace dîner sur le pont supérieur.

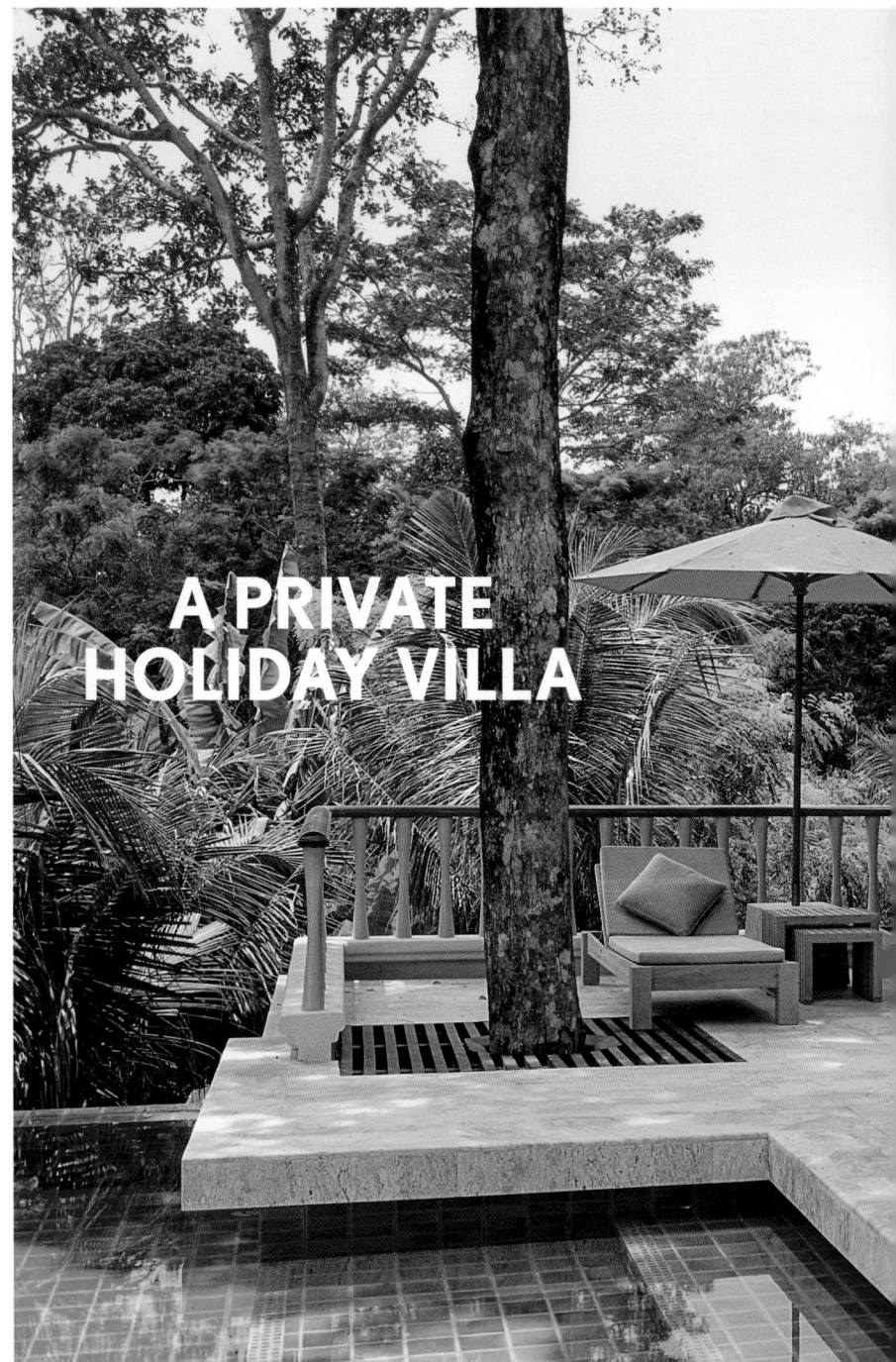

A PRIVATE
HOLIDAY VILLA

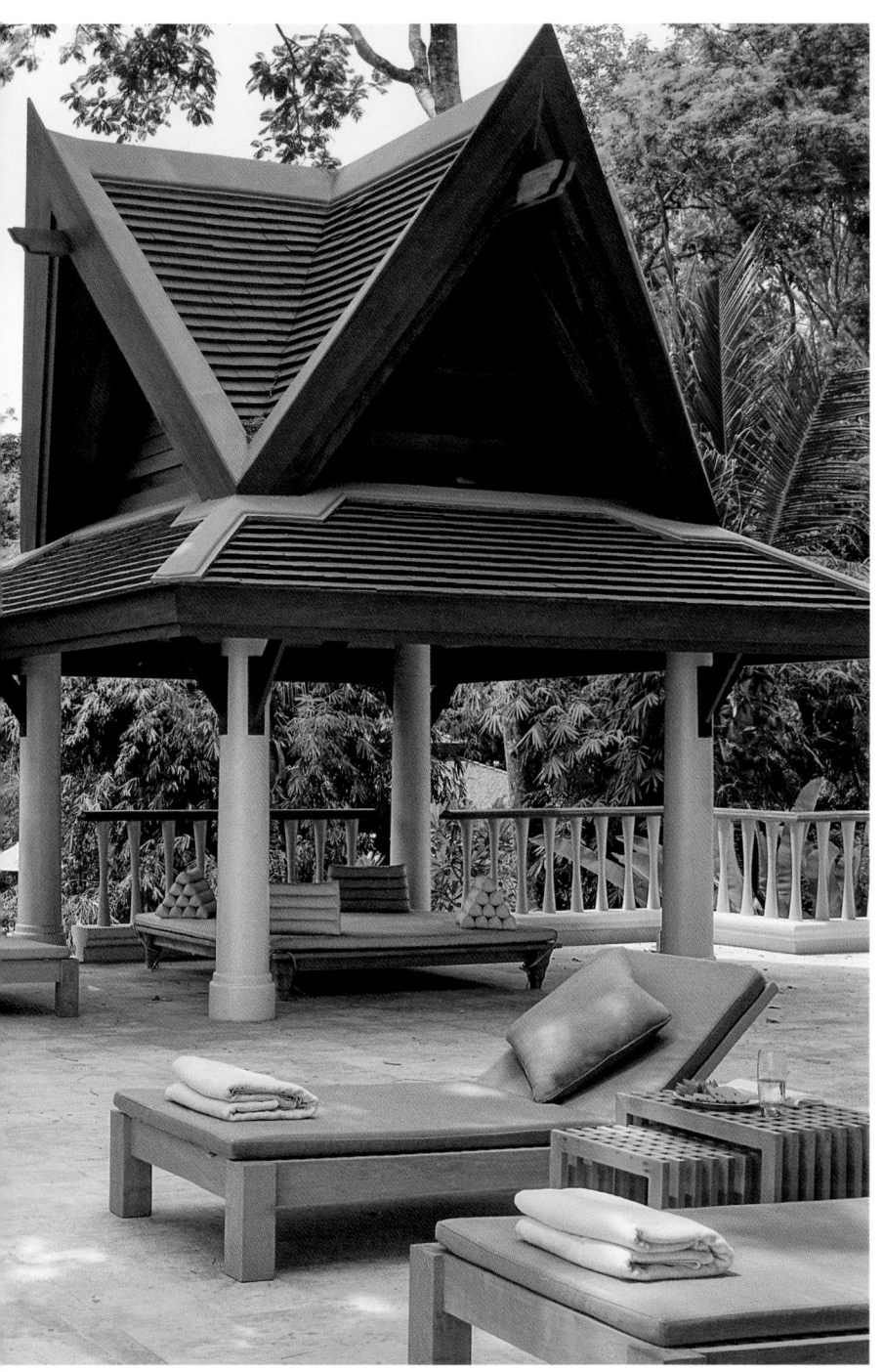

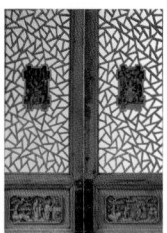

A PRIVATE HOLIDAY VILLA
PHUKET
THAILAND

Up until fifteen years ago, the land north of the tourist-filled resorts of Phuket was still wild open country. It was along this sparkling coastline – in what was once a rubber plantation – that a European couple bought into a development of villas promoted by a Thai architect. The couple is well-known for their fine taste and, in particular, their collection of contemporary Chinese, American and Russian art. After decades of travelling in Asia, when they began to consider a permanent holiday home, Thailand was the natural choice: as much for the friendliness of its people as its political stability and easy tax regime. They had the temple-like, three-story villa custom-built to their own design. A central teak and steel spiral staircase leads to the bedrooms and an office above. The floors of seasoned teak came from an old farmhouse, specially purchased for the purpose. Filled with a mixture of Asian antiques and contemporary art, it is a vacation villa that will one day they hope, become their retirement home.

Noch bis vor fünfzehn Jahren herrschte nördlich der Ferienanlagen von Phuket die reine Wildnis. An dieser paradiesischen Küste kaufte sich ein europäisches Ehepaar bei einem thailändischen Architekten in ein Villenprojekt am Standort einer ehemaligen Gummiplantage ein. Das Paar ist für seinen exquisiten Geschmack, vor allem aber wegen seiner Sammlung zeitgenössischer chinesischer, amerikanischer und russischer Kunst bekannt. Nachdem beide jahrzehntelang durch Asien gereist waren und ein festes Ferienhaus in Betracht zogen, kam als Standort nur Thailand infrage – der freundlichen Bevölkerung, der politischen Stabilität und der laxen Steuergesetze wegen. Die tempelähnliche, dreistöckige Villa wurde nach eigenen Entwürfen gebaut: In der Mitte führt eine Wendeltreppe aus Stahl und Teak zu den Schlafzimmern und einem Arbeitszimmer. Die Böden aus abgelagertem Teakholz stammen aus einem alten Bauernhaus, das die Eigentümer eigens für diesen Zweck kauften. In der Hoffnung, eines Tages als Rentner in ihrer Villa zu wohnen, kombinierten sie liebevoll asiatische Antiquitäten mit zeitgenössischer Kunst.

Il y a une quinzaine d'années, la région située au nord des stations balnéaires bondées de Phuket était encore sauvage. C'est sur son superbe littoral, où se trouvait autrefois une plantation d'hévéas, qu'un couple a acheté une villa dans un lotissement construit par un architecte et promoteur thaï. Ces Européens, connus pour leur goût raffiné et, plus particulièrement pour leur collection d'art contemporain chinois, américain et russe, se sont mis en quête, après des années à voyager en Asie, d'une résidence secondaire. Leur choix s'est tout naturellement porté sur la Thaïlande, paradis fiscal à l'hospitalité légendaire et d'une grande stabilité politique. Ils ont fait construire d'après leurs propres dessins cette villa de deux étages qui ressemble à un temple. Un escalier en colimaçon en teck et acier dessert les chambres et le bureau. Les planchers en teck séché proviennent d'une vieille ferme, achetée spécialement à cet effet. Un mélange d'antiquités asiatiques et d'art contemporain agrémente cette maison de vacances qui, espèrent-ils, deviendra un jour leur domicile permanent, l'heure de la retraite venue.

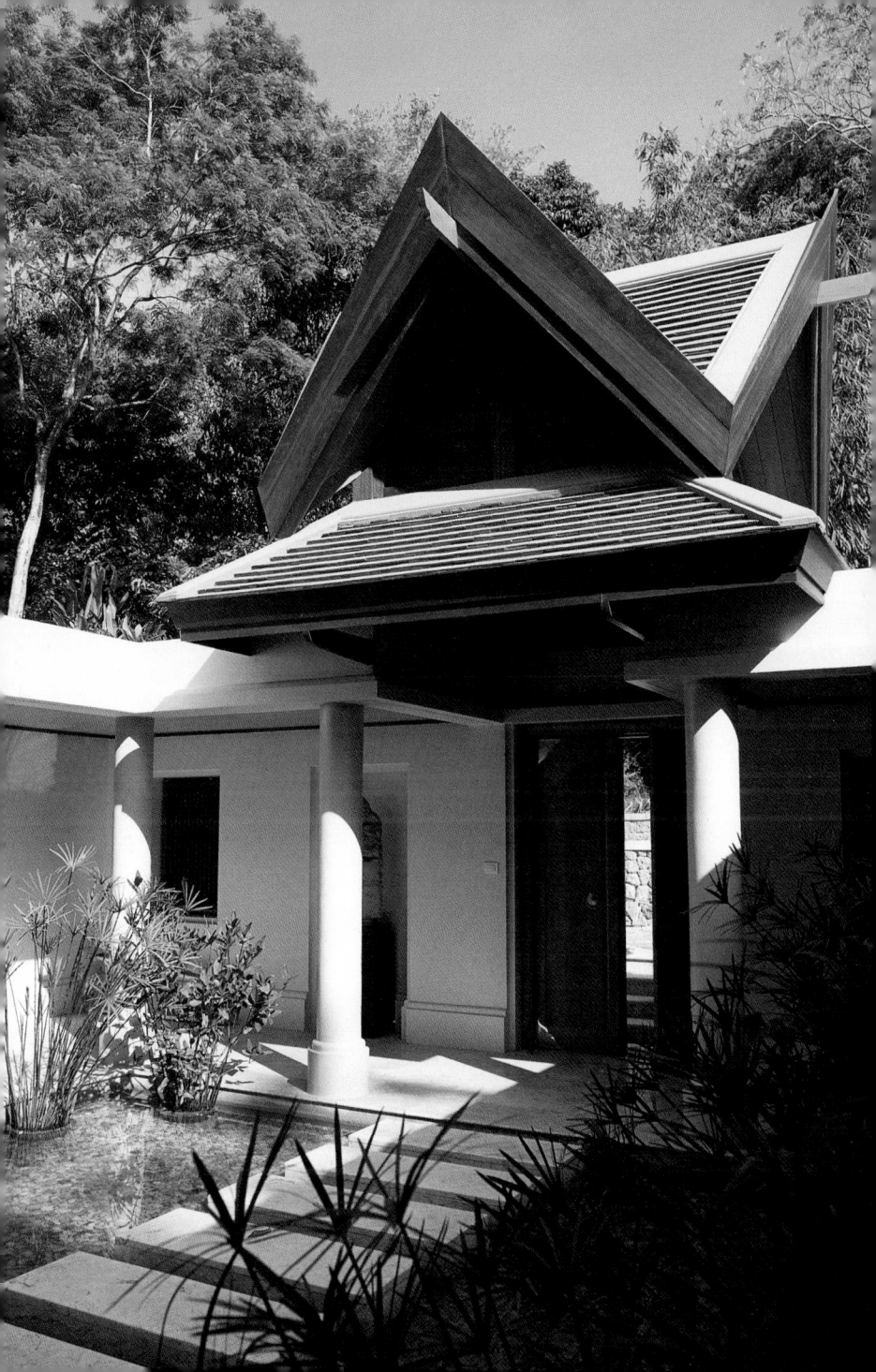

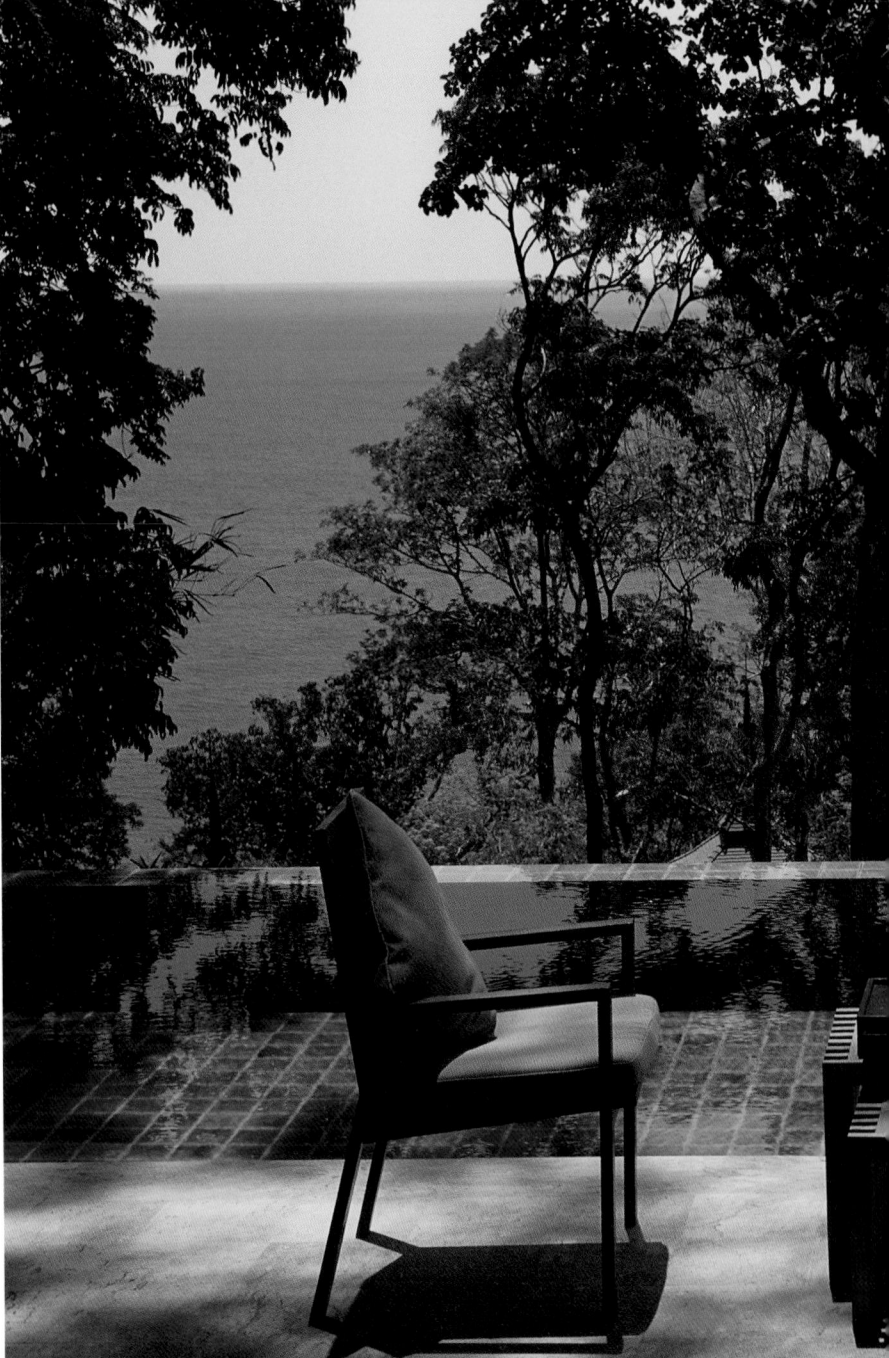

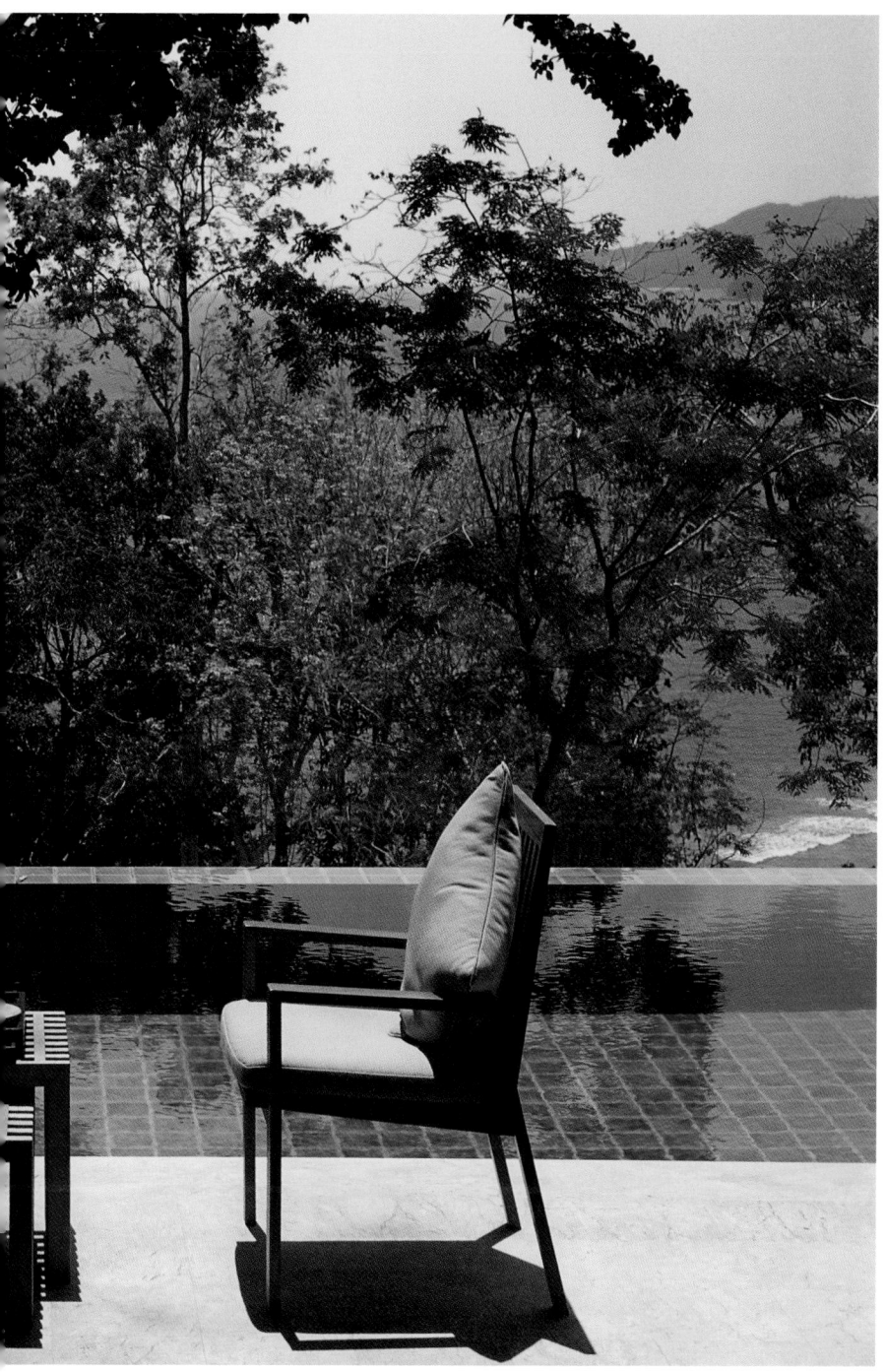

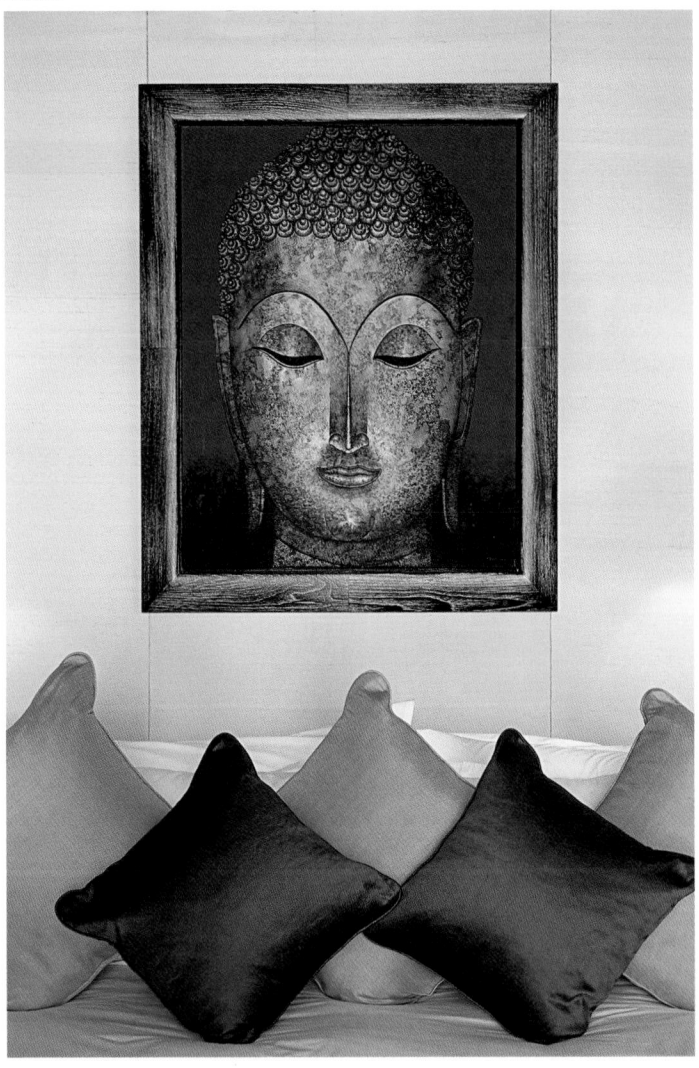

PP. 338–339 The house opens onto a swimming pool terrace with a shingle-roofed pavilion. • Das Haus verfügt über eine Terrasse mit Swimmingpool und einem Pavillon mit Schindeldach. • La maison donne sur la terrasse de la piscine et son pavillon couvert de bardeaux.

↑ A contemporary painting acquired in Phuket. • Zeitgenössisches Gemälde aus Phuket. • Un tableau contemporaine acheté à Phuket.

→ The 18th-century standing Buddha in the entrance hall is Burmese. • Die Buddhastatue aus dem 18. Jahrhundert in der Eingangshalle stammt aus Myanmar. • Le bouddha debout du 18ᵉ siècle dans l'entrée est originaire du Myanmar.

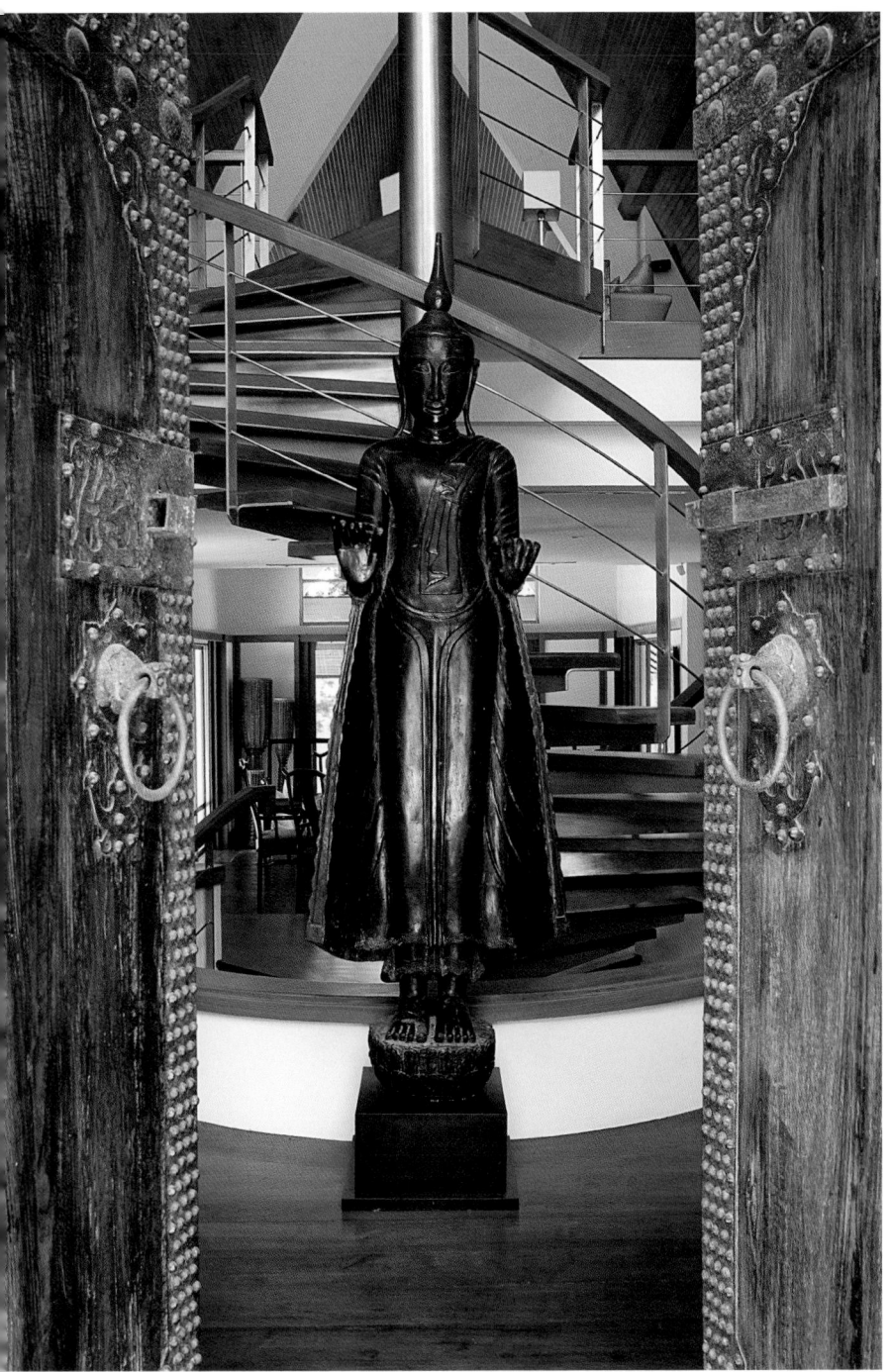

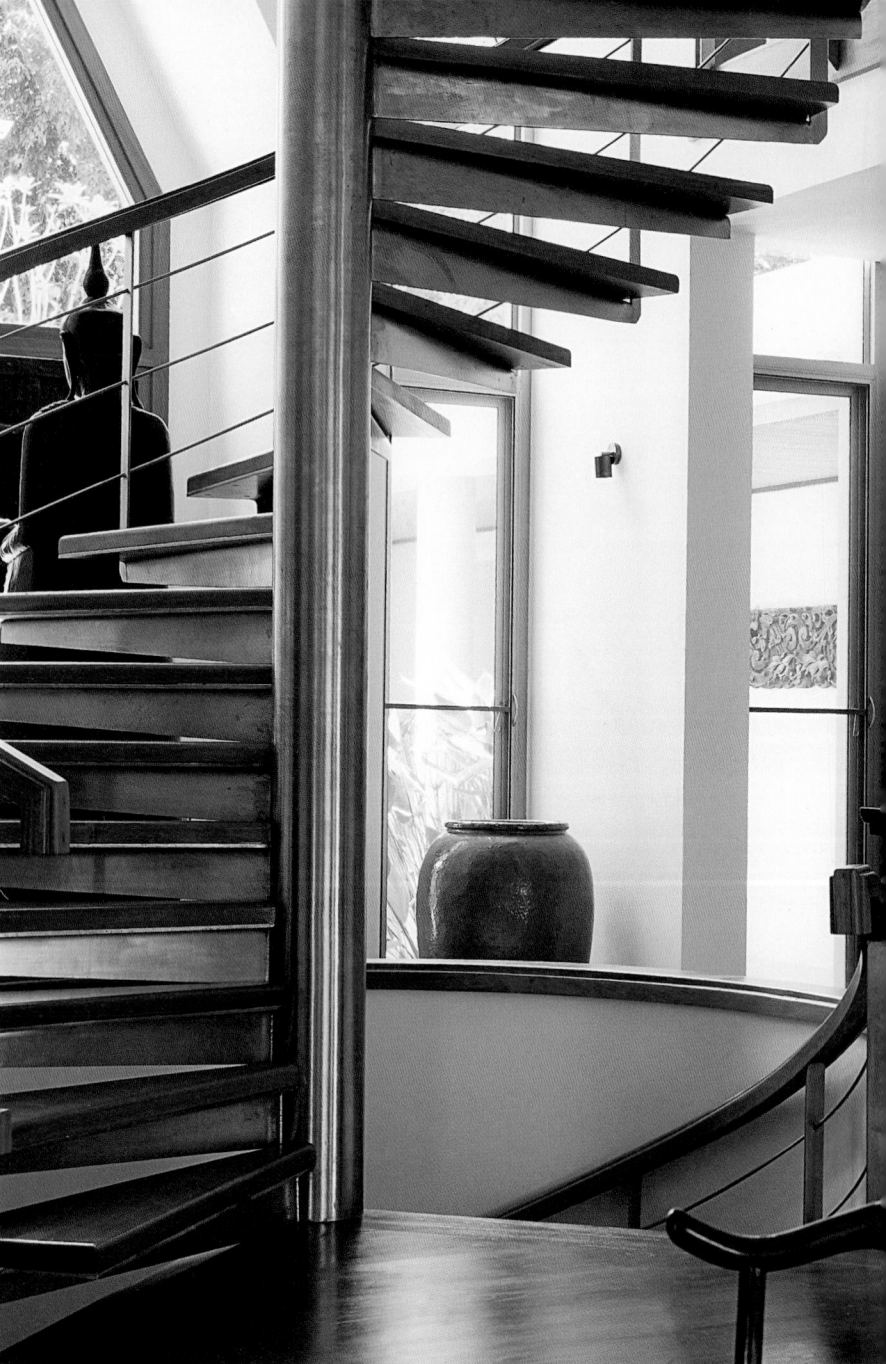

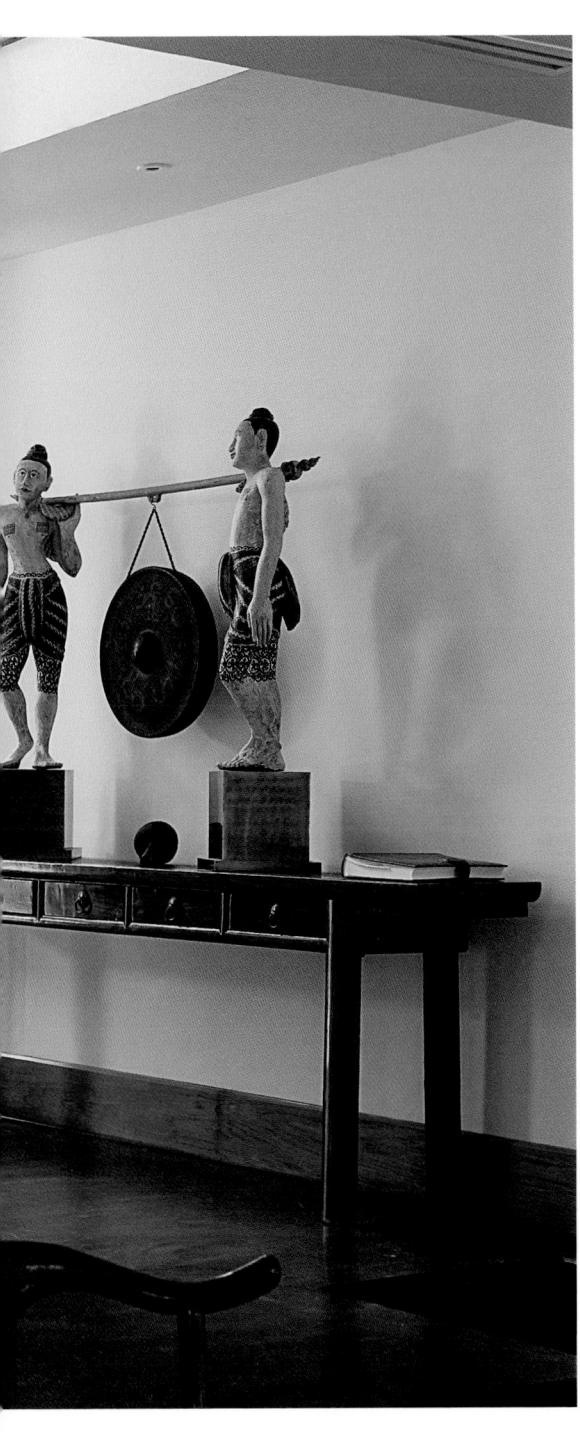

← In the entrance hall, a pair of 19th-century Burmese wooden figures carrying a gong stand on the long table from Shanxi province in China. • Zwei birmanische Holzfiguren aus dem 19. Jahrhundert halten einen Gong in der Eingangshalle. Der Tisch stammt aus der Provinz Shanxi (China). • Dans le hall d'entrée, deux figurines birmanes du 19ᵉ siècle en bois portant un gong sont posées sur une table provenant de la province chinoise de Shanxi.

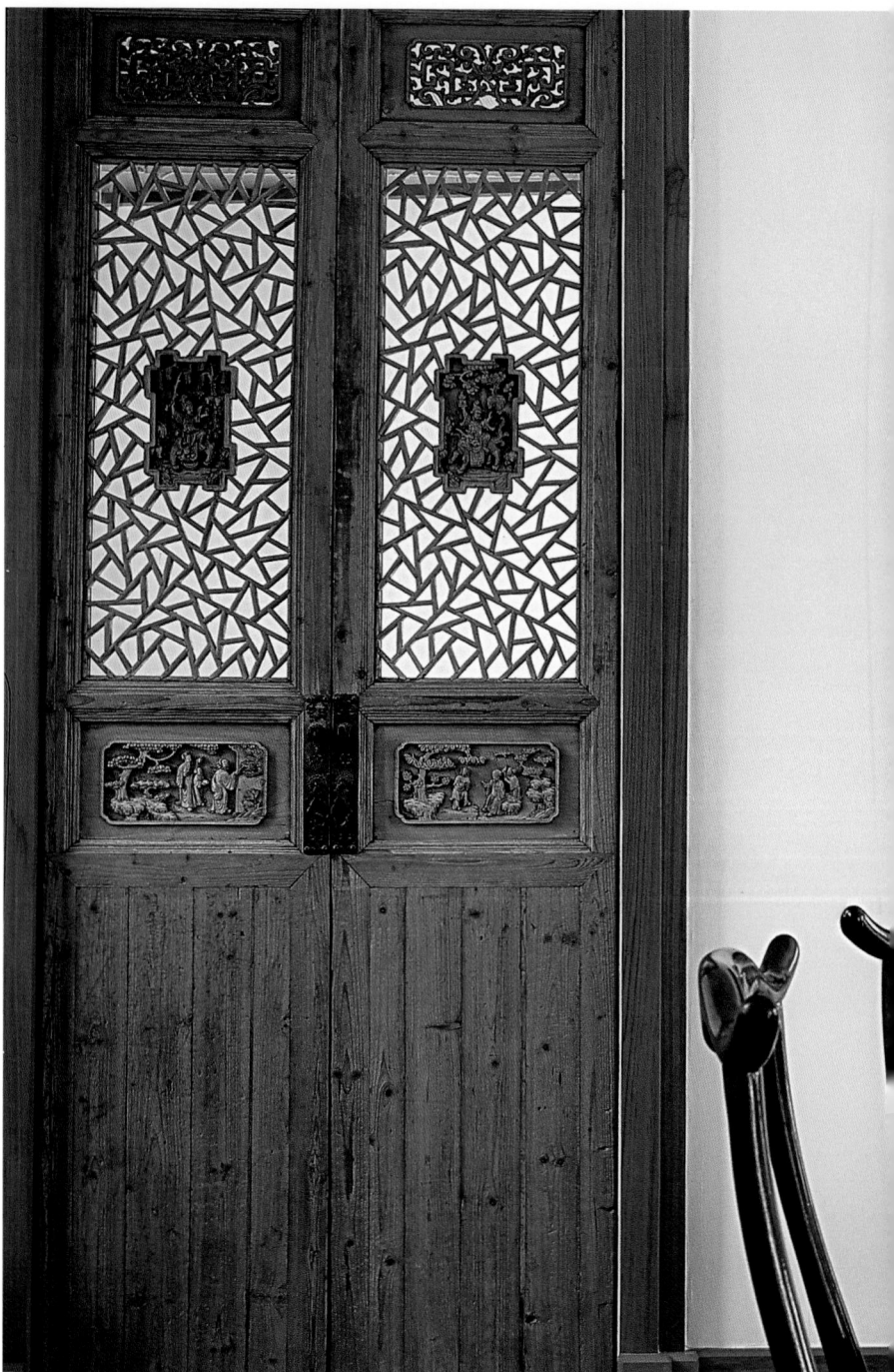

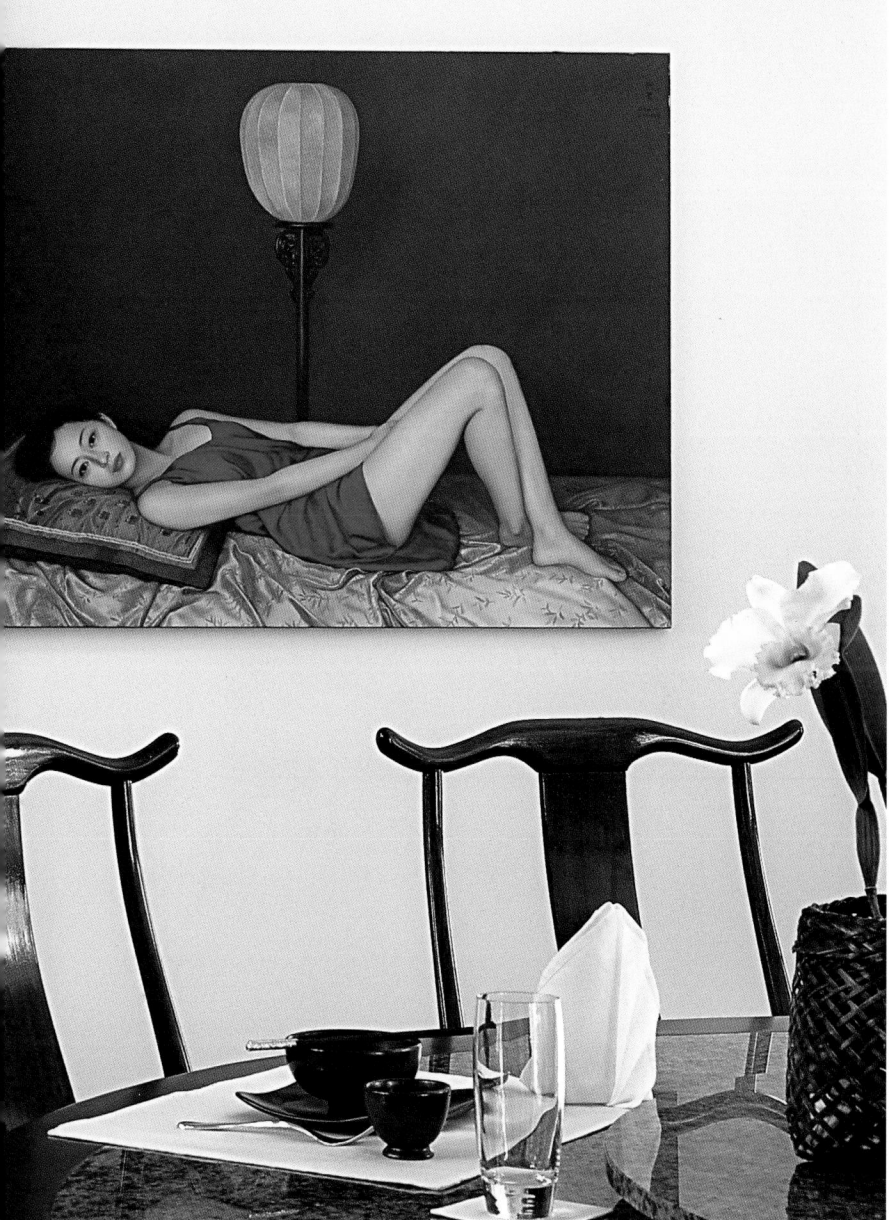

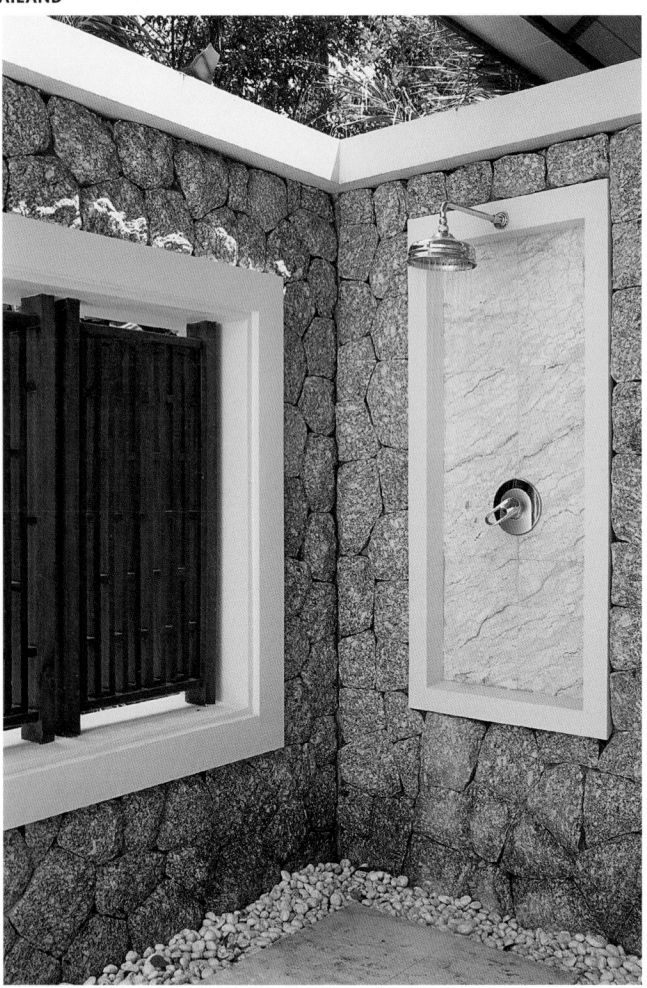

PP. 348–349 A pair of ornamental 19th-century Chinese doors lead into the dining room. A contemporary painting by Chinese artist Li Gui Jun titled "Warm Springs" hangs in the dining room. • Reich verzierte chinesische Türen aus dem 19. Jahrhundert führen ins Speisezimmer. Dort hängt das zeitgenössische Gemälde des chinesischen Malers Li Gui Jun „Warm Springs". • Deux portes décoratives chinoises du

19ᵉ siècle s'ouvrent sur la salle à manger. Dans la salle à manger, on peut admirer Warm Springs, un tableau moderne de l'artiste chinois Li Gui Jun.

↑ All bedrooms give onto open-air shower areas. • An jedes Schlafzimmer ist ein Badebereich mit Außendusche angeschlossen. • Toutes les chambres donnent sur un espace de douche en plein air.

→ The Buddha theme is continued with a locally-made model in the peak-roofed bedroom • Das Buddha-Motiv wird von der einheimischen Skulptur im Schlafzimmer unter dem Spitzdach aufgenommen. • Le thème du bouddha se retrouve dans une sculpture thaïe exposée dans la chambre à toit pointu.

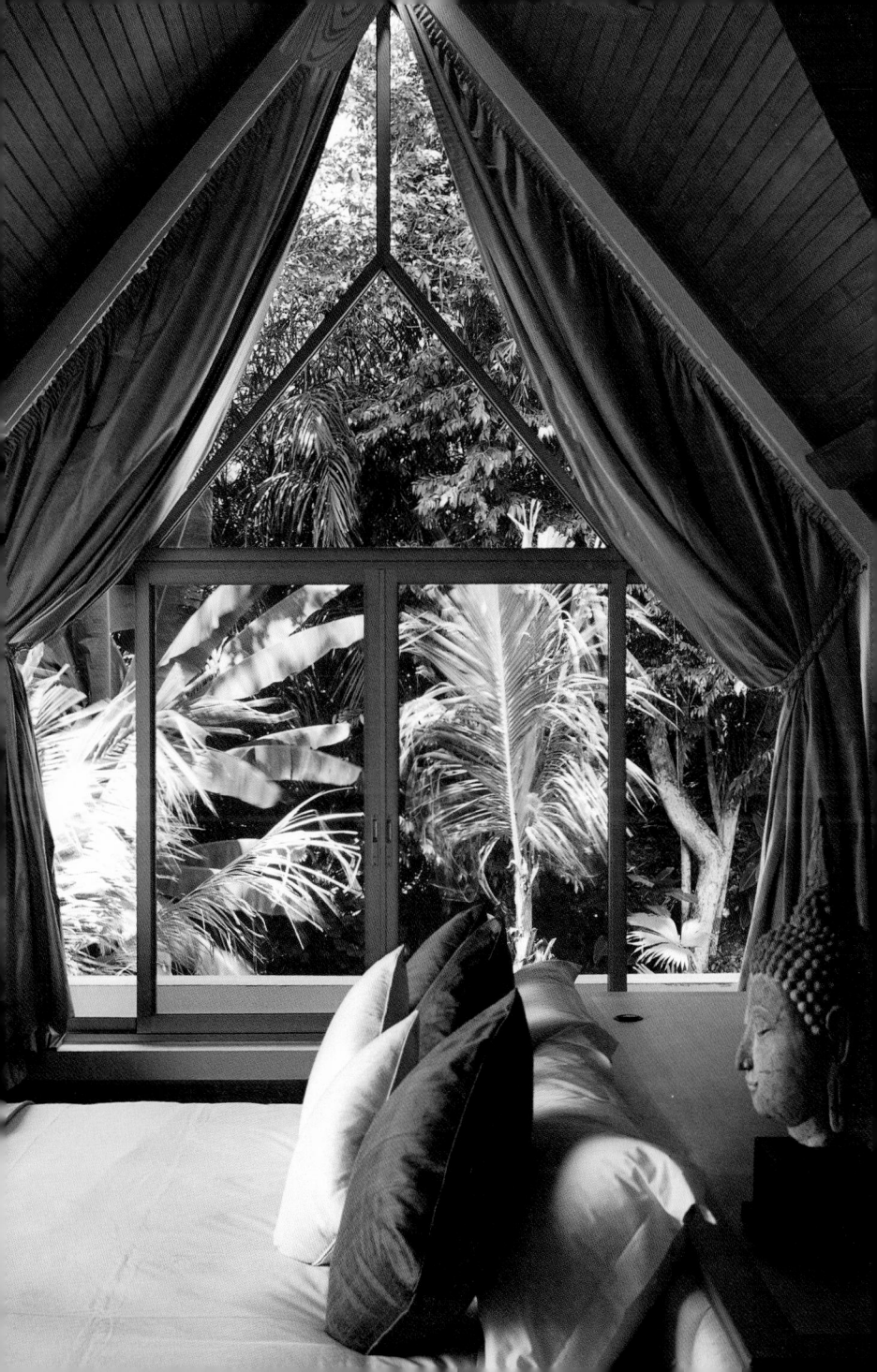

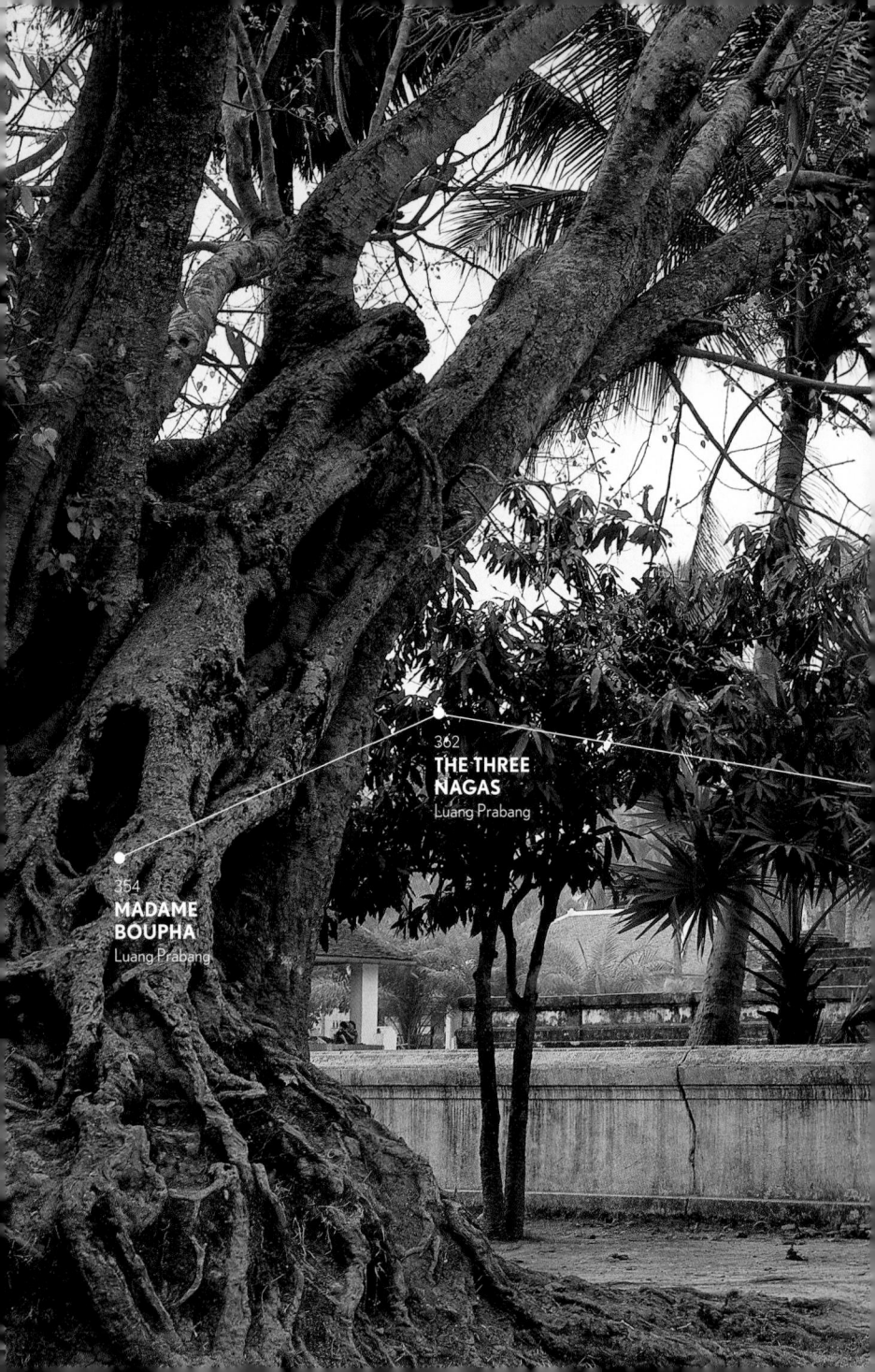

354
**MADAME
BOUPHA**
Luang Prabang

362
**THE THREE
NAGAS**
Luang Prabang

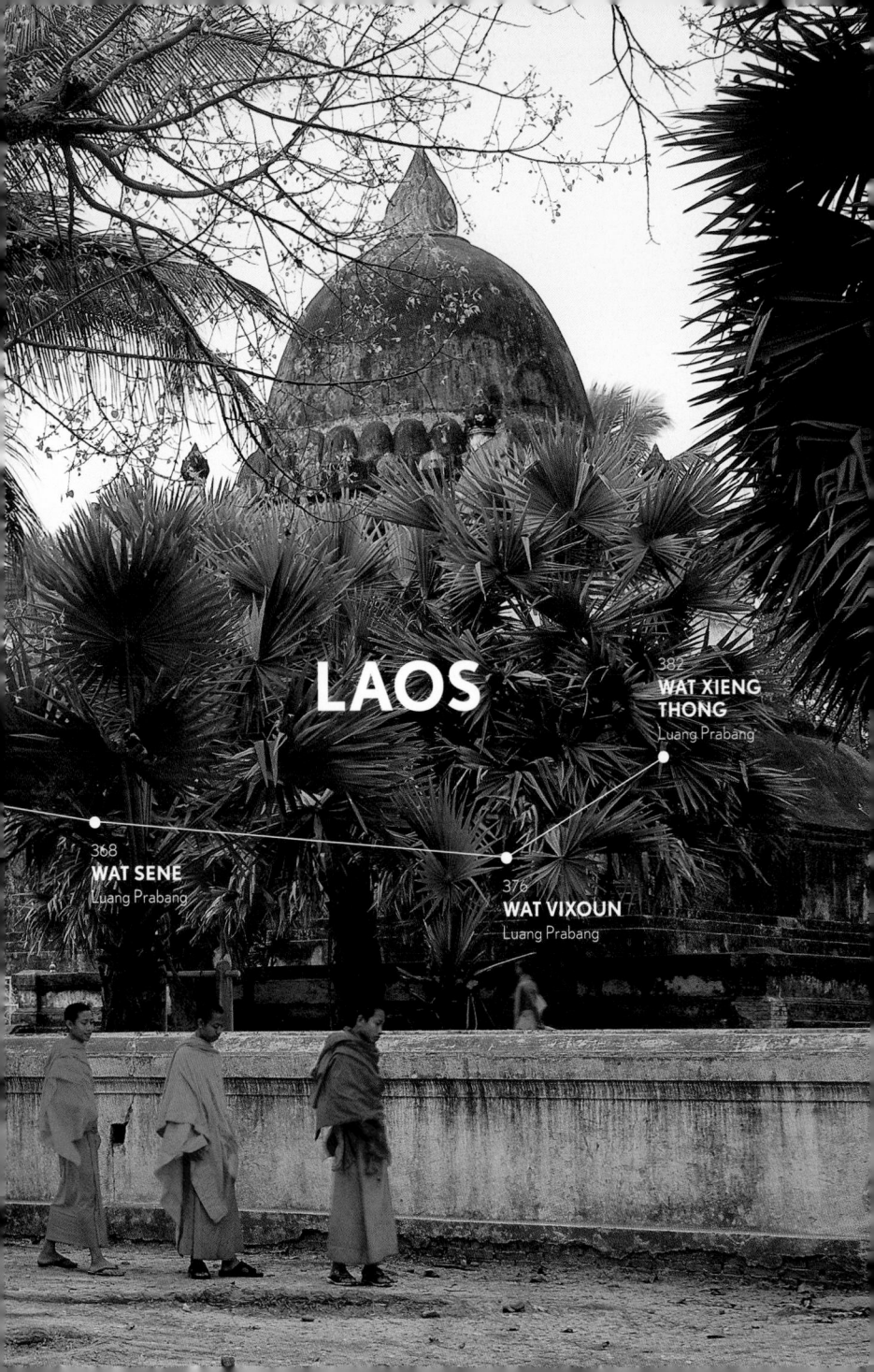

LAOS

382
WAT XIENG THONG
Luang Prabang

368
WAT SENE
Luang Prabang

376
WAT VIXOUN
Luang Prabang

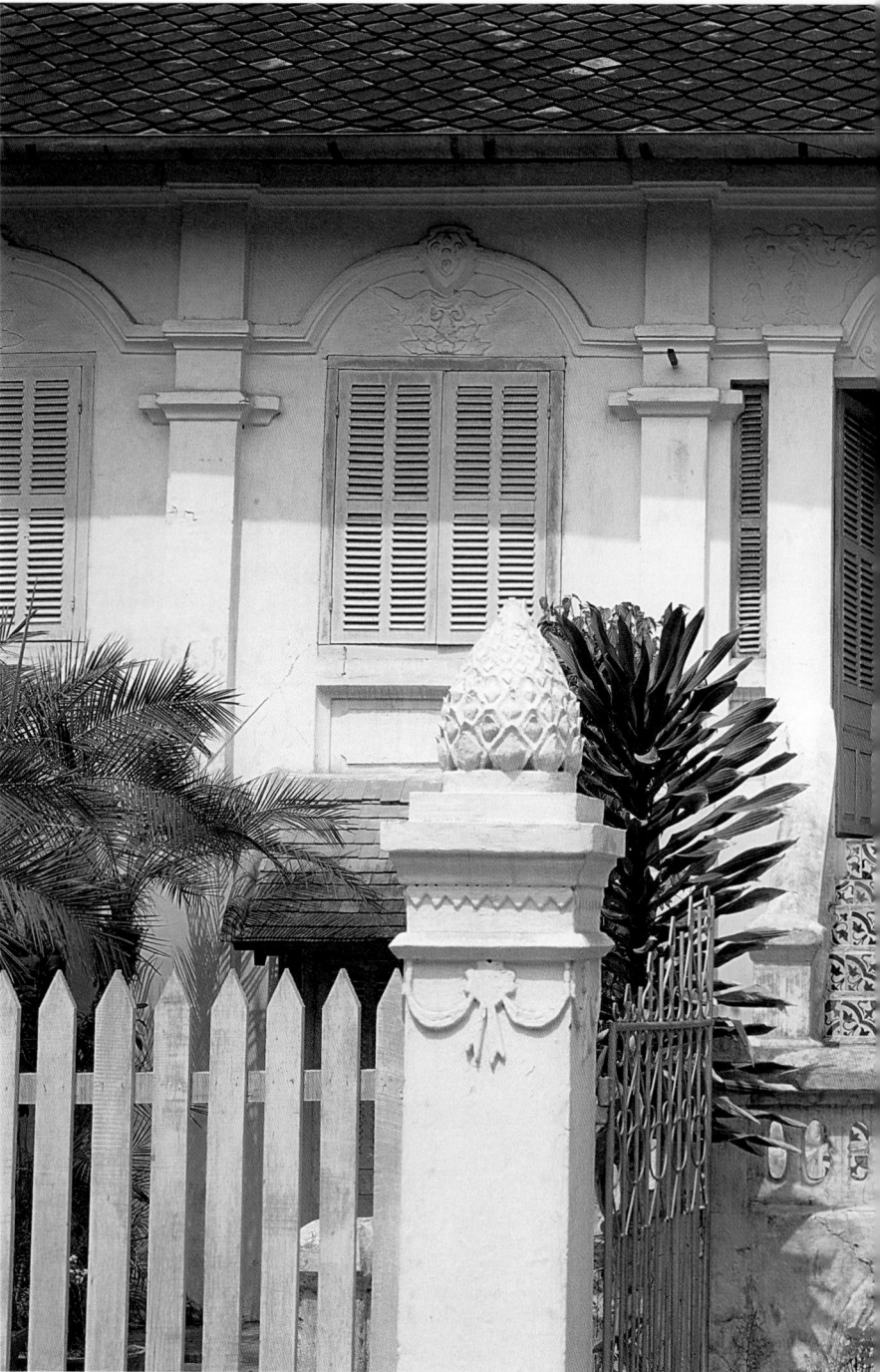

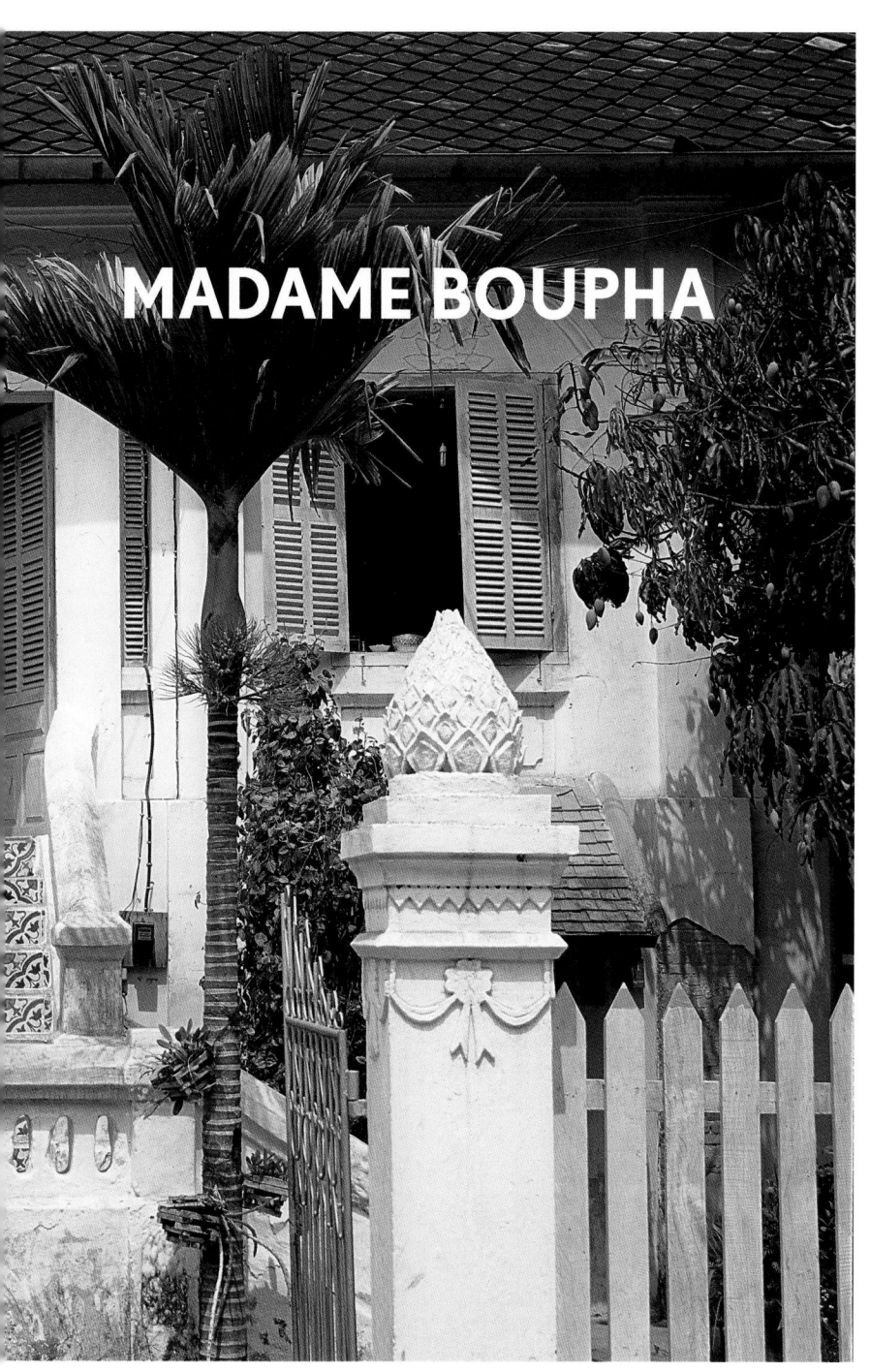

MADAME BOUPHA

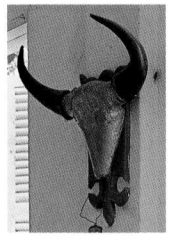

MADAME BOUPHA
LUANG PRABANG
LAOS

Even Madame Boupha, who has lived in the house since she was eight, is not quite sure how old it is. It was built by her grandfather and passed on to her through her mother. Little has changed in this house for more than a hundred years except the front entrance which once faced the river. A relative, the abbot of a Buddhist temple, preferred a street entrance. And, yes, he also replaced the terracotta roof tiles with cement ones, then considered modern, and put them on the front steps. He also added modern toilets but that was a long time ago. Madame Boupha was a primary school teacher but she got tired of talking to her pupils and became a housewife. She had a talent for needlework and covered clothes and curtains in gold embroidery. Her handiwork covers cushions, tablecloths and bed linen, which secured her a gradual accretion of possessions. The house has an ongoing life, like the ebb and flow of the nearby river.

Nicht einmal Madame Boupha, die seit ihrem achten Lebensjahr in diesem Haus wohnt, weiß, wie alt es ist. Ihr Großvater hat es gebaut und über ihre Mutter an sie weitervererbt. Mehr als hundert Jahre lang wurde in dem Haus nur wenig verändert, abgesehen vom Eingang, der einst zum Fluss hin lag. Ein Verwandter, Abt eines buddhistischen Klosters, bevorzugte einen Eingang zur Straße. Außerdem ersetzte er die Dachziegel aus Terrakotta durch solche aus Zement, die damals modern waren, und ließ auch die Eingangstreppe damit auslegen. Moderne Toiletten ließ er ebenfalls einbauen, doch das ist lange her. Madame Boupha war einst Grundschullehrerin, aber eines Tages hatte sie keine Lust mehr zu unterrichten und wurde Hausfrau. Sie entdeckte ihr Handarbeitstalent und verzierte Kleidung und Vorhänge mit goldener Stickerei. Sie bestickte Kissen, Tischdecken und Bettwäsche und wurde langsam wohlhabender. Das Leben im Haus ist beständig, wie Ebbe und Flut im nahen Fluss.

Même madame Boupha, qui habite cette maison depuis ses huit ans, n'est pas sûre de l'âge de celle-ci. Elle en a hérité de son grand-père maternel, qui l'a construite il y a un siècle. Peu de choses ont changé ici, si ce n'est qu'à l'origine l'entrée principale était face au fleuve. Un parent, supérieur d'un temple bouddhique, a un jour préféré que l'entrée donne sur la rue. Il a aussi remplacé les tuiles en terre cuite du toit par des tuiles en ciment, alors au goût du jour, et habillé le perron avec les tuiles d'origine. Il a aussi installé des toilettes modernes. Mais tout cela s'est passé il y a bien longtemps. Madame Boupha travaillait comme institutrice jusqu'au jour où elle en a eu assez d'enseigner et s'est retirée de la vie active. Très douée pour les travaux d'aiguille, elle brodait au fil d'or des vêtements et des rideaux. Elle brode aujourd'hui des coussins, des nappes, des draps et est devenue prospère. Sa maison est vivante, comme la rivière qui coule dans les parages.

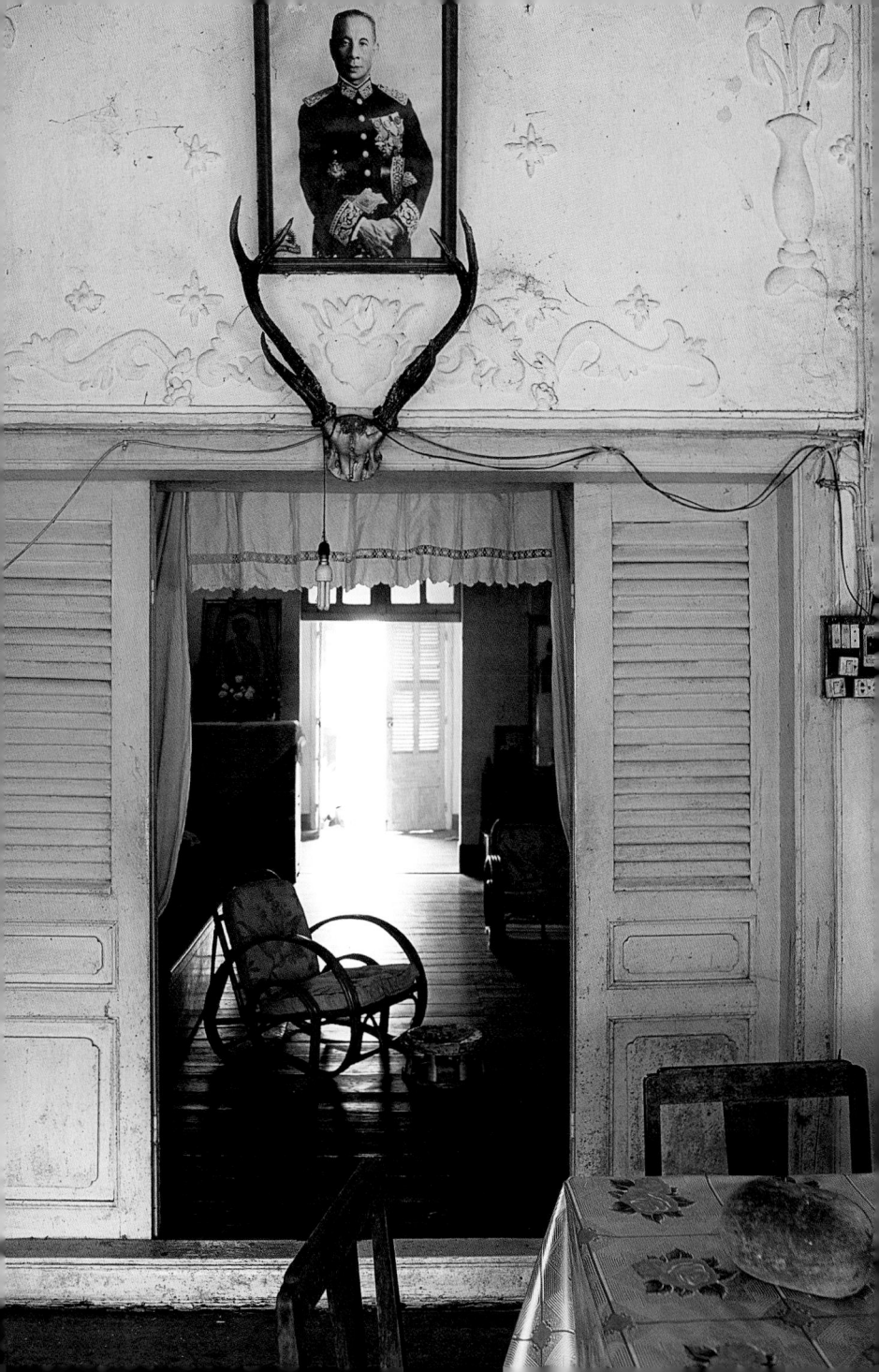

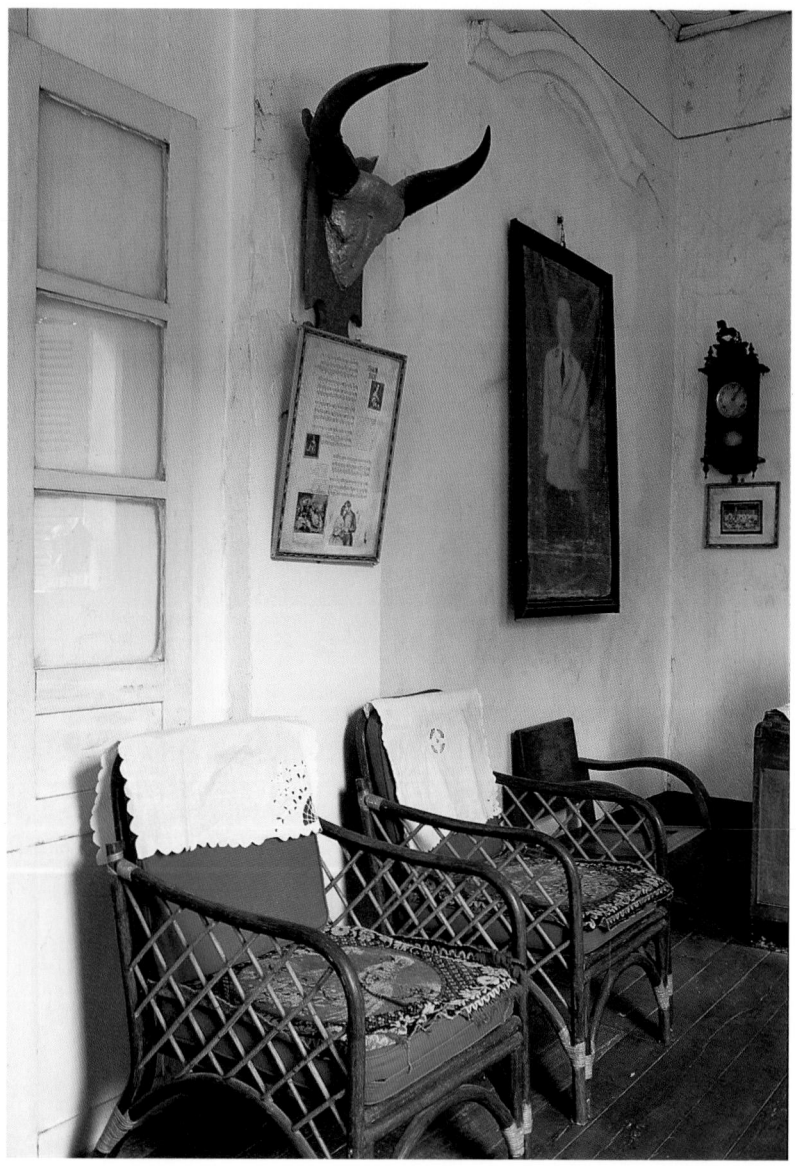

PP. 354–355 The entrance to
Madame Boupha's house. • Eingang
zu Madame Bouphas Haus. • L'entrée
de la maison de madame Boupha.

P. 357 and ↑ → The animal horns
were gifts to her father from villagers
in Phongsaly province where he was
governor. • Die Geweihe sind ein
Geschenk der Dorfbewohner aus der

Provinz Phongsaly an ihren Vater, den
Provinzgouverneur. • Les cornes
d'animaux sont des présents faits à son
père par des villageois de la province de
Phongsaly, dont il était gouverneur.

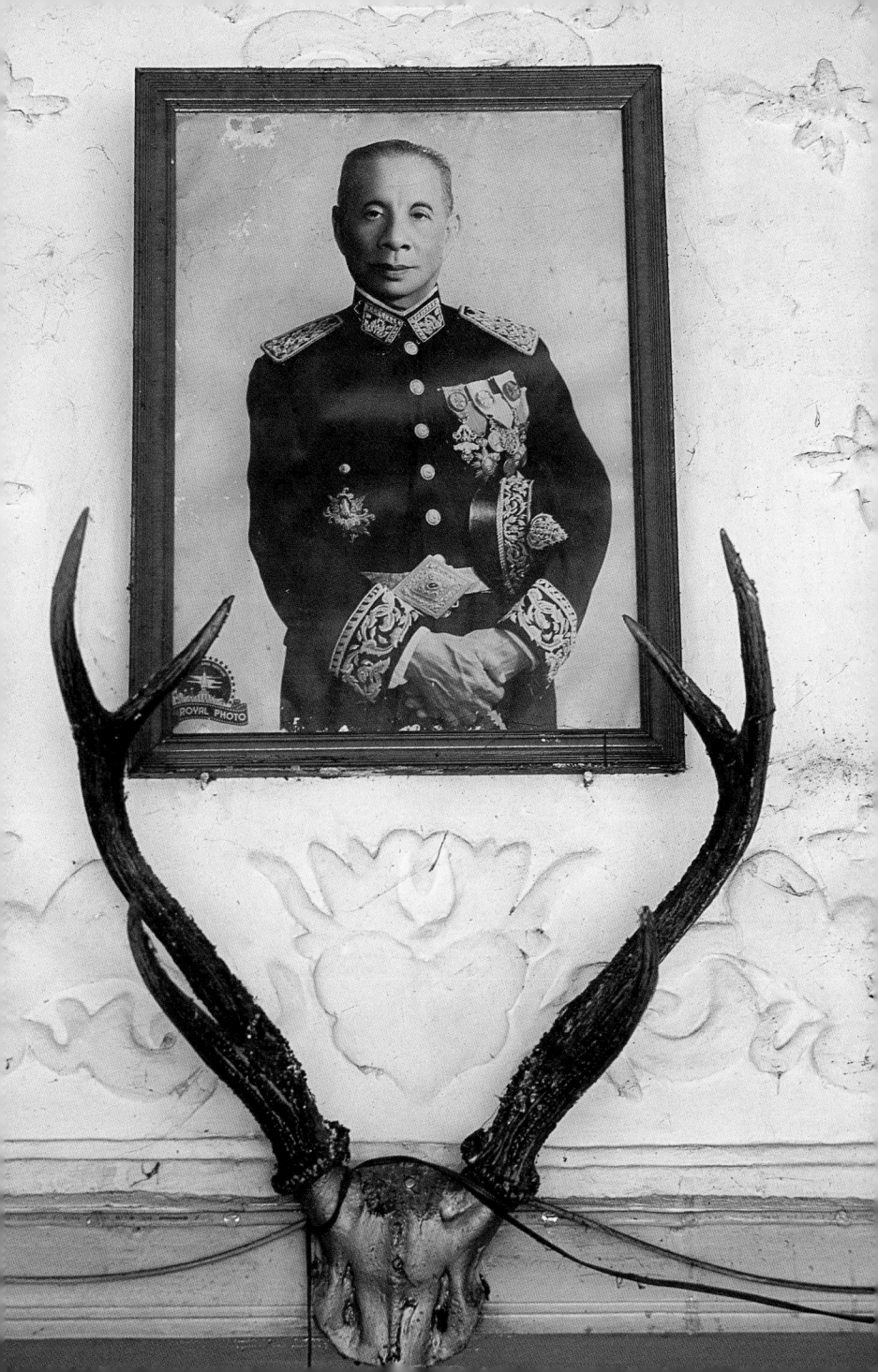

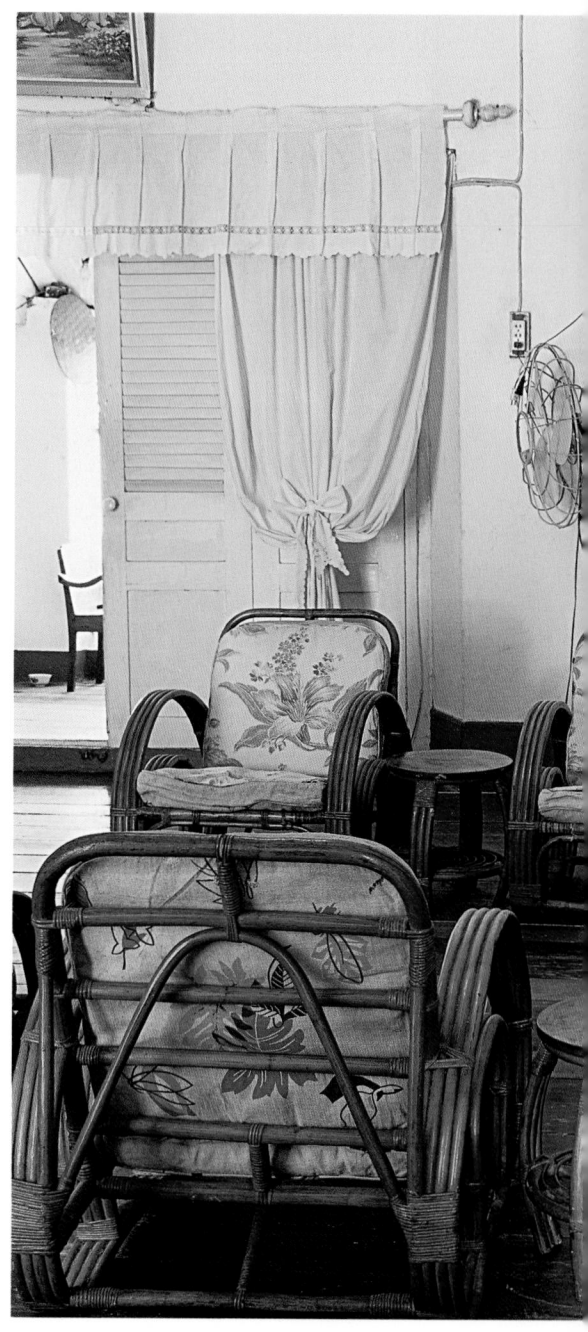

→ Living room and veranda. • Wohnzimmer und Veranda. • Le salon et la
véranda.

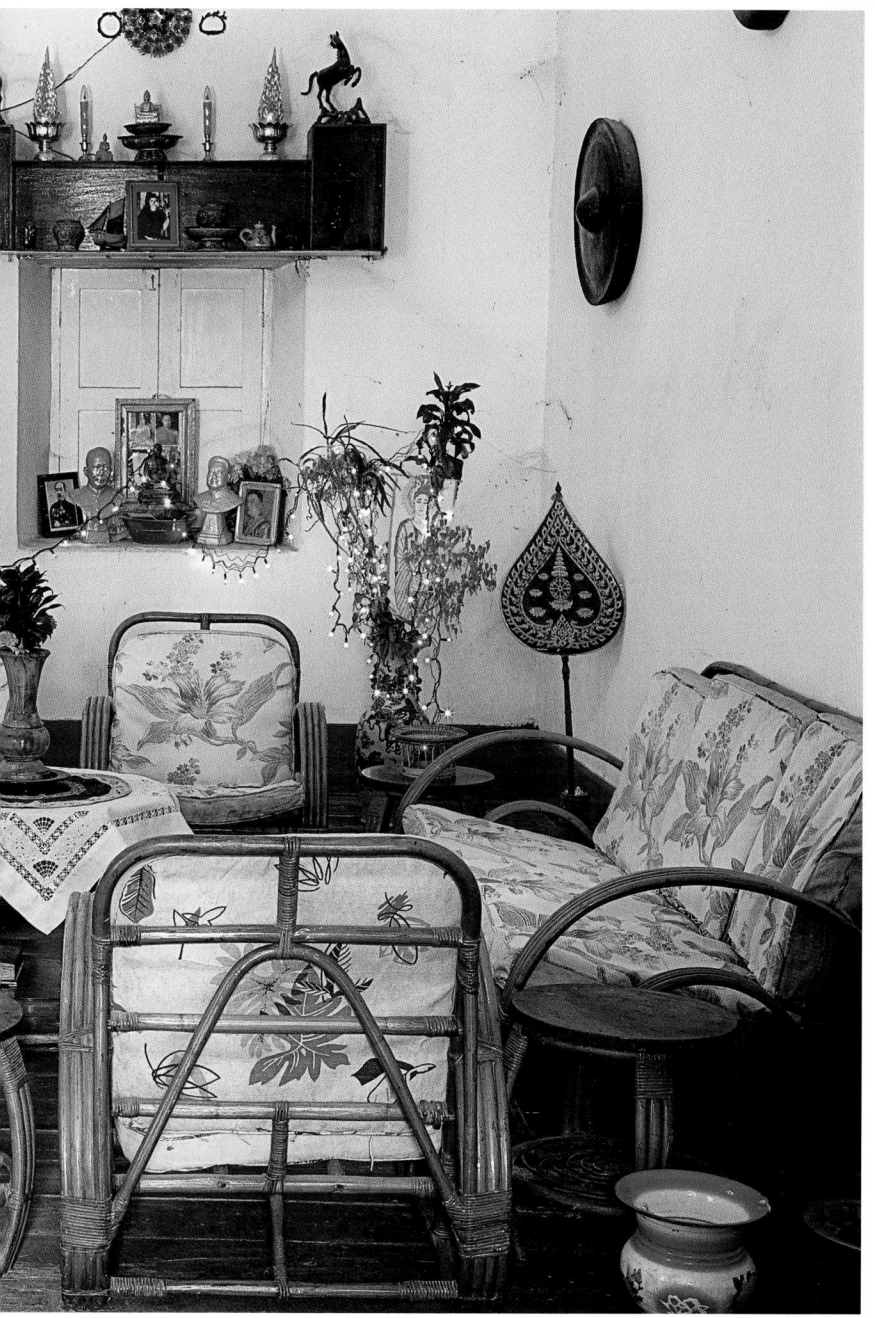

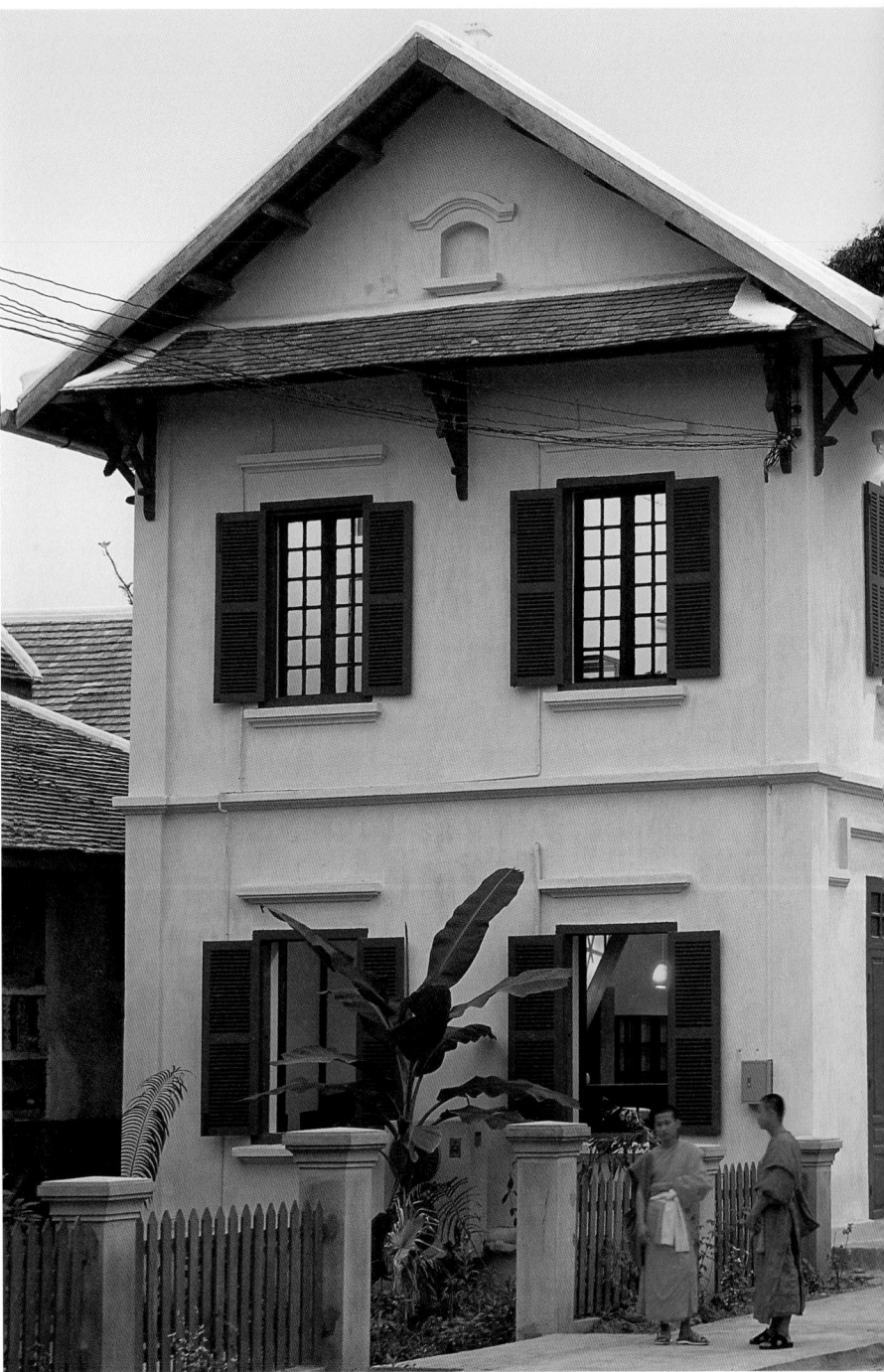

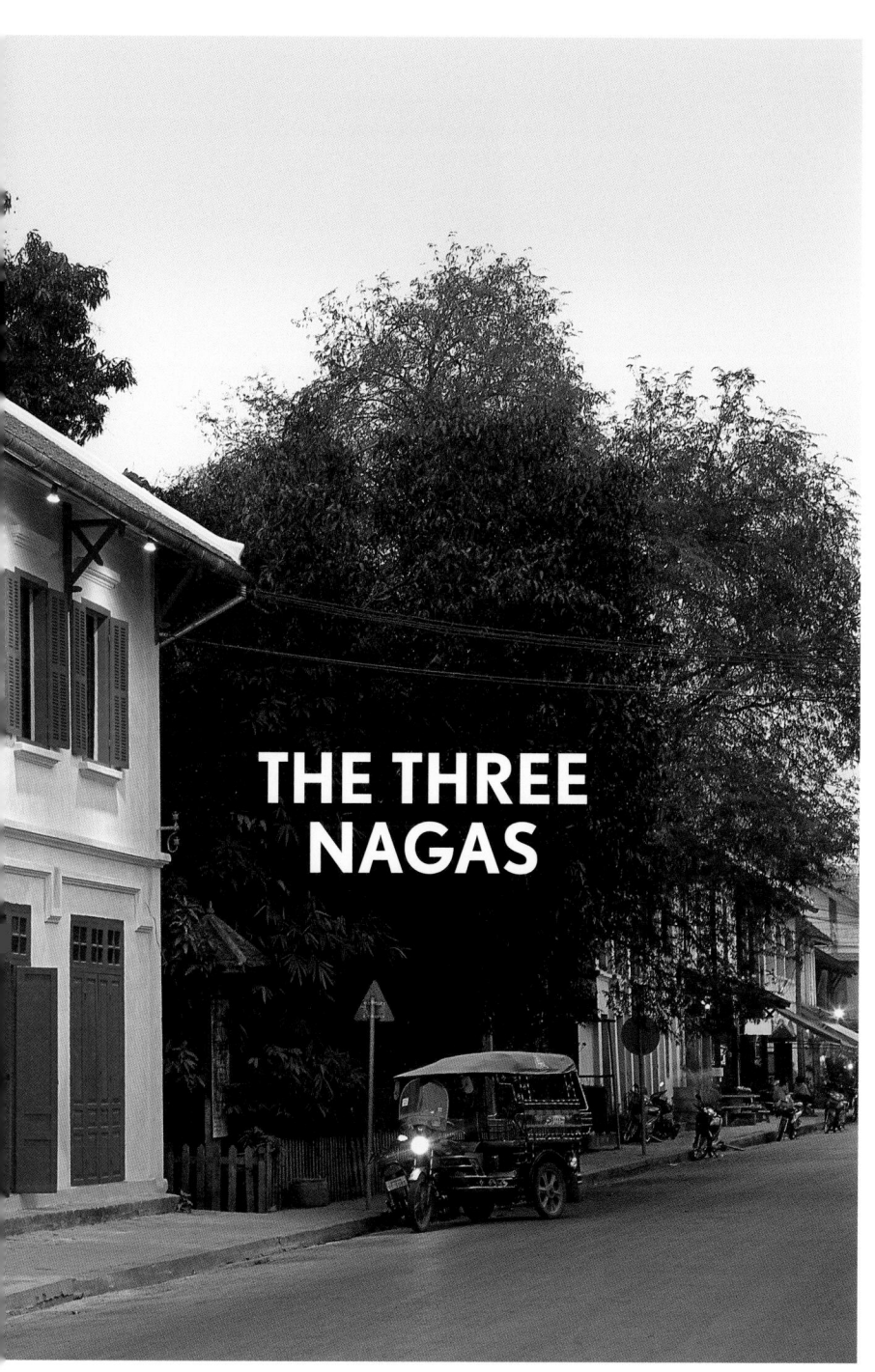

THE THREE
NAGAS

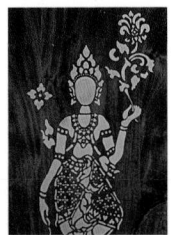

THE THREE NAGAS

LUANG PRABANG
LAOS

Pascal Trahan has a thing about Unesco's World Heritage cities. He studied architecture in Quebec, which is one, and eventually came to settle in Luang Prabang, which acquired World Heritage status in 1995 to preserve its unique blend of Buddhist temples and graceful French villas. Fifteen years ago, he took over a late 19th-century two-story house that had once served as a royal lodge and later as an ice-cream factory. Close to the Nam Khan River, in the heart of Luang Prabang's historic center, the Three Nagas, named after the guardian serpents that embellish the temples, is now an intimate hotel. Trahan worked with Lao artisans using strictly traditional architectural techniques: walls were composed of bamboo treads coated with layers of lime paste; flooring and furniture were fashioned from a local wood used in boat-building. Each room gives on to wooden terraces or private verandas that offer views of temples and monks at prayer – the spiritual life of a town unchanged since medieval times.

Pascal Trahan hat viel übrig für Städte, die von der Unesco zum Weltkulturerbe erklärt wurden. Er studierte in Quebec und ließ sich in Luang Prabang nieder, das diesen Status 1995 erhielt, damit die einzigartige Mischung aus buddhistischen Tempeln und anmutigen französischen Villen erhalten wird. Vor rund fünfzehn Jahren übernahm Trahan ein zweistöckiges Haus aus dem 19. Jahrhundert in der Nähe des Nam-Khan-Flusses – mitten in der Altstadt von Luang Prabang, das früher als königliche Behausung, später als Speiseeisfabrik diente. Das „Drei Nagas", das nach den dekorativen, schützenden Schlangen in den Tempeln benannt ist, wurde in ein gemütliches Hotel verwandelt. In Zusammenarbeit mit laotischen Handwerkern beschränkte sich Trahan auf traditionelle architektonische Techniken. Die Wände bestehen aus Bambusprofilen, die schichtweise mit Kalkpaste bedeckt wurden, und sowohl die Böden als auch die Möbel wurden aus einem Holz angefertigt, das sonst im Schiffsbau verwendet wird. An jedes Zimmer schließt sich eine Holzterrasse oder eine private Veranda an, von der aus die Gäste Tempel und Mönche beim Gebet – das spirituelle Leben einer Stadt, das sich seit dem Mittelalter kaum verändert hat – beobachten können.

Pascal Trahan est poursuivi par les villes patrimoine mondial de l'Humanité : il a fait ses études à Québec et s'est installé à Luang Prabang. Cette ville figure sur la liste du patrimoine mondial de l'Humanité depuis 1995 afin que soit préservé son syncrétisme unique en son genre de temples bouddhiques et de ravissantes villas coloniales françaises. Il y a quinze ans, Pascal Trahan a racheté un pavillon royal de la fin du 19e siècle – une construction de deux étages qui avait par la suite hébergé une usine de crème glacée. À proximité de la Nam Kahn, au cœur du centre historique de Luang Prabang, les Trois Nagas – ainsi nommé d'après les dieux serpents qui gardent les temples –, est maintenant un hôtel à l'ambiance familiale. Trahan a travaillé avec des artisans locaux qui utilisent des techniques de construction traditionnelles : les murs sont constitués de bandes de bambou chaulées, tandis que les sols et le mobilier ont été taillés dans un bois local utilisé en construction navale. Chaque pièce donne sur des terrasses en bois ou des vérandas privées d'où l'on peut contempler les temples et les moines en prière, témoignages de la vie spirituelle d'une ville inchangée depuis des siècles.

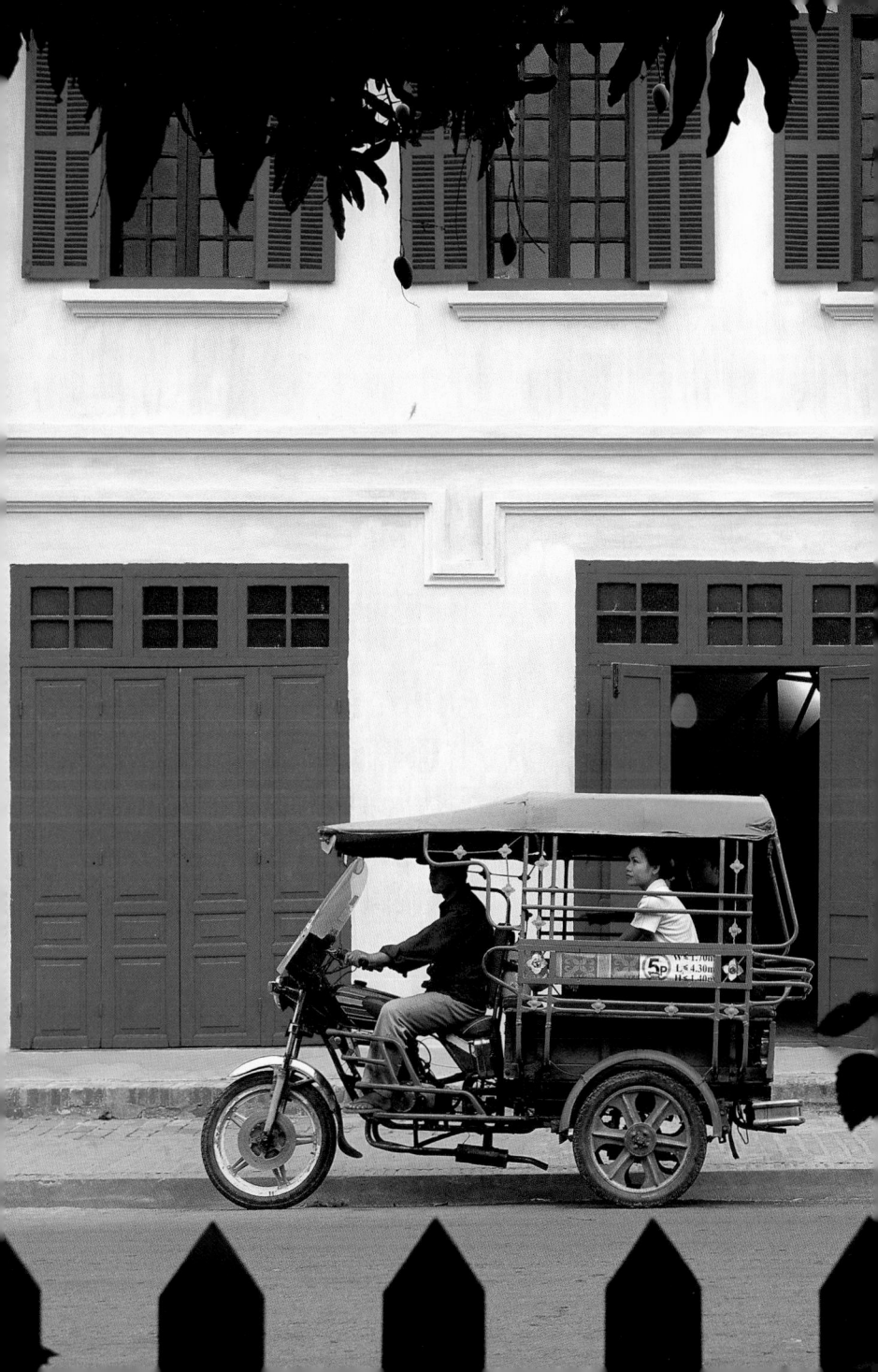

PP. 362–363 Monks strolling past the
Three Nagas. • Mönche vor dem Eingang des „Drei Nagas". • Les moines se
promènent aux abords des Trois Nagas.

↓ A dining corner in a suite decorated
with images of celestial nymphs. • Die
Essecke in einer Suite, mit Intarsien von

himmlischen Nymphen dekoriert. • Le
coin repas dans une suite décorée de
nymphes célestes.

→ The restored doors to a bedroom
are more than a century old. The suite is
decorated with silk and organza drapes
and a traditional umbrella. • Die

restaurierten Türen zum Schlafzimmer
sind mehr als hundert Jahre alt. Die Suite
ist mit Seiden- und Organzavorhängen
und einem traditionellen Schirm ausgestattet. • Ces portes de chambre
restaurées sont plus que centenaires.
Dans la suite, drapés de soie et d'organdi
et une ombrelle traditionnelle.

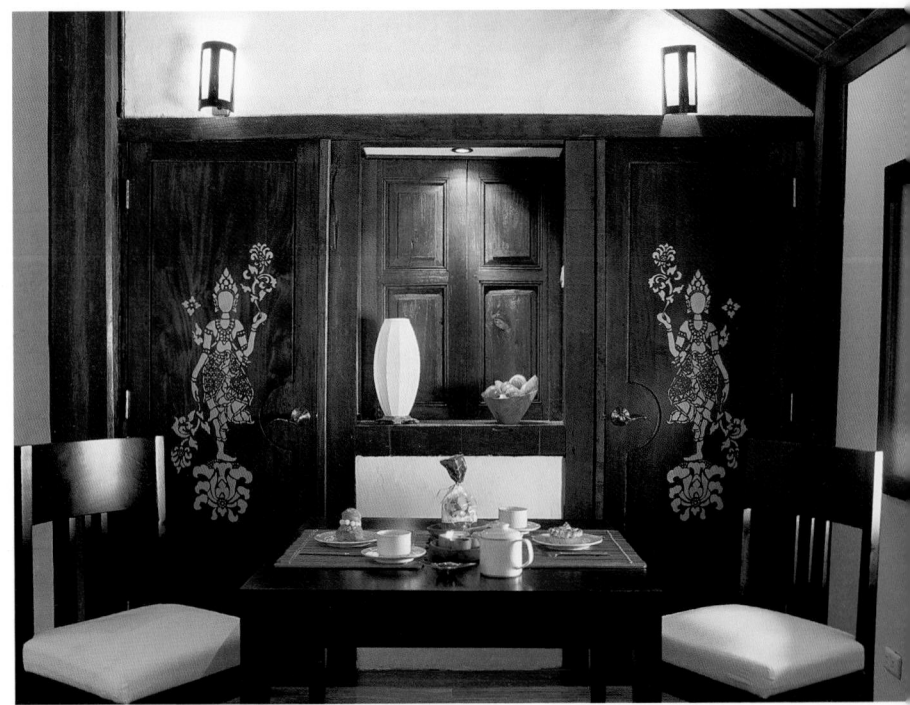

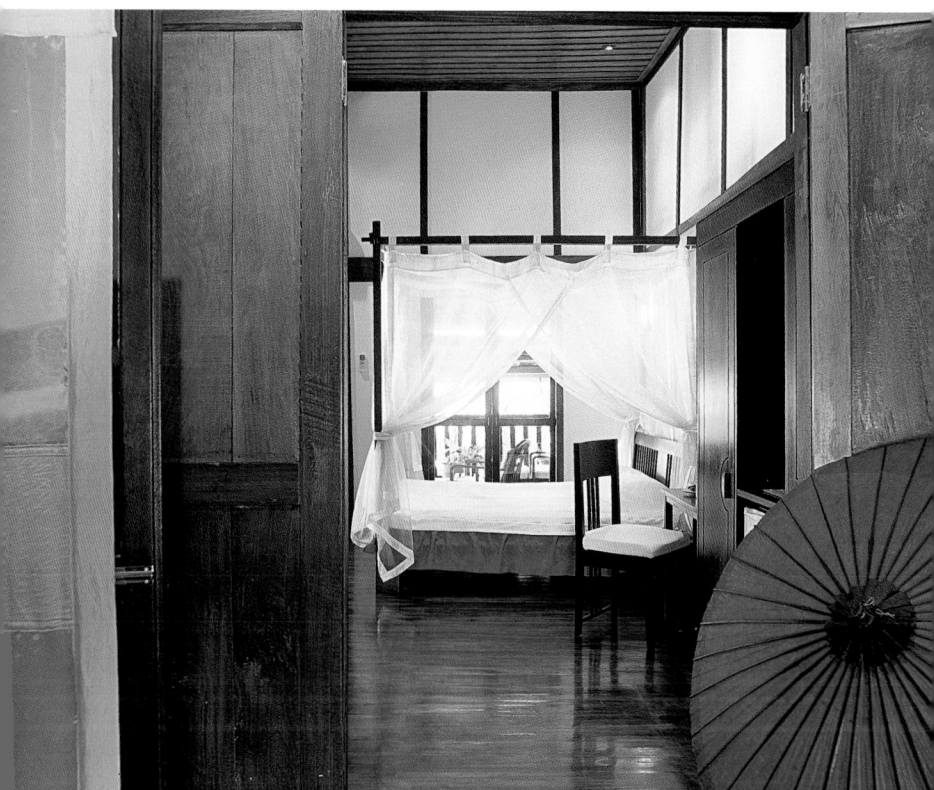

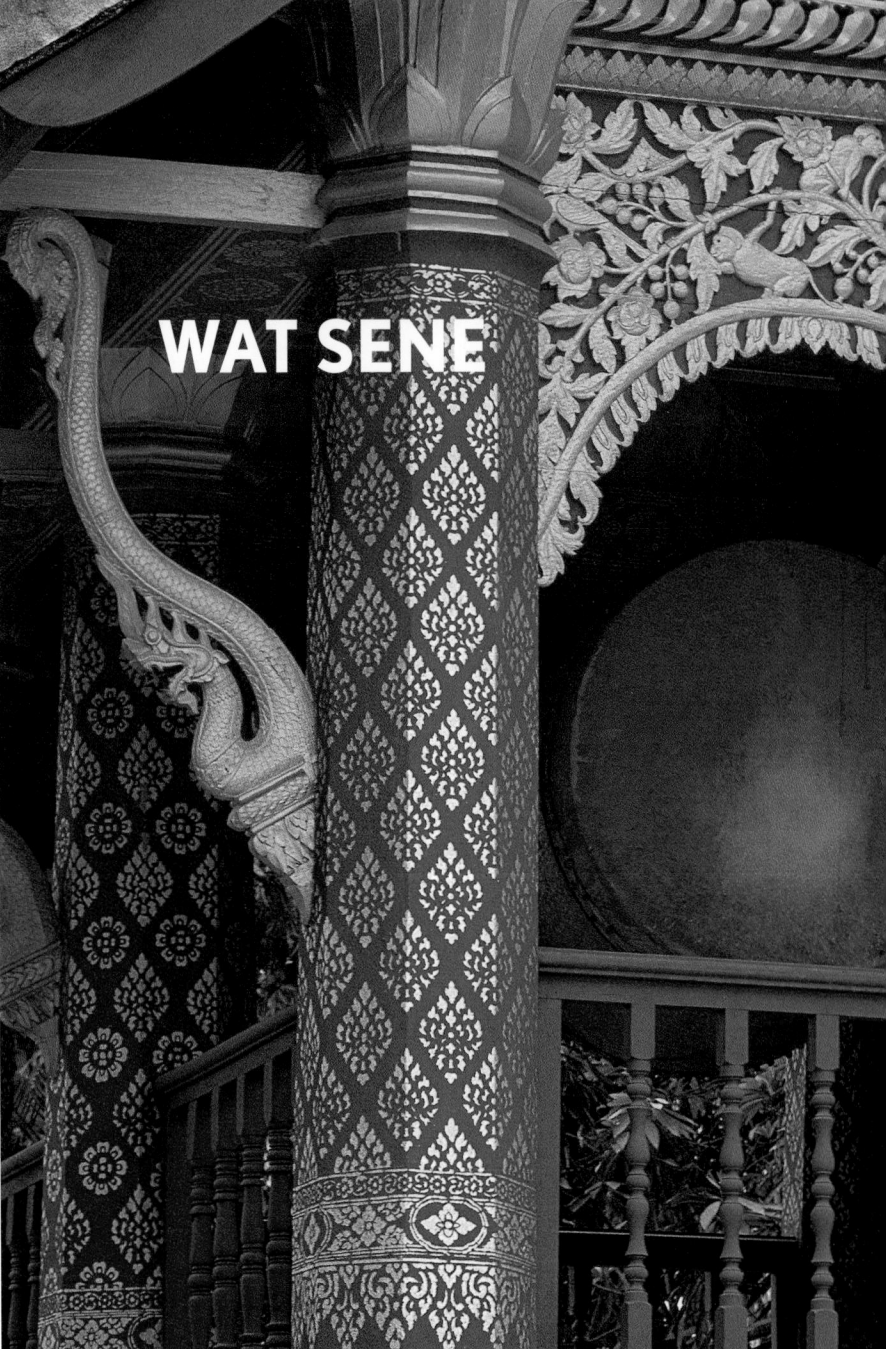

WAT SENE

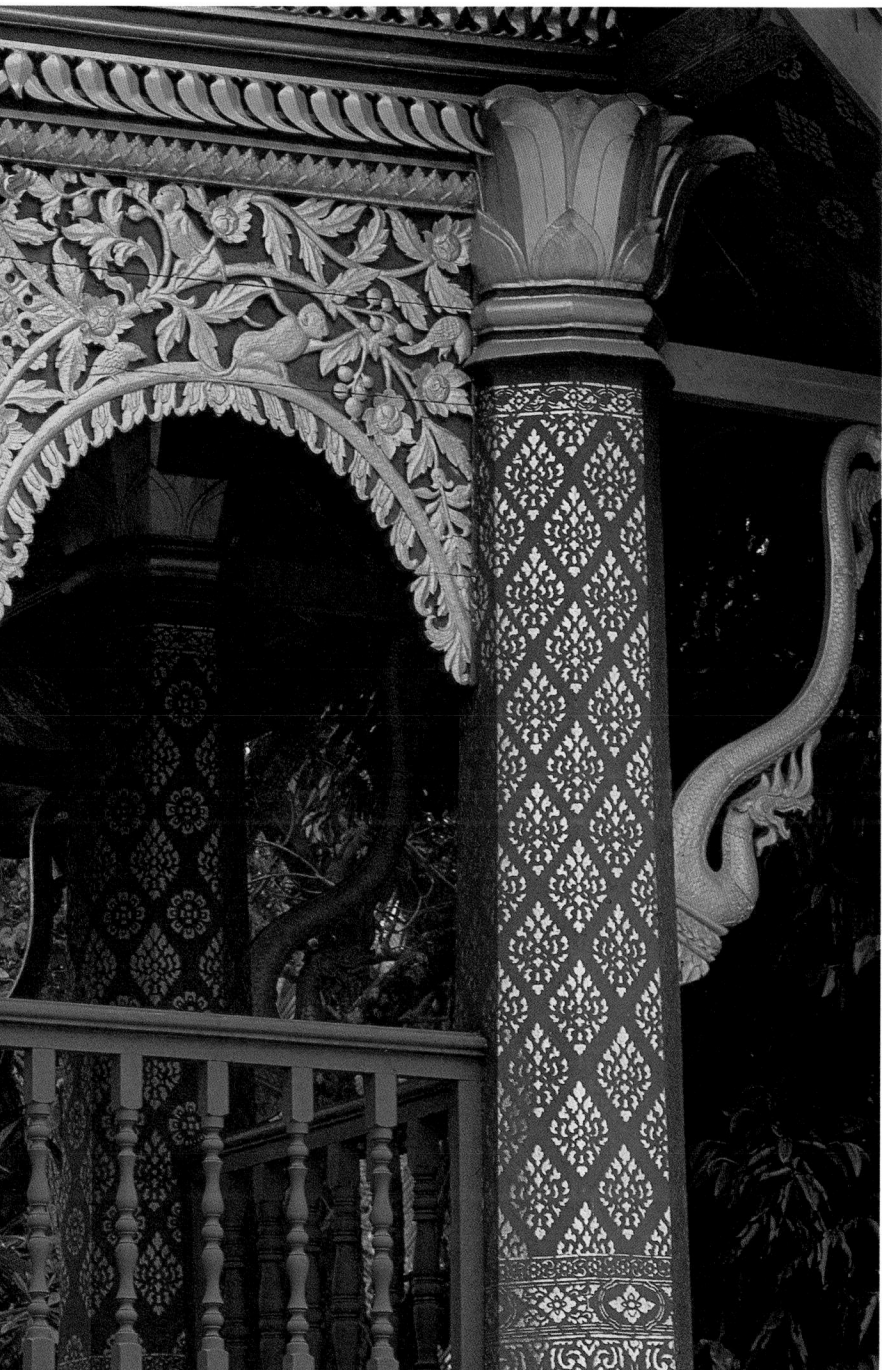

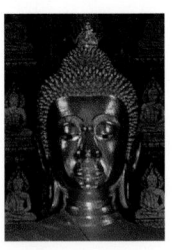

WAT SENE
LUANG PRABANG
LAOS

Wat Sene is one of Luang Prabang's lesser-known temples, amidst a profusion of more famous places of worship that dot the historic peninsula between two rivers and the large hill of Phu Si that forms a dramatic backdrop to the town. The monastery's full name is Wat Sene Soukharam and its importance derives from being the residence of Phra Sangkharath, the head abbot of the *sangha*, the community of monks (seen right). Like many Lao temples it was originally the gift of a king but has been restored several times, mostly recently in 1957. Wat Sene is famous for its red-painted walls, richly stencilled in gold, elaborate carved wooden decoration and fine mosaics. Built in the classic Luang Prabang temple style with curving, low-slung roofs, it is set inside an enclosed compound. A series of sublime Buddha images inside focus the mind. Small but jewel-like in its refinement and religious atmosphere, Wat Sene is Luang Prabang's little treasure.

Wat Sene, einer der weniger bekannten Tempel in Luang Prabang, liegt inmitten berühmter religiöser Stätten, die auf der historischen Halbinsel zwischen zwei Flüssen und dem großen Hügel Phu Si – dem aufregenden Hinterland der Stadt – verstreut sind. Die Bedeutung des Klosters – mit vollem Namen Wat Sene Soukharam – liegt darin begründet, dass der Phra Sangkharath (im Bild rechts), das Oberhaupt der *sangha*, der Gemeinschaft von Mönchen, hier lebt. Wie viele laotische Tempel ging auch dieser aus einem Geschenk des Königs hervor. Er wurde jedoch mehrmals restauriert, zuletzt im Jahr 1957. Heute ist Wat Sene berühmt wegen der rot gestrichenen, mit goldener Schablonenmalerei verschwenderisch verzierten Wände, der feinen Holzvertäfelung und der zarten Mosaike. Als Teil einer abgeschlossenen Tempelanlage wurde er im klassischen Tempelstil von Luang Prabang erbaut, mit gekrümmten, geneigten Dächern. Im Innern lenken zahlreiche erhabene Buddhabildnisse den Geist auf das Wesentliche. Der kleine Tempel Wat Sene erweist sich mit seiner Feinheit und seiner andächtigen Atmosphäre als Edelstein im großen Schatz von Luang Prabang.

Des nombreux temples bouddhiques de Luang Prabang, Vat Sene fait partie des lieux de culte les moins connus de cette ville située dans une péninsule historique entre deux cours d'eau et adossée à la spectaculaire colline de Phou Si. Ce monastère, dont le nom complet est Vat Sene Soukharam, est cependant important : il s'agit de la résidence de Phra Sangkharath (page de droite), le plus haut dignitaire de la *sangha*, la communauté des moines bouddhistes. À l'instar de nombreux temples lao, c'était à l'origine le cadeau fait par un roi à une communauté. Restauré à plusieurs reprises, la dernière fois en 1957, Vat Sene est connu pour ses murs rouges ornés de motifs à l'or réalisés au pochoir, de décorations élaborées en bois sculpté et de délicates mosaïques. Protégé par un mur d'enceinte, Vat Sene est construit dans le style des temples classiques de Luang Prabang, avec des toits superposés aux arbalétriers légèrement incurvés. Il abrite une collection de bouddhas sublimes qui invitent à la méditation. Concentré de beauté et de recueillement, Vat Sene est le joyau de Luang Prabang.

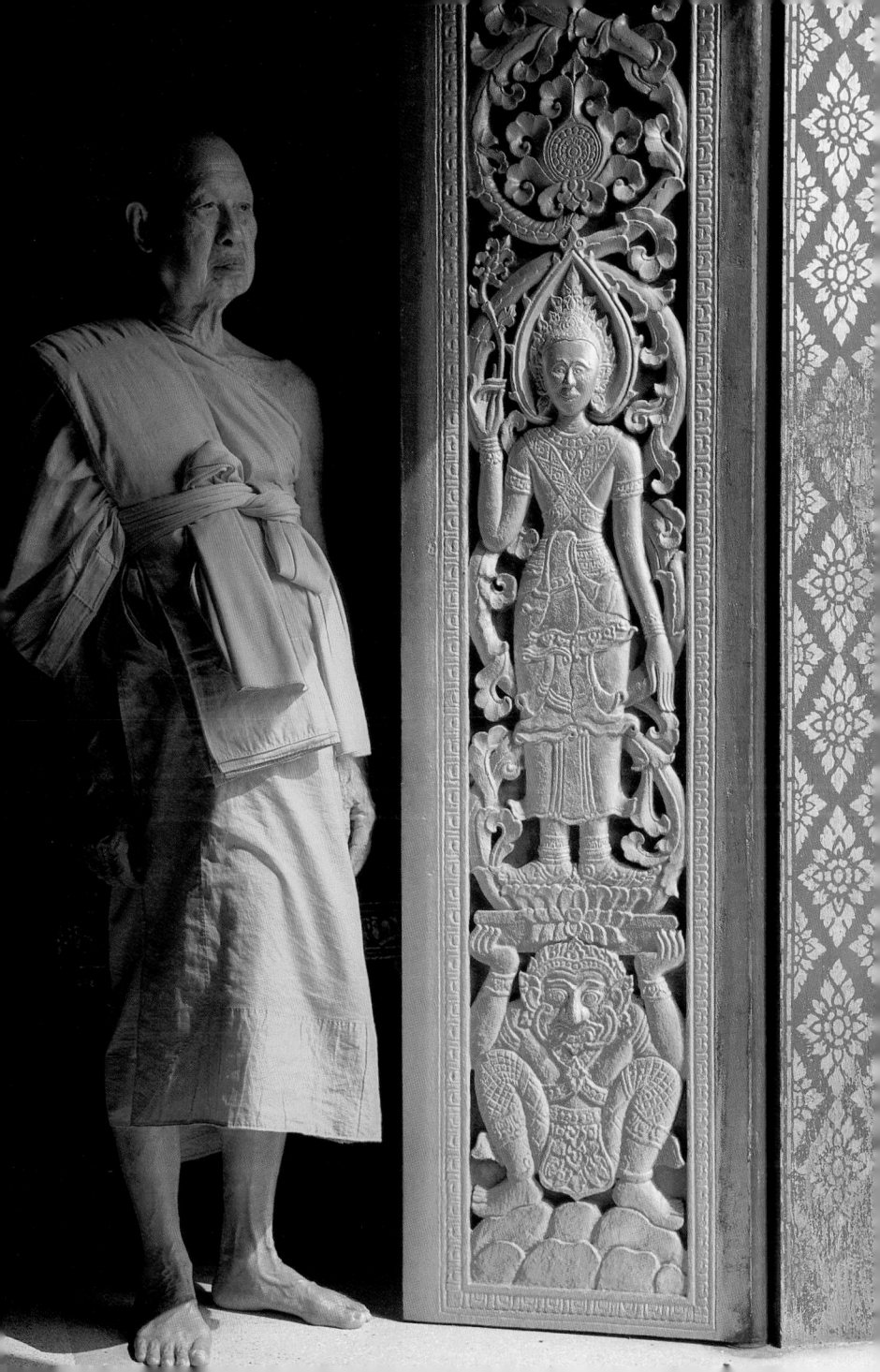

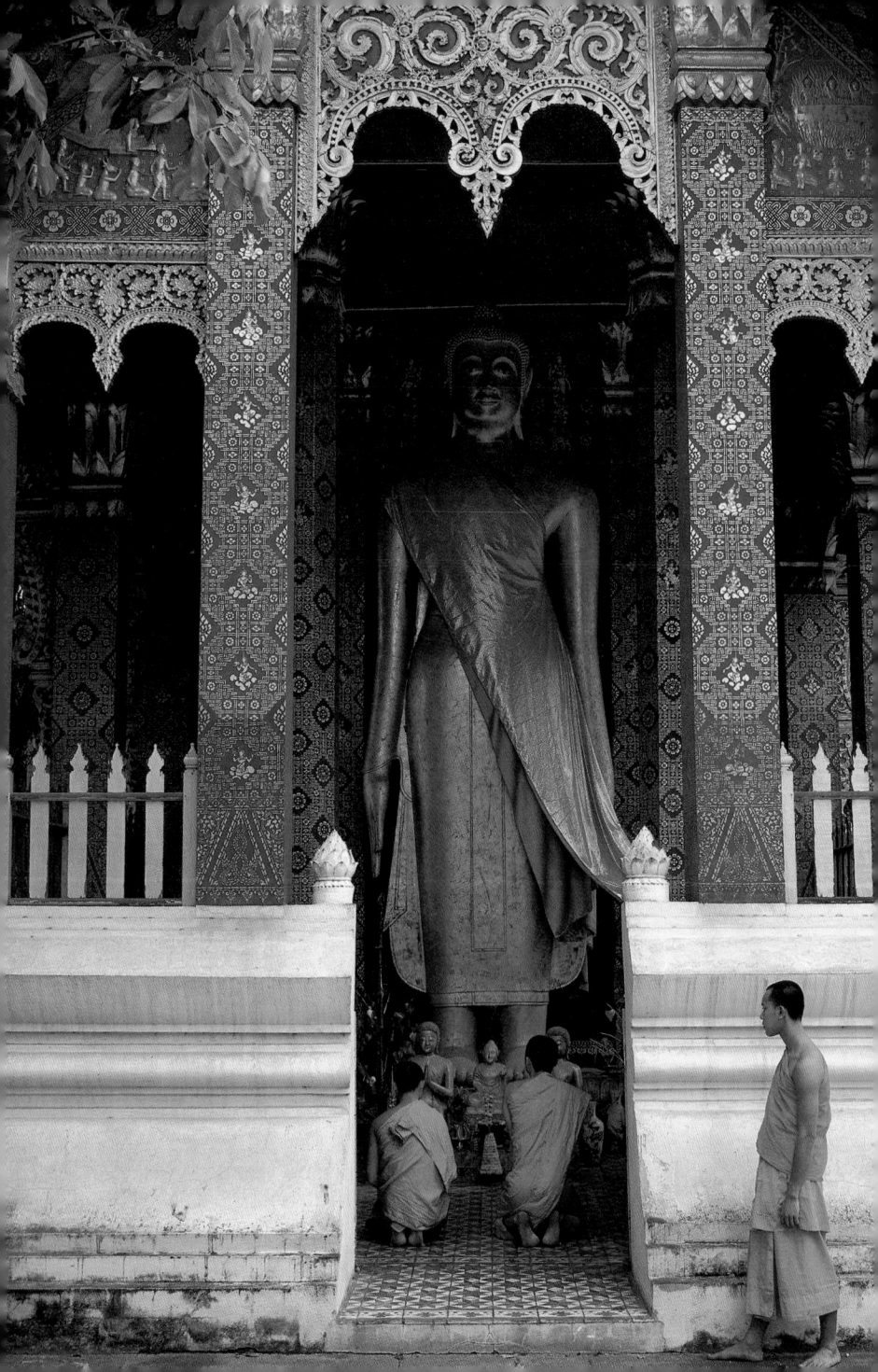

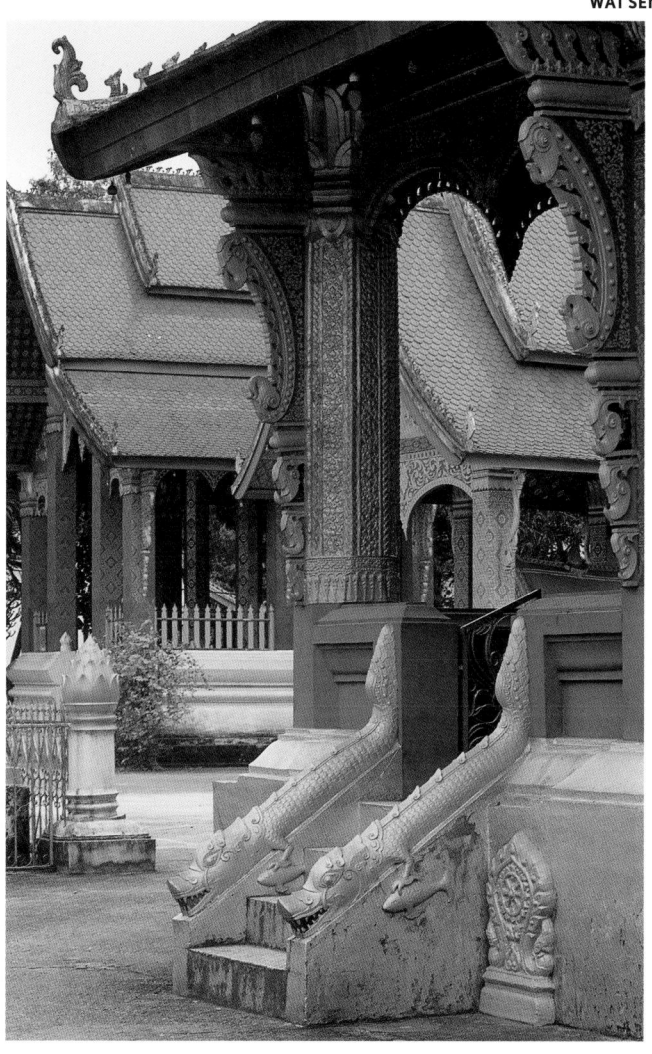

PP. 368–369 An elaborate shelter for a ritual drum used during lunar ceremonies • Unter diesem aufwendigen Baldachin wird die rituelle Trommel aufbewahrt, die bei den Mondzeremonien eingesetzt wird. • Cette niche de toute beauté abrite un tambour utilisé à l'occasion de cérémonies lunaires.

← Monks at prayer before a standing Buddha image. • Betende Mönche vor einer Buddha-Statue. • Les moines prient devant une statue de bouddha debout.

↑ Serpents embellish the balustrades of the entrance stairway. • Schützende Schlangen schmücken das Geländer der Eingangstreppe. • Des serpents montent la garde sur la main courante du perron.

P. 374 The main image of the Buddha in the sanctum. • Das Hauptbildnis Buddhas im Allerheiligsten. • Le plus grand bouddha du sanctuaire.

P. 375 The head abbot seated before his personal altar. • Das Oberhaupt der Mönche sitzt vor seinem privaten Altar. • Le chef de la communauté assis devant son autel personnel.

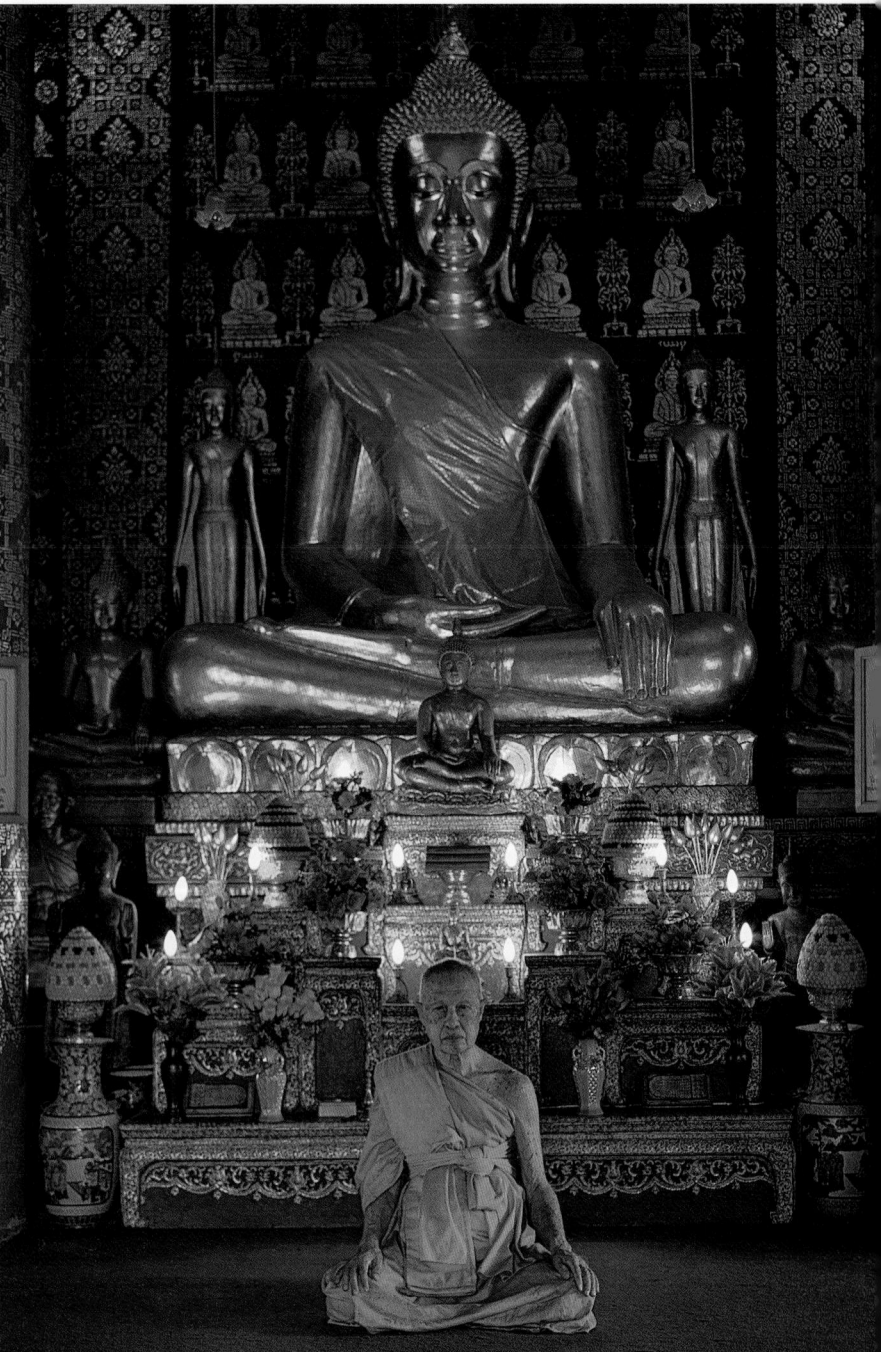

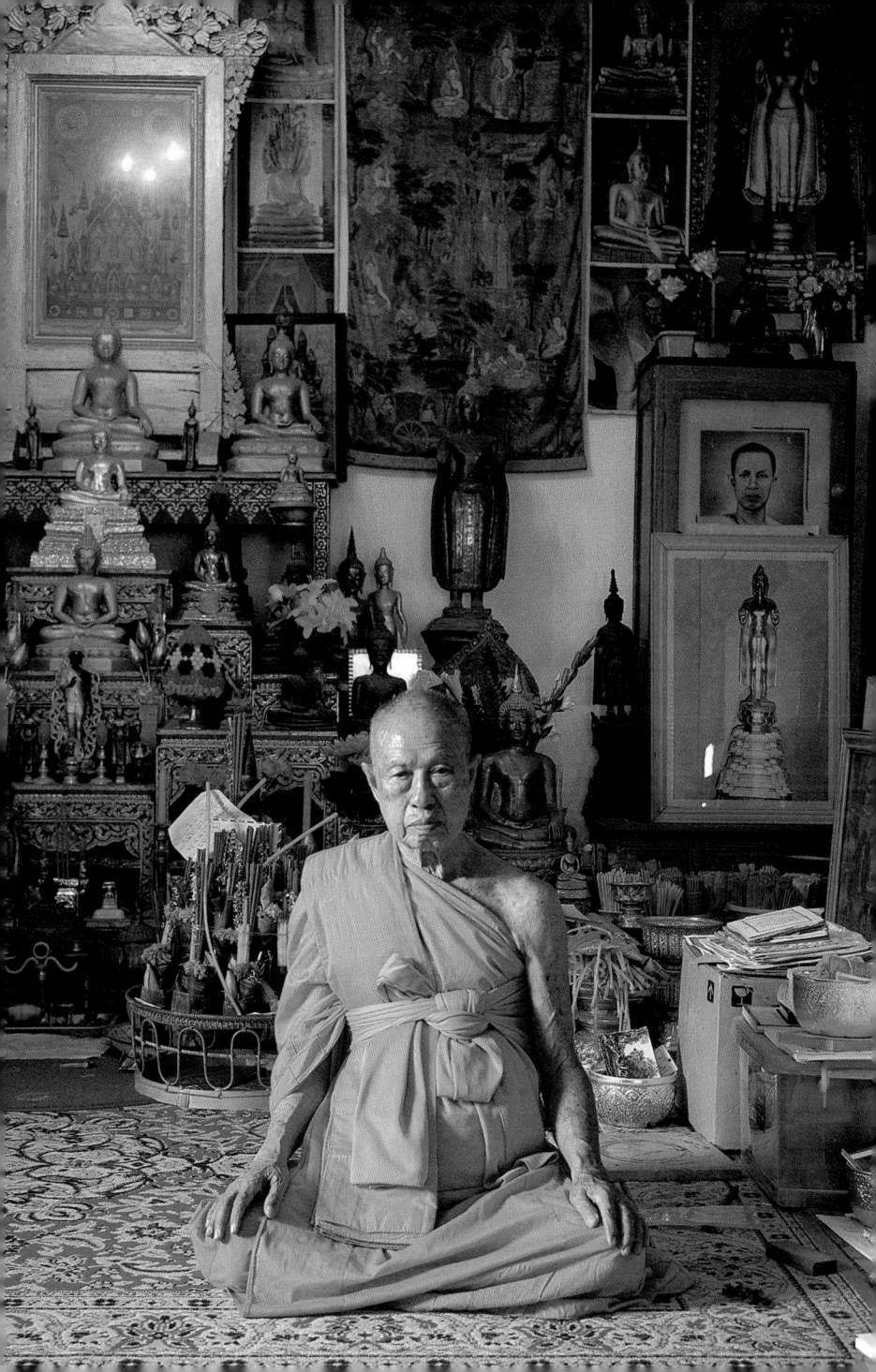

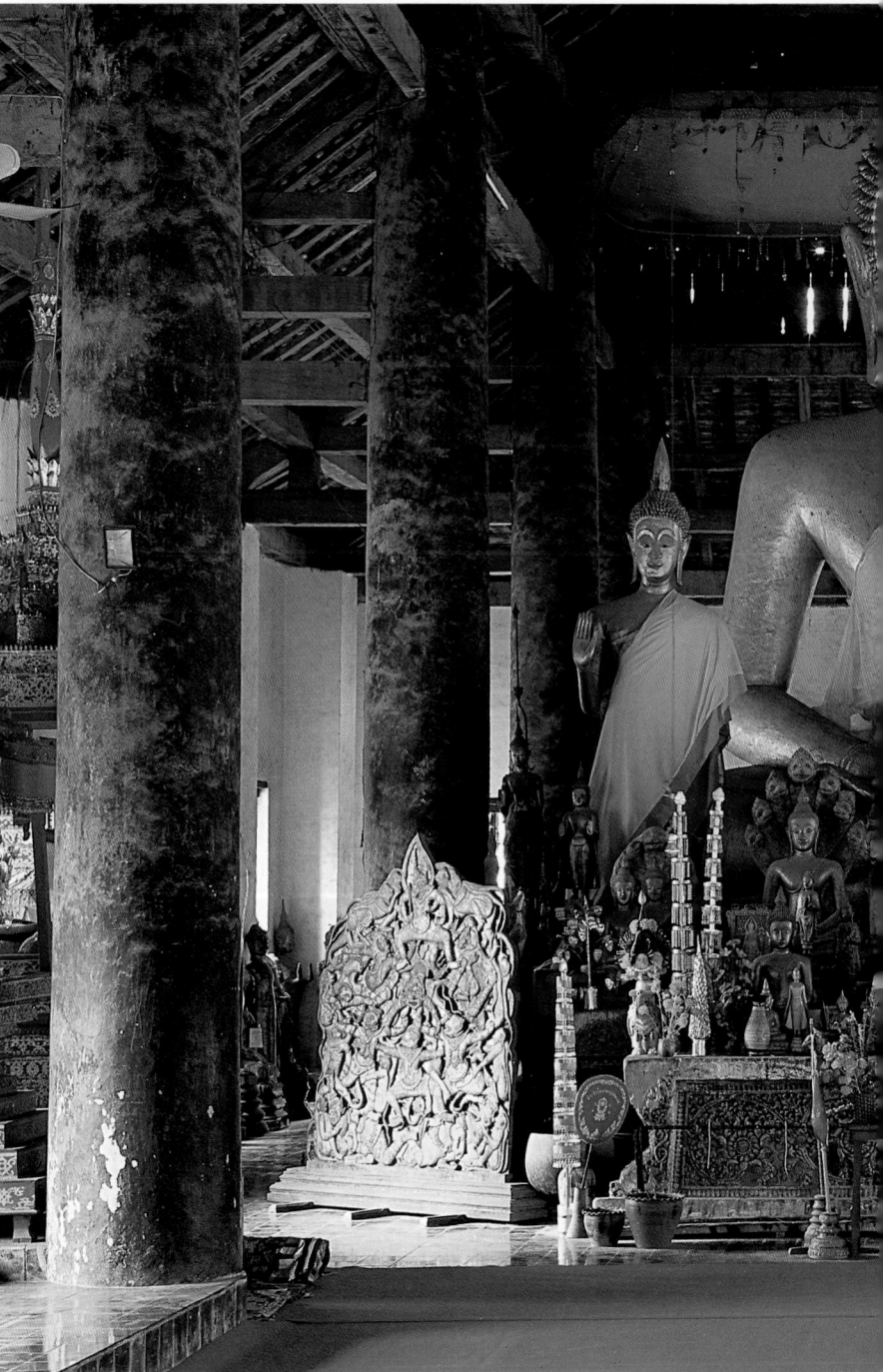

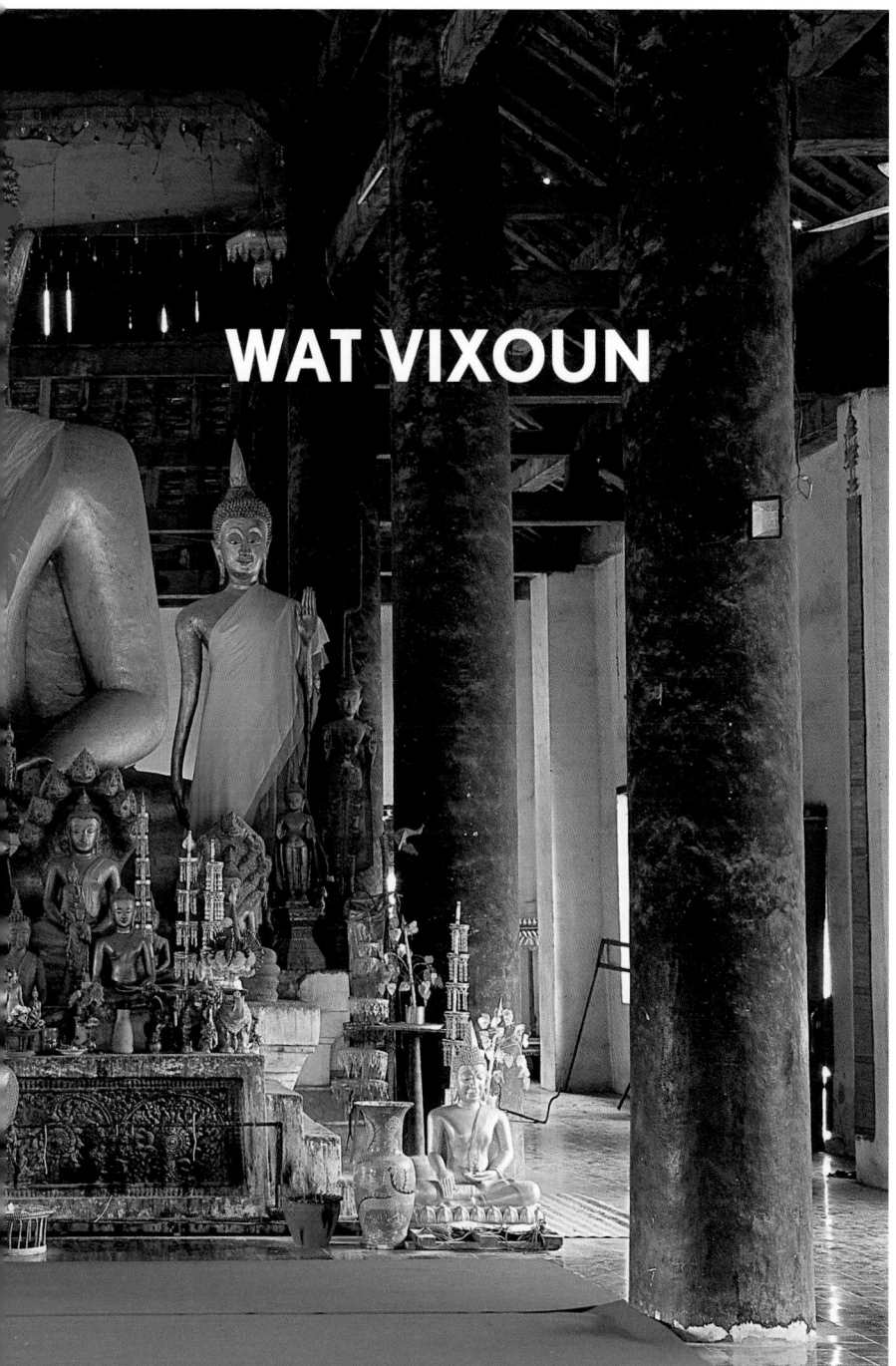

WAT VIXOUN

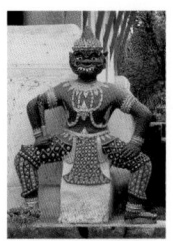

WAT VIXOUN
LUANG PRABANG
LAOS

Wat Vixoun, also known as Wat Wisunalat, was built by King Vixoun and is the oldest temple still in use in Luang Prabang. The original building, all in wood, burned down in 1887 when the city was attacked by "Black Banner" pirates from southern China. The present building dates from 1898, rebuilt in bricks, after the original wooden structure. Of special beauty are the sculpted doors. In 1942, a royal prince decided to transfer many antique works here and the temple became a museum. A superb collection of Buddhas in the Luang Prabang style, standing with hands by their side, are displayed in the temple. Yet another distinctive feature of the temple is the Mat Mo stupa within its precincts. *Mat Mo* means watermelon and refers to its spherical shape. King Vixoun's wife, Queen Phan Din Xieng, is said to have dedicated the original lotus-shaped stupa. The present stupa is an early 20th-century replacement. The temple is filled with the sounds of monks at prayer or going about their daily chores.

Wat Vixoun, auch unter dem Namen Wat Wisunalat bekannt, wurde im 16. Jahrhundert von König Vixoun errichtet. Er ist der älteste Tempel in Luang Prabang, in dem heute noch gebetet wird. 1887 brannte das ursprüngliche Holzgebäude ab, als die Stadt von "Schwarzflaggen"-Piraten aus Südchina angegriffen wurde. Das heutige Gebäude stammt aus dem Jahr 1898 und wurde dem Holzbau in Backstein nachempfunden. Die bildhauerisch gestalteten Türen sind besonders schön. 1942 beschloss ein königlicher Prinz, viele antike Kunstwerke in den Tempel zu schaffen. Das daraus entstandene Museum beherbergt eine einzigartige Sammlung von Buddhas im Luang-Prabang-Stil, stehend mit den Händen an den Seiten. Darüber hinaus steht auf dem Gelände der Tempelanlage der Mat-Mo-Stupa. Mat Mo bedeutet „Wassermelone" und bezieht sich auf die runde Form. Angeblich war der ehemals lotusförmige Stupa der Königin Phan Din Xieng, Vixouns Ehefrau, gewidmet. Im frühen 20. Jahrhundert wurde er durch den gegenwärtigen Stupa ersetzt. Der Tempel ist vom Klang der Gebete und den Geräuschen erfüllt, die die Mönche beim Verrichten der alltäglichen Arbeiten verursachen.

Vat Vixun, aussi connu sous le nom de Vat Visunalat, est le plus ancien temple en service de Luang Prabang. Il a été construit par le roi Vixun au 16ᵉ siècle. Le bâtiment d'origine, construit par le roi Vixun, a été réduit en cendres en 1887, lorsque la ville fut mise à sac par les « Pavillons noirs », faction de l'armée chinoise convertie dans le banditisme. En 1898, le temple a été reconstruit en briques sur le modèle de la construction d'origine en bois. Ses portes sculptées sont d'une très grande beauté. En 1942, un prince de sang royal a décidé d'y transférer une importante collection d'antiquités. Le temple est devenu un musée, dans lequel on peut admirer une superbe collection de bouddhas dans le style de Luang Prabang, bras le long du corps. Autre centre d'intérêt dans l'enceinte même du sanctuaire, un stupa sphérique appelé *Mat Mo*, ce qui signifie pastèque. Cette construction du début du 20ᵉ siècle est venue remplacer le stupa d'origine en forme de lotus, qui aurait été une donation de l'épouse du roi Visun, la reine Phan Din Xieng. Dans tout Vat Vixun on entend les moines prier ou vaquer à leurs occupations.

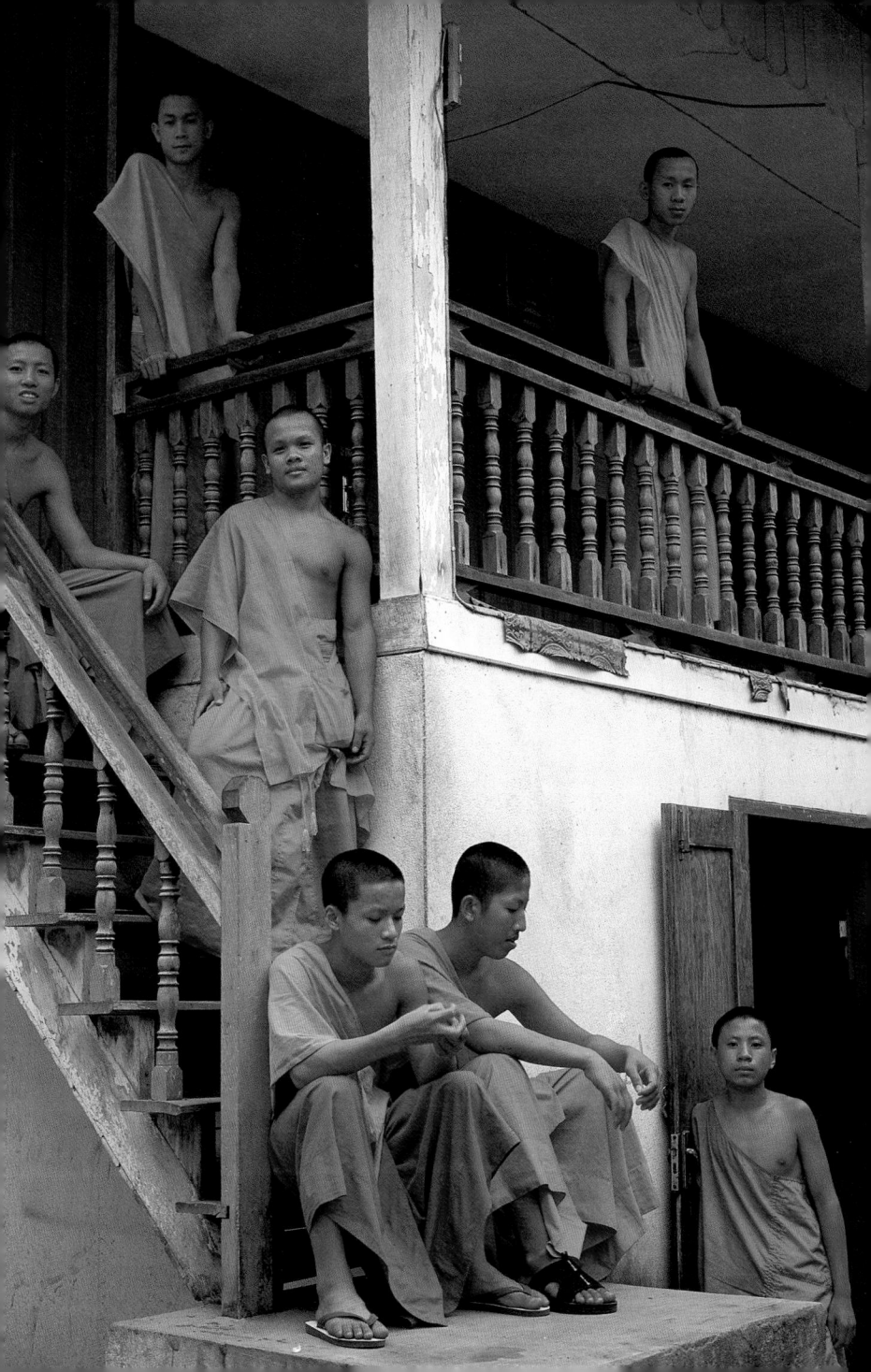

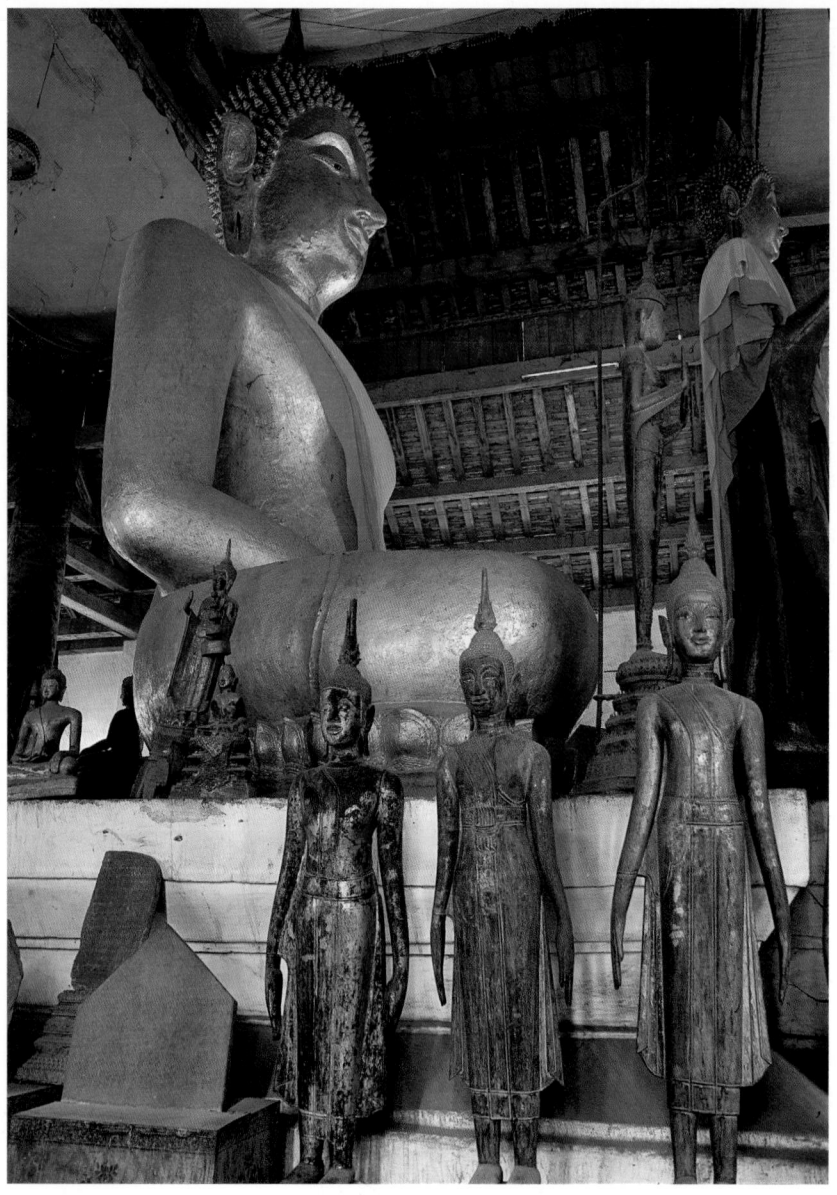

PP. 376–377 and ↑ → The great
Buddha image at the center of the altar
is the biggest in Luang Prabang and is
surrounded by smaller antique images. •

Die große Buddha-Statue in der Mitte
des Altars ist das größte in Luang
Prabang. Es ist von kleineren antiken
Statuen umgeben. • Le gigantesque

bouddha figurant au centre de l'autel
entouré de représentations anciennes
de dimensions plus modestes est le plus
grand de Luang Prabang.

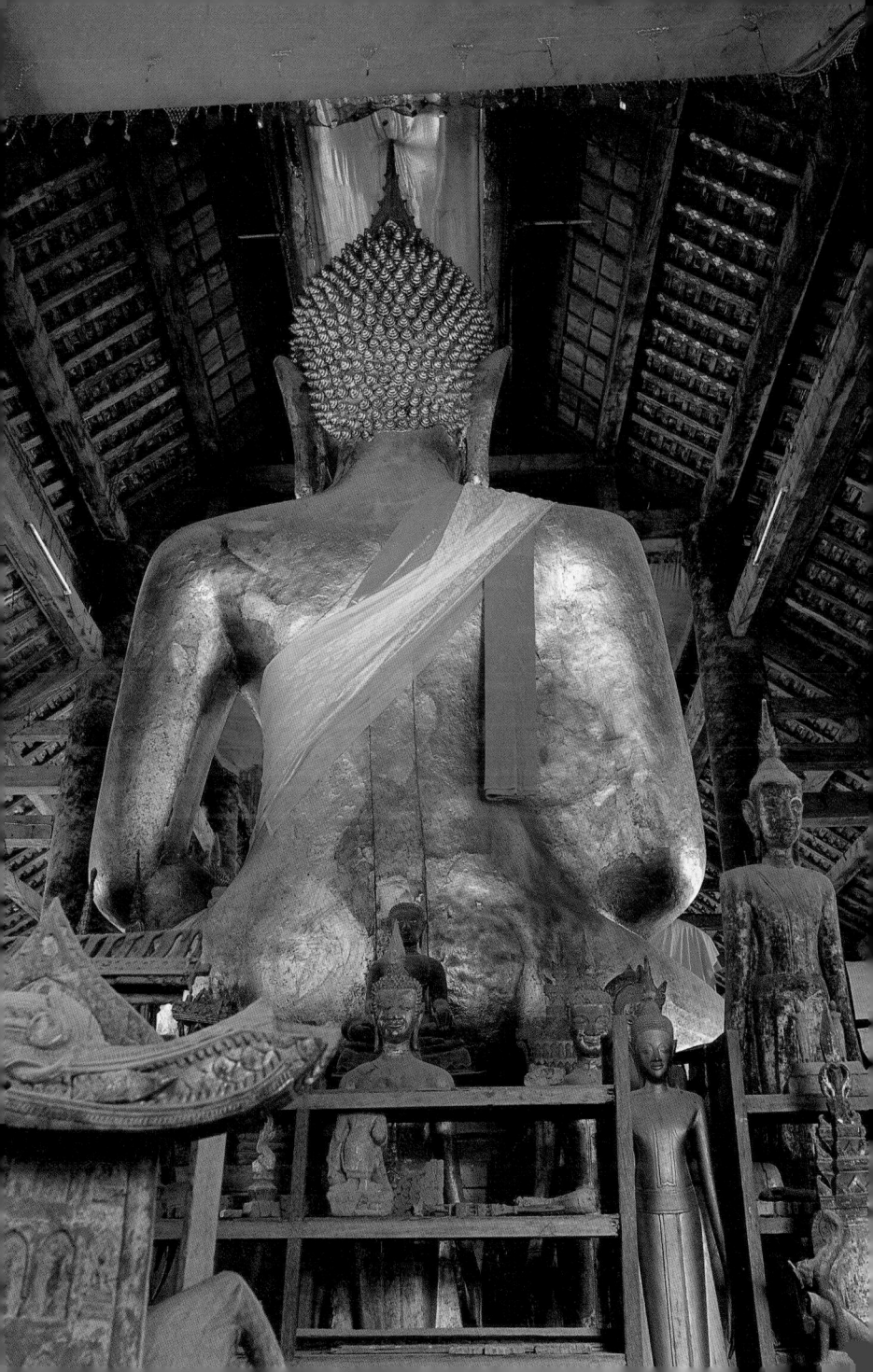

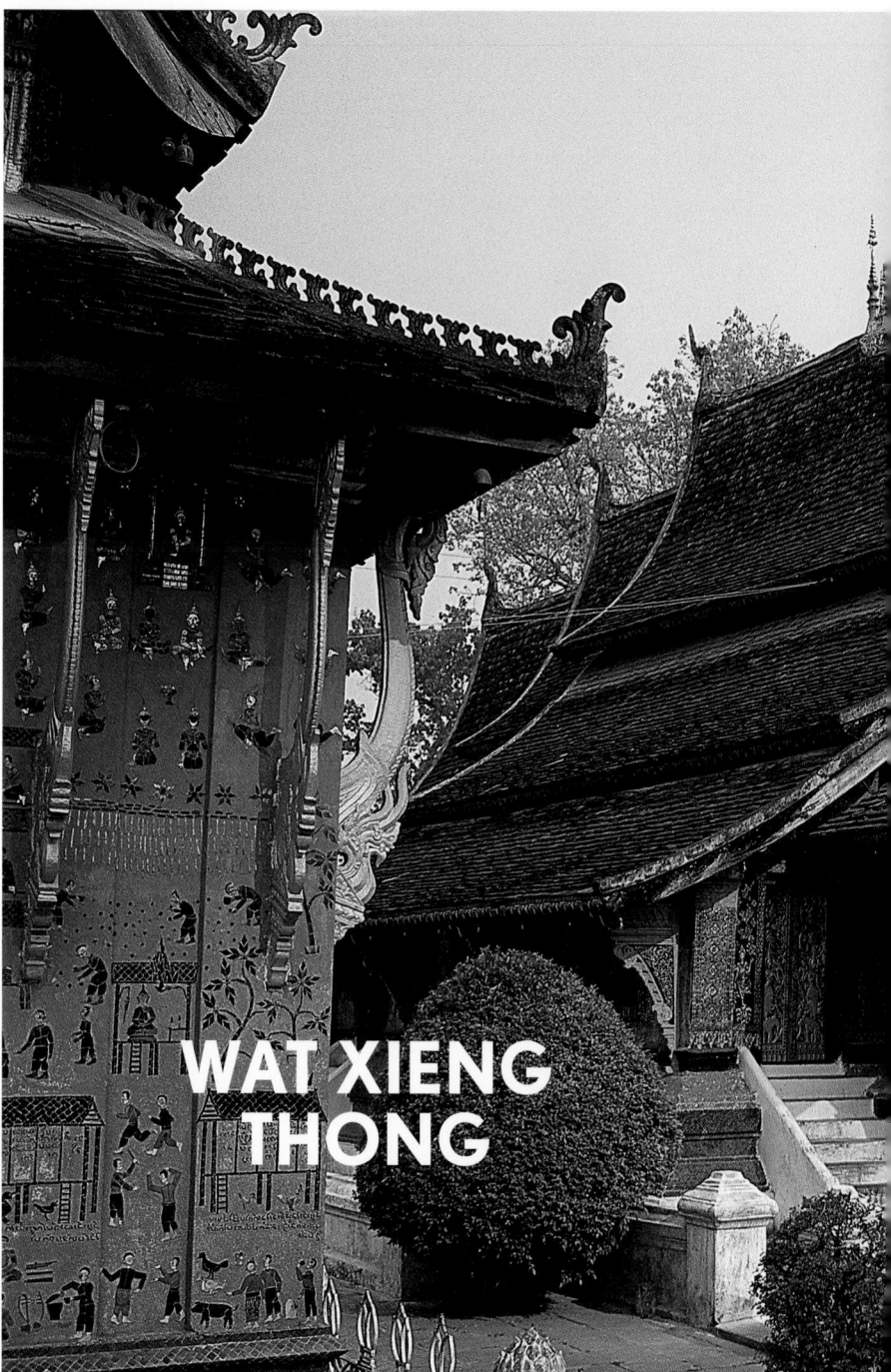

WAT XIENG
THONG

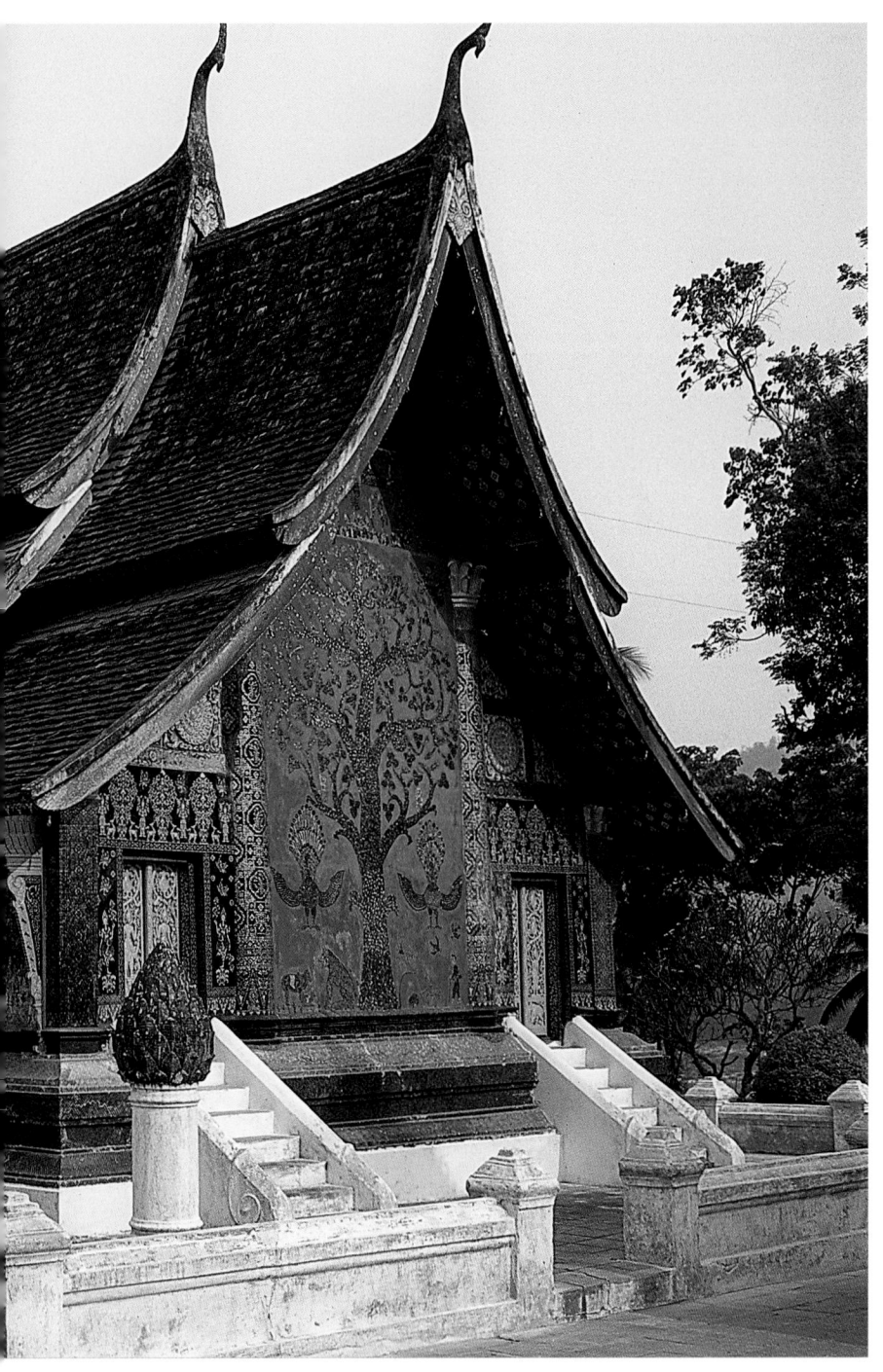

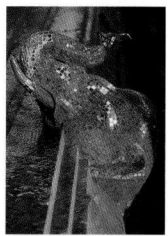

WAT XIENG THONG
LUANG PRABANG
LAOS

The meeting point of two rivers is a key point in sacred geography. Wat Xieng Thong, Temple of the Golden City, is located in a beautiful garden, where the smaller Nam Khan river runs into the waters of the majestic Mekong. It is one of the most important temples in Laos and layered with legend. One has it that this was the site where two hermits who founded Luang Prabang placed a boundary stone for the new settlement. The union of the Nam Khan and Mekong is also said to be the home of two nagas, sacred serpents, who are guardians of the river. The temple as it exists today was built in 1560 by King Setthathirat, a patron of Buddhism, and remained a royal preserve until 1975. It was where Lao kings were crowned and invested with power. Near the temple's eastern gate stands a royal funeral chapel with funerary urns that commemorate members of the royal family. Like many sacred spots, it is a place where, in the words of one scholar, "Buddhist, pre-Buddhist and royal traditions met, overlapped and meshed".

In der heiligen Geografie spielt der Zusammenfluss zweier Flüsse eine große Rolle. Wat Xieng Thong, der Tempel der Goldenen Stadt, liegt in einem wunderschönen Garten, wo der schmalere Fluss Nam Khan sich in den majestätischen Mekong ergießt. Er zählt zu den bedeutendsten Tempeln der Stadt, und es werden viele Legenden über ihn erzählt. Einer zufolge legten zwei Mönche, die Luang Prabang gegründet haben sollen, den Grenzstein für das neue Anwesen. Überdies heißt es, dass hier, wo Nam Khan und Mekong zusammenfließen, die beiden Nagas leben, heilige Schlangen und Schutzgöttinnen des Flusses. Der bis heute erhaltene Tempel wurde 1560 von König Setthathirat erbaut, einem Förderer des Buddhismus, und blieb bis 1975 im Besitz des Königshauses. Hier wurden die laotischen Könige gekrönt, hier wurde ihnen die Macht übertragen. Unweit des Osteingangs zum Tempel steht eine königliche Begräbniskapelle mit Urnen der königlichen Familie. Wie von vielen anderen heiligen Orten sagt man auch von diesem, dass hier „buddhistische, vorbuddhistische und königliche Traditionen eine ganz eigene Symbiose eingehen".

Le confluent de deux cours d'eau est toujours un endroit important dans la géographie sacrée. Vat Xieng Thong, temple de La Ville dorée, s'élève dans un superbe jardin où la modeste Nam Khan se jette dans les eaux du majestueux Mékong. Ce temple, un des plus importants du Laos, est auréolé de légendes. L'une d'elles rapporte que deux ermites auraient placé une borne à cet endroit, fondant ainsi la ville de Luang Prabang. Les eaux où le Mékong et la Nam Kahn se rejoignent seraient aussi la demeure de deux *nagas*, serpents sacrés et gardiens du fleuve. Le temple dans sa forme actuelle a été bâti en 1560 par le roi Setthathirat, un protecteur du bouddhisme, et est resté propriété royale jusqu'en 1975. C'est ici que les rois du Laos étaient couronnés et intronisés. Près de la porte est du temple, on peut voir une chapelle funéraire royale abritant des urnes à la mémoire de membres de la famille royale. Comme bien d'autres endroits disséminés dans le pays, c'est un lieu où, selon un érudit, « les traditions bouddhiques, prébouddhiques et royales se sont rencontrées, ont coexisté et ont fusionné ».

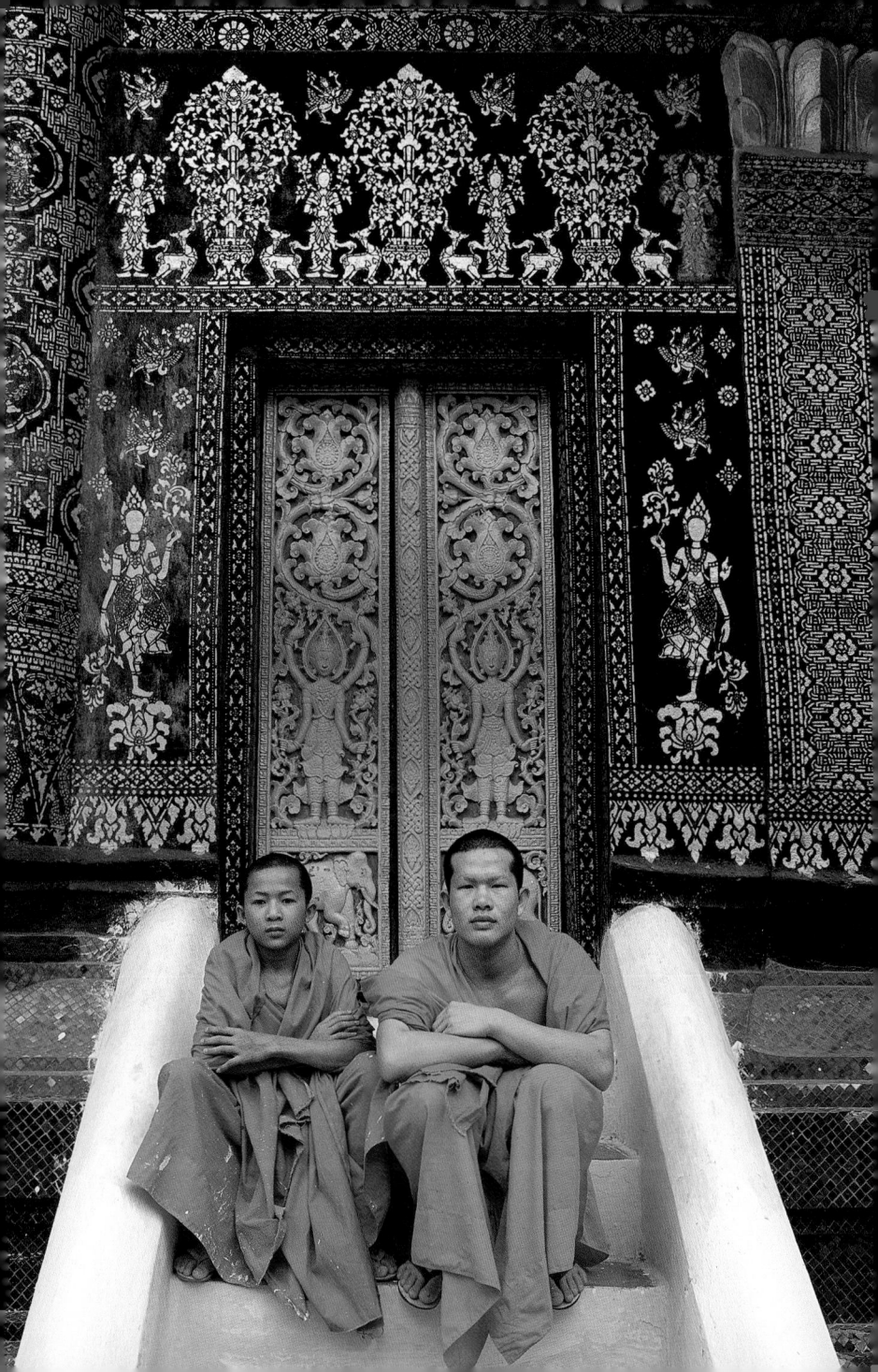

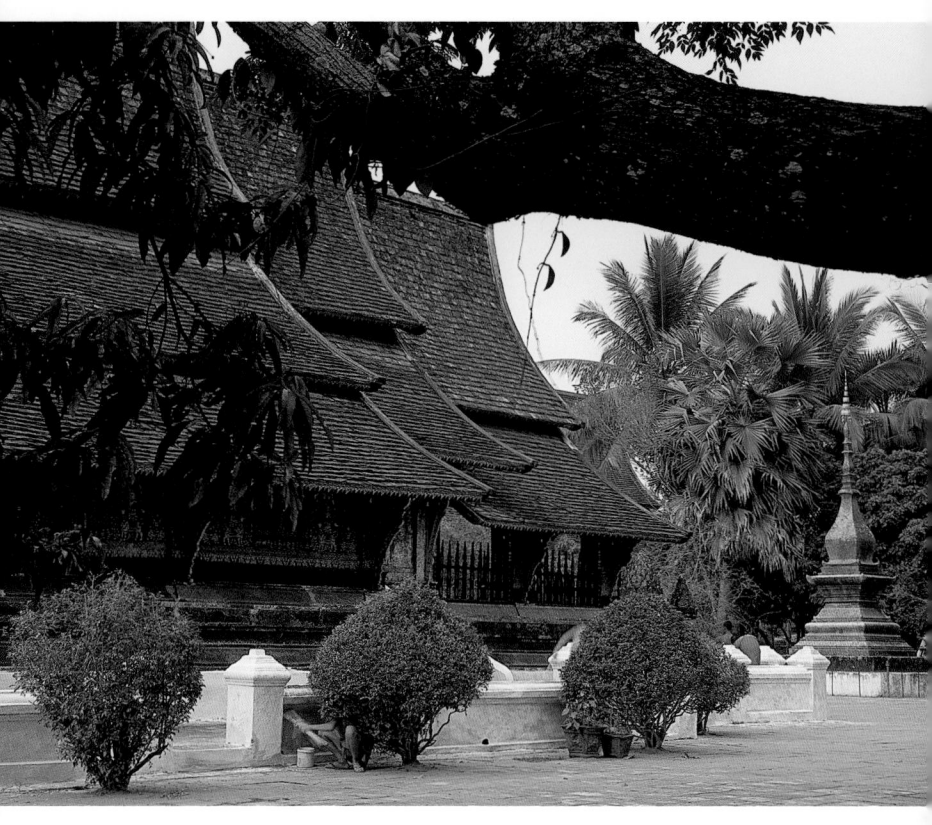

PP. 382–383 The rear wall of the
prayer chamber, in classical Luang
Prabang style, is embellished with a
"tree of life" mosaic. • Die Rückwand
der Gebetshalle wurde im klassischen
Luang-Prabang-Stil mit dem Mosaik

eines „Lebensbaums" verziert. •
La façade postérieure de la salle de
prière, dans le style classique de Luang
Prabang, est ornée d'une mosaïque
représentant l'« arbre de vie ».

↑ Exterior view of the prayer chamber
with its sloping roofs. • Außenansicht
einer Gebetshalle mit Gefälledächern. •
La salle de prière avec ses toits caractéristiques vue de l'extérieur.

↓ Monks at work, repainting the stupa, enclosure walls and staircases in preparation for new year celebrations. • Mönche bei der Arbeit – sie streichen den Stupa an und errichten Absperrungen für die laotische Neujahrsfeier. •

Les fêtes du Nouvel An lao approchent, les moines repeignent le stupa, les murets et les escaliers.

PP. 388–389 Young monks gaze longingly at coconuts during their afternoon break. • In der Nachmittagspause betrachten junge Mönche sehnsüchtig die hoch hängenden Kokosnüsse. • Les jeunes moines regardent avec envie des noix de coco pendant leur pause de l'après-midi.

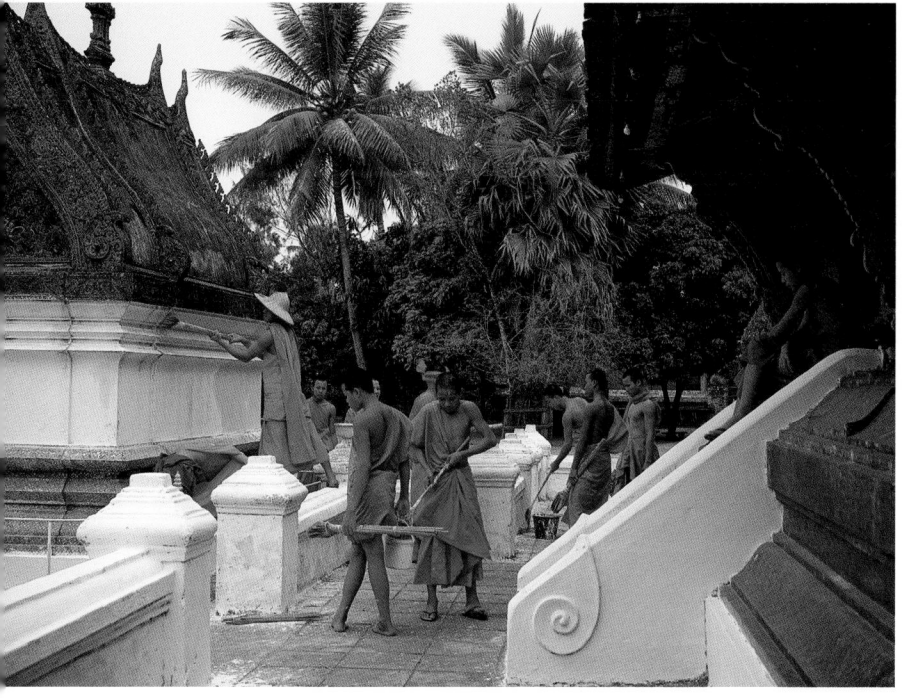

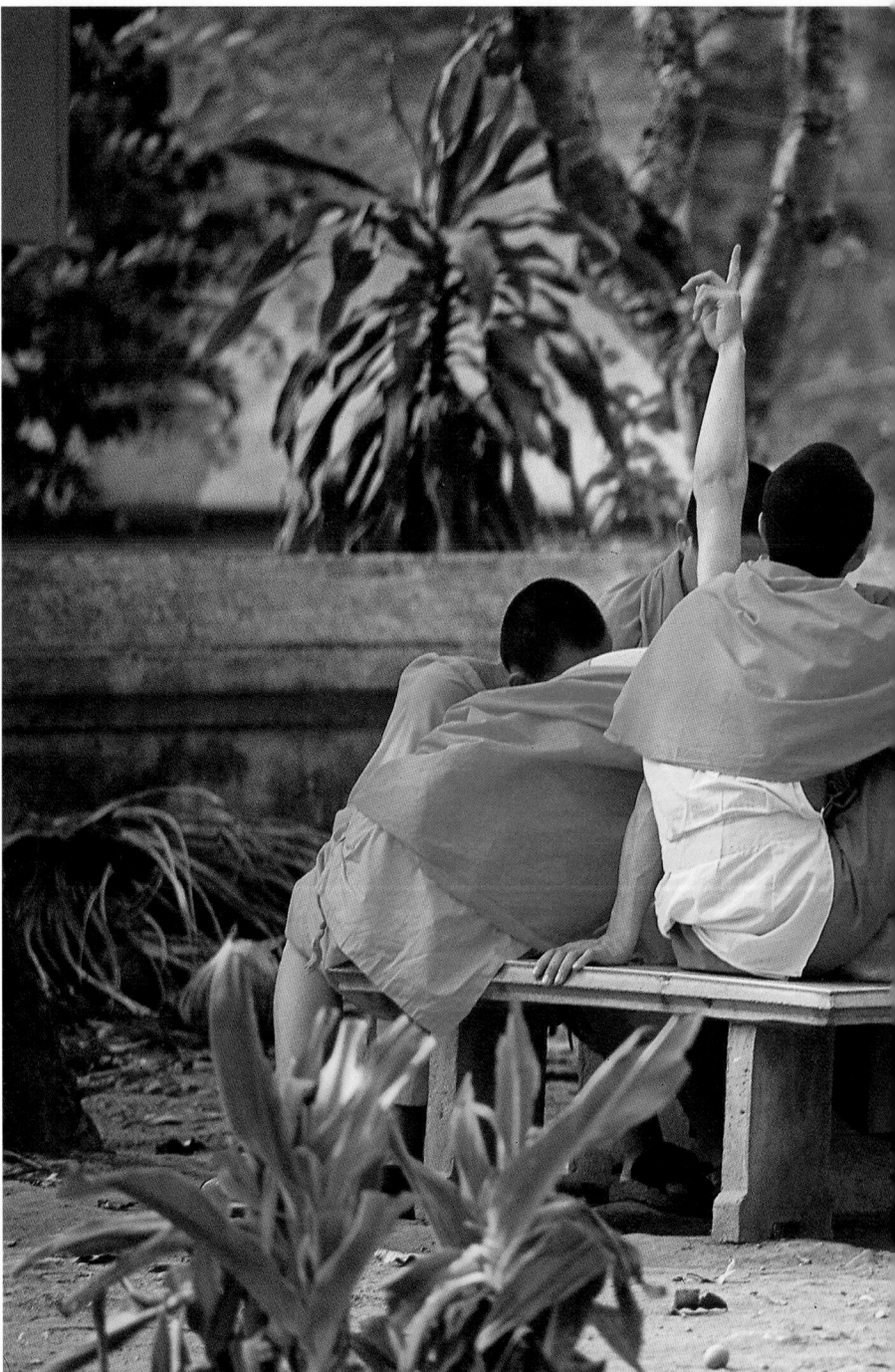

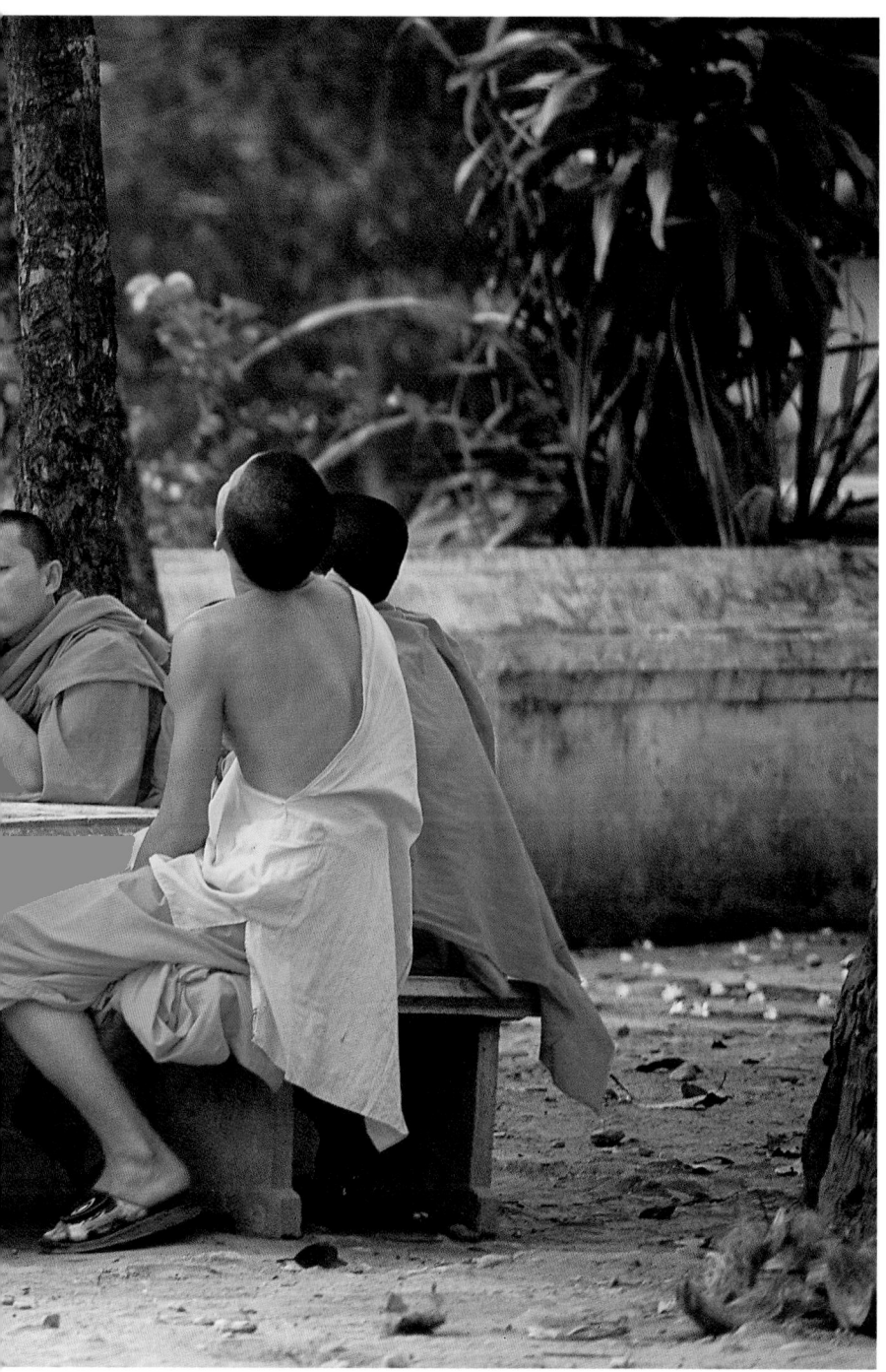

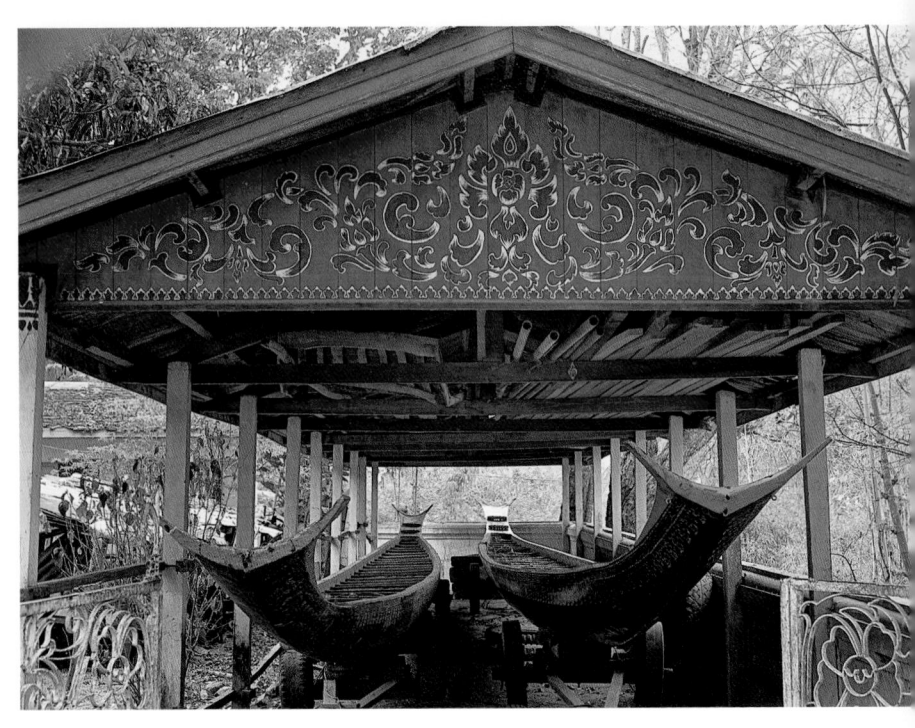

↑ A shelter for boats, each carved from a single tree trunk, that are used in a boat festival at the end of the rainy season. • Hier liegen die Boote bis zur Feier des Bootsfestes am Ende der Regenzeit sicher. • Les bateaux remisés sous cet abri ont été taillés dans des troncs d'arbre ; ils sont utilisés à l'occasion d'une fête nautique qui a lieu à la fin de la saison des pluies.

PP. 392–393 A detail of the exquisite "tree of life". • Details des erlesenen „Lebensbaums". • Le superbe « arbre de vie » (détail).

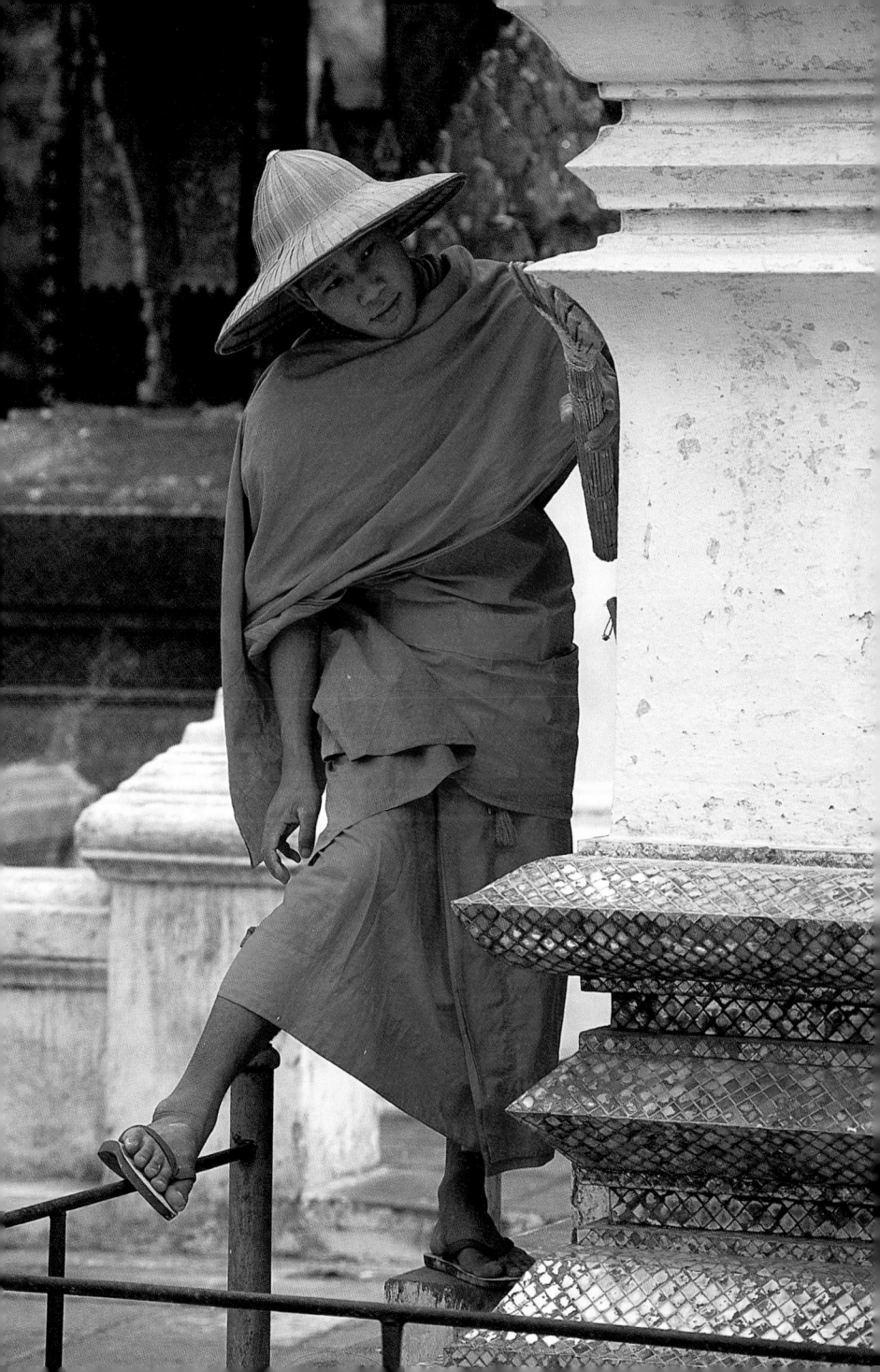

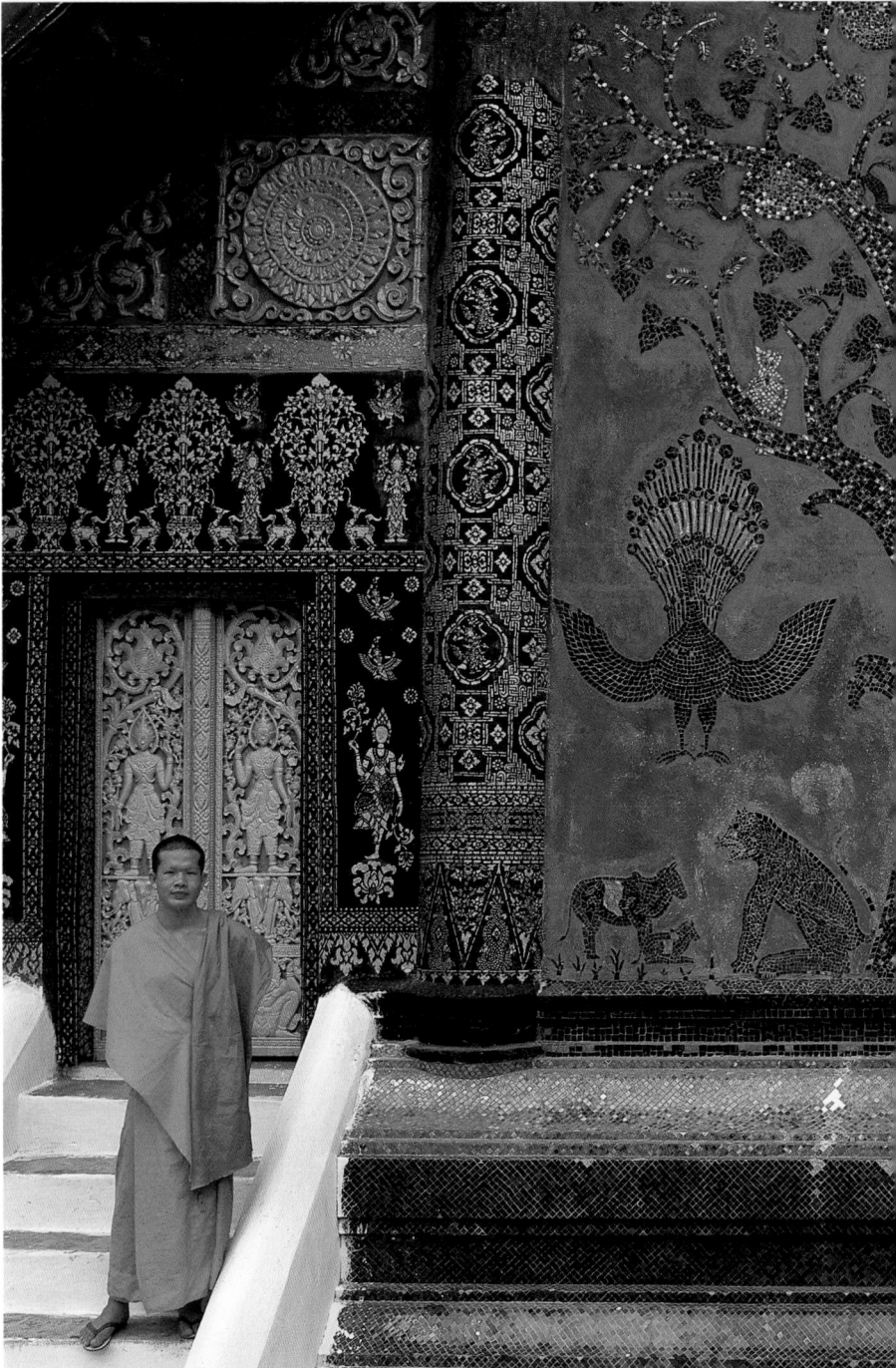

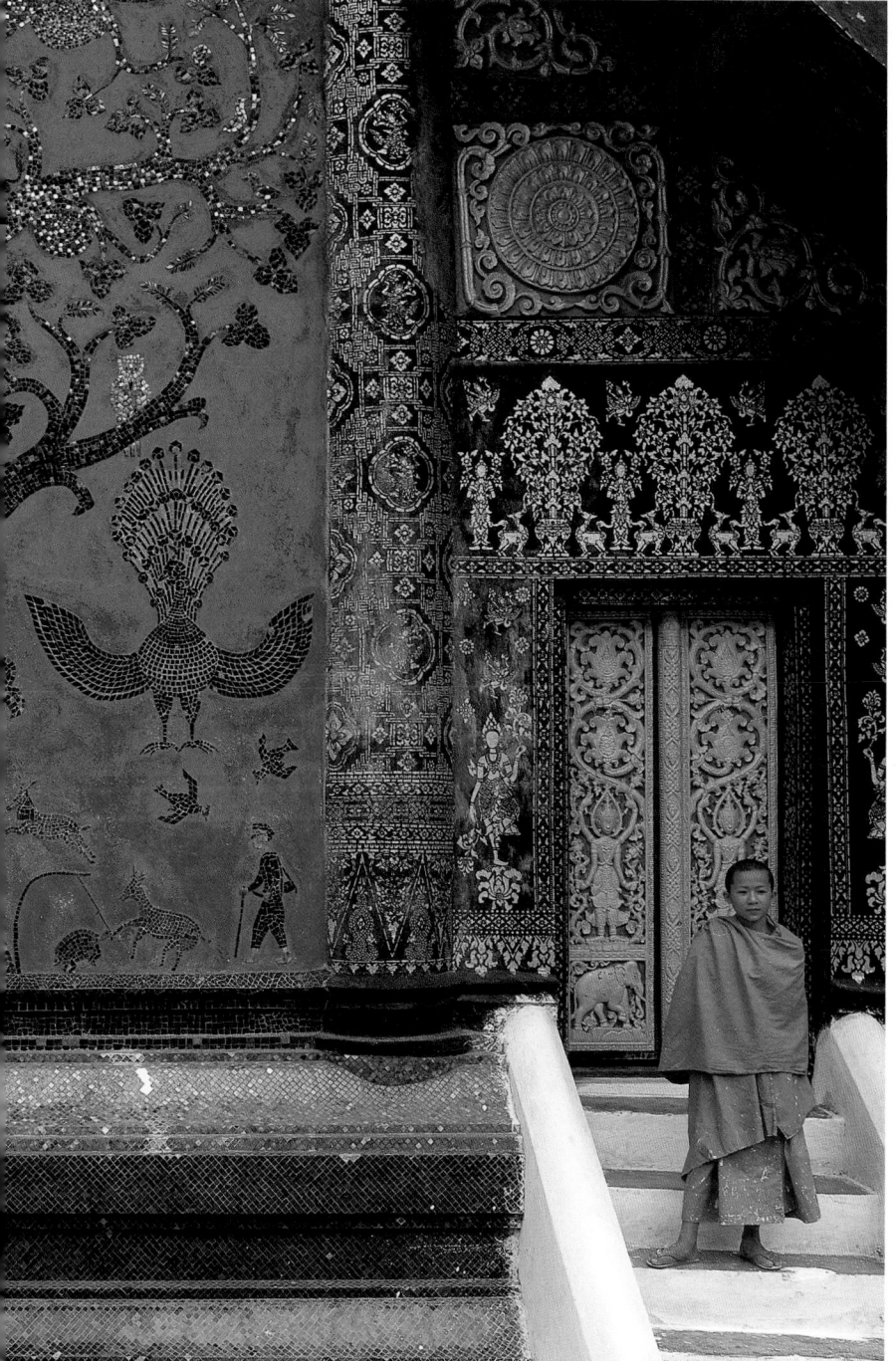

↓ Monks at study outside the prayer room with its richly stencilled walls and columns. • Studierende Mönche vor der Gebetshalle, die mit aufwendiger Schablonenbemalung auf Wänden und Säulen verziert ist. • Des moines se consacrant à l'étude à l'extérieur de la salle de prière dont les colonnes et les murs sont richement ornés de dessins au pochoir.

→ Monks at prayer before the gilded image of the Buddha inside the prayer room. • Betende Mönche in der Gebetshalle vor dem vergoldeten Bildnis Buddhas. • Dans la salle de prière, des moines prient devant un bouddha doré.

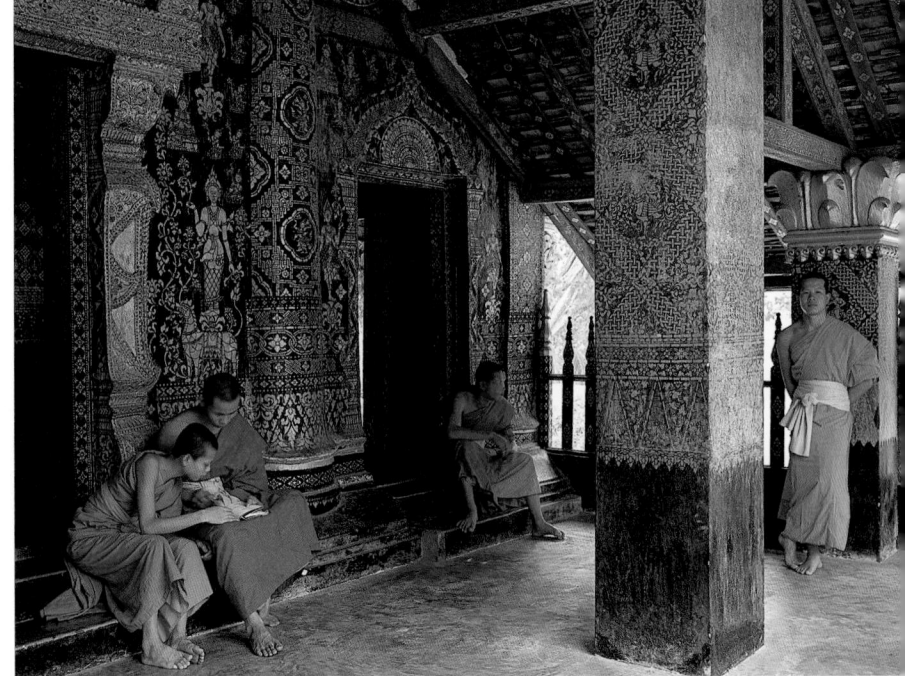

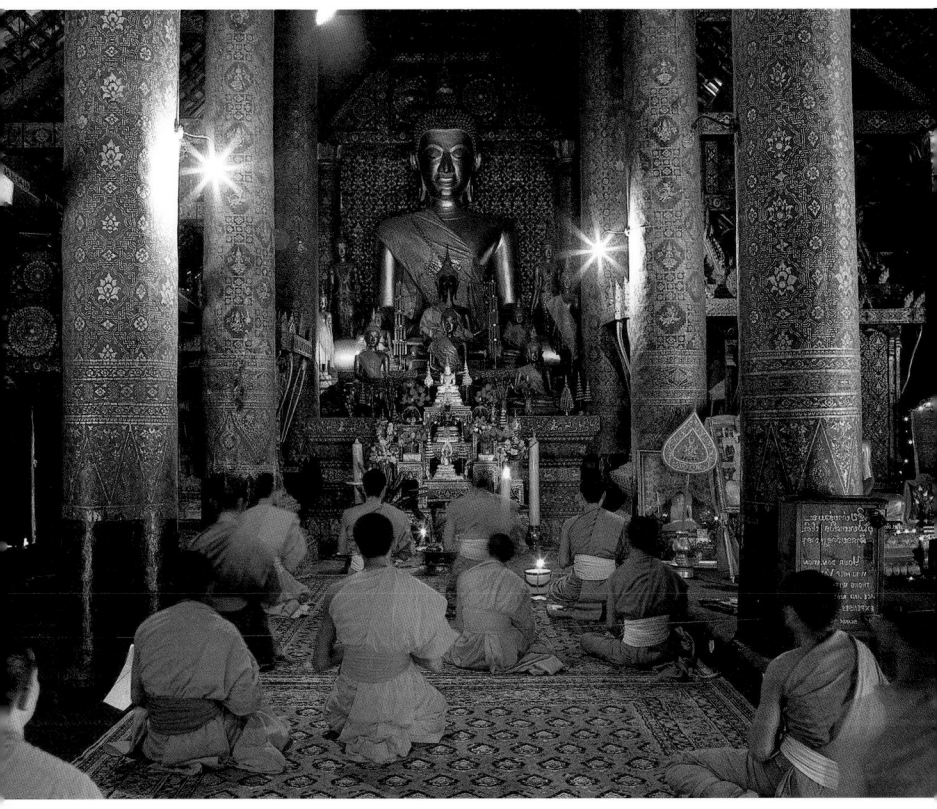

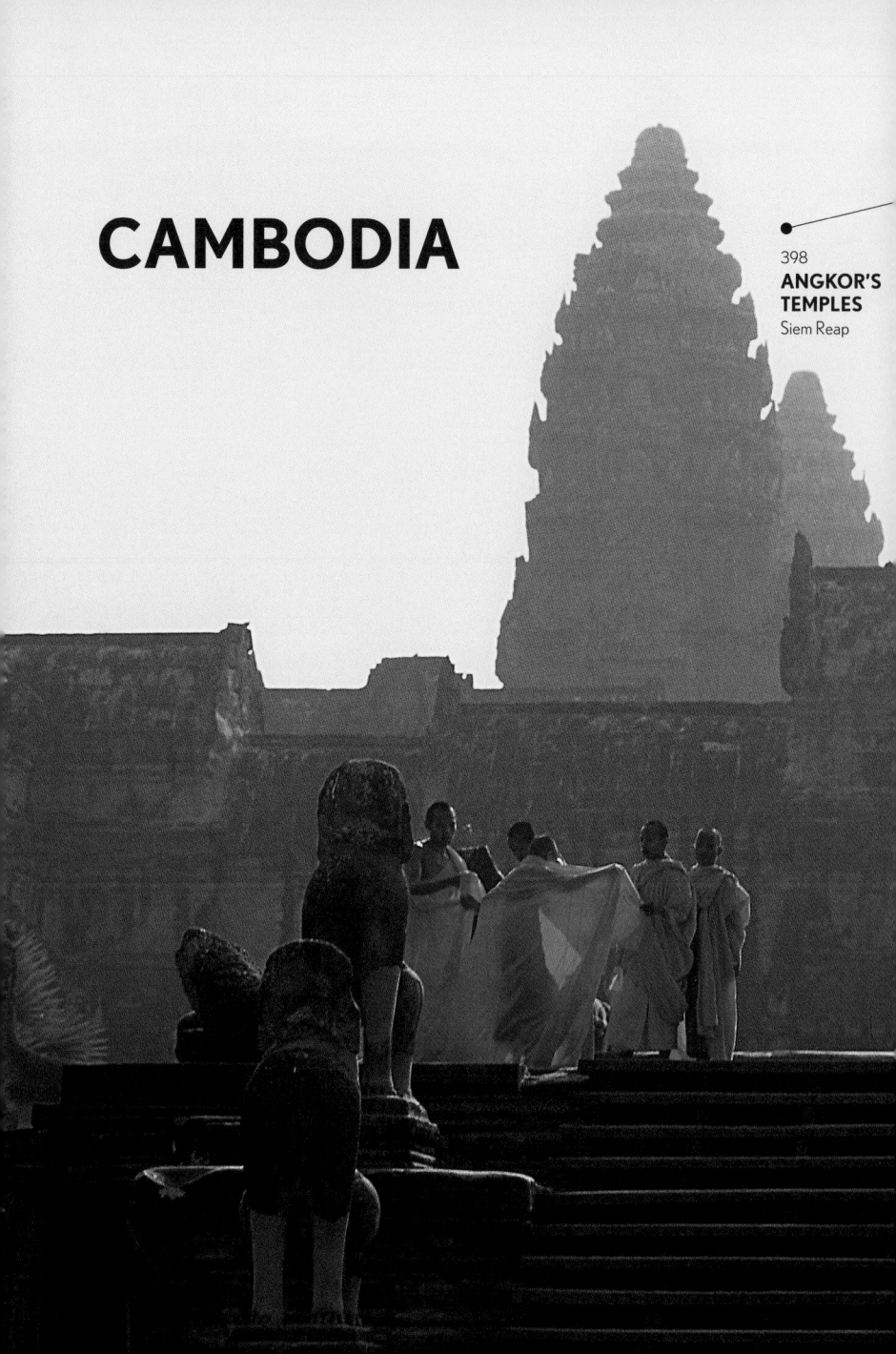

CAMBODIA

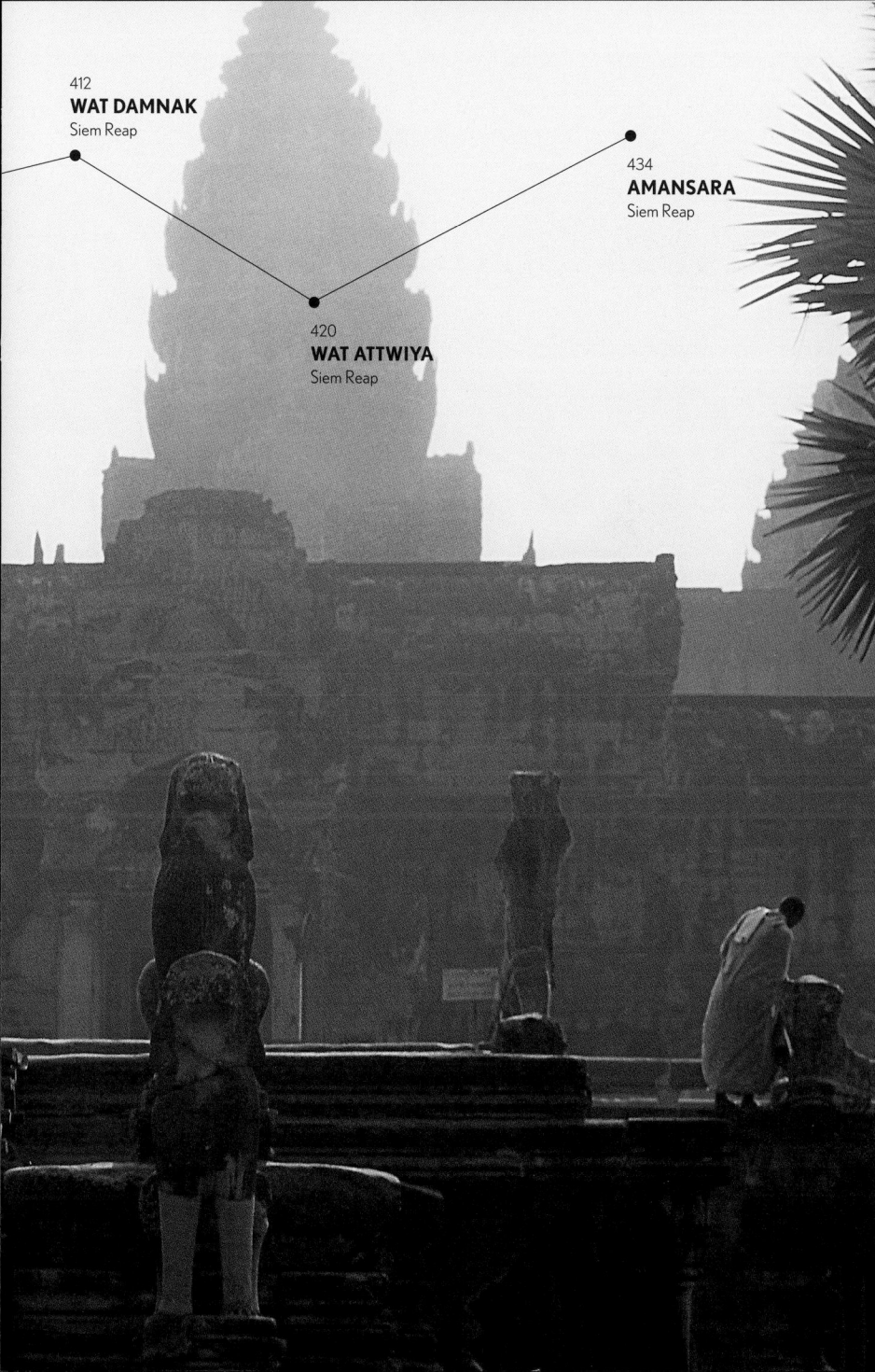

412
WAT DAMNAK
Siem Reap

434
AMANSARA
Siem Reap

420
WAT ATTWIYA
Siem Reap

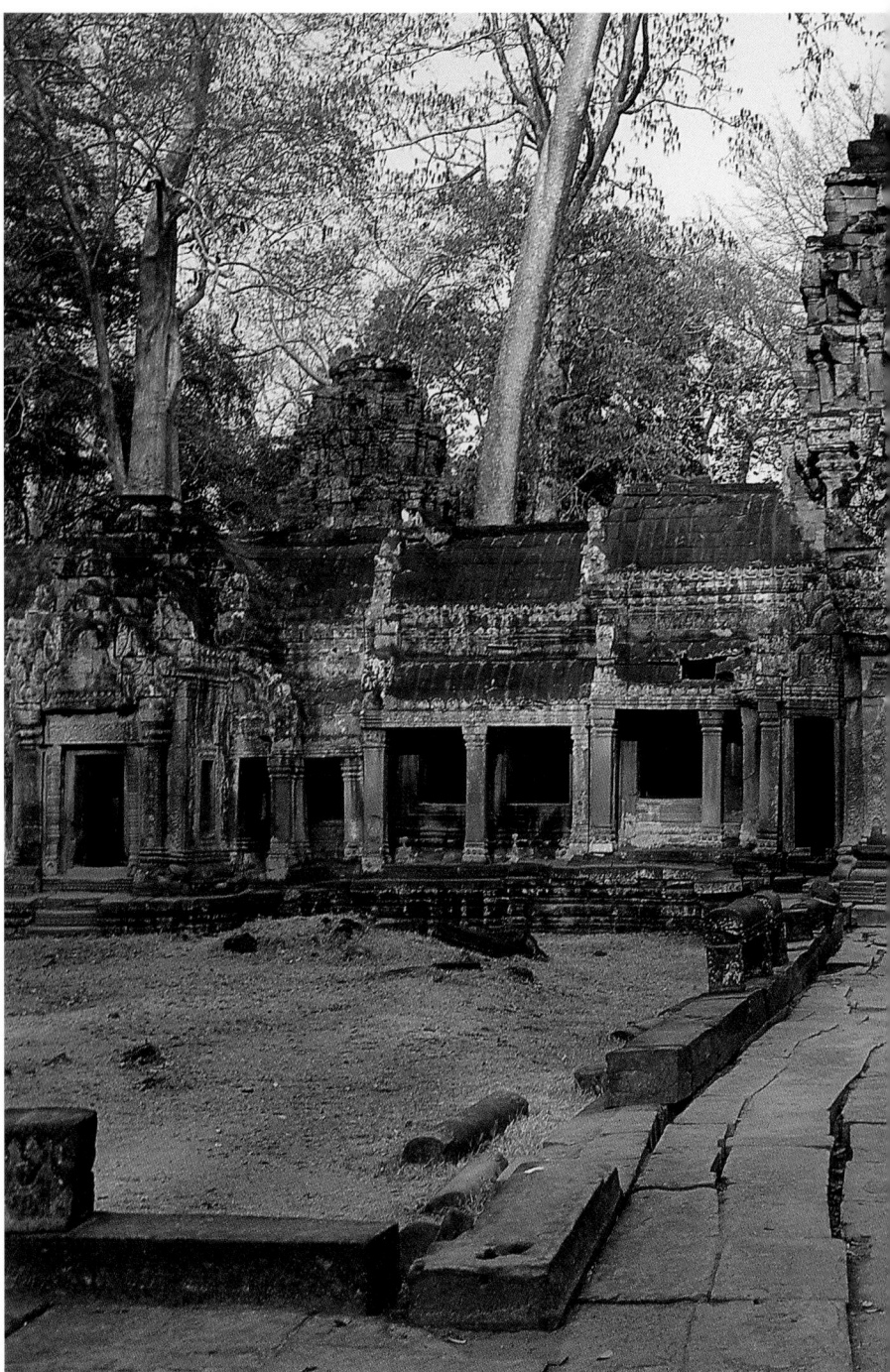

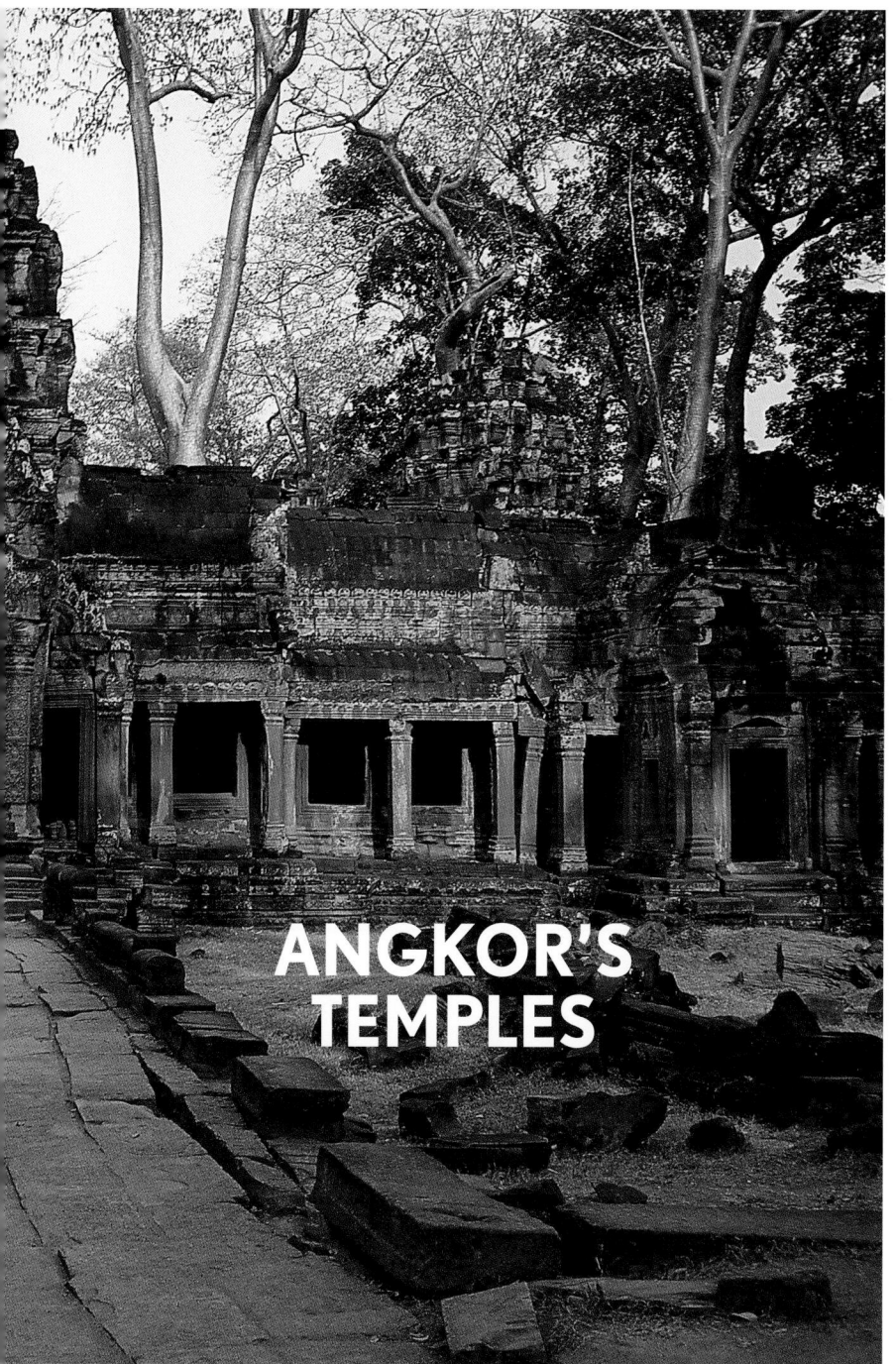

ANGKOR'S
TEMPLES

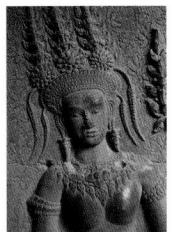

ANGKOR'S TEMPLES
SIEM REAP
CAMBODIA

When the French naturalist Henri Mouhot came upon the magnificent ruined temples of Angkor in 1860 he asked the local people who had built them. It is the work of giants, they said. Gigantic in scale and exquisite in sculptural detail, Angkor's temples had lain imprisoned by a tropical jungle for centuries. Mouhot's discovery created a sensation; it led to the establishment of the Ecole Française d'Extrême-Orient that since the late 19th century has tried to unlock the secrets of the powerful Khmer dynasty that built a series of royal capitals between the 9th and 13th centuries. "Unmatched in their fusion of art, architecture and philosophy," as Jon Ortner, the famous photographer of the Angkor temples put it, the citadels were built in the image of temples dedicated to Hindu gods. When the Angkor civilization declined, its temples too were abandoned, and the forest closed in. Despite decades of restoration, some monuments have been left in the embrace of nature. Roots and branches of ancient silk-cotton and strangler fig entwine the old stones, adding to Angkor's sepulchral magic.

Als der französische Naturkundler Henri Mouhot die beeindruckenden Ruinen der Tempel von Angkor 1860 entdeckte, erklärten die Einheimischen auf seine Fragen, Riesen hätten sie geschaffen. Als Mouhots Entdeckung weltweit Aufsehen erregte, waren die riesigen Tempel von Angkor, Terrassenanlagen mit detailreicher Bauornamentik, bereits seit Jahrhunderten vom tropischen Dschungel umschlossen. Daraufhin wurde die École Française d'Extrême-Orient gegründet, in deren Auftrag seit dem späten 19. Jahrhundert das Geheimnis der mächtigen Khmer-Dynastie erforscht wird, die zwischen dem 9. und 13. Jahrhundert mehrere königliche Hauptstädte erbauen ließ. Diese Zitadellen, die in „der Verschmelzung von Kunst, Architektur und Philosophie einzigartig" sind – wie Jon Ortner, der berühmte Fotograf der Angkor-Tempel, bemerkte –, wurden in Form von Hindu-Tempeln errichtet. Als die Angkor-Kultur unterging, wurden auch die Tempel verlassen und in der Folgezeit vom Dschungel überwuchert. Trotz der umfangreichen Restaurationsarbeiten sind einige Denkmäler noch immer der Natur überlassen. Wurzeln und Äste alter Kapokbäume und Würgefeigen umschlingen die alten Steine und tragen auf ihre Weise zu der zauberhaft düsteren Atmosphäre von Angkor bei.

Lorsqu'en 1860, le naturaliste français Henri Mouhot a découvert les impressionnantes ruines des temples d'Angkor, il a demandé aux habitants des alentours qui les avait construits. C'est l'œuvre de géants, ont-ils alors répondu. À la fois monumentaux et d'une grande recherche dans les détails, les temples d'Angkor étaient restés prisonniers de la jungle tropicale des siècles durant. La découverte de Mouhot a fait sensation et a entraîné la création, à la fin du 19ᵉ siècle, de l'École française d'Extrême-Orient. Celle-ci essaie de pénétrer les secrets de la puissante dynastie khmère qui a édifié sur ce site plusieurs capitales royales entre les 9ᵉ et 13ᵉ siècles. Ces citadelles, « sans égales dans leur fusion de l'art, de l'architecture et de la philosophie » – comme le dit Jon Ortner, le célèbre photographe des temples d'Angkor –, ont été construites sur le modèle des temples hindouistes. Avec le déclin de la civilisation d'Angkor, la forêt s'est refermée sur les temples laissés à l'abandon. Malgré un travail de restauration mené depuis des décennies, certains monuments subissent encore l'étreinte de la végétation : des racines et des branches de fromagers et de figuiers banians centenaires s'enroulent autour des vieilles pierres, ajoutant à la magie funèbre d'Angkor.

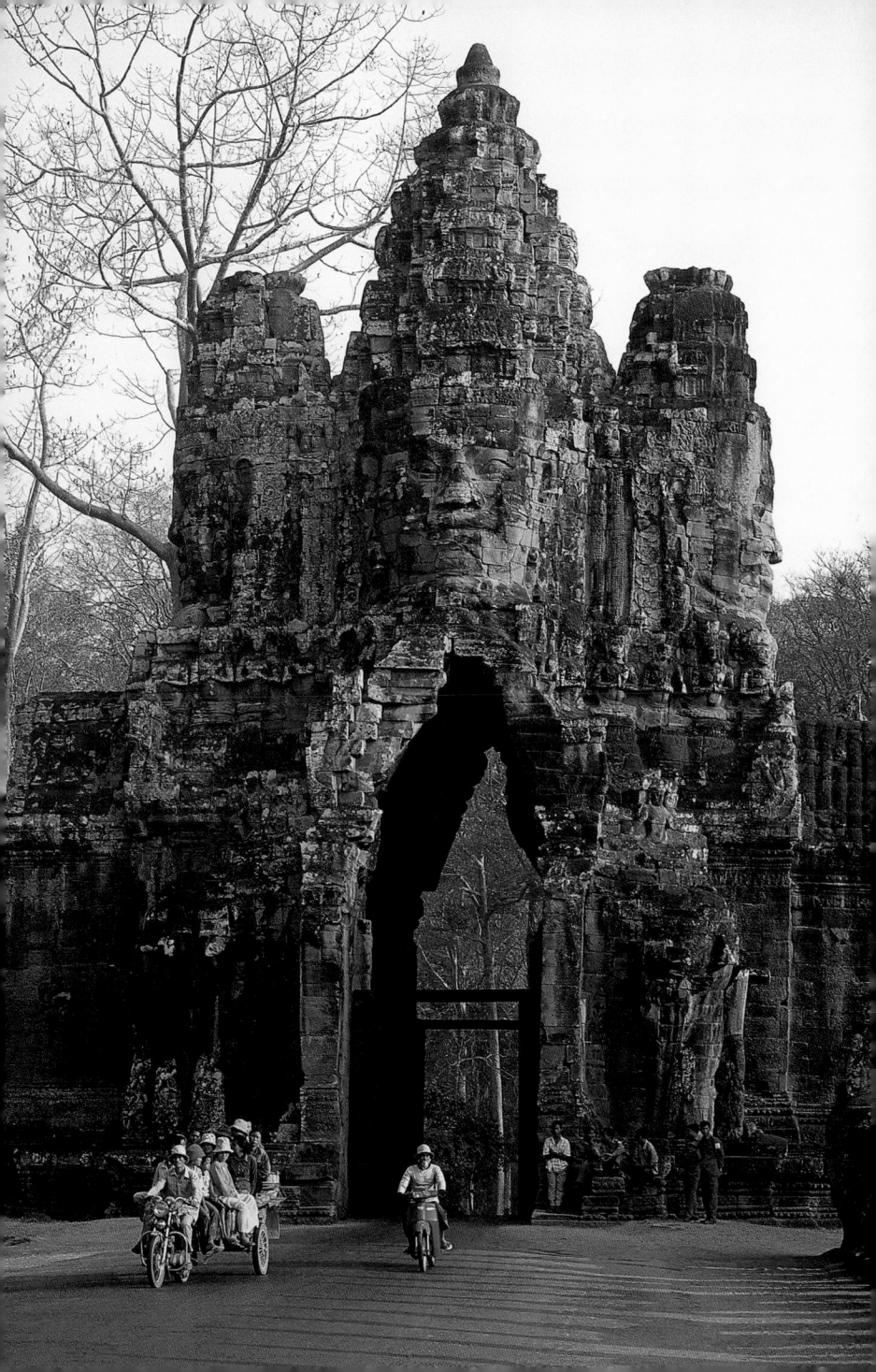

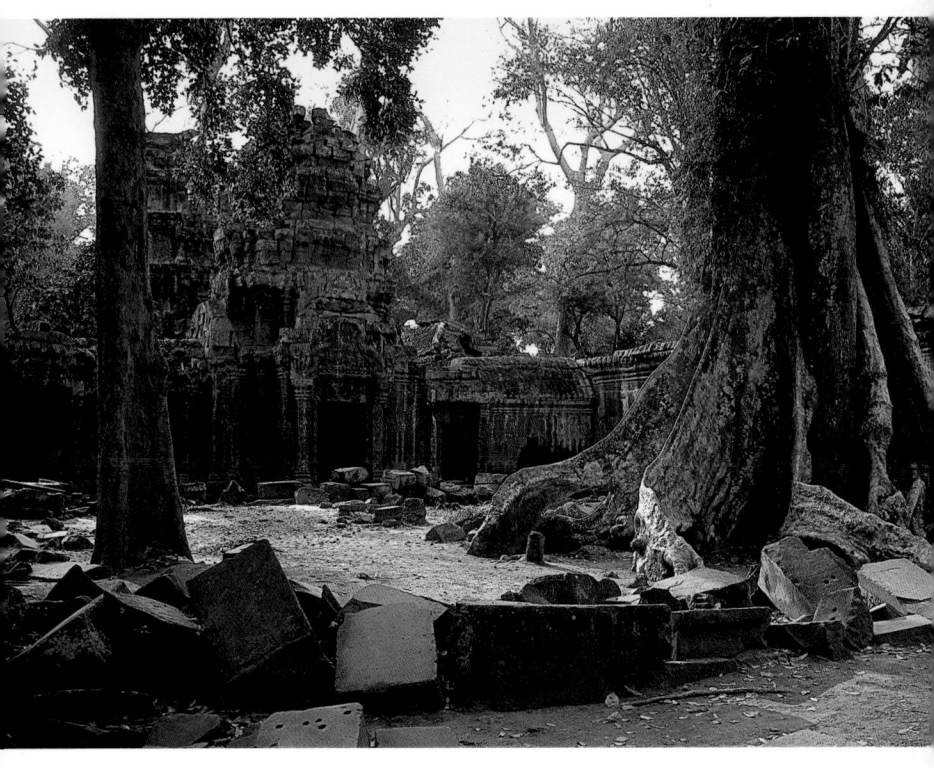

PP. 398-399 The entrance to the
12th-century Buddhist temple of Ta
Prohm. • Eingang zum buddhistischen
Tempel Ta Prohm. • Ta Prohm, l'entrée
du temple bouddhique du 12ᵉ siècle.

P. 401 The south gate of the citadel of
Angkor Thom. • Südliches Stadttor der
Zitadelle von Angkor Thom. • La porte
sud de la citadelle d'Angkor Thom.

→ 200 colossal faces of Avalokiteshvara adorn the Bayon temple. • 200
Avalokiteshvara schmücken den Bayon.
• 200 visages géants des avalokiteswa-
ras ornent le temple du Bayon.

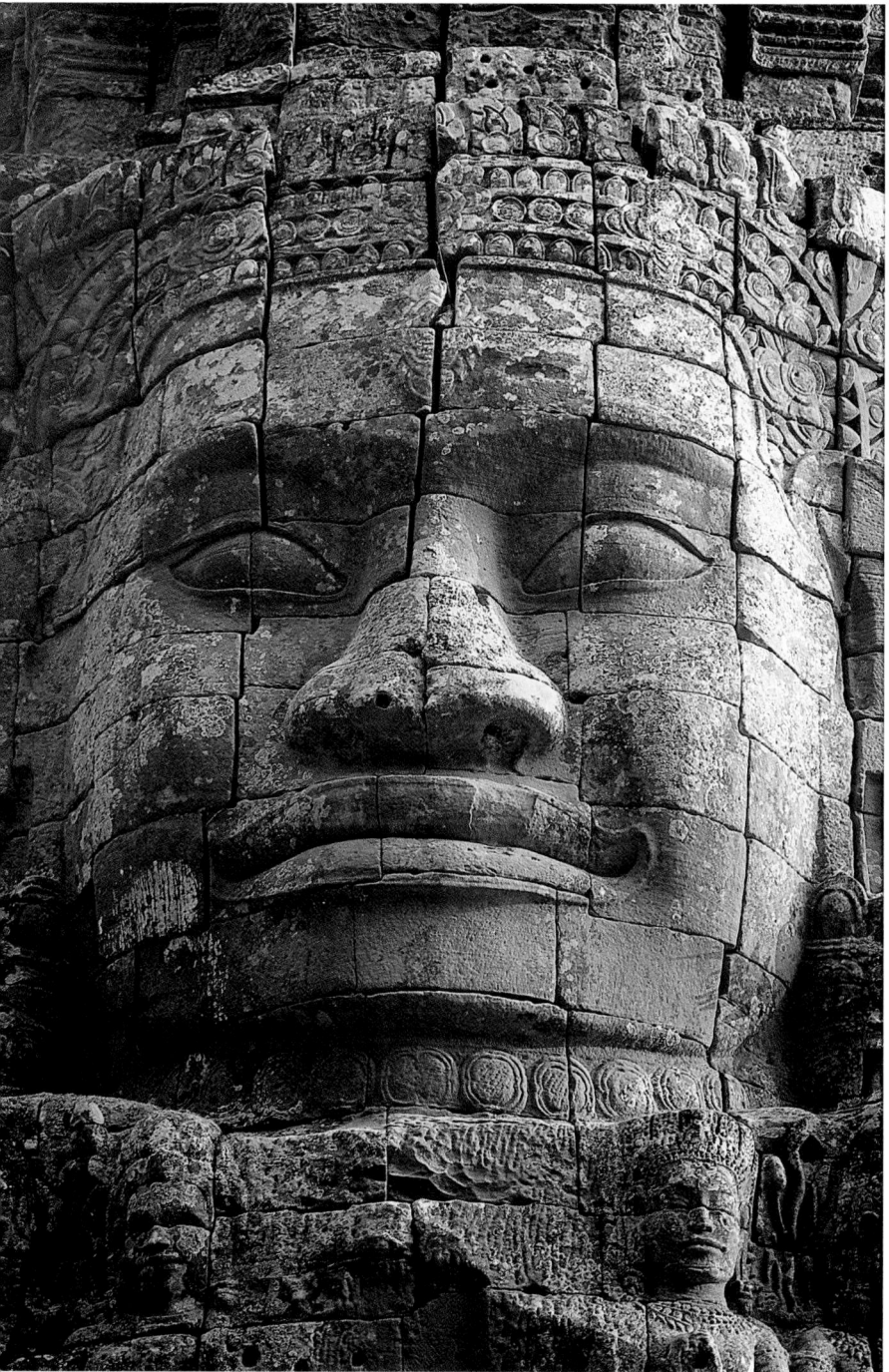

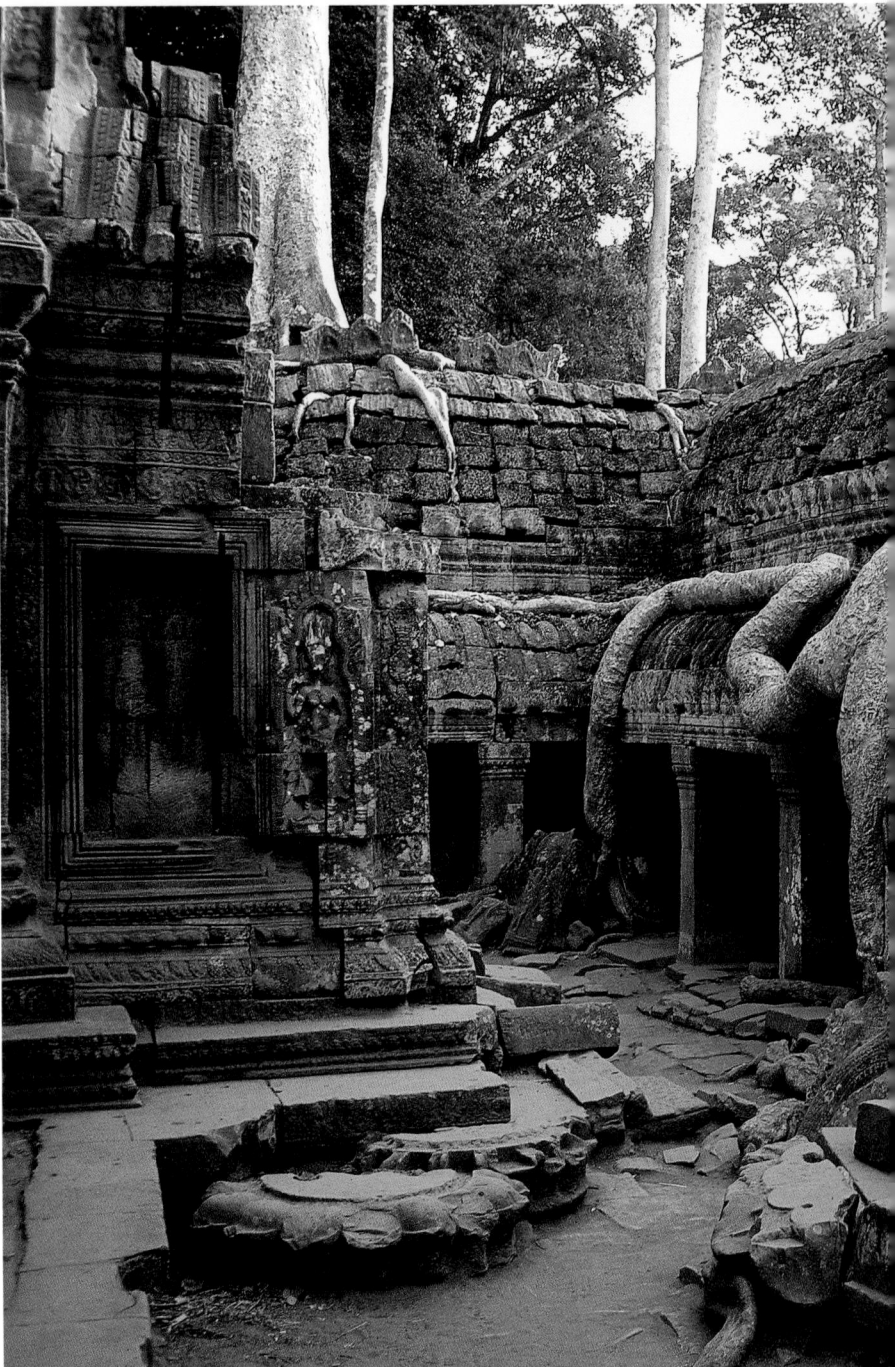

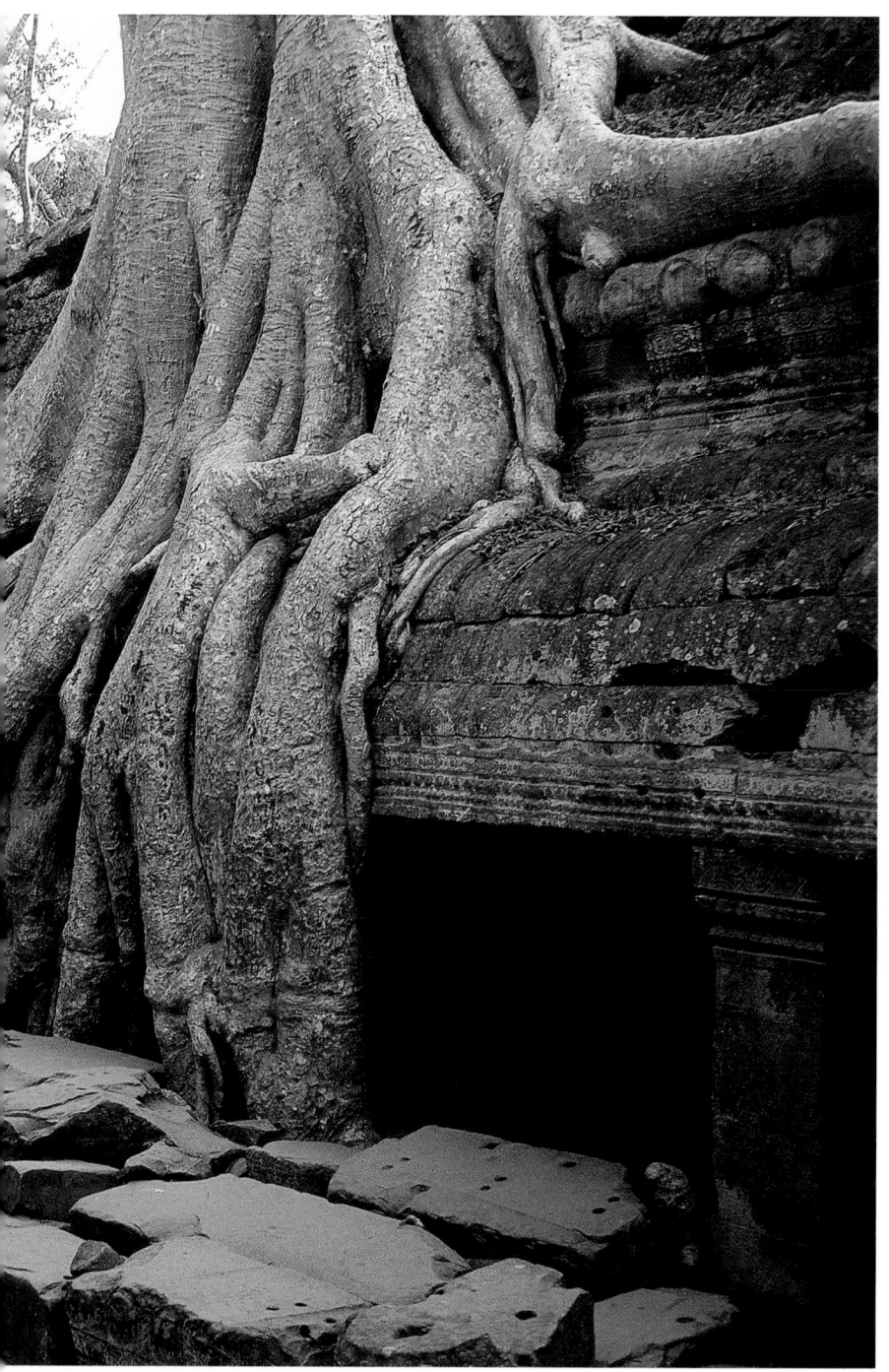

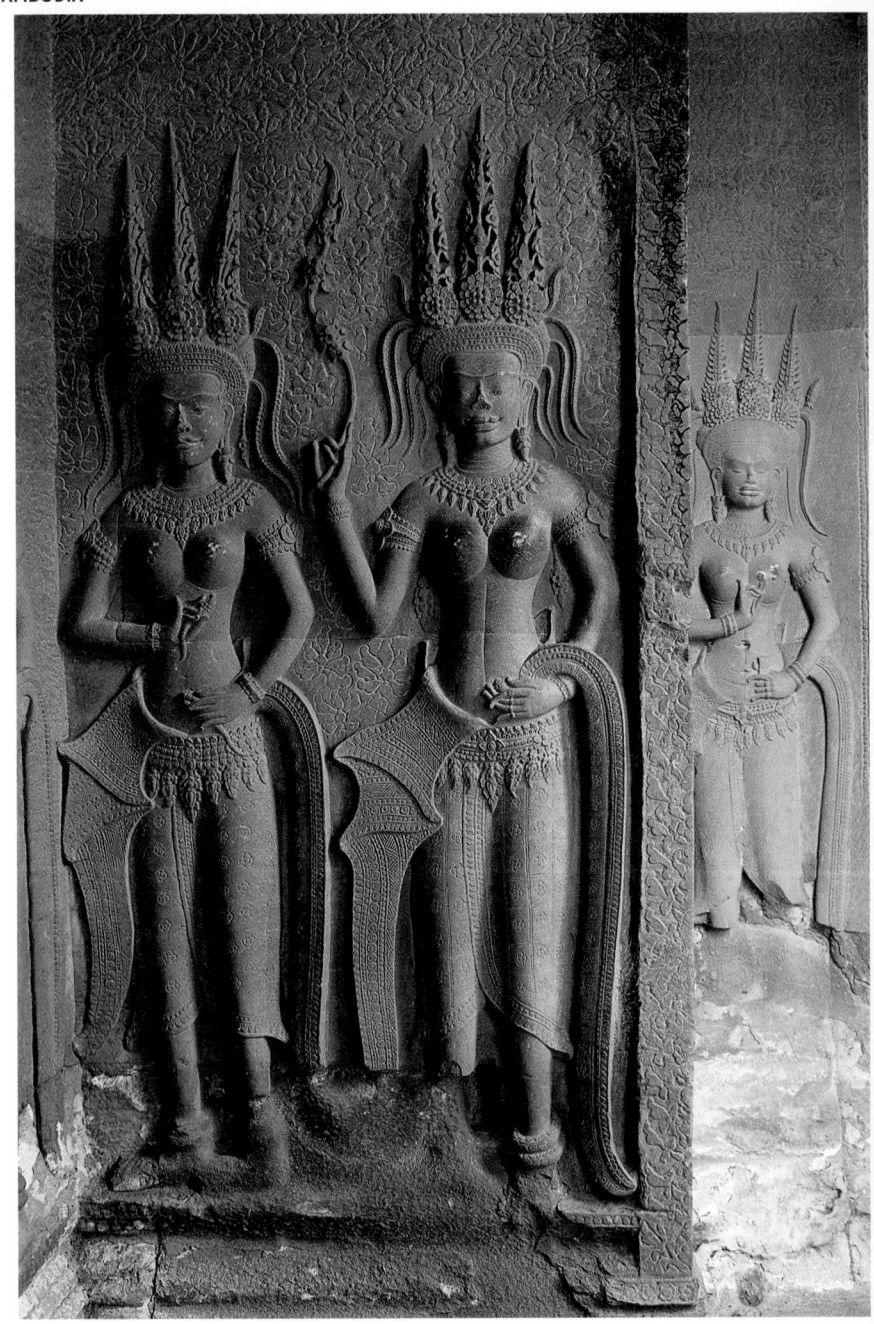

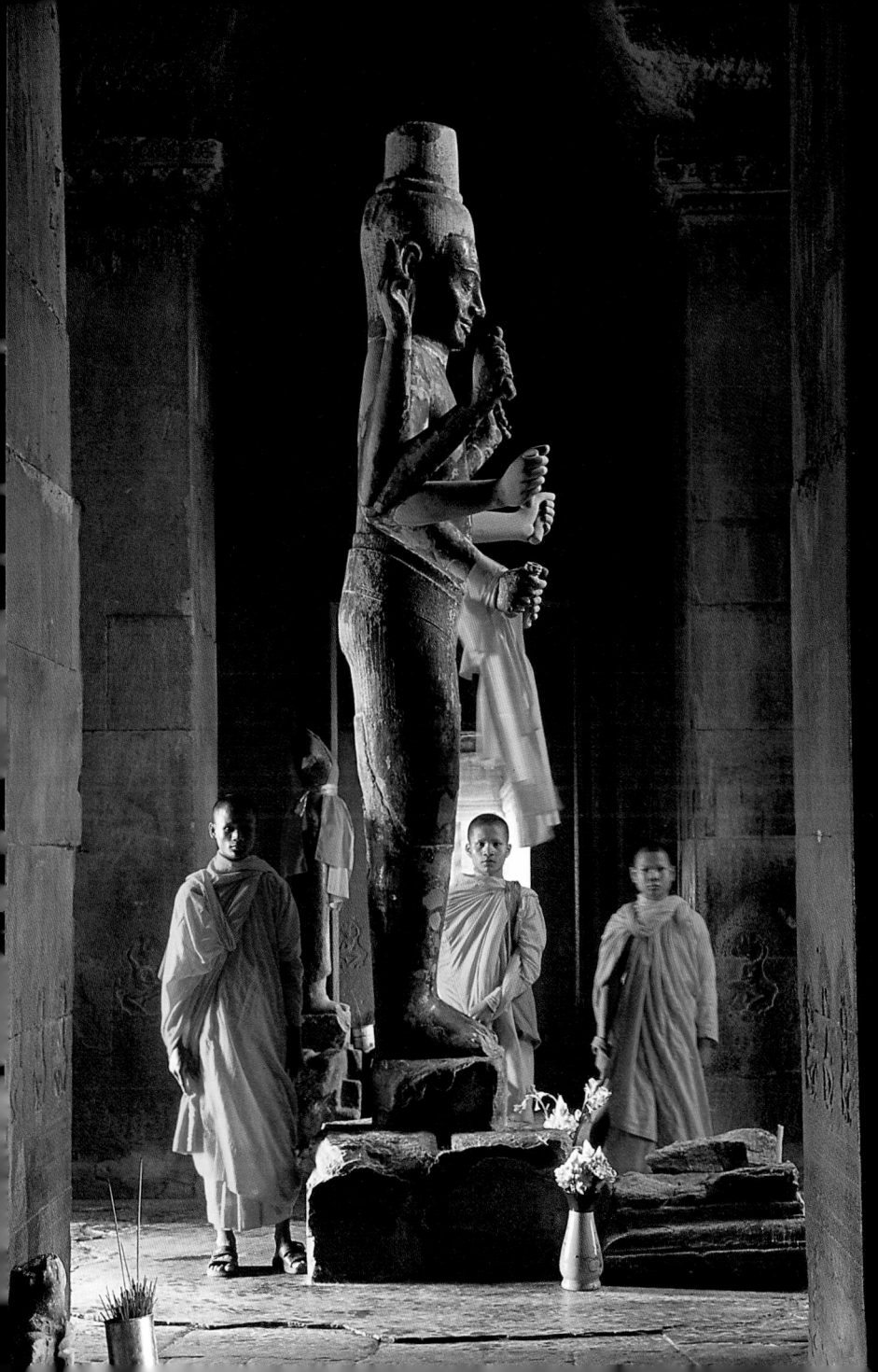

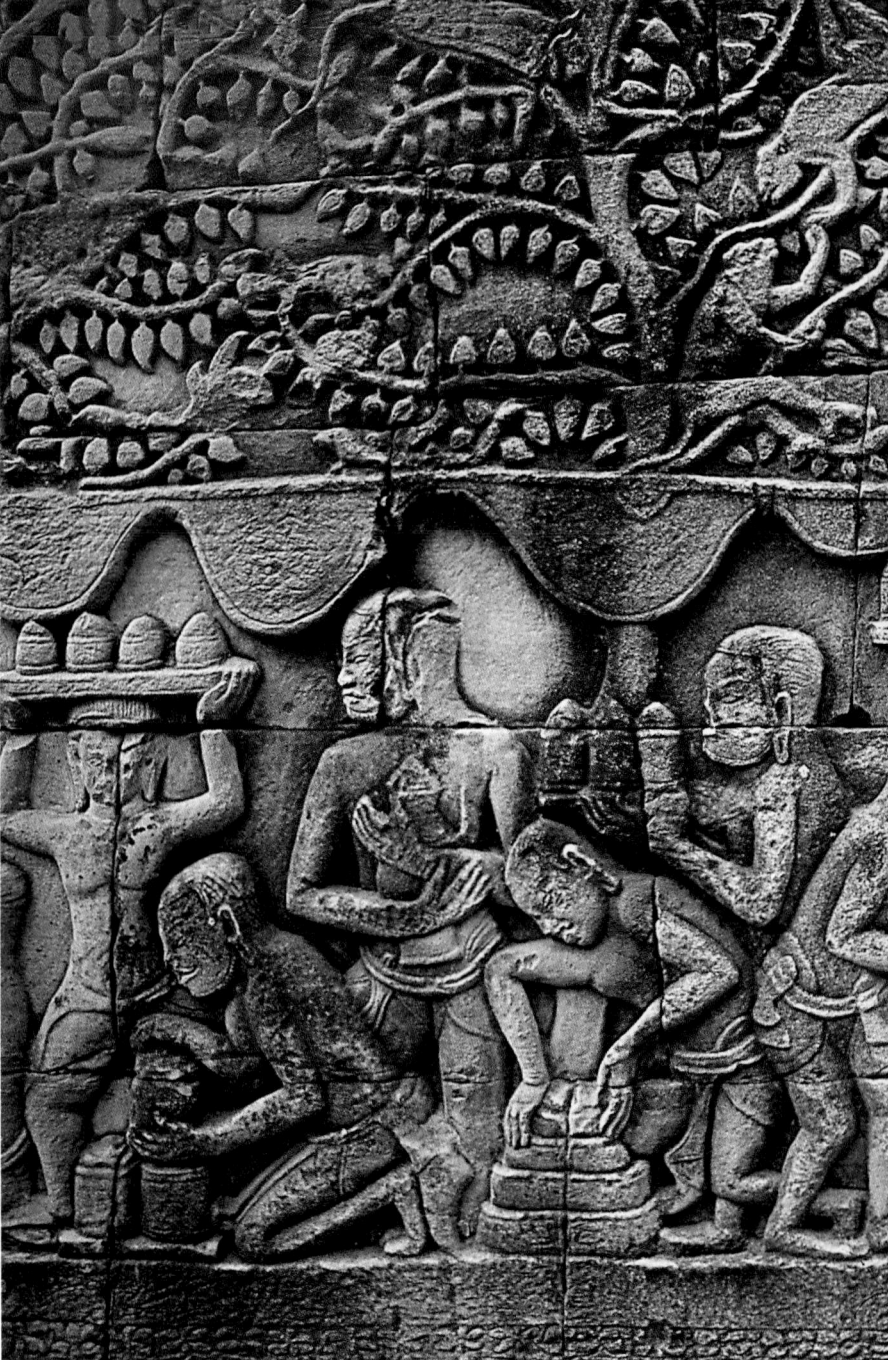

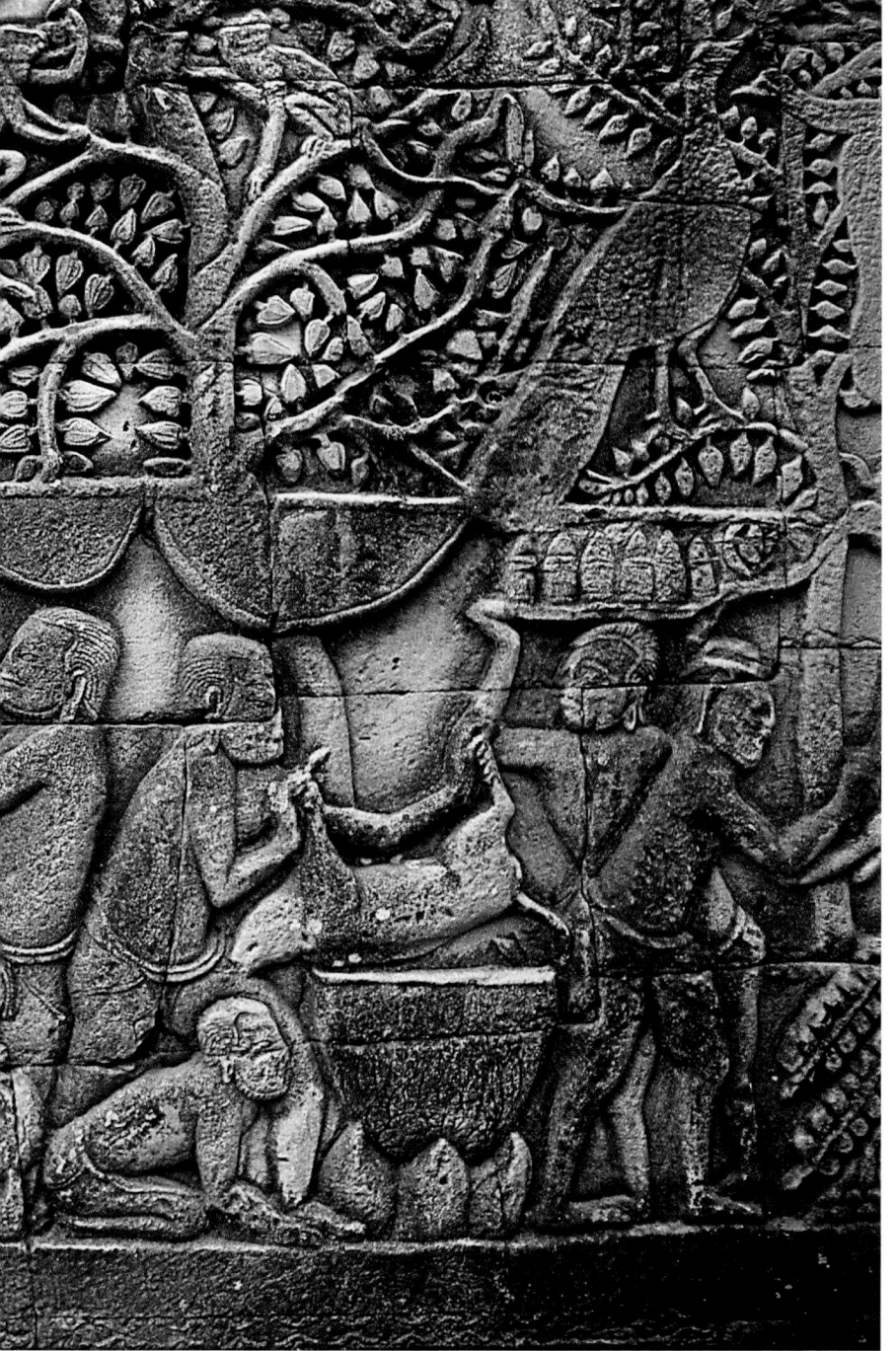

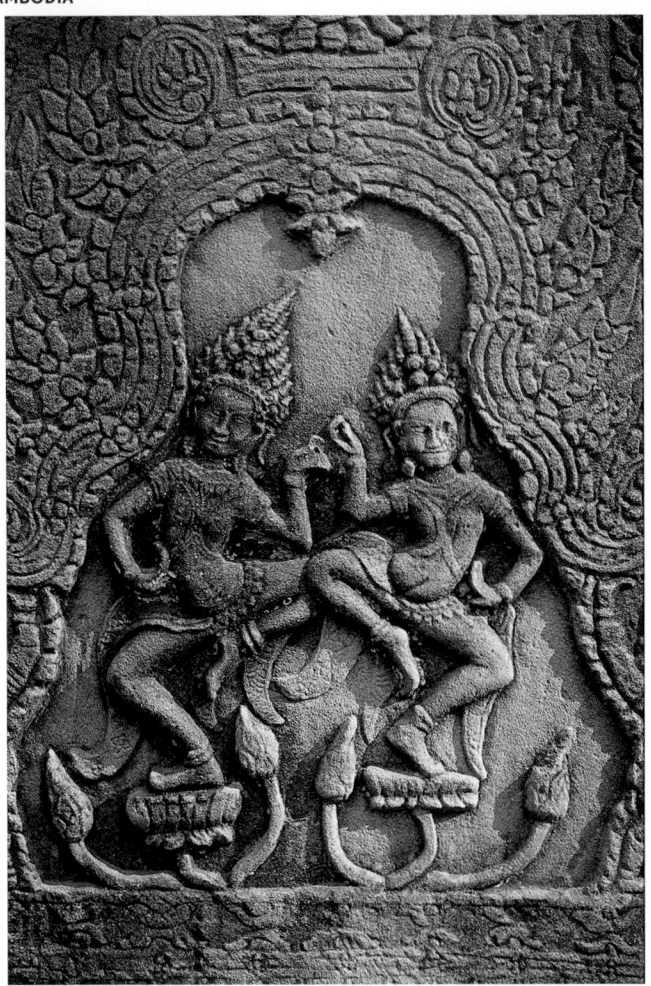

P. 406 and P. 407 A bas-relief of *apsaras*, celestial nymphs, and a statue of the Hindu god Vishnu. • *Apsaras*, weibliche Geister, im Flachrelief sowie eine Statue des Hindugottes Vishnu in Angkor Wat. • Un bas-relief représentant des *apsaras*, nymphes célestes, et une statue du dieu hindouiste Vishnou.

PP. 408–409 This bas-relief on the outer gallery of the Bayon temple shows cooks preparing an elaborate feast. • Flachreliefs der äußeren Galerie des

Bayon zeigen Köche bei der Vorbereitung eines großen Festes. • Sur ce bas-relief visible dans la galerie extérieure du temple du Bayon, des cuisiniers s'affairent à la préparation d'un festin.

↑ Friezes of exquisitely jeweled *devatas*, goddesses, and celestial dancers with ornamental headdresses line the galleries of the temple. • Weitere Flachreliefs der Bayon-Galerien präsentieren *devatas*, Göttinnen mit erlesenem Schmuck, sowie himmlische

Tänzerinnen mit verzierten Kopfbedeckungen. • Les galeries du Bayon sont ornées tout du long de frises représentant des *devatas* (divinités) parées de bijoux précieux et des danseuses célestes portant des coiffes ornementales.

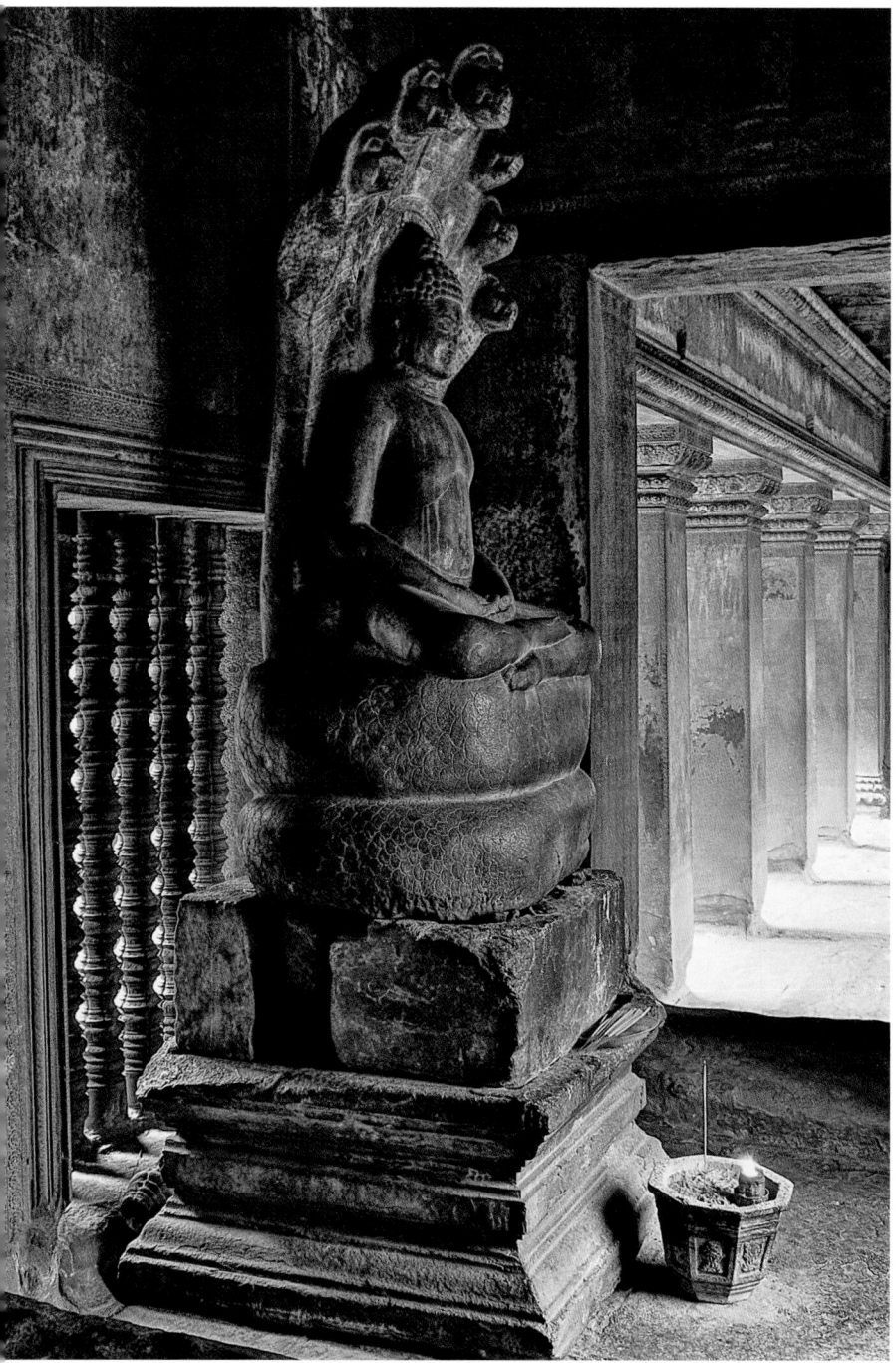

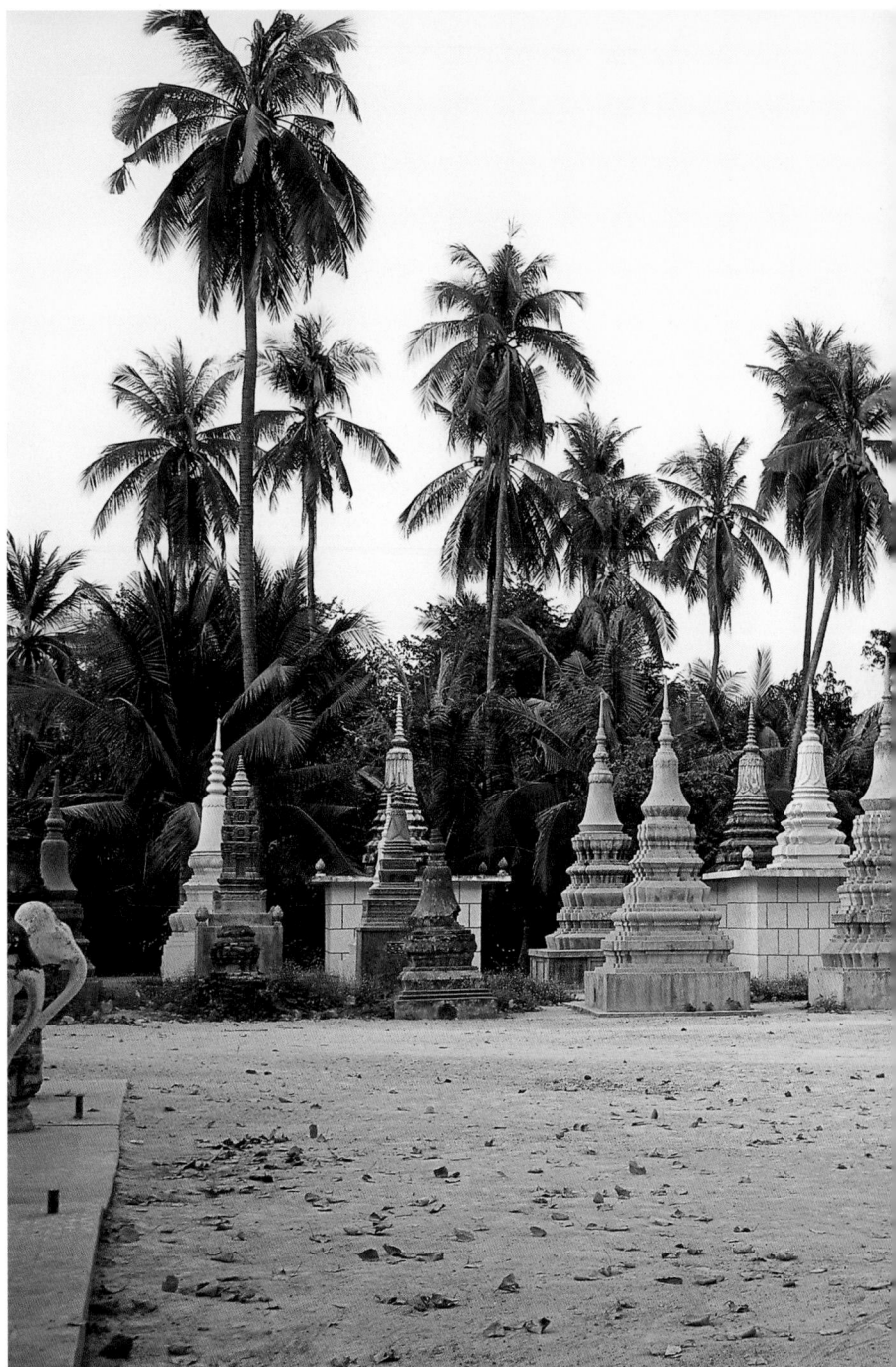

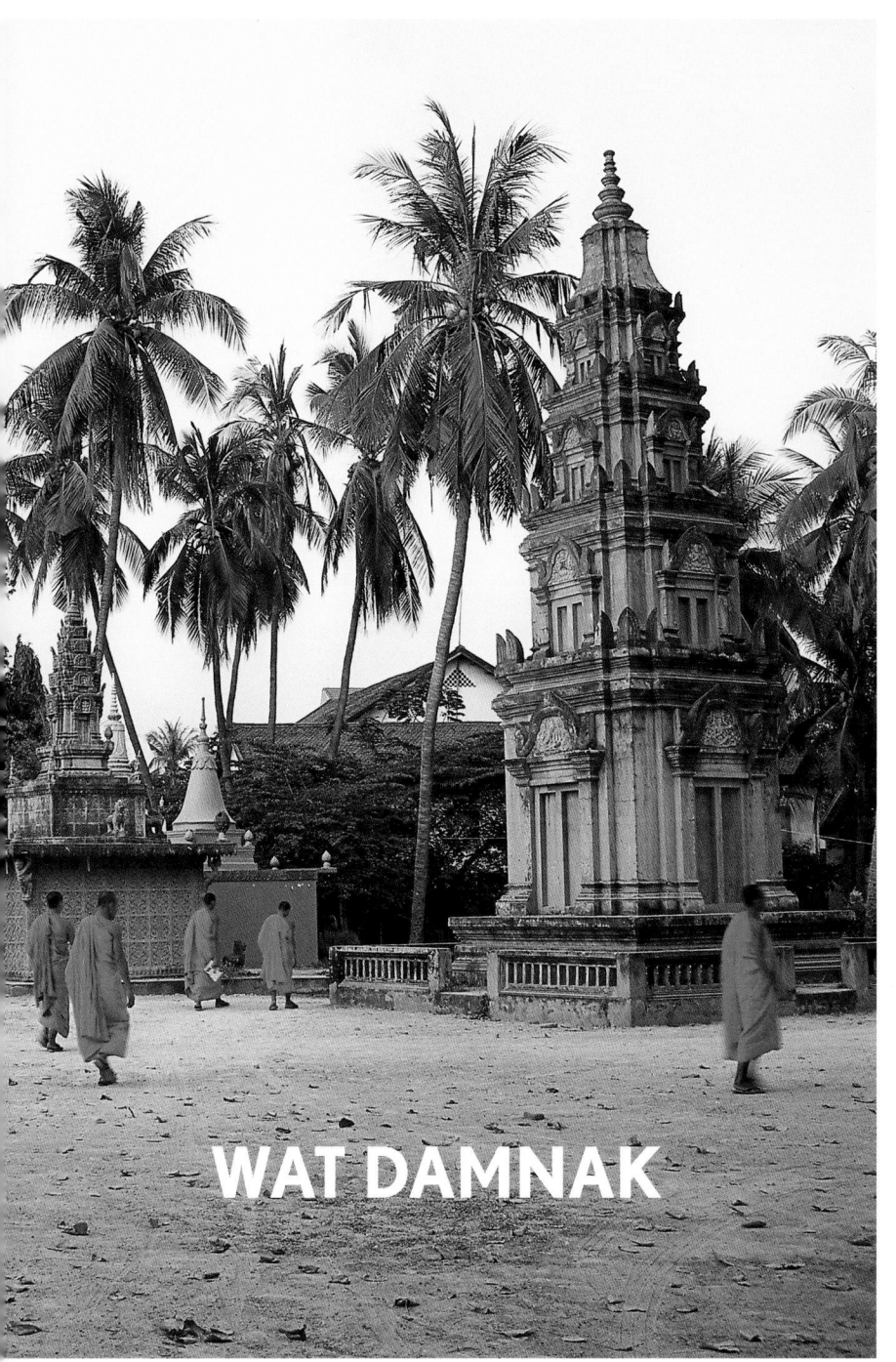

WAT DAMNAK

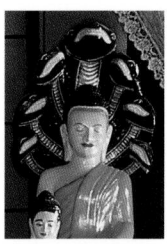

WAT DAMNAK
SIEM REAP
CAMBODIA

Wat Damnak is one of the principal pagodas in Siem Reap, a temple which has undergone a remarkable resurgence in recent years to incorporate an impressive Center for Khmer Studies. The word *wat* does not necessarily mean only a temple; it can refer to a complex of buildings that include the main temple, a monastery and wide collection of stupas, often a school and sometimes a cremation ground. In fact a wat can be a self-contained microcosm of the Buddhist way in its purest form – of living and learning, prayer, renunciation and salvation. A wat compound may be entered from any side, but the main entrance to the temple is from the east; the central image of the Buddha always faces eastwards – as did the Buddha at the moment of his enlightenment. Wat Damnak dates from the early 20th century and was mercifully left intact by the Khmer Rouge. The plain interior of the inner sanctum, its simple colonial-style buildings and cluster of old stupas, above all its atmosphere of modern scholarship, make it a bridge between the old and new.

Wat Damnak, eine der bedeutendsten Pagoden in Siem Reap, erfährt als Tempel seit einiger Zeit zunehmendes Interesse, seit dort ein renommiertes Khmer-Forschungszentrum eingerichtet wurde. Das Wort Wat bedeutet nicht zwangsläufig Tempel, sondern kann sich auch auf einen Gebäudekomplex mit Haupttempel, einem Kloster und zahlreichen Stupas beziehen. Häufig wurden auch noch eine Schule und ein Einäscherungsplatz angeschlossen. Tatsächlich kann ein Wat als ein in sich geschlossener Mikrokosmos des Buddhismus in Reinform betrachtet werden, wo sich das Leben um Lehre, Gebet, Entsagung und Heil dreht. Man kann einen Wat von allen Seiten betreten, der Haupteingang wird jedoch immer im Osten liegen, so wie auch die bedeutendste Buddha-Statue stets nach Osten blickt – wie einst Buddha im Augenblick seiner Erleuchtung. Wat Damnak wurde im frühen 20. Jahrhundert erbaut und glücklicherweise von den Roten Khmer verschont. Das karge zentrale Heiligtum mit den schlichten Gebäuden im Kolonialstil und zahlreichen alten Stupas strahlt eine Atmosphäre moderner Gelehrsamkeit aus, eine Verbindung von Alt und Neu.

Vat Damnak est l'une des principales pagodes de Siem Reap. Ce lieu de culte a connu une renaissance formidable et abrite désormais un impressionnant centre d'études khmères. Le mot *vat* ne signifie pas uniquement temple mais peut faire référence à un complexe comprenant un temple principal, un monastère, une kyrielle de stupas et, souvent une école, plus rarement un pavillon de crémation. En fait, un vat est souvent un microcosme du bouddhisme : le mode de vie, l'étude, la prière, le renoncement et le salut y sont visibles dans la plus pure tradition. Si les ensembles bouddhiques sont ouverts à tous les vents, l'entrée principale du temple est toujours orientée à l'est et la grande statue de Bouddha regarde toujours dans cette direction, comme jadis Bouddha au moment de son Éveil. Vat Damnak, construit au début du 20ᵉ siècle, a fort heureusement été épargné par les Khmers rouges. L'intérieur sobre du sanctuaire principal, ses bâtiments de style colonial et la ribambelle de stupas anciens, et surtout son atmosphère studieuse moderne font de lui un pont entre l'ancien et le moderne.

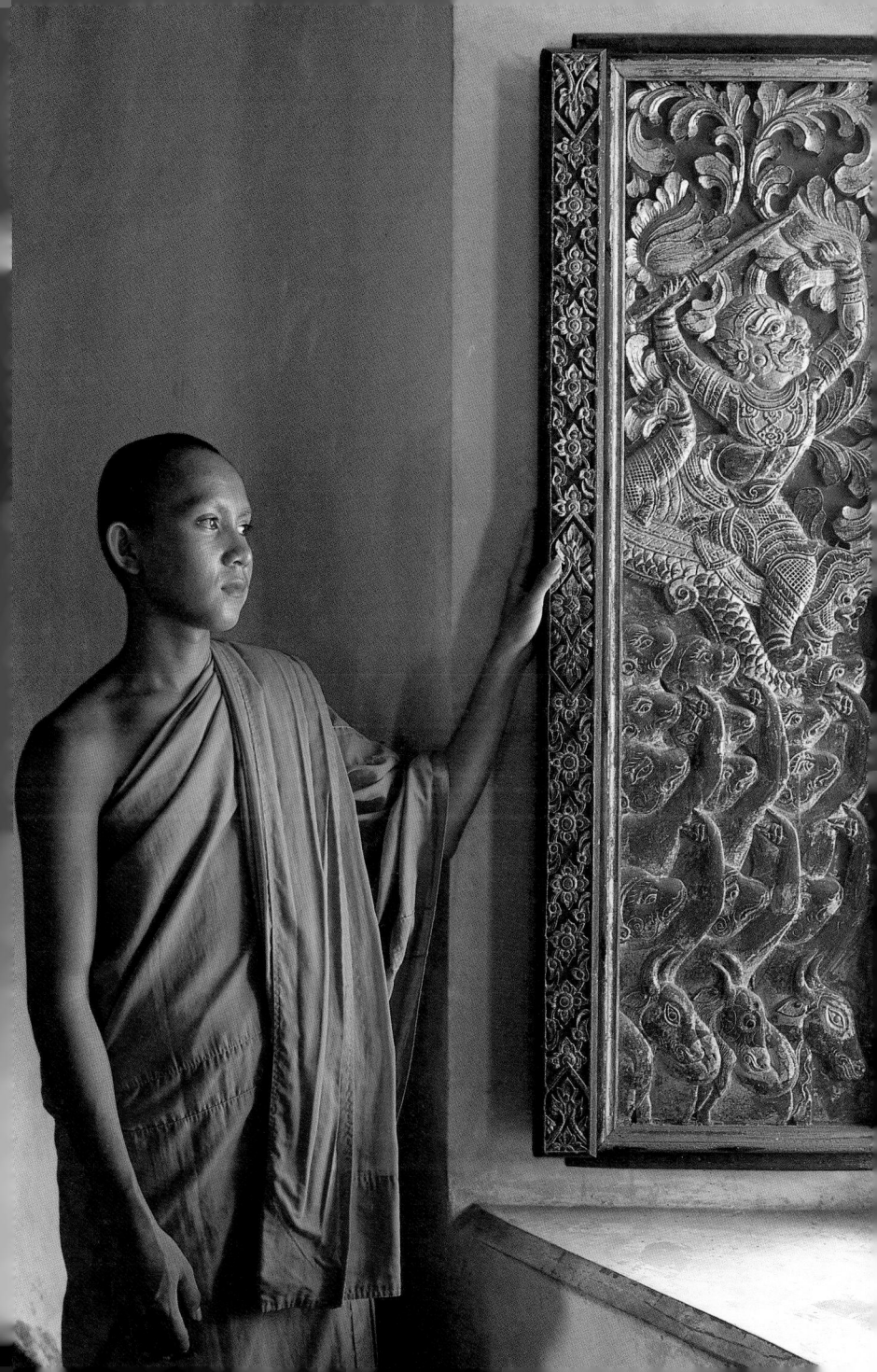

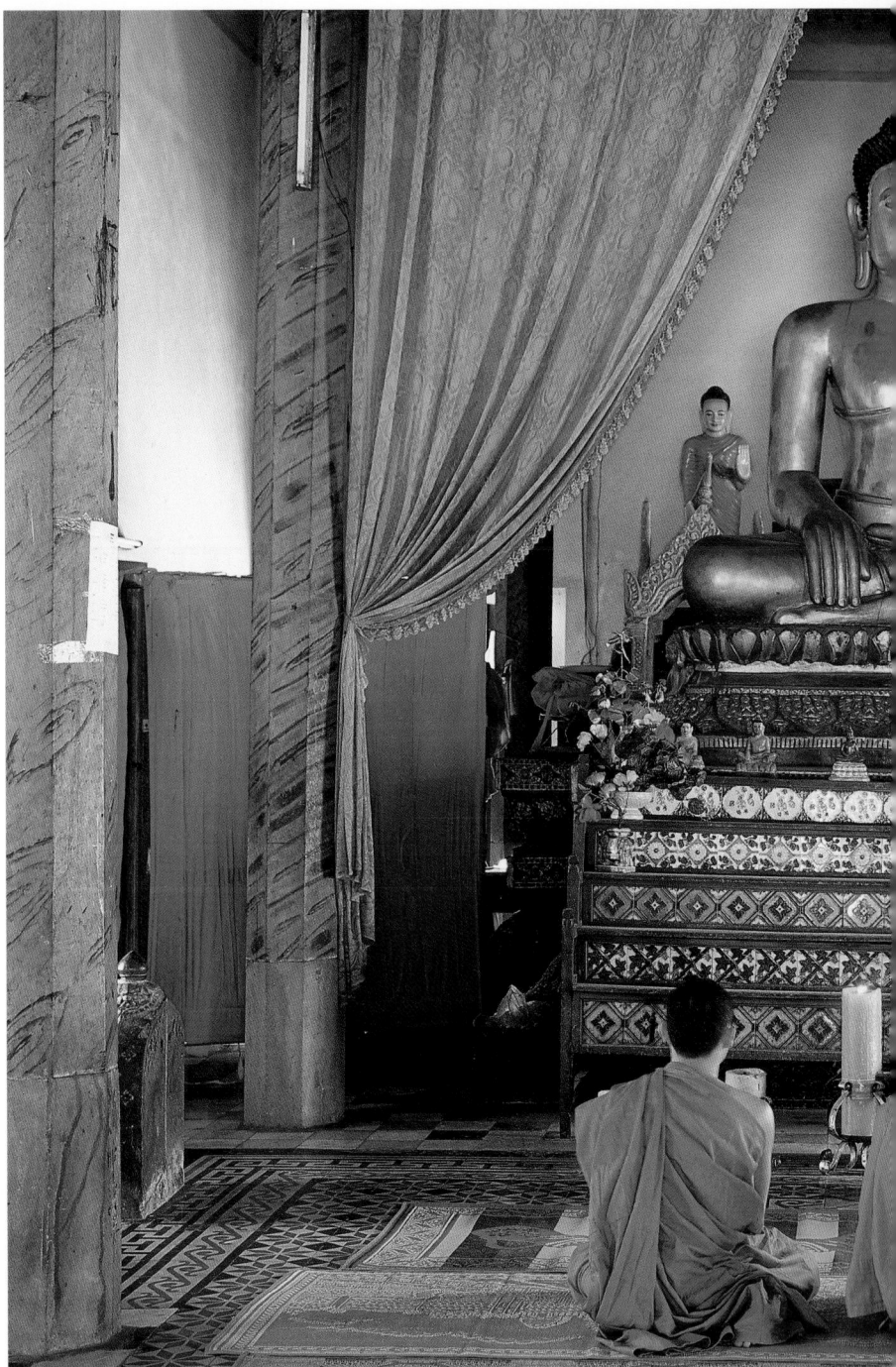

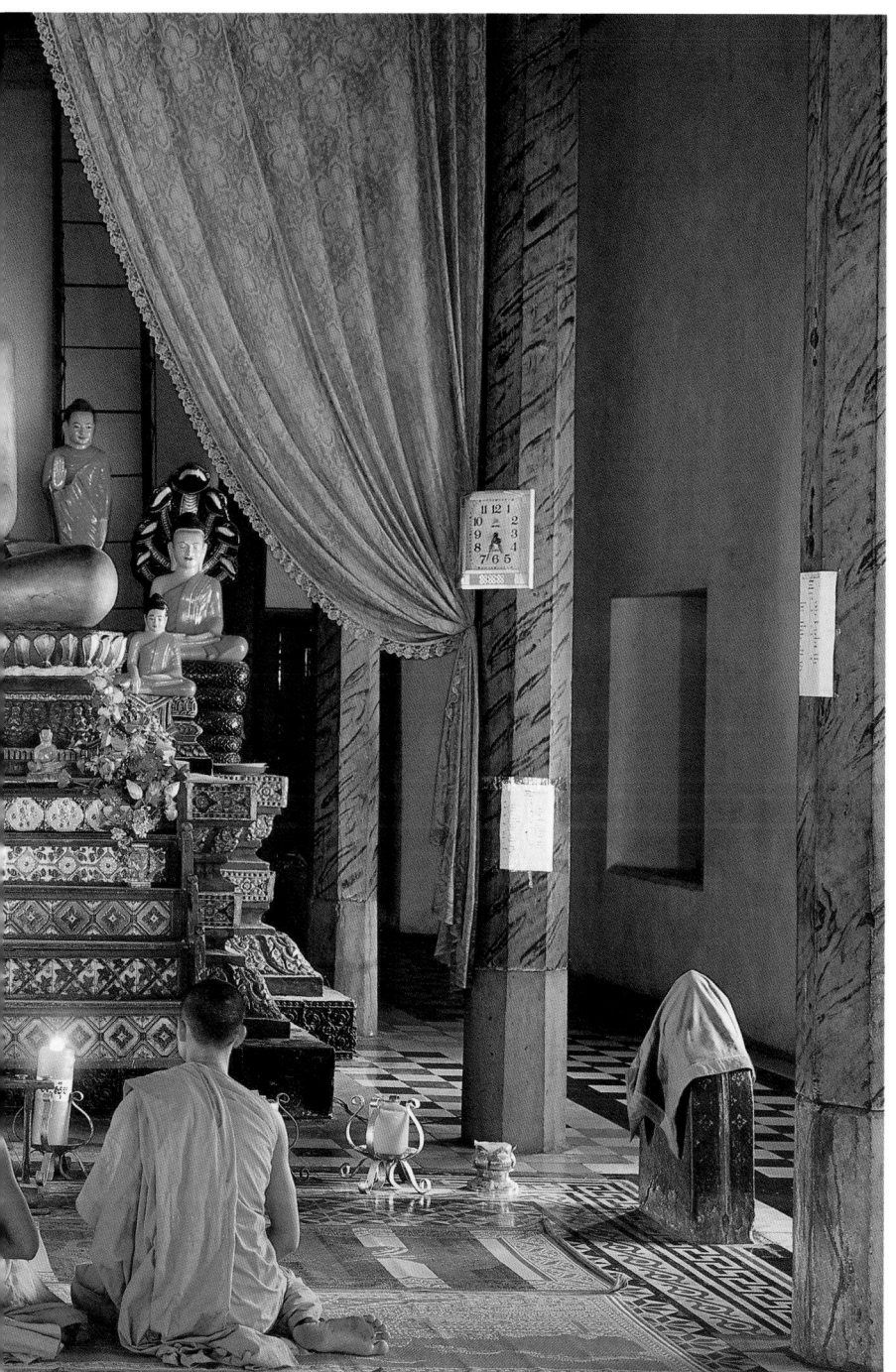

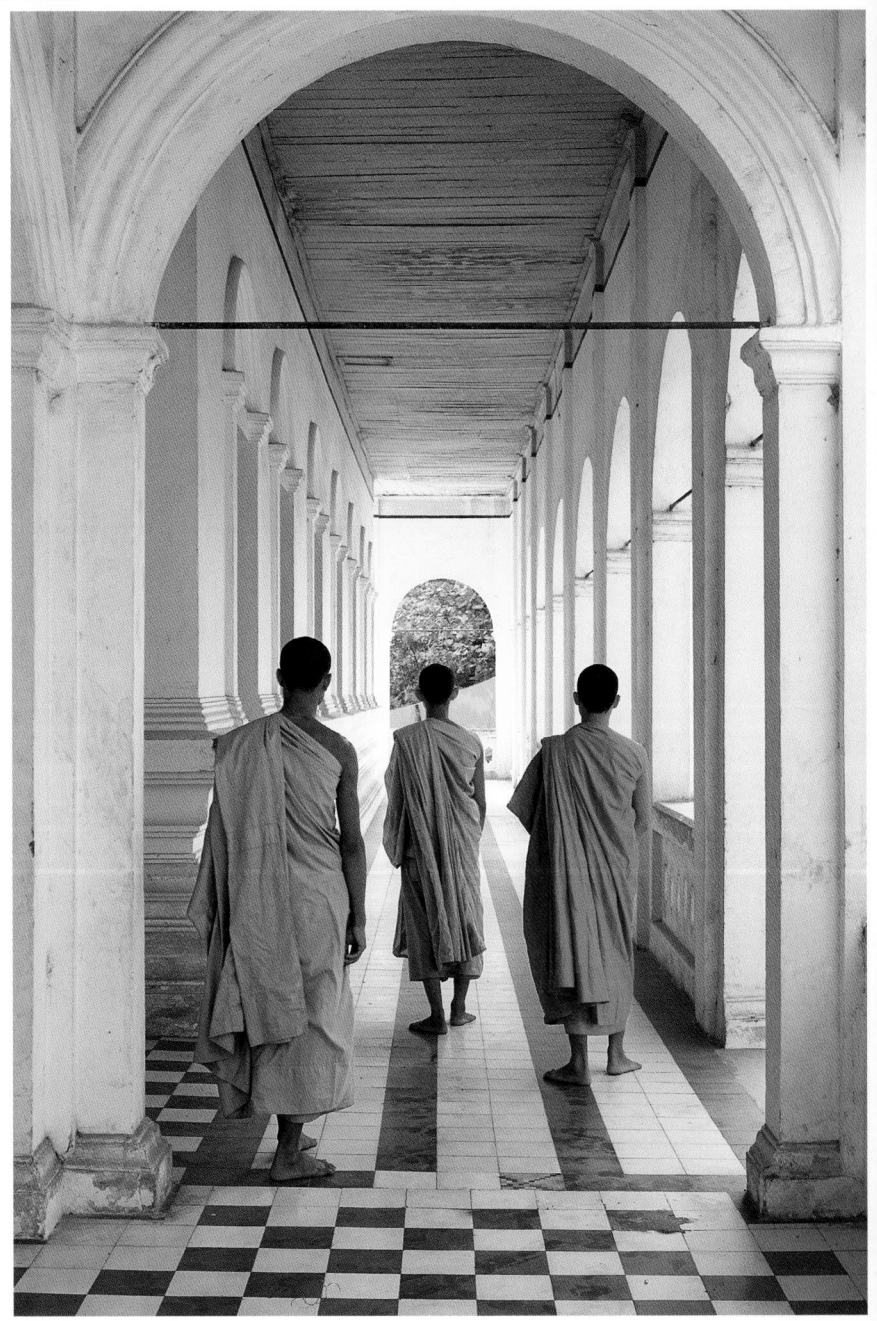

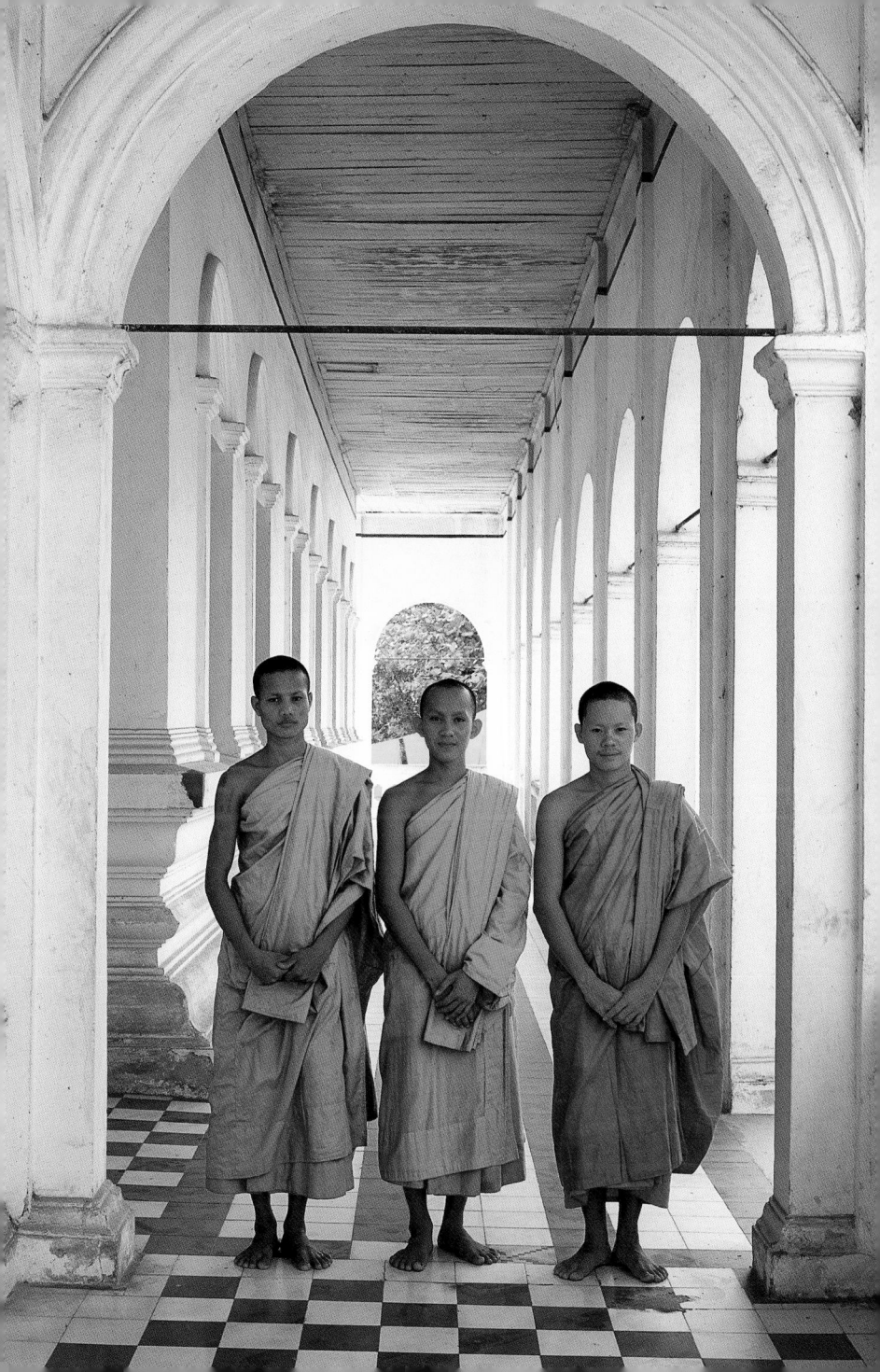

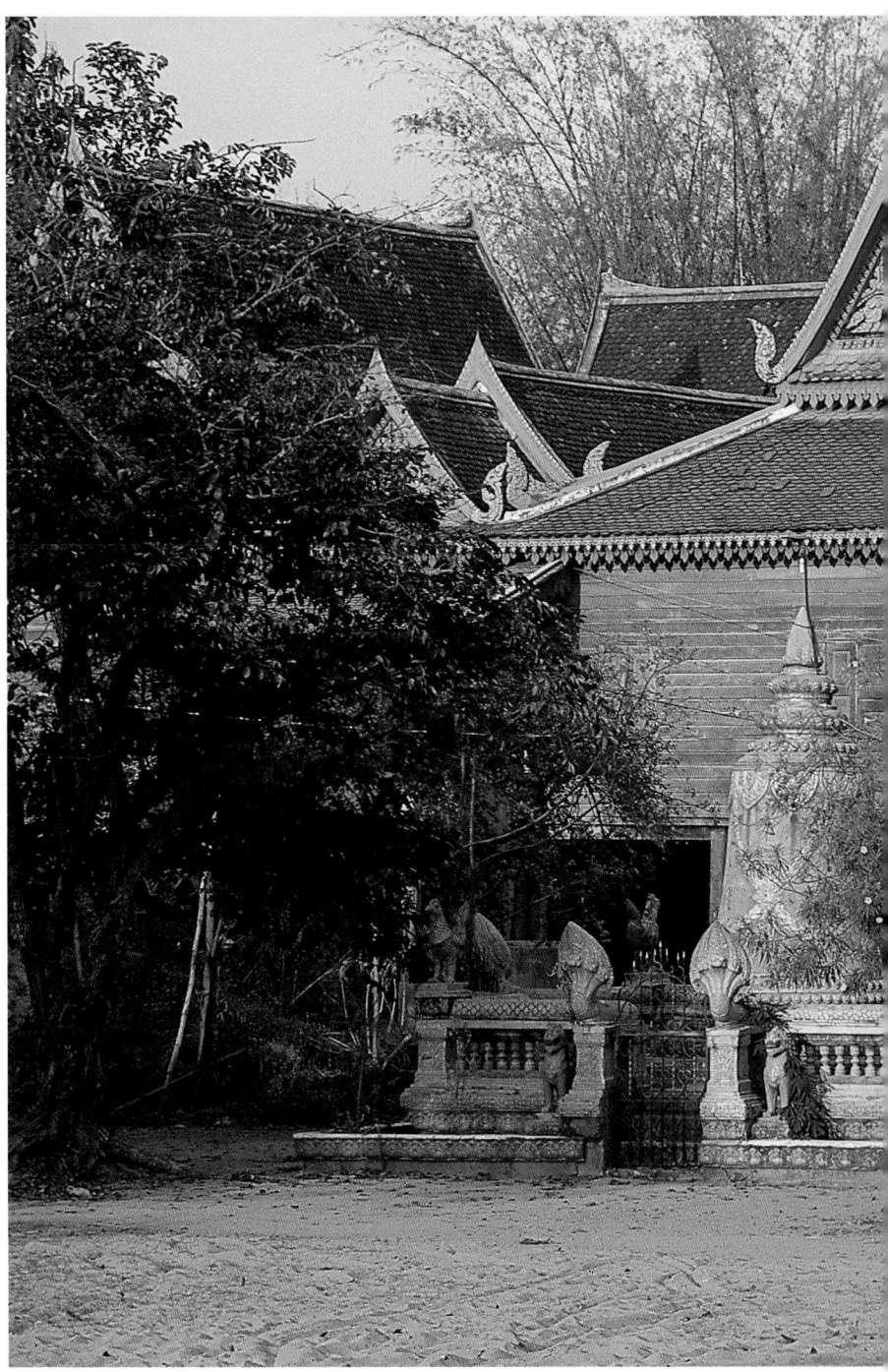

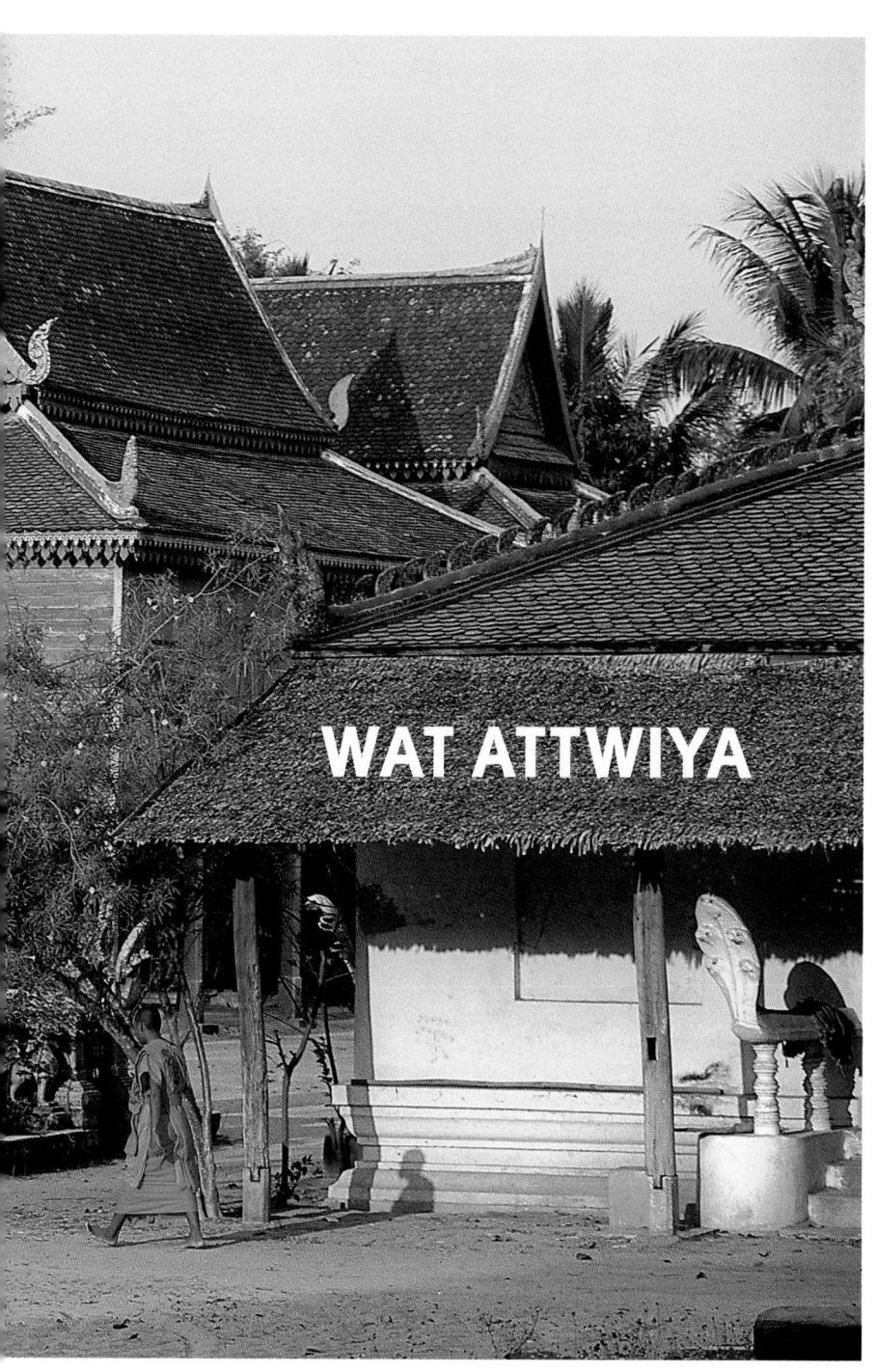

WAT ATTWIYA

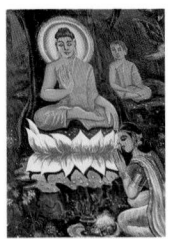

WAT ATTWIYA
SIEM REAP
CAMBODIA

Wat Attwiya is beautifully situated at the end of a winding road that runs alongside a shady stream before emerging into lush open countryside. After the grandeur of Angkor's many sites of antiquity, arriving at a relatively modern temple such as Wat Attwiya is to confront the continuity of a centuries-old unbroken Khmer tradition. The temple was founded around 1935 but was completely destroyed by the Khmer Rouge. It was only reconstructed in 1980. Behind the wat are the ruins of a large Angkor-era temple, a tranquil corner to reflect upon the power of Buddhism to triumph over the vicissitudes of a thousand years including some of the horrors of the previous century. About 25 monks live at Wat Attwiya and almost an equal number of novices under the age of 21. The canopy of trailing flags in the inner sanctum is said to convey prayers to heaven, carrying the souls of worshippers alongside. But perhaps the great joy of Wat Attwiya is a walk in the ruins: anonymous and rarely visited, they are witness to the rise and ebb of civilizations.

Wat Attwiya liegt idyllisch am Ende einer kurvigen Straße, die entlang eines schattigen Flüsschens verläuft, bevor es sich in der üppigen Vegetation der Landschaft verliert. Nach dem großartigen Eindruck, den Angkors antike Sehenswürdigkeiten hinterlassen, begegnet man in dem relativ modernen Tempel Wat Attwiya der ungebrochenen jahrhundertealten Tradition der Khmer. Der 1935 gegründete Tempel wurde von den Roten Khmer bis auf die Grundmauern zerstört und erst 1980 wieder aufgebaut. Hinter dem Wat liegen die Trümmer eines großen Tempels aus der Angkorzeit – ein geeignetes Plätzchen zum Nachdenken über die Kraft des Buddhismus, der über die Gräueltaten von tausend Jahren, insbesondere des letzten Jahrhunderts, triumphiert hat. In Wat Attwiya leben etwa fünfundzwanzig Mönche und fast ebenso viele Novizen unter einundzwanzig Jahren. Die vom Vordach herunterhängenden Gebetsfahnen im zentralen Heiligtum sollen Gebete in den Himmel tragen und gleichzeitig die Seelen der Gläubigen mitnehmen. Am meisten jedoch lohnt ein Spaziergang durch die Ruinen von Wat Attwiya, denn sie bezeugen namenlos und unbeachtet das Kommen und Gehen der Kulturen.

C'est au bout d'une route en lacets épousant le cours ombragé d'une rivière que s'élève Vat Attwiya, dans une plaine luxuriante. Après la magnificence et la profusion des sites antiques d'Angkor, la modernité relative de ce temple s'inscrit dans la continuité de la tradition khmère. Erigé vers 1935, puis complètement détruit par les Khmers rouges, il n'a été reconstruit qu'en 1980. Derrière le vat, on peut voir les ruines d'un grand temple datant de l'époque d'Angkor. Cet endroit paisible invite à réfléchir sur l'aptitude du bouddhisme à triompher des vicissitudes d'un millénaire, et plus particulièrement des tragédies du siècle écoulé. Vat Attwiya est habité par environ 25 moines et un nombre à peu près égal de novices âgés de moins de 21 ans. Les bannières formant une voûte dans le sanctuaire intérieur sont censées emmener les prières et les âmes des fidèles vers les cieux. Mais à Vat Attwiya, il faut surtout se promener dans les ruines : loin des sentiers battus, elles témoignent de la grandeur et du déclin des civilisations.

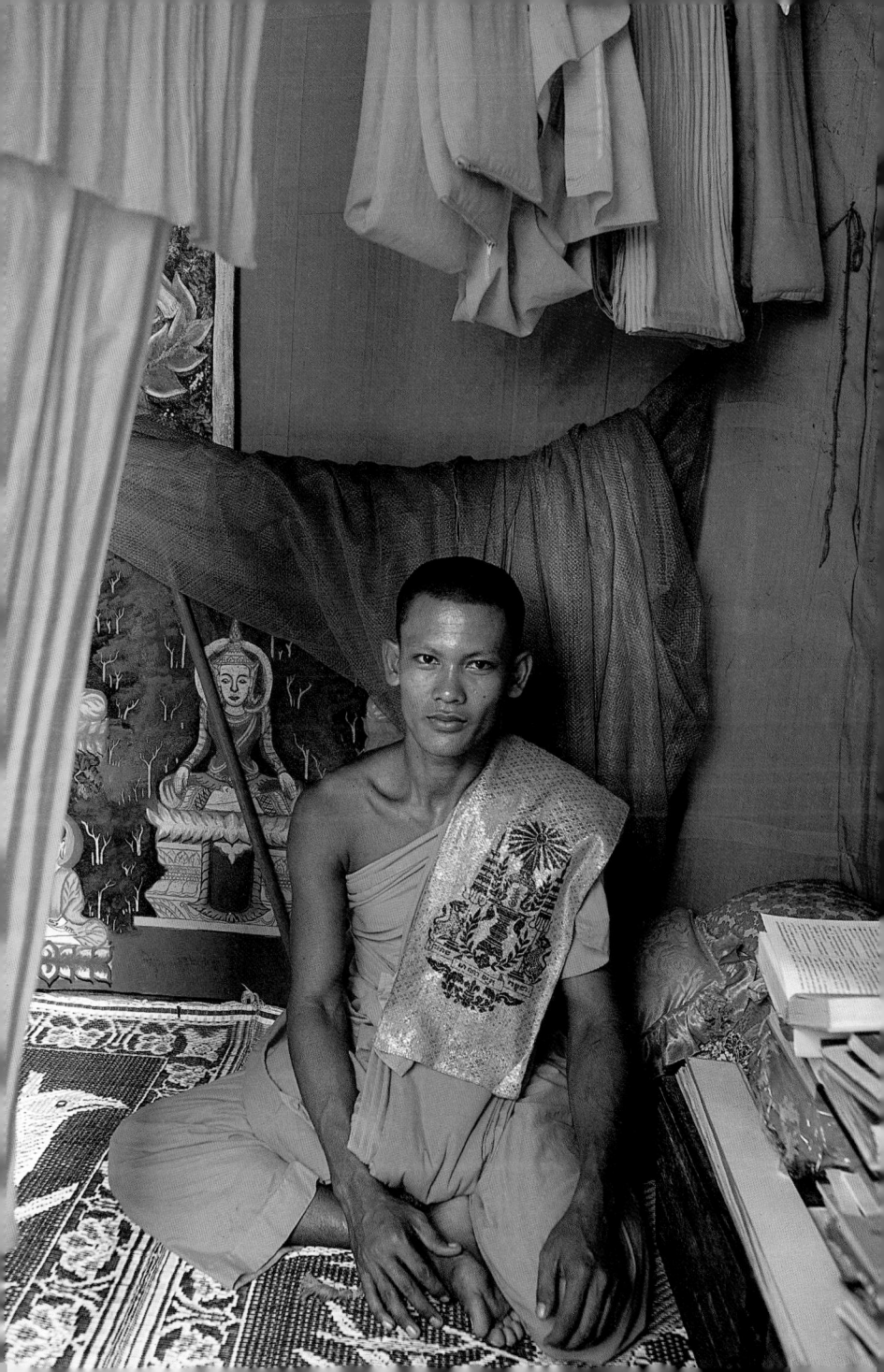

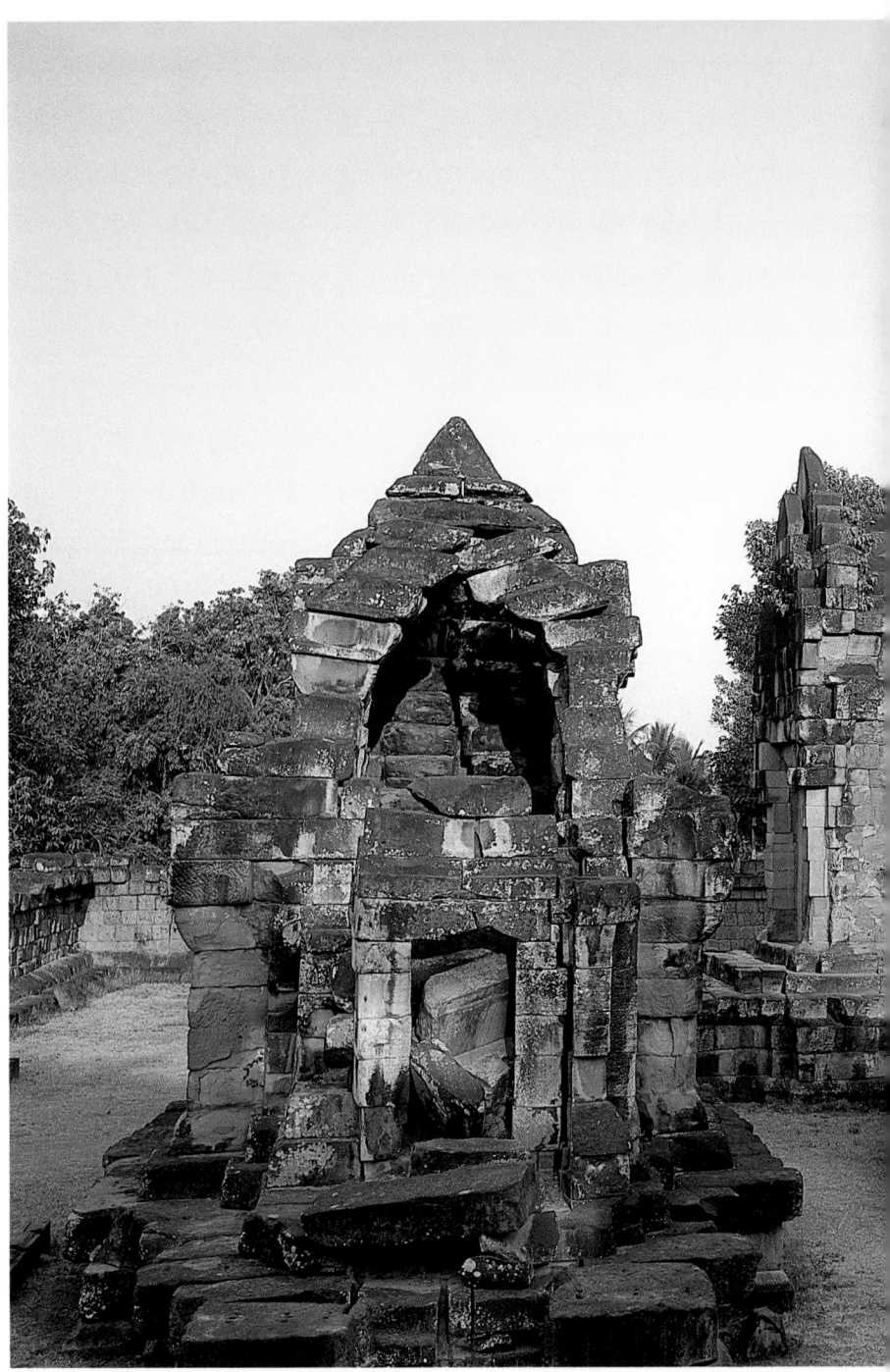

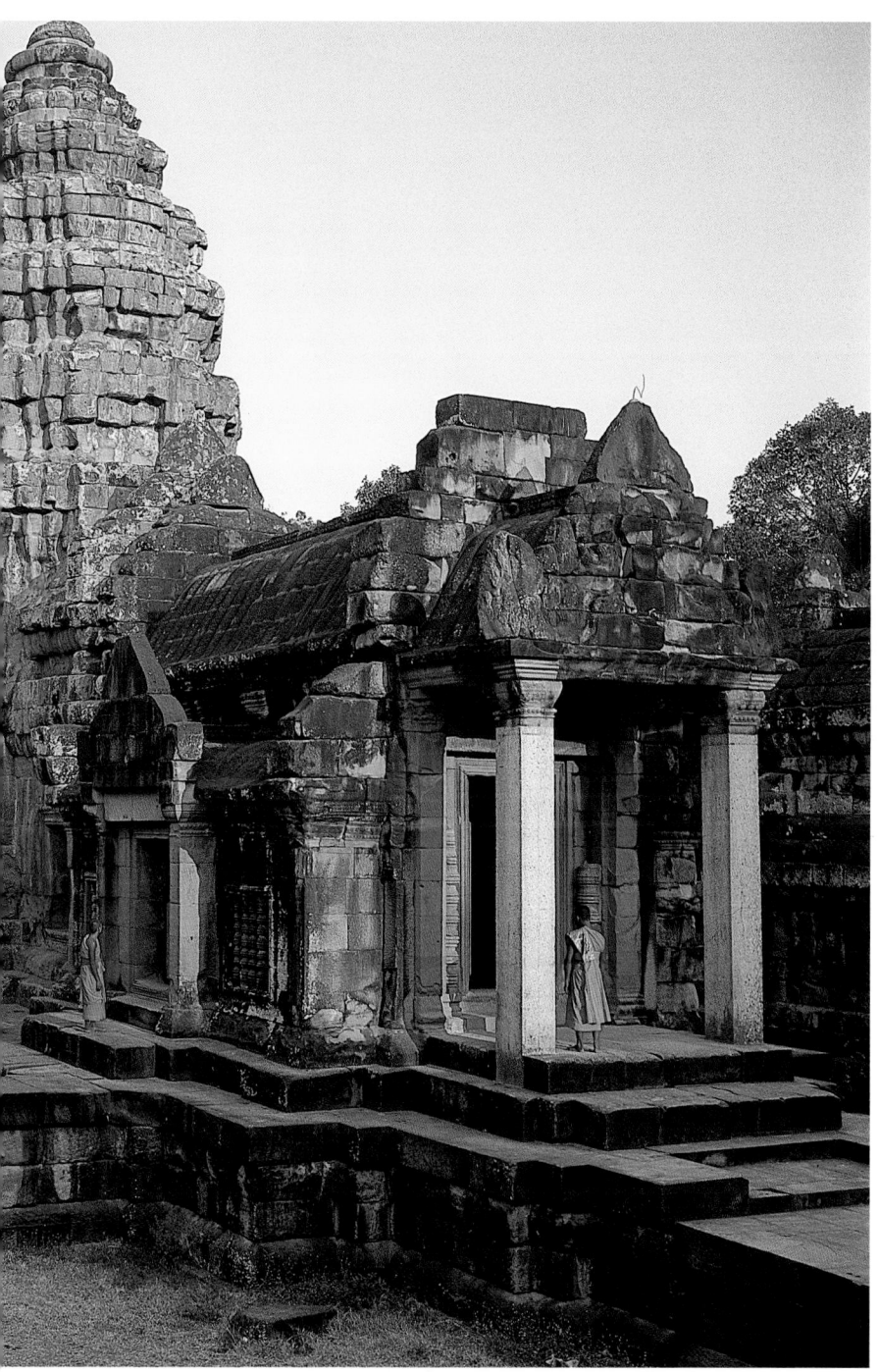

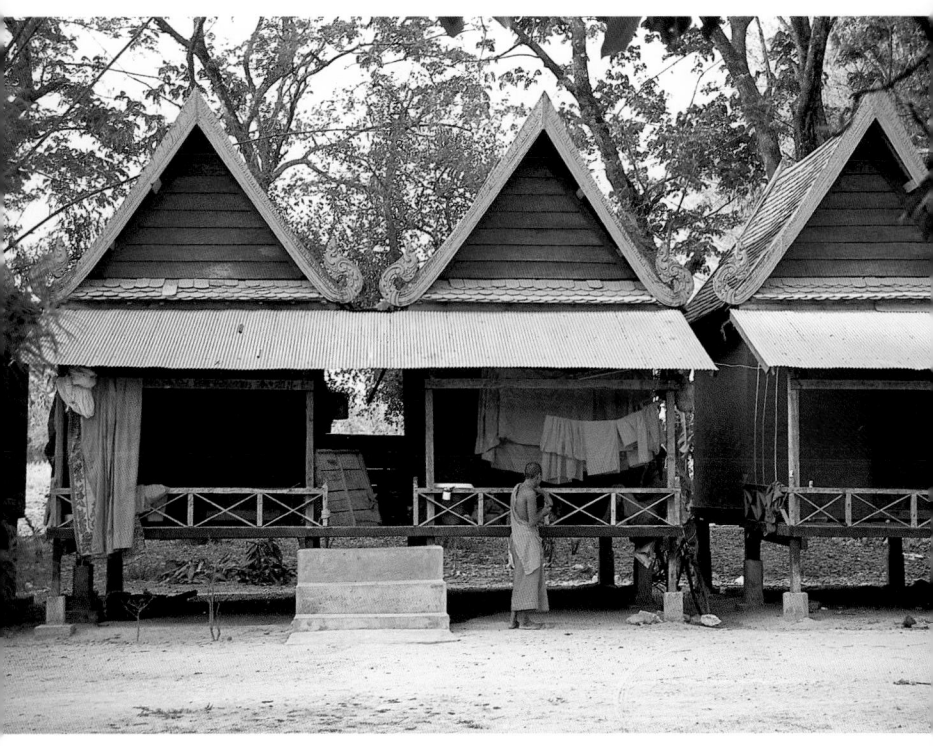

PP. 420–421 The double-peaked roofs of the wat's meeting hall. • Der Gemeinschaftsraum der Mönche wurde mit einem zweigiebeligen Dach gekrönt. • La salle commune du vat est surmontée d'un double toit.

PP. 424–425 A group of Angkor-period ruins just behind Wat Attwiya. • Diese Ruinen aus der Angkorzeit liegen direkt hinter dem Wat Attwiya. • Des ruines de l'époque d'Angkor derrière Vat Attwiya.

↑ The small houses are the monks private quarters. • In den kleineren Häusern leben die Mönche. • Les petits bâtiments sont les cellules des moines.

↓ A moped-powered trishaw parked outside the wat. • Eine Moped-Trishaw parkt vor dem Wat. • Un trishaw, un cyclopousse à moteur, garé devant le vat.

PP. 428–429 The meeting hall is decorated with paintings in a simple rustic style, possibly done by different artists at different times. • Die Wände des Gemeinschaftsraums sind mit naiven religiösen Motiven verziert, die

vermutlich von Künstlern aus diversen Epochen stammen. • La salle commune est ornée de peintures naïves, probablement réalisées par différents artistes au fil du temps.

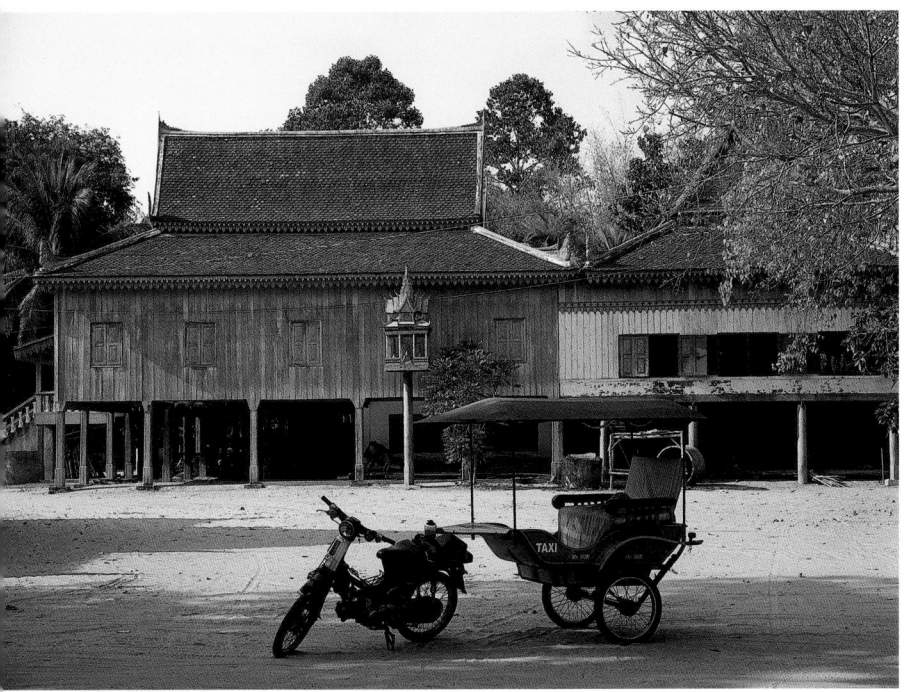

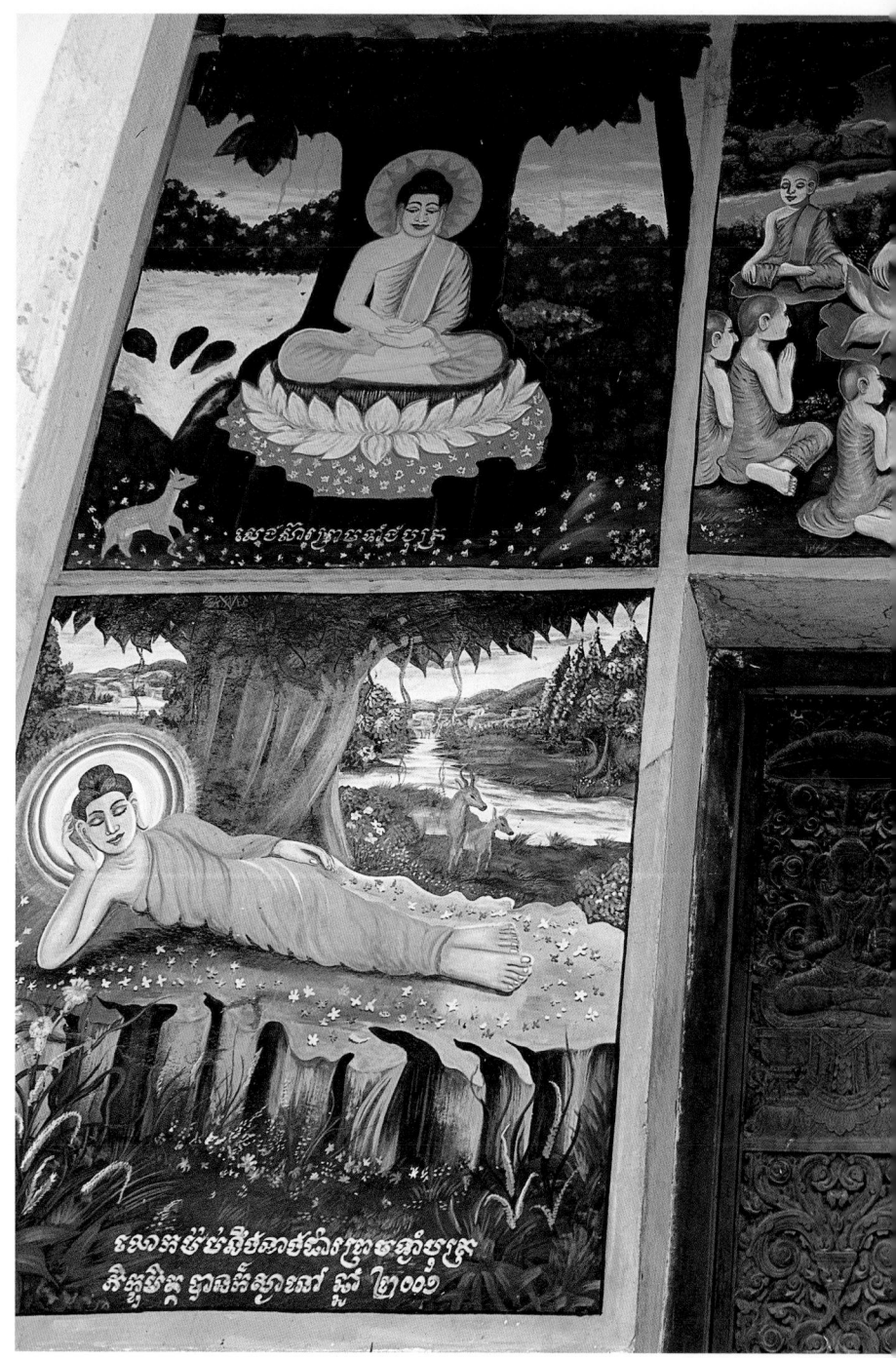

សេចក្តីប្រាថ្នាចុងក្រោយ

លោកម្ចាស់ធ្វើទីវាងគតបំរៀបឆ្មេបួត្រ
ភិក្ខុមិត្ត ឋានក់ស្មានៅ ឆ្នាំ ២០០១

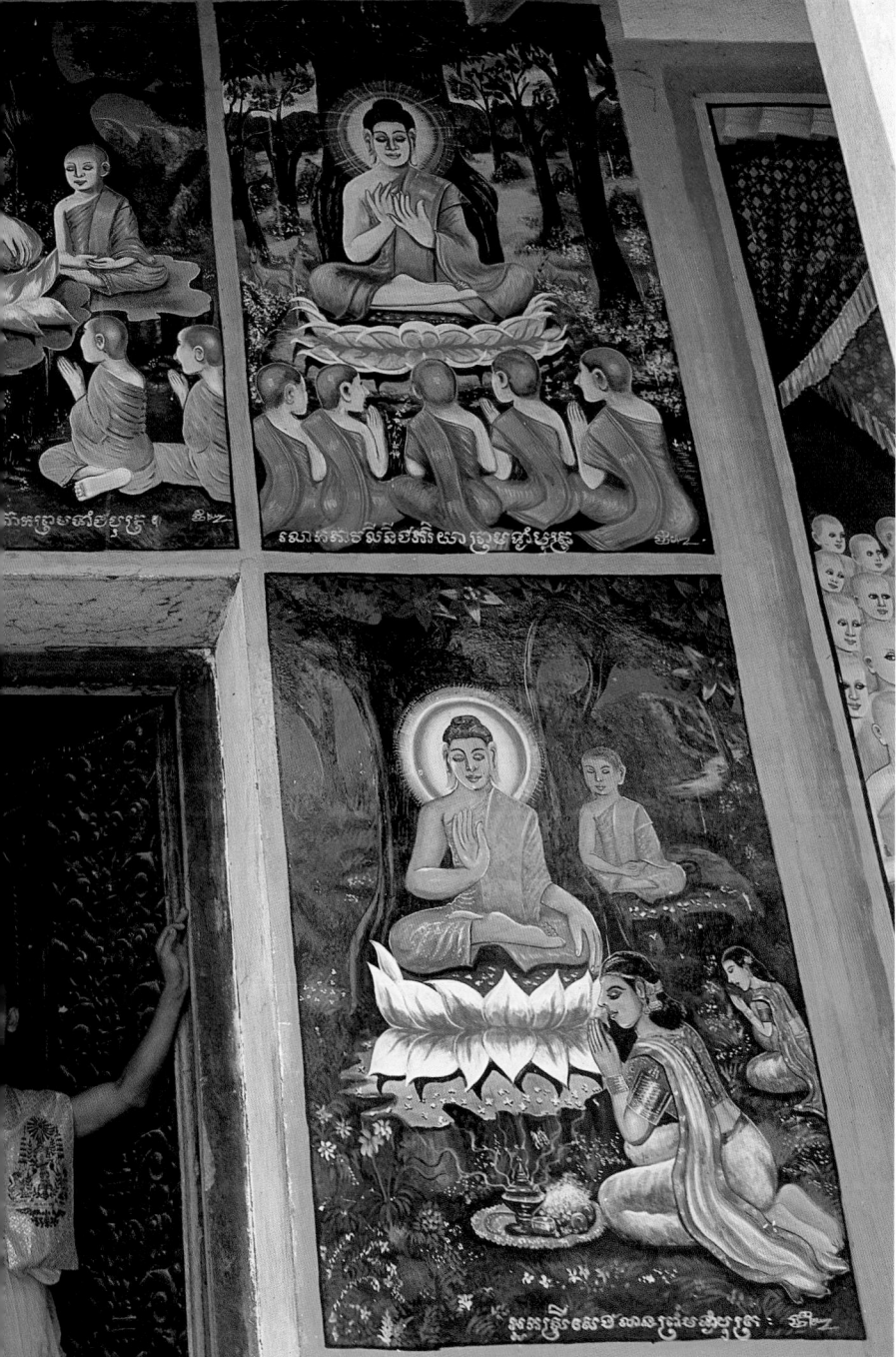

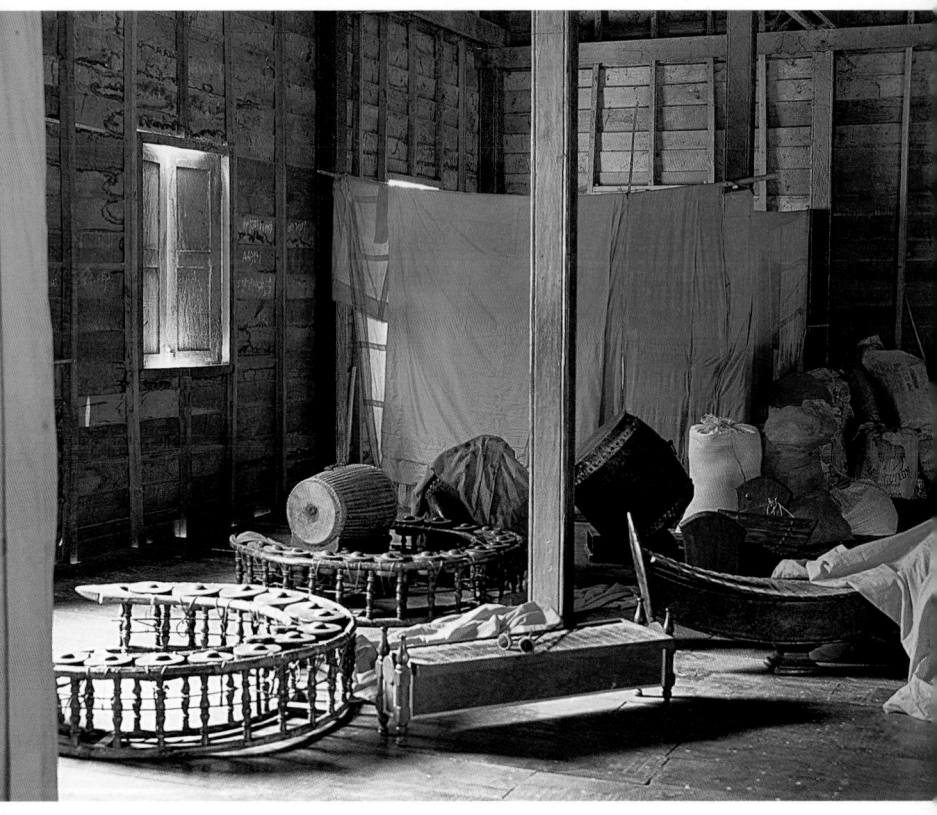

↑ Musical instruments, including a traditional xylophone and a pair of drums, in a corner of the meeting hall. • Musikinstrumente in einer Ecke des Gemeinschaftsraums, darunter Trommeln und ein traditionelles Xylophon. • Des instruments de musique, dont un xylophone traditionnel et des tambours dans un coin de la salle commune.

→ The flags hanging above the Buddhas in the main temple are believed to carry prayers as well as the souls of worshippers to heaven. • Die Gebetsfahnen über den Buddhafiguren im Haupt-

tempel sollen die Gebete und Seelen der Gläubigen in den Himmel bringen. • Les bannières qui pendent au-dessus des bouddhas du temple principal sont censées emmener aux cieux les prières et les âmes des fidèles.

P. 423 and P. 432 Monks in private quarters with their few possessions that include incense, Buddha images and stacks of prayer books. • In ihren Privaträumen zeigen die Mönche ihre geringen Besitztümer, darunter Räucherstäbchen, Buddhafiguren und stapelweise Gebetbücher. • Des

moines dans leur espace privé avec pour seuls objets personnels de l'encens, des statues du Bouddha et des livres de prière.

P. 433 Rows of Buddha images, candles and incense make up a private altar in a monk's chamber. • Zahlreiche Buddhafiguren, Kerzen und Räucherstäbchen bilden in dieser Mönchszelle einen privaten Altar. • Dans la cellule d'un moine, un autel privé avec des bouddhas, des bougies et des bâtonnets d'encens.

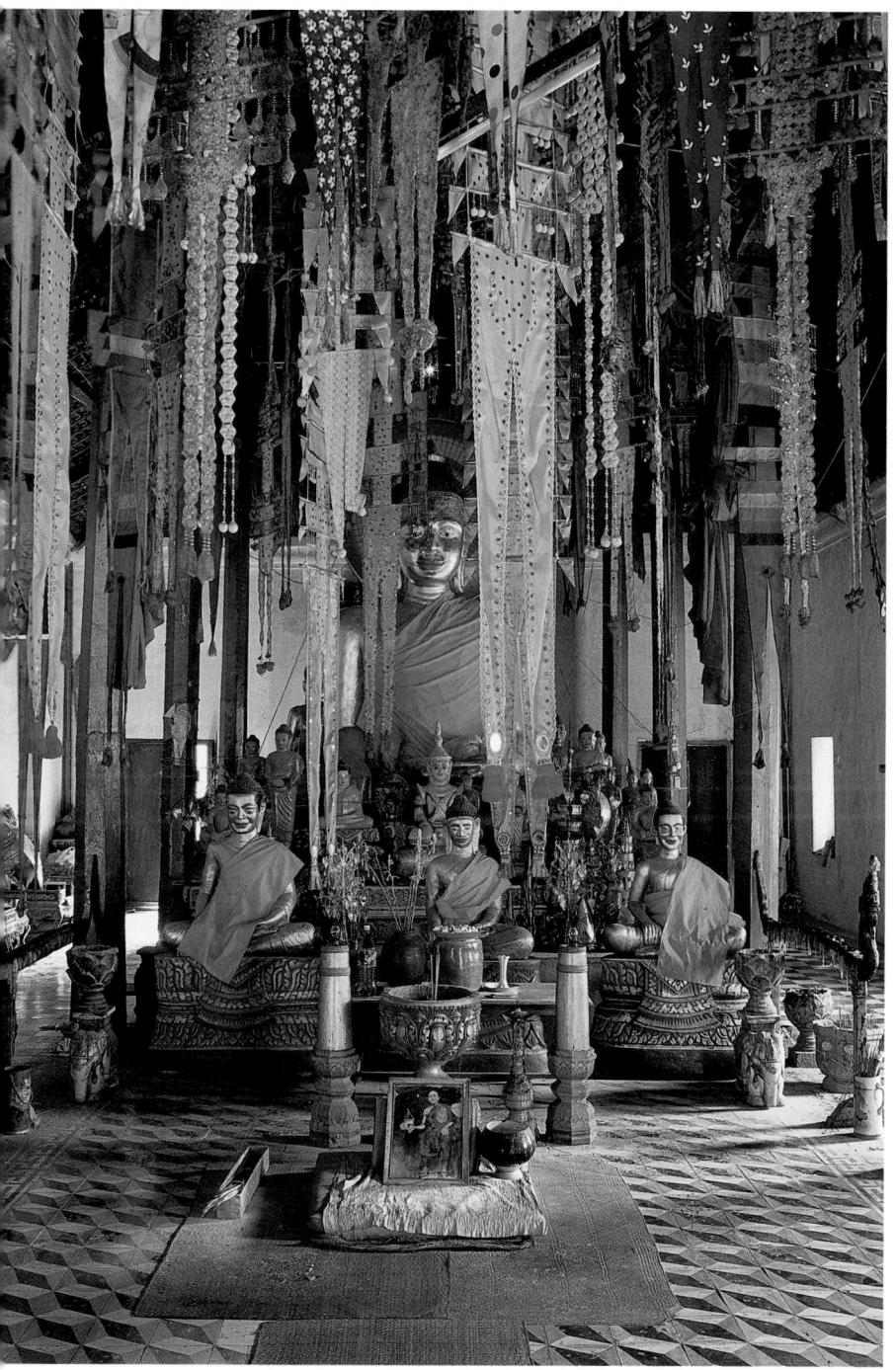

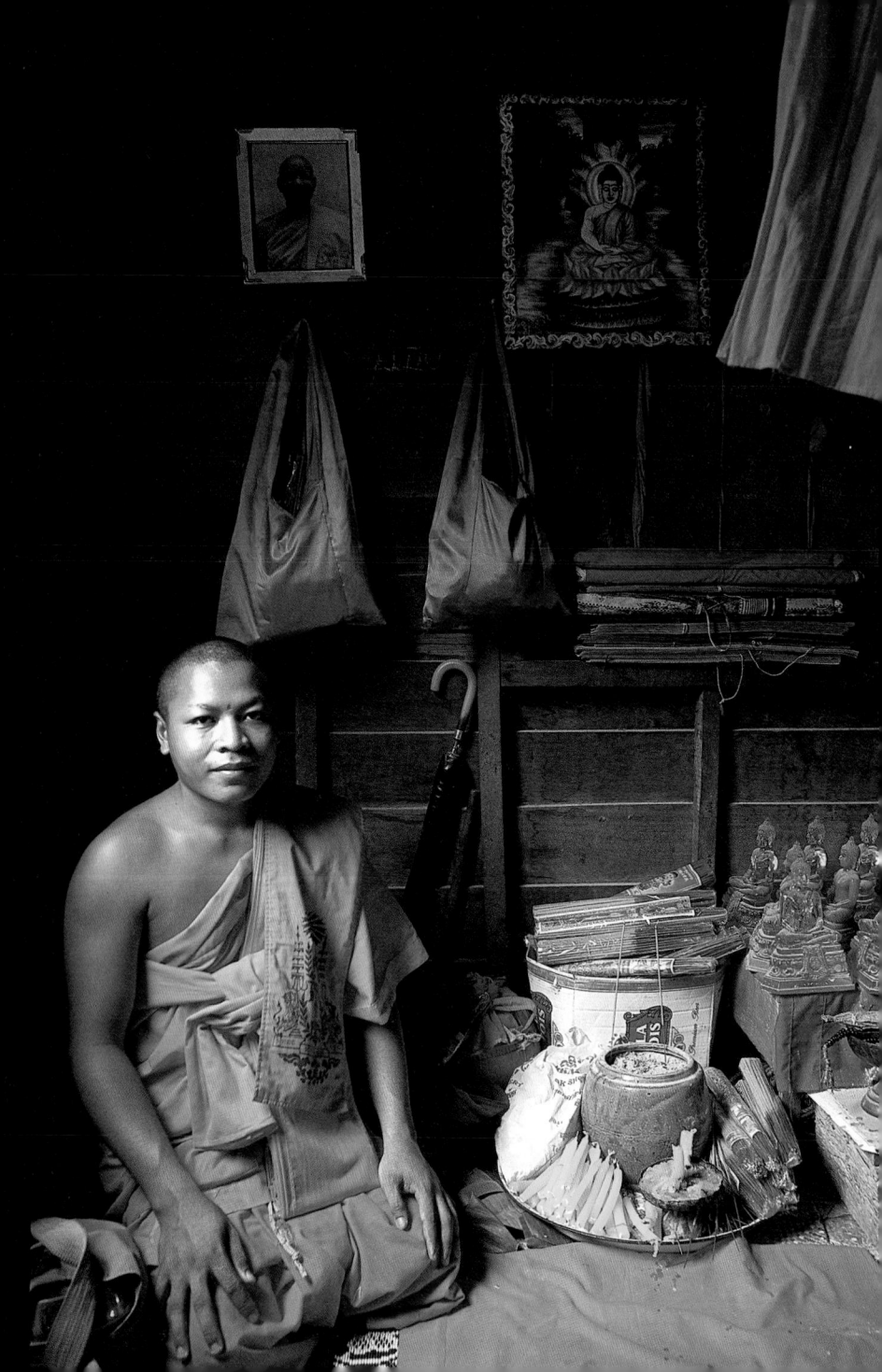

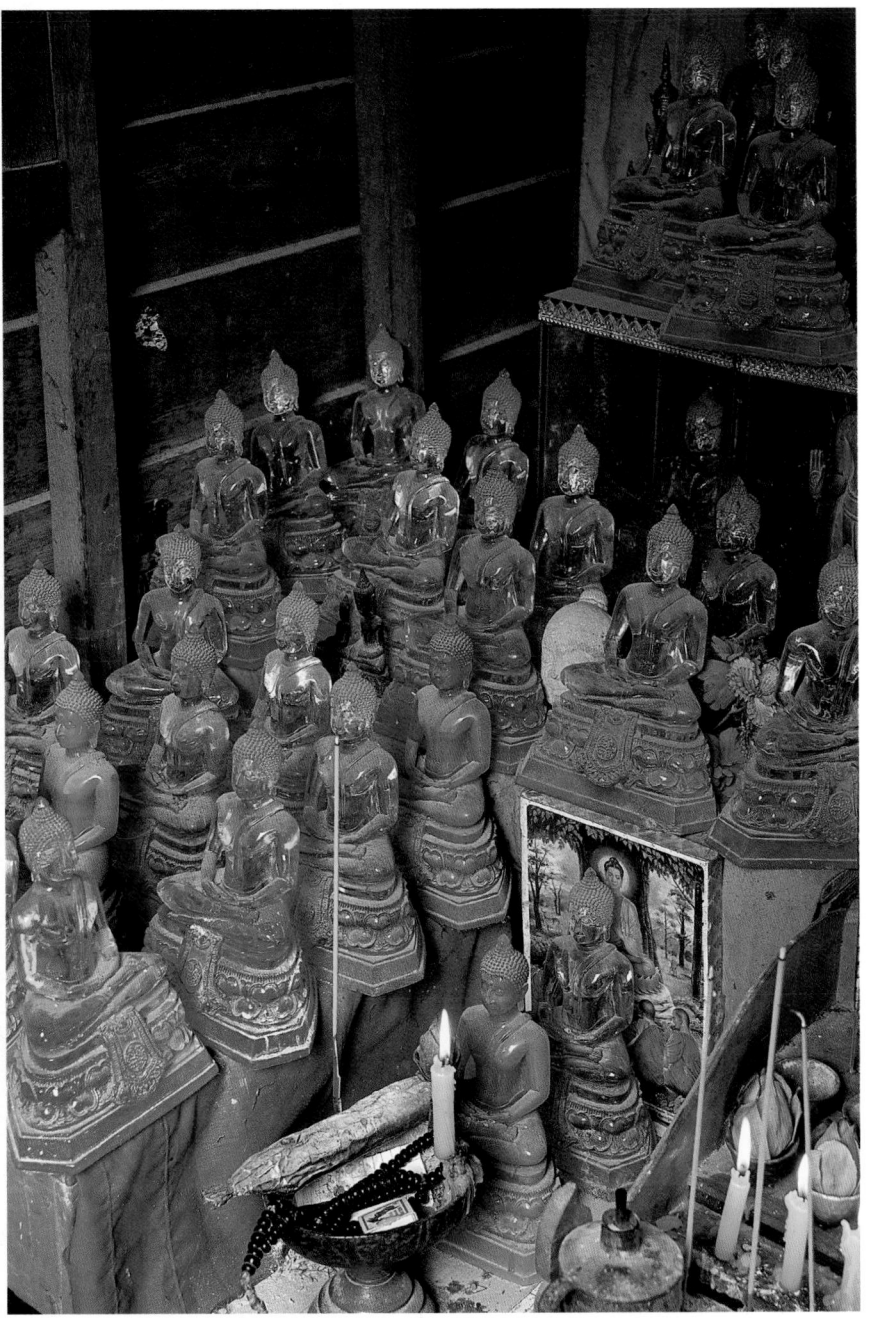

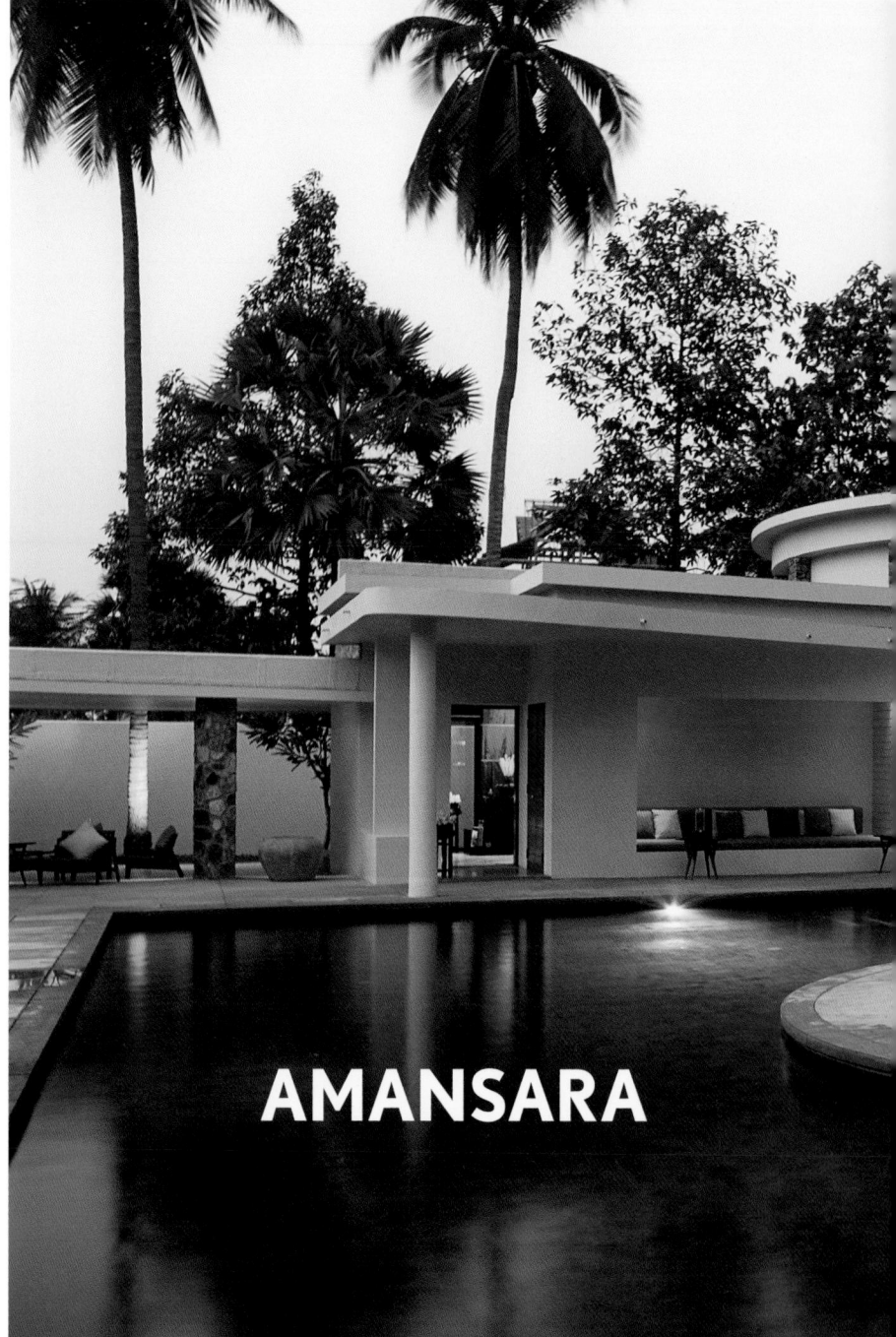

AMANSARA

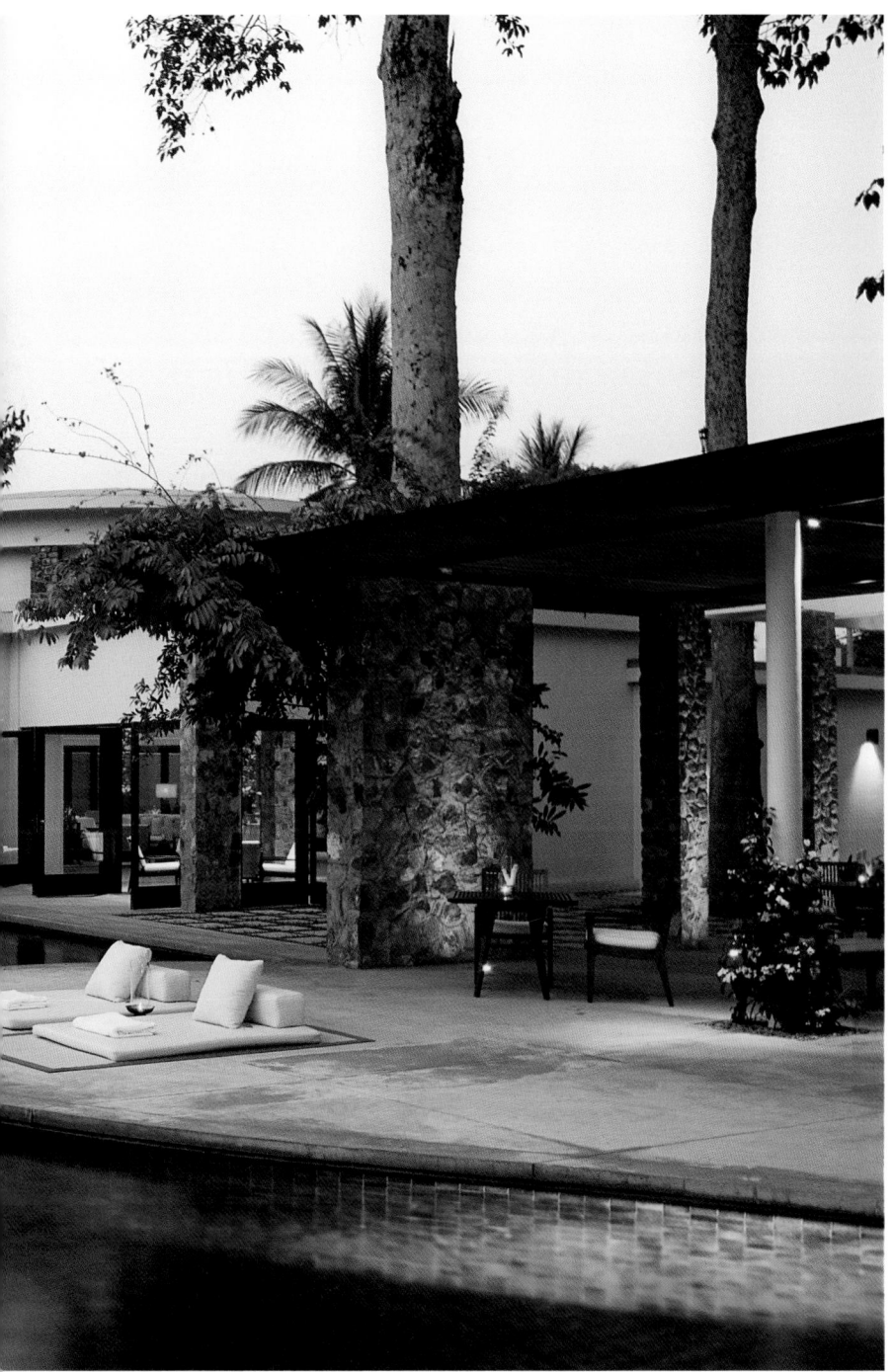

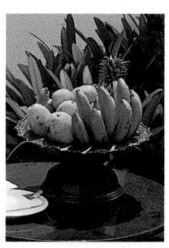

AMANSARA
SIEM REAP
CAMBODIA

Step aboard your own private *remork*, the moped-powered trishaw, and in ten minutes you are inside Angkor Wat's temple sanctuary. Amansara has its own fleet of custom-made remorks. Set in a garden with an irregular-shaped swimming pool, Amansara's twelve suites are arranged around a grassy courtyard, from which radiate the lounge, library and a dramatic, circular dining space. Built by the French architect Laurent Mondet in 1962 for King Sihanouk to house foreign dignitaries, it once hosted the likes of Charles de Gaulle, Jacqueline Kennedy, Marshal Tito and actor Peter O'Toole, who stayed here while filming "Lord Jim". Following several incarnations, the property was acquired by Aman Resorts in 2002 and carefully restored to preserve its Sixties style. The character of the Villa Princiere, as it was known, remains. Amansara derives its names from two Sanskrit words: *aman* means "peace" and *sara* is taken from apsara or "heavenly nymph". So it is the "peaceful garden of celestial nymphs".

Mit einem *remork*, einer Moped-Trishaw, gelangt man in zehn Minuten von Amansara zu den Tempeln von Angkor. Das kleine Hotel verfügt über einen eigenen kleinen Fuhrpark dieser eigens angefertigten Fahrzeuge. Die zwölf Suiten liegen in einem Garten mit einem Swimmingpool in ungewöhnlichem Format. Die Suiten gehen auf einen grasbewachsenen Innenhof hinaus, um den sich auch die Lounge, die Bibliothek und ein runder Speiseraum gruppieren. In dieser Anlage, die 1962 von dem französischen Architekten Laurent Mondet für König Sihanouk als Gästehaus für ausländische Würdenträger erbaut wurde, waren unter anderem Charles de Gaulle, Jacqueline Kennedy, Marschall Tito und Peter O'Toole zu Gast, Letzterer anlässlich der Dreharbeiten zu „Lord Jim". Nachdem es mehrfach anderweitig genutzt worden war, wurde das Haus schließlich 2002 von der Firma Aman Resorts gekauft und sorgfältig restauriert. Der Charakter der Villa Princière, wie das Haus genannt wurde, blieb im Stil der 1960er-Jahre erhalten. Der Name Amansara geht auf zwei Sanskritwörter zurück: *aman* heißt „Frieden", während *sara* dem Wort Apsara, „weiblicher Geist", entnommen ist.

Montez dans l'un des nombreux *reumok* qu'Amansara tient à la disposition de ses hôtes, et vous serez en dix minutes au cœur du sanctuaire d'Angkor Vat. Amansara, c'est un jardin doté d'une piscine aux contours irréguliers et 12 suites disposées autour d'une cour gazonnée à partir de laquelle rayonnent un salon, une bibliothèque et un spectaculaire espace circulaire destiné aux repas. Construit par l'architecte français Laurent Mondet en 1962 pour les visiteurs étrangers du roi Norodom Sihanouk, Amansara a accueilli des hôtes de marque tels que le général de Gaulle, Jackie Kennedy, Tito et l'acteur Peter O'Toole, qui y a séjourné pendant le tournage de « Lord Jim ». Après diverses utilisations, la propriété a été rachetée en 2002 par Aman Resorts, qui l'a rénovée avec soin de manière à préserver son style années soixante et son caractère de villa princière. Le nom d'Amansara est dérivé des mots sanscrits *aman*, la paix, et *apsara*, nymphe céleste. C'est ainsi que cet hôtel porte le nom poétique de « Jardin paisible des nymphes célestes ».

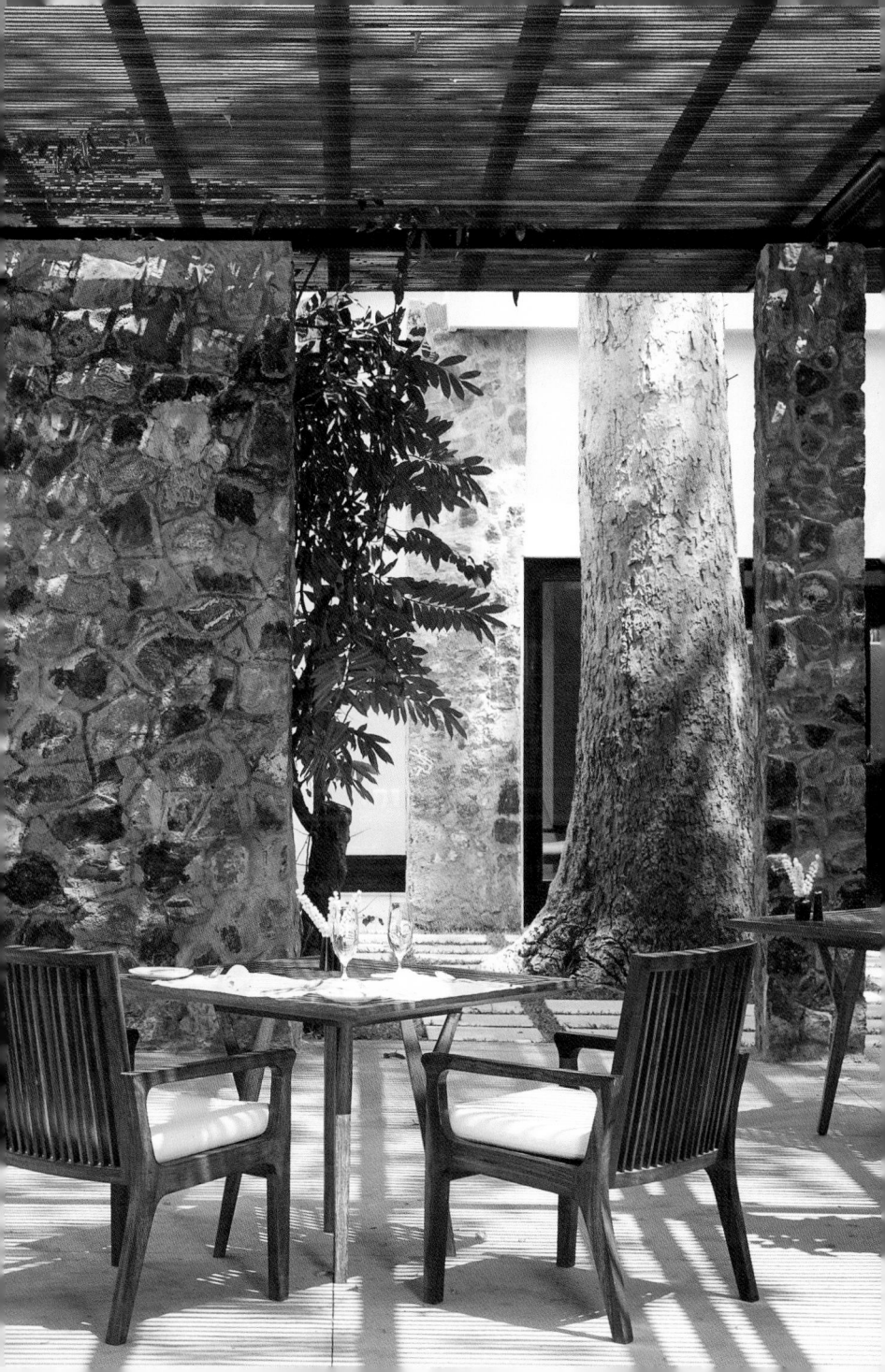

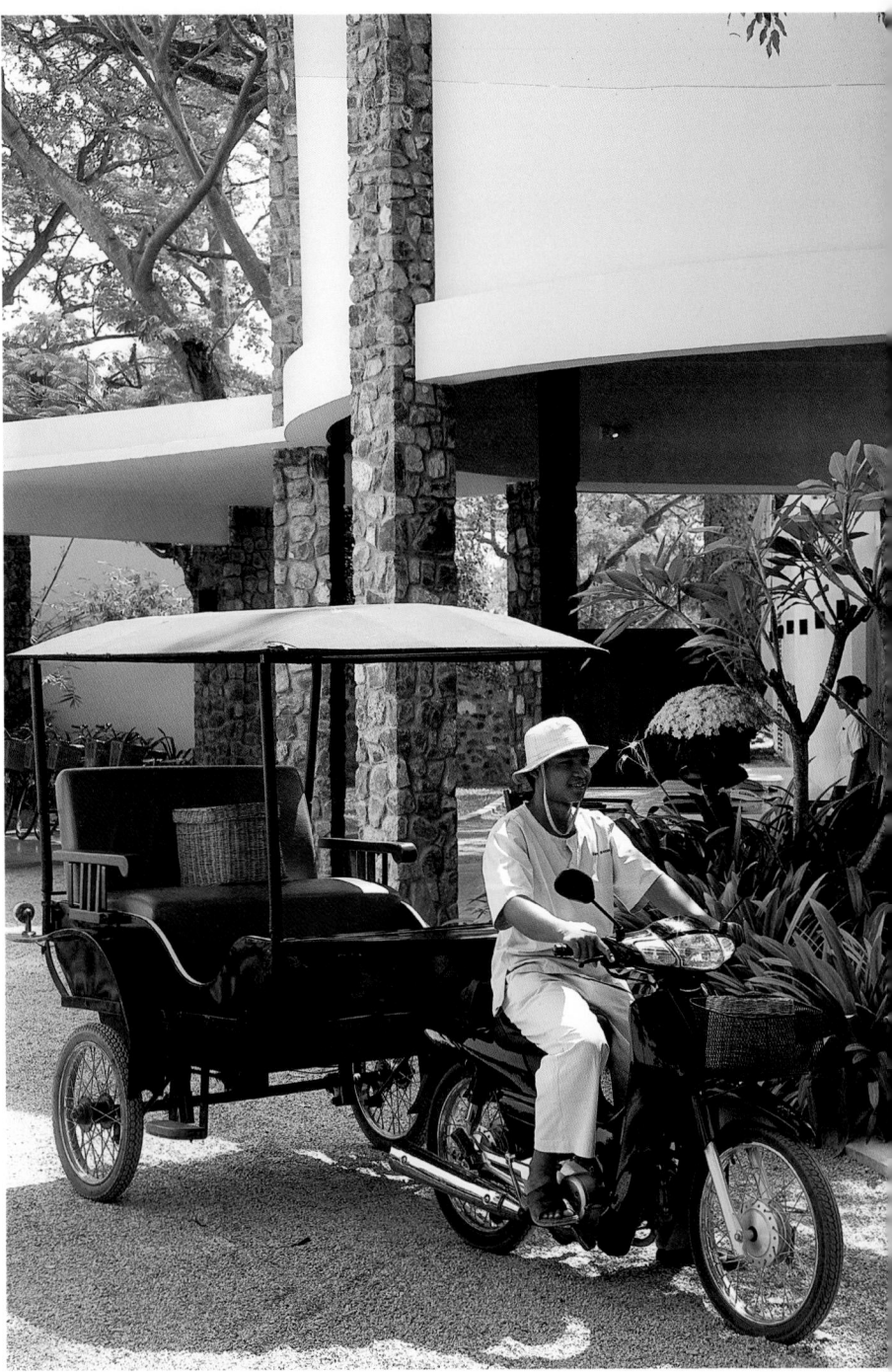

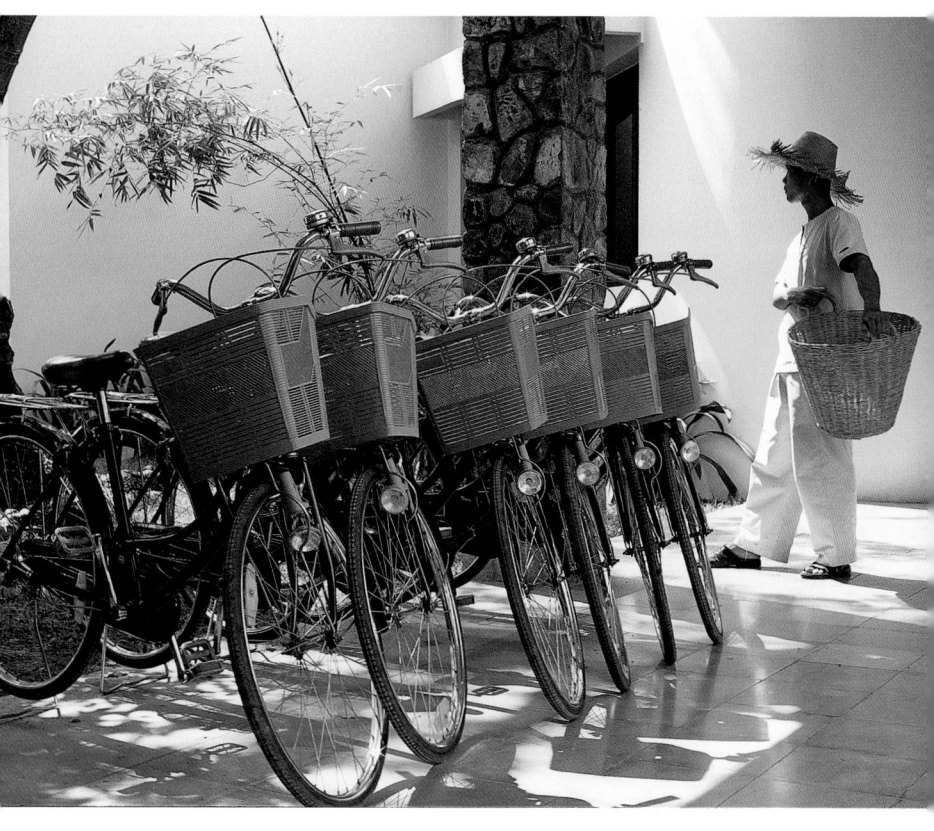

↑ A gardener strolls past a row of
bicycles reserved for guests to tour the
temples. • Ein Gärtner schlendert an
den Fahrrädern vorbei, mit denen die
Hotelgäste die Tempel erkunden. • Un
jardinier déambule près des bicyclettes
que les clients peuvent emprunter pour
visiter les temples.

PP. 440–441 Loungers on woven mats
by the swimming pool. • Matratzen auf
geflochtenen Matten am Swimmingpool. • Des lits de plage posés sur des
nattes au bord de la piscine.

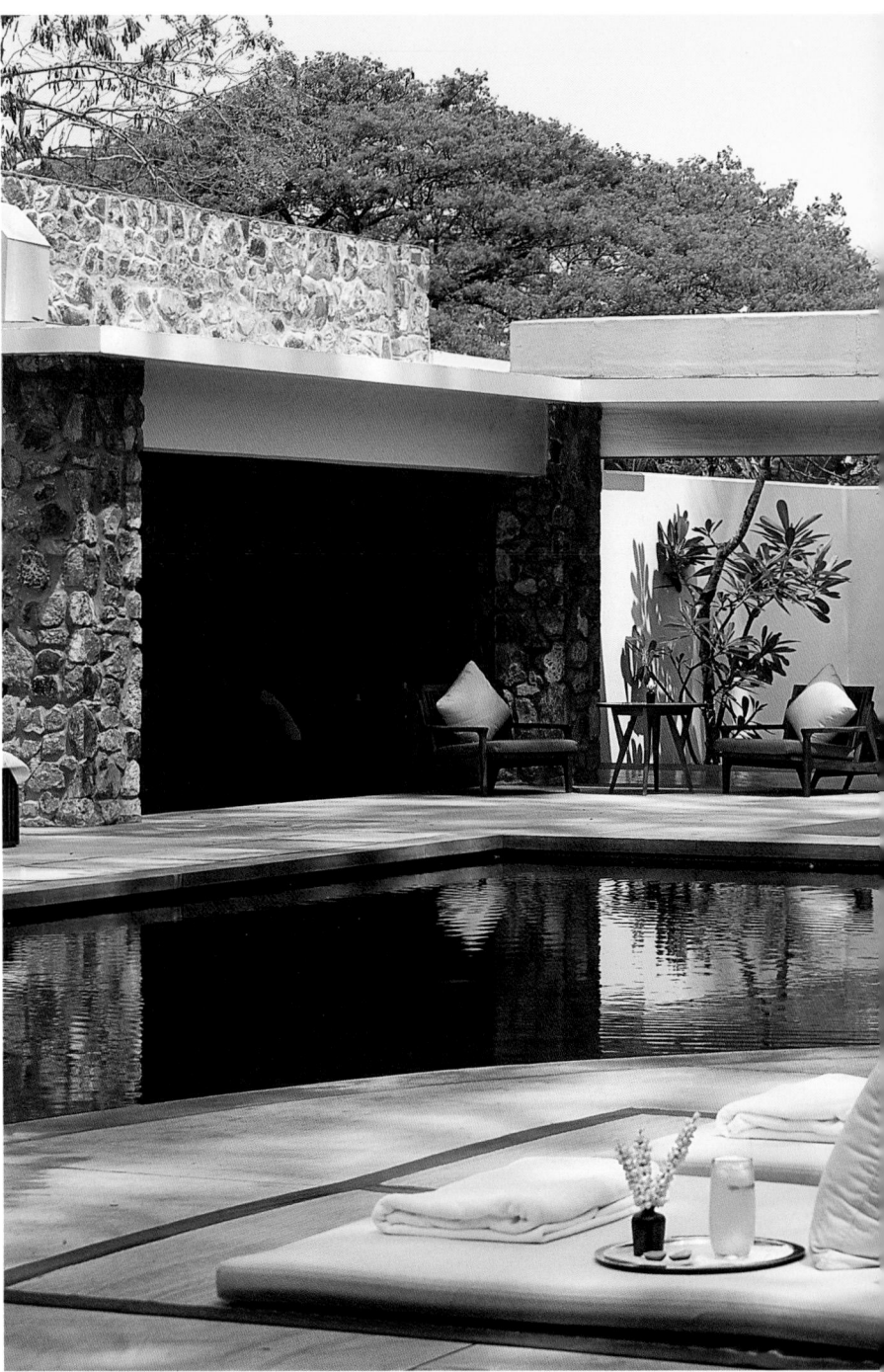

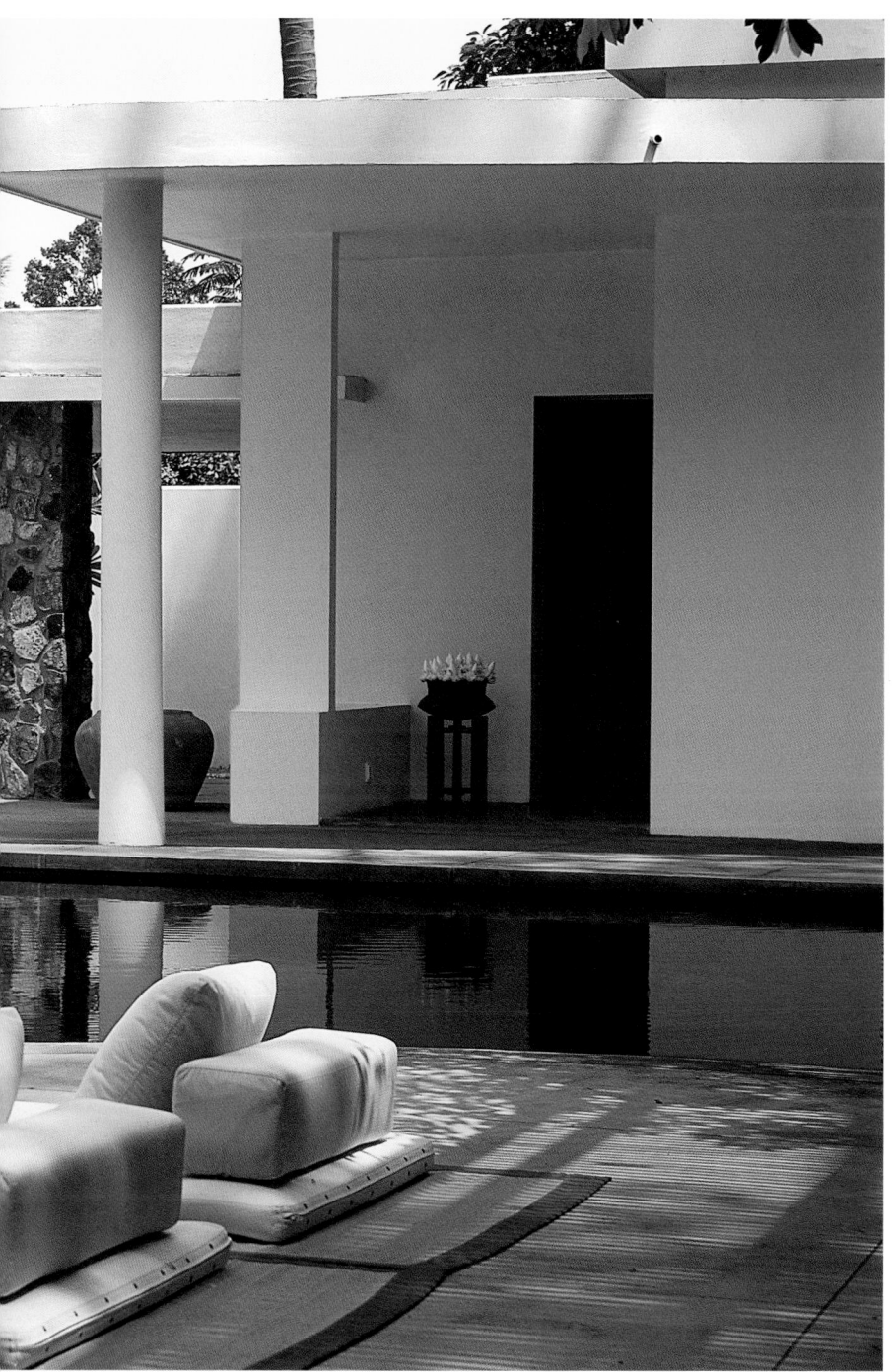

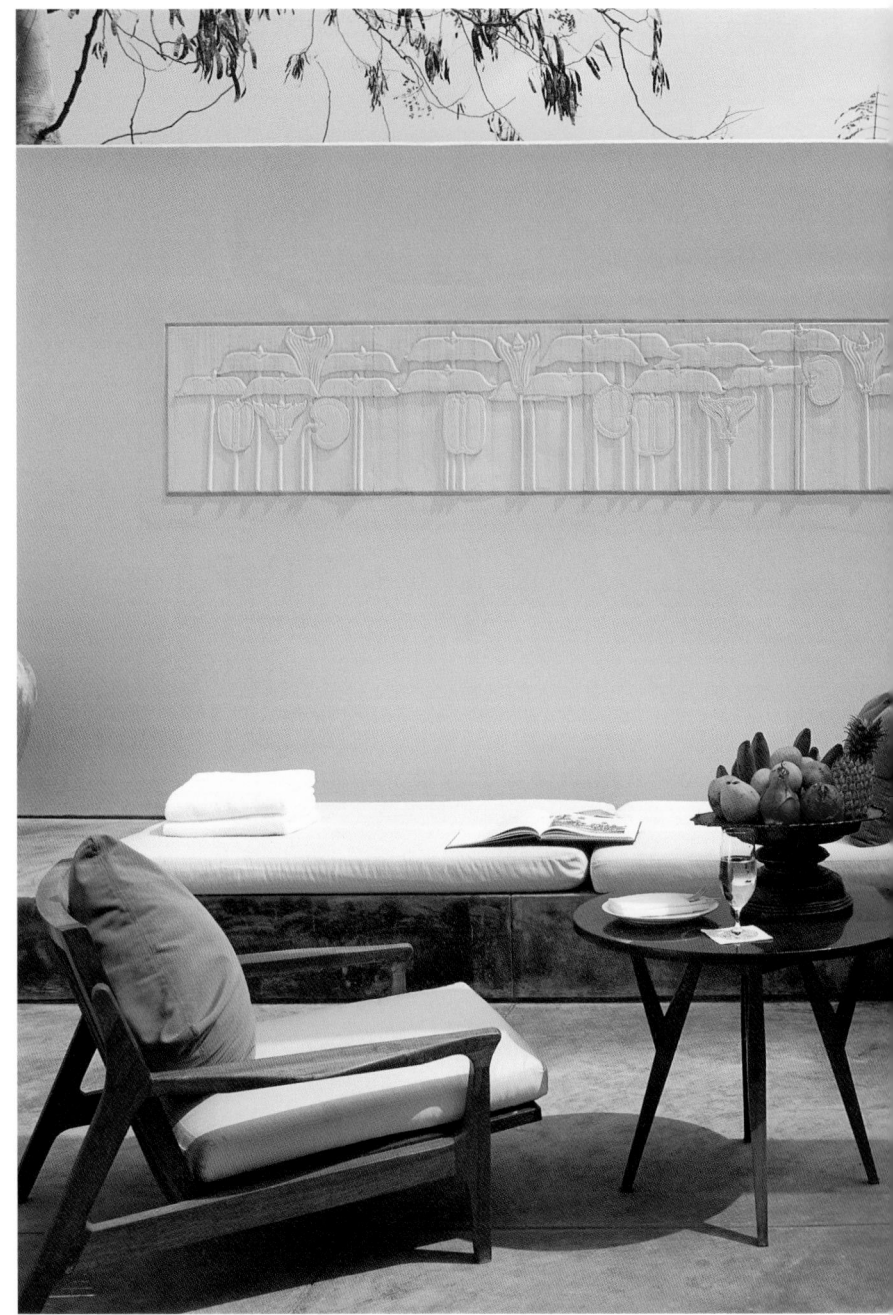

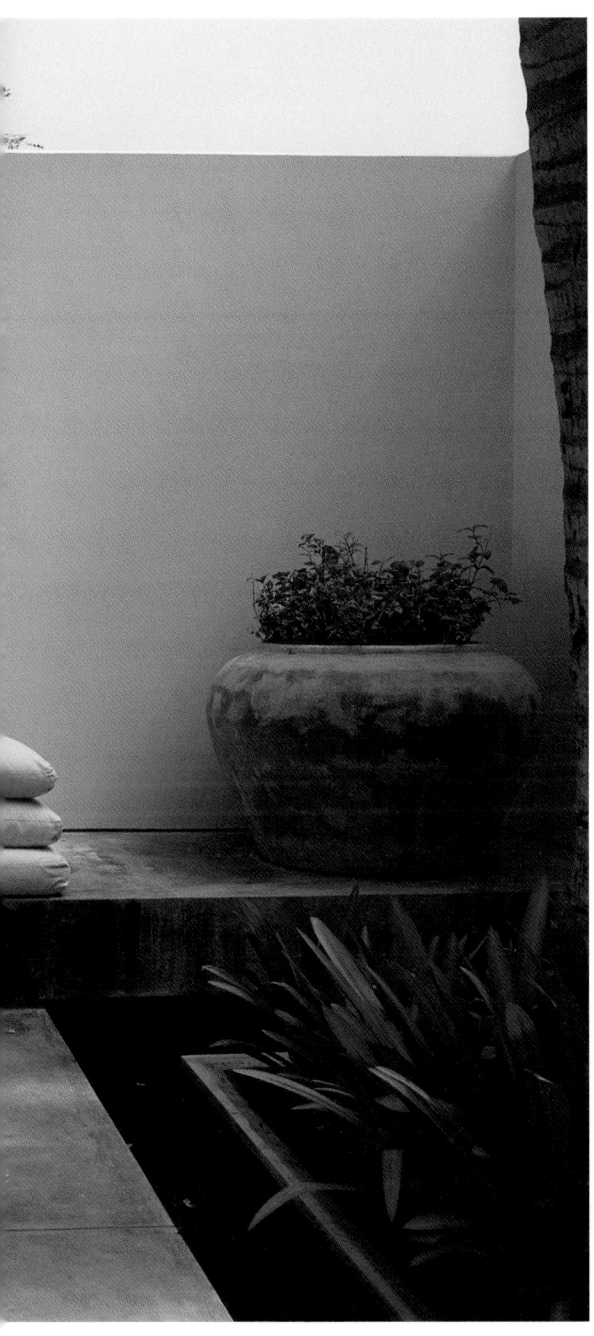

← Each suite opens on to an enclosed courtyard with a water garden. • An jede Suite schließt sich ein geschlossener Innenhof mit einem Wasserbecken an. • Chaque suite donne sur une courette fermée et un jardin d'eau.

PP. 444–445 The lounge is furnished with banquettes and Sixties-style furniture. • Die Lounge ist mit gepolsterten Bänken und Möbeln im Stil der 1960er-Jahre eingerichtet. • Dans le salon, des banquettes et des meubles années soixante invitent à la détente.

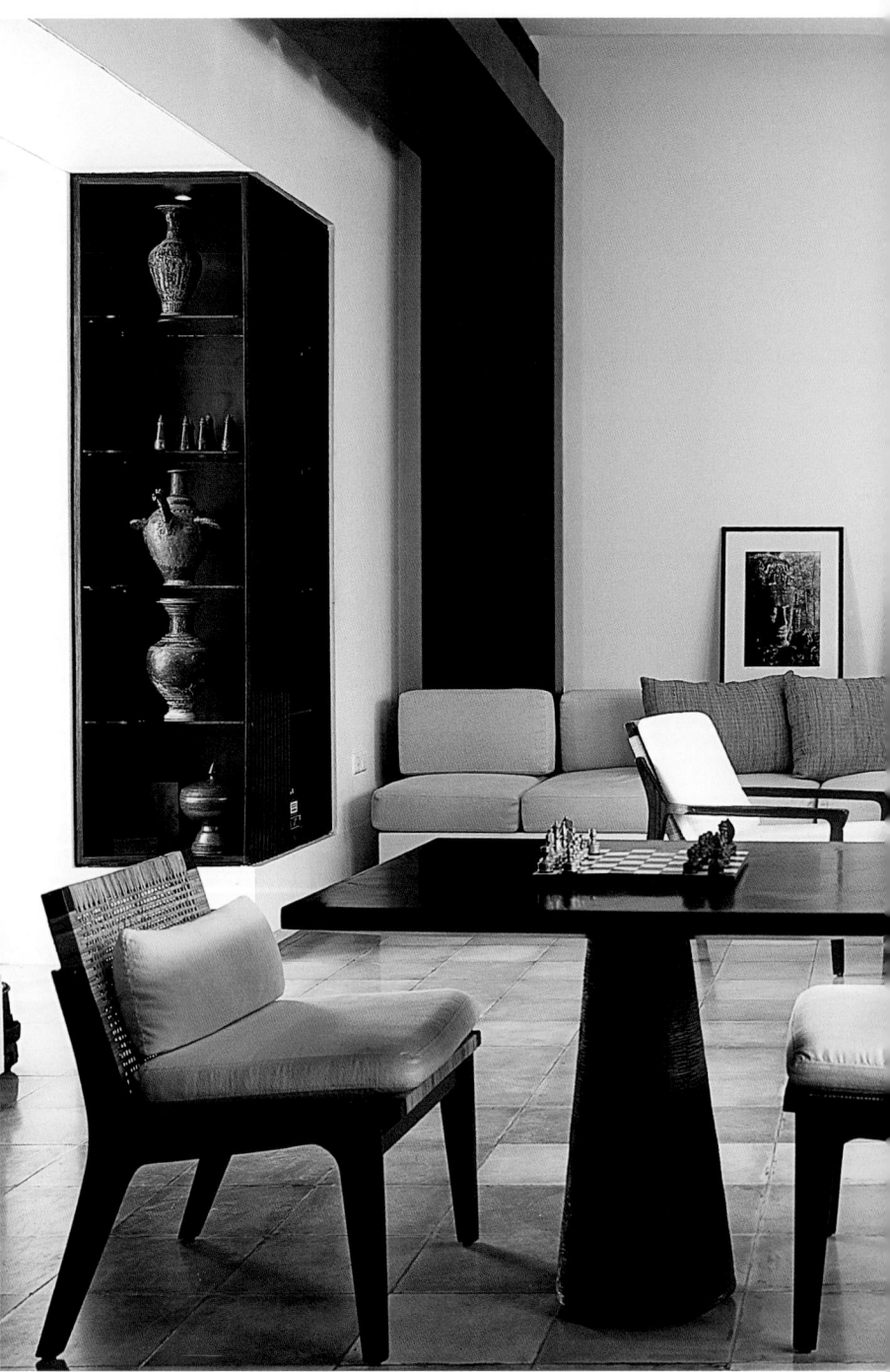

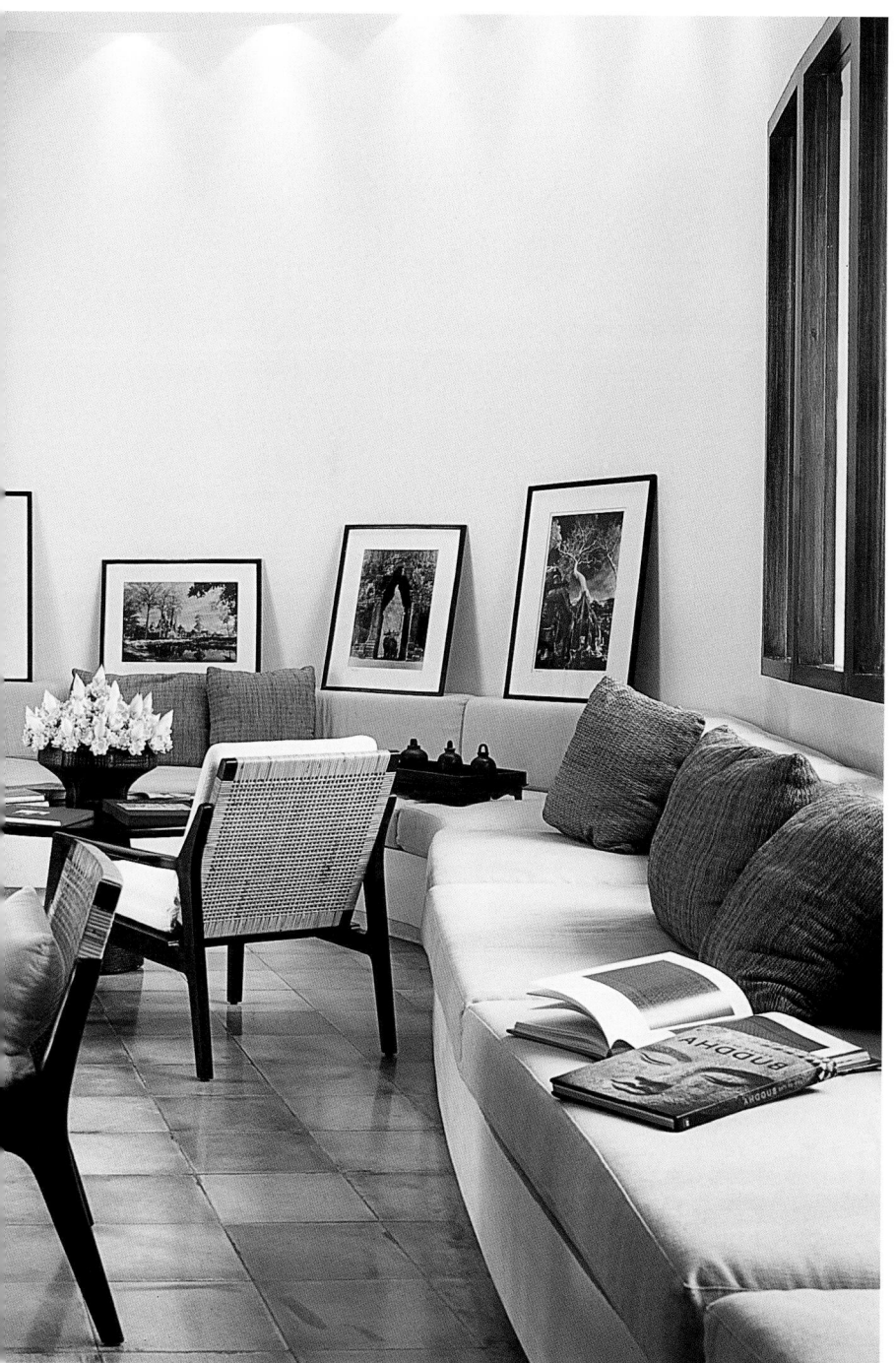

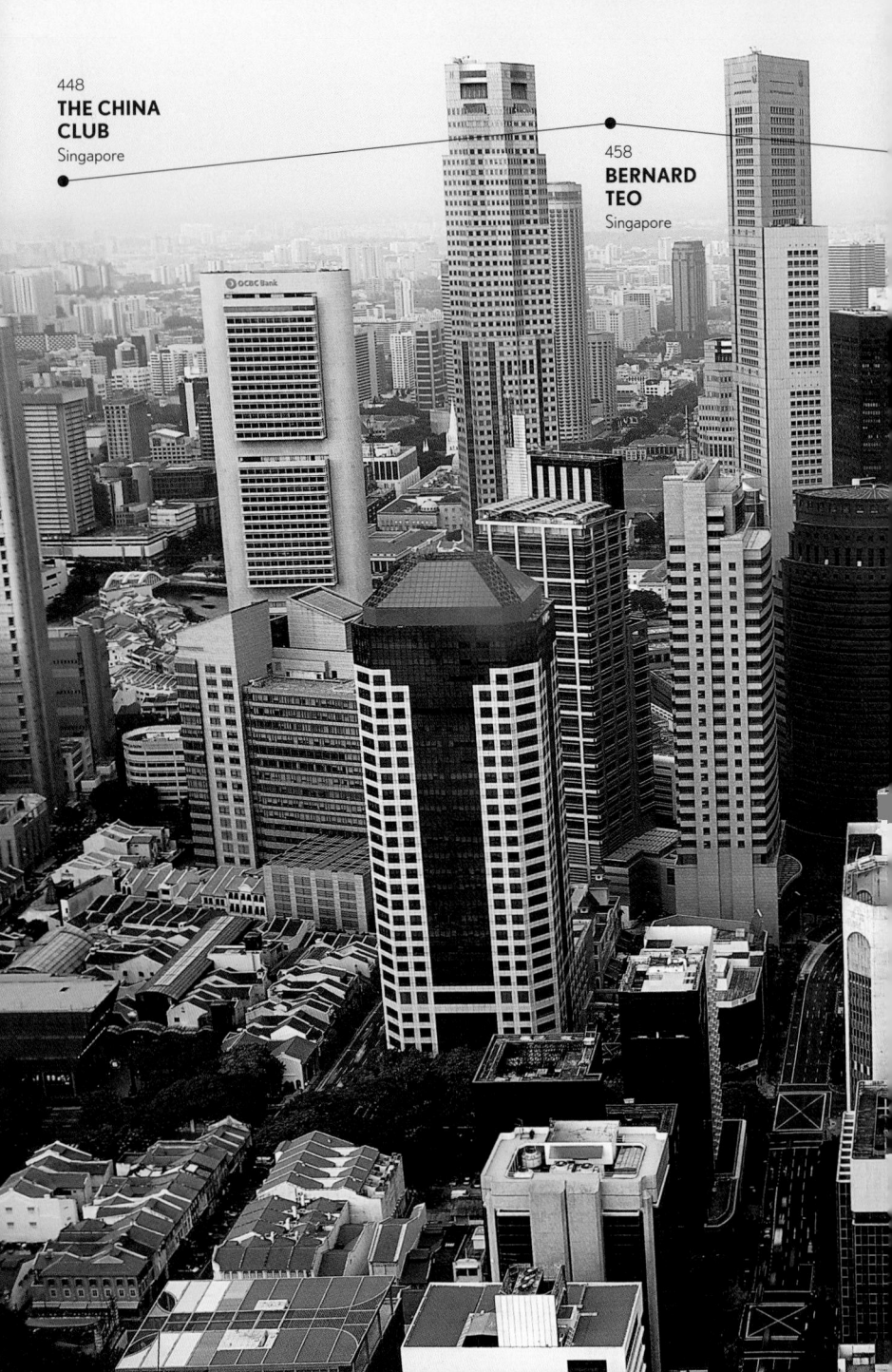

448
THE CHINA CLUB
Singapore

458
BERNARD TEO
Singapore

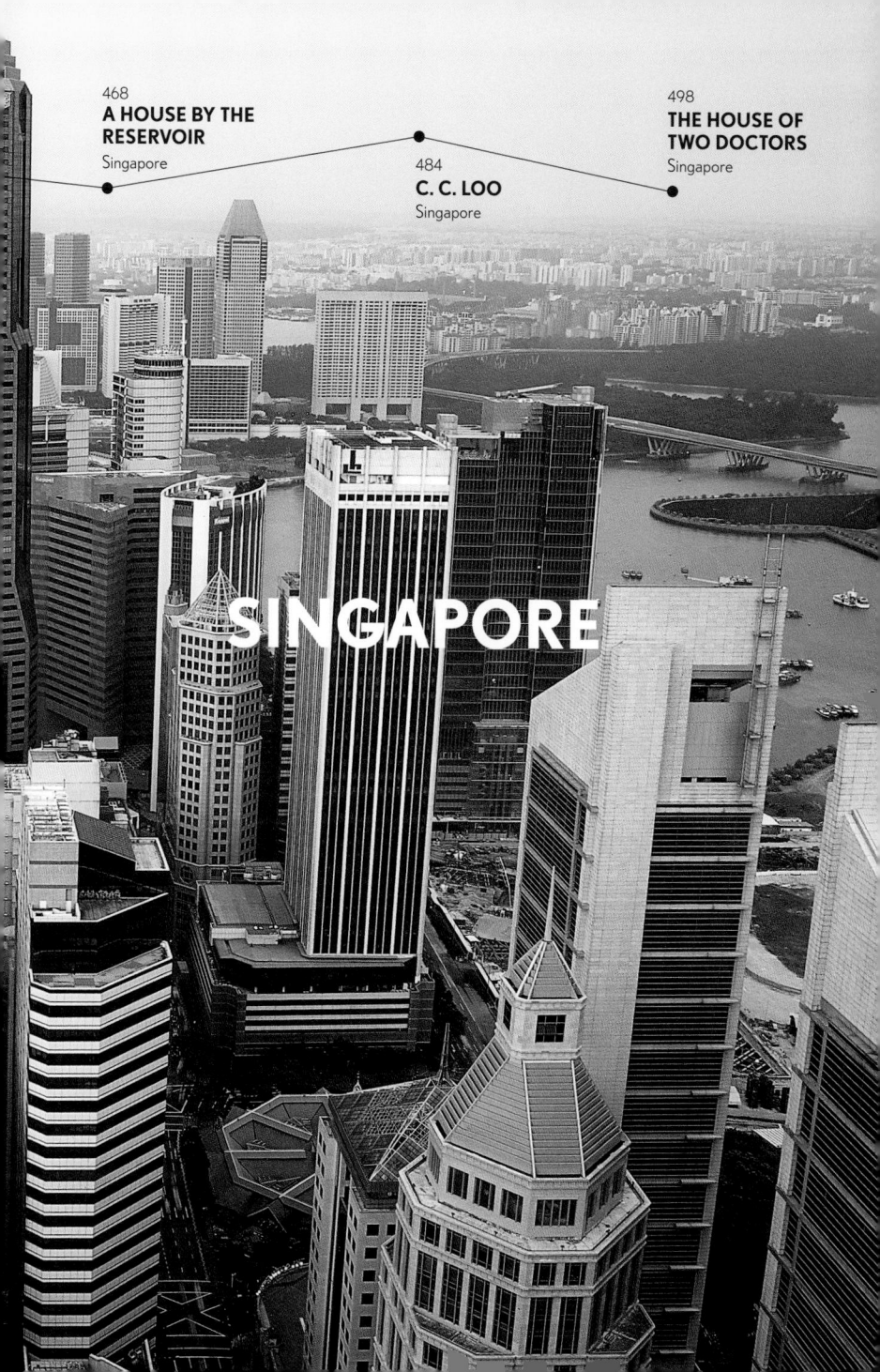

468
A HOUSE BY THE RESERVOIR
Singapore

484
C. C. LOO
Singapore

498
THE HOUSE OF TWO DOCTORS
Singapore

SINGAPORE

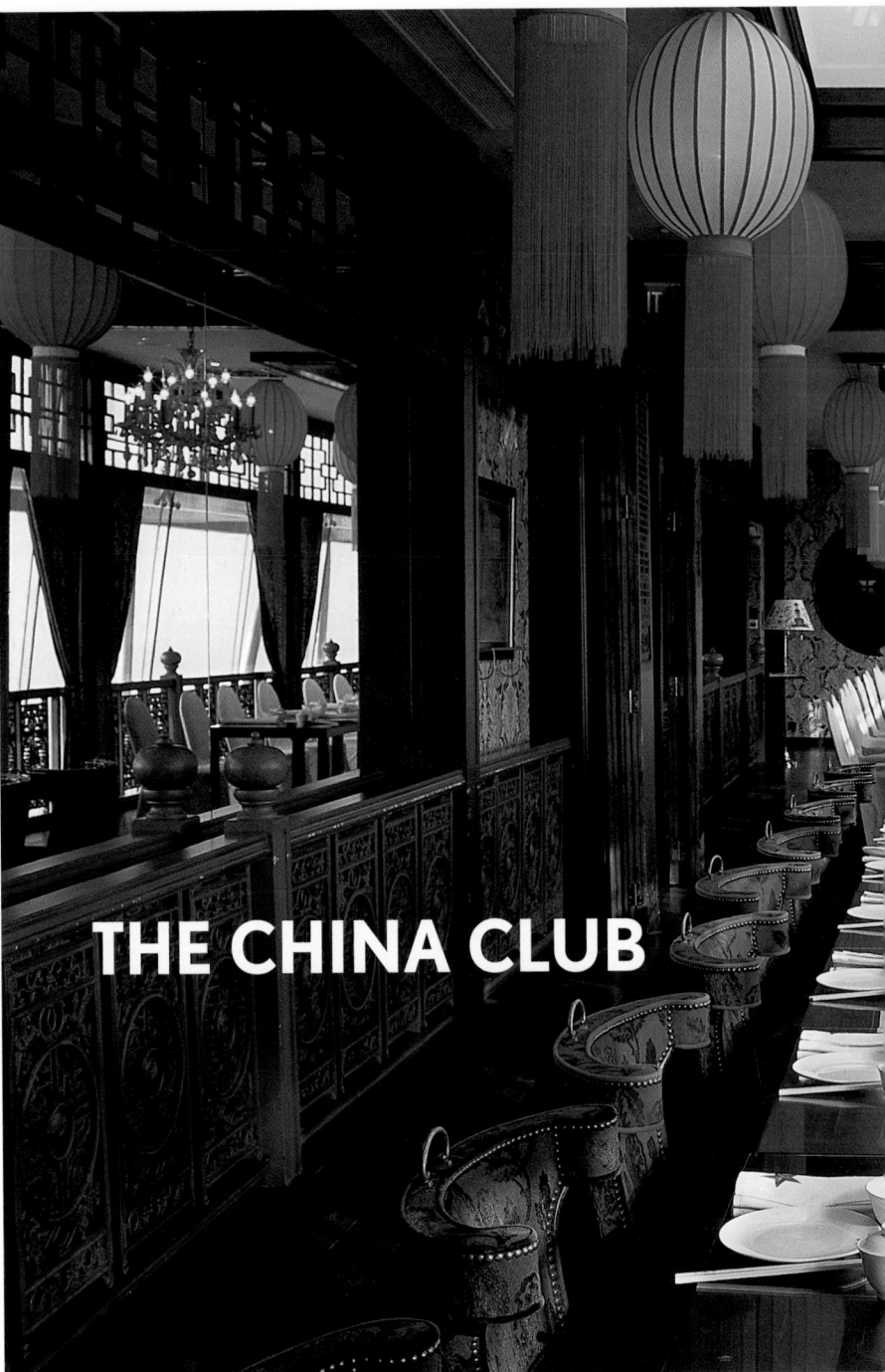

THE CHINA CLUB

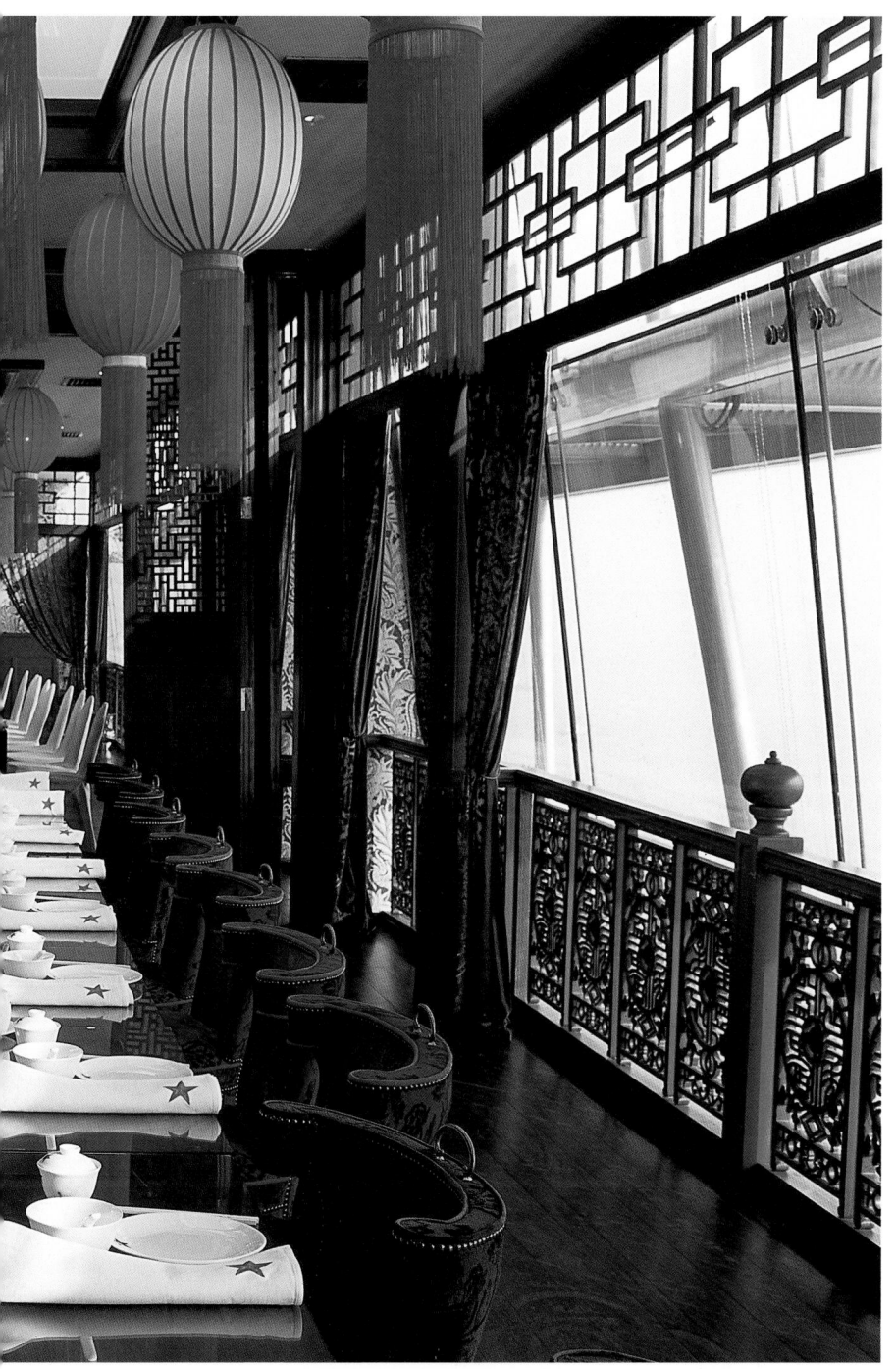

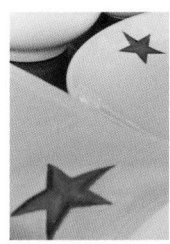

THE CHINA CLUB
SINGAPORE

High-speed lifts whizz you to a 12,000 square-foot rooftop dining club with 360-degree views of Singapore's skyline and the South China Sea. On a clear day you can see as far as Indonesia and Malaysia. In dazzling contrast to the long-distance vistas is the atmosphere of a 19th-century Chinese tea room, inspired in equal parts by old Shanghai and Mao memorabilia. Silk lanterns, French wallpaper and swathes of embroidered drapes in the dining room blend with statues and Warhol-inspired images of Chairman Mao in the Long March Bar. Underfoot, the rosewood flooring is stencilled with dragon, butterfly and floral motifs. The blackwood and marble inlaid furniture could have been transported from a warlord's house. Every accessory, from the tin ashtrays to the table china, is emblazoned with Mao's red star. Hong Kong entrepreneur David Tang made the tongue-in-cheek chinoiserie famous when he opened the first of the China Clubs in Hong Kong in 1991.

Der Hochgeschwindigkeitslift bringt einen hoch aufs Dach in einen 400 m² großen Dining Club mit Rundumsicht auf die Skyline von Singapur und das Südchinesische Meer. Bei gutem Wetter kann man bis nach Indonesien und Malaysia sehen. Die Aussicht steht in scharfem Kontrast zu der Atmosphäre eines chinesischen Teesalons aus dem 19. Jahrhundert, dessen Einrichtung vom alten Schanghai und Erinnerungsstücken aus der Zeit Maos inspiriert ist. Seidenlaternen, französische Tapeten und fein bestickte Gardinen im Speisesaal werden mit Statuen und Warhol-inspirierten Bildern des Vorsitzenden Mao in der „Bar des Langen Marsches" kombiniert. Der Boden aus Rosenholz ist mit Drachen-, Schmetterlings- und Blumenmustern, die Möbel mit Intarsien aus Palisanderholz und Marmor verziert. Maos roter Stern prangt auf jedem Accessoire, vom Blechaschenbecher bis zum Tafelservice. David Tang, ein Unternehmer aus Hongkong, machte diese nicht ganz ernst gemeinten Chinoiserien berühmt, als er den ersten China Club 1991 in Hongkong eröffnete.

Un ascenseur vous emmène à une allure vertigineuse au dernier étage, dans un club-restaurant de 400 m² offrant une vue panoramique sur Singapour et le sud de la mer de Chine. Quand le ciel est dégagé, vous pouvez apercevoir l'Indonésie et la Malaisie, et cela dans une ambiance de salon de thé chinois du 19e siècle, mêlant le style vieux Shanghai et les souvenirs de Mao. Des lanternes en soie, du papier peint français et des rideaux brodés dans la salle de restaurant se mêlent à des figurines et des représentations de Mao à la Andy Warhol dans le « Bar de la Longue Marche ». Sur le plancher en bois de rose, des dragons, des papillons et des motifs floraux ont été peints au pochoir. Le mobilier en marqueterie d'ébène et de marbre semble venir tout droit d'une demeure de seigneur de la guerre. Tous les accessoires, des cendriers en étain à la vaisselle, sont marqués de l'étoile rouge de Mao. David Tang, entrepreneur de Hong Kong, a mis les « chinoiseries » au goût du jour avec l'ouverture de son premier China Club à Hong Kong en 1991.

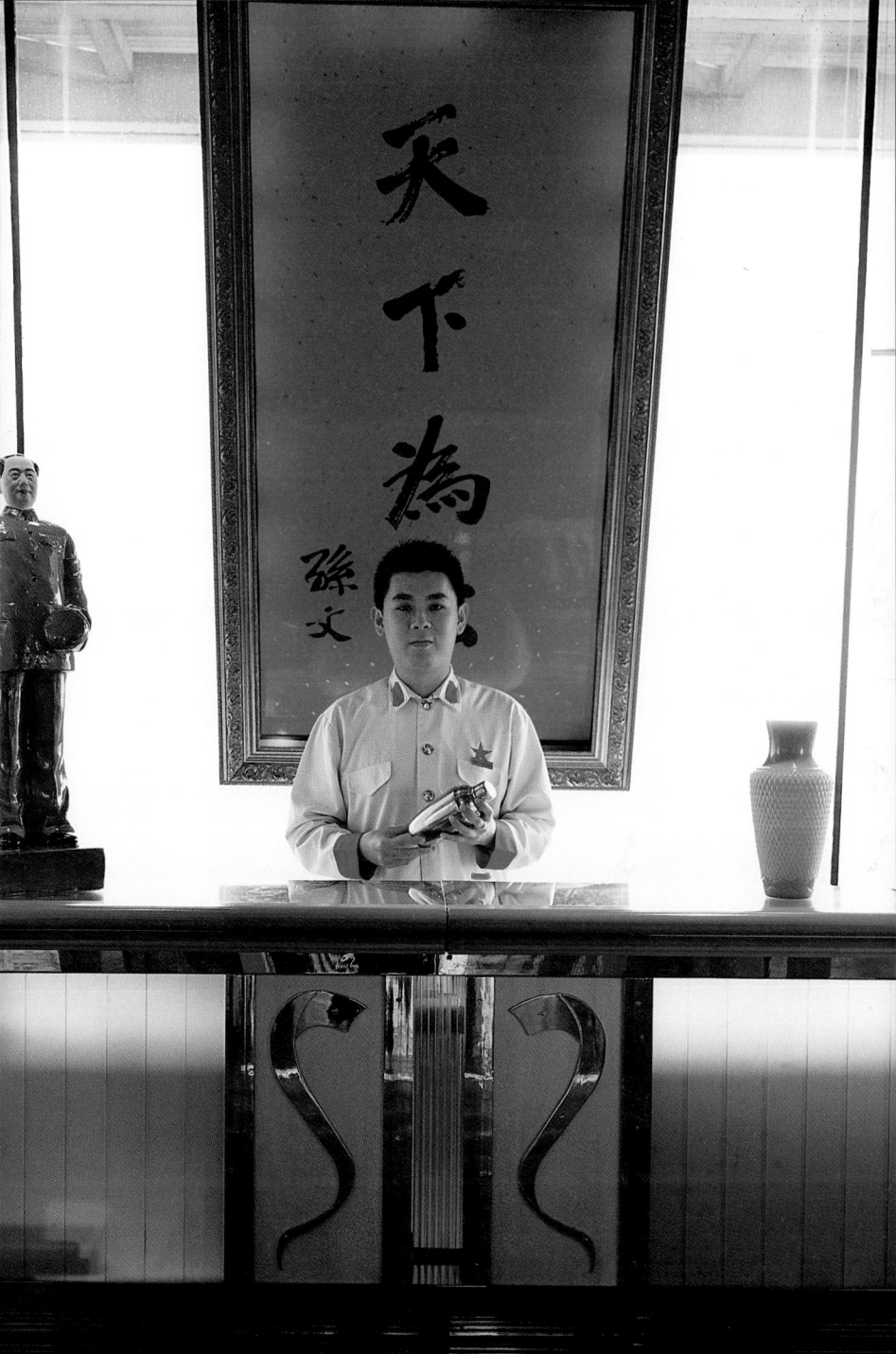

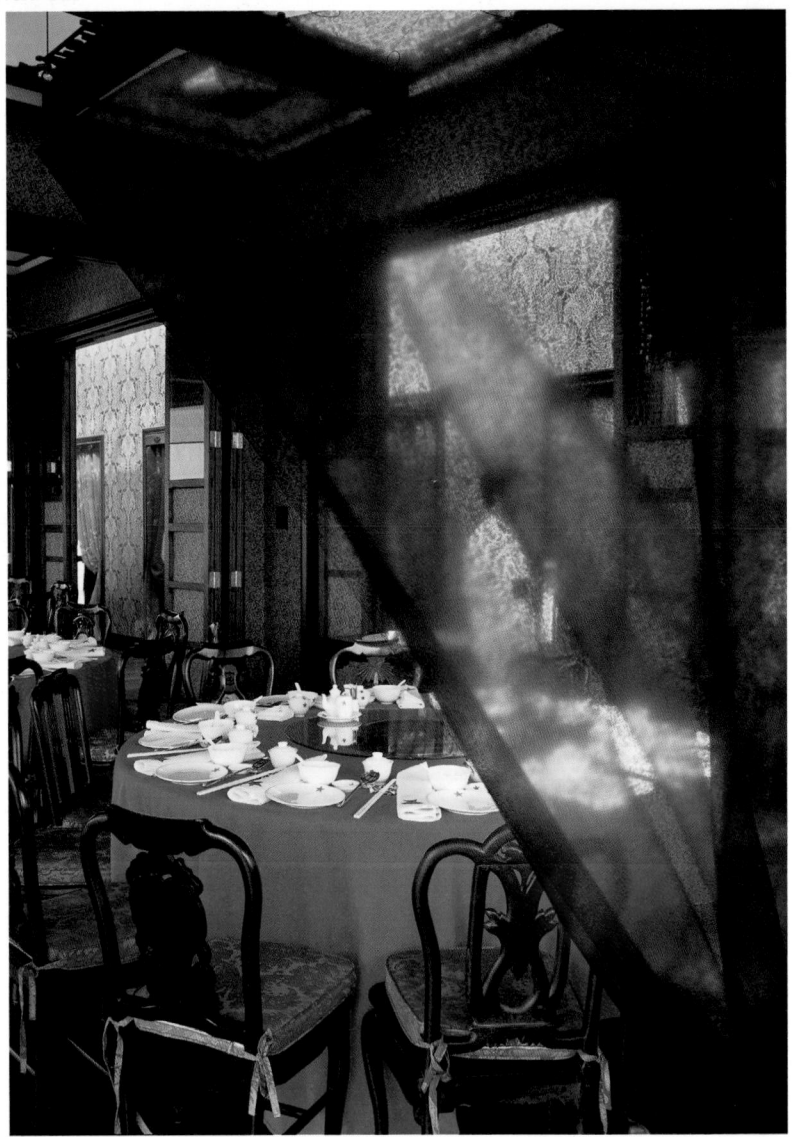

↑ French 19th-century wallpaper and flowing swathes of silk in a private dining room. • Französische Tapeten aus dem 19. Jahrhundert und Seide in verschwenderischem Ausmaß in einem der privaten Speiseräume. • Papier peint

français 19ᵉ et drapés de soie dans une salle à manger particulière.

→ Borrowed from Mao's army, the club's red star insignia is emblazoned on its china and napery. • Der China Club

hat den roten Stern der Armee Maos als Insignien ausgeliehen und Service und Tischwäsche damit verziert. • Emprunt à l'armée de Mao, l'étoile rouge symbole du club apparaît sur la porcelaine et le linge de table.

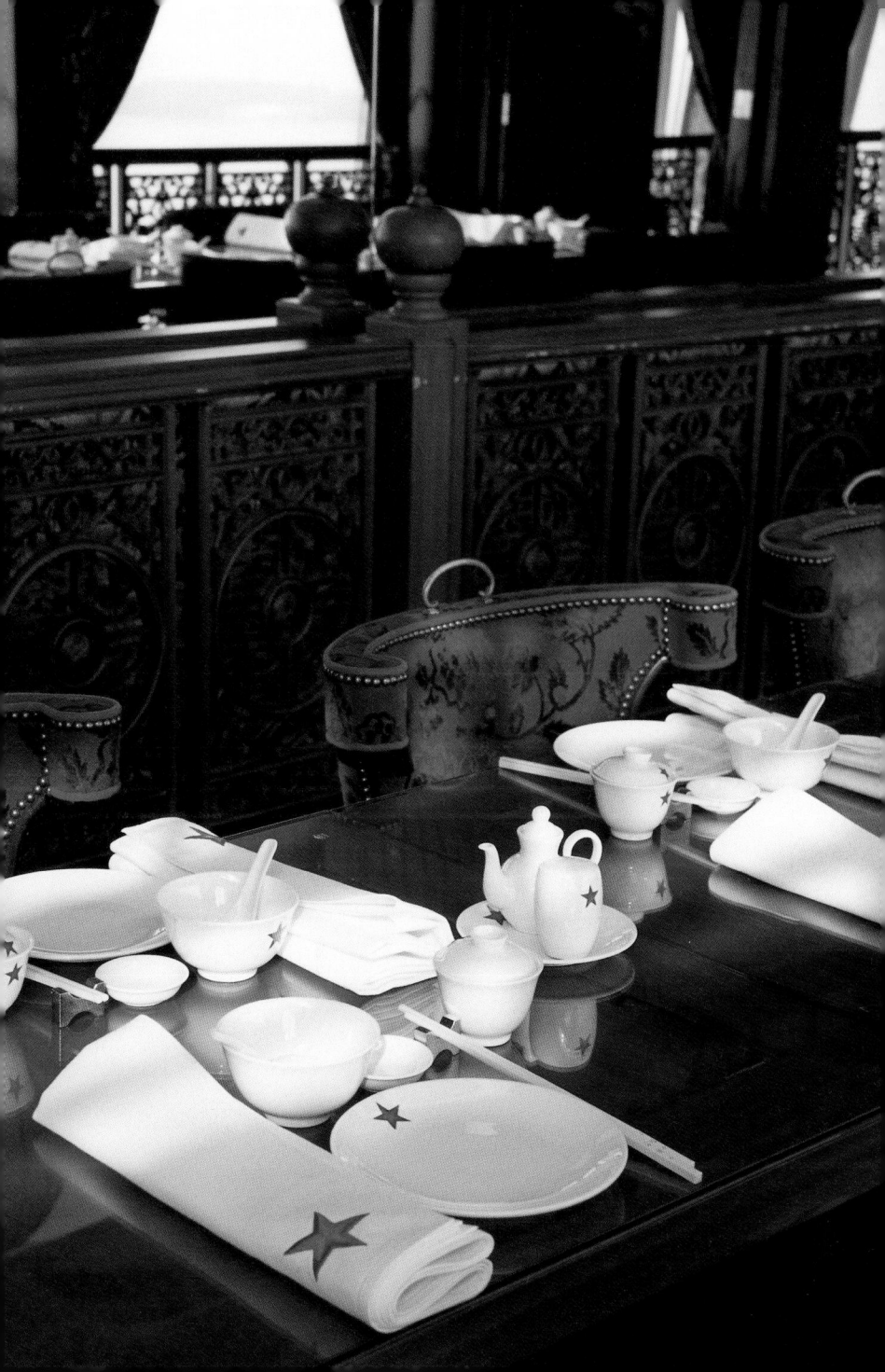

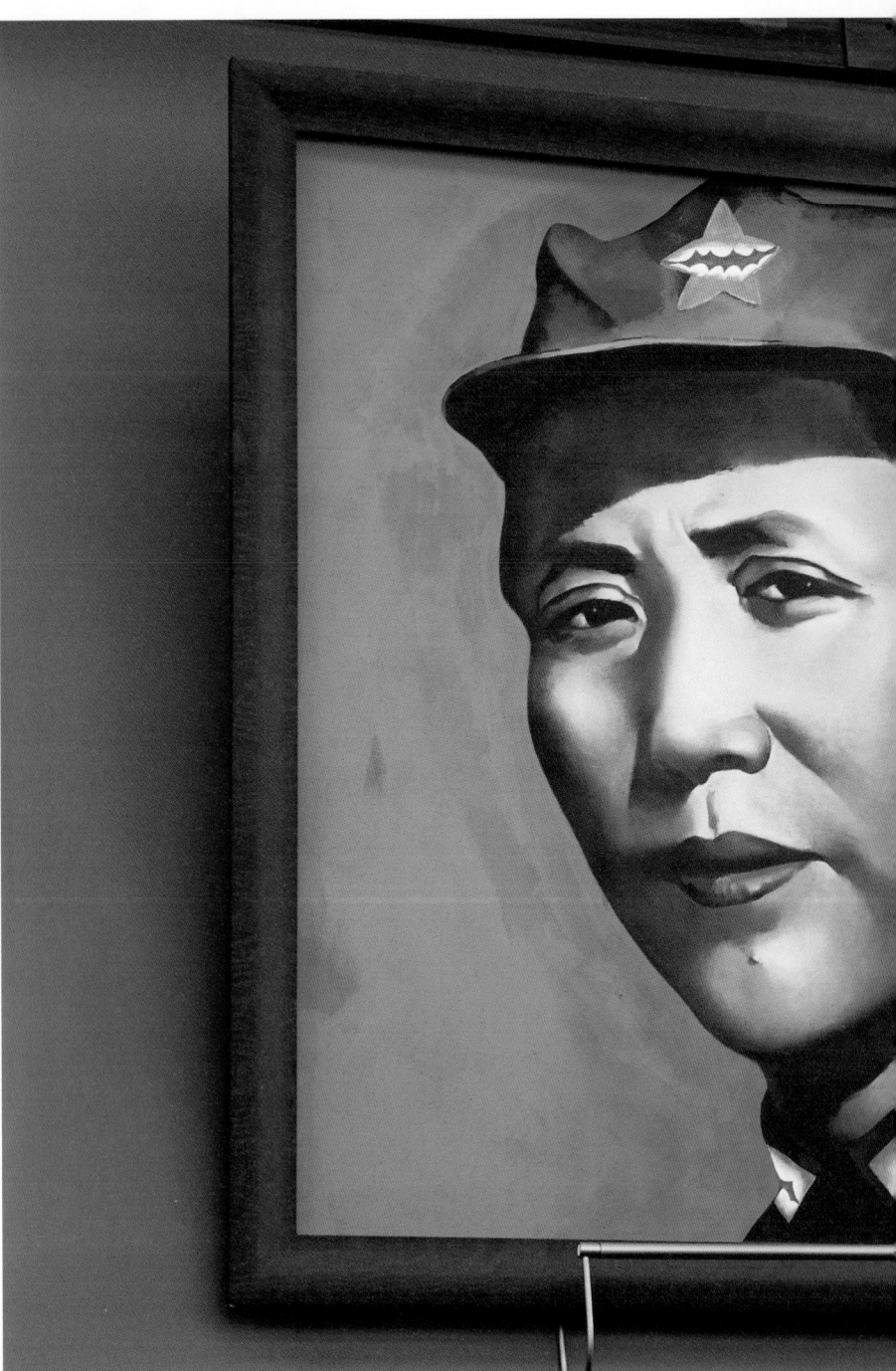

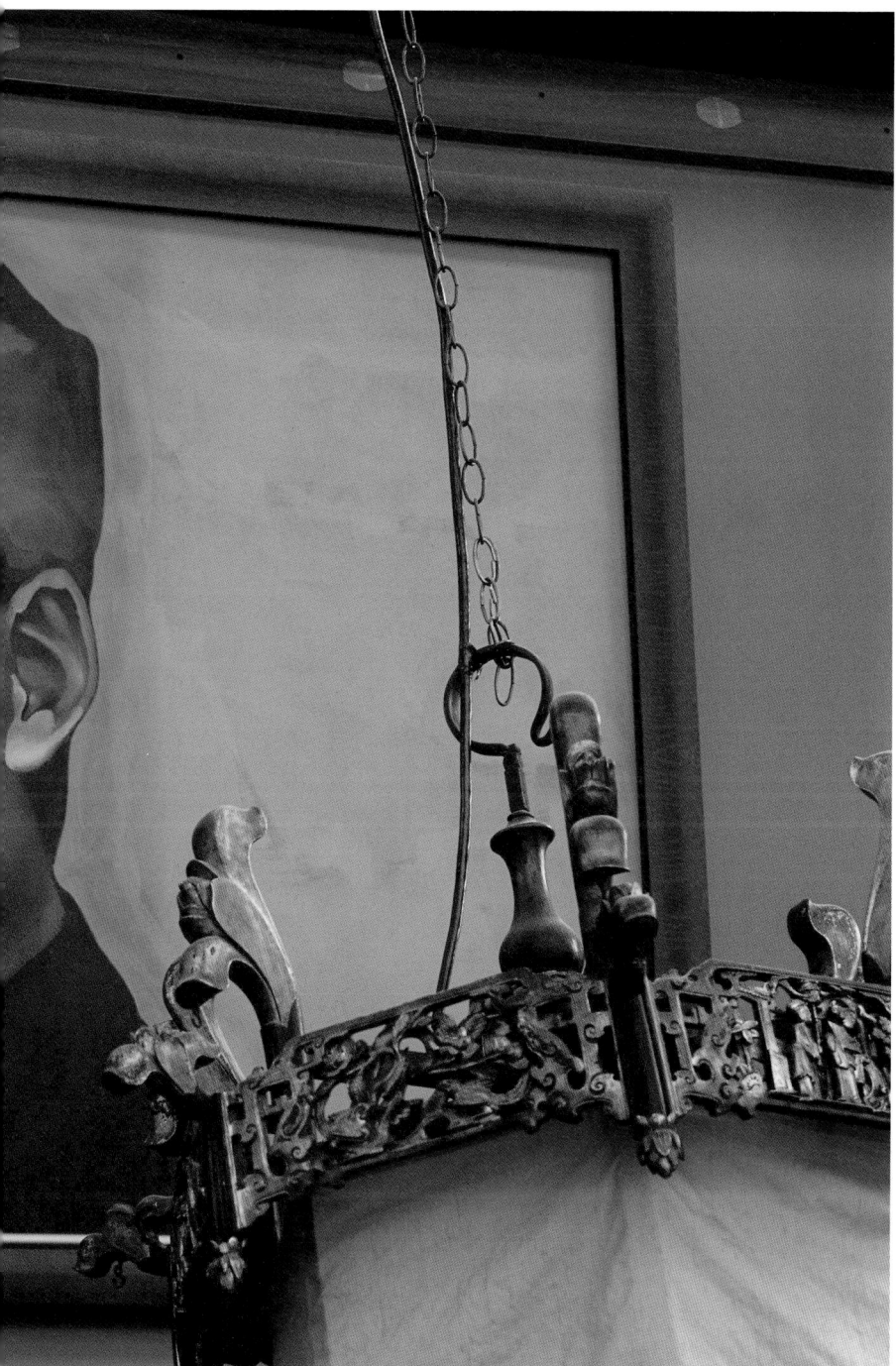

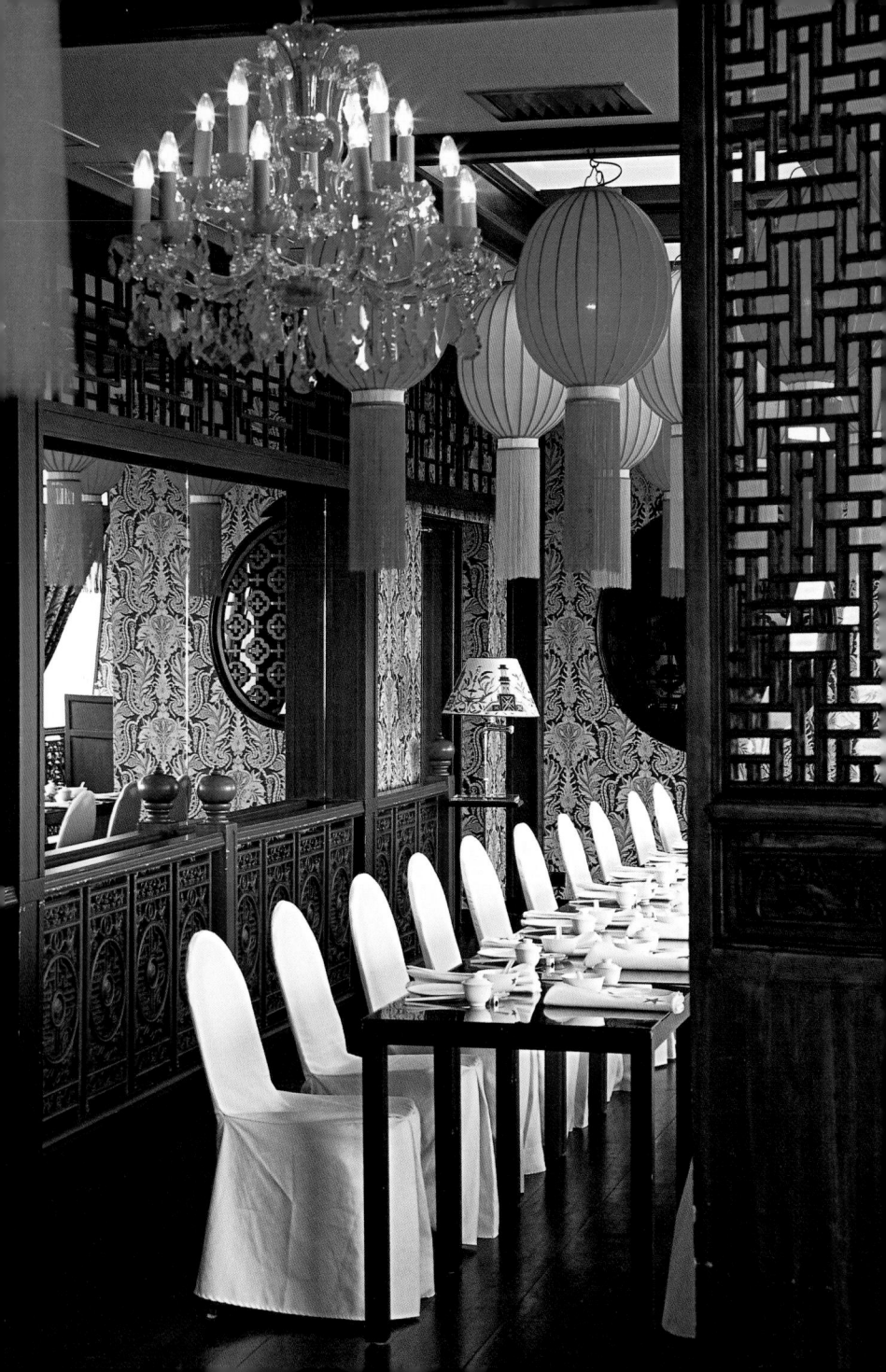

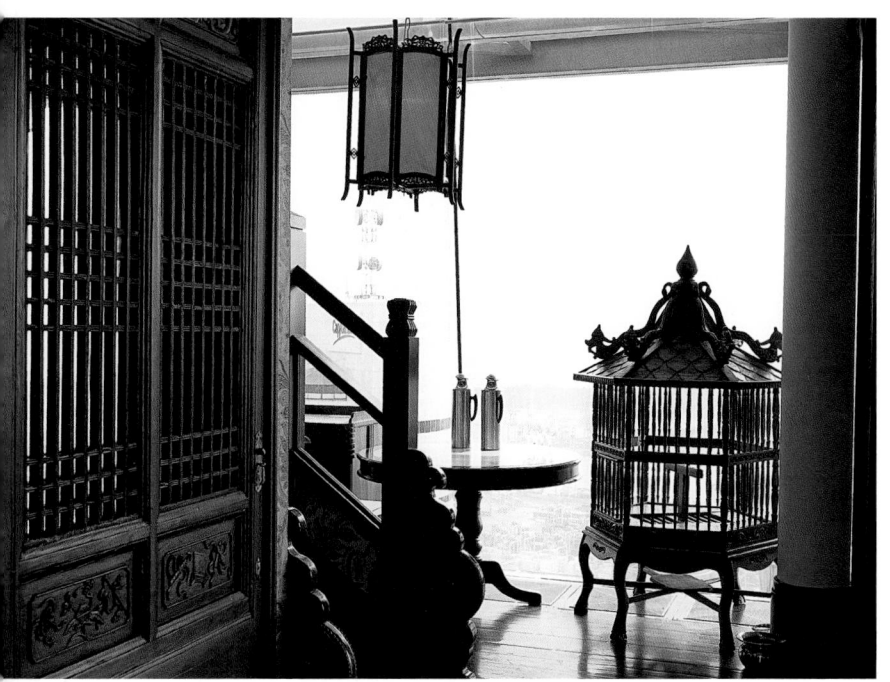

PP. 454–455 A youthful portrait of Mao in a Warhol-style silk-screen print. • Porträt Maos als junger Mann als Siebdruck im Stile Warhols. • Mao jeune homme, sérigraphie sur soie à la manière de Warhol.

← Gaudy Italian chandeliers and Chinese lattice doors recreate the atmosphere of old Shanghai. • Knallige italienische Kronleuchter und chinesi-sche Spaliertüren beschwören die Atmosphäre des alten Schanghai. • Ambiance Vieux Shanghai avec un lustre italien aux couleurs voyantes et des portes à claire-voie chinoises.

↑ A pagoda-shaped birdcage beside a floor-to-ceiling glass wall overlooking Singapore's skyline. • Ein pagoden-förmiger Vogelkäfig neben einem raum-hohen Panoramafenster mit Blick auf die Skyline Singapurs. • Une cage à oiseaux en forme de pagode devant une baie vitrée découvrant le panorama de Singapour.

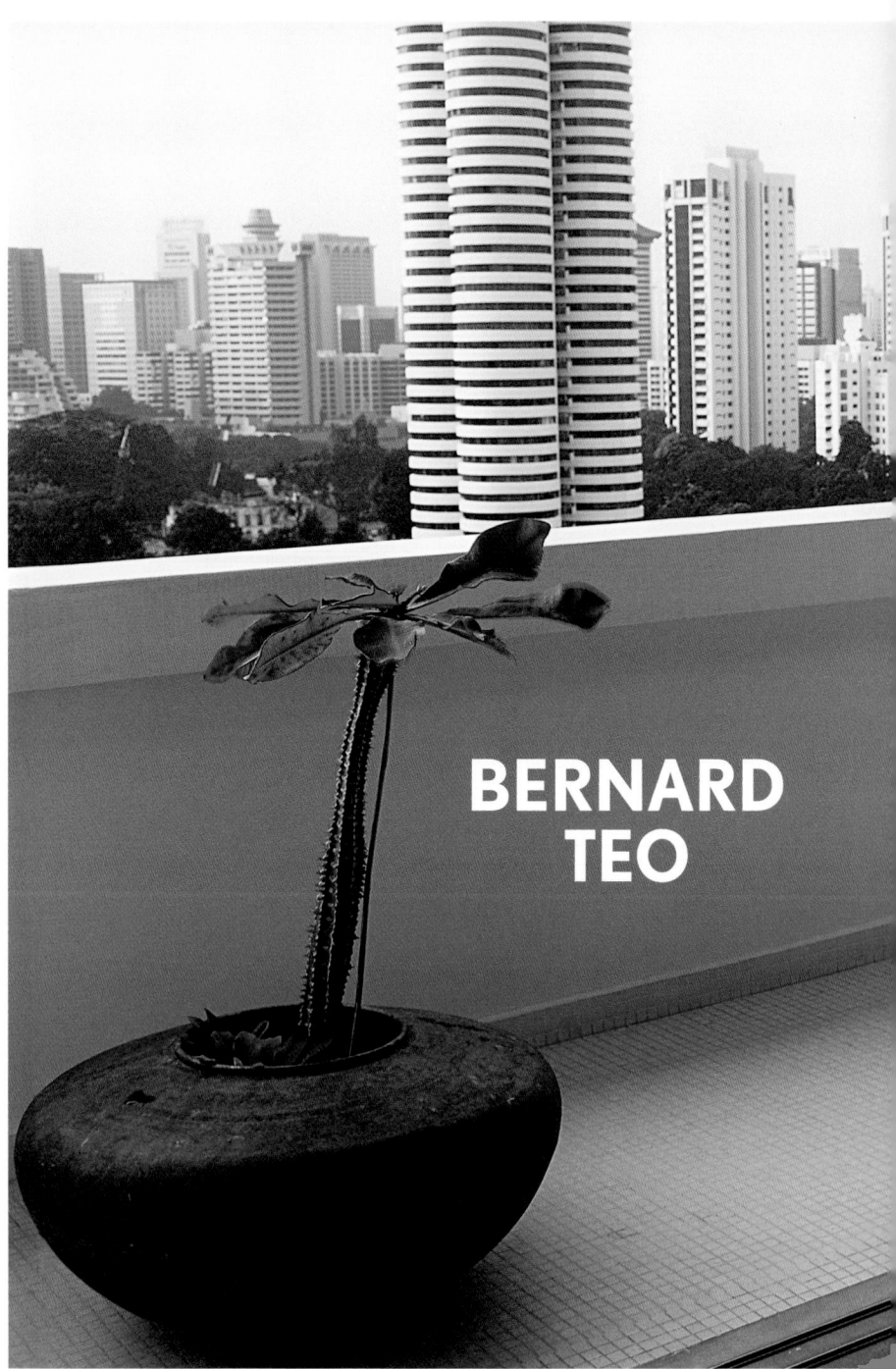

BERNARD
TEO

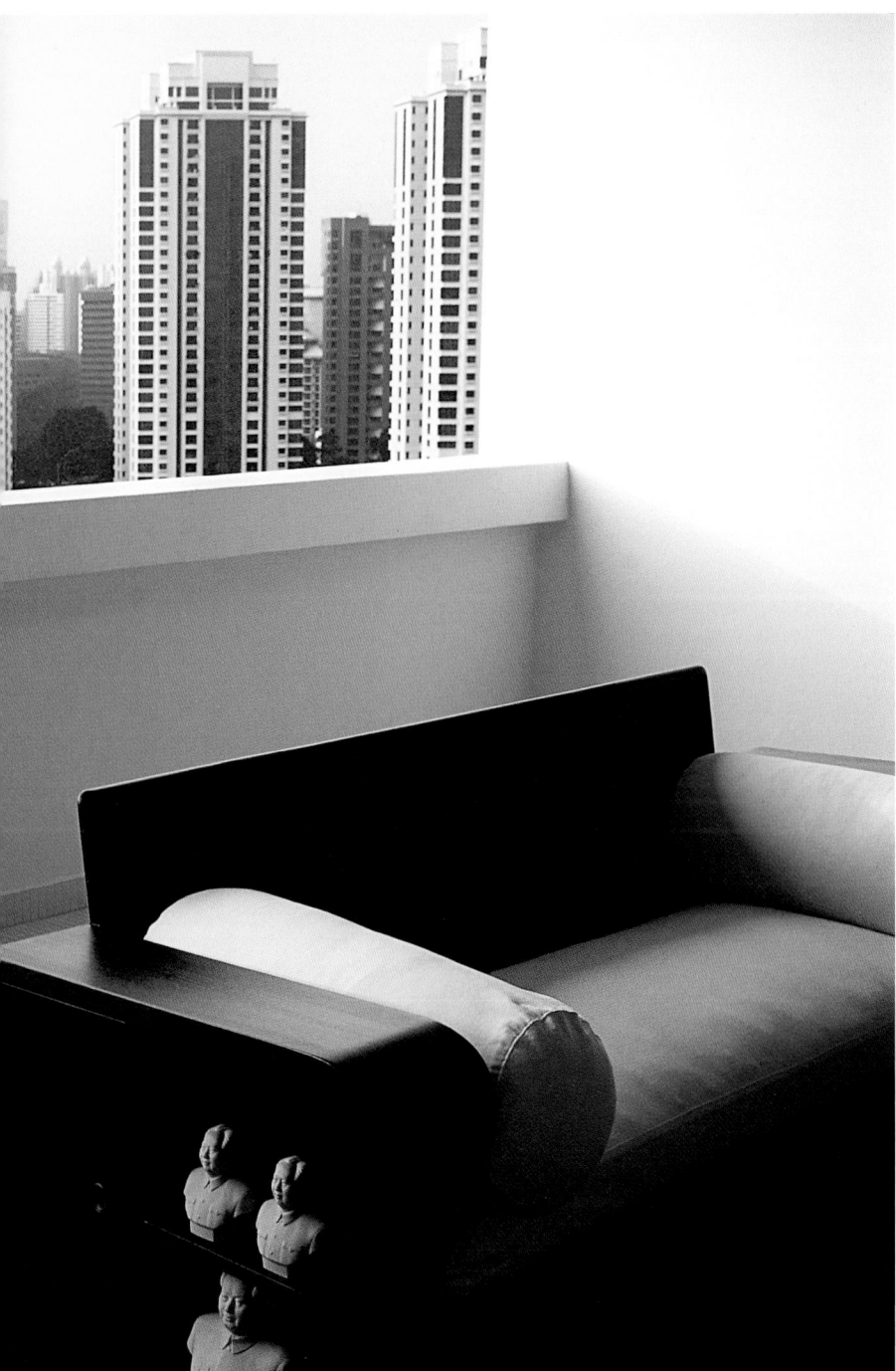

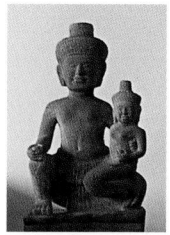

BERNARD TEO
SINGAPORE

High up on the fifteenth floor of an early 1960s modernist apartment block in the heart of Singapore, fashion retailer Bernard Teo's flat is a whimsical fusion of the old and new. The building sits on a hill, overlooking a green belt dotted with pre-war colonial bungalows. Finding it was a pursuit of love: Bernard first saw the flat thirty years ago, when it belonged to a girlfriend, and liked it so much that when it came up for sale six years later, he acquired it and literally took it apart. One of the bedrooms was sacrificed to extend the dining area and, over the years, he has reworked the place to suit his style. Modern art from Bali, industrial lighting saved from hospitals and schools, eclectic furniture, and a rare flowering cactus in an old Javanese copper container on the long terrace. Most amusing of all is the 175-piece collection of porcelain figures of Chairman Mao produced during the Cultural Revolution. Bernard started the collection because of his father's uncanny resemblance to the Great Helmsman.

Bernard Teos Wohnung liegt hoch oben im fünfzehnten Stock eines modernistischen Wohnblocks aus den frühen 1960er-Jahren mitten in Singapur. Der Boutiquenbesitzer verbindet in der Einrichtung Alt und Neu auf kuriose Weise. Das Gebäude steht auf einem Hügel, der Blick geht auf einen Grüngürtel mit Bungalows im Kolonialstil. Die Wohnung ging Teo nicht mehr aus dem Kopf, seit er sie vor über dreißig Jahren zum ersten Mal sah. Damals gehörte sie einer Freundin, aber als sie sechs Jahre später zum Verkauf stand, griff er sofort zu. Teo mochte die Wohnung sehr und nahm sie dennoch buchstäblich auseinander. Er opferte ein Schlafzimmer zugunsten einer Erweiterung des Esszimmers und gestaltete die Wohnung über die Jahre nach seinem Geschmack um. Eklektizistisch kombinierte er moderne Kunst aus Bali mit Werkslampen, die er aus Schulen oder Krankenhäusern rettete, und diversen Möbelstücken wie dem Wohnzimmersofa im Kolonialstil, das ihm die Bank of China im Zuge einer Renovierung verkaufte. Die kuriose 175 Exemplare umfassende Sammlung von Porzellanfiguren aus der Zeit der Kulturrevolution, die den Großen Vorsitzenden Mao darstellen, begann Bernard Teo wegen der verblüffenden Ähnlichkeit des Politikers mit seinem Vater.

Situé au quinzième étage d'un immeuble construit au début des années 1960 au centre de Singapour, l'appartement de Bernard Teo est un curieux mélange d'ancien et de neuf. L'immeuble est juché sur une colline, d'où il domine une ceinture verte émaillée de pavillons de style colonial remontant à l'avant-guerre. Son propriétaire est tombé amoureux de l'appartement il y a plus de trente ans, quand il l'a vu pour la première fois. Il appartenait alors à une de ses amies, et lorsqu'il a été mis en vente six ans plus tard, il en a fait l'acquisition parce qu'il l'aimait toujours autant – ce qui ne l'a pas empêché de le mettre littéralement en pièces. Il a sacrifié une des chambres pour agrandir le coin repas et, au fil des ans, il a remodelé le logement à son goût. De l'art moderne balinais et des éclairages industriels récupérés dans des hôpitaux ou des écoles côtoient des meubles hétéroclites. Le plus amusant de la décoration est la collection de 175 présidents Mao en porcelaine produits pendant la Révolution culturelle, collection que Bernard Teo avait commencée à cause de la troublante ressemblance entre son père et le Grand Timonier.

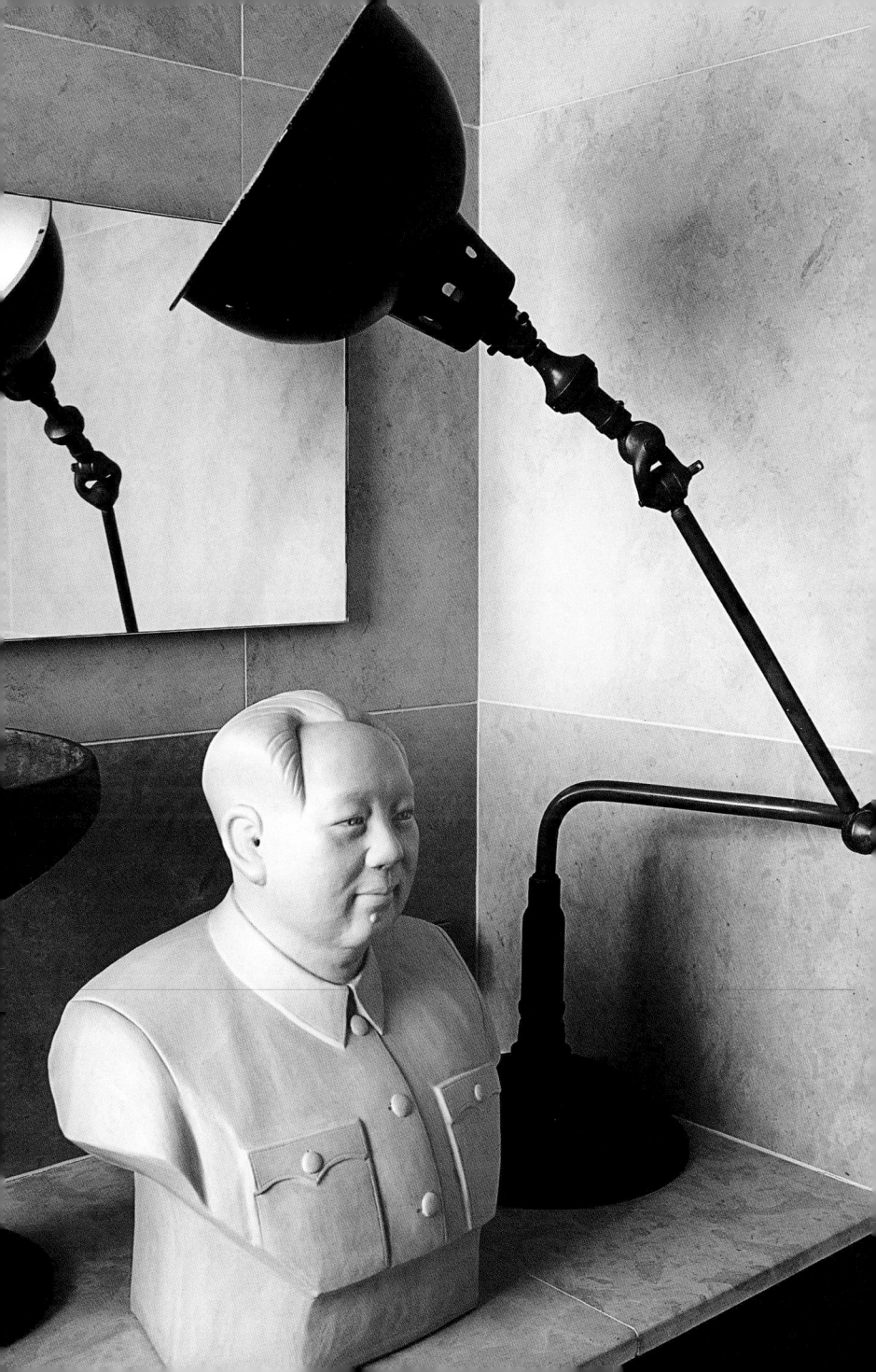

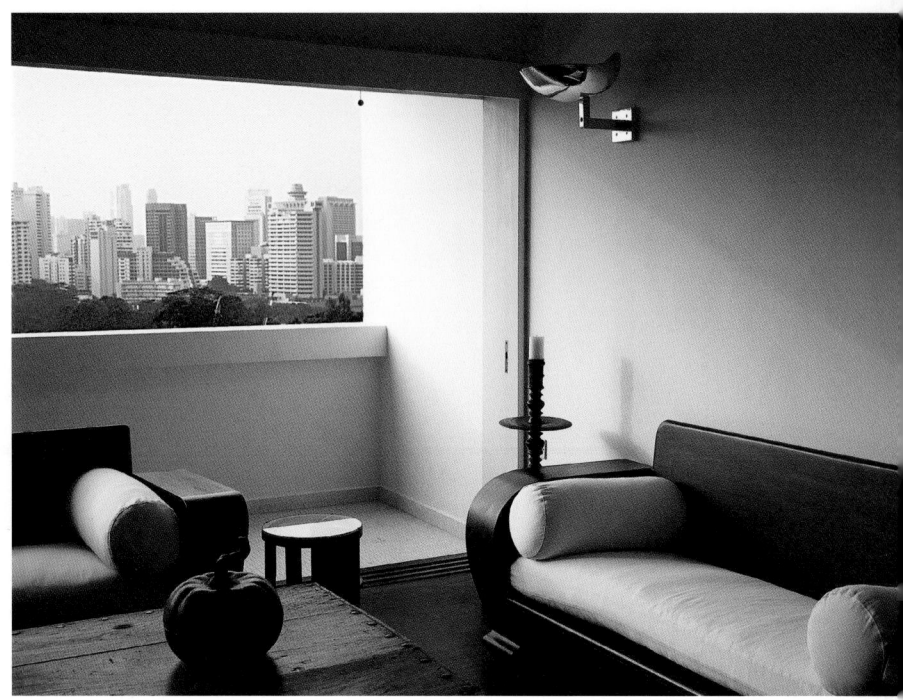

PP. 458–459 The terrace frames the city's skyline. • Durch das Fenster geht der Blick auf die Skyline der Stadt. • Les fenêtres encadrent la vue de la ville avec ses gratte-ciel.

↑ The colonial-style sofa was thrown out by the Bank of China when they were renovating their office. • Die Bank

of China entledigte sich im Zuge einer Renovierung dieses Kolonialstil-Sofas. • La Bank of China avait mis au rebut ce canapé de style colonial à l'occasion d'une rénovation.

→ A cabinet of curiosities is filled with Bernard Teo's collection of porcelain Mao figures which overflow into the

sofa's niche. • Das Kuriositätenkabinett enthält Bernard Teos Sammlung von Porzellanfiguren Maos, die bis in die Sofaecke vordringen. • À l'étroit dans un cabinet de curiosités, la collection de Mao en porcelaine de Bernard Teo se déverse dans la niche aménagée pour le sofa.

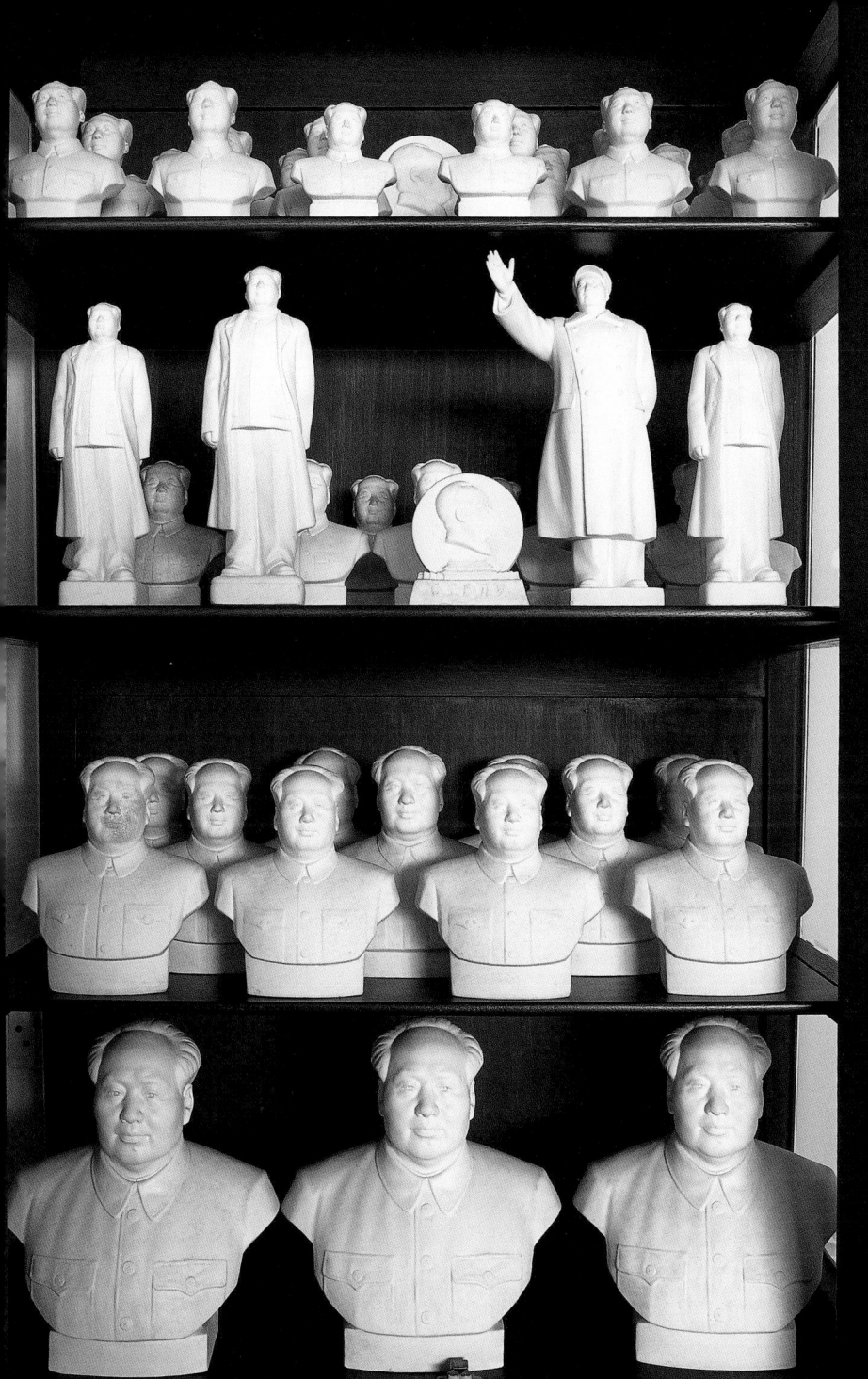

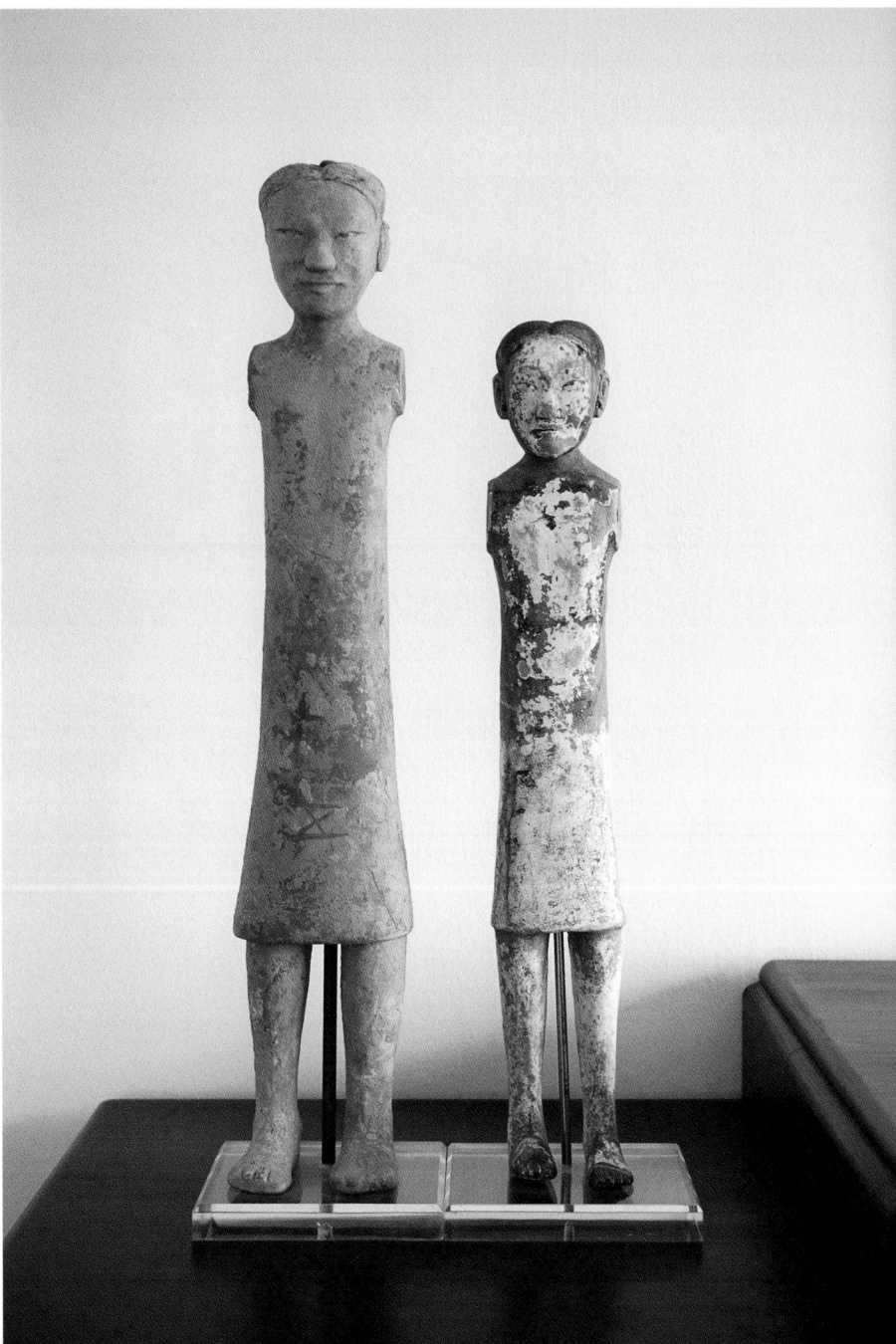

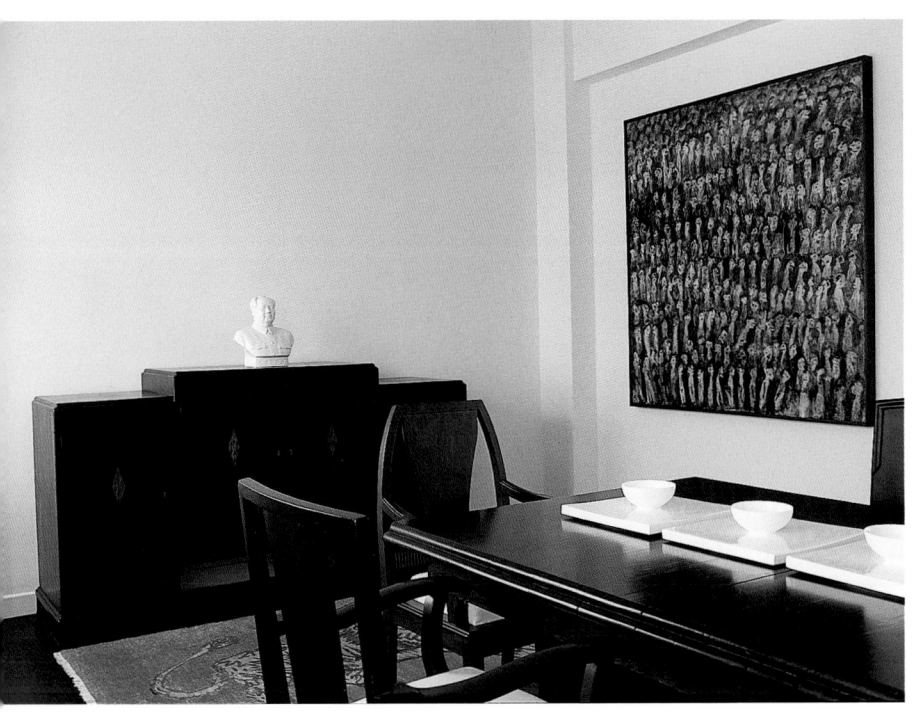

↑ A painting titled "Positive Negative" by Balinese artist Taman hangs above a 1940s Art Deco dining table. • Hinter dem Art-déco-Esstisch aus den 1940er-Jahren hängt das Bild „Positive Negative" des balinesischen Malers Taman. • Une œuvre de l'artiste balinais Taman intitulée « Positive Negative » est accrochée au-dessus d'une table Art déco des années 1940.

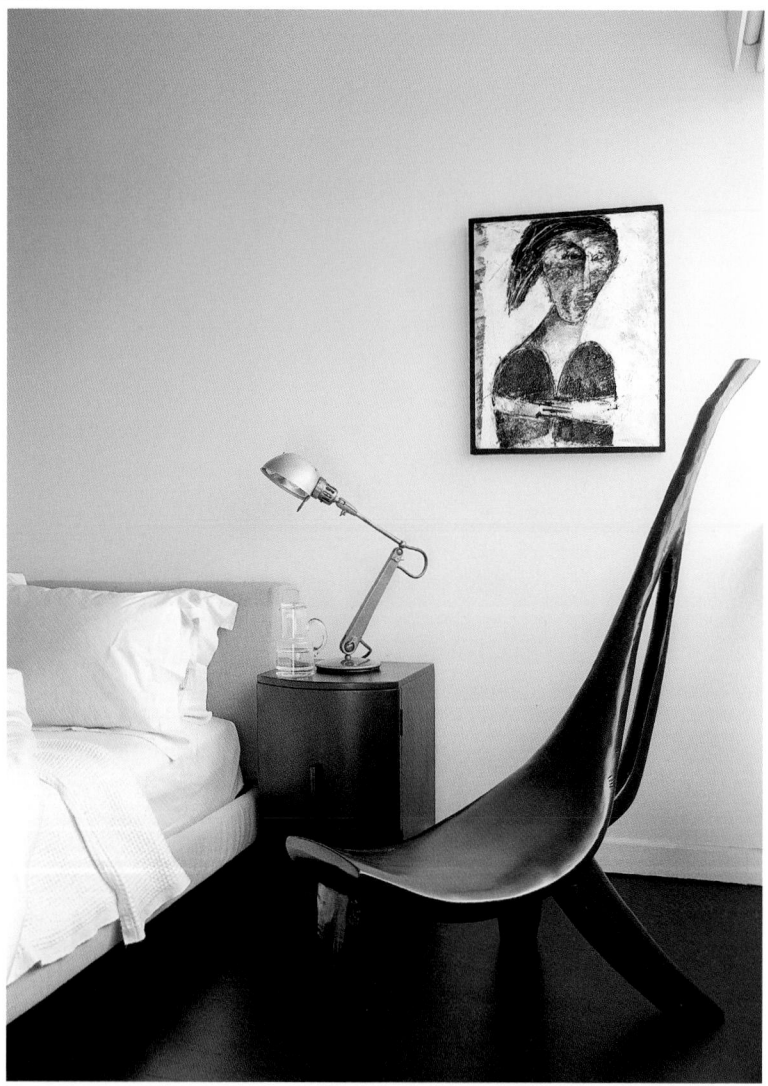

↑ In the bedroom an African chair with sensuous lines lends interest. The painting on the wall is a self-portrait by Balinese artist Made Djirna. • Der sinnlich anmutende afrikanische Stuhl steht im Schlafzimmer. An der Wand hängt ein Selbstporträt des balinesischen Künstlers Made

Djirna. • Une chaise africaine aux lignes sensuelles donne un petit quelque chose à la chambre. Le tableau au mur est un autoportrait de l'artiste balinais Made Djirna.

→ Photographs of Tibetan children by American photo journalist Phil Borges

hang above an Art-Deco style cabinet. • Die Fotos von tibetischen Kindern des amerikanischen Bildjournalisten Phil Borges hängen über einer Vitrine im Art-déco-Stil. • Au-dessus d'un meuble bas Art déco, photographies d'enfants tibétains prises par le photo-journaliste Phil Borges.

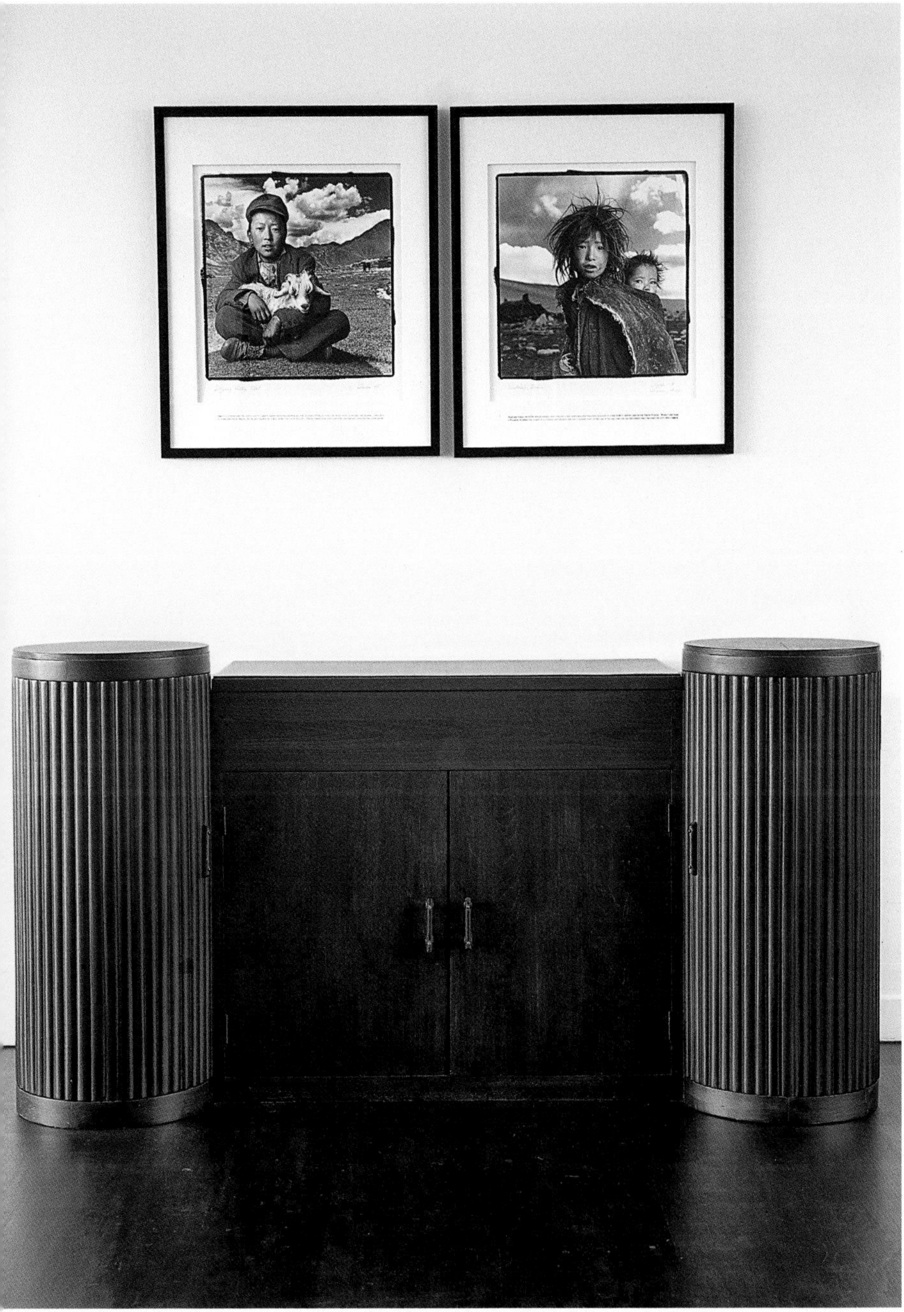

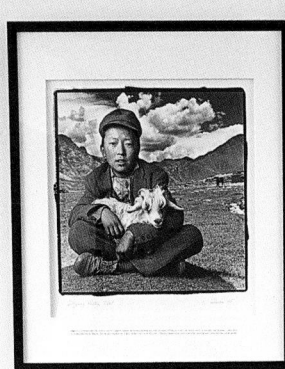
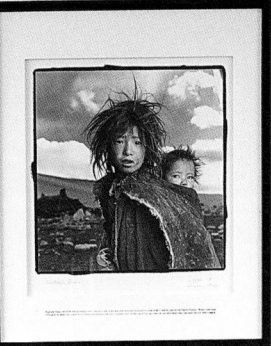

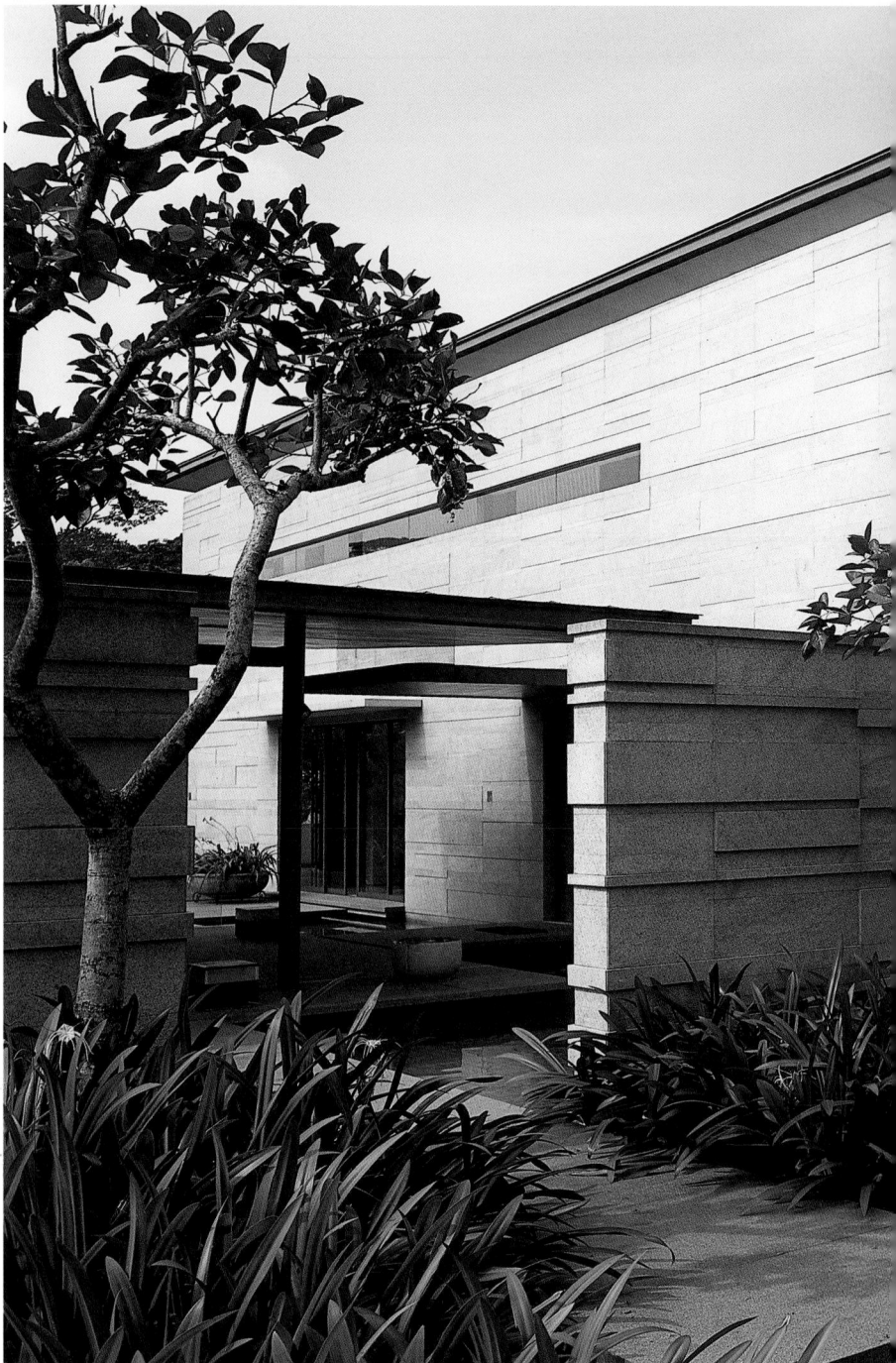

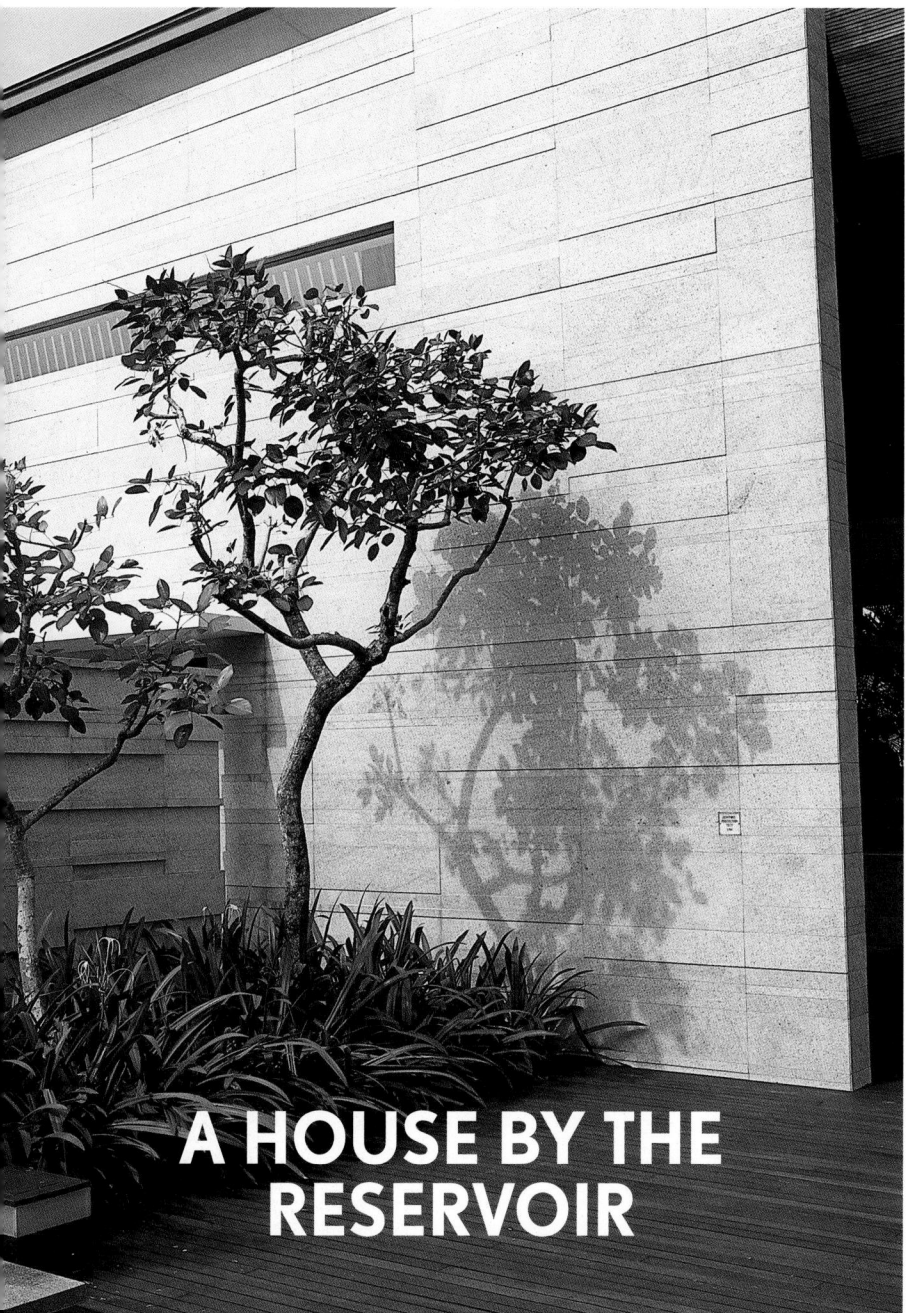

A HOUSE BY THE RESERVOIR

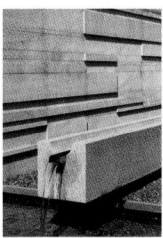

A HOUSE BY THE RESERVOIR

SINGAPORE

The house by the reservoir was commissioned by a businessman who finds many of the conventions of minimalism in modern architecture repetitive and predictable. Such houses often end up looking the same, a style he calls "straight-lined tropical". For the owner, the first achievement of his recently finished home was the plot's idyllic location near MacRitchie Reservoir, a green lung in the bustling commercial metropolis. The reservoir and its catchment area in fact became the inspired metaphor for the house. Architect Soo K. Chan extended the sense of greenery and water by providing two swimming pools, one of them infinity-edged, the overflow from which forms a running channel. The water features are flanked by granite walls skillfully built from stone blocks of varying sizes; like sculptural reliefs they break the monotony of line and surface. Double volume plate glass windows and an open-air atrium give the three wings of the house a well-proportioned lightness. Singapore's old reservoir has acquired a water pavilion in its vicinity.

Das Haus wurde von einem Geschäftsmann in Auftrag gegeben, der viele Elemente des Minimalismus in der modernen Architektur eintönig und vorhersehbar findet. Solche Häuser ähneln sich oft in einem Stil, den er „gradlinig tropisch" nennt. Für ihn selbst fing alles damit an, dass er das idyllische Grundstück in der Nähe des MacRitchie-Reservoirs fand, einer grünen Lunge in der geschäftigen Handelsmetropole. Das Wasserreservoir und sein Einzugsgebiet entwickelten sich zum Leitmotiv für das Haus. Der Architekt Soo K. Chan weitete die Vorstellung von Wasser und Grün aus und ließ zwei Swimmingpools bauen – der eine läuft an einem Ende stets über und strömt in einen fließenden Kanal. Um die Wasserbecken stehen Granitmauern, die geschickt aus unterschiedlich großen Steinblöcken gefertigt wurden. Wie die Reliefs eines Bildhauers brechen sie die Eintönigkeit der Begrenzungen und Oberflächen. Doppelglasfenster und ein Open-Air-Atrium verleihen den drei Flügeln des Hauses eine wohlproportionierte Leichtigkeit. Neben dem alten Wasserspeicher von Singapur steht jetzt ein Pavillon am Wasser.

Cette maison a été commandée par un homme d'affaires qui trouve que nombre des conventions du minimalisme en architecture moderne sont répétitives et prévisibles. Les maisons finissent toujours par être dans ce style qu'il appelle « tropical constant ». Pour le propriétaire, c'est la situation idyllique du terrain à proximité du MacRitchie Reservoir, un poumon vert dans la trépidante métropole commerçante, qui se trouve à l'origine du projet. La maison reprend la métaphore du réservoir et de son bassin hydrologique. Développant les thèmes de la verdure et de l'eau, l'architecte Soo K. Chan a prévu deux piscines, dont l'une s'écoule à l'infini : son trop-plein se déverse dans une rigole. Les pièces d'eau sont flanquées de murs habilement montés à partir de blocs de granite de différentes tailles, tels des reliefs rompant la monotonie de la ligne et de la surface. Des baies vitrées en double épaisseur et un atrium à ciel ouvert confèrent une légèreté équilibrée aux trois ailes de la maison. Le réservoir historique de Singapour a désormais son pavillon d'eau.

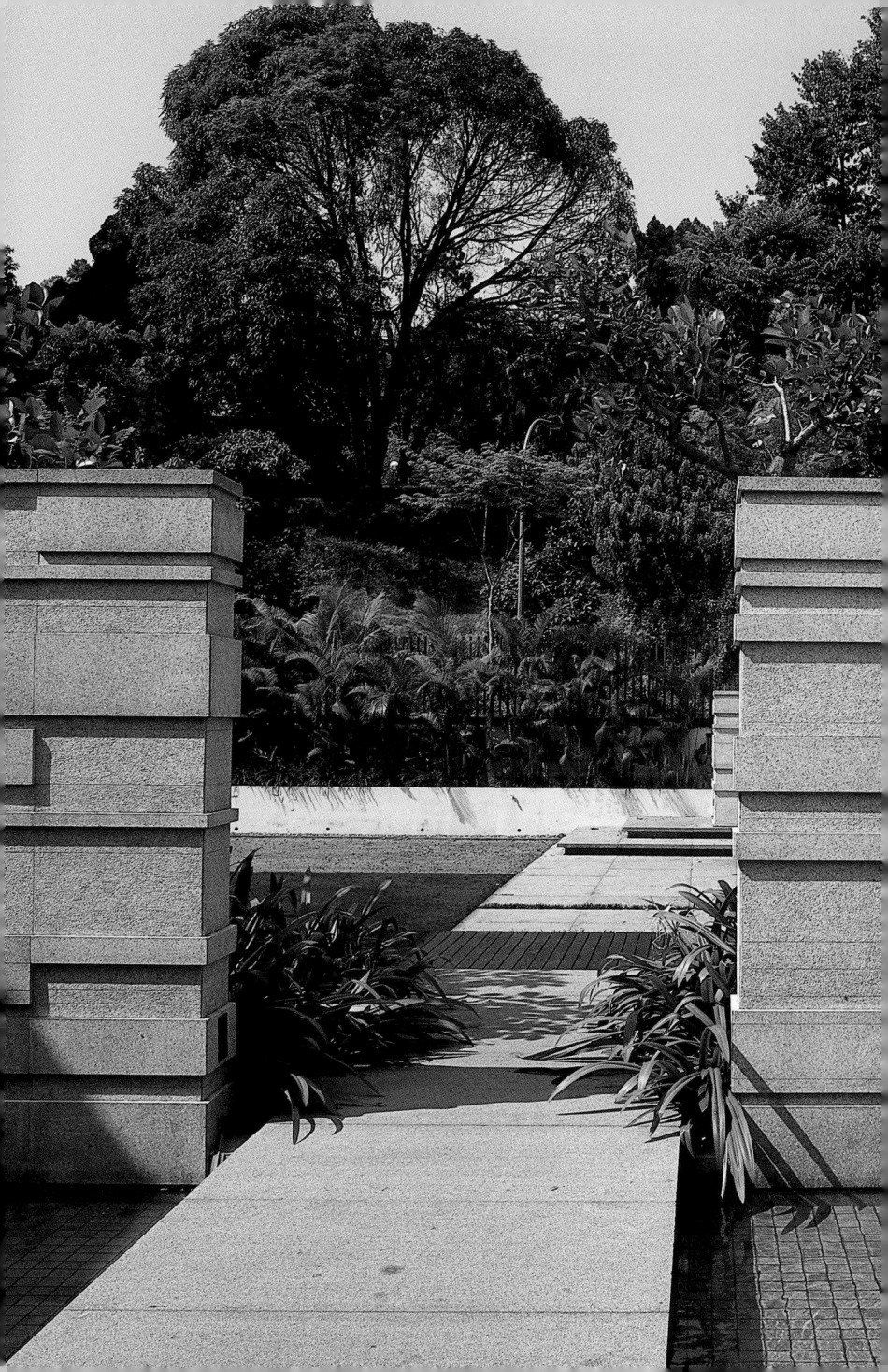

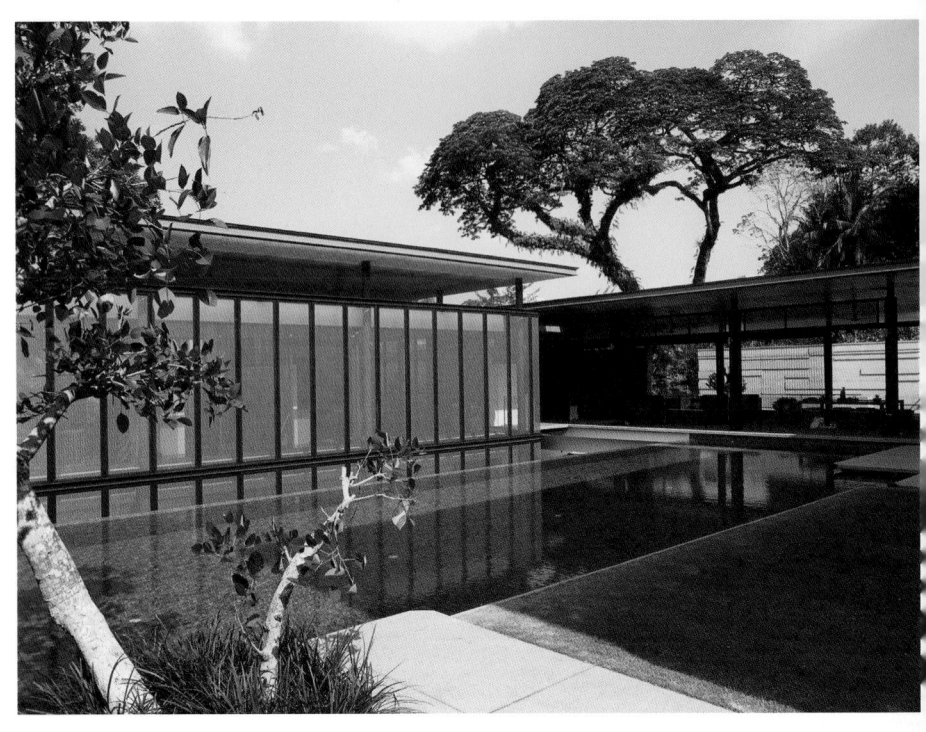

PP. 474–475 View from the pool looking towards the pavilion. • Blick vom Swimmingpool zum Pavillon. • De la piscine on voit très bien le pavillon.

→ A sense of water suffuses the courtyards of the house. A waterfall in the channel that runs along the house. •

Die Innenhöfe des Hauses sind von der Sinnlichkeit des Wassers erfüllt. Ein Wasserfall ergießt sich in den kleinen Kanal des Hauses. • L'eau est très présente dans les cours intérieures. Chute d'eau dans la rigole qui fait le tour de la maison.

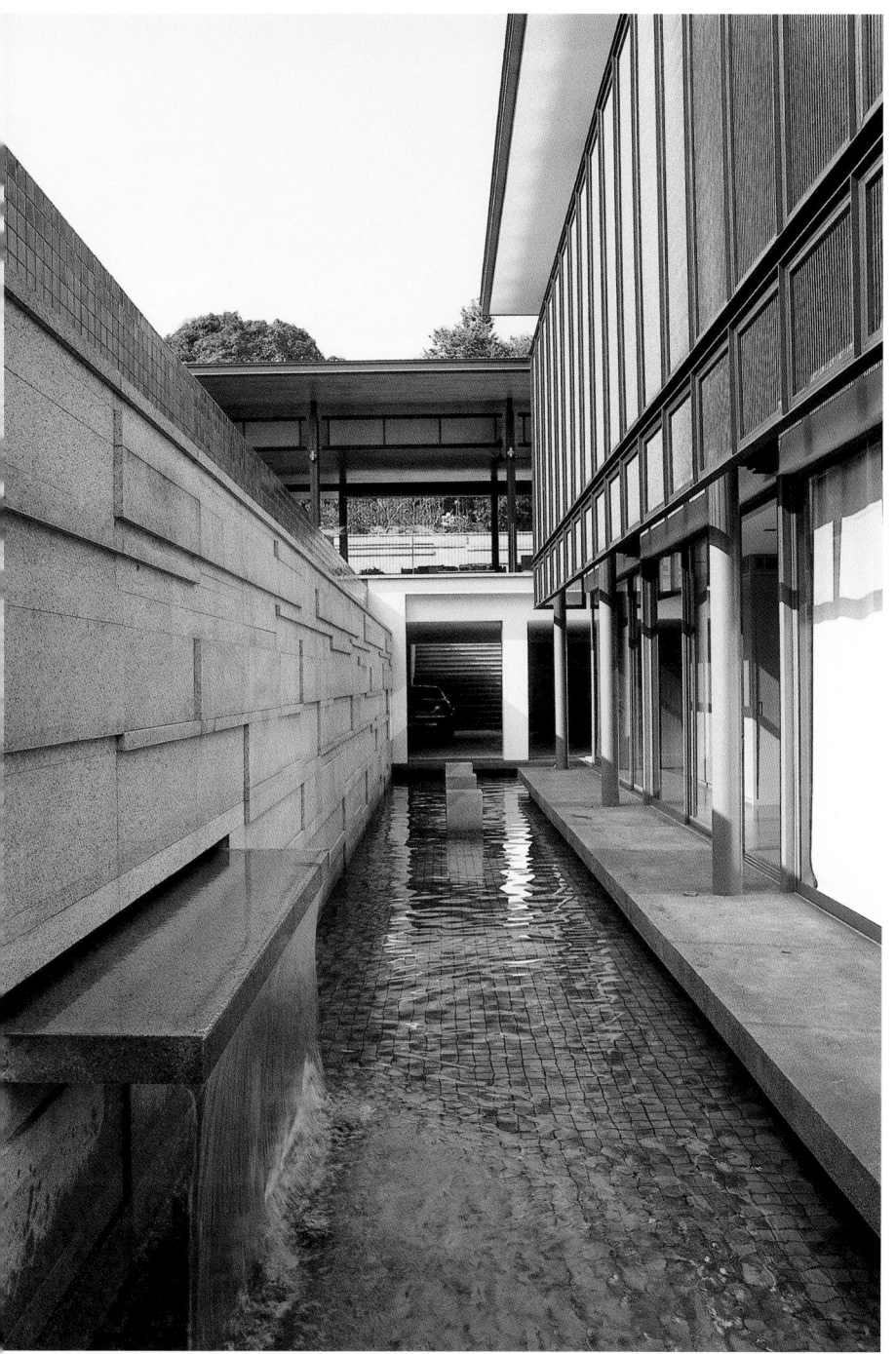

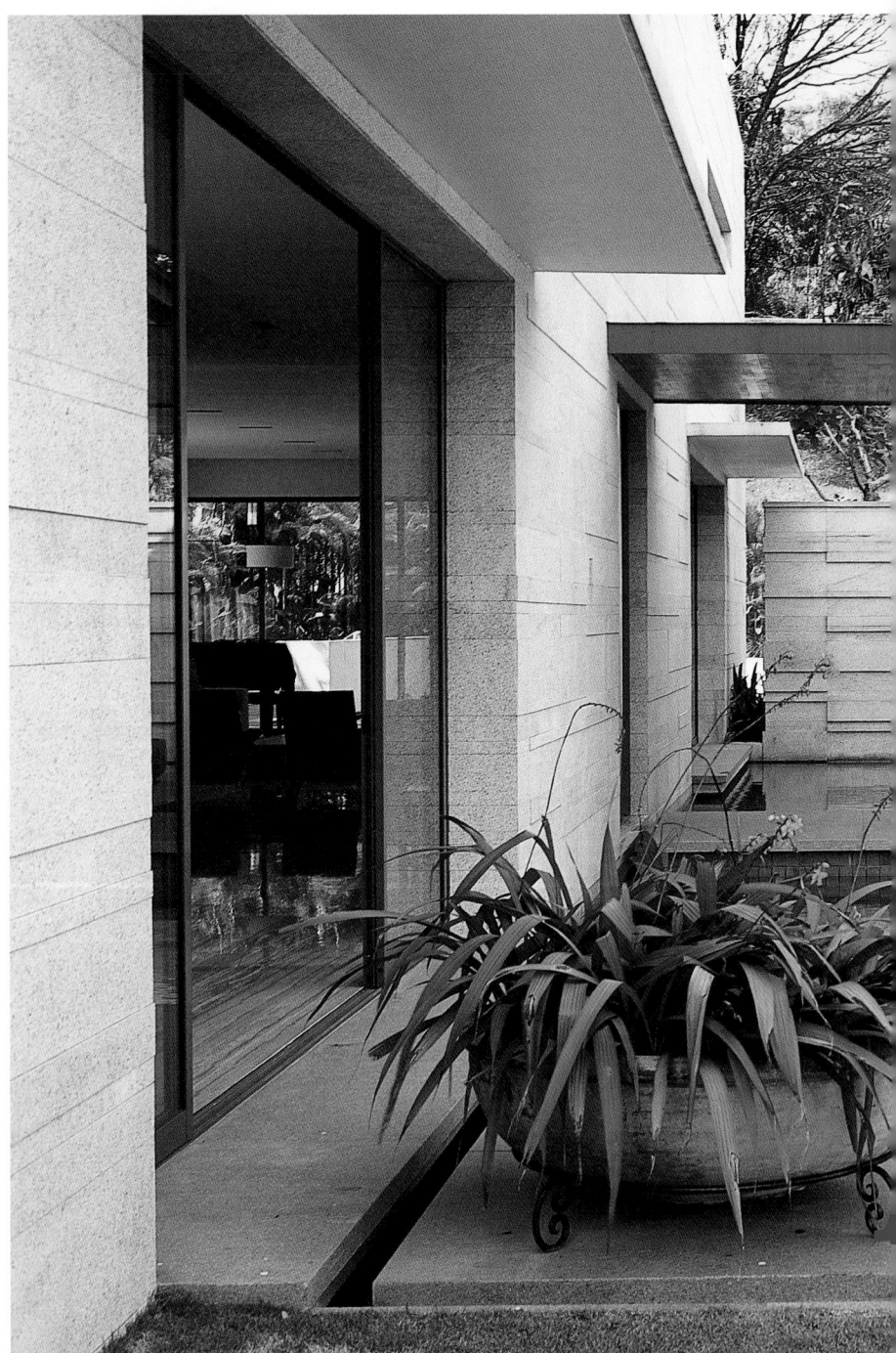

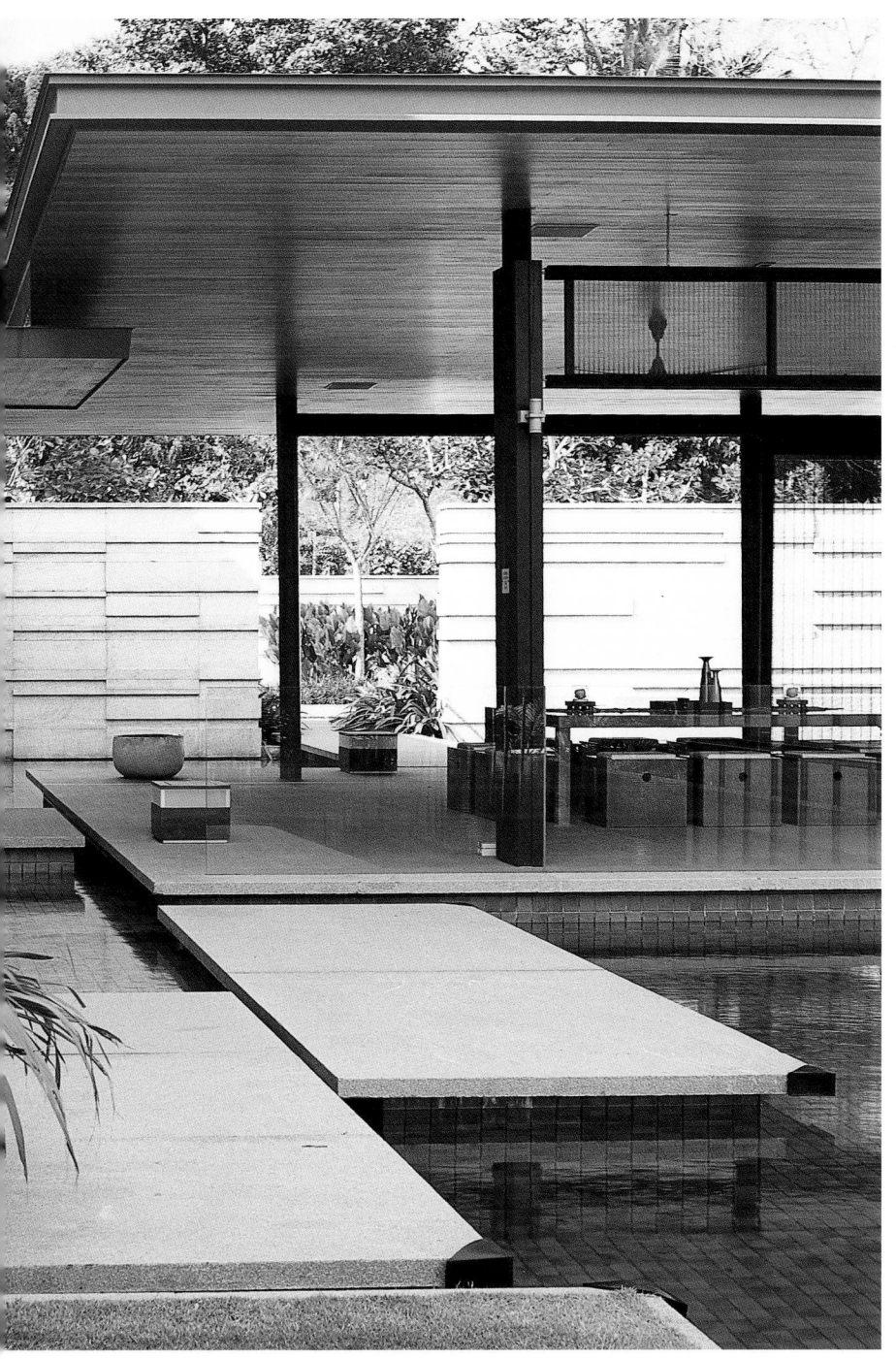

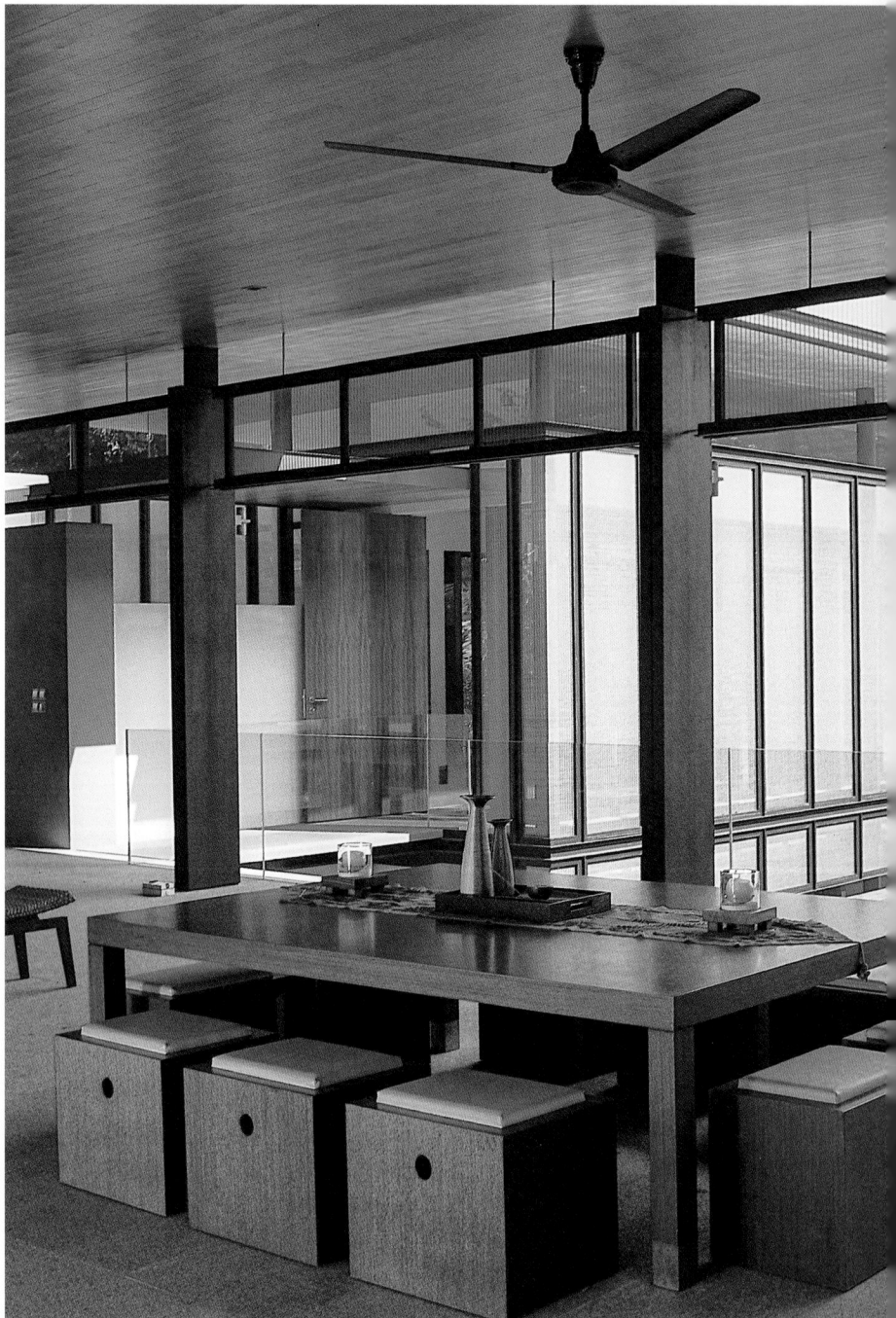

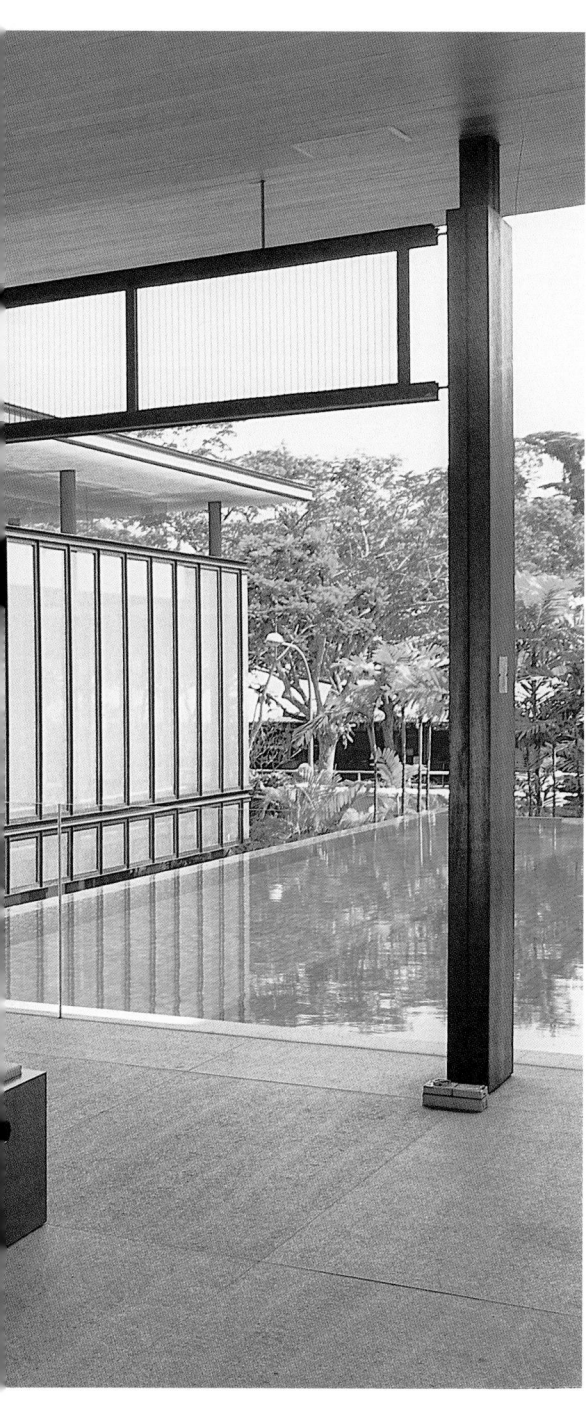

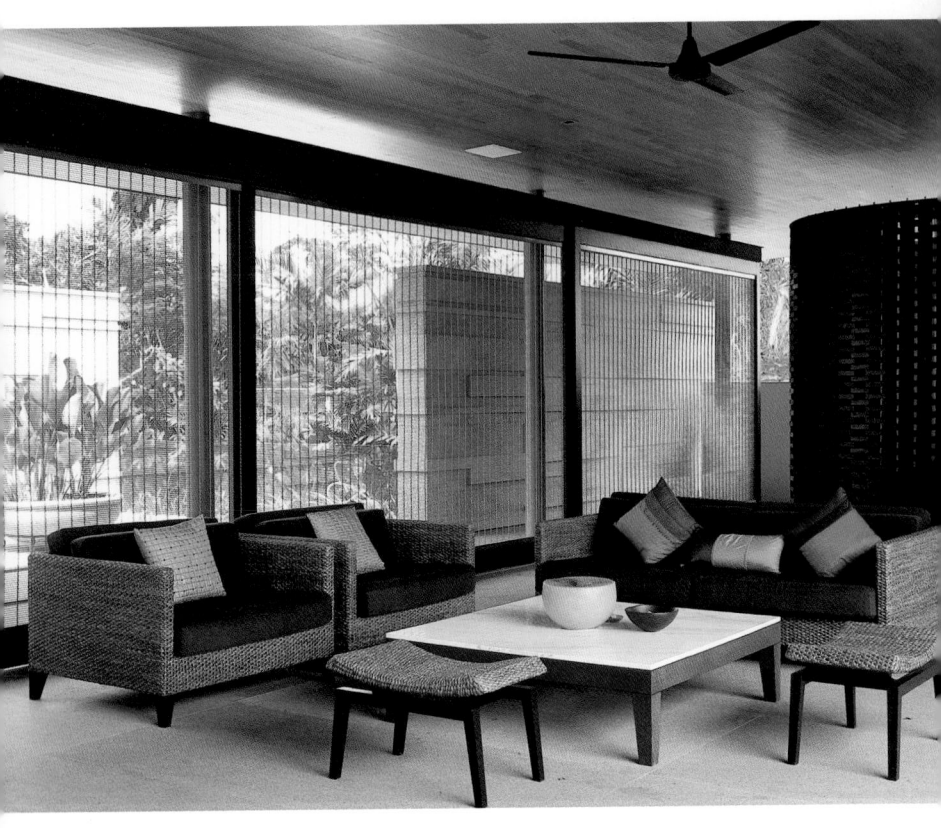

PP. 476–477 and ↑ Comfortable streamlined furniture adorns the rooms that open on to views of water features and garden terraces. • Bequeme stromlinienförmige Möblierung der Räume, die auf das Wasser und die terrassenförmig angelegten Gärten hinausgehen. • Mobilier aux lignes épurées dans les pièces donnant sur les bassins et les jardins en terrasse.

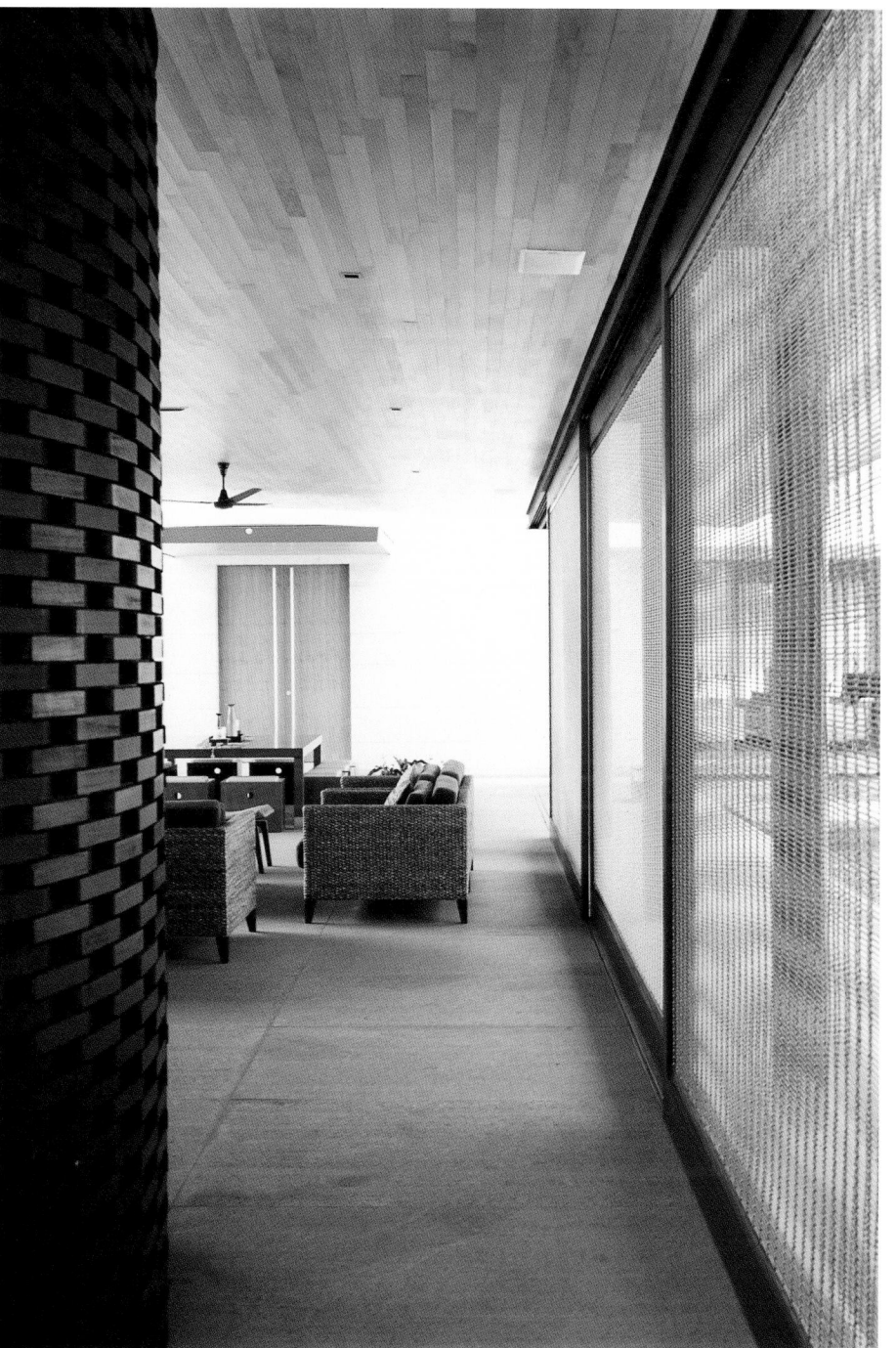

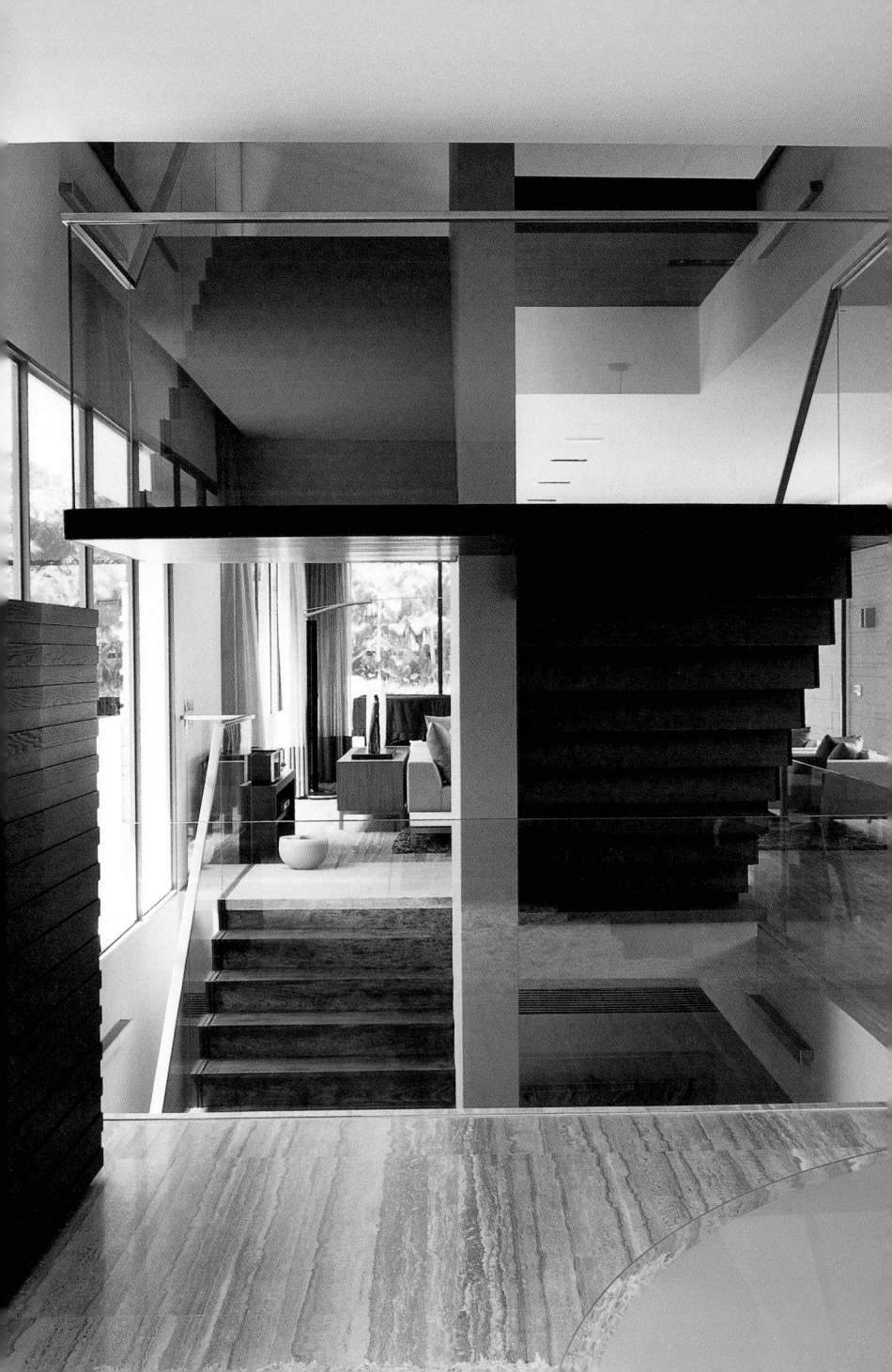

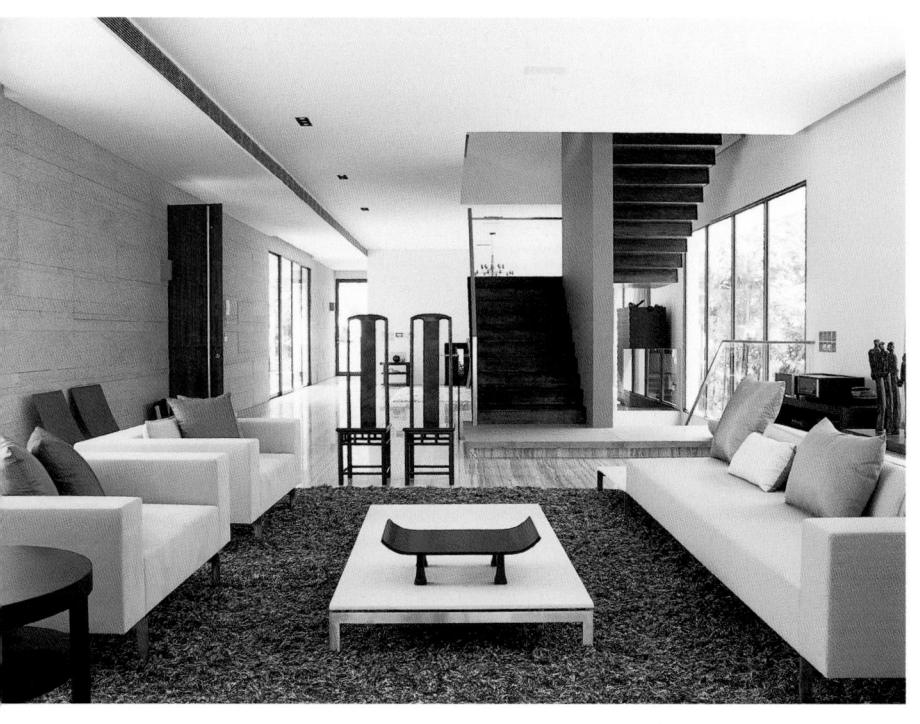

← A cantilevered staircase with a
glass and steel balustrade links the
living area to the private rooms above. ·
Die freitragende Treppe mit einem Geländer aus Stahl und Glas führt vom
Wohnbereich nach oben zu den Privatgemächern. · Un escalier suspendu
doté d'un garde-corps en verre et acier
fait le lien entre le séjour et les pièces
privées à l'étage.

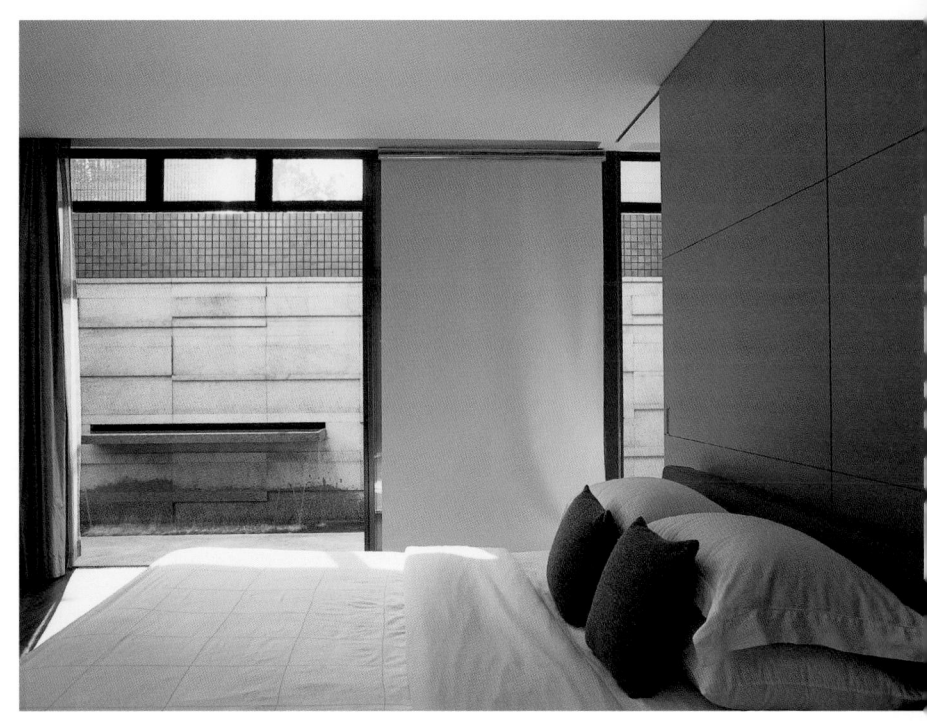

→ The main bathroom gives on to an
open-air shower area. • An das große
Badezimmer ist auch eine Außendusche
angeschlossen. • La salle de bains principale donne sur une douche en plein air.

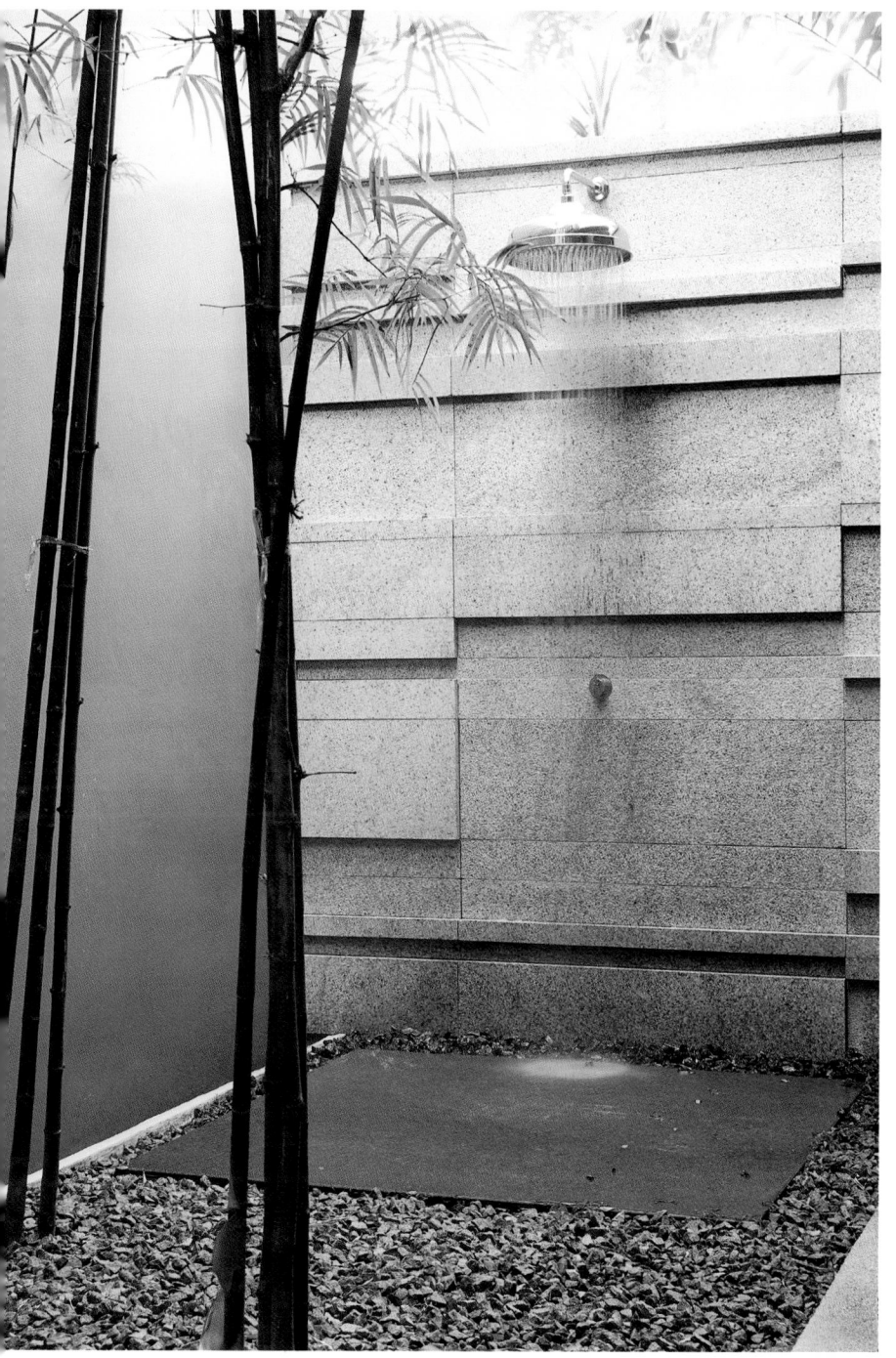

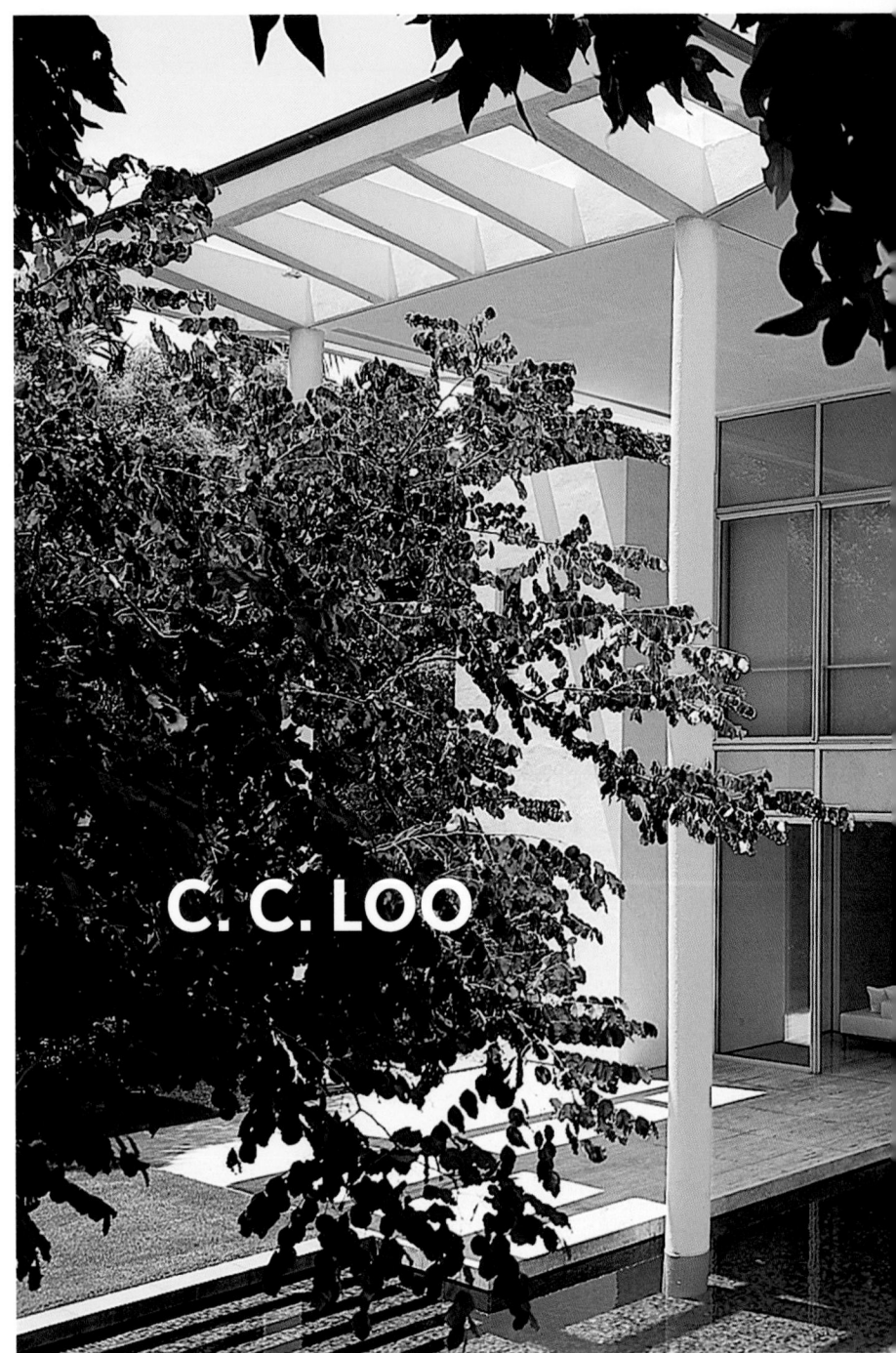

C. C. LOO

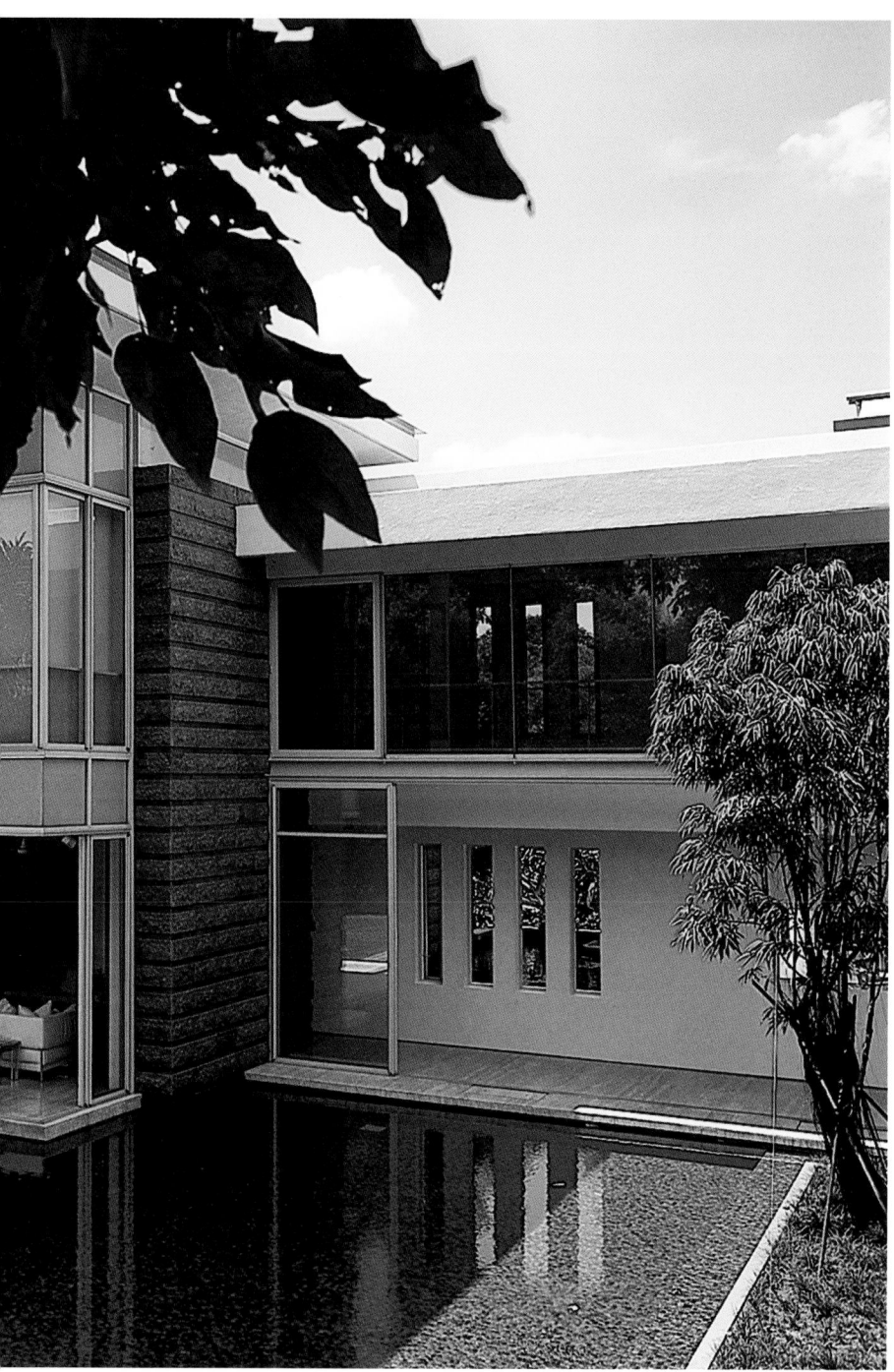

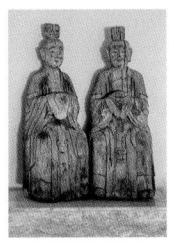

C. C. LOO

SINGAPORE

To preserve the stylish elegance of Singapore's Belmont Road residential district, the government decreed that each house must be built on a minimum plot size of 1,500 sq. meters. C. C. Loo, a barrister and third-generation Singaporean of Chinese origin, and his wife Sonia set their heart on a modern house that would somehow capture the essence of a classical Chinese garden. Commissioning the well-known architect Mok Wei Wei, they got a home that surpassed their expectations: a place of airy lightness and double volumes in which the slender supporting columns echo the stands of bamboo in the rock garden and indoor spaces evoke the feeling of Chinese water pavilions. Although many of the features – concrete, plate glass and a swimming pool – are modern, the house is built around traditional courtyards, pebbled paths and a pond filled with 99 koi. C. C. and Sonia Loo's contemporary home evokes an ancient spirit.

Per Gesetz will die Regierung die edle Eleganz des Wohngebiets um die Belmont Road bewahren. Demnach dürfen neue Häuser nur auf einer Grundfläche von mindestens 1500 m² errichtet werden. C. C. Loo, ein Anwalt chinesischer Abstammung, dessen Familie mittlerweile in der dritten Generation in Singapur ansässig ist, und seine Frau Sonia wünschten sich ein modernes Haus mit dem meditativen Charakter eines klassischen chinesischen Gartens. Sie beauftragten den bekannten Architekten Mok Wei Wei, dessen Entwurf ihre kühnsten Erwartungen übertraf. Ihr Haus zeichnet sich durch luftige Leichtigkeit und sehr hohe Räume aus, deren schlanke Stützpfeiler die Form der Bambusstauden im Steingarten wieder aufnehmen, während die Anordnung der Zimmer eine Vision chinesischer Wasserpavillons heraufbeschwört. Obwohl das Haus viele moderne Merkmale aufweist – Beton, Tafelglas und einen Swimmingpool –, ist es um traditionelle Innenhöfe, Kieswege und einen Teich mit 99 Koi herumgebaut. C. C. und Sonia Loo lieben das zeitgenössische Haus, das eine jahrhundertealte Spiritualität ausstrahlt.

Afin de préserver l'élégance raffinée du quartier résidentiel de Belmont Road, le gouvernement a décrété que chaque maison devait être construite sur une parcelle d'au minimum 1500 m². C. C. Loo, avocat et Singapourien de troisième génération d'origine chinoise, et son épouse Sonia voulaient à tout prix une maison moderne qui capte l'essence des jardins chinois classiques. Le célèbre architecte Mok Wei Wei leur a créé un chez-soi dépassant leurs espérances : un lieu de vie clair et spacieux, très haut de plafond, dont les graciles colonnes porteuses font écho aux bosquets de bambous dans le jardin de pierre, et dont les espaces intérieurs rappellent l'ambiance des pavillons d'eau chinois. Malgré la prépondérance d'éléments modernes – béton, vitrages et piscine –, la maison est construite autour de cours traditionnelles, de sentiers recouverts de galets et d'un bassin dans lequel évoluent 99 carpes koi. Aussi l'appartement de style contemporain de Sonia Loo est-il habité par l'esprit des temps passés.

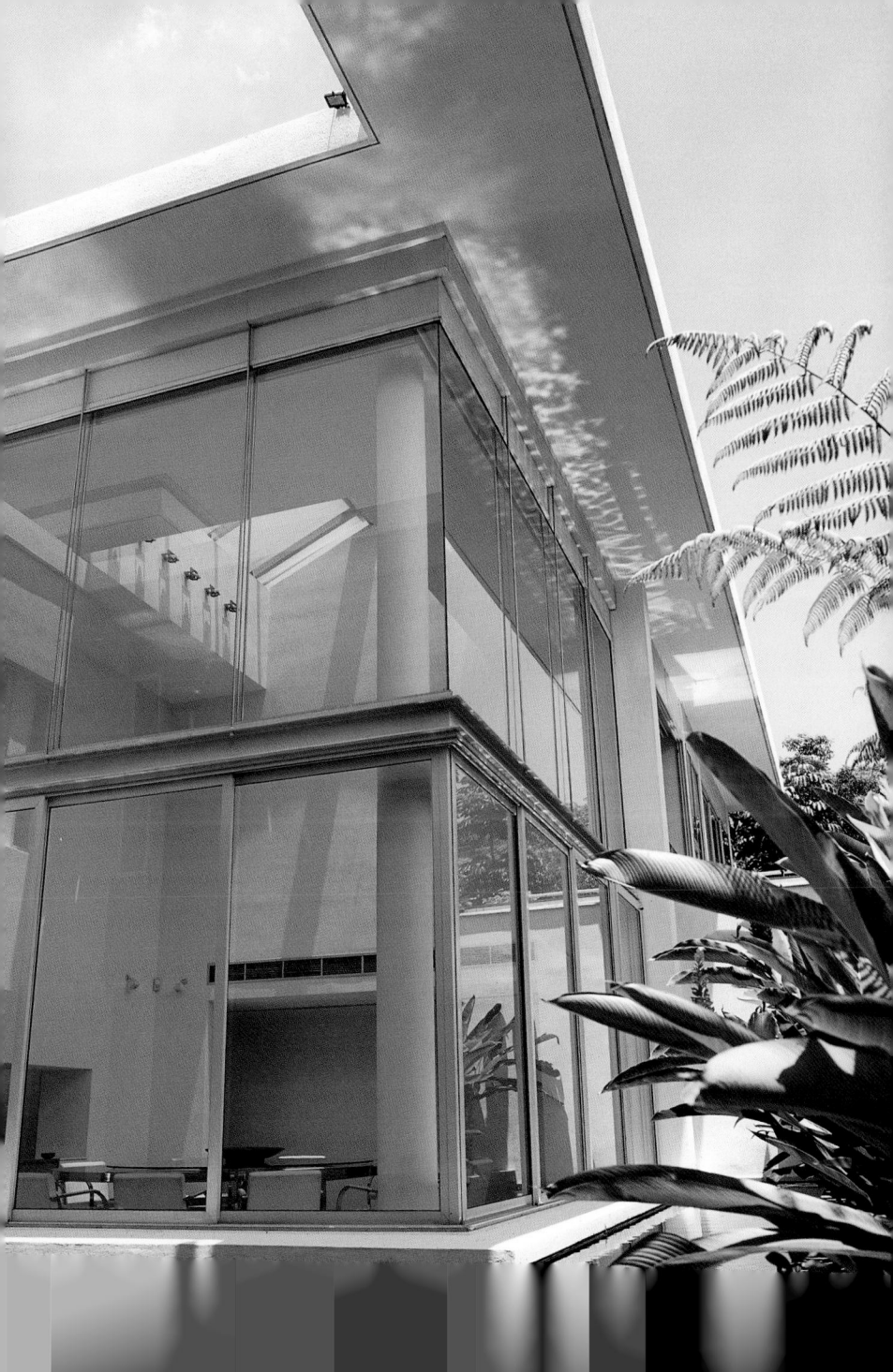

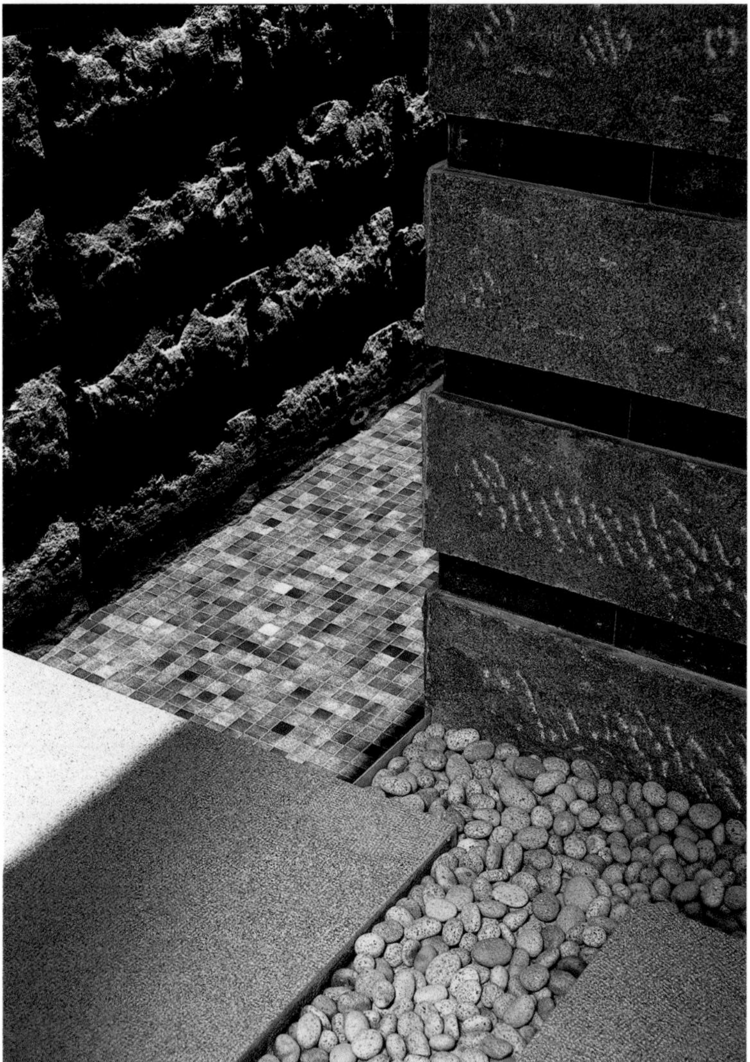

PP. 484-485 View from the garden of the elevation of the house. The bridge links the study to the dining room. • Der Blick vom Garten auf das Haus. Die Brücke verbindet das Arbeitszimmer mit dem Esszimmer. • La façade de la maison vue du jardin. Le pont relie le bureau à la salle à manger.

↑ Pebbles and mosaic tiles line the path from swimming pool to garden. • Der Weg vom Swimmingpool in den Garten ist mit Kies und Mosaik ausgelegt. • Un chemin de galets et de mosaïque relie la piscine au jardin.

→ The view between two overlapping Chinese-style granite walls is of the swimming pool and the dining room. • Durch die beiden versetzt stehenden Granitmauern in chinesischem Stil sieht man den Swimmingpool und das Esszimmer. • Entre deux murs en granite de style chinois, on peut contempler la piscine et la salle à manger.

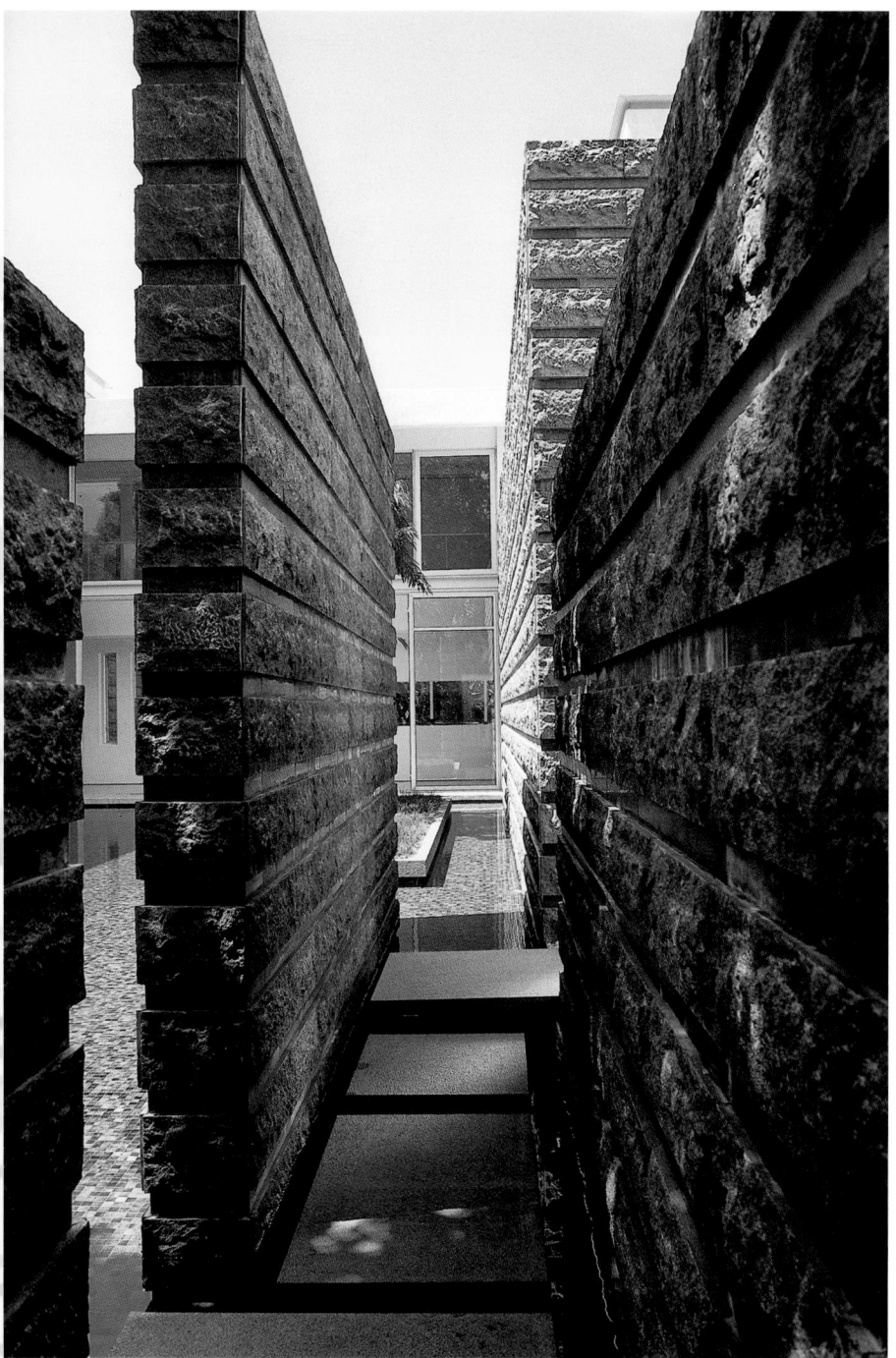

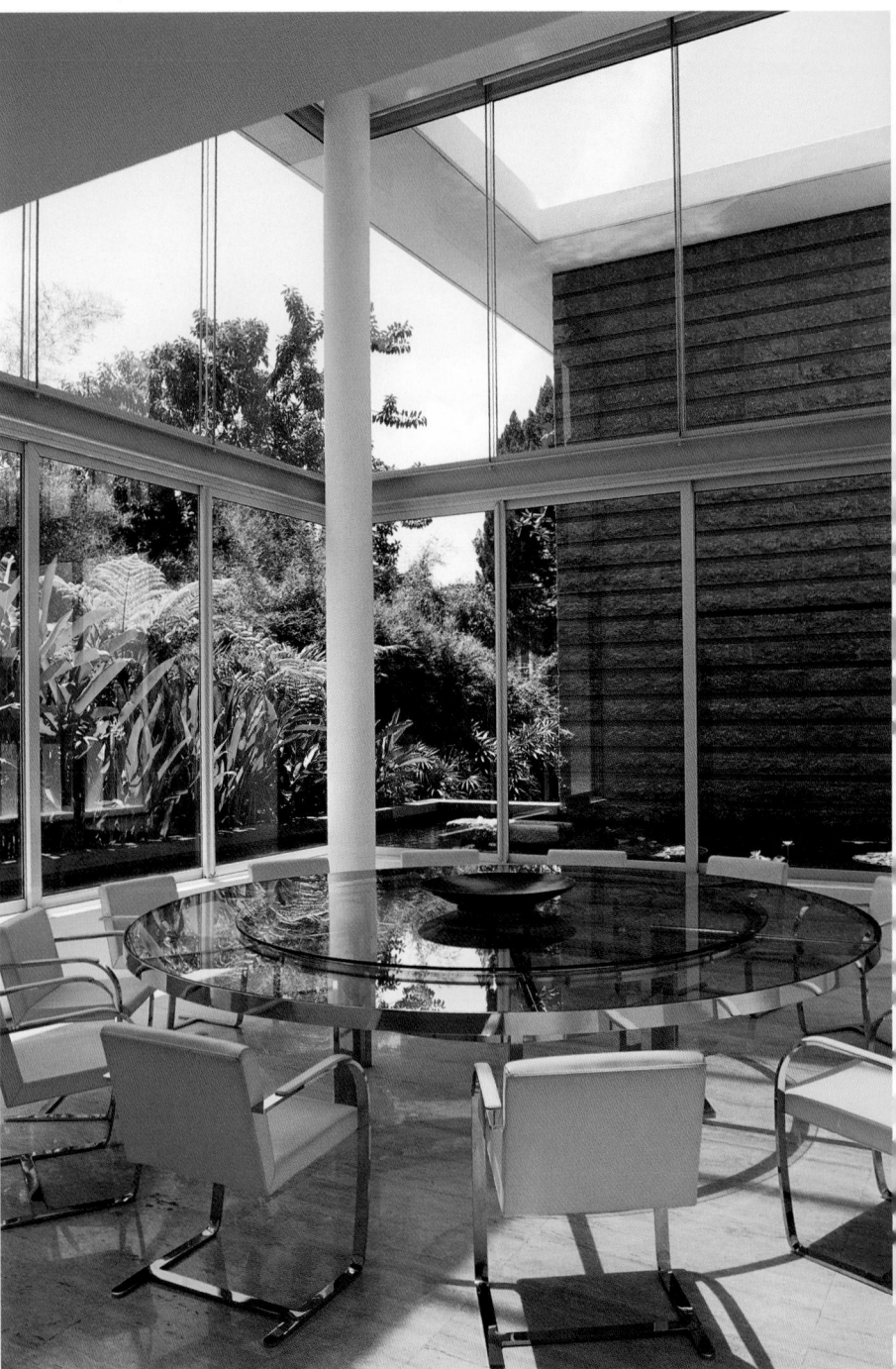

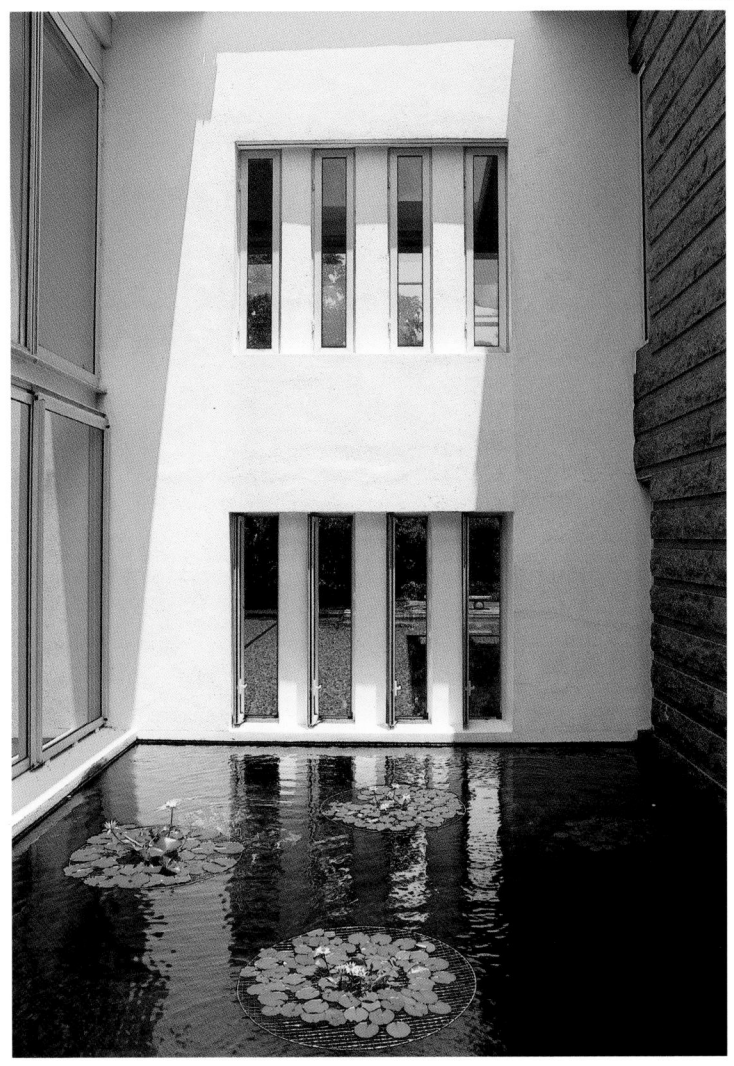

↑ Vertical windows overlook the koi pond afloat with water lilies. • Hohe schmale Fenster gehen auf den mit Seerosen geschmückten Koi-Teich hinaus. • De hautes fenêtres étroites donnent sur le bassin recouvert de nénuphars où s'ébattent les carpes koi.

PP. 492–493 Two Ming-dynasty mandarins carved in wood guard the long corridor dining room. • Die beiden holzgeschnitzten Mandarine aus der Ming-Dynastie bewachen den langen Korridor, in dem auch gegessen wird. • Deux mandarins Ming sculptés sur bois veillent sur la longue salle à manger-couloir.

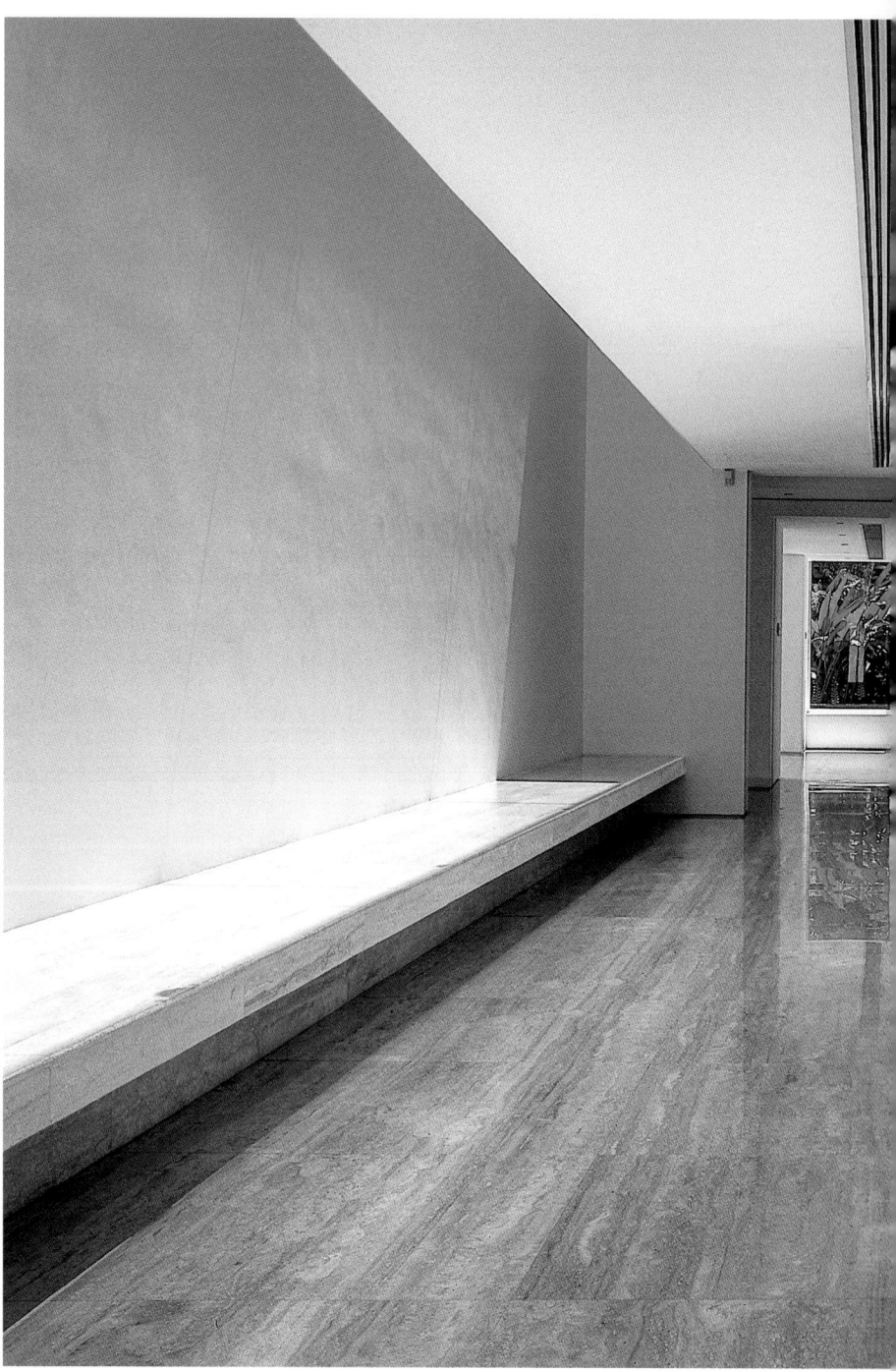

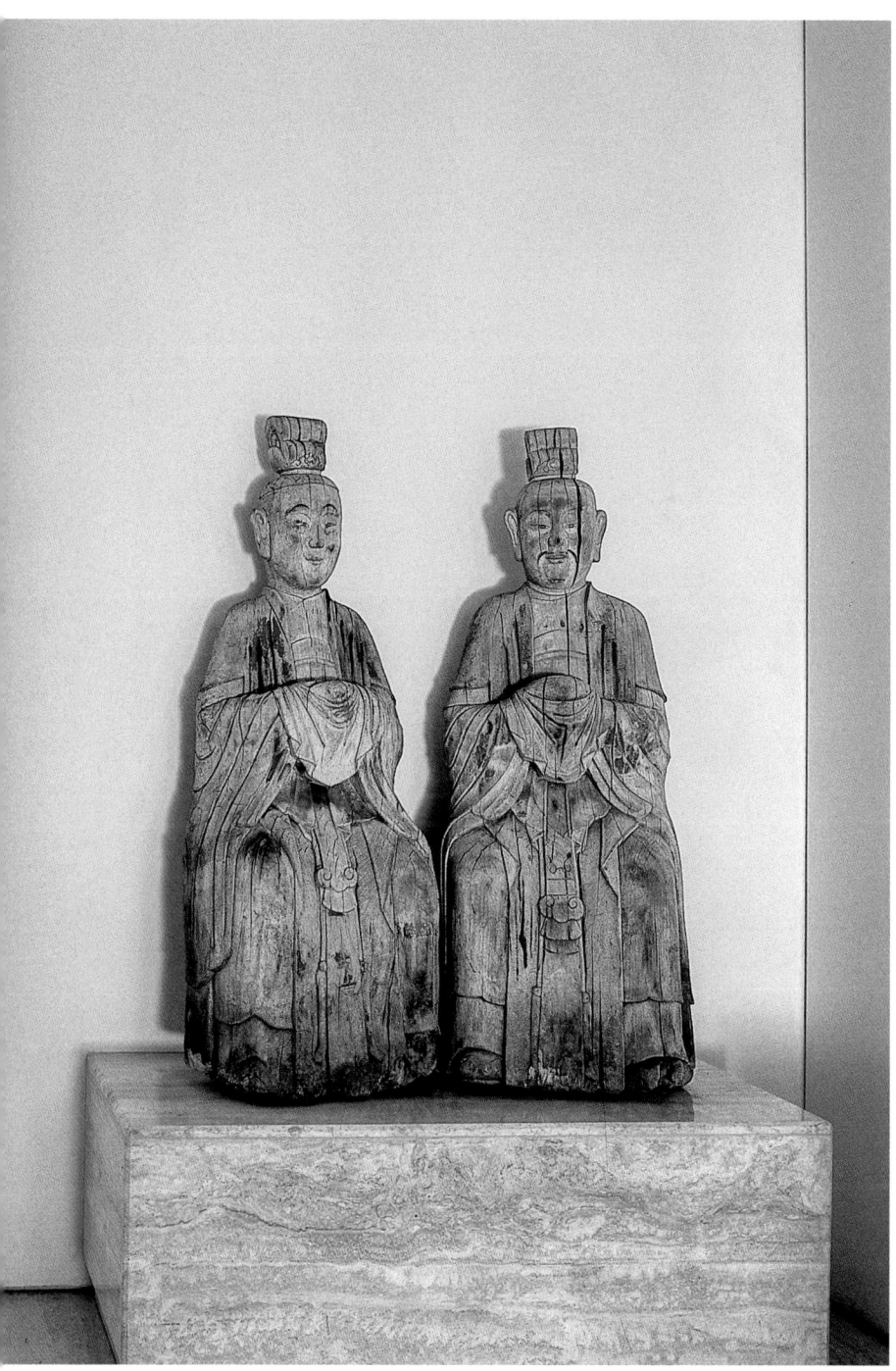

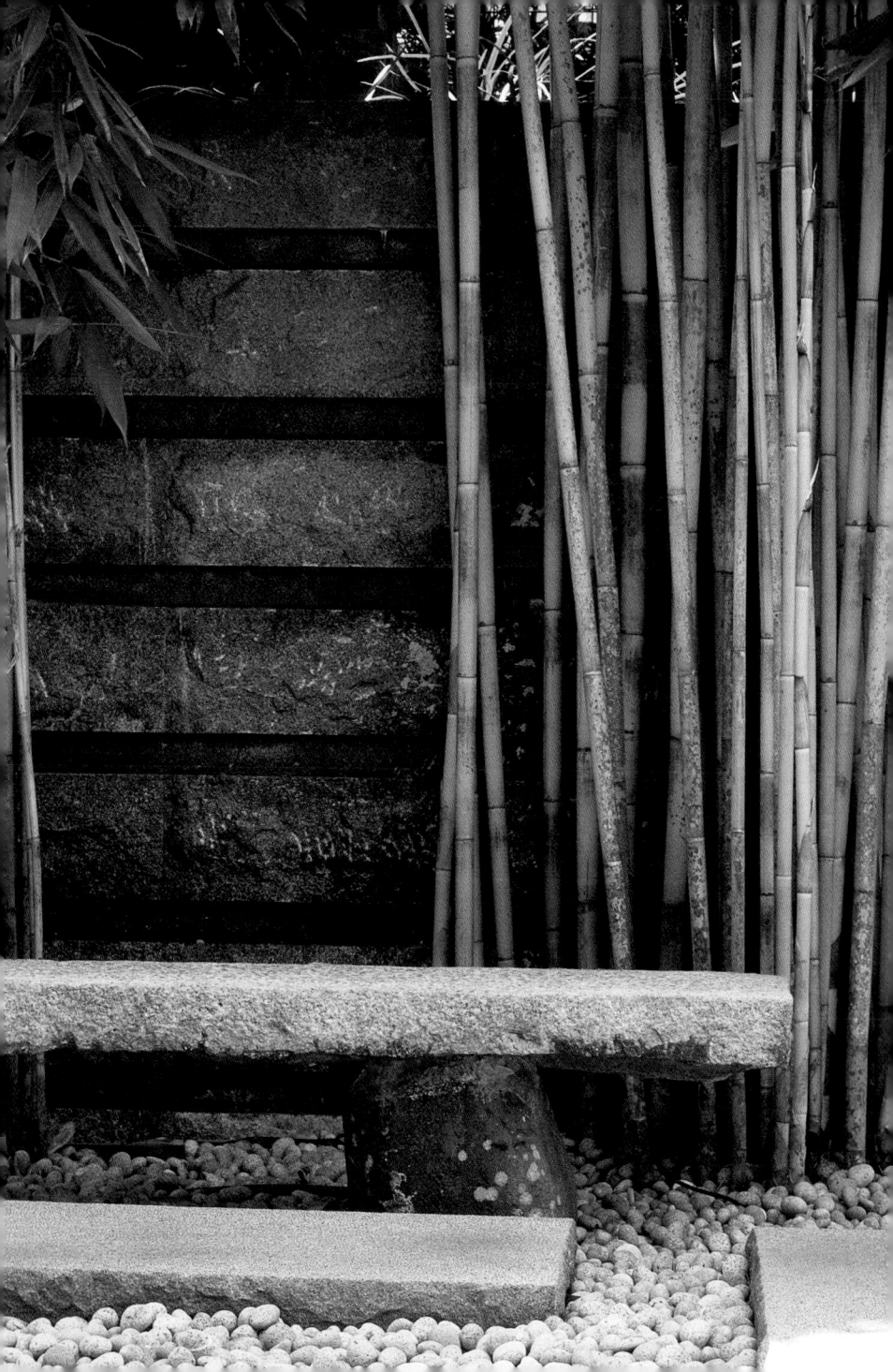

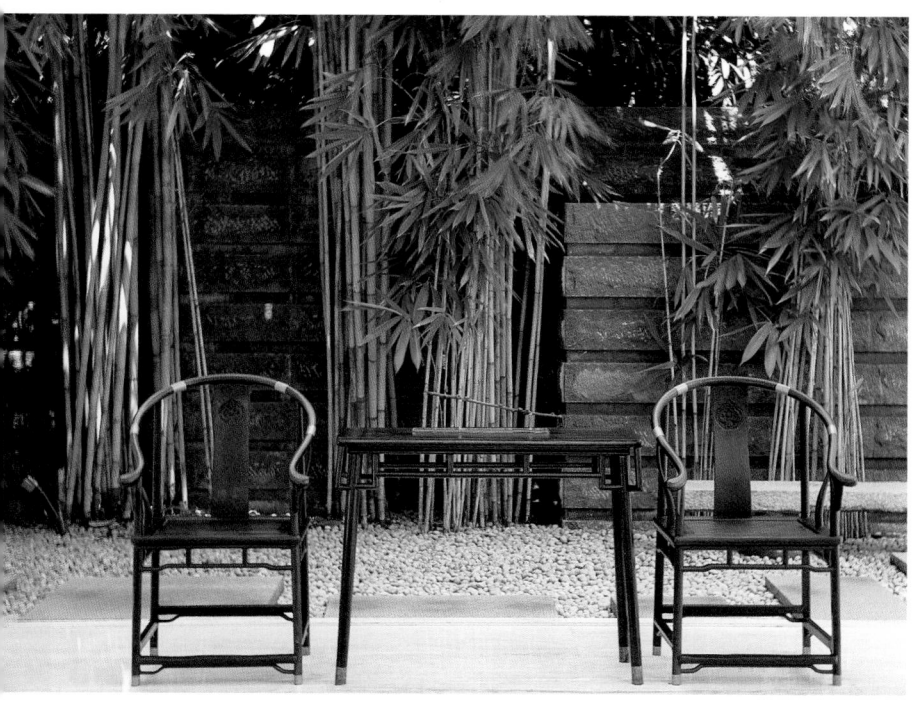

↑ Ming-dynasty chairs in the dining room are framed by views of bamboo in the rock garden. • Stühle aus der Ming-Dynastie im Esszimmer in Kombination mit Bambusstauden im Steingarten. • Dans la salle à manger, des chaises Ming se détachent sur un fond de bambous.

PP. 496–497 On the marble coffee table are two pieces of bronze sculpture by a contemporary Singapore artist. • Auf dem marmornen Couchtisch liegen zwei Bronzeskulpturen eines zeitgenössischen Singapurer Künstlers. • Les deux bronzes posés sur la table basse en marbre sont l'œuvre d'un artiste local contemporain.

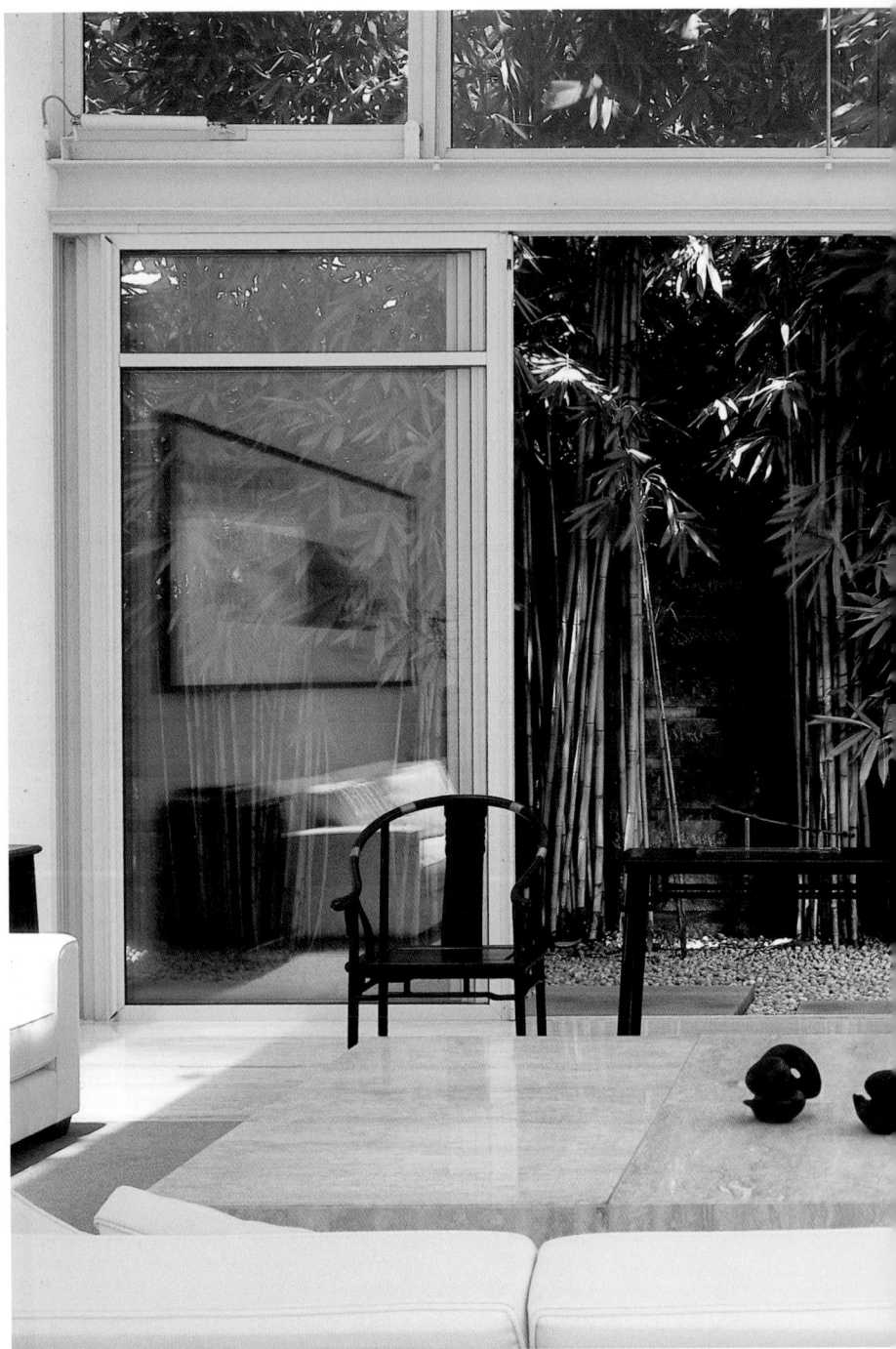

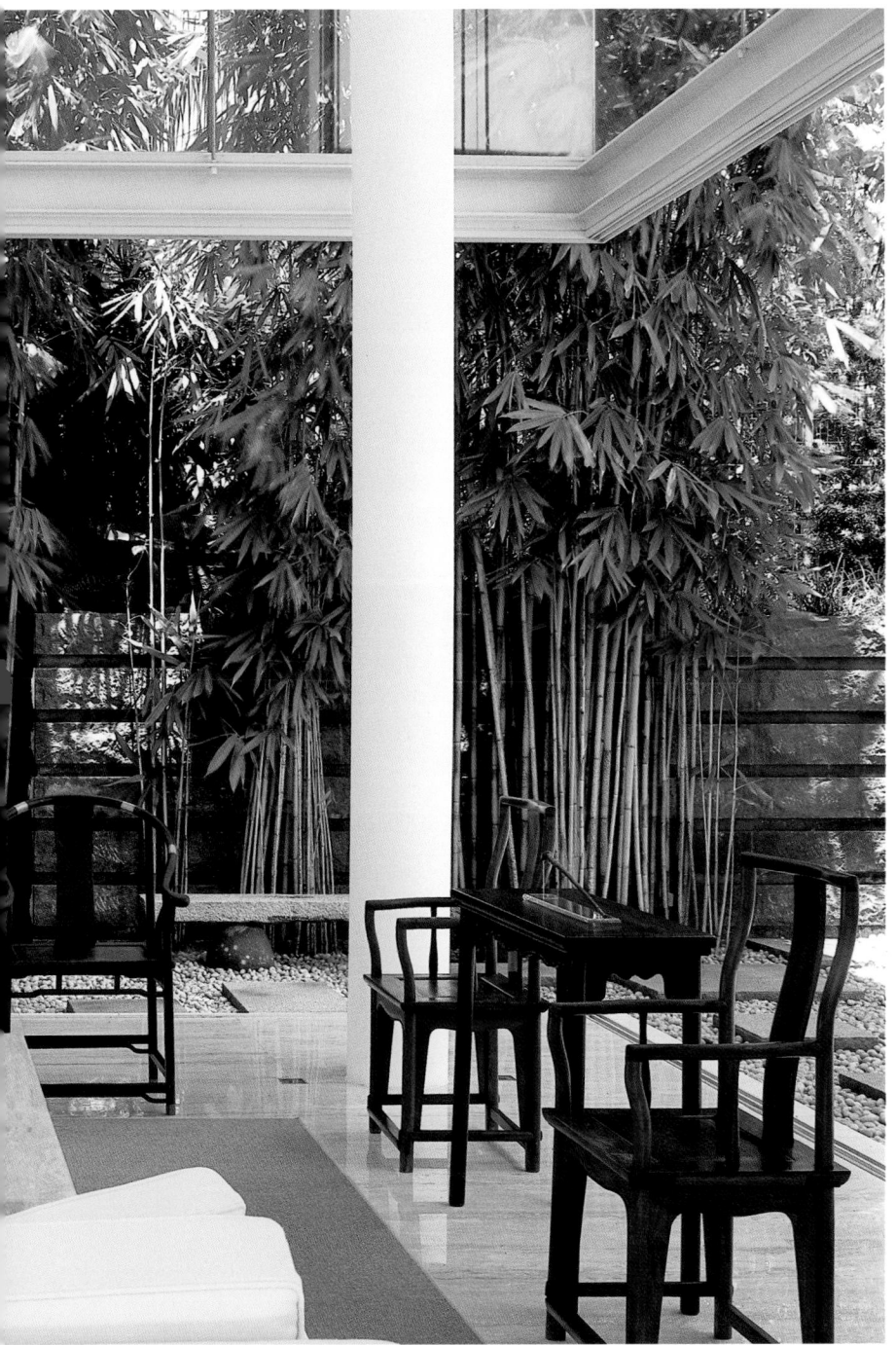

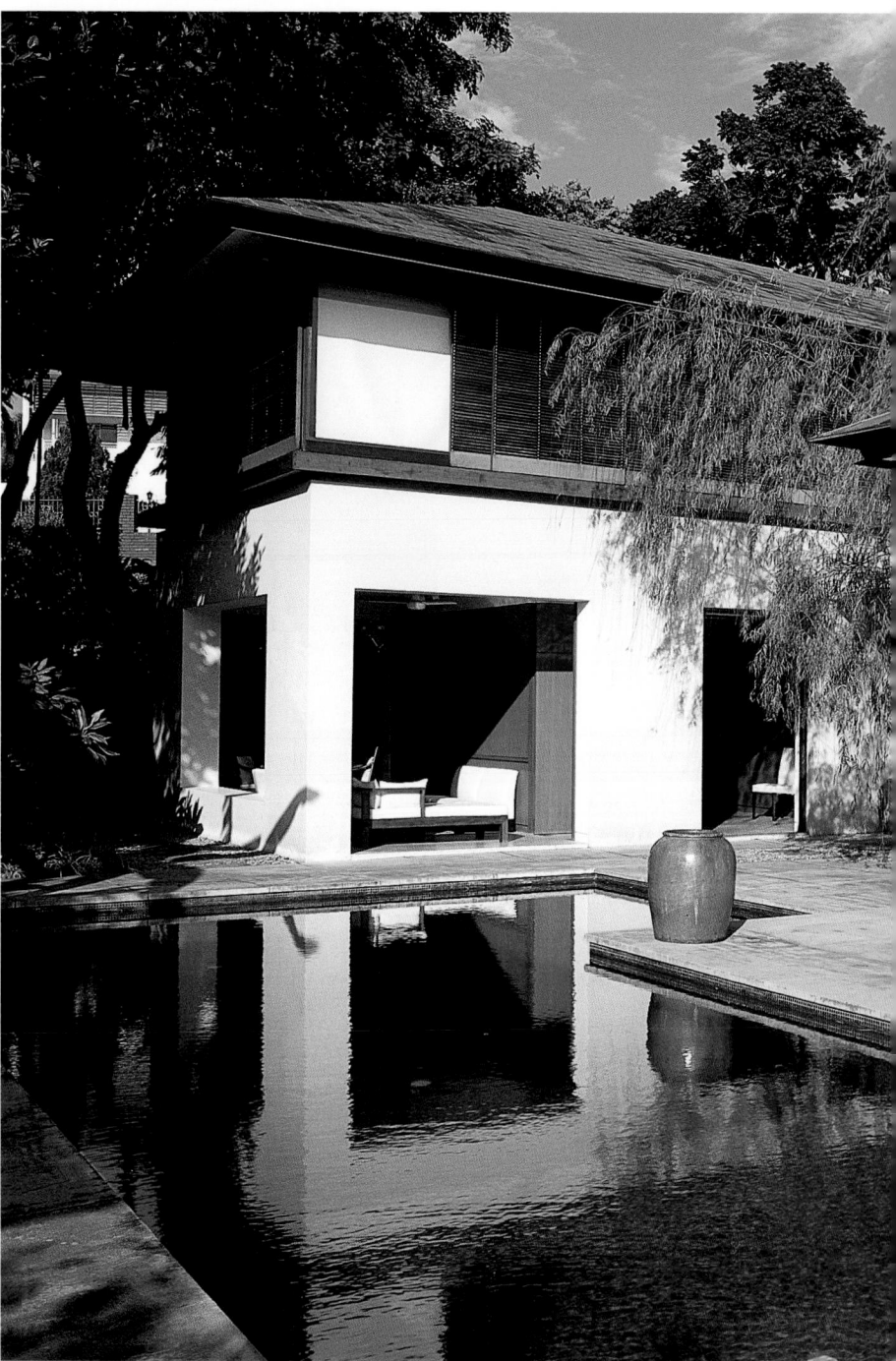

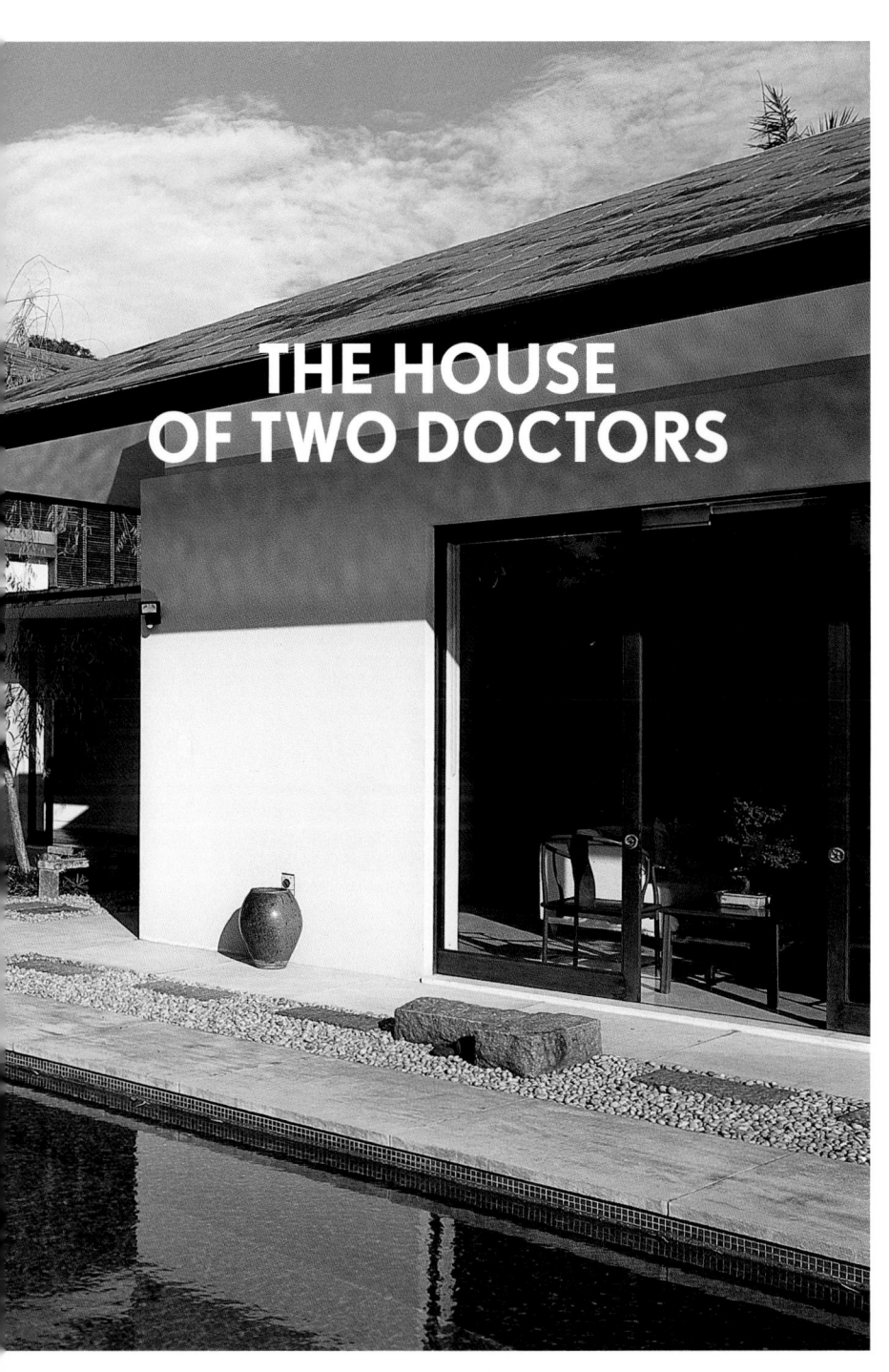

THE HOUSE
OF TWO DOCTORS

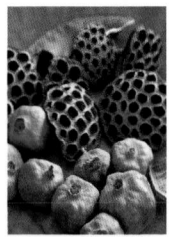

THE HOUSE OF TWO DOCTORS

SINGAPORE

Dr. Tong Ming Chuan is one of Singapore's leading cardiothoracic surgeons. His wife Dr. Geh Min is an eye surgeon. They wanted a house that was a peaceful counterpoint to their busy, often stressful professional lives – a timeless classic of understated, contemporary elegance. They approached the redoubtable Singapore-based architectural practice of Kerry Hill to design a family home around garden terraces and water features that would also house their fine collection of Chinese furniture, calligraphy and Sung porcelain. The two doctors dislike excessive ornamentation; music plays an important part in their lives. Kerry Hill's use of natural materials – slate roof, wooden shutters and limestone floors – and wide eaves and high ceilings keeps the house naturally cool. Much of the house is screened by delicate timber lattices that can be operated to modulate light. In some parts the screens are left open for cross ventilation. The play of light, water, sky and garden creates a unified space of contemplation.

Dr. Tong Ming Chuan ist einer der besten Herz-Lungen-Chirurgen in Singapur, seine Frau Dr. Geh Min arbeitet als Augenchirurgin. Die beiden sehnten sich nach einem Haus, das einen friedlichen Kontrapunkt zu ihrem stressigen Berufsleben bilden sollte – zeitlos klassisch und zurückhaltend, aber zeitgenössisch elegant. Sie gaben dem in Singapur ansässigen renommierten Architekturbüro Kerry Hill den Auftrag, ein Familienhaus um bepflanzte Terrassen und Wasserbecken herum zu bauen, das genügend Platz für ihre Sammlung chinesischer Möbel, von Kalligrafien und Sung-Porzellan bieten sollte. Die beiden Ärzte mögen keine überschwängliche Dekoration; Musik dagegen spielt eine große Rolle in ihrem Leben. Kerry Hill entschied sich für natürliche Baumaterialien – Schieferdach, hölzerne Fensterläden und Kalksteinböden – sowie Dachvorsprünge und hohe Decken, damit das Haus auf natürliche Weise kühl bleibt. Das Haus ist weitgehend mit hölzernen Spalieren ausgestattet, mit deren Hilfe man den Lichteinfall bestimmen kann. An einigen Stellen bleiben die Spaliere zum Querlüften offen. Das verspielte Zusammenwirken von Licht, Wasser, Himmel und Gärten schafft einen kontemplativen Raum.

Tong Ming Chuan, l'un des plus grands spécialistes de chirurgie cardio-thoracique, et son épouse Geh Min, spécialisée en chirurgie ophtalmique, ont une vie professionnelle chargée. Aussi voulaient-ils une maison qui soit un havre de paix, un classique intemporel d'élégance contemporaine discrète. C'est ainsi qu'ils ont commandé au redoutable cabinet d'architecture singapourien de Kerry Hill une maison organisée autour de terrasses-jardins et de bassins d'eau et qui soit susceptible d'accueillir leur collection de meubles chinois, de calligraphie et de porcelaine Song. Ce couple n'aime pas la décoration trop chargée et accorde une place importante à la musique dans sa vie. Les matériaux naturels – ardoise pour la toiture, bois pour les volets et calcaire pour les sols –, les avant-toits et la belle hauteur sous plafond maintiennent de manière naturelle une certaine fraîcheur dans la maison. La plupart des baies vitrées sont doublées de délicats panneaux en bois à lamelles orientables pour moduler l'éclairage. Certains de ces panneaux sont ouverts de façon à faire courant d'air. Le jeu de la lumière, de l'eau, du ciel et du jardin crée un espace harmonieux de contemplation.

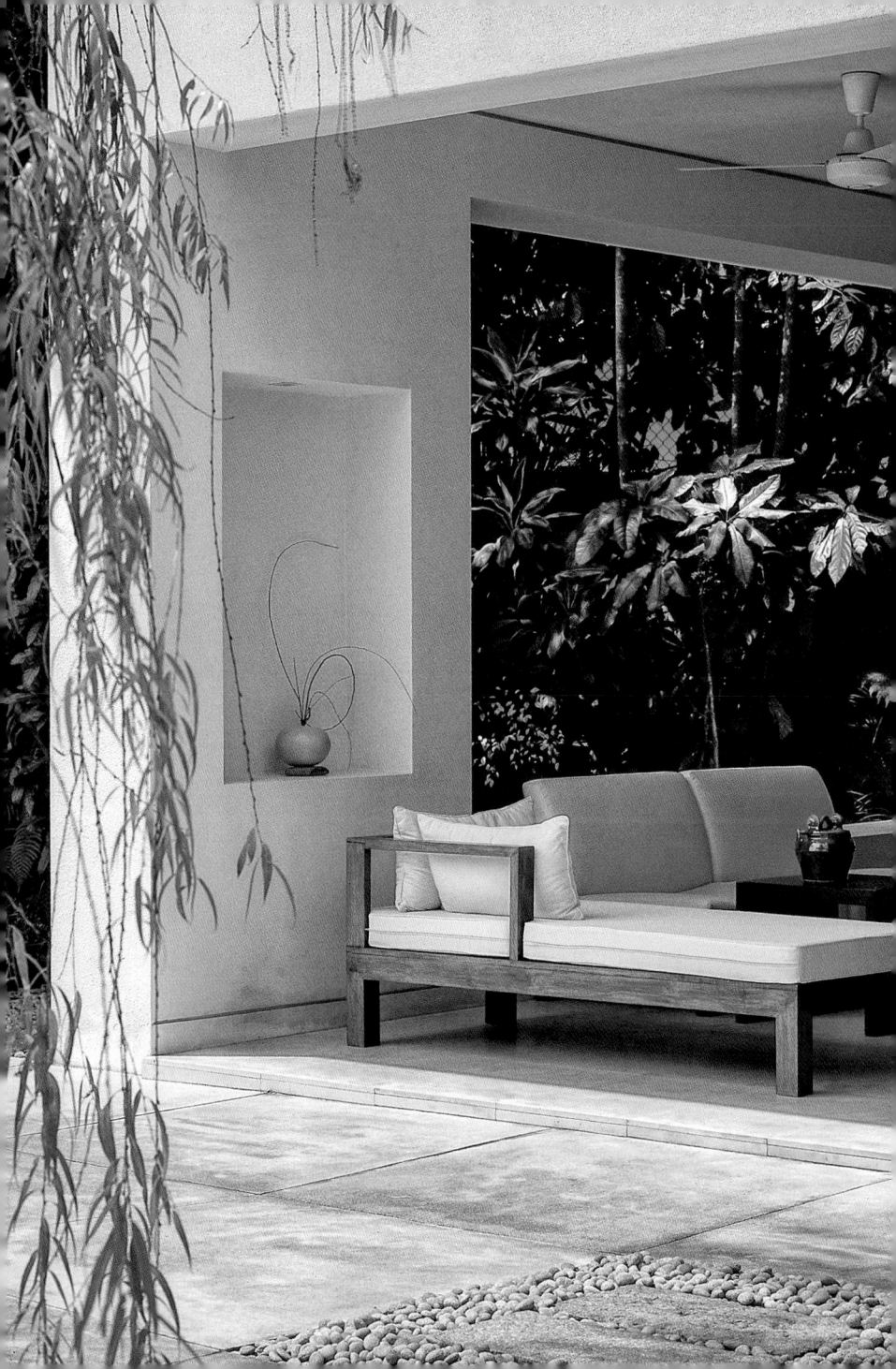

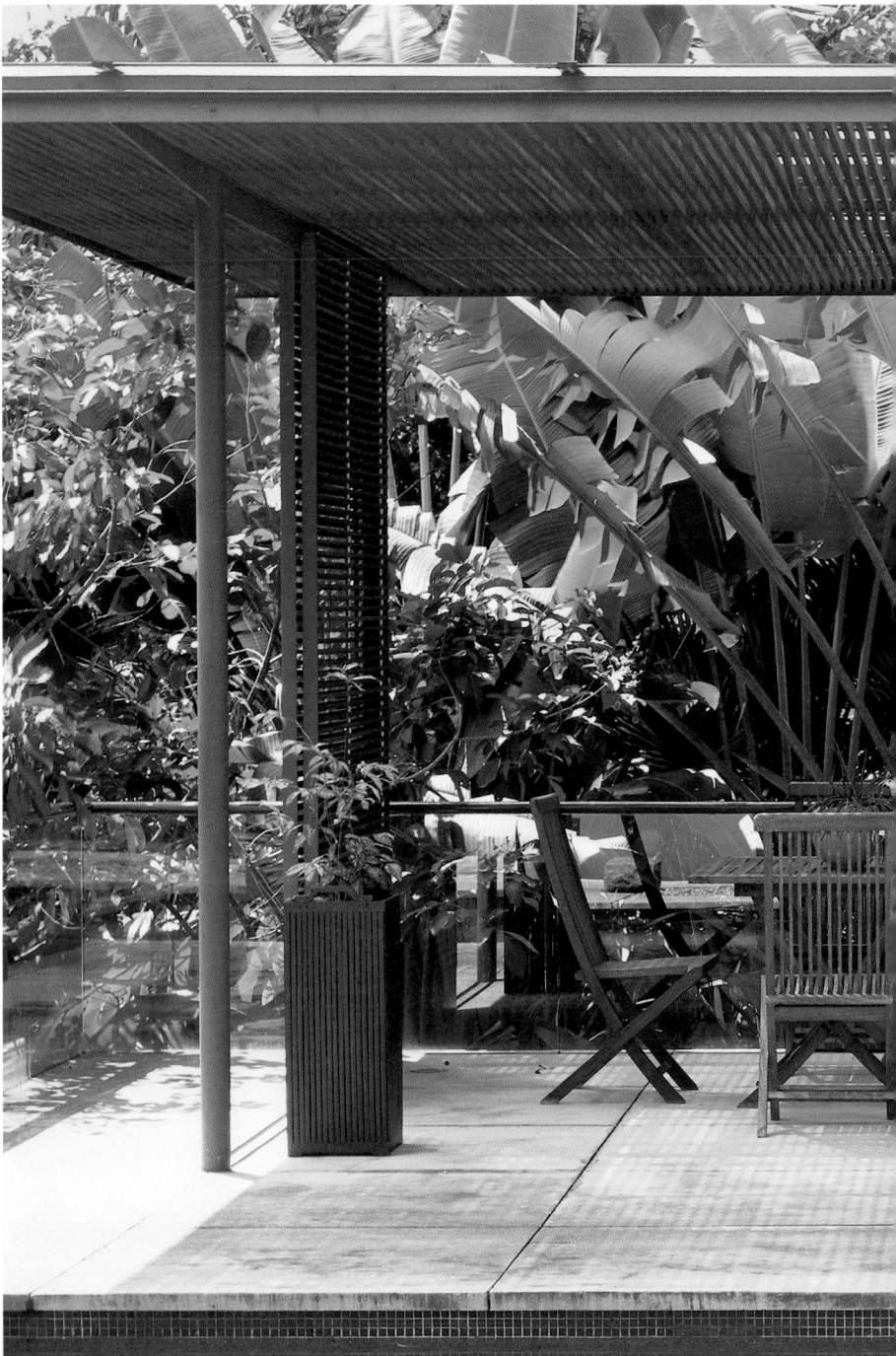

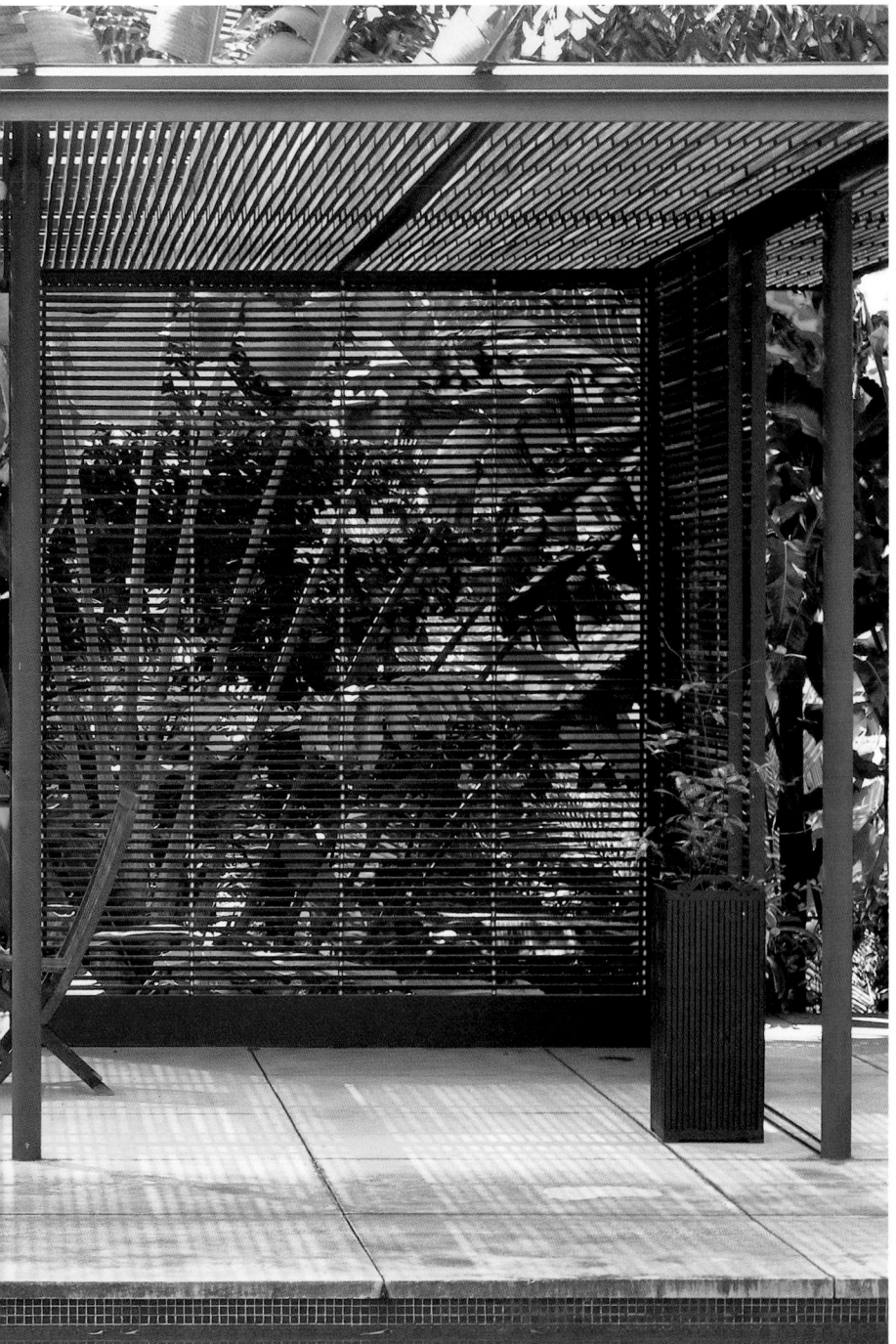

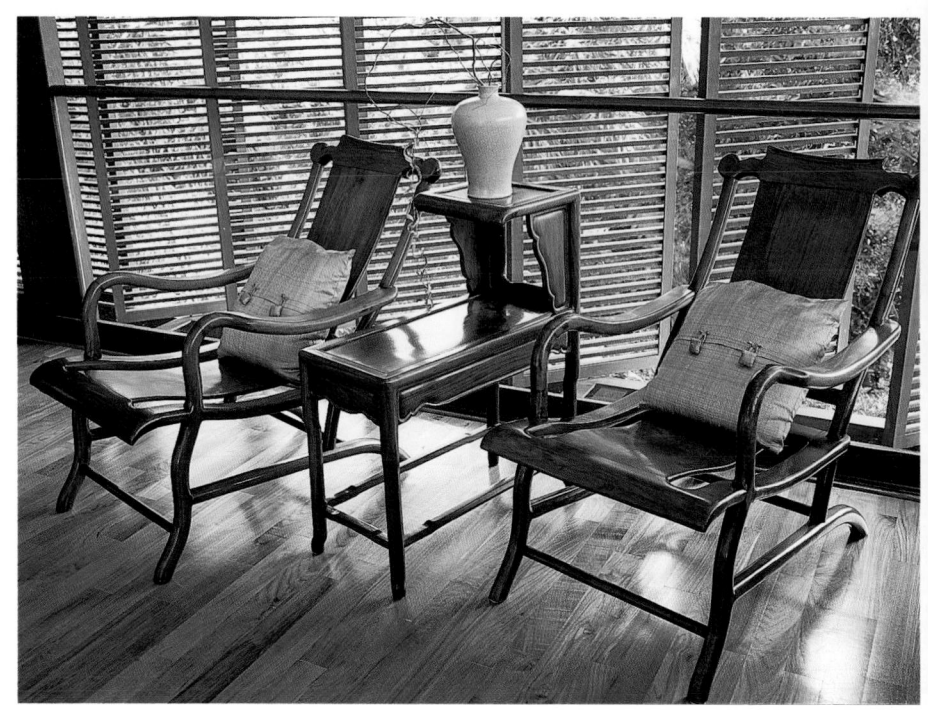

PP. 498-499 The terraced pool links two parts of the house. • Der terrassenförmig angelegte Swimmingpool verbindet zwei Seiten des Hauses. • La piscine en terrasse relie les deux parties de la maison.

P. 501 Willow branches frame the patio. • Weidenzweige rahmen den Patio ein. • Un patio à l'ombre d'un saule.

PP. 502-503 The pavilion overlooking the jade green swimming pool is screened by traveller's palms. • Der Pavillon am Rand des jadegrünen Swimmingpools wird von Palmen abgeschirmt. • Au bord de la piscine couleur de jade, le pavillon est encadré de verdure.

↑ Reading corner with Chinese reclining chairs. • Leseecke mit Ruhesesseln. • Un coin lecture équipé de chaises chinoises à dossier inclinable.

→ Cello and Chinese drum stool in the study. • Cello und chinesischer Schlagzeughocker im Arbeitszimmer. • Violoncelle et tabouret de batteur chinois dans le bureau.

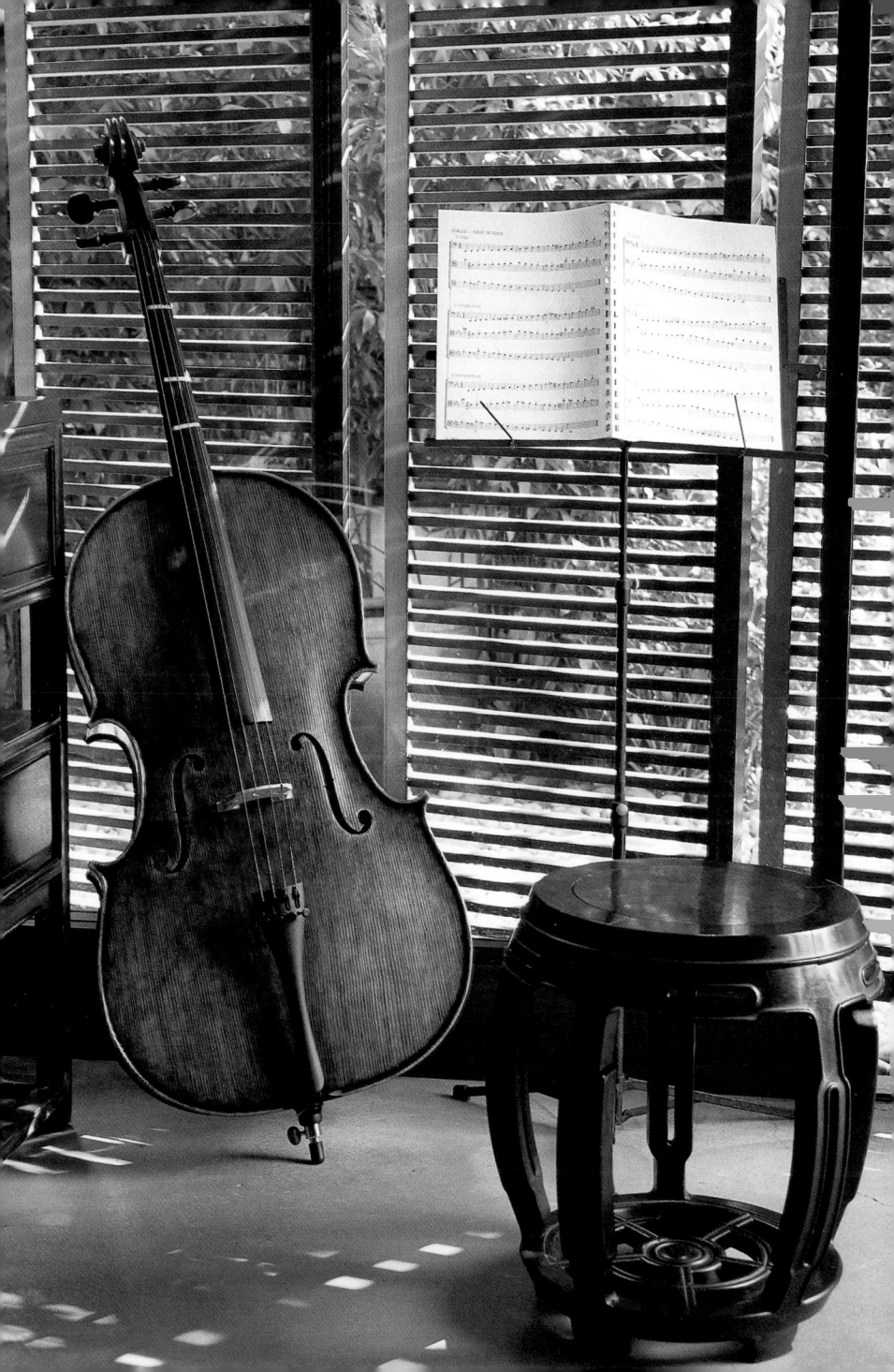

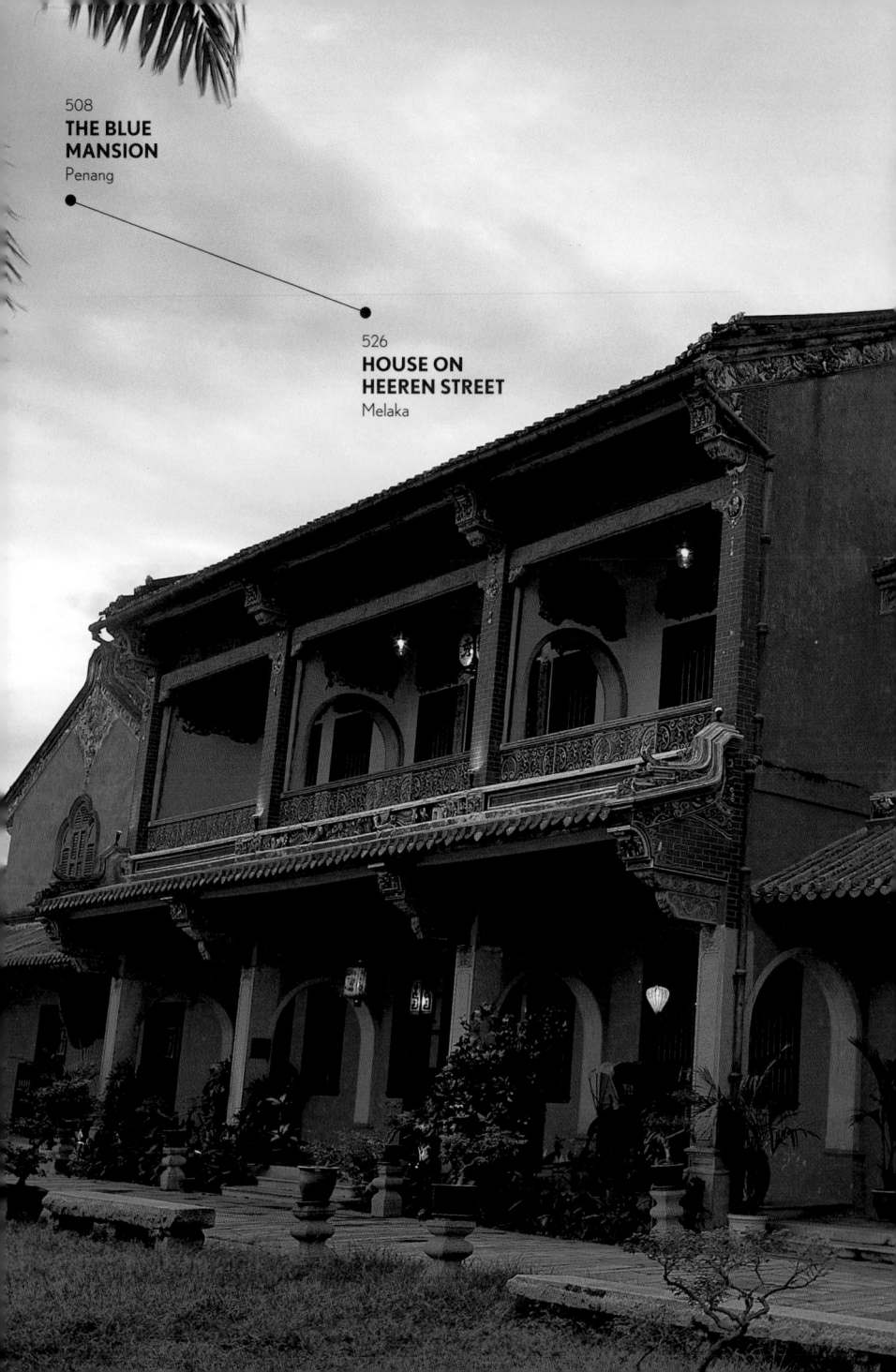

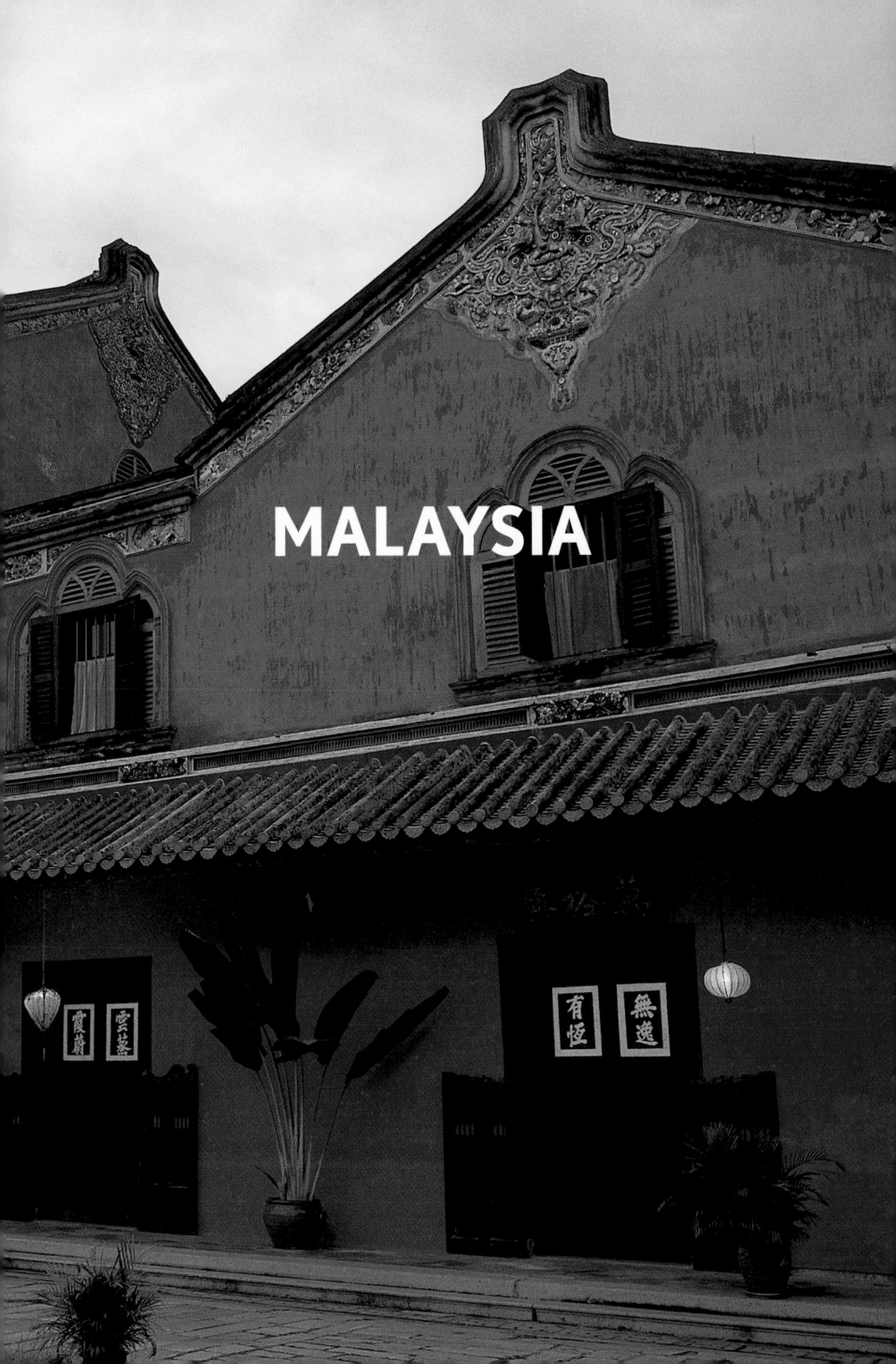

MALAYSIA

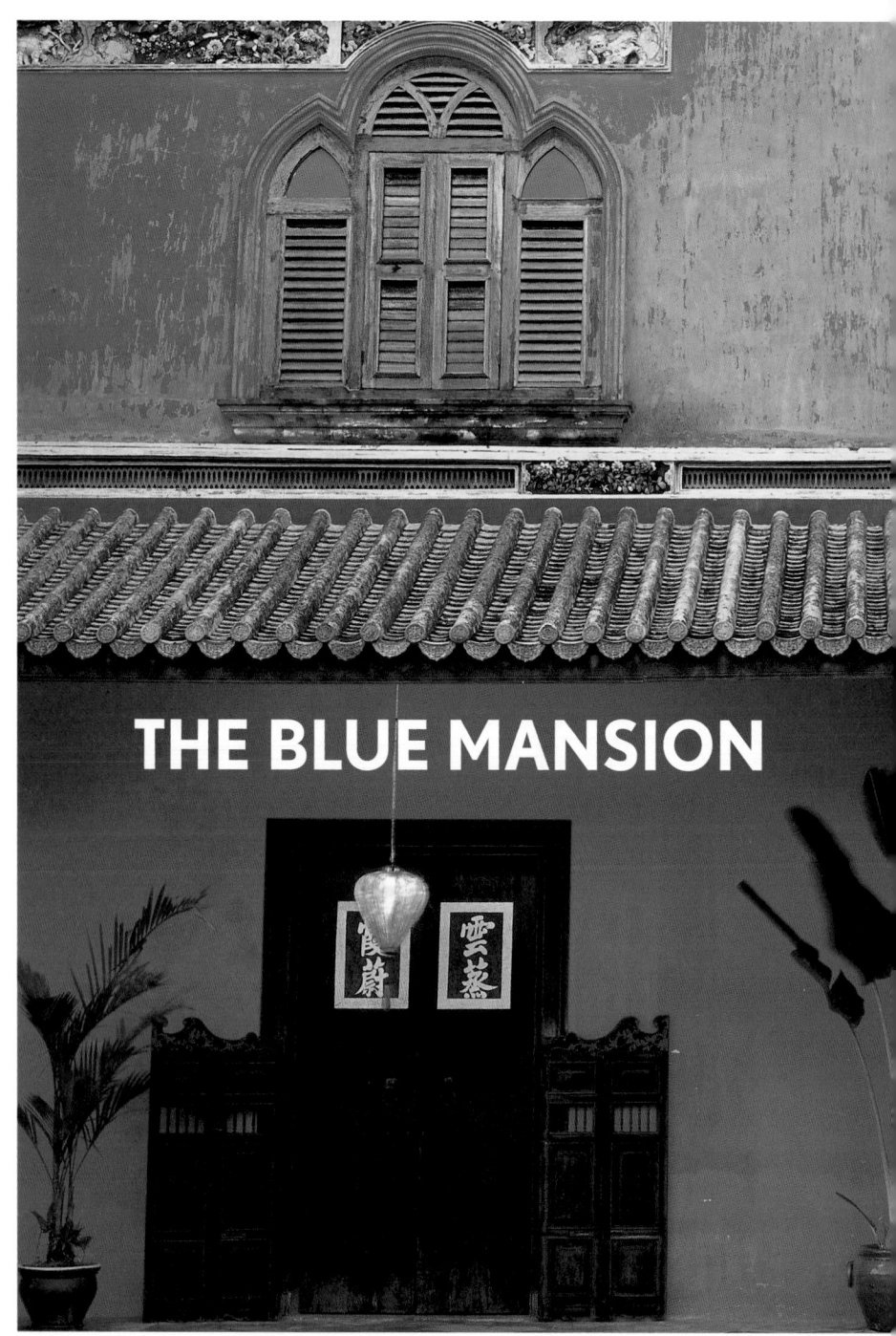

THE BLUE MANSION

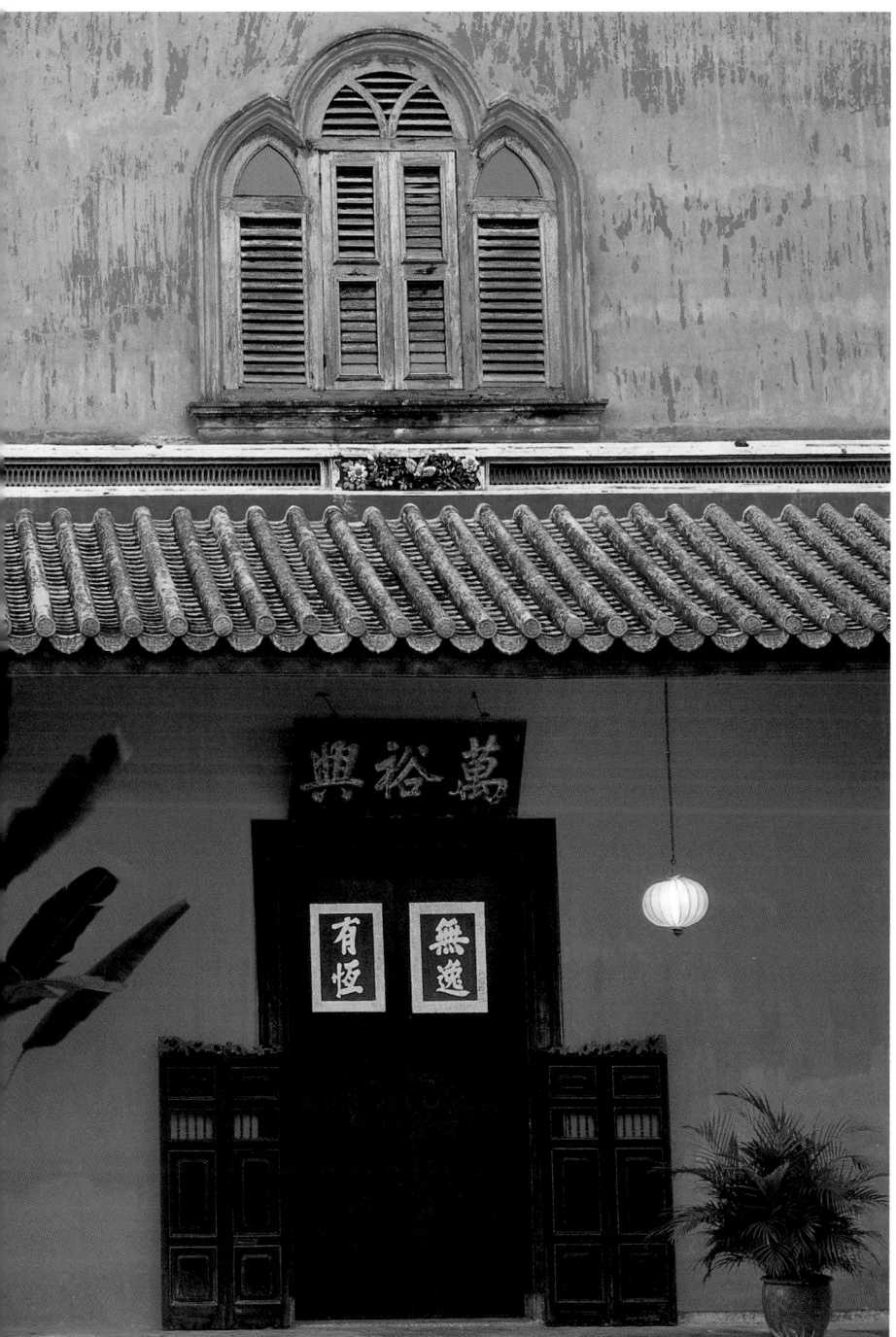

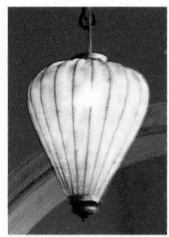

THE BLUE MANSION
PENANG
MALAYSIA

Two remarkable people gave the Blue Mansion its life and afterlife in historic George Town on the island of Penang. It was built by Cheong Fatt Tze, a late 19th-century Chinese merchant so wealthy he was called the "Rockefeller of the East". Architect Laurence Loh, who acquired the decaying mansion in 1990, spent a decade restoring it with his wife Lin Lee Loh-Lim. Cheong Fatt Tze owned other homes, in Singapore, Hong Kong and China, but he lavished riches on his showpiece, importing wrought-iron pillars and balcony grilles from Glasgow and shiploads of floor tiles from Stoke-on-Trent. Putting life back into the indigo-painted courtyard house became the Lohs' mission. Craftsmen were brought in from China to recreate porcelain mosaic decoration on the façade and every artifact, including a magnificent carved and gilded screen, is an authentic period piece. The award-winning conversion of the Blue Mansion into a 16-room boutique hotel is so impressive that it made a starring appearance in the film "Indochine" with Catherine Deneuve.

Das Blue Mansion im historischen George Town auf der Insel Penang verdankt seine Existenz und seinen Ruf zwei Persönlichkeiten. Gebaut hat es Cheong Fatt Tze, ein Kaufmann des späten 19. Jahrhunderts, der so reich war, dass er als „Rockefeller des Ostens" galt. Restauriert wurde es von dem Architekten Laurence Loh, der das Herrenhaus 1990 kaufte und in den folgenden Jahren mit seiner Frau von Grund auf renovierte. Cheong Fatt Tze besaß Häuser in Singapur, Hongkong und anderen chinesischen Städten, doch vor allem sein Paradestück ließ er prunkvoll ausstatten – mit aus Glasgow importierten schmiedeeisernen Säulen und Balkongittern und Fliesen aus Stoke-on-Trent. Dem blau getünchten, um einen Innenhof herum gebauten Haus neues Leben einzuhauchen, betrachteten die Lohs als ihre Mission. Handwerker wurden aus China eingeflogen, um die Mosaikverzierung aus Porzellan an der Fassade wiederherzustellen. Überdies stammt jedes Artefakt, darunter die herrliche holzgeschnitzte vergoldete Trennwand, aus dem 19. Jahrhundert. Die preisgekrönte Verwandlung des Blue Mansion in ein Hotel mit sechzehn Zimmern ist so überzeugend, dass es neben Catherine Deneuve eine Hauptrolle in dem Film „Indochine" spielen durfte.

Un couple remarquable a ramené la Villa bleue à la vie. Située dans la ville historique de George Town, sur l'île de Pinang, elle avait été construite à la fin du 19ᵉ siècle par Cheong Fatt Tze, dit le « Rockefeller de l'Orient ». L'architecte Laurence Loh, qui a fait l'acquisition en 1990 de cette maison tombant en ruine, a mis une dizaine d'années à la restaurer, secondé dans cette tâche par son épouse Lin Lee Loh-Lim. Cheong Fatt Tze possédait plusieurs autres maisons, à Singapour, Hong Kong et en Chine, mais c'est la Villa bleue qui avait sa préférence. Il n'a pas regardé à la dépense, important de Glasgow des colonnes et balustrades en fer forgé et de Stoke-on-Trent de pleines cargaisons de carreaux de faïence. Considérant que leur mission était de redonner vie à cette maison à patio, les Loh n'ont pas non plus ménagé leurs efforts. Ils ont fait venir de Chine des artisans qui ont reconstitué le décor en mosaïque de la façade, et ils ont veillé à ce que le moindre objet, dont un magnifique paravent en bois sculpté et doré à l'or fin, soit une authentique pièce d'époque. La transformation, primée par l'Unesco, de la Villa bleue en un hôtel proposant 16 suites à prix doux est si convaincante que la villa a servi de décor au tournage d'« Indochine » avec Catherine Deneuve.

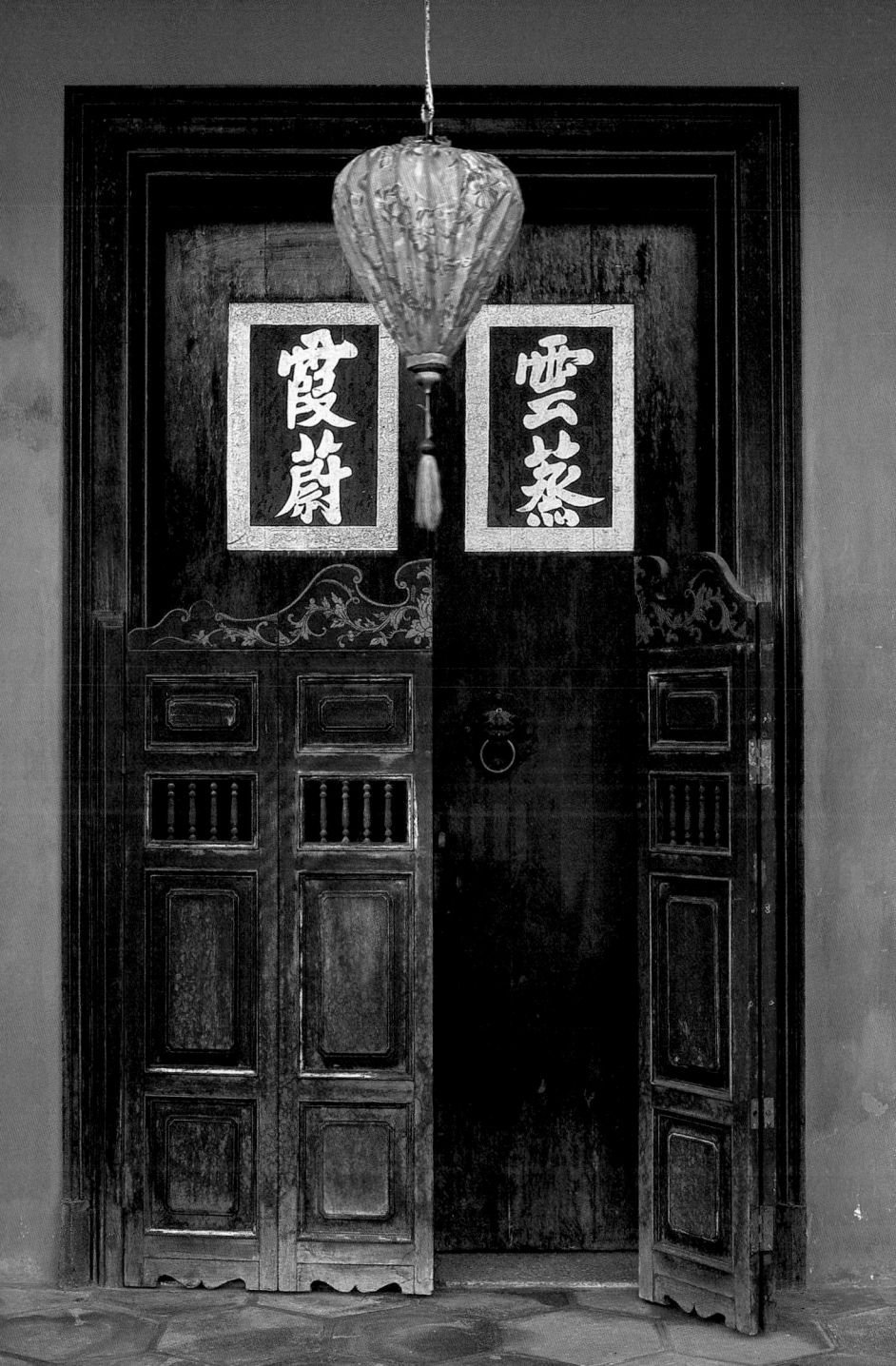

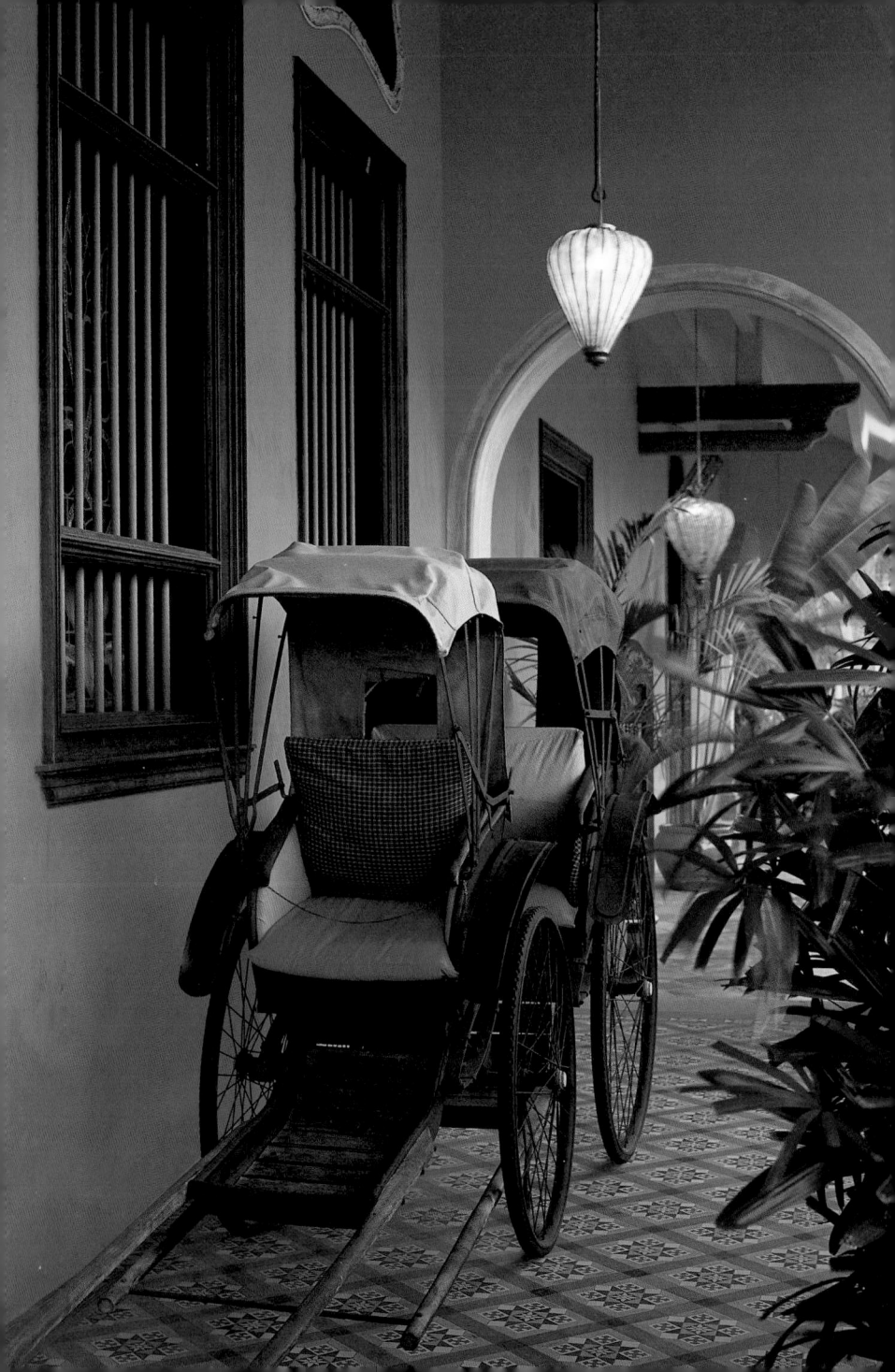

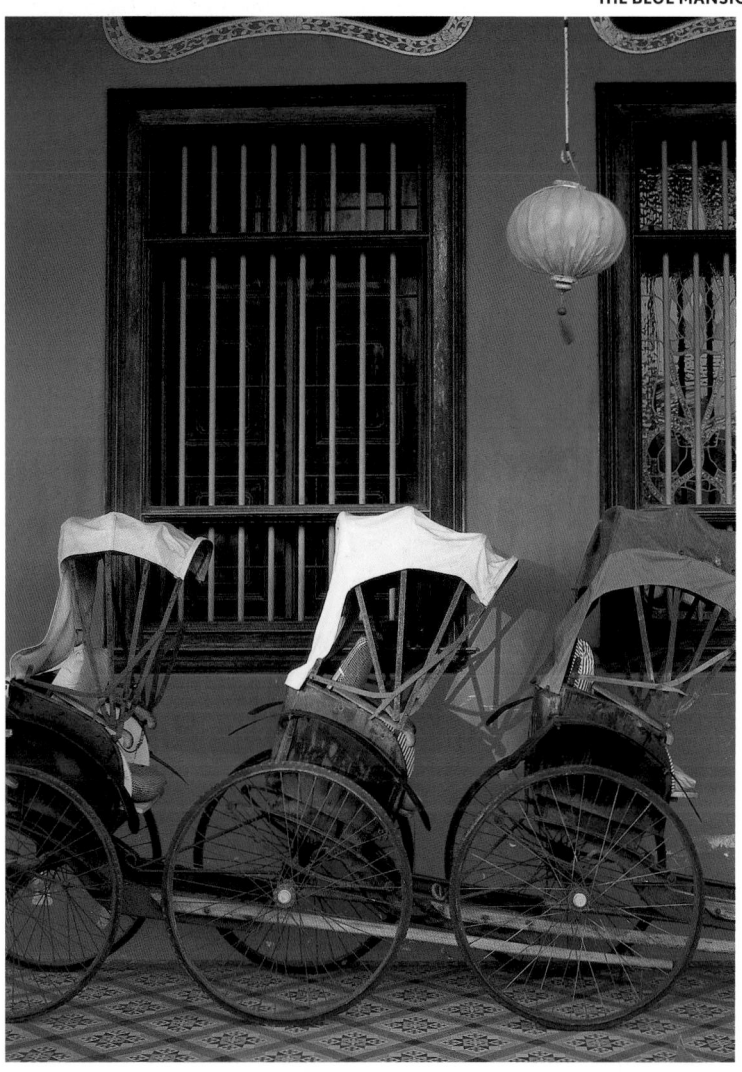

PP. 508–509 The mansion's indigo limewashed front elevation is set with shuttered Gothic windows, a sheltered walkway and double-layered timber doors. • Die Stirnansicht in blauem Kalkanstrich, mit gotischen Fenstern und Fensterläden, einem überdachten Gang und zweiflügeligen Holztüren. • La façade avant peinte à la chaux teinte à l'indigo est rythmée par des fenêtres gothiques fermées par des volets, un avant-toit sur toute sa longueur et des portes en bois à deux vantaux.

← ↑ The film crew of "Indochine" left three old rickshaws standing in the front. The shaded arcade is hung with Chinese lanterns and lined with floor tiles originally imported from Britain. • Die „Indochine"-Filmcrew ließ drei alte Rikschas vor dem Haus zurück. Der schattige Bogengang ist mit chinesischen Laternen und Bodenfliesen aus England geschmückt. • Ces trois rickshaws de collection ont été laissés sur place par l'équipe du tournage d'« Indochine ». Des lanternes chinoises et des carreaux de faïence importés d'Angleterre agrémentent l'arcade ombragée.

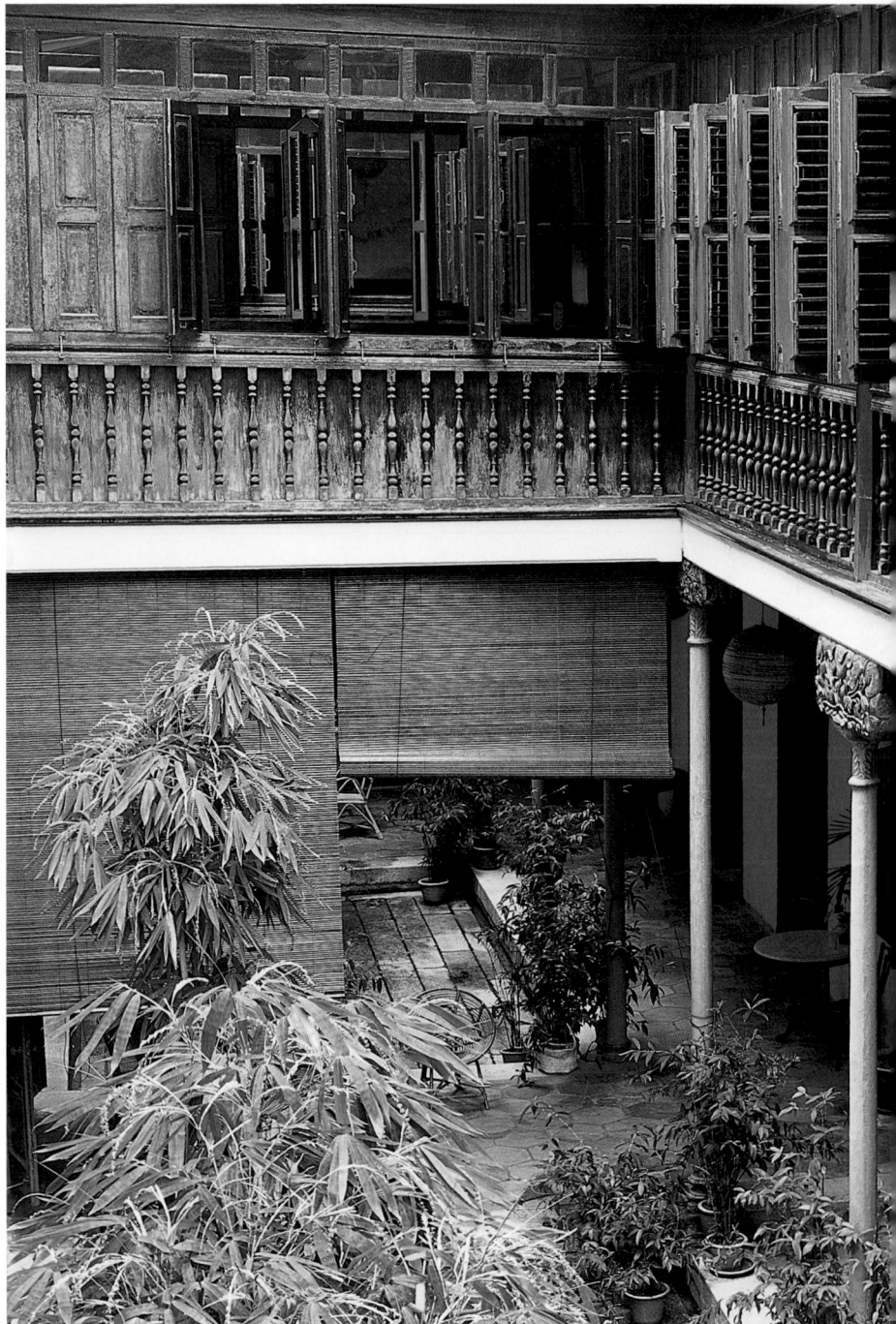

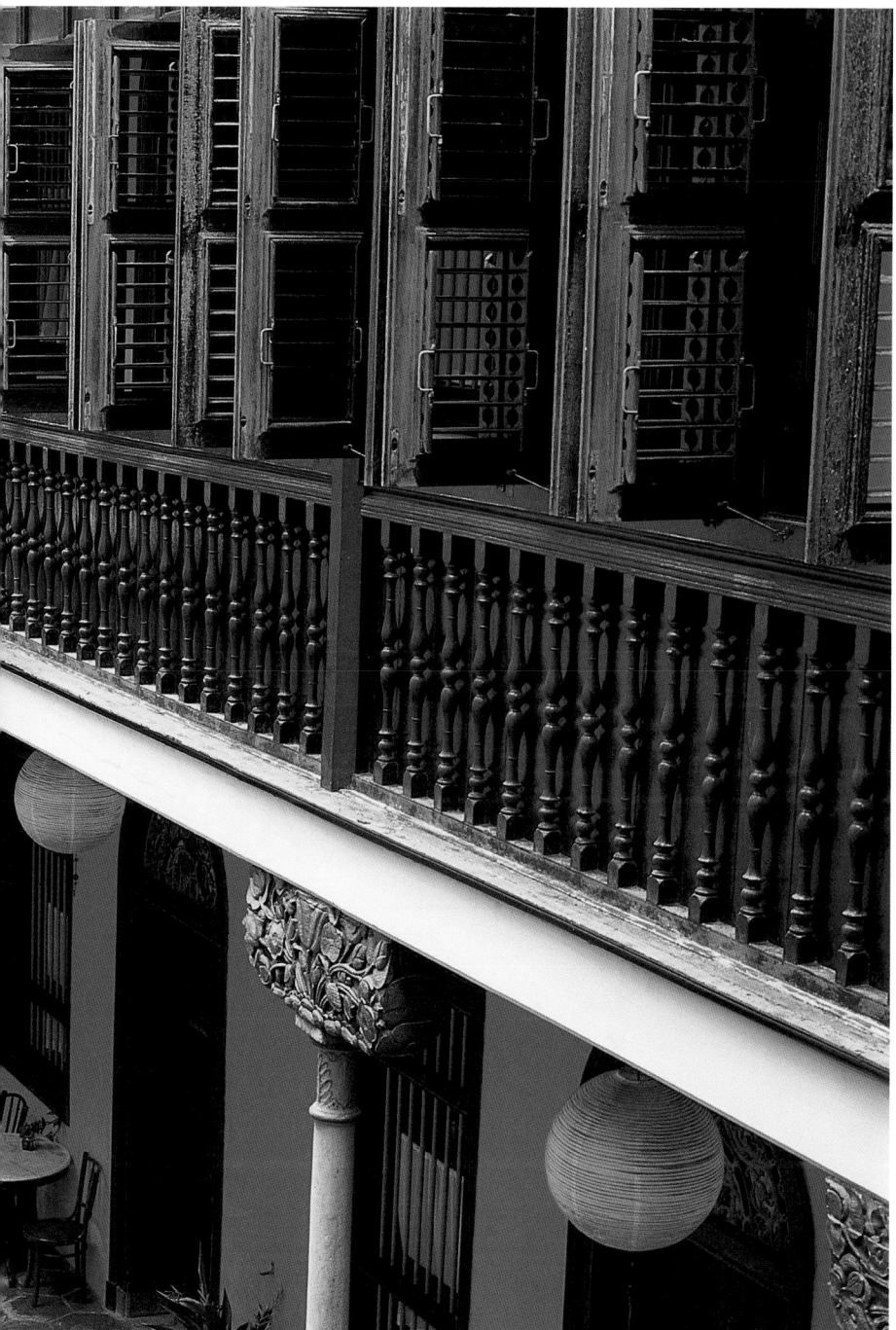

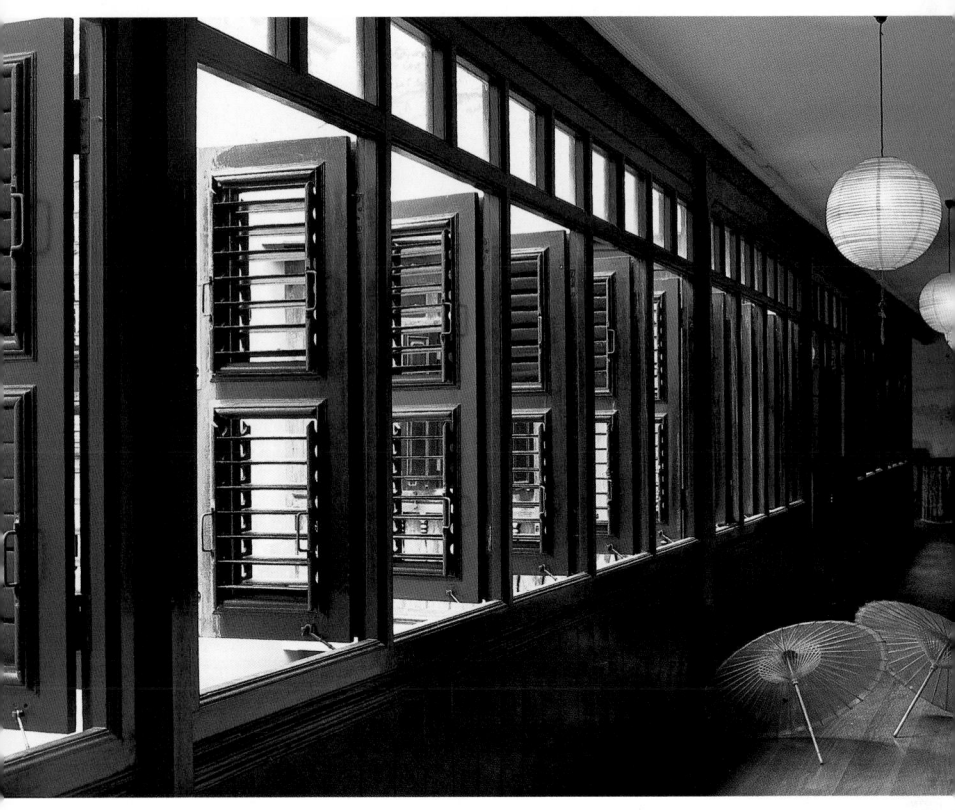

PP. 514–515 The open space acts as well for circulating air in the house. The louvred windows on the upper floor can be manoeuvred to modulate light. • Der große, hohe Innenhof sorgt für Lüftung im Haus. An den Jalousienfenstern im Obergeschoss kann man den Licht-einfall einstellen. • Cet espace ouvert

sert aussi à la circulation de l'air dans la maison. Il est possible de moduler la lumière filtrant par les fenêtres à claire-voie du premier étage.

↑ Louvred windows, typical of Penang's period architecture, line the corridors on the upper floor. • Die Jalousienfenster,

die reihenweise auf die oberen Flure hinausgehen, sind charakteristisch für Penang im 19. Jahrhundert. • Les couloirs du premier étage sont bordés de fenêtres à claire-voie, éléments caractéristiques de l'architecture de la période de Penang.

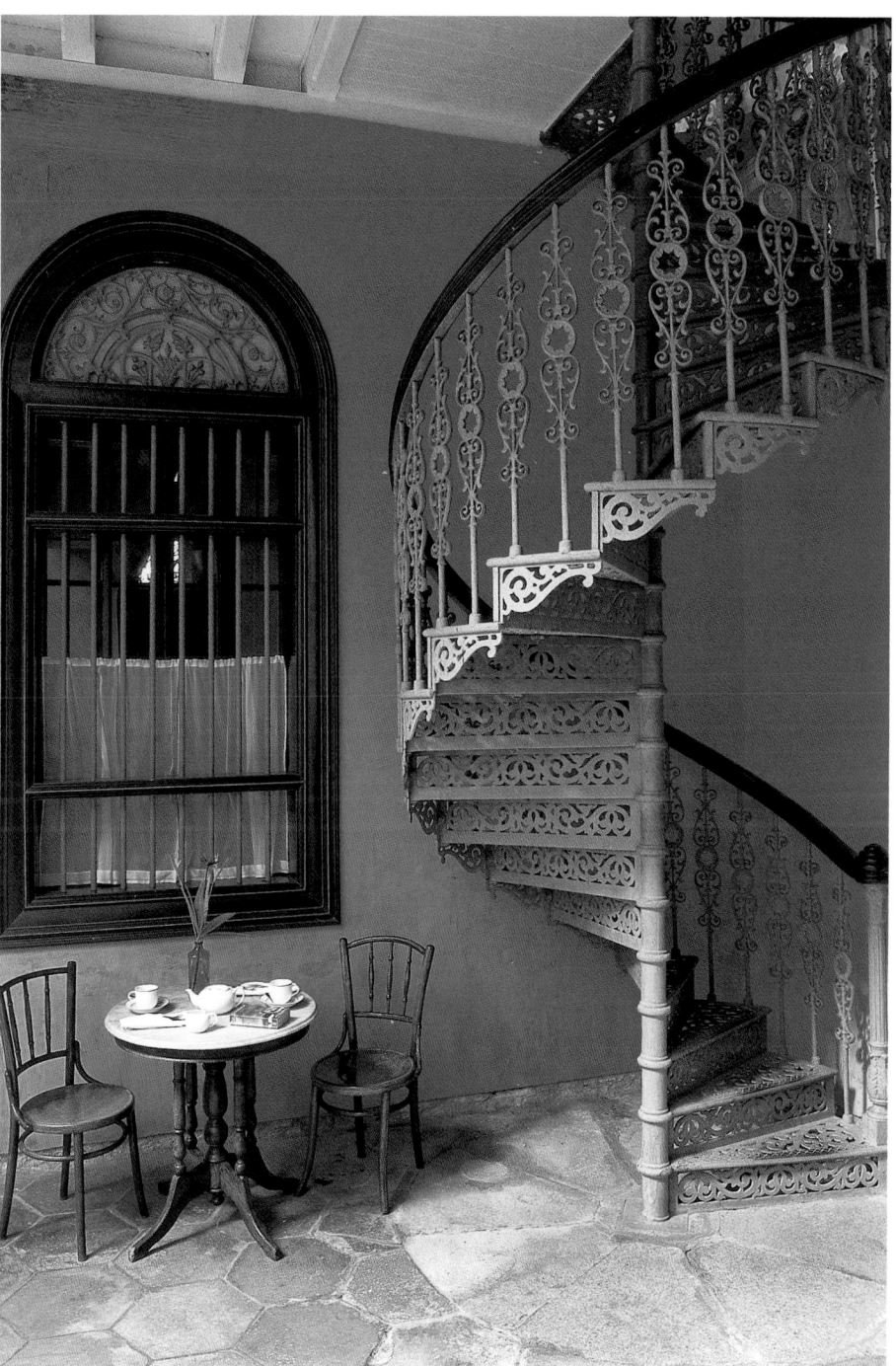

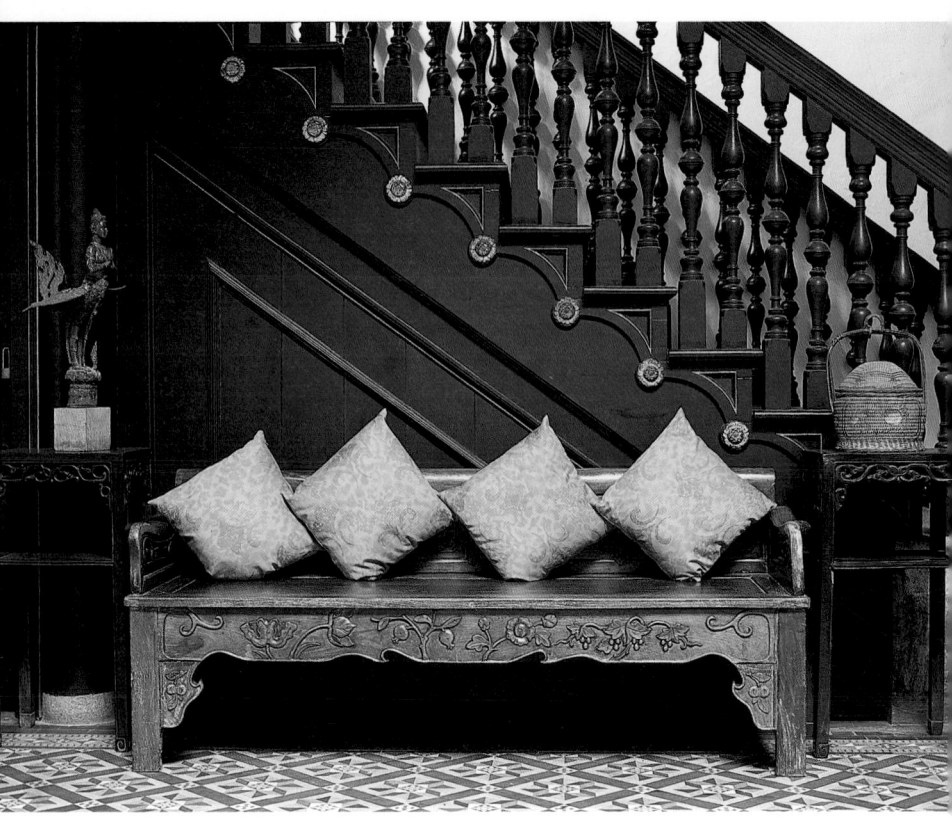

↑ An antique bench at the base of one of the seven staircases. • Eine antike Bank am Aufgang einer der sieben Treppen. • Un banc ancien au pied de l'un des sept escaliers de la maison.

→ The central courtyard is lined with painted wrought-iron pillars and balcony grilles made by the Victorian firm of MacFarlanes in Glasgow, Scotland. • Den zentralen Innenhof zieren bemalte schmiedeeiserne Säulen, die ebenso wie die Balkongitter von MacFarlane, einem viktorianischen Betrieb im schottischen Glasgow, angefertigt wurden. • La cour intérieure est bordée de colonnes et de balustrades en fer forgé peint, fabriquées à l'époque victorienne par l'entreprise écossaise MacFarlanes à Glasgow.

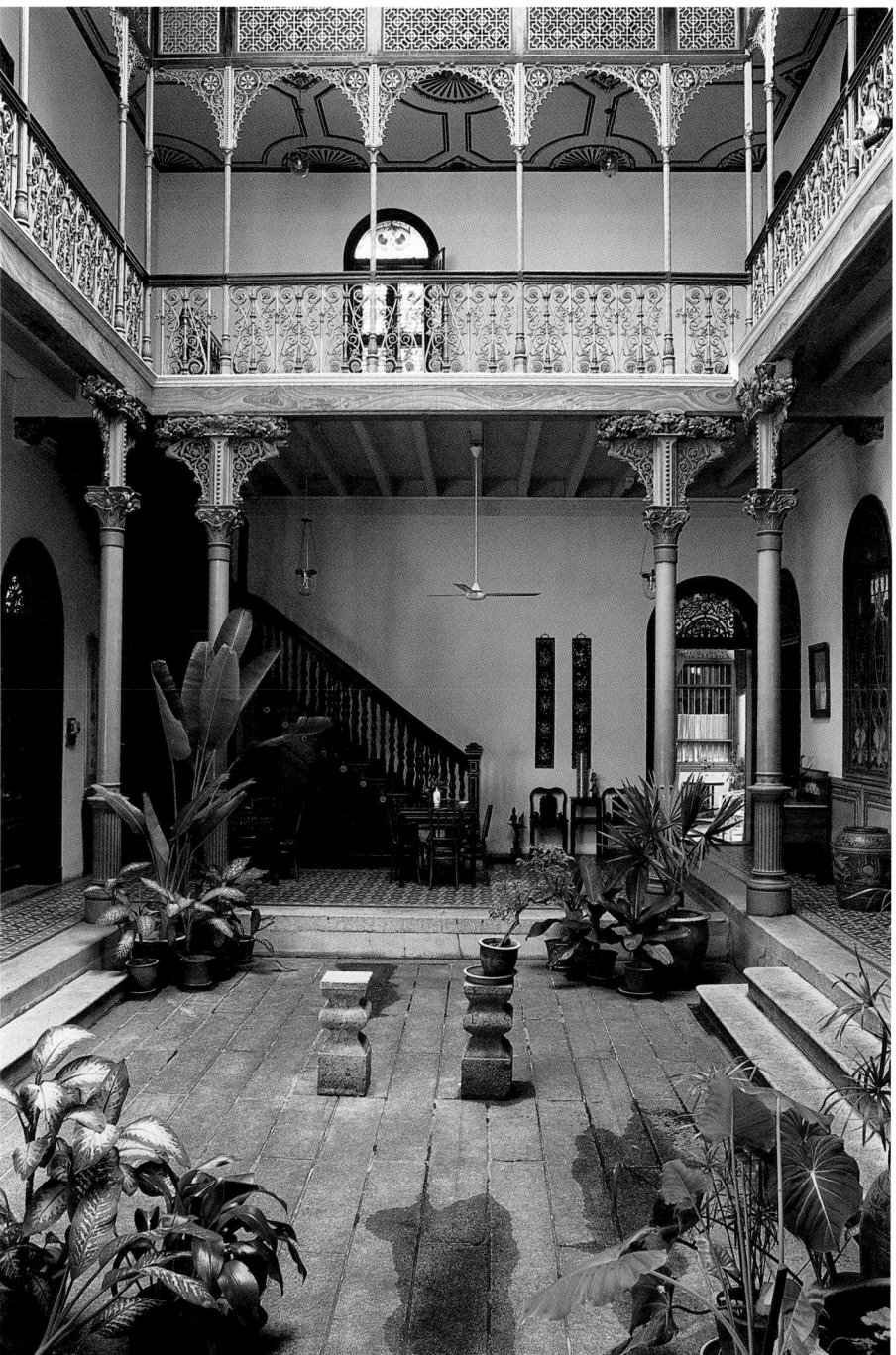

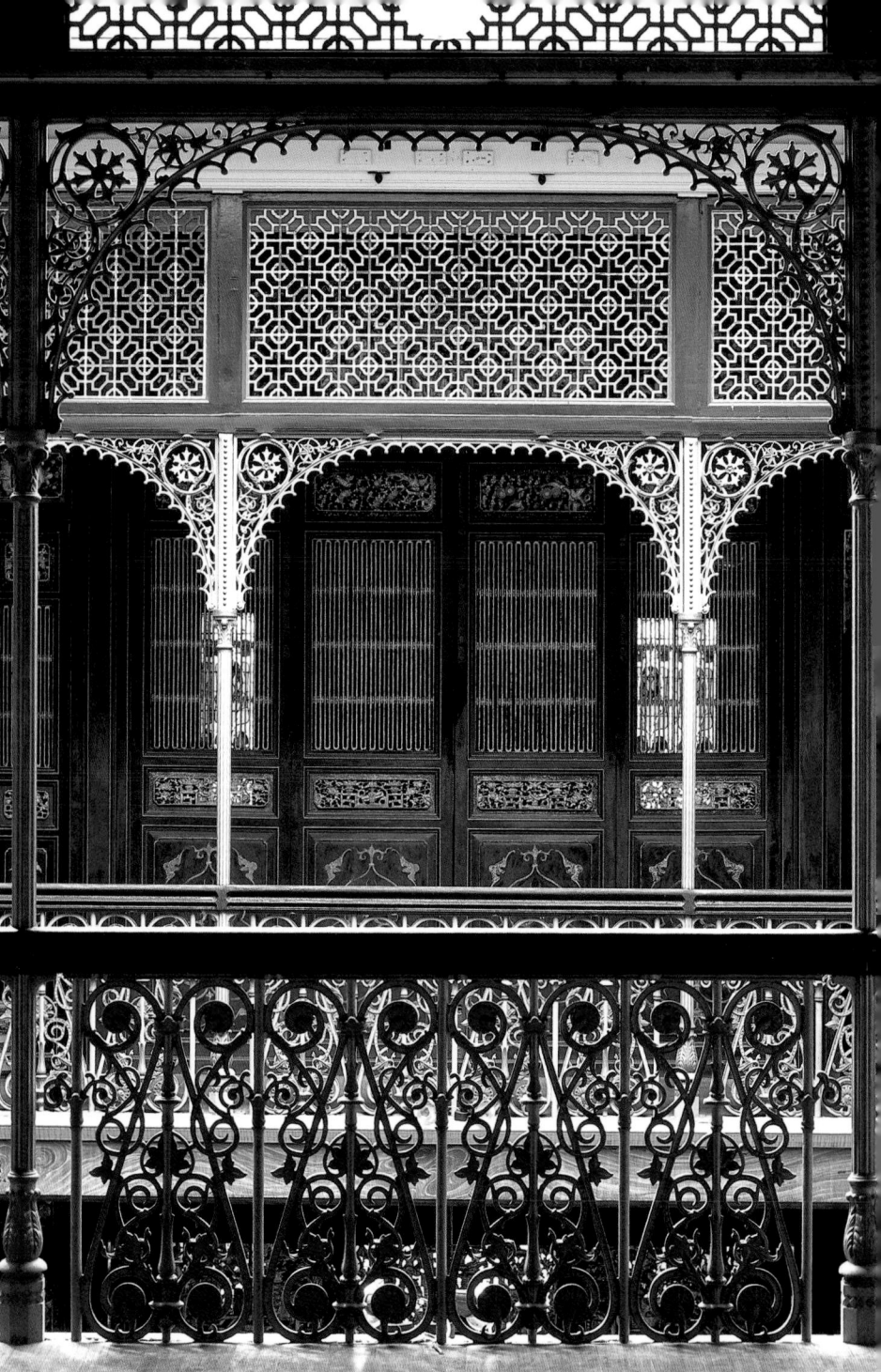

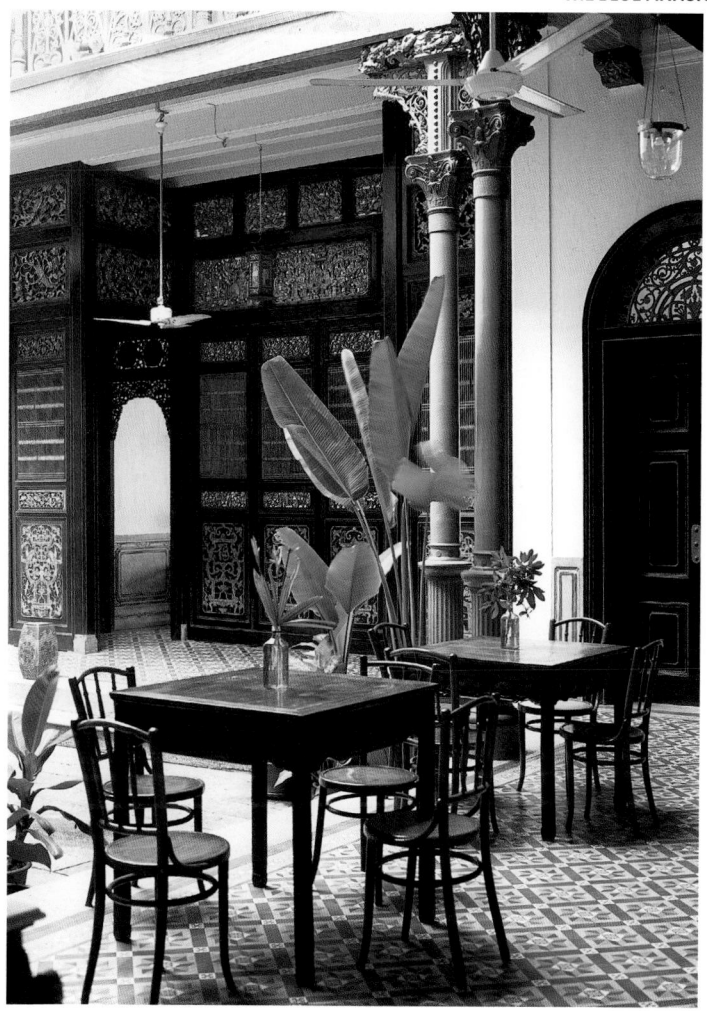

← Panels of filigreed wood carving are fitted above the wrought-iron grille-work of the balcony. A magnificent carved and gilded floor-to-ceiling screen divides the courtyard from the entrance hall. • Über dem schmiedeeisernen Balkongitter ist eine filigran geschnitzte Holzvertäfelung angebracht. Eine prächtig geschnitzte und vergoldete

Trennwand, die vom Boden bis zur Decke reicht, trennt den Innenhof von der Eingangshalle. • Des panneaux de bois finement sculptés font pendant aux éléments en fer forgé du balcon. Un magnifique claustra sculpté et doré sépare la cour intérieure du hall d'entrée.

↑ Breakfast is served along one side of the central courtyard. • An der einen Seite des zentralen Innenhofs wird das Frühstück serviert. • On sert le petit-déjeuner sous une des arcades de la cour centrale.

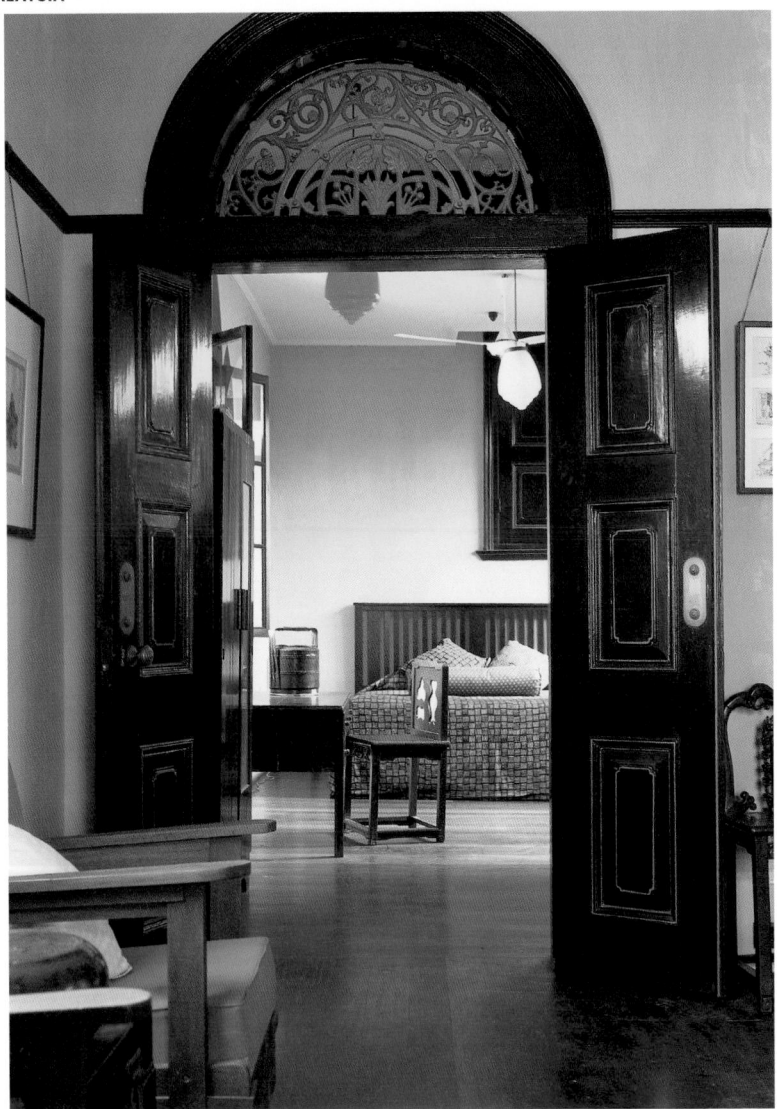

P. 524 A decorative wooden screen in a suite. Each carved panel has been gilded with gold leaf and protected with organic shellac. • Eine dekorative Trennwand aus Holz im Wohnbereich der Suite. Teile der Holzvertäfelung wurden mit Blattgold überzogen und mit Schellack versiegelt. • Un claustra

décoratif. Les panneaux sculptés ont été dorés à la feuille d'or et enduits de laque naturelle.

→ and P. 525 All 16 themed bedrooms are individually furnished with authentic period furniture, and named: this bedroom is called "Peony" (page

525). • Alle 16 thematisch gestalteten Hotelzimmer wurden mit historischen Möbeln eingerichtet: das Zimmer auf Seite 525 heißt „Pfingstrose". • Chacune des 16 chambres a une décoration, avec des meubles d'époque, et son nom : cette chambre (page 525) porte le nom « Pivoine ».

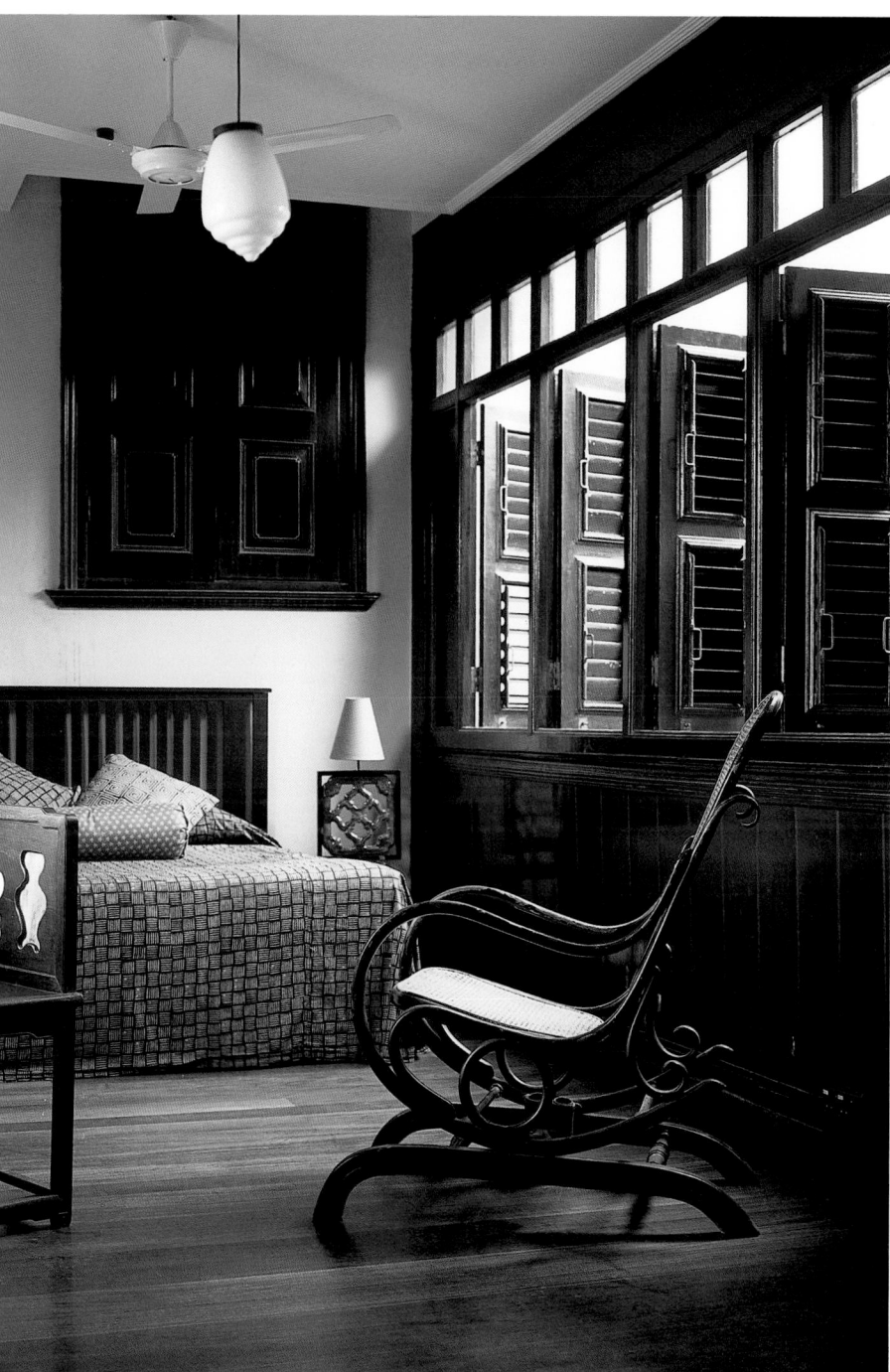

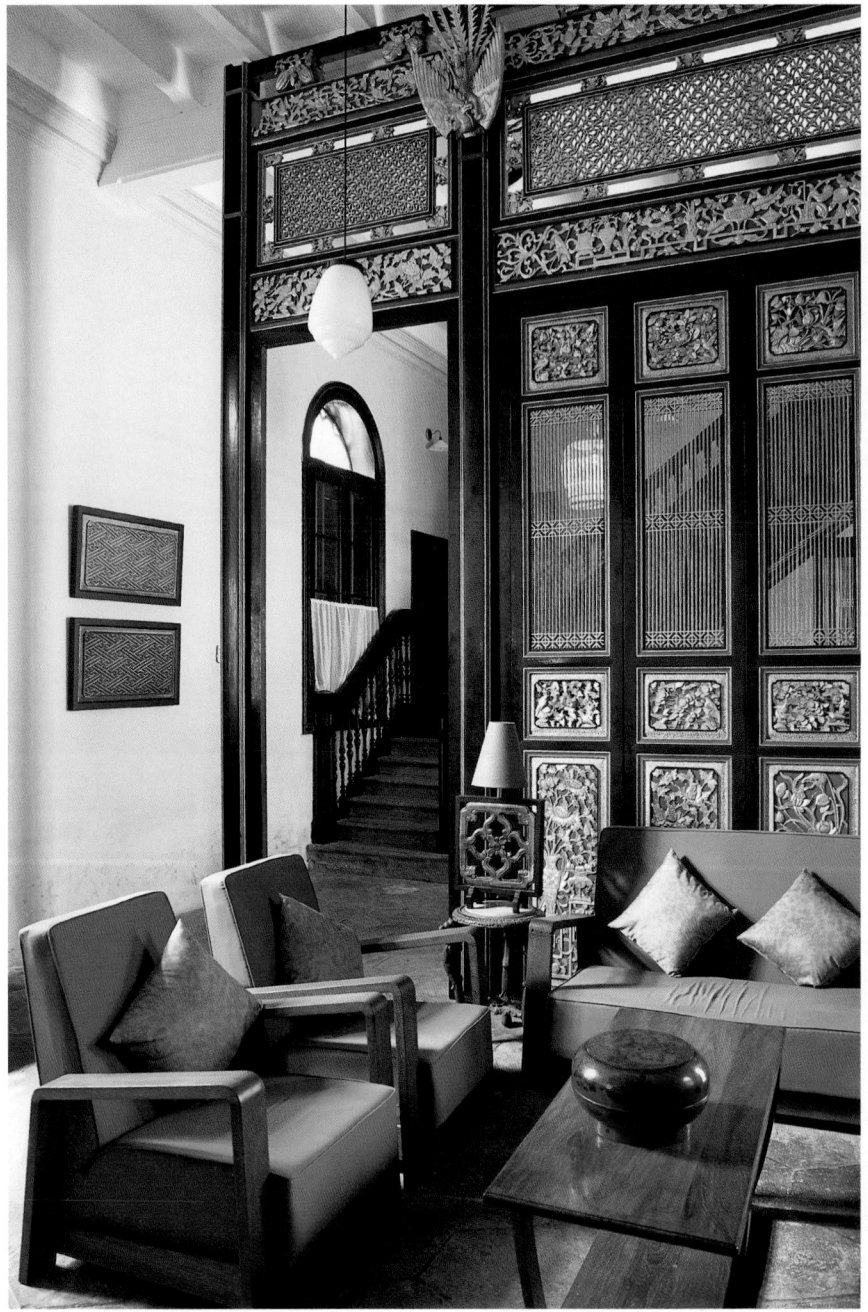

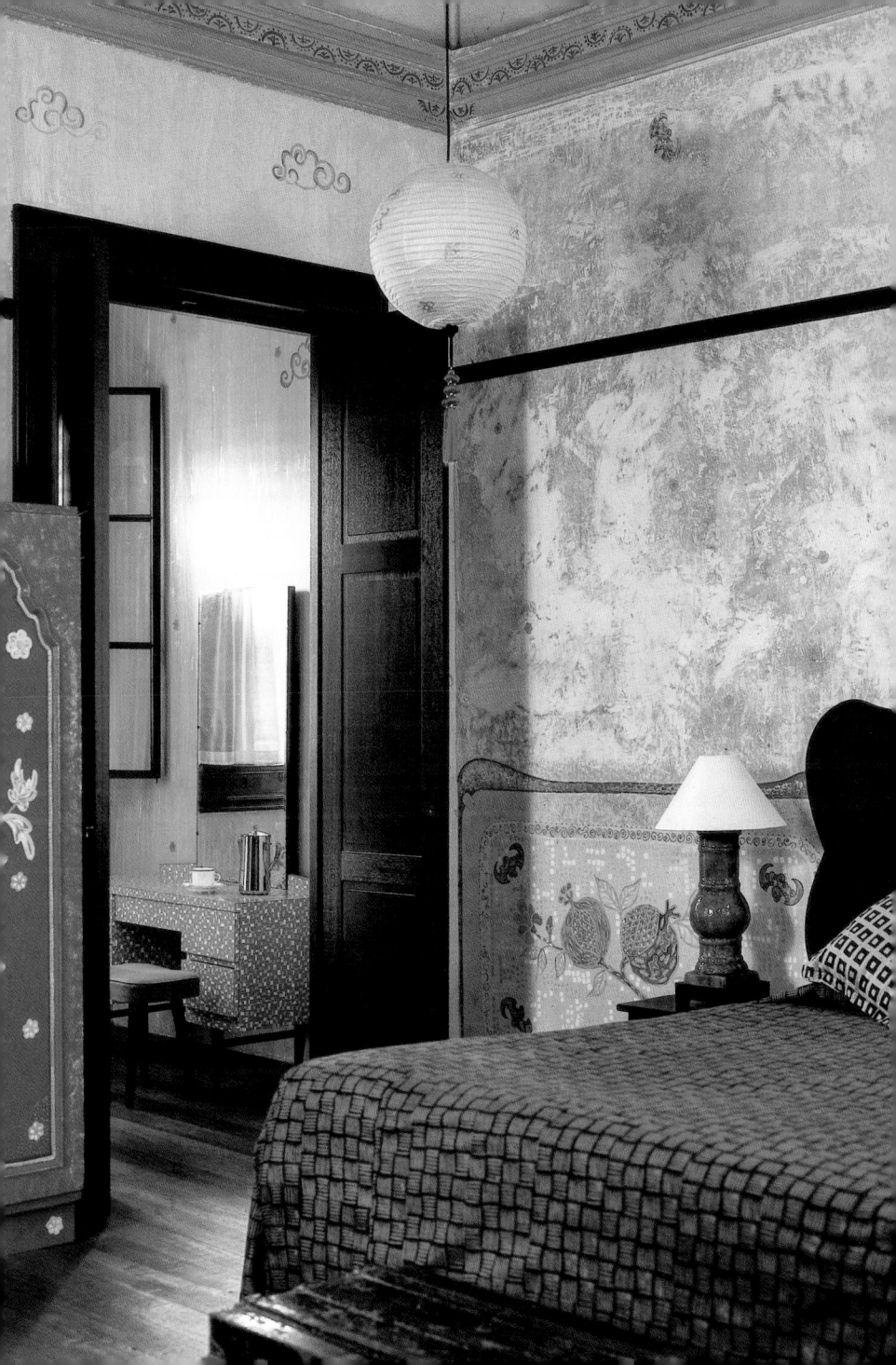

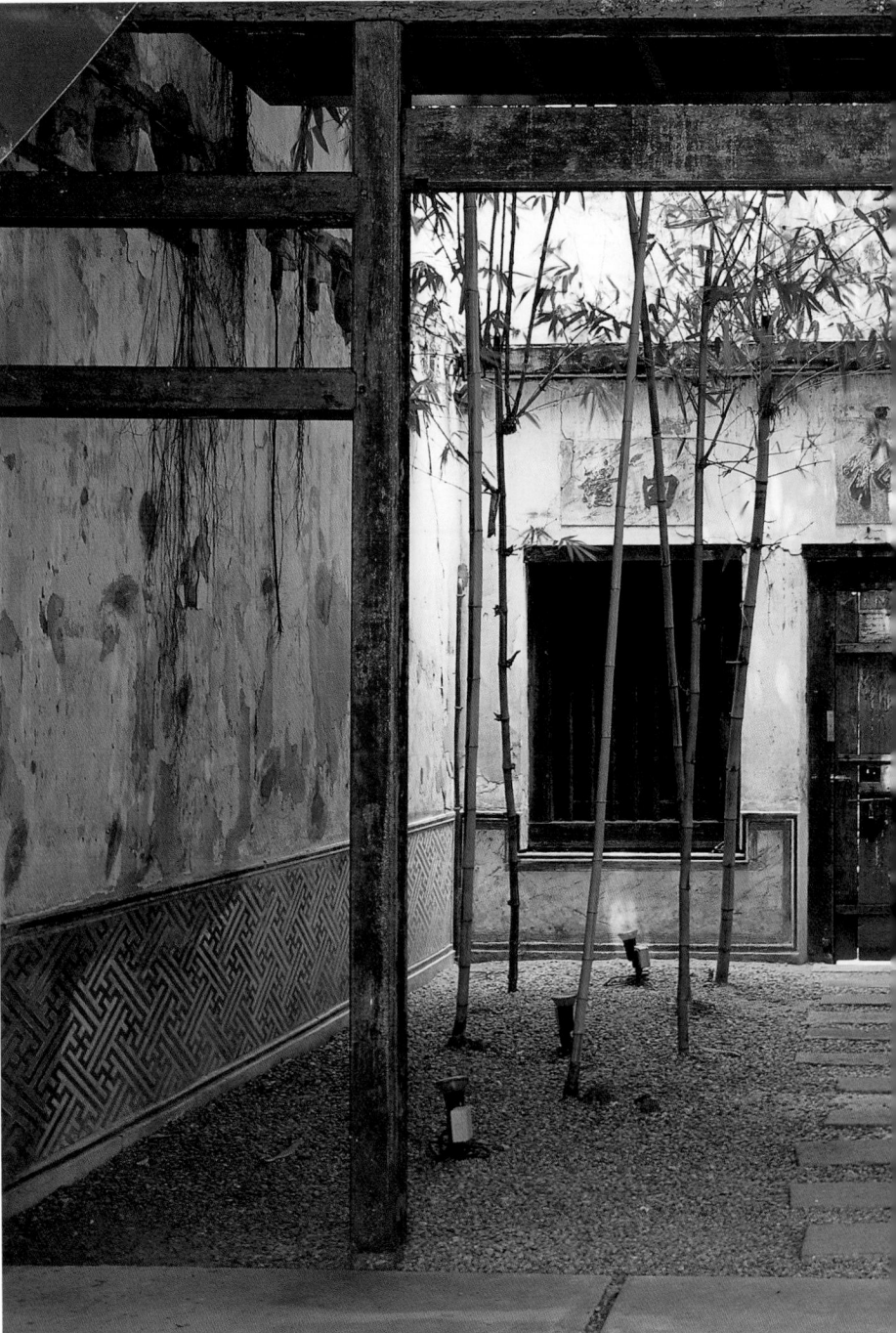

HOUSE ON HEEREN STREET

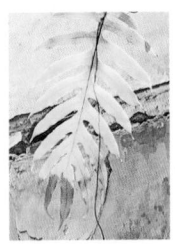

HOUSE ON
HEEREN STREET
MELAKA
MALAYSIA

Situated on the Malaysian peninsula with the island of Sumatra just across the narrow Strait of Melaka, the heyday of the town, once known as Malacca, began in the 15th century as a vital trading port on the spice route between India and China. For about 300 years the Portuguese, Dutch and the British jockeyed for control of this strategic entrepôt. By the early 20th century, though, what remained of Melaka was its layered history, a palimpsest of European, Chinese and Malay influences. Singapore-based architect Soo K. Chan was commissioned to resurrect a dilapidated pre-war building, a pastiche of Melaka's eclectic baroque style, as a meditative retreat by a client in Hong Kong. The idea was to preserve the building's atmosphere but prevent further structural decay and make it safe for occupancy. Soo Chan's solutions were minimal and spare: a series of steel frames to support the linked courtyards and a black reflecting pool to heighten its air of a lost oasis regained.

Die Stadt auf der Malaiischen Halbinsel, von der Insel Sumatra durch die enge Melakastraße getrennt, war im 15. Jahrhundert unter dem Namen Melaka als Handelshafen auf der Gewürzroute zwischen Indien und China weltbekannt. Portugiesen, Holländer und Briten wechselten sich 300 Jahre lang als Kolonialherren in diesem strategischen Handelshafen ab. Im frühen 20. Jahrhundert war von Melaka jedoch nur die vielschichtige Historie geblieben – ein Palimpsest europäischer, chinesischer und malaiischer Einflüsse. Soo K. Chan, ein Architekt aus Singapur, erhielt von einem Kunden aus Hongkong den Auftrag, ein baufälliges Gebäude in Melakas eklektizistischem Barockstil aus der Zeit vor dem Krieg in einen zur Meditation einladenden Zufluchtsort umzubauen. Der weitere Verfall sollte verhindert und das Haus in einen bewohnbaren Zustand versetzt werden, ohne die ursprüngliche Atmosphäre zu zerstören. In diesem Sinne beschränkte sich Soo Chan auf wenige sparsame Eingriffe: Stahlträger stützen nun die miteinander verbundenen Innenhöfe, und ein schwarzer Swimmingpool betont den Eindruck einer wiedergewonnenen Oase.

Située sur la péninsule malaise, qui n'est séparée de l'île de Sumatra que par le détroit de Malacca, la ville de Malacca a pris son essor au 15ᵉ siècle. C'était alors un comptoir florissant sur la route des épices reliant l'Inde à la Chine. Pendant près de trois siècles, Portugais, Hollandais et Britanniques se sont disputés le contrôle de cet entrepôt stratégique. Cependant, ce qui restait de Malacca au début du 20ᵉ siècle était une histoire marquée successivement par les influences européenne, chinoise et malaise, comme un palimpseste. Un client de Hong Kong a chargé l'architecte singapourien Soo K. Chan de relever de ses ruines un bâtiment datant de l'avant-guerre, pastiche du style éclectique baroque de la ville, et de le transformer en un refuge propice à la méditation. L'idée de départ était de préserver l'aura de l'édifice, tout en empêchant de nouvelles dégradations majeures et en assurant la sécurité de ses occupants. Soo K. Chan a donné dans le minimalisme et la sobriété : des profils métalliques assurent la stabilité du réseau de cours intérieures, et un bassin d'un noir réfléchissant la lumière accentue l'apparence d'oasis que la maison a retrouvée.

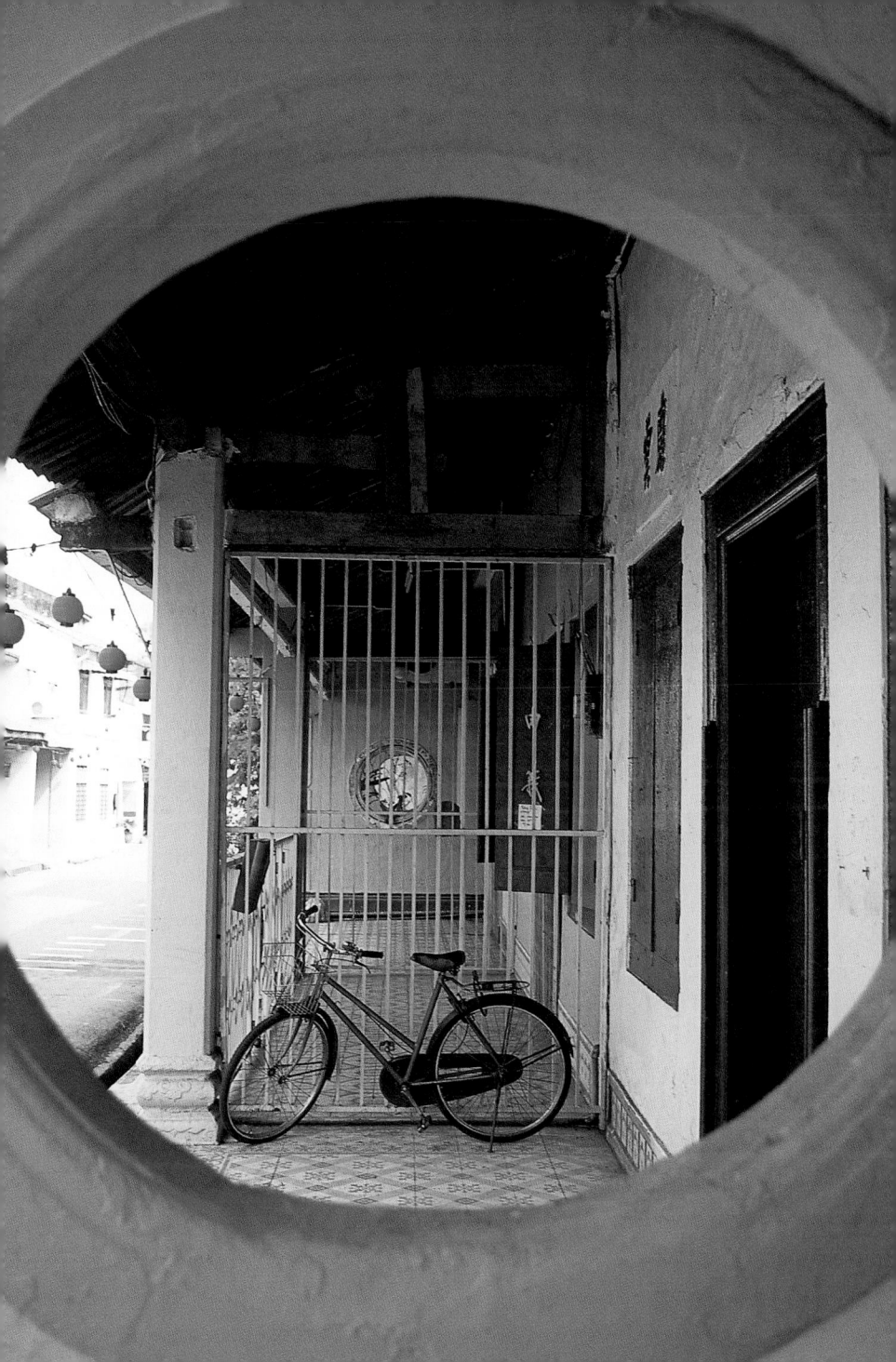

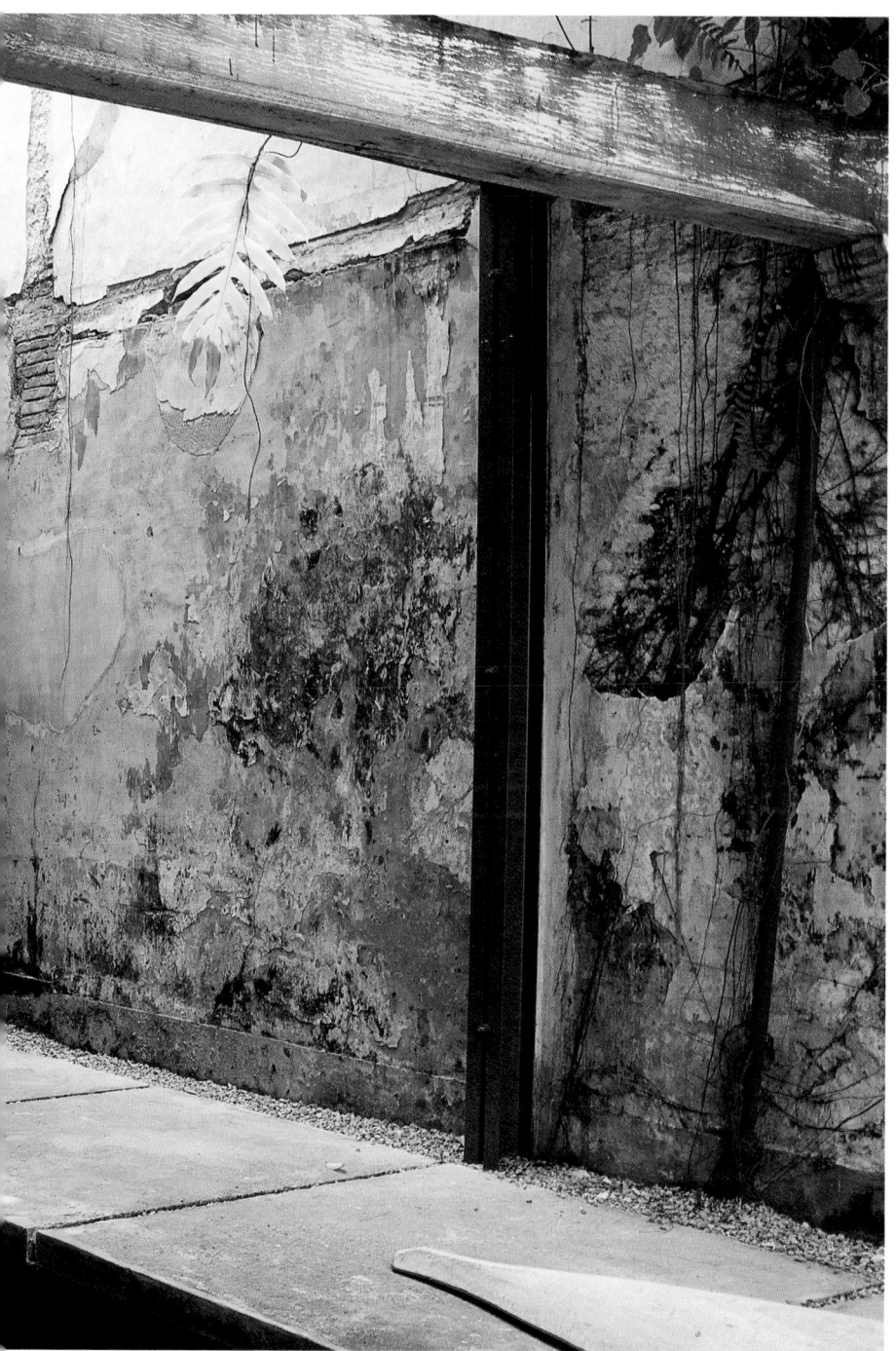

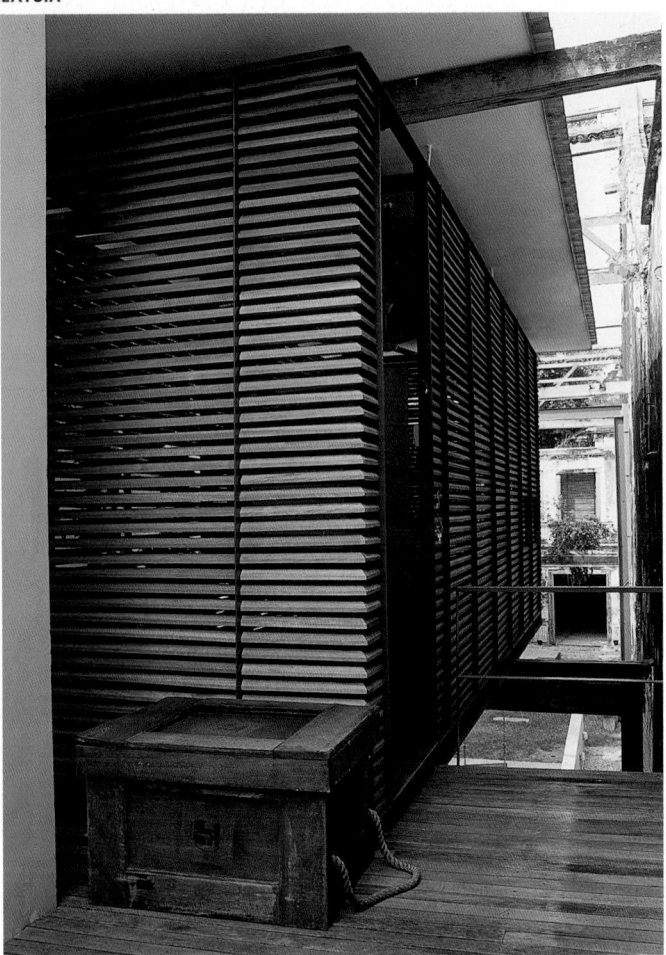

PP. 526-527 The pebbled bamboo courtyard leads to the living area. • Der mit Bambuspflanzen und Kies geschmückte Eingangshof. • La cour est couverte de galets et plantée de bambous.

PP. 530-531 The sleeping area is supported by steel frames by the pool. The existing walls have been left to weather naturally. • Der Schlafbereich wird von den Stahlträgern am Swimmingpool gehalten. Die bestehenden Mauern wurden der natürlichen

Verwitterung überlassen. • L'espace couchage à l'aplomb de la piscine repose sur des poutrelles métalliques. Les murs d'origine sont abandonnés aux outrages du temps.

↑ The sleeping area inside the wooden screen is set apart from the old walls. • Das Schlafzimmer innerhalb der hölzernen Trennwände wurde abseits der alten Mauern eingerichtet. • L'espace couchage enfermé dans un caisson à lattes forme une unité distincte.

→ The bench and swing were made from old timbers found on the site. • Bank und Schaukel wurden aus alten Balken hergestellt. • Le banc et la balançoire sont en bois de récupération.

PP. 534-535 Wooden lattices frame as well as screen views of the bamboo garden. • Durch das hölzerne Gitterwerk und die Trennwände blickt man in den Bambusgarten. • On aperçoit le jardin de bambous à travers les persiennes en bois.

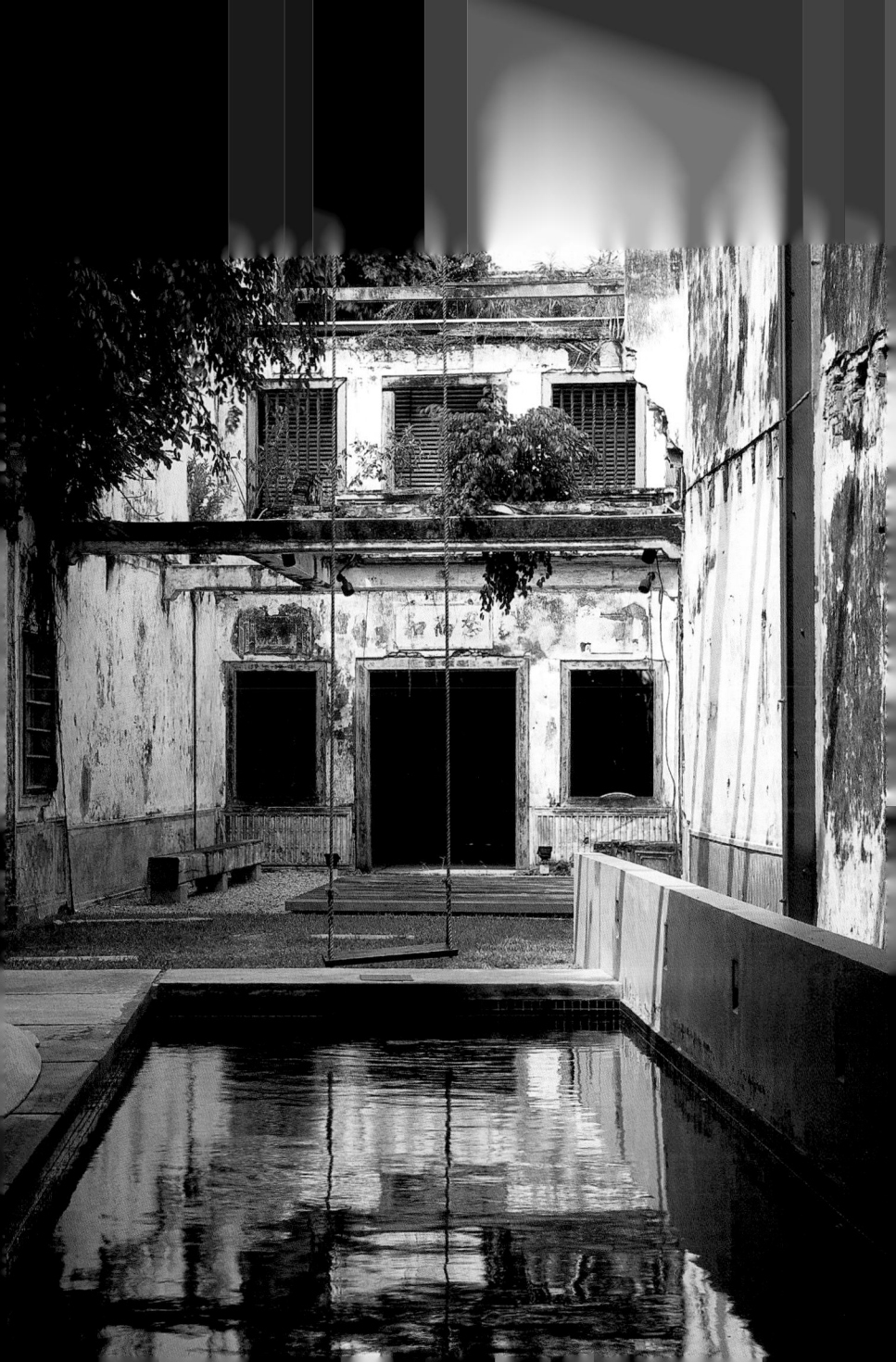

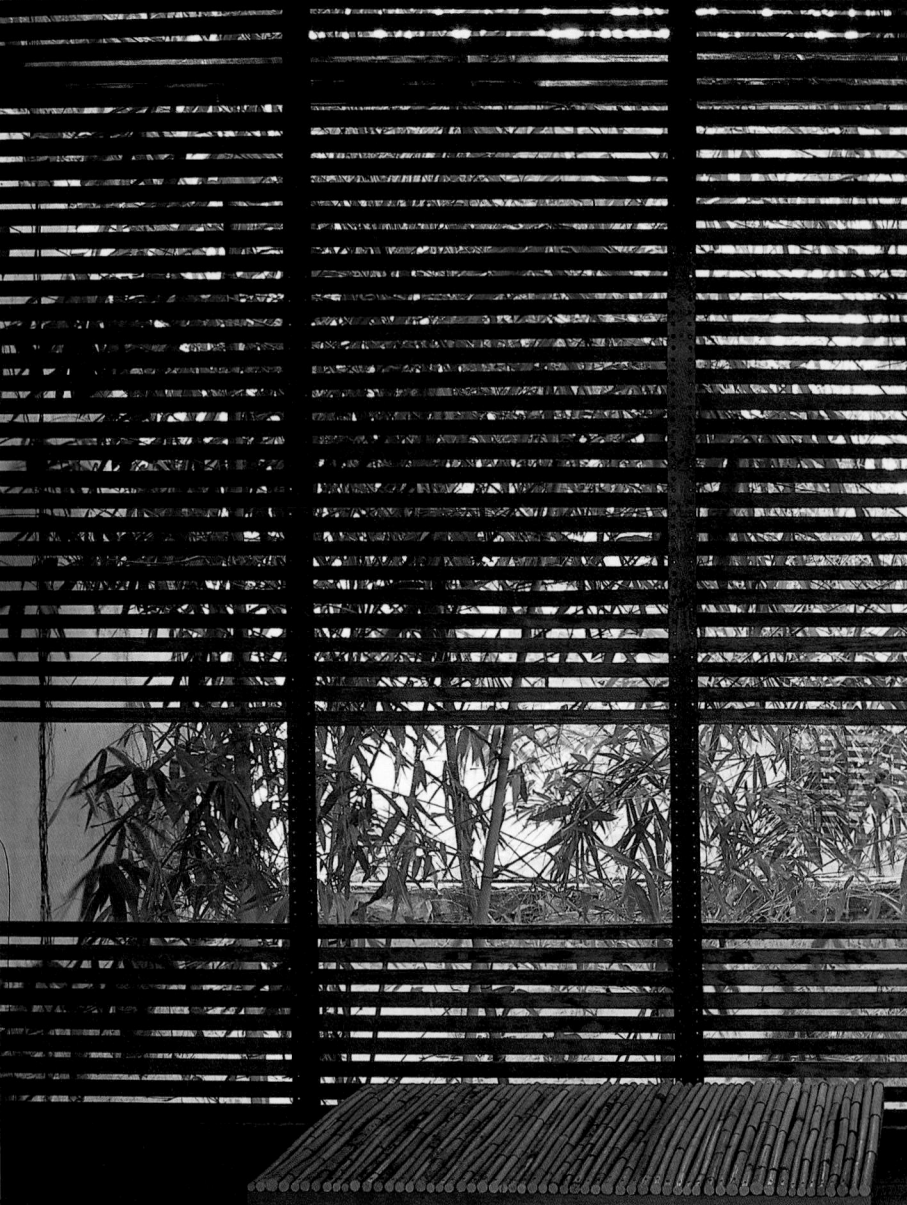

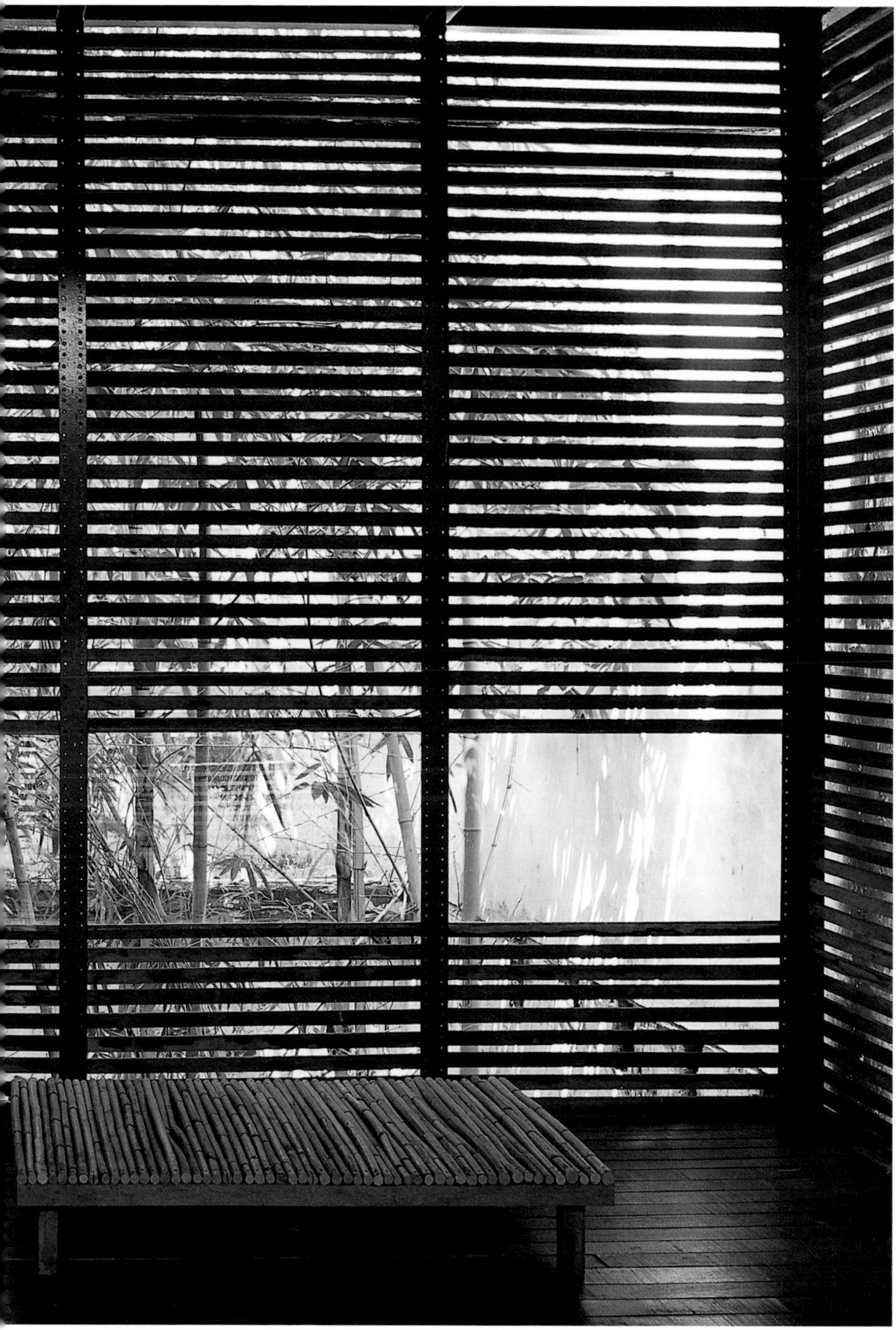

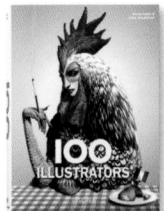

100 Illustrators

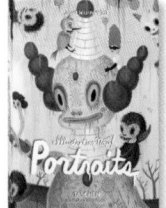

Illustration Now!
Portraits

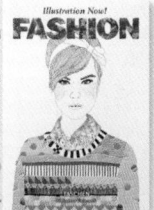

Illustration Now!
Fashion

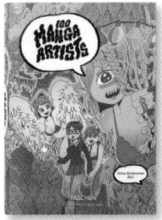

100 Manga Artists

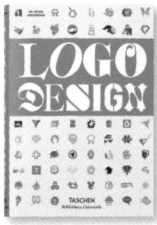

Logo Design

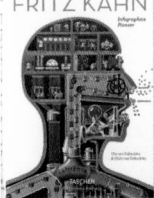

Fritz Kahn.
Infographics Pioneer

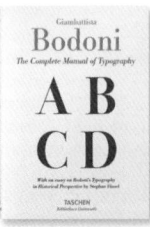

Bodoni. Manual of
Typography

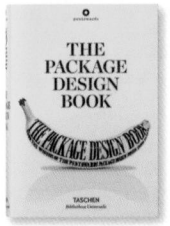

The Package Design
Book

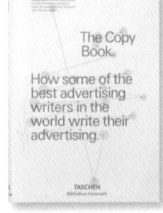

D&AD.
The Copy Book

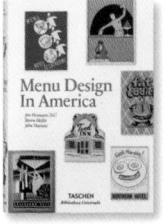

Menu Design
in America

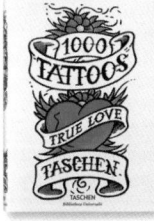

1000 Tattoos

Bookworm's delight:
never bore, always excite!

TASCHEN
Bibliotheca Universalis

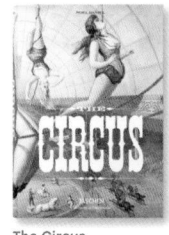

The Circus.
1870s–1950s

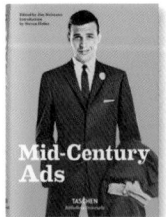

Mid-Century Ads

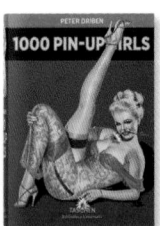

1000 Pin-Up Girls

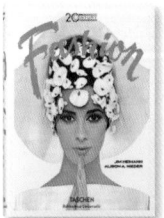

20th Century Fashion

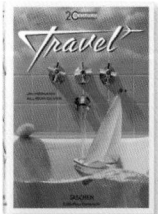

20th Century Travel

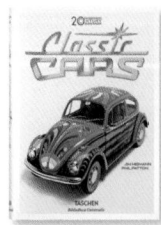

20th Century
Classic Cars

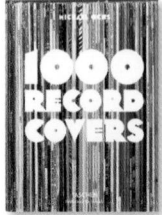

1000 Record Covers

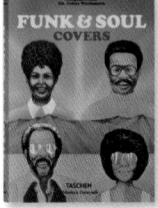

Funk & Soul Covers

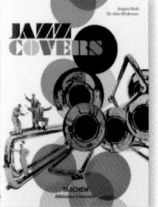

Jazz Covers

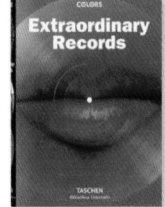

Extraordinary
Records

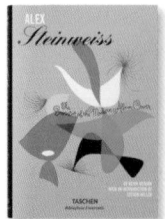

Steinweiss

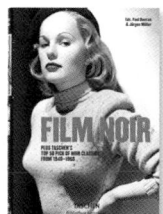
Film Noir

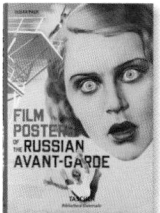
Film Posters of the
Russian Avant-Garde

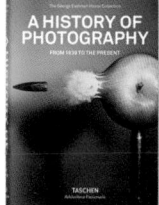
A History of
Photography

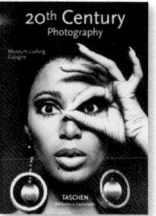
20th Century
Photography

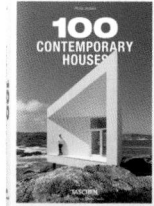
100 Contemporary
Houses

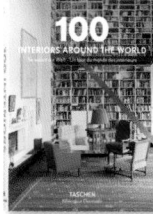
100 Interiors Around
the World

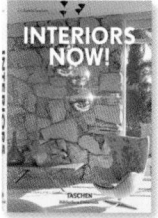
Interiors Now!

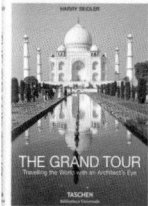
The Grand Tour

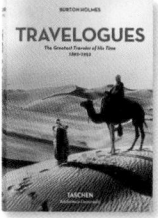
Burton Holmes.
Travelogues

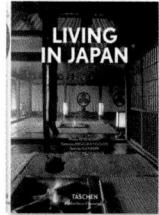
Living in Japan

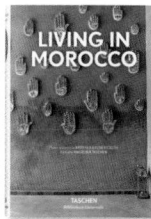
Living in Morocco

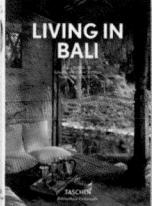
Living in Bali

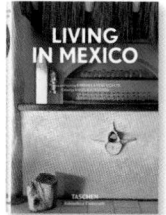
Living in Mexico

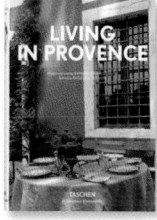
Living in Provence

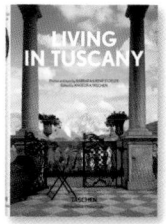
Living in Tuscany

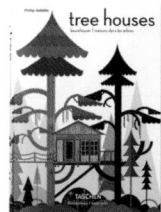
Tree Houses

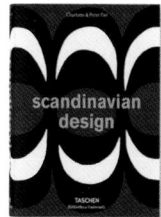
Scandinavian Design

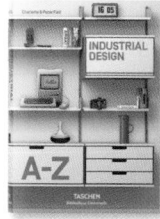
Industrial Design A-Z

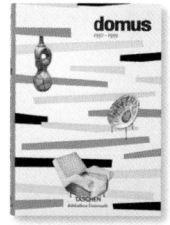
domus 1950s

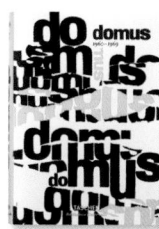
domus 1960s

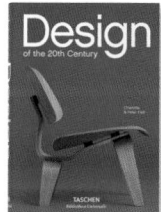
Design of the
20th Century

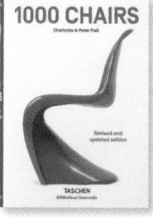
1000 Chairs

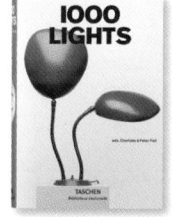
1000 Lights

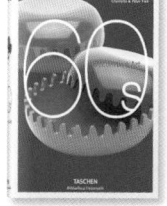
Decorative Art 60s

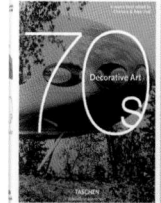
Decorative Art 70s

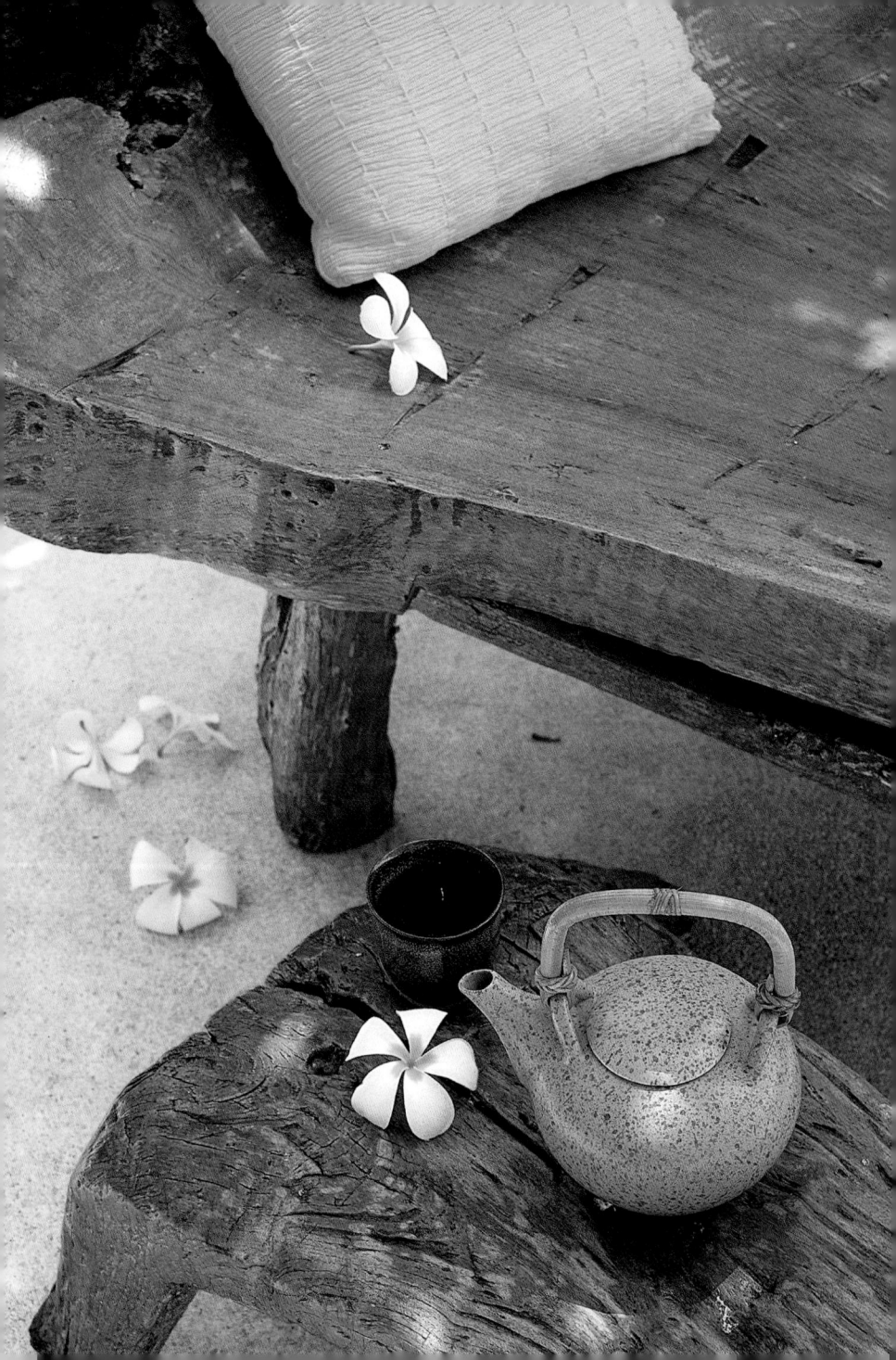

In a world without walls

Balinese homes in harmony with nature

Carved wood, secluded courtyards, and frangipani blossoms: soak up
the Eastern elegance of these heavenly Indonesian interiors. Opening onto
gorgeous green landscapes, majestic mountains, or beautiful coastlines,
these Balinese homes exude relaxing, contemplative vibes. Unwind and
refresh with this compact showcase of rustic paradises, updated with fresh,
never-before-seen images.

"A feast of color,
exquisite décor and
peaceful presence."

— *Style Magazine*, Cape Town

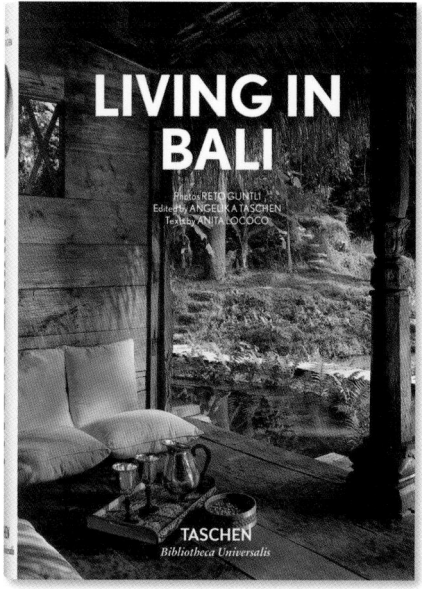

Living in Bali
Reto Guntli, Anita Lococo,
Angelika Taschen
472 pages

TRILINGUAL EDITIONS IN:
ENGLISH / DEUTSCH / FRANÇAIS &
ESPAÑOL / ITALIANO / PORTUGUÊS

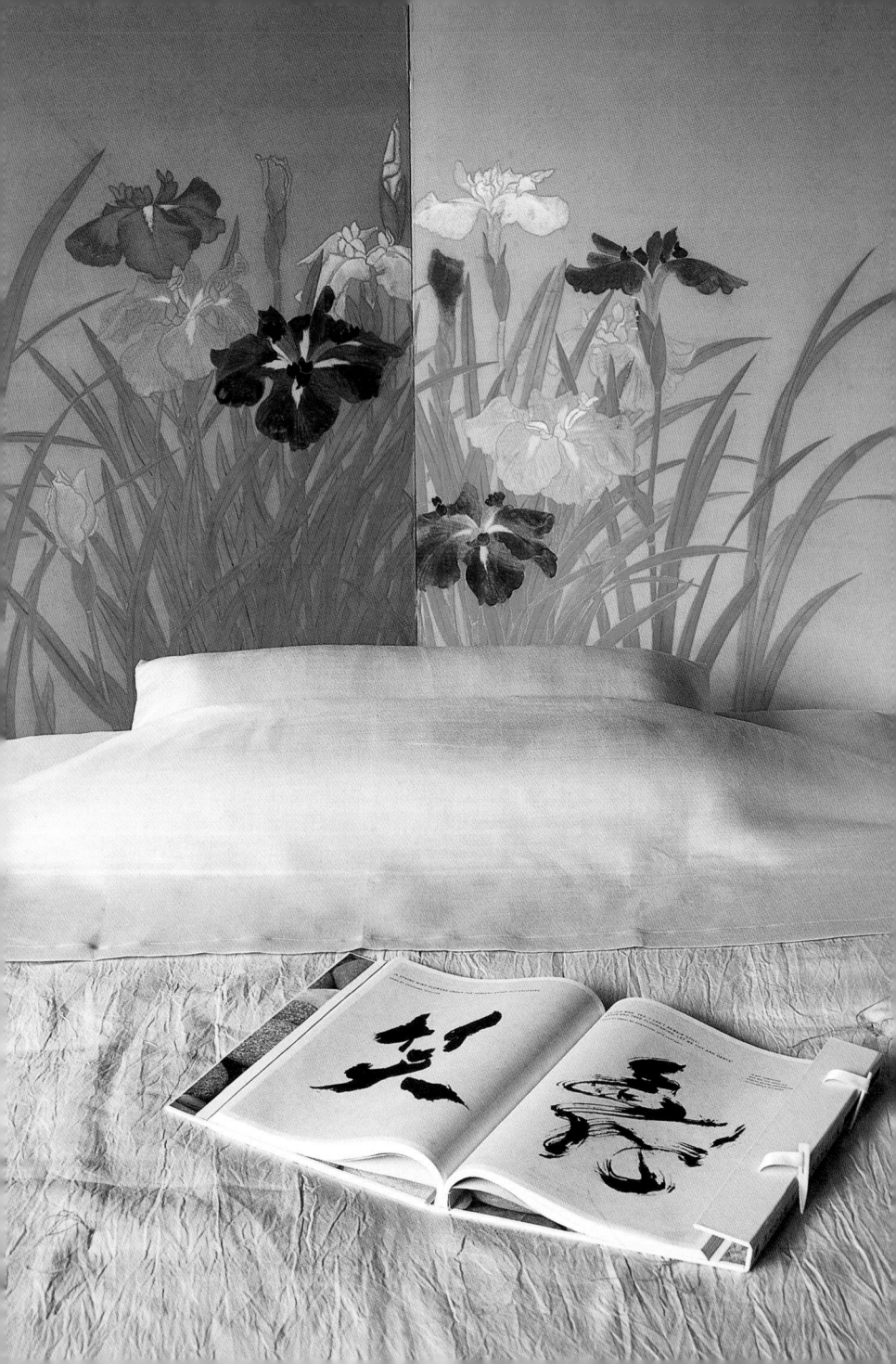

Nippon nests

Today's most exceptional Japanese homes

Carefully manicured gardens, sliding screens, and warm natural materials:
Japanese homes are refuges of tranquility, crafted in a unique domestic
aesthetic of Eastern minimalism. Traditional architecture features alongside
cutting-edge contemporary dwellings in this collection of homes, with many
never-before-seen photographs. Turn to the rising sun and discover the fluid
simplicity of these spaces where Zen philosophy breathes.

"The photographs alone
are enough to keep
readers entranced for
hours, but tear your
eyes away and the text
is equally enthralling."

— *Living & Homes*, Sydney

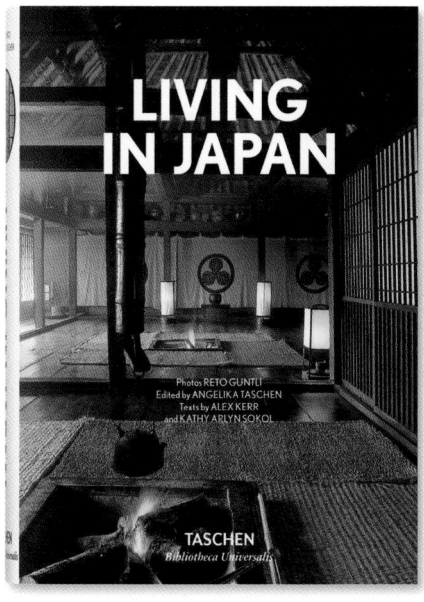

Living in Japan
Reto Guntli, Alex Kerr, Kathy Arlyn Sokol,
Angelika Taschen
512 pages

TRILINGUAL EDITIONS IN:
ENGLISH / DEUTSCH / FRANÇAIS &
ESPAÑOL / ITALIANO / PORTUGUÊS

YOU CAN FIND TASCHEN STORES IN

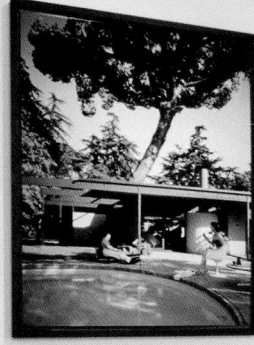
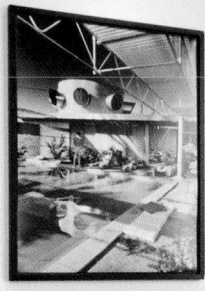
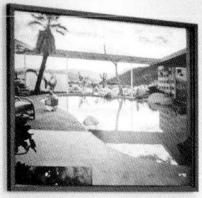

Amsterdam
P.C. Hooftstraat 44

Berlin
Schlüterstr. 39

Beverly Hills
354 N. Beverly Drive

Brussels
Rue Lebeaustraat 18

Cologne
Neumarkt 3

Hamburg
Bleichenbrücke 1-7

Hollywood
Farmers Market,
6333 W. 3rd Street, CT-10

Hong Kong
Shop 01-G02 Tai Kwun,
10 Hollywood Road,
Central

London
12 Duke of York Square

London Claridge's
49 Brook Street

Miami
1111 Lincoln Rd.

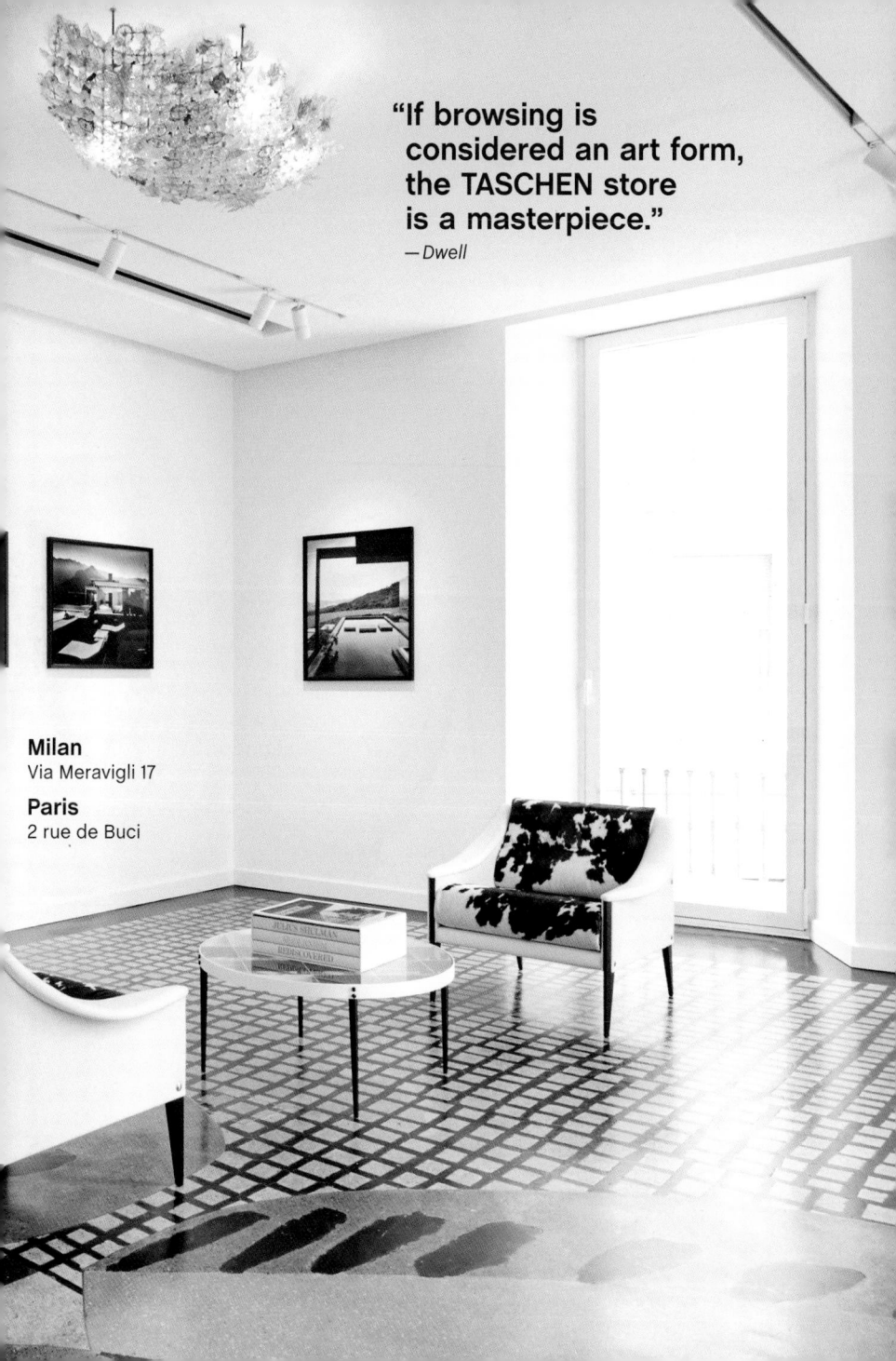

"If browsing is
considered an art form,
the TASCHEN store
is a masterpiece."
—*Dwell*

Milan
Via Meravigli 17

Paris
2 rue de Buci

IMPRINT

EACH AND EVERY TASCHEN BOOK PLANTS A SEED!

TASCHEN is a carbon neutral publisher. Each year, we offset our annual carbon emissions with carbon credits at the Instituto Terra, a reforestation program in Minas Gerais, Brazil, founded by Lélia and Sebastião Salgado. To find out more about this ecological partnership, please check: www.taschen.com/zerocarbon
Inspiration: unlimited. Carbon footprint: zero.

To stay informed about TASCHEN and our upcoming titles, please subscribe to our free magazine at www.taschen.com/magazine, follow us on Twitter, Instagram, and Facebook, or e-mail your questions to contact@taschen.com.

EDITING
Angelika Taschen, Berlin

PROJECT MANAGEMENT
Stephanie Paas and Inka Lohrmann, Cologne

DESIGN AND LAYOUT
Birgit Eichwede and Maximiliane Hüls, Cologne

PRODUCTION
Tina Ciborowius, Cologne

GERMAN TRANSLATION
Anne Brauner, Cologne

FRENCH TRANSLATION
Christèle Jany, Cologne

PAGE 1
A clay image of Ganesh, the Hindu god of auspicious beginnings, is adorned with jasmine garlands; Vip's Villa, Chiang Mai, Thailand.

PAGE 2
Monks from a nearby monastery have made the former minister's villa their own; a historic villa, Mandalay, Myanmar.

PAGE 6
Wat Attwiya, Siem Reap, Cambodia.

PAGE 9
The carpet and *thangka* are Tibetan; Vip's Villa, Chiang Mai, Thailand.

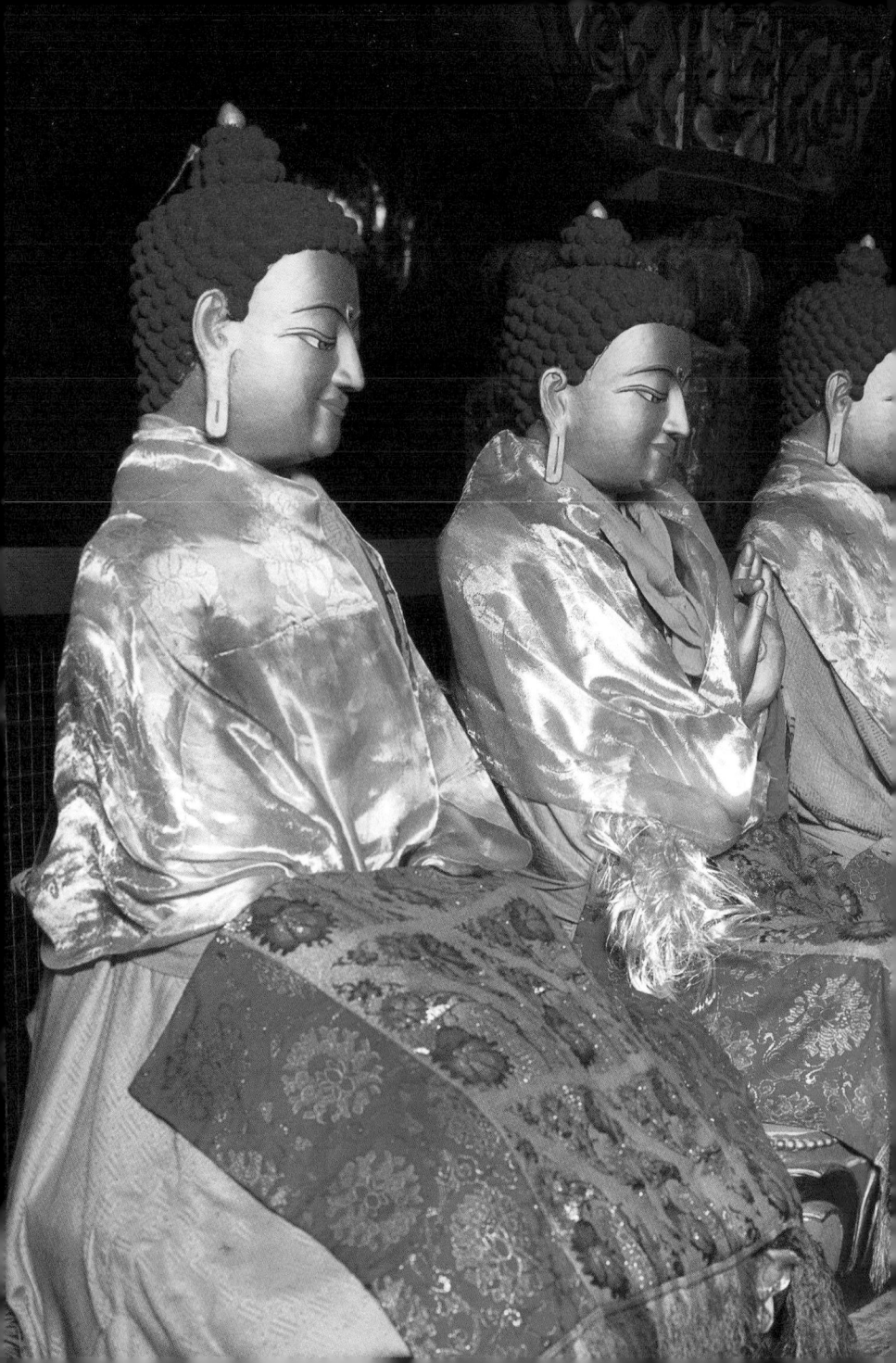